Metaphysics

Classic and Contemporary Readings

Metaphysics
Classic and Contemporary Readings

Edited by

RONALD C. HOY
California University of Pennsylvania

and

L. NATHAN OAKLANDER
The University of Michigan—Flint

Wadsworth Publishing Company
Belmont, California
A Division of Wadsworth, Inc.

PHILOSOPHY EDITOR: Kenneth King
EDITORIAL ASSISTANT: Cynthia Campbell
PRODUCTION: Cece Munson, The Cooper Company
PRINT BUYER: Martha Branch
DESIGNER: Cynthia Bassett
COPY EDITOR: Phyllis Cairns
COMPOSITOR: TCSystems, Shippensburg, Penn.
COVER: Al Burkhardt
SIGNING REPRESENTATIVE: David Leach

Printed in the United States of America

1 2 3 4 5 6 7 8 9 10—95 94 93 92 91

Library of Congress Cataloging in Publication Data

Metaphysics: classic and contemporary readings/edited
    by Ronald C. Hoy and L. Nathan Oaklander.
        p.   cm.
    Includes bibliographical references.
    ISBN 0-534-14580-9
    1. Metaphysics.   I. Hoy, Ronald C.
        II. Oaklander, L. Nathan, 1945–
BD111.M57   1990
110—dc20   90-41529
                                        CIP

Dedicated to our parents

Emaline A. and Erin H. Hoy

the late Fay and Isadore Oaklander

Contents

Part III Mind   189

Part IV Freedom   297

Part V *Knowing Reality* 395

Preface

Metaphysics is an ancient and honorable discipline that sometimes suffers from too much enthusiasm and sometimes from too much self-doubt. In the twentieth century, doubt has tended to dominate. Metaphysics has been declared meaningless or fruitless, and it has been analyzed, psychoanalyzed, deconstructed, and sometimes left for dead in the dust of "semantic ascent." Nevertheless, philosophers have continued to propose and debate arguments about what really exists—to wonder about how to achieve the best possible view of the world. And students and the general public show irrepressible interest in metaphysics, though this is sometimes evidenced only by the popularity of books on the occult, which offer entertaining views of reality beyond the ordinary. The common confusion of metaphysics with the study of the supernatural should be remedied by accessible books that show how fascinating and challenging the attempt to understand "ordinary" reality can be.

The working assumption of the editors of this anthology has been that professors who teach metaphysics have been poorly served by the scarcity of available texts. Professors have tended to resort to a historical approach, having their students read the work of classical authors, or they have tended to focus on specific contemporary problems as they are dealt with in journal articles that are collected in specialized anthologies that soon go out of print. The result is that it has been difficult to do two desirable things: ground the study of metaphysics in its history *and* motivate and

master contemporary theories, which are often quite technical. Accordingly, we have compiled an anthology that includes both classical and contemporary selections, and we have organized them around five topics of general and perennial interest. The readings represent alternative points of view and, hopefully, give some indication of the development of philosophical understanding.

Students taking metaphysics courses frequently have diverse backgrounds and preparation, so the anthology includes readings of varying degrees of difficulty. Enough material is included to allow professors flexibility in designing a variety of courses. For example, courses might be designed that follow the organization of the book and concentrate on selected problems, but it is also feasible to design a course by picking readings chronologically and using the problems covered as examples of how historically important philosophers dealt with metaphysical topics. Or a course might begin with a contemporary reading dealing with a popular topic like free will and then work backward, showing how the topic requires exploring theories of mind and time. Also, the variety of selections, and the relatedness of articles in different sections, should make the book useful in courses having a special focus, for example, philosophy of mind courses or seminars on free will or the nature of persons.

All the readings are from the Western philosophical tradition; many represent an analytic perspective, and many take seriously the metaphysical implications of advancing science. Selections by Augustine, Bergson, Hegel, and Heidegger, however, indicate other directions of metaphysical inquiry. To include other traditions or to explore very different idioms, and to do it well, would have required a much bigger book. There is no section devoted to the existence of God, a popular metaphysical topic. A number of good anthologies already cover this large subject, which is usually the main topic for philosophy of religion courses. Theological issues do surface, however, in some of the selections that deal, for example, with time, mind, or freedom. We have not devoted whole sections to such important topics as universals, or meaning and reference, or scientific realism; instead, they are integrating themes that recur throughout.

We begin the book with time because we have had success beginning our metaphysics courses by introducing puzzles about the nature of time. Not only do students have a great interest in this topic, but it leads naturally (as it has in the history of metaphysics) to further questions; for example, to questions about identity and freedom.

We would like to acknowledge the comments of the following reviewers: David Berlinski, San Jose State University and Santa Clara University; Lewis Ford, Old Dominion University; Gary Gurtler, Loyola University of Chicago; Arthur Herman, University of Wisconsin, Stevens Point; Daniel Kolak, William Paterson College; Bradford Petrie, Union College; and Steven L. Reynolds, Arizona State University.

R.C.H.
L.N.O.

Metaphysics

Classic and Contemporary Readings

Introduction

Metaphysics is the study of the general character of reality. What are the fundamental kinds of things that exist? Is reality logical? What is the true nature of familiar things? For example, are persons really material bodies or souls or minds or some combination of these things? Such questions are fascinating, but their boldness can be intimidating. And the diversity of exotic answers that philosophers have proposed can make one dizzy. This anthology focuses on five metaphysical topics that have natural interest to students: (1) What is time? (2) How can things change yet be the same—in particular, what constitutes the identity of a person? (3) What is the nature of mind? (4) If the structure of the world is fixed or determined, can people be free? (5) Can one know reality? These questions have been debated since the beginning of philosophy. Studying the diversity of answers that philosophers have proposed can enrich one's life by putting ordinary things in new perspectives. Hopefully, it will also show that philosophers have made some progress understanding reality.

Though everyone has probably wondered about metaphysical issues at some point, the study of metaphysics is bound to seem somewhat alien when compared with other subjects. Compare metaphysics with a familiar study, say, the study of rocks. Geologists ask, among other questions, What kinds of rocks exist? As they go about the business of classifying rocks, they can usually take it for granted they have working agreement about what counts as a rock. Philosophers would like to know, in most general terms, what kinds of things are real, but they do not always share working agreement about what counts as real. Instead of first agreeing about the criteria for reality and then looking to see what satisfies the criteria, philosophers spend much of their time proposing and debating different criteria. Thus, metaphysical theories can seem bewilderingly different from each other and difficult to evaluate.

To see how quickly metaphysical disagreements can escalate, consider the implications of endorsing the following two innocent-looking criteria for reality. Suppose one decides that for something to count as real it must be observable and have some definite location in space and time. Such things as individual rocks, trees, and birds meet these criteria, but what about abstract or ideal entities like numbers or justice? On reflection, most people will agree the square root of two, for example, cannot be seen and has no definite spatiotemporal location (though instances of its name can be seen and located). Should one conclude the square root of two does not exist? Similarly, though one might claim to be able to see people who are just, can one see justice itself, and, does it have a definite location? Some philosophers (for example, Plato) have denied justice can be seen or located in space and time, yet they have claimed since justice (like numbers) can be thought about and known, it must exist. An-

other example of something threatened by these innocent-looking criteria is God. God is often thought to be unobservable and to exist, somehow, beyond space and time. So would one's agreement with these criteria for reality (observability and spatiotemporal location) force one to deny the reality of God along with numbers and justice? If, however, one has good reasons for believing such things are real, then one should attack these criteria and propose some alternatives.

Suppose, on the other hand, you consider yourself to have a tough scientific temperament, and you are willing to hold onto the criteria and to deny the reality of numbers, justice, and God. Then you may still have cause to worry. You probably believe everyday objects are real and consist of matter. But physicists now explain matter in terms of strange subatomic things like quarks, virtual particles, or "superstrings." Many physicists claim these things are not observable and have no definite location. Are you then forced to deny the reality of these entities? Again, many scientists would answer affirmatively, saying the objects of quantum physics are merely parts of models, not much better than fictions that are useful only for making predictions. But if everyday material objects are not really, at their core, swarming clouds of subatomic particles, what are they?

After being introduced to puzzles about numbers, God, and theoretical scientific entities, it is tempting to try to take refuge in the reality of familiar, ordinary objects just as they appear. Surely, tables and trees are real; surely persons exist. It is an important historical fact, however, that metaphysics began in ancient Greece when people started asking simple but probing questions about ordinary things. For example, familiar things can change and yet still seem to be the same thing. But how can the *very same* thing have different, incompatible properties? Doesn't this involve a contradiction, and isn't being noncontradictory a minimum criterion for reality? Or can reality be contradictory? To avoid this problem, should one abandon the idea that self-identical things can endure change? (After all, are you *really* the same thing that had your name and social security number five years ago?) Or should one try to find some new view of things, change, and identity?

The early Greek philosophers were aware that ordinary objects present different appearances to different people. How are the different appearances of a table related to the table itself—to the *real* table? Once the distinction is made between appearance and reality, it is tempting to try to solve metaphysical puzzles by claiming they have their source in mistaking appearance for reality. In their different ways, thinkers like Parmenides, Zeno, and Plato used puzzles about change and identity to argue that the ordinary world of changing things is *mere* appearance. This is a disturbing conclusion, however, if you want to take refuge from questions about numbers, quarks, and God by holding fast to the reality of the ordinary world of perceived objects. So, one should not be too confident that even *that* world is real until one answers the challenges of those philosophers who maintain it is mere appearance.

Much of the history of metaphysics is the history of philosophers' claiming to find defects in some view of reality or claiming to find a new view that diagnoses and fixes the defects of earlier views. Often, the new theories are radical and fantastic. Imagine reality being entirely spiritual, consisting of an infinity of souls reflecting each other (a simplification of Leibniz's view). Or, imagine reality consisting only of dumb material atoms careening in the void (the view of some ancient and modern materialists). To read the history of metaphysics is to take a challenging journey, a journey where one is tempted to follow different ideas in different directions, and where each one offers some logic, some reason, to go in that direction.

The diversity of metaphysical theories may be entertaining, but it also can be confusing and disconcerting. How can intelligent people come to such different conclusions? How can each one be so sure his or her theory is correct? Why, after over 2,000 years of argumentation, does there appear to be so little agreement about which metaphysics is true?

Skepticism about metaphysics is itself a recurrent metaphysical theme, and it is usually accompanied by some analysis of the nature and limits of human knowledge. In the eighteenth century, for example, David Hume argued that all legitimate ideas must be analyzed in terms of sensations. He claimed that such metaphysical notions as ideas of causality and enduring substance could not be adequately grounded in experience. Skeptical critiques of metaphysics, however, eventually express or presuppose metaphysical theses of their own. Hume, for example, believed in the reality of sensations as inner, immediate objects of experience. Some later philosophers will try to understand perceptual experience without reifying sensations as inner objects, thereby denying the picture of consciousness on which Hume based his skepticism.

Closer to the present, early twentieth-century philosophers became skeptical about metaphysics for several reasons. First, some nineteenth-century metaphysics had become very flamboyant in maneuvering to try to sidestep skepticism. Hegel, for example, seemed to suggest reality is a mind evolving by having a contradictory dialogue with itself! Second, physics was undergoing a revolution in which the theory of relativity and quantum mechanics were radically altering the familiar mechanical view of the world, and these new theories were often advertized as being superior because they made fewer false or unverifiable metaphysical assumptions than did the old physics. Many philosophers became leery of taking either metaphysics or physics too literally, and they thought they might be able to use new tools invented in logic and semantics to explain how metaphysical thinking is often the result of some misuse of language. But here, too, skepticism was infected with metaphysical issues of its own. What kind of entities are meanings? How can the mind grasp them? To what kinds of objects do they refer? Philosophers continued to debate what is real, though their idiom became increasingly influenced by logical and linguistic concerns.

This book will not treat very general questions about whether it is possible to know what is real until the final section. And it will not survey chronologically the grand metaphysical systems that individual philosophers have constructed to try to solve all metaphysical problems. Instead, its strategy is to have the reader work through four specific topics—time, identity, mind, and freedom—seeing how earlier and contemporary philosophers have attempted to deal with them. Not only will this approach help one decide whether progress has been made in understanding these important topics, but also it will give the reader the opportunity to evaluate different philosophical perspectives by seeing them in action. Several themes will recur, for example, the influence of changing scientific beliefs on metaphysics and the tension between one's ordinary experience and theoretical views of reality. It will also become clear why a position on one subject, say the nature of mind, may lead naturally to a position on another subject, for example, freedom. After wrestling with these particular topics, the reader will be able to appreciate better the general reflections on metaphysics contained in Part V.

Part I

Time

Probably every reflective person has been struck by the importance of time and by its ellusive, puzzling character. People see time as important because their hopes and fears concern the coming and going of events they enjoy or dread. Birthdays celebrate years of growth and success, but they also mark one's approach to death. Since so much that is vital is ruled by time, one is bound to wonder what kind of sovereign it is. Myth and poetry occasionally personify time. The Hindu god Vishnu declared, "Know that I am time, that makes the worlds to perish, when ripe, and come to bring destruction." And in the West, the familiar figure of Father Time is thought to be a renaissance combination of Cronus (the reaper god who, in Greek myth, castrates his father), and Death. In some religions, people hope to escape time by trying to deny the importance of the transient events of life. Others use science and technology to wrestle with time, trying to win more free time and longer lives. But whether one battles, embraces, or flees time, one thereby acknowledges its significance.

When one wonders about time, each

question asked seems to lead to others. How should one interpret the question What is time? Should time be treated as an entity whose parts are the past, present, and future? But what are these parts? The past and future do not exist now, so what kind of entity is it that appears to consist largely of what does not exist now? Is time not a thing at all, but rather some kind of "movement," "flow," or "passage"? But movement seems to occur *in time*, so what is clarified by saying time itself is movement?

When early philosophers asked such questions about time, they not only found them very difficult to answer, but they also discovered their confusion spread to different topics. Time has something to do with change, but how can anything change? How can something be one way at one time and some other way at another time, yet still be the *same* thing? Thus, questions about the nature of time can lead to questions about the nature of change and identity. Here is another example. People frequently talk about future events, and presumably some of what is said about future events is true. Does this mean future events must have some kind of reality? And if future events are real, does this mean the future is fixed or "fated"? Therefore, questions about the nature of time can lead to questions about truth and about the freedom of actions.

Puzzles about time are central to metaphysics not only because they generate and are involved in additional philosophical problems, but also because their difficulty has called into question the whole philosophical project of trying to understand reality. Is the nature of time so problematic that any attempt to understand it leads to paradoxes—to contradictions? Some philosophers have come to this conclusion, and they have been then faced with a difficult choice: either time is real and our reason is incapable of compre-

hending an irrational world, or, if reality must conform to reason and logic, then time cannot be real. Important philosophers such as Parmenides, Plato, Kant, McTaggart, and Bergson wrestled with this dilemma, and all were driven to the conclusion that reality must be quite different from how we ordinarily think of it. Thus, the puzzling nature of time has repeatedly forced philosophers to deal with such bold and disturbing claims as "time is not real," and "there must be something drastically wrong with our ways of thinking." These general, skeptical challenges provide further motivation for philosophers to formulate a coherent metaphysics of time.

The study of time can take one in several different directions. The readings in Part I have been selected because they deal with central, perennial issues in the philosophy of time, and because they will be useful in motivating and understanding some of the other problems covered in this anthology. The articles in Part I concern two themes: (1) Is time real? (2) Should time be understood in terms of the passage of the present, or should time be viewed as a series of events standing in earlier-than and later-than relations? The first issue challenges one to formulate nonparadoxical accounts of change and identity. The second theme forces one to clarify the metaphysical status (the kind of reality) of the past and the future. It also has implications for analyses of change and identity, and it leads to further questions about truth and freedom.

Part I begins with the startling arguments of Parmenides and Zeno, according to whom time and motion are not real. Aristotle responded to this challenge, and his selection is a painstaking analysis of time that defends its reality. In the following article, Augustine is led to wonder about time by theological difficulties. But he, too, worries about the paradoxical character of time, and he is not content with Artistotle's analysis. Augustine hints that time has an important subjective aspect when he suggests it is some kind of "protraction" of mind. For Isaac Newton, on the other hand, time is the absolute flux of the present as it is represented by the true equations of mathematical physics. It is independent of both changing things and mind.

The remainder of the readings in Part I were originally published in the twentieth century. Bergson complains that logic and mathematics distort the true character of time, which he believes can be revealed in intuitive experience to be a *sui generis* flux of becoming (or the moving Now). McTaggart also worries that becoming does not obey logic, but he concludes that time, therefore, is not real.

Donald C. Williams argues that becoming is merely subjective—it is just the perspective from which consciousness views the four-dimensional world pictured by modern physics. D. Hugh Mellor continues to attack the alleged special metaphysical status of the moving present by arguing that only tenseless earlier-than and later-than statements are needed to describe time and change.

After studying Part I, the reader will appreciate how theories of time become intertwined with other philosophical topics and why there are many questions left to explore. For example, What gives time its apparent direction? What is the relation between temporal and timeless things (if any)? How are people able to apprehend durations?

1. *Being Is Not Temporal*

PARMENIDES

Parmenides of Elea lived during the dawn of Greek philosophy. Born about 515 B.C., he flourished in the generation before Socrates. He is given credit for focusing attention on the general question What is the nature of real being? Previous Presocratic thinkers had begun to break with the anthropomorphic explanation characteristic of early religions. Instead of being content to view the world in terms of the activities of human-like spiritual agencies, the Greek cosmologists had begun to speculate that the world might be intelligible in terms of generalizations like "everything is water" or "everything is fire." Parmenides did more than just debate or add to these theories. He purported to use only logic to argue for the startling view that reality is unchanging, undivided being—reality is One. Parmenides claimed to find something contradictory (and therefore impossible) in saying what exists is a created, changing, or diverse plurality of things.

Though Parmenides is not primarily concerned with the nature of time, it is appropriate to begin this section and this anthology with his writing. For in claiming reality has no beginning or end and does not change, he is denying that familiar temporal distinctions apply to it—in other words, time is not real. This implies that our familiar temporal world is an appearance or illusion. But do not appearances and illusions have some kind of reality? Is Parmenides' logic mistaken? Are there alternative strategies for analyzing time and change? Or should one conclude time is real, but not rational (or logical)? In this way, Parmenides' bold logic and implausible conclusion generated many of the metaphysical questions that concerned later philosophers.

Parmenides' metaphysics was expressed in a poem, fragments of which have survived and are reprinted here. In the poem, a goddess distinguishes the way of appearances from the way of truth, and she shows how the way of truth leads to the One. Readers should be aware that there are rival interpretations of the poem that are still debated by scholars.

The mares that draw me wherever my heart would go escorted me, when the goddesses who were driving set me on the renowned road that leads through all cities the man who knows. Along this I was borne; for along it the wise horses drew at full stretch the chariot, and maidens led the way.

The axle, urged round by the whirling wheels at either end, shrilled in its sockets and glowed, as the daughters of the sun, leaving the house of night and pushing the veils from their heads with their hands, hastened to escort me towards the light.

There are the gates of the ways of night and day, enclosed by a lintel and a threshold of stone; and these, high in the ether, are fitted with great doors, and avenging Justice holds the keys which control these ways. The maidens entreated her with gentle words, and wisely persuaded her to

From *An Introduction to Early Greek Philosophy* by John Mansley Robinson, trans. Copyright © 1968 by Houghton Mifflin. Reprinted by permission of the publisher.

thrust back quickly the bolts of the gate. The leaves of the door, swinging back, made a yawning gap as the brazen pins on either side turned in their sockets. Straight through them, along the broad way, the maidens guided mares and chariot; and the goddess received me kindly, and taking my right hand in hers spoke these words to me:

"Welcome, youth, who come attended by immortal charioteers and mares which bear you on your journey to our dwelling. For it is no evil fate that has set you to travel on this road, far from the beaten paths of men, but right and justice. It is meet that you learn all things—both the unshakable heart of well-rounded truth and the opinions of mortals in which there is no true belief. But these, too, you must learn completely, seeing that appearances have to be acceptable, since they pervade everything."

Come now, and I will tell you (and you, when you have heard my speech shall bear it away with you) the ways of inquiry which alone exist for thought. The one is the way of how it is, and how it is not possible for it not to be; this is the way of persuasion, for it attends Truth. The other is the way of how it is not, and how it is necessary for it not to be; this, I tell you, is a way wholly unknowable. For you could not know what is not—that is impossible—nor could you express it.

For thought and being are the same.

Thinking and the thought that it is are the same; for you will not find thought apart from what is, in relation to which it is uttered.

It is necessary to speak and to think what is; for being is, but nothing is not. These things I bid you consider. For I hold you back from this first way of inquiry; but also from that way on which mortals knowing nothing wander, of two minds. For helplessness guides the wandering thought in their breasts; they are carried along deaf and blind alike, dazed, beasts without judgment, convinced that to be and not to be are the same and not the same, and that the road of all things is a backward-turning one.

For never shall this prevail: that things that are not, are. But hold back your thought from this way of inquiry, nor let habit born of long experience force you to ply an aimless eye and droning ear along this road; but judge by reasoning the much-contested argument that I have spoken.

One way remains to be spoken of: the way how it is. Along this road there are very many indications that what is is unbegotten and imperishable; for it is whole and immovable and complete. Nor was it at any time, nor will it be, since it is now, all at once, one and continuous.

For what begetting of it would you search for? How and whence did it grow? I shall not let you say or think "from what is not"; for it is not possible either to say or to think how it is not. Again, what need would have driven it, if it began from nothing, to grow later rather than sooner? Thus it must exist fully or not at all. Nor will the force of conviction ever allow anything over and above itself to arise out of what is not; wherefore Justice does not loosen her fetters so as to allow it to come into being or pass away, but holds it fast.

Concerning these things the decision lies here: either it is, or it is not. But it has been decided, as was necessary, that the one way is unknowable and unnamable (for it is no true road) and that the other is real and true. How could what is perish? How could it have come to be? For if it came into being, it is not; nor is it if ever it is going to be. Thus coming into being is extinguished, and destruction unknown.

Nor is it divisible, since it is all alike; nor is there any more or less of it in one place which might prevent it from holding together, but all is full of what is.

Look steadfastly at those things which, though absent, are firmly present to the mind. For it cannot cut off what is from clinging to what is, either scattering it in every direction in order or bringing it together.

But motionless in the limits of mighty bonds, it is without beginning or end, since coming into being and passing away have been driven far off, cast out by true belief. Remaining the same, and in the same place, it lies in itself, and so abides firmly where it is. For strong Necessity holds it in the bonds of the limit which shuts it in on every side, because it is not right for what is to be incomplete. For it is not in need of anything, but not-being would stand in need of everything.

But since there is a furthest limit, it is complete on every side, like the body of a well-rounded sphere, evenly balanced in every direction from the middle; for it cannot be any greater or any less in one place than in another. For neither is there what is not, which would stop it from reaching its like, nor could what is possibly be more in one place and less than another, since it is all inviolable. For being equal to itself in every direction it nevertheless meets with its limits.

For there is not, nor will there be, anything other than what is, since indeed Destiny has fettered it to remain whole and immovable. Therefore those things which mortals have established, believing them to be true, will be mere names: "coming into being and passing away," "being and not-being," "change of place and alteration of bright color."

It is all one to me where I begin, for I shall come back there again.

Here I end my trustworthy account and thought concerning truth. Learn henceforth the beliefs of mortals, harkening to the deceitful ordering of my words. For they have made up their minds to name two forms, one of which it is not right to name—here is where they have gone astray—and have distinguished them as opposite in bodily form and have assigned to them marks distinguishing them from one another: to one ethereal flame of fire, which is gentle, very light, the same with itself in every direction but not the same with the other. That other too, in itself, is opposite: dark night, dense in bodily form and heavy. The whole arrangement of these I tell to you as it seems likely, so that no thought of mortals shall ever outstrip you.

You shall know the nature of the ether and all the signs in the ether, and the unseen works of the pure torch of the bright sun and whence they came into being. And you shall know the wandering works of the round-faced moon and its nature, and you shall know, too, the heaven which surrounds all, whence it grew, and how Necessity, guiding it, fettered it to keep the limits of the stars.

[And you shall learn] how sun and moon, the ether which is common to all, the Milky Way and outermost Olympos, and the burning might of the stars, began to arise.

But now that all things have been named light and night, and their powers have been assigned to each, everything is full at once of light and obscure night, both equally, since neither has a share in nothingness.

The narrower rings are filled with unmixed fire, those next to them with night; and into the midst of these a portion of fire is discharged. In the middle of these is the goddess who steers all things; for she is the beginner of all hateful birth and all begetting, sending the female to mix with the male and the male in turn to the female.

First of all the gods she devised Eros.

For as at any time the mixture of their much-wandering limbs is, so thought comes to men. For to all men and to each the nature of the bodily frame is the same as that which it thinks. For what predominates in it is the thought.

2. A *Contemporary Exposition of Zeno's Paradoxes*

WESLEY C. SALMON

Zeno of Elea was one of Parmenides' students. He defended the view that reality is a changeless One by devising additional arguments trying to show that to believe otherwise is to have beliefs infected with paradox. So, if it is hard to believe reality is changeless, it also should be difficult to believe it changes (at least, after reading Zeno's arguments). Although directly concerned with attacking motion, the arguments can be viewed as attacking change in general by attacking a simple case of change, namely, change of location in time. The paradoxes are pertinent to the study of time not merely because they were used to defend the thesis that reality is not temporal, but also because in attempting to resolve them philosophers have been forced to carefully analyze and develop their views of time. For example, the Dichotomy Paradox forces one to wonder whether a duration can consist of an infinite sequence of events, and the Arrow Paradox forces one to wonder about the character of the present. Is the Now momentary? If so, how does change occur? If, on the other hand, it is not momentary, how can the present consist of events some of which are *not* simultaneous?

Knowledge of Zeno's paradoxes derives from the comments of later philosophers, chiefly Aristotle. Reprinted here is a lucid contemporary exposition by Wesley Salmon, excerpted from his book *Space, Time, and Motion*. (Readers should consult Salmon's book for a discussion of mathematical resolutions of the paradoxes.) Salmon teaches at the University of Pittsburgh.

The intellectual heritage bequeathed to us by the ancient Greeks was rich indeed. The science of geometry and the entire course of Western philosophy, as we have noted, both had their beginnings with Thales. Both enjoyed fantastic development at the hands of his early successors, achieving a surprising degree of perfection during antiquity. During the same period, Aristotle provided the first systematic development of formal logic. But the fertile soil from which all of this grew also gave rise to a series of puzzles which have challenged successive generations of philosophers and scientists right down to the present. These are the famous paradoxes of Zeno of Elea who flourished about 500 B.C.

From *Space, Time, and Motion: A Philosophical Introduction* by Wesley C. Salmon. Copyright © 1980 by the University of Minnesota. Reprinted by permission of the University of Minnesota Press.

Zeno was a devoted disciple of the philosopher Parmenides, who had held that reality consisted of one undifferentiated, unchanging motionless whole which was devoid of any parts. Motion, change, and plurality were, according to him, mere illusions. Not too many philosophers could accept this view, and Parmenides was apparently the object of some ridicule from those who disagreed. Zeno's main purpose, it is reported, was to refute those who made fun of his master. His aim was to show that those who believed in motion, change, and plurality were involved in even greater absurdities. Out of perhaps forty such puzzles that he propounded, fewer than ten have come down to us, but they involve some very subtle difficulties. Since motion involves the occupation of different *places* at different *times*, these paradoxes strike at the heart of our concepts of space and time.

Bertrand Russell once remarked that "Zeno's arguments, in some form, have afforded grounds for almost all theories of space and time and infinity which have been constructed from his time to our own.'' This statement was made in 1914, in an essay which contains a penetrating analysis of the paradoxes, but as we shall see, there were problems inherent in these puzzles that escaped even Russell.

The following paradoxes fall into two main categories, paradoxes of *motion* and paradoxes of *plurality*. The paradoxes of motion are the more famous ones, and I shall begin with them.

The Paradoxes of Motion

Our knowledge of the paradoxes of motion comes from Aristotle who, in the course of his discussions, offers a paraphrase of each. Zeno's original formulations have not survived.

1. *Achilles and the Tortoise.* Imagine that Achilles, the fleetest of Greek warriors, is to run a footrace against a tortoise. It is only fair to give the tortoise a head start. Under these circumstances, Zeno argues, Achilles can never catch up with the tortoise, no matter how fast he runs. In order to overtake the tortoise, Achilles must run from his starting point A to the tortoise's original starting point T_0 (see Figure 1). While he is doing that, the tortoise will have moved ahead to T_1. Now Achilles must reach the point T_1. While Achilles is covering this new distance, the tortoise moves still farther to T_2.

Figure 1

Again, Achilles must reach this new position of the tortoise. And so it continues: whenever Achilles arrives at a point where the tortoise *was*, the tortoise has already moved a bit ahead. Achilles can narrow the gap, but he can never actually catch up with him. This is the most famous of all of Zeno's paradoxes. It is sometimes known simply as ''The Achilles.''

2. *The Dichotomy.* This paradox comes in two forms, progressive and regressive. According to the first, Achilles cannot get to the end of any racecourse, tortoise or no tortoise; indeed, he cannot even reach the original starting point T_0 of the tortoise in the previous paradox. Zeno argues as follows. Before the runner can cover the whole distance he must cover the first half of it (see Figure 2).

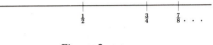

Figure 2

Then he must cover the first half of the remaining distance, and so on. In other words, he must first run one-half, then an additional one-fourth, then an additional one-eighth, etc., always remaining somewhere short of his goal. Hence, Zeno concludes, he can never reach it. This is the progressive form of the paradox, and it has very nearly the same force as Achilles and the Tortoise, the only difference being that in the Dichotomy the goal is stationary, while in Achilles and the Tortoise it moves, but at a speed much less than that of Achilles.

The regressive form of the Dichotomy attempts to show, worse yet, that the runner cannot even get started. Before he can complete the full distance, he must run half of it (see Figure 3). But before he can complete the first half, he must run half of that, namely, the first quarter.

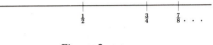

Figure 3

Before he can complete the first quarter, he must run the first eighth. And so on. In order to cover any distance no matter how short, Zeno concludes, the runner must already have completed an infinite number of runs. Since the sequence of runs he must already have completed has the form of a regression,

$$\ldots \cdot \tfrac{1}{16}, \tfrac{1}{8}, \tfrac{1}{4}, \tfrac{1}{2}$$

it has no first member, and hence, the runner cannot even get started.

3. *The Arrow.* In this paradox, Zeno argues that an arrow in flight is always at rest. At any given instant, he claims, the arrow is where it is, occupying a portion of space equal to itself. During the instant it cannot move, for that would require the instant to have parts, and an instant is by definition a minimal and indivisible element of time. If the arrow did move during the instant it would have to be in one place at one part of the instant, and in a different place at another part of the instant. Moreover, for the arrow to move during the instant would require that during the instant it must occupy a space larger than itself, for otherwise it has no room to move. As Russell says, "It is never moving, but in some miraculous way the change of position has to occur *between* the instants, that is to say, not at any time whatever." This paradox is more difficult to understand than Achilles and the Tortoise or either form of the Dichotomy, but another remark by Russell is apt: "The more the difficulty is meditated, the more real it becomes."

4. *The Stadium.* Consider three rows of objects A, B, and C, arranged as in the first position of Figure 4. Then, while row A remains at rest, imagine rows B and C moving in opposite directions until all three rows are lined up as shown in the second position. In the process, C_1 passes twice as many B's as A's; it lines up with the first A to its left, but with the second B to its left. According to

First Position

		A_1	A_2	A_3
B_1	B_2	B_3		
		C_1	C_2	C_3

Second Position

	A_1	A_2	A_3
	B_1	B_2	B_3
	C_1	C_2	C_3

Figure 4

Aristotle, Zeno concluded that "double the time is equal to half."

Some such conclusion would be warranted if we assume that the time it takes for a C to pass to the next B is the same as the time it takes to pass to the next A, but this assumption seems patently false. It appears that Zeno had no appreciation of relative speed, assuming that the speed of C relative to B is the same as the speed of C relative to A. If that were the only foundation for the paradox we would have no reason to be interested in it, except perhaps as a historical curiosity. It turns out, however, that there is an interpretation of this paradox which gives it serious import.

Suppose, as people occasionally do, that space and time are atomistic in character, being composed of space-atoms and time-atoms of non-zero size, rather than being composed of points and instants whose size is zero. Under these circumstances, motion would consist in taking up different discrete locations at different discrete instants. Now, if we suppose that the A's are not moving, but the B's move to the right at the rate of one place per instant while the C's move to the left at the same speed, some of the C's get past some of the B's without ever passing them. C_1 begins at the right of B_2 and it ends up at the left of B_2, but there is no instance at which it lines up with B_2; consequently, there is no time at which they pass each other—it never happens.

It has been suggested that Zeno's arguments fit into an overall pattern. Achilles and the Tortoise and the Dichotomy are designed to refute the doctrine that space and time are continuous, while the Arrow and the Stadium are intended to refute the view that space and time have an atomic structure. The paradox of plurality, which will be discussed later, also fits into the total schema. Thus, it has been argued, Zeno tries to cut off all possible avenues to escape from the conclusion that space, time, and motion are not real but illusory.

3. *Time Is a Measure of Change*

ARISTOTLE

Parmenides' view that the temporal world is not real had an influence on the two grandest metaphysical systems of ancient Greek philosophy, Plato's and Aristotle's. Plato basically agreed with Parmenides that real entities should be immune to puzzles surrounding time and change, and he claimed that only changeless, atemporal Forms (that is, ideal universals like circularity and justice) qualify as fully real objects. The ordinary particular things we perceive are only fleeting and imperfect instances of Forms. In this concession to Parmenides, Plato did not try to make time itself intelligible by developing a theory of time, though he did develop a picture of change according to which particulars "participate" in different Forms. Plato was content to poetically describe time as a (mere) moving image of eternity. (See his dialogue, *Timaeus* for remarks about time. Plato's *Phaedo* is reprinted in Part II; there Plato deals with the nature of change and the soul and claims that Forms cannot change).

In opposition to Plato (his teacher), Aristotle (384–322 B.C.) did not believe Forms existed separately from changing particulars. For him, ordinary objects (what he called "substances") were basic realities, and he tried to formulate a coherent account of change that did not cast doubt on their reality. As part of this effort, Aristotle wrestled with a variety of puzzles concerning time. What emerged was what might be viewed as the first relational theory of time. According to Aristotle, time is a measure (a way of numbering) change; so understanding time is a matter of understanding, in a particular way, how different states of substances are related. The selection reprinted here is from his *Physics*. Though Aristotle may have been trying to safeguard the world of common sense from views like Parmenides' and Plato's, his analyses are often technical and his writing style is compressed. It is believed that most of his surviving writings are not polished expositions, but rather notes for lectures. Readers should not be discouraged if they find this selection difficult.

Chapter 10

After what has been said, the next thing is to inquire into time. First, it is well to go through the problems about it, using the untechnical argu-

From *Aristotle's Physics, Book IV*, Edward Hussey, trans. Copyright © 1983 by Oxford University Press. Reprinted by permission of Oxford University Press.

ments as well [as technical ones]: whether it is among things that are or things that are not, and then what its nature is.

That it either is not at all or [only] scarcely and dimly is, might be suspected from the following considerations. (1) Some of it has been and is not, some of it is to be and is not yet. From these both infinite time and any arbitrary time are composed. But it would seem to be impossible that what is composed of things that are not should participate in being. (2) Further, it is necessary that, of everything that is resoluble into parts, if it is, either all the parts or some of them should be when it is. But of time, while it is resoluble into parts, some [parts] have been, some are to be, and none is. The now is not a part, for a part measures [the whole], and the whole must be composed of the parts, but time is not thought to be composed of nows. (3) Again, it is not easy to see whether the now, which appears to be the boundary between past and future, remains always one and the same or is different from time to time. (*a*) If it is always different, and if no two distinct parts of things that are in time are simultaneous—except those of which one includes the other, as the greater time includes the smaller—and if the now which is not but which previously was must have ceased to be at some time, then the nows too will not be simultaneous, and it must always be the case that the previous now has ceased-to-be. Now, that it has ceased-to-be in itself is not possible, because then it is; but it cannot be that the former now has ceased to be in another now, either. For we take it that it is impossible for the nows to be adjoining one another, as it is for a point to be adjoining a point; so, since the now has not ceased to be in the next now but in some other one, it will be simultaneously in the nows in between, which are infinitely many; but this is impossible. (*b*) Yet it is not possible either that the same now should always persist. For (*i*) nothing that is divisible and finite has [only] one limit, whether it is continuous in one direction or in more than one. But the now is a limit, and it is possible to take a finite time. Again (*ii*) if to be together in time and neither before or after, is to be in the one and the same now, and if both previous and subsequent [nows] are in this present now, then events of a thousand years ago will be simultaneous with those of today and none will be either previous or subsequent to any other.

Let this much, then, be our examination of difficulties about the properties of time. As to what time is and what its nature is, this is left equally unclear by the recorded opinions [of earlier thinkers] and by our own previous discussions. Some say it is the change of the universe, some the [celestial] sphere itself. Yet of the [celestial] revolution even a part is a time, though it is not a revolution. (The part considered is a part of a revolution, but not a revolution.) Again, if there were more than one world, time would equally be the change of any one whatever of them, so that there would be many times simultaneously. The sphere of the universe was thought to be time, by those who said it was, because everything is both in time and in the sphere of the universe; but this assertion is too simple-minded for us to consider the impossibilities it contains.

Since time is above all thought to be change, and a kind of alteration, this is what must be examined. Now the alteration and change of anything is only in the thing that is altering, or wherever the thing that is being changed and altering may chance to be; but time is equally everywhere and with everything. Again, alteration may be faster or slower, but not time; what is slow and what is fast is defined by time, fast being that which changes much in a short [time], slow that which changes little in a long [time]. But time is not defined by time, whether by its being so much or by its being of such a kind. It is manifest, then, that time is not change (let it make no difference to us, at present, whether we say 'change' or 'alteration').

Chapter 11

And yet [time is] not apart from alteration, either. When we ourselves do not alter in our mind or do not notice that we alter, then it does not seem to us that any time has passed, just as it does not seem so to the fabled sleepers in [the sanctuary of] the heroes in Sardinia, when they wake up; they join up the latter now to the former, and make it one, omitting what is in between because of failure to perceive it. So, just as, if the now were not different but one and the same, there would be no time, in the same way, even when the now *is* different but is not noticed to be different, what is in between does not seem to be any time. If, then, when we do not mark off any alteration, but the soul seems to remain in one indivisible, it happens as a consequence that we do not think there was any time, and if when we do perceive and mark off [an alteration], then we do say that some time has passed, then it is manifest that there is no time apart from change and alteration. It is manifest, then, that time neither is change nor is apart from change, and since we are looking for what time is we must start from this fact, and find what aspect of change it is. We perceive change and time together: even if it is dark and we are not acted upon through the body, but there is some change in the soul, it immediately seems to us that some time has passed together with the change. Moreover, whenever some time seems to have passed, some change seems to have occurred together with it. So that time is either change or some aspect of change; and since it is not change, it must be some aspect of change.

Now since what changes changes from something to something, and every magnitude is continuous, the change follows the magnitude: it is because the magnitude is continuous that the change is too. And it is because the change is that the time is. (For the time always seems to have been of the same amount as the change.)

Now the before and after is in place primarily; there, it is by convention. But since the before and after is in magnitude, it must also be in change, by analogy with what there is there. But in time, too, the before and after is present, because the one always follows the other of them. The before and after in change is, in respect of what makes it what it is, change; but its being is different and is not change.

But time, too, we become acquainted with when we mark off change, marking it off by the before and after, and we say that time has passed when we get a perception of the before and after in change. We mark off change by taking them to be different things, and some other thing between them; for whenever we conceive of the limits as other than the middle, and the soul says that the nows are two, one before and one after, then it is and this it is that we say time is. (What is marked off by the now is thought to be time: let this be taken as true.) So whenever we perceive the now as one, and not either as before and after in the change, or as the same but pertaining to something which is before and after, no time seems to have passed, because no change [seems to have occurred] either. But whenever [we do perceive] the before and after, then we speak of time.

For that is what time is: a number of change in respect of the before and after. So time is not change but in the way in which change has a number. An indication: we discern the greater and the less by number, and greater and less change by time; hence time is a kind of number. But number is [so called] in two ways: we call number both (*a*) that which is counted and countable, and (*b*) that by which we count. Time is that which is counted and not that by which we count. (That by which we count is different from that which is counted.)

Just as the change is always other and other, so the time is too, though the whole time in sum is the same. For the now is the same X, whatever X it may be which makes it what it is; but its being is not the same. It is the now that measures time, considered as before and after. The now is in a way the same, and in a way not the same: considered as being at different stages, it is different—that is what it is for it to be a now—but whatever it is that makes it a now is the same. For change follows magnitude, as was said, and time, we assert, follows change. As it is with the point, then, so it is with the moving thing, by which we become acquainted with change and the before and after in it. The moving thing is, in respect of what makes it what it is, the same (as the point is, so is a stone or something else of that sort); but in definition it is different, in the way in which the sophists assume that being Coriscus-in-the-Lyceum is different from being Coriscus-in-the-marketplace. That, then, is different by being in different places, and the now follows the moving thing as time does change. For it is by the moving thing that we become acquainted with the before and after in change, and the before and after, considered as countable, is the now. Here too, then, whatever it is that makes it the now is the same—it is the before and after in change. But its being is different: the now is the before and after, considered as countable. Moreover, it is this that is most familiar; for the change too is known by that which changes, and the motion by the moving thing, because the moving thing is a 'this,' but the change is not. So the now is in a way the same always, and in a way not the same, since the moving thing too [is so].

It is manifest too that, if time were not, the now would not be either, and if the now were not, time would not be. For just as the moving thing and the motion go together, so too do the number of the moving thing and the number of the motion. Time is the number of the motion, and the now is, as the moving thing is, like a unit of number.

Moreover, time is both continuous, by virtue of the now, and divided at the now—this too follows the motion and the moving thing. For the change and the motion too are one by virtue of the moving thing, because that is one (not [one] X, whatever X it may be that makes it what it is—for then it might leave a gap—but [one] in definition). And this bounds the change before and after. This too in a sense follows the point: the point, too, both makes the length continuous and bounds it, being the beginning of one and the end of another. But when one takes it in this way, treating the one [point] as two, one must come to a halt, if the same point is to be both beginning and end. But the now is always different, because the moving thing changes. Hence time is a number, not as [a number] of the same point, in that it is beginning and end, but rather in the way in which the extremes [are the number] of the line—and not as the parts [of the line] are, both because of what has been said (one will treat the middle point as two, so that there will be rest as a result), and further [because] it is manifest that the now is no portion of time, nor [is] the division [a portion] of the change, any more than the point is of the line (it is the two lines that are portions of the one). So, considered as a limit, the now is not time but is accidentally so, while, considered as counting, it is a number. (For limits are of that alone of which they are limits, but the number of these horses, the ten, is elsewhere too.)

It is manifest then that time is a number of change in respect of the before and after, and is continuous, for it is [a number] of what is continuous.

Chapter 12

The least number, without qualification, is the two; but [a least] particular number there in a way is and in a way is not, e.g., of a line, the number least in multiplicity is two lines or one line, but in magnitude there is no least number, for every line always gets divided. So it is, then, with time too: the least time in respect of number is one time or two times, but in respect of magnitude there is none.

It is manifest too that it is not said to be fast or slow, but is said to be much and little, and long and short. It is as being continuous that it is long and short, and as a number that it is much and little. But it is not fast or slow—nor indeed is any number by which we count fast or slow.

It is the same time, too, everywhere together, but before and after it is not the same [time], since the present alteration is one, but the past alteration and the future one are different, and time is not the number by which we count but the number which is counted, and this number turns out to be always different before and after, because the nows are different. (The number of a hundred horses and that of a hundred men is one and the same, but the things of which it is the number are different—the

horses are different from the men.) Again, in the sense in which it is possible for one and the same change to occur again and again, so too with time: e.g. a year, or spring or autumn.

Not only do we measure change by time, but time by change also, because they are defined by one another. The time defines the change, being its number, and the change the time. We speak of 'much time' and 'little time,' measuring it by change, just as we measure the number by what is countable: e.g. by the one horse we measure the number of the horses, for it is by number that we become acquainted with the multiplicity of the horses and, conversely, by the one horse that we become acquainted with the number of horses itself. Similarly, in the case of time and change, we measure the change by the time and the time by the change. It is reasonable that this should turn out so, because change follows magnitude, and time follows change, in being a quantity and continuous and divisible: for it is because the magnitude is of this kind that the change has these properties and because change is that time does. And we measure both magnitude by change and change by magnitude: we say the road is long, if the journey is long, and we say the journey is long, if the road is; and the time, if the change is, and the change, if the time is.

Since time is a measure of change and of being-in-change, and since it measures change by defining some change which will measure out the whole change (just as the cubit measures length by defining some magnitude which will measure off the whole magnitude), and since for a change the being in time is the being measured by time both of the change itself and of its being (time measures at once the change and the being of the change, and this is what it is, for the change, to be in time, viz. its being's being measured), it is clear, then, that for other things too this is what it is to be in time: their being's being measured by time. For to be in time is one or other of two things: *either*, to be when time is, *or*, [to be in it] in the way in which we say that some things are 'in number,' which means that [something is in number] *either* as a part or property of number, and, in general, that it is some aspect of number, *or* that there is a number of it. And since time is a number, the now and the before and everything of that kind are in time in the way in which the limit and the odd and the even are in number (they are aspects of number as the others are of time). But objects are [in time] as they are in number. If so, they are surrounded by time just as the things in number are by number and the things in place by place. It is manifest, too, that to be in time is not to be when time is, any more than to be in change or in place is to be when change is or place is. If this is what 'in something' is to mean, then all objects will be in anything whatever, and the world will be in the grain of millet, since when the grain is, the whole is too. This is accidentally so, but the other is a necessary consequence: for what is in time there must be some time when that too is, and for what is in change there must then be change.

Since what is in time is so as in a number, there will be found a time greater than anything that is in time, so that of necessity all things that are in time are surrounded by time, just like all other things that are in something: e.g. the things that are in place [are surrounded] by place. Moreover, they are acted upon in some respect by time, just as we are in the habit of saying 'time wears things away' and 'everything grows old through time' and 'forgets because of time'—but not 'learns because of time' or 'becomes young' or 'becomes beautiful.' For time, in itself, is responsible for ceasing-to-be rather [than for coming-to-be]; for it is the number of change, and change removes what is present. So it is manifest that the things that always are, considered as such, are not in time, for they are not surrounded by time, nor is their being measured by time, and an indication of this is that they are not acted on at all by time either, which shows that they are not in time.

And since time is the measure of change, it will be the measure of rest also. For all rest is in time; it is not the case that, as what is in change must change, so what is in time must, since time is not change but the number of change, and in the number of change there can also be that which is at rest. For it is not everything that is unchanging that is at rest, but that which, while deprived of change, has it in its nature to change, as was said earlier. For a thing to be in number is for there to be some number of the object, and for its being to be measured by the number in which it is, and so, if it is in time, by time. Time will measure what is changing and what is at rest, the one *qua* changing and the other *qua* at rest; for it will measure their change and their rest, [measuring] how great each is. Hence, what is changing is not measurable by time simply inasmuch as it is of some quantity, but inasmuch as its change is of some quantity. And so all that neither changes nor is at rest is not in time; for to be in time is to be measured by time, and time is a measure of change and rest.

It is manifest, therefore, that not everything that is not will be in time either; for example, all the things that cannot be otherwise [than not being], like the diagonal's being commensurate with the side. For in general, if time is a measure in itself of change and of other things accidentally, it is clear that all things of which it measures the being must have their being in being at rest or changing. Now all things that admit of ceasing-to-be and coming-to-be and, generally, that at some time are and at some time are not, must be in time—there will be some greater time which will exceed both their being and that [time] which measures their being. But, of things that are not, all that time surrounds either were (e.g. Homer once was) or will be (e.g. something future), on whichever side [of the present] it may surround them; and if on both sides, both. But all the things that it nowhere surrounds neither were nor are nor will be; and, among things that are not, such are all those that are such that their contraries always are: e.g. the diagonal's being incommensurable always is, and this will not be in time. So its being commensurable will not be [in time] either; so *that* always is not being opposite to what always is. But everything of which the opposite not always is, is capable of being and of not being, and there is coming-to-be of it and ceasing-to-be.

Chapter 13

The now is a link of time, as has been said, for it links together past and future time, and is a limit of time, since it is a beginning of one and an end of another. But this is not manifest, as it is in the case of the point at rest. It divides potentially, and *qua* such, the now is always different, but *qua* binding together it is always the same, just as in the case of mathematical lines: [a point is] not always the same point in thought, for if one divides the line it is different in different cases, but inasmuch as [the line] is one, [the point] is the same everywhere. So too the now is on the one hand a division of time, in potentiality, on the other hand the limit and union of both [times]; the division and the unification are the same thing and in respect of the same thing, but their being is not the same. This then is one sense of 'now'; another is when the time of a thing is close at hand: 'he will come now' because he will come today, 'he has now come,' because he came today. But it is not the case that the Trojan war has *now* occurred, or the deluge: the time *is* continuous [from now] to then, but they are not close at hand.

The 'at some time' is a time defined in relation to the now (in the former sense): e.g. 'Troy fell at some time,' 'the deluge will occur at some time'—the time must be finite in relation to the now. Therefore there will be a certain quantity of time from this to that, and there was [from this] to the past one. If there is no time which is not 'at some time,' every time will be finite. Will time then give out? Or not, if there always is change? Will it then be different, or the same many times over? It is clear that, as change is, so will time too be; if one and the same change comes to be at some time, the time too will be one and the same, and if not, not. Since the now is an end and a beginning of time, but not of the same time, being the end of past time and the beginning of future time, time will be like the circle—the convex and the concave are in what is in a sense the same—so too time is always at a beginning and at an end. And for this reason it is thought always different, for the now is not the beginning and the end of the same thing; otherwise opposites would hold simultaneously and in respect of the same thing. And so time will not give out, for it is always at a beginning.

The *just* is that which is close to the present indivisible now, whether it is a part of future time ('when are you taking a walk?' 'I'm just taking it'—because the time in which he is going to go is near) or of past time, when it is not far from the now ('when are you taking a walk?' 'I've just taken it'). But to say that Troy has just fallen—we do not say it, because that is too far from the now. The *recently* is the portion of the past which is close to the present now. ('When did you come?' 'Recently,' if the time is close to the actual now.) What is far away [from the now] is *long ago*. The *suddenly* is that which removes out of its previous state in a time which is so small as to be imperceptible.

It is in time that everything comes to be and ceases to be. For this reason some called it the wisest of things, but the Pythagorean Paron the most foolish, because people forget in time too; and he was more correct. It is clear, then, that it is, in itself, responsible for ceasing-to-be rather than for coming-to-be, as was stated earlier, because alteration, in itself, is productive of removal from a previous state—but it is, accidentally, responsible for coming-to-be and for being. A sufficient indication is that nothing comes to be without its being changed in some way and being acted upon, but a thing may cease to be even though it is not changed, and this is above all what we usually call ceasing-to-be by the agency of time. Yet even this is not produced by time, but it happens that this alteration too occurs in time.

It has now been stated that time is, and what it is, and in how many ways 'now' is said, and what 'at some time' and 'recently' and 'just' and 'long ago' and 'suddenly' are.

Chapter 14

Now that we have determined these matters in this way, it is manifest that every alteration and all that changes is in time. 'Faster' and 'slower' apply to every alteration, since in every case this is obviously true. (I say that changes faster which is earlier to alter into a given [state], changing over the same extension and with a uniform change (e.g. in the case of locomotion, if both things are changing along the curve or along the straight line, and in other cases similarly).) But the before is in time, for we use 'before' and 'after' according to the distance from the now, and the now is the boundary of the past and the future. So, since the nows are in time, the before and after will also be in time; for the distance from the now will be in that in which the now is. ('Before' is applied in opposite ways in relation to past time and to future time: in the past, we call 'before' what is further from the now, and 'after' what is nearer to it, but in the future we call 'before' what is nearer and 'after' what is further.) So, since the before is in time, and the before accompanies every change, it is manifest that every alteration and every change is in time.

It is also worth investigating how time is related to the soul, and for what reason it is that time is thought to be in everything—on earth and in the sea and in the heavens. Is it that it is a property or a state of change, being the number [of it], and all these things are changeable, since they are all in place, and time and change are together both in potentiality and in actual operation? One might find it a difficult question, whether if there were no soul there would be time or not. For if it is impossible that there should be something to do the counting, it is also impossible that anything should be countable, so that it is clear that there would be no number either, for number is either that which has been counted or that which can be. But if there is nothing that has it in its nature to count except soul, and of soul [the part which is] intellect, then it is impossible that there should be time if there is no soul, except that there could be that X which time is, whatever X makes it what it is; as for example if it is possible for there to be change without soul. The before and after are in change, and time is these *qua* countable.

One might also find it a difficult question: of what kind of change is time a number? Perhaps of any kind whatever? After all, [things] come to be and cease to be and increase in size and change qualitatively and move in time. So it is a number of each change, in as much as there is change. Hence it is, without qualification, a number of continuous change, not of a particular [kind of] change. But it is possible that now something else as well has been made to change: so it would be the number of either change. Is there then another time, and will there be two equal times together? Perhaps not, for the time which is equal and together is one and the same (and even those which are not together are the same in kind). Suppose there are some dogs and some horses, seven of each; the number is the same. In the same way, the time is the same of changes that reach a limit together, though one perhaps is fast and one not, one is locomotion and one a qualitative change. Still, the time is the same, if it is equal and together, of both the qualitative change and the locomotion. And this is why, while changes are various and in different places, time is everywhere the same, because the number, too, of things equal and together is one and the same everywhere.

Since there is locomotion, and, as a kind of locomotion, circular motion, and since each thing is counted by some one thing of the same kind (units by a unit, horses by a horse), and therefore time too by some definite time, and since, as we said, time is measured by change and change by time (that is, the quantity of the change and of the time is measured by the change defined by time)— if, then, that which is first is the measure of all things of the same sort, then uniform circular mo-

tion is most of all a measure, because the number of this is most easily known. (There is no uniform qualitative change or uniform increase in size or uniform coming-to-be, but there *is* uniform locomotion.) This is why time is thought to be the motion of the [celestial] sphere, because the other changes are measured by this one, and time by this change. And for this reason too, what is commonly said turns out true: people say that human affairs are a cycle, and so is what happens to the other things that have a natural motion and come to be and cease to be. This is so because all these things are discerned by means of time, and make an end and a beginning as if according to some circular course. Indeed, time itself is thought to be a kind of cycle, and this, in turn, is thought because it is the measure of what kind of motion and is itself measured by that kind. So that to say that those things that come to be are a cycle is to say that there is a kind of cycle of time; and this is so, because it is measured by circular motion. For, over and above the measure, nothing else is apparent which is obviously measured, but the whole is either one measure or more than one.

It is correct, too, to say that the number of the sheep and of the dogs is the same, if each number is equal, but that the ten is not the same [ten] nor [are there] ten of the same; just as the equilateral and the scalene are not the same triangles, though they are the same figure, in that both are triangles. For a thing is said to be the same X if it does not differ by the difference of an X, but not [the same X] if it does: e.g. a triangle differs from a triangle by the difference of a triangle, and therefore they are different triangles; but it does not [differ by the difference] of a figure, but the two are in one and the same division. For one kind of figure is a circle, another a triangle, and one kind of triangle is equilateral, another is scalene. So they are the same figure, namely a triangle, but not the same triangle. And so too it is the same number, since the number of them does not differ by the difference of a number, but not the same ten, since the things it is said of are different: dogs in one case, horses in another.

An account, then, has been given both of time itself and of the connected matters proper to our inquiry.

4. *What Is Time?*

ST. AUGUSTINE

Augustine (354–430) lived in North Africa, where he experienced the social transformations associated with the decline of the Roman Empire. He converted to Christianity in 386, became bishop of Hippo in 395, and died when the Vandals were attacking his city. Augustine worried about the nature of time in response to theological challenges. Christian doctrine had maintained that God created the world from nothing, but Manichaean objectors wondered what God was doing *before* creation and why the world was created at one time rather than another. For Augustine, the challenge was to answer these questions without making God subject to change (that is, without making God something less than eternally perfect). In dealing with these issues, he was led to consider additional problems. What kind of reality do the past and the future have? How can the future be known by God and the prophets unless it already exists? And, much as Zeno and Aristotle wondered, how can there be change in the present if the present is a moment that does not have earlier and later parts? Like Aristotle, Augustine maintained that time is not something prior to, or independent of, change; so he concluded there is no time "before" creation. Not being willing to identify time with the numbering of change, however, Augustine drew attention to the possibility that temporal distinctions are subjective when he suggested that time may be a "protraction" of mind.

Lo are they not full of their old leaven, who say to us, "What was God doing before *He made heaven and earth?*" "For if (say they) He were unemployed and wrought not, why does He not also hence-forth, and for ever, as He did heretofore? For did any new motion arise in God, and a new will to make a creature, which He had never before made, how then would that be a true eternity, where there ariseth a will, which was not? For the will of God is not a creature, but before the creature; see-ing nothing could be created, unless the will of the Creator had preceded. The will of God then be-longeth to His very Substance. And if aught have arisen in God's Substance, which before was not, that Substance cannot be truly called eternal. But if the will of God has been from eternity that the

From *Confessions*, St. Augustine, Book XI, sections X–XXXI, trans. E. B. Pusey. Copyright © 1948 by Regnery Gateway. Reprinted by permission of Regnery Gateway.

creature should be, why was not the creature also from eternity?"

Who speaks thus, do not yet understand Thee, O Wisdom of God, Light of souls, under-stand not yet how the things be made, which by Thee, and in Thee are made: yet they strive to comprehend things eternal, whilst their heart flut-tereth between the motions of things past and to come, and is still unstable. Who shall hold it, and fix it, that it be settled awhile, and awhile catch the glory of that ever-fixed Eternity, and compare it with the times which are never fixed, and see that it cannot be compared; and that a long time cannot become long, but out of many motions passing by, which cannot be prolonged altogether; but that in the Eternal nothing passeth, but the whole is present; whereas no time is all at once present: and that all time past, is driven on by time to come, and all to come followeth upon the past; and all past and to come, is created, and flows out of that which is ever present? Who shall hold the heart of man, that it may stand still, and see how eternity ever still-standing, neither past nor to come, uttereth the times past and to come? Can my hand do this, or the hand of my mouth by speech bring about a thing so great?

See, I answer him that asketh, "What did God before He *made heaven and earth?*" I answer not as one is said to have done merrily, (eluding the pressure of the question,) "He was preparing hell (saith he) for pryers into mysteries." It is one thing to answer enquiries, another to make sport of enquirers. So I answer not; for rather had I answer, "I know not," what I know not, than so as to raise a laugh at him who asketh deep things and gain praise for one who answereth false things. But I say that Thou, our God, art the Creator of every creature: and if by the name "heaven and earth," every creature be understood; I boldly say, "that before God made heaven and earth, He did not make any thing." For if He made, what did He make but a creature? And would I knew whatsoever I desire to know to my profit, as I know, that no creature was made, before there was made any creature.

But if any excursive brain rove over the images of forepassed times, and wonder that Thou the God Almighty and All-creating and All-supporting, Maker of heaven and earth, didst for innumerable ages forbear from so great a work, before Thou wouldest make it; let him awake and consider, that he wonders at false conceits. For whence could innumerable ages pass by, which Thou madest not, Thou the Author and Creator of all ages? or what times should there be, which were not made by Thee? or how should they pass by, if they never were? Seeing then Thou art the Creator of all times, if any time was before Thou *madest heaven and earth,* why say they that Thou didst forego working? For that very time didst Thou make, nor could times pass by, before Thou madest those times. But if before *heaven and earth* there was no time, why is it demanded, what Thou then didst? For there was no "then," when there was no time.

Nor dost Thou by time, precede time: else shouldest Thou not precede all times. But Thou precedest all things past, by the sublimity of an ever-present eternity; and surpassest all future because they are future, and when they come, they shall be past; *but Thou art the Same, and Thy years fail not.* Thy years neither come nor go; whereas ours both come and go, that they all may come. Thy years stand together, because they do stand; nor are departing thrust out by coming years, for they pass not away; but ours shall all be, when they shall no more be. Thy years are one day; and Thy day is not daily, but To-day, seeing Thy To-day gives not place unto to-morrow, for neither doth it replace yesterday. Thy To-day, is Eternity; therefore didst Thou beget The Coeternal, to whom Thou saidst, *This day have I begotten Thee.* Thou hast made all things; and before all times Thou art: neither in any time was time not.

At no time then hadst Thou not made any thing, because time itself Thou madest. And no times are coeternal with Thee, because Thou abidest; but if they abode, they should not be times. For what is time? Who can readily and briefly explain this? Who can even in thought comprehend it, so as to utter a word about it? But what in discourse do we mention more familiarly and knowingly, than time? And, we understand, when we speak of it; we understand also, when we hear it spoken of by another. What, then, is time? If no one asks me, I know: if I wish to explain it to one that asketh, I know not: yet I say boldly that I know, that if nothing passed away, time past were not; and if nothing were coming, a time to come were not; and if nothing were, time present were not. Those two times then, past and to come, how are they, seeing the past now is not, and that to come is not yet? But the present, should it always be present, and never pass into time past, verily it should not be time, but eternity. If time present (if it is to be time) only cometh into existence, because it passeth into time past, how can we say that either this is, whose cause of being is, that it shall not be; so, namely, that we cannot truly say that time is, but because it is tending not to be?

And yet we say, "a long time" and "a short time;" still, only of time past or to come. A long time past (for example) we call an hundred years since; and a long time to come, an hundred years hence. But a short time past, we call (suppose) ten days since; and a short time to come, ten days hence. But in what sense is that long or short, which is not? For the past, is not now; and the future, is not yet. Let us not then say, "it is long;" but of the past, "it hath been long;" and of the future, "it will be long." O my Lord, my Light, shall not here also Thy Truth mock at man? For that past time which was long, was it long when it was now past, or when it was yet present? For then might it be long, when there was, what could be long; but when past, it was no longer; wherefore neither could that be long, which was not at all. Let us not then say, "time past hath been long:" for we shall not find, what hath been long, seeing that since it was past, it is no more; but let us say, "that present time was long;" because, when it was present, it was long. For it had not yet passed away, so as not to be; and therefore there was, what could be long; but after it was past, that ceased also to be long, which ceased to be.

Let us see then, thou soul of man, whether present time can be long: for to thee it is given to feel and to measure length of time. What wilt thou answer me? Are an hundred years, when present, a long time? See first, whether an hundred years can be present. For if the first of these years be now current, it is present, but the other ninety and nine are to come, and therefore are not yet, but if the second year be current, one is now past, another present, the rest to come. And so if we assume any middle year of this hundred to be present, all before it, are past; all after it, to come; wherefore an hundred years cannot be present. But see at least whether that one which is now current, itself is present; for if the current month be its first, the rest are to come; if the second, the first is already past, and the rest are not yet. Therefore, neither is the year now current present; and if not present as a whole, then is not the year present. For twelve months are a year; of which whatever be the current month is present; the rest past, or to come. Although neither is that current month present; but one day only; the rest being to come, if it be the first; past, if the last; if any of the middle, then amid past and to come.

See how the present time, which alone we found could be called long, is abridged to the length scarce of one day. But let us examine that also; because neither is one day present as a whole. For it is made up of four and twenty hours of night and day: of which, the first hath the rest to come; the last hath them past; and any of the middle hath those before it past, those behind it to come. Yea, that one hour passeth away in flying particles. Whatsoever of it hath flown away, is past; whatsoever remaineth, is to come. If an instant of time be conceived, which cannot be divided into the smallest particles of moments, that alone is it, which may be called present. Which yet flies with such speed from future to past, as not to be lengthened out with the least stay. For if it be, it is divided into past and future. The present hath no space. Where then is the time, which we may call long? Is it to come? Of it we do not say, "it is long;" because

it is not yet, so as to be long; but we say, "it will be long." When therefore will it be? For if even then, when it is yet to come, it shall not be long, (because what can be long, as yet is not,) and so it shall then be long, when from future which as yet is not, it shall begin now to be, and have become present, that so there should exist what may be long; then does time present cry out in the words above, that it cannot be long.

And yet, Lord, we perceive intervals of times, and compare them, and say, some are shorter, and others longer. We measure also, how much longer or shorter this time is than that; and we answer, "This is double, or treble; and that, but once, or only just so much as that." But we measure times as they are passing, by perceiving them; but past, which now are not, or the future, which are not yet, who can measure? unless a man shall presume to say, that can be measured, which is not. When time is passing, it may be perceived and measured; but when it is past, it cannot, because it is not.

I ask, Father, I affirm not: O my God, rule and guide me. "Who will tell me that there are not three times, (as we learned when boys, and taught boys,) past, present, and future; but present only, because those two are not? Or are they also; and when from future it becometh present, doth it come out of some secret place; and so, when retiring, from present it becometh past? For where did they, who foretold things to come, see them, if as yet they be not? For that which is not, cannot be seen. And they who relate things past, could not relate them, if in mind they did not discern them, and if they were not, they could no way be discerned. Things then past and to come are."

Permit me, Lord, to seek further. O my hope, let not my purpose be confounded. For if times past and to come be, I would know where they be. Which yet if I cannot, yet I know, wherever they be, they are not there as future, or past, but present. For if there also they be future, they are not yet there; if there also they be past, they are no longer there. Wheresoever then is whatsoever is, it is only as present. Although when past facts are related, there are drawn out of the memory, not the things themselves which are past, but words which, conceived by the images of the things, they, in passing, have through the senses left as traces in the mind. Thus my childhood, which now is not, is in time past, which now is not: but now when I recall its image, and tell of it, I behold it in the present, because it is still in my memory. Whether there be a like cause of foretelling things to come also; that of things which as yet are not, the images may be perceived before, already existing, I confess, O my God, I know not. This indeed I know, that we generally think before on our future actions, and that that forethinking is present, but the action whereof we forethink is not yet, because it is to come. Which, when we have set upon, and have begun to do what we were forethinking, then shall that action be; because then it is no longer future, but present.

Which way soever then this secret fore-perceiving of things to come be; that only can be seen, which is. But what now is, is not future, but present. When then things to come are said to be seen, it is not themselves which as yet are not, (that is, which are to be,) but their causes perchance or signs are seen, which already are. Therefore they are not future but present to those who now see that, from which the future, being fore-conceived in the mind, is foretold. Which fore-conceptions again now are; and those who foretell those things, do behold the conceptions present before them. Let now the numerous variety of things furnish me some example. I behold the day-break, I foreshew, that the sun is about to rise. What I behold, is present; what I foresignify, to come; not the sun, which already is; but the sun-rising, which is not yet. And yet did I not in my mind imagine the sun-rising itself, (as now while I speak of it,) I could not foretell it. But neither is that daybreak which I discern in the sky, the sun-rising, although it goes before it; nor that imagination of my mind; which two are seen now present, that the other which is to be may be foretold. Future things then are not yet: and if they be not yet, they are not: and if they are not, they cannot be seen; yet foretold they may be from things present, which are already, and are seen.

Thou then, Ruler of Thy creation, by what way dost Thou teach souls things to come? For Thou didst teach Thy Prophets. By what way dost Thou, to whom nothing is to come, teach things to come, or rather of the future, dost teach things present? For, what is not, neither can it be taught. Too far is this way out of my ken: *it is too mighty for me, I cannot attain unto it*; but from Thee I can, when Thou shalt vouchsafe it, O sweet light of my hidden eyes.

What now is clear and plain is, that neither things to come nor past are. Nor is it properly said, "there be three times, past, present, and to come:" yet perchance it might be properly said, "there be three times; a present of things past, a present of things present, and a present of things future." For these three do exist in some sort, in the soul, but otherwhere do I not see them; present of things past, memory; present of things present, sight; present of things future, expectation. If thus we be permitted to speak, I see three times, and I confess there are three. Let it be said too, "there be three times, past, present, and to come:" in our incorrect way. See, I object not, nor gainsay, nor find fault, if what is so said be but understood, that neither what is to be, now is, nor what is past. For but few things are there, which we speak properly, most things improperly; still the things intended are understood.

I said then even now, we measure times as they pass, in order to be able to say, this time is twice so much as that one; or, this is just so much as that; and so of any other parts of time, which be measurable. Wherefore, as I said, we measure times as they pass. And if any should ask me, "How knowest thou?" I might answer, "I know, that we do measure, nor can we measure things that are not; and things past and to come, are not." But time present how do we measure, seeing it hath no space? It is measured while passing, but when it shall have passed, it is not measured; for there will be nothing to be measured. But whence, by what way, and whither passes it while it is a measuring? whence, but from the future? Which way, but through the present? whither, but into the past? From that therefore, which is not yet, through that, which hath no space, into that, which now is not. Yet what do we measure, if not time in some space? For we do not say, single, and double, and triple, and equal, or any other like way that we speak of time, except of spaces of times. In what space then do we measure time passing? In the future, whence it passeth through? But what is not yet, we measure not. Or in the present, by which it passes? but no space, we do not measure: or in the past, to which it passes? But neither do we measure that, which now is not.

My soul is on fire to know this most intricate enigma. Shut it not up, O Lord my God, good Father; through Christ I beseech Thee, do not shut up these usual, yet hidden things, from my desire, that it be hindered from piercing into them; but let them dawn through Thy enlightening mercy, O Lord. Whom shall I enquire of concerning these things? and to whom shall I more fruitfully confess my ignorance, than to Thee, to Whom these my studies, so vehemently kindled toward Thy Scriptures, are not troublesome? Give what I love; for I do love, and this hast Thou given me. Give, Father, Who *truly knowest to give good gifts unto Thy children.* Give, because I have taken upon me to know, and trouble is before me until Thou openest it. By Christ I beseech Thee, in His Name, Holy of holies, let no man disturb me. For *I believed, and therefore do I speak.* This is my hope, for this do I live, that *I may contemplate the delights of the Lord.* Behold, *Thou hast made my days* old, and they pass away, and how, I know not. And we talk of time, and time, and times, and times, "How long time is it since he said this;" "how long time since he did this;" and "how long time since I saw that;" and "this syllable hath double time to that single short syllable." These words we speak, and these we hear, and are understood, and understand. Most manifest and ordinary they are, and the self-same things again are but too deeply hidden, and the discovery of them were new.

I heard once from a learned man, that the motions of the sun, moon, and stars, constituted time, and I assented not. For why should not the motions of all bodies rather be times? Or, if the lights of heaven should cease, and a potter's wheel run round, should there be no time by which we might measure those whirlings, and say, that either it moved with equal pauses, or if it turned sometimes slower, otherwhiles quicker, that some rounds were longer, other shorter? Or, while we were saying this, should we not also be speaking in time? Or, should there in our words be some syllables short, others long, but because those sounded in a shorter time, these in a longer? God, grant to men to see in a small thing notices common to things great and small. The stars and lights of heaven, are also *for signs, and for seasons, and for years, and for days;* they are; yet neither should I say, that the going round of that wooden wheel was a day, nor yet he, that it was therefore no time.

I desire to know the force and nature of time, by which we measure the motions of bodies, and say (for example) this motion is twice as long as that. For I ask, seeing "day" denotes not the stay only of the sun upon the earth, (according to which day is one thing, night another;) but also its whole circuit from east to east again; according to which we say, "there passed so many days," the night being included when we say "so many days," and the nights not reckoned apart;—seeing then a day is completed by the motion of the sun and by his circuit from east to east again, I ask, does the motion alone make the day, or the stay in which that motion is completed, or both? For if the first be the day; then should we have a day, although the sun should finish that course in so small a space of time, as one hour comes to. If the second, then should not that make a day, if between one sunrise and another there were but so short a stay, as one hour comes to; but the sun must go four and twenty times about, to complete one day. If both, then neither could that be called a day, if the sun should run his whole round in the space of one hour; nor that, if, while the sun stood still, so much time should overpass, as the sun usually makes his whole course in, from morning to morning. I will not therefore now ask, what that is which is called day; but, what time is, whereby we, measuring the circuit of the sun, should say that it was finished in half the time it was wont, if so be it was finished in so small a space as twelve hours, and comparing both times, should call this a single time, that a double time; even supposing the sun to run his round from east to east, sometimes in that single, sometimes in that double time. Let no man then tell me, that the motions of the heavenly bodies constitute times, because, when at the prayer of one, the sun had stood still, till he could achieve his victorious battle, the sun stood still, but time went on. For in its own allotted space of time was that battle waged and ended. I perceive time then to be a certain extension. But do I perceive it, or seem to perceive it? Thou, Light and Truth, wilt shew me.

Dost Thou bid me assent, if any define time to be "motion of a body?" Thou dost not bid me. For that no body is moved, but in time, I hear; this Thou sayest; but that the motion of a body is time, I hear not; Thou sayest it not. For when a body is moved, I by time measure, how long it moveth, from the time it began to move, until it left off? And if I did not see whence it began; and it continue to move so that I see not when it ends, I cannot measure, save perchance from the time I began, until I cease to see. And if I took long, I can only pronounce it to be a long time, but not how long; because when we say "how long," we do it by comparison; as, "this is as long as that," or "twice so long as that," or the like. But when we can mark the distance of the places, whence and whither goeth the body moved, or his parts, if it moved as in a lathe, then can we say precisely, in how much time the motion of that body or his part, from this place unto that, was finished. Seeing therefore the motion of a body is one thing, that by which we measure how long it is, another; who sees not, which of the two is rather to be called time? For and if a body be sometimes moved, sometimes stands still, then we measure, not his motion only, but his standing still too by time; and we say, "it stood still, as much as it moved;" or "it stood still twice or thrice so long as it moved;" or any other space which our measuring hath either ascertained, or guessed; more or less, as we use to say. Time then is not the motion of a body.

And I confess to Thee, O Lord, that I yet know not what time is, and again I confess unto Thee, O Lord, that I know that I speak this in time, and that having long spoken of time, that very "long" is not long, but by the pause of time. How then know I this, seeing I know not what time is? or is it perchance that I know not how to express what I know? Woe is me, that do not even know, what I know not. Behold, O my God, before Thee I lie not; but as I speak so is my heart. *Thou shalt light my candle; Thou O Lord my God, wilt enlighten my darkness.*

Does not my soul most truly confess unto Thee, that I do measure times? Do I then measure, O my God, and know not what I measure? I measure the motion of a body in time; and the time itself do I not measure? Or could I indeed measure the motion of a body how long it were, and in how long space it could come from this place to that, without measuring the time in which it is moved? This same time then, how do I measure? do we by a shorter time measure a longer, as by the space of a cubit, the space of a rood? for so indeed we seem by the space of a short syllable, to measure the space of a long syllable, and to say that this is double the other. Thus measure we the spaces of stanzas, by the spaces of the verses, and the spaces of the verses, by the spaces of the feet, and the spaces of the feet, by the spaces of the syllables, and the spaces of long, by the spaces of short syllables; not measuring by pages, (for then we measure spaces, not times;) but when we utter the words and they pass by, and we say "it is a long stanza, because composed of so many verses; long verses, because consisting of so many feet; long feet, because prolonged by so many syllables; a long syllable because double to a short one." But neither do we this way obtain any certain measure of time; because it may be, that a shorter verse, pronounced more fully, may take up more time than a longer, pronounced hurriedly. And so for a verse, a foot, a syllable. Whence it seemed to me, that time is nothing else than protraction; but of what, I know not; and I marvel, if it be not of the mind itself? For what I beseech Thee, O my God, do I measure, when I say, either indefinitely "this is a longer time than that," or definitely "this is double that?" That I measure time, I know; and yet I measure not time to come, for it is not yet; nor present, because it is not protracted by any space; nor past, bcause it now is not. What then do I measure? Times passing, not past? for so I said.

Courage, my mind, and press on mightily. God is our helper, He *made us, and not we ourselves.* Press on where truth begins to dawn. Suppose, now, the voice of a body begins to sound, and does sound, and sounds on, and list, it ceases; it is silence now, and that voice is past, and is no more a voice. Before it sounded, it was to come, and could not be measured, because as yet it was not, and now it cannot, because it is no longer. Then therefore while it sounded, it might; because there then was what might be measured. But yet even then it was not at a stay; for it was passing on, and passing away. Could it be measured the rather, for that? For while passing, it was being extended into some space of time, so that it might be measured, since the present hath no space. If therefore then it might, then, lo, suppose another voice hath begun to sound, and still soundeth in one continued tenor without any interruption; let us measure it while it sounds; seeing when it hath left sounding, it will then be past, and nothing left to be measured; let us measure it verily, and tell how much it is. But it sounds still, nor can it be measured but from the instant it began in, unto the end it left in. For the very space between is the thing we measure, namely, from some beginning unto some end. Wherefore, a voice that is not yet ended, cannot be measured, so that it may be said how long, or short it is; nor can it be called equal to another, or double to a single, or the like. But when ended, it no longer is. How may it then be measured? And yet we measure times; but yet neither those which are not yet, nor those which no longer are, nor those which are not lengthened out by some pause, nor those which have no bounds. We measure neither times to come, nor past, nor present, nor passing; and yet we do measure times.

"Deus Creator omnium," this verse of eight syllables alternates between short and long syllables. The four short then, the first, third, fifth, and seventh, are but single, in respect of the four long, the second, fourth, sixth, and eighth. Every one of these, to every one of those, hath a double time: I pronounce them, report on them, and find it so, as one's plain sense perceives. By plain sense then, I measure a long syllable by a short, and I sensibly find it to have twice so much; but when one sounds after the other, if the former be short, the latter long, how shall I detain the short one, and how, measuring, shall I apply it to the long, that I may find this to have twice so much; seeing the long does not begin to sound, unless the short leaves sounding? And that very long one do I measure as present, seeing I measure it not till it be ended? Now his ending is his passing away. What then is it I measure? where is the short syllable by which I measure? where the long which I measure? Both have sounded, have flown, passed away, are no more; and yet I measure, and confidently answer (so far as is presumed on a practised sense) that as to space of time this syllable is but single, that double. And yet I could not do this, unless they were already past and ended. It is not then themselves, which now are not, that I measure, but something in my memory, which there remains fixed.

It is in thee, my mind, that I measure times. Interrupt me not, that is, interrupt not thyself with the tumults of thy impressions. In thee I measure times; the impression, which things as they pass by cause in thee, remains even when they are gone; this it is which, still present, I measure, not the things which pass by to make this impression. This I measure, when I measure times. Either then this is time, or I do not measure times. What when we measure silence, and say that this silence hath held as long time as did that voice? do we not stretch out our thought to the measure of a voice, as if it sounded that so we may be able to report of the intervals of silence in a given space of time? For though both voice and tongue be still, yet in thought we go over poems, and verses, and any other discourse, or dimensions of motions, and report as to the spaces of times, how much this is in respect of that, no otherwise than if vocally we did pronounce them. If a man would utter a lengthened sound, and had settled in thought how long it should be, he hath in silence already gone through a space of time, and committing it to memory, begins to utter that speech, which sounds on, until it be brought unto the end proposed. Yea it hath sounded, and will sound; for so much of it as is finished, hath sounded already, and the rest will sound. And thus passeth it on, until the present intent conveys over the future into the past; the past increasing by the diminution of the future, until by the consumption of the future, all is past.

But how is that future diminished or consumed, which as yet is not? or how that past increased, which is now no longer, save that in the mind which enacteth this, there be three things done? For it expects, it considers, it remembers; that so that which it expecteth, through that which it considereth, passeth into that which it remembereth. Who therefore denieth, that things to come are not as yet? and yet, there is in the mind an expectation of things to come. And who denies past things to be now no longer? and yet is there still in the mind a memory of things past. And who denieth that the present time hath no space, because it passeth away in a moment? and yet our consideration continueth, through which that which shall be present proceedeth to become absent. It is not then future time, that is long, for as yet it is not: but a "long future," is "a long expectation of the future," nor is it time past, which now is not, that is long; but a long past, is "a long memory of the past."

I am about to repeat a Psalm that I know. Before I begin, my expectation is extended over the whole; but when I have begun, how much soever of it I shall separate off into the past, is extended along my memory; thus the life of this action of mine is divided between my memory as to what I have repeated, and expectation as to what I am about to repeat; but "consideration" is present with me, that through it what was future, may be conveyed over, so as to become past. Which the more it is done again and again, so much the more the expectation being shortened, is the memory enlarged; till the whole expectation be at length exhausted, when that whole action being ended, shall have passed into memory. And this which takes place in the whole Psalm, the same takes place in each several portion of it, and each several syllable; the same holds in that longer action, whereof this Psalm may be a part; the same holds in the whole life of man, whereof all the actions of man are parts; the same holds through the whole age of the sons of men, whereof all the lives of men are parts.

But because *Thy loving kindness is better than* all *lives,* behold, my life is but a distraction, and *Thy right hand upheld me*, in my Lord the *Son of man*, the *Mediator betwixt Thee,* The One, and us many, many also through our manifold distractions amid many things, that by Him *I may apprehend in Whom I have been apprehended,* and may be re-collected from my old conversation, to follow The One, *forgetting what is behind, and* not distended, but *extended*, not to things which shall be and shall pass away, but *to those things which are before*, not distractedly but intently, *I follow on for the prize of my heavenly calling,* where I may *hear the voice* of Thy *praise*, and *contemplate* Thy *delights*, neither to come, nor to pass away. But now *are my years spent in mourning*. And Thou, O Lord, art my comfort, my Father everlasting, but I have been severed amid times, whose order I know not; and my thoughts, even the inmost bowels of my soul, are rent and mangled with tumultuous varieties, until I flow together into Thee, purified and molten by the fire of Thy love.

And now will I stand, and become firm in Thee, in my mould, Thy truth; nor will I endure the questions of men, who by a penal disease thirst for more than they can contain, and say, "what did God before He *made heaven and earth?*" "Or, how came it into His mind to make anything, having never before made any thing?" Give them, O Lord, well to bethink themselves what they say, and to find, that "never" cannot be predicated, when "time" is not. This then that He is said "never to have made;" what else is it to say, than "in 'no time' to have made?" Let them see therefore, that time cannot be without created being, and cease to *speak* that *vanity*. May they also be *extended towards those things which are before;* and understand Thee before all times, the eternal Creator of all times, and that no times be coeternal with Thee, nor any creature, even if there be any creature before all times.

O Lord my God, what a depth is that recess of Thy mysteries, and how far from it have the consequences of my transgressions cast me! Heal mine eyes, that I may share the joy of Thy light. Certainly, if there be a mind gifted with such vast knowledge and foreknowledge, as to know all things past and to come, as I know one well-known Psalm, truly that mind is passing wonderful, and fearfully amazing; in that nothing past, nothing to come in after-ages, is any more hidden from him, than when I sung that Psalm, was hidden from me what, and how much of it had passed away from the beginning, what, and how much there remined unto the end. But far be it that Thou the Creator of the Universe, the Creator of souls and bodies, far be it, that Thou shouldest in such wise know all things past and to come. Far, far more wonderfully, and far more mysteriously, dost thou know them. For not, as the feelings of one who singeth what he knoweth, or heareth some well-known song, are through expectation of the words to come, and the remembering of those that are past, varied, and his senses divided,—not so doth any thing happen unto Thee, unchangeably eternal, that is, the eternal Creator of minds. Like then as Thou *in the Beginning* knewest *the heaven and the earth*, without any variety of Thy knowledge, so *madest* Thou *in the Beginning heaven and earth*, without any distraction of Thy action. Whoso understandeth, let him confess unto Thee; and whoso understandeth not, let him confess unto Thee. Oh how high art Thou, and yet the humble in heart are Thy dwelling-place; for Thou *raisest up those that are bowed down*, and they fall not, whose elevation Thou art.

5. *Time Is Absolute*

ISAAC NEWTON

Isaac Newton (1642–1727) was the English mathematician and physicist whose work ensured the success of the Scientific Revolution. In previous generations, people like Copernicus, Galileo, and Descartes had advanced the use of mathematics as a tool for describing the natural world. Newton's invention of the mathematics of "fluxions" (that is, calculus), his formulation of the laws of motion, and his mathematical treatment of gravity successfully showed how both earthly and celestial phenomena could be viewed as the predictable behavior of matter in motion. The new theories made frequent reference to time because they dealt with the velocity and acceleration of objects and with the duration that objects were acted upon by forces. Newton was aware that not every "sensible" measurement of time led to the right results, so he made a distinction between absolute and relative time. He made a similar distinction between absolute and relative space, believing real forces were the ones that produced accelerations with respect to absolute space and time. These distinctions were rejected by Leibniz (Newton's contemporary) and abandoned in 1905 by Einstein in his special theory of relativity. (Philosophers, however, still debate whether the "spacetime" of later physics is in some way absolute.) Nonetheless, Newton's characterization of absolute time is important not only because it was a significant part of science for 200 years, but also because it gave voice to the common idea that time flows independently whether or not things change. In this view, time is something that changes occur "in," and the distinction between the past, present, and future is *sui generis*.

Hitherto I have laid down the definitions of such words as are less known, and explained the sense in which I would have them to be understood in the following discourse. I do not define time, space, place, and motion, as being well known to all. Only I must observe, that the common people conceive those quantities under no other notions but from the relation they bear to sensible objects. And thence arise certain prejudices, for the removing of which it will be convenient to distinguish them into absolute and relative, true and apparent, mathematical and common.

I. Absolute, true, and mathematical time, of itself, and from its own nature, flows equably without relation to anything external, and by another name is called duration: relative, apparent, and common time, is some sensible and external (whether accurate or unequable) measure of duration by the means of motion, which is commonly used instead of true time; such as an hour, a day, a month, a year.

II. Absolute space, in its own nature, without relation to anything external, remains always similar and immovable. Relative space is some movable dimension or measure of the absolute spaces; which our senses determine by its position to bodies; and which is commonly taken for immovable space; such is the dimension of a subterraneous, an aerial, or celestial space, determined by its position

From *Sir Isaac Newton's Mathematical Principles of Natural Philosophy and His System of the World*, Florian Cajori ed. Trans./ed. by Motte, Andrew, pages 6–12. Copyright © 1962 The Regents of the University of California. Reprinted by permission of the University of California Press.

in respect of the earth. Absolute and relative space are the same in figure and magnitude; but they do not remain always numerically the same. For if the earth, for instance, moves, a space of our air, which relatively and in respect of the earth remains always the same, will at one time be one part of the absolute space into which the air passes; at another time it will be another part of the same, and so, absolutely understood, it will be continually changed.

III. Place is a part of space which a body takes up, and is according to the space, either absolute or relative. I say, a part of space; not the situation, nor the external surface of the body. For the places of equal solids are always equal; but their surfaces, by reason of their dissimilar figures, are often unequal. Positions properly have no quantity, nor are they so much the places themselves, as the properties of places. The motion of the whole is the same with the sum of the motions of the parts; that is, the translation of the whole, out of its place, is the same thing with the sum of the translations of the parts out of their places; and therefore the place of the whole is the same as the sum of the places of the parts, and for that reason, it is internal, and in the whole body.

IV. Absolute motion is the translation of a body from one absolute place into another; and relative motion, the translation from one relative place into another. Thus in a ship under sail, the relative place of a body is that part of the ship which the body possesses; or that part of the cavity which the body fills, and which therefore moves together with the ship: and relative rest is the continuance of the body in the same part of the ship, or of its cavity. But real, absolute rest, is the continuance of the body in the same part of that immovable space, in which the ship itself, its cavity, and all that it contains, is moved. Wherefore, if the earth is really at rest, the body, which relatively rests in the ship, will really and absolutely move with the same velocity which the ship has on the earth. But if the earth also moves, the true and absolute motion of the body will arise, partly from the true motion of the earth, in immovable space, partly from the relative motion of the ship on the earth; and if the body moves also relatively in the ship, its true motion will arise, partly from the true motion of the earth, in immovable space, and partly from the relative motions as well of the ship on the earth, as of the body in the ship; and from these relative motions will arise the relative motion

of the body on the earth. As if that part of the earth, where the ship is, was truly moved towards the east, with a velocity of 10010 parts; while the ship itself, with a fresh gale, and full sails, is carried towards the west, with a velocity expressed by 10 of those parts; but a sailor walks in the ship towards the east, with 1 part of the said velocity; then the sailor will be moved truly in immovable space towards the east, with a velocity of 10001 parts, and relatively on the earth towards the west, with a velocity of 9 of those parts.

Absolute time, in astronomy, is distinguished from relative, by the equation or correction of the apparent time. For the natural days are truly unequal, though they are commonly considered as equal, and used for a measure of time; astronomers correct this inequality that they may measure the celestial motions by a more accurate time. It may be, that there is no such thing as an equable motion, whereby time may be accurately measured. All motions may be accelerated and retarded, but the flowing of absolute time is not liable to any change. The duration or perseverance of the existence of things remains the same, whether the motions are swift or slow, or none at all: and therefore this duration ought to be distinguished from what are only sensible measures thereof; and from which we deduce it, by means of the astronomical equation. The necessity of this equation, for determining the times of a phenomenon, is evinced as well from the experiments of the pendulum clock, as by eclipses of the satellites of Jupiter.

As the order of the parts of time is immutable, so also is the order of the parts of space. Suppose those parts to be moved out of their places, and they will be moved (if the expression may be allowed) out of themselves. For times and spaces are, as it were, the places as well of themselves as of all other things. All things are placed in time as to order of succession; and in space as to order of situation. It is from their essence or nature that they are places; and that the primary places of things should be movable, is absurd. These are therefore the absolute places; and translations out of those places, are the only absolute motions.

But because the parts of space cannot be seen, or distinguished from one another by our senses, therefore in their stead we use sensible measures of them. For from the positions and distances of things from any body considered as immovable, we define all places; and then with respect to such places, we estimate all motions, considering bodies as transferred from some of those places into others. And so, instead of absolute places and motions, we use relative ones; and that without any inconvenience in common affairs; but in philosophical disquisitions, we ought to abstract from our senses, and consider things themselves, distinct from what are only sensible measures of them. For it may be that there is no body really at rest, to which the places and motions of others may be referred.

But we may distinguish rest and motion, absolute and relative, one from the other by their properties, causes, and effects. It is a property of rest, that bodies really at rest do rest in respect to one another. And therefore as it is possible, that in the remote regions of the fixed stars, or perhaps far beyond them, there may be some body absolutely at rest; but impossible to know, from the position of bodies to one another in our regions, whether any of these do keep the same position to that remote body, it follows that absolute rest cannot be determined from the position of bodies in our regions.

It is a property of motion, that the parts, which retain given positions to their wholes, do partake of the motions of those wholes. For all the parts of revolving bodies endeavor to recede from the axis of motion; and the impetus of bodies moving forwards arises from the joint impetus of all the parts. Therefore, if surrounding bodies are moved, those that are relatively at rest within them will partake of their motion. Upon which account, the true and absolute motion of a body cannot be determined by the translation of it from those which only seem to rest; for the external bodies ought not only to appear at rest, but to be really at rest. For otherwise, all included bodies, besides their translation from near the surrounding ones, partake likewise of their true motions; and though that translation were not made, they would not be really at rest, but only seem to be so. For the surrounding bodies stand in the like relation to the surrounded as the exterior part of a whole does to the interior, or as the shell does to the kernel; but if the shell moves, the kernel will also move, as being part of the whole, without any removal from near the shell.

A property, near akin to the preceding, is this, that if a place is moved, whatever is placed therein moves along with it; and therefore a body, which is moved from a place in motion, partakes also of the motion of its place. Upon which account, all motions, from places in motion, are no other than

parts of entire and absolute motions; and every entire motion is composed of the motion of the body out of its first place, and the motion of this place out of its place; and so on, until we come to some immovable place, as in the before-mentioned example of the sailor. Wherefore, entire and absolute motions can be no otherwise determined than by immovable places; and for that reason I did before refer those absolute motions to immovable places, but relative ones to movable places. Now no other places are immovable but those that, from infinity to infinity, do all retain the same given position one to another; and upon this account must ever remain unmoved; and do thereby constitute immovable space.

The causes by which true and relative motions are distinguished, one from the other, are the forces impressed upon bodies to generate motion. True motion is neither generated nor altered, but by some force impressed upon the body moved; but relative motion may be generated or altered without any force impressed upon the body. For it is sufficient only to impress some force on other bodies with which the former is compared, that by their giving way, that relation may be changed, in which the relative rest or motion of this other body did consist. Again, true motion suffers always some change from any force impressed upon the moving body; but relative motion does not necessarily undergo any change by such forces. For if the same forces are likewise impressed on those other bodies, with which the comparison is made, that the relative position may be preserved, then that condition will be preserved in which the relative motion consists. And therefore any relative motion may be changed when the true motion remains unaltered, and the relative may be preserved when the true suffers some change. Thus, true motion by no means consists in such relations.

The effects which distinguish absolute from relative motion are, the forces of receding from the axis of circular motion. For there are no such forces in a circular motion purely relative, but in a true and absolute circular motion, they are greater or less, according to the quantity of the motion. If a vessel, hung by a long cord, is so often turned about that the cord is strongly twisted, then filled with water, and held at rest together with the water; thereupon, by the sudden action of another force, it is whirled about the contrary way, and while the cord is untwisting itself, the vessel continues for some time in this motion; the surface of the water will at first be plain, as before the vessel began to move; but after that, the vessel, by gradually communicating its motion to the water, will make it begin sensibly to revolve, and recede by little and little from the middle, and ascend to the sides of the vessel, forming itself into a concave figure (as I have experienced), and the swifter the motion becomes, the higher will the water rise, till at last, performing its revolutions in the same times with the vessel, it becomes relatively at rest in it. This ascent of the water shows its endeavor to recede from the axis of its motion; and the true and absolute circular motion of the water, which is here directly contrary to the relative, becomes known, and may be measured by this endeavor. At first, when the relative motion of the water in the vessel was greatest, it produced no endeavor to recede from the axis; the water showed no tendency to the circumference, nor any ascent towards the sides of the vessel, but remained of a plain surface, and therefore its true circular motion had not yet begun. But afterwards, when the relative motion of the water had decreased, the ascent thereof towards the sides of the vessel proved its endeavor to recede from the axis; and this endeavor showed the real circular motion of the water continually increasing, till it had acquired its greatest quantity, when the water rested relatively in the vessel. And therefore this endeavor does not depend upon any translation of the water in respect of the ambient bodies, nor can true circular motion be defined by such translation. There is only one real circular motion of any one revolving body, corresponding to only one power of endeavoring to recede from its axis of motion, as its proper and adequate effect; but relative motions, in one and the same body, are innumerable, according to the various relations it bears to external bodies, and, like other relations, are altogether destitute of any real effect, any otherwise than they may perhaps partake of that one only true motion. And therefore in their system who suppose that our heavens, revolving below the sphere of the fixed stars, carry the planets along with them; the several parts of those heavens, and the planets, which are indeed relatively at rest in their heavens, do yet really move. For they change their position one to another (which never happens to bodies truly at rest), and being carried together with their heavens, partake of their motions, and as parts of revolving wholes, endeavor to recede from the axis of their motions.

Wherefore relative quantities are not the quantities themselves, whose names they bear, but those sensible measures of them (either accurate or inaccurate), which are commonly used instead of the measured quantities themselves. And if the meaning of words is to be determined by their use, then by the names time, space, place, and motion, their [sensible] measures are properly to be understood; and the expression will be unusual, and purely mathematical, if the measured quantities themselves are meant. On this account, those violate the accuracy of language, which ought to be kept precise, who interpret these words for the measured quantities. Nor do those less defile the purity of mathematical and philosophical truths, who confound real quantities with their relations and sensible measures.

It is indeed a matter of great difficulty to discover, and effectually to distinguish, the true motions of particular bodies from the apparent; because the parts of that immovable space, in which those motions are performed, do by no means come under the observation of our senses. Yet the thing is not altogether desperate; for we have some arguments to guide us, partly from the apparent motions, which are the differences of the true motions; partly from the forces, which are the causes and effects of the true motions. For instance, if two globes, kept at a given distance one from the other by means of a cord that connects them, were revolved about their common centre of gravity, we might, from the tension of the cord, discover the endeavor of the globes to recede from the axis of their motion, and from thence we might compute the quantity of their circular motions. And then if any equal forces should be impressed at once on the alternate faces of the globes to augment or diminish their circular motions, from the increase or decrease of the tension of the cord, we might infer the increment or decrement of their motions; and thence would be found on what faces those forces ought to be impressed, that the motions of the globes might be most augmented; that is, we might discover their hindmost faces, or those which, in the circular motion, do follow. But the faces which follow being known, and consequently the opposite ones that precede, we should likewise know the determination of their motions. And thus we might find both the quantity and the determination of this circular motion, even in an immense vacuum, where there was nothing external or sensible with which the globes could be compared. But now, if in that space some remote bodies were placed that kept always a given position one to another, as the fixed stars do in our regions, we could not indeed determine from the relative translation of the globes among those bodies, whether the motion did belong to the globes or to the bodies. But if we observed the cord, and found that its tension was that very tension which the motions of the globes required, we might conclude the motion to be in the globes, and the bodies to be at rest; and then, lastly, from the translation of the globes among the bodies, we should find the determination of their motions. But how we are to obtain the true motions from their causes, effects, and apparent differences, and the converse, shall be explained more [later]. For to this end it was that I composed it.

6. *Time Is the Flux of Duration*

HENRI BERGSON

Henri Bergson (1859–1941) was a French philosopher who believed the mathematical picture of the world developed by science was incomplete and distorting. He wanted to base metaphysical knowledge on experience, but he felt language and concepts (especially scientific ones) were clumsy tools that evolved for practical purposes—not for expressing metaphysical knowledge. Bergson advocated an intuitive form of knowing that focused on immediate experience. With this intuition, Bergson claimed to find "pure duration," a kind of present or period of becoming that is not just the juxtapositioning of successive, momentary events. He claimed time is the flux of pure duration, and *concepts* of momentary states of things are like snapshots that freeze and misrepresent this flux. Influenced by theories of organic evolution, Bergson believed making time fundamental in this way would leave room for creative novelty and freedom (purportedly, in contrast to the mechanical world of physics). Though Bergson objected to the mathematical "spatialization" of time, it should be observed that he agreed with Newton that time is not just a relation among events. The article reprinted here is an early (1903) essay in which Bergson argues the way to know time is via intuition.

If we compare the various ways of defining metaphysics and of conceiving the absolute, we shall find, despite apparent discrepancies, that philosophers agree in making a deep distinction between two ways of knowing a thing. The first implies

going all around it, the second entering into it. The first depends on the viewpoint chosen and the symbols employed, while the second is taken from no viewpoint and rests on no symbol. Of the first kind of knowledge we shall say that it stops at the *relative;* of the second that, wherever possible, it attains the *absolute.*

Take, for example, the movement of an object in space. I perceive it differently according to the point of view from which I look at it, whether from that of mobility or of immobility. I express it differently, furthermore as I relate it to the system of axes or reference points, that is to say, according to the symbols by which I translate it. And I call it *relative* for this double reason: in either case, I place myself outside the object itself. When I speak of an absolute movement, it means that I attribute to the mobile an inner being and, as it were, states of soul; it also means that I am in harmony with these states and enter into them by an effort of imagination. Therefore, according to whether the object is mobile or immobile, whether it adopts one movement or another, I shall not have the same feeling about it. And what I feel will depend neither on the point of view I adopt toward the object, since I am in the object itself, nor on the symbols by which I translate it, since I have renounced all translation in order to possess the original. In short, the movement will not be grasped from without and, as it were, from where I am, but from within, inside it, in what it is in itself. I shall have hold of an absolute.

Or again, take a character whose adventures make up the subject of a novel. The novelist may multiply traits of character, make his hero speak and act as much as he likes: all this has not the same value as the simple and indivisible feeling I should experience if I were to coincide for a single moment with the personage himself. The actions, gestures and words would then appear to flow naturally, as though from their source. They would no longer be accidents making up the idea I had of the character, constantly enriching this idea without ever succeeding in completing it. The character would be given to me all at once in its entirety, and the thousand and one incidents which make it manifest, instead of adding to the idea and enriching it, would, on the contrary, seem to me to fall away from it without in any way exhausting or impoverishing its essence. I get a different point of view regarding the person with every added detail I am given. All the traits which describe it to me, yet which can only enable me to know it by comparisons with persons or things I already know, are signs by which it is more or less symbolically expressed. Symbols and points of view then place me outside it; they give me only what it has in common with others and what does not belong properly to it. But what is properly itself, what constitutes its essence, cannot be perceived from without, being internal by definition, nor be expressed by symbols, being incommensurable with everything else. Description, history and analysis in this case leave

me in the relative. Only by coinciding with the person itself would I possess the absolute.

It is in this sense, and in this sense alone, that *absolute* is synonymous with *perfection*. Though all the photographs of a city taken from all possible points of view indefinitely complete one another, they will never equal in value that dimensional object, the city along whose streets one walks. All the translations of a poem in all possible languages may add nuance to nuance and, by a kind of mutual retouching, by correcting one another, may give an increasingly faithful picture of the poem they translate, yet they will never give the inner meaning of the original. A representation taken from a certain point of view, a translation made with certain symbols still remain imperfect in comparison with the object whose picture has been taken or which the symbols seek to express. But the absolute is perfect in that it is perfectly what it is.

It is probably for the same reason that the *absolute* and the *infinite* are often taken as identical. If I wish to explain to someone who does not know Greek the simple impression that a line of Homer leaves upon me, I shall give the translation of the line, then comment on my translation, then I shall develop my commentary, and from explanation to explanation I shall get closer to what I wish to express; but I shall never quite reach it. When you lift your arm you accomplish a movement the simple perception of which you have inwardly; but outwardly, for me, the person who sees it, your arm passes through one point, then through another, and between these two points there will be still other points, so that if I begin to count them, the operation will continue indefinitely. Seen from within, an absolute is then a simple thing; but considered from without, that is to say relative to something else, it becomes, with relation to those signs which express it, the piece of gold for which one can never make up the change. Now what lends itself at the same time to an indivisible apprehension and to an inexhaustible enumeration is, by definition, an infinite.

It follows that an absolute can only be given in an *intuition*, while all the rest has to do with *analysis*. We call intuition here the *sympathy* by which one is transported into the interior of an object in order to coincide with what there is unique and consequently inexpressible in it. Analysis, on the contrary, is the operation which reduces the object to elements already known, that is, common to that object and to others. Analyzing then consists in expressing a thing in terms of what is not it. All analysis is thus a translation, a development into symbols, a representation taken from successive points of view from which are noted a corresponding number of contacts between the new object under consideration and others believed to be already known. In its eternally unsatisfied desire to embrace the object around which it is condemned to turn, analysis multiplies endlessly the points of view in order to complete the ever incomplete representation, varies interminably the symbols with the hope of perfecting the always imperfect translation. It is analysis ad infinitum. But intuition, if it is possible, is a simple act.

This being granted, it would be easy to see that for positive science analysis is its habitual function. It works above all with symbols. Even the most concrete of the sciences of nature, the sciences of life, confine themselves to the visible form of living beings, their organs, their anatomical elements. They compare these forms with one another, reduce the more complex to the more simple, in fact they study the functioning of life in what is, so to speak, its visual symbol. If there exists a means of possessing a reality absolutely, instead of knowing it relatively, of placing oneself within it instead of adopting points of view toward it, of having the intuition of it instead of making the analysis of it, in short, of grasping it over and above all expression, translation or symbolical representation, metaphysics is that very means. *Metaphysics is therefore the science which claims to dispense with symbols.*

There is at least one reality which we all seize from within, by intuition and not by simple analysis. It is our own person in its flowing through time, the self which endures. With no other thing can we sympathize intellectually, or if you like, spiritually. But one thing is sure: we sympathize with ourselves.

When, with the inner regard of my consciousness, I examine my person in its passivity, like some superficial encrustment, first I perceive all the perceptions which come to it from the material world. These perceptions are clear-cut, distinct, juxtaposed or mutually juxtaposable; they seek to group themselves into objects. Next I perceive memories more or less adherent to these perceptions and which serve to interpret them; these memories are, so to speak, as if detached from the depth of my person and drawn to the periphery by perceptions resembling them; they are fastened on

me without being absolutely myself. And finally, I become aware of tendencies, motor habits, a crowd of virtual actions more or less solidly bound to those perceptions and these memories. All these elements with their well-defined forms appear to me to be all the more distinct from myself the more they are distinct from one another. Turned outwards from within, together they constitute the surface of a sphere which tends to expand and loose itself in the external world. But if I pull myself in from the periphery toward the center, if I seek deep down within me what is the most uniformly, the most constantly and durably myself, I find something altogether different.

What I find beneath these clear-cut crystals and this superficial congelation is a continuity of flow comparable to no other flowing I have ever seen. It is a succession of states each one of which announces what follows and contains what precedes. Strictly speaking they do not constitute multiple states until I have already got beyond them, and turn around to observe their trail. While I was experiencing them they were so solidly organized, so profoundly animated with a common life, that I could never have said where any one of them finished or the next one began. In reality, none of them do begin or end; they all dove-tail into one another.

It is, if you like, the unrolling of a spool, for there is no living being who does not feel himself coming little by little to the end of his span; and living consists in growing old. But it is just as much a continual winding, like that of thread into a ball, for our past follows us, becoming larger and larger with the present it picks up on its way; and consciousness means memory.

To tell the truth, it is neither a winding nor an unwinding, for these two images evoke the representation of lines or surfaces whose parts are homogeneous to and superposable on one another. Now, no two moments are identical in a conscious being. Take for example the simplest feeling, suppose it to be constant, absorb the whole personality in it: the consciousness which will accompany this feeling will not be able to remain identical with itself for two consecutive moments, since the following moment always contains, over and above the preceding one, the memory the latter has left it. A consciousness which had two identical moments would be a consciousness without memory. It would therefore die and be re-born continually. How otherwise can unconsciousness be described?

We must therefore evoke a spectrum of a thousand shades, with imperceptible gradations leading from one shade to another. A current of feeling running through the spectrum, becoming tinted with each of these shades in turn, would suffer gradual changes, each of which would announce the following and sum up within itself the preceding ones. Even then the successive shades of the spectrum will always remain external to each other. They are juxtaposed. They occupy space. On the contrary, what is pure duration excludes all idea of juxtaposition, reciprocal exteriority and extension.

Instead, let us imagine an infinitely small piece of elastic, contracted, if that were possible, to a mathematical point. Let us draw it out gradually in such a way as to bring out of the point a line which will grow progressively longer. Let us fix our attention not on the line as line, but on the action which traces it. Let us consider that this action, in spite of its duration, is indivisible if one supposes that it goes on without stopping; that, if we intercalate a stop in it, we make two actions of it instead of one and that each of these actions will then be the indivisible of which we speak; that it is not the moving act itself which is never indivisible, but the motionless line it lays down beneath it like a track in space. Let us take our mind off the space subtending the movement and concentrate solely on the movement itself, on the act of tension or extension, in short, on pure mobility. This time we shall have a more exact image of our development in duration.

And yet that image will still be incomplete, and all comparison furthermore will be inadequate, because the unrolling of our duration in certain aspects resembles the unity of a movement which progresses, in others, a multiplicity of states spreading out, and because no metaphor can express one of the two aspects without sacrificing the other. If I evoke a spectrum of a thousand shades, I have before me a complete thing, whereas duration is the state of completing itself. If I think of an elastic being stretched, of a spring being wound or unwound, I forget the wealth of coloring characteristic of duration as something lived and see only the simple movement by which consciousness goes from one shade to the other. The inner life is all that at once, variety of qualities, continuity of progress, unity of direction. It cannot be represented by images.

But still less could it be represented by *concepts*, that is, by abstract ideas, whether general or simple. Doubtless no image will quite answer to the original feeling I have of the flowing of myself. But neither is it necessary for me to try to express it. To him who is not capable of giving himself the intuition of the duration constitutive of his being, nothing will ever give it, neither concepts nor images. In this regard, the philosopher's sole aim should be to start up a certain effort which the utilitarian habits of mind of everyday life tend, in most men, to discourage. Now the image has at least the advantage of keeping us in the concrete. No image will replace the intuition of duration, but many different images, taken from quite different orders of things, will be able, through the convergence of their action, to direct the consciousness to the precise point where there is a certain intuition to seize on. By choosing images as dissimilar as possible, any one of them will be prevented from usurping the place of the intuition it is instructed to call forth, since it would then be driven out immediately by its rivals. By seeing that in spite of their differences in aspect they all demand of our mind the same kind of attention and, as it were, the same degree of tension, one will gradually accustom the consciousness to a particular and definitely determined disposition, precisely the one it will have to adopt in order to appear unveiled to itself. But even then the consciousness must acquiesce in this effort; for we shall have shown it nothing. We shall simply have placed it in the attitude it must take to produce the desired effort and, by itself, to arrive at the intuition. On the other hand the disadvantage of too simple concepts is that they are really symbols which take the place of the object they symbolize and which do not demand any effort on our part. Upon close examination one would see that each of them retains of the object only what is common to that object and to others. Each of them is seen to express, even more than does the image, a *comparison* between the object and those objects resembling it. But as the comparison has brought out a resemblance, and as the resemblance is a property of the object, and as a property seems very much as though it were a *part* of the object possessing it, we are easily persuaded that by juxtaposing concepts to concepts we shall recompose the whole of the object with its parts and obtain from it, so to speak, an intellectual equivalent. We shall in this way think we are forming a faithful representation of duration by lining up the concepts of unity, multiplicity, continuity, finite or infinite divisibility, etc. That is precisely the illusion. And that, also, is the danger. In so far as abstract ideas can render service to analysis, that is, to a scientific study of the object in its relations with all others, to that very extent are they incapable of replacing intuition, that is to say, the metaphysical investigation of the object in what essentially belongs to it. On the one hand, indeed, these concepts placed end to end will never give us anything more than an artificial recomposition of the object of which they can symbolize only certain general and, as it were, impersonal aspects: therefore it is vain to believe that through them one can grasp a reality when all they present is its shadow. But on the other hand, alongside the illusion, there is also a very grave danger. For the concept generalizes at the same time that it abstracts. The concept can symbolize a particular property only by making it common to an infinity of things. Therefore it always more or less distorts this property by the extension it gives to it. A property put back into the metaphysical object to which it belongs coincides with the object, at least molds itself on it, adopting the same contours. Extracted from the metaphysical object and represented in a concept, it extends itself indefinitely, surpassing the object since it must henceforth contain it along with others. The various concepts we form of the properties of a thing are so many much larger circles drawn round it, not one of which fits it exactly. And yet, in the thing itself, the properties coincided with it and therefore with each other. We have no alternative then but to resort to some artifice in order to re-establish the coincidence. We shall take any one of these concepts and with it try to rejoin the others. But the junction will be brought about in a different way, depending upon the concept we start from. According to whether we start, for example, from unity or from multiplicity, we shall form a different conception of the multiple unity of duration. Everything will depend on the weight we assign to this or that concept, and this weight will always be arbitrary, since the concept, extracted from the object, has no weight, being nothing more than the shadow of a body. Thus a multiplicity of different *systems* will arise, as many systems as there are external viewpoints on the reality one is examining or as there are larger circles in which to enclose it. The simple concepts, therefore, not only have the disadvantage of dividing the concrete unity of the object into so many symbolical expressions; they also divide philosophy into distinct schools, each

of which reserves its place, chooses its chips, and begins with the others a game that will never end. Either metaphysics is only this game of ideas, or else, if it is a serious occupation of the mind, it must transcend concepts to arrive at intuition. To be sure, concepts are indispensable to it, for all the other sciences ordinarily work with concepts, and metaphysics cannot get along without the other sciences. But it is strictly itself only when it goes beyond the concept, or at least when it frees itself of the inflexible and ready-made concepts and creates others very different from those we usually handle, I mean flexible, mobile, almost fluid representations, always ready to mold themselves on the fleeting forms of intuition. I shall come back to this important point a little later. It is enough for us to have shown that our duration can be presented to us directly in an intuition, that it can be suggested indirectly to us by images, but that it cannot—if we give to the word *concept* its proper meaning—be enclosed in a conceptual representation.

Let us for an instant try to break it up into parts. We must add that the terms of these parts, instead of being distinguished like those of any multiplicity, encroach upon one another; that we can, no doubt, by an effort of imagination, solidify this duration once it has passed by, divide it into pieces set side by side and count all the pieces; but that this operation is achieved on the fixed memory of the duration, on the immobile track the mobility of the duration leaves behind it, not on the duration itself. Let us therefore admit that, if there is a multiplicity here, this multiplicity resembles no other. Shall we say then that this duration has unity? Undoubtedly a continuity of elements prolonged into one another partakes of unity as much as it does of multiplicity, but this moving, changing, colored and living unity scarcely resembles the abstract unity, empty and motionless, which the concept of pure unity circumscribes. Are we to conclude from this that duration must be defined by both unity and multiplicity at the same time? But curiously enough, no matter how I manipulate the two concepts, apportion them, combine them in various ways, practice on them the most delicate operations of mental chemistry, I shall never obtain anything which resembles the simple intuition I have of duration; instead of which, if I place myself back in duration by an effort of intuition, I perceive immediately how it is unity, multiplicity and many other things besides. These various concepts were therefore just so many external points of view on duration. Neither separated nor re-united have they made us penetrate duration itself.

We penetrate it, nevertheless, and the only way possible is by an intuition. In this sense, an absolute internal knowledge of the duration of the self by the self is possible. But if metaphysics demands and can obtain here an intuition, science has no less need of an analysis. And it is because of a confusion between the roles of analysis and intuition that the dissensions between schools of thought and the conflicts between systems will arise.

Psychology, in fact, like the other sciences, proceeds by analysis. It resolves the self, first given to it in the form of a simple intuition, into sensations, feelings, images, etc. which it studies separately. It therefore substitutes for the self a series of elements which are the psychological facts. But these *elements*, are they *parts*? That is the whole question, and it is because we have evaded it that we have often stated in insoluble terms the problem of the human personality. . . .

It is true that in order to do that one must institute a reversal of the habitual work of the intelligence. To think consists ordinarily in going from concepts to things, and not from things to concepts. To know a reality in the ordinary meaning of the word "to know," is to take ready-made concepts, apportion them, and combine them until one obtains a practical equivalent of the real. But it must not be forgotten that the normal work of the intelligence is far from being a disinterested work. We do not, in general, aim at knowing for the sake of knowing, but at knowing in order to take a stand, gain a profit, in fact to satisfy an interest. We try to find out up to what point the object to be known is *this* or *that*, into what known genus it fits, what kind of action, step or attitude it should suggest to us. These various possible actions and attitudes are so many *conceptual directions* of our thought, determined once and for all; nothing remains but for us to follow them; precisely in that consists the application of concepts to things. To try a concept on an object is to ask of the object what we have to do with it, what it can do for us. To label an object with a concept is to tell in precise terms the kind of action or attitude the object is to suggest to us. All knowledge properly so-called is, therefore, turned in a certain direction or taken from a certain point of view. It is true that our interest is often complex. And that is why we

sometimes manage to turn our knowledge of the same object in several successive directions and to cause view-points concerning it to vary. This is what, in the ordinary meaning of these terms, a "wide" and "comprehensive" knowledge of the object consists in: the object, then, is led back, not to a unique concept, but to several concepts in which it is deemed to "participate." How it is to participate in all these concepts at once is a question of no practical importance and one that need not be asked. It is, therefore, natural and legitimate that we proceed by juxtaposition and apportioning of concepts in every-day life: no philosophical difficulties will be born of this since, by tacit consent, we shall abstain from philosophizing. But to transfer this *modus operandi* to philosophy, to go—here again—from concepts to the thing, to employ for the disinterested knowledge of an object one now aims at attaining in itself, a manner of knowing inspired by a definite interest and consisting by definition in a view taken of the object externally, is to turn one's back on the goal at which one was aiming; it is to condemn philosophy to an eternal friction between the schools and set up a contradiction in the very heart of the object and the method. Either there is no philosophy possible and all knowledge of things is a practical knowledge turned to the profit to be gained from them, or philosophizing consists in placing oneself within the object itself by an effort of intuition.

But in order to comprehend the nature of this intuition, to determine precisely where intuition ends and analysis begins, we must return to what was said above concerning the flow of duration.

It is to be observed that the concepts or schemas, to which analysis leads, have the essential characteristic of being immobile while under consideration. I have isolated from the whole of the inner life that psychological entity which I call a simple sensation. So long as I study it I suppose it to remain what it is. If I were to find some change in it, I should say that it was not a single sensation, but several successive sensations; and it is to each one of the succeeding sensations that I should then transfer the immutability at first attributed to the whole sensation. In any case I shall, by carrying analysis far enough, be able to arrive at elements I shall hold to be immovable. It is there, and there only, that I shall find the solid base of operations which science needs for its proper development.

There is no mood, however, no matter how simple, which does not change at every instant, since there is no consciousness without memory, no continuation of a state without the addition, to the present feeling, of the memory of past moments. That is what duration consists of. Inner duration is the continuous life of a memory which prolongs the past into the present, whether the present distinctly contains the ever-growing image of the past, or whether, by its continual changing of quality, it attests rather the increasingly heavy burden dragged along behind one the older one grows. Without that survival of the past in the present there would be no duration but only instantaneity.

It is true that if I am criticized for abstracting the psychological state from duration by the mere fact of analyzing it, I shall defend myself against the charge by saying that each of these elementary psychological states to which my analysis leads is a state which still occupies time. "My analysis," I shall say, "easily resolves the inner life into states each of which is homogeneous to itself; only, since the homogeneity spreads out over a definite number of minutes or seconds, the elementary psychological state does not cease to have duration, though it does not change."

But who does not see that the definite number of minutes and seconds I attribute to the elementary psychological state, has no more than the value of an indication meant to remind me that the psychological state, supposedly homogeneous, is in reality a state which changes and endures? The state, taken in itself, is a perpetual becoming. I have extracted from this becoming a certain mean of quality which I have supposed invariable: I have thus constituted a state which is stable, and by that very fact, schematic. Again, I have extracted becoming in general, the becoming that would no more be the becoming of this than of that, and this is what I have called the *time* this state occupies. Were I to examine it closely, I should see that this abstract time is as immobile for me as the state I localize in it, that it could flow only by a continual changing of quality and that, if it is without quality, a simple theater of change, it thus becomes an immobile milieu. I should see that the hypothesis of this homogeneous time is simply meant to facilitate the comparison between the various concrete durations, to permit us to count simultaneities and to measure one flowing of duration in relation to another. And finally, I should understand that in fastening to the representation of an elementary psychological state the indication of a definite

number of minutes and seconds, I am merely recalling that the state has been detached from an ego which endures, and demarcating the place where it would have to be set in motion again in order to bring it, from the simple schema it has become, back to the concrete form it had at first. But I forget all that, having no use for it in analysis.

That is to say, analysis operates on immobility, while intuition is located in mobility or, what amounts to the same thing, in duration. That is the very clear line of demarcation between intuition and analysis. One recognizes the real, the actual, the concrete, by the fact that it is variability itself. One recognizes the element by the fact that it is invariable. And it is invariable by definition, being a schema, a simplified reconstruction, often a mere symbol, in any case, a view taken of the reality that flows.

But the mistake is to believe that with these schemas one could recompose the real. It cannot be too often repeated: from intuition one can pass on to analysis, but not from analysis to intuition.

With variability I shall make as many variations, as many qualities or modifications as I like because they are so many immobile views taken by analysis of the mobility given to intuition. But these modifications placed end to end will not produce anything resembling variability, because they were not parts of it but elements which is quite another thing.

Let us consider, for example, the variability nearest to homogeneity, movement in space. For the whole length of this movement I can imagine possible halts: they are what I call the positions of the mobile or the points through which the mobile passes. But with the positions, were they infinite in number, I shall not make movement. They are not parts of the movement; they are so many views taken of it; they are, we say, only halt suppositions. Never is the mobile really in any of these points; the most one can say is that it passes through them. But the passing, which is a movement, has nothing in common with a halt, which is immobility. A movement could not alight on an immobility for it would then coincide with it, which would be contradictory. The points are not *in* the movement as parts, nor even *under* the movement as places of the mobile. They are simply projected by us beneath the movement like so many places where, if it should stop, would be a mobile which by hypothesis does not stop. They are not, therefore, properly speaking, positions, but suppositions, views or mental viewpoints. How, with these points of view, could one construct a thing?

That, nevertheless, is what we try to do every time we reason about movement and also about time for which movement serves as representation. By an illusion deeply rooted in our mind, and because we cannot keep from considering analysis as equivalent to intuition, we begin by distinguishing, for the whole length of the movement, a certain number of possible halts or points which, willy-nilly, we make parts of the movement. Faced with our inability to recompose movement with these points we intercalate other points, in the belief that we are thus keeping closer to what mobility there is in movement. Then, as the mobility still escapes us, we substitute for a finite and definite number of points a number "infinitely increasing,"—trying thus, but vainly, through the movement of our thought, which indefinitely pursues the addition of points to points, to counterfeit the real and undivided movement of the mobile. Finally, we say that movement is made up of points, but that it comprises in addition the obscure, mysterious passing from one position to the next. As though the obscurity did not come wholly from the fact that we have assumed immobility to be clearer from mobility, the halt to precede movement! As though the mystery was not due to the fact that we claim to go from halts to movement by way of composition which is impossible, whereas we pass easily from movement to slowing down and to immobility! You have sought the meaning of a poem in the form of the letters which make it up, you have thought that in considering an increasing number of letters you would finally embrace the constantly fleeting meaning, and as a last resource, seeing that it was no use to seek a part of the meaning in each letter, you have assumed that between each letter and the one following was lodged the missing fragment of the mysterious meaning! But the letters, once more, are not parts of the thing, they are the elements of the symbol. The positions of the mobile are not parts of the movement: they are points of the space which is thought to subtend the movement. This empty and immobile space, simply *conceived*, never *perceived*, has exactly the value of a symbol. By manipulating symbols, how are you going to manufacture reality?

But in this case the symbol meets the demands of our most inveterate habits of thought. We install ourselves ordinarily in immobility, where we find a basis for practice, and with it we claim to recompose mobility. We obtain thus only a clumsy imitation, a counterfeit of real movement, but this imitation is of much greater use to us in life than the intuition of the thing itself would be. Now our mind has an irresistible tendency to consider the idea it most frequently uses to be the clearest. That is why immobility seems clearer to it than mobility, the halt preceding movement.

This explains the difficulties raised by the problem of movement from earliest antiquity. They are due to the fact that we claim to go from space to movement, from the trajectory to the flight, from immobile positions to mobility, and pass from one to the other by way of composition. But it is movement which precedes immobility, and between positions and a displacement there is not the relation of parts to the whole, but that of the diversity of possible viewpoints to the real indivisibility of the object.

Many other problems are born of the same illusion. What the immobile points are to the movement of a mobile, so are the concepts of various qualities to the qualitative change of an object. The different concepts into which a variation is resolved are therefore so many stable visions of the instability of the real. And to think an object, in the usual sense of the word "think," is to take one or several of these immobile views of its mobility. It is, in short, to ask oneself from time to time just where it is, in order to know what to do with it. Nothing is more legitimate than this method of procedure, as long as it is only a question of practical knowledge of reality. Knowledge, in so far as it is directed toward the practical, has only to enumerate the possible principal attitudes of the thing in relation to us, as also our best possible attitudes in respect to it. That is the ordinary role of ready-made concepts, those stations with which we mark out the passage of the becoming. But to desire, with them, to penetrate to the innermost nature of things, is to apply to the mobility of the real a method designed to give of it immobile points of view. It is to forget that if metaphysics is possible, it can only be an effort to re-ascend the slope natural to the work of thought, to place oneself immediately, through a dilation of the mind, in the thing one is studying, in short, to go from reality to concepts and not from concepts to reality. Is it surprising that philosophers so often see the object they claim to embrace recede from them, like children trying to catch smoke by closing their fists? A good many quarrels are thus perpetuated between the schools, in which each one accuses the others of having let the real escape them.

But if metaphysics is to proceed by intuition, if intuition has as its object the mobility of duration, and if duration is psychological in essence, are we not going to shut the philosopher up in exclusive self-contemplation? Will not philosophy consist simply in watching oneself live, "as a dozing shepherd watches the running water"? To speak in this fashion would be to return to the error I have not ceased to emphasize from the very beginning of this study. It would be to fail to recognize the particular nature of duration and at the same time the essentially active character of metaphysical intuition. It would be to fail to see that only the method of which we are speaking allows one to pass beyond idealism as well as realism, to affirm the existence of objects both inferior and superior to us, though nevertheless in a certain sense inferior to us, to make them coexistent without difficulty, and progressively to dispel the obscurities that analysis accumulates around great problems. Without taking up the study of these different points here, let us confine ourselves to showing how the intuition we are discussing is not a single act but an indefinite series of acts, all doubtless of the same genus but each one of a very particular species, and how this variety of acts corresponds to the degrees of being.

If I try to *analyze* duration, that is, to resolve it into ready-made concepts, I am certainly obliged by the very nature of the concept and the analysis, to take two opposing views of *duration in general,* views with which I shall then claim to recompose it. This combination can present neither a diversity of degrees nor a variety of forms: it is or it is not. I shall say, for example, that there is, on the one hand, a *multiplicity* of successive states of consciousness and, on the other hand, a *unity* which binds them together. Duration will be the "synthesis" of this unity and multiplicity, but how this mysterious operation can admit of shades or degrees—I repeat—is not quite clear. In this hypothesis there is, there can only be, a single duration, that in which our consciousness habitually operates. To make certain of what we mean, if we take duration under the simple aspect of a movement being accomplished in space and if we try to reduce to concepts movement considered as representative of time, we shall have on the one hand any desired number of points of the trajectory, and

on the other hand an abstract unity joining them, like a thread holding together the beads of a necklace. Between this abstract multiplicity and this abstract unity their combination, once assumed to be possible, is some strange thing in which we shall find no more shadings than the addition of given numbers in arithmetic would allow. But if, instead of claiming to analyze duration (that is, in reality, to make a synthesis of it with concepts), one first installs oneself in it by an effort of intuition, one has the feeling of a certain well-defined *tension,* whose very definiteness seems like a choice between an infinity of possible durations. This being so one perceives any number of durations, all very different from one another, even though each one of them, reduced to concepts, that is to say, considered externally from two opposite points of view, is always brought back to the indefinable combination of the multiple and the one.

Let us express the same idea more precisely. If I consider duration as a multiplicity of moments bound to one another by a unity which runs through them like a thread, these moments, no matter how short the chosen duration, are unlimited in number. I can imagine them as close together as I like; there will always be, between these mathematical points, other mathematical points, and so on, ad infinitum. Considered from the standpoint of multiplicity, duration will therefore disappear in a dust of moments not one of which has duration, each one being instantaneous. If on the other hand I consider the unity binding the moments together, it is evident that it cannot have duration either since, by hypothesis, everything that is changing and really durable in duration has been put to the account of the multiplicity of the moments. This unity, as I examine its essence, will then appear to me as an immobile substratum of the moving reality, like some intemporal essence of time: that is what I shall call eternity—the eternity of death, since it is nothing else than movement emptied of the mobility which made up its life. Examining closely the opinions of the schools antagonistic to the subject of duration, one would see that they differ simply in attributing to one or the other of these two concepts a capital importance. Certain of them are drawn to the point of view of the multiple; they set up as concrete reality the distance moments of a time which they have, so to speak, pulverized; they consider as being far more artificial the unity which makes a powder of these grains. The others, on the contrary, set up the unity of duration as concrete reality. They place themselves in the eternal. But as their eternity nevertheless remains abstract, being empty, as it is the eternity of a concept which by hypothesis excludes the opposite concept, one cannot see how this eternity could allow an indefinite multiplicity of moments to co-exist with it. In the first hypothesis one has a world suspended in mid-air which would have to end and begin again by itself each instant. In the second, one has an infinitely abstract eternity of which one can say that it is especially difficult to understand why it does not remain enveloped in itself and how it allows things to co-exist with it. But in either case, and no matter which one of the two metaphysics is chosen, time appears from the psychological point of view as a mixture of two abstractions neither one of which admits of either degrees or shadings. In either system, there is only a single duration which carries everything along with it, a river without bottom and without banks and flowing without assignable forces in a direction one cannot define. Even then it is a river and the river flows only because reality obtains this sacrifice from the two doctrines, taking advantage of an inadvertence in their logic. As soon as they regain possession of themselves, they congeal this flowing either into an immense solid sheet, or into an infinity of crystallized needles, but always in a *thing* which necessarily participates in the immobility of a *point of view.*

It is altogether different if one places oneself directly, by an effort of intuition, in the concrete flowing of duration. To be sure, we shall find no logical reason for positing multiple and diverse durations. Strictly speaking, there might exist no other duration than our own, as there might be no other color in the world than orange, for example. But just as a consciousness of color, which would harmonize inwardly with orange instead of perceiving it outwardly, would feel itself caught between red and yellow, would perhaps even have, beneath the latter color, a presentiment of a whole spectrum in which is naturally prolonged the continuity which goes from red to yellow, so the intuition of our duration, far from leaving us suspended in the void as pure analysis would do, puts us in contact with a whole continuity of durations which we should try to follow either downwardly or upwardly: in both cases we can dilate ourselves indefinitely by a more and more vigorous effort, in both cases transcend ourselves. In the first case, we advance toward a duration more and more scattered, whose palpitations, more rapid than ours, dividing our simple sensation, dilute its quality into quantity: at the limit would be the pure homogeneous, the pure *repetition* by which we shall define materiality. In advancing in the other direction, we go toward a duration which stretches, tightens, and becomes more and more intensified: at the limit would be eternity. This time not only conceptual eternity, which is an eternity of death, but an eternity of life. It would be a living and consequently still moving eternity where our own duration would find itself like the vibrations in light, and which would be the concretion of all duration as materiality is its dispersion. Between these two extreme limits moves intuition, and this movement is metaphysics itself.

7. *Time Is Not Real*

JOHN M. E. McTAGGART

John McTaggart (1866–1925) was a British philosopher who defended a variety of metaphysical idealism (that is, he believed reality consisted of minds and their contents). Like many turn-of-the-century philosophers, he was influenced by Hegel's idealism. McTaggart argued that space, time, and material objects, as we ordinarily conceive them, are not real. He believed they are misperceptions of spiritual entities. Though McTaggart's idealism has had few followers, his argument against the reality of time has been widely studied. He distinguishes two ways to think about time: we can view time either as a series of pasts, presents, and futures (what he calls the "*A* series") or as a series of events standing in earlier-than or later-than relations (the "*B* series"). McTaggart claimed that the *B* series does not capture the essence of time, namely, change. So for time to be real (for there to be real change), the *A* series must be real. Then McTaggart argues that time cannot be real because the *A* series leads to logical difficulties. McTaggart's position is doubly challenging. If one believes time is real and the distinction between the past, present, and future is the essence of time, then one should try to rescue the *A* series from the logical problems McTaggart claims to find. If, on the other hand, one believes time is real and adequately represented by earlier-later relations, then one must defend the *B* series from McTaggart's charge that it pictures a universe devoid of real change.

It will be convenient to begin our enquiry by asking whether anything existent can possess the characteristic of being in time. I shall endeavour to prove that it cannot.

It seems highly paradoxical to assert that time is unreal, and that all statements which involve its reality are erroneous. Such an assertion involves a departure from the natural position of mankind which is far greater than that involved in the assertion of the unreality of space or the unreality of matter. For in each man's experience there is a part—his own states as known to him by introspection—which does not even appear to be spatial or material. But we have no experience which does not appear to be temporal. Even our judgments that time is unreal appear to be themselves in time.

Yet in all ages and in all parts of the world the belief in the unreality of time has shown itself to be singularly persistent. In the philosophy and religion of the West—and still more, I suppose, in the philosophy and religion of the East—we find that the doctrine of the unreality of time continually recurs. Neither philosophy nor religion ever hold themselves apart from mysticism for any long period, and almost all mysticism denies the reality of time. In philosophy, time is treated as unreal by Spinoza, by Kant, and by Hegel. Among more modern thinkers, the same view is taken by Mr Bradley. Such a concurrence of opinion is highly significant, and is not the less significant because the doctrine takes such different forms, and is supported by such different arguments.

I believe that nothing that exists can be temporal, and that therefore time is unreal. But I believe it for reasons which are not put forward by any of the philosophers I have just mentioned.

Positions in time, as time appears to us *prima facie,* are distinguished in two ways. Each position is Earlier than some and Later than some of the other positions. To constitute such a series there is required a transitive asymmetrical relation, and a collection of terms such that, of any two of them, either the first is in this relation to the second, or the second is in this relation to the first. We may take here either the relation of "earlier than" or the relation of "later than," both of which, of course, are transitive and asymmetrical. If we take the first, then the terms have to be such that, of any two of them, either the first is earlier than the second, or the second is earlier than the first.

In the second place, each position is either Past, Present, or Future. The distinctions of the former class are permanent, while those of the latter are not. If M is ever earlier than N, it is always earlier. But an event, which is now present, was future, and will be past.

Since distinctions of the first class are permanent, it might be thought that they were more objective, and more essential to the nature of time, than those of the second class. I believe, however, that this would be a mistake, and that the distinction of past, present, and future is as *essential* to time as the distinction of earlier and later, while in a certain sense it may, as we shall see, be regarded as more *fundamental* than the distinction of earlier and later. And it is because the distinctions of past, present, and future seem to me to be essential for time, that I regard time as unreal.

For the sake of brevity I shall give the name of the A series to that series of positions which runs from the far past through the near past to the present, and then from the present through the near future to the far future, or conversely. The series of positions which runs from earlier to later, or conversely, I shall call the B series. The contents of any position in time form an event. The varied simultaneous contents of a single position are, of course, a plurality of events. But, like any other substance, they form a group, and this group is a compound substance. And a compound substance consisting of simultaneous events may properly be spoken of as itself an event.[1]

The first question which we must consider is whether it is essential to the reality of time that its events should form an A series as well as a B series. It is clear, to begin with, that, in present experience, we never *observe* events in time except as forming both these series. We perceive events in time as being present, and those are the only events which we actually perceive. And all other events which, by memory or by inference, we believe to be real, we regard as present, past, or future. Thus the events of time as observed by us form an A series.

It might be said, however, that this is merely subjective. It might be the case that the distinction of positions in time into past, present, and future, is only a constant illusion of our minds, and that the real nature of time contains only the distinctions of the B series—the distinctions of earlier and later. In that case we should not perceive time as it really is, though we might be able to *think* of it as it really is.

This is not a very common view, but it requires careful consideration. I believe it to be untenable, because, as I said above, it seems to me that the A series is essential to the nature of time, and that any difficulty in the way of regarding the A series as real is equally a difficulty in the way of regarding time as real.

It would, I suppose, be universally admitted that time involves change. In ordinary language, indeed, we say that something can remain unchanged through time. But there could be no time if nothing changed. And if anything changes, then all other things change with it. For its change must change some of their relations to it, and so their relational qualities. The fall of a sand-castle on the English coast changes the nature of the Great Pyramid.

If, then, a B series without an A series can constitute time, change must be possible without an A series. Let us suppose that the distinctions of past, present, and future do not apply to reality. In that case, can change apply to reality?

What, on this supposition, could it be that changes? Can we say that, in a time which formed a B series but not an A series, the change consisted in the fact that the event ceased to be an event, while another event began to be an event? If this were the case, we should certainly have got a change.

But this is impossible. If N is ever earlier than O and later than M, it will always be, and has always been, earlier than O and later than M, since the relations of earlier and later are permanent. N will thus always be in a B series. And as, by our present hypothesis, a B series by itself constitutes time, N will always have a position in a time-series, and always has had one. That is, it always has been an event, and always will be one, and cannot begin or cease to be an event.

Or shall we say that one event *M* merges itself into another event *N*, while still preserving a certain identity by means of an unchanged element, so that it can be said, not merely that *M* has ceased and *N* begun, but that it is *M* which has become *N*? Still the same difficulty recurs. *M* and *N* may have a common element, but they are not the same event, or there would be no change. If, therefore, *M* changed into *N* at a certain moment, then at that moment, *M* would have ceased to be *M*, and *N* would have begun to be *N*. This involves that, at that moment, *M* would have ceased to be an event, and *N* would have begun to be an event. And we saw, in the last paragraph, that, on our present hypothesis, this is impossible.

Nor can such change be looked for in the different moments of absolute time, even if such moments should exist. For the same argument will apply here. Each such moment will have its own place in the *B* series, since each would be earlier or later than each of the others. And, as the *B* series depends on permanent relations, no moment could ever cease to be, nor could it become another moment.

Change, then, cannot arise from an event ceasing to be an event, nor from one event changing into another. In what other way can it arise? If the characteristics of an event change, then there is certainly change. But what characteristics of an event can change? It seems to me that there is only one class of such characteristics. And that class consists of the determinations of the event in question by the terms of the *A* series.

Take any event—the death of Queen Anne, for example—and consider what changes can take place in its characteristics. That it is a death, that it is the death of Anne Stuart, that it has such causes, that it has such effects—every characteristic of this sort never changes. "Before the stars saw one another plain," the event in question was the death of a Queen. At the last moment of time—if time has a last moment—it will still be the death of a Queen. And in every respect but one, it is equally devoid of change. But in one respect it does change. It was once an event in the far future. It became every moment an event in the nearer future. At last it was present. Then it became past, and will always remain past, though every moment it becomes further and further past.[2]

Such characteristics as these are the only characteristics which can change. And, therefore, if there is any change, it must be looked for in the *A* series, and in the *A* series alone. If there is no real *A* series, there is no real change. The *B* series, therefore, is not by itself sufficient to constitute time, since time involves change.

The *B* series, however, cannot exist except as temporal, since earlier and later, which are the relations which connect its terms, are clearly time-relations. So it follows that there can be no *B* series when there is no *A* series, since without an *A* series there is no time.

We must now consider three objections which have been made to this position. The first is involved in the view of time which has been taken by Mr Russell, according to which past, present, and future do not belong to time *per se*, but only in relation to a knowing subject. An assertion that *N* is present means that it is simultaneous with that assertion, an assertion that it is past or future means that it is earlier or later than that assertion. Thus it is only past, present, or future, in relation to some assertion. If there were no consciousness, there would be events which were earlier and later than others, but nothing would be in any sense past, present, or future. And if there were events earlier than any consciousness, those events would never be future or present, though they could be past.

If *N* were ever present, past, or future in relation to some assertion *V*, it would always be so, since whatever is ever simultaneous to, earlier than, or later than, *V*, will always be so. What, then, is change? We find Mr Russell's views on this subject in his *Principles of Mathematics*. "Change is the difference, in respect of truth or falsehood, between a proposition concerning an entity and the time *T*, and a proposition concerning the same entity and the time *T'*, provided that these propositions differ only by the fact that *T* occurs in the one where *T'* occurs in the other." That is to say, there is change, on Mr Russell's view, if the proposition "at the time *T* my poker is hot" is true, and the proposition "at the time *T'* my poker is hot" is false.

I am unable to agree with Mr Russell. I should, indeed, admit that, when two such propositions were respectively true and false, there would be change. But then I maintain that there can be no time without an *A* series. If, with Mr Russell, we reject the *A* series, it seems to me that change goes with it, and that therefore time, for which change is essential, goes too. In other words, if the *A* series is rejected, no proposition of the type "at the time *T* my poker is hot'' can ever be true, because there would be no time.

It will be noticed that Mr Russell looks for change, not in the events in the time-series, but in the entity to which those events happen, or of which they are states. If my poker, for example, is hot on a particular Monday, and never before or since, the event of the poker being hot does not change. But the poker changes, because there is a time when this event is happening to it, and a time when it is not happening to it.

But this makes no change in the qualities of the poker. It is always a quality of that poker that it is one which is hot on that particular Monday. And it is always a quality of that poker that it is one which is not hot at any other time. Both these qualities are true of it at any time—the time when it is hot and the time when it is cold. And therefore it seems to be erroneous to say that there is any change in the poker. The fact that it is hot at one point in a series and cold at other points cannot give change, if neither of these facts change—and neither of them does. Nor does any other fact about the poker change, unless its presentness, pastness, or futurity change.

Let us consider the case of another sort of series. The meridian of Greenwich passes through a series of degrees of latitude. And we can find two points in this series, S and S', such that the proposition "at S the meridian of Greenwich is within the United Kingdom" is true, while the proposition "at S' the meridian of Greenwich is within the United Kingdom" is false. But no one would say that this gave us change. Why should we say so in the case of the other series?

Of course there is a satisfactory answer to this question if we are correct in speaking of the other series as a time-series. For where there is time, there is change. But then the whole question is whether it is a time-series. My contention is that if we remove the A series from the *prima facie* nature of time, we are left with a series which is not temporal, and which allows change no more than the series of latitudes does.

If, as I have maintained, there can be no change unless facts change, then there can be no change without an A series. For, as we saw with the death of Queen Anne, and also in the case of the poker, no fact about anything can change, unless it is a fact about its place in the A series. Whatever other qualities it has, it has always. But that

which is future will not always be future, and that which was past was not always past.

It follows from what we have said that there can be no change unless some propositions are sometimes true and sometimes false. This is the case of propositions which deal with the place of anything in the A series—"the battle of Waterloo is in the past," "it is now raining." But it is not the case with any other propositions.

Mr Russell holds that such propositions are ambiguous, and that to make them definite we must substitute propositions which are always true or always false—"the battle of Waterloo is earlier than this judgment," "the fall of rain is simultaneous with this judgment." If he is right, all judgments are either always true, or always false. Then, I maintain, no facts change. And then, I maintain, there is no change at all.

I hold, as Mr Russell does, that there is no A series. (My reasons for this will be given below.) And, as I shall explain, I regard the reality lying behind the appearance of the A series in a manner not completely unlike that which Mr Russell has adopted. The difference between us is that he thinks that, when the A series is rejected, change, time, and the B series can still be kept, while I maintain that its rejection involves the rejection of change, and, consequently, of time, and of the B series.

The second objection rests on the possibility of nonexistent time-series—such, for example, as the adventures of Don Quixote. This series, it is said, does not form part of the A series. I cannot at this moment judge it to be either past, present, or future. Indeed, I know that it is none of the three. Yet, it is said, it is certainly a B series. The adventure of the galley-slaves, for example, is later than the adventure of the windmills. And a B series involves time. The conclusion drawn is that an A series is not essential to time.

I should reply to this objection as follows. Time only belongs to the existent. If any reality is in time, that involves that the reality in question exists. This, I think, would be universally admitted. It may be questioned whether all of what exists is in time, or even whether anything really existent is in time, but it would not be denied that, if anything is in time, it must exist.

Now what is existent in the adventures of Don Quixote? Nothing. For the story is imaginary. The states of Cervantes' mind when he invented the story, the states of my mind when I think of the story—these exist. But then these form part of an *A* series. Cervantes' invention of the story is in the past. My thought of the story is in the past, the present, and—I trust—the future.

But the adventures of Don Quixote may be believed by a child to be historical. And in reading them I may, by an effort of my imagination, contemplate them as if they really happened. In this case, the adventures are believed to be existent, or are contemplated as existent. But then they are believed to be in the *A* series, or are contemplated as being in the *A* series. The child who believes them to be historical will believe that they happened in the past. If I contemplate them as existent, I shall contemplate them as happening in the past. In the same way, if I believed the events described in Jefferies' *After London* to exist, or contemplated them as existent, I should believe them to exist in the future, or contemplate them as existing in the future. Whether we place the object of our belief or of our contemplation in the present, the past, or the future, will depend upon the characteristics of that object. But somewhere in the *A* series it will be placed.

Thus the answer to the objection is that, just as far as a thing is in time, it is in the *A* series. If it is really in time, it is really in the *A* series. If it is believed to be in time, it is believed to be in the *A* series. If it is contemplated as being in time, it is contemplated as being in the *A* series.

The third objection is based on the possibility that, if time were real at all, there might be in reality several real and independent time-series. The objection, if I understand it rightly, is that every time-series would be real, while the distinctions of past, present, and future would only have a meaning within each series, and would not, therefore, be taken as absolutely real. There would be, for example, many presents. Now, of course, many points of time can be present. In each time-series many points are present, but they must be present successively. And the presents of the different time-series would not be successive, since they are not in the same time.[3] And different presents, it would be said, cannot be real unless they are successive. So the different time-series, which are real, must be able to exist independently of the distinction between past, present, and future.

I cannot, however, regard this objection as valid. No doubt in such a case, no present would

be *the* present—it would only be the present of a certain aspect of the universe. But then no time would be *the* time—it would only be the time of a certain aspect of the universe. It would be a real time-series, but I do not see that the present would be less real than the time.

I am not, of course, maintaining that there is no difficulty in the existence of several distinct *A* series. [Later] I shall endeavour to show that the existence of *any A* series is impossible. What I assert here is that, if there could be an *A* series at all, and if there were any reason to suppose that there were several distinct *B* series, there would be no additional difficulty in supposing that there should be a distinct *A* series for each *B* series.

We conclude, then, that the distinctions of past, present, and future are essential to time, and that, if the distinctions are never true of reality, then no reality is in time. This view, whether true or false, has nothing surprising in it. It was pointed out above that we always perceive time as having these distinctions. And it has generally been held that their connection with time is a real characteristic of time, and not an illusion due to the way in which we perceive it. Most philosophers, whether they did or did not believe time to be true of reality, have regarded the distinctions of the *A* series as essential to time.

When the opposite view has been maintained it has generally been, I believe, because it was held (rightly, as I shall try to show) that the distinctions of past, present, and future cannot be true of reality, and that consequently, if the reality of time is to be saved, the distinction in question must be shown to be unessential to time. The presumption, it was held, was for the reality of time, and this would give us a reason for rejecting the *A* series as unessential to time. But, of course, this could only give a presumption. If the analysis of the nature of time has shown that, by removing the *A* series, time is destroyed, this line of argument is no longer open.

I now pass to the second part of my task. Having, as it seems to me, succeeded in proving that there can be no time without an *A* series, it remains to prove that an *A* series cannot exist, and that therefore time cannot exist. This would involve that time is not real at all, since it is admitted that the only way in which time can be real is by existing.

Past, present, and future are characteristics

which we ascribe to events, and also to moments of time, if these are taken as separate realities. What do we mean by past, present, and future? In the first place, are they relations or qualities? It seems quite clear to me that they are not qualities but relations, though, of course, like other relations, they will generate relational qualities in each of their terms.[4] But even if this view should be wrong, and they should in reality be qualities and not relations, it will not affect the result which we shall reach. For the reasons for rejecting the reality of past, present, and future, which we are about to consider, would apply to qualities as much as to relations.

If, then, anything is to be rightly called past, present, or future, it must be because it is in relation to something else. And this something else to which it is in relation must be something outside the time-series. For the relations of the A series are changing relations, and no relations which are exclusively between members of the time-series can ever change. Two events are exactly in the same places in the time-series, relatively to one another, a million years before they take place, while each of them is taking place, and when they are a million years in the past. The same is true of the relation of moments to one another, if moments are taken as separate realities. And the same would be true of the relations of events to moments. The changing relation must be to something which is not in the time-series.

Past, present, and future, then, are relations in which events stand to something outside the time-series. Are these relations simple, or can they be defined? I think that they are clearly simple and indefinable. But, on the other hand, I do not think that they are isolated and independent. It does not seem that we can know, for example, the meaning of pastness, if we do not know the meaning of presentness or of futurity.

We must begin with the A series, rather than with past, present, and future, as separate terms. And we must say that a series is an A series when each of its terms has, to an entity X outside the series, one, and only one, of three indefinable relations, pastness, presentness, and futurity, which are such that all the terms which have the relation of presentness to X fall between all the terms which have the relation of pastness to X, on the one hand, and all the terms which have the relation of futurity to X, on the other hand.

We have come to the conclusion that an A series depends on relations to a term outside the A series. This term, then, could not itself be in time, and yet must be such that different relations to it determine the other terms of those relations, as being past, present, or future. To find such a term would not be easy, and yet such a term must be found, if the A series is to be real. But there is a more positive difficulty in the way of the reality of the A series.

Past, present, and future are incompatible determinations. Every event must be one or the other, but no event can be more than one. If I say that any event is past, that implies that it is neither present nor future, and so with the others. And this exclusiveness is essential to change, and therefore to time. For the only change we can get is from future to present, and from present to past.

The characteristics, therefore, are incompatible. But every event has them all.[5] If M is past, it has been present and future. If it is future, it will be present and past. If it is present, it has been future and will be past. Thus all the three characteristics belong to each event. How is this consistent with their being incompatible?

It may seem that this can easily be explained. Indeed, it has been impossible to state the difficulty without almost giving the explanation, since our language has verb-forms for the past, present, and future, but no form that is common to all three. It is never true, the answer will run, that M is present, past, and future. It is present, will be past, and has been future. Or it is past, and has been future and present, or again is future, and will be present and past. The characteristics are only incompatible when they are simultaneous, and there is no contradiction to this in the fact that each term has all of them successively.

But what is meant by "has been" and "will be"? And what is meant by "is," when, as here, it is used with a temporal meaning, and not simply for prediction? When we say that X has been Y, we are asserting X to be Y at a moment of past time. When we say that X will be Y, we are asserting X to be Y at a moment of future time. When we say that X is Y (in the temporal sense of "is"), we are asserting X to be Y at a moment of present time.

Thus our first statement about M—that it is present, will be past, and has been future—means that M is present at a moment of present time, past at some moment of future time, and future at some moment of past time. But every moment, like every event, is both past, present, and future. And so a similar difficulty arises. If M is present, there is no moment of past time at which it is past. But the moments of future time, in which it is past, are equally moments of past time, in which it cannot be past. Again, that M is future and will be present and past means that M is future at a moment of present time, and present and past at different moments of future time. In that case it cannot be present or past at any moments of past time. But all the moments of future time, in which M will be present or past, are equally moments of past time.

And thus again we get a contradiction, since the moments at which M has any one of the three determinations of the A series are also moments at which it cannot have that determination. If we try to avoid this by saying of these moments what had been previously said of M itself—that some moment, for example, is future, and will be present and past—then "is" and "will be" have the same meaning as before. Our statement, then, means that the moment in question is future at a present moment, and will be present and past at different moments of future time. This, of course, is the same difficulty over again. And so on infinitely.

Such an infinity is vicious. The attribution of the characteristics past, present, and future to the terms of any series leads to a contradiction, unless it is specified that they have them successively. This means, as we have seen, that they have them in relation to terms specified as past, present, and future. These again, to avoid a like contradiction, must in turn be specified as past, present, and future. And, since this continues infinitely, the first set of terms never escapes from contradiction at all.[6]

The contradiction, it will be seen, would arise in the same way supposing that pastness, presentness, and futurity were original qualities, and not, as we have decided that they are, relations. For it would still be the case that they were characteristics which were incompatible with one another, and that whichever had one of them would also have the other. And it is from this that the contradiction arises.

The reality of the A series, then, leads to a contradiction, and must be rejected. And, since we have seen that change and time require the A series, the reality of change and time must be rejected. And so must the reality of the B series, since that requires time. Nothing is really present, past, or future. Nothing is really earlier or later than anything else or temporally simultaneous with it.

Nothing really changes. And nothing is really in time. Whenever we perceive anything in time—which is the only way in which, in our present experience, we do perceive things—we are perceiving it more or less as it really is not.[7]

Dr Broad, in his admirable book *Scientific Thought,* has put forward a theory of time which he maintains would remove the difficulties which have led me to treat time as unreal.[8] It is difficult to do justice to so elaborate and careful a theory by means of extracts. I think, however, that the following passages will give a fair idea of Dr Broad's position. His theory, he tells us, "accepts the reality of the present and the past, but holds that the future is simply nothing at all. Nothing has happened to the present by becoming past except that fresh slices of existence have been added to the total history of the world. The past is thus as real as the present. On the other hand, the essence of a present event is, not that it precedes future events, but that there is quite literally *nothing* to which it has the relation of precedence. The sum total of existence is always increasing, and it is this which gives the time-series a sense as well as an order. A moment t is later than a moment t' if the sum total of existence at t includes the sum total of existence at t' together with something more."

Again, he says that "judgments which profess to be about the future do not refer to any fact, whether positive or negative, at the time when they are made. They are therefore at that time neither true nor false. They will become true or false when there is a fact for them to refer to; and after this they will remain true or false, as the case may be, for ever and ever. If you choose to define the word *judgment* in such a way that nothing is to be called a judgment unless it be either true or false, you must not, of course, count judgments that profess to be about the future as judgments. If you accept the latter, you must say that the Law of Excluded Middle does not apply to all judgments. If you reject them, you may say that the Law of Excluded Middle applies to all genuine judgments; but you must add that judgments which profess to be about the future are not genuine judgments when they are made, but merely enjoy a courtesy title by anticipation, like the elder sons of the higher nobility during the lifetime of their fathers." "I do not think that the laws of logic have anything to say against this kind of change; and, if they have, so much the worse for the laws of logic, for it is certainly a fact."

My first objection to Dr Broad's theory is that, as he says, it would involve that "it will rain to-morrow" is neither true nor false, and that "England will be a republic in 1920," was not false in 1919. It seems to me quite certain that "it will rain to-morrow" is either true or false, and that "England will be a republic in 1920," was false in 1919. Even if Dr Broad's theory did enable him to meet my objections to the reality of time (which I shall try to show later on is not the case) I should still think that my theory should be accepted in preference to his. The view that time is unreal is, no doubt, very different from the *prima facie* view of reality. And it involves that perception can be erroneous. But the *prima facie* view of reality need not be true, and erroneous perception is not impossible. And, I submit, it is quite impossible that "it will rain to-morrow" is neither true nor false.

In the second place it is to be noted that Dr Broad's theory must be false if the past ever intrinsically determines the future. If X intrinsically determines a subsequent Y, then (at any rate as soon as X is present or past, and therefore, on Dr Broad's theory, real) it will be true that, since there is an X, there must be a subsequent Y. Then it is true that there is a subsequent Y. And if that Y is not itself present or past, then it is true that there will be a future Y, and so something is true about the future.

Now is it possible to hold that the past never does intrinsically determine the future? It seems to me that there is just as much reason to believe that the past determines the future as there is to believe that the earlier past determines the later past or the present.

We cannot, indeed, usually get a positive statement as simple as "the occurrence of X intrinsically determines the occurrence of a subsequent Y." But the intrinsic determination of the events can often be summed up in a statement of only moderate complexity. If the moon was visible in a certain direction last midnight, this intrinsically determines that, either it will be visible in a rather different direction next midnight, or the night will be cloudy, or the universe will have come to an end, or the relative motions of the earth and moon will have changed. Thus it is true that in the future one of four things will happen. And thus a proposition about the future is true.

And there are other intrinsic determinations which can be summed up in very simple negative statements. If Smith has already died childless, this intrinsically determines that no future event will be a marriage of one of Smith's grandchildren.

It seems, then, impossible to deny that the truth of some propositions about the future is implied in the truth of some propositions about the past, and that, therefore, some propositions about the future are true. And we may go further. If no propositions abut the past implied propositions about the future, then no propositions about the past could imply propositions about the later past or the present.

If the proposition "the occurrence of X implies the occurrence of Y" is ever true, it is always true, while X is real, and, therefore, even according to Dr Broad's view of reality, it is always true while X is present and past. For it is dependent on the nature of X and the laws of implication. The latter are not changeable, and when an event has once happened, its nature remains unchangeable. Thus, if it were not true, in 1921, that the occurrence of any event in 1920 involved the occurrence of any event in 1922, then it could not be true in 1923, when both 1920 and 1922 are in the past. And this would apply to any two periods in time, as much as to 1920 and 1922.

There are, then, only two alternatives. Either propositions about the future are true, and Dr Broad's theory is wrong. Or else no proposition about any one period of time implies the truth of a proposition about any other period of time. From this it follows that no event at any point of time intrinsically determines any event at any other point of time, and that there is no causal determination except what is strictly simultaneous.

It is clear, from the rest of his book, that Dr Broad does not accept this last alternative, and it is difficult to conceive that anyone would do so, unless he were so complete a sceptic that he could have no theory as to the nature of time, or of anything else. For a person who accepted this alternative would not merely deny that complete causal determination could be proved, he would not merely deny that any causal determination could be proved, but he would assert that all causal determination, between non-simultaneous events, was proved to be impossible. But if this is not accepted, then some propositions about the future must be true[9].

In the third place, even if the two objections already considered should be disregarded, time would still, on Dr Broad's theory, involve the contradiction described above. For although, if Dr

Broad were right, no moment would have the three incompatible characteristics of past, present, and future, yet each of them (except the last moment of time, if there should be a last moment) would have the two incompatible characteristics of past and present. And this would be sufficient to produce the contradiction.

The words past and present clearly indicate different characteristics. And no one, I think, would suggest that they are simply compatible, in the way that the characteristics red and sweet are. If one man should say "strawberries are red," and another should reply "that is false, for they are sweet," the second man would be talking absolute nonsense. But if the first should say "you are eating my strawberries," and the second should reply "that is false, for I have already eaten them," the remark is admittedly not absolute nonsense, though its precise relation to the truth would depend on the truth about the reality of matter and time.

The terms can only be made compatible by a qualification. The proper statement of that qualification seems to me to be, as I have said, that, when we say that *M* is present, we mean that it is present at a moment of present time, and will be past at some moment of future time, and that, when we say that *M* is past we mean that it has been present at some moment of past time, and is past at a moment of present time. Dr Broad will, no doubt, claim to cut out "will be past at some moment of future time." But even then it would be true that, when we say *M* is past, we mean that it has been present at some moment of past time, and is past at a moment of present time, and that, when we say *M* is present, we mean that it is present at a moment of present time. As much as this Dr Broad can say, and as much as this he must say, if he admits that each event (except a possible last event) is both present and past.

Thus we distinguish the presentness and pastness of events by reference to past and present moments. But every moment which is past is also present. And if we attempt to remove this difficulty by saying that it *is* past and *has been* present, then we get an infinite vicious series.

For these three reasons it seems to me that Dr Broad's theory of time is untenable, and that the reality of time must still be rejected.

It is sometimes maintained that we are so immediately certain of the reality of time, that the certainty exceeds any certainty which can possibly be produced by arguments to the contrary, and that such arguments, therefore, should be rejected as false, even if we can find no flaw in them.

It does not seem to me that there is any immediate certainty of the reality of time. It is true, no doubt, that we perceive things as in time, and that therefore the unreality of time involves the occurrence of erroneous perception. But, as I have said, I hope to prove later that there is no impossibility in erroneous perception. It may be worth while, however, to point out that any theory which treated time as objectively real could only do so by treating time, *as we observe it*, as being either unreal or merely subjective. It would thus have no more claim to support from our perceptions than the theories which deny the reality of time.[10]

I perceive as present at one time whatever falls within the limits of one specious present. Whatever falls earlier or later than this, I do not perceive at all, though I judge it to be past or future. The time-series then, of which any part is perceived by me, is a time-series in which the future and the past are separated by a present which is a specious present.

Whatever is simultaneous with anything present, is itself present. If, therefore, the objective time-series, in which events really are, is the series which I immediately perceive, whatever is simultaneous with my specious present is present. But the specious present varies in length according to circumstances. And it is not impossible that there should be another conscious being existing besides myself, and that his specious present and mine may at the same time be of different lengths. Now the event *M* may be simultaneous both with *X*'s perception *Q*, and with *Y*'s perception *R*. At a certain moment *Q* may have ceased to be a part of *X*'s specious present. *M*, therefore, will at that moment be past. But at the same moment *R* may still be a part of *Y*'s specious present. And, therefore, *M* will be present at some moment at which it is past.

This is impossible. If, indeed, the *A* series was something purely subjective, there would be no difficulty. We could say that *M* was past for *X* and present for *Y*, just as we could say that it was pleasant for *X* and painful for *Y*. But we are now considering the hypothesis that time is objective. And, since the *A* series is essential to time, this involves that the *A* series is objective. And, if so, then at any moment *M* must be present, past, or future. It cannot be both present and past.

The present, therefore, through which events

are really to pass, cannot be determined as being simultaneous with a specious present. If it has a duration, it must be a duration which is independently fixed. And it cannot be independently fixed so as to be identical with the duration of all specious presents, since all specious presents have not the same duration. And thus an event may be past or future when I am perceiving it as present, and may be present when I am remembering it as past or anticipating it as future. The duration of the objective present may be the thousandth part of a second. Or it may be a century, and the coronations of George IV and of Edward VII may form part of the same present. What reasons can we find in the immediate certainties of our experience to believe in the existence of such a present, which we certainly do not observe to be a present, and which has no relation to what we do observe as a present?

If we take refuge from these difficulties in the view, which has sometimes been held, that the present in the A series is not a finite duration, but a single point, separating future from past, we shall find other difficulties as serious. For then the objective time, in which events are, would be something entirely different from the time in which we experience them as being. The time in which we experience them has a present of varying finite duration, and is therefore divided into three durations—the past, the present, and the future. The objective time has only two durations, separated by a present which has nothing but the name in common with the present of experience, since it is not a duration but a point. What is there in our perception which gives us the least reason to believe in such a time as this?

And thus the denial of the reality of time turns out not to be so very paradoxical. It was called paradoxical because it required us to treat our experience of time as illusory. But now we see that our experience of time—centring as it does about the specious present—would be no less illusory if there were a real time in which the realities we experience existed. The specious present of our observations cannot correspond to the present of the events observed. And consequently the past and future of our observations could not correspond to the past and future of the events observed. On either hypothesis—whether we take time as real or as unreal—everything is observed as in a specious present, but nothing, not even the observations themselves, can ever really *be* in a specious present. For if time is unreal, nothing can

be in any present at all, and, if time is real, the present in which things are will not be a specious present. I do not see, therefore, that we treat experience as much more illusory when we say that nothing is ever present at all, than when we say that everything passes through some present which is entirely different from the only present we experience.

It must further be noted that the results at which we have arrived do not give us any reason to suppose that *all* the elements in our experience of time are illusory. We have come to the conclusion that there is no real A series, and that therefore there is no real B series, and no real time-series. But it does not follow that when we have experience of a time-series we are not observing a real series. It is possible that, whenever we have an illusory experience of a time-series, we are observing a real series, and that all that is illusory is the appearance that it is a time-series. Such a series as this—a series which is not a time-series, but under certain conditions appears to us to be one—may be called a C series.

There are good reasons for supposing that such a C series does actually exist, in every case in which there is the appearance of a time-series. For when we consider how an illusion of time can come about, it is very difficult to suppose, either that all the elements in the experience are illusory, or that the element of the serial nature is so. And it is by no means so difficult to account for the facts if we suppose that there is an existent C series. In this case the illusion consists only in our applying the A series to it, and in the consequent appearance of the C series as a B series, the relation, whatever it may be, which holds between the terms of the C series, appearing as a relation of earlier and later.

The C series, then, can be real, while the A and B series are merely apparent. But when we consider how our experience is built up, we must class C and A together as primary, while B is only secondary. The real C series and the appearance of the A series must be given, separately and independently, in order to have the experience of time. For, as we have seen, they are both essential to it, and neither can be derived from the other. The B series, on the other hand, can be derived from the other two. For if there is a C series, where the terms are connected by permanent relations, and if the terms of this series appear also to form an A series, it will follow that the terms of the C series will also appear as a B series, those which are placed first, in the direction from past to future, appearing as earlier than those whose places are further in the direction of the future.

And thus, if there is a C series, it will follow that our experience of the time-series will not be entirely erroneous. Through the deceptive form of time, we shall grasp some of the true relations of what really exists. If we say that the events M and N are simultaneous, we say that they occupy the same position in the time-series. And there will be some truth in this, for the realities, which we perceive as the events M and N, do really occupy the same position in a series, though it is not a temporal series.

Again, if we assert that the events M, N, O are all at different times, and are in that order, we assert that they occupy different positions in the time-series, and that the position of N is between the positions of M and O. And it will be true that the realities which we see as these events will be in a series, though not in a temporal series, and that they will be in different positions in it, and that the position of the reality which we perceive as the event N will be between the positions of the realities which we perceive as the events M and O.

If this view is adopted, the result will so far resemble the views of Hegel rather than those of Kant. For Hegel regarded the order of the time-series as a reflection, though a distorted reflection, of something in the real nature of the timeless reality, while Kant does not seem to have contemplated the possibility that anything in the nature of the noumenon should correspond to the time-order which appears in the phenomenon.

Thus the C series will not be altogether unlike the time-series as conceived by Mr Russell. The C series will include as terms everything which appears to us as an event in time, and the C series will contain the realities in the same order as the events are ranged in by the relations of earlier and later. And the time-series, according to Mr Russell, does not involve the objective reality of the A series.

But there remain important differences. Mr Russell's series is a time-series, and the C series is not temporal. And although Mr Russell's time-series (which is identical with our B series) has a one-to-one correspondence with the C series, still the two series are very different. The terms of the B series are events, and the terms of the C series are not. And the relation which unites the terms of the B series is the relation of earlier and later, which is not the case with the C series.

Endnotes

[1] It is very usual to contemplate time by the help of a metaphor of spatial movement. But spatial movement in which direction? The movement of time consists in the fact that later and later terms pass into the present, or—which is the same fact expressed in another way—that presentness passes to later and later terms. If we take it the first way, we are taking the B series as sliding along a fixed A series. If we take it the second way, we are taking the A series as sliding along a fixed B series. In the first case time presents itself as a movement from future to past. In the second case it presents itself as a movement from earlier to later. And this explains why we say that events come out of the future, while we say that we ourselves move towards the future. For each man identifies himself especially with his present state, as against his future or his past, since it is the only one which he is directly perceiving. And this leads him to say that he is moving with the present towards later events. And as those events are now future, he says that he is moving towards the future.

Thus the question as to the movement of time is ambiguous. But if we ask what is the movement of either series, the question is not ambiguous. The movement of the A series along the B series is from earlier to later. The movement of the B series along the A series is from future to past.

[2] The past, therefore, is always changing, if the A series is real at all, since at each moment a past event is further in the past than it was before. This result follows from the reality of the A series, and is independent of the truth of our view that all change depends exclusively on the A series. It is worth while to notice this, since most people combine the view that the A series is real with the view that the past cannot change—a combination which is inconsistent.

[3] Neither would they be simultaneous, since that equally involves being in the same time. They would stand in no time-relation to one another.

[4] It is true, no doubt, that my anticipation of an experience M, the experience itself, and the memory of the experience, are three states which have different original qualities. But it is not the future M, the present M, and the past M, which have these three different qualities. The qualities are possessed by three different events—the anticipation of M, M itself, and the memory of M—each of which in its turn is future, present, and past. Thus this gives no support to the view that the changes of the A series are changes of original qualities.

[5] If the time-series has a first term, that term will never be future, and if it has a last term, that term will never be past. But the first term, in that case, will be present

and past, and the last term will be future and present. And the possession of two incompatible characteristics raises the same difficulty as the possession of three.

[6] It may be worth while to point out that the vicious infinite has not arisen from the impossibility of *defining* past, present, and future, without using the terms in their own definitions. On the contrary, we have admitted these terms to be indefinable. It arises from the fact that the nature of the terms involves a contradiction, and that the attempt to remove the contradiction involves the employment of the terms, and the generation of a similar contradiction.

[7] Even on the hypothesis that judgments are real it would be necessary to regard ourselves as perceiving things in time, and so perceiving them erroneously. And we shall see later that all cognition is perception, and that, therefore, all error is erroneous perception.

[8] I have published my views on time, pretty nearly in their present shape, in *Mind* for 1908.

[9] It might seem that the truth of propositions about the future would be as fatal to my theory as to Dr Broad's, since I am denying the reality of time. But, as will be explained later, although there is no time-series, there is a non-temporal series which is misperceived as a time-series. An assertion at one point of this series may be true of a fact at some other point in this series, which appears as a future point. And thus statements about the future might have phenomenal validity— they might have a one-to-one correspondence with true statements, and they might themselves be as true as any statements about the past could be. But Dr Broad's theory requires that they should have no truth whatever, while some statements about the past and present should be absolutely true.

[10] By objectively real time, I mean a common time in which all existent things exist, so that they stand in temporal relations to each other. By subjectively real time, I mean one in which only the different states of a single self exist, so that it does not connect any self with anything outside it.

8. The Myth of Passage

DONALD C. WILLIAMS

Donald C. Williams was an American philosopher who taught at Harvard University. His article, "The Myth of Passage," first appeared in the *Journal of Philosophy* in 1951. This article shows how empirically-minded philosophers were assimilating new ideas in physics and defending a relational view of time. Newton, Bergson, and McTaggart had maintained that there is something *sui generis* about the present, the Now. Whether called the "flux of absolute time" or "pure duration" or "Becoming," such thinkers believed time has a dynamic aspect that cannot be accounted for solely in terms of relations like earlier-than or later-than. But early in the twentieth century, Einstein's successful special theory of relativity rejected Newton's absolute time. Not only did Relativity take a relational approach to time, it said there is no unique cosmic Now: different observers in different "reference frames" could all be right when they disagreed about which events were past, present, or future. This led some people to believe reality is a four-dimensional "manifold" of "tenselessly existing" events. But how can such a view explain the deep-seated belief (and one's experience) that the present is unique and passing? Williams addresses this issue.

At every moment each of us finds himself the apparent center of the world, enjoying a little lit foreground of the here and now, while around him there looms, thing beyond thing, event beyond event, the plethora of a universe. Linking the furniture of the foreground are sets of relations which he supposes also to bind the things beyond and to bind the foreground with the rest. Noteworthy among them are those queerly obvious relations, peculiarly external to their terms, which compose the systems of space and time, modes of connection exhaustively specifiable in a scheme of four dimensions at right angles to one another. Within this manifold, for all that it is so firmly integrated, we are immediately struck by a disparity between the three-dimensional spread of space and the one dimension of time. The spatial dimensions are in a literal and precise sense perpendicular to one another, and the submanifold which they compose is

isotropic, the same in all directions. The one dimension of time, on the other hand, although it has the same formal properties as each of the other three, is at least sensuously different from them as they are not from one another, and the total manifold is apparently not isotropic. Whereas an object can preserve the same shape while it is so shifted that its height becomes its breadth, we cannot easily conceive how it could do so while being shifted so that its breadth becomes its duration.

The theory of the manifold, I think, is the one model on which we can describe and explain the foreground of experience, or can intelligibly and credibly construct our account of the rest of the world, and this is so because in fact the universe is spread out in those dimensions. There may be Platonic entities which are foreign to both space and time; there may be Cartesian spirits which are foreign to space; but the homely realm of natural existence, the total of world history, is a spatiotemporal volume of somewhat uncertain magnitude, chockablock with things and events. Logic, with its law of excluded middle and its tenseless operators, and natural science, with its secular world charts, concur inexorably with the vision of metaphysics

From "The Myth of Passage," *The Journal of Philosophy*, Vol. 48, 1951, pp. 457–472. Reprinted by permission of *The Journal of Philosophy* and the estate of Donald C. Williams.

and high religion that truth and fact are thus eternal.

I believe that the universe consists, without residue, of the spread of events in space-time, and that if we thus accept realistically the four-dimensional fabric of juxtaposed actualities we can dispense with all those dim nonfactual categories which have so bedeviled our race: the potential, the subsistential, and the influential, the noumenal, the numinous, and the nonnatural. But I am arguing here, not that there is nothing outside the natural world of events, but that the theory of the manifold is anyhow literally true and adequate to that world: true, in that the world contains no less than the manifold; adequate, in that it contains no more.

Since I think that this philosophy offers correct and coherent answers to real questions, I must think that metaphysical difficulties raised against it are genuine too. There are facts, logical and empirical, which can be described and explained only by the concept of the manifold; there are facts which some honest men deem irreconcilable with it. Few issues can better deserve adjudication. The difficulties which we need not take seriously are those made by primitive minds, and by new deliberate primitivists, who recommend that we follow out the Augustinian clue, as Augustine did not, that the man who best feels he understands time is he who refuses to think about it.

Among philosophical complainants against the manifold, some few raise difficulties about space—there are subjectivistic epistemologists, for example, who grant more reality to their own past and future than to things spatially beyond themselves. The temporal dimension of the manifold, however, bears the principal brunt. Sir James Jeans regretted that time is mathematically attached to space by so "weird" a function as the square root of minus one,[1] and the very word "weird," being cognate with "werden," to become, is a monument to the uncanniness of our fourth dimension. Maintaining that time is in its essence something wholly unique, a flow or passage, the "time snobs" (as Wyndham Lewis called them) either deny that the temporal spread is a reality at all, or think it only a very abstract phase of real time. Far from disparaging time itself, they conceive themselves thus to be "taking time seriously" in a profounder sense than our party who are content with the vasty reaches of what is, was, and will be.

The more radical opposition to the manifold takes time with such Spartan seriousness that almost none of it is left—only the pulse of the present, born virginally from nothing and devouring itself as soon as born, so that whatever past and future there be are strictly only the memory and anticipation of them in this Now.[2] One set of motives for this view is in the general romantic polemic against logic and the competence of concepts. The theory of the manifold is the logical account of events par excellence, the teeth by which the jaws of the intellect grip the flesh of occurrence. The Bergsonian, who thinks that concepts cannot convey the reality of time because they are "static," the Marxist who thinks that process defies the cadres of two-valued logic, and the Heideggerian who thinks that temporality, history, and existence are leagued outside the categories of the intellect, thus have incentives for denying, in effect, all the temporal universe beyond what is immanent in the present flare and urge.

To counter their attack, it is a nice and tempting question whether and how concepts are "static," whether and how, in any case, a true concept must be similar to its object, and whether and how history and existence are any more temporal than spatial. But we cannot here undertake the whole defense of the intellect against its most violent critics. We shall rather notice such doubters as trust and use conceptual analysis and still think there are cogent arguments against the manifold. One argument to that effect is an extreme sharpening of the positivistic argument from the egocentric predicament. For if it is impossible for my concepts to transcend experience in general, it may well be impossible for them to transcend the momentary experience in which they are entertained. Conversely, however, anybody who rejects the arguments for instantaneous solipsism, as most people do, must reject this argument for diminishing the manifold. The chief mode of argument is rather the finding of an intolerable anomaly in the statement that what was but has ceased, or what will be but has not begun, nevertheless is. This reflection has been used against the reality of the future, in particular, by philosophers as miscellaneous as Aristotle and neoscholastics, C. D. Broad, Paul Weiss, and Charles Hartshorne. In so far as it is an argument from logic, charging the manifold with self-contradiction, it would be as valid against the past as against the future; but, I have argued, it is by no means valid.[3]

The statement that a sea fight not present in time nevertheless exists is no more contradictory than that one not present in space nevertheless exists. If it seems so, this is only because there happens to be a temporal reference (tense) built into our verbs rather than a spatial reference (as in some languages) or than no locative reference (as in canonical symbolic transcriptions into logic).

I am not to contend now for the reality of the manifold, however, but against the extra *weirdness* alleged for time both by some champions who reject the manifold out of hand and by some who contend anyhow that it is not the whole story, both parties agreeing that the temporal dimension is not "real time," not "the genuine creative flux." If our temporalist means by this that the theory of temporal extension, along with the spatial models provided by calendars, kymographs, and statistical time charts, is in the last analysis fictitious, corresponding to nothing in the facts, he is reverting, under a thin cloak of dissimulation, to the mere rejection which we have agreed to leave aside. If he means, at the other extreme, no more than that the theory and the models themselves are not identical, either numerically or qualitatively, with the actual temporal succession which they represent, he is uttering a triviality which is true of every theory or representation. If he means that the temporal spread, though real and formally similar to a spatial spread, is qualitatively or intuitively very different from it, or lies in a palpably and absolutely unique direction, he says something plausible and important but not at all incompatible with the philosophy of the manifold.

He is most likely to mean, however, another proposition which is never more than vaguely expressed: that over and above the sheer spread of events, with their several qualities, along the time axis, which is analogous enough to the spread of space, there is something extra, something active and dynamic, which is often and perhaps best described as "passage." This something extra, I am going to plead, is a myth: not one of those myths which foreshadow a difficult truth in a metaphorical way, but altogether a false start, deceiving us about the facts, and blocking our understanding of them.

The literature of "passage" is immense, but it is naturally not very exact and lucid, and we cannot be sure of distinguishing in it between mere harmless allegorical phenomenology and the special metaphysical declaration which I criticize. But "passage," it would seem, is a character supposed to inhabit and glorify the present, "the passing present,"[4] "the moving present,"[5] the "travelling *now*."[6] It is "the passage of time as actual . . . given now with the jerky or whooshy quality of transience."[7] It is James' "passing moment."[8] It is what Broad calls "the transitory aspect" of time, in contrast with the "extensive."[9] It is Bergson's living felt duration. It is Heidegger's *Zeitlichkeit*. It is Tillich's "moment that is creation and fate."[10] It is "the act of becoming," the mode of potency and generation, which Hugh King finds properly appreciated only by Aristotle and Whitehead.[11] It is Eddington's "ongoing" and "the formality of taking place,"[12] and Dennes' "surge of process."[13] It is the dynamic essence which Ushenko believes that Einstein omits from the world.[14] It is the mainspring of McTaggart's "A-series" which puts movement in time,[15] and it is Broad's pure becoming.[16] Withal it is the flow and go of very existence, nearer to us than breathing, closer than hands and feet.

So far as one can interpret these expressions into a theory, they have the same purport as all the immemorial turns of speech by which we describe time as *moving*, with respect to the present or with respect to our minds. Time flows or flies or marches, years roll, hours pass. More explicitly we may speak as if the perceiving mind were stationary while time flows by like a river, with the flotsam of events upon it; or as if presentness were a fixed pointer under which the tape of happenings slides; or as if the time sequence were a moving-picture film, unwinding from the dark reel of the future, projected briefly on the screen of the present, and rewound into the dark can of the past. Sometimes, again, we speak as if the time sequence were a stationary plain or ocean on which we voyage, or a variegated river gorge down which we drift; or, in Broad's analogy, as if it were a row of house fronts along which the spotlight of the present plays. "The essence of nowness," Santayana says, "runs like fire along the fuse of time."[17]

Augustine pictures the present passing into the past, where the modern pictures the present as invading the future,[18] but these do not conflict, for Augustine means that the *events* which were present become past, while the modern means that *presentness* encroaches on what was previously the future. Sometimes the surge of presentness is conceived as a mere moving illumination by consciousness, sometimes as a sort of vivification and heightening, like an ocean wave heaving along beneath a stagnant expanse of floating seaweed, sometimes as no less than the boon of existence itself, reifying minute by minute a limbo of un-things.

Now, the most remarkable feature of all this is that while the modes of speech and thought which enshrine the idea of passage are universal and perhaps ineradicable, the instant one thinks about them one feels uneasy, and the most laborious effort cannot construct an intelligible theory which admits the literal truth of any of them. The obvious and notorious fault of the idea, as we have now localized it, is this. Motion is already defined and explained in the dimensional manifold as consisting of the presence of the same individual in different places at different times. It consists of bends or quirks in the world line, or the space-time worm, which is the four-dimensioned totality of the individual's existence. This is motion in space, if you like; but we can readily define a corresponding "motion in time." It comes out as nothing more dramatic than an exact equivalent: "motion in time" consists of being at different times in different places.

True motion then is motion at once in time and space. Nothing can "move" in time alone any more than in space alone, and time itself cannot "move" any more than space itself. "Does this road go anywhere?" asks the city tourist. "No, it stays right along here," replies the countryman. Time "flows" only in the sense in which a line flows or a landscape "recedes into the west." That is, it is an ordered extension. And each of us proceeds through time only as a fence proceeds across a farm: that is, parts of our being, and the fence's, occupy successive instants and points, respectively. There is passage, but it is nothing extra. It is the mere happening of things, their existence strung along in the manifold. The term "the present" is the conventional way of designating the cross section of events which are simultaneous with the uttering of the phrase, and "the present moves" only in that when similar words occur at successively different moments, they denote, by a twist of language essentially the same as that of all "egocentric particulars," like "here" and "this," different cross sections of the manifold.

Time travel, prima facie, then, is analyzable either as the banality that at each different moment we occupy a different moment from the one we occupied before, or the contradiction that at each different moment we occupy a different moment from the one which we are then occupying—that five minutes from now, for example, I may be a hundred years from now.[19]

The tragedy then of the extra idea of passage or absolute becoming, as a philosophical principle, is that it incomprehensibly doubles its world by reintroducing terms like "moving" and "becoming" in a sense which both requires and forbids interpretation in the preceding ways. For as soon as we say that time or the present or we move in the odd extra way which the doctrine of passage requires, we have no recourse but to suppose that this movement in turn takes time of a special sort: $time_1$ moves at a certain rate in $time_2$, perhaps one $second_1$ per one $second_2$, perhaps slower, perhaps faster. Or, conversely, the moving present slides over so many seconds of $time_1$ in so many seconds of $time_2$. The history of the new moving present, in $time_2$, then composes a new and higher time dimension again, which cries to be vitalized by a new level of passage, and so on forever.

We hardly needed to point out the unhappy regress to which the idea of time's motion commits us, for any candid philosopher, as soon as he looks hard at the idea, must *see* that it is preposterous. "Taking place" is not a formality to which an event incidentally submits—it is the event's very being. World history consists of actual concrete happenings in a temporal sequence; it is not necessary or possible that happening should happen to them all over again. The system of the manifold is thus "complete" in something like the technical logical sense, and any attempted addition to it is bound to be either contradictory or supererogatory.

Bergson, Broad, and some of the followers of Whitehead[20] have tried to soften the paradoxes of passage by supposing that the present does not move across the total time level, but that it is the very fountain where the river of time gushes out of nothingness (or out of the power of God). The past, then, having swum into being and floated away, is eternally real, but the future has no existence at all. This may be a more appealing figure, but logically it involves the same anomalies of metahappening and metatime which we observed in the other version.

What, then, we must ask, were the motives which drove men to the staggering philosophy of passage? One of them, I believe, we can dispose of at once. It is the innocent vertigo which inevitably besets a creature whose thinking is strung out in time, as soon as he tries to think of the time dimension itself. He finds it easiest to conceive and understand purely geometrical structures. Motion is more difficult, and generally remains vague, while time per se is very difficult indeed, but being now identified as the principle which imports motion into space, it is put down as a kind of quintessential motion itself. The process is helped by the fact that the mere further-along-ness of successive segments, either of a spatial or of a temporal stretch, can quite logically be conceived as a degenerate sort of change, as when we speak of the flow of a line or say that the scenery changes along the Union Pacific.

A rather more serious excuse for the idea of passage is that it is supposed necessary and sufficient for adding to the temporal dimension that intrinsic *sense* from earlier to later in which time is supposed to differ radically from any dimension of space.[21] A meridian of longitude has only a direction, but a river has a "sense," and time is in this like the river. It is, as the saying goes, irreversible and irrevocable. It has a "directed tension."[22] The mere dimension of time, on the other hand, would seem to be symmetrical. The principle of absolute passage is bidden to rectify this symmetry with what Eddington called "time's arrow."

It might be replied that science does not supply an arrow for time because it has no need of it. But I think it plain that time does have a sense, from early to late. I only think that it can be taken care of on much less draconian principles than absolute passage. There is nothing in the dimensional view of time to preclude its being generated by a uniquely asymmetrical relation, and experience suggests powerfully that it is so generated. But the fact is that every real series has a "sense" anyhow. This is provided, if by nothing else, then by the sheer numerical identity and diversity of terms.

In the line of individual things or events, a, b, c, . . . z, whether in space or in time, the "sense" from a to z is *ipso facto* other than the "sense" from z to a. Only because there is a difference between the ordered couple $a;z$ and the couple $z;a$ can we define the difference between a symmetrical and an asymmetrical relation. Only because there are already two distinguishable "ways" on a street, determined by its individual ends, can we decide to permit traffic to move one way and prohibit it the other. But a sufficient difference of sense, finally,

would appear to be constituted, if nothing else offered, by the inevitably asymmetrical distribution of properties along the temporal line (or any other). Eddington has been only one of many scientists who think the arrow is provided for the cosmos by the principle of entropy, and entropy has been only one principle thus advocated.[23]

In so far as what men mean by "the irrevocability of the past" is the causal circumstance that we can affect the future in a way we cannot affect the past, it is just a trait of the physicist's arrow. They often mean by it, however, only the inexorability of fact, that what is the case is the case, past, present, or future; or the triviality that the particular events of 1902, let us say, cannot also be the events of 1952. Very similar events might be so, however, and if very few of them are, this is the fault of the concrete nature of things and not of any grudge on the part of time.[24]

The final motive for the attempt to consummate or supplant the fourth dimension of the manifold with the special perfection, the grace and whiz, of passage is the vaguest but the most substantial and incorrigible. It is simply that we *find* passage, that we are immediately and poignantly involved in the whoosh of process, the felt flow of one moment into the next. Here is the focus of being. Here is the shore whence the youngster watches the golden mornings swing toward him like serried bright breakers from the ocean of the future. Here is the flood on which the oldster wakes in the night to shudder at its swollen black torrent cascading him into the abyss.

It would be futile to try to deny these experiences, but their correct description is another matter. If they are in fact consistent with our theory, they are no evidence against it; and if they are entailed by it, they are evidence in its favor. Since the theory was originally constructed to take account of them, it would be odd if they were inconsistent with it or even irrelevant to it. I believe that in fact they are neither, and that the theory of the manifold provides the true and literal description of what the enthusiastic metaphors of passage have deceptively garbled.

The principal reason why we are troubled to accommodate our experience of time to the intellectual theory of time goes very deep in the philosophy of philosophy. It is that we must here scrutinize the undoctored fact of perception, on the one hand, and must imagine our way into a conceptual scheme, and envisage the true intrinsic being of its objects, on the other hand, and then pronounce on the numerical identity of the first with the second. This is a very rare requirement. Even such apt ideas as those of space and of physical objects, as soon as we contemplate them realistically, begin to embarrass us, so that we slip into the assumption that the real objects of the conceptions, if they exist at all, exist on a different plane or in a different realm from the sensuous spread and lumpiness of experience. The ideas of time and of the mind, however, do not permit of such evasion. Those beings are given in their own right and person, filling the foreground. Here for once we must fit the fact directly into the intellectual form, without benefit of precedent or accustomed criteria. First off, then, comparing the calm conceptual scheme with the turbid event itself, we may be repelled by the former, not because it is not true to the latter, but because it *is* not the latter. When we see that this kind of diversity is inevitable to every concept and its object, and hence is irrelevant to the validity of any, we demur because the conceptual scheme is indifferently flat and third-personal, like a map, while the experienced reality is centripetal and perspectival, piled up and palpitating where we are, gray and retiring elsewhere.

But this is only because every occasion on which we compare the world map with experience has itself a single specific location, confronting part of the world, remote from the rest. The perspectivity of the view is exactly predictable from the map. The deception with respect to time is worse than with respect to space because our memories and desires run timewise and not spacewise. The jerk and whoosh of this moment, which are simply the real occurrence of one particular batch of events, are no different from the whoosh and being of any other patch of events up and down the eternal timestretch. Remembering some of the latter, however, and anticipating more, and bearing in mind that while they happen they are all called "the present," we mistakenly hypostatize *the* Present as a single surge of bigness which rolls along the time axis. There is in fact no more a single rolling Now than there is a single rolling Here along a spatial line—a standing line of soldiers, for example, though each of them has the vivid presentment of his own here.

Let us hug to us as closely as we like that there is real succession, that rivers flow and winds blow, that things burn and burst, that men strive and guess and die. All this is the concrete stuff of the manifold, the reality of serial happening, one event after another, in exactly the time spread which we have been at pains to diagram. What does the theory allege except what we find, and what do we find that is not accepted and asserted by the theory? Suppose a pure intelligence, bred outside of time, instructed in the nature of the manifold and the design of the human spacetime worm, with its mnemic organization, its particular delimited but overlapping conscious fields, and the strands of world history which flank them, and suppose him incarnated among us: what could he have expected the temporal experience to be like except just about what he actually discovers it to be? How, in brief, could processes and experiences which endure and succeed each other along the time line appear as anything other than enduring and successive processes and a stream of consciousness?

The theory of the manifold leaves abundant room for the sensitive observer to record any describable difference he may find, in intrinsic quality, relational texture, or absolute direction, between the temporal dimension and the spatial ones. He is welcome to mark it so on the map. The very singleness of the time dimension, over against the amalgamated three dimensions of space, may be an idiosyncrasy with momentous effects; its *fourthness*, so to speak, so oddly and immensely multiplying the degrees of freedom embodied in the familiar spatial complex, was bound to seem momentous too.

The theory has generally conceded or emphasized that time is unique in these and other respects, and I have been assuming that it was right to do so. In the working out of this thesis, however, and in considering the very lame demurrals which oppose it, I have come a little uneasily to the surmise that the idea of an absolute or intrinsic difference of texture or orientation is superfluous, and that the four dimensions of the manifold compose a perfectly homogeneous scheme of location relations, the same in all directions, and that the oddity of temporal distances is altogether a function of features which occupy them—a function of *de facto* pattern like the shape of an arrow, like the difference between the way in and the way out of a flytrap, and like the terrestrial difference between up and down.

Even a person who believes that temporal distances are a categorically peculiar mode of relation, intrinsically different from spatial distance, regardless of how they are filled, must grant that they nevertheless *are* filled differently: things, persons, and events, as a matter of natural fact, are strung along with respect to the time axis in rhythms and designs notably different from those in which they are deployed spacewise. Entropy and the other scientific criteria for the "sense" from past to future distinguish no less the whole temporal direction from the spatial ones. The very concept of "things" or "individual substances" derives from a peculiar kind of coherence and elongation of clumps of events in the time direction. Living bodies in particular have a special organized trend timewise, a *conatus sese conservandi*, which nothing has in spatial section. Characteristic themes of causation run in the same direction, and paralleling all these, and accounting for their importance and obviousness to us, is the pattern of mental events, the stream of consciousness, with its mnemic cumulation and that sad anxiety to *keep going* futureward which contrasts strangely with our comparative indifference to our spatial girth.

The same fact of the grain and configuration of events which, if it does not constitute, certainly accompanies and underlines the "senses" of space and time, has other virtues which help to naturalize experience in the manifold. It accounts for the apparent *rate* of happening, for example; for the span of the specious present; and for the way in which the future is comparatively malleable to our present efforts and correspondingly dark to our present knowledge. An easy interpretation would be that the world content is uniquely organized in the time direction because the time direction itself is aboriginally unique. Modern philosophical wisdom, however, consists mostly of trying the cart before the horse, and I find myself more than half convinced by the oddly repellent hypothesis that the peculiarity of the time dimension is not thus primitive but is wholly a resultant of those differences in the mere *de facto* run and order of the world's filling.

It is conceivable, then, though perhaps physically impossible, that one four-dimensional part of the manifold of events be slued around at right angles to the rest, so that the time order of that area, as composed by its interior lines of strain and structure, runs parallel with a spatial order in its environment. It is conceivable, indeed, that a single whole human life should lie thwartwise of the manifold, with its belly plump in time, its birth at the east and its death in the west, and its conscious stream perhaps running alongside somebody's garden path.[25]

It is conceivable too then that a human life be twisted, not 90° but 180°, from the normal temporal grain of the world. F. Scott Fitzgerald tells the story of Benjamin Button who was born in the last stages of senility and got younger all his life till he died a dwindling embryo.[26] Fitzgerald imagined the reversal to be so imperfect that Benjamin's stream of consciousness ran, not backward with his body's gross development, but in the common clockwise manner. We might better conceive a reversal of every cell twitch and electron whirl, and hence suppose that he experienced his own life stages in the same order as we do ours, but that he observed everyone around him moving backward from the grave to the cradle. True time travel, then, is conceivable after all, though we cannot imagine how it could be caused by beings whose lives are extended in the normal way: it would consist of a man's life-pattern, and the pattern of any appliances he employed, running at an abnormal rate or on an abnormal heading across the manifold.

As the dimensional theory accommodates what is true in the notion of passage, that is, the occurrence of events, in contrast with a mythical rearing and charging of time itself, so it accounts for what is true in the notions of "flux," "emergence," "creative advance," and the rest. Having learned the trick of mutual translation between theory and experience, we see where the utter misrepresentation lies in the accusation that the dimensional theory denies that time is "real," or that it substitutes a safe and static world, a block universe, a petrified *fait accompli*, a *totum simul*, for the actuality of risk and change.

Taking time with the truest seriousness, on the contrary, it calmly diagnoses "novelty" or "becoming," for example, as the existence of an entity, or kind of entity, at one time in the world continuum which does not exist at any previous time. No other sort of novelty than this, I earnestly submit, is discoverable or conceivable—or desirable. In practice, the modern sciences of the manifold have depicted it as a veritable caldron of force and action. Although the theory entails that it is true at every time that events occur at other times, it emphatically does not entail that all events happen at the same time or at every time, or at no time. It does not assert, therefore, that future things "already" exist or exist "forever." Emphatically also it does not, as is frequently charged, "make time a dimension of space,"[27] any more than it makes space a dimension of time.

The theory of the manifold, which is thus neutral with respect to the amount of change and permanence in the world, is surprisingly neutral also toward many other topics often broached as though they could be crucial between it and the extra idea of passage. It is neutral, so far, toward whether space and time are absolute and substantival in the Democritean and Newtonian way, or relative and adjectival in Spencer's and Whitehead's way, or further relativistic in Einstein's way. The theory of space does not, as Bergson pretended, have any preference for discontinuity over continuity, and while a time order in which nothing exists but the present would be fatal to any real continuity, the philosophy of the manifold is quite prepared to accept any verdict on whether space or time or both are continuous or discrete, as it is also on whether they are finite or infinite. Instead of "denying history," it preserves it, and is equally hospitable to all philosophies of history except such as themselves deny history by disputing the objectivity and irrevocability of historical truth. It does not care whether events eternally recur, or run along forever on the dead level as Aristotle thought, or enact the ringing brief drama of the Christian episode, or strive into the Faustian boundless. It is similarly neutral toward theories of causation and of knowledge.

The world manifold of occurrences, each eternally deter*minate* at its own place and date, may and may not be so deter*mined* in its texture that what occurs at one juncture has its sufficient reason at others. If it does evince such causal connections, these may be either efficient (as apparently they are) or final (as apparently they are not). The core of the causal nexus itself may be, so far as the manifold is concerned, either a real connection of Spinoza's sort, or Whitehead's, or the scholastics', or the mere regular succession admitted by Hume and Russell. It was a mistake for Spinoza to infer, if he did, that the eternal manifold and strict causation entail one another, as it is a worse mistake for the scholastics, Whitehead, Ushenko, and Weiss to infer the opposite (as they seem to), that "real time" and "real causation" entail one another.[28] The theory is similarly noncommittal toward metaphysical accounts of individual substances, which it can allow to be compounds of form and matter or mere sheaves of properties.

The theory of the manifold makes a man at home in the world to the extent that it guarantees that intelligence is not affronted at its first step into reality. Beyond that, the cosmos is as it is. If there is moral responsibility, if the will is free, if there is reasonableness in regret and hope in decision, these must be ascertained by more particular observations and hypotheses than the doctrine of the manifold. It makes no difference to our theory whether we are locked in an ice pack of fate, or whirled in a tornado of chance, or are firmfooted makers of destiny. It will accept benignly either the Christian Creator, or the organic and perfect Absolute, or Hume's sand pile of sensation, or the fluid melee of contextualism, or the structured world process of materialism.

The service which the theory performs with respect to all these problems is other than dictating solutions of them. It is the provision of a lucent frame or arena where they and their solutions can be laid out and clearheadedly appraised in view of their special classes of evidence. Once under this kind of observation, for example, the theories of change which describe becoming as a marriage of being and not-being, or an interpenetration of the present with the future and the past, become repulsive, not because they conflict especially with the philosophy of the manifold, but because if they are not mere incantations they contradict themselves. When we see that the problem how Achilles can overtake the tortoise is essentially the same as the problem how two lines can intersect one another obliquely, we are likely to be content with the simple mathematical intelligibility of both. When we see that the "change" of a leaf's color from day to day is of the same denomination as its "change" from inch to inch of its surface, we are less likely to hope that mysterious formulas about the actualization of the potential and the perdurance of a substratum are of any use in accounting for either of them.

If then there is some appearance of didactic self-righteousness in my effort here to save the pure theory of the manifold from being either displaced or amended by what I think is the disastrous myth of passage, this is because I believe that the theory of the manifold is the very paradigm of philosophic understanding. It grasps with a firm logic, so far as I can see, the most intimate and pervasive of facts; it clarifies the obscure and assimilates the apparently diverse.

Most of the effect of the prophets of passage, on the other hand, is to melt back into the primitive magma of confusion and plurality the best and sharpest instruments which the mind has forged. Some of those who do this have a deliberate preference for the melting pot of mystery as an end in itself. Others, I suppose, hope eventually to cast from it a finer metal and to forge a sharper point. No hope of that sort is altogether chimerical. But I suggest that if a tithe of the animus and industry invested in that ill-omened enterprise were spent on the refinement and imaginative use of the instrument we have, whatever difficulties still attend it would soon be dissipated.

Endnotes

[1] *The Mysterious Universe.* New York, 1930, p. 118.

[2] This I think is a fair description of G. H. Mead's doctrine in *The Philosophy of the Present.* See also, e.g., Schopenhauer: *The World as Will and Idea,* Bk. 4, Sec. 54.

[3] "The Sea Fight Tomorrow," Williams, *Principles of Empirical Realism.*

[4] W. R. Dennes, in California, University, Philosophical Union, *The Problem of Time.* Berkeley, Calif., 1935, p. 103.

[5] I. Stearns, in *Review of Metaphysics,* 4 (1950), 198.

[6] Santayana: *Realms of Being,* in *Works,* Vol. 14, p. 254.

[7] Lewis: *An Analysis of Knowledge and Valuation,* p. 19. This is pretty surely phenomenology, not metaphysics, but it is too good to omit.

[8] James: *A Pluralistic Universe,* p. 254.

[9] Broad: *An Examination of McTaggart's Philosophy,* Vol. 2, Pt. 1, p. 271.

[10] Paul Tillich: *The Interpretation of History.* New York, 1936, p. 129.

[11] H. R. King, in *Journal of Philosophy,* 46 (1949), 657–70. This is an exceptionally ingenious, serious, and explicit statement of the philosophy which I am opposing.

[12] Arthur S. Eddington: *Space, Time, and Gravitation,* New York, 1920, p. 51; *The Nature of the Physical World,* New York, 1928, p. 68.

[13] Dennes: op. cit., pp. 91, 93.

[14] Andrew P. Ushenko: *Power and Events.* Princeton, 1946, p. 146.

[15] John M. E. McTaggart: *The Nature of Existence.* Cambridge, 1927, Vol. 2, Bk. 5, Chap. 33.

[16] Broad: *Scientific Thought,* p. 67; *An Examination of McTaggart's Philosophy,* Vol. 2, Pt. 1, p. 277.

[17] *Realms of Being,* in *Works,* Vol. 15, p. 90.

[18] *Confessions,* Bk. 11, Chap. 14; cf. E. B. McGilvary, in *Philosophical Review,* 23 (1914), 121–45.

[19] "He may even now—if I may use the phrase—be wandering on some plesiosaurus-haunted oolitic coral reef, or beside the lonely saline seas of the Triassic Age"—H. G. Wells, *The Time Machine,* epilogue. This book, perhaps the best yarn ever written, contains such early and excellent accounts of the theory of the manifold that it has been quoted and requoted by scientific writers. Though it makes slips, its logic is better than that of later such stories.

[20] Bergson's theory of the snowball of time may be thus understood: the past abides in the center while ever new presents accrete around it. For Broad, see *Scientific Thought,* p. 66, and on Whitehead, see King, op. cit., esp. p. 663.

[21] See, for example, Broad: *Scientific Thought,* p. 57.

[22] Tillich, op. cit., p. 245.

[23] *The Nature of the Physical World,* Chap. 3. For the present scientific state of the question, see Adolf Grünbaum: *Philosophical Problems of Space and Time,* New York, 1963.

[24] Dennes argues thus, loc. cit.

[25] I should expect the impact of the environment on such a being to be so wildly queer and out of step with the way he is put together, that his mental life must be a dragged-out monstrous delirium. Professor George Burch has suggested to me that it might be the mystic's timeless illumination. Whether these diagnoses are different I shall not attempt to say.

[26] "The Curious Case of Benjamin Button," in *Tales of the Jazz Age.* New York, 1922.

[27] See Charles Hartshorne: *Man's Vision of God, and the Logic of Theism,* Chicago, 1941, p. 140, and Tillich, op. cit., pp. 132, 248; and remember Bergson's allegation that the principle of the manifold "spatializes" time.

[28] See, for example, Whitehead: *Process and Reality,* p. 363; Paul Weiss: *Nature and Man,* New York, 1947.

9. McTaggart, Fixity and Coming True*

D. HUGH MELLOR

Many twentieth-century philosophers have debated the metaphysical significance of language. This is in keeping with an ancient tradition that recognizes meaning is itself a puzzling phenomenon and philosophical disagreements and errors might result from faulty analyses of what people say. Modern logical and semantic theories have become quite technical in an effort to settle the question What exactly must exist if our statements are true? An important issue regarding time has been the significance of tense. Some philosophers have claimed tensed statements are indispensible and have no tenseless equivalents. They argue that this fact, if it is a fact, proves the Now is *sui generis* and, hence, tenseless views of time that reduce the present to earlier-later relations are false. The relevance of tense to the metaphysics of time is the central topic of D. Hugh Mellor's 1981 paper, "McTaggart, Fixity and Coming True."

Mellor is a British philosopher who teaches at Cambridge University. He explains his views at more length in his book *Real Time*.

1. *Introduction*

Some events are past, some present and some, I expect, are still to come. These are at once the most obvious, the most basic and the most disputed facts about time. I am one of those who dispute them. I maintain with McTaggart (1908; 1927:

From *Reduction, Time and Reality*, R. Healey, ed. Copyright © 1981 by Cambridge University Press. Reprinted by permission of Cambridge University Press.

* This paper developed out of classes given at Stanford University in the Fall of 1978, during a visit made possible by the grant of a Radcliffe Fellowship and a British Academy Overseas Visiting Fellowship, for which I owe thanks to the Radcliffe Trust and the British Academy. I am indebted for helpful comment and criticism to several Stanford students, to Professors John Perry, Nancy Cartwright and David Lewis, and to those taking part in the March 1979 meeting of the Thyssen U.K. Philosophy Group, at which the original version of it was discussed. In rewriting I have been further assisted by the replies of Professor Jeffrey and Mr Mackie to my critique, and also by detailed comments from Jeremy Butterfield.

ch. 33) that in reality nothing is either past, present or future. Since, however, I part from him by thinking that reality need not be tensed to be temporal, I am not led, as he is, to deny the reality of time itself. Indeed I believe that, paradoxically, time needs to be both real and tenseless to explain how and why people come to think of events as being past, present and future.

These propositions are, I fear, still contentious, so they will have to be defended in what follows. But my main object is not merely to promote and sugar McTaggart's pill. I want also to prescribe it: specifically, for R. C. Jeffrey's 'conceit that the world grows by accretion of facts'; or, in other words, that only when an event happens does the proposition saying so 'come true' (1980: 253). It will also serve to purge J. L. Mackie's closely related conceit that events become 'fixed and settled and unalterable' (1974: 178) as soon as their 'preceding sufficient causes . . . have occurred' (181). These are serious conceits, though not new ones: McTaggart himself (1927: §337) appeals to the second while disposing of Broad's (1923: ch. II) version of the first. But as they have been newly reconceived, so they need renewed purgation. They are, I shall argue, only trivially true if time is tenseless. And rather than tax my distinguished colleagues with triviality, I prefer to conclude that they are wrong.

2. *Time Without Tense*

First, however, we must get rid of tense, and I will not pretend that this is easy. Consider for example the fundamental relation '. . . is earlier than . . .' (or its converse, 'later than'). What makes this relation temporal? One persuasive answer is: one event, *e*, being earlier than another, *e'*, implies such tensed facts as that sometime *e'* is present and *e* past but never *vice versa*. What makes the 'earlier' relation temporal, in other words, is that it determines the order in which the events it relates become successively present and then past. But if there are in reality no such tensed facts as events being present or past, something else must make 'earlier' temporal—and it is no easy task to find something else that will do the job. As McTaggart saw, it is not enough for a tenseless relation between events merely to reproduce the order in which they appear to become present. If, for example, everything in the universe was always at the same temperature at the same time, but always cooling, the 'cooler' relation would do that: but that would not make 'cooler' a temporal relation.

Advocates of tenseless time have, I admit, mostly shirked the task, e.g. of saying what is temporal about the non-spatial dimension of their four-dimensional Minkowski manifolds. Their 'block' universes have no more real time in them than McTaggart's does—the difference being that McTaggart sees this and they, by and large, do not. I too will shirk the task here, but I do acknowledge it, since I am not willing to give up real time, and I undertake to tackle it elsewhere. All I can say here is that the materials I will use are the direct perception of one event being later than another, which occurs whenever we see something move or change in some other definite way, and the role causation plays in that perception.

There is another task, however, which I must attempt here: namely, to give a tenseless account of change. Time is essentially the dimension of change, and any theory of time has to account for that fact. Now McTaggart thought that change needed tense, since he thought change to be im-

possible without events moving from the future *via* the present to the past, a movement I shall call 'McTaggart change'. Without real tense, of course, McTaggart change does not exist, so a tenseless account of change must find a way of doing without it. My account derives from Russell (1903: §442): 'Change is the difference, in respect of truth or falsehood, between a proposition concerning an entity and the time *T*, and a proposition concerning the same entity and the time *T'*, provided that these propositions differ only by the fact that *T* occurs in the one where *T'* occurs in the other.' This is what Geach has called 'Cambridge change' and, as he says, actual change is only one species of it (1979: 90–2). To adapt an example of McTaggart's (1927: §309), 'the fall of a sand-castle on the English coast' effects a Cambridge change in the Great Pyramid, by changing a relation in which it stands to the sand; but clearly the Pyramid itself does not actually change as the sand does. The difference between actual and what Geach calls 'merely' Cambridge change is causal: actual changes are events, with spatiotemporally contiguous effects, and merely Cambridge changes are not.

I follow Davidson (1969) in taking events, including changes, to be individuated by their causes and effects. But not all events are changes; nor do events themselves change. Change occurs in things, i.e. individual substances, in one standard sense of that term. (The difference between things and events I take to be that whereas events, if extended in time, have temporal parts, things do not. People are things in this sense, and so are common objects such as tables, chairs—and McTaggart's (1927: §313) poker. For a longer list, and some reasons why the thing/event distinction matters, see my 1982: §6.) A thing may have a non-temporal property at one date incompatible with those it has at earlier or later dates; and when such a fact constitutes an event, with effects spatiotemporally contiguous to the thing, the thing has undergone an actual change between these dates. We may indeed use this as a criterion for distinguishing real from merely apparent properties of things, thus ruling out such spurious properties as being forty, famous, the tallest man in the room and 'grue' (Goodman 1965: ch. III). Real properties of things and people, loss or gain of which is actual change in them, rather than the merely Cambridge variety, include temperatures, masses, colours, shapes—and both physical dispositions such as solubility (Mellor 1974: §I–II), and mental states such as particular beliefs and desires (Mellor 1978: §II).

Now suppose some thing, a, has a pair, G and G^*, of such incompatible real properties (e.g. temperatures) during two separate stretches of time t and t^*: i.e.

$$a \text{ is } G \text{ during } t \qquad (1)$$

and

$$a \text{ is } G^* \text{ during } t^* \qquad (2)$$

If a were an event, it would have different temporal parts containing a-during-t and a-during-t^*, and the supposed change would reduce to these different parts having different properties:

$$G(a\text{-during-}t) \qquad (3)$$

and

$$G^*(a\text{-during-}t^*) \qquad (4)$$

But that different entities differ in their properties does not amount to change, even if one is earlier than the other and both are parts of something else. (3) and (4) would no more constitute a case of change than would a's spatial parts differing in their properties—e.g. McTaggart's poker being hot at one end and cool at the other.

I take change to require a difference between the state of a *whole* thing at two different times. That is, real changeable non-temporal properties of a thing are in fact relations it has to the various times and stretches of times at which it exists. I.e. (1) and (2) should be read as

$$G(a, t) \qquad (5)$$

and

$$G^*(a, t^*) \qquad (6)$$

Treating temperatures, colours, shapes etc. as relations between things and times may seem odd, but it is only a way of making two indubitable points about facts like (1):

(a) Both the contexts

$$. . . \text{is } G \text{ during } t'$$

and

$$\text{'}a \text{ is } G \text{ during } . . .$$

are transparent, i.e. (1) remains true however a and t are referred to.

(b) For (1) to be true, both a and t must exist. (This need not of course imply a Newtonian conception of absolute time: it does not follow that time could exist without events—times may still need specifying by events, such as Christ's birth, and their temporal relations, such as the earth's period of rotation on its axis and about the sun.)

I should emphasise at once that (5) and (6) in no way beg the question against tenses. Nothing prevents t and t^* taking tensed values like 'yesterday' and 'tomorrow' as well as tenseless ones like '9 January' and '10 January'. Nor do (5) and (6) conflict with the use of sentential operators which Prior's work has made usual in tense-logic; i.e., in this case,

$$\text{During } t, Ga \qquad (7)$$

and

$$\text{During } t^*, G^*a \qquad (8)$$

On the contrary, a relational reading of tensed facts is standardly used to supply 'semantics' for these operators (McArthur 1976: ch. 1.3). In other words, even tense-logicians take (7) and (8), with appropriately tensed t and t^*, to be made true by the corresponding relational facts as stated in (5) and (6).

However, as an advocate of tenseless time, I will restrict t and t^* to tenseless values. Change, I maintain, consists in a thing's having a real non-temporal property at one date which it lacks at others, i.e. respectively having and lacking, to those dates, the corresponding real non-temporal relation.

McTaggart would not agree; but not because he disputes—he does not draw—my distinctions between things and events and between actual and merely Cambridge change. For McTaggart, (1) and (2), however construed, would not constitute change because they are themselves unchanging facts about a. His poker being 'hot on a particular Monday' and cool thereafter (1927: §315) is no change in it, he says, since it always was and always will be a fact that it is hot that Monday and cool thereafter. And as McTaggart says, neither this 'nor any other fact about the poker change[s], unless its presentness, pastness, or futurity change'. McTaggart change, in other words, is the only kind of change tenseless facts are capable of. But why, in order for a change to be a fact, must that fact also change? I see no reason to believe it must, nor hence any good argument from real change to McTaggart change and hence real tense. We can quite well deny both, and still insist that McTaggart's poker changes as it cools.

3. *Tenses and Dates*

We can, I believe, account for time and change without real tense: but why should we try to? Because real tense implies McTaggart change, and that, as he showed, is a myth—the 'myth of passage' as it has been called (Williams 1951). But it is a very powerful myth, and undoubtedly expresses something real and important about time. As the persistent rejection of McTaggart's own sound and simple disproof of it shows, its grip will not be broken until something better is put in its place. In what follows, therefore, I shall put up a tenseless surrogate for it; to which end, I must first lay down more precisely the specification the surrogate has to satisfy.

The myth of time passing, i.e. of McTaggart change, combines two ways of locating events in time: by their dates, and by their temporal distance, past or future, from the present. These two ways locate events in two series of temporal positions which McTaggart called the '*B* series' and the '*A* series' respectively. McTaggart change consists in the relative motion of these two series. Events of given date become less future or more past, as the present time moves from earlier to later dates.

(There may in fact be several *A* and *B* series. In both, events get the same location just in case they are simultaneous; and relativity theory may make the simultaneity of distant events depend, within causal limits, on an arbitrary choice of a so-called 'reference frame', to settle what is to count as being at rest. Physical fact may fail to settle that question: so different but equally good reference frames may

make quite different celestial events simultaneous with the terrestrial events of 1 January 1984, for example, thus filling that *B* series position quite differently. But the same goes for the *A* series: whatever celestial events get that terrestrial date will *ipso facto* then count as temporally present. So there is, as McTaggart conjectured (1927: §323), a distinct *A* series corresponding to each distinct *B* series. For present purposes, however, I can afford to ignore these relativistic complications, since I am concerned only with the apparent relative movement of corresponding *A* and *B* series. In referring to 'the' *A* and *B* series, then, I shall henceforth mean any relativistically acceptable *B* series, and the *A* series corresponding to it.)

Positions in the *B* series I shall call 'dates', stretching that term to cover locations of all sizes from nanoseconds to millennia. Thus B.C. is a date, and so is the first p.m. second of 1 January 1984. (Events have any date that includes all their temporal parts, just as things have any spatial location that includes all their spatial parts. Thus, the end of World War II has, *inter alia*, the dates A.D., the twentieth century and 1945, just as London has the locations Earth, Europe and England. When I refer to 'the' date of an event, I mean the shortest date that includes all its temporal parts.) Dates may be regarded as intervals of *B* series instants, such as noon precisely on 1 January 1984, ordered by the 'earlier' relation. I do not of course mean by this that instants exist: if there are any such things, they will be spatiotemporal entities—spacetime points—not purely temporal ones. Instants are no more than convenient theoretical devices for generating indefinitely divisible systems for dating events.

Positions in the *A* series I shall reluctantly follow custom and call 'tenses', though they are mostly marked, not by verbal inflection but by adverbs and phrases such as 'today', 'ten days hence' and 'last year'; and given these, verbal tenses are redundant—'last year' already implies the past tense, as 'today' implies the present. Tense in the sense of *A* series position must therefore be sharply distinguished from verbal tense, which is merely one very crude way of marking it; and the former, not the latter, is what I shall mean by 'tense' hereafter unless I explicitly say otherwise.

Tenses, like dates in the *B* series, may be regarded as intervals of instants, and these are likewise ordered by the 'earlier' relation. McTaggart

(1927: §305) characterises the B series as ordered by 'earlier', as opposed to the A series, which is ordered by degrees of pastness or futurity; but this is a false contrast. 'Earlier' orders both series. Ten days ago, an A series position, is earlier than today in just the same sense in which 1 January is ten days earlier than 11 January. In fact, the A and B series have exactly the same temporal structure. They use the very same 'earlier' relation to order the very same collections of simultaneous events. Fix which B series instant is the A series' present instant, and either series is immediately definable in terms of the other. To every B series instant there then corresponds the A series instant which is that much earlier or later than the present instant; and hence to every date, i.e. interval of B series instants, there corresponds a tense, and *vice versa*. Thus, when it is now noon on 1 January 1984, 10 a.m. is two hours past, 11 January is ten days hence, and the next century is the twenty-first.

Seeing that the A and B series are so similar, and so simply interdefinable, what is the difference between them? The difference is that whereas an event's dates are fixed, its tenses are not. By this I mean that its tenses vary with time (this of course being just what McTaggart change is), and its dates do not. Suppose for example that it is now May 1984 and the Queen is 58. That is, she was born 58 years ago; in other words, that event has the tense: 58 years past. The tense of this event obviously varies with time: in 1974, the Queen was only 48 years old; in 1994, she will be 68. Note that the event's tense varies just the same if the time itself is reckoned by tense rather than by date: thus, ten years ago, the Queen's birth was 48 years past; ten years hence, it will be 68 years past. These facts, of course, follow from each other, the general study of such temporal entailments being the business of so-called 'tense-logic'. The reason there is no comparable 'date-logic' is simply that an event's dates, unlike its tenses, do not vary with time, whether the time be reckoned in tenses or dates. The fact now, in May 1984, is that the Queen was born on 21 April 1926; and that always was and always will be the date of her birth. (Some indeed think that before 1926, when the Queen's birth was future, it did not yet exist, and so had no date at all. But no one thinks it ever had, or ever will have, any date other than 21 April 1926.) Date-logic, then, is not studied, because it is too simple. Temporal operators, be they dated or tensed, and however they are

iterated, have no effect at all on the classical truth value (if any) of '*e* occurs at *T*'.

Dates, unlike tenses, are outright, temporally unqualified properties of events. That is the essential characteristic of the B, as opposed to the A, series—and why, provided tenseless sense can be made of 'earlier', it is the fundamental series. The B series is definable as the definite temporal structure of all the world's events (on a relational view of time), or of all instants (on an absolute view). The A series is neither: it has to be defined in terms of the B series plus a present instant. And the present instant has to move: there has to be McTaggart change, or the A series would be identical with the B series. Past, present and future, therefore, as aspects of reality, stand or fall with McTaggart change. They fall—as we shall see in the course of constructing something tenseless to put in their place. But first let us look at the reasons that support them.

4. *Tensed Truth, Tenseless Fact*

There are two chief reasons for believing in real tense, and in particular in a real present. One is experiential, the other linguistic. The former is what many take to be an irreducible experience of events being present as they happen to us (or, in the case of actions, as we perform them); in other words, its sheer presentness seems to be an undeniable part of our every experience. A credible surrogate is needed for this. To produce it, however, I must first dispose of the latter, linguistic reason for believing in real tense: namely, that our judgments about the tenses of events are generally either objectively true or objectively false, and real tenses are needed to make them so. In May 1984, for example, it is objectively true to think or say that the Queen is 58. What makes that true seems to be that she *is* then 58, i.e. that at that date her birth really does have the tense: 58 years past. But if reality has no tense, there is no such fact, and we must give this indisputably objective judgment alternative tenseless truth conditions. And once that has been done, explaining away the apparent presentness of our experience will turn out to pose no great problem.

The truth conditions I need are really quite

obvious, and also quite indisputable. Even if events have tenses, it turns out that these have nothing to do with making what I shall call 'tensed judgments' about them true or false. The truth value of a tensed judgment is determined entirely by how much earlier (or later) it is than the event it is about. A judgment that the Queen is N years old, for example, is objectively true just in case its date is between N and $N + 1$ years later than that of her birth. It is quite immaterial whether the Queen's birth, or the tensed judgment about it, is past, present or future.

The truth conditions of all tensed judgments are fixed in reality by dates. A present tense judgment is true if, and only if, it differs no more in date from the event it is about than the span of tense it ascribes to that event. E.g. 'e occurs today' is true just in case it is said or thought on the same day as e; 'e occurs this week' just in case it is said or thought the same week. Past and future tense judgments are true if and only if they have dates as much later or earlier respectively than the events they are about as the tenses they ascribe to them are than the present. Tensed judgments can of course be more complex than the simple ascription of an A series position to an event. There are, for example, the judgments commonly expressed in English by verbal tenses such as the future perfect. But the truth conditions of these too are fixed by how much earlier or later their dates are than those of events they are about and other dates definable from these. 'Next year the Queen will have reigned 33 years', for instance, is true just in case the Queen is still Queen the year after that judgment is made, and that year is 33 years later than her accession. And similarly for tensed judgments of any complexity. The real usefulness, indeed, of the standard 'semantics' of tense-logic referred to in Section 2, is that it shows how to derive any tensed judgment's truth conditions from its date in this sort of way.

Dates are not only sufficient to fix the truth conditions of tensed judgments, they are also necessary. Suppose a tensed judgment, e.g. that the Queen is 58, had no date—being, perhaps, one of God's judgments if, as some have said, He is 'outside time'. What could make it true? Not that the Queen really is 58 when the judgment is made; for, given that the Queen was born in 1926, that gives the judgment a date, namely 1984. Without a date, in short, a tensed judgment has no definite truth conditions; and with one, its truth conditions contain no tenses. These facts seem to me to make the idea of real tense not merely redundant, but incredible. Try to suppose that there really is in 1984 such a tensed fact as that the Queen is 58. This supposed fact turns out to be no part of what makes the corresponding judgment true: what does that job is simply the date of the Queen's birth being 58 years earlier. Now a fact which has nothing to do with making any tensed judgment true is surely no tensed fact. But these supposed facts are by definition tensed. Yet in reality no such supposedly tensed facts make any tensed judgment true. So I conclude that in reality there are no such facts: there is no real A series, and therefore no McTaggart change.

5. *Experience and Indexicals*

But what then of our experience of tense and of McTaggart change? Tenseless truth conditions seem not to dispose of that. Consider Prior's famous example: 'Thank goodness that's over!', said after a painful experience (Prior 1959). 'That's over' is indeed true if and only if said or thought later than whatever experience the 'that' refers to. But why thank goodness for such a tenseless fact, which could be recognised as such at any time, before or during, as well as after, the pain in question: surely the thanks are given in sheer relief for the pain's becoming past and thereby ceasing to be present?

Not necessarily. 'Thank goodness' certainly expresses relief, and is thus appropriately said or thought just when relief is appropriately felt. But when is that? Prior says it is when a pain is past, as opposed to present or future; whereas I say it is just after the pain, as opposed to during or before it. I cannot see that Prior's tensed account of when relief is appropriate is any better than my tenseless one. And mine does make sense of the whole remark: since 'thank goodness', said of a pain, is appropriate just when 'that's over', said of it, is true, it is always right to say both (or neither) at the same time.

This account of Prior's case gives the clue to a tenseless analysis of the apparent presentness of experience. Like his case, it involves selfconsciousness; only here one is making tensed judgments of experience as it occurs, rather than afterwards. Now simultaneity with its subject matter is the defining truth condition of a present tense judgment, as opposed to a past or future tense one; so if I am thinking of my actions or experiences as happening *while* I am thinking of them, I am *ipso facto* thinking of them as being present. And that, I suggest, is all there is to the much vaunted presentness of our experience. Experiences in themselves, like events of every other kind, are neither past, present nor future. It is only our simultaneous consciousness of them, as being simultaneous, which necessarily both has, and satisfies, the tenseless truth conditions of present tense judgments.

Our being trapped forever in the present is not a profound metaphysical constraint on our temporal location: it is a trivial consequence of the essential indexicality of tensed judgment. It is like everyone being condemned to be himself and, wherever he is, to being—as he sees it—here. The judgments 'I am X' and 'Here is Y', made respectively by person X and at place Y, are as objectively and inevitably true for all X and Y as 'It is now T', made at time T, is for all T: but not because X and Y have respectively such real properties as 'being me' and 'being here'. Obviously there are no such personal and spatial equivalents of our supposed tensed facts; and if there were, they would, like tensed facts, be no part of what makes the corresponding judgments true. 'I am X' is true if and only if X judges it; 'Here is Y' is true if and only if it is judged at Y. So anyone who judges, of the place that he is at, that it is here, is bound to be right, wherever he is; and similarly, *mutatis mutandis*, for judgments of one's own first person identity. That is all the inescapability of being oneself and being here amounts to: and so it is with the inescapability of the present.

I conclude that neither our experience of time nor the objective truth of tensed judgments requires, or indeed admits of, real tense. Tensed judgments are simply a kind of indexical judgment, with tenseless truth conditions. But this does not mean either that tensed judgments themselves are really tenseless, or that we could do without them. Tense may not be an aspect of the world; but, as Perry (1979) has shown, it is, like personal and spatial indexicality, an irreducible and indispensable aspect of our thought.

That a tensed judgment is not equivalent to any tenseless one is easily seen. If it were, it would be equivalent to the tenseless judgment that its own truth conditions obtain. For example, a particular judgment J, a 'token' of the 'type' 'It is now T', is true if and only if it is made at T. Let J' be the tenseless judgment that this is so, i.e. 'J is made at T'. J is true if and only if J' is. But they are not the same judgment. In particular, if J' is true at all, it is true whenever it is made, whereas J is only true at T.

In other words, as upholders of tense have rightly insisted, tensed truths cannot be translated into tenseless ones. Neither the sentence type 'It is now T', nor Prior's 'Thank goodness that's over', nor any other tensed sentence type, means the same as any tenseless sentence. That is because tensed sentence types are indexical: it is part of their meaning that the truth conditions of their tokens vary with time, which is not true of tokens of tenseless types. But there is no tense in the truth conditions themselves; just as the truth conditions of tokens of 'Here is Y' are (literally!) neither here nor there, despite its being different from any non-indexical spatial judgment.

Not only is indexical judgment untranslatable, it is also indispensable. To suppose that we could make do with a tenseless language is as much a mirage as is real tense itself. Suppose I want to do something at T. Some change in my state of mind is needed to prompt me to act at T rather than some other time. The change of course is my coming to judge 'It is now T', where before I judged, 'It is not yet T.' And for this kind of change of tensed belief there is no tenseless substitute. Because the truth value of tenseless beliefs does not change with time, mere lapse of time gives no cause to change them. But it does give us cause to change our tensed beliefs if we are to keep them true, which it is the object of all our belief to be. And these changes, especially changes of belief from the future to the present tense, are the immediate and indispensable causes of our actions. Whether they cause us to act in time is of course another matter: our mental clocks are as fallible as any others. But without them, i.e. without making tensed judgments, we should have no cause to act at all.

This is my surrogate for the myth of passage: the tensed judgments we need to have, and therefore continually to change, in order to be capable of timely action. This is the truth behind the myth. The error is to misread the tense of these judgments as part of their non-indexical content, and hence to see it as an extra, ever-changing aspect of the objective world. Having exposed the error, we may hope at last to break the myth, and begin to repair the havoc it has wreaked in the philosophy of time.

6. *Fixity and Coming True*

Tense has not wreaked all its havoc under its own name. Jeffrey's conceit of propositions about events 'coming true' as the events happen, is stated explicitly in tenseless terms; and Mackie's, of events acquiring 'fixity', easily can be. Nonetheless, these specious happenings are nothing if not kinds of McTaggart change. Without real tense they are trivial; and with it, impossible, as I will now attempt to show.

Jeffrey give events no tenses, only dates; but says that before the date of an event its happening is no fact. In other words, the corresponding tenseless proposition is not then true; though it may be 'ineluctable', if its 'final truth' is determined by the facts to date. As time goes on, therefore, propositions come true, and the number of facts increases: 'the world grows by accretion of facts'. What is wrong with this picture?

For a start, Jeffrey's use of 'true' and 'finally true'. In calling a tenseless proposition 'finally true', he means what most of us would mean by calling it plain 'true'. At any rate, what he calls 'final truth' is what our tenseless judgments aim at, and that is what matters. Given his 'final truth', what he calls 'truth' is entirely immaterial. Suppose I do not know whether the third Test in a (current) 1984 Australian series has finished yet, and so am unsure what tense to give my judgment that England win it. My judgment still has a perfectly definite tenseless content, and attains its object provided England do win, whether they have done so yet or not. That question, whose answer decides whether my judgment is 'true' in Jeffrey's sense, is of no interest to me whatever: 'final truth' is all I am after.

More seriously, suppose that at the end of 1984 I make some tenseless judgment about an event (picked out by a non-temporal description) that happens in a distant galaxy after the light I see left it and before its reflection would return there. If that event is as I judge it to be, my judgment attains

its object: it is 'finally true'. Whether, for Jeffrey, it is also 'true' depends on the event's date not being later than 1984, which, according to relativity, may be a matter of an arbitrary choice of reference frame (see Section 3 above): a matter which concerns me not at all, and is certainly not one I can credit with marking the boundaries of objective fact (see Mellor, 1974a; this objection is not met by the modification Jeffrey proposes in his n. 1, p. 259).

I propose to restore 'true' to its customary and proper use, for the intended attribute of all our judgments, tensed and tenseless alike. That is, I shall call 'true' what Jeffrey calls 'finally true'. So I need another term for what he calls 'true'. Since he applies the term to tenseless propositions just when it should be applied to the corresponding past and present tense ones, I shall take the liberty of saying instead that they have 'come to pass'.

I have no objection to Jeffrey's use of 'ineluctable'. By it he means 'necessary', in the sense in which 'it is necessary that p is true if the present state of affairs makes it certain that the p-event will occur, or again if the p-event has already occurred' (Ackrill 1963: 139). The peculiarity of this sense of 'necessary' (in which, for example, p entails its own necessity) is quite enough to justify Jeffrey's preference for 'ineluctable'. It is also what Mackie (1974: ch. 7) means in ascribing 'fixity' to past and present events and the future events they determine. Ackrill and Mackie put the matter in tensed terms, but that, as Jeffrey shows, is by no means essential: an event is 'fixed', we may say, only on and after the date it, or an earlier sufficient cause of it, happens. The tenseless proposition that it happens is likewise 'ineluctable' only on and after the date it, or some other true proposition that determines its truth, 'comes to pass'.

Events therefore, and true tenseless propositions about them, are credited with the ability to undergo at least two sorts of change: (i) the events happen, and the propositions come to pass; and (ii), then or earlier the events become fixed and the propositions ineluctable. What sort of sense can be made of these supposed changes? Tenseless propositions, after all, are normally thought to be unchanging; and while in Section 2 I have admitted that some events *are* changes, I have denied that events themselves change. Nevertheless, sense can be made of (i) and (ii)—only not, as we shall see in Section 7, a sense sufficient for their authors' needs.

Suppose an event e happens at date T. Let H be

the property of having happened, and let t and t^* be any dates entirely earlier or later respectively than (every temporal part of) e. Then the change (i) consists in the facts that

$$e \text{ is } \sim H \text{ during } t \qquad (9)$$

and

$$e \text{ is } H \text{ during } t^* \qquad (10)$$

for all t and t^*.

Do (9) and (10) constitute a change in the sense of Section 2? Certainly, even though e itself is an event and not a thing, (9) and (10) do not reduce to any difference between temporal parts. The parts that would be required, e-during-t and e-during-t^*, are not parts of e, since t is by definition earlier than every temporal part of e, and t^* is later. They would have to be parts of some *ersatz* e-thing, say E, which changes from being $\sim H$ to being H. But since t is *any* date before e, and t^* any date after it, E would have to span the whole history of the world (except perhaps when e itself is). And in reality there are obviously no such things. An everlasting whole of which World War II-during-5000 B.C., and World War II-during-20,000 A.D. are temporal parts, for example, is not a credible substitute for World War II itself.

So (9) and (10) must be read along the lines of (5) and (6), not (3) and (4): i.e. as

$$\sim H(e, t) \qquad (11)$$

and

$$H(e, t^*) \qquad (12)$$

H is thus some relation that any event e has to every date later than itself, but lacks to any earlier date. The relation is, of course, a familiar one: 'earlier' is its common name! For an event to 'happen' at a date is simply for it to be earlier than all later dates, and later than all earlier ones.

Now this is not of course a change in e, as it would be were H a real non-temporal relation. Instances of (5) and (6) are indeed taken to imply that a's temporal location includes both t and t^*: it exists at both dates, and at some time between them changes from being G to being G^*. But (11) and (12) imply no such thing about e: on the contrary, they imply that e is *not* located at t and t^*, or it would not

be later and earlier respectively than those dates. So e is not an everlasting thing, existing during all the dates t and t^* and changing at T in respect of having happened. Put like that, I dare say no one thinks it is. But there is evidently a recurrent temptation to harbour an equivalent thought: namely, that e's happening is another event, apart from e, and constituting some sort of change in it. Not so: e is all there is, and talk of it happening at T is just a way of saying that T is its date, its temporal location—i.e. that e is later than all times earlier than T and earlier than all later times.

T being e's date is also all there is to the proposition that says this 'coming to pass' (and hence all other true propositions about e doing so). Let p be this true tenseless proposition, and C be the supposed property of having come to pass (i.e. of being 'true' in Jeffrey's eccentric sense). As before, t and t^* are any dates earlier and later respectively than e. Then the facts are that

$$p \text{ is } \sim C \text{ during } t \qquad (13)$$

and

$$p \text{ is } C \text{ during } t^* \qquad (14)$$

Now Jeffrey in effect construes (13) along the lines of (3) and (4), not (5) and (6); i.e. he credits propositions with temporal parts:

$$\sim C(p\text{-during-}t) \qquad (15)$$

and

$$C(p\text{-during-}t^*) \qquad (16)$$

Once these temporal parts have come to pass, Jeffrey accumulates them into what he calls 'stages': 'Stages do duty (in the formal mode of speech) for all the facts so far' (253). We may reconstruct his stages from (15) and (16) as follows. For any t (before or after e), let p-through-t be the whole whose temporal parts are p-during-t' for all dates t' containing no instants later than t. Let C^* be the property such that p-through-t is C^* if and only if some temporal part of it is C. Then for any given t, the conjunction of all C^* p-through-t is the stage of the world at t's last instant. In other words, as true tenseless propositions come to pass, they become parts of all later stages of the world.

The mundane facts behind this formal farrago

are actually more visible in the relational reading of (13) and (14):

$$\sim C(p, t) \tag{17}$$

and

$$C(p, t^*) \tag{18}$$

Tenseless propositions, unlike events, admittedly have no dates; so C cannot just be the 'earlier' relation, i.e. H. But H suffices to define it:

$$C(p,t^*) =_{df} H(e,t^*) \tag{19}$$

In other words, e's being earlier than t^* is the fact that makes p have come to pass at that date. p's coming to pass at T, like e's happening then, is in reality nothing more than T being e's date.

So much for (i); what of (ii)? (ii) in fact depends on (i), since fixity depends on events happening, ineluctability on propositions coming to pass. The mere happening of an event fixes it, if the earlier happening of a sufficient cause has not already done so. And no event is fixed until it, or some preceding sufficient cause of it, has happened. Now we have seen that for an event to have happened by a certain date is simply for it to be earlier than that date. The supposed property, H, of having happened is in reality just the 'earlier' relation between events and dates. The supposed property, F, of being fixed is likewise in reality a relation events have to dates: a relation entailed by H but not entailing it, since the earlier happening of a sufficient cause may fix an event before it happens. F is thus definable by H, and by the relation S (= 'is a sufficient cause of'):

$$F(e,t) =_{df} H(e,t) \lor (\exists e^*)$$
$$[H(e^*, t) \,\&\, S(e^*, e)] \tag{20}$$

As for events, so for propositions. A proposition's coming to pass suffices to make it ineluctable, if it has not already been made so by the earlier coming to pass of a proposition that determines its truth. And no proposition is ineluctable until it, or some such determining proposition, has come to pass. The parallel between propositions and events here is obvious and exact. By definition, p becomes ineluctable just when e becomes fixed: i.e.

$$I(p,t) =_{df} F(e,t) \tag{21}$$

so the reality of ineluctability is just that of fixity, *viz* the conditions given in (20). All that fixity and ineluctability need are events, their dates, and the tenseless relations 'earlier' and 'sufficient cause'. (And if, as Hume thought, there is in reality no such relation as S, the second disjunct of (20) is always false, and both fixity and ineluctability reduce to events happening, i.e. to their having dates.)

7. Fixity, Coming True and Tense

I have given the simple relational conditions of happening, coming to pass, being fixed and being ineluctable. These conditions are undeniable, but they will hardly satisfy the authors of these conceits. Jeffrey, for example, is trying to conceive the world as 'growing by accretion of facts'. But the reality of his accretion turns out to be nothing more than the truism that the later a date is, the more events are earlier than it. There is no growth in that fact, any more than there is shrinkage in the fact that the earlier a date is, the more events are later than it. Jeffrey must be after something more.

So must Mackie. He hopes to find 'in this notion of fixity a basis for the concept of causal priority' (183). Specifically, causes are distinguished by being fixed at times when their effects are not, but not conversely (180). Since events are fixed at the latest when they happen, this is supposed to explain why causes mostly precede their effects (the exception being later causes fixed before their effects by the still earlier happening of sufficient causes of them). But for this to be an explanation, fixity must not itself be defined by the very fact Mackie wants to derive from it. But in (20) it is. When two causally related events e and e' have no preceding sufficient causes, e is fixed when e' is not just in case e is earlier than e'. So Mackie's definition of causal priority reduces in this case to the cause being the earlier of two causally related events, which is just what he is trying to explain. And when e does have sufficient causes, the arbitrary restriction in (20)'s second disjunct, to e^*s earlier than e, likewise begs the question it is supposed to answer. Later events, after all, exist no less than earlier ones, and are as capable of being sufficient causes of e. If any are, the restriction in

(20) discriminates without reason against them; and if none are, it is superfluous.

The fact is that Mackie's theory, like Jeffrey's, is useless and trivial unless having happened and being fixed are something more than the relations I have reduced them to. H and F must be real non-relational properties of events, acquired at times that are their, or their sufficient causes', dates, for the facts of causal priority to be explained by them. And similarly for C and I, the coming to pass and becoming ineluctable of Jeffrey's true tenseless propositions. Real accretion must be more than a relational fact: more, at any rate, than the different relations events have to different dates. Can we meet these seemingly modest demands?

Whatever these non-relational properties H, F, C and I are, their ascription will still have to satisfy the relational conditions I have stated. Maybe 'earlier', as a relation between events and dates, should be defined by 'has happened' rather than *vice versa:* but either way, their equivalence must follow. And even if (19), (20) and (21) will not do as definitions, they must still come out as necessary truths.

What this comes to is that, for example, any judgment to the effect that an event e has the property H must come out true just in case e is not later than the date of the judgment itself. But this is to say that the judgment is indexical: specifically, that its truth conditions are those of the simultaneous judgment that e is past or present. In other words, the nonrelational property H simply *is* that rather imprecise tense: to have happened is to be either past or present.

Ascriptions of fixity are indexical in a slightly more complex way. A judgment that an event e has the property F is true if and only if its date is not earlier than e or some sufficient cause of e. For e to be fixed, therefore, is just for it, or a sufficient cause of it, to be past or present.

Jeffrey's properties C and I likewise turn out to depend on tense, despite his tenseless pretensions. If p says that e's date is T, I judge truly that p is C if and only if I do so no earlier than e itself. So for p to have come to pass is for e to be past or present. Similarly, for p to be ineluctable, either e or a sufficient cause of e must be past or present.

Mackie and Jeffrey thus both require events to have positions in McTaggart's A series, and the changes they postulate are a species of McTaggart change. Events happen and become fixed, propo-sitions come to pass and become ineluctable, as the tense of events changes from future to present. Jeffrey's world growing by accretion of facts is Broad's (1923: ch. 11) world growing by accretion of present facts.

We can now, therefore, use the results of Sections 2–5 to extract the truth in Mackie's and Jeffrey's conceits from their error. The truth is that non-relational ascriptions of H, F, C and I, because they are indexical, do not mean the same as non-indexical statements of the relational facts to which I have reduced them. A judgment J, that e is H, is never the same as the simultaneous judgment J', that e is earlier than J. Yet they both have the same truth conditions, namely those stated by J'. And such truth conditions consist entirely of events, including judgments, having dates and being more or less earlier than, or simultaneous with, each other. In the real world that makes these judgments objectively true or false, the non-relational H, F, C and I do not figure at all. Because there is in reality no tense, so there is no real happening of events (apart from the events themselves) and no acquisition of fixity by them; no coming to pass, or becoming ineluctable, of true tenseless propositions.

Fixity, then, since it does not exist, cannot be the real basis of causal priority, nor can the world really grow by accretion of facts. In their intended substance, these conceits will have to go. Still, they will go in good company. Three quarters of a century after McTaggart demolished them, much writing, in many areas of philosophy, still appeals to real, non-relational non-indexical differences between past, present and future. All of that will have to go too. But not from here; despatching so great a multitude of errors must be matter for another place.

Endnotes

Ackrill, J. L., transl. 1963., *Aristotle: De Interpretatione.* London: Oxford University Press.

Broad, C. D. 1923. *Scientific Thought.* London: Kegan Paul, Trench and Trubner.

Davidson, Donald. 1969. 'The individuation of events.' *Essays in Honor of Carl G. Hempel,* ed. N. Rescher, pp. 216–34. Dordrecht: Reidel.

Geach, P. T. 1979. *Truth, Love and Immortality.* London: Hutchinson.

Goodman, Nelson. 1965. *Fact, Fiction and Forecast,* 2nd ed. New York: Bobbs-Merrill.

Jeffrey, R. C. 1980. 'Coming true.' *Intention and Intentionality,* ed. C. Diamond and J. Teichman, pp. 251–60. London: Harvester.

McArthur, R. P. 1976. *Tense Logic.* Dordrecht: Reidel.

Mackie, J. L. 1974. *The Cement of the Universe.* Oxford: Clarendon Press.

McTaggart, J. McT. E. 1908. 'The unreality of time.' *Mind* 18, 457–84.

McTaggart, J. McT. E. 1927. *The Nature of Existence,* vol. II. Cambridge: Cambridge University Press.

Mellor, D. H. 1974. 'In defense of dispositions.' *Philosophical Review* 83, 157–81.

Mellor, D. H. 1974a. 'Special relativity and present truth.' *Analysis* 34, 74–8.

Mellor, D. H. 1978. 'Conscious belief.' *Proceedings of the Aristotelian Society* 78, 87–101.

Mellor, D. H. 1982. 'The reduction of society.' *Philosophy* 57.

Perry, John. 1979. 'The problem of the essential indexical.' *Nous* 13, 3–21.

Prior, A. N. 1959. 'Thank goodness that's over.' *Philosophy* 34, 12–17.

Russell, B. 1903. *The Principles of Mathematics.* Cambridge: Cambridge University Press.

Williams, Donald C. 1951. 'The myth of passage.' *Journal of Philosophy* 48, 457–72.

Further Reading

Capek, M., ed., *The Concepts of Space and Time* (Dordrecht: D. Reidel, 1976).

Davies, P., *Space and Time in the Modern Universe* (Cambridge: Cambridge University Press, 1977).

Davies, P., *The Physics of Time Asymmetry* (Berkeley: University of California Press, 1977).*

Earman, J., et al., eds., *Foundations of Space-Time Theories, Minnesota Studies in the Philosophy of Science, VIII* (Minneapolis: University of Minnesota Press, 1977).*

Flood, R., and Lockwood, M., eds., *The Nature of Time* (Oxford: Blackwell, 1986).

Fraser, J., et al., eds., *The Study of Time,* Vol. 3 (New York: Springer-Verlag, 1978).

Friedman, M., *Foundations of Space-Time Theories* (Princeton: Princeton University Press, 1983).

Gale, R., *The Language of Time* (New York: Humanities, 1968).

Gale, R., ed., *The Philosophy of Time* (Garden City, N.Y.: Anchor, 1967).

Grünbaum, A., *Modern Science and Zeno's Paradoxes* (Middletown, Conn.: Wesleyan University Press, 1967).

Grünbaum, A., *Philosophical Problems of Space and Time,* 2d ed. (Dordrecht: Reidel, 1973).*

Hawking, S., *A Brief History of Time* (New York: Bantam, 1988).

Horwich, P., *Asymmetries in Time* (Cambridge: MIT Press, 1987).

Machamer, P., and Turnbull, R., eds., *Motion and Time, Space and Matter* (Columbus: Ohio University Press, 1976).

Mellor, D., *Real Time* (Cambridge: Cambridge University Press, 1981).

Newton-Smith, W., *The Structure of Time* (London: Routledge & Kegan Paul, 1980).

* May require familiarity with some advanced mathematics.

Oaklander, L., *Temporal Relations and Temporal Becoming* (Lanham, Md.: University Press of America, 1984).

Park, D., *The Image of Eternity* (Amherst: University of Massachusetts Press, 1980).

Prigogine, I., and Stenger, I., *Order out of Chaos* (New York: Bantam, 1984).

Prior, A., and Fine, K., *Worlds, Times, and Selves* (Amherst: University of Massachusetts Press, 1977).

Salmon, W., *Space, Time, and Motion,* 2d ed. (Minneapolis: University of Minnesota Press, 1980).

Schlesinger, G., *Aspects of Time* (Indianapolis: Hackett, 1980).

Sherover, C., ed., *The Human Experience of Time* (New York: New York University Press, 1975).

Sklar, L., *Space, Time and Space-Time* (Berkeley: University of California Press, 1974).*

Smart, J., ed., *Problems of Space and Time* (New York: Macmillan, 1964).

Sorabi, R., *Time, Creation, and the Continuum* (Ithaca, N.Y.: Cornell University Press, 1983).

Swinburne, R., ed., *Space, Time and Causality* (Dordrecht: D. Reidel, 1981).

van Fraassen, B., *An Introduction to the Philosophy of Time and Space* (New York: Random House, 1970).

van Inwagen, P., ed., *Time and Cause* (Dordrecht: Reidel, 1980).

Whitrow, G., *The Natural Philosophy of Time,* 2d ed. (Oxford: Oxford University Press, 1980).

* May require familiarity with some advanced mathematics.

Part II
Identity

In the fifth century B.C., the Greek philosopher Heraclitus said that you cannot step into the same river twice because rivers are constantly changing. He is also famous for such epigrams as "winter is summer" and "war is peace." Although little of Heraclitus' writings has been preserved, his brief remarks have ensured him a prominent place in the history of philosophy because he raised general problems about change and identity that stimulated later philosophers to try to find metaphysical solutions. Though he suggested there is some law governing change, Heraclitus used contradictory sentences to point to patterns of change. This might give the impression that change is contradictory; it is thought that Parmenides' belief that change is contradictory and therefore not real was, in part, a reaction to Heraclitus (see Chapter 1). The challenge to later philosophers was to explain how things could change yet, in some important sense, be the same; that is, retain their identity. Many of the problems of change and identity are still puzzling, and they are especially provocative when one considers *personal* identity. Part II begins with readings representing classic treatments of the general problem of change and identity, and proceeds to articles focusing on the nature of personal identity.

It will help explain some of the issues if you first reflect on the everyday experience of change. The experience of change is pervasive. Consider any object: an apple, a tree, a chair, this book, or yourself. There is one undeniable fact about them all—they change. Apples change color, trees grow taller, chairs become dirty, books become worn, and people change in more ways than can be described. If everything is constantly changing, then is there no permanence at all (is this Heraclitus' point)? Yet this cannot be entirely correct, because change also seems to require some permanence. Common sense says it is one and the same rose that was once in bloom and fragrant, but is now dry and odorless. Indeed, how could it be *the rose* that changes unless it is the same rose? Common sense seems to assume change involves identity, but how? How can the changing thing not be what it formerly was *and* be what it was?

Plato took very seriously the view that there is something contradictory about change, and this is the basis of his belief that a world of things that did not change would be perfectly real. Moreover, Plato claimed to discover such a world: the world of Forms (the world of general properties existing by themselves, "above" all change). Plato thought everyday objects (the objects of perceptual experience) were inferior entities infected by change. The best we can do, according to Plato, is to describe ordinary objects as at one time "participating" in (or exemplifying) one Form and later participating in another Form. For example, an apple changing from being green to red involves first participating in the Form, Greenness, and then participating in

Redness. Though Plato may have invented some of the logical distinctions useful for describing change, he left changing things themselves in metaphysical limbo. What, exactly, is it that participates in Forms?

Aristotle's answer was that changing things (or substances) are combinations of matter and form, and they—not the Forms themselves—are fundamental realities. As seen in Part I, Aristotle believed time is a property of change, and change is a property of substances. Without substances there would be no properties (or Forms), and without change there would be no time. But it is one thing to affirm the reality of change and time and another to give a coherent account of what constitutes the identity of something undergoing change. Here, though Aristotle starts with common sense, his analyses become complex and subtle. He claims individual things consist of some material having some essential form (some essential properties) and some accidental properties. When one asks whether an object is the same, the question can be ambiguous—it can be relative to whether one is asking about an object's essential properties, its accidental properties, or its matter.

Consider again the apple that changes from green to red. According to Aristotle, it is a substance having the essential property, being an apple. Its color is an accidental property. If, when one asks whether the apple is the same, one means *same apple*, then the answer is yes; because apples can change their color. Suppose, however, one means instead Is it the same *as it was* two weeks ago? Then, though it is the same apple, the answer is no, because it has changed its color. Suppose the apple is squashed so it becomes a puddle of apple juice. Now, even though the matter is the same matter, it is not the same apple because the matter no longer has the essential properties of an apple—the apple has ceased to exist altogether. Usually, for Aristotle, questions about the identity of an object involved determining whether some matter continued to have the same essential properties.

During the rise of modern science, Aristotle's notion of essential forms and their explanatory power came under attack. Materialists wanted to explain things in terms of their material constituents. From this perspective, the seventeenth-century philosopher Thomas Hobbes tried to solve an ancient puzzle: Suppose a ship's parts are gradually replaced over time so eventually the original ship no longer has any of the parts with which it began. And suppose the original parts are saved and gradually put together to make a second ship. Is the original ship identical with the one with new parts, or identical with the ship consisting of the old parts? Is the answer in some way arbitrary, to be decided by social conventions or laws?

Supposing that one could analyze the identity of such changing things as dogs or ships in the ways recommended by either Aristotle or Hobbes, many philosophers have nevertheless believed that the topic of personal identity raises new issues. Clearly, one's body changes dramatically during one's life: not only does its shape, size, and weight change, but also there are numerous complete replacements of its molecular constituents. Also, one's personality and memory can undergo significant changes. Yet, through all such changes it is common to believe that some identical person persists. It is not very helpful in understanding personal identity to be told that it is a matter of an individual maintaining the same essence. One would like to know what the exact *criteria* are for being the same person. Moreover, the issue of one's identity has ethical and value implications that make it seem vital in the way the identity of a ship is not. Whereas one might allow social or linguistic conventions to decide the identity of a ship, many believe that there must be more to personal identity. In this volume, Plato, Reid, and Chisholm represent the position that this something more is a unity (a soul, for example) that persists through all change. Other philosophers, however, are skeptical about this solution and try to formulate bodily or psychological criteria (see the articles by Williams, Parfit, and Nagel). Continuing to motivate and challenge much of this work is David Hume's skeptical worry that personal identity is a metaphysical illusion.

10. *Phaedo*

PLATO

Plato (470–347 B.C.) of Athens was closely associated with Socrates during the last years before his death. In his writings, which were primarily dialogues, Socrates is usually Plato's spokesperson. In the *Phaedo*, Plato is concerned with the question of immortality. The issue has dramatic significance, for the discussion takes place in the prison where Socrates is sentenced to die. Socrates expresses the view that the presence of the soul in the body is what gives it life, and that the soul is also crucial to personal identity. He argues that true philosophers should look forward to death because then, and only then, will they be able to attain their lifelong goal, namely, better knowledge of Reality. In order to render this view plausible Socrates considers several arguments for the immortality of the soul, all of which are included in this selection. Though the focus of the discussion is on the immortality of the soul, the *Phaedo* is also important because it shows how Plato analyzed change.

Socrates sat up on the bed, bent his leg and rubbed it with his hand, and as he rubbed he said: "What a strange thing that which men call pleasure seems to be, and how astonishing the relation it has with what is thought to be its opposite, namely pain! A man cannot have both at the same time. Yet if he pursues and catches the one, he is almost always bound to catch the other also, like two creatures with one head. I think that if Aesop had noted this he would have composed a fable that a god wished to reconcile their opposition but could not do so, so he joined their two heads together, and therefore when a man has the one, the other follows later. This seems to be happening to me. My bonds caused pain in my leg, and now pleasure seems to be following."

Cebes intervened and said: "By Zeus, yes, Socrates, you did well to remind me, Evenus asked me the day before yesterday, as others had done before, what induced you to write poetry after you came to prison, you who had never composed any poetry before, putting the fables of Aesop into verse and composing the hymn to Apollo. If it is of any concern to you that I should have an answer to give to Evenus when he repeats his question, as I know he will, tell me what to say to him."

Tell him the truth, Cebes, he said, that I did not do this with the idea of rivalling him or his poems, for I knew that would not be easy, but I tried to find out the meaning of certain dreams and to satisfy my conscience in case it was this kind of art they were frequently bidding me to practise. The dreams were something like this: the same dream often came to me in the past, now in one shape now in another, but saying the same thing: "Socrates," it said, "practise and cultivate the arts." In the past I imagined that it was instructing and advising me to do what I was doing, such as those who encourage runners in a race, that the dream was thus bidding me do the very thing I was doing, namely, to practise the art of philosophy, this being the highest kind of art, and I was doing that.

But now, after my trial took place, and the festival of the god was preventing my execution, I thought that, in case my dream was bidding me to practise this popular art, I should not disobey it but compose poetry. I thought it safer not to leave here until I had satisfied my conscience by writing poems in obedience to the dream. So I first wrote in

Plato's *Phaedo*, translated by G. M. A. Grube, 1977, pp. 8–31 and 46–58. Reprinted by permission of Hackett Publishing Company, Indianapolis, Ind., and Cambridge, Mass.

honour of the god of the present festival. After that I realized that a poet, if he is to be a poet, must compose fables, not arguments. Being no teller of fables myself, I took the stories I knew and had at hand, the fables of Aesop, and I versified the first ones I came across. Tell this to Evenus, Cebes, wish him well and bid him farewell, and tell him, if he is wise, to follow me as soon as possible. I am leaving today, it seems, as the Athenians so order it.

Said Simmias: "What kind of advice is this you are giving to Evenus, Socrates? I have met him many times, and from my observation he is not at all likely to follow it willingly."

How so, said he, is Evenus not a philosopher?

I think so, Simmias said.

Then Evenus will be willing, like every man who partakes worthily of philosophy. Yet perhaps he will not take his own life, for that, they say, is not right. As he said this, Socrates put his feet on the ground and remained in this position during the rest of the conversation.

Then Cebes asked: "How do you mean Socrates, that it is not right to do oneself violence, and yet that the philosopher will be willing to follow one who is dying?"

Come now, Cebes, have you and Simmias, who keep company with Philolaus, not heard about such things?

Nothing definite, Socrates.

Indeed, I too speak about this from hearsay, but I do not mind telling you what I have heard, for it is perhaps most appropriate for one who is about to depart yonder to tell and examine tales about what we believe that journey to be like. What else could one do in the time we have until sunset?

But whatever is the reason, Socrates, for people to say that it is not right to kill oneself? As to your question just now, I have heard Philolaus say this when staying in Thebes and I have also heard it from others, but I have never heard anyone give a clear account of the matter.

Well, he said, we must do our best, and you may yet hear one. And it may well astonish you if this subject, alone of all things, is simple, and it is never, as with everything else, better at certain times and for certain people to die than to live. And if this is so, you may well find it astonishing that those for whom it is better to die are wrong to help themselves, and that they must wait for someone else to benefit them.

And Cebes, lapsing into his own dialect laughed quietly and said: "Zeus knows it is."

Indeed, said Socrates, it does seem unreasonable when put like that, but perhaps there is reason to it. There is the explanation that is put in the language of the mysteries, that we men are in a kind of prison, and that one must not free oneself or run away. That seems to me an impressive doctrine and one not easy to understand fully. However, Cebes, this seems to me well expressed, that the gods are our guardians and that men are one of their possessions. Or do you not think so?

I do, said Cebes.

And would you not be angry if one of your possessions killed itself when you had not given any sign that you wished it to die, and if you had any punishment you could inflict, you would inflict it?

Certainly, he said.

Perhaps then, put in this way, it is not unreasonable that one should not kill oneself before a god had indicated some necessity to do so, like the necessity now put upon us.

That seems likely, said Cebes. As for what you were saying, that philosophers should be willing and ready to die, that seems strange, Socrates, if what we said just now is reasonable, namely, that a god is our protector and that we are his possessions. It is not logical that the wisest of men should not resent leaving this service in which they are governed by the best of masters, the gods, for a wise man cannot believe that he will look after himself better when he is free. A foolish man might easily think so, that he must escape from his master; he would not reflect that one must not escape from a good master but stay with him as long as possible, because it would be foolish to escape. But the sensible man would want always to remain with one better than himself. So, Socrates, the opposite of what was said before is likely to be true; the wise would resent dying, whereas the foolish would rejoice at it.

I thought that when Socrates heard this he was pleased by Cebes' argumentation. Glancing at us, he said: "Cebes is always on the track of some arguments; he is certainly not willing to be at once convinced by what one says."

Said Simmias: "But actually, Socrates, I think myself that Cebes has a point now. Why should truly wise men want to avoid the service of masters better than themselves, and leave them easily? And I think Cebes is aiming his argument at you, because you are bearing leaving us so lightly, and leaving those good masters, as you say yourself, the gods."

You are both justified in what you say, and I think you mean that I must make a defence against this, as if I were in court.

You certainly must, said Simmias.

Come then, he said, let me try to make my defence to you more convincing than it was to the jury. For, Simmias and Cebes, I should be wrong not to resent dying if I did not believe that I should go first to other wise and good gods, and then to men who have died and are better than men are here. Be assured that, as it is, I expect to join the company of good men. This last I would not altogether insist on, but if I insist on anything at all in these matters, it is that I shall come to gods who are very good masters. That is why I am not so resentful, because I have good hope that some future awaits men after death, as we have been told for years, a much better future for the good than for the wicked.

Well now, Socrates, said Simmias, do you intend to keep this belief to yourself as you leave us, or would you share it with us? I certainly think it would be a blessing for us too, and at the same time it would be your defence if you convince us of what you say.

I will try, he said, but first let us see what it is that Crito here has, I think, been wanting to say for quite a while.

What else, Socrates, said Crito, but what the man who is to give you the poison has been telling me for some time, that I should warn you to talk as little as possible. People get heated when they talk, he says, and one should not be heated when taking the poison, as those who do must sometimes drink it two or three times.

Socrates replied: "Take no notice of him; only let him be prepared to administer it twice or, if necessary, three times."

I was rather sure you would say that, Crito said, but he has been bothering me for some time.

Let him be, he said. I want to make my argument before you, my judges, as to why I think that a man who has spent his life in philosophy is probably right to be of good cheer in the face of death and to be very hopeful that after death he will attain the greatest blessings yonder. I will try to tell you, Simmias and Cebes, how this may be so. I am afraid that other people do not realize that the one aim of those who practise philosophy in the proper

manner is to practise for dying and death. Now if this is true, it would be strange indeed if they were eager for this all their lives and then resent it when what they have wanted and practised for a long time comes upon them.

Simmias laughed and said: "By Zeus, Socrates, you made me laugh, though I was in no laughing mood just now. I think that the majority, on hearing this, will think that it describes the philosophers very well, and our people in Thebes would thoroughly agree that philosophers are nearly dead and that the majority of men is well aware that they deserve to be."

And they would be telling the truth, Simmias, except for their being aware. They are not aware of the way true philosophers are nearly dead, nor of the way they deserve to be, nor of the sort of death they deserve. But never mind them, he said, let us talk among ourselves. Do we believe that there is such a thing as death?

Certainly, said Simmias.

Is it anything else than the separation of the soul from the body? Do we believe that death is this, namely, that the body comes to be separated by itself apart from the soul, and the soul comes to be separated by itself apart from the body? Is death anything else than that?

No, that is what it is, he said.

Consider then, my good sir, whether you share my opinion, for this will lead us to a better knowledge of what we are investigating. Do you think it is the part of a philosopher to be concerned with such so-called pleasures as those of food and drink?

By no means.

What about the pleasures of sex?

Not at all.

What of the other pleasures concerned with the service of the body? Do you think such a man prizes them greatly, the acquisition of distinguished clothes and shoes and the other bodily ornaments? Do you think he values these or despises them, except in so far as one cannot do without them?

I think the true philosopher despises them.

Do you not think, he said, that in general such a man's concern is not with the body but that, as far as he can, he turns away from the body towards the soul?

I do.

So in the first place, such things show clearly that the philosopher more than other men frees the soul from association with the body as much as possible?

Apparently.

A man who finds no pleasure in such things and has no part in them is thought by the majority not to deserve to live and to be close to death; the man, that is, who does not care for the pleasures of the body.

What you say is certainly true.

Then what about the actual acquiring of knowledge? Is the body an obstacle when one associates with it in the search for knowledge? I mean, for example, do men find any truth in sight or hearing, or are not even the poets forever telling us that we do not see or hear anything accurately, and surely if those two physical senses are not clear or precise, our other senses can hardly be accurate, as they are all inferior to these. Do you not think so?

I certainly do, he said.

When then, he asked, does the soul grasp the truth? For whenever it attempts to examine anything with the body, it is clearly deceived by it.

True.

Is it not in reasoning if anywhere that any reality becomes clear to the soul?

Yes.

And indeed the soul reasons best when none of these senses troubles it, neither hearing nor sight, nor pain nor pleasure, but when it is most by itself, taking leave of the body and as far as possible having no contact or association with it in its search for reality.

That is so.

And it is then that the soul of the philosopher most disdains the body, flees from it and seeks to be by itself?

It appears so.

What about the following, Simmias? Do we say that there is such a thing as the Just itself, or not?

We do say so, by Zeus.

And the Beautiful, and the Good?

Of course.

And have you ever seen any of these things with your eyes?

In no way, he said.

Or have you ever grasped them with any of your bodily senses? I speaking of all things such as Size, Health, Strength and, in a word, the reality of all other things, that which each of them essentially is. Is what is most true in them contemplated through the body, or is this the position: whoever

of us prepares himself best and most accurately to grasp that thing itself which he is investigating will come closest to the knowledge of it?

Obviously.

Then he will do this most perfectly who approaches the object with thought alone, without associating any sight with his thought, or dragging in any sense perception with his reasoning, but who, using pure thought alone, tries to track down each reality pure and by itself, freeing himself as far as possible from eyes and ears, and in a word, from the whole body, because the body confuses the soul and does not allow it to acquire truth and wisdom whenever it is associated with it. Will not that man reach reality, Simmias, if anyone does?

What you say, said Simmias, is indeed true.

All these things will necessarily make the true philosophers believe and say to each other something like this: "There is likely to be something such as a path to guide us out of our confusion, because as long as we have a body and our soul is fused with such an evil we shall never adequately attain what we desire, which we affirm to be the truth. The body keeps us busy in a thousand ways because of its need for nurture. Moreover, if certain diseases befall it, they impede our search for the truth. It fills us with wants, desires, fears, all sorts of illusions and much nonsense, so that, as it is said, in truth and in fact no thought of any kind ever comes to us from the body. Only the body and its desires cause war, civil discord and battles, for all wars are due to the desire to acquire wealth, and it is the body and the care of it, to which we are enslaved, which compel us to acquire wealth, and all this makes us too busy to practice philosophy. Worst of all, if we do get some respite from it and turn to some investigation, everywhere in our investigations the body is present and makes for confusion and fear, so that it prevents us from seeing the truth.

It really has been shown to us that, if we are ever to have pure knowledge, we must escape from the body and observe matters in themselves with the soul by itself. It seems likely that we shall, only then, when we are dead, attain that which we desire and of which we claim to be lovers, namely, wisdom, as our argument shows, not while we live; for if it is impossible to attain any pure knowledge with the body, then one of two things is true: either we can never attain knowledge or we can do so after death. Then and not before, the soul is by itself apart from the body. While we live, we shall be closest to knowledge if we refrain as much as possible from association with the body or join with it more than we must, if we are not infected with its nature but purify ourselves from it until the god himself frees us. In this way we shall escape the contamination of the body's folly; we shall be likely to be in the company of people of the same kind, and by our own efforts we shall know all that is pure, which is presumably the truth, for it is not permitted to the impure to attain the pure."

Such are the things, Simmias, that all those who love learning in the proper manner must say to one another and believe. Or do you not think so?

I certainly do, Socrates.

And if this is true, my friend, said Socrates, there is good hope that on arriving where I am going, if anywhere, I shall acquire what has been our chief preoccupation in our past life, so that the journey that is now ordered for me is full of good hope, as it is also for any other man who believes that his mind has been prepared and, as it were, purified.

It certainly is, said Simmias.

And does purification not turn out to be what we mentioned in our argument some time ago, namely, to separate the soul as far as possible from the body and accustom it to gather itself and collect itself out of every part of the body and to dwell by itself as far as it can both now and in the future, freed, as it were, from the bonds of the body?

Certainly, he said.

And that freedom and separation of the soul from the body is called death?

That is altogether so.

It is only those who practise philosophy in the right way, we say, who always most want to free the soul; and this release and separation of the soul from the body is the preoccupation of the philosophers?

So it appears.

Therefore, as I said at the beginning, it would be ridiculous for a man to train himself in life to live in a state as close to death as possible, and then to resent it when it comes?

Ridiculous, of course.

In fact, Simmias, he said, those who practise philosophy in the right way are in training for dying and they fear death least of all men. Consider it from this point of view: if they are altogether estranged from the body and desire to have their soul by itself, would it not be quite absurd for them to be afraid and resentful when this happens? If they did

not gladly set out for a place, where, on arrival, they may hope to attain that for which they had yearned during their lifetime, that is, wisdom, and where they would be rid of the presence of that from which they are estranged?

Many men, at the death of their lovers, wives or sons, were willing to go to the underworld, driven by the hope of seeing there those for whose company they longed, and being with them. Will then a true lover of wisdom, who has a similar hope and knows that he will never find it to any extent except in Hades, be resentful of dying and not gladly undertake the journey thither? One must surely think so, my friend, if he is a true philosopher, for he is firmly convinced that he will not find pure knowledge anywhere except there. And if this is so, then, as I said just now, would it not be highly unreasonable for such a man to fear death?

It certainly would, by Zeus, he said.

Then you have sufficient indication, he said, that any man whom you see resenting death was not a lover of wisdom but a lover of the body, and also a lover of wealth or of honours, either or both.

It is certainly as you say.

And, Simmias, he said, does not what is called courage belong especially to men of this disposition?

Most certainly.

And the quality of moderation which even the majority call by that name, that is, not to get swept off one's feet by one's passions, but to treat them with disdain and orderliness, is this not suited only to those who most of all despise the body and live the life of philosophy?

Necessarily so, he said.

If you are willing to reflect on the courage and moderation of other people, you will find them strange.

In what way, Socrates?

You know that they all consider death a great evil?

Definitely, he said.

And the brave among them face death, when they do, for fear of greater evils?

That is so.

Therefore, it is fear and terror that make all men brave, except the philosophers. Yet it is illogical to be brave through fear and cowardice.

It certainly is.

What of the moderate among them? Is their experience not similar? Is it licence of a kind that makes them moderate? We say this is impossible, yet their experience of this unsophisticated moderation turns out to be similar: they fear to be deprived of other pleasures which they desire, so they keep away from some pleasures because they are overcome by others. Now to be mastered by pleasure is what they call licence, but what happens to them is that they master certain pleasures because they are mastered by others. This is like what we mentioned just now, that in some way it is a kind of licence that has made them moderate.

That seems likely.

My good Simmias, I fear this is not the right exchange to attain virtue, to exchange pleasures for pleasures, pains for pains and fears for fears, the greater for the less like coins, but that the only valid currency for which all these things should be exchanged is wisdom. With this we have real courage and moderation and justice and, in a word, true virtue, with wisdom, whether pleasures and fears and all such things be present or absent. Exchanged for one another without wisdom such virtue is only an illusory appearance of virtue; it is in fact fit for slaves, without soundness or truth, whereas, in truth, moderation and courage and justice are a purging away of all such things, and wisdom itself is a kind of cleansing or purification. It is likely that those who established the mystic rites for us were not inferior persons but were speaking in riddles long ago when they said that whoever arrives in the underworld uninitiated and unsanctified will wallow in the mire, whereas he who arrives there purified and initiated will dwell with the gods. There are indeed, as those concerned with the mysteries say, many who carry the thyrsus but the Bacchants are few. These latter are, in my opinion, no other than those who have practised philosophy in the right way. I have in my life left nothing undone in order to be counted among these as far as possible, as I have been eager to be in every way. Whether my eagerness was right and we accomplished anything we shall, I think, know for certain in a short time, god willing, on arriving yonder.

This is my defence, Simmias and Cebes, that I am likely to be right to leave you and my masters here without resentment or complaint, believing that there, as here, I shall find good masters and good friends. If my defence is more convincing to you than to the Athenian jury, it will be well.

When Socrates finished, Cebes intervened: "Socrates," he said, "everything else you said is excellent, I think, but men find it very hard to believe what you said about the soul. They think that after it has left the body it no longer exists anywhere, but that it is destroyed and dissolved on the day the man dies, as soon as it leaves the body; and that, on leaving it, it is dispersed like breath or smoke, has flown away and gone and is no longer anything anywhere. If indeed it gathered itself together and existed by itself and escaped those evils you were recently enumerating, there would then be much good hope, Socrates, that what you say is true; but to believe this requires a good deal of faith and persuasive argument, to believe that the soul still exists after a man has died and that it still possesses some capability and intelligence."

What you say is true, Cebes, Socrates said, but what shall we do? Do you want to discuss whether this is likely to be true or not?

Personally, said Cebes, I should like to hear your opinion on the subject.

I do not think, said Socrates, that anyone who heard me now, not even a comic poet, could say that I am babbling and discussing things that do not concern me, so we must examine the question thoroughly, if you think we should do so. Let us examine it in some such a manner as this: whether the souls of men who have died exist in the underworld or not. We recall an ancient theory that souls arriving there come from here, and then again that they arrive here and are born here from the dead. If that is true, that the living come back from the dead, then surely our souls must exist there, for they could not come back if they did not exist, and this is a sufficient proof that these things are so if it truly appears that the living never come from any other source than from the dead. If this is not the case we should need another argument.

Quite so, said Cebes.

Do not, he said, confine yourself to humanity if you want to understand this more readily, but take all animals and all plants into account, and, in short, for all things which come to be, let us see whether they come to be in this way, that is, from their opposites if they have such, as the beautiful is the opposite of the ugly and the just of the unjust, and a thousand other things of the kind. Let us examine whether those that have an opposite must necessarily come to be from their opposite and from nowhere else, as for example when something comes to be larger it must necessarily become larger from having been smaller before.

Yes.

Then if something smaller comes to be, it will come from something larger before, which became smaller?

That is so, he said.

And the weaker comes to be from the stronger, and the swifter from the slower?

Certainly.

Further, if something worse comes to be, does it not come from the better, and the juster from the more unjust?

Of course.

So we have sufficiently established that all things come to be in this way, opposites from opposites?

Certainly.

There is a further point, something such as this, about these opposites: between each of those pairs of opposites there are two processes: from the one to the other and then again from the other to the first; between the larger and the smaller there is increase and decrease, and we call the one increasing and the other decreasing?

Yes, he said.

And so too there is separation and combination, cooling and heating, and all such things, even if sometimes we do not have a name for the process, but in fact it must be everywhere that they come to be from one another, and that there is a process of becoming from each into the other?

Assuredly, he said.

Well then, is there an opposite to living, as sleeping is the opposite of being awake?

Quite so, he said.

What is it?

Being dead, he said.

Therefore, if these are opposites, they come to be from one another, and there are two processes of generation between the two?

Of course.

I will tell you, said Socrates, one of the two pairs I was just talking about, the pair itself and the two processes, and you will tell me the other. I mean, to sleep and to be awake; to be awake comes from sleeping, and to sleep comes from being awake. Of the two processes one is going to sleep, the other is waking up. Do you accept that, or not?

Certainly.

You tell me in the same way about life and death. Do you not say that to be dead is the opposite of being alive?

I do.

And they come to be from one another?

Yes.

What comes to be from being alive?

Being dead.

What comes to be from being dead?

One must agree that it is being alive.

Then, Cebes, living creatures and things come to be from the dead?

So it appears, he said.

Then our souls exist in the underworld.

That seems likely.

Then in this case one of the two processes of becoming is clear, for dying is clear enough, is it not?

It certainly is.

What shall we do then? Shall we not supply the opposite process of becoming? Is nature to be lame in this case? Or must we provide a process of becoming opposite to dying?

We surely must.

And what is that?

Coming to life again.

Therefore, he said, if there is such a thing as coming to life again, it would be a process of coming from the dead to the living?

Quite so.

It is agreed between us then that the living come from the dead in this way no less than the dead from the living and, if that is so, it seems to be a sufficient proof that the souls of the dead must be somewhere whence they can come back again.

I think, Socrates, he said, that this follows from what we have agreed on.

Consider in this way, Cebes, he said, that, as I think, we were not wrong to agree. If the two processes of becoming did not always balance each other as if they were going round in a circle, but generation proceeded from one point to its opposite in a straight line and it did not turn back again to the other opposite or take any turning, do you realize that all things would ultimately have the same form, be affected in the same way, and cease to become?

How do you mean? he said.

It is not hard to understand what I mean. If, for example, there was such a process as going to sleep, but no corresponding process of waking up, you realize that in the end everything would show the story of Endymion to have no meaning. There would be no point to it because everything would have the same experience as he, be asleep. And if everything were combined and nothing separated, the saying of Anaxagoras would soon be true, "that all things were mixed together." In the same way, my dear Cebes, if everything that partakes of life were to die and remain in that state and not come to life again, would not everything ultimately have to be dead and nothing alive? Even if the living came from some other source, and all that lived died, how could all things avoid being absorbed in death?

It could not be, Socrates, said Cebes, and I think what you say is altogether true.

I think, Cebes, said he, that this is very definitely the case and that we were not deceived when we agreed on this: coming to life again in truth exists, the living come to be from the dead, and the souls of the dead exist.

Furthermore, Socrates, Cebes rejoined, such is also the case if that theory is true that you are accustomed to mention frequently, that for us learning is no other than recollection. According to this, we must at some previous time have learned what we now recollect. This is possible only if our soul existed somewhere before it took on this human shape. So according to this theory too, the soul is likely to be something immortal.

Cebes, Simmias interrupted, what are the proofs of this? Remind me, for I do not quite recall them at the moment.

There is one excellent argument, said Cebes, namely that when men are interrogated in the right manner, they always give the right answer of their own accord, and they could not do this if they did not possess the knowledge and the right explanation inside them. Then if one shows them a diagram or something else of that kind, this will show most clearly that such is the case.

If this does not convince you, Simmias, said Socrates, see whether you agree if we examine it in some such way as this, for you doubt that what we call learning is recollection.

It is not that I doubt, said Simmias, but I want to experience the very thing we are discussing, recollection, and from what Cebes undertook to say, I am now remembering and am pretty nearly convinced. Nevertheless, I should like to hear now the way you were intending to explain it.

This way, he said. We surely agree that if anyone recollects anything, he must have known it before.

Quite so, he said.

Do we not also agree that when knowledge comes to mind in this way, it is recollection? What way do I mean? Like this: when a man sees or hears or in some other way perceives one thing and not only knows that thing but also thinks of another thing of which the knowledge is not the same but different, are we not right to say that he recollects the second thing that comes into his mind?

How do you mean?

Things such as this: to know a man is surely a different knowledge from knowing a lyre.

Of course.

Well, you know what happens to lovers: whenever they see a lyre, a garment or anything else that their beloved is accustomed to use, they know the lyre, and the image of the boy to whom it belongs comes into their mind. This is recollection, just as someone, on seeing Simmias, often recollects Cebes, and there are thousands of other such occurrences.

Thousands indeed, said Simmias.

Is this kind of thing not recollection of a kind? he said, especially so when one experiences it about things that one had forgotten, because one had not seen them for some time?—Quite so.

Further, he said, can a man seeing the picture of a horse or a lyre recollect a man, or seeing a picture of Simmias recollect Cebes?—Certainly.

Or seeing a picture of Simmias, recollect Simmias himself?—He certainly can.

In all these cases the recollection is occasioned by things that are similar, but it can also be occasioned by things that are dissimilar?—It can.

When the recollection is caused by similar things, must one not of necessity also experience this: to consider whether the similarity to that which one recollects is deficient in any respect or complete?—One must.

Consider, he said, whether this is the case: we say that there is something that is equal. I do not mean a stick equal to a stick or a stone to a stone, or anything of that kind, but something else beyond all these, the Equal itself. Shall we say that this exists or not?

Indeed we shall, by Zeus, said Simmias, most definitely.

And do we know what this is?—Certainly.

Whence have we acquired the knowledge of it? Is it not from the things we mentioned just now, from seeing sticks or stones or some other things that are equal we come to think of that other which is different from them? Or doesn't it seem to you to be different? Look at it also this way: do not equal stones and sticks sometimes, while remaining the same, appear to one person to be equal and to another to be unequal?—Certainly they do.

But what of the equals themselves? Have they ever appeared unequal to you, or Equality to be Inequality?

Never, Socrates.

These equal things and the Equal itself are therefore not the same?

I do not think they are the same at all, Socrates.

But it is definitely from the equal things, though they are different from that Equal, that you have derived and grasped the knowledge of equality?

Very true, Socrates.

Whether it be like them or unlike them?

Certainly.

It makes no difference. As long as the sight of one thing makes you think of another, whether it be similar or dissimilar, this must of necessity be recollection?

Quite so.

Well then, he said, do we experience something like this in the case of equal sticks and the other equal objects we just mentioned? Do they seem to us to be equal in the same sense as what is Equal itself? Is there some deficiency in their being such as the Equal, or is there not?

A considerable deficiency, he said.

Whenever someone, on seeing something, realizes that that which he now sees wants to be like some other reality but falls short and cannot be like that other since it is inferior, do we agree that the one who thinks this must have prior knowledge of that to which he says it is like, but deficiently so?

Necessarily.

Well, do we also feel this about the equal objects and the Equal itself, or do we not?

Very definitely.

We must then possess knowledge of the Equal before that time when we first saw the equal objects and realized that all these objects strive to be like the Equal but are deficient in this.

That is so.

Then surely we also agree that this conception of ours derives from seeing or touching or some other sense perception, and cannot come into our mind in any other way, for all these senses, I say, are the same.

They are the same, Socrates, at any rate in respect to that which our argument wishes to make plain.

Our sense perceptions must surely make us realize that all that we perceive through them is striving to reach that which is Equal but falls short of it; or how do we express it?

Like that.

Then before we began to see or hear or otherwise perceive, we must have possessed knowledge of the Equal itself if we were about to refer our sense perceptions of equal objects to it, and realized that all of them were eager to be like it, but were inferior.

That follows from what has been said, Socrates.

But we began to see and hear and otherwise perceive right after birth?

Certainly.

We must then have acquired the knowledge of the Equal before this.

Yes.

It seems then that we must have possessed it before birth.

It seems so.

Therefore, if we had this knowledge, we knew before birth and immediately after not only the Equal, but the Greater and the Smaller and all such things, for our present argument is no more about the Equal than about the Beautiful itself, the Good itself, the Just, the Pious and, as I say, about all those things to which we can attach the word "itself," both when we are putting questions and answering them. So we must have acquired knowledge of them all before we were born.

That is so.

If, having acquired this knowledge in each case, we have not forgotten it, we remain knowing and have knowledge throughout our life, for to know is to acquire knowledge, keep it and not lose it. Do we not call the losing of knowledge forgetting?

Most certainly, Socrates, he said.

But, I think, if we acquired this knowledge before birth, then lost it at birth, and then later by the use of our senses in connection with those objects we mentioned, we recovered the knowledge we had before, would not what we call learning be the recovery of our own knowledge, and we are right to call this recollection?

Certainly.

It was seen to be possible for someone to see or hear or otherwise perceive something, and by this to be put in mind of something else which he had forgotten and which is related to it by similarity or difference. One of two things follows, as I say: either we were born with the knowledge of it, and all of us know it throughout life, or those who later, we say, are learning, are only recollecting, and learning would be recollection.

That is certainly the case, Socrates.

Which alternative do you choose Simmias? That we are born with this knowledge or that we recollect later the things of which we had knowledge previously?

I have no means of choosing at the moment, Socrates.

Well, can you make this choice? What is your opinion about it? A man who has knowledge would be able to give an account of what he knows, or would he not?

He must certainly be able to do so, Socrates, he said.

And do you think everybody can give an account of the things we were mentioning just now?

I wish they could, said Simmias, but I'm afraid it is much more likely that by this time tomorrow there will be no one left who can do so adequately.

So you do not think that everybody has knowledge of those things?

No indeed.

So they recollect what they once learned?

They must.

When did our souls acquire the knowledge of them? Certainly not since we were born as men.

Indeed no.

Before that then?

Yes.

So then, Simmias, our souls also existed apart from the body before they took on human form, and they had intelligence.

Unless we acquire the knowledge at the moment of birth, Socrates, for that time is still left to us.

Quite so, my friend, but at what other time do we lose it? We just now agreed that we are not born with that knowledge. Do we then lose it at the very time we acquire it, or can you mention any other time?

I cannot, Socrates. I did not realize that I was talking nonsense.

So this is our position, Simmias? he said. If those realities we are always talking about exist, the Beautiful and the Good and all that kind of reality, and we refer all the things we perceive to that reality, discovering that it existed before and is ours, and we compare these things with it, then,

just as they exist, so our soul must exist before we are born. If these realities do not exist, then this argument is altogether futile. Is this the position, that there is an equal necessity for those realities to exist, and for our souls to exist before we were born? If the former do not exist, neither do the latter?

I do not think, Socrates, said Simmias, that there is any possible doubt that it is equally necessary for both to exist, and it is opportune that our argument comes to the conclusion that our soul exists before we are born, and equally so that reality of which you are now speaking. Nothing is so evident to me personally as that all such things must certainly exist, the Beautiful, the Good, and all those you mentioned just now. I also think that sufficient proof of this has been given.

Then what about Cebes? said Socrates, for we must persuade Cebes also.

He is sufficiently convinced I think, said Simmias, though he is the most difficult of men to persuade by argument, but I believe him to be fully convinced that our soul existed before we were born. I do not think myself, however, that it has been proved that the soul continues to exist after death; the opinion of the majority which Cebes mentioned still stands, that when a man dies his soul is dispersed and this is the end of its existence. What is to prevent the soul coming to be and being constituted from some other source, existing before it enters a human body and then, having done so and departed from it, itself dying and being destroyed?

You are right, Simmias, said Cebes. Half of what needed proof has been proved, namely, that our soul existed before we were born, but further proof is needed that it exists no less after we have died, if the proof is to be complete.

It has been proved even now, Simmias and Cebes, said Socrates, if you are ready to combine this argument with the one we agreed on before, that every living thing must come from the dead. If the soul exists before, it must, as it comes to life and birth, come from nowhere else than death and being dead, so how could it avoid existing after death since it must be born again? What you speak of has then even now been proved. However, I think you and Simmias would like to discuss the argument more fully. You seem to have this childish fear that the wind would really dissolve and scatter the soul, as it leaves the body, especially if one happens to die in a high wind and not in calm weather.

Cebes laughed and said: "Assuming that we were afraid, Socrates, try to change our minds, or rather do not assume that we are afraid, but perhaps there is a child in us who has these fears; try to persuade him not to fear death like a bogey."

You should, said Socrates, sing a charm over him every day until you have charmed away his fears.

Where shall we find a good charmer for these fears, Socrates, he said, now that you are leaving us?

Greece is a large country, Cebes, he said, and there are good men in it; the tribes of foreigners are also numerous. You should search for such a charmer among them all, sparing neither trouble nor expense, for there is nothing on which you could spend your money to greater advantage. You must also search among yourselves, for you might not easily find people who could do this better than yourselves.

That shall be done, said Cebes, but let us, if it pleases you, go back to the argument where we left it.

Of course it pleases me.

Splendid, he said.

We must then ask ourselves something like this: what kind of thing is likely to be scattered? On behalf of what kind of thing should one fear this, and for what kind of thing should one not fear it? We should then examine to which class the soul belongs, and as a result either fear for the soul or be of good cheer.

What you say is true.

Is not anything that is composite and a compound by nature liable to be split up into its component parts, and only that which is noncomposite, if anything, is not likely to be split up?

I think that is the case, said Cebes.

Are not the things that always remain the same and in the same state most likely not to be composite, whereas those that vary from one time to another and are never the same are composite?

I think that is so.

Let us then return to those same things with which we were dealing earlier, to that reality of whose existence we giving an account in our questions and answers; are they ever the same and in the same state, or do they vary from one time to another; can the Equal itself, the Beautiful itself, each thing in itself, the real, ever be affected by any change whatever? Or does each of them that really is, being simple by itself, remain the same and never in any way tolerate any change whatever?

It must remain the same, said Cebes, and in the same state, Socrates.

What of the many beautiful particulars, be they men, horses, clothes, or other such things, or the many equal particulars, and all those which bear the same name as those others? Do they remain the same or, in total contrast to those other realities, one might say, never in any way remain the same as themselves or in relation to each other?

The latter is the case, they are never in the same state.

These latter you could touch and see and perceive with the other senses, but those that always remain the same can only be grasped by the reasoning power of the mind? They are not seen but are invisible?

That is altogether true, he said.

Do you then want us to assume two kinds of existences, the visible and the invisible?

Let us assume this.

And the invisible always remains the same, whereas the visible never does?

Let us assume that too.

Now one part of ourselves is the body, another part is the soul?

Quite so.

To which class of existence do we say the body is more alike and akin?

To the visible, as anyone can see.

What about the soul? Is it visible or invisible?

It is not visible to men, Socrates, he said.

Well, we meant visible and invisible to human eyes; or to any others, do you think?

To human eyes.

Then what do we say about the soul? Is it visible or not visible?

Not visible.

So it is invisible?—Yes.

So the soul is more like the invisible than the body, and the body more like the visible?—Without any doubt, Socrates.

Haven't we also said some time ago that when the soul makes use of the body to investigate something, be it through hearing or seeing or some other sense—for to investigate something through the senses is to do it through the body—it is dragged by the body to the things that are never the same, and the soul itself strays and is confused and dizzy, as if it were drunk, in so far as it is in contact with that kind of thing?

Certainly.

But when the soul investigates by itself it passes into the realm of what is pure, ever existing, immortal and unchanging, and being akin to this, it always stays with it whenever it is by itself and can do so; it ceases to stray and remains in the same state as it is in touch with things of the same kind, and its experience then is what is called wisdom?

Altogether well said and very true, Socrates, he said.

Judging from what we have said before and what we are saying now, to which of these two kinds do you think that the soul is more alike and more akin?

I think, Socrates, he said, that on this line of argument any man, even the dullest, would agree that the soul is altogether more like that which always exists in the same state rather than like that which does not.

What of the body?

That is like the other.

Look at it also this way: when the soul and the body are together, nature orders the one to be subject and to be ruled, and the other to rule and be master. Then again, which do you think is like the divine and which like the mortal? Do you not think that the nature of the divine is to rule and to lead, whereas it is that of the mortal to be ruled and be subject?

I do.

Which does the soul resemble?

Obviously, Socrates, the soul resembles the divine, and the body resembles the mortal.

Consider then, Cebes, whether it follows from all that has been said that the soul is most like the divine, deathless, intelligible, uniform, indissoluble, always the same as itself, whereas the body is most like that which is human, mortal, multiform, unintelligible, soluble and never consistently the same. Have we anything else to say to show, my dear Cebes, that this is not the case?

We have not.

Well then, that being so, is it not natural for the body to dissolve easily, and for the soul to be altogether indissoluble, or nearly so?

Of course. . . .

The sum of your problem is this: you consider that the soul must be proved to be immortal and indestructible before a philosopher on the point of death, who is confident that he will fare much better in the underworld than if he had led any other kind of life, can avoid being foolish and simpleminded in this confidence. To prove that the soul is strong, that it is divine, that it existed before we were born as men, all this, you say, does not show the soul to be immortal but only long-lasting. That it existed for a very long time before, that it knew much and acted much, makes it no more immortal because of that; indeed, its very entering into a human body was the beginning of its destruction, like a disease; it would live that life in distress and would in the end be destroyed in what we call death. You say it makes no difference whether it enters a body once or many times as far as the fear of each of us is concerned, for it is natural for a man who is no fool to be afraid, if he does not know and cannot prove that the soul is immortal. This, I think, is what you maintain, Cebes; I deliberately repeat it often, in order that no point may escape us, and that you may add or subtract something if you wish.

And Cebes said: "There is nothing that I want to add or subtract at the moment. That is what I say."

Socrates paused for a long time, deep in thought. He then said: "This is no unimportant problem that you raise, Cebes, for it requires a thorough investigation of the cause of generation and destruction. I will, if you wish, give you an account of my experience in these matters. Then if something I say seems useful to you, make use of it to persuade us of your position."

I surely do wish that, said Cebes.

Listen then, and I will, Cebes, he said. When I was a young man I was wonderfully keen on that wisdom which they call natural science, for I thought it splendid to know the causes of everything, why it comes to be, why it perishes and why it exists. I was often changing my mind in the investigation, in the first instance, of questions such as these: Are living creatures nurtured when heat and cold produce a kind of putrefaction, as some say? Do we think with our blood, or air, or fire, or none of these, and does the brain provide our senses of hearing and sight and smell, from which come memory and opinion, and from memory and opinion which has become stable, comes knowledge? Then again, as I investigated how these things perish and what happens to things in the sky and on the earth, finally I became convinced that I had no natural aptitude at all for that kind of investigation, and of this I will give you sufficient proof. This investigation made me quite blind even to those things which I and others thought that I clearly knew before, so that I unlearned what I thought I knew before, about many other things and specifically about how men grew. I thought before that it was obvious to anybody that men grew through eating and drinking, for food adds flesh to flesh and bones to bones, and in the same way appropriate parts were added to all other parts of the body, so that the man grew from an earlier small bulk to a large bulk later, and so a small man became big. That is what I thought then. Do you not think it was reasonable?

I do, said Cebes.

Then further consider this: I thought my opinion was satisfactory, that when a large man stood by a small one he was taller by a head, and so a horse was taller than a horse. Even clearer than this, I thought that ten was more than eight because two had been added, and that a two-cubit length was larger than a cubit because it surpasses it by half its length.

And what do you think now about these things?

That I am far, by Zeus, from believing that I know the cause of any of those things. I will not even allow myself to say that where one is added to one either the one to which it is added or the one that is added becomes two, or that the one added and the one to which it is added become two because of the addition of the one to the other. I wonder that, when each of them is separate from the other, each of them is one, nor are they then two, but that, when they come near to one another, this is the cause of their becoming two, the coming together and being placed closer to one another. Nor can I any longer be persuaded that when one thing is divided, this division is the cause of its becoming two, for just now the cause of becoming two was the opposite. At that time it was their coming close together and one was added to the other, but now it is because one is taken and separated from the other.

I do not any longer persuade myself that I know why a unit or anything else comes to be, or perishes or exists by the old method of investigation, and I do not accept it, but I have a confused method of my own. One day I heard someone reading, as he said, from a book of Anaxagoras, and saying that it is Mind that directs and is the cause of everything. I was delighted with this cause and it seemed to me good, in a way, that Mind should be the cause of all. I thought that if this were so, the directing Mind would direct everything and arrange each thing in the way that was best. If then one wished to know the cause of each thing, why it comes to be or perishes or exists, one had to find what was the best way for it to be,

or to be acted upon, or to act. On these premises then it befitted a man to investigate only, about this and other things, what is best. The same man must inevitably also know what is worse, for that is part of the same knowledge. As I reflected on this subject I was glad to think that I had found in Anaxagoras a teacher about the cause of things after my own heart, and that he would tell me, first, whether the earth is flat or round, and then would explain why it is so of necessity, saying which is better, and that it was better to be so. If he said it was in the middle of the universe, he would go on to show that it was better for it to be in the middle, and if he showed me those things I should be prepared never to desire any other kind of cause. I was ready to find out in the same way about the sun and the moon and the other heavenly bodies, about their relative speed, their turnings and whatever else happened to them, how it is best that each should act or be acted upon. I never thought that Anaxagoras, who said that those things were directed by Mind, would bring in any other cause for them than it was best for them to be as they are. Once he had given the best for each as the cause for each and the general cause of all, I thought he would go on to explain the common good for all, and I would not have exchanged my hopes for a fortune. I eagerly acquired his books and read them as quickly as I could in order to know the best and the worst as soon as possible.

This wonderful hope was dashed as I went on reading and saw that the man made no use of Mind, nor gave it any responsibility for the management of things, but mentioned as causes air and ether and water and many other strange things. That seemed to me much like saying that Socrates' actions are all due to his mind, and then in trying to tell the causes of everything I do, to say that the reason that I am sitting here is because my body consists of bones and sinews, because the bones are hard and are separated by joints, that the sinews are such as to contract and relax, that they surround the bones along with flesh and skin which hold them together, then as the bones are hanging in their sockets, the relaxation and contraction of the sinews enable me to bend my limbs, and that is the cause of my sitting here with my limbs bent.

Again, he would mention other such causes for my talking to you: sounds and air and hearing, and a thousand other such things, but he would neglect to mention the true causes, that, after the

Athenians decided it was better to condemn me, for this reason it seemed best to me to sit here and more right to remain and to endure whatever penalty they ordered. For by the dog, I think these sinews and bones could long ago have been in Megara or among the Boeotians, taken there by my belief as to the best course, if I had not thought it more right and honourable to endure whatever penalty the city ordered rather than escape and run away. To call those things causes is too absurd. If someone said that without bones and sinews and all such things, I should not be able to do what I decided, he would be right, but surely to say that they are the cause of what I do, and not that I have chosen the best course, even though I act with my mind, is to speak very lazily and carelessly. Imagine not being able to distinguish the real cause from that without which the cause would not be able to act as a cause. It is what the majority appear to do, like people groping in the dark; they call it a cause, thus giving it a name that does not belong to it. That is why one man surrounds the earth with a vortex to make the heavens keep it in place, another makes the air support it like a wide lid. As for their capacity of being in the best place they could possibly be put, this they do not look for, nor do they believe it to have any divine force, but they believe that they will some time discover a stronger and more immortal Atlas to hold everything together more, and they do not believe that the truly good and "binding" binds and holds them together. I would gladly become the disciple of any man who taught the workings of that kind of cause. However, since I was deprived and could neither discover it myself nor learn it from another, do you wish me to give you an explanation of how, as a second best, I busied myself with the search for the cause, Cebes?

I would wish it above all else, he said.

After this, he said, when I had wearied of investigating things, I thought that I must be careful to avoid the experience of those who watch an eclipse of the sun, for some of them ruin their eyes unless they watch its reflection in water or some such material. A similar thought crossed my mind, and I feared that my soul would be altogether blinded if I looked at things with my eyes and tried to grasp them with each of my senses. So I thought I must take refuge in discussions and investigate the truth of things by means of words. However, perhaps this analogy is inadequate, for I certainly do not admit that one who investigates things by means of words is dealing with images, any more than one who looks at facts. However, I started in this manner: taking as my hypothesis in each case the theory that seemed to me the most compelling, I would consider as true, about cause and everything else, whatever agreed with this, and as untrue whatever did not so agree. But I want to put my meaning more clearly for I do not think that you understand me now.

No, by Zeus, said Cebes, not very well.

This, he said, is what I mean. It is nothing new, but what I have never stopped talking about, both elsewhere and in the earlier part of our conversation. I am going to try to show you the kind of cause with which I have concerned myself. I turn back to those oft-mentioned things and proceed from them. I assume the existence of a Beautiful, itself by itself, of a Good and a Great and all the rest. If you grant me these and agree that they exist, I hope to show you the cause as a result, and to find the soul to be immortal.

Take it that I grant you this, said Cebes, and hasten to your conclusion.

Consider then, he said, whether you share my opinion as to what follows, for I think that, if there is anything beautiful besides the Beautiful itself, it is beautiful for no other reason than that it shares in that Beautiful, and I say so with everything. Do you agree to this sort of cause?—I do.

I no longer understand or recognize those other sophisticated causes, and if someone tells me that a thing is beautiful because it has a bright colour or shape or any such thing, I ignore these other reasons—for all these confuse me—but I simply, naively and perhaps foolishly cling to this, that nothing else makes it beautiful other than the presence of, or the sharing in, or however you may describe its relationship to that Beautiful we mentioned, for I will not insist on the precise nature of the relationship, but that all beautiful things are beautiful by the Beautiful. That, I think, is the safest answer I can give myself or anyone else. And if I stick to this I think I shall never fall into error. This is a safe answer for me or anyone else to give, namely, that it is through Beauty that beautiful things are made beautiful. Or do you not think so too?—I do.

And that it is through Bigness that big things are big and the bigger are bigger, and that smaller things are made small by Smallness?—Yes.

And you would not accept the statement that one man is taller than another by a head and the shorter man shorter by the same, but you would bear witness that you mean nothing else than that everything that is bigger is made bigger by nothing else than by Bigness, and that is the cause of its being bigger, and the smaller is made smaller only by Smallness and this is why it is smaller. I think you would be afraid that some opposite argument would confront you if you said that someone is bigger or smaller by a head, first, because the bigger is bigger and the smaller smaller by the same, then because the bigger is bigger by a head which is small, and this would be strange, namely, that someone is made bigger by something small. Would you not be afraid of this?

I certainly would, said Cebes, laughing.

Then you would be afraid to say that ten is more than eight by two, and that this is the cause of the excess, and not magnitude and because of magnitude, or that two cubits is bigger than one cubit by half and not by Bigness, for this is the same fear.—Certainly.

Then would you not avoid saying that when one is added to one it is the addition and when it is divided it is the division that is the cause of two? And you would loudly exclaim that you do not know how else each thing can come to be except by sharing in the particular reality in which it shares, and in these cases you do not know of any other cause of becoming two except by sharing in Twoness, and that the things that are to be two must share in this, as that which is to be one must share in Oneness, and you would dismiss these additions and divisions and other such subtleties, and leave them to those wiser than yourself to answer. But you, afraid, as they say, of your own shadow and your inexperience, would cling to the safety of your own hypothesis and give that answer. If someone then attacked your hypothesis itself, you would ignore him and would not answer until you had examined whether the consequences that follow from it agree with one another or contradict one another. And when you must give an account of your hypothesis itself you will proceed in the same way: you will assume another hypothesis, the one which seems to you best of the higher ones until you come to something acceptable, but you will not jumble the two as the debaters do by discussing the hypothesis and its consequences at the same time, if you wish to discover any truth. This they do not discuss at all nor give any thought to, but their wisdom enables them to mix everything up and yet to be pleased with themselves,

but if you are a philosopher I think you will do as I say.

What you say is very true, said Simmias and Cebes together.

ECHECRATES: Yes, by Zeus, Phaedo, and they were right, I think he made these things wonderfully clear to anyone of even small intelligence.

PHAEDO [who is narrating the dialogue]: Yes indeed, Echecrates, and all those present thought so too.

ECHECRATES: And so do we who were not present but hear of it now. What was said after that?

PHAEDO: As I recall it, when the above had been accepted, and it was agreed that each of the Forms existed, and that other things acquired their name by having a share in them, he followed this up by asking: If you say these things are so, when you then say that Simmias is taller than Socrates but shorter than Phaedo, do you not mean that there is in Simmias both tallness and shortness?—I do.

But, he said, do you agree that the words of the statement 'Simmias is taller than Socrates' do not express the truth of the matter? It is not, surely, the nature of Simmias to be taller than Socrates because he is Simmias but because of the tallness he happens to have? Nor is he taller than Socrates because Socrates is Socrates, but because Socrates has smallness compared with the tallness of the other?—True.

Nor is he shorter than Phaedo because Phaedo is Phaedo, but because Phaedo has tallness compared with the shortness of Simmias?—That is so.

So then Simmias is called both short and tall, being between the two, presenting his shortness to be overcome by the tallness of one, and his tallness to overcome the shortness of the other. He smilingly added, I seem to be going to talk like a book, but it is as I say. The other agreed.

My purpose is that you may agree with me. Now it seems to me that not only Tallness itself is never willing to be tall and short at the same time, but also that that tallness in us will never admit the short or be overcome, but one of two things happens: either it flees and retreats whenever its opposite, the short, approaches, or it is destroyed by its approach. It is not willing to endure and admit shortness and be other than it was, whereas I admit and endure shortness and still remain the same person and am this short man. But Tallness, being tall, cannot venture to be small. In the same way, the short in us is unwilling to become or to be tall ever, nor does any other of the opposites become or be its opposite while still being what it was; either it goes away or is destroyed when that happens.—I altogether agree, said Cebes.

When he heard this, someone of those present—I have no clear memory of who it was—said: "By the gods, did we not agree earlier in our discussion to the very opposite of what is now being said, namely, that the larger came from the smaller and the smaller from the larger, and that this simply was how opposites came to be, from their opposites, but now I think we are saying that this would never happen?"

On hearing this, Socrates inclined his head towards the speaker and said: "You have bravely reminded us, but you do not understand the difference between what is said now and what was said then, which was that an opposite thing came from its opposite thing; now we say that the opposite itself could never become its opposite, neither that in us or that in nature. Then, my friend, we were talking of things that have opposite qualities and naming these after them, but now we say that these opposites themselves, from the presence of which in them things get their name, never can tolerate the coming to be from one another." At the same time he looked to Cebes and said: "Does anything of what this man says also disturb you?"

Not at the moment, said Cebes, but I do not deny that many things do disturb me.

We are altogether agreed then, he said, that an opposite will never be its own opposite.—Entirely agreed.

Consider then whether you will agree to this further point. There is something you call hot and something you call cold.—There is.

Are they the same as what you call snow and fire?—By Zeus, no.

So the hot is something other than fire, and the cold is something other than snow?—Yes.

You think, I believe, that being snow it will not admit the hot, as we said before, and remain what it was and be both snow and hot, but when the hot approaches it will either retreat before it or be destroyed.—Quite so.

So fire, as the cold approaches, will either go away or be destroyed; it will never venture to admit coldness and remain what it was, fire and cold.—What you say is true.

It is true then about some of these things that not only the Form itself deserves its own name for all time, but there is something else that is not the Form but has its character whenever it exists. Perhaps I can make my meaning clearer: the Odd must always be given this name we now mention. Is that not so?—Certainly.

Is it the only one of existing things to be called odd?—this is my question—or is there something else than the Odd which one must nevertheless also always call odd, as well as by its own name, because it is such by nature as never to be separated from the Odd? I mean, for example, the number three and many others. Consider three: do you not think that it must always be called both by its own name and by that of the Odd, which is not the same as three? That is the nature of three, and of five, and of half of all the numbers; each of them is odd, but it is not the Odd. Then again, two and four and the whole other column of numbers; each of them, while not being the same as the Even, is always even. Do you not agree?—Of course.

Look now. What I want to make clear is this: not only do those opposites not admit each other, but this is also true of those things which, while not being opposite to each other yet always contain the opposites, and it seems that these do not admit that Form which is opposite to that which is in them; when it approaches them, they either perish or give way. Shall we not say that three will perish or undergo anything before, while remaining three, becoming even?—Certainly, said Cebes.

Yet surely two is not the opposite of three?—Indeed it is not.

It is then not only opposite Forms that do not admit each other's approach, but also some other things that do not admit the onset of opposites.—Very true.

Do you then want us, if we can, to define what these are?—I surely do.

Would they be the things that are compelled by whatever occupies them not only to contain their own Form but also always that of some opposite?—How do you mean?

As we were saying just now, you surely know that what the Form of three occupies must not only be three but also odd.—Certainly.

And we say that the opposite Form to the Form that achieves this result could never come to it.—It could not.

Now it is Oddness that has done this?—Yes.

And opposite to this is the Form of the Even?—Yes.

So then the Form of the Even will never come to three?—Never.

Then three has no share in the Even?—Never. So three is uneven?—Yes.

As for what I said we must define, that is, what kind of things, while not being opposites to something, yet do not admit the opposite, as for example the triad, though it is not the opposite of the Even, yet does not admit it because it always brings along the opposite of the Even, and so the dyad in relation to the Odd, fire to the Cold, and very many other things, see whether you would define it thus: Not only does the opposite not admit its opposite, but that which brings along some opposite into that which it occupies, that which brings this along will not admit the opposite to that which it brings along. Refresh your memory, it is no worse for being heard often. Five does not admit the form of the Even, nor will ten, which is twice five, admit the form of the Odd. It is the opposite of something else, yet it will not admit the form of the Odd. Nor does one-and-a-half and other such fractions admit the form of the Whole, nor will one-third, and so on, if you follow me and agree to this.

I certainly agree, he said, and I follow you.

Tell me again from the beginning, he said, and do not answer in the words of the question, but do as I do. I say that beyond that safe answer, which I spoke of first, I see another safe answer. If you should ask me what, coming into a body, makes it hot, my reply would not be that safe and ignorant one, that it is heat, but our present argument provides a more sophisticated answer, namely, fire, and if you ask me what, on coming into a body, makes it sick, I will not say sickness but fever. Nor, if asked the presence of what in a number makes it odd, I will not say oddness but oneness, and so with other things. See if you now sufficiently understand what I want.—Quite sufficiently.

Answer me then, he said, what is it that, present in a body, makes it living?—A soul.

And is that always so?—Of course.

Whatever the soul occupies, it always brings life to it?—It does.

Is there, or is there not, an opposite to life?— There is.

What is it?—Death.

So the soul will never admit the opposite of that which it brings along, as we agree from what has been said?

Most certainly, said Cebes.

Well, and what do we call that which does not admit the form of the even?—The uneven.

What do we call that which will not admit the just and that which will not admit the musical?

The unmusical, and the other the unjust.

Very well, what do we call that which does not admit death?

The deathless, he said.

Now the soul does not admit death?—No.

So the soul is deathless?—It is.

Very well, he said. Shall we say that this has been proved, do you think?

Quite adequately proved, Socrates.

Well now, Cebes, he said, if the uneven were of necessity indestructible, surely three would be indestructible?—Of course.

And if the non-hot were of necessity indestructible, then whenever anyone brought heat to snow, the snow would retreat safe and unthawed, for it could not be destroyed, nor again could it stand its ground and admit the heat?—What you say is true.

In the same way, if the non-cold were indestructible, then when some cold attacked the fire, it would neither be quenched nor destroyed, but retreat safely.—Necessarily.

Must then the same not be said of the deathless? If the deathless is also indestructible, it is impossible for the soul to be destroyed when death comes upon it. For it follows from what has been said that it will not admit death or be dead, just as three, we said, will not be even nor will the odd; nor will fire be cold, nor the heat that is in the fire. But, someone might say, what prevents the odd, while not becoming even as has been agreed, from being destroyed, and the even to come to be instead? We could not maintain against the man who said this that it is not destroyed, for the uneven is not indestructible. If we had agreed that it was indestructible we could easily have maintained that at the coming of the even, the odd and the three have gone away and the same would hold for fire and the hot and the other things.— Surely.

And so now, if we are agreed that the deathless is indestructible, the soul, besides being deathless, is indestructible. If not, we need another argument.

There is no need for one as far as that goes, for hardly anything could resist destruction if the deathless, which lasts forever, would admit destruction.

All would agree, said Socrates, that the god, and the Form of life itself, and anything that is deathless, are never destroyed.—All men would agree, by Zeus, to that, and the gods, I imagine, even more so.

If the deathless is indestructible, then the soul, if it is deathless, would also be indestructible?—Necessarily.

Then when death comes to man, the mortal part of him dies, it seems, but his deathless part goes away safe and indestructible, yielding the place to death.—So it appears.

Therefore the soul, Cebes, he said, is most certainly deathless and indestructible and our souls will really dwell in the underworld.

I have nothing more to say against that, Socrates, said Cebes, nor can I doubt your arguments. If Simmias here or someone else has something to say, he should not remain silent, for I do not know to what further occasion other than the present he could put it off if he wants to say or to hear anything on these subjects.

Certainly, said Simmias, I myself have no remaining grounds for doubt after what has been said; nevertheless, in view of the importance of our subject and my low opinion of human weakness, I am bound still to have some private misgivings about what we have said.

You are not only right to say this, Simmias, Socrates said, but our first hypotheses require clearer examination, even though we find them convincing. And if you analyze them adequately, you will, I think, follow the argument as far as a man can and if the conclusion is clear, you will look no further.—That is true.

11. *On Substance*

ARISTOTLE

Aristotle entered Plato's Academy when he was seventeen and remained there as a student and then teacher, for twenty years. Naturally, Plato had an enormous influence on Aristotle's thought, but like the brilliant student he was, Aristotle came to repudiate some central theses of his teacher. For Aristotle, ordinary individual things (what he calls "primary substances") are fundamental realities—not Plato's Forms.

Plato's distinction between an individual thing and its qualities is essential to his account of change, but he has little confidence that changing things can be known the way the Forms can. Aristotle, on the other hand, says a great deal about particular things. In the *Categories*, Aristotle approaches the question What is a substance? through a consideration of the role that words referring to individual things play in ordinary language. Thus, he distinguishes between primary substances (this man, this horse), which are subjects but never predicates, and secondary substances (man, horse), which can be predicated of a subject. He further claims the most distinctive mark of primary sustance is that "while remaining numerically one and the same, it is capable of admitting contrary qualities." In *On Generation and Corruption*, Aristotle explains the difference between a substance coming to be (or ceasing to be) and its coming to have different qualities. In *Metaphysics Z*, he analyzes substances in a way that sheds light on questions about their identity.

Categories

Things are said to be named 'equivocally' when, though they have a common name, the definition corresponding with the name differs for each. Thus, a real man and a figure in a picture can both lay claim to the name 'animal'; yet these are equivocally so named, for, though they have a common name, the definition corresponding with the name differs for each. For should any one define in what sense each is an animal, his definition in the one case will be appropriate to that case only.

On the other hand, things are said to be named 'univocally' which have both the name and the definition answering to the name in common. A man and an ox are both 'animal', and these are univocally so named, inasmuch as not only the name, but also the definition, is the same in both cases: for if a man should state in what sense each is an animal, the statement in the one case would be identical with that in the other.

Things are said to be named 'derivatively', which derive their name from some other name, but differ from it in termination. Thus the grammarian derives his name from the word 'grammar', and the courageous man from the word 'courage'.

Forms of speech are either simple or composite. Examples of the latter are such expressions as 'the man runs', 'the man wins'; of the former 'man', 'ox', 'runs', 'wins'.

Of things themselves some are predicable of a subject, and are never present in a subject. Thus 'man' is predicable of the individual man, and is never present in a subject.

By being 'present in a subject' I do not mean present as parts are present in a whole, but being

Excerpts from *Categories, On Generation and Corruption,* and *Metaphysics Z* are from Richard McKeon, ed., *The Basic Works of Aristotle* (New York: Random House, 1941). Copyright © by Oxford: Clarendon Press. Reprinted by permission of the Clarendon Press.

incapable of existence apart from the said subject.

Some things, again, are present in a subject, but are never predicable of a subject. For instance, a certain point of grammatical knowledge is present in the mind, but is not predicable of any subject; or again, a certain whiteness may be present in the body (for colour requires a material basis), yet it is never predicable of anything.

Other things, again, are both predicable of a subject and present in a subject. Thus while knowledge is present in the human mind, it is predicable of grammar.

There is, lastly, a class of things which are neither present in a subject nor predicable of a subject, such as the individual man or the individual horse. But, to speak more generally, that which is individual and has the character of a unit is never predicable of a subject. Yet in some cases there is nothing to prevent such being present in a subject. Thus a certain point of grammatical knowledge is present in a subject.

When one thing is predicated of another, all that which is predicable of the predicate will be predicable also of the subject. Thus 'man' is predicated of the individual man; but 'animal' is predicated of 'man'; it will, therefore, be predicable of the individual man also: for the individual man is both 'man' and 'animal'.

If genera are different and co-ordinate, their differentiae are themselves different in kind. Take as an instance the genus 'animal' and the genus 'knowledge'. 'With feet', 'two-footed', 'winged', 'aquatic', are differentiae of 'animal'; the species of knowledge are not distinguished by the same differentiae. One species of knowledge does not differ from another in being 'two-footed'.

But where one genus is subordinate to another, there is nothing to prevent their having the same differentiae: for the greater class is predicated of the lesser, so that all the differentiae of the predicate will be differentiae also of the subject.

Expressions which are in no way composite signify substance, quantity, quality, relation, place, time, position, state, action, or affection. To sketch my meaning roughly, examples of substance are 'man' or 'the horse', of quantity, such terms as 'two cubits long' or 'three cubits long', of quality, such attributes as 'white', 'grammatical'. 'Double', 'half', 'greater', fall under the category of relation; 'in the market place', 'in the Lyceum', under that of place; 'yesterday', 'last year', under that of time. 'Lying', 'sitting', are terms indicating position; 'shod', 'armed', state; 'to lance', 'to cauterize', action; 'to be lanced', 'to be cauterized', affection.

No one of these terms, in and by itself, involves an affirmation; it is by the combination of such terms that positive or negative statements arise. For every assertion must, as is admitted, be either true or false, whereas expressions which are not in any way composite, such as 'man', 'white', 'runs', 'wins', cannot be either true or false.

Substance, in the truest and primary and most definite sense of the word, is that which is neither predicable of a subject nor present in a subject; for instance, the individual man or horse. But in a secondary sense those things are called substances within which, as species, the primary substances are included; also those which, as genera, include the species. For instance, the individual man is included in the species 'man', and the genus to which the species belongs is 'animal'; these, therefore—that is to say, the species 'man' and the genus 'animal'—are termed secondary substances.

It is plain from what has been said that both the name and the definition of the predicate must be predicable of the subject. For instance, 'man' is predicated of the individual man. Now in this case the name of the species 'man' is applied to the individual, for we use the term 'man' in describing the individual; and the definition of 'man' will also be predicated of the individual man, for the individual man is both man and animal. Thus, both the name and the definition of the species are predicable of the individual.

With regard, on the other hand, to those things which are present in a subject, it is generally the case that neither their name nor their definition is predicable of that in which they are present. Though, however, the definition is never predicable, there is nothing in certain cases to prevent the name being used. For instance, 'white' being present in a body is predicated of that in which it is present, for a body is called white: the definition, however, of the colour 'white' is never predicable of the body.

Everything except primary substances is either predicable of a primary substance or present in a primary substance. This becomes evident by reference to particular instances which occur. 'Animal' is predicated of the species 'man', therefore of the individual man, for if there were no individual man of whom it could be predicated, it could not be predicated of the species 'man' at all. Again, colour is present in body, therefore in individual bodies, for if there were no individual body in which it was present, it could not be present in body at all. Thus everything except primary substances is either predicated of primary substances, or is present in them, and if these last did not exist, it would be impossible for anything else to exist.

Of secondary substances, the species is more truly substance than the genus, being more nearly related to primary substance. For if any one should render an account of what a primary substance is, he would render a more instructive account, and one more proper to the subject, by stating the species than by stating the genus. Thus, he would give a more instructive account of an individual man by stating that he was man than by stating that he was animal, for the former description is peculiar to the individual in a greater degree, while the latter is too general. Again, the man who gives an account of the nature of an individual tree will give a more instructive account by mentioning the species 'tree' than by mentioning the genus 'plant'.

Moreover, primary substances are most properly called substances in virtue of the fact that they are the entities which underlie everything else, and that everything else is either predicated of them or present in them. Now the same relation which subsists between primary substance and everything else subsists also between the species and the genus: for the species is to the genus as subject is to predicate, since the genus is predicated of the species, whereas the species cannot be predicated of the genus. Thus we have a second ground for asserting that the species is more truly substance than the genus.

Of species themselves, except in the case of such as are genera, no one is more truly substance than another. We should not give a more appropriate account of the individual man by stating the species to which he belonged, than we should of an individual horse by adopting the same method of definition. In the same way, of primary substances, no one is more truly substance than another; an individual man is not more truly substance than an individual ox.

It is, then, with good reason that of all that remains, when we exclude primary substances, we concede to species and genera alone the name 'secondary substance', for these alone of all the predicates convey a knowledge of primary substance. For it is by stating the species or the genus that we appropriately define any individual man; and we

shall make our definition more exact by stating the former than by stating the latter. All other things that we state, such as that he is white, that he runs, and so on, are irrelevant to the definition. Thus it is just that these alone, apart from primary substances, should be called substances.

Further, primary substances are most properly so called, because they underlie and are the subjects of everything else. Now the same relation that subsists between primary substance and everything else subsists also between the species and the genus to which the primary substance belongs, on the one hand, and every attribute which is not included within these, on the other. For these are the subjects of all such. If we call an individual man 'skilled in grammar', the predicate is applicable also to the species and to the genus to which he belongs. This law holds good in all cases.

It is a common characteristic of all substance that it is never present in a subject. For primary substance is neither present in a subject nor predicated of a subject; while, with regard to secondary substances, it is clear from the following arguments (apart from others) that they are not present in a subject. For 'man' is predicated of the individual man, but is not present in any subject: for manhood is not present in the individual man. In the same way, 'animal' is also predicated of the individual man, but is not present in him. Again, when a thing is present in a subject, though the name may quite well be applied to that in which it is present, the definition cannot be applied. Yet of secondary substances, not only the name, but also the definition, applies to the subject: we should use both the definition of the species and that of the genus with reference to the individual man. Thus substance cannot be present in a subject.

Yet this is not peculiar to substance, for it is also the case that differentiae cannot be present in subjects. The characteristics 'terrestrial' and 'two-footed' are predicated of the species 'man', but not present in it. For they are not *in* man. Moreover, the definition of the differentia may be predicated of that of which the differentia itself is predicated. For instance, if the characteristic 'terrestrial' is predicated of the species 'man', the definition also of that characteristic may be used to form the predicate of the species 'man': for 'man' is terrestrial.

The fact that the parts of substances appear to be present in the whole, as in a subject, should not make us apprehensive lest we should have to admit that such parts are not substances: for in explaining the phrase 'being present in a subject', we stated that we meant 'otherwise than as parts of a whole'.

It is the mark of substances and of differentiae that, in all propositions of which they form the predicate, they are predicated univocally. For all such propositions have for their subject either the individual or the species. It is true that, inasmuch as primary substance is not predicable of anything, it can never form the predicate of any proposition. But of secondary substances, the species is predicated of the individual, the genus both of the species and of the individual. Similarly the differentiae are predicated of the species and of the individuals. Moreover, the definition of the species and that of the genus are applicable to the primary substance, and that of the genus to the species. For all that is predicated of the predicate will be predicated also of the subject. Similarly, the definition of the differentiae will be applicable to the species and to the individuals. But it was stated above that the word 'univocal' was applied to those things which had both name and definition in common. It is, therefore, established that in every proposition, of which either substance or a differentia forms the predicate, these are predicated univocally.

All substance appears to signify that which is individual. In the case of primary substance this is indisputably true, for the thing is a unit. In the case of secondary substances, when we speak, for instance, of 'man' or 'animal', our form of speech gives the impression that we are here also indicating that which is individual, but the impression is not strictly true; for a secondary substance is not an individual, but a class with a certain qualification; for it is not one and single as a primary substance is; the words 'man', 'animal', are predicable of more than one subject.

Yet species and genus do not merely indicate quality, like the term 'white'; 'white' indicates quality and nothing further, but species and genus determine the quality with reference to a substance: they signify substance qualitatively differentiated. The determinate qualification covers a larger field in the case of the genus than in that of the species: he who uses the word 'animal' is herein using a word of wider extension than he who uses the word 'man'.

Another mark of substance is that it has no contrary. What could be the contrary of any primary substance, such as the individual man or animal? It has none. Nor can the species or the genus have a contrary. Yet this characteristic is not peculiar to substance, but is true of many other things, such as quantity. There is nothing that forms the contrary of 'two cubits long' or of 'three cubits long', or of 'ten', or of any such term. A man may contend that 'much' is the contrary of 'little', or 'great' of 'small', but of definite quantitative terms no contrary exists.

Substance, again, does not appear to admit of variation of degree. I do not mean by this that one substance cannot be more or less truly substance than another, for it has already been stated that this is the case; but that no single substance admits of varying degrees within itself. For instance, one particular substance, 'man', cannot be more or less man either than himself at some other time or than some other man. One man cannot be more man than another, as that which is white may be more or less white than some other white object, or as that which is beautiful may be more or less beautiful than some other beautiful object. The same quality, moreover, is said to subsist in a thing in varying degrees at different times. A body, being white, is said to be whiter at one time than it was before, or, being warm, is said to be warmer or less warm than at some other time. But substance is not said to be more or less that which it is: a man is not more truly a man at one time than he was before, nor is anything, if it is substance, more or less what it is. Substance, then, does not admit of variation of degree.

The most distinctive mark of substance appears to be that, while remaining numerically one and the same, it is capable of admitting contrary qualities. From among things other than substance, we should find ourselves unable to bring forward any which possessed this mark. Thus, one and the same colour cannot be white and black. Nor can the same one action be good and bad: this law holds good with everything that is not substance. But one and the self-same substance, while retaining its identity, is yet capable of admitting contrary qualities. The same individual person is at one time white, at another black, at one time warm, at another cold, at one time good, at another bad. This capacity is found nowhere else, though it might be maintained that a statement or opinion was an exception to the rule. The same statement, it is agreed, can be both true and false. For if the statement 'he is sitting' is true, yet, when the person in question has risen, the same statement will be false. The same applies to opinions. For if any one thinks truly that a person is sitting, yet, when that person has risen, this same opinion, if still held, will be false. Yet although this exception may be allowed, there is, nevertheless, a difference in the manner in which the thing takes place. It is by themselves changing that substances admit contrary qualities. It is thus that that which was hot becomes cold, for it has entered into a different state. Similarly that which was white becomes black, and that which was bad good, by a process of change; and in the same way in all other cases it is by changing that substances are capable of admitting contrary qualities. But statements and opinions themselves remain unaltered in all respects: it is by the alteration in the facts of the case that the contrary quality comes to be theirs. The statement 'he is sitting' remains unaltered, but it is at one time true, at another false, according to circumstances. What has been said of statements applies also to opinions. Thus, in respect of the manner in which the thing takes place, it is the peculiar mark of substance that it should be capable of admitting contrary qualities; for it is by itself changing that it does so.

If, then, a man should make this exception and contend that statements and opinions are capable of admitting contrary qualities, his contention is unsound. For statements and opinions are said to have this capacity, not because they themselves undergo modification, but because this modification occurs in the case of something else. The truth or falsity of a statement depends on facts, and not on any power on the part of the statement itself of admitting contrary qualities. In short, there is nothing which can alter the nature of statements and opinions. As, then, no change takes place in themselves, these cannot be said to be capable of admitting contrary qualities.

But it is by reason of the modification which takes place within the substance itself that a substance is said to be capable of admitting contrary qualities; for a substance admits within itself either disease or health, whiteness or blackness. It is in this sense that it is said to be capable of admitting contrary qualities.

To sum up, it is a distinctive mark of substance, that, while remaining numerically one and the same, it is capable of admitting contrary qualities, the modification taking place through a change in the substance itself.

Let these remarks suffice on the subject of substance.

On Generation and Corruption

So much, then, on these topics. Next we must state what the difference is between coming-to-be and 'alteration'—for we maintain that these changes are distinct from one another.

Since, then, we must distinguish (*a*) the *substratum*, and (*b*) the property whose nature it is to be predicated of the *substratum;* and since change of each of these occurs; there is 'alteration' when the *substratum* is perceptible and persists, but changes in its own properties, the properties in question being opposed to one another either as contraries or as intermediates. The body, e.g., although persisting as the same body, is now healthy and now ill; and the bronze is now spherical and at another time angular, and yet remains the same bronze. But when nothing perceptible persists in its identity as a *substratum,* and the thing changes as a whole (when e.g., the seed as a whole is converted into blood, or water into air, or air as a whole into water), such an occurrence is no longer 'alteration'. It is a coming-to-be of one substance and a passing-away of the other—especially if the change proceeds from an imperceptible something to something perceptible (either to touch or to all the senses), as when water comes-to-be out of, or passes-away into, air: for air is pretty well imperceptible. If, however, in such cases, any property (being one of a pair of contraries) persists, in the thing that has come-to-be, the same as it was in the thing which has passed-away—if, e.g., when water comes-to-be out of air, both are transparent or cold—the *second* thing, into which the *first* changes, must not be a property of this persistent identical something. Otherwise the change will be 'alteration'.

Suppose, e.g., that *the musical man* passed-away and *an unmusical man* came-to-be, and that *the man* persists as something identical. Now, if 'musicalness and unmusicalness' had not been a property essentially inhering in man, these changes would have been a coming-to-be of unmusicalness and a passing-away of musicalness: but in fact 'musicalness and unmusicalness' are a property of the persistent identity, viz. man. (Hence, as regards *man,* these changes are 'modifications'; though, as regards *musical man* and *unmusical man,* they are a passing-away and a coming-to-be.) Consequently such changes are 'alteration'.

When the change from contrary to contrary is *in quantity*, it is 'growth and diminution'; when it is *in place*, it is 'motion'; when it is in property, i.e., *in quality*, it is 'alteration'; but when nothing persists, of which the resultant is a property (or an 'accident' in any sense of the term), it is 'coming-to-be', and the converse change is 'passing-away'.

'Matter', in the most proper sense of the term is to be identified with the *substratum* which is receptive of coming-to-be and passing-away: but the *substratum* of the remaining kinds of change is also, in a certain sense, 'matter', because all these *substrata* are receptive of 'contrarieties' of some kind. So much, then, as an answer to the questions (i) whether coming-to-be 'is' or 'is not'—i.e., what are the precise conditions of its occurrence—and (ii) what 'alteration' is; but we have still to treat of growth.

Metaphysics Z

There are several senses in which a thing may be said to 'be', as we pointed out previously in our book on the various senses of words; for in one sense the 'being' meant is 'what a thing is' or a 'this', and in another sense it means a quality or quantity or one of the other things that are predicated as these are. While 'being' has all these senses, obviously that which 'is' primarily is the 'what', which indicates the substance of the thing. For when we say of what quality a thing is, we say that it is good or bad, not that it is three cubits long or that it is a man; but when we say *what* it is, we do not say 'white' or 'hot' or 'three cubits long', but 'a man' or 'a god'. And all other things are said to be because they are, some of them, quantities of that which *is* in this primary sense, others qualities of it, others affections of it, and others some other determination of it. And so one might even raise the question whether the words 'to walk', 'to be healthy', 'to sit' imply that each of these things is existent, and similarly in any other case of this sort; for none of them is either self-subsistent or capable of being separated from substance, but rather, if anything, it is that which walks or sits or is healthy that is an existent thing. Now these are seen to be more real because there is something definite which underlies them (i.e., the substance or individual), which is implied in such a predicate; for we never use the word 'good' or 'sitting' without implying this. Clearly then it is in virtue of this category that each of the others also *is*. Therefore that which is primarily, i.e., not in a qualified sense but without qualification, must be substance.

Now there are several senses in which a thing is said to be first; yet substance is first in every sense—(1) in definition, (2) in order of knowledge, (3) in time. For (3) of the other categories none can exist independently, but only substance. And (1) in definition also this is first; for in the definition of each term the definition of its substance must be present. And (2) we think we know each thing most fully, when we know what it is, e.g., what man is or what fire is, rather than when we know its quality, its quantity, or its place; since we know each of these predicates also, only when we know *what* the quantity or the quality *is*.

And indeed the question which was raised of old and is raised now and always, and is always the subject of doubt, viz. what being is, is just the question, what is substance? For it is this that some assert to be one, others more than one, and that some assert to be limited in number, others unlimited. And so we also must consider chiefly and primarily and almost exclusively what that is which *is* in *this* sense.

Substance is thought to belong most obviously to bodies; and so we say that not only animals and plants and their parts are substances, but also natural bodies such as fire and water and earth and everything of the sort, and all things that are either parts of these or composed of these (either of parts or of the whole bodies), e.g., the physical universe and its parts, stars and moon and sun. But whether these alone are substances, or there are also others, or only some of these, or others as well, or none of these but only some other things, are substances, must be considered. Some think the limits of body, i.e., surface, line, point, and unit, are substances, and more so than body or the solid.

Further, some do not think there is anything substantial besides sensible things, but others think there are eternal substances which are more in number and more real; e.g., Plato posited two kinds of substance—the Forms and the objects of mathematics—as well as a third kind, viz. the substance of sensible bodies. And Speusippus made still more kinds of substance, beginning with the One, and assuming principles for each kind of substance, one for numbers, another for spatial magnitudes, and then another for the soul; and by going on in this way he multiplies the kinds of substance. And some say Forms and numbers have the same nature, and the other things come after them— lines and planes—until we come to the substance of the material universe and to sensible bodies.

Regarding these matters, then, we must inquire which of the common statements are right and which are not right, and what substances there are, and whether there are or are not any besides sensible substances, and how sensible substances exist, and whether there is a substance capable of separate existence (and if so why and how) or no such substance, apart from sensible substances; and we must first sketch the nature of substance.

The word 'substance' is applied, if not in more senses, still at least to four main objects; for both the essence and the universal and the genus are thought to be the substance of each thing, and fourthly the substratum. Now the substratum is that of which everything else is predicated, while it is itself not predicated of anything else. And so we must first determine the nature of this; for that which underlies a thing primarily is thought to be in the truest sense its substance. And in one sense matter is said to be of the nature of substratum, in another, shape, and in a third, the compound of these. (By the matter I mean, for instance, the bronze, by the shape the pattern of its form, and by the compound of these the statue, the concrete whole.) Therefore if the form is prior to the matter and more real, it will be prior also to the compound of both, for the same reason.

We have now outlined the nature of substance, showing that it is that which is not predicated of a stratum, but of which all else is predicated. But we must not merely state the matter thus; for this is not enough. The statement itself is obscure, and further, on this view, *matter* becomes substance. For if this is not substance, it baffles us to say what else is. When all else is stripped off evidently nothing but matter remains. For while the rest are affections, products, and potencies of bodies, length, breadth, and depth are quantities and not substances (for a quantity is not a substance), but the substance is rather that to which these belong primarily. But when length and breadth and depth are taken away we see nothing left unless there is something that is bounded by these; so that to those who consider the question thus matter alone must seem to be substance. By matter I mean that which in itself is neither a particular thing nor of a certain quantity nor assigned to any other of the categories by which being is determined. For there is something of which each of these is predicated, whose being is different from that of each of the predicates (for the predicates other than substance are predicated of substance, while substance is predicated of matter). Therefore the ultimate substratum is of itself neither a particular thing nor of a particular quantity nor otherwise positively characterized; nor yet is it the negations of these, for negations also will belong to it only by accident.

If we adopt this point of view, then, it follows that matter is substance. But this is impossible; for both separability and 'thisness' are thought to belong chiefly to substance. And so form and the compound of form and matter would be thought to be substance, rather than matter. The substance compounded of both, i.e., of matter and shape, may be dismissed; for it is posterior and its nature is obvious. And matter also is in a sense manifest. But we must inquire into the third kind of substance; for this is the most perplexing.

Some of the sensible substances are generally admitted to be substances, so that we must look first among these. For it is an advantage to advance to that which is more knowable. For learning proceeds for all in this way—through that which is less knowable by nature to that which is more knowable; and just as in conduct our task is to start from what is good for each and make what is without qualification good good for each, so it is our task to start from what is more knowable to oneself and make what is knowable by nature knowable to oneself. Now what is knowable and primary for particular sets of people is often knowable to a very small extent, and has little or nothing of reality. But yet one must start from that which is barely knowable but knowable to oneself, and try to know what is knowable without qualification, passing, as has been said, by way of those very things which one does know.

Since at the start we distinguished the various marks by which we determine substance, and one of these was thought to be the essence, we must investigate this. And first let us make some linguistic remarks about it. The essence of each thing is what it is said to be *propter se*. For being you is not being musical, since you are not by your very nature musical. What, then, you are by your very nature is your essence.

Nor yet is the whole of this the essence of a thing; not that which is *propter se* as white is to a surface, because being a surface is not *identical* with being white. But again the combination of both—'being a white surface'—is not the essence of surface, because 'surface' itself is added. The formula, therefore, in which the term itself is not present but its meaning is expressed, this is the formula of the essence of each thing. Therefore if to be a white surface is to be a smooth surface, to be white and to be smooth are one and the same.

But since there are also compounds answering to the other categories (for there is a substratum for each category, e.g., for quality, quantity, time, place, and motion), we must inquire whether there is a formula of the essence of each of them, i.e., whether to these compounds also there belongs an essence, e.g., to 'white man'. Let the compound be denoted by 'cloak'. What is the essence of cloak? But, it may be said, this also is not a *propter se* expression. We reply that there are just two ways in which a predicate may fail to be true of a subject *propter se,* and one of these results from the addition, and the other from the omission, of a determinant. *One* kind of predicate is not *propter se* because the term that is being defined is combined with another determinant, e.g., if in defining the essence of white one were to state the formula of white *man;* the *other* because in the subject another determinant is combined with that which is expressed in the formula, e.g., of 'cloak' meant 'white man', and one were to define cloak as white; white man is white indeed, but its essence is not to be white.

But is being-a-cloak an essence at all? Probably not. For the essence is precisely what something *is;* but when an attribute is asserted of a subject other than itself, the complex is not precisely what some 'this' *is,* e.g., white man is not precisely what some 'this' *is,* since thisness belongs only to substances. Therefore there is an essence only of those things whose formula is a definition. But we have a definition not where we have a word and a formula identical in meaning (for in that case all formulae or sets of words would be definitions; for there will be some name for any set of words whatever, so that even the *Iliad* will be a definition), but where there is a formula of something primary; and primary things are those which do not imply the predication of one element in them of another element. Nothing, then, which is not a species of a genus will have an *essence*—only species will have it, for these are thought to imply not merely that the subject participates in the attribute and has it as

an affection, or has it by accident; but for everything else as well, if it has a name, there will be a *formula of its meaning*—viz., that this attribute belongs to this subject; or instead of a simple formula we shall be able to give a more accurate one; but there will be no definition nor essence.

Or has 'definition', like 'what a thing is', several meanings? 'What a thing is' in one sense means substance and the 'this', in another one or other of the predicates, quantity, quality, and the like. For as 'is' belongs to all things, not however in the same sense, but to one sort of thing primarily and to others in a secondary way, so too 'what a thing is' belongs in the simple sense to substance, but in a limited sense to the other categories. For even of a quality we might ask what it is, so that quality also is a 'what a thing is'—not in the simple sense, however, but just as, in the case of that which is not, some say, emphasizing the linguistic form, that that which is not *is*—not *is* simply, but *is* nonexistent; so too with quality.

We must no doubt inquire how we should express ourselves on each point, but certainly not more than how the facts actually stand. And so now also, since it is evident what language we use, essence will belong, just as 'what a thing is' does, primarily and in the simple sense to substance, and in a secondary way to the other categories also—not essence in the simple sense, but the essence of a quality or of a quantity. For it must be either by an equivocation that we say these *are,* or by adding to and taking from the meaning of 'are' (in the way in which that which is not known may be said to be known)—the truth being that we use the word neither ambiguously nor in the same sense, but just as we apply the word 'medical' by virtue of a *reference* to one and the same thing, not *meaning* one and the same thing, nor yet speaking ambiguously; for a patient and an operation and an instrument are called medical neither by an ambiguity nor with a single meaning, but with reference to a common end. But it does not matter at all in which of the two ways one likes to describe the facts; this is evident, that definition and essence in the primary and simple sense belong to substances. Still they belong to other things as well, only not in the primary sense. For if we suppose this it does not follow that there is a definition of every word which means the same as any formula; it must mean the same as a particular kind of formula; and this condition is satisfied if it is a formula of something which is one, not by continuity like the *Iliad* or the things that are one by being bound together, but in one of the main senses of 'one', which answer to the senses of 'is'; now 'that which is' in one sense denotes a 'this', in another a quantity, in another a quality. And so there can be a formula or definition even of white man, but not in the sense in which there is a definition either of white or of a substance.

It is a difficult question, if one denies that a formula with an added determinant is a definition, whether any of the terms that are not simple but coupled will be definable. For we *must* explain them by adding a determinant. E.g., there is the nose, and concavity, and snubness, which is compounded out of the two by the presence of the one in the other, and it is not by *accident* that the nose has the attribute either of concavity or of snubness, but in virtue of its nature; nor do they attach to it as whiteness does to Callias, or to man (because Callias, who happens to be a man, is white), but as 'male' attaches to animal and 'equal' to quantity, and as all so-called 'attributes *propter se*' attach to their subjects. And such attributes are those in which is involved either the *formula* or the *name* of the subject of the particular attribute, and which cannot be explained without this; e.g., white can be explained apart from man, but not female apart from animal. Therefore there is either no essence and definition of any of these things, or if there is, it is in another sense, as we have said.

But there is also a second difficulty about them. For if snub nose and concave nose are the same thing, snub and concave will be the same thing; but if snub and concave are not the same (because it is impossible to speak of snubness apart from the thing of which it is an attribute *propter se*, for snubness is concavity-*in-a-nose*), either it is impossible to say 'snub nose' or the same thing will have been said twice, concave-nose nose; for snub nose will be concave-nose nose. And so it is absurd that such things should have an essence; if they have, there will be an infinite regress; for in snub-nose nose yet another 'nose' will be involved.

Clearly, then, only substance is definable. For if the other categories also are definable, it must be by addition of a determinant, e.g., the qualitative is defined thus, and so is the odd, for it cannot be defined apart from number; nor can female be defined apart from animal. (When I say 'by addition' I mean the expression in which it turns out that we are saying the same thing twice, as in these instances.) And if this is true, coupled terms also, like 'odd number', will not be definable (but this es-

capes our notice because our formulae are not accurate). But if these also are definable, either it is in some other way or, as we said, definition and essence must be said to have more than one sense. Therefore in one sense nothing will have a definition and nothing will have an essence, except substances, but in another sense other things will have them. Clearly, then, definition is the formula of the essence, and essence belongs to substances either alone or chiefly and primarily and in the unqualified sense.

We must inquire whether each thing and its essence are the same or different. This is of some use for the inquiry concerning substance; for each thing is thought to be not different from its substance, and the essence is said to be the substance of each thing.

Now in the case of accidental unities the two would be generally thought to be different, e.g., white man would be thought to be different from the essence of white man. For if they are the same, the essence of man and that of white man are also the same; for a man and a white man are the same thing, as people say, so that the essence of white man and that of man would be also the same. But perhaps it does not follow that the essence of accidental unities should be the same as that of the simple terms. For the extreme terms are not in the same way identical with the middle term. But perhaps *this* might be thought to follow, that the extreme terms, the accidents, should turn out to be the same, e.g., the essence of white and that of musical; but this is not actually thought to be the case.

But in the case of so-called self-subsistent things, is a thing necessarily the same as its essence? E.g., if there are some substances which have no other substances nor entities prior to them—substances such as some assert the Ideas to be?—If the essence of good is to be different from good-itself, and the essence of animal from animal-itself, and the essence of being from being-itself, there will, firstly, be other substances and entities and Ideas besides those which are asserted, and, secondly, these others will be prior substances, if essence is substance. And if the posterior substances and the prior are severed from each other (*a*) there will be no knowledge of the former, and (*b*) the latter will have no being. (By 'severed' I mean, if the good-itself has not the essence of good, and the latter has not the property of being good.) For (*a*) there is knowledge of each thing only when we know its essence. And (*b*) the case is the same for other things as for the good; so that if the essence of good is not good, neither is the essence of reality real, nor the essence of unity one. And all essences alike exist or none of them does; so that if the essence of reality is not real, neither is any of the others. Again, that to which the essence of good does not belong is not good.—The good, then, must be one with the essence of good, and the beautiful with the essence of beauty, and so with all things which do not depend on something else but are self-subsistent and primary. For it is enough if they are this, even if they are not Forms; or rather, perhaps, even if they *are* Forms. (At the same time it is clear that if there are Ideas such as some people say there are, it will not be substratum that is substance; for these must be substances, but not predicable of a substratum; for if they were they would exist only by being participated in.)

Each thing itself, then, and its essence are one and the same in no merely accidental way, as is evident both from the preceding arguments and because to *know* each thing, at least, is just to know its essence, so that even by the exhibition of instances it becomes clear that both must be one.

(But of an accidental term, e.g., 'the musical' or 'the white', since it has two meanings, it is not true to say that it itself is identical with its essence; for both that to which the accidental quality belongs, and the accidental quality, are white, so that in a sense the accident and its essence are the same, and in a sense they are not; for the essence of white is not the same as the man or the white man, but it is the same as the attribute white.)

The absurdity of the separation would appear also if one were to assign a name to each of the essences; for there would be yet another essence besides the original one, e.g., to the essence of horse there will belong a second essence. Yet why should not some things be their essences from the start, since essence is substance? But indeed not only are a thing and its essence one, but the formula of them is also the same, as is clear even from what has been said; for it is not by accident that the essence of one, and the one, are one. Further, if they are to be different, the process will go on to infinity; for we shall have (1) the essence of one, and (2) the one, so that to terms of the former kind the same argument will be applicable.

Clearly, then, each primary and self-subsistent thing is one and the same as its essence. The sophistical objections to this position, and the question whether Socrates and to be Socrates are the same thing, are obviously answered by the same solution; for there is no difference either in the standpoint from which the question would be asked, or in that from which one could answer it successfully. We have explained, then, in what sense each thing is the same as its essence and in which sense it is not.

Of things that come to be, some come to be by nature, some by art, some spontaneously. Now everything that comes to be comes to be by the agency of something and from something and comes to be something. And the something which I say it comes to be may be found in any category; it may come to be either a 'this' or of some size or of some quality or somewhere.

Now natural comings to be are the comings to be of those things which come to be by nature; and that out of which they come to be is what we call matter; and that by which they come to be is something which exists naturally; and the something which they come to be is a man or a plant or one of the things of this kind, which we say are substances if anything is—all things produced either by nature or by art have matter; for each of them is capable both of being and of not being, and this capacity is the matter in each—and, in general, both that from which they are produced is nature, and the type according to which they are produced is nature (for that which is produced, e.g., a plant or an animal, has a nature), and so is that by which they are produced—the so-called 'formal' nature, which is specifically the same (though this is in another individual); for man begets man.

Thus, then, are natural products produced; all other productions are called 'makings'. And all makings proceed either from art or from a faculty or from thought. Some of them happen also spontaneously or by luck just as natural products sometimes do; for there also the same things sometimes are produced without seed as well as from seed. Concerning these cases, then, we must inquire later, but from art proceed the things of which the form is in the soul of the artist. (By form I mean the essence of each thing and its primary substance.) For even contraries have in a sense the same form; for the substance of a privation is the opposite substance, e.g., health is the substance of disease (for disease is the absence of health); and health is the formula in the soul or the knowledge of it. The healthy subject is produced as the result of the following train of thought: since *this* is health, if the subject is to be healthy *this* must first be present, e.g., a uniform state of body, and if this is to be present, there must be heat; and the physician goes on thinking thus until he reduces the matter to a final something which he himself can produce. Then the process from this point onward, i.e., the process towards health, is called a 'making'. Therefore it follows that in a sense health comes from health and house from house, that with matter from that without matter; for the medical art and the building art are the form of health and of the house, and when I speak of substance without matter I mean essence.

Of the productions or processes one part is called thinking and the other making—that which proceeds from the starting-point and the form is thinking, and that which proceeds from the final step of the thinking is making. And each of the other, intermediate, things is produced in the same way. I mean, for instance, if the subject is to be healthy his bodily state must be made uniform. What then does being made uniform imply? This or that. And this depends on his being made warm. What does this imply? Something else. And this something is present potentially; and what is present potentially is already in the physician's power.

The active principle then and the starting-point for the process of becoming healthy is, if it happens by art, the form in the soul, and if spontaneously, it is that, whatever it is, which starts the making, for the man who makes by art, as in healing the starting-point is perhaps the production of warmth (and this the physician produces by rubbing). Warmth in the body, then, is either a part of health or is followed (either directly or through several intermediate steps) by something similar which is a part of health; and this, viz. that which produces the part of health, is the limiting-point— and so too with a house (the stones are the limiting-point here) and in all other cases.

Therefore, as the saying goes, it is impossible that anything should be produced if there were nothing existing before. Obviously then some part of the result will pre-exist of necessity; for the matter is a part; for this is present in the process and it is this that becomes something. But is the matter an element even in the *formula*? We certainly describe in both ways what brazen circles are; we describe both the matter by saying it is brass, and the form by saying that it is such and such a figure; and

figure is the proximate genus in which it is placed. The brazen circle, then, has its matter *in its formula.*

As for that out of which as matter they are produced, some things are said, when they have been produced, to be not that but 'that-en'; e.g., the statue is not gold but golden. And a healthy man is not said to be that from which he has come. The reason is that though a thing comes both from its privation and from its substratum, which we call its matter (e.g., what becomes healthy is both a man and an invalid), it is said to come rather from its privation (e.g., it is from an invalid rather than from a man that a healthy subject is produced). And so the healthy subject is not said to *be* an invalid, but to be a man, and the man is said to be healthy. But as for the things whose privation is obscure and nameless, e.g., in brass the privation of a particular shape or in bricks and timber the privation of arrangement as a house, the thing is thought to be produced *from* these materials, as in the former case the healthy man is produced *from* an invalid. And so, as there also a thing is not said to be that from which it comes, here the statue is not said to be wood but is said by a verbal change to be wooden, not brass but brazen, not gold but golden, and the house is said to be not bricks but bricken (though we should not say without qualification, if we looked at the matter carefully, even that a statue is produced from wood or a house from bricks, because coming to be implies change in that from which a thing comes to be, and not permanence). It is for this reason, then, that we use this way of speaking.

Since anything which is produced is produced by something (and this I call the starting-point of the production), and from something (and let this be taken to be not the privation but the matter; for the meaning we attach to this has already been explained), and since something is produced (and this is either a sphere or a circle or whatever else it may chance to be), just as we do not make the substratum (the brass), so we do not make the sphere, except incidentally, because the brazen sphere is a sphere and we make the former. For to make a 'this' is to make a 'this' out of the substratum in the full sense of the word. (I mean that to make the brass round is not to make the round or the sphere, but something else, i.e., to produce this form in something different from itself. For if we make the form, we must make it out of something else; for this was assumed. E.g., we make a brazen sphere; and that in the sense that out of this, which is brass, we make this other, which is a sphere.) If, then, we also make the substratum itself, clearly we shall make it in the same way, and the processes of making will regress to infinity. Obviously then the form also, or whatever we ought to call the shape present in the sensible thing, is not produced, nor is there any production of it, nor is the essence produced; for this is that which is made to be in something else either by art or by nature or by some faculty. But that there is a *brazen sphere*, this we make. For we make it out of brass and the sphere; we bring the form into this particular matter, and the result is a brazen sphere. But if the essence of sphere in general is to be produced, something must be produced out of something. For the product will always have to be divisible, and one part must be this and another that; I mean the one must be matter and the other form. If then, a sphere is 'the figure whose circumference is at all points equidistant from the centre', part of this will be the medium in which the thing made will be, and part will be in that medium, and the whole will be the thing produced, which corresponds to the brazen sphere. It is obvious, then, from what has been said, that that which is spoken of as form or substance is not produced, but the concrete thing which gets its name from this is produced, and that in everything which is generated matter is present, and one part of the thing is matter and the other form.

Is there, then, a sphere apart from the individual spheres or a house apart from the bricks? Rather we may say that no 'this' would ever have been coming to be, if this had been so, but that the 'form' means the 'such', and is not a 'this'—a definite thing; but the artist makes, or the father begets a 'such' out of a 'this'; and when it has been begotten, it is a 'this such'. And the whole 'this', Callias or Socrates, is analogous to 'this brazen sphere', but man and animal to 'brazen sphere' in general. Obviously, then, the cause which consists of the Forms (taken in the sense in which some maintain the existence of the Forms, i.e., if they are something apart from the individuals) is useless, at least with regard to comings-to-be and to substances; and the Forms need not, for this reason at least, be self-subsistent substances. In some cases indeed it is even obvious that the begetter is of the same kind as the begotten (not, however, the *same* nor one in number, but in form), i.e., in the case of natural products (for man begets man), unless something happens contrary to nature, e.g., the production of a mule by a horse. (And even these cases are similar; for that which would be found to be common to horse and ass, the genus next above them, has not received a name, but it would doubtless be both, in fact something like a mule.) Obviously, therefore, it is quite unnecessary to set up a Form as a pattern (for we should have looked for Forms in these cases if in any; for these are substances if anything is so); the begetter is adequate to the making of the product and to the causing of the form in the matter. And when we have the whole, such and such a form in this flesh and in these bones, this is Callias or Socrates; and they are different in virtue of their matter (for that is different), but the same in form; for their form is indivisible.

12. Of *Identity and Diversity*

THOMAS HOBBES

Thomas Hobbes (1588–1679) was an English philosopher who attempted to extend mechanistic explanations to people and society. Impressed by the new physics of the Scientific Revolution, he tried to view everything in terms of material bodies and their interactions. As a nominalist, he believed meanings are just a matter of the interactions among particular signs. He attempted to diagnose many traditional philosophical problems as stemming from a misunderstanding of meaning (and for this reason some have wanted to call him the first "analytic" philosopher). His discussion of an ancient puzzle about identity—the ship of Theseus puzzle, in which a ship's parts are gradually replaced while the old parts are reassembled—is an example of his concern about clarity. Which ship qualifies as the *same* ship? Hobbes insisted that one specify "by what name [sign]" the ship is called. In other words, is one asking about the same matter, about the same form, or about the same aggregate of parts? For persons, he indicated that the same form is usually what one is interested in. Later philosophers, however, worry that analogs of the ship of Theseus puzzle that apply to persons may require a different solution. (See Chapter 16, Chisholm's "Problems of Identity.")

1. *What it is for one thing to differ from another.* Hitherto I have spoken of body simply, and accidents common to all bodies, *as magnitude, motion, rest, action, passion, power, possible, &c.*; and I should now descend to those accidents by which one body is distinguished from another, but that it is first to be declared what it is to be *distinct* and *not distinct*, namely, what are the SAME and DIFFERENT; for this also is common to all bodies, that they may be distinguished and differenced from one another. Now, two bodies are said to *differ* from one another, when something may be said of one of them, which cannot be said of the other at the same time.

2. *To differ in number, magnitude, species, and genus, what.* And, first of all, it is manifest that no two bodies are the *same;* for seeing they are two, they are in two places at the same time; as that, which is the *same,* is at the same time in one and the same place. All bodies therefore differ from one another in *number,* namely, as one and another; so

that the *same* and *different in number,* are names opposed to one another by contradiction.

In *magnitude* bodies differ when one is greater than another, as *a cubit long,* and *two cubits long,* of *two pound weight,* and of *three pound weight.* And to these, *equals* are opposed.

Bodies, which differ more than in magnitude, are called *unlike;* and those, which differ only in magnitude, *like.* Also, of unlike bodies, some are said to differ in the *species,* others in the *genus;* in the *species,* when their difference is perceived by one and the same sense, as *white* and *black;* and in the *genus,* when their difference is not perceived but by divers senses, as *white* and *hot.*

3. *What is relation, proportion, and relatives.* And the *likeness,* or *unlikeness, equality,* or *inequality* of one body to another, is called their RELATION; and the bodies themselves *relatives* or *correlatives; Aristotle* calls them τὰ πρὸς τί; the first whereof is usually named the *antecedent,* and the second the *consequent;* and the *relation* of the antecedent to the consequent, according to magnitude, namely, the equality, the excess or defect thereof, is called the PROPORTION of the antecedent to the consequent; so that *proportion* is nothing but the equality

From Hobbes's *Elements of Philosophy,* Section I, Part II, Chapter 11, first published in 1839.

or inequality of the magnitude of the antecedent compared to the magnitude of the consequent by their difference only, or compared also with their difference. For example, the *proportion* of three to two consists only in this, that three *exceeds* two by unity; and the proportion of two to five in this, that two, compared with five, is *deficient* of it by three, either simply, or compared with the numbers different; and therefore in proportion of unequals, the proportion of the less to the greater, is called DE-FECT; and that of the greater to the less, EXCESS.

4. *Proportionals, what.* Besides, of unequals, some are more, some less, and some equally unequal; so that there is *proportion of proportions*, as well as of *magnitudes;* namely, where two unequals have relation to two other unequals; as, when the inequality which is between 2 and 3, is compared with the inequality which is between 4 and 5. In which comparison there are always four magnitudes; or, which is all one, if there be but three, the middlemost is twice numbered; and if the proportion of the first to the second, be equal to the proportion of the third to the fourth, then the four are said to be *proportionals;* otherwise they are not proportionals.

5. *The proportion of magnitudes to one another, wherein it consists.* The proportion of the antecedent to the consequent consists in their difference, not only simply taken, but also as compared with one of the relatives; that is, either in that part of the greater, by which it exceeds the less, or in the remainder, after the less is taken out of the greater; as the proportion of two to five consists in the three by which five exceeds two, not in three simply only, but also as compared with five or two. For though there be the same difference between two and five, which is between nine and twelve, namely three, yet there is not the same inequality; and therefore the proportion of two to five is not in all relation the same with that of nine to twelve, but only in that which is called arithmetical.

6. *Relation is no new accident, but one of those that were in the relative, before the relation or comparison was made. Also the causes of accidents in correlatives are the cause of relation.* But we must not so think of relation, as if it were an accident differing from all the other accidents of the relative; but one of them, namely, that by which the comparison is made. For example, the likeness of one *white* to another *white,* or its unlikeness to *black,* is the same accident with its *whiteness;* and *equality* and *inequality,* the same accident with the *magnitude* of the thing compared,

though under another name: for that which is called *white* or *great,* when it is not compared with something else, the same when it is compared, is called *like* or *unlike, equal* or *unequal.* And from this it follows that the causes of the accidents, which are in relatives, are the causes also of *likeness, unlikeness, equality* and *inequality;* namely, that he, that makes two unequal bodies, makes also their inequality; and he, that makes a rule and an action, makes also, if the action be congruous to the rule, their congruity; if incongruous, their incongruity. And thus much concerning *comparison* of one body with another.

7. *Of the beginning of individuation.* But the same body may at different times be compared with itself. And from hence springs a great controversy among philosophers about the *beginning of individuation,* namely, in what sense it may be conceived that a body is at one time the same, at another time not the same it was formerly. For example, whether a man grown old be the same man he was whilst he was young, or another man; or whether a city be in different ages the same, or another city. Some place *individuity* in the unity of *matter;* others, in the unity of *form;* and one says it consists in the unity of the *aggregate of all the accidents together.* For *matter,* it is pleaded that a lump of wax, whether it be spherical or cubical, is the same wax, because the same matter. For *form,* that when a man is grown from an infant to be an old man, though his matter be changed, yet he is still the same numerical man; for that *identity,* which cannot be attributed to the matter, ought probably to be ascribed to the form. For the *aggregate of accidents,* no instance can be made; but because, when any new accident is generated, a new name is commonly imposed on the thing, therefore he, that assigned this cause of *individuity,* thought the thing itself also was become another thing. According to the first opinion, he that sins, and he that is punished, should not be the same man, by reason of the perpetual flux and change of man's body; nor should the city, which makes laws in one age and abrogates them in another, be the same city; which were to confound all civil rights. According to the second opinion, two bodies existing both at once, would be one and the same numerical body. For if, for example, that ship of Theseus, concerning the difference whereof made by continual reparation in taking out the old planks and putting in new, the sophisters of Athens were wont to dispute, were, after all the planks were changed, the same

numerical ship it was at the beginning; and if some man had kept the old planks as they were taken out, and by putting them afterwards together in the same order, had again made a ship of them, this, without doubt, had also been the same numerical ship with that which was at the beginning; and so there would have been two ships numerically the same, which is absurd. But, according to the third opinion, nothing would be the same it was; so that a man standing would not be the same he was sitting; nor the water, which is in the vessel, the same with that which is poured out of it. Wherefore the beginning of *individuation* is not always to be taken either from matter alone, or from form alone.

But we must consider by what name anything is called, when we inquire concerning the *identity* of it. For it is one thing to ask concerning Socrates, whether he be the same man, and another to ask whether he be the same body; for his body, when he is old, cannot be the same it was when he was an infant, by reason of the difference of magnitude; for one body has always one and the same magnitude; yet, nevertheless, he may be the same man. And therefore, whensoever the name, by which it is asked whether a thing be the same it was, is given it for the matter only, then, if the matter be the same, the thing also is *individually* the same; as

the water, which was in the sea, is the same which is afterwards in the cloud; and any body is the same, whether the parts of it be put together, or dispersed; or whether it be congealed, or dissolved. Also, if the name be given for such form as is the beginning of motion, then, as long as that motion remains, it will be the same *individual* thing; as that man will be always the same, whose actions and thoughts proceed all from the same beginning of motion, namely, that which was in his generation; and that will be the same river which flows from one and the same fountain, whether the same water, or other water, or something else than water, flow from thence; and that the same city, whose acts proceed continually from the same institution, whether the men be the same or no. Lastly, if the name be given for some accident, then the *identity* of the thing will depend upon the matter; for, by the taking away and supplying of matter, the accidents that were, are destroyed, and other new ones are generated, which cannot be the same numerically; so that a ship, which signifies matter so figured, will be the same as long as the matter remains the same; but if no part of the matter be the same, then it is numerically another ship; and if part of the matter remain and part be changed, then the ship will be partly the same, and partly not the same.

13. *Of Identity and Diversity*

JOHN LOCKE

John Locke (1632–1704) is considered an empiricist because of his commitment to the doctrine that all knowledge (ideas) about the world is based on sensory experience and introspection. The selection below is from Locke's most important work, *Essay Concerning Human Understanding.* Like Hobbes, Locke maintains that questions of identity can be answered only by specifying the *kind* of thing we are inquiring about. Thus, he gives different accounts of the identity of inanimate substances, living things, and persons. Furthermore, Locke uses a thought experiment or "puzzle case" to support his conception of personal identity. Locke considers the possibility of a prince having his consciousness transferred to a cobbler's body and vice versa. He uses this case, variations of which have become common fare in recent discussions of personal identity, to lend support to his thesis that memory, not bodily identity, is constitutive of personal identity. Another innovative feature of Locke's view is his attempt to analyze personal identity in terms of a *relation* (memory) between diverse things and not in terms of a continuing underlying substance or Platonic soul. Much of the current discussion of personal identity consists of criticisms and modifications of Locke's views. (See the selections by Williams and Parfit, Chapters 18 and 19, respectively.)

1. *Wherein Identity Consists.* Another occasion the mind often takes of comparing, is the very being of things; when, considering anything as existing at any determined time and place, we compare it with itself existing at another time, and thereon form the ideas of identity and diversity. When we see anything to be in any place in any instant of time, we are sure (be it what it will) that it is that very thing, and not another, which at that same time exists in another place, how like and undistinguishable soever it may be in all other respects: and in this consists identity, when the ideas it is attributed to vary not at all from what they were that moment wherein we consider their former existence, and to which we compare the present. For we never finding, nor conceiving it possible, that two things of the same kind should exist in the same place at the same time, we rightly conclude, that, whatever exists anywhere at any time, excludes all of the same kind, and is there itself alone. When therefore we demand whether anything be the same or no, it refers always to something that existed such a time in such a place, which it was certain at that instant was the same with itself, and no other. From whence it follows, that one thing cannot have two beginnings of existence, nor two things one beginning; it being impossible for two things of the same kind to be or exist in the same instant, in the very same place, or one and the same thing in different places. That, therefore, that had one beginning, is the same thing; and that which had a different beginning in time and place from that, is not the same, but diverse. That which had made the difficulty about this relation has been the little care and attention used in having precise notions of the things to which it is attributed.

2. *Identity of Substances.* We have the ideas but of three sorts of substances: (1) God, (2) finite intelligences, (3) bodies. First, God is without beginning, eternal, unalterable, and everywhere; and therefore concerning his identity there can be no

From Locke's *Essay Concerning Human Understanding,* 2nd ed., Chapter 27, first published in 1694.

doubt. Secondly, finite spirits having had each its determinate time and place of beginning to exist, the relation to that time and place will always determine to each of them its identity, as long as it exists. Thirdly, the same will hold of every particle of matter, to which no addition or subtraction of matter being made, it is the same. For, though these three sorts of substances, as we term them, do not exclude one another out of the same place, yet we cannot conceive but that they must necessarily each of them exclude any of the same kind out of the same place; or else the notions and names of identity and diversity would be in vain, and there could be no such distinctions of substances, or anything else one from another. For example: could two bodies be in the same place at the same time, then those two parcels of matter must be one and the same, take them great or little; nay, all bodies must be one and the same. For, by the same reason that two particles of matter may be in one place, all bodies may be in one place; which, when it can be supposed, takes away the distinction of identity and diversity of one and more, and renders it ridiculous. But it being a contradiction that two or more should be one, identity and diversity are relations and ways of comparing well founded, and of use to the understanding.

Identity of Modes. All other things being but modes or relations ultimately terminated in substances, the identity and diversity of each particular existence of them too will be by the same way determined: only as to things whose existence is in succession, such as are the actions of finite beings, v.g., motion and thought, both which consist in a continued train of succession: concerning their diversity there can be no question; because each perishing the moment it begins, they cannot exist in different times, or in different places, as permanent beings can at different times exist in distant places; and therefore no motion or thought, considered as at different times, can be the same, each part thereof having a different beginning of existence.

3. *Principium Individuationis.* From what has been said, it is easy to discover what is so much inquired after, the *principium individuationis*; and that, it is plain, is existence itself, which determines a being of any sort to a particular time and place, incommunicable to two beings of the same kind. This, though it seems easier to conceive in simple substances or modes, yet, when reflected on, is not more difficult in compound ones, if care

be taken to what it is applied: v.g., let us suppose an atom, i.e., a continued body under one immutable superfices, existing in a determined time and place; it is evident, that considered in any instant of its existence, it is in that instant the same with itself. For, being at that instant what it is, and nothing else, it is the same, and so must continue as long as its existence is continued; for so long it will be the same, and no other. In like manner, if two or more atoms be joined together into the same mass, every one of those atoms will be the same, by the foregoing rule: and whilst they exist united together, the mass, consisting of the same atoms, must be the same mass, or the same body, let the parts be ever so differently jumbled. But if one of these atoms be taken away, or one new one added, it is no longer the same mass or the same body. In the state of living creatures, their identity depends not on a mass of the same particles, but on something else. For in them the variation of great parcels of matter alters not the identity: an oak growing from a plant to a great tree, and then lopped, is still the same oak; and a colt grown up to a horse, sometimes fat, sometimes lean, is all the while the same horse: though, in both these cases, there may be a manifest change of the parts; so that truly they are not either of them the same masses of matter, though they be truly one of them the same oak, and the other the same horse. The reason whereof is, that, in these two cases, a mass of matter, and a living body, identity is not applied to the same thing.

4. *Identity of Vegetables.* We must therefore consider wherein an oak differs from a mass of matter, and that seems to me to be in this, that the one is only the cohesion of particles of matter any how united, the other such a disposition of them as constitutes the parts of an oak; and such an organization of those parts as is fit to receive and distribute nourishment, so as to continue and frame the wood, bark, and leaves, etc., of an oak, in which consists the vegetable life. That being then one plant which has such an organization of parts in one coherent body, partaking of one common life, it continues to be the same plant as long as it partakes of the same life, though that life be communicated to new particles of matter vitally united to the living plant, in a like continued organization comformable to that sort of plants. For this organization being at any one instant in any one collection of matter, is in that particular concrete distinguished from all other, and is that individual life,

which existing constantly from that moment both forwards and backwards, in the same continuity of insensibly succeeding parts united to the living body of the plant, it has that identity which makes the same plant, and all the parts of it, parts of the same plant, during all the time that they exist united in that continued organization, which is fit to convey that common life to all the parts so united.

5. *Identity of Animals.* The case is not so much different in brutes, but that any one may hence see what makes an animal and continues it the same. Something we have like this in machines, and may serve to illustrate it. For example, what is a watch? It is plain it is nothing but a fit organization or construction of parts to a certain end, which, when a sufficient force is added to it, it is capable to attain. If we would suppose this machine one continued body, all whose organized parts were repaired, increased, or diminished by a constant addition or separation of insensible parts, with one common life, we should have something very much like the body of an animal; with this difference, that, in an animal the fitness of the organization, and the motion wherein life consists, begin together, the motion coming from within; but in machines, the force coming sensibly from without, often away when the organ is in order, and well fitted to receive it.

6. *The Identity of Man.* This also shows wherein the identity of the same man consists; viz., in nothing but a participation of the same continued life, by constantly fleeting particles of matter, in succession vitally united to the same organized body. He that shall place the identity of man in anything else, but like that of other animals, in one fitly organized body, taken in any one instant, and from these continued, under one organization of life, in several successively fleeting particles of matter united to it, will find it hard to make an embryo, one of years, mad and sober, the same man, by any supposition, that will not make it possible for Seth, Ismael, Socrates, Pilate, St. Austin, and Caesar Borgia, to be the same man. For, if the identity of soul alone makes the same man, and there be nothing in the nature of matter why the same individual spirit may not be united to different bodies, it will be possible that those men living in distant ages, and of different tempers, may have been the same man: which way of speaking must be, from a very strange use of the word man, applied to an idea, out of which body

and shape are excluded. And that way of speaking would agree yet worse with the notions of those philosophers who allow of transmigration, and are of opinion that the souls of men may, for their miscarriages, be detruded into the bodies of beasts, as fit habitations, with organs suited to the satisfaction of their brutal inclinations. But yet I think nobody, could he be sure that the soul of Heliogabalus were in one of his hogs, would yet say that hog were a man or Heliogabalus.

7. *Identity Suited to the Idea.* It is not therefore unity of substance that comprehends all sorts of identity, or will determine it in every case; but to conceive and judge of it aright, we must consider what idea the word it is applied to stands for: it being one thing to be the same substance, another the same man, and a third the same person, if person, man, and substance, are three names standing for three different ideas; for such as is the idea belonging to that name, such must be the identity; which, if it had been a little more carefully attended to, would possibly have prevented a great deal of that confusion which often occurs about this matter, with no small seeming difficulties, especially concerning personal identity, which therefore we shall in the next place a little consider.

8. *Same Man.* An animal is living organized body; and consequently the same animal, as we have observed, is the same continued life communicated to different particles of matter, as they happen successively to be united to that organized living body. And whatever is talked of other definitions, ingenious observation puts it past doubt, that the idea in our minds, of which the sound man in our mouths is the sign, is nothing else but of an animal of such a certain form: since I think I may be confident, that, whoever should see a creature of his own shape or make, though it had no more reason all its life than a cat or a parrot, would call him still a man; or whoever should hear a cat or a parrot discourse, reason, and philosophize, would call or think it nothing but a cat or a parrot; and say, the one was a dull irrational man, and the other a very intelligent rational parrot. A relation we have in an author of great note, is sufficient to countenance the supposition of a rational parrot. His words are:

I had a mind to know, from Prince Maurice's own mouth, the account of a common, but much credited story, that I had heard so often from many others, of an old parrot he had in Brazil, during his government there, that spoke, and asked, and answered common questions, like a reasonable creature: so that those of his train there generally concluded it to be witchery or possession; and one of his chaplains, who lived long afterwards in Holland, would never from that time endure a parrot, but said they all had a devil in them. I had heard many particulars of this story, and assevered by people hard to be discredited, which made me ask Prince Maurice what there was of it. He said, with his usual plainness and dryness in talk, there was something true, but a great deal false of what had been reported. I desired to know of him what there was of the first. He told me short and coldly, that he had heard of such an old parrot when he had been at Brazil; and though he believed nothing of it, and it was a good way off, yet he had so much curiosity as to send for it: that it was a very great and a very old one; and when it came first into the room where the prince was, with a great many Dutchmen about him, it said presently, What a company of white men are here! They asked it, what it thought that man was, pointing to the prince. It answered, Some General or other. When they brought it close to him, he asked it, D'ou venez-vous? It answered, De Marinnan. The Prince, A qui estes-vous? The parrot, A un Portugais. The Prince, Que fais-tu là? Je garde les poulles. The Prince laughed, and said, Vous gardez les poulles? The parrot answered, Oui, moi, et je sçai bein faire; and made the chuck four or five times that people use to make to chickens when they call them. I set down the words of this worthy dialogue in French, just as Prince Maurice said them to me. I asked him in what language the parrot spoke, and he said in Brazilian. I asked whether he understood Brazilian; he said no: but he had taken care to have two interpreters by him, the one a Dutchman that spoke Brazilian, and the other a Brazilian that spoke Dutch; that he asked them separately and privately, and both of them agreed in telling him just the same thing that the parrot had said. I could not but tell this odd story, because it is so much out of the way, and from the first hand, and what may pass for a good one; for I dare say this prince at least believed himself in all he told me, having ever passed for a very honest and pious man: I leave it to naturalists to reason, and to other men to believe, as they please upon it; however, it is not, perhaps, amiss to relieve or enliven a busy scene sometimes with such digressions, whether to the purpose or no.

Same Man. I have taken care that the reader should have the story at large in the author's own words, because he seems to me not to have thought it incredible; for it cannot be imagined that so able a man as he, who had sufficiency enough to warrant all the testimonies he gives of himself, should take so much pains, in a place where it had nothing to do, to pin so close not only on a man whom he mentions as his friend, but on a prince in whom he acknowledges very great honesty and piety, a story which, if he himself thought incredible, he could not but also think ridiculous. The prince, it is plain, who vouches this story, and our author, who relates it from him, both of them call this talker a parrot: and I ask any one else who thinks such a story fit to be told, whether—if this parrot, and all of its kind, had always talked, as we have a prince's word for it this one did—whether, I say, they would not have passed for a race of rational animals; but yet, whether, for all that, they would have been allowed to be men, and not parrots? For I presume it is not the idea of a thinking or rational being alone that makes the idea of a man in most people's sense, but of a body, so and so shaped, joined to it; and if that be the idea of a man, the same successive body not shifted all at once, must, as well as the same immaterial spirit, go to the making of the same man.

9. *Personal Identity*. This being premised, to find wherein personal identity consists, we must consider what person stands for; which, I think, is a thinking intelligent being, that has reason and reflection, and can consider itself as itself, the same thinking thing, in different times and places; which it does only by that consciousness which is inseparable from thinking, and, as it seems to me, essential to it: it being impossible for any one to perceive without perceiving that he does perceive. When

we see, hear, smell, taste, feel, meditate, or will anything, we know that we do so. Thus it is always as to our present sensations and perceptions: and by this every one is to himself that which he calls self; it not being considered, in this case, whether the same self be continued in the same or divers substances. For, since consciousness always accompanies thinking, and it is that which makes every one to be what he calls self, and thereby distinguishes himself from all other thinking things: in this alone consists personal identity, i.e., the sameness of a rational being; and as far as this consciousness can be extended backwards to any past action or thought, so far reaches the identity of that person; it is the same self now it was then; and it is by the same self with this present one that now reflects on it, that that action was done.

10. *Consciousness Makes Personal Identity.* But it is further inquired, whether it be the same identical substance? This, few would think they had reason to doubt of, if these perceptions, with their consciousness, always remained present in the mind, whereby the same thinking thing would be always consciously present, and, as would be thought, evidently the same to itself. But that which seems to make the difficulty is this, that this consciousness being interrupted always by forgetfulness, there being no moment of our lives wherein we have the whole train of all our past actions before our eyes in one view, but even the best memories losing the sight of one part whilst they are viewing another; and we sometimes, and that the greatest part of our lives, not reflecting on our past selves, being intent on our present thoughts, and in sound sleep having no thoughts at all, or at least none with that consciousness which remarks our waking thoughts; I say, in all these cases, our consciousness being interrupted, and we losing the sight of our past selves, doubts are raised whether we are the same thinking thing, i.e., the same substance or no. Which, however reasonable or unreasonable, concerns not personal identity at all: the question being, what makes the same person, and not whether it be the same identical substance, which always thinks in the same person; which, in this case, matters not at all: different substances, by the same consciousness (where they do partake in it) being united into one person, as well as different bodies by the same life are united into one animal, whose identity is preserved in that change of substances by the unity of one continued life. For it being the same consciousness that makes a man be

himself to himself, personal identity depends on that only, whether it be annexed solely to one individual substance, or can be continued in a succession of several substances. For as far as any intelligent being can repeat the idea of any past action with the same consciousness it had of it at first, and with the same consciousness it has of any present action; so far it is the same personal self. For it is by the consciousness it has of its present thoughts and actions, that it is self to itself now, and so will be the same self, as far as the same consciousness can extend to actions past or to come; and would be by distance of time, or change of substance, no more two persons, than a man be two men by wearing other clothes today than he did yesterday, with a long or a short sleep between: the same consciousness uniting those distant actions into the same person, whatever substances contributed to their production.

11. *Personal Identity in Change of Substances.* That this is so, we have some kind of evidence in our very bodies, all whose particles, whilst vitally united to this same thinking conscious self, so that we feel when they are touched, and are affected by, and conscious of good or harm that happens to them, are a part of ourselves; i.e., of our thinking conscious self. Thus, the limbs of his body are to every one a part of himself; he sympathizes and is concerned for them. Cut off a hand, and thereby separate it from that consciousness he had of its heat, cold, and other affections, and it is then no longer a part of that which is himself, any more than the remotest part of matter. Thus, we see the substance whereof personal self consisted at one time may be varied at another, without the change of personal identity; there being no question about the same person, though the limbs which but now were a part of it, be cut off.

12. But the question is, "Whether, if the same substance, which thinks, be changed, it can be the same person; or, remaining the same, it can be different persons?"

Whether in the Change of Thinking Substances. And to this I answer: First, This can be no question at all to those who place thought in a purely material animal constitution, void of an immaterial substance. For, whether their supposition be true or no, it is plain they conceive personal identity preserved in something else than identity of substance; as animal identity is preserved in identity of life, and not of substance. And therefore those who place thinking in an immaterial substance only, before they can come to deal with these men, must show why personal identity cannot be preserved in the change of immaterial substances, or variety of particular immaterial substances, as well as animal identity is preserved in the change of material substances, or variety of particular bodies: unless they will say, it is one immaterial spirit that makes the same life in brutes, as it is one immaterial spirit that makes the same person in men; which the Cartesians at least will not admit, for fear of making brutes thinking things too.

13. But next, as to the first part of the question, "Whether, if the same thinking substance (supposing immaterial substances only to think) be changed, it can be the same person?" I answer, that cannot be resolved, but by those who know what kind of substances they are that do think, and whether the consciousness of past actions can be transferred from one thinking substance to another. I grant, were the same consciousness the same individual action, it could not: but it being a present representation of a past action, why it may not be possible that that may be represented to the mind to have been, which really never was, will remain to be shown. And therefore how far the consciousness of past actions is annexed to any individual agent, so that another cannot possibly have it, will be hard for us to determine, till we know what kind of action it is that cannot be done without a reflex act of perception accompanying it, and how performed by thinking substances, who cannot think without being conscious of it. But that which we call the same consciousness, not being the same individual act, why one intellectual substance may not have represented to it, as done by itself, what it never did, and was perhaps done by some other agent; why, I say, such a representation may not possibly be without reality of matter of fact, as well as several representations in dreams are, which yet whilst dreaming we take for true, will be difficult to conclude from the nature of things. And that it never is so, will by us, till we have clearer views of the nature of thinking substances, be best resolved into the goodness of God, who, as far as the happiness or misery of any of his sensible creatures is concerned in it, will not, by a fatal error of theirs, transfer from one to another that consciousness which draws reward or punishment with it. How far this may be an argument against those who would place thinking in a system of fleeting animal spirits, I leave to be considered. But yet, to return to the question before us,

it must be allowed, that, if the same consciousness (which, as has been shown, is quite a different thing from the same numerical figure or motion in body) can be transferred from one thinking substance to another, it will be possible that two thinking substances may make but one person. For the same consciousness being preserved, whether in the same or different substances, the personal identity is preserved.

14. As to the second part of the question, "Whether the same immaterial substance remaining, there may be two distinct person?" which question seems to me to be built on this, whether the same immaterial being, being conscious of the action of its past duration, may be wholly stripped of all the consciousnes of its past existence, and lose it beyond the power of ever retrieving it again; and so as it were beginning a new account from a new period, have a consciousness that cannot reach beyond this new state. All those who hold pre-existence are evidently of this mind, since they allow the soul to have no remaining consciousness of what it did in that pre-existent state, either wholly separate from body, or informing any other body; and if they should not, it is plain experience would be against them. So that personal identity reaching no further than consciousness reaches, a pre-existent spirit not having continued so many ages in a state of silence, must needs make different persons. Suppose a Christian Platonist or a Pythagorean should, upon God's having ended all his works of creation the seventh day, think his soul hath existed ever since; and would imagine it has revolved in several human bodies, as I once met with one, who was persuaded his had been the soul of Socrates; (how reasonably I will not dispute; this I know, that in the post he filled, which was no inconsiderable one, he passed for a very rational man, and the press has shown that he wanted not parts or learning); would any one say, that he, being not conscious of any of Socrates' actions or thoughts, could be the same person with Socrates? Let any one reflect upon himself, and conclude that he has in himself an immaterial spirit, which is that which thinks in him, and, in the constant change of his body keeps him the same: and is that which he calls himself: let him also suppose it to be the same soul that was in Nestor or Thersites, at the siege of Troy (for souls being, as far as we know anything of them, in their nature indifferent to any parcel of matter, the supposition has no apparent absurdity in it), which it may have been, as well as it is now

the soul of any other man: but he now having no consciousness of any of the actions either of Nestor or Thersites, does or can he conceive himself the same person with either of them? Can he be concerned in either of their actions? attribute them to himself, or think them his own, more than the actions of any other men that ever existed? So that this consciousness not reaching to any of the actions of either of those men, he is no more one self with either of them, than if the soul or immaterial spirit that now informs him had been created, and began to exist, when it began to inform his present body, though it were ever so true, that the same spirit that informed Nestor's or Thersites' body were numerically the same that now informs his. For this would no more make him the same person with Nestor, than if some of the particles of matter that were once a part of Nestor, were now a part of this man; the same immaterial substance, without the same consciousness, no more making the same person by being united to any body, than the same particle of matter, without consciousness united to any body, makes the same person. But let him once find himself conscious of any of the actions of Nestor, he then finds himself the same person with Nestor.

15. And thus may we be able, without any difficulty, to conceive the same person at the resurrection, though in a body not exactly in make or parts the same which he had here, the same consciousness going along with the soul that inhabits it. But yet the soul alone, in the change of bodies, would scarce to any one but to him that makes the soul the man, be enough to make the same man. "For should the soul of a prince, carrying with it the consciousness of the prince's past life, enter and inform the body of a cobbler, as soon as deserted by his own soul, every one sees he would be the same person with the prince," accountable only for the prince's actions: but who would say it was the same man? The body too goes to the making the man, and would, I guess, to everybody determine the man in this case; wherein the soul, with all its princely thoughts about it, would not make another man: but he would be the same cobbler to every one besides himself. I know that, in the ordinary way of speaking, the same person, and the same man, stand for one and the same thing. And indeed every one will always have a liberty to speak as he pleases, and to apply what articulate sounds to what ideas he thinks fit, and change them as often as he pleases. But yet, when

we will inquire what makes the same spirit, man, or person, we must fix the ideas of spirit, man, or person in our minds, and having resolved with ourselves what we mean by them, it will not be hard to determine in either of them, or the like, when it is the same, and when not.

16. *Consciousness Makes the Same Person.* But though the same immaterial substance or soul does not alone, wherever it be, and in whatsoever state, make the same man; yet it is plain, consciousness, as far as ever it can be extended, should it be to ages past, unites existences and actions, very remote in time into the same person, as well as it does the existences and actions of the immediately preceding moment: so that whatever has the consciousness of present and past actions, is the same person to whom they both belong. Had I the same consciousness that I saw the ark and Noah's flood, as that I saw an overflowing of the Thames last winter, or as that I write now; I could no more doubt that I who write this now, that saw the Thames overflowed last winter, and that viewed the flood at the general deluge, was the same self, place that self in what substance you please, than that I who write this am the same myself now whilst I write (whether I consist of all the same substance, material or immaterial, or no) that I was yesterday; for as to this point of being the same self, it matters not whether this present self be made up of the same or other substances; I being as much concerned, and as justly accountable for any action that was done a thousand years since, appropriated to me now by this self-consciousness, as I am for what I did the last moment.

17. *Self Depends on Consciousness.* Self is that conscious thinking thing, whatever substance made up of (whether spiritual or material, simple or compounded, it matters not), which is sensible or conscious of pleasure and pain, capable of happiness or misery, and so is concerned for itself, as far as that consciousness extends. Thus every one finds, that whilst comprehended under that consciousness, the little finger is as much a part of himself as what is most so. Upon separation of this little finger, should this consciousness go along with the little finger, and leave the rest of the body, it is evident the little finger would be the person, the same person, and self then would have nothing to do with the rest of the body. As in this case it is the consciousness that goes along with the substance, when one part is separate from another, which makes the same person, and constitutes this

inseparable self; so it is in reference to substances remote in time. That with which the consciousness of this present thinking thing can join itself, makes the same person, and is one self with it, and with nothing else; and so attributes to itself, and owns all the actions of that thing as its own, as far as that consciousness reaches, and no further; as every one who reflects will perceive.

18. *Objects of Reward and Punishment*. In this personal identity is founded all the right and justice of reward and punishment; happiness and misery being that for which every one is concerned for himself, and not mattering what becomes of any substance not joined to, or affected with that consciousness. For as it is evident in the instance I gave but now, if the consciousness went along with the little finger when it was cut off, that would be the same self which was concerned for the whole body yesterday, as making part of itself, whose actions then it cannot but admit as its own now. Though, if the same body should still live, and immediately from the separation of the little finger have its own peculiar consciousness, whereof the little finger knew nothing; it would not at all be concerned for it, as a part of itself, or could own any of its actions, or have any of them imputed to him.

19. This may show us wherein personal identity consists: not in the identity of substance, but, as I have said, in the identity of consciousness; wherein if Socrates and the present mayor of Queenborough agree, they are the same person: if the same Socrates waking and sleeping do not partake of the same consciousness, Socrates waking and sleeping is not the same person. And to punish Socrates waking for what sleeping Socrates thought, and waking Socrates was never conscious of, would be no more of right, than to punish one twin for what his brother-twin did, whereof he knew nothing, because their outsides were so like, that they could not be distinguished; for such twins have been seen.

20. But yet possibly it will still be objected, suppose I wholly lose the memory of some parts of my life, beyond a possibility of retrieving them, so that perhaps I shall never be conscious of them again; yet am I not the same person that did those actions, had those thoughts that I once was conscious of, though I have now forgot them? To which I answer, that we must here take notice what the word I is applied to; which, in this case, is the man only. And the same man being presumed to be the same person, I is easily here supposed to stand also for the same person. But if it be possible for the same man to have distinct incommunicable consciousness at different times, it is past doubt the same man would at different times make different persons; which, we see, is the sense of mankind in the solemnest declaration of their opinions; human laws not punishing the mad man for the sober man's actions, nor the sober man for what the mad man did, thereby making them two persons: which is somewhat explained by our way of speaking in English, when we say such an one is not himself, or is beside himself; in which phrases it is insinuated, as if those who now, or at least first used them, thought that self was changed, the selfsame person was no longer in that man.

21. *Difference Between Identity of Man and Person*. But yet it is hard to conceive that Socrates, the same individual man, should be two persons. To help us a little in this, we must consider what is meant by Socrates, or the same individual man.

First, it must be either the same individual, immaterial, thinking substance; in short, the same numerical soul, and nothing else.

Secondly, or the same animal, without any regard to an immaterial soul.

Thirdly, or the same immaterial spirit united to the same animal.

Now, take which of these suppositions you please, it is impossible to make personal identity to consist in anything but consciousness, or reach any further than that does.

For, by the first of them, it must be allowed possible that a man born of different women, and in distant times, may be the same man. A way of speaking, which whoever admits, must allow it possible for the same man to be two distinct persons, as any two that have lived in different ages, without the knowledge of one another's thoughts.

By the second and third, Socrates, in this life and after it, cannot be the same man any way, but by the same consciousness; and so making human identity to consist in the same thing wherein we place personal identity, there will be no difficulty to allow the same man to be the same person. But then they who place human identity in consciousness only, and not in something else, must consider how they will make the infant Socrates the same man with Socrates after the resurrection. But whatsoever to some men makes a man, and consequently the same individual man, wherein perhaps few are agreed, personal identity can by us be placed in nothing but consciousness (which is that alone which makes what we call self), without involving us in great absurdities.

22. But is not a man drunk and sober the same person? Why else is he punished for the fact he commits when drunk, though he be never afterwards conscious of it? Just as much the same person as a man that walks, and does other things in his sleep, is the same person, and is answerable for any mischief he shall do in it. Human laws punish both, with a justice suitable to their way of knowledge; because, in these cases, they cannot distinguish certainly what is real, what counterfeit: and so the ignorance in drunkenness or sleep is not admitted as a plea. For, though punishment be annexed to personality, and personality to consciousness, and the drunkard perhaps be not conscious of what he did, yet human judicatures justly punish him, because the fact is proved against him, but want of consciousness cannot be proved for him. But in the great day, wherein the secrets of all hearts shall be laid open, it may be reasonable to think, no one shall be made to answer for what he knows nothing of; but shall receive his doom, his conscience accusing or excusing him.

23. *Consciousness Alone Makes Self.* Nothing but consciousness can unite remote existences into the same person: the identity of substance will not do it; for whatever substance there is, however framed, without consciousness there is no person: and a carcass may be a person, as well as any sort of substance be so without consciousness.

Could we suppose two distinct incommunicable consciousnesses acting the same body, the one constantly by day, the other by night; and, on the other side, the same consciousness, acting by intervals, two distinct bodies; I ask, in the first case, whether the day and the night man would not be two as distinct persons as Socrates and Plato? And whether, in the second case, there would not be one person in two distinct bodies, as much as one man is the same in two distinct clothings? Nor is it at all material to say, that this same, and this distinct consciousness, in the cases above mentioned, is owing to the same and distinct immaterial substances, bringing it with them to those bodies; which, whether true or no, alters not the case; since it is evident the personal identity would equally be determined by the consciousness, whether that consciousness were annexed to some individual immaterial substance or no. For, granting that the thinking substance in man must be necessarily

supposed immaterial, it is evident that immaterial thinking thing may sometimes part with its past consciousness, and be restored to it again, as appears in the forgetfulness men often have of their past actions: and the mind many times recovers the memory of a past consciousness, which it had lost for twenty years together. Make these intervals of memory and forgetfulness to take their turns regularly by day and night, and you have two persons with the same immaterial spirit, as much as in the former instance two persons with the same body. So that self is not determined by identity or diversity of substance, which it cannot be sure of, but only by identity of consciousness.

24. Indeed it may conceive the substance whereof it is now made up to have existed formerly, united in the same conscious being; but, consciousness removed, that substance is no more itself, or makes no more a part of it, than any other substance; as is evident in the instance we have already given of a limb cut off, of whose heat, or cold, or other affections, having no longer any consciousness, it is no more of a man's self, than any other matter of the universe. In like manner it will be in reference to any immaterial substance, which is void of that consciousness whereby I am myself to myself: if there be any part of its existence which I cannot upon recollection join with that present consciousness, whereby I am now myself, it is in that part of its existence no more myself, than any other immaterial being. For whatsoever any substance has thought or done, which I cannot recollect, and by my consciousness make my own thought and action, it will no more belong to me, whether a part of me thought or did it, than if it had been thought or done by any other immaterial being anywhere existing.

25. I agree, the more probable opinion is, that this consciousness is annexed to, and the affection of, one individual immaterial substance.

But let men, according to their diverse hypotheses, resolve of that as they please; this very intelligent being, sensible of happiness or misery, must grant that there is something that is himself that he is concerned for, and would have happy; that this self has existed in a continued duration more than one instant, and therefore it is possible may exist, as it has done, months and years to come, without any certain bounds to be set to its duration; and may be the same self by the same consciousness continued on for the future. And thus, by this consciousness, he finds himself to be the same self which did such and such an action some years since, by which he comes to be happy or miserable now. In all which account of self, the same numerical substance is not considered as making the same self; but the same continued consciousness, in which several substances may have been united, and again separated from it; which, whilst they continued in a vital union with that wherein this consciousness then resided, made a part of that same self. Thus any part of our bodies vitally united to that which is conscious in us, makes a part of ourselves: but upon separation from the vital union by which that consciousness is communicated, that which a moment since was part of ourselves, is now no more so than a part of another man's self is a part of me: and it is not impossible but in a little time may become a real part of another person. And so we have the same numerical substance become a part of two different persons; and the same person preserved under the change of various substances. Could we suppose any spirit wholly stripped of all its memory or consciousness of past actions, as we find our minds always are of a great part of ours, and sometimes of them all; the union or separation of such a spiritual substance would make no variation of personal identity, and more than that of any particle of matter does. Any substance vitally united to the present thinking being, is a part of that very same self which now is; anything united to it by a consciousness of former actions, makes also a part of the same self, which is the same both then and now.

26. *Person a Forensic Term.* Person, as I take it, is the name for this self. Wherever a man finds what he calls himself there, I think, another may say is the same person. It is a forensic term, appropriating actions and their merit; and so belongs only to intelligent agents capable of a law, and happiness, and misery. This personality extends itself beyond present existence to what is past, only by consciousness, whereby it becomes concerned and accountable, owns and imputes to itself past actions, just upon the same ground and for the same reason that it does the present. All which is founded in a concern for happiness, the unavoidable concomitant of consciousness; that which is conscious of pleasure and pain, desiring that that self that is conscious should be happy. And therefore whatever past actions it cannot reconcile or appropriate to that present self by consciousness, it can be no more concerned in, than if they had never been done; and to receive pleasure or pain,

i.e., reward or punishment, on the account of any such action, is all one as to be made happy or miserable in its first being, without any demerit at all: for supposing a man punished now for what he had done in another life, whereof he could be made to have no consciousness at all, what difference is there between that punishment, and being created miserable? And therefore, conformable to this, the apostle tells us, that, at the great day, when every one shall "receive according to his doings, the secrets of all hearts shall be laid open." The sentence shall be justified by the consciousness all persons shall have, that they themselves, in what bodies soever they appear, or what substances soever that consciousness adheres to, are the same that committed those actions, and deserve that punishment for them.

27. I am apt enough to think I have, in treating of this subject, made some suppositions that will look strange to some readers, and possibly they are so in themselves. But yet, I think they are such as are pardonable, in this ignorance we are in of the nature of that thinking thing that is in us, and which we look on as ourselves. Did we know what it was, or how it was tied to a certain system of fleeting animal spirits; or whether it could or could not perform its operations of thinking and memory out of a body organized as ours is: and whether it has pleased God, that no one such spirit shall ever be united to any one but such body, upon the right constitution of whose organs its memory should depend; we might see the absurdity of some of these suppositions I have made. But, taking as we ordinarily now do, (in the dark concerning these matters,) the soul of a man for an immaterial substance, independent from matter, and indifferent alike to it all, there can, from the nature of things, be no absurdity at all to suppose that the same soul may at different times be united to different bodies, and with them make up for that time one man, as well as we suppose a part of a sheep's body yesterday should be a part of a man's body tomorrow, and in that union make a vital part of Meliboeus himself, as well as it did of his ram.

28. *The Difficulty from Ill Use of Names.* To conclude: Whatever substance begins to exist, it must, during its existence, necessarily be the same: whatever compositions of substances begin to exist, during the union of those substances the concrete must be the same; whatsoever mode begins to exist, during its existence it is the same; and so if the composition be of distinct substances and different

modes, the same rule holds: whereby it will appear, that the difficulty or obscurity that has been about this matter rather rises from the names ill used, than from any obscurity in things themselves. For whatever makes the specific idea to which the name is applied, if that idea be steadily kept to, the distinction of anything into the same, and divers, will easily be conceived, and there can arise no doubt about it.

29. *Continued Existence Makes Identity*. For, supposing a rational spirit be the idea of a man, it is easy to know what is the same man, viz., the same spirit, whether separate or in a body, will be the same man. Supposing a rational spirit vitally united to a body of a certain conformation of parts to make a man, whilst that rational spirit, with that vital conformation of parts, though continued in a fleeting successive body, remain, it will be the same man. But if to any one the idea of a man be but the vital union of parts in a certain shape, as long as that vital union and shape remain in a concrete no otherwise the same, but by a continued succession of fleeting particles, it will be the same man. For, whatever be the composition whereof the complex idea is made, whenever existence makes it one particular thing under any denomination, the same existence continued, preserves it the same individual under the same denomination.

14. Of Identity and On Mr. Locke's Theory of Personal Identity

THOMAS REID

Thomas Reid (1710–1796), the founder of the Scottish School of Common Sense, was born in Aberdeen. He was an insightful, albeit critical, interpreter of the empiricists and a staunch defender of the view that the mind and the body are two different substances (mind-body dualism). In the first selection, Reid maintains that the idea or concept of identity is univocal and involves "continued, uninterrupted existence." Since physical objects are continually changing their parts, they do not, according to the strict and philosophical sense of the term, have strict identity through time. A person, on the other hand, is a simple indivisible substance that remains, in the strict and philosophical sense, identical through time. In the second selection, Reid raises several objections to Locke's views on personal identity.

Of Identity

The conviction which every man has of his identity, as far back as his memory reaches, needs no aid of philosophy to strengthen it; and no philosophy can weaken it, without first producing some degree of insanity.

The philosopher, however, may very properly consider this conviction as a phenomenon of human nature worthy of his attention. If he can discover its cause, an addition is made to his stock of knowledge; if not, it must be held as a part of our original constitution, or an effect of that constitution produced in a manner unknown to us.

We may observe, first of all, that this conviction is indispensably necessary to all exercise of reason. The operations of reason, whether in action or in speculation, are made up of successive parts. The antecedent are the foundation of the consequent, and, without the conviction that the antecedent have been seen or done by me, I could

From Reid's *Essays on the Intellectual Powers of Man,* first published in 1785. "Of Identity" is Essay III, Chapter 4; "Of Mr. Locke's Account of Our Personal Identity" is Essay III, Chapter 6.

have no reason to proceed to the consequent, in any speculation, or in any active project whatever.

There can be no memory of what is past without the conviction that we existed at the time remembered. There may be good arguments to convince me that I existed before the earliest thing I can remember; but to suppose that my memory reaches a moment farther back than my belief and conviction of my existence, is a contradiction.

The moment a man loses this conviction, as if he had drunk the water of Lethe, past things are done away; and, in his own belief, he then begins to exist. Whatever was thought, or said, or done, or suffered before that period, may belong to some other person; but he can never impute it to himself, or take any subsequent step that supposes it to be his doing.

From this it is evident that we must have the conviction of our own continued existence and identity, as soon as we are capable of thinking or doing anything, on account of what we have thought, or done, or suffered before; that is, as soon as we are reasonable creatures.

That we may form as distinct a notion as we are able of this phenomenon of the human mind, it is proper to consider what is meant by identity in general, what by our own personal identity, and how we are led into that invincible belief and conviction which every man has of his own personal identity, as far as his memory reaches.

Identity in general I take to be a relation between a thing which is known to exist at one time, and a thing which is known to have existed at another time. If you ask whether they are one and the same, or two different things, every man of common sense understands the meaning of your question perfectly. Whence we may infer with certainty, that every man of common sense has a clear and distinct notion of identity.

If you ask a definition of identity, I confess I can give none; it is too simple a notion to admit of logical definition: I can say it is a relation, but I cannot find words to express the specific difference between this and other relations, though I am in no danger of confounding it with any other. I can say that diversity is a contrary relation, and that similitude and dissimilitude are another couple of contrary relations, which every man easily distinguishes in his conception from identity and diversity.

I see evidently that identity supposes an uninterrupted continuance of existence. That which has ceased to exist cannot be the same with that which afterwards begins to exist; for this would be to suppose a being to exist after it ceased to exist, and to have had existence before it was produced, which are manifest contradictions. Continued uninterrupted existence is therefore necessarily implied in identity.

Hence we may infer, that identity cannot, in its proper sense, be applied to our pains, our pleasures, our thoughts, or any operation of our minds. The pain felt this day is not the same individual pain which I felt yesterday, though they may be *similar* in kind and degree, and have the same cause. The same may be said of every feeling, and of every operation of mind. They are all successive in their nature, like time itself, no two moments of which can be the same moment.

It is otherwise with the parts of absolute space. They always are, and were, and will be the same. So far, I think, we proceed upon clear ground in fixing the notion of identity in general.

It is perhaps more difficult to ascertain with precision the meaning of personality; but it is not necessary in the present subject: it is sufficient for our purpose to observe, that all mankind place their personality in something that cannot be divided, or consist of parts.

A part of a person is a manifest absurdity.

When a man loses his estate, his health, his strength, he is still the same person, and has lost nothing of his personality. If he has a leg or an arm cut off, he is the same person he was before. The amputated member is no part of his person, otherwise it would have a right to a part of his estate, and be liable for a part of his engagements. It would be entitled to a share of his merit and demerit, which is manifestly absurd. A person is something indivisible, and is what Leibnitz calls a *monad*.

My personal identity, therefore, implies the continued existence of that indivisible thing which I call *myself*. Whatever this self may be, it is something which thinks, and deliberates, and resolves, and acts, and suffers. I am not thought, I am not action, I am not feeling; I am something that thinks, and acts, and suffers. My thoughts, and actions, and feelings, change every moment; they have no continued, but a successive, existence; but that *self*, or *I*, to which they belong, is permanent, and has the same relation to all the succeeding thoughts, actions, and feelings which I call mine.

Such are the notions that I have of my personal identity. But perhaps it may be said, this may all be fancy without reality. How do you know—what evidence have you—that there is such a permanent self which has a claim to all the thoughts, actions, and feelings which you call yours?

To this I answer, that the proper evidence I have of all this is remembrance. I remember that twenty years ago I conversed with such a person; I remember several things that passed in that conversation: my memory testifies, not only that this was done, but that it was done by me who now remember it. If it was done by me, I must have existed at that time, and continued to exist from that time to the present: if the identical person whom I call myself had not a part in that conversation, my memory is fallacious; it gives a distinct and positive testimony of what is not true. Every man in his senses believes what he distinctly remembers, and every thing he remembers convinces him that he existed at the time remembered.

Although memory gives the most irresistible evidence of my being the identical person that did such a thing, at such a time, I may have other good evidence of things which befell me, and which I do not remember: I know who bare me, and suckled me, but I do not remember these events.

It may here be observed (though the observation would have been unnecessary, if some great philosophers had not contradicted it), that it is not my remembering any action of mine that makes me to be the person who did it. This remembrance makes me to know assuredly that I did it; but I might have done it, though I did not remember it. That relation to me, which is expressed by saying that I did it, would be the same, though I had not the least remembrance of it. To say that my remembering that I did such a thing, or, as some choose to express it, my being conscious that I did it, makes me to have done it, appears to me as great an absurdity as it would be to say, that my belief that the world was created made it to be created.

When we pass judgment on the identity of other persons than ourselves, we proceed upon other grounds, and determine from a variety of circumstances, which sometimes produce the firmest assurance, and sometimes leave room for doubt. The identity of persons has often furnished matter of serious litigation before tribunals of justice. But no man of a sound mind ever doubted of his own identity, as far as he distinctly remembered.

The identity of a person is a perfect identity: wherever it is real, it admits of no degrees; and it is impossible that a person should be in part the same, and in part different; because a person is a *monad,* and is not divisible into parts. The evidence of identity in other persons than ourselves does indeed admit of all degrees, from what we account certainty, to the least degree of probability. But still it is true, that the same person is perfectly the same, and cannot be so in part, or in some degree only.

For this cause, I have first considered personal identity, as that which is perfect in its kind, and the natural measure of that which is imperfect.

We probably at first derive our notion of identity from that natural conviction which every man has from the dawn of reason of his own identity and continued existence. The operations of our minds are all successive, and have no continued existence. But the thinking being has a continued existence, and we have an invincible belief, that it remains the same when all its thoughts and operations change.

Our judgments of the identity of objects of sense seem to be formed much upon the same grounds as judgments of the identity of other persons than ourselves.

Wherever we observe great similarity, we are apt to presume identity, if no reason appears to the contrary. Two objects ever so like, when they are perceived at the same time, cannot be the same; but if they are presented to our senses at different times, we are apt to think them the same, merely from their similarity.

Whether this be a natural prejudice, or from whatever cause it proceeds, it certainly appears in children from infancy; and when we grow up, it is confirmed in most instances by experience: for we rarely find two individuals of the same species that are not distinguishable by obvious differences.

A man challenges a thief whom he finds in possession of his horse or his watch, only on similarity. When the watchmaker swears that he sold this watch to such a person, his testimony is grounded on similarity. The testimony of witnesses to the identity of a person is commonly grounded on no other evidence.

Thus it appears, that the evidence we have of our own identity, as far back as we remember, is totally of a different kind from the evidence we have of the identity of other persons, or of objects of sense. The first is grounded on memory, and gives undoubted certainty. The last is grounded on similarity, and on other circumstances, which in many cases are not so decisive as to leave no room for doubt.

It may likewise be observed, that the identity of objects of sense is never perfect. All bodies, as they consist of innumerable parts that may be disjoined from them by a great variety of causes, are subject to continual changes of their substance, increasing, diminishing, changing insensibly. When such alterations are gradual, because language could not afford a different name for every different state of such a changeable being, it retains the same name, and is considered as the same thing. Thus we say of an old regiment, that it did such a thing a century ago, though there now is not a man alive who then belonged to it. We say a tree is the same in the seed-bed and in the forest. A ship of war, which has successively changed her anchors, her tackle, her sails, her masts, her planks, and her timbers, while she keeps the same name, is the same.

The identity, therefore, which we ascribe to bodies, whether natural or artificial, is not perfect identity; it is rather something which, for the conveniency of speech, we call identity. It admits of a great change of the subject, providing the change be gradual; sometimes, even of a total change. And the changes which in common language are made consistent with identity differ from those that are thought to destroy it, not in kind, but in number and degree. It has no fixed nature when applied to bodies; and questions about the identity of a body are very often questions about words. But identity, when applied to persons, has no ambiguity, and admits not of degrees, or of more and less. It is the foundation of all rights and obligations, and of all accountableness; and the notion of it is fixed and precise.

Of Mr. Locke's Account of Our Personal Identity

In a long chapter upon Identity and Diversity, Mr. Locke has made many ingenious and just observations, and some which I think cannot be defended. I shall only take notice of the account he gives of our own personal identity. His doctrine upon this subject has been censured by Bishop Butler, in a short essay subjoined to his *Analogy*, with whose sentiments I perfectly agree.

Identity, as was observed, supposes the continued existence of the being of which it is affirmed, and therefore can be applied only to things which have a continued existence. While any being continues to exist, it is the same being; but two beings which have a different beginning or a different ending of their existence cannot possibly be the same. To this, I think, Mr. Locke agrees.

He observes, very justly, that, to know what is meant by the same person, we must consider what the word *person* stands for; and he defines a person to be an intelligent being, endowed with reason and with consciousness, which last he thinks inseparable from thought.

From this definition of a person, it must necessarily follow, that, while the intelligent being continues to exist and to be intelligent, it must be the same person. To say that the intelligent being is the person, and yet that the person ceases to exist while the intelligent being continues, or that the person continues while the intelligent being ceases to exist, is to my apprehension a manifest contradiction.

One would think that the definition of a per-

son should perfectly ascertain the nature of personal identity, or wherein it consists, though it might still be a question how we come to know and be assured of our personal identity.

Mr. Locke tells us, however, "that personal identity, that is, the sameness of a rational being, consists in consciousness alone, and, as far as this consciousness can be extended backwards to any past action or thought, so far reaches the identity of that person. So that whatever has the consciousness of present and past actions is the same person to whom they belong."

This doctrine has some strange consequences, which the author was aware of. Such as, that if the same consciousness can be transferred from one intelligent being to another, which he thinks we cannot show to be impossible, *then two or twenty intelligent beings may be the same person*. And if the intelligent being may lose the consciousness of the actions done by him, which surely is possible, then he is not the person that did those actions; so that *one intelligent being may be two or twenty different persons*, if he shall so often lose the consciousness of his former actions.

There is another consequence of this doctrine, which follows no less necessarily, though Mr. Locke probably did not see it. It is, *that a man may be, and at the same time not be, the person that did a particular action*.

Suppose a brave officer to have been flogged when a boy at school for robbing an orchard, to have taken a standard from the enemy in his first campaign, and to have been made a general in advanced life; suppose, also, which must be admitted to be possible, that, when he took the standard, he was conscious of his having been flogged at school, and that, when made a general, he was conscious of his taking the standard, but had absolutely lost the consciousness of his flogging.

These things being supposed, it follows, from Mr. Locke's doctrine, that he who was flogged at school is the same person who took the standard, and that he who took the standard is the same person who was made a general. Whence it follows, if there be any truth in logic, that the general is the same person with him who was flogged at school. But the general's consciousness does not reach so far back as his flogging; therefore, according to Mr. Locke's doctrine, he is not the person who was flogged. Therefore the general is, and at the same time is not, the same person with him who was flogged at school.

Leaving the consequences of this doctrine to those who have leisure to trace them, we may observe, with regard to the doctrine itself:

First, that Mr. Locke attributes to consciousness the conviction we have of our past actions, as if a man may now be conscious of what he did twenty years ago. It is impossible to understand the meaning of this, unless by consciousness be meant memory, the only faculty by which we have an immediate knowledge of our past actions.

Sometimes, in popular discourse, a man says he is conscious that he did such a thing, meaning that he distinctly remembers that he did it. It is unnecessary, in common discourse, to fix accurately the limits between consciousness and memory. This was formerly shown to be the case with regard to sense and memory: and therefore distinct remembrance is sometimes called sense, sometimes consciousness, without any inconvenience.

But this ought to be avoided in philosophy, otherwise we confound the different powers of the mind, and ascribe to one what really belongs to another. If a man can be conscious of what he did twenty years or twenty minutes ago, there is no use for memory, nor ought we to allow that there is any such faculty. The faculties of consciousness and memory are chiefly distinguished by this, that the first is an immediate knowledge of the present, the second an immediate knowledge of the past.

When, therefore, Mr. Locke's notion of personal identity is properly expressed, it is, that personal identity consists in distinct remembrance; for, even in the popular sense, to say that I am conscious of a past action means nothing else than that I distinctly remember that I did it.

Secondly, it may be observed, that, in this doctrine, not only is consciousness confounded with memory, but, which is still more strange, personal identity is confounded with the evidence which we have of our personal identity.

It is very true, that my remembrance that I did such a thing is the evidence I have that I am the identical person who did it. And this, I am apt to think, Mr. Locke meant. But to say that my remembrance that I did such a thing, or my consciousness, makes me the person who did it, is, in my apprehension, an absurdity too gross to be entertained by any man who attends to the meaning of it; for it is to attribute to memory or consciousness a strange magical power of producing its object,

though that object must have existed before the memory or consciousness which produced it.

Consciousness is the testimony of one faculty; memory is the testimony of another faculty; and to say that the testimony is the cause of the thing testified, this surely is absurd, if any thing be, and could not have been said by Mr. Locke, if he had not confounded the testimony with the thing testified.

When a horse that was stolen is found and claimed by the owner, the only evidence he can have, or that a judge or witnesses can have, that this is the very identical horse which was his property, is similitude. But would it not be ridiculous from this to infer that the identity of a horse consists in similitude only? The only evidence I have that I am the identical person who did such actions is, that I remember distinctly I did them; or, as Mr. Locke expresses it, I am conscious I did them. To infer from this, that personal identity consists in consciousness, is an argument which, if it had any force, would prove the identity of a stolen horse to consist solely in similitude.

Thirdly, is it not strange that the sameness or identity of a person should consist in a thing which is continually changing, and is not any two minutes the same?

Our consciousness, our memory, and every operation of the mind, are still flowing like the water of a river, or like time itself. The consciousness I have this moment can no more be the same consciousness I had last moment, than this moment can be the last moment. Identity can only be affirmed of things which have a continued existence. Consciousness, and every kind of thought, are transient and momentary, and have no continued existence; and, therefore, if personal identity consisted in consciousness, it would certainly follow, that no man is the same person any two moments of his life; and as the right and justice of reward and punishment are founded on personal identity, no man could be responsible for his actions.

But though I take this to be the unavoidable consequence of Mr. Locke's doctrine concerning personal identity, and though some persons may have liked the doctrine the better on this account, I am far from imputing any thing of this kind to Mr. Locke. He was too good a man not to have rejected with abhorrence a doctrine which he believed to draw this consequence after it.

Fourthly, there are many expressions used by Mr. Locke, in speaking of personal identity, which to me are altogether unintelligible, unless we suppose that he confounded that sameness or identity which we ascribe to an individual with the identity which, in common discourse, is often ascribed to many individuals of the same species.

When we say that pain and pleasure, consciousness and memory, are the same in all men, this sameness can only mean similarity, or sameness of kind. That the pain of one man can be the same individual pain with that of another man is no less impossible, than that one man should be another man: the pain felt by me yesterday can no more be the pain I feel to-day, than yesterday can be this day; and the same thing may be said of every passion and of every operation of the mind. The same kind or species of operation may be in different men, or in the same man at different times; but it is impossible that the same individual operation should be in different men, or in the same man at different times.

When Mr. Locke, therefore, speaks of "the same consciousness being continued through a succession of different substances"; when he speaks of "repeating the idea of a past action, with the same consciousness we had of it at the first," and of "the same consciousness extending to actions past and to come"; these expressions are to me unintelligible, unless he means not the same individual consciousness, but a consciousness that is similar, or of the same kind.

If our personal identity consists in consciousness, as this consciousness cannot be the same individually any two moments, but only of the same kind, it would follow, that we are not for any two moments the same individual persons, but the same kind of persons.

As our consciousness sometimes ceases to exist, as in sound sleep, our personal identity must cease with it. Mr. Locke allows, that the same thing cannot have two beginnings of existence, so that our identity would be irrecoverably gone every time we ceased to think, if it was but for a moment.

15. *On Identity and Personal Identity*

DAVID HUME

David Hume (1711–1776), a Scottish philosopher and historian, was born in Edinburgh. His philosophy was based on the empiricist dictum that all ideas are copies of prior impressions (experiences). He recommended skepticism about many metaphysical topics (see his selection in Part V). What follows are three excerpts from Hume's *Treatise of Human Nature*. In the first on identity, Hume elucidates a view that accords well with Reid's position, since for Hume identity involves an "invariable uninterrupted existence." Where he differs from Reid is in maintaining that neither persons nor nonpersons have a perfect identity through change. In the second, after rejecting the view of the self as a substance (see Plato and Reid above and Descartes in Part III), Hume offers his own account of the self as a bundle of perceptions, that is, thoughts, feelings, and experiences. In the third selection, he gives up hope of ever achieving an adequate account of the relation that would tie the successive perceptions into a *single* self.

On Identity[1]

First, as to the principle of individuation; we may observe, that the view of any one object is not sufficient to convey the idea of identity. For in that proposition, *an object is the same with itself*, if the idea express'd by the word, *object*, were no ways distinguish'd from that meant by *itself*; we really shou'd mean nothing, nor wou'd the proposition contain a predicate and a subject, which however are imply'd in this affirmation. One single object conveys the idea of unity, not that of identity.

On the other hand, a multiplicity of objects can never convey this idea, however resembling they may be suppos'd. The mind always pronounces the one not to be the other, and considers them as forming two, three, or any determinate number of objects, whose existences are entirely distinct and independent.

Since then both number and unity are incompatible with the relation of identity, it must lie in something that is neither of them. But to tell the truth, at first sight this seems utterly impossible. Betwixt unity and number there can be no me-dium; no more than betwixt existence and non-existence. After one object is suppos'd to exist, we must either suppose another also to exist; in which case we have the idea of number: Or we must suppose it not to exist; in which case the first object remains at unity.

To remove this difficulty, let us have recourse to the idea of time or duration. I have already observ'd,[2] that time, in a strict sense, implies succession, and that when we apply its idea to any unchangeable object, 'tis only by a fiction of the imagination, by which the unchangeable object is suppos'd to participate of the changes of the co-existent objects, and in particular of that of our perceptions. The fiction of the imagination almost universally takes place; and 'tis by means of it, that a single object, plac'd before us, and survey'd for any time without our discovering in it any interruption or variation, is able to give us a notion of identity. For when we consider any two points of this time, we may place them in different lights: We may either survey them at the very same instant; in which case they give us the idea of number, both by themselves and by the object; which must be multiply'd, in order to be conceiv'd at once, as existent in these two different points of time: Or on the other hand, we may trace the succession of time by a like succession of ideas, and conceiving first one moment, along with the object then existent, imagine afterwards a change in the time without any *variation* or *interruption* in the object; in which case it gives us the idea of unity. Here then is an idea, which is a medium betwixt unity and number; or more properly speaking, is either of them, according to the view, in which we take it: And this idea we call that of identity. We cannot, in any propriety of speech, say, that an object is the same with itself, unless we mean, that the object existent at one time is the same with itself existent at another. By this means we make a difference, betwixt the idea meant by the word, *object,* and that meant by *itself,* without going the length of number, and at the same time without restraining ourselves to a strict and absolute unity.

Thus the principle of individuation is nothing but the *invariableness* and *uninterruptedness* of any object, thro' a suppos'd variation of time, by which the mind can trace it in the different periods of its existence, without any break of the view, and without being oblig'd to form the idea of multiplicity or number.

Of Personal Identity[3]

There are some philosophers, who imagine we are every moment intimately conscious of what we call our *self;* that we feel its existence and its continuance in existence; and are certain, beyond the evidence of a demonstration, both of its perfect identity and simplicity. The strongest sensation, the most violent passion, say they, instead of distracting us from this view, only fix it the more intensely, and make us consider their influence on *self* either by their pain or pleasure. To attempt a farther proof of this were to weaken its evidence; since no proof can be deriv'd from any fact, of which we are so intimately conscious; nor is there any thing, of which we can be certain, if we doubt of this.

Unluckily all these positive assertions are contrary to that very experience, which is pleaded for them, nor have we any idea of *self,* after the manner it is here explain'd. For from what impression cou'd this idea be deriv'd? This question 'tis impossible to answer without a manifest contradiction and absurdity; and yet 'tis a question, which must

necessarily be answer'd, if we wou'd have the idea of self pass for clear and intelligible. It must be some one impression, that gives rise to every real idea. But self or person is not any one impression, but that to which our several impressions and ideas are suppos'd to have a reference. If any impression gives rise to the idea of self, that impression must continue invariably the same, thro' the whole course of our lives; since self is suppos'd to exist after that manner. But there is no impression constant and invariable. Pain and pleasure, grief and joy, passions and sensations succeed each other, and never all exist at the same time. It cannot, therefore, be from any of these impressions, or from any other, that the idea of self is deriv'd; and consequently there is no such idea.

But farther, what must become of all our particular perceptions upon this hypothesis? All these are different, and distinguishable, and separable from each other, and may be separately consider'd, and may exist separately, and have no need of any thing to support their existence. After what manner, therefore, do they belong to self; and how are they connected with it? For my part, when I enter most intimately into what I call *myself,* I always stumble on some particular perception or other, of heat or cold, light or shade, love or hatred, pain or pleasure. I never can catch *myself* at any time without a perception, and never can observe any thing but the perception. When my perceptions are remov'd for any time, as by sound sleep; so long am I insensible of *myself,* and may truly be said not to exist. And were all my perceptions remov'd by death, and cou'd I neither think, nor feel, nor see, nor love, nor hate after the dissolution of my body, I shou'd be entirely annihilated, nor do I conceive what is farther requisite to make me a perfect nonentity. If any one upon serious and unprejudic'd reflexion, thinks he has a different notion of *himself,* I must confess I can reason no longer with him. All I can allow him is, that he may be in the right as well as I, and that we are essentially different in this particular. He may, perhaps, perceive something simple and continu'd, which he calls *himself;* tho' I am certain there is no such principle in me.

But setting aside some metaphysicians of this kind, I may venture to affirm the rest of mankind, that they are nothing but a bundle or collection of different perceptions, which succeed each other with an inconceivable rapidity, and are in a perpetual flux and movement. Our eyes cannot turn in their sockets without varying our perceptions. Our thought is still more variable than our sight; and all our other senses and faculties contribute to this change; nor is there any single power of the soul, which remains unalterably the same, perhaps for one moment. The mind is a kind of theatre, where several perceptions successively make their appearance; pass, re-pass, glide away, and mingle in an infinite variety of postures and situations. There is properly no *simplicity* in it at one time, nor *identity* in different; whatever natural propension we may have to imagine that simplicity and identity. The comparison of the theatre must not mislead us. They are the successive perceptions only, that constitute the mind; nor have we the most distant notion of the place, where these scenes are represented, or of the materials, of which it is compos'd.

What then gives us so great a propension to ascribe an identity to these successive perceptions, and to suppose ourselves possest of an invariable and uninterrupted existence thro' the whole course of our lives? In order to answer this question, we must distinguish betwixt personal identity, as it regards our thought or imagination, and as it regards our passions or the concern we take in ourselves. The first is our present subject; and to explain it perfectly we must take the matter pretty deep, and account for that identity, which we attribute to plants and animals: there being a great analogy betwixt it, and the identity of a self or person.

We have a distinct idea of an object, that remains invariable and uninterrupted thro' a suppos'd variation of time; and this idea we call that of *identity* or *sameness*. We have also a distinct idea of several different objects existing in succession, and connected together by a close relation; and this to an accurate view affords as perfect a notion of *diversity*, as if there was no manner of relation among the objects. But tho' these two ideas of identity, and a succession of related objects be in themselves perfectly distinct, and even contrary, yet 'tis certain, that in our common way of thinking they are generally confounded with each other. That action of the imagination, by which we consider the uninterrupted and invariable object, and that by which we reflect on the succession of related objects, are almost the same to the feeling, nor is there much more effort of thought requir'd in the latter case than in the former. The relation facilitates the transition of the mind from one object to another, and renders its passage as smooth as if it contemplated one continu'd object. This resemblance is the cause of the confusion and mistake, and makes us substitute the notion of identity, instead of that of related objects. However at one instant we may consider the related succession as variable or interrupted, we are sure the next to ascribe to it a perfect identity, and regard it as invariable and uninterrupted. Our propensity to this mistake is so great from the resemblance above-mention'd, that we fall into it before we are aware; and tho' we incessantly correct ourselves by reflexion, and return to a more accurate method of thinking, yet we cannot long sustain our philosophy, or take off this biass from the imagination. Our last resource is to yield to it, and boldly assert that these different related objects are in effect the same, however interrupted and variable. In order to justify to ourselves this absurdity, we often feign some new and unintelligible principle, that connects the objects together, and prevents their interruption or variation. Thus we feign the continu'd existence of the perceptions of our senses, to remove the interruption; and run into the notion of a *soul*, and *self*, and *substance*, to disguise the variation. But we may farther observe, that where we do not give rise to such a fiction, our propension to confound identity with relation is so great, that we are apt to imagine[4] something unknown and mysterious, connecting the parts, beside their relation; and this I take to be the case with regard to the identity we ascribe to plants and vegetables. And even when this does not take place, we still feel a propensity to confound these ideas, tho' we are not able fully to satisfy ourselves in that particular, nor find any thing invariable and uninterrupted to justify our notion of identity.

Thus the controversy concerning identity is not merely a dispute of words. For when we attribute identity, in an improper sense, to variable or interrupted objects, our mistake is not confin'd to the expression, but is commonly attended with a fiction, either of something invariable and uninterrupted, or of something mysterious and inexplicable, or at least with a propensity to such fictions. What will suffice to prove this hypothesis to the satisfaction of every fair enquirer, is to shew from daily experience and observation, that the objects, which are variable or interrupted, and yet are suppos'd to continue the same, are such only as consist of a succession of parts, connected together by resemblance, contiguity, or causation. For as such a succession answers evidently to our notion of diversity, it can only be by mistake we ascribe to it an identity; and as the relation of parts, which leads us into this mistake, is really nothing but a quality, which produces an association of ideas, and an easy transition of the imagination from one to another, it can only be from the resemblance, which this act of the mind bears to that, by which we contemplate one continu'd object, that the error arises. Our chief business, then, must be to prove, that all objects, to which we ascribe identity, without observing their invariableness and uninterruptedness, are such as consist of a succession of related objects.

In order to this, suppose any mass of matter, of which the parts are contiguous and connected, to be plac'd before us; 'tis plain we must attribute a perfect identity to this mass, provided all the parts continue uninterruptedly and invariably the same, whatever motion or change of place we may observe either in the whole or in any of the parts. But supposing some very *small* or *inconsiderable* part to be added to the mass, or subtracted from it; tho' this absolutely destroys the identity of the whole, strictly speaking; yet as we seldom think so accurately, we scruple not to pronounce a mass of matter the same, where we find so trivial an alteration. The passage of the thought from the object before the change to the object after it, is so smooth and easy, that we scarce perceive the transition, and are apt to imagine that 'tis nothing but a continu'd survey of the same object.

There is a very remarkable circumstance, that attends this experiment; which is, that tho' the change of any considerable part in a mass of matter destroys the identity of the whole, yet we must measure the greatness of the part, not absolutely, but by its *proportion* to the whole. The addition or diminution of a mountain wou'd not be sufficient to produce a diversity in a planet; tho' the change of a very few inches wou'd be able to destroy the identity of some bodies. 'Twill be impossible to account for this, but by reflecting that objects operate upon the mind, and break or interrupt the continuity of its actions not according to their real greatness, but according to their proportion to each other: And therefore, since this interruption makes an object cease to appear the same, it must be the uninterrupted progress of the thought, which constitutes the imperfect identity.

This may be confirm'd by another phænomenon. A change in any considerable part of a body destroys its identity; but 'tis remarkable, that where the change is produc'd *gradually* and *insensibly* we are less apt to ascribe to it the same effect.

The reason can plainly be no other, than that the mind, in following the successive changes of the body, feels an easy passage from the surveying its condition in one moment to the viewing of it in another, and at no particular time perceives any interruption in its actions. From which continu'd perception, it ascribes a continu'd existence and identity to the object.

But whatever precaution we may use in introducing the changes gradually, and making them proportionable to the whole, 'tis certain, that where the changes are at last observ'd to become considerable, we make a scruple of ascribing identity to such different objects. There is, however, another artifice, by which we may induce the imagination to advance a step farther; and that is, by producing a reference of the parts to each other, and a combination to some *common end* or purpose. A ship, of which a considerable part has been chang'd by frequent reparations, is still consider'd as the same; nor does the difference of the materials hinder us from ascribing an identity to it. The common end, in which the parts conspire, is the same under all their variations, and affords an easy transition of the imagination from one situation of the body to another.

But this is still more remarkable, when we add a *sympathy* of parts to their *common end*, and suppose that they bear to each other, the reciprocal relation of cause and effect in all their actions and operations. This is the case with all animals and vegetables; where not only the several parts have a reference to some general purpose, but also a mutual dependance on, and connexion with each other. The effect of so strong a relation is, that tho' every one must allow, that in a very few years both vegetables and animals endure a *total* change, yet we still attribute identity to them, while their form, size, and substance are entirely alter'd. An oak, that grows from a small plant to a large tree, is still the same oak; tho' there be not one particle of matter, or figure of its parts the same. An infant becomes a man, and is sometimes fat, sometimes lean, without any change in his identity.

We may also consider the two following phænomena, which are remarkable in their kind. The first is, that tho' we commonly be able to distinguish pretty exactly betwixt numerical and specific identity, yet it sometimes happens, that we confound them, and in our thinking and reasoning employ the one for the other. Thus a man, who hears a noise, that is frequently interrupted and renew'd, says, it is still the same noise; tho' 'tis evident the sounds have only a specific identity or resemblance, and there is nothing numerically the same, but the cause, which produc'd them. In like manner it may be said without breach of the propriety of language, that such a church, which was formerly of brick, fell to ruin, and that the parish rebuilt the same church of free-stone, and according to modern architecture. Here neither the form nor materials are the same, nor is there any thing common to the two objects, but their relation to the inhabitants of the parish; and yet this alone is sufficient to make us denominate them the same. But we must observe, that in these cases the first object is in a manner annihilated before the second comes into existence; by which means, we are never presented in any one point of time with the idea of difference and multiplicity; and for that reason are less scrupulous in calling them the same.

Secondly, We may remark, that tho' in a succession of related objects, it be in a manner requisite, that the change of parts be not sudden nor entire, in order to preserve the identity, yet where the objects are in their nature changeable and inconstant, we admit of a more sudden transition, than wou'd otherwise be consistent with that relation. Thus as the nature of a river consists in the motion and change of parts; tho' in less than four and twenty hours these be totally alter'd; this hinders not the river from continuing the same during several ages. What is natural and essential to any thing is, in a manner, expected; and what is expected makes less impression, and appears of less moment, than what is unusual and extraordinary. A considerable change of the former kind seems really less to the imagination, than the most trivial alteration of the latter; and by breaking less the continuity of the thought, has less influence in destroying the identity.

We now proceed to explain the nature of *personal identity*, which has become so great a question in philosophy, especially of late years in *England*, where all the abstruser sciences are study'd with a peculiar ardour and application. And here 'tis evident, the same method of reasoning must be continu'd, which has so successfully explain'd the identity of plants, and animals, and ships, and houses, and of all the compounded and changeable productions either of art or nature. The identity, which we ascribe to the mind of man, is only a fictitious one, and of a like kind with that which we ascribe to vegetables and animal bodies. It cannot,

therefore, have a different origin, but must proceed from a like operation of the imagination upon like objects.

But lest this argument shou'd not convince the reader; tho' in my opinion perfectly decisive; let him weigh the following reasoning, which is still closer and more immediate. 'Tis evident, that the identity, which we attribute to the human mind, however perfect we may imagine it to be, is not able to run the several different perceptions into one, and make them lose their characters of distinction and difference, which are essential to them. 'Tis still true, that every distinct perception, which enters into the composition of the mind, is a distinct existence, and is different, and distinguishable, and separable from every other perception, either contemporary or successive. But, as, notwithstanding this distinction and separability, we suppose the whole train of perceptions to be united by identity, a question naturally arises concerning this relation of identity; whether it be something that really binds our several perceptions together, or only associates their ideas in the imagination. That is, in other words, whether in pronouncing concerning the identity of a person, we observe some real bond among his perceptions, or only feel one among the ideas we form of them. This question we might easily decide, if we wou'd recollect what has been already prov'd at large, that the understanding never observes any real connexion among objects, and that even the union of cause and effect, when strictly examin'd, resolves itself into a customary association of ideas. For from thence it evidently follows, that identity is nothing really belonging to these different perceptions, and uniting them together; but is merely a quality, which we attribute to them, because of the union of their ideas in the imagination, when we reflect upon them. Now the only qualities, which can give ideas an union in the imagination, are these three relations above-mention'd. These are the uniting principles in the ideal world, and without them every distinct object is separable by the mind, and may be separately consider'd, and appears not to have any more connexion with any other object, than if disjoin'd by the greatest difference and remoteness. 'Tis, therefore, on some of these three relations of resemblance, contiguity and causation, that identity depends; and as the very essence of these relations consists in their producing an easy transition of ideas; it follows, that our notions of personal identity, proceed entirely from the smooth and uninterrupted progress of the thought along a train of connected ideas, according to the principles above-explain'd.

The only question, therefore, which remains, is, by what relations this uninterrupted progress of our thought is produc'd, when we consider the successive existence of a mind or thinking person. And here 'tis evident we must confine ourselves to resemblance and causation, and must drop contiguity, which has little or no influence in the present case.

To begin with *resemblance;* suppose we cou'd see clearly into the breast of another, and observe that succession of preceptions, which constitutes his mind or thinking principle, and suppose that he always preserves the memory of a considerable part of past perceptions; 'tis evident that nothing cou'd more contribute to the bestowing a relation on this succession amidst all its variations. For what is the memory but a faculty, by which we raise up the images of past perceptions? And as an image necessarily resembles its object, must not the frequent placing of these resembling perceptions in the chain of thought, convey the imagination more easily from one link to another, and make the whole seem like the continuance of one object? In this particular, then, the memory not only discovers the identity, but also contributes to its production, by producing the relation of resemblance among the perceptions. The case is the same whether we consider ourselves or others.

As to *causation;* we may observe, that the true idea of the human mind, is to consider it as a system of different perceptions or different existences, which are link'd together by the relation of cause and effect, and mutually produce, destroy, influence, and modify each other. Our impressions give rise to their correspondent ideas; and these ideas in their turn produce other impressions. One thought chases another, and draws after it a third, by which it is expell'd in its turn. In this respect, I cannot compare the soul more properly to any thing than to a republic or commonwealth, in which the several members are united by the reciprocal ties of government and subordination, and give rise to other persons, who propagate the same republic in the incessant changes of its parts. And as the same individual republic may not only change its members, but also its laws and constitutions; in like manner the same person may vary his character and disposition, as well as his impressions and ideas, without losing his identity. What-

ever changes he endures, his several parts are still connected by the relation of causation. And in this view our identity with regard to the passions serves to corroborate that with regard to the imagination, by the making our distant perceptions influence each other, and by giving us a present concern for our past or future pains and pleasures.

As memory alone acquaints us with the continuance and extent of this succession of perceptions, 'tis to be considered, upon that account chiefly, as the source of personal identity. Had we no memory, we never shou'd have any notion of causation, nor consequently of that chain of causes and effects, which constitute our self or person. But having once acquir'd this notion of causation from the memory, we can extend the same chain of causes, and consequently the identity of our persons beyond our memory, and can comprehend times, and circumstances, and actions, which we have entirely forgot, but suppose in general to have existed. For how few of our past actions are there, of which we have any memory? Who can tell me, for instance, what were his thoughts and actions on the first of January 1715, the 11th of March 1719, and the 3d of August 1733? Or will he affirm, because he has entirely forgot the incidents of these days, that the present self is not the same person with the self of that time; and by that means overturn all the most establish'd notions of personal identity? In this view, therefore, memory does not so much *produce* as *discover* personal identity, by shewing us the relation of cause and effect among our different perceptions. 'Twill be incumbent on those, who affirm that memory produces entirely our personal identity, to give a reason why we can thus extend our identity beyond our memory.

The whole of this doctrine leads us to a conclusion, which is of great importance in the present affair, viz., that all the nice and subtile questions concerning personal identity can never possibly be decided, and are to be regarded rather as grammatical than as philosophical difficulties. Identity depends on the relations of ideas; and these relations produce identity, by means of that easy transition they occasion. But as the relations, and the easiness of the transition may diminish by insensible degrees, we have no just standard, by which we can decide any dispute concerning the time, when they acquire or lose a title to the name of identity. All the disputes concerning the identity of connected objects are merely verbal, except so far as the relation of parts gives rise to some fiction or imaginary principle of union, as we have already observ'd.

What I have said concerning the first origin and the uncertainty of our notion of identity, as apply'd to the human mind, may be extended with little or no variation to that of *simplicity*. An object, whose different co-existent parts are bound together by a close relation, operates upon the imagination after much the same manner as one perfectly simple and indivisible, and requires not a much greater stretch of thought in order to its conception. From this similarity of operation we attribute a simplicity to it, and feign a principle of union as the support of this simplicity, and the center of all the different parts and qualities of the object.

Appendix[5]

I had entertain'd some hopes, that however deficient our theory of the intellectual world might be, it wou'd be free from those contradictions, and absurdities, which seem to attend every explication, that human reason can give of the material world. But upon a more strict review of the section concerning *personal identity*, I find myself involv'd in such a labyrinth, that, I must confess, I neither know how to correct my former opinions, nor how to render them consistent. If this be not a good *general* reason for scepticism, 'tis at least a sufficient one (if I were not already abundantly supplied) for me to entertain a diffidence and modesty in all my decisions. I shall propose the arguments on both sides, beginning with those that induc'd me to deny the strict and proper identity and simplicity of a self or thinking being.

When we talk of *self* or *substance*, we must have an idea annex'd to these terms, otherwise they are altogether unintelligible. Every idea is deriv'd from preceding impressions; and we have no impression of self or substance, as something simple and individual. We have, therefore, no idea of them in that sense.

Whatever is distinct, is distinguishable; and whatever is distinguishable, is separable by the thought or imagination. All perceptions are distinct. They are, therefore, distinguishable, and separable, and may be conceiv'd as separately exis-

tent, and may exist separately, without any contradiction or absurdity.

When I view this table and that chimney, nothing is present to me but particular perceptions, which are of a like nature with all the other perceptions. This is the doctrine of philosophers. But this table, which is present to me, and that chimney, may and do exist separately. This is the doctrine of the vulgar, and implies no contradiction. There is no contradiction, therefore, in extending the same doctrine to all the perceptions.

In general, the following reasoning seems satisfactory. All ideas are borrow'd from preceding perceptions. Our ideas of objects, therefore, are deriv'd from that source. Consequently no proposition can be intelligible or consistent with regard to objects, which is not so with regard to perceptions. But 'tis inteillgible and consistent to say, that objects exist distinct and independent, without any common *simple* substance or subject of inhesion. This proposition, therefore, can never be absurd with regard to perceptions.

When I turn my reflexion on *myself*, I never can perceive this *self* without some one or more perceptions; nor can I ever perceive any thing but the perceptions. 'Tis the composition of these, therefore, which forms the self.

We can conceive a thinking being to have either many or few perceptions. Suppose the mind to be reduc'd even below the life of an oyster. Suppose it to have only one perception, as of thirst or hunger. Consider it in that situation. Do you conceive any thing but merely that perception? Have you any notion of *self* or *substance*? If not, the addition of other perceptions can never give you that notion.

The annihilation, which some people suppose to follow upon death, and which entirely destroys this self, is nothing but an extinction of all particular perceptions; love and hatred, pain and pleasure, thought and sensation. These therefore must be the same with self; since the one cannot survive the other.

Is *self* the same with *substance*? If it be, how can that question have place, concerning the subsistence of self, under a change of substance? If they be distinct, what is the difference betwixt them? For my part, I have a notion of neither, when conceiv'd distinct from particular perceptions.

Philosophers begin to be reconcil'd to the principle, *that we have no idea of external substance, distinct from the ideas of particular qualities.* This must pave the way for a like principle with regard to the mind, *that we have no notion of it, distinct from the particular perceptions.*

So far I seem to be attended with sufficient evidence. But having thus loosen'd all our particular perceptions, when[6] I proceed to explain the principle of connexion, which binds them together, and makes us attribute to them a real simplicity and identity; I am sensible, that my account is very defective, and that nothing but the seeming evidence of the precedent reasonings cou'd have induc'd me to receive it. If perceptions are distinct existences, they form a whole only by being connected together. But no connexions among distinct existences are ever discoverable by human understanding. We only *feel* a connexion or determination of the thought, to pass from one object to another. It follows, therefore, that the thought alone finds personal identity, when reflecting on the train of past perceptions, that compose a mind, the ideas of them are felt to be connected together, and naturally introduce each other. However extraordinary this conclusion may seem, it need not surprise us. Most philosophers seem inclin'd to think, that personal identity *arises* from consciousness; and consciousness is nothing but a reflected thought or perception. The present philosophy, therefore, has so far a promising aspect. But all my hopes vanish, when I come to explain the principles, that unite our successive perceptions in our thought or consciousness. I cannot discover any theory, which gives me satisfaction on this head.

In short there are two principles, which I cannot render consistent; nor is it in my power to renounce either of them, viz., *that all our distinct perceptions are distinct existences,* and *that the mind never perceives any real connexion among distinct existences.* Did our perceptions either inhere in something simple and individual, or did the mind perceive some real connexion among them, there wou'd be no difficulty in the case. For my part, I must plead the privilege of a sceptic, and confess, that this difficulty is too hard for my understanding. I pretend not, however, to pronounce it absolutely insuperable. Others, perhaps, or myself, upon more mature reflexions, may discover some hypothesis, that will reconcile those contradictions.

Endnotes

[1] This selection is a part of "Of Skepticism With Regard to the Senses," which is section 2 of Part IV of Book I of Hume's *Treatise of Human Nature*, first published in 1739.

[2] Sect. 5, Part II, Book I, *Treatise of Human Nature.*

[3] This selection is section 6 of Part IV of Book I of Hume's *Treatise of Human Nature*, first published in 1739.

[4] If the reader is desirous to see how a great genius may be influenc'd by these seemingly trivial principles of the imagination, as well as the mere vulgar, let him read my Lord *Shaftsbury*'s reasonings concerning the uniting principle of the universe, and the identity of plants and animals. See his *Moralists* or *Philosophical rhapsody.*

[5] This selection is from the appendix Hume attached to the first edition of Book III of his *Treatise of Human Nature*, which was first published in 1740.

[6] Book I.

16. *Problems of Identity*

RODERICK M. CHISHOLM

In "Problems of Identity," Roderick Chisholm, emeritus professor of philosophy at Brown Univeristy, attempts to show why many of the traditional metaphysical approaches to identity (e.g., Hobbes') will not work for persons. Basically, he defends Reid's intuition that personal identity requires the persistence of some "unity." But unlike Hume, Chisholm claims to find some experienced basis for personal identity. Referring to the work of Brentano (see his essay in Part III), Chisholm suggests the complex diversity of experience (for example, seeing and hearing something at the same time) demands that the different components of the experience be united in the experience of a single self. Similarly, Chisholm claims it must be the same self that can have different experiences at different times. In the course of his discussion, Chisholm considers and rejects the "doctrine of temporal parts." This view, which is congenial to the tenseless analysis of time (see Part I), analyses change and identity in terms of the relations among the temporal parts of an object's history (see the following article by Armstrong). Chisholm feels this kind of analysis is contrary to experience and not needed to account for the fact that the same object can have different properties at different times.

Identity and Persistence

I shall discuss what is, for me at least, an extraordinarily difficult and puzzling topic: that of persistence, or identity through time. I have discussed this topic on other occasions when, I regret to say, I have been even more confused than I am now. But I find that other philosophers are confused too. I think I have made some progress. And so I feel justified, therefore, in taking up the topic once again.

I will begin by formulating three different puzzles, Puzzle A, Puzzle B, and Puzzle C, and by describing a uniform way of treating all three puzzles. The treatment in question is reasonably plausible in connection with Puzzle A, which has to do with identity through space. It is fairly plausible in

connection with Puzzle B, which has to do with the identity of a familiar type of physical thing through time. But, I will try to suggest, the treatment is entirely implausible in connection with Puzzle C, which has to do with the identity of persons through time. I will also try to suggest that by contemplating the nature of a person, or, better, by contemplating upon the nature of *oneself*, we will be led to a more adequate view of the nature of persistence, or identity through time. My approach to these questions is very much like that of Leibniz, Bishop Butler, and Thomas Reid.[1]

We begin, then, with Puzzle A. We will depict, somewhat schematically, a dispute about the identity of roads. In the northern part of the city, there is a road composed of two parts: *A*, which is the

$$
\begin{array}{cc}
AB & \\
CD & \\
EF & GH \\
IJ & KL \\
\end{array}
$$

south-bound lane, and *B*, which is the north-bound lane. Proceeding down the south-bound lane, we come to another area where the road is composed, in a similar way, of C and D. Then we arrive at a fork in the road: one can go in a southeasterly direction through GH to KL, or one can go in a southwesterly direction through EF to IJ. The road from AB to IJ is called "Elm Street" and the road from AB to KL is called "Route 42." Elm Street has been in approximately the same place for more than 100 years, while Route 42 is less than 10 years old. But Route 42 is a three-lane highway with the same kind of topping from one end to the other, while Elm Street switches at the fork from tar to concrete and from three lanes to two. We can imagine now that a dispute could develop over the question: "If you start out at AB and stay on the same road, will you end up at IJ or at KL?" The Elm Street faction insists that you will end up at IJ and the Route 42 group insists that it will be at KL. They consult a metaphysician and he gives them this advice:

"Your dispute has to do with the following six objects among others: (1) the northern stretch of road AB; (2) the southwestern stretch IJ; (3) the southeastern stretch KL; (4) a road which begins at AB and ends at IJ, that is, Elm Street; (5) a road which begins at AB and ends up at KL, that is, Route 42; and (6) a Y-shaped object with AB as its handle and IJ and KL as the ends of its forks. These objects overlap in various ways but they are six different things. IJ is not identical with KL; neither of these is identical with AB or with Elm Street or with Route 42 or with the Y-shaped object; and Elm Street, Route 42, and the Y-shaped object are different things despite their overlap. These six different things are equally respectable ontologically. No one of them is any less genuine an entity than any of the others.

"Now there is no dispute about any observational data. You have agreed about what it is that is called 'Elm Street', about what it is that is called 'Route 42', about the number of lanes in the various places, and about what parts are composed of what. Your dispute, then, has to do with criteria for *constituting the same road* or, as we may also put it, with criteria for applying the expression 'x constitutes the same road as does y'. Both groups should be able to see that the members of the other side have correctly *applied* the criterion they happen to be using. That is to say, given the criterion of the Elm Street faction, it would be true to say that if you start at AB and continue on the same road you will end up at IJ. And given the criterion of the

Route 42 group, it would be true to say that you would end up instead at KL. It's just a matter, therefore, of your employing conflicting criteria. You have different standards for applying such expressions as 'the same road' and 'x constitutes the same road as does y'.

"I realize you may be inclined to say that you have the 'right' criterion and that the other people have the 'wrong' one. But think more carefully and try to see just what it is you would be trying to express if you talk that way. For once you see what it is, we can call in other experts—in all probability nonphilosophers this time—and they will settle the dispute for you.

"Thus if you think you are using the expression 'the same road' the way the majority of people do or the way the traffic experts of our culture circle or some other more select group uses it and if you think the other group is not using the expression that way, then we can call in the linguists. They can work up questionnaires and conduct surveys and, it may be hoped, you will soon find out who is right. Or perhaps your concern is not with the ways in which other people may happen to use 'the same road'. You may think only that your way of using it is the most convenient one. If you think, say, that we can handle traffic problems more efficiently by using the expression your way than by using it the other way, then the traffic experts and psychologists should be able to help. Or if you think that your use is the better one for promoting some other kind of good, there will be some expert who will know better than any of us.

"Finally, keep in mind that if people had quite different interests from those that any of us now happen to have and if we had been brought up to play some language game very different from this one, there might be no temptation at all to use *either* of the present criteria. If you were grasshoppers, for example, you might be arguing whether the road from C to K goes through E or goes through I."

I think now we can leave the dispute about the road. As philosophers, surely, we have little or no interest in the outcome. I hope we can agree that, in this instance, the metaphysician's advice is fairly reasonable and that there is little more to be said.

But let us now consider what happens when he applies a similar treatment to two analogous problems having to do with identity or persistence through time. I will formulate Puzzle B and Puzzle C. It may be tempting to follow the metaphysician in his treatment of Puzzle B, but something is clearly wrong, I think, with his treatment of Puzzle C. I suggest that, it is not until we have seen what is wrong with his treatment of Puzzle C, that we can really appreciate the problem of identity through time.

Puzzle B is a version of the ancient problem of the Ship of Theseus. We now consider a dispute that might arise about the identity of ships through time. The ship when it first set sail was composed of two parts *A* and *B*. Parts of parts were replaced and at a later point in its history it was composed of *C* and *D* where previously it had been composed of *A* and *B*. At a certain point it underwent fission and went off, so to speak, in two different directions—one ship being composed of *E* and *F* going off toward the southwest and another ship being composed of *G* and *H* going off toward the southeast. The ship that went southwest ended up being composed of *I* and *J* and the one that went southeast

being composed of *K* and *L*. This time the question arises: "Had you boarded *AB* when it first set sail and remained on the same ship, would you now be on the southwesterly *IJ* or on the southeasterly *KL*?" The *IJ* faction may point out that, if you end up on *IJ*, you will have remained throughout on a wooden ship called *Theseus* and that, if you end up on *KL*, you will now be on an aluminum ship called *The East Coast Ferry*. The *KL* group may point out, to the contrary, that if you end up on *KL*, you will have remained throughout on a ship having the same daily schedule, the same crew, and the same traditions and that, if you end up on *IJ*, you will be on a weekend cruise ship having an amateur crew and nothing worth calling a tradition. Being impressed by the way in which our metaphysician handled the problem of the roads, the two parties turn to him for advice. And this is what he tells them:

"There is no difference in principle between the present problem and the problem of the roads. For just as an object that is extended through space at a given time has, for each portion of space that it occupies, a *spatial part* that is unique to that portion of space at that time, so, too, any object that persists through a period of time has, for each sub-

period of time during which it exists, a *temporal part* that is unique to that subperiod of time.

"Taking our cue from the problem of the roads, we see that in this case, too, there are six objects which are of special concern. Just as a road that extends through space has different spatial parts at the different places at which it exists, a ship that persists through time has different temporal parts at the different times at which it exists. So we may distinguish (1) the earlier temporal part *AB*; (2) the present southwestern part *IJ*; (3) the present southeastern part *KL*; (4) that temporally extended object now called the *Theseus* with the early part *AB*, the later part *IJ*, and *CD* and *EF* falling in between; (5) that temporally extended object now called *The East Coast Ferry* with the early part *AB*, the later part *KL*, and *CD* and *GH* falling in between; and (6), what you may not have noticed, a Y-shaped temporal object with *AB* as its root and *IJ* and *KL* as the ends of its forks. As in the previous case, these are different things despite their overlap and they are all on a par ontologically.

"There is no dispute about any of the observational data. You are in agreement about crews, schedules, stuff, and traditions, and about what things are called what. Your dispute has to do with *criteria* for constituting the same ship, or, as we may now also put it, with criteria for applying the expression '*x* constitutes the same ship as does *y*'. The members of each faction have correctly applied their own criteria. If you are inclined to say that your criterion is the right one and that the other one is the wrong one, reflect a little further and I'm sure we can find some nonphilosophical expert who can help you settle the question. Do you think, for example, that you are using 'the same ship' the way the majority of people do or the way the nautical people do? The linguists can check on that for you. Or do you think you are using it the way it's used in the courts? Then we can call in the lawyers. Or do you think that your way of using it is the most convenient one given your purposes or given the purposes of most people? State as clearly as you can what the purposes in question are and then we can find an expert who will help you out.

"Keep in mind that, if people had quite different interests and played a different language game, then there might be no temptation to use either of the present criteria. After all there are still other temporal objects involved here: for example, the temporally scattered object made up of *A*, *F*, and *L*, the one made up of *C*, *H*, and *J*, and so on. Some one of those might be what you would call a ship—if *you* were a different type of temporal object."

Let us not pause to evaluate this advice. For our interest in Puzzle B and its treatment is only transitional. I have spelled out the account only to prepare us for Puzzle C.

Puzzle C: Mr. Jones has learned somehow that he is about to undergo fission. Or, more accurately, he has learned that his body will undergo fission. It is now made up of parts *A* and *B*. Presently it will be made up of *C* and *D*. Then there will be fission; one body will go off as *EF* and end up as *IJ*, and the other will go off as *GH* and end up as *KL*. Then there will be the two men, *IJ* and *KL*. Or, to be more cautious, there will be a man who has *IJ* as his body and there will be a man who has *KL* as his body.

Mr. Jones knows that the man who ends up with *IJ* will have the distinctive physical characteristics—brain waves, fingerprints, and all the rest—that he, Mr. Jones, now has, and that the man who ends up as *KL* will not. He also knows that the inner parts of *IJ* will have evolved in the usual manner from the inner parts he has now, that is, from the inner parts of *AB*, whereas a number of the crucial organs within *KL* will have been transplanted from outside. But he knows further that the man who has *KL* as his body will have the memories, or a significant part of the memories, that he, Mr. Jones, now has, and what is more that the man will remember doing things that only Mr. Jones has ever done. Or perhaps we should say, more cautiously, that the man will *seem* to himself to remember—will *think he remembers*—having done those things. And the memory, or ostensible memory, will be extraordinarily accurate in points of detail. Mr. Jones now puts this question: "Will I be the one who ends up as *IJ* or will I be the one who ends up as *KL*?"

It has been said that there are "two main competing answers" to the question "What are the criteria for the identity of a person through time?" One of these is that "the criterion of the identity of a person is the identity of the body that he has." And the other is that "the criterion of the identity of a person is the set of memories which he has."[2] We will suppose that, according to the first of these

criteria ("the bodily criterion") the man who has *IJ* as his body is the same person as Mr. Jones; and according to the second of these criteria ("the memory criterion") the man who has *KL* as his body is the same person as Mr. Jones.

To make sure that Mr. Jones's interest in the question is not purely theoretical, let us suppose further that he has the following information: Though both men will languish during their final phases, the *IJ* and the *KL* phases, the man who ends up as *KL* will lead the most wretched of lives during his *GH* phase, and the man who ends up as *IJ* will lead a life of great happiness and value during his *EF* phase. And so Mr. Jones asks with some concern: "Which one am I going to be?"

The approach of the metaphysician should now be familiar. He will note that, for each portion of space that Mr. Jones's body now occupies there is a spatial part of Mr. Jones's body that is now unique to that portion of space. He will then point out that, for any period of time during which Mr. Jones will have existed, there is a *temporal part* of Mr. Jones that is unique to that period of time. Turning to the problem at hand, he will distinguish the following things among others: *AB*; *IJ*; *KL*; the thing that begins as *AB* and ends as *LJ*; the thing that begins as *AB* and ends as *KL*; and the Y-shaped object that begins as *AB* and ends as *IJ* in one place and *KL* in another. He will note that Mr. Jones is raising a question about criteria: "Is 'the memory criterion' or 'the bodily criterion' the correct criterion of what it is for someone at one time to constitute the same person as does someone at some other time?" He will point out to Mr. Jones that, in asking which is the correct criterion, he is in fact concerned with some more specific question. If he is asking how the majority of people, or how certain people, use the expression "same person," he should consult the linguists. If he is asking how the courts would deal with the question, he should look up the law books. And if he is asking, with respect to certain definite ends, what linguistic uses would best promote those ends, there will be authorities who can give him at least a probable answer. (*We* might remind Mr. Jones, however, that if he asks these empirical authorities how he, Mr. Jones, could best promote certain ends after the fission has taken place, then he should look very carefully at the answer.)

As before, the metaphysician will conclude with some general advice: "Keep in mind that, if people had quite different interests and played a different language game, there might be no temptation to use either the bodily criterion or the memory criterion. After all, there are still other temporal objects involved in your problem. With different interests and a different makeup, you might be more concerned with two of *them* instead of with the two that you happen to have singled out. You claim to know that the *EF* phase is going to be good and that the *GH* phase is going to be bad. You haven't noticed, apparently, that there is more than one person who will go through the *EF* phase and more than one person who will go through the *GH* phase. What other persons? For example, there is the one that goes from *AB* to *EF* to *KL*, and then there is the one that goes from *CD* through *GH* to *IJ*. If you had a different makeup, you might wish you were one of *those* and hope you're not the other."

If Mr. Jones is at all reasonable, he will feel at this point that something has gone wrong. However many persons the problem involves, if there is a person who starts out as *AB*, goes through *CD* and *EF* to *IJ*, there is not also *another* person who starts out as *AB*, goes through *EF*, and ends up as *KL*. And if there is a person who starts out as *AB*, goes through *CD* and *GH* to *KL*, there is not *another* person who goes through *GH* and ends up as *IJ*. (It would hardly be just to punish *two* persons for the sins that someone committed during the *GH* phase.) And, what is more important, after Mr. Jones has consulted the various empirical authorities, he will still wonder whether he has an answer to his question: "Which one am I going to be?"

Where did the metaphysician go wrong?

Going back for a moment to Route 42 in Puzzle A, consider what is involved when we say there is a Buick and an Oldsmobile on the road, the former a mile behind the latter. We are saying, of course, that there exists an x, namely, Route 42, which is such that a Buick is on x and an Oldsmobile is on x, a mile in front of the Buick. But this is to say that there is a y and a z which are distinct from x and from each other and which are such that the Buick is on y and not on z and the Oldsmobile is on z and not on y. And so we are referring to *three* different things in addition to the Oldsmobile and the Buick. We are referring, first, to Route 42 which both the Oldsmobile and the Buick are on; we are referring, secondly, to that portion of Route 42 which the Oldsmobile but not the Buick is on; and we are

referring, thirdly, to that portion of Route 42 which the Buick but not the Oldsmobile is on. Our metaphysician assumes that temporal differences are analogous.

What is involved when we say that a ship had been red and then subsequently became blue? According to our metaphysician we are, once again, referring to three different things. We are saying, of course, that there was an x, namely, the ship, which was such that x was red and then x became blue. And this, according to our metaphysician, is to say that there was a y and a z, each distinct from x and from each other, which were such that y was red and not blue and z was blue and not red. In addition to the ship, there was that "temporal part" of it which was red and that other "temporal part" of it which was blue.

It is very important to note that, according to the metaphysician, his thesis will be true whether or not any of the parts of the ship are ever replaced—or, more exactly, it will be true whether or not anything occurs that would *ordinarily* be described as replacement of the parts of the ship. Let the ship be such that we could describe it in our ordinary language by saying it has kept all its parts intactly, down to the smallest particles. Our metaphysician will nevertheless say that that temporal part of the ship which is red is other than that temporal part of the ship which is blue and that each of these is other than the ship itself.

And he maintains a similar thesis with respect to Puzzle C. Consider now the man who began with the body made up of *A* and *B* and ended up with *I* and *J*. What is involved in saying that he is sad one day and happy the next? Again, there will be an x, the man, such that x is sad and subsequently x is happy. And to say this, according to our metaphysician, is to say that there is also a y and a z each distinct from x and from each other and such that y is sad and z is happy. But is this true?

It may be instructive to compare the doctrine of our metaphysician with what Jonathan Edwards says in defense of the doctrine of original sin. Edwards is concerned with the question whether it is just to impute to you and me the sins that were committed by Adam. And he wishes to show that it is *as* just to attribute Adam's sins to us now as it is to attribute any *other* past sins to us now.

He appeals to the doctrine, which he accepts, that God not only created the world *ex nihilo* but constantly preserves or upholds the things which he creates. Without God's continued preservation of the world, all created things would fall into nothingness. Now Edwards says that "God's upholding created substance, or causing its existence in each successive moment, is altogether equivalent to an immediate *production out of nothing*, at each moment." In preserving the table in its being a moment from now, God will get no help from the table. It isn't as though the table will be there waiting to be upheld. If it were there waiting to be upheld, if it were available to God and ready for preservation, he would not *need* to uphold or preserve it. God does not uphold the table by making use of matter that is left over from an earlier moment. Edwards compares the persistence of such things as the table with that of the reflection or image on the surface of a mirror. "The image that exists this moment, is not at all *derived* from the image which existed the last preceding moment. . . . If the succession of new *rays* be intercepted, by something interposed between the object and the glass, the image immediately ceases; the *past existence* of the image has no influence to uphold it, so much as for one moment. Which shows that the image is altogether completely remade every moment; and strictly speaking, is in no part numerically the same with that which existed in the moment preceding. And truly so the matter must be with the *bodies* themselves, as well as their images. They also cannot be the same, with an absolute identity, but must be wholly renewed every moment. . . ." Edwards summarizes his doctrine of preservation this way: "If the existence of created *substance*, in each successive moment, be wholly the effect of God's immediate power, in *that* moment, without any dependence on prior existence, as much as the first creation out of *nothing*, then what exists at this moment, by this power, is a *new effect*, and simply and absolutely considered, not the same with any past existence. . . ."[3]

This conception of persisting physical things, though not its theological basis, is also defended by a number of contemporary philosophers. It may be found, for example, in the axiom system concerning things and their parts that is developed in Carnap's *Introduction to Symbolic Logic*.[4] Carnap's system is derived from the systems developed by J. H. Woodger and Alfred Tarski, in Woodger's *The Axiomatic Method in Biology*.[5] These authors say that, for every moment at which a thing exists there

is a set of momentary parts of the thing; none of these parts exists at any other moment; and the thing itself is the sum of its momentary parts.[6]

The thing that constitutes you now, according to this view, is diverse from the things that have constituted you at any other moment, just as you are diverse from every other person who exists now. But God, according to Jonathan Edwards, can contemplate a collection of objects existing at different times and "treat them as one." He can take a collection of various individuals existing at different times and think of them as all constituting a single individual. Edwards appeals to a doctrine of truth by divine convention; he says that God *"makes truth* in affairs of this nature." Like our metaphysician, God could regard temporally scattered individuals—you this year, me last year, and General De Gaulle the year before that—as comprising a single individual. And then he could justly punish you this year and me last year for the sins that General De Gaulle committed the year before that. And so, Edwards concludes, "No solid reason can be given, why God . . . may not establish a constitution whereby the natural posterity of Adam . . . should be treated as *one* with him, for the derivation, either of righteousness, and communion in rewards, or of the loss of righteousness, and consequent corruption and guilt."

Like our metaphysician, Edwards is impressed by what he takes to be the analogy between space and time. To persuade his reader that God could reasonably regard Adam's posterity as being one with Adam, he asserts that there would be no problem at all if Adam's posterity *coexisted* with Adam. If Adam's posterity had "somehow *grown out of him*, and yet remained *contiguous* and literally *united to him*, as the branches to a tree, or the members of the body to the head; and had all, before the fall, existed together at the *same time*, though in *different places*, as the head and members are in different places," surely then, Edwards says, God could treat the whole collection as "one moral whole" with each of us as its parts. And if a collection of persons existing in different places can be thought of as a single moral whole, why not also a collection of persons existing at different times?

What are we to say of all this? What Jonathan Edwards and our metaphysician have left out, if I am not mistaken, is what has traditionally been called the *unity* of every real thing. Leibniz said that we acquire this notion of unity by reflecting upon our own nature.[7] I suggest that this is so and that if we reflect "upon our own nature," we will see what is wrong with the Edwardian doctrine and with the solution to Puzzle C.

Edwards was even mistaken in his spatial figure. If we think of Adam's posterity as growing out of Adam's body, with me here and you there and Adam some place in between, we cannot properly regard the resulting whole as "a moral unity." Though there may be just one body involved there will be irreducibly many persons if one of them is me, another you, and a third Adam.

Let me quote to you from the chapter "On the Unity of Consciousness" from Franz Brentano's *Psychologie vom empirischen Standpunkt.* Brentano asks whether when we consider our own consciousness at any moment we find a real unified whole or a bare multiplicity—what he called a mere *collectivum* and not a unity or unitary whole. Suppose you find yourself hearing a certain sound and seeing a certain color, as you do now, and you realize that these are two different experiences. Could one conceivably say that the thing that is doing the seeing is *other* than the thing that is doing the hearing? "If the presentation of the color is to be ascribed to one thing and the presentation of the sound to another, is the presentation of the difference to be ascribed to the one, or to the other, or to both together, or to a third thing?" If one thing is doing the hearing and another thing is doing the seeing, how would either of *those* things become aware of the fact that there are two different experiences going on, one the hearing and the other the seeing? It wouldn't do, Brentano says, to attribute the perception of the difference to some *third* thing—some thing other than the thing that's doing the seeing and other than the thing that's doing the hearing. Should we ascribe the perception of the difference then to the *two* different things—to the seer and to the hearer? "This, too, would be ridiculous. It would be as though one were to say that, although neither a blind man nor a deaf man can perceive the difference between a color and a tone, the two of them can perceive it together when the one sees and the other hears. . . . When we combine the activities of the blind man and the deaf man, we have only a *collectivum*, not a real unitary thing [*immer nur ein Kollektiv, niemals ein einheitliches wirkliches Ding*]. Whether the blind man and the deaf man are close together or far apart makes no difference. It wouldn't make any difference

whether they lived in the same house, or whether they were Siamese twins, or whether they had developed even more inseparably together. It is only when the color and the sound are presented to one and the same individual thing, that it is thinkable that they may be compared with each other."[8]

In short, when you see and hear something at the same time, the experience cannot be adequately described by saying "There exists an x and a y such that x sees something, y hears something, and x is other than y." We can use just one personal variable ("There exists an x such that x sees something and x also hears it") or if we use two ("There exists an x such that x hears something and there exists a y such that y hears it"), then we must add that their values are one and the same ("x is identical with y").

Brentano discussed the kind of unity that is involved when we are aware of ourselves as having two different experiences, seeing and hearing, at the same time. Let us now consider, analogously, the kind of unity that is involved when we are aware of ourselves as having different experiences throughout an interval of time. This is what happens when, as now, you are listening to someone talking, or what happens when you are listening to a melody. But consider an experience of even shorter duration: one hears the birdcall "Bob White." The experience might be described by saying "There exists an x such that x hears 'Bob' and x hears 'White'." But we want to make sure we are not talking about the experience wherein one hears two sounds at once—'Bob' from one bird and 'White' from another. And so we might say "There exists an x and two times, t^1 *and* t^2, such that t^2 is later than t^1, and such that x hears 'Bob' at t^1 and x hears 'White' at t^2." If we are not to reify times, we will put the matter another way, perhaps as "There exists an x such that x hears 'Bob' *before* x hears 'White' or as "There exists an x such that x hears 'Bob' *and then* x hears 'White'." But we are not now concerned with what is philosophically the best way to describe the passage of time. Our present concern is with the variable 'x' and the thing that it refers to.

We will say, then, "There exists an x such that x hears 'Bob' and then x hears 'White'." Jonathan Edwards and our metaphysician would say that the experience could be adequately described by using two variables: "There exists a y and a z such that y hears 'Bob' and z hears 'White'." But the latter sentence is *not* adequate to the experience in question. The man who has the experience knows not only (1) that there is someone who hears 'Bob' and someone who hears 'White'. He also knows (2) that the one who hears 'Bob' is *identical with* the one who hears 'White'. And, what is crucial to the present problem, he knows (3) that his experience of hearing 'Bob' and his experience of hearing 'White' were not *also* had by two other things, each distinct from himself and from each other.

What are we to say, then, of the doctrine of "temporal parts," of the doctrine according to which, for every period of time during which an individual thing exists, there is a temporal part of that thing which is unique to that period of time? We can point out, as I have tried to do, that it is not adequate to the experience we have of ourselves. We can also point out that the doctrine multiplies entities beyond necessity. And, finally, we can criticize the case *for* the doctrine of temporal parts.

What is this case? It is based, presumably, upon the assumption that whatever may be said about spatial continuity and identity may also be said, *mutatis mutandis*, about temporal continuity and identity. If this assumption is correct, then the doctrine of temporal parts would seem to be true. We may say, as our metaphysician did: "Just as an object that is extended through space at a given time has, for each portion of space that it occupies, a *spatial part* that is unique to that portion of space at that time, so, too, any object that persists through a period of time has, for each subperiod of time during which it exists, a *temporal part* that is unique to that subperiod of time." But is it correct to assume that whatever may be said about spatial continuity and identity may also be said, *mutatis mutandis*, about temporal continuity and identity? I would say that there is a fundamental *disanalogy* between space and time.

The disanalogy may be suggested by saying simply: "One and the same thing cannot be in two different places at one and the same time. But one and the same thing can be at two different times in one and the same place." Let us put the point of disanalogy, however, somewhat more precisely.

When we say, "A thing cannot be in two different places at one and the same time," we mean that it is not possible for *all* the parts of the thing to be in one of the places at that one time and *also* to be in the other of the places at that same time. It *is* possible, of course, for *some* part of the thing to be

in place at a certain time and *another* part of the thing to be in another place at that time. And to remove a possible ambiguity in the expression "all the parts of a thing," let us spell it out to "all the parts that the thing ever will have had."

Instead of saying simply, "a thing cannot be in two different places at one and the same time," let us say this: "It is *not* possible for there to be a thing which is such that all the parts it ever will have had are in one place at one time and also in another place at that same time." And instead of saying "a thing can be at two different times in one and the same place," let us say this: "It *is* possible for there to be a thing which is such that all the parts it ever will have had are in one place at one time and also in that same place at another time."

It seems to me to be clear that each of these two theses is true and therefore that there is a fundamental disanalogy between space and time. And so if the case *for* the doctrine of temporal parts presupposes that there is no such disanalogy, then the case is inadequate. (We may, of course, appeal to the doctrine of temporal parts in order to *defend* the view that there is no such disanalogy. We may use it, in particular, to criticize the second of the two theses I set forth above, the thesis according to which it is possible for there to be a thing which is such that all the parts it ever will have had are in one place at one time and also in that same place at another time. But what, then, is the case *for* the doctrine of temporal parts?)

The doctrine of temporal parts is sometimes invoked as a solution to this type of puzzle. "(i) Johnson was President five years ago but is not President now. Therefore (ii) something can be truly said of the Johnson of five years ago that cannot be truly said of the Johnson of now. Hence (iii) the Johnson of five years ago is other than the Johnson of now. How, then, are they related?" The proposed solution is "they are different temporal parts of the same person." But it is simpler just to note that (ii) is false. *Nothing* can truly be said of the Johnson of five years ago that cannot be truly said of the Johnson of now. The Johnson of now, like the Johnson of five years ago, *was* President five years ago, and the Johnson of five years ago, like the Johnson of now, is *not* President now. But if (ii) is false, then the derivation of (iii) is invalid. And so the puzzle disappears.

Mr. Jones's problem, the problem of Puzzle C, is much more difficult than our metaphysician thought it was. I fear that we cannot help him either, but we may point out, in conclusion, certain considerations which would be relevant to the solution of his problem.

Let us say that an "Edwardian object" is an individual thing such that, for any two different moments at which it exists, there is a set of things making it up at the one moment and another set of things making it up at the other moment and the two sets of things have no members in common. According to Jonathan Edwards and to the doctrine of temporal parts, *every* individual thing is Edwardian. I have suggested that some things that persist through time, namely, we ourselves, are *not* Edwardian. Some persisting things have a kind of *unity* through time that Edwardian objects, if there *are* any Edwardian objects, do not have.[9] How are we to characterize this unity?

We might characterize it by reference to "intact persistence." Let us say that a thing "persists intactly" if it has continued, uninterrupted existence through a period of time and if, at any moment of its existence, it has precisely the same parts it has at any other moment of its existence. Thus a thing that persists intactly would exist at at least two different times; for any two times during which it exists, it also exists at any time between those times; and at no time during which it exists does it have any part it does not have at any other time during which it exists. We might now define a "primary thing" as a thing that persists intactly during every moment of its existence. The simplest type of unity through time, then, would be that possessed by primary things. Other types of unity could then be described by reference to it.

It is tempting to say, in Leibnizian fashion: "There are things. Therefore there are primary things." But a somewhat more modest thesis would be this: Every extended period of time, however short, is such that some primary thing exists during some part of that time. I would suggest that it is only by presupposing this thesis that we can make sense of the identity or persistence of any individual thing through time.

So far as Mr. Jones's problem is concerned, we may note that it is at least possible that persons are primary things and hence that Mr. Jones is a primary thing. This would mean, of course, that we could not identify Mr. Jones with that object that persists without remaining intact which is his body. But for all anyone knows he might be identical with some physical thing which is a *part* of that body. We should also note that it is logically possible for a primary thing to persist from one time to another without there being any *criterion* by means of which anyone who had identified it at the earlier time could also identify it at the later time. Hence if Mr. Jones is a primary thing, it is possible that *he* will be the one who has bodily parts *IJ* even though neither he nor anyone else will ever know, or even have good reason to believe, that the man who now has bodily parts *AB* is also the man who will have bodily parts *IJ*.[10]

Endnotes

[1] See Leibniz' *New Essays Concerning Human Understanding*, Book II, Chapter XXVII ("What Identity or Diversity Is"); Bishop Butler's dissertation "Of Personal Identity"; and Thomas Reid, *Essays on the Intellectual Powers of Man*, Essay III, Chapters IV and VI. I have discussed these questions in "The Loose and Popular and the Strict and Philosophical Senses of Identity," in Norman S. Care and Robert H. Grimm, eds., *Perception and Personal Identity* (Cleveland: The Press of Western Reserve University, 1969); and in "Identity Through Time," in Howard Keifer and Milton K. Munitz, eds., *Language, Belief, and Metaphysics* (Albany: State University of New York Press, 1970).

[2] See Terence Penelhum's article, "Personal Identity," in *The Encyclopedia of Philosophy*, ed. Paul Edwards (New York: Macmillan, 1967), Vol. VI.

[3] The quotations are from Edwards' *Doctrine of Original Sin Defended* (1758), Part IV, Chapter II.

[4] Rudolf Carnap, *Introduction to Symbolic Logic* (New York: Dover Publications, 1958), p. 213 ff.

[5] J. H. Woodger, *The Axiomatic Method in Biology* (Cambridge: Cambridge University Press, 1937); see especially pp. 55–63, and Appendix E by Alfred Tarski (pp. 161–172).

[6] A thing *a* is said to be the *sum* of a class *F*, provided only every member of the class *F* is a part of *a*, and every part of *a* has a part in common with some member of the class. If, as these authors postulate, every nonempty class has a sum, there would be, for example, an *individual thing* which is the sum of the class of men: Every man would be a part of this collective man and every part of this collective man would share a part with some individual man. The same would hold for that class the only members of which are this man and that horse. An opposing view is that of Boethius: A man and a horse are not one thing. See D. P. Henry, *The Logic of Saint Anselm* (Oxford: The Clarendon Press, 1967), p. 56.

[7] *New Essays Concerning Human Understanding,* Book II, Ch. 1, sec. 8.

[8] Franz Brentano, *Psychologie vom empirischen Standpunkt,* Vol. 1 (Leipzig: Felix Meiner, 1924), pp. 226–227.

[9] I have attributed to Carnap the view that every individual thing is Edwardian; see Carnap, *op. cit.,* p. 213 ff. I should note, however, that he is quite aware of what I have called the problem of the unity of a persisting thing through time. He is aware, for example, that such an object as the one that is composed of my temporal parts of this year, yours of last year, and General De Gaulle's of the year before that does not have the type of unity through time that other objects do. To secure the latter type of unity he introduces the concept of *genidentity.* "Following Kurt Lewin, we say that world-points [temporal slices] of *the same particle* are *genidentical"; op. cit.,* p. 198. (I have italicized "the same particle.") But if we do not multiply entities by assuming that every concrete individual is Edwardian, we need not multiply relations by supposing that there is a concept of *genidentity* in addition to that of identity, or persistence through time.

[10] Compare Sydney S. Shoemaker, "Comments," and Roderick M. Chisholm, "Reply," in *Perception and Personal Identity,* Norman S. Care and Robert H. Grimm, eds. (Cleveland: The Press of Case Western Reserve University, 1969).

17. *Identity Through Time*

DAVID M. ARMSTRONG

In this article, David M. Armstrong, professor of philosophy at the University of Sydney, distinguishes what he calls the "identity analysis" and the "relational analysis" of identity through time. These analyses provide different answers to the question In virtue of what are X and Y stages (or phases) of one and the same object P? Armstrong attempts to defend a relational analysis, according to which the identity of a thing is composed of suitably related temporal parts. He appeals to *causality* as the glue that unites the diverse parts into a single whole.

Some philosophers in their work are led on to ever greater complexity; others seek simplicity and clarity of argument and vision. Each type of mind serves to check the shortcomings of the other. In our age philosophy is more professionalized than ever before, so as a result the first sort of mind is in the ascendant. All the more important, therefore, is the role of those who will not let their thought be dissipated in endless ramifications. Richard Taylor's particular intellectual contribution has been to discover, or to restate, simple and direct, yet profound and forceful, arguments which lead to important conclusions about major philosophical issues. He has done this in a way which involves no sacrifice of contemporary standards of rigor and exactness.

From Peter van Inwagen, ed., *Time and Cause: Essays Presented to Richard Taylor,* pp. 67–78. Copyright © 1980 by D. Reidel Publishing Company. Reprinted by permission of Kluwer Academic Publishers.

Identity Through Time: The Identity and the Relational View

Two views may be taken of the identity of particulars through time. We may call them the identity view and the relational view. Many, but not all, contemporary analytical philosophers accept the relational view. So do I. Recently, however, as a result of working on the problem of universals, I have come to have more sympathy with the identity view. I still think it is false, but I do not think, as I used to think, that it is nonsense. In this paper I want to consider again the dispute between the two views.

It is to be understood that neither of these views challenges the truism that if X and Y are different phases of an object, P, then they are phases of one identical thing. The identity and the relational views are, rather, different philosophical analyses of the situations referred to in the previous sentence. I oppose an "identity" to a "relational" view because I believe that identity is not a genuine relation. If this is an incorrect belief, however, for our present purposes it means no more than that my terminology is ill-chosen.

I begin by trying to characterize the relational view. If we consider nonoverlapping phases in the history of the same particular, P, then, according to the relational view, such phases are in no way identical. What we have is simply a particular case of different *parts* of the same thing. They are temporal parts rather than spatial parts, but the adjectives 'temporal' and 'spatial' do not modify the meaning of the word 'parts.' These parts, themselves particulars, are related in various ways to each other and to further particulars. The holding of some of these relations *constitutes* what it is for the parts to be different temporal parts of P.

Consider, by way of comparison, nonoverlapping spatial parts of P at a certain instant of time. Very few philosophers would want to argue that such spatial parts are in any way identical with each other. These parts, themselves particulars, are related in various ways, to each other and to further particulars. The holding of some of these relations *constitutes* what it is for the parts to be different spatial parts of P. Just what these constituting relations are will depend upon what sort of thing P is. The relations between the handle of a cup and the rest of the cup which make the two particulars into a cup are rather different from the relations which make the soldiers of an army into an army. But the unity of P at a time seems secured simply by uniting relations between P's spatial parts at that time, or, in some cases, their relations to some further particular or particulars.

If we accept this view about the spatial case, it is natural to conclude that the temporal parts, that is, the phases, of P are also united to form P by nothing more than relations.

Nevertheless, we do have a sense that non-

overlapping phases of the history of the one particular are not mere different parts of the same particular, but are actually *identical* with each other in some deeper way. It is the same thing which existed yesterday and today, we are inclined to think, in a way that the different spatial parts of the same thing are not identical with each other in any way. We do have some intuitive sense that a relational analysis of identity through time is false and that an identity theory is true.

Is this feeling just nonsense, nonsense which, perhaps, appeals to us because of our deep emotional interest in the continuing of ourselves and other things which we cherish? I think that Hume thought it was nonsense, although he recognized that it was nonsense to which we are instinctively attracted. He spoke of the way in which we 'feign' an identity between the different phases of the same thing.[1]

A strong argument can be advanced in support of Hume's view that the identity account of identity through time is nonsense. Consider again two nonoverlapping phases of the particular P. However intimately they may be related, it seems impossible to deny that they are two wholly distinct particulars. This becomes clear when we consider that we can attribute properties and relations to both phases, and that these properties and relations may be different from (and even incompatible with) each other. P may be at one temperature during the first phase, another temperature during the second. Things which differ in their properties are different things. But if the two phases are different things, then they are not the same thing.

I think that this argument does show that nonoverlapping phases of the same particular are distinct particulars. What it fails to show, however, is that they are *wholly* distinct particulars. It leaves open the possibility that they are distinct, but not wholly distinct.

In thinking about identity there is a tendency for one's thought to be dominated by the two extreme cases. These cases may be illustrated by the complete identity of the morning star with the evening star, on the one hand, and the complete nonidentity of the morning star with the Red Planet, on the other. But we need to remember that there are intermediate cases: for instance, terraced houses which have a party wall in common, or unseparated Siamese twins. Another sort of case is that where phases of the same particular overlap but do not coincide completely. Wherever things overlap or stand as part to whole we have merely partial identity.

But what is the relevance of all this to the case, which we are considering, of *nonoverlapping* phases of a particular? The answer is that, given certain further assumptions, even different particulars of this sort may be partially identical. Suppose, in particular, that one rejects nominalism, the doctrine that nothing exists which is not a particular. Suppose that, as I do, one accepts the objective reality of (instantiated) universals. Suppose one holds that different particulars may have the very same, the *identical*, property, for instance, the same mass. One is then committed to saying that such particulars are (at least partially) identical in nature. And if identity is a univocal notion, as I believe it is, partial identity of nature entails partial identity.

To think along these lines is to have one's ideas about the complete nonidentity of nonoverlapping particulars shaken up in a fruitful way. But it is hardly to accept that nonoverlapping phases of the same particular could be identical *as particulars*.

To understand this latter possibility we need to consider what a particular is. The view which I accept is the orthodox view among those who are realists, that is, are believers in universals. A particular is, essentially, a particular-having-certain-properties-and-relations. Its particularity is distinguishable but not separable from its properties and relations. Following Scotus, we can say that it involves both thisness and nature, or with Aristotle that it is a this-such.

Against the background of this view we can now characterize the identity analysis of the identity of particulars through time. We may note as a preliminary that identity analyses are normally restricted to certain favored particulars, such as atoms and spiritual substances.[2] Suppose that X and Y are nonoverlapping phases of a particular P. X and Y are particulars themselves, particulars having certain properties and relations. The identity view is that the particularity or thisness of X is identical with the particularity or thisness of Y. The relational view is that they are distinct.

My present inclination is to say that both identity and relational analyses are intelligible hypotheses. I reject the identity analysis, looking rather to relations between different phases to secure the unity of a particular over time. But I do not think

that the identity view can be rejected as illogical. If it is to be rejected, then I think it must be rejected for Occamist reasons. The different phases exist, and so do their relations. These phases so related, it seems, are sufficient to secure identity through time for all particulars.

Locke on Identity Through Time

I suggest, then, that the identity view of identity through time is not illogical. The question is rather whether it is a postulation which is fruitful, or expedient, or which we are compelled, to make. I shall try now to illuminate the difficulties faced by an identity theory by a discussion of Locke's views.[3] Locke, I believe, accepted the identity view, at any rate for certain sorts of entity. I think that this is what he meant when he spoke of "identity of substance": ". . . whatever substance begins to exist, it must, during its existence, necessarily be the same".[4] Such identity appears to be one of the notions involved in the Lockean notion of a *substratum* which underlies and supports the properties and relations of things. Among other things, the substratum is that which is identical in the different phases of a thing's existence. However, this function does not seem to be an essential part of the doctrine of substratum. It is possible to have a less rich conception of substratum which could be combined with a relational theory of identity through time. Contrariwise, it would be possible to take an identity view and yet reject the notion of an underlying substratum. Locke's substratum, however, both underlies properties and relations and is also identical through different phases. It is the latter function only which we are interested in here.

But there is a difficulty for the identity view, a difficulty of which Locke is well aware:

> . . . if two or more atoms be joined
> together into the same mass, every one of
> those atoms will be the same, . . . and
> whilst they exist united together, the mass,
> consisting of the same atoms, must be the
> same mass, or the same body, let the parts
> be never so differently jumbled. *But if one
> of these atoms be taken away, or one new one*

added, it is no longer the same mass or the same body.[5]

From the perspective of a relational view of identity through time this can only seem to be extreme pedantry. For the relational theorist is not saddled with any very strict rules as to what will constitute 'the very same thing at a later time'. The rules may differ for different sorts of things. But Locke has less room for maneuver. On the basis of the science of his day Locke assumes, as we still assume, that ordinary physical objects are made up of atoms. Further he adopts an identity view of their identity through time. (Unlike our atoms, they are physically indivisible.) Now suppose that an ordinary physical object loses a few atoms and gains others over a period of time. The atoms which it loses continue their career elsewhere. What object at the latter time is identical with the object at the earlier time? For an identity theorist the best candidate *must be* the collection of the original atoms with which the object started out, in however scattered a state those atoms are at the later time. There the identity is complete. By comparison, the collection of atoms actually adhering together is only *partially* identical with the original collection. This, I believe, is why Locke wrote as he did in Section 4. The difficulty he is in is a difficulty only for one who holds an identity view. This in turn is evidence that, with respect to atoms, Locke did hold an identity view.

The situation is still more paradoxical for Locke in cases of objects all of whose matter is replaced over a period of time, as is said to occur in the case of the human body. Since the body in its later state does not contain a single one of the original atoms, it cannot even be partially identical with the body in its earlier state. They are two completely different substances.

What is Locke to do? He is well aware of this problem faced by an identity theory. He wants to give a nonskeptical account of identity through time for human and animal bodies, trees and so on. One solution for him would be to fall back on a relational analysis for such objects. And, indeed, when it comes to giving an account of *personal* identity Locke does embrace a relational analysis. In the case of the bodies of animals and men, however, his view appears to be different. He says of the bodies of animals that ". . . animal identity is preserved in identity of *life* and not of substance."[6] What is meant by "identity of life"? Locke, I believe, thinks of life here as a certain property which the animal possesses. In particular, it is a structural property, a way in which the (spatial) parts of the animal are related and organized.[7] Locke calls such a property a "mode", and, when summing up his position, after having said that ". . . whatever substance begins to exist, it must, during its existence, necessarily be the same; . . ." he also says that ". . . whatsoever mode begins to exist, during its existence it is the same."[8]

I think that what he is suggesting here is an identity theory for properties as well as substances. Suppose that particular a has property L at t_1 and that b has L at t_2. Suppose, also, that a and b are not even partially 'identical in substance.' It may nevertheless be the case that L at t_1 is identical with L at t_2. If so, then it can be said that a and b, although not different phases of the same *substance*, are different phases in the existence of the same L. Suppose L to be the property of *being a living thing*. Then a at t_1 and b at t_2 are different phases in the existence of the same living thing. It might have been a caterpillar at t_1 and a butterfly at t_2.

It seems that a restriction will have to be put upon the sort of property which L is. It will have to be the sort of property which 'divides its instantiations' so that, at a given time, there is a certain definite number, finite or infinite, of instances of L in the universe. But, given this restriction to the sort of property L is, may not Locke postulate such an identity to account for the identity through time of such things as oaks?

There is, however, a difficulty which Locke must face here. If L is a property, and a property is a universal, then it is all too easy for L to be identical with itself at different times. For it is the same property wherever it is instantiated. This has the consequence, contrary to what Locke requires, that no special identity is set up between L, the property of a at t_1, and L, the property of b at t_2.

What this makes clear is that the conception of a property which Locke requires if he is to make good his notion of property identity through time is not that of a property as a universal but that of a property-instance. Certain philosophers, G. F. Stout was a prominent Anglo-Saxon example, hold that where two billiard balls are red or are spherical each of the balls has its own redness or sphericity. These properties are not universals, but are as particular as the billiard balls themselves. This position may or may not be combined with the admission that these particular properties themselves have universal properties ('This redness is red').

Let it now be given that the *L*-ness of *a* at t_1 and the *L*-ness of *b* at t_2 are particulars. Might they not be different phases of the same property-instance? And might we not give an identity rather than a relational account of what makes the two phases phases of the same property-instance? It is difficult to see how the distinction between particularity and nature could be drawn in the case of property-instances. But perhaps it could be said that the different phases in the existence of a property-instance are not numerically diverse, as a relational theorist would assert, but are instead completely identical.

When Locke asserts that "whatsoever mode begins to exist, during its existence it is the same", he appears to be asserting that we must give an identity analysis of the situation. I do not see that an identity analysis is required, but granted the conception of a property-instance, it seems to be a possible analysis.

Whether or not Locke explicitly holds to the notion of property-instance, I do not know. But it may be noted that it would fit in well with his general position. Locke talks freely of modes and qualities. Yet at the same time he is an explicit nominalist, holding that everything there is is a particular. If he is to be consistent, then he should hold that modes and qualities are particulars. And we have seen that this doctrine is required if he is to have any show of maintaining his doctrine of the identity of modes over time.

Locke's building, however, is only as strong as its foundations. And here I am given pause. It would take me too far afield to argue the matter in detail, but I am convinced that the notion of a property-instance turns out in the end to be an incoherent one. The idea of property is the idea of a nature, a nature which is different for different properties. I do not think that we can make any sense of the notion of nature unless we conceive of properties as universals. If this is correct, then Locke's ingenious attempt to supplement his identity view of the identity of substances through time with an identity view of the identity of modes through time, does not succeed.

The Relational View Defended

Relational theorists are inclined to argue that identity theories of identity through time are unintelligible. I have argued, however, that identity views are in good logical order. Perhaps postulating such identities is to fall into an abyss of nonsense but I cannot at present see that this is so. I have argued that Locke's notion of the identity of modes through time rests upon the notion of a property-instance, and the latter notion, I believe, is an untenable one. But if property-instances are acceptable, as I think they are not, then perhaps an identity theorist can even deal with the identity through time of things which 'change their substance' during that time.

But to show that the identity theory is in good logical order is not to show that we should adopt it. We can distinguish between, and refer to, different phases in the existence of the same particular. Since the different phases will, in general at least, have different properties, we must recognize them as different particulars. Such difference is compatible with partial identity, and to the extent that particulars have common properties they are partially identical. But why should we say that different phases of a particular are identical in their *particularity*? It is clear from our discussion of Locke's difficulties that, at best, it is plausible to say this only of certain favored individuals which do not change their substance, such as Newtonian atoms. But even in such a case it seems that unity can be secured for the enduring individual simply by relations between the phases. To extend the relational analysis to all enduring particulars is therefore economy of theory.

As already mentioned, one very powerful intellectual motive here is our unwillingness to contemplate an identity view with respect to the different spatial parts of the same thing. As Hume points out in his satirical way, in spatial cases we find the scholastic maxim, "*totum in toto, et totum in qualibet parte*" [the whole in the whole and in each part], quite unacceptable.[9] I should still want to argue, against Hume, that this identity view is, or can be presented as, an intelligible hypothesis. But surely an adequate account of spatial unities can be given without appealing to anything except the relations which the spatial parts of the object, be it nation, plant, animal, or stone, bear to each other? Any other account seems to be extravagance. But if a relational account is possible in the case of spatial unities, that is surely a strong reason for thinking that a similar account can be given of the different *phases* of the same thing. To deny the parallel is to set up a very dubious distinction between space and time.

I note here in passing that it has been a major theme in Richard Taylor's metaphysical reflection to reject various asymmetries between space and time. In this particular case, to combine an indentity view of identity through time with a relational view of identity across space seems even to involve scientific difficulty. For how is the combination to be effected if the simultaneity of spatially separated things is a relative rather than an absolute notion (a three-termed rather than a two-termed relation)?

If we are looking for relations to bind together the spatial parts of a thing so that it constitutes a thing of a certain sort, then, in general, we must appeal to different relations in the case of different sorts of things. But there is one relation which seems to be of quite peculiar importance in the case of the spatial parts. It is causation. In the case of solid objects, and particularly in the case of organisms, reciprocal causal relations between the spatial parts are all-important. By contrast, in the case of identity through time it is fashionable to set great store by spatiotemporal continuity. Again, however, I believe that we ought to set greater store by causal relations.

Hume was well aware of the importance of causality for relational accounts of identity through time. Ironically, it is probably the ontological downgrading of causality involved in Humean analyses of causality which has brought about the modern neglect of causal relation as a cement for different phases of the same thing. In the case of spatial parts the causal relation stares us in the face, so that it cannot be ignored.

I reject all Humean analyses of the causal relation. I do accept the Humean view that causal connection is a species of nomic connection. But I reject the view that nomic connection is nothing more than a regularity. In my view it is a regularity determined by a relation between universals. Causal connection *so conceived* seems capable of welding different phases of the same particular much more closely together than mere spatiotemporal continuity.

We do not normally speak of an earlier phase of an object as being the cause of a succeeding phase. But, in general at least, the earlier phase will be one of the nomically necessary conditions for the existence of the latter phase. Quite often, it will be absolutely nomically necessary. For instance, there is no known method, at least, of creating an adult human being except by creating an embryo and letting it develop under appropriate conditions. Embryonic and childhood phases appear, at least, to be absolutely nomically necessary for the existence of adult phases. But even where there is no such absolute nomical necessity, the earlier phases of an object may still be nomically necessary for later phases in a given particular situation. Given the concrete situation, the recent existence of this desk I write on is nomically necessary for the current existence of this desk. For consider the concrete situation which obtained in this room a few minutes ago, but subtract from it the desk. It is nomically impossible that in that situation a desk should come to be in my room now having the same properties as the original desk. In all probability, it is nomically impossible that in that situation a desk should come to be in my room now having rather similar properties to my desk.

So we seem justified in saying that, for the vast majority of cases at least, preceding phases of a thing are a necessary part of the total cause which brings the succeeding phases to be. The succeeding phases are got by way of the preceding phases, even if for many things (plants and animals especially) much cooperation from the environment is also needed. All this paves the way for the suggestion that, for most sorts of things at least, this causal relation between phases is a logically necessary condition for the *identity* of that thing through time.

The suggestion may be supported by considering a case where the usually suggested marks of identity through time, such as spatiotemporal continuity, are present but it is given that there is no causal connection between an earlier and a later 'phase'. (I call this method of arguing for a logically necessary condition 'the method of subtraction'.) Suppose, then, that there are two very powerful deities, each able to annihilate and create, who operate quite independently of each other. The first deity decides to annihilate Richard Taylor and does so at place *p*, time *t*. The second deity has not been watching what was happening. He decides to create a man at *p* and *t*. By a coincidence which can only be described as cosmic, he decides to give this man exactly the same physical and mental characteristics that Taylor had at p and t. Life goes on as usual.

The question is 'Did Taylor survive?'; 'Is Taylor$_2$ identical with Taylor$_1$?' I hope that the reader will agree with my intuition that he did not and is not. It is true, of course, that everybody earthly, including Taylor$_2$, will take for granted (because they will not even raise the question) that Taylor$_2$ is Taylor$_1$. But I think that that only shows that, given the right stage setting, it is logically possible that we should be deceived about anything at all, including Taylor about Taylor's identity.

We may note, incidentally, that a spatiotemporal gap seems quite unimportant provided the proper causal connection is present. If Taylor$_1$ appears to be annihilated at t_1 and p_1, and Taylor$_2$ comes into existence at t_2 and p_2 as, or much as, Taylor$_1$ was at t_1 and p_1, and if further the coming-to-be of Taylor$_2$ stands in a suitable causal relation to Taylor$_1$, then Taylor$_2$ would appear to be simply a later phase of the existence of Taylor$_1$. (It will be noticed that I say 'suitable' causal relation. I am far from thinking that I have adequately characterized the particular nature of the causal relation which holds between different phases of the same thing.) Spatiotemporal continuity of phases of things appears to be a mere result of, an observable sign of, the existence of a certain sort of causal relation between the phases.

I will finish this paper by considering another imaginary case which I think brings out quite strongly the attraction of an identity view of identity through time. But I will then argue that the puzzle which it creates for the relational view can be resolved by an appeal to causation.

In general, we can distinguish between a spherical object rotating on its own axis and that same object stationary. Consider, however, an exactly spherical object of completely homogeneous material containing no empty space at all. (Perhaps the situation is no more than logically possible.) Can a relational theory make the distinction between such a sphere stationary and the same sphere rotating on its own axis? Let it be granted that there is no way of telling whether rotation is occuring or not. It seems natural still to say that it might rotate or not rotate.

However, the difficulty for a relational theory of identity through time is that if the sphere is considered at any instant, its nature, including its relations to other things, appears to be exactly the same whether the sphere is rotating or not. But if the nature of the sphere supposedly stationary and the nature of the sphere supposedly rotating are the same at every instant, then it seems that, contrary to intuition, no distinction can be drawn between the sphere stationary and the sphere rotating.

It is here that the identity view becomes attractive, as enabling us to draw the distinction. Suppose that the sphere is not rotating. Consider, then, the eastern portion of the sphere from t_1 to t_2. The phases of the eastern portion will not merely remain identical in nature (as they would if the sphere were rotating), but will at all times be phases of the very same thing, in the sense which an identity analysis would yield. If, however, the sphere starts to rotate, then such an identity of the eastern portion will not be maintained except at the instants when the sphere has made exactly N revolutions, for any whole number N. On the relational analysis, however, it seems that there is no difference between the stationary and the rotating sphere.

But I suggest that a relational view can appeal to causality here as a means of differentiating the two cases, though it will certainly have to be causality conceived of in a non-Humean manner. If the sphere is stationary, then the phases of the eastern portion from t_1 to t_2 will bear to each other that particular causal relationship which is required for phases of the same thing to constitute phases of the same thing. In particular, the existence of the earlier phases will be nomically required for the existence of the later phases in a way which will not be so for different temporal phases of spatially separate portions of the sphere. If the sphere is rotating, the causal relations will at once be different.

The point may be brought out by considering the sphere with a segment removed. If the sphere is stationary, the empty segment stays stationary, because nothing comes from nothing. If the sphere rotates, then the empty segment moves round for exactly the same reason. The hypothesis that the sphere is really stationary but that the empty segment moves round is logically possible. But it demands annihilations and creations at every moment of revolution which we believe to be nomically impossible.

So I suggest that we should continue to favor a relational account of identity through time, appealing in particular to the relation of causality between the successive phases. Causality does seem to furnish a powerful enough cement to bond together different phases of the same thing. Only if this program encounters insuperable difficulties need we consider falling back upon an identity analysis.

Endnotes

[1] *A Treatise of Human Nature* 1. 4. 2, 6, ed. by L. A. Selby-Bigge, Oxford University Press, London, 1888, pp. 187–218, 251–263.

[2] One contemporary philosopher who appears to accept an identity analysis of identity through time, at any rate with respect to the *self*, is Roderick Chisholm. See Section 1 of his 'Problems of Identity' in *Identity and Individuation*, ed. by Milton K. Munitz, New York University Press, 1971, pp. 3–30.

[3] Presented in his rich though difficult Chap. 27 ('Of Identity and Diversity') in Book 2 of *An Essay Concerning Human Understanding*, 2 vols., ed. by A. C. Fraser, Oxford University Press, Oxford, 1894, Vol. 1, pp. 439–470.

[4] *Essay* 2. 27. 28; Fraser edition, Vol. 1, p. 469.

[5] *Essay* 2. 27. 4; Fraser edition, Vol. 1, pp. 442; emphasis added.

[6] *Essay* 2. 27. 12; Fraser edition, Vol. 1, p. 453; emphasis added.

[7] Section 5 may be quoted here (Fraser, Vol. 1, p. 443): "We must therefore consider wherein an oak differs from a mass of matter, and that seems to me to be in this, that the one is only the cohesion of particles of matter any how united, the other such a disposition of them as constitutes the parts of an oak; and such an organization of those parts as is fit to receive and distribute nourishment, so as to continue and frame the wood, bark, and leaves, etc., of an oak, in which consists the vegetable life. That being then one plant which has such an organization of parts in one coherent body, partaking of one common life, it continues to be the same plant as long as it partakes of the same life, though that life be communicated to new particles of matter vitally united to the living plant."

[8] *Essay* 2. 27. 28; Fraser, Vol. 1, p. 469.

[9] *Treatise* 1. 4. 5; Selby-Bigge edition, p. 238.

18. *Personal Identity and Individuation*

BERNARD WILLIAMS

In "Personal Identity and Individuation," Bernard Williams, professor of philosophy at the University of California at Berkeley, argues that bodily identity is a necessary condition of personal identity. Williams presents a challenge to the Lockean memory criterion. He envisions a situation in which two future persons remember having had the experiences of one Guy Fawkes. What should one say about this case? According to Williams, if personal identity is analyzed solely in terms of memory, there is no satisfactory answer. The following paper by Parfit and the earlier paper by Chisholm can both be read as suggesting different responses to the duplication or fission case that Williams raises.

There is a special problem about personal identity for two reasons. The first is self-consciousness— the fact that there seems to be a peculiar sense in which a man is conscious of his own identity. This I shall consider in Section 3 of this paper. The second reason is that a question of personal identity is evidently not answered merely by deciding the identity of a certain physical body. If I am asked whether the person in front of me is the same person as one uniquely present at place *a* at time *t*, I shall not necessarily be justified in answering 'yes' merely because I am justified in saying that this human body is the same as that present at *a* at *t*. Identity of body is at least not a sufficient condition of personal identity, and other considerations, of personal characteristics and, above all, memory, must be invoked.

Some have held, further, that bodily identity is not a necessary condition of personal identity. This, however, is ambiguous, and yields either a weak or a strong thesis, depending on one's view of the necessity and sufficiency of the other conditions. The weaker thesis asserts merely that at least one case can be consistently constructed in which bodily identity fails, but in which the other condi-tions will be sufficient for an assertion of personal identity; even though there may be some other imaginable case in which, some other condition failing, bodily identity is a necessary condition of personal identity. The stronger thesis asserts that there is no conceivable situation in which bodily identity would be necessary, some other condi-tions being always both necessary and sufficient. I take it that Locke's theory[1] is an example of this latter type.

I shall try to show that bodily identity is always a necessary condition of personal identity, and hence that both theses fail. In this connexion I shall discuss in detail a case apparently favourable to the weaker thesis (Section 1). I shall also be concerned with the stronger thesis, or rather with something that follows from it—the idea that we can give a sense to the concept of *a particular personality* with-out reference to a body. This I shall consider chiefly in Section 4, where the individuation of personali-ties will be discussed; the notion occurs, however, at various other places in the paper. The criterion of bodily identity itself I take for granted. I assume that it includes the notion of spatio-temporal conti-nuity, however that notion is to be explained.

In discussions of this subject, it is easy to fall into ways of speaking that suggest that 'bodily' and other considerations are easily divorced. I have regrettably succumbed to this at some points, but I certainly do not believe that this easy divorce is possible; I hope that both the general tenor of my thesis and some more direct remarks on the subject (Section 2) will show why.

"Personal Identity and Individuation" originally ap-peared in the *Proceedings of the Aristotelian Society*, 57 (1956–57), pp. 229–52. Copyright © by the Aristotelian Society, 1957. Reprinted by courtesy of the editor and the author.

1. *Deciding Another's Identity.* Suppose someone undergoes a sudden and violent change of character. Formerly quiet, deferential, church-going and home-loving, he wakes up one morning and has become, and continues to be, loud-mouthed, blasphemous and bullying. Here we might ask the question (a) Is he the same person as he used to be?

There seem to be two troubles with the formulation of this question, at least as an *identity* question. The first is a doubt about the reference of the second 'he': if asked the question 'as *who* used to be?' we may well want to say 'this person', which answers the original question (a) for us. This is not a serious difficulty, and we can easily avoid it by rephrasing the question in some such way as (b) Is this person the same as the person who went to sleep here last night?

We do not, however, *have* to rephrase the question in any such way; we can understand (a) perfectly well, and avoid paradox, because our use of personal pronouns and people's names is malleable. It is a reflection of our concept of 'a person' that some references to *him* cannot be understood as references to *his body* or to parts of it, and that others can; and that these two sorts of reference can readily occur in one statement ('He was embarrassed and went red'.) In the case of (a), the continuity of reference for 'he' can be supplied by the admitted continuity of reference of 'his body', and the more fundamental identity question can be discussed in these terms without any serious puzzlement.

The second difficulty with (a) is that it is too readily translated into (c) Is he the same sort of person as he used to be? or possibly (d) Has he the same personality as he used to have? But (c) and (d) are not identity questions in the required sense. For on any interpretation, 'sort of person', and on one interpretation, 'personality', are quality-terms, and we are merely asking whether the same subject now has different qualities, which is too easy to answer.

But this is only one interpretation of 'personality'. It corresponds interestingly to a loose sense of 'identity', which is found for instance in Nigel Dennis' novel *Cards of Identity*. There 'identity' is often used to mean 'a set of characteristics', and 'giving someone an identity' means 'convincing someone that he is a certain sort of person.' It does not, however, only mean this; for Dennis' Identity Clubs do not stop at giving someone a new character—they give him a new background as

well, and a local sponger is made by their persuasive methods not just into a submissive old-style butler, but into such a butler who used to be at sea and has deserted his wife.

We might feel that this was the point at which something specially uncanny was beginning to happen, and that this was the kind of anomalous example we were really looking for—the uncanniness of someone's acquiring a new past is connected with our increasing reluctance to describe the situation as one in which the same man has acquired a new set of qualities. Here we have one powerful motive for the introduction of memory. It can be put by saying that there are, or we can imagine, cases where we want to use some term like 'personality' in such a way that it is not a type-expression, meaning 'set of characteristics', but is a particular term meaning something like *individual* personality. It may seem that this particularity is attained by reference to memory—the possession of a particular past. Thus we are concerned here with cases more drastic than those in which for instance people say 'it has made a new man of him', or even 'he is not the same person as he used to be' in the sense suggested by a change of character; these cases we can too readily redescribe. Thus we may put our question in the barbarous form (e) Is the (particular) personality he has now the same as the one he had before?

We must now see whether we can make sense, in terms of memory, of the idea of a particular personality; and whether there can be personal identity without bodily identity.

In doing this, two obvious but important features of memory have to be borne in mind.

> (I) To say 'A remembers *x*', without irony or inverted commas, is to imply that *x* really happened; in this respect 'remember' is parallel to 'know'.

> (II) It does not follow from this, nor is it true, that all claims to remember, any more than all claims to know, are veridical; or, not everything one seems to remember is something one really remembers.

So much is obvious, although Locke[2] was forced to invoke the providence of God to deny the latter. These points have been emphasised by Flew in his discussion of Locke's views on personal identity.[3] In formulating Locke's thesis, however, Flew makes a mistake; for he offers Locke's thesis in the form 'if X can remember Y's doing such-and-such, then X and Y are the same person'. But this obviously will not do, even for Locke, for we constantly say things like 'I remember my brother joining the army' without implying that I and my brother are the same person. So if we are to formulate such a criterion, it looks as though we have to say something like 'if X remembers doing such-and-such, then he is the person who did that thing'. But since 'remembers doing' means 'remembers himself doing', this is trivially tautologous, and moreover lends colour to Butler's famous objection that memory, so far from constituting personal identity, presupposed it. Hence the criterion should rather run: 'if X claims to remember doing such-and-such. . . .' We must now ask how such a criterion might be used.

Suppose the man who underwent the radical change of character—let us call him Charles—claimed, when he woke up, to remember witnessing certain events and doing certain actions which earlier he did not claim to remember; and that under questioning he could not remember witnessing other events and doing other actions which earlier he did remember. Would this give us grounds for saying that he now was or had, in some particular sense, a different personality? An argument to show that it did give us such grounds might be constructed on the following lines.

Any token event E, and any token action A, are by definition particulars. Moreover, the description 'the man who did the action A' necessarily individuates some one person; for it is logically impossible that two persons should do the same *token* action.[4] In the case of events, it is possible that two persons should witness the same token event; but nevertheless the description 'the man who witnessed E' may happen to individuate some one person, and 'the man who witnessed E_1, E_2 . . . E_n' has a proportionately greater chance of so doing. Thus if our subject Charles now claims to remember doing certain actions A_1, A_2, etc., and witnessing certain events E_1, E_2, etc., which are themselves suitably identified, we have good grounds for saying that he is some particular person or has some particular personality.

Now by principle (II), we have no reason without corroborative evidence of some kind to believe Charles when he now claims to remember A or E; so we must set about checking. How are we to do this in the present case? Ordinarily if some person X claims to have witnessed E, and we wish to check this, we must find out whether there is any record, or anyone has any memory, of X's witnessing E.

This is evidently inapplicable to the present case. For either the evidence shows that Charles was *bodily* present at E, or it does not. If it does, then Charles is remembering in the ordinary way, which is contrary to the hypothesis. If it does not, then there is no corroboration. Here we have a first important step. We are trying to prise apart 'bodily' and 'mental' criteria; but we find that the normal operation of one 'mental' criterion involves the 'bodily' one.

However, the situation may not be quite as desperate as this makes it appear. We can examine Charles' putative memories, and we may find that he can offer detailed information which there is no reason to believe he would ordinarily have known, and which strongly suggests the reports of an eye-witness of some particular events. What we can do with this information in the present case depends on a number of considerations. I shall now examine these, first in connexion with events, and then with actions. Events can in principle be witnessed by any number of persons, or by none. Some of the events which Charles claims to remember witnessing may be events of which we have other eye-witness accounts; others may be events which we believe to have occurred, though we do not know whether or not anyone witnessed them; others again may be events which we believe to have occurred, but which we believe no-one to have witnessed.

For all these, there is an hypothesis about—or, perhaps, description of—Charles' present condition which has nothing to do with a change of personality: the hypothesis of clairvoyance (together, of course, with the loss of his real memories). To describe Charles as clairvoyant is certainly not to advance very far towards an *explanation* of his condition; it amounts to little more than saying that he has come to know, by no means what, what other people know by evidence. But so long as Charles claimed to remember events which were supposedly or certainly unwitnessed, such a description might be the best we could offer. We might do better than this, however, if the events Charles claimed to remember were witnessed; in this case we could begin to advance to the idea that Charles had a new identity, because we would have the chance of finding someone for him to be identical *with*. Thus if the events were witnessed, we might say that Charles was (now) identical with a witness of these events. This is ambiguous; it might mean that he was identical with anyone who witnessed the events, or with some particular person who witnessed the events. The former of these is no advance, since it comes to a roundabout way of saying that he claims to have witnessed the events, i.e., is possibly clairvoyant. The situation is different, however, if we can identify some one person who, it is plausible to suppose, witnessed all the events that Charles now claims to remember. That this should be possible is, indeed, a necessary condition of describing what has happened to Charles as a *change of identity*; I shall return to this point a little later.

If we now turn to actions, it looks as though we can find even better grounds for describing the case in terms of a change of identity. While there can be unwitnessed token events, there can be no unwitnessed token actions; moreover, as we noticed above, each token action can be performed by only one person. So if we can find out who performed the actions that Charles now claims to remember performing, it looks as if we can find out who he now is. These supposed advantages, however, are largely illusory. We may say, crudely, that there are many features of actions in which they are just like events—which, from another point of view, they indeed are. What differentiates actions from events are rather certain features of the agent, such as his intentions. In a particular case, some of these latter features may be known to, or inferred by, observers, while others may remain private to the agent. In neither case, however, do these special features of actions much help our investigation of Charles' identity. In so far as these special features may be known to observers, they are still, for the purposes of the investigation, in the class of events, and Charles' claim to remember them may still be plausibly described as clairvoyance; and in so far as these features remain private to the performer of the actions in question, we can have no ground for saying whether Charles' claims to remember them are even correct.

Again, the logical truth that a description of the form 'the person who did the (token) action A' individuates some one person, does not give unfailing help. How much help it gives depends on how effectively, and by what means, we can identify the action in question. Suppose that several men at a certain time and place are each sharpening a pencil. In these circumstances the description 'the man sharpening a pencil' fails to individuate: the action of sharpening a pencil is common to

them all. If, however, the pencils were of different colours, I might be able to identify a particular pencil, and through this a token action of sharpening; thus 'the man sharpening the red pencil' may individuate. But such methods of identifying token actions are not always available. In particular, there are some cases in which a token action can be effectively identified only through a reference to the agent. Thus if several men were all dancing the czardas, I might be able to identify a token dancing only as e.g., 'Josef's dancing of the czardas'. In such a case reference to a token action cannot help in identifying its agent, since I must identify him in order to identify it.

However, we often can effectively identify actions without actually identifying the agents, and so have a use for descriptions like 'the person who murdered the Duchess, whoever it was'. It is obvious that such descriptions can play a peculiarly useful role in an enquiry into identity; and this role may, for several reasons, be more useful than that played by descriptions like 'the man who witnessed the event E'. For, first, granted that I have identified *an action*, the description cannot fail of reference because there is no such agent; while the mere fact that I have identified a certain event E of course does not guarantee the description 'the man who *witnessed* the event E' against failure of reference. Secondly, it is inherently less likely that the description referring to an action should fail of unique reference because of multiplicity, than it is that the description referring to an event should so fail. For it is in general less probable that a certain action should have been co-operatively undertaken than that a certain event should have been multiply witnessed; and, as we noticed above, for every description of a co-operative action, we can produce a series of descriptions of constituent actions which have progressively greater chance of unique reference. Last, knowledge of a particular action can give one knowledge not only of the location, but of the character, of its agent, but knowledge of a particular event will standardly give one knowledge only of the location of its witnesses.

Let us now go back to the case of Charles. We may suppose that our enquiry has turned out in the most favourable possible way, and that all the events he claims to have witnessed and all the actions he claims to have done point unanimously to the life-history of some one person in the past—for instance, Guy Fawkes. Not only do all Charles' memory-claims that can be checked fit the pattern of Fawkes' life as known to historians, but others that cannot be checked are plausible, provide explanations of unexplained facts, and so on. Are we to say that Charles is now Guy Fawkes, that Guy Fawkes has come to life again in Charles' body, or some such thing?

Certainly the temptation to say something on this pattern is very strong. It is difficult to insist that we *couldn't* say that Charles (or sometime Charles) had become Guy Fawkes; this is certainly what the newspapers would say if they heard of it. But newspapers are prone to exaggeration, and this might be an exaggeration. For why shouldn't we say that Charles had, except for his body, become just like Guy Fawkes used to be; or perhaps that Charles clairvoyantly—i.e., mysteriously— knows all about Guy Fawkes and his *ambiance*? In answer to this, it will be argued that this is just what memory was introduced to rule out; granted that we need similar personal characteristics, skills, and so on as necessary conditions of the identification, the final—and, granted these others, sufficient—condition is provided by memories of seeing just *this*, and doing just *that*, and it is these that pick out a particular man. But perhaps this point is fundamentally a logical trick. Granted that in a certain context the expressions 'the man who did A', 'the man who saw E', do effectively individuate, it is logically impossible that two different persons should (correctly) remember being the man who did A or saw E; but it is not logically impossible that two different persons should *claim* to remember being this man, and this is the most we can get.

This last argument is meant to show only that we are not forced to accept the description of Charles' condition as his being identical with Guy Fawkes. I shall now put forward an argument to strengthen this contention and to suggest that we should not be justified in accepting this description. If it is logically possible that Charles should undergo the changes described, then it is logically possible that some other man should simultaneously undergo the same changes; e.g., that both Charles and his brother Robert should be found in this condition. What should we say in that case? They cannot both be Guy Fawkes; if they were, Guy Fawkes would be in two places at once, which is absurd. Moreover, if they were both identical with Guy Fawkes, they would be identical with each other, which is also absurd. Hence we could

not say that they were both identical with Guy Fawkes. We might instead say that one of them was identical with Guy Fawkes, and that the other was just like him; but this would be an utterly vacuous manoeuvre, since there would be *ex hypothesi* no principle determining which description was to apply to which. So it would be best, if anything, to say that both had mysteriously become like Guy Fawkes, clairvoyantly knew about him, or something like this. If this would be the best description of each of the two, why would it not be the best description of Charles if Charles alone were changed?

Perhaps this last rhetorical question too readily invites an answer. It might be said that there is a relevant difference beween the case in which two persons are changed and the case in which only one is changed, the difference being just this difference in numbers; and that there is no guarantee that what we would say in one of these situations would be the same as what we would say in the other. In the more complicated situation our linguistic and conceptual resources would be taxed even more severely than in the simpler one, and we might not react to the demands in the same way. Moreover, there is a reason why we should not react in the same way. The standard form of an identity question is 'Is this x the same x as that x which . . . ?' and in the simpler situation we are at least presented with just the materials for constructing such a question; but in the more complicated situation we are baffled even in asking the question, since both the transformed persons are equally good candidates for being its subject, and the question 'Are these two x's the same $(x?)$ as the x which . . . ?' is not a recognisable form of identity question. Thus, it might be argued, the fact that we could not speak of identity in the latter situation is no kind of proof that we could not do so in the former.

Certainly it is not a proof. Yet the argument does indicate that to speak of identity in the simpler case would be at least quite vacuous. The point can be made clearer in the following way. In the case of material objects, we can draw a distinction between identity and exact similarity; it is clearly not the same to say that two men live in the same house, and that they live in exactly similar houses. This notion of identity is given to us primarily, though not completely, by the notion of spatio-temporal continuity. In the case of character, however, this distinction cannot be drawn, for to say that *A* and *B* have the same character is just to say that *A*'s character is exactly similar to *B*'s. Nor can this distinction be drawn in the case of memories—if you could say that two men had the same memories, this would be to say that their memories were exactly similar. There is, however, an extreme difficulty in saying these things about memories at all; it is unclear what it would mean to say that there were *two* men who had exactly similar, or the same, memories, since to call them real memories is to imply their correctness. Thus if we are to describe Charles' relations to Guy Fawkes in terms of *exact similarity* of everything except the body, we are going to have difficulty in finding a suitable description in these terms of his memory claims. We cannot say that he has the same memories as Guy Fawkes, as this is to imply, what we want to deny, that he really is Guy Fawkes; nor can we say that the memory claims he makes are the same as those made by Guy Fawkes, as we have little idea of what memory claims Fawkes in fact made, or indeed of how much he at various times remembered. All we actually know is that Charles' claims fit Fawkes' life.

These difficulties, in applying the concept of exact similarity in the matter of the supposed memories, are (I suspect) a motive for the thought that we *must* describe the situation in terms of identity. This is where the reduplicated situation of Charles and Robert gives some help. In that situation it is quite obvious that the idea of identity cannot be applied, and that we must fall back on similarity; and that one respect in which the trio are similar is—however we are to express it—that of 'memory'. (If the situation sometimes occurred, we might find an expression; we might speak of 'similarity of one's supposed past'.) This eases the way for doing the same thing in the case of Charles alone, whose relation to Fawkes in his unique case is exactly the same as both his and Robert's in the reduplicated one. We can then say that Charles has the same character, and the same supposed past, as Fawkes; which is just the same as to say that they are in these respects exactly similar. This is not to say that they are identical at all. The only case in which identity and exact similarity could be distinguished, as we have just seen, is that of the body— 'same body' and 'exactly similar body' really do mark a difference. Thus I should claim that the omission of the body takes away all content from the idea of personal *identity*.

I should like to make one last point about this example. This turns on the fact, mentioned before, that in order to describe Charles' change of identity, we must be able to identify some one person who might plausibly be supposed to have seen and done all the things that Charles' now claims to remember having seen and done; otherwise there would be nothing to pin down Charles' memory claims as other than random feats of clairvoyance. We succeeded in doing this, just by discovering that Charles' memory claims fitted Fawkes' life. This could be done only by knowing what Fawkes did, and what Fawkes did could be known only by reference to witnesses of Fawkes' activities, and these witnesses must have seen Fawkes' *body*. In order for their accounts to be connected into the history of one person, it is necessary to rely on the continuity of this body.

Now the fact that Fawkes is in this sense identified through his body does not rule out the possibility that Charles should later be identified with Fawkes without reference to a body; i.e., this fact does not rule out the weaker thesis about the nonnecessity of bodies. To illustrate this, one might compare the case of someone's going to a crowded party, where he sees a girl who is very like all the other girls at the party except that she has red hair. This girl sings various songs and quarrels with the band; she is easily identified on each occasion by the colour of her hair. The man later meets a platinum blonde who recalls singing songs at a party and quarrelling with the band. He can identify her as the red-haired girl at the party, even though she has changed the colour of her hair in the meantime. There is an important difference, however, between this case and that of Fawkes. If the girl had remarkably changed the colour of her hair between songs and before the quarrel, identifying her at the various stages of the party would have been more difficult, but not in principle impossible; but if the Fawkes-personality changed bodies frequently, identification would become not just difficult but impossible. For the only other resource would be the memory criterion, and the operation of this would once more make exactly the same requirements. Hence, it is a necessary condition of making the supposed identification on non-bodily grounds that at some stage identifications should be made on bodily grounds. Hence any claim that bodily considerations can be absolutely omitted from the criteria of personal identity must fail, i.e., these facts do rule out the stronger thesis.

2. *Some Remarks on Bodily Interchange.* Anyone who believed that personalities could be identified without reference to bodies might be expected to make sense of the idea of bodily interchange; and anyone who thought that they might always be identified in this way would presumably require that for any two contemporaneous persons we should be able to make sense of the idea that their bodies should be interchanged. It is worth considering how far we can make sense of it, if we look at it closely.

Suppose a magician is hired to perform the old trick of making the emperor and the peasant become each other. He gets the emperor and the peasant in one room, with the emperor on his throne and the peasant in the corner, and then casts the spell. What will count as success? Clearly not that after the smoke has cleared the old emperor should be in the corner and the old peasant on the throne. That would be a rather boring trick. The requirement is presumably that the emperor's body, with the peasant's personality, should be on the throne, and the peasant's body with the emperor's personality, in the corner. What does this mean? In particular, what has happened to the voices? The voice presumably ought to count as a bodily function; yet how would the peasant's gruff blasphemies be uttered in the emperor's cultivated tones, or the emperor's witticisms in the peasant's growl? A similar point holds for the features; the emperor's body might include the sort of face that just *could not* express the peasant's morose suspiciousness, the peasant's a face no expression of which could be taken for one of fastidious arrogance. These 'could's' are not just empirical—such expressions on these features might be unthinkable.

The point need not be elaborated; I hope I have said enough to suggest that the concept of bodily interchange cannot be taken for granted, and that there are even logical limits to what we should be prepared to say in this direction. What these limits are, cannot be foreseen—one has to consider the cases, and for this one has to see the cases. The converse is also true, that it is difficult to tell in advance how far certain features may suddenly seem to express something quite unexpected. But there are limits, and when this is recognised, the idea of the interchange of personalities seems very odd. There might be something like a logical impossibility of the magician's trick's succeeding. However much of the emperor's past the sometime peasant now claimed to remember, the trick would not have succeeded if he could not satisfy the simpler requirement of being the same *sort* of person as the sometime emperor. Could he do this, if he could not smile royally? Still less, could he be the same person, if he could not smile the characteristic smile of the emperor?

These considerations are relevant to the present question in two ways. First, the stronger view about the identification implies that an interchange is always conceivable; but there are many cases in which it does not seem to be conceivable at all. Secondly, there is connected with this the deeper point, that when we are asked to distinguish a man's personality from his body, we do not really know what to distinguish from what. I take it that this was part of what Wittgenstein meant when he said that the best picture of the human soul was the human body.[5]

3. *A Criterion for Oneself?* I now turn to a different supposed use of a criterion of identity for persons. It may be objected that I have been discussing all the time the use of memory and other criteria of personal identity as applied to one man by others; but that the real role of memory is to be seen in the way it reveals a man to *himself*. Thus Locke speaks of 'consciousness' (and by this he means here memory) as 'what makes a man be himself to himself'.[6]

It is difficult to see what this can mean. If we take it to mean that a man could use memory as a criterion in deciding whether he was the same person, in the particular sense, as he used to be, the suggestion is demonstrably absurd. I hope that a short and schematised argument will be enough to show this point. Suppose a man to have had previously some set of memories S, and now a different set S_1. This should presumably be the situation in which he should set about using the criterion to decide the question of his identity. But this cannot be so, for when he has memories S, and again when he has memories S_1, he is in no doubt about his identity, and so the question does not even occur to him. For it to occur to him, he would have to have S and S_1 at the same time, and so S would be included in S_1, which is contrary to the hypothesis that they are, in the relevant sense, different.

Alternatively, let S_1 include a general memory to the effect that he used to remember things that he no longer remembers. This would again present no question to him, for it is the condition of most of us. So let us strengthen this into the requirement that S_1 include a general memory Σ to the effect that he used to remember things empirically incompatible with memories in S_1. In this situation he might set about trying to find out what kind of illusion he was under. His most economical hypothesis would be that Σ itself was an illusion. If he were not satisfied with this, or if some parts of S were left over in S_1, so that he seemed to have definitely incompatible 'memories', there would be nothing he could do with the help of his own memory; he would have to ask others about his past. In doing this, he would be relying on other people's memories of his past; but this is certainly not what was meant by the suggestion of memory as a criterion for the man himself. It is just a reversion to the case of such a criterion being used by some persons about another. Thus there is no way in which memory could be used by a man as a criterion of his own identity.

A criterion, however, must be used by someone. This is a point that has been notably and unhappily neglected by theorists of personal identity. Thus Hume, for instance, in the course of his account revealingly says, 'Suppose we could see clearly into the breast of another, and observe that succession of perceptions, which constitutes his mind or thinking principle, and suppose that he always preserves the memory of a considerable part of past perceptions. . . .'[7] Others, in criticising or expanding Hume's account, have written in terms that similarly require an externalised view of the contents of a man's mind, a view obtainable from no conceivable vantage-point. Theorising which is in this sense abstract must be vacuous, because this privileged but positionless point of view can mean nothing to us.

At this point it might be objected that if what has been said is true about a criterion of identity, then it was not a *criterion* that memory was supposed uniquely to provide. 'You have argued', it might be said, 'that no man can use memory as a criterion of his own identity. But this is just what shows that memory is the essence of personal identity; figuratively speaking, memory is so much what makes him a certain person that when provided with certain memories, he cannot doubt who he is. This is just the heart of the thesis.' Or the objection might be put by saying that a man might conceivably have occasion to look into a mirror and say 'this is not my body', but could never have

occasion to say 'these are not my memories'. Or, again, a man who has lost his memory cannot say who he is.

If this is what the thesis asserts, however, it comes to little. A man who has lost his memory cannot say who anyone else is, either, nor whether any object is the same as one previously presented, since he will not remember the previous presentation. So the last argument shows nothing about personal identity as such; it just shows that identifying anything is a process that involves memory. Nor is the first argument more illuminating. It comes really to no more than the trivialities that in order to remember, you have to have something you can remember, and that if you are remembering everything you can remember, there is nothing else you can remember. Again, the example of the man looking into the mirror does not do what is required. In order to sustain the objection it would be necessary to show not just that a man might say 'this is not my body', but that if he said it, he would necessarily be right; or at least that the question whether he was right or not did not involve any reference to other people's memories. It is obvious that neither is the case, because the situation of the example *might* be best described by saying that this was a man who misremembered what he looked like, and the question whether this was the best description of the situation would have to be decided by other people conducting the kind of enquiry into identity that was earlier discussed at length.

It is not part of my aim to discuss in general consciousness of self. I have tried in this section to show in a limited way that although we may have the feeling that, by consideration of it alone, we may be given the clue to personal identity, this is in fact an illusion. That it is an illusion is disguised by those theories of personal identity which, by assuming no particular point of view, try to get the best of both worlds, the inner and the outer. If we abandon this for a more realistic approach, the facts of self-consciousness prove incapable of yielding the secret of personal identity, and we are forced back into the world of public criteria.

If we accept those conclusions, together with the earlier ones, it may seem that the attempt to give a sense to 'particular personality' that omits reference to the body has failed. However, there is another and familiar class of cases that seems to provide strong independent grounds for the view that such a sense can be given: these are the cases in which more than one personality is associated with one body. I shall end by discussing this type of case and some related questions.

4. *Multiple Personality and Individuation.* Examples of multiple personality, such as the notorious case of Miss Beauchamp,[8] raise identity questions interestingly different from those that arose in the case of Charles. In that case, we identified, by means that turned out to involve the body, what would normally, if tendentiously, be called a different person, and asked whether the person in front of us was identical with him. In the cases of multiple personality, we are in a sense more directly confronted with personalities, and naturally make direct reference to them in order to ask our identity questions at all. The standard type of identity question about Miss Beauchamp is whether the personality that is now being manifested in her behaviour (or some such description) is the same as that which was being manifested two hours ago. In asking a question of this type, we may in fact feel a doubt about the reference of descriptions like 'the personality now manifesting itself', because the principal question here just is what personalities there are to be referred to—how many personalities there are, and how the subject's behaviour is to be 'sorted out' into the manifestations of different personalities.

For this reason, there is a strong motive for not putting our questions about Miss Beauchamp in the form of identity questions at all. Instead of asking something of the form 'Is this personality the same as that?' we may prefer to ask, 'Do these two pieces of behaviour belong to one personality or to two?'; that is, instead of referring to personalities *through* their manifestations and asking whether they are identical, we may refer to manifestations and ask how they are to be allocated to personalities. A parallel to this would be the case of a tangled skein of wool, where, catching hold of a piece at each end, we might ask either 'Is this thread the same as that?' or 'Are these pieces parts of one thread?' The second formulation in each case might seem to be strictly preferable to the first, because the references that are being made are more determinate; I can tell you exactly which *part* or which *manifestation* I am referring to in the second formulation, but can tell you much less exactly which *thread* or which *personality* I am referring to in

the first. It is useful to distinguish these sorts of questions, and I shall call the first, questions of identity, and the second, questions of individuation. I shall also in this section speak of our having individuated a personality when, roughly, we have answered enough questions of this type for us to have picked out a certain personality from the pattern of manifestations. I shall not here examine the complexities involved in a proper formulation of these concepts.

We have just seen that it might be preferable to put our questions about Miss Beauchamp in the form of individuation, and not of identity, questions. It might seem, indeed, that it is essential to do this. Because asking an identity question about personalities involves referring to personalities, and this involves knowing what personalities one is referring to, it is tempting to think that we could not use the identity form in a case where our problem was just what, and how many, personalities there were. This, however, would be an exaggeration. I do not have to be able to answer the question 'Which personality are you referring to?' in the thorough-going way suggested by this argument. I may do enough to establish the reference by saying 'I just mean the personality now being manifested, whichever that is', without committing myself thereby to more than the belief that there is at least one personality to be referred to, and possibly more. I should be *debarred* from using the identity form only in a situation where I was in doubt whether there was even one personality to be referred to.

The case of Miss Beauchamp is more relevant to the discussion of the role of the body in the individuation of personalities than it is to the straightforward question whether bodily identity is a necessary condition of personal identity; since bodily identity is granted, this case can have no tendency to show that bodily identity is not a necessary condition (though it will of course tend to show that it is not a sufficient condition). It will, however, lend colour to the idea that we can individuate particular personalities, and not through bodies; if there are here four different particular personalities, and only one body, it is clear that there can be some principle for distinguishing personalities without at least *distinguishing* bodies. There is such a principle; but it does not yield as exciting a result from this case as might be hoped.

Miss Beauchamp's striking different personalities were individuated in the first place by reference to personal characteristics, in which they were largely opposed; also by tastes and preferences (B_1 and B_4 hated smoking, for instance, and B_3 loved it); and by skills (B_3, unlike the others, knew no French or shorthand). Memory did not serve straightforwardly to individuate them, because their memories were asymmetrical. B_1 and B_4, for instance, knew only what they were told by the investigator about the others, but B_3 knew, without being told, everything that B_4 did, and in the case of B_1 knew all her thoughts as well; she referred to them both in the third person.[9] These remarkable and systematic discontinuities in Miss Beauchamp's behaviour, together with the violent and active conflict between her various selves, who abused and tricked each other, make the reference to different particular personalities completely natural. Thus we have individuated various personalities by reference to character, attainments and (up to a point) memories, and without reference to bodies.

This claim, however, is liable to serious misinterpretation. There has been no reference to bodies only in the sense that no such reference came into the principles used; but it does not follow from this that there was no reference to a body in starting to individuate at all. Obviously there was, because too many and too various things were going on in connexion with one body; if Miss Beauchamp had been four sisters, there would have been no problem. Thus the individuation by reference to character and so on alone, was individuation in the context of the continuity of a certain body; and the fact that these principles were successful in individuating in this case does not show that they would be successful in so doing generally. The point may be put by saying that what we have succeeded in doing on these principles is individuating particular personalities *of Miss Beauchamp*, who is bodily identified; this is not to say that they provide us with a principle for individuating particular personalities without any reference to bodies at all.

This is quite obvious if we look at the principles themselves. Leaving aside memory, which only partially applies to the case, character and attainments are quite clearly general things. *Jones'* character is, in a sense, a particular; just because 'Jones' character' refers to the instantiation of certain properties by a particular (and bodily) man.[10] Even so, the sense in which it is a particular is

peculiar and limited. This can be seen from the odd workings of its criterion of identity. Consider the statement

(i) He has the same character as his father (*or* he has his father's character)

and compare the two statements

(ii) He wears the same clothes as his father.

(iii) He has his father's watch.

Of these, (ii) is ambiguous, the expression, 'the same clothes' see-sawing over the line between particular and general (though its companion 'he wears his father's clothes' seems to allow only the particular interpretation). Neither (i) nor (iii) is ambiguous in this way; and in (iii) 'his father's watch' obviously refers to a particular. But (i) is quite different from (iii). If (iii) is true, then if the watch he has is going to be pawned tomorrow, his father's watch is going to be pawned; but it does not similarly follow from (i) that if his character is going to be ruined by the Army, his father's character is going to be ruined. This illustrates how little weight can be laid on the idea of Jones' character being a particular, and throws us back on the familiar point that to talk of Jones' character is a way of talking about what Jones is like.

Miss Beauchamp's various personalities are particulars only in the weak sense that Jones' character is a particular, a sense which is grounded in the particular body. In using character and attainments to individuate them, I am telling the difference between them in just the sense that I tell the difference between sets of characteristics; Miss Beauchamp was peculiar in having more than one set of characteristics. Her personalities, like more normal people's, each had *peculiarities,* the combination of which might well have been, as a matter of fact, uniquely instantiated; but this does not affect the fundamental logical issue. About her memories, it need only be said that if different personalities have the same memories, memory is not being used to individuate; if they have different memories, the bodily identity connecting the various remembered occasions makes it easy to describe the situation as one of Miss Beauchamp's sometimes being able to remember what at other times she could not.

When Miss Beauchamp was nearly cured, and only occasionally lapsed into dissociation, she spoke freely of herself as having been B_1 or B_4. 'These different states seem to her very largely differences of moods. She regrets them, but does not attempt to excuse them, because, as she says, "After all, it is always myself." '[11]

Endnotes

[1] *Essay Concerning Human Understanding*, II, 27.

[2] *Loc. cit.*, Section 13. He is speaking, however, only of the memories of actions.

[3] *Philosophy*, xxvi (1951) pp. 53 *seq.*

[4] This is to ignore the case of joint or co-operative actions. Thus when three persons *A, B* and *C* jointly fell a tree, it might be said that each of them has done the same action, that of felling the particular tree. But this would not be quite accurate. They have *all* felled the tree; what *each* of them has done is to share in the felling of the tree, or to have felled the tree with the help of the other two. When the variables implicit in this last expression are replaced with names, we obtain descriptions of token actions which indeed individuate; thus it is true of *A*, but not of *B* or *C*, that he is the man who felled the tree *with the help of B and C.*

[5] *Philosophical Investigations*, II, iv.

[6] *Loc. cit.*, Section 10.

[7] Hume, *Treatise of Human Nature*, Bk. I, Pt. IV, Sec. VI.

[8] See Morton Prince, *The Dissociation of a Personality* (New York: Longmans, 1906).

[9] Prince, *Dissociation of a Personality*, p. 181. The extent of memory discontinuity in such cases varies cf., e.g., William James, *Principles of Psychology*, I (London: Macmillan, 1890), pp. 379 *seq.*

[10] Cf. P. F. Strawson, 'Particular and General,' PAS LIV (1953–4). pp. 250 *seq.*

[11] Prince, *Dissociation of a Personality*, p. 525.

19. *Personal Identity*[1]

DEREK PARFIT

In this selection, Derek Parfit, senior research fellow at All Souls College, Oxford, attempts to show how a sophisticated but essentially Lockean view of personal identity against the objections of Reid and Williams. Parfit's view is richer than Locke's since it includes, in addition to memory, a person's character (for example, beliefs, intentions, goals, and ambitions) as pertinent to the relations that unite different stages of one life. Parfit guards against Williams's duplication argument by maintaining that personal identity requires *non-branching* psychological continuity. Thus, in a duplication where two people are psychologically continuous with an earlier pre-duplicated person, *neither* of the resulting people would be identical to the original. But in the end, according to Parfit, psychological connections and continuities, whether one-one or one-many, are what matter when discussing questions of survival and responsibility. The views expressed in "Personal Identity" have been elaborated in Part III of Parfit's much discussed book, *Reasons and Persons*.

We can, I think, describe cases in which, though we know the answer to every other question, we have no idea how to answer a question about personal identity. These cases are not covered by the criteria of personal identity that we actually use.

Do they present a problem?

It might be thought that they do not, because they could never occur. I suspect that some of them could. (Some, for instance, might become scientifically possible.) But I shall claim that even if they did they would present no problem.

My targets are two beliefs: one about the nature of personal identity, the other about its importance.

The first is that in these cases the question about identity must have an answer.

No one thinks this about, say, nations or machines. Our criteria for the identity of these do not cover certain cases. No one thinks that in these cases the questions "Is it the same nation?" or "Is it the same machine?" must have answers.

Some people believe that in this respect they are different. They agree that our criteria of personal identity do not cover certain cases, but they believe that the nature of their own identity through time is, somehow, such as to guarantee that in these cases questions about their identity must have answers. This belief might be expressed as follows: "Whatever happens between now and any future time, either I shall still exist, or I shall not. Any future experience will either be *my* experience, or it will not."

This first belief—in the special nature of personal identity—has, I think, certain effects. It makes people assume that the principle of self-interest is more rationally compelling than any moral principle. And it makes them more depressed by the thought of aging and of death.

I cannot see how to disprove this first belief. I shall describe a problem case. But this can only make it seem implausible.

Another approach might be this. We might suggest that one cause of the belief is the projection of our emotions. When we imagine ourselves in a problem case, we do feel that the question "Would it be me?" must have an answer. But what we take to be a bafflement about a further fact may be only the bafflement of our concern.

Derek Parfit, "Personal Identity," *Philosophical Review*, 80 (1971): 3–27. Reprinted by permission of the *Philosophical Review* and the author.

It shall not pursue this suggestion here. But one cause of our concern is the belief which is my second target. This is that unless the question about identity has an answer, we cannot answer certain important questions (questions about such matters as survival, memory, and responsibility).

Against this second belief my claim will be this. Certain important questions do presuppose a question about personal identity. But they can be freed of this presupposition. And when they are, the question about identity has no importance.

I

We can start by considering the much discussed case of the man who, like an amoeba, divides.[2]

Wiggins has recently dramatized this case.[3] He first referred to the operation imagined by Shoemaker.[4] We suppose that my brain is transplanted into someone else's (brainless) body, and that the resulting person has my character and apparent memories of my life. Most of us would agree, after thought, that the resulting person is me. I shall here assume such agreement.[5]

Wiggins then imagined his own operation. My brain is divided, and each half is housed in a new body. Both resulting people have my character and apparent memories of my life.

What happens to me? There seem only three possibilities: (1) I do not survive; (2) I survive as one of the two people; (3) I survive as both.

The trouble with (1) is this. We agreed that I could survive if my brain were successfully transplanted. And people have in fact survived with half their brains destroyed. It seems to follow that I could survive if half my brain were successfully transplanted and the other half were destroyed. But if this is so, how could I *not* survive if the other half were also successfully transplanted? How could a double success be a failure?

We can move to the second description. Perhaps one success is the maximum score. Perhaps I shall be one of the resulting people.

The trouble here is that in Wiggins' case each half of my brain is exactly similar, and so, to start with, is each resulting person. So how can I survive as only one of the two people? What can make me one of them rather than the other?

It seems clear that both of these descriptions—that I do not survive, and that I survive as one of the people—are highly implausible. Those who have accepted them must have assumed that they were the only possible descriptions.

What about our third description: that I survive as both people?

It might be said, "If 'survive' implies identity, this description makes no sense—you cannot be two people. If it does not, the description is irrelevant to a problem about identity."

I shall later deny the second of these remarks. But there are ways of denying the first. We might say, "What we have called 'the two resulting people' are not two people. They are one person. I do survive Wiggins' operation. Its effect is to give me two bodies and a divided mind."

It would shorten my argument if this were absurd. But I do not think it is. It is worth showing why.

We can, I suggest, imagine a divided mind. We can imagine a man having two simultaneous experiences, in having each of which he is unaware of having the other.

We may not even need to imagine this. Certain actual cases, to which Wiggins referred, seem to be best described in these terms. These involve the cutting of the bridge between the hemispheres of the brain. The aim was to cure epilepsy. But the result appears to be, in the surgeon's words, the creation of "two separate spheres of consciousness,"[6] each of which controls one half of the patient's body. What is experienced in each is, presumably, experienced by the patient.

There are certain complications in these actual cases. So let us imagine a simpler case.

Suppose that the bridge between my hemispheres is brought under my voluntary control. This would enable me to disconnect my hemispheres as easily as if I were blinking. By doing this I would divide my mind. And we can suppose that when my mind is divided I can, in each half, bring about reunion.

This ability would have obvious uses. To give an example: I am near the end of a maths exam, and see two ways of tackling the last problem. I decide to divide my mind, to work, with each half, at one of two calculations, and then to reunite my mind and write a fair copy of the best result.

What shall I experience?

When I disconnect my hemispheres, my consciousness divides into two streams. But this division is not something that I experience. Each of my two streams of consciousness seems to have been straightforwardly continuous with my one stream of consciousness up to the moment of division. The only changes in each stream are the disappearance of half my visual field and the loss of sensation in, and control over, half my body.

Consider my experiences in what we can call my "right-handed" stream. I remember that I assigned my right hand to longer calculation. This I now begin. In working at this calculation I can see, from the movements of my left hand, that I am also working at the other. But I am not aware of working at the other. So I might, in my right-handed stream, wonder how, in my left-handed stream, I am getting on.

My work is now over, I am about to reunite my mind. What should I, in each stream, expect? Simply that I shall suddenly seem to remember just having thought out two calculations, in thinking out each of which I was not aware of thinking out the other. This, I submit, we can imagine. And if my mind was divided, these memories are correct.

In describing this episode, I assumed that there were two series of thoughts, and that they were both mine. If my two hands visibly wrote out two calculations, and if I claimed to remember two corresponding series of thoughts, this is surely what we should want to say.

If it is, then a person's mental history need not be like a canal, with only one channel. It could be like a river, with islands, and with separate streams.

To apply this to Wiggins' operation: we mentioned the view that it gives me two bodies and a divided mind. We cannot now call this absurd. But it is, I think, unsatisfactory.

There were two features of the case of the exam that made us want to say that only one person was involved. The mind was soon reunited, and there was only one body. If a mind was permanently divided and its halves developed in different ways, the point of speaking of one person would start to disappear. Wiggins' case, where there are also two bodies, seems to be over the borderline. After I have had his operation, the two "products" each have all the attributes of a person. They could live at opposite ends of the earth. (If they later met, they might even fail to recognize each other.) It would become intolerable to deny that they were different people.

Suppose we admit that they are different people. Could we still claim that I survived as both, using "survive" to imply identity?

We could. For we might suggest that two people could compose a third. We might say, "I do survive Wiggins' operation as two people. They can be different people, and yet be me, in just the way in which the Pope's three crowns are one crown."[7]

This is a possible way of giving sense to the claim that I survive as two different people, using "survive" to imply identity. But it keeps the language of identity only by changing the concept of a person. And there are obvious objections to this change.[8]

The alternative, for which I shall argue, is to give up the language of identity. We can suggest that I survive as two different people without implying that I am these people.

When I first mentioned this alternative, I mentioned this objection: "If your new way of talking does not imply identity, it cannot solve our problem. For that is about identity. The problem is that all the possible answers to the question about identity are highly implausible."

We can now answer this objection.

We can start by reminding ourselves that this is an objection only if we have one or both of the beliefs which I mentioned at the start of this paper.

The first was the belief that to any question about personal identity, in any describable case, there must be a true answer. For those with this belief, Wiggins' case is doubly perplexing. If all the possible answers are implausible, it is hard to decide which of them is true, and hard even to keep the belief that one of them must be true. If we give up this belief, as I think we should, these problems disappear. We shall then regard the case as like many others in which, for quite unpuzzling reasons, there is no answer to a question about identity. (Consider "Was England the same nation after 1066?")

Wiggins' case makes the first belief implausible. It also makes it trivial. For it undermines the second belief. This was the belief that important questions turn upon the question about identity. (It is worth pointing out that those who have only this second belief do not think that there must be an answer to this question, but rather that we must decide upon an answer.)

Against this second belief my claim is this. Certain questions do presuppose a question about personal identity. And because these questions are important, Wiggins' case does present a problem. But we cannot solve this problem by answering the question about identity. We can solve this problem only by taking these important questions and prizing them apart from the question about identity. After we have done this, the question about identity (though we might for the sake of neatness decide it) has no further interest.

Because there are several questions which presuppose identity, this claim will take some time to fill out.

We can first return to the question of survival. This is a special case, for survival does not so much presuppose the retaining of identity as seem equivalent to it. It is thus the general relation which we need to prize apart from identity. We can then consider particular relations, such as those involved in memory and intention.

"Will I survive?" seems, I said, equivalent to "Will there be some person alive who is the same person as me?"

If we treat these questions as equivalent, then the least unsatisfactory description of Wiggins' case is, I think, that I survive with two bodies and a divided mind.

Several writers have chosen to say that I am neither of the resulting people. Given our equivalence, this implies that I do not survive, and hence, presumably, that even if Wiggins' operation is not literally death, I ought, since I will not survive it, to regard it *as* death. But this seemed absurd.

It is worth repeating why. An emotion or attitude can be criticized for resting on a false belief, or for being inconsistent. A man who regarded Wiggins' operation as death must, I suggest, be open to one of these criticisms.

He might believe that his relation to each of the resulting people fails to contain some element which is contained in survival. But how can this be true? We agreed that he *would* survive if he stood in this very same relation to only *one* of the resulting people. So it cannot be the nature of this relation which makes it fail, in Wiggins' case, to be survival. It can only be its duplication.

Suppose that our man accepts this, but still regards division as death. His reaction would now seem wildly inconsistent. He would be like a man who, when told of a drug that could double his years of life, regarded the taking of this drug as death. The only difference in this case of division is that the extra years are to run concurrently. This is an interesting difference. But it cannot mean that there are *no* years to run.

I have argued this for those who think that there must, in Wiggins' case, be a true answer to the question about identity. For them, we might add, "Perhaps the original person does lose his identity. But there may be other ways to do this than to die. One other way might be to multiply. To regard these as the same is to confuse nought with two."

For those who think that the question of identity is up for decision, it would be clearly absurd to regard Wiggins' operation as death. These people would have to think, "We could have chosen to say that I should be one of the resulting people. If we had, I should not have regarded it as death. But since we have chosen to say that I am neither person, I *do*." This is hard even to understand.[9]

My first conclusion, then, is this. The relation of the original person to each of the resulting people contains all that interests us—all that matters—in any ordinary case of survival. This is why we need a sense in which one person can survive as two.[10]

One of my aims in the rest of this paper will be to suggest such a sense. But we can first make some general remarks.

II

Identity is a one-one relation. Wiggins' case serves to show that what matters in survival need not be one-one.

Wiggins' case is of course unlikely to occur. The relations which matter are, in fact, one-one. It is because they are that we can imply the holding of these relations by using the language of identity.

This use of language is convenient. But it can lead us astray. We may assume that what matters *is* identity and, hence, has the properties of identity.

In the case of the property of being one-one, this mistake is not serious. For what matters is in fact one-one. But in the case of another property, the mistake *is* serious. Identity is all-or-nothing. Most of the relations which matter in survival are, in fact, relations of degree. If we ignore this, we shall be led into quite ill-grounded attitudes and beliefs.

The claim that I have just made—that most of what matters are relations of degree—I have yet to support. Wiggins' case shows only that these relations need not be one-one. The merit of the case is not that it shows this in particular, but that it makes the first break between what matters and identity. The belief that identity *is* what matters is hard to overcome. This is shown in most discussions of the problem cases which actually occur: cases, say, of amnesia or of brain damage. Once Wiggins' case has made one breach in this belief, the rest should be easier to remove.[11]

To turn to a recent debate: most of the relations which matter can be provisionally referred to under the heading "psychological continuity" (which includes causal continuity). My claim is thus that we use the language of personal identity in order to imply such continuity. This is close to the view that psychological continuity provides a criterion of identity.

Williams has attacked this view with the following argument. Identity is a one-one relation. So any criterion of identity must appeal to a relation which is logically one-one. Psychological continuity is not logically one-one. So it cannot provide a criterion.[12]

Some writers have replied that it is enough if the relation appealed to is always in fact one-one.[13]

I suggest a slightly different reply. Psychological continuity is a ground for speaking of identity when it is one-one.

If psychological continuity took a one-many or branching form, we should need, I have argued, to abandon the language of identity. So this possibility would not count against this view.

We can make a stronger claim. This possibility would count in its favor.

The view might be defended as follows. Judgments of personal identity have great importance. What gives them their importance is the fact that they imply psychological continuity. This is why, whenever there is such continuity, we ought, if we can, to imply it by making a judgment of identity.

If psychological continuity took a branching form, no coherent set of judgments of identity could correspond to, and thus be used to imply, the branching form of this relation. But what we ought to do, in such a case, is take the importance which would attach to a judgment of identity and attach this importance directly to each limb of the branching relation. So this case helps to show that judgments of personal identity do derive their importance from the fact that they imply psychological continuity. It helps to show that when we can, usefully, speak of identity, this relation is our ground.

This argument appeals to a principle which Williams put forward.[14] The principle is that an important judgment should be asserted and denied only on importantly different grounds.

Williams applied this principle to a case in which one man is psychologically continuous with the dead Guy Fawkes, and a case in which two men are. His argument was this. If we treat psychological continuity as a sufficient ground for speaking of identity, we shall say that the one man is Guy Fawkes. But we could not say that the two men are, although we should have the same ground. This disobeys the principle. The remedy is to deny that the one man is Guy Fawkes, to insist that sameness of the body is necessary for identity.

Williams' principle can yield a different answer. Suppose we regard psychological continuity as more important than sameness of the body.[15] And suppose that the one man really is psychologically (and causally) continuous with Guy Fawkes. If he is, it would disobey the principle to deny that he is Guy Fawkes, for we have the same important ground as in a normal case of identity. In the case of the two men, we again have the same important ground. So we ought to take the importance from the judgment of identity and attach it directly to this ground. We ought to say, as in Wiggins' case, that each limb of the branching relation is as good as survival. This obeys the principle.

To sum up these remarks: even if psychological continuity is neither logically, nor always in fact, one-one, it can provide a criterion of identity. For this can appeal to the relation of *non-branching* psychological continuity, which is logically one-one.[16]

The criterion might be sketched as follows. "X and Y are the same person if they are psychologically continuous and there is no person who is contemporary with either and psychologically continuous with the other." We should need to explain what we mean by "psychologically continuous" and say how much continuity the criterion requires. We should then, I think, have described a sufficient condition for speaking of identity.[17]

We need to say something more. If we admit that psychological continuity might not be one-one, we need to say what we ought to do if it were not one-one. Otherwise our account would be open to the objections that it is incomplete and arbitrary.[18]

I have suggested that if psychological continuity took a branching form, we ought to speak in a new way, regarding what we describe as having the same significance as identity. This answers these objections.[19]

We can now return to our discussion. We have three remaining aims. One is to suggest a sense of "survive" which does not imply identity. Another is to show that most of what matters in survival are relations of degree. A third is to show that none of these relations needs to be described in a way that presupposes identity.

We can take these aims in the reverse order.

III

The most important particular relation is that involved in memory. This is because it is so easy to believe that its description must refer to identity.[20] This belief about memory is an important cause of the view that personal identity has a special nature. But it has been well discussed by Shoemaker[21] and by Wiggins.[22] So we can be brief.

It may be a logical truth that we can only remember our own experiences. But we can frame a new concept for which this is not a logical truth. Let us call this "*q*-memory."

To sketch a definition[23] I am *q*-remembering an experience if (1) I have a belief about a past experience which seems in itself like a memory belief, (2) someone did have such an experience, and (3) my belief is dependent upon this experience in the same way (whatever that is) in which a memory of an experience is dependent upon it.

According to (1) *q*-memories seem like memories. So I *q*-remember *having* experiences.

This may seem to make *q*-memory presuppose identity. One might say, "My apparent memory of *having* an experience is an apparent memory of *my* having an experience. So how could I *q*-remember my having other people's experiences?"

This objection rests on a mistake. When I seem to remember an experience, I do indeed seem to remember *having* it.[24] But it cannot be a part of what I seem to remember about this experience that I, the person who now seems to remember it, am the person who had this experience.[25] That I am is something that I automatically assume. (My apparent memories sometimes come to me simply as the belief that *I* had a certain experience.) But it is something that I am justified in assuming only

because I do not in fact have *q*-memories of other people's experiences.

Suppose that I did start to have such *q*-memories. If I did, I should cease to assume that my apparent memories must be about my own experiences. I should come to assess an apparent memory by asking two questions: (1) Does it tell me about a past experience? (2) If so, whose?

Moreover (and this is a crucial point) my apparent memories would now come to me *as q*-memories. Consider those of my apparent memories which do come to me simply as beliefs about my past: for example, "I did that." If I knew that I could *q*-remember other people's experiences, these beliefs would come to me in a more guarded form: for example, "Someone—probably I—did that." I might have to work out who it was.

I have suggested that the concept of *q*-memory is coherent. Wiggins' case provides an illustration. The resulting people, in his case, both have apparent memories of living the life of the original person. If they agree that they are not this person, they will have to regard these as only *q*-memories. And when they are asked a question like "Have you heard this music before?" they might have to answer "I am sure that I *q*-remember hearing it. But I am not sure whether I remember hearing it. I am not sure whether it was I who heard it, or the original person."

We can next point out that on our definition every memory is also a *q*-memory. Memories are, simply, *q*-memories of one's own experiences. Since this is so, we could afford now to drop the concept of memory and use in its place the wider concept *q*-memory. If we did, we should describe the relation between an experience and what we now call a "memory" of this experience in a way which does not presuppose that they are had by the same person.[26]

This way of describing this relation has certain merits. It vindicates the "memory criterion" of personal identity against the charge of circularity.[27] And it might, I think, help with the problem of other minds.

But we must move on. We can next take the relation between an intention and a later action. It may be a logical truth that we can intend to perform only our own actions. But intentions can be redescribed as *q*-intentions. And one person could *q*-intend to perform another person's actions.

Wiggins' case again provides the illustration. We are supposing that neither of the resulting people is the original person. If so, we shall have to agree that the original person can, before the operation, q-intend to perform their actions. He might, for example, q-intend, as one of them, to continue his present career, and, as the other, to try something new.[28] (I say "q-intend as one of them" because the phrase "q-intend that one of them" would not convey the directness of the relation which is involved. If I intend that someone else should do something, I cannot get him to do it simply by forming this intention. But if I am the original person, and he is one of the resulting people, I can.)

The phrase "q-intend as one of them" reminds us that we need a sense in which one person can survive as two. But we can first point out that the concepts of q-memory and q-intention give us our model for the others that we need: thus, a man who can q-remember could q-recognize, and be a q-witness of, what he has never seen; and a man who can q-intend could have q-ambitions, make q-promises, and be q-responsible for.

To put this claim in general terms: many different relations are included within, or are a consequence of, psychological continuity. We describe these relations in ways which presuppose the continued existence of one person. But we could describe them in new ways which do not.

This suggests a bolder claim. It might be possible to think of experiences in a wholly "impersonal" way. I shall not develop this claim here. What I shall try to describe is a way of thinking of our own identity through time which is more flexible, and less misleading, than the way in which we now think.

This way of thinking will allow for a sense in which one person can survive as two. A more important feature is that it treats survival as a matter of degree.

IV

We must first show the need for this second feature. I shall use two imaginary examples.

The first is the converse of Wiggins' case: fusion. Just as division serves to show that what matters in survival need not be one-one, so fusion serves to show that it can be a question of degree.

Physically, fusion is easy to describe. Two people come together. While they are unconscious, their two bodies grow into one. One person then wakes up.

The psychology of fusion is more complex. One detail we have already dealt with in the case of the exam. When my mind was reunited, I remembered just having thought out two calculations. The one person who results from a fusion can, similarly, q-remember living the lives of the two original people. None of their q-memories need be lost.

But some things must be lost. For any two people who fuse together will have different characteristics, different desires, and different intentions. How can these be combined?

We might suggest the following. Some of these will be compatible. These can coexist in the one resulting person. Some will be incompatible. These, if of equal strength, can cancel out, and if of different strengths, the stronger can be made weaker. And all these effects might be predictable.

To give examples—first, of compatibility: I like Palladio and intend to visit Venice. I am about to fuse with a person who likes Giotto and intends to visit Padua. I can know that the one person we shall become will have both tastes and both intentions. Second, of incompatibility: I hate red hair, and always vote Labour. The other person loves red hair, and always votes Conservative. I can know that the one person we shall become will be indifferent to red hair, and a floating voter.

If we were about to undergo a fusion of this kind, would we regard it as death?

Some of us might. This is less absurd than regarding division as death. For after my division the two resulting people will be in every way like me, while after my fusion the one resulting person will not be wholly similar. This makes it easier to say, when faced with fusion, "I shall not survive," thus continuing to regard survival as a matter of all-or-nothing.

This reaction is less absurd. But here are two analogies which tell against it.

First, fusion would involve the changing of some of our characteristics and some of our desires. But only the very self-satisfied would think of this as death. Many people welcome treatments with these effects.

Second, someone who is about to fuse can have, beforehand, just as much "intentional control" over the actions of the resulting individual as someone who is about to marry can have, beforehand, over the actions of the resulting couple.

And the choice of a partner for fusion can be just as well considered as the choice of a marriage partner. The two original people can make sure (perhaps by "trial fusion") that they do have compatible characters, desires, and intentions.

I have suggested that fusion, while not clearly survival, is not clearly failure to survive, and hence that what matters in survival can have degrees.

To reinforce this claim we can now turn to a second example. This is provided by certain imaginary beings. These beings are just like ourselves except that they reproduce by a process of natural division.

We can illustrate the histories of these imagined beings with the aid of a diagram. The lines on the diagram represent the spatiotemporal paths which would be traced out by the bodies of these beings. We can call each single line (like the double line) a "branch"; and we can call the whole structure a "tree." And let us suppose that each "branch" corresponds to what is thought of as the life of one individual. These individuals are referred to as "A," "B^{+1}," and so forth.

Now, each single division is an instance of Wiggins' case. So A's relation to both B^{+1} and B^{+2} is just as good as survival. But what of A's relation to B^{+30}?

I said earlier that what matters in survival could be provisionally referred to as "psychological continuity." I must now distinguish this relation from another, which I shall call "psychological connectedness."

Let us say that the relation between a q-memory and the experience q-remembered is a "direct" relation. Another "direct" relation is that which holds between a q-intention and the q-intended action. A third is that which holds between different expressions of some lasting q-characteristic.

"Psychological connectedness," as I define it, requires the holding of these direct psychological relations. "Connectedness" is not transitive, since these relations are not transitive. Thus, if X q-remembers most of Y's life, and Y q-remembers most of Z's life, it does not follow that X q-remembers most of Z's life. And if X carries out the q-intentions of Y, and Y carries out the q-intentions of Z, it does not follow that X carries out the q-intentions of Z.

"Psychological continuity," in contrast, only requires overlapping chains of direct psychological relations. So "continuity" is transitive.

To return to our diagram. A is psychologically continuous with B^{+30}. There are between the two continuous chains of overlapping relations. Thus, A has q-intentional control over B^{+2}, B^{+2} has q-intentional control over B^{+6}, and so on up to B^{+30}. Or B^{+30} can q-remember the life of B^{+14}, B^{+14} can q-remember the life of B^{+6}, and so on back to A.[29]

A, however, need *not* be psychologically connected to B^{+30}. Connectedness requires direct relations. And if these beings are like us, A cannot stand in such relations to every individual in his indefinitely long "tree." Q-memories will weaken with the passage of time, and then fade away. Q-ambitions, once fulfilled, will be replaced by others. Q-characteristics will gradually change. In general, A stands in fewer and fewer direct psychological relations to an individual in his "tree" the more remote that individual is. And if the individual is (like B^{+30}) sufficiently remote, there may be between the two *no* direct psychological relations.

Now that we have distinguished the general relations of psychological continuity and psychological connectedness, I suggest that connectedness is a more important element in survival. As a claim about our own survival, this would need more arguments than I have space to give. But it seems clearly true for my imagined beings. A is as close psychologically to B^{+1} as I today am to myself tomorrow. A is as distant from B^{+30} as I am from my great-great-grandson.

Even if connectedness is not more important than continuity, the fact that one of these is a relation of degree is enough to show that what matters in survival can have degrees. And in any case the two relations are quite different. So our imagined

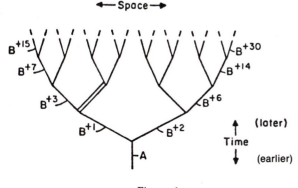

Figure 1

beings would need a way of thinking in which this difference is recognized.

V

What I propose is this.

First, A can think of any individual, anywhere in his "tree," as "a descendant self." This phrase implies psychological continuity. Similarity, any later individual can think of any earlier individual on the single path[30] which connects him to A as "an ancestral self."

Since psychological continuity is transitive, "being an ancestral self of" and "being a descendant self of" are also transitive.

To imply psychological connectedness I suggest the phrases "one of my future selves" and "one of my past selves."

These are the phrases with which we can describe Wiggins' case. For having past and future selves is, what we needed, a way of continuing to exist which does not imply identity through time. The original person does, in this sense, survive Wiggins' operation: the two resulting people are his later selves. And they can each refer to him as "my past self." (They can share a past self without being the same self as each other.)

Since psychological connectedness is not transitive, and is a matter of degree, the relations "being a past self of" and "being a future self of" should themselves be treated as relations of degree. We allow for this series of descriptions: "my most recent self," "one of my earlier selves," "one of my distant selves," "hardly one of *my* past selves (I can only *q*-remember a few of his experiences)," and, finally, "not in any way one of *my* past selves—just an ancestral self."

This way of thinking would clearly suit our first imagined beings. But let us now turn to a second kind of being. These reproduce by fusion as

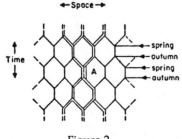

Figure 2

well as by division.[31] And let us suppose that they fuse every autumn and divide every spring. This yields the following diagram:

If A is the individual whose life is represented by the three-lined "branch," the two-lined "tree" represents those lives which are psychologically continuous with A's life. (It can be seen that each individual has his own "tree," which overlaps with many others.)

For the imagined beings in this second world, the phrases "an ancestral self" and "a descendant self" would cover too much to be of much use. (There may well be pairs of dates such that every individual who ever lived before the first date was an ancestral self of every individual who ever will live after the second date.) Conversely, since the lives of each individual last for only half a year, the word "I" would cover too little to do all of the work which it does for us. So part of this work would have to be done, for these second beings, by talk about past and future selves.

We can now point out a theoretical flaw in our proposed way of thinking. The phrase "a past self of" implies psychological connectedness. Being a past self of is treated as a relation of degree, so that this phrase can be used to imply the varying degrees of psychological connectedness. But this phrase can imply only the degrees of connectedness between different lives. It cannot be used within a single life. And our way of delimiting successive lives does not refer to the degrees of psychological connectedness. Hence there is no guarantee that this phrase, "a past self of," could be used whenever it was needed. There is no guarantee that psychological connectedness will not vary in degree within a single life.

This flaw would not concern our imagined beings. For they divide and unite so frequently, and their lives are in consequence so short, that within a single life psychological connectedness would always stand at a maximum.

But let us look, finally, at a third kind of being.

In this world there is neither division nor union. There are a number of everlasting bodies, which gradually change in appearance. And direct psychological relations, as before, hold only over limited periods of time. This can be illustrated with a third diagram (Figure 3). In this diagram the two shadings represent the degrees of psychological connectedness to their two central points.

These beings could not use the way of thinking that we have proposed. Since there is no

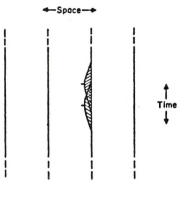

Figure 3

branching of psychological continuity, they would have to regard themselves as immortal. It might be said that this is what they are. But there is, I suggest, a better description.

Our beings would have one reason for thinking of themselves as immortal. The parts of each "line" are all psychologically continuous. But the parts of each "line" are not all psychologically connected. Direct psychological relations hold only between those parts which are close to each other in time. This gives our beings a reason for *not* thinking of each "line" as corresponding to one single life. For if they did, they would have no way of implying these direct relations. When a speaker says, for example, "I spent a period doing such and such," his hearers would not be entitled to assume that the speaker has any memories of this period, that his character then and now are in any way similar, that he is now carrying out any of the plans or intentions which he then had, and so forth. Because the word "I" would carry none of these implications, it would not have for these "immortal" beings the usefulness which it has for us.[32]

To gain a better way of thinking, we must revise the way of thinking that we proposed above. The revision is this. The distinction between successive selves can be made by reference, not to the branching psychological continuity, but to the degrees of psychological connectedness. Since this connectedness is a matter of degree, the drawing of these distinctions can be left to the choice of the speaker and be allowed to vary from context to context.

On this way of thinking, the word "I" can be used to imply the greatest degree of psychological connectedness. When the connections are reduced, when there has been any marked change of character or style of life, or any marked loss of memory, our imagined beings would say, "It was not I who did that, but an earlier self." They could then describe in what ways, and to what degree, they are related to this earlier self.

This revised way of thinking would suit not only our "immortal" beings. It is also the way in which we ourselves could think about our lives. And it is, I suggest, surprisingly natural.

One of its features, the distinction between successive selves, has already been used by several writers. To give an example, from Proust: "We are incapable, while we are in love, of acting as fit predecessors of the next persons who, when we are in love no longer, we shall presently have become. . . ."[33]

Although Proust distinguished between successive selves, he still thought of one person as being these different selves. This we would not do on the way of thinking that I propose. If I say, "It will not be me, but one of my future selves," I do not imply that I will be that future self. He is one of my later selves, and I am one of his earlier selves. There is no underlying person who we both are.

To point out another feature of this way of thinking. When I say, "There is no person who we both are," I am only giving my decision. Another person could say, "It will be you," thus deciding differently. There is no question of either of these decisions being a mistake. Whether to say "I," or "one of my future selves," or "a descendant self" is entirely a matter of choice. The matter of fact, which must be agreed, is only whether the disjunction applies. (The question "Are X and Y the same person?" thus becomes "Is X *at least* an ancestral [or descendant] self of Y?")

VI

I have tried to show that what matters in the continued existence of a person are, for the most part, relations of degree. And I have proposed a way of thinking in which this would be recognized.

I shall end by suggesting two consequences and asking one question.

It is sometimes thought to be especially rational to act in our own best interests. But I suggest that the principle of self-interest has no force. There are only two genuine competitors in this particular field. One is the principle of biased rationality: do what will best achieve what you actually want. The other is the principle of impartiality: do what is in the best interests of everyone concerned.

The apparent force of the principle of self-interest derives, I think, from these two other principles.

The principle of self-interest is normally supported by the principle of biased rationality. This is because most people care about their own future interests.

Suppose that this prop is lacking. Suppose that a man does not care what happens to him in, say, the more distant future. To such a man, the principle of self-interest can only be propped up by an appeal to the principle of impartiality. We must say, "Even if you don't care, you ought to take what happens to you then equally into account." But for this, as a special claim, there seem to me no good arguments. It can only be supported as part of the general claim, "You ought to take what happens to everyone equally into account."[34]

The special claim tells a man to grant an *equal* weight to all the parts of his future. The argument for this can only be that all the parts of his future are *equally* parts of *his* future. This is true. But it is a truth too superficial to bear the weight of the argument. (To give an analogy: The unity of a nation is, in its nature, a matter of degree. It is therefore only a superficial truth that all of a man's compatriots are *equally* his compatriots. This truth cannot support a good argument for nationalism.)[35]

I have suggested that the principle of self-interest has no strength of its own. If this is so, there is no special problem in the fact that what we ought to do can be against our interests. There is only the general problem that it may not be what we want to do.

The second consequence which I shall mention is implied in the first. Egoism, the fear not of near but of distant death, the regret that so much of one's *only* life should have gone by—these are not, I think, wholly natural or instinctive. They are all strengthened by the beliefs about personal identity which I have been attacking. If we give up these beliefs, they should be weakened.

My final question is this. These emotions are bad, and if we weaken them we gain. But can we achieve this gain without, say, also weakening loyalty to, or love of, other particular selves? As Hume warned, the "refined reflections which philosophy suggests . . . cannot diminish . . . our vicious passions . . . without diminishing . . . such as are virtuous. They are . . . applicable to all our affec-

tions. In vain do we hope to direct their influence only to one side."[36]

That hope *is* vain. But Hume had another: that more of what is bad depends upon false belief. This is also my hope.[37]

Endnotes

[1] I have been helped in writing this by D. Wiggins, D. F. Pears, P. F. Strawson, A. J. Ayer, M. Woods, N. Newman, and (through his publications) S. Shoemaker.

[2] Implicit in John Locke, *Essay Concerning Human Understanding*, ed. by John W. Yolton, vol. 2, chap. 27, sec. 18 (London, 1961) and discussed by (among others) A. N. Prior in "Opposite Number," *Review of Metaphysics*, 11 (1957–1958), and "Time, Existence and Identity," *Proceedings of the Aristotelian Society*, vol. 57 (1965–1966); J. Bennett in "The Simplicity of the Soul," *Journal of Philosophy*, vol. 64 (1967); and R. Chisholm and S. Shoemaker in "The Loose and Popular and the Strict and the Philosophical Senses of Identity," in *Perception and Personal Identity: Proceeding of the 1967 Oberlin Colloquium in Philosophy*, ed. Norman Care and Robert H. Grimm (Cleveland, 1967).

[3] David Wiggins, *Identity and Spatio-Temporal Continuity* (Oxford, 1967), p. 50.

[4] Sydney S. Shoemaker, *Self-Knowledge and Self-Identity* (Ithaca, N.Y., 1963), p. 22.

[5] Those who would disagree are not making a mistake. For them my argument would need a different case. There must be some multiple transplant, faced with which these people would both find it hard to believe that there must be an answer to the question about personal identity, and be able to be shown that nothing of importance turns upon this question.

[6] R. W. Sperry, in *Brain and Conscious Experience*, ed. J. C. Eccles (New York, 1966), p. 299.

[7] Cf. David Wiggins, *op. cit*, p. 40.

[8] Suppose the resulting people fight a duel. Are there three people fighting, one on each side, and one on both? And suppose one of the bullets kills. Are there two acts, one murder and one suicide? How many people are left alive? One? Two? (We could hardly say, "One and a half.") We could talk in this way. But instead of saying that the resulting people are the original person—so that the pair is a trio—it would be far simpler to treat them as a pair, and describe their relation to the original person in some new way. (I owe this suggested way of talking, and the objections to it, to Michael Woods.)

[9] Cf. Sydney Shoemaker, in *Perception and Personal Identity*, p. 54.

[10] Cf. David Wiggins, *op. cit.*

[11] Bernard Williams' "The Self and the Future," *Philosophical Review*, 79 (1970), 161–180, is relevant here. He asks the question "Shall I survive?" in a range of problem cases, and he shows how natural it is to believe (1) that this question must have an answer, (2) that the answer must be all-or-nothing, and (3) that there is a "risk" of our reaching the wrong answer. Because these beliefs are so natural, we should need in undermining them to discuss their causes. These, I think, can be found in the ways in which we misinterpret what it is to remember and to anticipate (cf. Williams' "Imagination and the Self," *Proceedings of the British Academy*, 52 [1966], 105–124); and also in the way in which certain features of our egoistic concern—e.g., that it is simple, and applies to all imaginable cases—are "projected" onto its object. (For another relevant discussion, see Terence Penelhum's *Survival and Disembodied Existence* [London, 1970], final chapters.)

[12] "Personal Identity and Individuation," *Proceedings of the Aristotelian Society*, 57 (1956–1957), 229–253; also *Analysis*, 21 (1960–1961), 43–48.

[13] J. M. Shorter, "More about Bodily Continuity and Personal Identity," *Analysis*, 22 (1961–1962), 79–85; and Mrs. J. M. R. Jack (unpublished), who requires that this truth be embedded in a causal theory.

[14] *Analysis*, 21 (1960–1961), 44.

[15] For the reasons given by A. M. Quinton in "The Soul," *Journal of Philosophy*, 59 (1962), 393–409.

[16] Cf. S. Shoemaker, "Persons and Their Pasts," *American Philosophical Quarterly*, 7 (1970), 269; and "Wiggins on Identity," *Philosophical Review*, 79 (1970), 542.

[17] But not a necessary condition, for in the absence of psychological continuity bodily identity might be sufficient.

[18] Cf. Bernard Williams, "Personal Identity and Individuation," *Proceedings of the Aristotelian Society*, 57 (1956–1957), 240–241, and *Analysis*, 21 (1960–1961), 44; and also Wiggins, *op. cit.*, p. 38: "if coincidence under [the concept] *f* is to be *genuinely* sufficient we must not withhold identity . . . simply because transitivity is threatened."

[19] Williams produced another objection to the "psychological criterion," that it makes it hard to explain the difference between the concepts of identity and exact similarity (*Analysis*, 21 [1960–1961], 48). But if we include the requirement of causal continuity we avoid this objection (and one of those produced by Wiggins in his note 47).

[20]Those philosophers who have held this belief, from Butler onward, are too numerous to cite.

[21]*Op. cit.*

[22] In a paper on Butler's objection to Locke (not yet published).

[23] I here follow Shoemaker's "quasi-memory." Cf. also Penelhum's "retrocognition," in his article on "Personal Identity," in the *Encyclopedia of Philosophy*, ed. Paul Edwards.

[24] As Shoemaker put it, I seem to remember the experience "from the inside" (*op. cit.*).

[25] This is what so many writers have overlooked. Cf. Thomas Reid: "My memory testifies not only that this was done, but that it was done by me who now remember it" ("Of Identity," in *Essays on the Intellectual Powers of Man*, ed. A. D. Woozley [London, 1941], p. 203). This mistake is discussed by A. B. Palma in "Memory and Personal Identity," *Australasian Journal of Philosophy*, 42 (1964), 57.

[26] It is not logically necessary that we only *q*-remember our own experiences. But it might be necessary on other grounds. This possibility is intriguingly explored by Shoemaker in his "Persons and Their Pasts" (*op. cit.*). He shows that *q*-memories can provide a knowledge of the world only if the observations which are *q*-remembered trace out fairly continuous spatiotemporal paths. If the observations which are *q*-remembered traced out a network of frequently interlocking paths, they could not, I think, be usefully ascribed to persisting observers, but would have to be referred to in some more complex way. But in fact the observations which are *q*-remembered trace out single separate paths; so we can ascribe them to ourselves. In other words, it is epistemologically necessary that the observations which are *q*-remembered should satisfy a certain general condition, one particular form of which allows them to be usefully self-ascribed.

[27] Cf. Wiggins' paper on Butler's objection to Locke.

[28] There are complications here. He could form *divergent* *q*-intentions only if he could distinguish, in advance, between the resulting people (e.g., as "the left-hander" and "the right-hander"). And he could be confident that such divergent *q*-intentions would be carried out only if he had reason to believe that neither of the resulting people would change their (inherited) mind. Suppose he was torn between duty and desire. He could not solve this dilemma by *q*-intending, as one of the resulting people, to do his duty, and, as the other, to do what he desires. For the one he *q*-intended to do his duty would face the same dilemma.

[29] The chain of continuity must run in one direction of time. B^{+2} is not, in the sense I intend, psychologically continuous with B^{+1}.

[30] Cf. David Wiggins, *op. cit.*

[31] Cf. Sydney Shoemaker in "Persons and Their Pasts," *op. cit.*

[32] Cf. Austin Duncan Jones, "Man's Mortality," *Analysis*, 28 (1967–1968), 65–70.

[33] *Within a Budding Grove* (London, 1949), I, 226 (my own translation).

[34] Cf. Thomas Nagel's *The Possibility of Altruism* (Oxford, 1970), in which the special claim is in effect defended as part of the general claim.

[35] The unity of a nation we seldom take for more than what it is. This is partly because we often think of nations, not as units, but in a more complex way. If we thought of ourselves in the way that I proposed, we might be less likely to take our own identity for more than what it is. We are, for example, sometimes told, "It is irrational to act against your own interests. After all, it will be you who will regret it." To this we could reply, "No, not me. Not even one of my future selves. Just a descendant self."

[36] "The Sceptic," in "Essays Moral, Political and Literary," *Humes's Moral and Political Philosophy* (New York, 1959), p. 349.

[37] (Footnote added in 1976.) Of the many things which I now regret in this paper, I shall briefly mention three. (1) Talk about 'successive selves' is only a *façon de parler*; taken as anything more it can be misleading. (2) I should not have claimed that connectedness was more important than continuity. I now think that neither relation can be shown to be more important than the other. (3) The real issue seems to me now this. Does personal identity just consist in bodily and psychological continuity, or is it a further fact, independent of the facts about these continuities? Our reactions to the 'problem cases' show, I think, that we believe the latter. And we seem inclined to believe that this further fact is peculiarly deep, and is all-or-nothing—we believe that in any describable case it must hold either completely or not at all. My main claim is the *denial of this further fact*. This is what may make a difference. (No one needs to be told that psychological continuity is, in part, a matter of degree.) For some further remarks, see 'On "The Importance of Self-identity," ' *Journal of Philosophy*, 21 Oct. 1971, 'Later Selves and Moral Principles,' in *Philosophy and Personal Relations*, ed. Alan Montefiore (Routledge & Kegan Paul, 1973), and 'Lewis, Perry, and What Matters', in *The Identities of Persons*, ed. Amelie Rorty (University of California Press, 1976).

20. *The Self as Private Object*

THOMAS NAGEL

According to Thomas Nagel, professor of philosophy at New York University, the concept of the self is essentially a psychological concept. It is the concept of a *subject* that has various mental states and is aware of the world from a particular (first-person) point of view. He sides with Locke against Reid in maintaining that one can conceive of the same self as having a different soul from time to time. But he also sides with Reid in maintaining that psychological discontinuity is compatible with sameness of self. Thus, he finds no solution to the problem of personal identity in either the persistent unity view of Reid or Chisholm, or the psychological continuity theories of Locke and Parfit. Nagel's own gambit is to treat the self as "whatever persisting individual in the objective order underlies the subjective continuities of that mental life that I call mine." Essentially, he believes the entity that fills that criterion is the brain, and so he maintains that one is essentially one's brain.

The concept of the self seems suspiciously pure—too pure—when we look at it from inside. The self is the ultimate private object, apparently lacking logical connections to anything else, mental or physical. When I consider my own individual life from inside, it seems that my existence in the future or the past—the existence of the same 'I' as this one—depends on nothing but itself. To capture my own existence it seems enough to use the word "I", whose meaning is entirely revealed on any occasion of its use. "I know what I mean by 'I.' I mean *this*!" (as one might think that the concept of a phenomenological quality like sweetness is fully captured in the thought "the same as *this*").

My nature then appears to be at least conceptually independent not only of bodily continuity but also of all other subjective mental conditions, such as memory and psychological similarity. It can seem, in this frame of mind, that whether a past or future mental state is mine or not is a fact not analyzable in terms of any relations of continuity, psychological or physical, between that state and my present state. The migration of the self from one body to another seems conceivable, even if it is not in fact possible. So does the persistence of the self over a total break in psychological continuity—as in the fantasy of reincarnation without memory. If all these things really are possible, I certainly can't be an organism: I must be a pure, featureless mental receptacle.

The apparently strict, perfect, and unanalyzable identity of self has tempted some to objectify its existence by postulating a similarly disconnected soul designed expressly for the purpose, and otherwise characterized negatively. But such a thing seems inadequate to bear the weight of personal identity, which seems to escape all attempts to define it. We can see this in the classical debates about personal identity between Locke on the one hand and Reid and Butler on the other. Both sides seem to be right in their rejection of the other side, but wrong in their positive theories.

Locke seems right in asserting that a divergence of same self from either same soul or same body is conceivable. This reflects the truth that the self cannot be defined as a kind of object, either physical or nonphysical, but must be understood as same subjective consciousness. What Locke claimed was that if a soul were postulated as the individual that gave identity to the self, it would drop out as irrelevant to the actual operation of that

From Thomas Nagel, *The View from Nowhere* (Oxford University Press, 1986), pp. 32–45. Copyright © 1986 by Thomas Nagel. Reprinted by permission of Oxford University Press.

idea. Kant makes a similar point in the third paralogism.

On the other hand, Butler and Reid seem right in arguing that sameness of self cannot be adequately defined in terms of memory continuity. And even more sophisticated analyses in terms of qualitative psychological continuity seem not to capture the essence of the idea of same consciousness, which seems to be something additional and not complex at all. Discontinuity in the self seems compatible with any amount of continuity in psychological content, and vice versa. But Reid and Butler are wrong in thinking that a nonphysical substance is therefore what the self must be. That after all is just another occupant of the objective order. An individual consciousness may depend for its existence on either a body or a soul, but its identity is essentially that of a psychological subject, and not equivalent to anything else—not even anything else psychological.

At the same time it seems to be something determinate and nonconventional. That is, the question with regard to any future experience, "Will it be mine or not?" seems to require a definite yes or no answer. And the answer must be determined by the facts, and not by an externally motivated and optional decision about how a word is to be used or how it is convenient to cut up the world into pieces (as might be possible with 'same nation', 'same restaurant', or 'same automobile').

This seems to leave us with the conclusion that being mine is an irreducible, unanalyzable characteristic of all my mental states, and that it has no essential connection with anything in the objective order or any connection among those states over time.[1] Even if it is causally dependent on something else, such as the continued existence of my brain, there is no way of finding this out on the basis of the idea of the self. The question of whether a future experience will be mine or not demands a definite answer without providing any way of determining what that answer is, even if all other facts are known.

There must be something wrong with this picture, but it is not easy to say what or to suggest a better one that admits essential connections between personal identity and anything else. Like other psychological concepts, the ordinary concept of the self breeds philosophical illusions that are difficult to resist without falling into errors that are at least as bad, and often shallower.

The apparent impossibility of identifying or essentially connecting the self with anything comes from the Cartesian conviction that its nature is fully revealed to introspection, and that our immediate subjective conception of the thing in our own case contains everything essential to it, if only we could extract it. But it turns out that we can extract nothing, not even a Cartesian soul. And the very bareness and apparent completeness of the concept leaves no room for the discovery that it refers to something that has other essential features which would figure in a richer account of what I really am. Identification of myself with an objectively persisting thing of whatever kind seems to be excluded in advance.

The first step in resisting this conclusion is to deny that the concept of myself, or any other psychological concept, is or could be as purely subjective as the Cartesian assumption takes it to be. As I said earlier, picking up a famous point of Wittgenstein's, even subjective concepts have their appropriate objectivity. I [have] discussed the possibility of extending the idea of mental objectivity to cover more than the range of mental phenomena with which we are subjectively familiar, but here I want to concentrate on the more limited objectivity that characterizes even those ordinary mental concepts, including personal identity, which we can all apply in the first person to ourselves.

Some of the more radical experiments of imagination that lead to the apparent detachment of the self from everything else result from delusions of conceptual power. It is an error, though a natural one, to think that a psychological concept like personal identity can be understood through an examination of my first-person concept of self, apart from the more general concept of 'someone' of which it is the essence of 'I' to be the first-person form. I would add only that the full conditions of personal identity cannot be extracted from the concept of a person at all: they cannot be arrived at a priori.

The concept of 'someone' is not a generalization of the concept of 'I'. Neither can exist without the other, and neither is prior to the other. To possess the concept of a subject of consciousness an individual must be able in certain circumstances to identify himself and the states he is in without external observation. But these identifications must correspond by and large to those that can be made on the basis of external observation, both by others and by the individual himself. In this respect 'I' is like other psychological concepts, which are applicable to states of which their subjects can be aware without the observational evidence used by others to ascribe those states to them.

As with other concepts, however, we cannot immediately infer the nature of the thing referred to from the conditions of our possession of the concept. Just as adrenalin would exist even if no one had ever thought about it, so conscious mental states and persisting selves could exist even if the concepts didn't. Given that we have these concepts, we apply them to other beings, actual and possible, who lack them. The natural (and treacherous) question then becomes, what *are* these things, apart from the concepts which enable us to refer to them? In particular, what is this self which I can reidentify without the observational evidence used by others to reidentify it? The problem, with regard to the self as with regard to sensations, is how to avoid the error of false objectification, or objectification of the wrong form, of something that does not conform to the physical conception of objective reality.

There must be a notion of objectivity which applies to the self, to phenomenological qualities, and to other mental categories, for it is clear that the idea of a mistake with regard to my own personal identity, or with regard to the phenomenological quality of an experience, makes sense. I may falsely remember making a witty remark that in fact was made in my presence by someone else, I may think falsely that the way something tastes to me now is the same as it tasted to me yesterday; I may think that I am someone I am not. There is a distinction between appearance and reality in this domain as elsewhere. Only the objectivity underlying this distinction must be understood as objectivity with regard to something subjective—mental rather than physical objectivity.

In the case of sensation, the reality is itself a form of appearance, and the distinction one between real appearance and apparent appearance. This cannot be captured by something which is just like an ordinary object or physical property, except that it is visible to only one person. But the correct account of it is extremely difficult, because the conditions of objectivity in the application of psychological concepts do not enter noticeably into each application of those concepts, especially in the first person. They are hidden, because the concepts seem perfectly simple.

When a mental concept seems simple and unanalyzable, there is a philosophical temptation to interpret it as referring to a privately accessible something, which the subjective appearance of the self, or of phenomenological sameness, is the appearance *of*. I believe Wittgenstein in the *Investigations* has made a convincing case that if we construe mental concepts this way, the private something drops out as irrelevant, which shows that there is something wrong with the construal (secs. 200–300, approximately). His argument was offered with respect to sensations: it was designed to show that sensation terms were not the names of private features or objects of experience such as sense data were supposed to be. Similarity or difference of sensations is similarity or difference of sensory appearances, not of something that appears.

The argument is in part a *reductio*: Even if every sensation were the perception of a private object or feature, the sensation would be not the thing itself but its appearing to us in a certain way. Even if the thing changed, the sensation would be the same if it appeared the same. Thus the object drops out as irrelevant to the operation of the concept. (This need not imply incorrigibility with regard to our sensations, since there can be divergence between an appearance and our beliefs about it. It is the appearance itself to which the sensation term refers.)

The other aspect of the argument—the general private language argument—is too complex to discuss adequately here. Wittgenstein claims that there could be no concept of a necessarily private object of experience—that is, a type of thing that was in principle detectable by only one person— since no distinction could exist between the correct and incorrect sincere application of such a concept: adherence to or deviation from the rule for its application by its sole user. All concepts, including concepts of how things appear to us, must admit this distinction. The rule for their use cannot collapse into the individual user's sincere application of them. Otherwise there is nothing he is *saying about* a thing in applying the term to it. To mean something by a term I must be able to make sense of the possibility that my actual use of the term has deviated from that meaning without my knowing it. Otherwise my use doesn't bring with it any meaning apart from itself.

Wittgenstein believes that psychological concepts meet the condition of being governed by objective rules, in virtue of the connection between first-person and third-person ascription. That is the sort of objectivity appropriate to what is essentially subjective.

Whether or not we accept his positive account, with its famous obscurity and reticence, I believe his point that mental concepts are sui generis is correct. They refer not to private objects like souls and sense data but to subjective points of view and their modifications—even though the range of mental phenomena is not limited to those we ourselves can identify subjectively. The question is how to apply to the problem of personal identity this general idea that mental concepts do not refer to logically private objects of awareness.

Personal Identity and Reference

Identity is not similarity. The conditions of objectivity for sensations cannot be directly transferred to the self, because being mine is not a phenomenological quality of my experiences and, as with other types of thing, qualitative similarity is here neither a necessary nor a sufficient condition of numerical identity. Still, some sort of objectivity must characterize the identity of the self, otherwise the subjective question whether a future experience will be mine or not will be contentless: *nothing* will make an answer right or wrong. What kind of objectivity can this be?

There are two possible types of answer. One explains the identity of the self in terms of other psychological concepts, thus making its objectivity parasitic on theirs. This is the family of explanations of personal identity in terms of some form or other of psychological continuity—psychological continuity broadly conceived to include action, emotion, and intention as well as thought, memory, and perception. The other type of answer treats personal identity as an independent psychological concept, so that the self is something that underlies the psychological continuities where they exist but has no necessary or sufficient conditions specifiable in terms of them.

This second type of answer is what I shall defend. I believe that whatever we are told about continuity of mental content between two stages of experience, the issue logically remains open whether they have the same subject or not. In addition, it is clearly part of the idea of my identity that I could have led a completely different mental life,

from birth. This would have happened, for example, if I had been adopted at birth and brought up in Argentina. The question is how this idea of the same subject can meet the conditions of objectivity appropriate for a psychological concept: how it can express an identity that is subjective (not merely biological) but at the same time admits the distinction between correct and incorrect self-identification.

Even if such a thing cannot be defined in terms of psychological continuities, it will be closely connected with them. Most of my self-reidentifications, and most reidentifications of me by others, refer to stages linked to the present directly or indirectly by memory, intention, and so forth. But here as elsewhere the reality can diverge from the evidence. The idea of myself is the idea of something to which memory and externally observable continuity of mental life stand in an evidential relation—something which can at one time subjectively reidentify itself in memory, expectation, and intention, and can be observationally reidentified as the same person by others, but which *is* something in its own right. In other words, I am rejecting the view that the person is merely the grammatical or logical subject of mental and physical predicates ascribed on the usual grounds. Those grounds provide only evidence of personal identity, rather than criteria of it.

The question is whether this reach of the concept beyond the introspective and observational evidence and the correlation between them permits us to interpret it as referring to something with still further features—something with a nature of its own. If so, then those features can supply further conditions of personal identity which may determine an answer to the question whether someone will be me, in cases where the usual psychological evidence leaves the question unsettled. The idea is that the ordinary conditions of application of the concept point to something further to which the concept refers but whose essence it does not capture.

This is possible only on the assumption that the concept of the self does not tell us fully what kind of things we are. But that assumption seems to me to be true. Our idea of ourselves is one whose exact extension is determined in part by things we don't necessarily know simply in virtue of, or as a condition of, having the concept: our true nature and the principle of our identity may be partly hidden from us. This is a familiar enough situation with regard to other concepts. It is obviously true of definite descriptions, and Kripke and Putnam have argued that it is also true of proper names and natural kind terms, even if they cannot be analyzed as definite descriptions in disguise.[2] But it is harder to accept with respect to the self, because of the apparent subjective completeness of that idea. It does not immediately seem, like the concept of 'gold' or the concept of 'cat' or the concept of 'Cicero', to have any blank space which can be filled in by discoveries as to the true internal constitution of the thing. Nothing seems to correspond here to our general idea of a kind of substance or a kind of living creature whose complete nature we do not know. The idea of the self seems not to be a partial specification of anything.

In general, when a term refers to something whose real nature is not fully captured by the subjective conditions for the term's application, those conditions will nevertheless dictate what kind of thing it is about the world that determines the real nature of the referent. Thus before the development of chemistry, gold already referred to a type of metal, and this determined which kinds of further discoveries about its material composition would reveal the true nature of gold. Specifically it determined that certain common observable properties of gold would have to be explained by its true nature, and that the explanation would have to be uniform for different samples of gold, in terms of something of which they were all composed.

What might perform the function of the idea of a 'type of metal,' or 'type of material substance' in the case of ourselves? Subjects of experience are not like anything else. While they do have observable properties, the most important thing about them is that they are subjects, and it is their subjective mental properties that must be explained if we are to be able to identify them with anything in the objective order. As with gold, there is also an implication of generality—that the self in my case is something of the same kind as it is for other persons.

I suggest that the concept of the self is open to objective "completion" provided something can be found which straddles the subjective-objective gap. That is, the concept contains the possibility that it refers to something with further objective essential features beyond those included in the psychological concept itself—something whose objective persistence is among the necessary con-

ditions of personal identity—but only if this objectively describable referent is in a strong sense the basis for those subjective features that typify the persistent self.

This is where dual aspect theory comes in. The concept of the self does not of course imply the truth of dual aspect theory. The concept implies only that if it refers at all, it must refer to something essentially subjective, often identifiable nonobservationally in the first person and observationally in the third, which is the persisting locus of mental states and activities and the vehicle for carrying forward familiar psychological continuities when they occur. So far as the *concept* is concerned, this might turn out to be any of a number of things or there might be no such thing. But if dual aspect theory is correct, then it is as a matter of fact the intact brain—customarily found in a living animal of a certain kind but not in principle inseparable from it. I could lose everything but my functioning brain and still be me, and it might even be possible by some monstrosity of genetic engineering to produce a brain that had never been part of an animal but was nevertheless an individual subject.

Let me repeat that this is not offered as an analysis of the concept of the self but as an empirical hypothesis about its true nature. My concept of myself contains the blank space for such an objective completion, but does not fill it in. I am whatever persisting individual in the objective order underlies the subjective continuities of that mental life that I call mine. But a type of objective identity can settle questions about the identity of the self only if the thing in question is both the bearer of mental states and the cause of their continuity when there is continuity. If my brain meets these conditions then the core of the self—what is essential to my existence—is my functioning brain. As things are, the rest of my body is integrally attached to it and is also part of me, so I am not just my brain: I weigh more than three pounds, am more than six inches high, have a skeleton, etc. But the brain is the only part of me whose destruction I could not possibly survive. The brain, but not the rest of the animal, is essential to the self.

Let me express this with mild exaggeration as the hypothesis that I am my brain, and let me leave aside for now problems that could be raised about what counts as the same brain (for example, about its dependence on the sameness of the organism). On the evidence, the intact brain seems to be responsible for the maintenance of memory and other psychological continuities and for the unity of consciousness. If in addition the mental states are themselves states of the brain, which is therefore not just a physical system, then the brain is a serious candidate for being the self—even though, as I shall admit, it does not meet all the intuitive conditions on the idea of the self.

What I am is whatever is in fact the seat of the person TN's experiences and his capacity to identify and reidentify himself and his mental states, in memory, experience, and thought, without relying on the sort of observational evidence that others must use to understand him. That I am a person requires that I have this capacity, but not that I know what makes it possible. In fact, I do not know in any detail what is responsible for it, and others need not know it either in order to know that I am a person. So far as their concept of me and my conception of myself as a self are concerned, the possibility of my subjective identification of myself could depend on a soul, or on the activity of a part of my brain, or on something else that I can't even imagine. If it depended on a soul, then my identity would be the identity of that soul, so long as the soul persisted in the condition which, when it occupies TN, allows it to undergo TN's experiences and enables TN to identify himself and his states subjectively. If it could persist thus after the death of the body, I could exist after death. (Perhaps I could even exist without memory of my present life.)

If, on the other hand, my mental life depends entirely on certain states and activities of my brain, and if some form of dual aspect theory is correct, then that brain in those states (not just in its physical states) is what I am, and my survival of the destruction of my brain is not conceivable. However, I may not know that it is not conceivable, because I may not know the conditions of my own identity. That knowledge is not provided by my subjective idea of myself. It is not provided by the idea others have of me either. Something is left open by the idea which has to be discovered.

The point is a familiar one, taken from Kripke's views about reference. The essence of what a term refers to depends on what the world is actually like, and not just on what we have to know in order to use and understand the term. I may understand and be able to apply the term "gold" without knowing what gold really is—what physical and chemical conditions anything must meet to be gold. My prescientific idea of gold, including my knowledge of the perceptible features by which I identify samples of it, includes a blank space to be filled in by empirical discoveries about its intrinsic nature. Similarly I may understand and be able to apply the term "I" to myself without knowing what I really am. In Kripke's phrase, what I use to *fix the reference* of the term does not tell me everything about the nature of the referent.

This can give rise to those illusions, discussed earlier, concerning the detachability of the self from everything else. Since I do not know what I really am, it seems possible so far as what I *do* know is concerned—epistemically possible—that I may really be any of a variety of things (soul, brain, etc.) that could underlie my capacity for subjective self-identification. Various accounts of my real nature, and therefore various conditions of my identity over time, are compatible with my concept of myself as a self, for that concept leaves open the real nature of what it refers to. This is equally true of other people's concept of me as a self, since it is true of the concept of a self or continuing subject of consciousness in general.

Now this may lead me to think I can imagine myself surviving the death of my brain even if that is not in fact imaginable. On the other hand, it may equally well lead me to think I can imagine myself surviving the destruction of my soul—or anything else. What I imagine may be possible so far as what I know about my nature is concerned, but may not be possible so far as my actual nature is concerned. In that case I will not have imagined *myself* surviving the death of my brain, but will merely have confused epistemic with metaphysical possibility. In trying to conceive of my survival after the destruction of my brain, I will not succeed in referring to myself in such a situation if I am in fact my brain. Even if I conceive of a soul with the appropriate memories surviving the death of my body, that will not be to conceive of myself surviving, if in fact I am not a soul.[3]

It is the mistake of thinking that my concept of myself alone can reveal the objective conditions of my identity that leads to the giddy sense that personal identity is totally independent of everything else, so that it might even be possible for you and me to switch selves although *nothing* else changed, either physically or psychologically, or in any other respect. Adding in the third person and second person conditions of application of the concept doesn't complete the specification of its reference either, though. The fact that I can reidentify persons by looking at them, tracing their movements, and listening to what they say does not mean that I know their true nature. I do not know it (though I may conjecture about it), unless I know not only what makes them the organisms they are, but also what makes them capable of subjective, nonobservational self-knowledge extending over time. Without this information, the concept of personal identity will not tell me what I am or what they are.

Parfit

This approach to personal identity is not without its problems. If what we are depends not only on our concept of ourselves but on the world, the possibility arises that nothing in the world satisfies the concept perfectly. The best candidate may be in various ways defective.

To what extent could it turn out that our true nature diverges from our intuitive conception of ourselves? More specifically, does the hypothesis that I am my brain require the abandonment of central features of my conception of myself; and if so, does this cast doubt on the hypothesis? If the best candidate for what I am is my brain, the best candidate may not be good enough; in that case the proper conclusion would be that the self which we intuitively take ourselves to be does not exist at all.

The problems I have in mind are those which have led Derek Parfit to conclude that the most natural prereflective concept of the self does not apply to us. To say that I am, as a matter of fact rather than of definition, essentially my brain does not solve those acute puzzles he has posed, concerning the apparent unique simplicity and indivisibility of the self.

Parfit begins by describing a natural conception of the self which he calls the Simple View.[4] This says that nothing can be me unless (a) it determines a completely definite answer to the question whether any given experience—past, present, or future—is mine or not (the all-or-nothing condition); and (b) it excludes the possibility that two experiences both of which are mine should occur in subjects that are not identical with each other (the one-one condition). Subjectively, these seem like nonnegotiably essential features of myself.

But the brain is a complex organ, neither simple nor indivisible. While there are no examples of gradual replacement of its cells over time, for example by grafting, there are the famous examples

of its division by commissurotomy, with striking psychological effects.[5] As Parfit points out, if my survival depends on the continued functioning of my brain, it seems that I might be able to survive as two distinct selves, not identical with each other, and this would violate the one-one condition. Similarly, he has observed, if the cells of my brain could be gradually replaced, with accompanying gradual transformation of my personality and memories, then a future experience might belong to someone about whom there was *no answer* to the question whether he was me or not, and this would violate the all-or-nothing condition.

Parfit himself concludes that the conditions of the ordinary concept of personal identity cannot be met if such things are possible. Our ordinary concept is so tied to the Simple View that it can actually apply only if the mental life of each of us has a subject that makes such things impossible—something like a simple, indivisible soul. If, as appears to be the case, the subject of our mental lives is a complex, divisible brain, then it is not a suitable bearer of the identity of the self, and we should adopt instead a more complex view of our own nature. His suggestion is that we should withdraw our special self-interested concern from the identity of the organ that underlies our mental lives, and be concerned instead about the psychological continuities themselves, however they are produced, which may hold to different degrees and need not be one-one.

I believe, however, that the actual cause is what matters—even if it doesn't satisfy the conditions of the Simple View. This would be one of those cases where some of our most important beliefs about the referent of one of our concepts may be false, without its following that there is no such thing. In ordinary circumstances, the brain satisfies the one-one and all-or-nothing conditions, but it does not do so necessarily. Nevertheless, it seems to me to be something without which I could not survive—so that if a physically distinct replica of me were produced who was psychologically continuous with me though my brain had been destroyed, it would not be me and its survival would not be as good (for me) as my survival. This assumes that there can be an empirically discoverable answer to the question what I in fact am which falsifies some of my fundamental beliefs about what kind of thing I am.[6]

The difficult issue is whether the answer I propose falsifies such fundamental beliefs that it is disqualified. The brain does not guarantee an absolutely definite and unique answer to the question whether any of the centers of consciousness existing at some past or future time are mine or not. The possibility of its being split or partially replaced implies this. It is therefore hard to internalize a conception of myself as identical with my brain: if I am told that my brain is about to be split, and that the left half will be miserable and the right half euphoric, there is no form that my subjective expectations can take, because my idea of myself doesn't allow for divisibility—nor do the emotions of expectation, fear, and hope.

It might be asked, if I am prepared to abandon the Simple View over such resistance, why not go all the way with Parfit and abandon the identification of the self with the typical underlying cause of the mental life—regarding psychological continuity, however maintained, as what is really important? What is the advantage of continuing to identify myself with a *thing* whose survival need be neither one-one nor all-or-nothing? Why isn't it enough to identify myself as a person in the weaker sense in which this is the subject of mental predicates but not a separately existing thing—more like a nation than a Cartesian ego?

I don't really have an answer to this, except the question-begging answer that one of the conditions that the self should meet if possible is that it be something in which the flow of consciousness and the beliefs, desires, intentions, and character traits that I have all take place—something beneath the contents of consciousness, which might even survive a radical break in the continuity of consciousness. If there were no such thing, then the idea of personal identity would be an illusion, but we are not in that situation. Even if nothing can be found to fill this role which satisfies the condition of the Simple View, the brain with its problematic conditions of identity in certain cases is still better than nothing. And it is a possible hypothesis that I am my brain, since it is not ruled out by the apparent subjective conceivability of my moving to a different brain. That seems conceivable, to the extent that it does, only so far as what my incomplete concept of myself tells me; and that isn't a reliable basis for deciding what is possible. If a dual aspect theory is correct, then it is not possible for my mental life to go on in a different brain.[7]

Endnotes

[1] The conclusion is accepted by Madell [*The Identity of the Self*, Edinburgh University Press, 1983]. What unites all my experiences, he says, is simply that they all have the irreducible and unanalyzable property of "mineness."

[2] Kripke [*Naming and Necessity*, Harvard University Press, 1980]; Putnam ["The Meaning of 'Meaning,'" *Mind, Language, and Reality: Philosophical Papers*, Vol 2, Cambridge University Press, 1975]; see Searle [*Intentionality*, Cambridge University Press, 1983] for an argument that this view doesn't involve as big a departure from the Fregean tradition of analysis of sense and reference as is often supposed.

[3] Cf. Williams ["Imagination and the Self," *Proceedings of the British Academy*, 1966, p. 44]: "At least with regard to the self, the imagination is too tricky a thing to provide a reliable road to the comprehension of what is logically possible."

[4] This term appears in Parfit ["Later Selves and Moral Principles," in A. Montefiore, ed., *Philosophy and Personal Relations*, London, Routledge & Kegan Paul, 1973], and I shall use it for convenience here, even though in the much more elaborate treatment of Parfit [*Reasons and Persons*, Oxford University Press, 1984], several different non-reductionist views are distinguished. See p. 210, for example.

[5] Parfit [*Reasons and Persons*, sec. 87]. I have discussed these cases in Nagel ["Brain Bisection and the Unity of Consciousness," *Synthese*, 1971].

[6] My position is rather like Mackie's, except that he recommends it as a conceptual reform, inconsistent with our present concept of personal identity. He also thinks that further reform might be in order if it turned out that we could produce exact physical and psychological replicas of people: then even brain identity could be dropped as a condition of personal identity. See Mackie [*Problems from Locke*, Oxford University Press, 1976], pp 201–3.

[7] I have not begun to do justice here to the Proustian exhaustiveness of Parfit's arguments. Among other things, he comments on some remarks in an earlier draft of the present chapter which I have since abandoned—having to do with possible "series-persons" whose bodies are destroyed and replicated regularly. I said there that they could reasonably regard replication as survival, though we could not. Parfit replies that we can choose what type of beings to think of ourselves as—and he defines "Phoenix Parfit" as the individual he is who *would* survive replication. This is an ingenious suggestion, but there must be some objective limits to the freedom to reconstrue oneself, or it will become hollow. I can't defeat death by

identifying myself as "Proteus Nagel", the being who survives if *anyone* survives. "Phoenix Parfit" seems to me also an abuse, though clearly a lesser one, of the privilege of choosing one's own identity.

But I also think now that the series-persons themselves, if they were of human origin, might simply be deluded to think they survive replication—and that like us, they would not be entitled to the "Phoenix" concept of themselves.

Further Reading

Ayer, A. J. *The Concept of a Person and Other Essays*. New York: Macmillan, 1964.

Brennan, A. *Conditions of Identity*. New York: Oxford University Press, 1988.

Brody, B. *Identity and Essence*. Princeton: Princeton University Press, 1980.

Butchvarov, P. *Being Qua Being*. Bloomington: Indiana University Press, 1979.

Care, N., and Grimm, R. H., eds. *Perception and Personal Identity*. Cleveland: Ohio University Press, 1969.

Carruthers, P. *Introducing Persons*. London: Routledge, 1989.

Chisholm, R. D. *Person and Object*. Chicago: Open Court, 1976.

Flew, A., ed. *Body, Mind and Death*. New York: Macmillan, 1964.

Flew, A. *The Logic of Mortality: On Personal Identity*. Oxford: Blackwell, 1987.

Hirsch, E. *The Concept of Identity*. New York: Oxford University Press, 1982.

Lewis, H. D. *The Elusive Self*. London: Macmillan, 1982.

Loux, M. *Substance and Attribute*. Dördrecht: D. Reidel, 1978.

Mackie, J. *Problems from Locke*, Chapter 6. New York: Oxford University Press, 1976.

Madell, G. *The Identity of the Self*. Edinburgh: Edinburgh University Press, 1981.

Marks, C. E. *Commissurotomy, Consciousness, and Unity of Mind*. Cambridge, Mass.: MIT Press, 1986.

Noonan, H. *Personal Identity*. New York: Routledge & Kegan Paul, 1989.

Nozick, R. *Philosophical Explanations*, Chapter I. Cambridge, Mass.: Harvard University Press, 1981.

Peacocke, A., and Gillett, G., eds. *Persons and Personality*. Oxford: Blackwell, 1987.

Penelhum, T. *Survival and Disembodied Existence*. London: Routledge & Kegan Paul, 1970.

Perry, J., ed. *Personal Identity*. Berkeley: University of California Press, 1976.

Perry, J. *A Dialogue on Personal Identity and Immortality*. Indianapolis: Hackett, 1978.

Rorty, A., ed. *The Identities of Persons*. Berkeley: University of California Press, 1976.

Shalom, A. *The Body/Mind Conceptual Framework and the Problem of Personal Identity: Some Theories in Philosophy, Psychoanalysis and Neurology*. Atlantic Highlands, N.J.: Humanities Press International, 1985.

Shoemaker, S. *Self-Knowledge and Self-Identity*. Ithaca, N.Y.: Cornell University Press, 1963.

Shoemaker, S. *Identity, Cause and Mind*. Cambridge: Cambridge University Press, 1984.

Shoemaker S., and Swinburne, R. G. *Personal Identity*. Oxford: Blackwell, 1984.

Strawson, P. F. *Individuals*. London: Methuen, 1959.

Swinburne, R. G. *The Evolution of the Soul*. Oxford: Oxford Clarendon Press, 1986.

Vesey, G. *Personal Identity*. New York: Macmillan, 1974.

Wiggins, D. *Identity and Spatio-Temporal Continuity*. Oxford: Blackwell, 1967.

Wiggins, D. *Sameness and Substance*. Oxford: Blackwell, 1980.

Wilkes, K. *Real People*. Cambridge: Cambridge University Press, 1989.

Williams, B. *Problems of the Self*. Cambridge: Cambridge University Press, 1973.

Wittgenstein, L. *The Blue and Brown Books*. Oxford: Blackwell, 1958.

Wollheim, R. *The Thread of Life*. Cambridge, Mass.: Harvard University Press, 1984.

Part III
Mind

What are persons? In Part II, this question was raised in the context of wondering what constituted the *identity* of a person through change. Most answers assume a person is a conscious, thinking being (or a being able to be conscious). In other words, it is assumed a person has a *mind*. Though one can be certain one is conscious, at least when thinking about thinking, the *nature* of consciousness has often struck philosophers as most puzzling. Minds are quite different from rocks or trees, but how exactly should the differences be de-scribed and understood? When philosophers ask this question they are often wondering whether an explanation of mental phenomena must posit basic kinds of entities that are very different from the basic entities used to explain the rest of nature. For example, are minds so different from rocks and trees that they cannot be understood to be arrangements of matter and energy in the way rocks and trees are so understood?

Debates about the nature of mind often center on what is called the mind-body problem. Is the mind some part or aspect of the body? Are mental phenomena in the brain? Are they some process in the nervous system? Mental life involves a variety of feelings, qualitative perceptions, and an ability to grasp meaning. Assuming one's body is made of physical stuff (namely, collections of molecules), how can all these mental phenomena be just the electrochemical activity of molecules in one's head? Some philosophers claim they cannot be, so they argue that the mind is not physical. They believe it is something altogether different from the body as it is understood by science. Other philosophers, however, are impressed by the underlying unity of nature as revealed in science, and they argue that mental phenomena can in some way be identified with, or reduced to, physical phenomena.

Formulated in this way, the mind-body problem is a relatively recent problem. It came into sharp focus in the context of the development of modern science. It was not until the seventeenth century (during the Scientific Revolution) that physics held out the real promise of developing a complete theory of nature in terms of the mechanical properties of matter. In the seventeenth century, while contributing to the advancement of mechanistic physics, Descartes nevertheless argued that minds are distinct things, quite different from material bodies. Descartes's dualistic views, expressed in his second and sixth *Meditations*, mark the beginning of the modern mind-body problem.

Prior to the rise of mechanistic physics, it was common to try to explain the behavior of all things using either persons or organisms as explanatory models. For example, ancient myths viewed natural objects and forces anthropomorphically. Minds were everywhere, so to speak, directing all action—from storms to the movement of the stars. Minds and willful actions were not viewed as needing to be

explained in terms of something better understood. Even when people began to abandon explicitly anthropomorphic explanations, their conceptions of the elements (including matter) often remained more organic than mechanical. Aristotle, for example, thought things made of earth (for example, rocks) tended to move toward the center of the universe because they have in them the potential for such directed movement, just as an acorn has in it the potential to become an oak tree.

Though versions of the mind-body problem that are inspired by developments in science may be comparatively recent, nonetheless, arguments about the nature of mind frequently rely on views of the mind or soul that were articulated long ago. The ancient Greek idea of the soul (or *psyche*) was that it is whatever is responsible for life, and mind was regarded as a part or aspect of the soul. Some philosophers tried to identify soul with something elemental like air (breath) or fire (the heat of the body). Sometimes it was imagined that the soul might journey from the body and continue to be conscious, but this did not mean the soul was not a part of (or like) the rest of nature. It was Plato who voiced the idea that the soul might be totally different from things in nature, and this was, in part, because he was skeptical about the reality of the temporal world of changing things. The excerpt in Part II from Plato's *Phaedo* should also be read in conjunction with the selections in Part III. In the *Phaedo*, Plato argues that the soul is eternal and separable from the chaotic flux of ordinary things.

Aristotle offered what was, perhaps, the most influential analysis of soul prior to Descartes. Aristotle thought the soul was just the form (in his technical sense of "form") of a living body, and he rejected Plato's belief that forms could exist separately from matter. Aristotle's analyses of thinking and perceiving (as aspects of the soul) are subtle, and they incorporate much of the scientific opinion of his time. Yet, they have a down-to-earth quality that has made Aristotle's views attractive to people who find Plato's world of transcendent forms too removed from experience. (For example, the traditional Christian conception of personal immortality has often been interpreted as requiring resurrection of the body, and this is more Aristotelian than Platonic.)

The writings in Part III that follow the selections from Aristotle and Descartes were chosen because they highlight contemporary issues pertinent to the mind-body problem and illustrate recent philosophical strategies for dealing with them. What exactly are the properties of mental phenomena that make it seem that mind cannot be understood in physical terms? The readings cover at least three features that have been at the center of recent controversies: (1) the intentionality (or aboutness) of mental states; (2) the qualitative features of sensations; and (3) the subjectivity of consciousness. The selections also represent four strategies: (1) nonreductionism (Brentano and Nagel); (2) identity theories (Armstrong); (3) functionalism (Dennett and Putnam); and (4) eliminative materialism (Churchland). Finally, the rapid evolution of computer technology and neuroscience has allowed the mind-body problem to be expressed in a new idiom: Will it be possible to build a computer that can be programmed to be conscious? Can human consciousness or the operation of the brain be understood in terms of computer architecture and programs? The last two articles in Part III debate these questions.

21. *On the Soul*

ARISTOTLE

The ancient Greeks viewed the soul as the principle, or cause, of life, but they disagreed about its nature. Some speculated it was something elemental, like fire or air. Is it what leaves the body at death (like heat or breath)? What implications does the absence or departure of the soul have for questions about personal immortality? In the *Phaedo* selections in Part II, Plato argues that the soul is eternal and cannot die. Plato maintains that the soul can exist apart from the body; and, in thus being eternal and separable from matter, it is akin to (and can know) ideal Forms. In "On the Soul," Aristotle examines and rejects the views of his predecessors. Aristotle does not posit soul as a separate entity. Instead, it is just the form or actuality of a material body having the potential for life. For Aristotle, describing the form and function (or "formal" and "final causes") of things was part of a systematic explanation of their nature. As an aspect of being alive, living things are more or less capable of sensation, perception, and thought. Thus, the investigation of the soul (or the forms of living things) leads Aristotle to an analysis of perceiving and thinking. In "On the Soul," Aristotle explores the idea that perceiving occurs when some of the forms of the objects of perception come to be embodied in the different material of a person's sensory or cognitive faculties. Though Aristotle's general position is that souls cannot exist without being embodied, there are passages hinting he entertained the idea that the thinking part of the soul might, in some sense, be able to do so. (For Aristotle's disagreement with Plato about the existence of Forms apart from matter and about their explanatory power, the reader should study Book I of Aristotle's *Metaphysics*.)

Book I

Holding as we do that, while knowledge of any kind is a thing to be honoured and prized, one kind of it may, either by reason of its greater exactness or of a higher dignity and greater wonderfulness in its objects, be more honourable and precious than another, on both accounts we should naturally be led to place in the front rank the study of the soul. The knowledge of the soul admittedly contributes

From Jonathan Barnes, ed., *Complete Works of Aristotle: The Revised Oxford Translations*. Bollingen Series 71, J. A. Smith, trans. Copyright © 1984 Jowett Copyright Trustees. Excerpt, pp. 642–87. Reprinted with permission of Princeton University Press.

greatly to the advance of truth in general, and, above all, to our understanding of Nature, for the soul is in some sense the principle of animal life. Our aim is to grasp and understand, first its essential nature, and secondly its properties; of these some are thought to be affections proper to the soul itself, while others are considered to attach to the animal owing to the presence of soul.

To attain any knowledge about the soul is one of the most difficult things in the world. As the form of question which here presents itself, viz., the question 'What is it?' recurs in other fields, it might be supposed that there was some single method of inquiry applicable to all objects whose essential nature we are endeavouring to ascertain (as there *is* for incidental properties the single method of demonstration); in that case what we should have to seek for would be this unique method. But if there is no such single and general method for solving the question of essence, our task becomes still more difficult; in the case of each different subject we shall have to determine the appropriate process of investigation. If to this there be a clear answer, e.g., that the process is demonstration or division, or some other known method, many difficulties and hesitations still beset us— with what facts shall we begin the inquiry? For the facts which form the starting-points in different subjects must be different, as e.g., in the case of numbers and surfaces.

First, no doubt, it is necessary to determine in which of the *summa genera* soul lies, what it *is*; is it 'a this-somewhat', a substance, or is it a quale or a quantum, or some other of the remaining kinds of predicates which we have distinguished? Further, does soul belong to the class of potential existents, or is it not rather an actuality? Our answer to this question is of the greatest importance.

We must consider also whether soul is divisible or is without parts, and whether it is everywhere homogeneous or not; and if not homogeneous, whether its various forms are different specifically or generically: up to the present time those who have discussed and investigated soul seem to have confined themselves to the human soul. We must be careful not to ignore the question whether soul can be defined in a single account, as is the case with animal, or whether we must not give a separate account for each sort of it, as we do for horse, dog, man, god (in the latter case the universal, animal—and so too every other common predicate—is either nothing or posterior). Further, if what exists is not a plurality of souls, but a plurality of parts of one soul, which ought we to investigate first, the whole soul or its parts? It is also a difficult problem to decide which of these parts are in nature distinct from one another. Again, which ought we to investigate first, these parts or their functions, mind or thinking, the faculty or the act of sensation, and so on? If the investigation of the functions precedes that of the parts, the further question suggests itself: ought we not before either to consider the correlative objects, e.g., of sense or thought? It seems not only useful for the discovery of the causes of the incidental properties of substances to be acquainted with the essential nature of those substances (as in mathematics it is useful for the understanding of the property of the equality of the interior angles of a triangle to two right angles to know the essential

nature of the straight and the curved or of the line and the plane) but also conversely, for the knowledge of the essential nature of a substance is largely promoted by an acquaintance with its properties: for, when we are able to give an account conformable to experience of all or most of the properties of a substance, we shall be in the most favourable position to say something worth saying about the essential nature of that subject; in all demonstration a definition of the essence is required as a starting-point, so that definitions which do not enable us to discover the incidental properties, or which fail to facilitate even a conjecture about them, must obviously, one and all, be dialectical and futile.

A further problem presented by the affections of soul is this: are they all affections of the complex of body and soul, or is there any one among them peculiar to the soul by itself? To determine this is indispensable but difficult. If we consider the majority of them, there seems to be no case in which the soul can act or be acted upon without involving the body; e.g., anger, courage, appetite, and sensation generally. Thinking seems the most probable exception; but if this too proves to be a form of imagination or to be impossible without imagination, it too requires a body as a condition of its existence. If there is any way of acting or being acted upon proper to soul, soul will be capable of separate existence; if there is none, its separate existence is impossible. In the latter case, it will be like what is straight, which has many properties arising from the straightness in it, e.g., that of touching a bronze sphere at a point, though straightness divorced from the other constituents of the straight thing cannot touch it in this way; it cannot be so divorced at all, since it is always found in a body. It seems that all the affections of soul involve a body—passion, gentleness, fear, pity, courage, joy, loving, and hating; in all these there is a concurrent affection of the body. In support of this we may point to the fact that, while sometimes on the occasion of violent and striking occurrences there is no excitement or fear felt, on others faint and feeble stimulations produce these emotions, viz., when the body is already in a state of tension resembling its condition when we are angry. Here is a still clearer case: in the absence of any external cause of terror we find ourselves experiencing the feelings of a man in terror. From all this it is obvious that the affections of soul are enmattered accounts.

Consequently their definitions ought to correspond, e.g., anger should be defined as a certain mode of movement of such and such a body (or part or faculty of a body) by this or that cause and for this or that end. That is precisely why the study of the soul—either every soul or souls of this sort—must fall within the science of nature. Hence a physicist would define an affection of soul differently from a dialectician; the latter would define e.g., anger as the appetite for returning pain for pain, or something like that, while the former would define it as a boiling of the blood or warm substance surrounding the heart. The one assigns the material conditions, the other the form or account; for what he states is the account of the fact, though for its actual existence there must be embodiment of it in a material such as is described by the other. Thus the essence of a house is assigned in such an account as 'a shelter against destruction by wind, rain, and heat'; the physicist would describe it as 'stones, bricks, and timbers'; but there is a third possible description which would say that it was that form in that material with that purpose or end. Which, then, among these is entitled to be regarded as the genuine physicist? The one who confines himself to the material, or the one who restricts himself to the account alone? Is it not rather the one who combines both? If this is so, how are we to characterize the other two? Must we not say that there is no type of thinker who concerns himself with those qualities or attributes of the material which are in fact inseparable from the material, and without attempting even in thought to separate them? The physicist is he who concerns himself with all the properties active and passive of bodies or materials thus or thus defined; attributes not considered as being of this character he leaves to others, in certain cases it may be to a specialist, e.g., a carpenter or a physician, in others (a) where they are inseparable in fact, but are separable from any particular kind of body by an effort of abstraction, to the mathematician, (b) where they are separate, to the First Philosopher. But we must return from this digression, and repeat that the affections of soul, insofar as they are such as passion and fear, are inseparable from the natural matter of animals in this way and not in the same way as a line or surface.

For our study of soul it is necessary, while formulating the problems of which in our further advance we are to find the solutions, to call into council the views of those of our predecessors who have declared any opinion on this subject, in order that we may profit by whatever is sound in their suggestions and avoid their errors.

The starting-point of our inquiry is an exposition of those characteristics which have chiefly been held to belong to soul in its very nature. Two characteristic marks have above all others been recognized as distinguishing that which has soul in it from that which has not—movement and sensation. It may be said that these two are what our predecessors have fixed upon as characteristic of soul.

Some say that what originates movement is both pre-eminently and primarily soul; believing that what is not itself moved cannot originate movement in another, they arrived at the view that soul belongs to the class of things in movement. This is what led Democritus to say that soul is a sort of fire or hot substance; his 'forms' or atoms are infinite in number; those which are spherical he calls fire and soul, and compares them to the motes in the air which we see in shafts of light coming through windows; the mixture of seeds of all sorts he calls the elements of the whole of nature (Leucippus gives a similar account); the spherical atoms are identified with soul because atoms of that shape are most adapted to permeate everywhere, and to set all the others moving by being themselves in movement. This implies the view that soul is identical with what produces movement in animals. That is why, further, they regard respiration as the characteristic mark of life; as the environment compresses the bodies of animals, and tends to extrude those atoms which impart movement to them, because they themselves are never at rest, there must be a reinforcement of these by similar atoms coming in from without in the act of respiration; for they prevent the extrusion of those which are already within by counteracting the compressing and consolidating force of the environment; and animals continue to live only so long as they are able to maintain this resistance.

The doctrine of the Pythagoreans seems to rest upon the same ideas; some of them declared the motes in air, others what moved them, to be soul. These motes were referred to because they are seen always in movement, even in a complete calm.

The same tendency is shown by those who define soul as that which moves itself; all these seem to hold the view that movement is what is closest to the nature of soul, and that while all else is moved by soul, it alone moves itself. This belief arises from their never seeing anything originating movement which is not first itself moved.

Similarly also Anaxagoras (and whoever agrees with him in saying that thought set the whole in movement) declares the moving cause of things to be soul. His position must, however, be distinguished from that of Democritus. Democritus roundly identifies soul and mind, for he identifies what appears with what is true—that is why he commends Homer for the phrase 'Hector lay with thought distraught'; he does not employ mind as a special faculty dealing with truth, but identifies soul with thought. What Anaxagoras says about them is less clear; in many places he tells us that the cause of beauty and order is thought, elsewhere that it is soul; it is found, he says, in all animals, great and small, high and low, but thought (in the sense of intelligence) appears not to belong alike to all animals, and indeed not even to all human beings.

All those, then, who had special regard to the fact that what has soul in it is moved, adopted the view that soul is to be identified with what is eminently originative of movement. All, on the other hand, who looked to the fact that what has soul in it knows or perceives what is, identify soul with the principle or principles of Nature, according as they admit several such principles or one only. Thus Empedocles declares that it is formed out of all his elements, each of them also being his soul; his words are:

For 'tis by Earth we see Earth, by Water
    Water,
By Ether Ether divine, by Fire destructive
    Fire,
By Love Love, and Hate by cruel Hate.

In the same way Plato in the *Timaeus* fashions the soul out of his elements; for like, he holds, is known by like, and things are formed out of the principles or elements. Similarly also in the lectures 'On Philosophy' it was set forth that the Animal-itself is compounded of the Idea itself of the One together with the primary length, breadth, and depth, everything else being similarly constituted. Again he puts his view in yet other terms: Mind is the monad, science or knowledge the dyad (because it goes undeviatingly from one point to another), opinion the number of the plane, sensation the number of the solid; the numbers are by him expressly identified with the Forms themselves or principles, and are formed out of the elements; now things are apprehended either by mind or science or opinion or sensation, and these same numbers are the Forms of things.

Some thinkers, accepting both premisses, viz., that the soul is both originative of movement and cognitive, have compounded it of both and declared the soul to be a self-moving number.

As to the nature and number of the first principles opinions differ. The difference is greatest between those who regard them as corporeal and those who regard them as incorporeal, and from both dissent those who make a blend and draw their principles from both sources. The number of principles is also in dispute; some admit one only, others assert several. There is a consequent diversity in their several accounts of soul; they assume, naturally enough, that what is in its own nature originative of movement must be among what is primordial. That has led some to regard it as fire, for fire is the subtlest of the elements and nearest to incorporeality; further, in the primary sense, fire both is moved and originates movement in all the others.

Democritus has expressed himself more ingeniously than the rest on the grounds for ascribing each of these two characters to soul; soul and thought are, he says, one and the same thing, and this thing must be one of the primary and indivisible bodies, and its power of originating movement must be due to its fineness of grain and the shape of its atoms; he says that of all the shapes the spherical is the most mobile, and that this is the shape of the particles of both fire and thought.

Each of the elements has thus found its partisan, except earth—earth has found no supporter unless we count as such those who have declared soul to be, or to be compounded of, *all* the elements. All, then, it may be said, characterize the soul by three marks. Movement, Sensation, Incorporeality, and each of these is traced back to the first principles. That is why (with one exception) all those who define the soul by its power of knowing make it either an element or constructed out of the elements. The language they all use is similar; like, they say, is known by like; as the soul knows everything, they construct it out of all the principles. Hence all those who admit but one cause or element, make the soul also one (e.g., fire or air), while those who admit a multiplicity of principles make the soul also multiple. The exception is Anaxagoras; he alone says that thought is impassible and has nothing in common with any-thing else. But, if this is so, how or in virtue of what cause can it know? That Anaxagoras has not ex-plained, nor can any answer be inferred from his words. All who acknowledge pairs of opposites among their principles, construct the soul also out of these contraries, while those who admit as prin-ciples only one contrary of each pair, e.g., either hot or cold, likewise make the soul some one of these. That is why they allow themselves to be guided by the names; those who identify soul with the hot argue that to live is derived from to boil, while those who identify it with the cold say that soul (ψυχή) is so called from the process of respira-tion and refrigeration.

Such are the traditional opinions concerning soul, together with the grounds on which they are maintained. . . .

The view we have just been examining, in company with most theories about the soul, in-volves the following absurdity: they all join the soul to a body, or place it in a body, without adding any specification of the reason of their union, or of the bodily conditions required for it. Yet such ex-planation can scarcely be omitted; for some com-munity of nature is presupposed by the fact that the one acts and the other is acted upon, the one moves and the other is moved; but it is not the case that *any* two things are related to one another in these ways. All, however, that these thinkers do is to describe the specific characteristics of the soul; they do not try to determine anything about the body which is to contain it, as if it were possible, as in the Pythagorean myths, that any soul could be clothed in any body—an absurd view, for each body seems to have a form and shape of its own. It is as absurd as to say that the art of carpentry could embody itself in flutes; each art must use its tools, each soul its body.

There is yet another opinion about soul, which has commended itself to many as no less probable than any of those we have hitherto mentioned, and has rendered public account of itself in the court of popular discussion. Its supporters say that the soul is a kind of harmony; for harmony is a blend or composition of contraries, and the body is com-pounded out of contraries. Harmony, however, is a certain proportion or composition of the constitu-ents blended, and soul can be neither the one nor the other of these. Further, the power of originat-ing movement cannot belong to a harmony, while

all concur in regarding this pretty well as a prin-cipal attribute of soul. It is more appropriate to call health (or generally one of the good states of the body) a harmony than to predicate it of the soul. The absurdity becomes most apparent when we try to attribute the active and passive affections of the soul to a harmony—it is difficult to harmonize them. Further, in using the word 'harmony' we have one or other of two cases in mind: the most proper sense is in relation to magnitudes which have motion and position, where harmony means their being compounded and harmonized in such a manner as to prevent the introduction of anything homogeneous; and the derived sense is that in which it means the ratio between the constituents so blended; in neither of these senses is it plausible to predicate it of soul. That soul is a harmony in the sense of the composition of the parts of the body is a view easily refutable; for there are many and various compoundings of the parts; of what is thought or the sensitive or the appetitive faculty the composition? And what *is* the composition which constitutes each of them? It is equally absurd to identify the soul with the ratio of the mixture; for the mixture of the elements which makes flesh has a different ratio from that which makes bone. The consequence of this view will therefore be that dis-tributed throughout the whole body there will be many souls, since every one of the bodily parts is a mixture of the elements, and the ratio of mixture is in each case a harmony, i.e., a soul.

From Empedocles at any rate we might de-mand an answer to the following question—for he says that each of the parts of the body is what it is in virtue of a ratio between the elements: is the soul identical with this ratio, or is it not rather some-thing over and above this which is formed in the parts? Is love the cause of any and every mixture, or only of those that are in the right ratio? Is love this ratio itself, or is love something over and above this? Such are the problems raised by this account. But, on the other hand, if the soul is different from the mixture, why does it disappear at one and the same moment with that relation between the ele-ments which constitutes flesh or the other parts of the animal body? Further, if the soul is not identical with the ratio of mixture, and it is consequently not the case that each of the parts has a soul, what is that which perishes when the soul quits the body?

That the soul cannot either be a harmony, or be moved in a circle, is clear from what we have said. Yet that it can be moved incidentally is, as we said above, possible, and even that it can move itself, i.e., in the sense that *the vehicle* in which it is can be moved, and moved by it; in no other sense can the soul be moved in space.

More legitimate doubts might remain as to its movement in view of the following facts. We speak of the soul as being pained or pleased, being bold or fearful, being angry, perceiving, thinking. All these are regarded as modes of movement, and hence it might be inferred that the soul is moved. This, however, does not necessarily follow. We may admit to the full that being pained or pleased, or thinking, are movements (each of them a being moved), and that the movement is originated by the soul. For example we may regard anger or fear as such and such movements of the heart, and thinking as such and such another movement of that organ, or of some other; these modifications may arise either from changes of place in certain parts or from qualitative alterations (the special nature of the parts and the special modes of their changes being for our present purpose irrelevant). Yet to say that it is the soul which is angry is as if we were to say that it is the soul that weaves or builds houses. It is doubtless better to avoid saying that the soul pities or learns or thinks, and rather to say that it is the man who does this with his soul. What we mean is not that the movement is in the soul, but that sometimes it terminates in the soul and sometimes starts from it, sensation e.g., coming from without, and reminiscence starting from the soul and terminating with the movements or states of rest in the sense organs.

But thought seems to be an independent substance implanted within us and to be incapable of being destroyed. If it could be destroyed at all, it would be under the blunting influence of old age. What really happens is, however, exactly parallel to what happens in the case of the sense organs; if the old man could recover the proper kind of eye, he would see just as well as the young man. The incapacity of old age is due to an affection not of the soul but of its vehicle, as occurs in drunkenness or disease. Thus it is that thinking and reflecting decline through the decay of some other inward part and are themselves impassible. Thinking, loving, and hating are affections not of thought, but of that which has thought, so far as it has it. That is why, when this vehicle decays, memory and love cease; they were activities not of thought, but of the composite which has perished; thought is, no doubt, something more divine and impassible. That the

soul cannot be moved is therefore clear from what we have said, and if it cannot be moved at all, manifestly it cannot be moved by itself. . . .

Such are the three ways in which soul has traditionally been defined: one group of thinkers declared it to be that which is most originative of movement because it moves itself, another group to be the subtlest and most incorporeal of all kinds of body. We have now sufficiently set forth the difficulties and inconsistencies to which these theories are exposed. It remains now to examine the doctrine that soul is composed of the elements.

The reason assigned for this doctrine is that thus the soul may perceive and come to know everything that is; but the theory necessarily involves itself in many impossibilities. Its upholders assume that like is known by like, as though they were assuming that the soul is identical with the objects. But the elements are not the only things; there are many others, or, more exactly, an infinite number of others, formed out of the elements. Let us admit that the soul knows and perceives the elements out of which each of these composites is made up; but by what means will it know or perceive the composite whole, e.g., what god, man, flesh, bone (or any other compound) is? For each *is*, not merely the elements of which it is composed, but those elements combined in a determinate mode or ratio, as Empedocles himself says of bone,

> The kindly Earth in its broad-bosomed moulds
> Won of clear Water two parts out of eight
> And four of Fire; and so white bones were formed.

Nothing, therefore, will be gained by the presence of the elements of the soul, unless there be also present there the ratios and the composition. Each element will indeed know its like, but there will be no knowledge of bone or man, unless they too are present in it. The impossibility of this needs no pointing out; for who would suggest that a stone or a man is in the soul? The same applies to the good and the not-good, and so on.

Further, things are said to be in many ways: 'be' signifies of a 'this' or substance, or a quantum, or a quale, or any other of the kinds of predicates we have distinguished. Does the soul consist of all of these or not? It does not appear that all have common elements. Is the soul formed out of those elements alone which enter into substances? If so, how will it be able to know each of the other kinds of thing? Will it be said that each kind of thing has elements or principles of its own, and that the soul is formed out of these? In that case, the soul must be a quantum *and* a quale *and* a substance. But all that can be made out of the elements of a quantum is a quantum, not a substance. These (and others like them) are the consequences of the view that the soul is composed of all the elements. . . .

From what has been said it is now clear that knowing as an attribute of soul cannot be explained by soul's being composed of the elements, and that it is neither sound nor true to speak of soul as moved. But since knowing, perceiving, opining, and further desiring, wishing, and generally all other modes of appetition, belong to soul, and the local movements of animals, and growth, maturity, and decay are produced by the soul, we must ask whether each of these is an attribute of the soul as a whole, i.e., whether it is with the whole soul we think, perceive, move ourselves, act or are acted upon, or whether each of them requires a different part of the soul? So too with regard to life. Does it depend on one of the parts of soul? Or is it dependent on more than one? Or on all? Or has it some quite other cause?

Some hold that the soul is divisible, and that we think with one part and desire with another. If, then, its nature admits of its being divided, what can it be that holds the parts together? Surely not the body; on the contrary it seems rather to be the soul that holds the body together; at any rate when the soul departs the body disintegrates and decays. If, then, there is something else which makes the soul one, this would have the best right to the name of soul, and we shall have to repeat for it the question: Is *it* one or multipartite? If it is one, why not at once admit that *the soul* is one? If it has parts, once more the question must be put: What holds *its* parts together, and so *ad infinitum*?

The question might also be raised about the parts of the soul: What is the separate role of each in relation to the body? For, if the whole soul holds together the whole body, we should expect each part of the soul to hold together a part of the body. But this seems an impossibility; it is difficult even to imagine what sort of bodily part thought will hold together, or how it will do this.

It is a fact of observation that plants and certain insects go on living when divided into segments; this means that each of the segments has a soul in it identical in species, though not numerically; for both of the segments for a time possess the power of sensation and local movement. That this does not last is not surprising, for they no longer possess the organs necessary for self-maintenance. But, all the same, in each of the parts there are present all the parts of soul, and the souls so present are homogeneous with one another and with the whole—the several parts of the soul being inseparable from one another, although the whole soul is divisible. It seems that the principle found in plants is also a kind of soul; for this is the only principle which is common to both animals and plants; and this exists in isolation from the principle of sensation, though there is nothing which has the latter without the former.

Book II

Let the foregoing suffice as our account of the views concerning the soul which have been handed on by our predecessors; let us now make as it were a completely fresh start, endeavouring to answer the question, What is soul? i.e., to formulate the most general possible account of it.

We say that substance is one kind of what is, and that in several senses: in the sense of matter or that which in itself is not a this, and in the sense of form or essence, which is that precisely in virtue of which a thing is called a this, and thirdly in the sense of that which is compounded of both. Now matter is potentiality, form actuality; and actuality is of two kinds, one as e.g., knowledge, the other as e.g., reflecting.

Among substances are by general consent reckoned bodies and especially natural bodies; for they are the principles of all other bodies. Of natural bodies some have life in them, others not; by life we mean self-nutrition and growth and decay. It follows that every natural body which has life in it is a substance in the sense of a composite.

Now given that there are bodies of such and such a kind, viz., having life, the soul cannot be a body; for the body is the subject or matter, not what is attributed to it. Hence the soul must be a substance in the sense of the form of a natural body having life potentially within it. But substance is actuality, and thus soul is the actuality of a body as above characterized. Now there are two kinds of actuality corresponding to knowledge and to reflecting. It is obvious that the soul is an actuality like knowledge; for both sleeping and waking presuppose the existence of soul, and of these waking corresponds to reflecting, sleeping to knowledge possessed but not employed, and knowledge of something is temporally prior.

That is why the soul is an actuality of the first kind of a natural body having life potentially in it. The body so described is a body which is organized. The parts of plants in spite of their extreme simplicity are organs; e.g., the leaf serves to shelter the pericarp, the pericarp to shelter the fruit, while the roots of plants are analogous to the mouth of animals, both serving for the absorption of food. If, then, we have to give a general formula applicable to all kinds of soul, we must describe it as an actuality of the first kind of a natural organized body. That is why we can dismiss as unnecessary the question whether the soul and the body are one: it is as though we were to ask whether the wax and its shape are one, or generally the matter of a thing and that of which it is the matter. Unity has many senses (as many as 'is' has), but the proper one is that of actuality.

We have now given a general answer to the question, What is soul? It is substance in the sense which corresponds to the account of a thing. That means that it is what it is to be for a body of the character just assigned. Suppose that a tool, e.g., an axe, were a *natural* body, then being an axe would have been its essence, and so its soul; if this disappeared from it, it would have ceased to be an axe, except in name. As it is, it is an axe; for it is not of a body of that sort that what it is to be, i.e., its account, is a soul, but of a natural body of a particular kind, viz., one having in itself the power of setting itself in movement and arresting itself. Next, apply this doctrine in the case of the parts of the living body. Suppose that the eye were an animal—sight would have been its soul, for sight is the substance of the eye which corresponds to the account, the eye being merely the matter of seeing; when seeing is removed the eye is no longer an eye, except in name—no more than the eye of a statue or of a painted figure. We must now extend our consideration from the parts to the whole living body; for what the part is to the part, that the whole faculty of sense is to the whole sensitive body as such.

We must not understand by that which is potentially capable of living what has lost the soul it had, but only what still retains it; but seeds and fruits are bodies which are potentially of that sort.

Consequently, while waking is actuality in a sense corresponding to the cutting and the seeing, the soul is actuality in the sense corresponding to sight and the power in the tool; the body corresponds to what is in potentiality; as the pupil *plus* the power of sight constitutes the eye, so the soul *plus* the body constitutes the animal.

From this it is clear that the soul is inseparable from its body, or at any rate that certain parts of it are (if it has parts)—for the actuality of some of them is the actuality of the parts themselves. Yet some may be separable because they are not the actualities of any body at all. Further, we have no light on the problem whether the soul may not be the actuality of its body in the sense in which the sailor is the actuality of the ship.

This must suffice as our sketch or outline of the nature of soul.

Since what is clear and more familiar in account emerges from what in itself is confused but more observable by us, we must reconsider our results from this point of view. For it is not enough for a definitional account to express as most now do the mere fact; it must include and exhibit the cause also. At present definitions are given in a form analogous to the conclusion of an argument; e.g., What is squaring? The construction of an equilateral rectangle equal to a given oblong rectangle. Such a definition is in form equivalent to a conclusion. One that tells us that squaring is the discovery of a mean proportional discloses the cause of what is defined.

We resume our inquiry from a fresh starting-point by calling attention to the fact that what has soul in it differs from what has not in that the former displays life. Now this word has more than one sense, and provided any one alone of these is found in a thing we say that thing is living—viz., thinking or perception or local movement and rest, or movement in the sense of nutrition, decay and growth. Hence we think of plants also as living, for they are observed to possess in themselves an originative power through which they increase or decrease in all spatial directions; they do not grow up but not down—they grow alike in both, indeed in all, directions; and that holds for everything which is constantly nourished and continues to live, so long as it can absorb nutriment.

This power of self-nutrition can be separated from the other powers mentioned, but not they from it—in mortal beings at least. The fact is obvious in plants; for it is the only psychic power they possess.

This is the originative power the possession of which leads us to speak of things as *living* at all, but it is the possession of sensation that leads us for the first time to speak of living things as *animals*; for even those beings which possess no power of local movement but do possess the power of sensation we call animals and not merely living things.

The primary form of sense is touch, which belongs to all animals. Just as the power of self-nutrition can be separated from touch and sensation generally, so touch can be separated from all other forms of sense. (By the power of self-nutrition we mean that part of the soul which is common to plants and animals: all animals whatsoever are observed to have the sense of touch.) What the explanation of these two facts is, we must discuss later. At present we must confine ourselves to saying that soul is the source of these phenomena and is characterized by them, viz., by the powers of self-nutrition, sensation, thinking, and movement.

Is each of these a soul or a part of a soul? And if a part, a part merely distinguishable by definition or a part distinct in local situation as well? In the case of certain of these powers, the answers to these questions are easy, in the case of others we are puzzled what to say. Just as in the case of plants which when divided are observed to continue to live though separated from one another (thus showing that in *their* case the soul of each individual plant was actually one, potentially many), so we notice a similar result in other varieties of soul, e.g., in insects which have been cut in two; each of the segments possesses both sensation and local movement; and if sensation, necessarily also imagination and appetition; for, where there is sensation, there is also pleasure and pain, and, where these, necessarily also desire.

We have no evidence as yet about thought or the power of reflexion; it seems to be a different kind of soul, differing as what is eternal from what is perishable; it alone is capable of being separated. All the other parts of soul, it is evident from what we have said, are, in spite of certain statements to the contrary, incapable of separate existence though, of course, distinguishable by definition. If opining is distinct from perceiving, to be capable of opining and to be capable of perceiving must be distinct, and so with all the other forms of living

above enumerated. Further, some animals possess all these parts of soul, some certain of them only, others one only (this is what enables us to classify animals); the cause must be considered later. A similar arrangement is found also within the field of the senses; some classes of animals have all the senses, some only certain of them, others only one, the most indispensable, touch.

Since the expression 'that whereby we live and perceive' has two meanings, just like the expression 'that whereby we know'—that may mean either knowledge or the soul, for we can speak of knowing *by* either, and similarly that whereby we are in health may be either health or the body or some part of the body; and since of these knowledge or health is a form, essence, or account, or if we so express it an activity of a recipient matter—knowledge of what is capable of knowing, health of what is capable of being made healthy (for the activity of that which is capable of originating change seems to take place in what is changed or altered); further, since it is the soul by which primarily we live, perceive, and think:—it follows that the soul must be an account and essence, not matter or a subject. For, as we said, the word substance has three meanings—form, matter, and the complex of both—and of these matter is potentiality, form actuality. Since then the complex here is the living thing, the body cannot be the actuality of the soul; it is the soul which is the actuality of a certain kind of body. Hence the rightness of the view that the soul cannot be without a body, while it cannot *be* a body; it is not a body but something relative to a body. That is why it is *in* a body, and a body of a definite kind. It was a mistake, therefore, to do as former thinkers did, merely to fit it into a body without adding a definite specification of the kind or character of that body, although evidently one chance thing will not receive another. It comes about as reason requires: the actuality of any given thing can only be realized in what is already potentially that thing, i.e., in a matter of its own appropriate to it. From all this it is plain that soul is an actuality or account of something that possesses a potentiality of being such. . . .

The soul is the cause or source of the living body. The terms cause and source have many senses. But the soul is the cause of its body alike in all three senses which we explicitly recognize. It is the source of movement, it is the end, it is the essence of the whole living body.

That it is the last, is clear; for in everything the essence is identical with the cause of its being, and here, in the case of living things, their being is to live, and of their being and their living the soul in them is the cause or source. Further, the actuality of whatever is potential is identical with its account.

It is manifest that the soul is also the final cause. For nature, like thought, always does whatever it does for the sake of something, which something is its end. To that something corresponds in the case of animals the soul and in this it follows the order of nature; all natural bodies are organs of the soul. This is true of those that enter into the constitution of plants as well as of those which enter into that of animals. This shows that that for the sake of which they are is soul. That for the sake of which has two senses, viz., the end to achieve which, and the being in whose interest, anything is or is done.

The soul is also the cause of the living body as the original source of local movement. The power of locomotion is not found, however, in all living things. But change of quality and change of quantity are also due to the soul. Sensation is held to be a qualitative alteration, and nothing except what has soul in it is capable of sensation. The same holds of growth and decay; nothing grows or decays naturally except what feeds itself, and nothing feeds itself except what has a share in life in it. . . .

In dealing with each of the senses we shall have first to speak of the objects which are perceptible by each. The term 'object of sense' covers three kinds of objects, two kinds of which we call perceptible in themselves, while the remaining one is only incidentally perceptible. Of the first two kinds one consists of what is special to a single sense, the other of what is common to any and all of the senses. I call by the name of special object of this or that sense that which cannot be perceived by any other sense than that one and in respect of which no error is possible; in this sense colour is the special object of sight, sound of hearing, flavour of taste. Touch, indeed, discriminates more than one set of different qualities. Each sense has one kind of object which it discerns, and never errs in reporting that what is before it is colour or sound (though it may err as to what it is that is coloured or where that is, or what it is that is sounding or where that is). Such objects are what we call the special objects of this or that sense.

Common sensibles are movement, rest, number, figure, magnitude; these are not special to any one sense, but are common to all. There are at any rate certain kinds of movement which are perceptible both by touch and by sight.

We speak of an incidental object of sense where e.g., the white object which we see is the son of Diares; here because being the son of Diares is incidental to the white which is perceived, we speak of the son of Diares as being incidentally perceived. That is why it in no way as such affects the senses. Of the things perceptible in themselves, the special objects are properly called perceptible and it is to them that in the nature of things the structure of each several sense is adapted. [Omitted Chapters 7–11 deal with how the senses might work.]

Generally, about all perception, we can say that a sense is what has the power of receiving into itself the sensible forms of things without the matter, in the way in which a piece of wax takes on the impress of a signet-ring without the iron or gold; what produces the impression is a signet of bronze or gold, but not *qua* bronze or gold; in a similar way the sense is affected by what is coloured or flavoured or sounding not insofar as each is what it is, but insofar as it is of such and such a sort and according to its form.

A primary sense-organ is that in which such a power is seated. The sense and its organ are the same in fact, but their essence is not the same. What perceives is, of course, a spatial magnitude, but we must not admit that either the having the power to perceive or the sense itself is a magnitude; what they are is a certain form or power in a magnitude. This enables us to explain why excesses in objects of sense destroy the organs of sense; if the movement set up by an object is too strong for the organ, the form which is its sensory power is disturbed; it is precisely as concord and tone are destroyed by too violently twanging the strings of a lyre. This explains also why plants cannot perceive, in spite of their having a portion of soul in them and being affected by tangible objects themselves; for their temperature can be lowered or raised. The explanation is that they have no mean, and so no principle in them capable of taking on the forms of sensible objects but are affected together with their matter.

Book III

. . . There are two distinctive peculiarities by reference to which we characterize the soul—(1) local movement and (2) thinking, understanding, and perceiving. Thinking and understanding are regarded as akin to a form of perceiving; for in the one as well as the other the soul discriminates and is cognizant of something which is. Indeed the ancients go so far as to identify thinking and perceiving; e.g., Empedocles says 'For 'tis in respect of what is present that man's wit is increased', and again 'Whence it befalls them from time to time to think diverse thoughts', and Homer's phrase, 'For suchlike is man's mind' means the same. They all look upon thinking as a bodily process like perceiving, and hold that like is understood as well as perceived by like, as I explained at the beginning of our discussion. Yet they ought at the same time to have accounted for error also; for it is more intimately connected with animal existence and the soul continues longer in the state of error. They cannot escape the dilemma: either whatever seems is true (and there are some who accept this) or error is contact with the unlike: for that is the opposite of the knowing of like by like.

But it seems that error as well as knowledge in respect to contraries is one and the same.

That perceiving and understanding are not identical is therefore obvious; for the former is universal in the animal world, the latter is found in only a small division of it. Further, thinking is also distinct from perceiving—I mean that in which we find rightness and wrongness—rightness in understanding, knowledge, true opinion, wrongness in their opposites; for perception of the special objects of sense is always free from error, and is found in all animals, while it is possible to think falsely as well as truly, and thought is found only where there is discourse of reason. For imagination is different from either perceiving or discursive thinking, though it is not found without sensation, or judgement without it. That this activity is not the same kind of thinking as judgement is obvious. For imagining lies within our own power whenever we wish (e.g., we can call up a picture, as in the practice of mnemonics by the use of mental images), but in forming opinions we are not free: we cannot escape the alternative of falsehood or truth. Further, when we think something to be fearful or

threatening, emotion is immediately produced, and so too with what is encouraging; but when we merely imagine we remain as unaffected as persons who are looking at a painting of some dreadful or encouraging scene. Again within the field of judgement itself we find varieties— knowledge, opinion, understanding, and their opposites; of the differences between these I must speak elsewhere.

Thinking is different from perceiving and is held to be in part imagination, in part judgement: we must therefore first mark off the sphere of imagination and then speak of judgement. If then imagination is that in virtue of which an image arises for us, excluding metaphorical uses of the term, is it a single faculty or disposition relative to images, in virtue of which we discriminate and are either in error or not? The faculties in virtue of which we do this are sense, opinion, knowledge, thought.

Turning now to the part of the soul with which the soul knows and (whether this is separable from the others in definition only, or spatially as well) we have to inquire what differentiates this part, and how thinking can take place.

If thinking is like perceiving, it must be either a process in which the soul is acted upon by what is capable of being thought, or a process different from but analogous to that. The thinking part of the soul must therefore be, while impassible, capable of receiving the form of an object; that is, must be potentially identical in character with its object without being the object. Thought must be related to what is thinkable, as sense is to what is sensible.

Therefore, since everything is a possible object of thought, mind in order, as Anaxagoras says, to dominate, that is, to know, must be pure from all admixture; for the co-presence of what is alien to its nature is a hindrance and a block: it follows that it can have no nature of its own, other than that of having a certain capacity. Thus that in the soul which is called thought (by thought I mean that whereby the soul thinks and judges) is, before it thinks, not actually any real thing. For this reason it cannot reasonably be regarded as blended with the body: if so, it would acquire some quality, e.g., warmth or cold, or even have an organ like the sensitive faculty: as it is, it has none. It was a good idea to call the soul 'the place of forms,' though this description holds only of the thinking soul, and even this is the forms only potentially, not actually.

Observation of the sense-organs and their employment reveals a distinction between the impassibility of the sensitive faculty and that of the faculty of thought. After strong stimulation of a sense we are less able to exercise it than before, as e.g., in the case of a loud sound we cannot hear easily immediately after, or in the case of a bright colour or a powerful odour we cannot see or smell, but in the case of thought thinking about an object that is highly thinkable renders it more and not less able afterwards to think of objects that are less thinkable: the reason is that while the faculty of sensation is dependent upon the body, thought is separable from it.

When thought has become each thing in the way in which a man who actually knows is said to do so (this happens when he is now able to exercise the power on his own initiative), its condition is still one of potentiality, but in a different sense from the potentiality which preceded the acquisition of knowledge by learning or discovery; and thought is then able to think of itself.

Since we can distinguish between a magnitude and what it is to be a magnitude, and between water and what it is to be water, and so in many other cases (though not in all; for in certain cases the thing and its form are identical), flesh and what it is to be flesh are discriminated either by different faculties, or by the same faculty in two different states; for flesh necessarily involves matter and is like what is snub-nosed, a *this* in a *this*. Now it is by means of the sensitive faculty that we discriminate the hot and the cold, i.e., the factors which combined in a certain ratio constitute flesh: the essential character of flesh is apprehended by something different either wholly separate from the sensitive faculty or related to it as a bent line to the same line when it has been straightened out.

Again in the case of abstract objects what is straight is analogous to what is snub-nosed; for it necessarily implies a continuum: its constitutive essence is different, if we may distinguish between straightness and what is straight: let us take it to be two-ness. It must be apprehended, therefore, by a different power or by the same power in a different state. To sum up, in so far as the realities it knows are capable of being separated from their matter, so it is also with the powers of thought.

The problem might be suggested: if thinking is a passive affection, then if thought is simple and impassible and has nothing in common with anything else, as Anaxagoras says, how can it come to think at all? For interaction between two factors is held to require a precedent community of nature between the factors. Again it might be asked, is thought a possible object of thought to itself? For if thought is thinkable *per se* and what is thinkable is in kind one and the same, then either thought will belong to everything, or it will contain some element common to it with all other realities which makes them all thinkable.

Have not we already disposed of the difficulty about interaction involving a common element, when we said that thought is in a sense potentially whatever is thinkable, though actually it is nothing until it has thought? What it thinks must be in it just as characters may be said to be on a writing-table on which as yet nothing actually stands written: this is exactly what happens with thought.

Thought is itself thinkable in exactly the same way as its objects are. For in the case of objects which involve no matter, what thinks and what is thought are identical; for speculative knowledge and its object are identical. (Why thought is not always thinking we must consider later.) In the case of those which contain matter each of the objects of thought is only potentially present. It follows that while they will not have thought in them (for thought is a potentiality of them only in so far as they are capable of being disengaged from matter) thought may yet be thinkable.

Since in every class of things, as in nature as a whole, we find two factors involved, a matter which is potentially all the particulars included in the class, a cause which is productive in the sense that it makes them all (the latter standing to the former, as e.g., an art to its material), these distinct elements must likewise be found within the soul.

And in fact thought, as we have described it, is what it is by virtue of becoming all things, while there is another which is what it is by virtue of making all things: this is a sort of positive state like light; for in a sense light makes potential colours into actual colours.

Thought in this sense of it is separable, impassible, unmixed, since it is in its essential nature activity (for always the active is superior to the passive factor, the originating force to the matter).

Actual knowledge is identical with its object: in the individual, potential knowledge is in time prior to actual knowledge, but absolutely it is not prior even in time. It does not sometimes think and sometimes not think. When separated it is alone just what it is, and this above is immortal and eternal (we do not remember because, while this is impossible, passive thought is perishable); and withou. this nothing thinks.

Let us now summarize our results about soul, and repeat that the soul is in a way all existing things; for existing things are either sensible or thinkable, and knowledge is in a way what is knowable, and sensation is in a way what is sensible: in *what* way we must inquire.

Knowledge and sensation are divided to correspond with the realities, potential knowledge and sensation answering to potentialities, actual knowledge and sensation to actualities. Within the soul the faculties of knowledge and sensation are *potentially* these objects, the one what is knowable, the other what is sensible. They must be either the things themselves or their forms. The former alternative is of course impossible: it is not the stone which is present in the soul but its form.

It follows that the soul is analogous to the hand; for as the hand is a tool of tools, so thought is the form of forms and sense the form of sensible things.

Since it seems that there is nothing outside and separate in existence from sensible spatial magnitudes, the objects of thought are in the sensible forms, viz., both the abstract objects and all the states and affections of sensible things. Hence no one can learn or understand anything in the absence of sense, and when the mind is actively aware of anything it is necessarily aware of it along with an image; for images are like sensuous contents except in that they contain no matter.

Imagination is different from assertion and denial; for what is true or false involves a synthesis of thoughts. In what will the primary thoughts differ from images? Must we not say that neither these nor even our other thoughts are images, though they necessarily involve them?

22. *Meditations on First Philosophy*

RENÉ DESCARTES

René Descartes (1596–1650), French mathematician and philosopher, is commonly called the father of modern philosophy. He lived during a time of great intellectual upheaval. In 1543, Copernicus published his radical, non-Aristotelian view that the earth rotates on its axis and revolves around the sun. Galileo was supporting the Copernican theory by attacking Aristotle's physics. His famous slogan said that God wrote the book of nature in the language of mathematics, and the picture of nature that was to emerge during the Scientific Revolution was a picture that increasingly emphasized the mechanistic causality of matter in motion. Descartes took part in this revolution by, for example, inventing analytic geometry and proposing mechanistic models of planetary motion and for the operation of the nervous system. The new scientific ideas were controversial, and they became mixed with disputes in religion. The Protestant Reformation was attacking the authority of the Roman Catholic Church on theological matters; and by 1633, the church (through the Inquisition) tried to suppress Galileo's work by banning it and by putting him under house arrest. It is against this background of doubt and dispute that Descartes tried to find a new foundation for philosophy.

In *Meditations on First Philosophy*, Descartes proposes to base knowledge of nature and God on a foundation of indubitable beliefs about thinking: one can be certain one is thinking, and some of one's ideas reveal the essences of things. As a by-product of his theory of knowledge, Descartes posed the modern mind-body problem: he claims an examination of the ideas of mind and body show that they must be metaphysically distinct substances.

Are Descartes' arguments in support of mind-body dualism correct? If so, how do mind and body interact? If not, how can the apparently incompatible properties of mind and body be explained or accommodated in a comprehensive metaphysics?

Meditation 2: Concerning the Nature of the Human Mind: That the Mind Is More Known Than the Body

Yesterday's meditation filled my mind with so many doubts that I can no longer forget about

From René Descartes, *Meditations on First Philosophy*, D. A. Cress, trans. (Indianapolis: Hackett Publishing, 1980), pp. 61–67 and 89–100. Reprinted by permission of Hackett Publishing Company, Indianapolis, Ind., and Cambridge, Mass.

them—nor yet do I see how they are to be resolved. But, as if I had suddenly fallen into a deep whirlpool, I am so disturbed that I can neither touch my foot to the bottom, nor swim up to the top. Nevertheless, I will work my way up, and I will follow the same path I took yesterday, putting aside everything which admits of the least doubt, as if I had discovered it to be absolutely false. I will go forward until I know something certain—or, if nothing else, until I at least know for certain that nothing is certain. Archimedes sought only a firm and immovable point in order to move the entire earth from one place to another. Surely great things are to be hoped for if I am lucky enough to find at least one thing that is certain and indubitable.

Therefore I will suppose that all I see is false. I will believe that none of those things that my deceitful memory brings before my eyes ever existed. I thus have no senses: body, shape, extension, movement, and place are all figments of my imagination. What then will count as true? Perhaps only this one thing: that nothing is certain.

But on what grounds do I know that there is nothing over and above all those which I have just reviewed, concerning which there is not even the least cause for doubt? Is there not a God (or whatever name I might call him) who instills these thoughts in me? But why should I think that, since perhaps I myself could be the author of these things? Therefore am I not at least something? But I have already denied that I have any senses and any body. Still, I hesitate; for what follows from that? Am I so tied to the body and to the senses that I cannot exist without them? But I have persuaded myself that there is nothing at all in the world: no heaven, no earth, no minds, no bodies. Is it not then true that I do not exist? But certainly I should exist, if I were to persuade myself of something. But there is a deceiver (I know not who he is) powerful and sly in the highest degree, who is always purposely deceiving me. Then there is no doubt that I exist, if he deceives me. And deceive me as he will, he can never bring it about that I am nothing so long as I shall think that I am something. Thus it must be granted that, after weighing everything carefully and sufficiently, one must come to the considered judgment that the statement "I am, I exist" is necessarily true every time it is uttered by me or conceived in my mind.

But I do not yet understand well enough who I am—I, who now necessarily exist. And from this point on, I must take care lest I imprudently substitute something else in place of myself; and thus be mistaken even in that knowledge which I claim to be the most certain and evident of all. To this end, I shall meditate once more on what I once believed myself to be before having embarked upon these deliberations. For this reason, then, I will set aside whatever can be refuted even to a slight degree by the arguments brought forward, so that at length there shall remain precisely nothing but what is certain and unshaken.

What therefore did I formerly think I was? A man, of course. But what is a man? Might I not say a rational animal? No, because then one would have to inquire what an "animal" is and what "rational" means. And then from only one question we slide into many more difficult ones. Nor do I now have enough free time that I want to waste it on subtleties of this sort. But rather here I pay attention to what spontaneously and at nature's lead came into my thought beforehand whenever I pondered what I was. Namely, it occurred to me first that I have a face, hands, arms, and this entire mechanism of bodily members, the very same as are discerned in a corpse—which I referred to by the name "body." It also occurred to me that I eat, walk, feel and think; these actions I used to assign to the soul as their cause. But what this soul was I either did not think about or I imagined it was something terribly insubstantial—after the fashion of a wind, fire, or ether—which has been poured into my coarser parts. I truly was not in doubt regarding the body; rather I believed that I distinctly knew its nature, which, were I perhaps tempted to describe it such as I mentally conceived it, I would explain it thus: by "body," I understand all that is suitable for being bounded by some shape, for being enclosed in some place, and thus for filling up space, so that it excludes every other body from that space; for being perceived by touch, sight, hearing, taste, or smell; for being moved in several ways, not surely by itself, but by whatever else that touches it. For I judged that the power of self-motion, and likewise of sensing or of thinking, in no way pertains to the nature of the body. Nonetheless, I used to marvel especially that such faculties were found in certain bodies.

But now what am I, when I suppose that some deceiver—omnipotent and, if I may be allowed to say it, malicious—takes all the pains he can in order to deceive me? Can I not affirm that I possess at least a small measure of all those traits which I already have said pertain to the nature of the body? I pay attention, I think, I deliberate—but nothing happens. I am wearied of repeating this in vain. But which of these am I to ascribe to the soul? How about eating or walking? These are surely nothing but illusions, because I do not have a body. How about sensing? Again, this also does not happen without a body, and I judge that I really did not sense those many things I seemed to have sensed in my dreams. How about thinking? Here I discover that thought is an attribute that really does belong to me. This alone cannot be detached from me. I am; I exist; this is certain. But for how long? For as long as I think. Because perhaps it could also come to pass that if I should cease from all thinking I would then utterly cease to exist. I now admit nothing that is not necessarily true. I am therefore precisely only a thing that thinks; that is, a mind, or soul, or intellect, or reason—words the meaning of which I was ignorant before. Now, I am a true thing, and truly existing; but what kind of thing? I have said it already: a thing that thinks.

What then? I will set my imagination going to see if I am not something more. I am not that connection of members which is called the human body. Neither am I some subtle air infused into these members, not a wind, not a fire, not a vapor, not a breath—nothing that I imagine to myself, for I have supposed all these to be nothing. The assertion stands: the fact still remains that I am something. But perhaps is it the case that, nevertheless, these very things which I take to be nothing (because I am ignorant of them) in reality do not differ from that self which I know? This I do not know. I shall not quarrel about it right now; I can make a judgment only regarding things which are known to me. I know that I exist; I ask now who is this "I" whom I know. Most certainly the knowledge of this matter, thus precisely understood, does not depend upon things that I do not yet know to exist. Therefore, it is not dependent upon any of those things that I feign in my imagination. But this word "feign" warns me of my error. For I would be feigning if I should "imagine" that I am something, because imagining is merely the contemplation of the shape or image of a corporeal thing. But I know now with certainty that I am, and at the same time it could happen that all these images—and, generally, everything that pertains to the nature of the body—are nothing but dreams. When these things are taken into account, I would speak no less foolishly were I to say: "I will imagine so that I might recognize more distinctly who I am," than were I to say: "Now I surely am awake, and I see something true, but because I do not yet see it with sufficient evidence, I will take the trouble of going to sleep so that my dreams might show this to me more truly and more evidently." Thus I know that none of what I can comprehend by means of the imagination pertains to this understanding that I have of myself. Moreover, I know that I must be most diligent about withdrawing my mind from these things so that it can perceive its nature as distinctly as possible.

But what then am I? A thing that thinks. What is that? A thing that doubts, understands, affirms, denies, wills, refuses, and which also imagines and senses.

It is truly no small matter if all of these things pertain to me. But why should they not pertain to me? Is it not I who now doubt almost everything, I who nevertheless understand something, I who affirm that this one thing is true, I who deny other things, I who desire to know more things, I who wish not to be deceived, I who imagine many things against my will, I who take note of many things as if coming from the senses? Is there anything in all of this which is not just as true as it is that I am, even if I am always dreaming or even if the one who created me tries as hard as possible to delude me? Are any of these attributes distinct from my thought? What can be said to be separate from myself? For it is so obvious that it is I who doubt, I who understand, I who will, that there is nothing through which it could be more evidently explicated. But indeed I am also the same one who imagines; for, although perhaps as I supposed before, no imagined thing would be wholly true, the very power of imagining does really exist, and constitutes a part of my thought. Finally, I am the same one who senses or who takes note of bodily things as if through the senses. For example, I now see a light, I hear a noise, I feel heat. These are false, since I am asleep. But I certainly seem to see, hear, and feel. This cannot be false: properly speaking, this is what is called "sensing" in me. But this is, to speak precisely, nothing other than thinking.

From these considerations I begin to know a little better who I am. But it still seems that I cannot hold back from believing that bodily things—whose images are formed by thought, and which the senses themselves examine—are much more distinctly known than this unknown aspect of myself which does not come under the imagination. And yet it would be quite strange if the very things which I consider to be doubtful, unknown, and foreign to me are comprehended by me more distinctly than what is true, what is known—than, in fine, myself. But I see what is happening: my mind loves to wander and does not allow itself to be restricted to the confines of truth. Let it be that way then: let us allow it the freest rein in every respect, so that, when we pull in the reins at the right time a little later, the mind may suffer itself to be ruled more easily.

Let us consider those things which are commonly believed to be the most distinctly comprehended of all: namely the bodies which we touch and see. But not bodies in general, for these generic perceptions are often somewhat more confused; rather let us consider one body in particular. Let us take, for instance, this piece of wax. It has very recently been taken from the honeycombs; it has not as yet lost all the flavor of its honey. It retains some of the smell of the flowers from which it was collected. Its color, shape, and size are obvious. It is hard and cold. It can easily be touched, and if you rap on it with a knuckle it makes a sound. In short, everything is present in it that appears to be needed in order that a body can be known as distinctly as possible. But notice that while I am speaking, it is brought close to the fire; the remaining traces of the honey flavor are purged; the odor vanishes; the color is changed; the original shape disappears. Its magnitude increases, it becomes liquid and hot, and can hardly be touched; and now, when you knock on it, it does not emit any sound. Up to this point, does the same wax remain? One must confess that it does: no one denies it; no one thinks otherwise. What was there then in the wax that was so distinctly comprehended? Certainly none of the things that I reached by means of the senses. For whatever came under taste or smell or sight or touch or hearing by now has changed, yet the wax remains.

Perhaps the wax was what I now think it is: namely that it really never was the sweetness of the honey or the fragrance of the flowers, not this whiteness, not a figure, not a sound, but a body which a little earlier manifested itself to me in these ways, and now does so in other ways. But just what precisely is this thing which I imagine thus? Let us direct our attention to this and see what remains after we have removed everything which does not belong to the wax: only that it is something extended, flexible, and subject to change. What is this flexible and mutable thing? Is it not the fact that I imagine that this wax can change from a round to a square shape, or from the latter to a rectangular shape? Not at all: for I comprehend that the wax is capable of innumerable changes, yet I cannot survey these innumerable changes by imagining them. Therefore this comprehension is not accomplished by the faculty of imagination. What is this extended thing? Is this thing's extension also unknown? For it becomes larger in wax that is beginning to liquify, greater in boiling wax, and greater still as the heat is increased. And I would not judge rightly what the wax is if I did not believe that this wax can take on even more variet-

ies of extension than I could ever have grasped by the imagination. It remains then for me to concede that I in no way imagine what this wax is, but perceive it by the mind only. I am speaking about this piece of wax in particular, for it is clearer in the case of wax in general. But what is this wax which is perceived only by the mind? It is the same that I see, touch, and imagine; in short it is the same as I took it to be from the very beginning. But we must take note of the fact that the perception of the wax is neither by sight, nor touch, nor imagination, nor was it ever so (although it seemed so before), but rather an inspection on the part of the mind alone. This inspection can be imperfect and confused, as it was before, or clear and distinct, as it is now, according to whether I pay greater or less attention to those things of which the wax consists.

But meanwhile I marvel at how prone my mind is to errors; for although I am considering these things within myself silently and without words, nevertheless I latch onto words themselves and I am very nearly deceived by the ways in which people speak. For we say that we see the wax itself, if it is present, and not that we judge it to be present from its color or shape. Whence I might conclude at once: the wax is therefore known by eyesight, and not by an inspection on the part of the mind alone, unless I perhaps now might have looked out the window at the men crossing the street whom I say I am no less wont to see than the wax. But what do I see over and above the hats and clothing? Could not robots be concealed under these things? But I judge them to be men; thus what I believed I had seen with my eyes, I actually comprehend with nothing but the faculty of judgment which is in my mind.

But a person who seeks to know more than the common crowd should be ashamed of himself if he has come upon doubts as a result of an encounter with the forms of speech devised by the common crowd. Let us then go forward, paying attention to the following question: did I perceive more perfectly and evidently what the wax was when I first saw it and believed I had known it by the external sense—or at least by the common sense, as they say, that is, the imaginative power—than I know it now, after having examined more diligently both what the wax is and how it is known. Surely it is absurd to doubt this matter. For what was there in the first perception that was distinct? What was there that any animal could not have seemed capable of possessing? But when I distinguish the wax from its external forms, as if having taken off its clothes, as it were, I look at the naked wax, even though at this point there can be an error in my judgment; nevertheless I could not perceive it without a human mind.

But what am I to say about this mind, or about myself? For as yet I admit nothing else to be in me over and above my mind. What, I say, am I who seem to perceive this wax so distinctly? Do I not know myself not only much more truly and with more certainty, but also much more distinctly and evidently? For if I judge that the wax exists from the fact that I see it, certainly it follows much more evidently that I myself exist, from the fact that I see the wax. For it could happen that what I see is not truly wax. It could happen that I have no eyes with which to see anything. But it could not happen that, while I see or think I see (I do not now distinguish these two), I who think am not something. Likewise, if I judge that the wax exists from the fact that I touch it, the same thing will again follow: I exist. If from the fact that I imagine, or from whatever other cause, the same thing readily follows. But what I noted regarding the wax applies to all the other things that are external to me. Furthermore, if the perception of the wax seemed more distinct after it became known to me not only from sight or touch, but from many causes, how much more distinctly I must be known to myself; for there are no considerations that can aid in the perception of the wax or any other body without these considerations demonstrating even better the nature of my mind. But there are still so many other things in my mind from which one can draw a more distinct knowledge of the mind, so that those things which emanate from a body seem hardly worth enumerating.

But lo and behold, I have arrived on my own at the place I wanted. Since I know that bodies are not, properly speaking, perceived by the senses or by the faculty of imagination, but only by the intellect, and since, moreover, I know that they are not perceived by being touched or seen, but only insofar as they are expressly understood, nothing can be more easily and more evidently perceived by me than my mind. But because an established habit of belief cannot be put aside so quickly, it is appropriate to stop here, so that by the length of my meditation this new knowledge may be more deeply impressed on my memory. . . .

Meditation 6: *Concerning the Existence of Material Things, and the Real Distinction of the Mind from the Body*

It remains for me to examine whether material things exist. Indeed I now know that they can exist, at least insofar as they are the object of pure mathematics, because I clearly and distinctly perceive them. For no doubt God is capable of bringing about everything that I am thus capable of perceiving. And I have never judged that God was incapable of something, except when it was incompatible with being perceived by me distinctly. Moreover, from the faculty of imagination, which I observe that I use while I am engaged in dealing with these material things, it seems to follow that they exist; to someone paying very close attention to what imagination is, it appears to be nothing else but an application of the knowing faculty to a body intimately present to it—hence, a body that exists.

And to make this very clear, I first examine the difference between imagination and pure intellection. So, for example, when I imagine a triangle, I not only understand that it is a figure bounded by three lines, but at the same time I also intuit by my powers of discernment these three lines as present—this is what I call "imagining." But if I want to think about a chiliagon, I certainly understand just as well that it is a figure consisting of a thousand sides, and that a triangle is a figure consisting of three lines; but I do not imagine those thousand sides in the same way, that is, I do not intuit them as being present. Albeit that when I think of a chiliagon I may perchance represent to myself some figure confusedly—because whenever I think about something corporeal, I always, out of force of habit, imagine something—nevertheless it is evident that it is not a chiliagon. This is so because it is not really different from the figure I would represent to myself if I were to think of a myriagon or any other figure with a large number of sides. Nor is imagination of any help in knowing the properties that differentiate the chiliagon from other polygons. But if it is a question of a pentagon, I surely can understand its form, just as was the case with the chiliagon, without the help of my imagination. But I can also imagine it, that is, by applying the powers of discernment both to its five sides and, at the same time, to the area bounded by those sides; clearly I am aware at this point that I need a peculiar sort of effort on the part of the mind in order to imagine, one that I do not employ in order to understand. This new effort on the part of the mind clearly shows the difference between imagination and pure intellection.

Besides, I believe that this power of imagining that is in me, insofar as it differs from the power of understanding, is not a necessary element of my essence, that is, of the essence of my mind; for although I might lack this power, nonetheless I would undoubtedly remain the same person as I am now. Thus it seems to follow that the power of imagining depends upon something different from me. And I readily understand that were a body to exist to which a mind is so joined that it might direct itself to look at it anytime it wishes, it could happen that by means of this body I intuit corporeal things. The result would be that this mode of thinking differs from pure intellection only in the fact that the mind, when it understands, in a sense turns itself toward itself and gazes upon one of the ideas that are in it. But when it imagines, it turns itself toward the body, and intuits something in the body similar to an idea either understood by the mind or perceived by sense. I say I easily understand that the imagination can function in this way, provided a body does exist. But this is only a probability; although I may investigate everything carefully, nevertheless, I do not yet see how, from the distinct idea of corporeal nature that I find in my imagination, I can draw up an argument that necessarily concludes that some body exists.

But I am in the habit of imagining many other things—over and above the corporeal nature that is the object of pure mathematics—such as colors, sounds, tastes, pain, and so on, but not so distinctly. Inasmuch as I perceive these things better with those senses from which, with the aid of the memory, they seem to have come to the imagination, the same trouble should also be taken concerning the senses, so that I might deal with them more appropriately. It must be seen whether I can obtain any certain argument for the existence of corporeal things from those things that are perceived by the way of thinking that I call "sense."

First I will repeat to myself here what those things were that I believed to be true because I had perceived them by means of the senses and what the grounds were for so believing. Next I will assess the reasons why I called them into doubt.

Finally, I will consider what I must now believe concerning these things.

So, first, I sensed that I have a head, hands, feet, and other members that composed this body; I viewed it as a part of me, or perhaps even as the whole of me. I sensed that this body is frequently amid many other bodies, and that these bodies can affect my body in pleasant and unpleasant ways; I gauged what was pleasant by a certain sense of pleasure, and what was unpleasant by a sense of pain. In addition to pain and pleasure, I also sensed in me hunger, thirst, and other such appetites, as well as certain corporeal tendencies to mirth, sadness, anger, and other such feelings. But, as for things external to me—besides the extension, shapes, and motions of bodies—I also sensed their roughness, heat, and other tactile qualities; I sensed, too, the light, colors, odors, tastes, and sounds from whose variety I distinguished the heavens, the earth, the seas, and the other bodies one from the other. Indeed, because of the ideas of all these qualities that presented themselves to my thought and that alone I properly and immediately sensed, it was not wholly without reason that I believed that I sensed things clearly different from my thought, namely, the bodies from which these ideas might proceed. For I knew by experience that they come upon me without my consent, to the extent that, wish as I may, I cannot sense any object unless it be present to the organ of sense, and I cannot fail to sense it when it is present. Since the ideas perceived by sense are much more vivid and clear-cut, and even, in their own way, more "distinct," than any of those that I willingly and knowingly formed by meditation or those that I found impressed on my memory, it seems impossible that they come from myself. Therefore, it remained that they came from other things. Since I had no knowledge of such things except from these ideas themselves, I could not help entertaining the view that these things were similar to those ideas. Also, because I recalled that I had used my senses earlier than my reason, and I saw that the ideas that I myself constructed were not as clear-cut as those that I perceived by means of the senses, I saw that these former ideas were for the most part composed of parts of these latter ideas; I easily convinced myself that I plainly have no idea in the intellect that I did not have beforehand in the sense. Not without reason did I judge that this body, which by a special right I called "mine," belongs more to me than to any other thing, for I could never be separated from it in the same way as I could be from the rest. I sensed all appetites and feelings in it and for it. Finally, I have noticed pain and pleasurable excitement in its parts, but not in other bodies external to it. But why a certain sadness of spirit arises from one feeling of pain or another, and why a certain elation arises from a feeling of excitement, or why some sort of twitching of the stomach, which I call hunger, should warn me to take in nourishment, or why dryness of throat should warn me to take something to drink, and so on—for all these I plainly had no explanation other than that I have been taught so by nature. For there is clearly no affinity, at least none I am aware of, between the twitching of the stomach and the will to take in nourishment, or between the sense of something that causes pain and the thought of the sadness arising from this sense. But nature seems to have taught me everything else that I judged concerning the objects of the senses, because I convinced myself—even before having spent time on any of the arguments that might prove it—that things were this way.

But afterwards many experiences gradually caused all faith that I had in the senses to totter; occasionally towers, which had seemed round from afar, appeared square at close quarters; very large statues, standing on their pinnacles, did not seem large to someone looking at them from ground level; in countless other such things I detected that judgments of the external senses deceived me—not just the external senses, but also the internal senses. What can be more intimate than pain? But I had once heard it said by people whose leg or arm had been amputated that it seems to them that they occasionally sense pain in the very limb that they lacked. Therefore, even in me, it did not seem to be clearly certain that some part of my body was causing me pain, although I did sense pain in it. To these causes of doubt I recently added two quite general ones: first, I believed I never sensed anything while I was awake that I could not believe I also sometimes perceive while asleep. Since I do not believe that what I seem to sense in my dreams comes to me from things external to me, I did not see any reason why I should have these beliefs about things that I seem to sense while I am awake. The second cause of doubt was that, since I was ignorant of the cause of my coming into being (or at least pretended that I was ignorant of it), I saw that nothing prevented my

having been so constituted by nature that I should be deceived about even what appeared to me most true. As to the arguments by which I formerly convinced myself of the truth of sensible things, I found no difficulty in responding to them. Since I seemed driven by nature toward many things opposed to reason, I did not think what was taught by nature deserved much credence. Although the perceptions of the senses did not depend on my will, I did not think that we must therefore conclude that they came from things external to me, because perhaps there is in me some faculty, as yet unknown to me, that produces these perceptions.

However, now, after having begun to know better the cause of my coming to be, I believe that I must not rashly admit everything that I seem to derive from the senses. But, then, neither should I call everything into doubt.

First, because I know that all the things that I clearly and distinctly understand can be made by God exactly as I understand them, it is enough that I can clearly and distinctly understand one thing without the other in order for me to be certain that the one thing is different from the other, because at least God can establish them separately. The question of the power by which this takes place is not relevant to their being thought to be different. For this reason, from the fact that I know that I exist, and that meanwhile I judge that nothing else clearly belongs to my nature or essence except that I am a thing that thinks, I rightly conclude that my essence consists in this alone: that I am only a thing that thinks. Although perhaps (or rather, as I shall soon say, to be sure) I have a body that is very closely joined to me, nevertheless, because on the one hand I have a clear and distinct idea of myself—insofar as I am a thing that thinks and not an extended thing—and because on the other hand I have a distinct idea of a body—insofar as it is merely an extended thing, and not a thing that thinks—it is therefore certain that I am truly distinct from my body, and that I can exist without it.

Moreover, I find in myself faculties endowed with certain special modes of thinking—namely the faculties of imagining and sensing—without which I can clearly and distinctly understand myself in my entirety, but not vice versa: I cannot understand them clearly and distinctly without me, that is, without the knowing substance to which they are attached. For in their formal concept they include an act of understanding; thus I perceive that they are distinguished from me just as modes are to be distinguished from the thing of which they are modes. I also recognize certain other faculties—like those of moving from one place to another, of taking on various shapes, and so on—that surely no more can be understood without the substance to which they are attached than those preceding faculties; for that reason they cannot exist without the substance to which they are attached. But it is clear that these faculties, if in fact they exist, must be attached to corporeal or extended substances, but not to a knowing substance, because extension—but certainly not understanding—is contained in a clear and distinct concept of them. But now there surely is in me a passive faculty of sensing, that is, of receiving and knowing the ideas of sensible things; but I cannot use it unless there also exists, either in me or in something else, a certain active faculty of producing or bringing about these ideas. This faculty surely cannot be in me, since it clearly presupposes no intellection, and these ideas are produced without my cooperation and often against my will. Because this faculty is in a substance other than myself, in which ought to be contained—formally or eminently—all the reality that is objectively in the ideas produced by this faculty (as I have just now taken notice), it thus remains that either this substance is a body (or corporeal nature) in which is contained formally all that is contained in ideas objectively or it is God—or some other creature more noble than a body—in which it is all contained eminently. But, since God is not a deceiver, it is absolutely clear that he sends me these ideas neither directly and immediately—nor even through the mediation of any creature, in which the objective reality of these ideas is contained not formally but only eminently. Since he plainly gave me no faculty for making this discrimination— rather, he gave me a great inclination to believe that these ideas proceeded from things—I fail to see why God cannot be understood to be a deceiver, if they proceeded from a source other than corporeal things. For this reason, corporeal things exist. Be that as it may, perhaps not all bodies exist exactly as I grasp them by sense, because this grasp by the senses is in many cases very obscure and confused. But at least everything is in these bodies that I clearly and distinctly understand—that is, everything, considered in a general sense, that is encompassed in the object of pure mathematics.

But as to how this point relates to the other remaining matters that are either merely particular—as, for example, that the sun is of such and such a size or shape, and so on—or less clearly understood—as, for example, light, sound, pain, and so on—although they are very doubtful and uncertain, still, because God is not a deceiver, and no falsity can be found in my opinions, unless there is also in me a faculty given me by God for the purpose of rectifying this falsity, these features provide me with a certain hope of reaching the truth in them. And plainly it cannot be doubted that whatever I am taught by nature has some truth to it; for by "nature," taken generally, I understand only God himself or the coordination, instituted by God, of created things. I understand nothing else by my nature in particular than the totality of all the things bestowed on me by God.

There is nothing that this nature teaches me in a more clear-cut way than that I have a body that is ill-disposed when I feel pain, that it needs food and drink when I suffer hunger or thirst, and so on. Therefore, I ought not to doubt that there is some truth in this.

By means of these feelings of pain, hunger, thirst and so on, nature also teaches that I am present to my body not merely in the way a seaman is present to his ship, but that I am tightly joined and, so to speak, mingled together with it, so much so that I make up one single thing with it. For otherwise, when the body is wounded, I, who am nothing but a thing that thinks, would not then sense the pain. Rather, I would perceive the wound by means of the pure intellect, just as a seaman perceives by means of sight whether anything in the ship is broken. When the body lacks food or drink, I would understand this in a clear-cut fashion; I would not have confused feelings of hunger and thirst. For certainly these feelings of thirst, hunger, pain, and so on are nothing but confused modes of thinking arising from the union and, as it were, the mingling of the mind with the body.

Moreover, I am also taught by nature that many other bodies exist around my body; some of them are to be pursued, and others are to be avoided. And to be sure, from the fact that I sense widely different colors, sounds, odors, tastes, heat, roughness, and so on, I rightly conclude that in the bodies from which these different perceptions of the senses proceed, there are differences corresponding to the different perceptions—

although perhaps the former are not similar to the latter. But from the fact that some of these perceptions are pleasant and others unpleasant, it is plainly certain that my body—or rather my whole self, insofar as I am composed of a body and a mind—can be affected by the various agreeable and disagreeable bodies in the vicinity.

But I have accepted many other things, and, although I seem to have been taught them by nature, still it was not really nature that taught them to me, but a certain habit of making unconsidered judgments. And thus it could easily happen that they are false, as, for example, the belief that any space where there is nothing that moves my senses is empty; or, for example, the belief that in a hot body there is something plainly similar to the idea of heat which is in me; or that in a white or green body there is the same whiteness or greeness that I sense; or in a bitter or sweet thing the same taste, and so on; or the belief that stars and towers, and any other distant bodies have only the same size and shape that they present to the senses—and other examples of the same sort. But lest I not perceive distinctly enough something about this matter, I ought to define more carefully what I properly understand when I say that I am "taught something by nature." For I am using "nature" here in a stricter sense than the totality of everything bestowed on me by God. For in this totality there are contained many things that pertain only to my mind, as, for example, that I perceive that what has been done cannot be undone, and everything else that is known by the light of nature. At the moment the discussion does not center on these matters. There are also many things that pertain only to the body, as, for example, that it tends downward, and so on. I am not dealing with these either, but only with what has been bestowed on me by God, insofar as I am composed of mind and body. Therefore it is nature, thus understood, that teaches me to flee what brings a sense of pain and to pursue what brings a sense of pleasure, and the like. But it does not appear that nature, so conceived, teaches that we conclude from these perceptions of the senses anything in addition to this regarding things external to us unless there previously be an inquiry by the intellect; for it pertains to the mind alone, and not to the composite, to know the truth in these matters. Thus, although a star affects my eye no more than the flame from a small torch, still there is no real or positive tendency in my eye toward believing that the star is any bigger than the flame; rather, ever since my youth, I have made this judgment without reason. Although I feel heat upon drawing closer to the fire, and I feel pain upon drawing even closer to it, there is indeed no argument that convinces me that there is something in the fire that is similar either to the heat or to the pain, but only that there is something in the fire that causes in us these feelings of heat or pain. Although there be nothing in a given space that moves the sense, it does not therefore follow that there is no body in it. I use the perceptions of the senses that properly have been given by nature only for the purpose of signifying to the mind what is agreeable and disagreeable to the composite, of which the mind is a part; within those limits these perceptions are sufficiently clear and distinct. However, I see that I have been in the habit of subverting the order of nature in these and many other matters, because I use the perceptions of the senses as certain rules for immediately discerning what the essence is of the bodies external to us; yet, in respect to this essence, these perceptions still show me nothing but obscurity and confusion.

I have already examined in sufficient detail how it could happen that my judgments are false, the goodness of God notwithstanding. But a new difficulty now comes on the scene concerning those very things that are shown to me by nature as things to be either sought or avoided, as well as concerning the internal senses in which I seem to have detected errors: for example, when a person, deluded by the pleasant taste of food, ingests a poison hidden inside it. But in this case he is impelled by nature only toward desiring the thing in which the pleasant taste is located, but not toward the poison, of which he obviously is unaware. Nothing else can be concluded here except that this nature is not all-knowing. This is not remarkable, since man is a limited being; thus only limited perfection is appropriate to man.

But we often err even in those things to which nature impels us; for example, when those who are ill desire food or drink that will soon be injurious to them. Perhaps it could have been said here that they erred because their nature was corrupt. But this does not remove our difficulty, because a sickly man is no less a creature of God than a healthy one; for that reason it does not seem any less repugnant that the sickly man got a deceiving nature from God. And just as a clock made of wheels and counter-weights follows all the laws of nature no less closely when it has been badly constructed and does not tell time accurately than when it satisfies on all scores the wishes of its maker, just so, if I should consider the body of a man—insofar as it is a kind of mechanism composed of and outfitted with bones, nerves, muscles, veins, blood and skin—even if no mind existed in it, the man's body would still have all the same motions that are in it now except for those motions that proceed either from a command of the will or, consequently, from the mind. I readily recognize that it would be natural for this body, were it, say, suffering from dropsy, to suffer dryness of the throat, which commonly brings a feeling of thirst to the mind, and thus too its nerves and other parts are so disposed by the mind to take a drink with the result that the sickness is increased. It would be no more natural for this body, when there is no such infirmity in it and it is moved by the same dryness, to drink something useful to it. And, from the point of view of the intended purpose of the watch, I could say that it turns away from its nature when it does not tell the right time. Similarly, considering the mechanism of the human body as equipped for the motions that typically occur in it, I might think that it too turns away from its nature, if its throat were dry, when taking a drink would not be beneficial to its continued existence. Nevertheless, I realize well enough that this latter usage of the term "nature" differs greatly from the former. For this latter "nature" is only an arbitrary denomination, extrinsic to the things on which it is predicated and dependent upon my thought, because it compares a man in poor health and a poorly constructed clock with the idea of a man in good health and a well-made clock. But by "nature" taken in the former sense, I understand something that really is in things, and thus it is not without some truth.

When it is said, in the case of the dropsical body, that its "nature" is corrupt—from the fact that this body has a parched throat, and yet does not need a drink—it certainly is only an extrinsic denomination of nature. But be that as it may, in the case of the composite, that is, of a mind joined to such a body, it is not a pure denomination, but a true error of nature that this body should thirst when a drink would be harmful to it. Therefore it remains here to inquire how the goodness of God

does not stand in the way of "nature," thus considered, being deceptive.

Now, first, I realize at this point that there is a great difference between a mind and a body, because the body, by its very nature, is something divisible, whereas the mind is plainly indivisible. Obviously, when I consider the mind, that is, myself insofar as I am only a thing that thinks, I cannot distinguish any parts of me; rather, I take myself to be one complete thing. Although the whole mind seems to be united to the whole body, nevertheless, were a foot or an arm or any other bodily part amputated, I know that nothing would be taken away from the mind; nor can the faculties of willing, sensing, understanding, and so on be called its "parts," because it is one and the same mind that wills, senses, and understands. On the other hand, no corporeal or extended thing can be thought by me that I did not easily in thought divide into parts; in this way I know that it is divisible. If I did not yet know it from any other source, this consideration alone would suffice to teach me that the mind is wholly different from the body.

Next, I observe that my mind is not immediately affected by all the parts of the body, but merely by the brain, or perhaps even by just one small part of the brain—namely, by that part in which the "common sense" is said to be found. As often as it is disposed in the same manner, it presents the same thing to the mind, although the other parts of the body can meanwhile orient themselves now this way, now that way, as countless experiments show—none of which need be reviewed here.

I also notice that the nature of the body is such that none of its parts can be moved by another part a short distance away, unless it is also moved in the same direction by any of the parts that stand between them, even though this more distant part does nothing. For example, in the cord ABCD, if the final part D is pulled, the first part A would be moved in exactly the same direction as it could be moved if one of the intermediate parts, B or C, were pulled and the last part D remained motionless. Just so, when I sense pain in the foot, physics teaches me that this feeling took place because of nerves scattered throughout the foot. These nerves, like cords, are extended from that point all the way to the brain; when they are pulled in the foot, they also pull on the inner parts of the brain to which they are stretched, and produce a certain motion in these parts of the brain. This motion has been constituted by nature so as to affect the mind with a feeling of pain, as if it existed in the foot. But because these nerves need to pass through the tibia, thigh, loins, back, and neck, with the result that they extend from the foot to the brain, it can happen that the part that is in the foot is not stretched; rather, one of the intermediate parts is thus stretched, and obviously the same movement will occur in the brain that happens when the foot was badly affected. The necessary result is that the mind feels the same pain. And we must believe the same regarding any other sense.

Finally, I observe that, since each of the motions occurring in that part of the brain that immediately affects the mind occasions only one sensation in it, there is no better way to think about this than that it occasions the sensation that, of all that could be occasioned by it, is most especially and most often conducive to the maintenance of a healthy man. Moreover, experience shows that such are all the senses bestowed on us by nature; therefore, clearly nothing is to be found in them that does not bear witness to God's power and goodness. Thus, for example, when the nerves in the foot are violently and unusually agitated, their motion, which extends through the marrow of the spine to the inner reaches of the brain, gives the mind at that point a sign to feel something—namely, the pain as if existing in the foot. This pain provokes it to do its utmost to move away from the cause, since it is harmful to the foot. But the nature of man could have been so constituted by God that this same motion in the brain might have displayed something else to the mind: either the motion itself as it is in the brain, or as it is in the foot, or in some place in between—or somewhere else entirely different. But nothing else serves so well the maintenance of the body. Similarly, when we need a drink, a certain dryness arises in the throat that moves its nerves, and, by means of them, the inner recesses of the brain. This motion affects the mind with a feeling of thirst, because in this situation nothing is more useful for us to know than that we need a drink to sustain our health; the same holds for the other matters.

From these considerations it is totally clear that, notwithstanding the immense goodness of God, the nature of man—insofar as it is composed of mind and body, cannot help but sometimes be deceived. For if some cause, not in the foot but in some other part through which the nerves are stretched from the foot to the brain—or perhaps even in the brain itself—were to produce the same motion that would normally be produced by a badly affected foot, then the pain will be felt as if it were in the foot, and the senses will naturally be deceived, because it is reasonable that the motion should always show the pain to the mind as something belonging to the foot rather than to some other part, since an identical motion in the brain can bring about only the identical effect and this motion more frequently is wont to arise from a cause that harms the foot than from something existing elsewhere. And if the dryness of the throat does not, as is the custom, arise from the fact that drink aids in the health of the body, but from a contrary cause—as happens in the case of the person with dropsy—then it is far better that it should deceive, than if, on the contrary, it were always deceptive when the body is well constituted. The same goes for the other cases.

This consideration is most helpful, not only for noticing all the errors to which my nature is liable, but also for easily being able to correct or avoid them. To be sure, I know that every sense more frequently indicates what is true than what is false regarding those things that concern the advantage of the body, and I can almost always use more than one sense in order to examine the same thing. Furthermore, I can use memory, which connects present things with preceding ones, plus the intellect, which now has examined all the causes of error. I should no longer fear lest those things that are daily shown me by the senses, are false; rather, the hyperbolic doubts of the last few days ought to be rejected as worthy of derision—especially the principle doubt regarding sleep, which I did not distinguish from being awake. For I now notice that a very great difference exists between these two; dreams are never joined with all the other actions of life by the memory, as is the case with those actions that occur when one is awake. For surely, if someone, while I am awake, suddenly appears to me, and then immediately disappears, as happens in dreams, so that I see neither where he came from or where he went, it is not without reason that I would judge him to be a ghost or a phantom conjured up in my brain, rather than a true man. But when these things happen, regarding which I notice distinctly where they come from, where they are now, and when they come to me, and I connect the perception of them without any interruption with the rest of my life, obviously I am certain that these perceptions have occurred not in sleep but in a waking state. Nor ought I to have even a little doubt regarding the truth of these things, if, having mustered all the senses, memory, and intellect in order to examine them, nothing is announced to me by one of these sources that conflicts with the others. For from the fact that God is no deceiver, it follows that I am in no way deceived in these matters. But because the need to get things done does not always give us the leisure time for such a careful inquiry, one must believe that the life of man is vulnerable to errors regarding particular things, and we must acknowledge the infirmity of our nature.

23. *The Distinction Between Mental and Physical Phenomena*

FRANZ BRENTANO

Descartes's confidence that ideas (that is, what is in the mind) can yield knowledge of reality beyond the mind was challenged by empiricists like Berkeley and Hume. Berkeley argued that the idea of matter as something existing independently of mind was incoherent, and he concluded that reality was entirely mental or mind-dependent (metaphysical idealism). Hume felt only sensory ideas (sense impressions) could provide knowledge about what exists, but he argued that these ideas could not adequately support beliefs about matter, causality, or even enduring minds (see Hume's essays in Part II and Part V). Thus, Hume advocated metaphysical skepticism. Yet, whether they were idealists, empiricists, or skeptics, eighteenth- and nineteenth-century philosophers tended to adopt Descartes' starting point: what is indubitable is something mental given in present consciousness. Compared to the phemonena of experience, concepts of matter remained philosophically problematic throughout the nineteenth century: Mill tried to construct things out of sensations, and Bergson and James tried to construct them out of the stream of experience (see Bergson's essay in Part I).

Franz Brentano (1838–1917) was a German philosopher and psychologist who taught at the University of Vienna. He believed psychologists and philosophers had become muddled in their talk about what is mental and what is physical. He attempted to clarify matters by rejecting part of Descartes's legacy: the assumption that consciousness is always just an inspection of mental entities (ideas, images, or sensations). It is this view that risks turning all phenomena into mental phenomena. As an alternative, Brentano recommends that we identify the mental as the "acts" that are "directed upon" (or about) objects (or, using Scholastic terminology, the mental is what can have "intentionally inexistent objects"). This characteristic of "mental acts" (like wanting a million dollars or believing in Santa Claus) later came to be called their "intentionality." (Note that "intentionality" in this sense is a technical term that should not be confused with "intentionally," or doing something purposely.)

Brentano's work has been influential and has led philosophers to debate the correct metaphysical analysis of mental acts and their objects. Through his student, Husserl, it helped spawn Phenomenology (the philosophical movement that recommends "reflection" on mental acts as a means to knowledge of the necessary structure of experience). And in claiming nothing physical is characterized by intentionality, it has challenged twentieth-century philosophers who want to show that the mind is, at bottom, something physical.

1

The data of our consciousness make up a world which, taken in its entirety, falls into two great classes, the class of *physical* and the class of *mental* phenomena. . . .

The fact that neither unity nor complete clarity has yet been achieved regarding the line of demarcation between the two areas seems to make this all the more necessary. We have already had occasion to see how physical phenomena which appear in the imagination have been taken to be mental. But there are many other cases of confusion as well. Even psychologists of considerable importance may find it difficult to vindicate themselves against the charge of self-contradiction. We occasionally encounter such assertions as that sensation and imagination are differentiated by the fact that one occurs as the result of a physical phenomenon, while the other is evoked, according to the laws of association, by means of a mental phenomenon. But along with this the same psychologists admit that what appears in sensation does not correspond to its efficient cause. Accordingly, it turns out that what they call physical phenomena never appear to us in actual fact, and that we have no presentation of them whatsoever; surely this is a strange way in which to misuse the term "phenomenon"! When affairs are in such a state, we can not refrain from taking a somewhat closer look at the problem.

From *Introduction to the Philosophy of Mind*, Harold Morick, ed., trans., D. Terrell (New York: Scott, Foresman and Company, 1970). Reprinted by permission of Humanities Press International, Inc., Atlantic Highlands, N.J.

2

. . . Our object is the elucidation of the two terms: physical phenomenon—mental phenomenon. We wish to exclude misunderstanding and confusion in connection with them. And for this we needn't be concerned about the means used, if only they really serve to produce clarity.

Giving more general, superordinate definitions is not the only useful means that can be employed for such an end. Just as induction is contrasted with deduction in the sphere of demonstration, here definition by way of the specific, i.e., by way of an example, is contrasted with definition by means of the more general. And the former method will be more appropriate as long as the particular term is more intelligible than the general. Hence, it may be a more effective procedure to define the term "color" by saying that it designates the general class for red, blue, green, and yellow, than to choose to give an account of red—following the opposite procedure—as a particular species of color. Definition by way of particular cases will perform still more useful service in connection with terms, such as those involved in our case, which are not at all common in ordinary life, while the names of the particular phenomena comprehended under them are familiar enough. So let us start with an attempt to make our concepts clear by way of examples.

Every presentation (*Vorstellung*) of sensation or imagination offers an example of the mental phenomenon; and here I understand by presentation not that which is presented, but the act of presentation. Thus, hearing a sound, seeing a colored object, sensing warm or cold, and the comparable states of imagination as well, are examples of what I mean; but thinking of a general concept, provided such a thing does actually occur, is equally so. Furthermore, every judgment, every recollection, every expectation, every inference, every conviction or opinion, every doubt, is a mental phenomenon. And again, every emotion, joy, sorrow, fear, hope, pride, despair, anger, love, hate, desire, choice, intention, astonishment, wonder, contempt, etc., is such a phenomenon.

Examples of physical phenomena, on the other hand, are a color, a shape, a landscape, which I see; a musical chord, which I hear; heat, cold, odor, which I sense; as well as comparable images, which appear to me in my imagination.

These examples may suffice as concrete illustrations of the distinction between the two classes.

━━

3

Nevertheless, we will attempt to give a definition of the mental phenomenon in another, more unified way. For this, there is available a definition we have used before, when we said that by the term, mental phenomena, we designate presentations and, likewise, all those phenomena which are based on presentations. It scarcely requires notice that, once again, by presentation we understand here not what is presented but the presenting of it. This presentation forms the basis not merely of judgments, but also of desires, as well as of every other mental act. We cannot judge of anything, cannot desire anything, cannot hope for anything, or fear anything, if it is not presented. Hence, the definition which we gave embraces all of the examples just introduced and, in general, all of the phenomena belonging to this domain.

It is a sign of the immature state in which psychology finds itself that one can scarcely utter a single sentence about mental phenomena which would not be disputed by many. Still, the great majority agree with what we just said; presentations are the basis for the other mental phenomena. Thus, Herbart is quite correct in saying: "In every case of emotion, something, no matter how diversified and complicated, must be in consciousness as something presented; so that this particular presentation is included in this particular feeling. And every time we have a desire . . . [we] also have in our thoughts that which we desire." As we

use the word "to present," "to be presented" comes to the same thing as "to appear." . . . Still, we may surely find that, as regards some kinds of sensual feelings of pleasure and displeasure, [some] actually hold the opinion that there is no presentation, even in our sense, on which they are based. We cannot deny a certain temptation in that direction, at least. This holds, for example, in regard to feelings which are caused by a cut or a burn. If someone is cut, then for the most part he has no further perception of touch; if he is burned, no further perception of heat; but pain alone seems to be present in the one case and the other.

Nonetheless, there is no doubt that even here the feeling is based on a presentation. In such cases we always have the presentation of a definite spatial location, which we ordinarily specify in relation to one or the other of the visible and palpable parts of our body. We say that our foot hurts, or our hand hurts, this or the other place on our body is in pain. In the first place, then, those who look on such a spatial presentation as something originally given by means of the neural stimulation itself will therefore be unable to deny that a presentation is the basis of this feeling. But others, too, cannot avoid making the same assumption. For we have within us not merely the presentation of a definite spatial location, but also that of a particular sensory quality, analogous to color, sound, and other so-called sensory qualities, a quality which belongs among the physical phenomena and which is definitely to be distinguished from the accompanying feeling. If we hear a pleasant, mild sound or a shrill one, a harmonious chord or a discord, it will occur to no one to identify the sound with the accompanying feeling of pleasure or pain. But, likewise, when a cut, a burn, or a tickle arouses a feeling of pain or pleasure in us, we must maintain in a similar manner the distinction between a physical phenomenon, which enters in as the object of outer perception, and a mental phenomenon of feeling, which accompanies its appearance, even though the superficial observer is rather inclined to confusion here. . . .

A further basis of the illusion is that the quality on which the feeling ensues, and the feeling itself, do not bear two distinct names. We call the physical phenomenon, which occurs along with the feeling of pain, itself pain in this case. We do not say that this or that phenomenon in the foot is experienced with pain so much as we say that pain is experienced in the foot. To be sure, this is an equivocation such as we find elsewhere, whenever things stand in a close relationship to each other. We call the body healthy, and in connection with it, the air, food, facial color, and so on, but plainly in different senses. In our case, a physical phenomenon itself is called pleasure or pain, after the feeling of pleasure or pain which accompanies its appearance, and here too the sense is modified. It is as if we should say of a harmonious sound that it is a pleasure to us, because we experience a feeling of pleasure on its occurrence; or that the loss of a friend is a great sorrow to us. Experience shows that equivocation is one of the foremost hindrances to our knowledge of distinctions. It must necessarily be very much so here, where a danger of being deluded exists in and of itself, and the transference of the term was perhaps itself the result of a confusion. Hence, many psychologists were deceived, and further errors were tied up with this one. Many arrived at the false conclusion that the experiencing subject must be present at the place of the injured limb in which a painful phenomenon is localized in perception. For, insofar as they identified the phenomenon with the accompanying feeling of pain, they regarded it as a mental, not as a physical, phenomenon. And for just that reason, they believed its perception in the limb to be an inner, and consequently, an evident and infallible perception. But their opinion is contradicted by the fact that the same phenomena often appear in the same way after the limb has been amputated. Others accordingly argued rather to the opposite effect, skeptically opposing the self-evidence (*Evidenz*) of inner perception. This is all resolved, if one has learned to distinguish between the pain in the sense in which the term designates the apparent property of a part of our body and the feeling of pain which is tied up with sensing it. But if one has done this, then one is no longer inclined to hold that the feeling of sensory pain which one experiences on being injured is not based on any presentation.

We may, accordingly, regard it as an indubitably correct definition of mental phenomena that they are either presentations or (in the sense which has been explained) rest on presentations as their basis. In this we would thus have a second definition of the concept [of mental phenomena] which breaks down into fewer terms. Yet it is not entirely unified, since it presents mental phenomena as divided into two groups.

4

The attempt has been made to give a perfectly unified definition which distinguishes all of the mental phenomena, as contrasted with the physical, by means of negation. All physical phenomena, it is said, manifest extension and definite spatial location, whether they are appearances to sight or another sense, or products of the imagination, which presents similar objects to us. The opposite, however, is true of mental phenomena; thinking, willing, and so on appear as unextended and without a situation in space.

According to this view, we would be in a position to characterize the physical phenomena easily and rigorously in contrast to the mental, if we were to say that they are those which appear extended and spatial. And, with the same exactitude, the mental phenomena would then be definable, as contrasted with the physical, as those which exhibit no extension or definite spatial location. One could call on Descartes and Spinoza in support of such a differentiation, but particularly on Kant, who declares space to be the form of intuition of outer sensation. . . .

But here, too, unanimity does not prevail among the psychologists, and for diverse reasons we often hear it denied that extension and the absence of extension are differentiating characteristics distinguishing physical and mental phenomena.

Many believe that the definition is false because not only mental, but also many physical phenomena, appear without extension. Thus, a large number of not unimportant psychologists teach that the phenomena of certain senses, or even of the senses in general, originally manifest themselves free of all extension and definite spatial character. This is very generally believed [to be true] of sounds and of the phenomena of smell. According to Berkeley, the same holds true of colors, and according to Platner, of the phenomena of the sense of touch. . . .

Others, as I have said, will reject the definition for contrary reasons. It is not so much the claim that all physical phenomena appear extended that arouses their opposition. It is the claim, rather, that all mental phenomena lack extension; according to them, certain mental phenomena also manifest themselves as extended. Aristotle appears to have been of this opinion when, in the first chapter of his treatise on sensation and the object of sense, he regards it as evident, immediately and without previous proof, that sense perception is the act of a physical organ. . . .

So we see that the stated distinction is assailed with regard to both physical and mental phenomena. Perhaps both points raised against it are equally unfounded.[1] Nevertheless, a further definition common to mental phenomena is still desirable in any case. For conflict over the question whether certain mental and physical phenomena appear extended or not shows at once that the alleged attribute does not suffice for a distinct differentiation; furthermore, for the mental phenomena it is negative only.

5

What positive attribute will we now be able to advance? Or is there, perhaps, no positive definition at all which holds true of all mental phenomena generally?

A. Bain says that in fact there is none. Nonetheless, psychologists of an earlier period have already directed attention to a particular affinity and analogy which exists among all mental phenomena, while the physical do not share in it. Every mental phenomenon is characterized by what the scholastics of the Middle Ages called the intentional (and also mental)[2] inexistence (Inexistenz) of an object (Gegenstand), and what we could call, although in not entirely unambiguous terms, the reference to a content, a direction upon an object (by which we are not to understand a reality in this case), or an immanent objectivity. Each one includes something as object within itself, although not always in the same way. In presentation something is presented, in judgment something is affirmed or denied, in love [something is] loved, in hate [something] hated, in desire [something] desired, etc.[3]

This intentional inexistence is exclusively characteristic of mental phenomena. No physical phenomenon manifests anything similar. Consequently, we can define mental phenomena by saying that they are such phenomena as include an object intentionally within themselves.

But here, too, we come up against conflict and contradiction. And it is Hamilton in particular who denies the alleged property of a whole broad class of mental phenomena, namely, of all those which he designates as feelings, of pleasure and pain in their most diverse shades and varieties. He is in agreement with us concerning the phenomena of thinking and desire. Obviously, there would be no thinking without an object which is thought, no desire without an object which is desired. "In the phenomena of Feeling—the phenomena of Pleasure and Pain—on the contrary, consciousness does not place the mental modification or state before itself; it does not contemplate it apart—as separate from itself—but is, as it were, fused into one. The peculiarity of Feeling, therefore, is that there is nothing but what is subjectively subjective; there is no object different from self—no objectification of any mode of self." In the first case, there would be something there which, according to Hamilton's way of expression, is "objective"; in the second, something which is "objectively subjective," as in self-knowledge, whose object Hamilton therefore calls subject-object; Hamilton, in denying both with regard to feeling, most definitely denies any intentional inexistence to it.

However, what Hamilton says is surely not entirely correct. Certain feelings are unmistakably referred to objects, and language itself indicates these through the expressions it uses. We say that a person rejoices in or about something, that a person sorrows or grieves about something. And once again: that delights me, that pains me, that hurts me, and so on. Joy and sorrow, like affirmation and denial, love and hate, desire and aversion, distinctly ensue upon a presentation and are referred to what is presented in it.

At the utmost, one could be inclined to agree with Hamilton in those cases in which one succumbs most easily, as we saw before, to the illusion that feeling is not based on any presentation: the case of the pain which is aroused by a cut or burn, for example. But its basis is none other than the very temptation toward this hypothesis, which, as we saw, is erroneous. Moreover, even Hamilton recognizes with us the fact that, without exception, presentations form that basis of feelings, and consequently [do so] in these cases as well. Therefore, his denial that feelings have an object seems so much the more striking.

To be sure, one thing is to be granted. The object to which a feeling refers is not always an external object. Even when I hear a harmonious chord, the pleasure which I feel is not really a pleasure in the sound, but a pleasure in the hearing [of it]. Indeed, one might not be mistaken in saying that it even refers to itself in a certain way and, therefore, that what Hamilton asserts, namely, that the feeling is "fused into one" with its object, *does* occur more or less. But this is nothing which does not likewise hold true of many phenomena of presentation and knowledge, as we shall see in our study of inner consciousness. Nevertheless, in them there is still a mental inexistence, a subject-object, to speak Hamilton's language; and the same will therefore hold true of these feelings as well. Hamilton is mistaken when he says that, in them, everything is "subjectively subjective," an expression which is indeed really self-contradictory; for where we can no longer speak of an object, we can no longer speak of a subject either. Even when Hamilton spoke of a fusion-into-one of the feeling with the mental modification, he gave witness against himself if we consider the matter exactly. Every fusion is a unification of several things; and consequently the pictorial expression, which is intended to make us concretely aware of the distinctive character of feeling, still indicates a certain duality in the unity.

We may thus take it to be valid that the intentional inexistence of an object is a general distinguishing characteristic of mental phenomena, which differentiates this class of phenomena from the class of physical phenomena.

6

It is a further general characteristic of all mental phenomena that they are perceived only in inner consciousness, while only outer perception is possible for the physical.

One could believe that such a definition says little, since it would seem more natural to take the opposite course, defining the act by reference to its object, and so defining inner perception, in contrast to all others, as perception of mental phenomena. But inner perception has still another characteristic, apart from the special nature of its object, which distinguishes it: namely, that immediate, infallible self-evidence, which pertains to it alone among all the cases in which we know objects of experience. Thus, if we say that mental phenomena are those which are grasped by means of inner perception, we have accordingly said that their perception is immediately evident.

Still more! Inner perception is not merely unique as immediately evident perception; it is really unique as perception *(Wahrmehmung)* in the strict sense of the word. We have seen that the phenomena of so-called outer perception can in no way be demonstrated to be true and real, even by means of indirect reasoning. Indeed, we have seen that anyone who placed confidence in them and took them to be what they presented themselves as being is misled by the way the phenomena hang together. Strictly speaking, so-called outer perception is thus not perception; and mental phenomena can accordingly be designated as the only ones of which perception in the strict sense of the word is possible.

Mental phenomena are also adequately characterized by means of this definition. It is not as if all mental phenomena are introspectively perceivable for everyone, and therefore that everything which a person cannot perceive he is to count among the physical phenomena. On the contrary, it is obvious, and was already expressly remarked by us earlier, that no mental phenomenon is perceived by more than a single individual; but on that occasion we also saw that every type of mental phenomenon is represented in the psychical life of every fully developed human being. For this reason, reference to the phenomena which constitute the realm of inner perception serves our purpose satisfactorily.

7

We said that mental phenomena are the only ones of which a perception in the strict sense is possible. We could just as well say that they are the only phenomena to which actual, as well as intentional, existence pertains. Knowledge, joy, desire, exist actually; color, sound, heat, only phenomenally and intentionally.

There are philosophers who go so far as to say that it is self-evident that no actuality *could* correspond to a phenomenon such as we call a physical one. They maintain that anyone who assumes this and ascribes to physical phenomena any existence other than mental holds a view which is self-contradictory in itself. Bain, for example, says that some people have attempted to explain the phenomena of outer perception by the hypothesis of a material world, "in the first instance, detached from perception, and, afterwards, coming into perception, by operating upon the mind." "This view," he says, "involves a contradiction. The prevailing doctrine is that a tree is something in itself apart from all perception; that, by its luminous emanations, it impresses our mind and is then perceived; the perception being an effect, and the unperceived tree [i.e., the one which exists outside of perception] the cause. But the tree is known only through perception; what it may be anterior to, or independent of, perception, we cannot tell; we can think of it as perceived but not as unperceived. There is a manifest contradiction in the supposition; we are required at the same moment to perceive the thing and not to perceive it. We know the touch of iron, but we cannot know the touch apart from the touch."[4]

I must confess that I am not in a position to be convinced of the correctness of this argument. As certain as it is that a color only appears to us when it is an object of our presentation [*wenn wir sie vorstellen*], it is nevertheless not to be inferred from this that a color could not exist without being presented. Only if being persented were included as one factor in the color, just as a certain quality and intensity is included in it, would a color which is not presented signify a contradiction, since a whole without one of its parts is truly a contradiction. This, however, is obviously not the case. Otherwise it would be strictly inconceivable how the belief in the actual existence of the physical phenomenon outside of our presentation of it could have, not to say originated, but achieved the most general dissemination, been maintained with the utmost tenacity, and, indeed, even long been shared by thinkers of the first rank. If what Bain says were correct: "We can think of [a tree] as perceived, but not as unperceived. There is manifest contradiction in the supposition," then his fur-

ther conclusion would surely no longer be subject to objection. But it is precisely this which is not to be granted. Bain explains his dictum by saying: "We are required at the same moment to perceive the thing and not to perceive it." But it is not true that this is required: For, in the first place, not every case of thinking is a perception; and further, even if this were the case, it would only follow that a person could only think of trees perceived by him, but not that he could only think of trees *as perceived by him*. To taste a white piece of sugar does not mean to taste a piece of sugar *as white*. The fallacy reveals itself quite distinctly when it is applied to mental phenomena. If one should say: "I cannot think of a mental phenomenon without thinking of it; and so I can only think of mental phenomena as thought by me; hence no mental phenomena exists outside of my thinking," this mode of inference would be exactly like the one Bain uses. Nonetheless, Bain himself will not deny that his individual mental life is not the only thing to which actual existence belongs. When Bain adds, "We know the touch of iron, but it is not possible that we should know the touch apart from the touch," he uses the word "touch," in the first place, obviously, in the sense of what is felt, and then in the sense of the feeling of it. These are different concepts even if they have the same name. Accordingly, only someone who permits himself to be deceived by the equivocation could make the concession of immediate evidence required by Bain.

It is not true, then, that the hypothesis that a physical phenomenon like those which exist intentionally in us exists outside of the mind in actuality includes a contradiction. It is only that, when we compare one with the other, conflicts are revealed, which show clearly that there is no actual existence corresponding to the intentional existence in this case. And even though this holds true in the first instance only as far as our experience extends, we will, nevertheless, make no mistake if we quite generally deny to physical phenomena any existence other than intentional existence. . . .

9

In conclusion, let us summarize the results of our comments on the distinction between physical and mental phenomena. First of all, we made ourselves concretely aware of the distinctive nature of the two classes by means of *examples.* We then defined mental phenomena as *presentations* and such phenomena which are *based upon presentations;* all the rest belong to the physical. We next spoke of the attribute of *extension,* which was taken by psychologists to be a distinctive characteristic of all physical phenomena; all mental phenomena were supposed to lack it. The contention had not remained uncontested, however, and only later investigations could decide the issue; that in fact mental phenomena do invariably appear unextended was all that could be confirmed now. We next found *intentional inexistence,* the reference to something as an object, to be a distinguishing feature of all mental phenomena; no physical phenomenon manifests anything similar. We further defined mental phenomena as the exclusive *object of inner perception;* they alone are therefore perceived with immediate evidence; indeed, they alone are perceived in the strict sense of the word. And with this there was bound up the further definition, that they alone are phenomena which posses *actual* existence besides their intentional existence. Finally, we advanced it as a distinguishing [feature] that the mental phenomena which someone perceives *always* appear *as a unity* despite their variety, while the physical phenomena which he may perceive simultaneously are not all presented in the same way as partial phenomena within a single phenomenon.

There can be no doubt but that the characteristic which is more distinctive of mental phenomena than any of the others is intentional inexistence. We may now regard them as distinctly defined, over against the physical phenomena, by this, as well as by the other properties which were introduced.

The definitions of mental and physical phenomena which have been given cannot fail to throw a brighter light on our earlier definitions of mental science and physical science *(psychischer und Naturwissenschaft):* indeed, we said of the latter that it is the science of physical phenomena and of the former that it is the science of mental phenomena. It is now easy to see that both definitions implicitly include certain limitations.

This holds true principally of the definition of physical science. For it is not concerned with all physical phenomena; not with those of imagination, but only with those which appear in sensation. And it determines laws for these only insofar as they depend upon physical stimulation of the sense organs. We could express the scientific task of physical science precisely by saying that physical science is the science which attempts to explain the succession of physical phenomena which are normal and pure (not influenced by any particular psychological states and events) on the basis of the hypothesis [that they are the effect] of the stimulation of our sense organs by a world which is quasi-spatially *(raumähnlich)* extended in three dimensions and which proceeds quasi-temporally *(zeitähnlich)* in *one* direction.[5] Without giving any particulars concerning the absolute nature of this world, [physical science] is satisfied to ascribe to it powers which evoke the sensations and mutually influence each other in their working, and to determine the laws of coexistence and succession for these powers. In those laws, it then indirectly gives the laws governing the succession of the physical phenomena of sensation when, by means of scientific abstraction from concomitant psychological conditions, these are regarded as pure and as occurring in relation to a constant sensory capacity. Hence, "science of physical phenomena" must be interpreted in this somewhat complicated way, if it is made synonymous with physical science.[6]

We have seen, along the way, how the expression "physical phenomenon" is sometimes misused by being applied to the above-mentioned powers themselves. And, since the object of a science is naturally designated as the one for which it determines laws directly and explicitly, I believe I make no mistake in also assuming with respect to the definition of physical science as the science of physical phenomena that there is ordinarily bound up with this term the concept of powers belonging to a world which is quasi-spatially extended and which proceeds quasi-temporally, powers which evoke sensations by their effect on the sense organs and which reciprocally influence one another, and for which physical science investigates the laws of coexistence and succession. If one regards these powers as the object [of physical science], this also has the convenient feature that something which truly and actually exists appears as object of the science. This last would be just as attainable if we defined physical science as the science of sensations, implicitly adding the same limitation of which we just spoke. What made the expression "physical phenomenon" seem preferable was, probably, primarily the fact that the external causes of sensation were thought of as corresponding to the physical phenomena appearing in it, (whether this be in every respect, as was originally the case, or whether it be, as now, in respect at least to extension in three dimensions). From this, there also arose the otherwise inappropriate term, "outer perception." It is pertinent, however, that the act of sensation manifests, along with the intentional inexistence of the physical phenomenon, still other properties with which the physical scientist *(Naturforscher)* is not at all concerned, since sensation does not give through them similar information about the distinctive relationships of the external world.

With respect to the definition of psychology, it may be apparent in the first place that the concept of mental phenomena is to be broadened rather than narrowed. For the physical phenomena of imagination, at least, fall completely within its scope just as much as do mental phenomena, in the sense defined earlier; and those which appear in sensation can also not remain unconsidered in the theory of sensation. But it is obvious that they come into consideration only as the content of mental phenomena, when the characteristics of those phenomena are being described. And the same holds true of all mental phenomena which possess exclusively phenomenal existence. It is only mental phenomena in the sense of actual states which we shall have to regard as the true object of psychology. And it is exclusively with reference to them that we say psychology is the science of mental phenomena.

Endnotes

[1] The claim that even mental phenomena appear extended rests plainly on a confusion between physical and mental phenomena similar to the one we became convinced of above, when we established that even sensory feelings are necessarily based on a presentation.

[2] They also use the expression "to be in something objectively," which, if we should wish to make use of it now, could possibly be taken in just the opposite

sense, as the designation of a real existence outside of the mind. Nevertheless, it reminds one of the expression "to be immanently objective," which we sometimes use in a similar sense, and in which the "immanently" is intended to exclude the misunderstanding that was to be feared.

[3] Aristotle has already spoken of this mental inherence. In his books on the soul, he says that what is experienced, insofar as it is experienced, is in the one experiencing it, that sense contains what is experienced without its matter, that what is thought is in the thinking intellect. In Philo we likewise find the doctrine of mental existence and inexistence. In confusing this, however, with existence in the strict sense, he arrives at his doctrine of the Logos and Ideas, with its wealth of contradictions. The like holds true of the Neo-Platonists. Augustine touches on the same fact in his theory of the *Verbum mentis* and its internal origin. Anselm does so in his well-known ontological argument; and many have alleged the basis of his fallacy to be the fact that he regarded mental existence as if it were actual existence (see Ueberweg, *History of Philosophy*, Vol. II). Thomas Aquinas teaches that what is thought is intentionally in the one thinking, the object of love in the person loving, what is desired in the person desiring, and uses this for theological purposes. When the scripture speaks of an indwelling of the Holy Ghost, he explains this as an intentional indwelling by way of love. And he also seeks to find in intentional inexistence, in the cases of thinking and loving, a certain analogy for the mystery of the Trinity and the procession of the Word and Spirit.

[4] *Mental Science*, 3d ed., p. 198.

[5] On this point see Ueberweg (*System der Logik*), in whose analysis, to be sure, not everything is deserving of approval. He is mistaken particularly when he considers the external causes to be spatial instead of quasi-spatial, temporal instead of quasi-temporal.

[6] The interpretation would not be quite as Kant would have it; nevertheless, it approximates his interpretations as far as is feasible. In a certain sense, it comes closer to the viewpoint of Mill in his book against Hamilton, but still without agreeing with him in all the essential respects. What Mill calls permanent possibilities of sensations has a close relationship with what we call powers. The relationship to, as well as the most important departure from, Ueberweg's view was already touched upon in the preceding note.

24. *Intentional Systems*

DANIEL C. DENNETT

In the previous selection, Brentano claims that nothing physical exhibits intentionality, the feature of consciousness whereby mind is "directed upon an object." This thesis has been championed by dualists and idealists who want to deny that minds are really physical brains or aspects of the nervous system. Many twentieth-century philosophers, however, have been impressed by progress in science whereby things (like heat, genes, or molecules) turn out to be complex properties or configurations of basic physical entities, and they suspect that the mind, too, will turn out to be physical (see the following essay by Armstrong). Also, along with many psychologists, many philosophers doubt the mind has the ability to intuit (or to introspect) its own essence. For these philosophers, the challenge is to account for intentionality in a way that leaves the door open for a physicalist understanding of the mind. Dennett argues that it is useful in explanations of behavior to ascribe intentionality to a variety of systems, including physical ones. Similarly, physicalists have suggested, the attribution of intentionality to persons may not indicate the presence of a preternatural power of mind, but instead just be part of an explanation of behavior. Dennett, an American philosopher who teaches at Tufts University, further develops this strategy in his 1987 book, *The Intentional Stance.*

I wish to examine the concept of a system whose behavior can be—at least sometimes—explained and predicted by relying on ascriptions to the system of beliefs and desires (and hopes, fears, intentions, hunches, . . .). I will call such systems *intentional systems,* and such explanations and predictions intentional explanations and predictions, in virtue of the intentionality of the idioms of belief and desire (and hope, fear, intention, hunch, . . .).

I used to insist on capitalizing "intentional" wherever I meant to be using Brentano's notion of *intentionality,* in order to distinguish this technical term from its cousin, e.g., "an intentional shove," but the technical term is now in much greater currency, and since almost everyone else who uses the term seems content to risk this confusion, I have decided, with some trepidation, to abandon my typographical eccentricity. But let the uninitiated reader beware: "intentional" as it occurs here is *not* the familiar term of layman's English. For me, as for many recent authors, intentionality is primarily a feature of linguistic entities—idioms, contexts—and for my purposes here we can be satisfied that an idiom is intentional if substitution of codesignative terms do not preserve truth or if the "objects" of the idiom are not capturable in the usual way by quantifiers.

I

The first point to make about intentional systems as I have just defined them is that a particular thing is an intentional system only in relation to the strategies of someone who is trying to explain and predict its behavior. What this amounts to can best be brought out by example. Consider the case of a chess-playing computer, and the different

From *Journal of Philosophy* 68, No. 4 (February 1971): 87–101 and 106. Reprinted by permission of the author and the *Journal of Philosophy.*

strategies or stances one might adopt as its opponent in trying to predict its moves. There are three
different stances of interest to us. First there is the
design stance. If one knows exactly how the computer is designed (including the impermanent part
of its design: its program) one can predict its designed response to any move one makes by following the computation instructions of the program.
One's prediction will come true provided only that
the computer performs as designed—that is, without breakdown. Different varieties of design-
stance predictions can be discerned, but all of them
are alike in relying on the notion of *function*, which
is purpose-relative or teleological. That is, a design
of a system breaks it up into larger or smaller functional parts, and design-stance predictions are generated by assuming that each functional part will
function properly. For instance, the radio engi-
neer's schematic wiring diagrams have symbols for
each resistor, capacitor, transistor, etc.—*each with
its task to perform*—and he can give a design-stance
prediction of the behavior of a circuit by assuming
that each element performs its task. Thus one can
make design-stance predictions of the computer's
response at several different levels of abstraction,
depending on whether one's design treats as
smallest functional elements strategy-generators
and consequence-testers, multipliers and dividers,
or transistors and switches. (It should be noted that
not all diagrams or pictures are designs in this
sense, for a diagram may carry no information
about the functions—intended or observed—of
the elements it depicts.)

We generally adopt the design stance when
making predictions about the behavior of mechanical objects, e.g., "As the typewriter carriage approaches the margin, a bell will ring (provided the
machine is in working order)," and more simply,
"Strike the match and it will light." We also often
adopt this stance in predictions involving natural
objects: "Heavy pruning will stimulate denser fo-
liage and stronger limbs." The essential feature of
the design stance is that we make predictions
solely from knowledge or assumptions about the
system's functional design, irrespective of the
physical constitution or condition of the innards of
the particular object.

Second, there is what we may call the *physical
stance*. From this stance our predictions are based
on the actual physical state of the particular object,
and are worked out by applying whatever knowledge we have of the laws of nature. It is from this
stance alone that we can predict the malfunction of
systems (unless, as sometimes happens these
days, a system is *designed* to malfunction after a
certain time, in which case malfunctioning in one
sense becomes a part of its proper functioning).
Instances of predictions from the physical stance
are common enough: "If you turn on the switch
you'll get a nasty shock," and, "When the snows
come that branch will break right off." One seldom
adopts the physical stance in dealing with a computer just because the number of critical variables
in the physical constitution of a computer would
overwhelm the most prodigious calculator. Significantly, the physical stance is generally reserved for
instances of breakdown, where the condition preventing normal operation is generalized and easily
locatable, e.g., "Nothing will happen when you
type in your questions, because it isn't plugged
in," or, "It won't work with all that flood water in
it." Attempting to give a physical account or prediction of the chess-playing computer would be a
pointless and herculean labor, but it would work in
principle. One could predict the response it would
make in a chess game by tracing out the effects of
the input energies all the way through the computer until once more type was pressed against
paper and a response was printed. (Because of the
digital nature of computers, quantum-level indeterminacies, if such there be, will cancel out rather
than accumulate, unless of course a radium "ran-
domizer" or other amplifier of quantum effects is
built into the computer).

The best chess-playing computers these days
are practically inaccessible to prediction from either
the design stance or the physical stance; they have
become too complex for even their own designers
to view from the design stance. A man's best hope
of defeating such a machine in a chess match is to
predict its responses by figuring out as best he can
what the best or most rational move would be,
given the rules and goals of chess. That is, one
assumes not only (1) that the machine will function
as designed, but (2) that the design is optimal as
well, that the computer will "choose" the most
rational move. Predictions made on these assumptions may well fail if either assumption proves un-
warranted in the particular case, but still this *means*
of prediction may impress us as the most fruitful
one to adopt in dealing with a particular system.
Put another way, when one can no longer hope to
beat the machine by utilizing one's knowledge of
physics or programming to anticipate its re-

sponses, one may still be able to avoid defeat by treating the machine rather like an intelligent human opponent.

We must look more closely at this strategy. A prediction relying on the assumption of the system's rationality is relative to a number of things. First, rationality here so far means nothing more than optimal design relative to a goal or optimally weighted hierarchy of goals (checkmate, winning pieces, defense, etc., in the case of chess) and a set of constraints (the rules and starting position). Prediction itself is, moreover, relative to the nature and extent of the information the system has at the time about the field of endeavor. The question one asks in framing a prediction of this sort is: What is the most rational thing for the computer to do, given goals $x, y, z, . . .$, constraints $a, b, c, . . .$ and information (including misinformation, if any) about the present state of affairs $p, q, r, . . . ?$ In predicting the computer's response to my chess move, my assessment of the computer's most rational move may depend, for instance, not only on my assumption that the computer has information about the present disposition of all the pieces, but also on whether I believe the computer has information about my inability to see four moves ahead, the relative powers of knights and bishops, and my weakness for knight-bishop exchanges. In the end I may not be able to frame a very good prediction, if I am unable to determine with any accuracy what information and goals the computer has, or if the information and goals I take to be given do not dictate any one best move, or if I simply am not so good as the computer is at generating an optimal move from this given. Such predictions then are very precarious; not only are they relative to a set of postulates about goals, constraints, and information, and not only do they hinge on determining an optimal response in situations where we may have no clear criteria for what is optimal, but also they are vulnerable to short-circuit falsifications that are in principle unpredictable from this stance. Just as design-stance predictions are vulnerable to malfunctions (by depending on the assumption of no malfunction), so these predictions are vulnerable to design weaknesses and lapses (by depending on the assumption of optimal design). It is a measure of the success of contemporary program designers that these precarious predictions turn out to be true with enough regularity to make the method useful.

The denouement of this extended example

should now be obvious: this third stance, with its assumption of rationality, is the *intentional stance*; the predictions one makes from it are intentional predictions; one is viewing the computer as an intentional system. One predicts behavior in such a case by ascribing to the system *the possession of certain information* and supposing it to be *directed by certain goals*, and then by working out the most reasonable or appropriate action on the basis of these ascriptions and suppositions. It is a small step to calling the information possessed the computer's *beliefs*, its goals and subgoals its *desires*. What I mean by saying that this is a small step, is that the notion of possession of information or misinformation is just as intentional a notion as that of belief. The "possession" at issue is hardly the bland and innocent notion of storage one might suppose; it is, and must be, "epistemic possession"—an analogue of belief. Consider: the Frenchman who possesses the *Encyclopedia Britannica* but knows no English might be said to "possess" the information in it, but if there is such a sense of possession, it is not strong enough to serve as the sort of possession the computer must be supposed to enjoy, relative to the information it *uses* in "choosing" a chess move. In a similar way, the goals of a goal-directed computer must be specified intentionally, just like desires.

Lingering doubts about whether the chess-playing computer *really* has beliefs and desires are misplaced; for the definition of intentional systems I have given does not say that intentional systems *really* have beliefs and desires, but that one can explain and predict their behavior by *ascribing* beliefs and desires to them, and whether one calls what one ascribes to the computer beliefs or belief-analogues or information complexes or intentional whatnots makes no difference to the nature of the calculation one makes on the basis of the ascriptions. One will arrive at the same predictions whether one forthrightly thinks in terms of the computer's beliefs and desires, or in terms of the computer's information-store and goal-specifications. The inescapable and interesting fact is that for the best chess-playing computers of today, intentional explanation and prediction of their behavior is not only common, but works when no other sort of prediction of their behavior is manageable. We do quite successfully treat these computers as intentional systems, and we do this independently of any considerations about what substance they are composed of, their origin, their position or lack of position in the community of moral agents, their consciousness or self-consciousness, or the determinacy or indeterminacy of their operations. The decision to adopt the strategy is pragmatic, and is not intrinsically right or wrong. One can always refuse to adopt the intentional stance toward the computer, and accept its checkmates. One can switch stances at will without involving oneself in any inconsistencies or inhumanities, adopting the intentional stance in one's role as opponent, the design stance in one's role as redesigner, and the physical stance in one's role as repairman.

This celebration of our chess-playing computer is not intended to imply that it is a completely adequate model or simulation of Mind, or intelligent human or animal activity; nor am I saying that the attitude we adopt toward this computer is precisely the same that we adopt toward a creature we deem to be conscious and rational. All that has been claimed is that on occasion, a purely physical system can be so complex, and yet so organized, that we find it convenient, explanatory, pragmatically necessary for prediction, to treat it as if it had beliefs and desires and was rational. The chess-playing computer is just that, a machine for playing chess, which no man or animal is; and hence its "rationality" is pinched and artificial.

Perhaps we could straightforwardly expand the chess-playing computer into a more faithful model of human rationality, and perhaps not. I prefer to pursue a more fundamental line of inquiry first.

When should we expect the tactic of adopting the intentional stance to pay off? Whenever we have reason to suppose the assumption of optimal design is warranted, and doubt the practicality of prediction from the design or physical stance. Suppose we travel to a distant planet and find it inhabited by things moving about its surface, multiplying, decaying, apparently reacting to events in the environment, but otherwise as unlike human beings as you please. Can we make intentional predictions and explanations of their behavior? If we have reason to suppose that a process of natural selection has been in effect, then we can be assured that the populations we observe have been selected in virtue of their design: they will respond to at least some of the more common event-types in this environment in ways that are normally appropriate—that is, conducive to propagation of the species.[1] Once we have tentatively identified the

perils and succors of the environment (relative to the constitution of the inhabitants, not ours), we shall be able to estimate which goals and which weighting of goals will be optimal relative to the creatures' *needs* (for survival and propagation), which sorts of information about the environment will be *useful* in guiding goal-directed activity, and which activities will be appropriate given the environmental circumstances. Having doped out these conditions (which will always be subject to revision) we can proceed at once to ascribe beliefs and desires to the creatures. Their behavior will "manifest" their beliefs by being seen as the actions which, given the creatures' desires, would be appropriate to such beliefs as would be appropriate to the environmental stimulation. Desires, in turn, will be "manifested" in behavior as those appropriate desires (given the needs of the creature) to which the actions of the creature would be appropriate, given the creature's beliefs. The circularity of these interlocking specifications is no accident. Ascriptions of beliefs and desires must be interdependent, and the only points of anchorage are the demonstrable needs for survival, the regularities of behavior, and the assumption, grounded in faith in natural selection, of optimal design. Once one has ascribed beliefs and desires, however, one can at once set about predicting behavior on their basis, and if evolution has done its job—as it must over the long run—our predictions will be reliable enough to be useful.

It might at first seem that this tactic unjustifiably imposes human categories and attributes (belief, desire, and so forth) on these alien entities. It is a sort of anthropomorphizing, to be sure, but it is conceptually innocent anthropomorphizing. We do not have to suppose these creatures share with us any peculiarly human inclinations, attitudes, hopes, foibles, pleasures, or outlooks; their actions may not include running, jumping, hiding, eating, sleeping, listening, or copulating. All we transport from our world to theirs are the categories of rationality, perception (information input by some "sense" modality or modalities—perhaps radar or cosmic radiation), and action. The question of whether we can expect them to share any of our beliefs or desires is tricky, but there are a few points that can be made at this time; in virtue of their rationality they can be supposed to share our belief in logical truths,[2] and we cannot suppose that they normally desire their own destruction, for instance.

II

When one deals with a system—be it man, machine, or alien creature—by explaining and predicting its behavior by citing its beliefs and desires, one has what might be called a "theory of behavior" for the system. Let us see how such intentional theories of behavior relate to other putative theories of behavior.

One fact so obvious that it is easily overlooked is that our "common-sense" explanations and predictions of the behavior of both men and animals are intentional. We start by assuming rationality. We do not *expect* new acquaintances to react irrationally to particular topics or eventualities, but when they do we learn to adjust our strategies accordingly, just as, with a chess-playing computer, one sets out with a high regard for its rationality and adjusts one's estimate downward wherever performance reveals flaws. The presumption of rationality is so strongly entrenched in our inference habits that when our predictions prove false, we at first cast about for adjustments in the information-possession conditions (he must not have heard, he must not know English, he must not have seen x, been aware that y, etc.) or goal weightings, before questioning the rationality of the system as a whole. In extreme cases personalities may prove to be so unpredictable from the intentional stance that we abandon it, and if we have accumulated a lot of evidence in the meanwhile about the nature of response patterns in the individual, we may find that a species of design stance can be effectively adopted. This is the fundamentally different attitude we occasionally adopt toward the insane. To watch an asylum attendant manipulate an obsessively countersuggestive patient, for instance, is to watch something radically unlike normal interpersonal relations.

Our prediction of animal behavior by "common sense" is also intentional. Whether or not sentimental folk go overboard when they talk to their dogs or fill their cats' heads with schemes and worries, even the most hardboiled among us predict animals' behavior intentionally. If we observe a mouse in a situation where it can see a cat waiting at one mousehole and cheese at another, we know which way the mouse will go, providing it is not deranged; our prediction is not based on our familiarity with maze-experiments or any assumptions about the sort of special training the mouse has been through. We suppose the mouse can see the cat and the cheese, and hence has beliefs (belief-analogues, intentional whatnots) to the effect that there is a cat to the left, cheese to the right, and we ascribe to the mouse also the desire to eat the cheese and the desire to avoid the cat (subsumed, appropriately enough, under the more general desires to eat and to avoid peril); so we predict that the mouse will do what is appropriate to such beliefs and desires, namely, go to the right in order to get the cheese and avoid the cat. Whatever academic allegiances or theoretical predilections we may have, we would be astonished if, in the general run, mice and other animals falsified such intentional predictions of their behavior. Indeed, experimental psychologists of every school would have a hard time devising experimental situations to support their various theories without the help of their intentional expectations of how the test animals will respond to circumstances.

Earlier I alleged that even creatures from another planet would share with us our beliefs in logical truths; light can be shed on this claim by asking whether mice and other animals, in virtue of being intentional systems, also believe the truths of logic. There is something bizarre in the picture of a dog or mouse cogitating a list of tautologies, but we can avoid that picture. The assumption that something is an intentional system is the assumption that it is rational; that is, one gets nowhere with the assumption that entity x has beliefs $p,q,r, \ldots$ unless one also supposes that x believes what follows from $p,q,r, \ldots$; otherwise there is no way of ruling out the prediction that x will, in the face of its beliefs $p,q,r, \ldots$ do something utterly stupid, and, if we cannot rule out *that* prediction, we will have acquired no predictive power at all. So whether or not the animal is said to *believe* the *truths* of logic, it must be supposed to *follow* the *rules* of logic. Surely our mouse follows or believes in *modus ponens*, for we ascribed to it the beliefs: (a) *there is a cat to the left*, and (b) *if there is a cat to the left, I had better not go left*, and our prediction relied on the mouse's ability to get to the conclusion. In general there is a trade-off between rules and truths; we can suppose x to have an inference rule taking A to B or we can give x the belief in the "theorem"; *if A then B*. As far as our predictions are concerned, we are free to ascribe to the mouse either a few inference rules and belief in many logical propositions, or many inference rules and few if any logical beliefs.[3] We can even take a patently nonlogical belief like (b) and recast it as an inference rule taking (a) to the desired conclusion.

Will all logical truths appear among the beliefs of any intentional system? If the system were ideally or perfectly rational, all logical truths would appear, but any actual intentional system will be imperfect, and so not all logical truths must be ascribed as beliefs to any system. Moreover, not all the inference rules of an actual intentional system may be valid; not all its inference-licensing beliefs may be truths of logic. Experience may indicate where the shortcomings lie in any particular system. If we found an imperfectly rational creature whose allegiance to *modus ponens*, say, varied with the subject matter, we could characterize that by excluding *modus ponens* as a rule and ascribing in its stead a set of nonlogical inference rules covering the *modus ponens* step for each subject matter where the rule was followed. Not surprisingly, as we discover more and more imperfections (as we banish more and more logical truths from the creature's beliefs), our efforts at intentional prediction become more and more cumbersome and undecidable, for we can no longer count on the beliefs, desires, and actions going together that *ought* to go together. Eventually we end up, following this process, by predicting from the design stance; we end up, that is, dropping the assumption of rationality.[4]

This migration from common-sense intentional explanations and predictions to more reliable design-stance explanations and predictions that is forced on us when we discover that our subjects are imperfectly rational is, independently of any such discovery, the proper direction for theory builders to take whenever possible. In the end, we want to be able to explain the intelligence of man, or beast, in terms of his design, and this in turn in terms of the natural selection of this design; so whenever we stop in our explanations at the intentional level we have left over an unexplained instance of intelligence or rationality. This comes out vividly if we look at theory building from the vantage point of economics.

Any time a theory builder proposes to call any event, state, structure, etc., in any system (say the brain of an organism) a *signal* or *message* or *command* or otherwise endows it with content, he *takes out a loan* of intelligence. He implicitly posits along with his signals, messages, or commands, something that can serve as a signal-*reader, message-understan-*der, or *commander*, else his "signals" will be for naught, will decay unreceived, uncomprehended. This loan must be repaid eventually by finding and analyzing away these readers or comprehenders; for, failing this, the theory will have among its elements unanalyzed man-analogues endowed with enough intelligence to read the signals, etc., and thus the theory will *postpone* answering the major question: what makes for intelligence? The intentionality of all such talk of signals and commands reminds us that rationality is being taken for granted, and in this way shows us where a theory is incomplete. It is this feature that, to my mind, puts a premium on the yet unfinished task of devising a rigorous definition of intentionality, for if we can lay claim to a purely formal criterion of intentional discourse, we will have what amounts to a medium of exchange for assessing theories of behavior. Intentionality *abstracts* from the inessential details of the various forms intelligence-loans can take (e.g., signal-readers, volition-emitters, librarians in the corridors of memory, egos and superegos) and serves as a reliable means of detecting exactly where a theory is *in the red* relative to the task of explaining intelligence; wherever a theory relies on a formulation bearing the logical marks of intentionality, there a little man is concealed.

This insufficiency of intentional explanation from the point of view of psychology has been widely felt and as widely misconceived. The most influential misgivings, expressed in the behaviorism of Skinner and Quine, can be succinctly characterized in terms of our economic metaphor. Skinner's and Quine's adamant prohibitions of intentional idioms at all levels of theory is the analogue of rock-ribbed New England conservatism: no deficit spending when building a theory! In Quine's case, the abhorrence of loans is due mainly to his fear that they can never be repaid, whereas Skinner stresses rather that what is borrowed is worthless to begin with. Skinner's suspicion is that intentionally couched claims are empirically vacuous, in the sense that they are altogether too easy to accommodate to the data, like the *virtus dormitiva* Molière's doctor ascribes to the sleeping powder. Questions can be begged on a temporary basis, however, permitting a mode of prediction and explanation not totally vacuous. Consider the following intentional prediction: if I were to ask a thousand American mathematicians how much seven times five is, more than nine hundred would respond by saying that it was thirty-five. (I have allowed for a few to mis-hear my question, a few others to be obstreperous, a few to make slips of the tongue.) If you doubt the prediction, you can test it; I would bet good money on it. It seems to have empirical content because it can, in a fashion, be tested, and yet it is unsatisfactory as a prediction of an empirical theory of psychology. It works, of course, because of the contingent, empirical—but evolution-guaranteed—fact that men in general are well enough designed both to get the answer right and to want to get it right. It will hold with as few exceptions for any group of Martians with whom we are able to converse, for it is not a prediction just of *human* psychology, but of the "psychology" of intentional systems generally.

Deciding on the basis of available empirical evidence that something is a piece of copper or a lichen permits one to make predictions based on the empirical theories dealing with copper and lichens, but deciding on the basis of available evidence that something is (may be treated as) an intentional system permits predictions having a normative or logical basis rather than an empirical one, and hence the success of an intentional prediction, based as it is on no particular picture of the system's design, cannot be construed to confirm or disconfirm any particular pictures of the system's design.

Skinner's reaction to this has been to try to frame predictions purely in non-intentional language, by predicting bodily responses to physical stimuli, but to date this has not provided him with the alternative mode of prediction and explanation he has sought, as perhaps an extremely cursory review can indicate. To provide a setting for non-intentional prediction of behavior, he invented the Skinner box, in which the rewarded behavior of the occupant—say, a rat—is a highly restricted and stereotypic bodily motion—usually pressing a bar with the front paws.

The claim that is then made is that once the animal has been trained, a law-like relationship is discovered to hold between non-intentionally characterized events: controlling stimuli and bar-pressing responses. A regularity is discovered to hold, to be sure, but the fact that it is between non-intentionally defined events is due to a property of the Skinner box and not of the occupant. For let us turn our prediction about mathematicians into a Skinnerian prediction: strap a mathematician in a Skinner box so he can move only his head; display in front of him a card on which appear the marks: "How much is seven times five?"; move into the range of his head-motions two buttons, over one of which is the mark "35" and over the other "34"; place electrodes on the soles of his feet and give him a few quick shocks; the controlling stimulus is then to be the sound: "Answer now!" I predict that in a statistically significant number of cases, even *before* training trials to condition the man to press button "35" with his forehead, he will do this when given the controlling stimulus. Is this a satisfactory scientific prediction just because it eschews the intentional vocabulary? No, it is an intentional prediction disguised by so restricting the environment that only one bodily motion is available to fulfill the intentional *action* that anyone would prescribe as appropriate to the circumstances of perception, belief, desire. That it is action, not merely motion, that is predicted can also be seen in the case of subjects less intelligent than mathematicians. Suppose a mouse were trained, in a Skinner box with a food reward, to take exactly four steps forward and press a bar with its nose; if Skinner's laws truly held between stimuli and responses defined in terms of bodily motion, were we to move the bar an inch farther away, so four steps did not reach it, Skinner would have to predict that the mouse would jab its nose into the empty air rather than take a fifth step.

A variation of Skinnerian theory designed to meet this objection acknowledges that the trained response one predicts is not truly captured in a description of skeletal motion alone, but rather in a description of an environmental effect achieved: the bar going down, the "35" button being depressed. This will also not do. Suppose we could in fact train a man or animal to achieve an environmental effect, as this theory proposes. Suppose, for instance, we train a man to push a button under the longer of two displays, such as drawings or simple designs, that is, we reward him when he pushes the button under the longer of two pictures of pencils, or cigars, etc. The miraculous consequence of this theory, were it correct, would be that if, after training him on simple views, we were to present him with the Müller-Lyer arrow-head illusion, he would be immune to it, for *ex hypothesi* he has been trained to achieve an *actual* environmental effect (choosing the display that *is* longer), not a *perceived* or *believed* environmental effect (choosing the display that *seems* longer). The reliable prediction, again, is the intentional one.[5]

Skinner's experimental design is supposed to eliminate the intentional, but it merely masks it. Skinner's non-intentional predictions work to the extent they do, not because Skinner has truly found non-intentional behavioral laws, but because the highly reliable intentional predictions underlying his experimental situations (the rat desires food and believes it will get food by pressing the bar—something for which it has been given good evidence—so it will press the bar) are disguised by leaving virtually no room in the environment for more than one bodily motion to be the appropriate action and by leaving virtually no room in the environment for discrepancy to arise between the subject's beliefs and the reality.

Where, then, should we look for a satisfactory theory of behavior? Intentional theory is vacuous as psychology because it presupposes and does not explain rationality or intelligence. The apparent successes of Skinnerian behaviorism, however, rely on hidden intentional predictions. Skinner is right in recognizing that intentionality can be no *foundation* for psychology, and right also to look for purely mechanistic regularities in the activities of his subjects, but there is little reason to suppose they will lie on the surface in gross behavior— except, as we have seen, when we put an artificial straitjacket on an intentional regularity. Rather, we will find whatever mechanistic regularities there are in the functioning of internal systems whose design approaches the optimal (relative to some ends). In seeking knowledge of internal design our most promising tactic is to take out intelligence-loans, endow peripheral and internal events with content, and then look for mechanisms that will function appropriately with such "messages" so that we can pay back the loans. This tactic is hardly untried. Research in artificial intelligence, which has produced, among other things, the chess-playing computer, proceeds by working from an intentionally characterized problem (how to get the computer to consider the right sorts of information, make the right decisions) to a design-stance solution—an approximation of optimal design. Psychophysicists and neurophysiologists who routinely describe events in terms of the transmission of information within the nervous system are similarly borrowing intentional capital—even if they are often inclined to ignore or disavow their debts.

Finally, it should not be supposed that, just because intentional theory is vacuous as psychology, in virtue of its assumption of rationality, it is vacuous from all points of view. Game theory, for example, is inescapably intentional, but as a formal normative theory and not a psychology this is nothing amiss. Game-theoretical predictions applied to human subjects achieve their accuracy in virtue of the evolutionary guarantee that man is well designed as a game player, a special case of rationality. Similarly, economics, the social science of greatest predictive power today, is not a psychological theory and presupposes what psychology must explain. Economic explanation and prediction is intentional (although some is disguised) and succeeds to the extent that it does because individual men are in general good approximations of the optimal operator in the marketplace.

III

The concept of an intentional system is a relatively uncluttered and unmetaphysical notion, abstracted as it is from questions of the composition, constitution, consciousness, morality, or divinity of the entities falling under it. Thus, for example, it is much easier to decide whether a machine can be an intentional system than it is to decide whether a machine can *really* think, or be conscious, or morally responsible. This simplicity makes it ideal as a source of order and organization in philosophical analyses of "mental" concepts. Whatever else a person might be—embodied mind or soul, self-conscious moral agent, "emergent" form of intelligence—he is an intentional system, and whatever follows just from being an intentional system is thus true of a person. It is interesting to see just how much of what we hold to be the case about persons or their minds follows directly from their being intentional systems. To revert for a moment to the economic metaphor, the guiding or challenging question that defines work in the philosophy of mind is this: are there mental treasures that cannot be purchased with intentional coin? If not, a considerable unification of science can be foreseen in outline. Of special importance for such an examination is the subclass of intentional systems that have language, that can communicate; for these provide a framework for a theory of consciousness. . . .

What will be true of human believers just in virtue of their being intentional systems with the capacity to communicate?

Just as not all intentional systems currently known to us can fly or swim, so not all intentional systems can talk, but those which can do this raise special problems and opportunities when we come to ascribe beliefs and desires to them. That is a massive understatement; without the talking intentional systems, of course, there would be no ascribing beliefs, no theorizing, no assuming rationality, no predicting. The capacity for language is without doubt the crowning achievement of evolution, an achievement that feeds on itself to produce ever more versatile and subtle rational systems, but still it can be looked at as an adaptation which is subject to the same conditions of environmental utility as any other behavioral talent. When it is looked at in this way several striking facts emerge. One of the most pervasive features of evolutionary histories is the interdependence of distinct organs and capacities in a species. Advanced eyes and other distance receptors are of no utility to an organism unless it develops advanced means of locomotion; the talents of a predator will not accrue to a species that does not evolve a carnivore's digestive system. The capacities of belief and communication have prerequisites of their own. We have already seen that there is no point in ascribing beliefs to a system unless the beliefs ascribed are in general appropriate to the environment, and the system responds appropriately to the beliefs. An eccentric expression of this would be: the capacity to believe would have no survival value unless it were a capacity to believe truths. What is eccentric and potentially misleading about this is that it hints at the picture of a species "trying on" a faculty giving rise to beliefs most of which were false, having its inutility demonstrated, and abandoning it. A species might "experiment" by mutation in any number of inefficacious systems, but none of these systems would deserve to be called belief systems precisely because of their defects, their nonrationality, and hence a false belief system is a conceptual impossibility. To borrow an example from a short story by MacDonald Harris, a soluble fish is an evolutionary impossibility, but a system for false beliefs cannot even be given a coherent description. The same evolutionary bias in favor of truth prunes the capacity to communicate as it develops; a capacity for false communication would not be a capacity for communication at all, but just an emission proclivity of no systematic value to

the species. The faculty of communication would not gain ground in evolution unless it was by and large the faculty of transmitting true beliefs, which means only: the faculty of altering other members of the species in the direction of more optimal design. . . .

The concept of an intentional system explicated in these pages is made to bear a heavy load. It has been used here to form a bridge connecting the intentional domain (which includes our "commonsense" world of persons and actions, game theory, and the "neural signals" of the biologist) to the non-intentional domain of the physical sciences. That is a lot to expect of one concept, but nothing less than Brentano himself expected when, in a day of less fragmented science, he proposed intentionality as the mark that sunders the universe in the most fundamental way: dividing the mental from the physical.

Endnotes

[1] Note that what is *directly* selected, the gene, is a diagram and not a design; it is selected, however, because it happens to ensure that its bearer has a certain (functional) design. This was pointed out to me by Woodruff.

[2] Cf. Quine's argument about the necessity of "discovering" our logical connectives in any language we can translate in *Word and Object* (Cambridge, Mass.: MIT, 1960), Section 13. More will be said in defense of this below.

[3] Accepting the argument of Lewis Carroll, in "What the Tortoise Said to Achilles," *Mind* (1895), reprinted in I. M. Copi and J. A. Gould, *Readings on Logic* (New York: MacMillan, 1964), we cannot allow all the rules for a system to be replaced by beliefs, for this would generate an infinite and unproductive nesting of distinct beliefs about what can be inferred from what.

[4] This paragraph owes much to discussion with John Vickers, whose paper "Judgment and Belief," in K. Lambert, *The Logical Way of Doing Things* (New Haven, Conn.: Yale, 1969), goes beyond the remarks here by considering the problems of the relative strength or weighting of beliefs and desires.

[5] R. L. Gregory, *Eye and Brain* (London: World University Library, 1966): p. 137, reports that pigeons and fish given just this training are, not surprisingly, susceptible to visual illusions of length.

25. *The Nature of Mind*

DAVID M. ARMSTRONG

During the middle third of the twentieth century, many philosophers
who rejected dualism were influenced by some form of behaviorism. In
1913, the psychologist J. B. Watson had begun to argue that psychology
could ignore consciousness and should not rely on introspection. For
some, behaviorism was primarily a methodological recommendation:
one should investigate psychological phenomena by studying behavior.
For others, behaviorism was a metaphysical thesis: behavior is all there
is to psychological phenomena. It eventually became clear that metaphysical behaviorism faced serious problems. It proved impossible to
classify behavior as belonging to interesting psychological categories
without making some use of "mentalistic" concepts. And it proved fruitful to posit "inner" states as causes of behavior and as the basis of tendencies to behave. Some philosophers who still wanted to reject dualism
proposed identity theories: mental states are neurophysiological states
that cause behavior. Armstrong, an Australian philosopher who teaches
at the University of Sydney, proposed a version of the identity theory
that attempts to specify mental states in terms of their causal or functional character.

Men have minds, that is to say, they perceive, they
have sensations, emotions, beliefs, thoughts, purposes, and desires.[1] What is it to have a mind?
What is it to perceive, to feel emotion, to hold a
belief, or to have a purpose? In common with many
other modern philosophers, I think that the best
clue we have to the nature of mind is furnished by
the discoveries and hypotheses of modern science
concerning the nature of man.

What does modern science have to say about
the nature of man? There are, of course, all sorts of
disagreements and divergencies in the views of
individual scientists. But I think it is true to say that
one view is steadily gaining ground, so that it bids
fair to become established scientific doctrine. This
is the view that we can give a complete account of
man *in purely physico-chemical terms.* This view has
received a tremendous impetus in the last decade

from the new subject of molecular biology, a subject which promises to unravel the physical and
chemical mechanisms which lie at the basis of life.
Before that time, it received great encouragement
from pioneering work in neurophysiology pointing to the likelihood of a purely electro-chemical
account of the working of the brain. I think it is fair
to say that those scientists who still reject the
physico-chemical account of man do so primarily
for philosophical, or moral, or religious reasons,
and only secondarily, and halfheartedly, for reasons of scientific detail. This is not to say that in
the future new evidence and new problems may
not come to light which will force science to reconsider the physico-chemical view of man. But at
present, the drift of scientific thought is clearly set
towards the physico-chemical hypothesis. And we
have nothing better to go on than the present.

For me, then, and for many philosophers who
think like me, the moral is clear. We must try to
work out an account of the nature of mind which is
compatible with the view that man is nothing but a
physico-chemical mechanism.

And in this paper I shall be concerned to do
just this: to sketch (in barest outline) what may be

called a Materialist or Physicalist account of the mind.

But before doing this I should like to go back and consider a criticism of my position which must inevitably occur to some. What reason have I, it may be asked, for taking my stand on science? Even granting that I am right about what is the currently dominant scientific view of man, why should we concede science a special authority to decide questions about the nature of man? What of the authority of philosophy, of religion, of morality, or even of literature and art? Why do I set the authority of science above all these? Why this 'scientism'?

It seems to me that the answer to this question is very simple. If we consider the search for truth, in all its fields, we find that it is only in science that men versed in their subject can, after investigation that is more or less prolonged, and which may in some cases extend beyond a single human lifetime, reach substantial agreement about what is the case. It is only as a result of scientific investigation that we ever seem to reach an intellectual consensus about controversial matters.

In the Epistle Dedicatory to his *De Corpore*, Hobbes wrote of William Harvey, the discoverer of the circulation of the blood, that he was 'the only man I know, that conquering envy, hath established a new doctrine in his life-time'.

Before Copernicus, Galileo and Harvey, Hobbes remarks, 'There was nothing certain in natural philosophy.' And, we might add, with the exception of mathematics, there was nothing certain in any other learned discipline.

These remarks of Hobbes are incredibly revealing. They show us what a watershed in the intellectual history of the human race the seventeenth century was. Before that time inquiry proceeded, as it were, in the dark. Men could not hope to see their doctrine *established*, that is to say, accepted by the vast majority of those properly versed in the subject under discussion. There was no intellectual consensus. Since that time, it has become a commonplace to see new doctrines, sometimes of the most far-reaching kind, established to the satisfaction of the learned, often within the lifetime of their first proponents. Science has provided us with a method of deciding disputed questions. This is not to say, of course, that the consensus of those who are learned and competent in a subject cannot be mistaken. Of

course such a consensus can be mistaken. Sometimes it has been mistaken. But, granting fallibility, what better authority have we than such a consensus?

Now this is of the utmost importance. For in philosophy, in religion, in such disciplines as literary criticism, in moral questions in so far as they are thought to be matters of truth and falsity, there has been a notable failure to achieve an intellectual consensus about disputed questions among the learned. Must we not then attach a peculiar authority to the discipline that can achieve a consensus? And if it presents us with a certain vision of the nature of man, is this not a powerful reason for accepting that vision?

I will not take up here the deeper question *why* it is that the methods of science have enabled us to achieve an intellectual consensus about so many disputed matters. That question, I think, could receive no brief or uncontroversial answer. I am resting my argument on the simple and uncontroversial fact that, as a result of scientific investigation, such a consensus has been achieved.

It may be replied—it often is replied—that while science is all very well in its own sphere—the sphere of the physical, perhaps—there are matters of fact on which it is not competent to pronounce. And among such matters, it may be claimed, is the question what is the whole nature of man. But I cannot see that this reply has much force. Science has provided us with an island of truths, or, perhaps one should say, a raft of truths, to bear us up on the sea of our disputatious ignorance. There may have to be revisions and refinements, new results may set old findings in a new perspective, but what science has given us will not be altogether superseded. Must we not therefore appeal to these relative certainties for guidance when we come to consider uncertainties elsewhere? Perhaps science cannot help us to decide whether or not there is a God, whether or not human beings have immortal souls, or whether or not the will is free. But if science cannot assist us, what can? I conclude that it is the scientific vision of man, and not the philosophical or religious or artistic or moral vision of man, that is the best clue we have to the nature of man. And it is rational to argue from the best evidence we have.

Having in this way attempted to justify my procedure, I turn back to my subject: the attempt to work out an account of mind, or, if you prefer, of mental process, within the framework of the physico-chemical, or, as we may call it, the Materialist view of man.

Now there is one account of mental process that is at once attractive to any philosopher sympathetic to a Materialist view of man: this is Behaviourism. Formulated originally by a psychologist, J. B. Watson, it attracted widespread interest and considerable support from scientifically oriented philosophers. Traditional philosophy had tended to think of the mind as a rather mysterious inward arena that lay behind, and was responsible for, the outward or physical behaviour of our bodies. Descartes thought of this inner arena as a *spiritual substance*, and it was this conception of the mind as spiritual object that Gilbert Ryle attacked, apparently in the interest of Behaviourism, in his important book *The Concept of Mind*. He ridiculed the Cartesian view as the dogma of 'the ghost in the machine'. The mind was not something behind the behaviour of the body, it was simply part of that physical behaviour. My anger with you is not some modification of a spiritual substance which somehow brings about aggressive behaviour; rather it is the aggressive behaviour itself; my addressing strong words to you, striking you, turning my back on you, and so on. Thought is not an inner process that lies behind, and brings about, the words I speak and write: it is my speaking and writing. The mind is not an inner arena, it is outward act.

It is clear that such a view of mind fits in very well with a completely Materialistic or Physicalist view of man. If there is no need to draw a distinction between mental processes and their expression in physical behaviour, but if instead the mental processes are identified with their so-called 'expressions,' then the existence of mind stands in no conflict with the view that man is nothing but a physico-chemical mechanism.

However, the version of Behaviourism that I have just sketched is a very crude version, and its crudity lays it open to obvious objections. One obvious difficulty is that it is our common experience that there can be mental processes going on although there is no behaviour occurring that could possibly be treated as expressions of these processes. A man may be angry, but give no bodily sign; he may think, but say or do nothing at all.

In my view, the most plausible attempt to refine Behaviourism with a view to meeting this objection was made by introducing the notion of *a disposition to behave*. (Dispositions to behave play a particularly important part in Ryle's account of the mind.) Let us consider the general notion of disposition first. Brittleness is a disposition, a disposition possessed by materials like glass. Brittle materials are those which, when subjected to relatively small forces, break or shatter easily. But breaking and shattering easily is not brittleness, rather it is the *manifestation* of brittleness. Brittleness itself is the tendency or liability of the material to break or shatter easily. A piece of glass may never shatter or break throughout its whole history, but it is still the case that it is brittle: it is liable to shatter or break if dropped quite a small way or hit quite lightly. Now a disposition to *behave* is simply a tendency or liability of a person to behave in a certain way under certain circumstances. The brittleness of glass is a disposition that the glass retains throughout its history, but clearly there could also be dispositions that come and go. The dispositions to behave that are of interest to the Behaviourist are, for the most part, of this temporary character.

Now how did Ryle and others use the notion of a disposition to behave to meet the obvious objection to Behaviourism that there can be mental processes going on although the subject is engaging in no relevant behaviour? Their strategy was to argue that in such cases, although the subject was not behaving in any relevant way, he or she was *disposed* to behave in some relevant way. The glass does not shatter, but it is still brittle. The man does not behave, but he does have a disposition to behave. We can say he thinks although he does not speak or act because at that time he was disposed to speak or act in a certain way. *If* he had been asked, perhaps, he would have spoken or acted. We can say he is angry although he does not behave angrily, because he is disposed so to behave. *If* only one more word had been addressed to him, he would have burst out. And so on. In this way it was hoped that Behaviourism could be squared with the obvious facts.

It is very important to see just how these thinkers conceived of dispositions. I quote from Ryle:

> To possess a dispositional property *is not to be in a particular state, or to undergo a particular change*; it is to be bound or liable to be in a particular state, or to undergo a particular change, when a particular condition is realised. (*The Concept of Mind*, p. 43, my italics.)

So to explain the breaking of a lightly struck glass on a particular occasion by saying it was brittle is, on this view of dispositions, simply to say that the glass broke because it is the sort of thing that regularly breaks when quite lightly struck. The breaking was the normal behaviour, or not abnormal behaviour, of such a thing. The brittleness is not to be conceived of as a *cause* for the breakage, or even, more vaguely, a *factor* in bringing about the breaking. Brittleness is just the fact that things of that sort break easily.

But although in this way the Behaviourists did something to deal with the objection that mental processes can occur in the absence of behaviour, it seems clear, now that the shouting and the dust have died, that they did not do enough. When I think, but my thoughts do not issue in any action, it seems as obvious as anything is obvious that there is something actually going on in me which constitutes my thought. It is not simply that I would speak or act if some conditions that are unfulfilled were to be fulfilled. Something is currently going on, in the strongest and most literal sense of 'going on', and this something is my thought. Rylean Behaviourism denies this, and so it is unsatisfactory as a theory of mind. Yet I know of no version of Behaviourism that is more satisfactory. The moral for those of us who wish to take a purely physicalistic view of man is that we must look for some other account of the nature of mind and of mental processes.

But perhaps we need not grieve too deeply about the failure of Behaviourism to produce a satisfactory theory of mind. Behaviourism is a profoundly unnatural account of mental processes. If somebody speaks and acts in certain ways it is natural to speak of this speech and action as the *expression* of his thought. It is not at all natural to speak of his speech and action as identical with his thought. We naturally think of the thought as something quite distinct from the speech and action which, under suitable circumstances, brings the speech and action about. Thoughts are not to be identified with behaviour, we think, they lie behind behaviour. A man's behaviour constitutes the *reason* we have for attributing certain mental processes to him, but the behaviour cannot be identified with the mental processes.

This suggests a very interesting line of thought about the mind. Behaviourism is certainly wrong, but perhaps it is not altogether wrong. Perhaps the Behaviourists are wrong in identifying the mind and mental occurrences with behaviour, but perhaps they are right in thinking that our notion of a mind and of individual mental states is *logically tied to behaviour*. For perhaps what we mean by a mental state is some state of the person which, under suitable circumstances, *brings about* a certain range of behaviour. Perhaps mind can be defined not as behaviour, but rather as the inner *cause* of certain behaviour. Thought is not speech under suitable circumstances, rather it is something within the person which, in suitable circumstances, brings about speech. And, in fact, I believe that this is the true account, or, at any rate, a true first account, of what we mean by a mental state.

How does this line of thought link up with a purely physicalist view of man? The position is, I think, that while it does not make such a physicalist view inevitable, it does make it *possible*. It does not entail, but it is compatible with, a purely physicalist view of man. For if our notion of the mind and mental states is nothing but that of a cause within the person of certain ranges of behaviour, then it becomes a scientific question, and not a question of logical analysis, what in fact the intrinsic nature of that cause is. The cause might be, as Descartes thought it was, a spiritual substance working through the pineal gland to produce the complex bodily behaviour of which men are capable. It might be breath, or specially smooth and mobile atoms dispersed throughout the body; it might be many other things. But in fact the verdict of modern science seems to be that the sole cause of mind-betokening behaviour in man and the higher animals is the physico-chemical workings of the central nervous system. And so, assuming we have correctly characterised our concept of a mental state as nothing but the cause of certain sorts of behaviour, then we can identify these mental states with purely physical states of the central nervous system.

At this point we may stop and go back to the Behaviourists' dispositions. We saw that, according to them, the brittleness of glass or, to take another example, the elasticity of rubber, is not a state of the glass or the rubber, but is simply the fact that things of that sort behave in the way they do. But now let us consider how a scientist would think about brittleness or elasticity. Faced with the phenomenon of breakage under relatively small impacts, or the phenomenon of stretching when a force is applied followed by contraction when the force is removed, he will assume that there is some current *state* of the glass or the rubber which is responsible for the characteristic behaviour of samples of these two materials. At the beginning he will not know what this state is, but he will endeavour to find out, and he may succeed in finding out. And when he has found out he will very likely make remarks of this sort: 'We have discovered that the brittleness of glass is in fact a certain sort of pattern in the molecules of the glass.' That is to say, he will *identify* brittleness with the state of the glass that is responsible for the liability of the glass to break. For him, a disposition of an object is a state of the object. What makes the state a state of brittleness is the fact that it gives rise to the characteristic manifestations of brittleness. But the disposition itself is distinct from its manifestations: it is the state of the glass that gives rise to these manifestations in suitable circumstances.

You will see that this way of looking at dispositions is very different from that of Ryle and the Behaviourists. The great difference is this: If we treat dispositions as actual states, as I have suggested that scientists do, even if states whose intrinsic nature may yet have to be discovered, then we can say that dispositions are actual *causes*, or causal factors, which, in suitable circumstances, actually bring about those happenings which are the manifestations of the disposition. A certain molecular constitution of glass which constitutes its brittleness is actually *responsible* for the fact that, when the glass is struck, it breaks.

Now I shall not argue the matter here, because the detail of the argument is technical and difficult,[2] but I believe that the view of dispositions as states, which is the view that is natural to science, is the correct one. I believe it can be shown quite strictly that, to the extent that we admit the notion of dispositions at all, we are committed to the view that they are actual *states* of the object that has the disposition. I may add that I think that the same holds for the closely connected notions of capacities and powers. Here I will simply assume this step in my argument.

But perhaps it can be seen that the rejection of the idea that mind is simply a certain range of man's behaviour in favour of the view that mind is rather the inner *cause* of that range of man's behaviour is bound up with the rejection of the Rylean view of dispositions in favour of one that treats disposition as states of objects and so as having actual causal power. The Behaviourists were wrong to identify the mind with behaviour. They were not so far off the mark when they tried to deal with cases where mental happenings occur in the absence of behaviour by saying that these are dispositions to behave. But in order to reach a correct view, I am suggesting, they would have to conceive of these dispositions as actual *states* of the person who has the disposition, states that have actual power to bring about behaviour in suitable circumstances. But to do this is to abandon the central inspiration of Behaviourism: that in talking about the mind we do not have to go behind outward behaviour to inner states.

And so two separate but interlocking lines of thought have pushed me in the same direction. The first line of thought is that it goes profoundly against the grain to think of the mind as behaviour. The mind is, rather, that which stands behind and brings about our complex behaviour. The second line of thought is that the Behaviourists' dispositions, properly conceived, are really states that underlie behaviour, and, under suitable circumstances, bring about behaviour. Putting these two together, we reach the conception of a mental state as *a state of the person apt for producing certain ranges of behaviour.* This formula: a mental state is a state of the person apt for producing certain ranges of behaviour, I believe to be a very illuminating way of looking at the concept of a mental state. I have found it very fruitful in the search for detailed logical analyses of the individual mental concepts.

Now, I do not think that Hegel's dialectic has much to tell us about the nature of reality. But I think that human thought often moves in a dialectical way, from thesis to antithesis and then to the synthesis. Perhaps thought about the mind is a case in point. I have already said that classical philosophy tended to think of the mind as an inner arena of some sort. This we may call the Thesis. Behaviourism moved to the opposite extreme: the mind was seen as outward behaviour. This is the Antithesis. My proposed Synthesis is that the mind is properly conceived as an inner principle, but a principle that is identified in terms of the outward behaviour it is apt for bringing about. This way of looking at the mind and mental states does not itself entail a Materialist or Physicalist view of man, for nothing is said in this analysis about the intrinsic nature of these mental states. But if we have, as I have asserted that we do have, general scientific grounds for thinking that man is nothing but a physical mechanism, we can go on to argue that the mental states are in fact nothing but physical states of the central nervous system.

Along these lines, then, I would look for an account of the mind that is compatible with a purely Materialist theory of man. I have tried to carry out this programme in detail in *A Materialist Theory of the Mind*. There are, as may be imagined, all sorts of powerful objections that can be made to this view. But in the rest of this paper I propose to do only one thing. I will develop one very important objection to my view of the mind—an objection felt by many philosophers—and then try to show how the objection should be met.

The view that our notion of mind is nothing but that of an inner principle apt for bringing about certain sorts of behaviour may be thought to share a certain weakness with Behaviourism. Modern philosophers have put the point about Behaviourism by saying that although Behaviourism may be a satisfactory account of the mind from an *other-person point of view*, it will not do as a *first-person* account. To explain. In our encounters with other people, all we ever observe is their behaviour: their actions, their speech, and so on. And so, if we simply consider other people, Behaviourism might seem to do full justice to the facts. But the trouble about Behaviourism is that it seems so unsatisfactory as applied to our *own* case. In our own case, we seem to be aware of so much more than mere behaviour.

Suppose that now we conceive of the mind as an inner principle apt for bringing about certain sorts of behaviour. This again fits the other-person cases very well. Bodily behaviour of a very sophisticated sort is observed, quite different from the behaviour that ordinary physical objects display. It is inferred that this behaviour must spring from a very special sort of inner cause in the object that exhibits this behaviour. This inner cause is christened 'the mind', and those who take a physicalist view of man argue that it is simply the central nervous system of the body observed. Compare this with the case of glass. Certain characteristic behaviour is observed: the breaking and shattering of the material when acted upon by relatively small forces. A special inner state of the glass is postulated to explain this behaviour. Those who take a purely physicalist view of glass then argue that this state is a *natural* state of the glass. It is, perhaps, an arrangement of its molecules, and not, say, the peculiarly malevolent disposition of the demons that dwell in glass.

But when we turn to our own case, the position may seem less plausible. We are conscious, we have experiences. Now can we say that to be conscious, to have experiences, is simply for something to go on within us apt for the causing of certain sorts of behaviour? Such an account does not seem to do any justice to the phenomena. And so it seems that our account of the mind, like Behaviourism, will fail to do justice to the first-person case.

In order to understand the objection better it may be helpful to consider a particular case. If you have driven for a very long distance without a break, you may have had experience of a curious state of automatism, which can occur in these conditions. One can suddenly 'come to' and realise that one has driven for long distances without being aware of what one was doing, or indeed, without being aware of anything. One has kept the car on the road, used the brake and the clutch perhaps, yet all without any awareness of what one was doing.

Now, if we consider this case it is obvious that *in some sense* mental processes are still going on when one is in such an automatic state. Unless one's will was still operating in some way, and unless one was still perceiving in some way, the car would not still be on the road. Yet, of course, *something* mental is lacking. Now, I think, when it is alleged that an account of mind as an inner principle apt for the production of certain sorts of behaviour leaves out consciousness or experience, what is alleged to have been left out is just whatever is missing in the automatic driving case. It is conceded that an account of mental processes as states of the person apt for the production of certain sorts of behaviour may very possibly be adequate to deal with such cases as that of automatic driving. It may be adequate to deal with most of the mental processes of animals, who perhaps spend a good deal of their lives in this state of automatism. But, it is contended, it cannot deal with the consciousness that we normally enjoy.

I will now try to sketch an answer to this important and powerful objection. Let us begin in an apparently unlikely place, and consider the way that an account of mental processes of the sort I am giving would deal with *sense-perception*.

Now psychologists, in particular, have long realised that there is a very close logical tie between sense-perception and *selective behaviour*. Suppose we want to decide whether an animal can perceive the difference between red and green. We might give the animal a choice between two pathways, over one of which a red light shines and over the other of which a green light shines. If the animal happens by chance to choose the green pathway we reward it; if it happens to choose the other pathway we do not reward it. If, after some trials, the animal systematically takes the green-lighted pathway, and if we become assured that the only relevant differences in the two pathways are the differences in the colour of the lights, we are entitled to say that the animal can see this colour difference. Using its eyes, it selects between red-lighted and green-lighted pathways. So we say it can see the difference between red and green.

Now a Behaviourist would be tempted to say that the animal's regularly selecting the green-lighted pathway *was* its perception of the colour difference. But this is unsatisfactory, because we all want to say that perception is something that goes on within the person or animal—within its mind—although, of course, this mental event is normally *caused* by the operation of the environment upon the organism. Suppose, however, that we speak instead of *capacities* for selective behaviour towards the current environment, and suppose we think of these capacities, like dispositions, as actual inner states of the organism. We can then think of the animal's perception as a state within the animal apt, if the animal is so impelled, for selective behaviour between the red- and green-lighted pathways.

In general, we can think of perceptions as inner states or events apt for the production of certain sorts of selective behaviour towards our environment. To perceive is like acquiring a key to a door. You do not have to use the key: you can put it in your pocket and never bother about the door. But if you do want to open the door the key may be essential. The blind man is a man who does not acquire certain keys, and, as a result, is not able to operate in his environment in the way that somebody who has his sight can operate. It seems, then, a very promising view to take of perceptions that they are inner states defined by the sorts of selective behaviour that they enable the perceiver to exhibit, if so impelled.

Now how is this discussion of perception related to the question of consciousness or experience, the sort of thing that the driver who is in a state of automatism has not got, but which we normally do have? Simply this. My proposal is that consciousness, in this sense of the word, is nothing but *perception or awareness of the state of our own mind.* The driver in a state of automatism perceives, or is aware of, the road. If he did not, the car would be

in a ditch. But he is not currently aware of his awareness of the road. He perceives the road, but he does not perceive his perceiving, or anything else that is going on in his mind. He is not, as we normally are, conscious of what is going on in his mind.

And so I conceive of consciousness or experience, in this sense of the words, in the way that Locke and Kant conceived it, as like perception. Kant, in a striking phrase, spoke of 'inner sense'. We cannot directly observe the minds of others, but each of us has the power to observe directly our own minds, and 'perceive' what is going on there. The driver in the automatic state is one whose 'inner eye' is shut: who is not currently aware of what is going on in his own mind.

Now if this account is along the right lines, why should we not give an account of this inner observation along the same lines as we have already given of perception? Why should we not conceive of it as an inner state, a state in this case directed towards other inner states and not to the environment, which enables us, if we are so impelled, to behave in a selective way *towards our own states of mind?* One who is aware, or conscious, of his thoughts or his emotions is one who has the capacity to make discriminations between his different mental states. His capacity might be exhibited in words. He might say that he was in an angry state of mind when, and only when, he *was* in an angry state of mind. But such verbal behaviour would be the mere *expression* or *result* of the awareness. The awareness itself would be an inner state: the sort of inner state that gave the man a capacity for such behavioural expressions.

So I have argued that consciousness of our own mental state may be assimilated to *perception* of our own mental state, and that, like other perceptions, it may then be conceived of as an inner state or event giving a capacity for selective behaviour, in this case selective behaviour towards our own mental state. All this is meant to be simply a logical analysis of consciousness, and none of it entails, although it does not rule out, a purely physicalist account of what these inner states are. But if we are convinced, on general scientific grounds, that a purely physical account of man is likely to be the true one, then there seems to be no bar to our identifying these inner states with purely physical states of the central nervous system. And so consciousness of our own mental state becomes simply the scanning of one part of our central nervous system by another. Consciousness is a self-scanning mechanism in the central nervous system.

As I have emphasised before, I have done no more than sketch a programme for a philosophy of mind. There are all sorts of expansions and elucidations to be made, and all sorts of doubts and difficulties to be stated and overcome. But I hope I have done enough to show that a purely physicalist the-

ory of the mind is an exciting and plausible intellectual option.

Endnotes

[1] Inaugural lecture of the Challis Professor of Philosophy at the University of Sydney (1965); slightly amended (1968).

[2] It is presented in my book *A Materialist Theory of the Mind* (1968) ch. 6, sec. VI.

---

26. *Philosophy and Our Mental Life*

HILARY PUTNAM

In the previous selection, Armstrong proposed that mental states be understood as functionally (or causally) described states of the central nervous system. In the philosophy of mind, "functionalism" has come to refer to the view that mental entities are functional states. Many philosophers who find dualism implausible are attracted to some variety of functionalism because, like Armstrong, they want to identify mental states with the physical states that play a functional role. Interest in functionalism has also been influenced by computer science. In understanding computers, it often suffices to describe their states functionally (that is, in terms of their program or software) without making any reference to their specific physical nature (their hardware). In "Philosophy and Our Mental Life," Hilary Putnam claims functionalism should free us from worrying about whether or not our mental states are physical. He claims it is the functional character of psychological states—not what they are embodied in—that leads to understanding the nature and autonomy of our mental lives. Putnam teaches philosophy at Harvard University.

The question which troubles laymen, and which has long troubled philosophers, even if it is somewhat disguised by today's analytic style of writing philosophy, is this: are we made of matter or soulstuff?[1] To put it as bluntly as possible, are we just material beings, or are we 'something more'? In this paper, I will argue as strongly as possible that this whole question rests on false assumptions. My purpose is not to dismiss the question, however, so much as to speak to the real concern which is behind the question. The real concern is, I believe, with the autonomy of our mental life.

People are worried that we may be debunked, that our behavior may be exposed as really

From Hilary Putnam, *Philosophical Papers, Vol. II: Mind, Language, and Reality*, pp. 291–303. Copyright © 1975 by Cambridge University Press. Reprinted by permission of Cambridge University Press.

explained by something mechanical. Not, to be sure, mechanical in the old sense of cogs and pulleys, but in the newer sense of electricity and magnetism and quantum chemistry and so forth. In this paper, part of what I want to do is to argue that this can't happen. Mentality is a real and autonomous feature of our world.

But even more important, at least in my feeling, is the fact that this whole question has nothing to do with our substance. Strange as it may seem to common sense and to sophisticated intuition alike, the question of the autonomy of our mental life does not hinge on and has nothing to do with that all too popular, all too old question about matter or soul-stuff. We could be made of Swiss cheese and it wouldn't matter.

Failure to see this, stubborn insistence on formulating the question as *matter or soul*, utterly prevents progress on these questions. Conversely, once we see that our substance is not the issue, I do not see how we can help but make progress.

The concept which is key to unravelling the mysteries in the philosophy of mind, I think, is the concept of *functional isomorphism*. Two systems are functionally isomorphic if *there is a correspondence between the states of one and the states of the other that preserves functional relations*. To start with computing machine examples, if the functional relations are just sequence relations, e.g., *state A is always followed by state B,* then, for F to be a functional isomorphism, it must be the case that state A is followed by state B in system 1 if and only if state *F(A)* is followed by state *F(B)* in system 2. If the functional relations are, say, data or printout relations, e.g., *when symbol S is scanned on the tape, system 1 goes into state A,* these must be preserved. *When symbol S is scanned on the tape, system 2 goes into state F(A),* if F is a functional isomorphism between system 1 and system 2. More generally, if T is a correct theory of the functioning of system 1, at the functional or psychological level, then an isomorphism between system 1 and system 2 must map each property and relation defined in system 2 in such a way that T comes out true when all references to system 1 are replaced by references to system 2, and all property and relation symbols in T are reinterpreted according to the mapping.

The difficulty with the notion of functional isomorphism is that it *presupposes the notion of a thing's being a functional or psychological description*. It is for this reason that, in various papers on this subject, I introduced and explained the notion in terms of Turing machines. And I felt constrained, therefore, to defend the thesis that *we* are Turing machines. Turing machines come, so to speak, with a normal form for their functional description, the so-called machine table—a standard style of program. But it does not seem fatally sloppy to me, although it is sloppy, if we apply the notion of functional isomorphism to systems for which we have no detailed idea at present what the normal form description would look like—systems like ourselves. The point is that even if we don't have any idea what a comprehensive psychological theory would look like, I claim that we know enough (and here analogies from computing machines, economic systems, games and so forth are helpful) to point out illuminating differences between any possible psychological theory of a human being, or even a functional description of a computing machine or an economic system, and a physical or chemical description. Indeed, Dennett and Fodor have done a great deal along these lines in recent books.

This brings me back to the question of *copper, cheese, or soul*. One point we can make immediately as soon as we have the basic concept of functional isomorphism is this: two systems can have quite different constitutions and be functionally isomorphic. For example, a computer made of electrical components can be isomorphic to one made of cogs and wheels. In other words, for each state in the first computer there is a corresponding state in the other, and, as we said before, the sequential relations are the same—if state S is followed by state B in the case of the electronic computer, state A would be followed by state B in the case of the computer made of cogs and wheels, and it doesn't matter at all that the *physical realizations* of those states are totally different. So a computer made of electrical components can be isomorphic to one made of cogs and wheels or to human clerks using paper and pencil. A computer made of one sort of wire, say copper wire, or one sort of relay, etc. will be in a different physical and chemical state when it computes than a computer made of a different sort of wire and relay. But the functional description may be the same.

We can extend this point still further. Assume that one thesis of materialism (I shall call it the 'first thesis') is correct, and we are, as wholes, just material systems obeying physical laws. Then the second thesis of classical materialism cannot be correct—namely, our mental states, e.g., *thinking about next summer's vacation,* cannot be *identical* with any physical or chemical states. For it is clear from what we already know about computers etc., that whatever the program of the brain may be, it must be physically possible, though not necessarily feasible, to produce something with that same program but quite a different physical and chemical constitution. Then to identify the state in question with its physical or chemical realization would be quite absurd, given that that realization is in a sense quite accidental, from the point of view of psychology, anyway (which is the relevant science).[2] It is as if we met Martians and discovered that they were in all functional respects isomorphic to us, but we refused to admit that they could feel pain because their C fibers were different.

Now, imagine two possible universes, perhaps 'parallel worlds,' in the science fiction sense, in one of which people have good old fashioned souls, operating through pineal glands, perhaps, and in the other of which they have complicated brains. And suppose that the souls in the soul world are functionally isomorphic to the brains in the brain world. Is there any more sense to attaching importance to this difference than to the difference between copper wires and some other wires in the computer? Does it matter that the soul people have, so to speak, immaterial brains, and that the brain people have material souls? What matters is the common structure, the theory T of which we are, alas, in deep ignorance, and not the hardware, be it ever so etheral.

One may raise various objections to what I have said. I shall try to reply to some of them.

One might, for example, say that if the souls of the soul people are isomorphic to the brains of the brain people, then their souls must be automata-like, and that's not the sort of soul we are interested in. 'All your argument really shows is that there is no need to distinguish between a brain and an automaton-like soul.' But what precisely does that objection come to?

I think there are two ways of understanding it. It might come to the claim that the notion of functional organization or functional isomorphism only makes sense for automata. But that is totally false. Sloppy as our notions are at present, we at least know this much, that the notion of functional organization applies to anything to which the notion of a psychological theory applies. I explained the

most general notion of functional isomorphism by saying that two systems are functionally isomorphic if there is an isomorphism that makes both of them models for the same psychological theory. (That is stronger than just saying that they are both models for the same psychological theory—they are isomorphic realizations of the same abstract structure.) To say that real old fashioned souls would not be in the domain of definition of the concept of functional organization or of the concept of functional isomorphisms would be to take the position that whatever we mean by the soul, it is something for which there can be no theory. That seems pure obscurantism. I will assume, henceforth, that it is not built into the notion of mind or soul or whatever that it is unintelligible or that there couldn't be a theory of it.

Secondly, someone might say more seriously that even if there is a theory of the soul or mind, the soul, at least in the full, rich old fashioned sense, is supposed to have powers that no mechanical system could have. In the latter part of this chapter I shall consider this claim.

If it is built into one's notions of the soul that the soul can do things that violate the laws of physics, then I admit I am stumped. There cannot be a soul which is isomorphic to a brain, if the soul can read the future clairvoyantly, in a way that is not in any way explainable by physical law. On the other hand, if one is interested in more modest forms of magic like telepathy, it seems to me that there is no reason in principle why we couldn't construct a device which would project subvocalized thoughts from one brain to another. As to reincarnation, if we are, as I am urging, a certain kind of functional structure (my identity is, as it were, my functional structure), there seems to be in principle no reason why that could not be reproduced after a thousand years or a million years or a billion years. Resurrection: as you know, Christians believe in resurrection in the flesh, which completely bypasses the need for an immaterial vehicle. So even if one is interested in those questions (and they are not my concern in this paper, although I am concerned to speak to people who have those concerns), even then one doesn't need an immaterial brain or soul-stuff.

So if I am right, and the question of matter or soul-stuff is really irrelevant to any question of philosophical or religious significance, why so much attention to it, why so much heat? The crux of the matter seems to be that both the Diderots of this world and the Descartes of this world have agreed that if we are matter, then there is a physical explanation for how we behave, disappointing or exciting. I think the traditional dualist says *'wouldn't it be terrible if we turned out to be just matter, for then there is a physical explanation for everything we do'*. And the traditional materialist says *'if if we are just matter, then there is a physical explanation for everything we do. Isn't that exciting!'* (It is like the distinction between the optimist and the pessimist: an optimist is a person who says 'this is the best of all possible worlds'; and a pessimist is a person who says 'you're right'.)[3]

I think they are both wrong. I think Diderot and Descartes were both wrong in assuming that if we are matter, or our souls are material, then there is a physical explanation for our behavior.

Let me try to illustrate what I mean by a very simple analogy. Suppose we have a very simple physical system—a board in which there are two holes, a circle one inch in diameter and a square one inch high, and a cubical peg one-sixteenth of an inch less than one inch high. We have the following very simple fact to explain: *the peg passes through the square hole, and it does not pass through the round hole.*

In explanation of this, one might attempt the following. One might say that the peg is, after all, a cloud or, better, a rigid lattice of atoms. One might even attempt to give a description of that lattice, compute its electrical potential energy, worry about why it does not collapse, produce some quantum mechanics to explain why it is stable, etc. The board is also a lattice of atoms. I will call the peg 'system A,' and the holes 'region 1' and 'region 2.' One could compute all possible trajectories of system A (there are, by the way, very serious questions about these computations, their effectiveness, feasibility, and so on, but let us assume this), and perhaps one could deduce from just the laws of particle mechanics or quantum electrodynamics that system A never passes through region 1, but that there is at least one trajectory which enables it to pass through region 2. Is this an explanation of the fact that the peg passes through the square hole and not the round hole?

Very often we are told that if something is made of matter, its behavior must have a physical explanation. And the argument is that if it is made of matter (and we make a lot of assumptions), then there should be a deduction of its behavior from its material structure. *What makes you call this deduction an explanation?*

On the other hand, if you are not 'hipped' on the idea that *the* explanation must be at the level of the ultimate constituents, and that in fact the explanation might have the property that *the ultimate constituents don't matter*, that *only the higher level structure matters*, then there is a very simple explanation here. The explanation is that the board is rigid, the peg is rigid, and as a matter of geometrical fact, the round hole is smaller than the peg, the square hole is bigger than the cross-section of the peg. The peg passes through the hole that is large enough to take its cross-section, and does not pass through the hole that is too small to take its cross-section. That is a correct explanation whether the peg consists of molecules, or continuous rigid substance, or whatever. (If one wanted to amplify the explanation, one might point out the geometrical fact that a square one inch high is bigger than a circle one inch across.)

Now, one can say that in this explanation certain *relevant structural features of the situation* are brought out. The geometrical features are brought out. It is *relevant* that a square one inch high is bigger than a circle one inch around. And the relationship between the size and shape of the peg and the size and shape of the holes is *relevant.* It is *relevant* that both the board and the peg are *rigid* under transportation. And nothing else is relevant. The same explanation will go in any world (whatever the microstructure) in which those *higher level structural features* are present. In that sense *this explanation is autonomous.*

People have argued that I am wrong to say that the microstructural deduction is not an explanation. I think that in terms of the *purposes for which we use the notion of explanation,* it is not an explanation. If you want to, let us say that the deduction *is* an explanation, it is just a terrible explanation, and why look for terrible explanations when good ones are available?

Goodness is not a subjective matter. Even if one agrees with the positivists who saddled us with the notion of explanation as deduction from laws, one of the things we do in science is to look for laws. Explanation is superior not just subjectively, but *methodologically,* in terms of facilitating the aims of scientific inquiry, if it brings out relevant laws. An explanation is superior if it is more general.

Just taking those two features, and there are

many many more one could think of, compare the explanation at the higher level of this phenomenon with the atomic explanation. The explanation at the higher level brings out the relevant geometrical relationships. The lower level explanation conceals those laws. Also notice that the higher level explanation applies to a much more interesting class of systems (of course that has to do with what we are interested in).

The fact is that we are much more interested in generalizing to other structures which are rigid and have various geometrical relations, than we are in generalizing to *the next peg that has exactly this molecular structure,* for the very good reason that there is not going to *be* a next peg that has exactly this molecular structure. So in terms of real life disciplines, real life ways of slicing up scientific problems, the higher level explanation is far more general, which is why it is *explanatory.*

We were only able to deduce a statement which is lawful at the *higher* level, that the peg goes through the hole which is larger than the cross-section of the peg. When we try to deduce the possible trajectories of 'system *A*' from statements about the individual atoms, we use premises which are totally accidental—this atom is here, this carbon atom is there, and so forth. And that is one reason that it is very misleading to talk about a reduction of a science like economics to the level of the elementary particles making up the players of the economic game. In fact, their motions—buying this, selling that, arriving at an equilibrium price—these motions cannot be deduced from just the equations of motion. Otherwise they would be *physically necessitated,* not *economically necessitated,* to arrive at an equilibrium price. They play that game because they are particular systems with particular boundary conditions which are totally accidental from the point of view of physics. This means that the derivation of the laws of economics from *just* the laws of physics is *in principle* impossible. The derivation of the laws of economics from the laws of physics and *accidental statements about which particles were where when* by a Laplacian supermind might be in principle possible, but why want it? A few chapters of, e.g., von Neumann, will tell one far more about regularities at the level of economic structure than such a deduction ever could.

The conclusion I want to draw from this is that we do have the kind of autonomy that we are looking for in the mental realm. Whatever our

mental functioning may be, there seems to be no serious reason to believe that it is *explainable* by our physics and chemistry. And what we are interested in is not: given that we consist of such and such particles, could someone have predicted that we would have this mental functioning? because such a prediction is not *explanatory,* however great a feat it may be. What we are interested in is: can we say at this autonomous level that since we have this sort of structure, this sort of program, it follows that we will be able to learn this, we will tend to like that, and so on? These are the problems of mental life—the description of this autonomous level of mental functioning—and that is what is to be discovered.

In previous papers, I have argued for the hypothesis that (1) a whole human being is a Turing machine, and (2) that psychological states of a human being are Turing machine states or disjunctions of Turing machine states. In this section I want to argue that this point of view was essentially wrong, and that I was too much in the grip of the reductionist outlook.

Let me begin with a technical difficulty. A *state* of a Turing machine is described in such a way that a Turing machine can be in exactly one state at a time. Moreover, memory and learning are not represented in the Turing machine model as acquisition of new states, but as acquisition of new information printed on the machine's tape. Thus, if human beings have any states at all which resemble Turing machine states, those states must (1) be states the human can be in at any time, independently of learning and memory; and (2) be *total* instantaneous states of the human being—states which determine, together with learning and memory, what the next state will be, as well as totally specifying the present condition of the human being ('totally' from the standpoint of psychological theory, that means).

These characteristics establish that *no* psychological state in any customary sense can be a Turing machine state. Take a particular kind of pain to be a 'psychological state'. If I *am* a Turing machine, then my present 'state' must determine not only whether or not I am having that particular kind of pain, but also whether or not I am about to say 'three', whether or not I am hearing a shrill whine, etc. So the psychological state in question (the pain) is not the same as my 'state' in the sense of *machine state,* although it is possible (so far) that my machine state *determines* my psychological state. Moreover, *no* psychological theory would pretend that having a pain of a particular kind, being about to say 'three,' or hearing a shrill whine, etc., all belong to *one* psychological state, although there could well be a machine state characterized by the fact that I was in it only when simultaneously having that pain, being about to say 'three', hearing a shrill whine, etc. So, even if I am a Turing machine, my machine states are *not* the same as my psychological states. My description *qua* Turing machine (machine table) and my description *qua* human being (*via* a psychological theory) are descriptions at two totally different levels of organization.

So far it is still possible that a psychological state is a large disjunction (practically speaking, an almost infinite disjunction) of machine states, although no *single* machine state is a psychological state. But this is very unlikely when we move away from states like 'pain' (which are almost *biological*) to states like 'jealousy' or 'love' or 'competitiveness'. Being jealous is certainly not an *instantaneous* state, and it depends on a great deal of information and on many learned facts and habits. But Turing machine states are instantaneous and are independent of learning and memory. That is, learning and memory may cause a Turing machine to go into a state, but the identity of the state does not depend on learning and memory, whereas, no matter what state I am in, identifying that state as 'being jealous of X's regard for Y' involves specifying that I have learned that X and Y are persons and a good deal about social relations among persons. Thus jealousy can neither be a machine state nor a disjunction of machine states.

One might attempt to modify the theory by saying that being jealous = either being in State A and having tape c_1 or being in State A and having tape c_2 or . . . being in State B and having tape d_1 or being in State B and having tape d_2 . . . or being in State Z and having tape y_1 . . . or being in State Z and having tape y_n—i.e., define a psychological state as a disjunction, the individual disjuncts being not Turing machine states, as before, but conjunctions of a machine state and a tape (i.e., a total description of the content of the memory bank). Besides the fact that such a description would be literally infinite, the theory is now without content, for the original purpose was to use the machine table as a model of a psychological theory, whereas it is now clear that the machine table description, although different from the description at the elementary particle level, is as removed from the description *via* a psychological theory as the physico-chemical description is.

What is the importance of machines in the philosophy of mind? I think that machines have both a positive and a negative importance. The positive importance of machines was that it was in connection with machines, computing machines in particular, that the notion of functional organization first appeared. Machines forced us to distinguish between an abstract structure and its concrete realization. Not that that distinction came into the world for the first time with machines. But in the case of computing machines, we could not avoid rubbing our noses against the fact that what we had to count as to all intents and purposes the same structure could be realized in a bewildering variety of different ways; that the important properties were not physical-chemical. That the machines made us catch on to the idea of functional organization is extremely important. The negative importance of machines, however, is that they tempt us to oversimplification. The notion of functional organization became clear to us through systems with a very restricted, very specific functional organization. So the temptation is present to assume that we must have that restricted and specific kind of functional organization.

Now I want to consider an example—an example which may seem remote from what we have been talking about, but which may help. This is not an example from the philosophy of mind at all. Consider the following fact. The earth does not go around the sun in a circle, as was once believed, it goes around the sun in an ellipse, with the sun at one of the foci, not in the center of the ellipse. Yet one statement which would hold true if the orbit was a circle and the sun was at the centre still holds true, surprisingly. That is the following statement: the radius vector from the sun to the earth sweeps out equal areas in equal times. If the orbit were a circle, and the earth were moving with a constant velocity, that would be trivial. But the orbit is not a circle. Also the velocity is not constant—when the earth is farthest away from the sun, it is going most slowly, when it is closest to the sun, it is going fastest. The earth is speeding up and slowing down. But the earth's radius vector sweeps out equal areas in equal times.[4] Newton deduced that law in his *Principia*, and his deduction shows that the only thing on which that law depends is that the force acting on the earth is in the direction of the sun. That is absolutely the only fact one needs to deduce that law. Mathematically it is equivalent to that law.[5] That is all well and good when the gravitational law is that every body attracts every other body according to an inverse square law, because then there is always a force on the earth in the direction of the sun. If we assume that we can neglect all the other bodies, that their influence is slight, then that is all we need, and we can use Newton's proof, or a more modern, simpler proof.

But today we have very complicated laws of gravitation. First of all, we say what is really going is that the world lines of freely falling bodies in space-time are geodesics. And the geometry is determined by the mass-energy tensor, and the ankle bone is connected to the leg bone, etc. So, one might ask, how would a modern relativity theorist explain Kepler's law? He would explain it very simply. *Kepler's laws are true because Newton's laws are approximately true.* And, in fact, an attempt to replace that argument by a deduction of Kepler's laws from the field equations would be regarded as almost as ridiculous (but not quite) as trying to deduce that the peg will go through one hole and not the other from the positions and velocities of the individual atoms.

I want to draw the philosophical conclusion that Newton's laws *have a kind of reality in our world* even though they are not *true*. The point is that it will be necessary to appeal to Newton's laws in order to explain Kepler's laws. Methodologically, I can make that claim at least plausible. One remark—due to Alan Garfinkel—is that *a good explanation is invariant under small perturbations of the assumptions.* One problem with deducing Kepler's laws from the gravitational field equations is that if we do it, tomorrow the gravitational field equations are likely to be different. Whereas the explanation which consists in showing that whichever equation we have implies Newton's equation to a first approximation is invariant under even moderate perturbations, quite big perturbations, of the assumptions. One might say that every explanation of Kepler's laws 'passes through' Newton's laws.

Let me come back to the philosophy of mind, now. If we assume a thorough atomic structure of matter, quantization and so forth, then, at first blush, it looks as if *continuities* cannot be relevant to our brain functioning. Mustn't it all be discrete? Physics says that the deepest level is discrete.

There are two problems with this argument. One is that there are continuities even in quantum mechanics, as well as discontinuities. But ignore that, suppose quantum mechanics were a thoroughly discrete theory.

The other problem is that if that were a good argument, it would be an argument against the utilizability of the model of air as a continuous liquid, which is the model on which aeroplane wings are constructed, at least if they are to fly at anything less than supersonic speeds. There are two points: one is that a discontinuous structure, a discrete structure, can approximate a continuous structure. The discontinuities may be irrelevant, just as in the case of the peg and the board. The fact that the peg and the board are not continuous solids is irrelevant. One can say that the peg and the board only approximate perfectly rigid continuous solids. But if the error in the approximation is irrelevant to the level of description, so what? It is not just that discrete systems can approximate continuous systems; the fact is that the system may behave in the way it does *because* a continuous system would behave in such and such a way, and the system approximates a continuous system.

This is not a Newtonian world. Tough. Kepler's law comes out true because the sun-earth system approximates a Newtonian system. And the error in the approximation is quite irrelevant at that level.

This analogy is not perfect because physicists are interested in laws to which the error in the approximation is relevant. It seems to me that in the psychological case the analogy is even better, that continuous models (for example, Hull's model for rote learning which used a continuous potential) could perfectly well be correct, whatever the ultimate structure of the brain is. We cannot deduce that a digital model has to be the correct model from the fact that ultimately there are neurons. The brain may work the way it does because it approximates some system whose laws are best conceptualized in terms of continuous mathematics. What is more, the errors in that approximation may be irrelevant at the level of psychology.

What I have said about *continuity* goes as well for many other things. Let us come back to the question of the soul people and the brain people, and the isomorphism between the souls in one world and the brains in the other. One objection was, if there is a functional isomorphism between souls and brains, wouldn't the souls have to be rather simple? The answer is no. Because brains can be essentially infinitely complex. A system with as many degrees of freedom as the brain can imitate to within the accuracy relevant to psychological theory any structure one can hope to describe. It might be, so to speak, that the ultimate physics of the soul will be quite different from the ultimate physics of the brain, but that at the level we are interested in, the level of functional organization, the same description might go for both. And also that that description might be formally incompatible with the actual physics of the brain, in the way that the description of the air flowing around an aeroplane wing as a continuous incompressible liquid is *formally incompatible with the actual structure of the air.*

Let me close by saying that these examples support the idea that our substance, what we are made of, places almost no first order restrictions on our form. And that what we are really interested in, as Aristotle saw,[6] is form and not matter. *What is our intellectual form?* is the question, not what the matter is. And whatever our substance may be, soul-stuff, or matter or Swiss cheese, it is not going to place any interesting first order restrictions on the answer to this question. It may, of course, place interesting higher order restrictions. Small effects may have to be explained in terms of the actual physics of the brain. But when we are not even at the level of an *idealized* description of the functional organization of the brain, to talk about the importance of small perturbations seems decidedly premature. My conclusion is that we have what we always wanted—an autonomous mental life. And we need no mysteries, no ghostly agents, no *élan vital* to have it.

Endnotes

[1] This paper was presented as a part of a Foerster symposium on 'Computers and the Mind' at the University of California (Berkeley) in October, 1973. I am indebted to Alan Garfinkel for comments on earlier versions of this paper.

[2] Even if it were not physically possible to realize human psychology in a creature made of anything but the usual protoplasm, DNA, etc., it would still not be correct to say that psychological states are identical with their physical realizations. For, as will be argued below, such an identification has no *explanatory* value *in psychology.*

[3] Joke Credit: Joseph Weizenbaum.

[4] This is one of Kepler's laws.

[5] Provided that the two bodies—the sun and the earth—are the whole universe. If there are other forces, then, of course, Kepler's law cannot be *exactly* correct.

[6] E.g., Aristotle says: '. . . we can wholly dismiss as unnecessary the question whether the soul and the body are one: it is as meaningless to ask whether the wax and the shape given to it by the stamp are one, or generally the matter of a thing and that of which it is the matter.' (See *De Anima*, 412 a6–b9.)

27. *What Is It Like to Be a Bat?*

THOMAS NAGEL

Science attempts to understand the world objectively—in a way that abstracts from, and does not depend on, the peculiarities of a subjective point of view. During the rise of the mechanistic view of nature in the Scientific Revolution, discovering mathematical relations among material things became a paradigm of objective understanding. On the other hand, things like appearances, sensations, and feelings were considered subjective and relegated to the mind—the mind viewed dualistically as a dualistic container or stage for the phenomenal world. Contemporary physicalists and functionalists who want to understand mind objectively must find some way to analyze or dismiss such ostensibly nonphysical entities. In "What Is It Like to Be a Bat?" Thomas Nagel claims the objective strategies of physical science cannot capture the subjective points of view of conscious creatures, and he argues that to leave them out of an account of mind means the physicalist and functionalist theories are incomplete. Nagel is a member of the Philosophy Department at New York University. He further develops his point of view in his 1986 book, *The View from Nowhere*.

Consciousness is what makes the mind-body problem really intractable. Perhaps that is why current discussions of the problem give it little attention or get it obviously wrong. The recent wave of reductionist euphoria has produced several analyses of mental phenomena and mental concepts designed to explain the possibility of some variety of materialism, psychophysical identification, or reduction.[1] But the problems dealt with are those common to this type of reduction and other types, and what makes the mind-body problem unique, and unlike the water-H_2O problem or the Turing machine-IBM machine problem or the lightning-electrical discharge problem or the gene-DNA problem or the oak tree–hydrocarbon problem, is ignored.

Every reductionist has his favorite analogy from modern science. It is most unlikely that any of these unrelated examples of successful reduction will shed light on the relation of mind to brain. But philosophers share the general human weakness for explanations of what is incomprehensible in terms suited for what is familiar and well understood, though entirely different. This has led to the acceptance of implausible accounts of the mental largely because they would permit familiar kinds of reduction. I shall try to explain why the usual examples do not help us to understand the relation between mind and body—why, indeed, we have at present no conception of what an explanation of the physical nature of a mental phenomenon would be. Without consciousness the mind-body problem would be much less interesting. With consciousness it seems hopeless. The most important and characteristic feature of conscious mental phenomena is very poorly understood. Most reductionist theories do not even try to explain it. And careful examination will show that no currently available concept of reduction is applicable to it. Perhaps a new theoretical form can be devised for the purpose, but such a solution, if it exists, lies in the distant intellectual future.

Conscious experience is a widespread phenomenon. It occurs at many levels of animal life, though we cannot be sure of its presence in the simpler organisms, and it is very difficult to say in general what provides evidence of it. (Some

From Thomas Nagel, "What Is It Like to Be a Bat?" *Philosophical Review* 83 (1974): 435–50. Reprinted by permission of the author and *Philosophical Review*.

extremists have been prepared to deny it even of mammals other than man.) No doubt it occurs in countless forms totally unimaginable to us, on other planets in other solar systems throughout the universe. But no matter how the form may vary, the fact that an organism has conscious experience *at all* means, basically, that there is something it is like to *be* that organism. There may be further implications about the form of the experience; there may even (though I doubt it) be implications about the behavior of the organism. But fundamentally an organism has conscious mental states if and only if there is something that it is like to *be* that organism—something it is like *for* the organism.

We may call this the subjective character of experience. It is not captured by any of the familiar, recently devised reductive analyses of the mental, for all of them are logically compatible with its absence. It is not analyzable in terms of any explanatory system of functional states, or intentional states, since these could be ascribed to robots or automata that behaved like people though they experienced nothing.[2] It is not analyzable in terms of the causal role of experiences in relation to typical human behavior—for similar reasons.[3] I do not deny that conscious mental states and events cause behavior, nor that they may be given functional characterizations. I deny only that this kind of thing exhausts their analysis. Any reductionist program has to be based on an analysis of what is to be reduced. If the analysis leaves something out, the problem will be falsely posed. It is useless to base the defense of materialism on any analysis of mental phenomena that fails to deal explicitly with their subjective character. For there is no reason to suppose that a reduction which seems plausible when no attempt is made to account for consciousness can be extended to include consciousness. Without some idea, therefore, of what the subjective character of experience is, we cannot know what is required of a physicalist theory.

While an account of the physical basis of mind must explain many things, this appears to be the most difficult. It is impossible to exclude the phenomenological features of experience from a reduction in the same way that one excludes the phenomenal features of an ordinary substance from a physical or chemical reduction of it—namely, by explaining them as effects on the minds of human observers.[4] If physicalism is to be defended, the phenomenological features must themselves be given a physical account. But when we examine their subjective character it seems that such a result is impossible. The reason is that every subjective phenomenon is essentially connected with a single point of view, and it seems inevitable that an objective, physical theory will abandon that point of view.

Let me first try to state the issue somewhat more fully than by referring to the relation between the subjective and the objective, or between the *pour-soi* and the *en-soi*. This is far from easy. Facts about what it is like to be an *X* are very peculiar, so peculiar that some may be inclined to doubt their reality, or the significance of claims about them. To illustrate the connection between subjectivity and a point of view, and to make evident the importance of subjective features, it will help to explore the matter in relation to an example that brings out clearly the divergence between the two types of conception, subjective and objective.

I assume we all believe that bats have experience. After all, they are mammals, and there is no more doubt that they have experience than that mice or pigeons or whales have experience. I have chosen bats instead of wasps or flounders because if one travels too far down the phylogenetic tree, people gradually shed their faith that there is experience there at all. Bats, although more closely related to us than those other species, nevertheless present a range of activity and a sensory apparatus so different from ours that the problem I want to pose is exceptionally vivid (though it certainly could be raised with other species). Even without the benefit of philosophical reflection, anyone who has spent some time in an enclosed space with an excited bat knows what it is to encounter a fundamentally *alien* form of life.

I have said that the essence of the belief that bats have experience is that there is something that it is like to be a bat. Now we know that most bats (the microchiroptera, to be precise) perceive the external world primarily by sonar, or echolocation, detecting the reflections, from objects within range, of their own rapid, subtly modulated, high-frequency shrieks. Their brains are designed to correlate the outgoing impulses with the subsequent echoes, and the information thus acquired enables bats to make precise discriminations of distance, size, shape, motion, and texture comparable to those we make by vision. But bat sonar, though clearly a form of perception, is not similar in its operation to any sense that we possess, and there is no reason to suppose that it is subjectively like anything we can experience or imagine. This appears to create difficulties for the notion of what it is like to be a bat. We must consider whether any method will permit us to extrapolate to the inner life of the bat from our own case,[5] and if not, what alternative methods there may be for understanding the notion.

Our own experience provides the basic material for our imagination, whose range is therefore limited. It will not help to try to imagine that one has webbing on one's arms, which enables one to fly around at dusk and dawn catching insects in one's mouth; that one has very poor vision, and perceives the surrounding world by a system of reflected high-frequency sound signals; and that one spends the day hanging upside down by one's feet in an attic. In so far as I can imagine this (which is not very far), it tells me only what it would be like for *me* to behave as a bat behaves. But that is not the question. I want to know what it is like for a *bat* to be a bat. Yet if I try to imagine this, I am restricted to the resources of my own mind, and those resources are inadequate to the task. I cannot perform it either by imagining additions to my present experience, or by imagining segments gradually subtracted from it, or by imagining some combination of additions, subtractions, and modifications.

To the extent that I could look and behave like a wasp or a bat without changing my fundamental structure, my experiences would not be anything like the experiences of those animals. On the other hand, it is doubtful that any meaning can be attached to the supposition that I should possess the internal neurophysiological constitution of a bat. Even if I could by gradual degrees be transformed into a bat, nothing in my present constitution enables me to imagine what the experiences of such a future stage of myself thus metamorphosed would be like. The best evidence would come from the experiences of bats, if we only knew what they were like.

So if extrapolation from our own case is involved in the idea of what it is like to be a bat, the extrapolation must be incompletable. We cannot form more than a schematic conception of what it *is* like. For example, we may ascribe general *types* of experience on the basis of the animal's structure and behavior. Thus we describe bat sonar as a form of three-dimensional forward perception; we believe that bats feel some versions of pain, fear, hunger, and lust, and that they have other, more familiar types of perception besides sonar. But we

believe that these experiences also have in each case a specific subjective character, which it is beyond our ability to conceive. And if there is conscious life elsewhere in the universe, it is likely that some of it will not be describable even in the most general experiential terms available to us.[6] (The problem is not confined to exotic cases, however, for it exists between one person and another. The subjective character of the experience of a person deaf and blind from birth is not accessible to me, for example, nor presumably is mine to him. This does not prevent us each from believing that the other's experience has such a subjective character.)

If anyone is inclined to deny that we can believe in the existence of facts like this whose exact nature we cannot possibly conceive, he should reflect that in contemplating the bats we are in much the same position that intelligent bats or Martians[7] would occupy if they tried to form a conception of what it was like to be us. The structure of their own minds might make it impossible for them to succeed, but we know they would be wrong to conclude that there is not anything precise that it is like to be us: that only certain general types of mental state could be ascribed to us (perhaps perception and appetite would be concepts common to us both; perhaps not). We know they would be wrong to draw such a skeptical conclusion because we know what it is like to be us. And we know that while it includes an enormous amount of variation and complexity, and while we do not possess the vocabulary to describe it adequately, its subjective character is highly specific, and in some respects describable in terms that can be understood only by creatures like us. The fact that we cannot expect ever to accommodate in our language a detailed description of Martian or bat phenomenology should not lead us to dismiss as meaningless the claim that bats and Martians have experiences fully comparable in richness of detail to our own. It would be fine if someone were to develop concepts and a theory that enabled us to think about those things; but such an understanding may be permanently denied to us by the limits of our nature. And to deny the reality or logical significance of what we can never describe or understand is the crudest form of cognitive dissonance.

This brings us to the edge of a topic that requires much more discussion than I can give it here: namely, the relation between facts on the one hand and conceptual schemes or systems of representation on the other. My realism about the subjective domain in all its forms implies a belief in the existence of facts beyond the reach of human concepts. Certainly it is possible for a human being to believe that there are facts which humans never *will* possess the requisite concepts to represent or comprehend. Indeed, it would be foolish to doubt this, given the finiteness of humanity's expectations. After all, there would have been transfinite numbers even if everyone had been wiped out by the Black Death before Cantor discovered them. But one might also believe that there are facts which *could* not ever be represented or comprehended by human beings, even if the species lasted forever—simply because our structure does not permit us to operate with concepts of the requisite type. This impossibility might even be observed by other beings, but it is not clear that the existence of such beings, or the possibility of their existence, is a precondition of the significance of the hypothesis that there are humanly inaccessible facts. (After all, the nature of beings with access to humanly inaccessible facts is presumably itself a humanly inaccessible fact.) Reflection on what it is like to be a bat seems to lead us, therefore, to the conclusion that there are facts that do not consist in the truth of propositions expressible in a human language. We can be compelled to recognize the existence of such facts without being able to state or comprehend them.

I shall not pursue this subject, however. Its bearing on the topic before us (namely, the mind-body problem) is that it enables us to make a general observation about the subjective character of experience. Whatever may be the status of facts about what it is like to be a human being, or a bat, or a Martian, these appear to be facts that embody a particular point of view.

I am not adverting here to the alleged privacy of experience to its possessor. The point of view in question is not one accessible only to a single individual. Rather it is a *type*. It is often possible to take up a point of view other than one's own, so the comprehension of such facts is not limited to one's own case. There is a sense in which phenomenological facts are perfectly objective: one person can know or say of another what the quality of the other's experience is. They are subjective, however, in the sense that even this objective ascription of experience is possible only for someone sufficiently similar to the object of ascription to be able to adopt his point of view—to understand the ascription in the first person as well as in the third,

so to speak. The more different from oneself the other experiencer is, the less success one can expect with this enterprise. In our own case we occupy the relevant point of view, but we will have as much difficulty understanding our own experience properly if we approach it from another point of view as we would if we tried to understand the experience of another species without taking up *its* point of view.[8]

This bears directly on the mind-body problem. For if the facts of experience—facts about what it is like *for* the experiencing organism—are accessible only from one point of view, then it is a mystery how the true character of experiences could be revealed in the physical operation of that organism. The latter is a domain of objective facts *par excellence*—the kind that can be observed and understood from many points of view and by individuals with differing perceptual systems. There are no comparable imaginative obstacles to the acquisition of knowledge about bat neurophysiology by human scientists, and intelligent bats or Martians might learn more about the human brain than we ever will.

This is not by itself an argument against reduction. A Martian scientist with no understanding of visual perception could understand the rainbow, or lightning, or clouds as physical phenomena, though he would never be able to understand the human concepts of rainbow, lightning, or cloud, or the place these things occupy in our phenomenal world. The objective nature of the things picked out by these concepts could be apprehended by him because, although the concepts themselves are connected with a particular point of view and a particular visual phenomenology, the things apprehended from that point of view are not: they are observable from the point of view but external to it; hence they can be comprehended from other points of view also, either by the same organisms or by others. Lightning has an objective character that is not exhausted by its visual appearance, and this can be investigated by a Martian without vision. To be precise, it has a *more* objective character than is revealed in its visual appearance. In speaking of the move from subjective to objective characterization, I wish to remain noncommittal about the existence of an end point, the completely objective intrinsic nature of the thing, which one might or might not be able to reach. It may be more accurate to think of objectivity as a direction in which the understanding can travel. And in understanding a phenomenon like lightning, it is legitimate to go as far away as one can from a strictly human viewpoint.[9]

In the case of experience, on the other hand, the connection with a particular point of view seems much closer. It is difficult to understand what could be meant by the *objective* character of an experience, apart from the particular point of view from which its subject apprehends it. After all, what would be left of what it was like to be a bat if one removed the viewpoint of the bat? But if experience does not have, in addition to its subjective character, an objective nature that can be apprehended from many different points of view, then how can it be supposed that a Martian investigating my brain might be observing physical processes which were my mental processes (as he might observe physical processes which were bolts of lightning), only from a different point of view? How, for that matter, could a human physiologist observe them from another point of view?[10]

We appear to be faced with a general difficulty about psychophysical reduction. In other areas the process of reduction is a move in the direction of greater objectivity, toward a more accurate view of the real nature of things. This is accomplished by reducing our dependence on individual or species-specific points of view toward the object of investigation. We describe it not in terms of the impressions it makes on our senses, but in terms of its more general effects and of properties detectable by means other than the human senses. The less it depends on a specifically human viewpoint, the more objective is our description. It is possible to follow this path because although the concepts and ideas we employ in thinking about the external world are initially applied from a point of view that involves our perceptual apparatus, they are used by us to refer to things beyond themselves—toward which we *have* the phenomenal point of view. Therefore we can abandon it in favor of another, and still be thinking about the same things.

Experience itself, however, does not seem to fit the pattern. The idea of moving from appearance to reality seems to make no sense here. What is the analogue in this case to pursuing a more objective understanding of the same phenomena by abandoning the initial subjective viewpoint toward them in favor of another that is more objective but concerns the same thing? Certainly it *appears* unlikely that we will get closer to the real nature of human experience by leaving behind the particularity of our human point of view and striving for a description in terms accessible to beings that could not imagine what it was like to be us. If the subjective character of experience is fully comprehensible only from one point of view, then any shift to greater objectivity—that is, less attachment to a specific viewpoint—does not take us nearer to the real nature of the phenomenon: it takes us farther away from it.

In a sense, the seeds of this objection to the reducibility of experience are already detectable in successful cases of reduction; for in discovering sound to be, in reality, a wave phenomenon in air or other media, we leave behind one viewpoint to take up another, and the auditory, human or animal viewpoint that we leave behind remains unreduced. Members of radically different species may both understand the same physical events in objective terms, and this does not require that they understand the phenomenal forms in which those events appear to the senses of members of the other species. Thus it is a condition of their referring to a common reality that their more particular viewpoints are not part of the common reality that they both apprehend. The reduction can succeed only if the species-specific viewpoint is omitted from what is to be reduced.

But while we are right to leave this point of view aside in seeking a fuller understanding of the external world, we cannot ignore it permanently, since it is the essence of the internal world, and not merely a point of view on it. Most of the neobehaviorism of recent philosophical psychology results from the effort to substitute an objective concept of mind for the real thing, in order to have nothing left over which cannot be reduced. If we acknowledge that a physical theory of mind must account for the subjective character of experience, we must admit that no presently available conception gives us a clue how this could be done. The problem is unique. If mental processes are indeed physical processes, then there is something it is like, intrinsically,[11] to undergo certain physical processes. What it is for such a thing to be the case remains a mystery.

What moral should be drawn from these reflections, and what should be done next? It would be a mistake to conclude that physicalism must be false. Nothing is proved by the inadequacy of physicalist hypotheses that assume a faulty objective analysis of mind. It would be truer to say that physicalism is a position we cannot understand because we do not at present have any conception of how it might be true. Perhaps it will be thought unreasonable to require such a conception as a condition of understanding. After all, it might be said, the meaning of physicalism is clear enough: mental states are states of the body; mental events are physical events. We do not know *which* physical states and events they are, but that should not prevent us from understanding the hypothesis. What could be clearer than the words "is" and "are"?

But I believe it is precisely this apparent clarity of the word "is" that is deceptive. Usually, when we are told that *X* is *Y* we know *how* it is supposed to be true, but that depends on a conceptual or theoretical background and is not conveyed by the "is" alone. We know how both "*X*" and "*Y*" refer, and the kinds of things to which they refer, and we have a rough idea how the two referential paths might converge on a single thing, be it an object, a person, a process, an event, or whatever. But when the two terms of the identification are very disparate it may not be so clear how it could be true. We may not have even a rough idea of how the two referential paths could converge, or what kind of things they might converge on, and a theoretical framework may have to be supplied to enable us to understand this. Without the framework, an air of mysticism surrounds the identification.

This explains the magical flavor of popular presentations of fundamental scientific discoveries, given out as propositions to which one must subscribe without really understanding them. For example, people are now told at an early age that all matter is really energy. But despite the fact that they know what "is" means, most of them never form a conception of what makes this claim true, because they lack the theoretical background.

At the present time the status of physicalism is similar to that which the hypothesis that matter is energy would have had if uttered by a pre-Socratic philosopher. We do not have the beginnings of a conception of how it might be true. In order to understand the hypothesis that a mental event is a physical event, we require more than an understanding of the word "is." The idea of how a mental and a physical term might refer to the same thing is lacking, and the usual analogies with theoretical identification in other fields fail to supply it. They fail because if we construe the reference of mental terms to physical events on the usual model, we either get a reappearance of separate

subjective events as the effects through which mental reference to physical events is secured, or else we get a false account of how mental terms refer (for example, a causal behaviorist one).

Strangely enough, we may have evidence for the truth of something we cannot really understand. Suppose a caterpillar is locked in a sterile safe by someone unfamiliar with insect metamorphosis, and weeks later the safe is reopened, revealing a butterfly. If the person knows that the safe has been shut the whole time, he has reason to believe that the butterfly is or was once the caterpillar, without having any idea in what sense this might be so. (One possibility is that the caterpillar contained a tiny winged parasite that devoured it and grew into the butterfly.)

It is conceivable that we are in such a position with regard to physicalism. Donald Davidson has argued that if mental events have physical causes and effects, they must have physical descriptions. He holds that we have reason to believe this even though we do not—and in fact *could* not—have a general psychophysical theory.[12] His argument applies to intentional mental events, but I think we also have some reason to believe that sensations are physical processes, without being in a position to understand how. Davidson's position is that certain physical events have irreducibly mental properties, and perhaps some view describable in this way is correct. But nothing of which we can now form a conception corresponds to it; nor have we any idea what a theory would be like that enabled us to conceive of it.[13]

Very little work has been done on the basic question (from which mention of the brain can be entirely omitted) whether any sense can be made of experiences' having an objective character at all. Does it make sense, in other words, to ask what my experiences are *really* like, as opposed to how they appear to me? We cannot genuinely understand the hypothesis that their nature is captured in a physical description unless we understand the more fundamental idea that they *have* an objective nature (or that objective processes can have a subjective nature).[14]

I should like to close with a speculative proposal. It may be possible to approach the gap between subjective and objective from another direction. Setting aside temporarily the relation between the mind and the brain, we can pursue a more objective understanding of the mental in its own right. At present we are completely unequipped to think about the subjective character of experience without relying on the imagination—without taking up the point of view of the experiential subject. This should be regarded as a challenge to form new concepts and devise a new method—an objective phenomenology not dependent on empathy or the imagination. Though presumably it would not capture everything, its goal would be to describe, at least in part, the subjective character of experiences in a form comprehensible to beings incapable of having those experiences.

We would have to develop such a phenomenology to describe the sonar experiences of bats; but it would also be possible to begin with humans. One might try, for example, to develop concepts that could be used to explain to a person blind from birth what it was like to see. One would reach a blank wall eventually, but it should be possible to devise a method of expressing in objective terms much more than we can at present, and with much greater precision. The loose intermodal analogies—for example, "Red is like the sound of a trumpet"—which crop up in discussions of this subject are of little use. That should be clear to anyone who has both heard a trumpet and seen red. But structural features of perception might be more accessible to objective description, even though something would be left out. And concepts alternative to those we learn in the first person may enable us to arrive at a kind of understanding even of our own experience which is denied us by the very ease of description and lack of distance that subjective concepts afford.

Apart from its own interest, a phenomenology that is in this sense objective may permit questions about the physical[15] basis of experience to assume a more intelligible form. Aspects of subjective experience that admitted this kind of objective description might be better candidates for objective explanations of a more familiar sort. But whether or not this guess is correct, it seems unlikely that any physical theory of mind can be contemplated until more thought has been given to the general problem of subjective and objective. Otherwise we cannot even pose the mind-body problem without sidestepping it.[16]

Endnotes

[1] Examples are J. J. C. Smart, *Philosophy and Scientific Realism* (London, 1963); David K. Lewis, "An Argument for the Identity Theory," *Journal of Philosophy*, 63 (1966), reprinted with addenda in David M. Rosenthal,

Materialism and the Mind-Body Problem (Englewood Cliffs, N.J., 1971); Hilary Putnam, "Psychological Predicates" in Capitan and Merrill, *Art, Mind, and Religion* (Pittsburgh, 1967), reprinted in Rosenthal, op. cit., as "The Nature of Mental States"; D. M. Armstrong, *A Materialist Theory of the Mind* (London, 1968); D. C. Dennett, *Content and Consciousness* (London, 1969). I have expressed earlier doubts in "Armstrong on the Mind," *Philosophical Reivew*, 79 (1970), 394–403; "Brain Bisection and the Unity of Consciousness," *Synthese*, 22 (1971); and a review of Dennett, *Journal of Philosophy*, 69 (1972). See also Saul Kripke, "Naming and Necessity" in Davidson and Harman, *Semantics of Natural Language* (Dordrecht, 1972), esp. pp. 334–342; and M. T. Thornton, "Ostensive Terms and Materialism," *The Monist*, 56 (1972).

[2] Perhaps there could not actually be such robots. Perhaps anything complex enough to behave like a person would have experiences. But that, if true, is a fact which cannot be discovered merely by analyzing the concept of experience.

[3] It is not equivalent to that about which we are incorrigible, both because we are not incorrigible about experience and because experience is present in animals lacking language and thought, who have no beliefs at all about their experiences.

[4] Cf. Richard Rorty, "Mind-Body Identity, Privacy, and Categories," *The Review of Metaphysics*, 19 (1965), esp. 37–38.

[5] By "our own case" I do not mean just "my own case," but rather the mentalistic ideas that we apply unproblematically to ourselves and other human beings.

[6] Therefore the analogical form of the English expression "what it is *like*" is misleading. It does not mean "what (in our experience) it *resembles*," but rather "how it is for the subject himself."

[7] Any intelligent extraterrestrial beings totally different from us.

[8] It may be easier than I suppose to transcend interspecies barriers with the aid of the imagination. For example, blind people are able to detect objects near them by a form of sonar, using vocal clicks or taps of a cane. Perhaps if one knew what that was like, one could by extension imagine roughly what it was like to possess the much more refined sonar of a bat. The distance between oneself and other persons and other species can fall anywhere on a continuum. Even for other persons the understanding of what it is like to be them is only partial, and when one moves to species very different from oneself, a lesser degree of partial understanding may still be available. The imagination is remarkably flexible. My point, however, is not that we cannot *know* what it is like to be a bat. I am not raising that epistemological problem. My point is rather that even to form a *conception* of what it is like to be a

bat (and a fortiori to know what it is like to be a bat) one must take up the bat's point of view. If one can take it up roughly, or partially, then one's conception will also be rough or partial. Or so it seems in our present state of understanding.

[9] The problem I am going to raise can therefore be posed even if the distinction between more subjective and more objective descriptions or viewpoints can itself be made only within a larger human point of view. I do not accept this kind of conceptual relativism, but it need not be refuted to make the point that psychophysical reduction cannot be accommodated by the subjective-to-objective model familiar from other cases.

[10] The problem is not just that when I look at the "Mona Lisa," my visual experience has a certain quality, no trace of which is to be found by someone looking into my brain. For even if he did observe there a tiny image of the "Mona Lisa," he would have no reason to identify it with the experience.

[11] The relation would therefore not be a contingent one, like that of a cause and its distinct effect. It would be necessarily true that a certain physical state felt a certain way. Saul Kripke (op. cit.) argues that causal behaviorist and related analyses of the mental fail because they construe, e.g., "pain" as a merely contingent name of pains. The subjective character of an experience ("its immediate phenomenological quality" Kripke calls it [p. 340]) is the essential property left out by such analyses, and the one in virtue of which it is, necessarily, the experience it is. My view is closely related to his. Like Kripke, I find the hypothesis that a certain brain state should *necessarily* have a certain subjective character incomprehensible without further explanation. No such explanation emerges from theories which view the mind-brain relation as contingent, but perhaps there are other alternatives, not yet discovered.

A theory that explained how the mind-brain relation was necessary would still leave us with Kripke's problem of explaining why it nevertheless appears contingent. That difficulty seems to me surmountable, in the following way. We may imagine something by representing it to ourselves either perceptually, sympathetically, or symbolically. I shall not try to say how symbolic imagination works, but part of what happens in the other two cases is this. To imagine something perceptually, we put ourselves in a conscious state resembling the state we would be in if we perceived it. To imagine something sympathetically, we put ourselves in a conscious state resembling the thing itself. (This method can be used only to imagine mental events and states—our own or another's.) When we

try to imagine a mental state occurring without its associated brain state, we first sympathetically imagine the occurrence of the mental state: that is, we put ourselves into a state that resembles it mentally. At the same time, we attempt to perceptually imagine the non-occurrence of the associated physical state, by putting ourselves into another state unconnected with the first: one resembling that which we would be in if we perceived the non-occurrence of the physical state. Where the imagination of physical features is perceptual and the imagination of mental features is sympathetic, it appears to us that we can imagine any experience occurring without its associated brain state, and vice versa. The relation between them will appear contingent even if it is necessary, because of the independence of the disparate types of imagination.

(Solipsism, incidentally, results if one misinterprets sympathetic imagination as if it worked like perceptual imagination: it then seems impossible to imagine any experience that is not one's own.)

[12] See "Mental Events" in Foster and Swanson, *Experience and Theory* (Amherst, 1970); though I don't understand the argument against psychophysical laws.

[13] Similar remarks apply to my paper "Physicalism," *Philosophical Review* 74 (1965), 339–356, reprinted with postscript in John O'Connor, *Modern Materialism* (New York, 1969).

[14] This question also lies at the heart of the problem of other minds, whose close connection with the mind-body problem is often overlooked. If one understood how subjective experience could have an objective nature, one would understand the existence of subjects other than oneself.

[15] I have not defined the term "physical." Obviously it does not apply just to what can be described by the concepts of contemporary physics, since we expect further developments. Some may think there is nothing to prevent mental phenomena from eventually being recognized as physical in their own right. But whatever else may be said of the physical, it has to be objective. So if our idea of the physical ever expands to include mental phenomena, it will have to assign them an objective character—whether or not this is done by analyzing them in terms of other phenomena already regarded as physical. It seems to me more likely, however, that mental-physical relations will eventually be expressed in a theory whose fundamental terms cannot be placed clearly in either category.

[16] I have read versions of this paper to a number of audiences, and am indebted to many people for their comments.

28. *Epiphenomenal Qualia*

FRANK JACKSON

Frank Jackson, professor of philosophy at Monash University, argues there are features of bodily sensations and perceptual experiences which no amount of physical information adequately describes. Jackson takes the existence of such "qualia" to show the incompleteness of physicalism. He goes on to defend qualia against the charge they might not be able to causally affect physical events—that is, they might be epiphenomena caused by physical entities.

It is undeniable that the physical, chemical and biological sciences have provided a great deal of information about the world we live in and about ourselves. I will use the label 'physical information' for this kind of information, and also for information that automatically comes along with it. For example, if a medical scientist tells me enough about the processes that go on in my nervous system, and about how they relate to happenings in the world around me, to what has happened in the past and is likely to happen in the future, to what happens to other similar and dissimilar organisms, and the like, he or she tells me—if I am clever enough to fit it together appropriately—about what is often called the functional role of those states in me (and in organisms in general in similar cases). This information, and its kin, I also label 'physical'.

I do not mean these sketchy remarks to constitute a definition of 'physical information', and of the correlative notions of physical property, process, and so on, but to indicate what I have in mind here. It is well known that there are problems with giving a precise definition of these notions, and so of the thesis of Physicalism that all (correct) information is physical information.[1] But—unlike some—I take the question of definition to cut across the central problems I want to discuss in this paper.

I am what is sometimes known as a "qualia freak". I think that there are certain features of the bodily sensations especially, but also of certain perceptual experiences, which no amount of purely physical information includes. Tell me everything physical there is to tell about what is going on in a living brain, the kind of states, their functional role, their relation to what goes on at other times and in other brains, and so on and so forth, and be I as clever as can be in fitting it all together, you won't have told me about the hurtfulness of pains, the itchiness of itches, pangs of jealousy, or about the characteristic experience of tasting a lemon, smelling a rose, hearing a loud noise or seeing the sky.

There are many qualia freaks, and some of them say that their rejection of Physicalism is an unargued intuition.[2] I think that they are being unfair to themselves. They have the following argument. Nothing you could tell of a physical sort captures the smell of a rose, for instance. Therefore, Physicalism is false. By our lights this is a perfectly good argument. It is obviously not to the point to question its validity, and the premise is intuitively obviously true both to them and to me.

I must, however, admit that it is weak from a polemical point of view. There are, unfortunately for us, many who do not find the premise intuitively obvious. The task then is to present an argument whose premises are obvious to all, or at least to as many as possible. This I try to do in §I with what I will call "the Knowledge argument". In §II I contrast the Knowledge argument with the Modal argument and in §III with the "What is it like to be" argument. In §IV I tackle the question of the causal role of qualia. The major factor in stopping people from admitting qualia is the belief that they would

From *Philosophical Quarterly*, 1982, Vol. 32, pp. 127–136.

have to be given a causal role with respect to the physical world and especially the brain;[3] and it is hard to do this without sounding like someone who believes in fairies. I seek in §IV to turn this objection by arguing that the view that qualia are epiphenomenal is a perfectly possible one.

I. *The Knowledge Argument for Qualia*

People vary considerably in their ability to discriminate colours. Suppose that in an experiment to catalogue this variation Fred is discovered. Fred has better colour vision than anyone else on record; he makes every discrimination that anyone has ever made, and moreover he makes one that we cannot even begin to make. Show him a batch of ripe tomatoes and he sorts them into two roughly equal groups and does so with complete consistency. That is, if you blindfold him, shuffle the tomatoes up, and then remove the blindfold and ask him to sort them out again, he sorts them into exactly the same two groups.

We ask Fred how he does it. He explains that all ripe tomatoes do not look the same colour to him, and in fact that this is true of a great many objects that we classify together as red. He sees two colours where we see one, and he has in consequence developed for his own use two words 'red$_1$' and 'red$_2$' to mark the difference. Perhaps he tells us that he has often tried to teach the difference between red$_1$ and red$_2$ to his friends but has got nowhere and has concluded that the rest of the world is red$_1$-red$_2$ colour-blind—or perhaps he has had partial success with his children, it doesn't matter. In any case he explains to us that it would be quite wrong to think that because 'red' appears in both 'red$_1$' and 'red$_2$' that the two colours are shades of the one colour. He only uses the common term 'red' to fit more easily into our restricted usage. To him red$_1$ and red$_2$ are as different from each other and all the other colours as yellow is from blue. And his discriminatory behaviour bears this out: he sorts red$_1$ from red$_2$ tomatoes with the greatest of ease in a wide variety of viewing circumstances. Moreover, an investigation of the physiological basis of Fred's exceptional ability reveals that Fred's optical system is able to separate

out two groups of wave-lengths in the red spectrum as sharply as we are able to sort out yellow from blue.[4]

I think that we should admit that Fred can see, really see, at least one more colour than we can; red$_1$ is a different colour from red$_2$. We are to Fred as a totally red-green colour-blind person is to us. H. G. Wells' story "The Country of the Blind" is about a sighted person in a totally blind community.[5] This person never manages to convince them that he can see, that he has an extra sense. They ridicule this sense as quite inconceivable, and treat his capacity to avoid falling into ditches, to win fights and so on as precisely that capacity and nothing more. We would be making their mistake if we refused to allow that Fred can see one more colour than we can.

What kind of experience does Fred have when he sees red$_1$ and red$_2$? What is the new colour or colours like? We would dearly like to know but do not; and it seems that no amount of physical information about Fred's brain and optical system tells us. We find out perhaps that Fred's cones respond differentially to certain light waves in the red section of the spectrum that make no difference to ours (or perhaps he has an extra cone) and that this leads in Fred to a wider range of those brain states responsible for visual discriminatory behaviour. But none of this tells us what we really want to know about his colour experience. There is something about it we don't know. But we know, we may suppose, everything about Fred's body his behaviour and dispositions to behaviour and about his internal physiology, and everything about his history and relation to others that can be given in physical accounts of persons. We have all the physical information. Therefore, knowing all this is *not* knowing everything about Fred. It follows that Physicalism leaves something out.

To reinforce this conclusion, imagine that as a result of our investigations into the internal workings of Fred we find out how to make everyone's physiology like Fred's in the relevant respects; or perhaps Fred donates his body to science and on his death we are able to transplant his optical system into someone else—again the fine detail doesn't matter. The important point is that such a happening would create enormous interest. People would say, "At last we will know what it is like to see the extra colour, at last we will know how Fred has differed from us in the way he has struggled to tell us about for so long". Then it cannot be that we knew all along all about Fred. But *ex hypothesi* we did know all along everything about Fred that features in the physicalist scheme; hence the physicalist scheme leaves something out.

Put it this way. *After* the operation, we will know *more* about Fred and especially about his colour experiences. But beforehand we had all the physical information we could desire about his body and brain, and indeed everything that has ever featured in physicalist accounts of mind and consciousness. Hence there is more to know than all that. Hence Physicalism is incomplete.

Fred and the new colour(s) are of course essentially rhetorical devices. The same point can be made with normal people and familiar colours. Mary is a brilliant scientist who is, for whatever reason, forced to investigate the world from a black and white room *via* a black and white television monitor. She specialises in the neurophysiology of vision and acquires, let us suppose, all the physical information there is to obtain about what goes on when we see ripe tomatoes, or the sky, and use terms like 'red', 'blue', and so on. She discovers, for example, just which wave-length combinations from the sky stimulate the retina, and exactly how this produces *via* the central nervous system the contraction of the vocal chords and expulsion of air from the lungs that results in the uttering of the sentence ''The sky is blue'. (It can hardly be denied that it is in principle possible to obtain all this physical information from black and white television, otherwise the Open University would *of neccessity* need to use colour television.)

What will happen when Mary is released from her black and white room or is given a colour television monitor? Will she *learn* anything or not? It seems just obvious that she will learn something about the world and our visual experience of it. But then it is inescapable that her previous knowledge was incomplete. But she had *all* the physical information. *Ergo* there is more to have than that, and Physicalism is false.

Clearly the same style of Knowledge argument could be deployed for taste, hearing, the bodily sensations and generally speaking for the various mental states which are said to have (as it is variously put) raw feels, phenomenal features or qualia. The conclusion in each case is that the qualia are left out of the physicalist story. And the polemical strength of the Knowledge argument is that it is so hard to deny the central claim that one

can have all the physical information without having all the information there is to have.

II. *The Modal Argument*

By the Modal Argument I mean an argument of the following style.[6] Sceptics about other minds are not making a mistake in deductive logic, whatever else may be wrong with their position. No amount of physical information about another *logically entails* that he or she is conscious or feels anything at all. Consequently there is a possible world with organisms exactly like us in every physical respect (and remember that includes functional states, physical history, *et al.*) but which differ from us profoundly in that they have no conscious mental life at all. But then what is it that we have and they lack? Not anything physical *ex hypothesi*. In all physical regards we and they are exactly alike. Consequently there is more to us than the purely physical. Thus Physicalism is false.[7]

It is sometimes objected that the Modal argument misconceives Physicalism on the ground that that doctrine is advanced as a *contingent* truth.[8] But to say this is only to say that physicalists restrict their claim to *some* possible worlds, including especially ours; and the Modal argument is only directed against this lesser claim. If we in *our* world, let alone beings in any others, have features additional to those of our physical replicas in other possible worlds, then we have non-physical features or qualia.

The trouble rather with the Modal argument is that it rests on a disputable modal intuition. Disputable because it is disputed. Some sincerely deny that there can be physical replicas of us in other possible worlds which nevertheless lack consciousness. Moreover, at least one person who once had the intuition now has doubts.[9]

Head-counting may seem a poor approach to a discussion of the Modal argument. But frequently we can do no better when modal intuitions are in question, and remember our initial goal was to find the argument with the greatest polemical utility.

Of course, *qua* protagonists of the Knowledge argument we may well accept the modal intuition in question; but this will be a *consequence* of our already having an argument to the conclusion that qualia are left out of the physicalist story, not our ground for that conclusion. Moreover, the matter is complicated by the possibility that the connection between matters physical and qualia is like that sometimes held to obtain between aesthetic qualities and natural ones. Two possible worlds which agree in all "natural" respects (including the experiences of sentient creatures) must agree in all aesthetic qualities also, but it is plausibly held that the aesthetic qualities cannot be reduced to the natural.

III. The "What Is It Like to Be" Argument

In "What is it like to be a bat?" Thomas Nagel argues that no amount of physical information can tell us what it is like to be a bat, and indeed that we, human beings, cannot imagine what it is like to be a bat.[10] His reason is that what this is like can only be understood from a bat's point of view, which is not our point of view and is not something capturable in physical terms which are essentially terms understandable equally from many points of view.

It is important to distinguish this argument from the Knowledge argument. When I complained that all the physical knowledge about Fred was not enough to tell us what his special colour experience was like, I was not complaining that we weren't finding out what it is like to *be* Fred. I was complaining that there is something *about* his experience, a property of it, of which we were left ignorant. And if and when we come to know what this property is we still will not know what it is like to *be* Fred, but we will know more *about* him. No amount of knowledge about Fred, be it physical or not, amounts to knowledge "from the inside" concerning Fred. We are not Fred. There is thus a whole set of items of knowledge expressed by forms of words like 'that it is *I myself* who is . . .' which Fred has and we simply cannot have because we are not him.[11]

When Fred sees the colour he alone can see, one thing he knows is the way his experience of it differs from his experience of seeing red and so on, *another* is that he himself is seeing it. Physicalist and qualia freaks alike should acknowledge that no amount of information of whatever kind that *others* have *about* Fred amounts to knowledge of the second. My complaint though concerned the first and

was that the special quality of his experience is certainly a fact about it, and one which Physicalism leaves out because no amount of physical information told us what it is.

Nagel speaks as if the problem he is raising is one of extrapolating from knowledge of one experience to another, of imagining what an unfamiliar experience would be like on the basis of familiar ones. In terms of Hume's example, from knowledge of some shades of blue we can work out what it would be like to see other shades of blue. Nagel argues that the trouble with bats *et al.* is that they are too unlike us. It is hard to see an objection to Physicalism here. Physicalism makes no special claims about the imaginative or extrapolative powers of human beings, and it is hard to see why it need do so.[12]

Anyway, our Knowledge argument makes no assumptions on this point. If Physicalism were true, enough physical information about Fred would obviate any need to extrapolate or to perform special feats of imagination or understanding in order to know all about his special colour experience. *The information would already be in our possession.* But it clearly isn't. That was the nub of the argument.

IV. The Bogey of Epiphenomenalism

Is there any really *good* reason for refusing to countenance the idea that qualia are causally impotent with respect to the physical world? I will argue for the answer no, but in doing this I will say nothing about two views associated with the classical epiphenomenalist position. The first is that mental *states* are inefficacious with respect to the physical world. All I will be concerned to defend is that it is possible to hold that certain *properties* of certain mental states, namely those I've called qualia, are such that their possession or absence makes no difference to the physical world. The second is that the mental is *totally* causally inefficacious. For all I will say it may be that you have to hold that the instantiation of *qualia* makes a difference to *other mental states* though not to anything physical. Indeed general considerations to do with how you could come to be aware of the instantiation of qualia suggest such a position.[13]

Three reasons are standardly given for holding that a quale like the hurtfulness of a pain must be causally efficacious in the physical world, and so, for instance, that its instantiation must sometimes make a difference to what happens in the brain. None, I will argue, has any real force. (I am much indebted to Alec Hyslop and John Lucas for convincing me of this.)

(i) It is supposed to be just obvious that the hurtfulness of pain is partly responsible for the subject seeking to avoid pain, saying 'It hurts' and so on. But, to reverse Hume, anything can fail to cause anything. No matter how often B follows A, and no matter how initially obvious the causality of the connection seems, the hypothesis that A causes B can be overturned by an over-arching theory which shows the two as distinct effects of a common underlying causal process.

To the untutored the image on the screen of Lee Marvin's fist moving from left to right immediately followed by the image of John Wayne's head moving in the same general direction looks as causal as anything.[14] And of course throughout countless Westerns images similar to the first are followed by images similar to the second. All this counts for precisely nothing when we know the over-arching theory concerning how the relevant images are both effects of an underlying causal process involving the projector and the film. The epiphenomenalist can say exactly the same about the connection between, for example, hurtfulness and behaviour. It is simply a consequence of the fact that certain happenings in the brain cause both.

(ii) The second objection relates to Darwin's Theory of Evolution. According to natural selection the traits that evolve over time are those conducive to physical survival. We may assume that qualia evolved over time—we have them, the earliest forms of life do not—and so we should expect qualia to be conducive to survival. The objection is that they could hardly help us to survive if they do nothing to the physical world.

The appeal of this argument is undeniable, but there is a good reply to it. Polar bears have particularly thick, warm coats. The Theory of Evolution explains this (we suppose) by pointing out that having a thick, warm coat is conducive to survival in the Arctic. But having a thick coat goes along with having a heavy coat, and having a heavy coat is *not* conducive to survival. It slows the animal down.

Does this mean that we have refuted Darwin because we have found an evolved trait—having a heavy coat—which is not conducive to survival? Clearly not. Having a heavy coat is an unavoidable concomitant of having a warm coat (in the context, modern insulation was not available), and the advantages for survival of having a warm coat outweighed the disadvantages of having a heavy one. The point is that all we can extract from Darwin's theory is that we should expect any evolved characteristic to be *either* conducive to survival *or* a by-product of one that is so conducive. The epiphenomenalist holds that qualia fall into the latter category. They are a by-product of certain brain processes that are highly conducive to survival.

(iii) The third objection is based on a point about how we come to know about other minds. We know about other minds by knowing about other behaviour, at least in part. The nature of the inference is a matter of some controversy, but it is not a matter of controversy that it proceeds from behaviour. That is why we think that stones do not feel and dogs do feel. But, runs the objection, how can a person's behaviour provide any reason for believing he has qualia like mine, or indeed any qualia at all, unless this behaviour can be regarded as the *outcome* of the qualia. Man Friday's footprint was evidence of Man Friday because footprints are causal outcomes of feet attached to people. And an epiphenomenalist cannot regard behaviour, or indeed anything physical, as an outcome of qualia.

But consider my reading in *The Times* that Spurs won. This provides excellent evidence that *The Telegraph* has also reported that Spurs won, despite the fact that (I trust) *The Telegraph* does not get the results from *The Times*. They each send their own reporters to the game. *The Telegraph*'s report is in no sense an outcome of *The Times*', but the latter provides good evidence for the former nevertheless.

The reasoning involved can be reconstructed thus. I read in *The Times* that Spurs won. This gives me reason to think that Spurs won because I know that Spurs' winning is the most likely candidate to be what caused the report in *The Times*. But I also know that Spurs' winning would have had many effects, including almost certainly a report in *The Telegraph*.

I am arguing from one effect back to its cause and out again to another effect. The fact that neither effect causes the other is irrelevant. Now the epiphenomenalist allows that qualia are effects of what goes on in the brain. Qualia cause nothing physical but are caused by something physical. Hence the epiphenomenalist can argue from the behaviour of others to the qualia of others by arguing from the behaviour of others back to its causes in the brains of others and out again to their qualia.

You may well feel for one reason or another that this is a more dubious chain of reasoning than its model in the case of newspaper reports. You are right. The problem of other minds is a major philosophical problem, the problem of other newspaper reports is not. But there is no special problem of Epiphenomenalism as opposed to, say, Interactionism here.

There is a very understandable response to the three replies I have just made. "All right, there is no knockdown refutation of the existence of epiphenomenal qualia. But the fact remains that they are an excrescence. They *do* nothing, they *explain* nothing, they serve merely to soothe the intuitions of dualists, and it is left a total mystery how they fit into the world view of science. In short we do not and cannot understand the how and why of them."

This is perfectly true; but is no objection to qualia, for it rests on an overly optimistic view of the human animal, and its powers. We are the products of Evolution. We understand and sense what we need to understand and sense in order to survive. Epiphenomenal qualia are totally irrelevant to survival. At no stage of our evolution did natural selection favour those who could make sense of how they are caused and the laws governing them, or in fact why they exist at all. And that is why we can't.

It is not sufficiently appreciated that Physicalism is an extremely optimistic view of our powers. If it is true, we have, in very broad outline admittedly, a grasp of our place in the scheme of things. Certain matters of sheer complexity defeat us—there are an awful lot of neurons—but in principle we have it all. But consider the antecedent probability that everything in the Universe be of a kind that is relevant in some way or other to the survival of *homo sapiens*. It is very low surely. But then one must admit that it is very likely that there is a part of the whole scheme of things, maybe a big part, which no amount of evolution will ever bring us near to knowledge about or understanding. For the simple reason that such knowledge and understanding is irrelevant to survival.

Physicalists typically emphasise that we are a part of nature on their view, which is fair enough. But if we are a part of nature, we are as nature has left us after however many years of evolution it is, and each step in that evolutionary progression has been a matter of chance constrained just by the need to preserve or increase survival value. The wonder is that we understand as much as we do, and there is no wonder that there should be matters which fall quite outside our comprehension. Perhaps exactly how epiphenomenal qualia fit into the scheme of things is one such.

This may seem an unduly pessimistic view of our capacity to articulate a truly comprehensive picture of our world and our place in it. But suppose we discovered living on the bottom of the deepest oceans a sort of sea slug which manifested intelligence. Perhaps survival in the conditions required rational powers. Despite their intelligence, these sea slugs have only a very restricted conception of the world by comparison with ours, the explanation for this being the nature of their immediate environment. Nevertheless they have developed sciences which work surprisingly well in these restricted terms. They also have philosophers, called slugists. Some call themselves tough-minded slugists, others confess to being soft-minded slugists.

The tough-minded slugists hold that the restricted terms (or ones pretty like them which may be introduced as their sciences progress) suffice in principle to describe everything without remainder. These tough-minded slugists admit in moments of weakness to a feeling that their theory leaves something out. They resist this feeling and their opponents, the soft-minded slugists, by pointing out—absolutely correctly—that no slugist has ever succeeded in spelling out how this mysterious residue fits into the highly successful view that their sciences have and are developing of how their world works.

Our sea slugs don't exist, but they might. And there might also exist super beings which stand to us as we stand to the sea slugs. We cannot adopt the perspective of these super beings, because we are not them, but the possibility of such a perspective is, I think, an antidote to excessive optimism.[15]

Endnotes

[1] See, e.g., D. H. Mellor, "Materialism and Phenomenal Qualities", *Aristotelian Society Supp. Vol. 47* (1973),

107–19; and J. W. Cornman, *Materialism and Sensations* (New Haven and London, 1971).

[2] Particularly in discussion, but see, e.g., Keith Campbell, *Metaphysics* (Belmont, 1976), p. 67.

[3] See, e.g., D. C. Dennett, "Current Issues in the Philosophy of Mind", *American Philosophical Quarterly*, 15 (1978), 249–61.

[4] Put this, and similar simplifications below, in terms of Land's theory if you prefer. See, e.g., Edwin H. Land, "Experiments in Color Vision", *Scientific American*, 200 (5 May 1959), 84–99.

[5] H. G. Wells, *The Country of the Blind and Other Stories* (London, n.d.).

[6] See, e.g., Keith Campbell, *Body and Mind* (New York, 1970); and Robert Kirk, "Sentience and Behaviour", *Mind*, 83 (1974), 43–60.

[7] I have presented the argument in an inter-world rather than the more usual intra-world fashion to avoid inessential complications to do with supervenience, causal anomalies and the like.

[8] See, e.g., W. G. Lycan, "A New Lilliputian Argument Against Machine Functionalism", *Philosophical Studies*, 35 (1979), 279–87, p. 280; and Don Locke, "Zombies, Schizophrenics and Purely Physical Objects", *Mind*, 85 (1976), 97–9.

[9] See R. Kirk, "From Physical Explicability to Full-Blooded Materialism", *The Philosophical Quarterly*, 29 (1979), 229–37. See also the arguments against the modal intuition in, e.g., Sydney Shoemaker, "Functionalism and Qualia", *Philosophical Studies*, 27 (1975), 291–315.

[10] *The Philosophical Review*, 83 (1974), 435–50. Two things need to be said about this article. One is that, despite my dissociations to come, I am much indebted to it. The other is that the emphasis changes through the article, and by the end Nagel is objecting not so much to Physicalism as to all extant theories of mind for ignoring points of view, including those that admit (irreducible) qualia.

[11] Knowledge *de se* in the terms of David Lewis, "Attitudes De Dicto and De Se", *The Philosophical Review*, 88 (1979), 513–43.

[12] See Laurence Nemirow's comments on "What is it . . ." in his review of T. Nagel, *Mortal Questions*, in *The Philosophical Review*, 89 (1980), 473–7. I am indebted here in particular to a discussion with David Lewis.

[13] See my review of K. Campbell, *Body and Mind*, in *Australasian Journal of Philosophy*, 50 (1972), 77–80.

[14] Cf. Jean Piaget, "The Child's Conception of Physical Causality", reprinted in *The Essential Piaget* (London, 1977).

[15] I am indebted to Robert Pargetter for a number of comments and, despite his dissent, to §IV of Paul E. Meehl, "The Compleat Autocerebroscopist" in *Mind, Matter, and Method*, ed. Paul Feyerabend and Grover Maxwell (Minneapolis, 1966).

29. *Reduction, Qualia, and the Direct Introspection of the Brain*

PAUL M. CHURCHLAND

Dualists typically claim to know that the mind has properties that are not physical, and physicalists (like Armstrong) have often tried to identify those properties with physical ones. Some functionalists (like Putnam in "Philosophy and Our Mental Life") may be content to argue that mental properties are functional properties that could have (and in the human case probably do have) realization in systems of physical things. Recently, physicalists have explored another strategy, called "eliminative materialism." These philosophers contend that beliefs about the mind are shaped by learned systems of beliefs, or theories, and that the dualists' view of mind just expresses the beliefs of common sense—or so-called "folk psychology." But what if much of folk psychology is false and could be replaced by a better theory? Then, the eliminativists argue, there may be no need to try to *identify* mental states or properties with physical ones because, as traditionally conceived, they may not exist at all. In other words, new and better theories will *eliminate* them.

In this article, Paul Churchland, professor of philosophy at the University of California, San Diego, applies this strategy to beliefs about the qualitative features of sensations, taking as a focus the argument of Frank Jackson in the preceding selection, "Epiphenomenal Qualia." The debate about qualia is ongoing; for further developments the reader should consult Churchland's *A Neurocomputational Perspective: The Nature of Minds and the Structure of Science* (MIT, 1989). For more background, see Wilfrid Sellars's "Philosophy and the Scientific Image of Man" reprinted in Part V of this book.

Do the phenomenological or qualitative features of our sensations constitute a permanent barrier to the reductive aspirations of any materialistic neuroscience? I here argue that they do not. Specifically, I wish to address the recent anti-reductionist arguments posed by Thomas Nagel,[1] Frank Jackson,[2] and Howard Robinson.[3] And I wish to explore the possibility of human subjective consciousness within a conceptual environment constituted by a matured and successful neuroscience.

If we are to deal sensibly with the issues here at stake, we must approach them with a general theory of scientific reduction already in hand, a theory motivated by and adequate to the many instances and varieties of interconceptual reduction displayed *elsewhere* in our scientific history. With an independently based account of the nature and grounds of intertheoretic reduction, we can approach the specific case of subjective qualia, free from the myopia that results from trying to divine the proper conditions on reduction by simply staring long and hard at the problematic case at issue.

I. *Intertheoretic Reduction*

We may begin by remarking that the classical account of intertheoretic reduction[4] now appears to be importantly mistaken, though the repairs necessary are quickly and cleanly made. Suppressing

From Paul M. Churchland, *Journal of Philosophy*, 82, no. 1 (January 1985): 8–28. Reprinted by permission of the author and the *Journal of Philosophy*.

niceties, we may state the original account as follows. A new and more comprehensive theory *reduces* an older theory just in case the new theory, when conjoined with appropriate correspondence rules, logically entails the principles of the older theory. (The point of the correspondence rules, or "bridge laws," is to connect the disparate ontologies of the two theories: often these are expressed as identity statements, such as *Temperature = $mv^2/2k$.*) Schematically,

$$T_N \& \text{ (Correspondence Rules)}$$

logically entails

$$T_O$$

Difficulties with this view begin with the observation that most reduced theories turn out to be, strictly speaking and in a variety of respects, *false*. (Real gases don't really obey $PV = \mu RT$, as in classical thermodynamics; the planets don't really move in ellipses, as in Keplerian astronomy; the acceleration of falling bodies isn't really uniform, as in Galilean dynamics; etc.) If reduction is *deduction*, modus tollens would thus require that the premises of the new reducing theories (statistical thermodynamics in the first case, Newtonian dynamics in the second and third) be somehow false as well, in contradiction to their assumed truth.

This complaint can be temporarily deflected by pointing out that the premises of a reduction must often include not just the new reducing theory but also some limiting assumptions or counterfactual boundary conditions (such as that the molecules of a gas enjoy only mechanical energy, or that the mass of the planets is negligible compared to the sun's, or that the distance any body falls is negligibly different from zero). Falsity in the reducing premises can thus be conceded, since it is safely confined to those limiting or counterfactual assumptions.

This defense will not deal with all cases of falsity, however, since in some cases the reduced theory is so radically false that some or all of its ontology must be rejected entirely, and the "correspondence rules" connecting that ontology to the newer ontology therefore display a problematic status. Newly conceived features cannot be identical with, nor even nomically connected with, old features, if the old features are illusory and uninstantiated. For example, relativistic mass is not identical with Newtonian mass, nor even coextensive with it, even at low velocities. Nevertheless, the reduction of Newtonian by Einsteinian mechanics is a paradigm of a successful reduction. For a second example, neither is caloric-fluid-pressure identical with, nor even coextensive with, mean molecular kinetic energy. But an overtly *fluid* thermodynamics (i.e., one committed to the existence of caloric) still finds a moderately impressive reduction within statistical thermodynamics. In sum, even theories with a *nonexistent* ontology can enjoy reduction, and this fact is problematic on the traditional account at issue.

What cases like these invite us to give up is the idea that what gets *deduced* in a reduction is the theory to be *reduced*. A more accurate, general, and illuminating schema for intertheoretic reduction is as follows:

$$T_N \& \text{ (Limiting Assumptions \& Boundary Conditions)}$$

logically entails

$$I_N \text{ [a set of theorems of (restricted) } T_N]$$
$$\text{e.g., } (x) (Ax \supset Bx)$$
$$(x) ((Bx \& Cx) \supset Dx)$$

which is relevantly isomorphic with

$$T_O \text{ (the older theory)}$$
$$\text{e.g., } (x) (Jx \supset Kx)$$
$$(x) ((Kx \& Lx) \supset Mx)$$

That is to say, a reduction consists in the deduction, within T_N, not of T_O itself, but rather of a roughly equipotent *image* of T_O, an image still expressed in the vocabulary proper to T_N. The correspondence rules play no part whatever in the *deduction*. They show up only later, and not necessarily as material-mode statements, but as mere ordered pairs: $\langle Ax, Jx \rangle$, $\langle Bx, Kx \rangle$, $\langle Cx, Lx \rangle$, $\langle Dx, Mx \rangle$. Their function is to indicate which term substitutions in the image I_N will yield the principles of T_O. The older theory, accordingly, is never deduced; it is just the target of a relevantly adequate *mimicry*. Construed in this way, a correspondence rule is entirely consistent with the assumption that the older predicate it encompasses has no extension whatever. This allows that a true theory might reduce even a substantially false theory.

The point of a reduction, according to this view, is to show that the new or more comprehensive theory contains explanatory and predictive resources that parallel, to a relevant degree of exactness, the explanatory and predictive resources of the reduced theory. The in*tra*-theoretic deduction (of I_N within T_N), and the in*ter*-theoretic mapping (of T_O into I_N), constitute a fell-swoop demonstration that the older theory can be displaced wholesale by the new, without significant explanatory or predictive loss.[5]

Material-mode statements of identity can occasionally be made, of course. We do wish to assert that visible light = EM waves between .35 μm and .75 μm, that sound = atmospheric compression waves, that temperature = mean molecular KE, and that electric current = net motion of charged particles. But a correspondence rule does not itself make such a claim: at best, it records the fact that the new predicate applies in all those cases where its T_O-doppelganger predicate was normally *thought* to apply. On this view, full-fledged *identity* statements are licensed by the comparative *smoothness* of the relevant reduction (i.e., the limiting assumptions or boundary conditions on T_N are not wildly counterfactual, all or most of T_O's principles find close analogues in I_N, etc.). This smoothness permits the comfortable assimilation of the old ontology within the new and thus allows the old theory to retain all or most of its ontological integrity. *It is smooth intertheoretic reductions that motivate and sustain statements of cross-theoretic identity, not the other way around.*

The preceding framework allows us to frame a useful conception of reduction for specific *properties*, as opposed to entire theories, and it allows us to frame a useful conception of the contrary notion of "emergent" properties. A property F, postulated by an older theory or conceptual framework T_O, is reduced to a property G in some new theory T_N just in case

1. T_N reduces T_O;

2. F and G are correspondence-rule paired in the reduction; and

3. the reduction is sufficiently smooth to sustain the ontology of T_O, and thus to sustain the identity claim, "F-ness = G-ness."

Intuitively, and in the material mode, this means that F-ness reduces to G-ness just in case the "causal powers" of F-ness (as outlined in the laws of T_O) are a subset of the "causal powers" of G-ness (as outlined in the laws of T_N).

Finally, a property F will be said to be an *emergent* property (relative to T_N) just in case

1. F is definitely real and instantiated;

2. F is co-occurrent with some feature or complex circumstance recognized in T_N; but

3. F cannot be *reduced* to any property postulated by or definable within T_N.

Intuitively, this will happen when T_N does not have the resources adequate to define a property with all the "causal powers" possessed by F-ness. Claims about the emergence of certain properties are therefore claims about the relative poverty in the resources of certain aspirant theories.[6] Having outlined these notions, we shall turn to address substantive questions of emergence and irreducibility in a few moments.

Before we do so, several points about reduction need to be emphasized. The first is that, in arguing for the emergence of a given property F relative to some theory T_N, it is not sufficient to point out that the existence or appearance of F-ness cannot be deduced from T_N. It is occasionally claimed, for example, that the objective features of warmth or blueness must be irreducibly emergent properties, since, however much one bends and squeezes the molecular theory concerning H_2O, one cannot deduce from it that water will be *blue*, but only that water will scatter electromagnetic radiation at such-and-such wavelengths. And however much one wrings from the mechanics of molecular motion, one cannot deduce from it that a roaring hearth will be warm, but only that its molecules will have such-and-such a mean kinetic energy and will collectively emit EM radiation at longish wavelengths.

These premises about nondeducibility are entirely true, but the conclusion against reducibility does not follow. It is a serious mistake even to make *in*direct deducibility (i.e., deducibility with the help of correspondence rules) a requirement on successful reduction, as we saw at the beginning of this section. And there are additional reasons why it would be even more foolish to insist on the much stronger condition of direct deducibility. For example, formal considerations alone guarantee that, for any predicate 'F' not already in the proprietary lexicon of the aspirant reducing theory T_N, no statements whatever involving 'F' (beyond tautol- /

ogies and other trivial exceptions) will be deducible from T_N. The deducibility requirement would thus trivialize the notion of reduction by making it impossible for *any* conceptual framework to reduce any other, distinct conceptual framework. Even temperature—that paradigm of a successfully reduced property—would be rendered irreducible, since the term 'temperature' does not appear in the lexicon of statistical mechanics.

There is a further reason why the demand for direct deducibility is too strong. It is a historical accident that we humans currently use precisely the conceptual framework we do use. We might have used any one of an infinite number of other conceptual frameworks to describe the observable world, each one of which could have been roughly adequate to common experience and many of which would be roughly isomorphic (each in its different way) with some part of the correct account that a utopian theory will eventually provide. Accordingly, we can legitimately ask of a putatively correct theory of a given objective domain that it account for the phenomena in (= function successfully in) that domain. But we cannot insist that it also be able to predict how this, that, or the other conceptually idiosyncratic human culture is going to *conceive* of that domain. That would be to insist that the new theory do *predictive cultural anthropology* for us, as well as mechanics, or electromagnetic theory, or what have you. The demand that molecular theory directly entail *our* thermal or color concepts is evidently this same unreasonable demand.

All we can properly ask of a reducing theory is that it have the resources to conjure up a set of properties whose nomological powers/roles/features are systematic *analogues* of the powers/roles/features of the set of properties postulated by the old theory. Since both theories presume to describe the same empirical domain, these systematic nomological parallels constitute the best grounds there can be for concluding that both theories have managed to latch onto the *same* set of objective properties. The hypothesized identity of the properties at issue explains why I_N and T_O are taxonomically and nomically parallel: they are both at least partially correct accounts of the very same objective properties. I_N merely frames that account within a much more penetrating conceptual system—that of T_N.

Moreover, it is to be expected that existing conceptual frameworks will eventually be reduced

or displaced by new and better ones, and those in turn by frameworks better still; for who will be so brash as to assert that the feeble conceptual achievements of our adolescent species comprise an exhaustive account of anything at all? If we put aside this conceit, then the only alternatives to intertheoretic reduction are epistemic stagnation or the outright elimination of old frameworks as wholly false and illusory.

II. *Theoretical Change and Perceptual Change*

Esoteric properties and arcane theoretical frameworks are not the only things that occasionally enjoy intertheoretic reduction. Observable properties and common-sense conceptual frameworks can also enjoy smooth reduction. Thus, being a middle-A sound is identical with being an oscillation in air pressure at 440 hz; being red is identical with having a certain triplet of electromagnetic reflectance efficiencies; being warm is identical with having a certain mean level of microscopically embodied energies, and so forth.

Moreover, the relevant reducing theory is capable of replacing the old framework not just in contexts of calculation and inference. *It should be appreciated that the reducing theory can displace the old framework in all its observational contexts as well.* Given the reality of the property identities just listed, it is quite open to us to begin framing our spontaneous perceptual reports in the language of the more sophisticated reducing theory. It is even desirable that we begin doing this, since the new vocabulary observes distinctions that are in fact within the discriminatory reach of our native perceptual systems, though those objective distinctions go unmarked and unnoticed from within the old framework. We can thus make more penetrating use of our native perceptual equipment. Such displacement is also desirable for a second reason: the greater inferential or computational power of the new conceptual framework. We can thus make better inferential *use* of our new perceptual judgments than we made of our old ones.

It is difficult to convey in words the vastness of such perceptual transformations and the naturalness of the new conceptual regime, once established. A nonscientific example may help to get the initial point across.

Consider the enormous increase in discriminatory skill that spans the gap between an untrained child's auditory apprehension of a symphony and the same person's apprehension of the same symphony forty years later, heard in his capacity as conductor of the orchestra performing it. What was before a seamless voice is now a mosaic of distinguishable elements. What was before a dimly apprehended tune is now a rationally structured sequence of distinguishable and identifiable chords supporting an appropriately related melody line. The matured musician hears an entire world of structured detail, concerning which the child is both dumb and deaf.

Other modalities provide comparable examples. Consider the practiced and chemically sophisticated wine taster, for whom the "red wine" classification used by most of us divides into a network of fifteen or twenty distinguishable elements: ethanol, glycol, fructose, sucrose, tannin, acid, carbon dioxide, and so forth, whose relative concentrations he can estimate with accuracy.

Or consider the astronomer, for whom the speckled black dome of her youth has become a visible abyss, scattering nearby planets, yellow dwarf stars, blue and red giants, distant globular clusters, and even a remote galaxy or two, all discriminable as such and locatable in three-dimensional space with her unaided (repeat: *unaided*) eye.

In each of these cases, what is finally mastered is a conceptual framework—whether musical, chemical, or astronomical—a framework that embodies far more wisdom about the relevant sensory domain than is immediately apparent to untutored discrimination. Such frameworks are characteristically a cultural heritage, pieced together over many generations, and their mastery supplies a richness and penetration to our sensory lives that would be impossible in their absence.[7]

Our *introspective* lives are already the extensive beneficiaries of this phenomenon. The introspective discriminations we make are for the most part learned; they are acquired with practice and experience, often quite slowly. And the specific discriminations we learn to make are those it is useful for us to make. Generally, those are the discriminations that others are already making, the discriminations embodied in the psychological vocabulary of the language we learn. The conceptual framework for

psychological states that is embedded in ordinary language is a modestly sophisticated theoretical achievement in its own right, and it shapes our matured introspection profoundly. If it embodied substantially *less* wisdom in its categories and connecting generalizations, our introspective apprehension of our internal states and activities would be much diminished, though our native discriminatory mechanisms remain the same. Correlatively, if folk psychology embodied substantially *more* wisdom about our inner nature than it actually does, our introspective discrimination and recognition could be very much *greater* than it is, though our native discriminatory mechanisms remain unchanged.

This brings me to the central positive suggestion of this paper. Consider now the possibility of learning to describe, conceive, and introspectively apprehend the teeming intricacies of our inner lives within the conceptual framework of a matured neuroscience, a neuroscience that successfully reduces, either smoothly or roughly, our common-sense folk psychology. Suppose we trained our native mechanisms to make a new and more detailed set of discriminations, a set that corresponded not to the primitive psychological taxonomy of ordinary language, but to some more penetrating taxonomy of states drawn from a completed neuroscience. And suppose we trained ourselves to respond to that reconfigured discriminative activity with judgments that were framed, as a matter of course, in the appropriate concepts from neuroscience.[8]

If the examples of the symphony conductor (who can hear the Am7 chords), the oenologist (who can see and taste the glycol), and the astronomer (who can see the temperature of a blue giant star) provide a fair parallel, then the enhancement in our introspective vision could approximate a revelation. Dopamine levels in the limbic system, the spiking frequencies in specific neural pathways, resonances in the nth layer of the occipital cortex, inhibitory feedback to the lateral geniculate nucleus, and countless other neurophysical niceties could be moved into the objective focus of our introspective discrimination, just as Gm7 chords and Adim chords are moved into the objective focus of a trained musician's auditory discrimination. We will of course have to *learn* the conceptual framework of a matured neuroscience in order to pull this off. And we will have to *practice* its noninferential application. But that seems a small price to pay for the quantum leap in self-apprehension.

All of this suggests that there is no problem at all in conceiving the eventual reduction of mental states and properties to neurophysiological states and properties. A matured and successful neuro-science need only include, or prove able to define, a taxonomy of kinds with a set of embedding laws that faithfully mimics the taxonomy and causal generalizations of *folk* psychology. Whether future neuroscientific theories will prove able to do this is a wholly empirical question, not to be settled a priori. The evidence for a positive answer is substantial and familiar, centering on the growing explanatory success of the several neurosciences.

But there is negative evidence as well: I have even urged some of it myself ("Eliminative Materialism and the Propositional Attitudes," op. cit.). My negative arguments there center on the explanatory and predictive poverty of folk psychology, and they question whether it has the categorial integrity to *merit* the reductive preservation of its familiar ontology. That line suggests substantial revision or outright elimination as the eventual fate of our mentalistic ontology. The qualia-based arguments of Nagel, Jackson, and Robinson, however, take a quite different line. They find no fault with folk psychology. Their concern is with the explanatory and descriptive poverty of any possible *neuro-science*, and their line suggests that emergence is the correct story for our mentalistic ontology. Let us now examine their arguments.

III. *Thomas Nagel's Arguments*

For Thomas Nagel, it is the phenomological features of our experiences, the properties or *qualia* displayed by our sensations, that constitute a problem for the reductive aspirations of any materialistic neuroscience. In his classic position paper (op. cit.) I find three distinct arguments in support of the view that such properties will never find any plausible or adequate reduction within the framework of a matured neuroscience. All three arguments are beguiling, but all three, I shall argue, are unsound.

First Argument. What makes the proposed reduction of mental phenomena different from reductions elsewhere in science, says Nagel, is that

It is impossible to exclude the phenomenological features of experience from a reduction, in the same way that one excludes the phenomenal features of an ordinary substance from a physical or chemical reduction of it—namely, by explaining them as effects on the minds of human observers.

The reason it is impossible to exclude them, continues Nagel, is that the phenomenological features are essential to experience and to the subjective point of view. But this is not what interests me about this argument. What interests me is the claim that reductions of various substances elsewhere in science *exclude the phenomenal features of the substance.*

This is simply false, and the point is extremely important. The phenomenal features at issue are those such as the objective redness of an apple, the warmth of a coffee cup, and the pitch of a sound. These properties are not excluded from our reductions. Redness, an objective phenomenal property of apples, is identical with a certain wavelength triplet of electromagnetic reflectance efficiencies. Warmth, an objective phenomenal property of objects, is identical with the mean level of the objects' microscopically embodied energies. Pitch, an objective phenomenal property of a sound, is identical with its oscillatory frequency. These electromagnetic and micromechanical properties, out there in the objective world, are genuine phenomenal properties. Despite widespread ignorance of their dynamical and microphysical details, it is these objective physical properties to which everyone's perceptual mechanisms are keyed.

The reductions whose existence Nagel denies are in fact so complete that one can already displace entirely large chunks of our common-sense vocabulary for observable properties and learn to frame one's perceptual judgments directly in terms of the reducing theory. The mean KE of the molecules in this room, for example, is currently about . . . 6.2×10^{-21} joules. The oscillatory frequency of this sound (I here whistle C one octave above middle C) is about 524 hz. And the three critical electromagnetic reflectance efficiencies (at .45, .53, and .63 μm) of this (white) piece of paper are all above 80 per cent. These microphysical and electromagnetic properties can be felt, heard, and seen, respectively. Our native sensory mechanisms can easily discriminate such properties, one from another, and their presence from their absence. They have been doing so for millennia. The "resolution" of these mechanisms is inadequate, of course, to reveal the microphysical details and the extended causal roles of the properties thus discriminated. But they are abundantly adequate to permit the reliable discrimination of the properties at issue.[9]

On this view, the standard perceptual properties are not "secondary" properties at all, in the standard sense which implies that they have no real existence save *inside* the minds of human observers. On the contrary, they are as objective as you please, with a wide variety of objective causal properties. Moreover, it would be a mistake even to try to "kick the phenomenal properties inwards," since that would only postpone the problem of reckoning their place in nature. We would only confront them again later, as we address the place in nature of mental phenomena. And, as Nagel correctly points out, the relocation dodge is no longer open to us, once the problematic properties are already located within the mind.

Nagel concludes from this that subjective qualia are unique in being immune from the sort of reductions found elsewhere in science. I draw a very different conclusion. The *objective* qualia (redness, warmth, etc.) should never have been "kicked inwards to the minds of observers" in the first place. They should be confronted squarely, and they should be reduced where they stand: *out*side the human observer. As we saw, this can and has in fact been done. If objective phenomenal properties are so treated, then *subjective* qualia can be confronted with parallel forthrightness, and can be reduced where *they* stand: *in*side the human observer. So far then, the external and the internal case are not different: they are parallel after all.

Second Argument. A second argument urges the point that the intrinsic character of experiences, the qualia of sensations, are essentially accessible from only a single point of view, the subjective point of view of the experiencing subject. The properties of physical brain states, by contrast, are accessible from a variety of entirely objective points of view. We cannot hope adequately to account for the former, therefore, in terms of properties appropriate to the latter domain (cf. Nagel).

This somewhat diffuse argument appears to be an instance of the following argument:

1. The qualia of my sensations are directly known by me, by introspection, as elements of my conscious self.

2. The properties of my brain states are *not* directly known by me, by introspection, as elements of my conscious self.

∴**3.** The qualia of my sensations ≠ the properties of my brain states.

And perhaps there is a second argument here as well, a complement to the first:

1. The properties of my brain states are known-by-the-various-external-senses, as having such-and-such physical properties.

2. The qualia of my sensations are *not* known-by-the-various-external-senses, as having such-and-such physical properties.

∴**3.** The qualia of my sensations ≠ the properties of my brain states.

The argument form here is apparently

1. Fa

2. $\sim Fb$

∴**3.** $a \neq b$

Given Leibniz's law and the extensional nature of the property F, this is a valid argument form. But, in the examples at issue, F is obviously not an extensional property. The fallacy committed in both cases is amply illustrated in the following parallel arguments.

1. Hitler is widely recognized as a mass murderer.

2. Adolf Schicklgruber is *not* widely recognized as a mass murderer.

∴**3.** Hitler ≠ Adolf Schicklgruber.

or

1. Aspirin is known by John to be a pain reliever.

2. Acetylsalicylic acid is *not* known by John to be a pain reliever.

∴**3.** Aspirin ≠ acetylsalicylic acid.

or, to cite an example very close to the case at issue,

1. Temperature is known by me, by tactile sensing, as a feature of material objects.

2. Mean molecular kinetic energy is *not* known by me, by tactile sensing, as a feature of material objects.

∴**3.** Temperature ≠ mean molecular kinetic energy.

The problem with all these arguments is that the "property" ascribed in premise 1 and withheld in premise 2 consists only in the subject item's being *recognized, perceived,* or *known* as something, *under some specific description or other.* Such apprehension is not a genuine feature of the item itself, fit for divining identities, since one and the same subject may be successfully recognized under one description (e.g., "qualia of my mental state"), and yet fail to be recognized under another, equally accurate, coreferential description (e.g., "property of my brain state"). In logician's terms, the propositional function:

x is known (perceived, recognized) by me, as an F

is one of a large number of *intensional contexts* whose distinguishing feature is that they do not always retain the same truth value through substitution of a coreferential or coextensive term for whatever holds the place of 'x.' Accordingly, that such a context (i.e., the one at issue) should show a difference in truth value for two terms 'a' and 'b' (i.e., 'qualia of my sensations' and 'property of my brain-states') is therefore hardly grounds for concluding that 'a' and 'b' cannot be coreferential or coextensive terms![10]

This objection is decisive, I think, but it does not apply to a different version of the argument, which we must also consider. It may be urged that one's brain states are more than merely not (yet) known by introspection: they are not knowa*ble* by introspection under any circumstances. In correspondence, Thomas Nagel has advised me that what he wishes to defend is the following *modalized* version of the argument:

1. My mental states are knowable by me by introspection.

2. My brain states are *not* knowable by me by introspection.

∴**3.** My mental states ≠ my brain states.

Here Nagel will insist that being knowable-by-me-by-introspection is a genuine relational property of a thing and that this version of the argument is free of the intensional fallacy discussed above.

And so it is. But now the reductionist is in a position to insist that the argument contains a false premise: premise 2. At the very least, he can insist that (2) begs the question. For if mental states are indeed identical with brain states, then it is really brain states that we have been introspecting all along, though without appreciating their fine-grained nature. And if we can learn to think of and recognize those states under their familiar mentalistic descriptions—*as all of us have*—then we can certainly learn to think of and recognize them under their more pentrating neurophysiological descriptions. Brain states, that is, are indeed knowa*ble* by introspection, and Nagel's argument commits the same error instanced below.

1. Temperature is knowable by tactile sensing.

2. Mean molecular kinetic energy is *not* knowable by tactile sensing.

∴**3.** Temperature ≠ mean molecular kinetic energy.

Here the conclusion is known to be false. Temperature is indeed mean molecular kinetic energy. Since the argument is valid, it must therefore have a false premise. Premise 2 is clearly the stinker. Just as one can learn to feel that the summer air is about 70°F, or 21°C, so one can learn to feel that the mean KE of its molecules is about 6.2×10^{-21} joules; for, whether we realize it or not, that is the property our native discriminatory mechanisms are keyed to. And if one can come to know, by feeling, the mean KE of atmospheric molecules, why is it unthinkable that one might come to know, by introspection, the states of one's brain? (What would that feel like? It would feel exactly the same as introspecting the states of one's mind, since they are one and the same states. One would simply employ a different and more penetrating conceptual framework in their description.)

One must be careful, in evaluating the plausibility of Nagel's second premise, to distinguish it from the second premise of the very first version of the argument, the version that commits the intensional fallacy. My guess is that Nagel has profited somewhat from the ambiguity here. For, in the first version, both premises are true. And in the second version, the argument is valid. Neither version, however, meets both conditions.

The matter of introspecting one's brain states will arise once more in the final section of this paper. For now, let us move on.

Third Argument. The last argument here is the one most widely associated with Nagel's paper. The leading example is the (mooted) character of the experiences enjoyed by an alien creature such as a bat. The claim is that, no matter how much one knew about the bat's neurophysiology and its interaction with the physical world, one could still not know, nor perhaps even imagine, what it is like to be a bat. Even total knowledge of the physical details still leaves something out. The lesson drawn is that the reductive aspirations of neurophysiology are doomed to dash themselves, unrealized, against the impenetrable keep of subjective qualia.

This argument is almost identical with an argument put forward in a recent paper by Frank Jackson.[11] Since Jackson's version deals directly with humans, I shall confront the problem as he formulates it.

IV. *Jackson's Knowledge Argument*

Imagine a brilliant neuroscientist named Mary, who has lived her entire life in a room that is rigorously controlled to display only various shades of black, white, and grey. She learns about the outside world by means of a black/white television monitor, and, being brilliant, she manages to transcend these obstacles. She becomes the world's greatest neuroscientist, all from within this room. In particular, she comes to know everything there is to know about the physical structure and activity of the brain and its visual system, of its actual and possible states.

But there would still be something she did *not* know, and could not even imagine, about the actual experiences of all the other people who live outside her black/white room, and about her possible experiences were she finally to leave her room: the nature of the experience of seeing a ripe tomato, what it is like to see red or have a sensation-of-red. Therefore, complete knowledge of the physical facts of visual perception and its related brain activity *still leaves something out*. Therefore, materialism cannot give an adequate reductionist account of all mental phenomena.

To give a conveniently tightened version of this argument:

1. Mary knows everything there is to know about brain states and their properties.

2. It is not the case that Mary knows everything there is to know about sensations and their properties.

Therefore, by Leibniz's law,

3. Sensations and their properties $\neq$ brain states and their properties.

It is tempting to insist that we here confront just another instance of the intensional fallacy discussed earlier, but Jackson's defenders[12] insist that 'knows *about*' is a perfectly transparent, entirely extensional context. Let us suppose that it is. We can, I think, find at least two other shortcomings in this sort of argument.

The First Shortcoming. This defect is simplicity itself. 'Knows about' may be transparent in both premises, but it is not *univocal* in both premises. (David Lewis[13] and Laurence Nemirow[14] have both raised this same objection, though their analysis of the ambiguity at issue differs from mine.) Jackson's argument is valid only if 'knows about' is univocal in both premises. But the kind of knowledge addressed in premise 1 seems pretty clearly to be different from the kind of knowledge addressed in (2). Knowledge in (1) seems to be a matter of having mastered a set of sentences or propositions, the kind one finds written in neuroscience texts, whereas knowledge in (2) seems to be a matter of having a representation of redness in some prelinguistic or sublinguistic medium of representation for sensory variables, or to be a matter of being able to *make* certain sensory discriminations, or something along these lines.

Lewis and Nemirow plump for the "ability" analysis of the relevant sense of 'knows about', but they need not be so narrowly committed, and the complaint of equivocation need not be so narrowly based. As my alternative gloss illustrates, other analyses of 'knowledge by acquaintance' are possible, and the charge of equivocation will be sustained so long as the type of knowledge invoked in premise 1 is distinct from the type invoked in premise 2. Importantly, they do seem very different, even in advance of a settled analysis of the latter.

In short, the difference betwen a person who knows all about the visual cortex but has never enjoyed a sensation of red, and a person who knows no neuroscience but knows well the sensation of red, may reside not in *what* is respectively known by each (brain states by the former, qualia by the latter), but rather in the different *type* of knowledge each has *of exactly the same thing*. The difference is in the manner of the knowing, not in the nature of the thing(s) known. If one replaces the ambiguous occurrences of 'knows about' in Jackson's argument with the two different expansions suggested above, the resulting argument is a clear non sequitur.

a. Mary has mastered the complete set of true propositions about people's brain states.

b. Mary does *not* have a representation of redness in her prelinguistic medium of representation for sensory variables.

Therefore, by Leibniz's law,

c. The redness sensation ≠ any brain state.

Premises a and b are compossible, even on a materialist view. But they do not entail (c).

In sum, there are pretty clearly more ways of "having knowledge" than having mastered a set of sentences. And nothing in materialism precludes this. The materialist can freely admit that one has "knowledge" of one's sensations in a way that is independent of the scientific theories one has learned. This does not mean that sensations are beyond the reach of physical science. *It just means that the brain uses more modes and media of representation than the simple storage of sentences.* And this proposition is pretty obviously true: almost certainly the brain uses a considerable variety of modes and media of representation, perhaps hundreds of them. Jackson's argument, and Nagel's, exploit this variety illegitimately: both arguments equivocate on 'knows about.'

This criticism is supported by the observation that, if Jackson's form of argument were sound, it would prove far too much. Suppose that Jackson were arguing, not against materialism, but against dualism: against the view that there exists a nonmaterial substance—call it "ectoplasm"—whose

hidden constitution and nomic intricacies ground all mental phenomena. Let our cloistered Mary be an "ectoplasmologist" this time, and let her know₁ everything there is to know about the ectoplasmic processes underlying vision. There would still be something she did not know₂: what it is like to see red. Dualism is therefore inadequate to account for all mental phenomena!

This argument is as plausible as Jackson's, and for the same reason: it exploits the same equivocation. But the truth is, such arguments show nothing, one way or the other, about how mental phenomena might be accounted for.

The Second Shortcoming. There is a further shortcoming with Jackson's argument, one of profound importance for understanding one of the most exciting consequences to be expected from a successful neuroscientific account of mind. I draw your attention to the assumption that even a utopian knowledge of neuroscience *must* leave Mary hopelessly in the dark about the subjective qualitative nature of sensations not-yet-enjoyed. It is true, of course, that no sentence of the form "x is a sensation-of-red" will be deducible from premises restricted to the language of neuroscience. But this is no point against the reducibility of phenomenological properties. As we saw in section I, direct deducibility is an intolerably strong demand on reduction, and if this is all the objection comes to, then there is no objection worth addressing. What the defender of emergent qualia must have in mind here, I think, is the claim that Mary could not even *imagine* what the relevant experience would be like, despite her exhaustive neuroscientific knowledge, and hence must still be missing certain crucial information.

This claim, however, is simply false. Given the truth of premise 1, premise 2 seems plausible to Jackson, Nagel, and Robinson only because none of these philosophers has adequately considered how much one might know if, as premise 1 asserts, one knew *everything* there is to know about the physical brain and nervous system. In particular, none of these philosophers has even begun to consider the changes in our introspective apprehension of our internal states that could follow upon a wholesale revision in our conceptual framework for our internal states.

The fact is, we can indeed imagine how neuroscientific information would give Mary detailed information about the qualia of various sensations.

Recall our earlier discussion of the transformation of perception through the systematic reconceptualization of the relevant perceptual domain. In particular, suppose that Mary has learned to conceptualize her inner life, even in introspection, in terms of the completed neuroscience we are to imagine. So she does not identify her visual sensations crudely as "a sensation-of-black," "a sensation-of-grey," or "a sensation-of-white"; rather she identifies them more revealingly as various spiking frequencies in the nth layer of the occipital cortex (or whatever). If Mary has the relevant neuroscientific concepts for the sensational states at issue (viz., sensations-of-*red*), but has never yet been *in* those states, she may well be able to imagine being in the relevant cortical state, and imagine it with substantial success, even in advance of receiving external stimuli that would actually produce it.

One test of her ability in this regard would be to give her a stimulus that would (finally) produce in her the relevant state (viz., a spiking frequency of 90 hz in the gamma network: a "sensation-of-red" to us), and see whether she can identify it correctly *on introspective grounds alone*, as "a spiking frequency of 90 hz: the kind a tomato would cause." It does not seem to me to be impossible that she should succeed in this, and do so regularly on similar tests for other states, conceptualized clearly by her, but not previously enjoyed.

This may seem to some an outlandish suggestion, but the following will show that it is not. Musical chords are auditory phenomena that the young and unpracticed ear hears as undivided wholes, discriminable one from another, but without elements or internal structure. A musical education changes this, and one comes to hear chords as groups of discriminable notes. If one is sufficiently practiced to have absolute pitch, one can even name the notes of an apprehended chord. And the reverse is also true: if a set of notes is specified verbally, a trained pianist or guitarist can identify the chord and recall its sound in auditory imagination. Moreover, a really skilled individual can construct, in auditory imagination, the sound of a chord he may never have heard before, and certainly does not remember. Specify for him a relatively unusual one—an F#9th*add* 13th for example—and let him brood for a bit. Then play for him three or four chords, one of which is the target, and see whether he can pick it out as the sound that meets the description. Skilled musicians can do

this. Why is a similar skill beyond all possibility for Mary?

"Ah," it is tempting to reply, "musicians can do this only because chords are audibly structured sets of elements. Sensations of color are not."

But neither did chords seem, initially, to be structured sets of elements. They also seemed to be undifferentiated wholes. Why should it be unthinkable that sensations of color possess a comparable internal structure, unnoticed so far, but awaiting our determined and informed inspection? Jackson's argument, to be successful, must rule this possibility out, and it is difficult to see how he can do this *a priori*. Especially since there has recently emerged excellent empirical evidence to suggest that *our sensations of color are indeed structured sets of elements*.

The retinex theory of color vision recently proposed by Edwin Land[15] represents any color apprehendable by the human visual system as being uniquely specified by its joint position along three vertices—its reflectance efficiences at three critical wavelengths, those wavelengths to which the retina's triune cone system is selectively responsive. Since colors are apprehended by us, it is a good hypothesis that those three parameters are represented in our visual systems and that our sensations of color are in some direct way determined by them. Sensations of color may turn out literally to *be* three-element chords in some neural medium! In the face of all this, I do not see why it is even briefly plausible to insist that it is utterly impossible for a conceptually sophisticated Mary accurately to imagine, and subsequently to pick out, color sensations she has not previously enjoyed. We can already foresee how it might actually be done.

The preceding argument does not collapse the distinction (between knowledge-by-description and knowledge-by-acquaintance) urged earlier in the discussion of equivocation. But it does show that the "taxonomies" that reside in our prelinguistic media of representation can be profoundly shaped by the taxonomies that reside in the linguistic medium, especially if one has had long practice at the observational discrimination of items that answer to those linguistically embodied categories. This is just a further illustration of the plasticity of human perception.

I do not mean to suggest, of course, that there will be no limits to what Mary can imagine. Her brain is finite, and its specific anatomy will have specific limitations. For example, if a bat's brain includes computational machinery that the human brain simply lacks (which seems likely), then the subjective character of *some* of the bat's internal states may well be beyond human imagination. Clearly, however, the elusiveness of the bat's inner life here stems not from the metaphysical "emergence" of its internal qualia, but only from the finite capacities of our idiosyncratically human brains. Within those sheerly structural limitations, our imaginations may soar far beyond what Jackson, Nagel, and Robinson suspect, if we possess a neuroscientific conceptual framework that is at last adequate to the intricate phenomena at issue.

I suggest then, that those of us who prize the flux and content of our subjective phenomenological experience need not view the advance of materialistic neuroscience with fear and foreboding. Quite the contrary. The genuine arrival of a materialist kinematics and dynamics for psychological states and cognitive processes will constitute not a gloom in which our inner life is suppressed or eclipsed, but rather a dawning, in which its marvelous intricacies are finally *revealed*—most notably, if we apply ourselves, in direct self-conscious introspection.

Endnotes

[1] "What Is It Like to Be a Bat?" *Philosophical Review*, I., XXXXIII. 4 (October 1974): 435–450; page references to Nagel are to this paper.

[2] "Epiphenomenal Qualia," *Philosophical Quarterly*, XXXII. 127 (April 1982): 127–136.

[3] *Matter and Sense* (New York: Cambridge, 1982), p. 4.

[4] Ernest Nagel, *The Structures of Science* (New York: Harcourt, Brace & World, 1961), ch. 11.

[5] This sketch of intertheoretic reduction is drawn from my *Scientific Realism and the Plasticity of Mind* (New York: Cambridge, 1979), section 11. For a more detailed account see Clifford A. Hooker, "Towards a General Theory of Reduction," *Dialogue*, xx, 1, 2, 3 (March, June, September 1981): 38–59, 201–236, 496–529.

[6] A word of caution is perhaps in order here, since the expression 'emergent property' is often used in two diametrically opposed senses. In scientific contexts, one frequently hears it used to apply to what might be called a "network property," a property that appears exactly when the elements of some substrate are suitably organized, a property that *consists* in the elements of that substrate standing in certain relations to one another, a set of relations that collectively sustain the set of causal powers ascribed to the "emergent" property. In this innocent sense of 'emergent,' there are a great many emergent properties, and quite probably the qualia of our sensations should be numbered among them. But in philosophical contexts one more often encounters a different sense of 'emergent,' one that implies that an "emergent" property does *not* consist in any collective or organizational feature of its substrate. The first sense positively implies reducibility; the second implies *ir*reducibility. It is emergence in the second sense that is at issue in this paper.

[7] The role of theory in perception, and the systematic enhancement of perception through theoretical progress, are examined at length in my *Scientific Realism and the Plasticity of Mind*, op. cit. secs. 1–6.

[8] I believe it was Paul K. Feyerabend and Richard Rorty who first identified and explored this suggestion. See Feyerabend, "Materialism and the Mind-Body Problem," *Review of Metaphysics*, XVIII.1, 65 (September 1963); 49–66: and Rorty, "Mind-Body Identity, Privacy, and Categories", ibid. XIX.1, 73 (September 1965): 24–54. This occurred in a theoretical environment prepared largely by Wilfrid Sellars in "Empiricism and the Philosophy of Mind," in Herbert Feigl and Michael Scriven, eds., *Minnesota Studies in the Philosophy of Mind*, vol. I (Minneapolis: University of Minnesota Press, 1956): secs. 45–63. The idea has been explored more recently in my "Eliminative Materialism and the Propositional Attitudes," *Journal of Philosophy*, I.XXVIII, 2 (February 1981): 67–90.

[9] See again my *Scientific Realism and the Plasticity of Mind*, op. cit., specs. 2–6. See also Paul and Patricia Churchland, "Functionalism, Qualia, and Intentionality", *Philosophical Topics*, XII, 1 (October 1981): 121–145. Reprinted in J. I. Biro and R. W. Shahan, eds., in *Mind, Brain, and Function* (Norman: U. of Oklahoma Press, 1982): 121–145.

[10] I believe it was Richard Brandt and Jaegwon Kim who first identified this fallacy specificially in connection with the identity theory, in "The Logic of the Identity Theory," *Journal of Philosophy* 64, no. 7 (September 1967): 515–537.

[11] "Epiphenomenal Qualia," op. cit. Howard Robinson runs a very similar argument in *Matter and Sense*, op. cit., p. 4.

[12] See, for example, Keith Campbell, "Abstract Particulars and the Philosophy of Mind," *Australasian Journal of Philosophy*, LXI, 2 (June 1983): 129–141.

[13] "Postscript to "Mad Pain and Martian Pain," *Philosophical Papers*, vol. I (New York: Oxford, 1983).

[14] Review of Thomas Nagel, *Mortal Questions*, *Philosophical Review*, LXXXIX, 3 (July 1980): 473–477.

[15] "The Retinex Theory of Color Vision," *Scientific American* (December 1977): 108–128.

30. Is *the Brain's Mind a Computer Program?*

JOHN R. SEARLE

It is commonplace knowledge that computers can perform numerical calculations, win chess games, and govern the complex behavior of robots. They are able to do so because they embody a program—a set of instructions that governs their transitions from one information processing state to another. It has long been appreciated that programs (and the states of computers) need only be described in functional terms if one wants to understand what they are doing (e.g., calculating, playing chess, or maneuvering a satellite); in this regard, they are provocatively similar to functional descriptions of mental states (see the earlier selections by Dennett and Putnam). Thus, the questions have naturally arisen: Could a computer with a sufficiently sophisticated program actually be conscious? and Might not our consciousness be understandable in terms of our brains having a program of some complex kind? In this article, John Searle, professor of philosophy at the University of California, Berkeley, answers no to the second question. He claims programs merely manipulate symbols, while consciousness involves the apprehension of their meaning.

Can a machine think? Can a machine have conscious thoughts in exactly the same sense that you and I have? If by "machine" one means a physical system capable of performing certain functions (and what else can one mean?), then humans are machines of a special biological kind, and humans can think, and so of course machines can think. And, for all we know, it might be possible to produce a thinking machine out of different materials altogether—say, out of silicon chips or vacuum tubes. Maybe it will turn out to be impossible, but we certainly do not know that yet.

In recent decades, however, the question of whether a machine can think has been given a different interpretation entirely. The question that has been posed in its place is, Could a machine think just by virtue of implementing a computer program? Is the program by itself constitutive of thinking? This is a completely different question because it is not about the physical, causal properties of actual or possible physical systems but rather about the abstract, computational properties of formal computer programs that can be implemented in any sort of substance at all, provided only that the substance is able to carry the program.

A fair number of researchers in artificial intelligence (AI) believe the answer to the second question is yes; that is, they believe that by designing the right programs with the right inputs and outputs, they are literally creating minds. They believe furthermore that they have a scientific test for determining success or failure: the Turing test devised by Alan M. Turing, the founding father of artificial intelligence. The Turing test, as currently understood, is simply this: if a computer can perform in such a way that an expert cannot distinguish its performance from that of a human who has a certain cognitive ability—say, the ability to do addition or to understand Chinese—then the computer also has that ability. So the goal is to design programs that will simulate human cognition in such a way as to pass the Turing test. What is more, such a program would not merely be a model of the mind; it would literally be a mind, in the same sense that a human mind is a mind.

"Is the Brain's Mind a Computer Program?" originally appeared in *Scientific American* (January 1990). Reprinted with permission. Copyright © 1990 by Scientific American, Inc. All rights reserved.

By no means does every worker in artificial intelligence accept so extreme a view. A more cautious approach is to think of computer models as being useful in studying the mind in the same way that they are useful in studying the weather, economics or molecular biology. To distinguish these two approaches, I call the first strong AI and the second weak AI. It is important to see just how bold an approach strong AI is. Strong AI claims that thinking is merely the manipulation of formal symbols, and that is exactly what the computer does: manipulate formal symbols. This view is often summarized by saying, "The mind is to the brain as the program is to the hardware" . . .

Strong AI is unusual among theories of the mind in at least two respects: it can be stated clearly, and it admits of a simple and decisive refutation. The refutation is one that any person can try for himself or herself. Here is how it goes. Consider a language you don't understand. In my case, I do not understand Chinese. To me Chinese writing looks like so many meaningless squiggles. Now suppose I am placed in a room containing baskets full of Chinese symbols. Suppose also that I am given a rule book in English for matching Chinese symbols with other Chinese symbols. The rules identify the symbols entirely by their shapes and do not require that I understand any of them. The rules might say such things as, "Take a squiggle-squiggle sign from basket number one and put it next to a squoggle-squoggle sign from basket number two."

Imagine that people outside the room who understand Chinese hand in small bunches of symbols and that in response I manipulate the symbols according to the rule book and hand back more small bunches of symbols. Now, the rule book is the "computer program." The people who wrote it are "programmers," and I am the "computer." The baskets full of symbols are the "data base," the small bunches that are handed in to me are "questions" and the bunches I then hand out are "answers."

Now suppose that the rule book is written in such a way that my "answers" to the "questions" are indistinguishable from those of a native Chinese speaker. For example, the people outside might hand me some symbols that unknown to me mean, "What's your favorite color?" and I might after going through the rules give back symbols that, also unknown to me, mean, "My favorite is

blue, but I also like green a lot." I satisfy the Turing test for understanding Chinese. All the same, I am totally ignorant of Chinese. And there is no way I could come to understand Chinese in the system as described, since there is no way that I can learn the meanings of any of the symbols. Like a computer, I manipulate symbols, but I attach no meaning to the symbols.

The point of the thought experiment is this: if I do not understand Chinese solely on the basis of running a computer program for understanding Chinese, then neither does any other digital computer solely on that basis. Digital computers merely manipulate formal symbols according to rules in the program.

What goes for Chinese goes for other forms of cognition as well. Just manipulating the symbols is not by itself enough to guarantee cognition, perception, understanding, thinking and so forth. And since computers, qua computers, are symbol-manipulating devices, merely running the computer program is not enough to guarantee cognition.

This simple argument is decisive against the claims of strong AI. The first premise of the argument simply states the formal character of a computer program. Programs are defined in terms of symbol manipulations, and the symbols are purely formal, or "syntactic." The formal character of the program, by the way, is what makes computers so powerful. The same program can be run on an indefinite variety of hardwares, and one hardware system can run an indefinite range of computer programs. Let me abbreviate this "axiom" as

Axiom 1. *Computer programs are formal (syntactic).*

This point is so crucial that it is worth explaining in more detail. A digital computer processes information by first encoding it in the symbolism that the computer uses and then manipulating the symbols through a set of precisely stated rules. These rules constitute the program. For example, in Turing's early theory of computers, the symbols were simply 0's and 1's, and the rules of the program said such things as, "Print a 0 on the tape, move one square to the left and erase a 1." The astonishing thing about computers is that any information that can be stated in a language can be encoded in such a system, and any information-processing task that can be solved by explicit rules can be programmed.

Two further points are important. First, symbols and programs are purely abstract notions: they have no essential physical properties to define them and can be implemented in any physical medium whatsoever. The 0's and 1's, qua symbols, have no essential physical properties and a fortiori have no physical, causal properties. I emphasize this point because it is tempting to identify computers with some specific technology—say, silicon chips—and to think that the issues are about the physics of silicon chips or to think that syntax identifies some physical phenomenon that might have as yet unknown causal powers, in the way that actual physical phenomena such as electromagnetic radiation or hydrogen atoms have physical, causal properties. The second point is that symbols are manipulated without reference to any meanings. The symbols of the program can stand for anything the programmer or user wants. In this sense the program has syntax but no semantics.

The next axiom is just a reminder of the obvious fact that thoughts, perceptions, understandings and so forth have a mental content. By virtue of their content they can be about objects and states of affairs in the world. If the content involves language, there will be syntax in addition to semantics, but linguistic understanding requires at least a semantic framework. If, for example, I am thinking about the last presidential election, certain words will go through my mind, but the words are about the election only because I attach specific meanings to these words, in accordance with my knowledge of English. In this respect they are unlike Chinese symbols for me. Let me abbreviate this axiom as

Axiom 2. *Human minds have mental contents (semantics).*

Now let me add the point that the Chinese room demonstrated. Having the symbols by themselves—just having the syntax—is not sufficient for having the semantics. Merely manipulating symbols is not enough to guarantee knowledge of what they mean. I shall abbreviate this as

Axiom 3. *Syntax by itself is neither constitutive of nor sufficient for semantics.*

At one level this principle is true by definition. One might, of course, define the terms syntax and semantics differently. The point is that there is a distinction between formal elements, which have no intrinsic meaning or content, and those phenomena that have intrinsic content. From these premises it follows that

I satisfy the Turing test for understanding Chinese

Conclusion 1. *Programs are neither constitutive of nor sufficient for minds.*

And that is just another way of saying that strong AI is false.

It is important to see what is proved and not proved by this argument.

First, I have not tried to prove that "a computer cannot think." Since anything that can be simulated computationally can be described as a computer, and since our brains can at some levels be simulated, it follows trivially that our brains are computers and they can certainly think. But from the fact that a system can be simulated by symbol manipulation and the fact that it is thinking, it does not follow that thinking is equivalent to formal symbol manipulation.

Second, I have not tried to show that only biologically based systems like our brains can think. Right now those are the only systems we know for a fact can think, but we might find other systems in the universe that can produce conscious thoughts, and we might even come to be able to create thinking systems artificially. I regard this issue as up for grabs.

Third, strong AI's thesis is not that, for all we know, computers with the right programs might be thinking, that they might have some as yet undetected psychological properties; rather it is that they must be thinking because that is all there is to thinking.

Fourth, I have tried to refute strong AI so defined. I have tried to demonstrate that the program by itself is not constitutive of thinking because the program is purely a matter of formal symbol manipulation—and we know independently that symbol manipulations by themselves are not sufficient to guarantee the presence of meanings. That is the principle on which the Chinese room argument works.

I emphasize these points here partly because it seems to me the Churchlands [see (following article), "Could a Machine Think?"] have not quite understood the issues. They think that strong AI is claiming that computers might turn out to think and that I am denying this possibility on commonsense grounds. But that is not the claim of strong AI, and my argument against it has nothing to do with common sense.

I will have more to say about their objections later. Meanwhile I should point out that, contrary to what the Churchlands suggest, the Chinese room argument also refutes any strong-AI claims made for the new parallel technologies that are inspired by and modeled on neural networks. Unlike the traditional von Neumann computer, which proceeds in a step-by-step fashion, these systems have many computational elements that operate in parallel and interact with one another according to rules inspired by neurobiology. Although the results are still modest, these "parallel distributed processing," or "connectionist," models raise useful questions about how complex, parallel network systems like those in brains might actually function in the production of intelligent behavior.

The parallel, "brainlike" character of the processing, however, is irrelevant to the purely computational aspects of the process. Any function that can be computed on a parallel machine can also be computed on a serial machine. Indeed, because parallel machines are still rare, connectionist programs are usually run on traditional serial machines. Parallel processing, then, does not afford a way around the Chinese room argument.

What is more, the connectionist system is subject even on its own terms to a variant of the objection presented by the original Chinese room argument. Imagine that instead of a Chinese room, I have a Chinese gym: a hall containing many monolingual, English-speaking men. These men would carry out the same operations as the nodes and synapses in a connectionist architecture as described by the Churchlands, and the outcome would be the same as having one man manipulate symbols according to a rule book. No one in the gym speaks a word of Chinese, and there is no way for the system as a whole to learn the meanings of any Chinese words. Yet with appropriate adjustments, the system could give the correct answers to Chinese questions.

There are, as I suggested earlier, interesting properties of connectionist nets that enable them to simulate brain processes more accurately than traditional serial architecture does. But the advantages of parallel architecture for weak AI are quite irrelevant to the issues between the Chinese room argument and strong AI.

The Churchlands miss this point when they say that a big enough Chinese gym might have higher-level mental features that emerge from the size and complexity of the system, just as whole brains have mental features that are not had by individual neurons. That is, of course, a possibility, but it has nothing to do with computation.

Computationally, serial and parallel systems are equivalent: any computation that can be done in parallel can be done in serial. If the man in the Chinese room is computationally equivalent to both, then if he does not understand Chinese solely by virtue of doing the computations, neither do they. The Churchlands are correct in saying that the original Chinese room argument was designed with traditional AI in mind but wrong in thinking that connectionism is immune to the argument. It applies to any computational system. You can't get semantically loaded thought contents from formal computations alone, whether they are done in serial or in parallel; that is why the Chinese room argument refutes strong AI in any form.

Many people who are impressed by this argument are nonetheless puzzled about the differences between people and computers. If humans are, at least in a trivial sense, computers, and if humans have a semantics, then why couldn't we give semantics to other computers? Why couldn't

we program a Vax or a Cray so that it too would have thoughts and feelings? Or why couldn't some new computer technology overcome the gulf between form and content, between syntax and semantics? What, in fact, are the differences between animal brains and computer systems that enable the Chinese room argument to work against computers but not against brains?

The most obvious difference is that the processes that define something as a computer—computational processes—are completely independent of any reference to a specific type of hardware implementation. One could in principle make a computer out of old beer cans strung together with wires and powered by windmills.

But when it comes to brains, although science is largely ignorant of how brains function to produce mental states, one is struck by the extreme specificity of the anatomy and the physiology. Where some understanding exists of how brain processes produce mental phenomena—for example, pain, thirst, vision, smell—it is clear that spe-

Computer programs are formal (syntactic).
Human minds have mental contents (semantics)

cific neurobiological processes are involved. Thirst, at least of certain kinds, is caused by certain types of neuron firings in the hypothalamus, which in turn are caused by the action of a specific peptide, angiotensin II. The causation is from the "bottom up" in the sense that lower-level neuronal processes cause higher-level mental phenomena. Indeed, as far as we know, every "mental" event, ranging from feelings of thirst to thoughts of mathematical theorems and memories of childhood, is caused by specific neurons firing in specific neural architectures.

But why should this specificity matter? After all, neuron firings could be simulated on computers that had a completely different physics and chemistry from that of the brain. The answer is that the brain does not merely instantiate a formal pattern or program (it does that, too), but it also *causes* mental events by virtue of specific neurobiological processes. Brains are specific biological organs, and their specific biochemical properties enable them to cause consciousness and other sorts of mental phenomena. Computer simulations of brain processes provide models of the formal aspects of these processes. But the simulation should not be confused with duplication. The computational model of mental processes is no more real than the computational model of any other natural phenomenon.

One can imagine a computer simulation of the action of peptides in the hypothalamus that is accurate down to the last synapse. But equally one can imagine a computer simulation of the oxidation of hydrocarbons in a car engine or the action of digestive processes in a stomach when it is digesting pizza. And the simulation is no more the real thing in the case of the brain than it is in the case of the car or the stomach. Barring miracles, you could not run your car by doing a computer simulation of the oxidation of gasoline, and you could not digest pizza by running the program that simulates such digestion. It seems obvious that a simulation of cognition will similarly not produce the effects of the neurobiology of cognition.

All mental phenomena, then, are caused by neurophysiological processes in the brain. Hence,

Axiom 4. *Brains cause minds.*

In conjunction with my earlier derivation, I immediately derive, trivially,

Conclusion 2. *Any other system capable of causing minds would have to have causal powers (at least) equivalent to those of brains.*

This is like saying that if an electrical engine is to be able to run a car as fast as a gas engine, it must have (at least) an equivalent power output. This conclusion says nothing about the mechanisms. As a matter of fact, cognition is a biological phenomenon: mental states and processes are caused by brain processes. This does not imply that only a biological system could think, but it does imply that any alternative system, whether made of silicon, beer cans or whatever, would have to have the relevant causal capacities equivalent to those of brains. So now I can derive

Conclusion 3. *Any artifact that produced mental phenomena, any artificial brain, would have to be able to duplicate the specific causal powers of brains, and it could not do that just by running a formal program.*

Furthermore, I can derive an important conclusion about human brains:

Conclusion 4. *The way that human brains actually produce mental phenomena cannot be solely by virtue of running a computer program.*

I first presented the Chinese room parable in the pages of *Behavioral and Brain Sciences* in 1980, where it appeared, as is the practice of the journal, along with peer commentary, in this case, 26 commentaries. Frankly, I think the point it makes is rather obvious, but to my surprise the publication was followed by a further flood of objections that—more surprisingly—continues to the present day. The Chinese room argument clearly touched some sensitive nerve.

The thesis of strong AI is that any system whatsoever—whether it is made of beer cans, silicon chips or toilet paper—not only might have thoughts and feelings but *must* have thoughts and feelings, provided only that it implements the right program, with the right inputs and outputs. Now, that is a profoundly antibiological view, and one would think that people in AI would be glad to abandon it. Many of them, especially the younger generation, agree with me, but I am amazed at the number and vehemence of the defenders. Here are some of the common objections.

a. In the Chinese room you really do understand Chinese, even though you don't know it. It is, after all, possible to understand something without knowing that one understands.

Which semantics is the system giving off now?

b. You don't understand Chinese, but there is an (unconscious) subsystem in you that does. It is, after all, possible to have unconscious mental states, and there is no reason why your understanding of Chinese should not be wholly unconscious.

c. You don't understand Chinese, but the whole room does. You are like a single neuron in the brain, and just as such a single neuron by itself cannot understand but only contributes to the understanding of the whole system, you don't understand, but the whole system does.

d. Semantics doesn't exist anyway; there is only syntax. It is a kind of prescientific illusion to suppose that there exist in the brain some mysterious "mental contents," "thought processes" or "semantics." All that exists in the brain is the same sort of syntactic symbol manipulation that goes on in computers. Nothing more.

e. You are not really running the computer program—you only think you are. Once you have a conscious agent going through the steps of the program, it ceases to be a case of implementing a program at all.

f. Computers would have semantics and not just syntax if their inputs and outputs were put in appropriate causal relation to the rest of the world. Imagine that we put the computer into a robot, attached television cameras to the robot's head, installed transducers connecting the television messages to the computer and had the computer

output operate the robot's arms and legs. Then the whole system would have a semantics.

g. If the program simulated the operation of the brain of a Chinese speaker, then it would understand Chinese. Suppose that we simulated the brain of a Chinese person at the level of neurons. Then surely such a system would understand Chinese as well as any Chinese person's brain.

And so on.

All of these arguments share a common feature: they are all inadequate because they fail to come to grips with the actual Chinese room argument. That argument rests on the distinction between the formal symbol manipulation that is done by the computer and the mental contents biologically produced by the brain, a distinction I have abbreviated—I hope not misleadingly—as the distinction between syntax and semantics. I will not repeat my answers to all of these objections, but it will help to clarify the issues if I explain the weaknesses of the most widely held objection, argument c—what I call the systems reply. (The brain simulator reply, argument g, is another popular one, but I have already addressed that one in the previous section.)

The systems reply asserts that of course *you* don't understand Chinese but the whole system—you, the room, the rule book, the bushel baskets full of symbols—does. When I first heard this explanation, I asked one of its proponents, "Do you

How could anyone have supposed that a computer simulation
of a mental process must be the real thing?

mean the room understands Chinese?'' His answer was yes. It is a daring move, but aside from its implausibility, it will not work on purely logical grounds. The point of the original argument was that symbol shuffling by itself does not give any access to the meanings of the symbols. But this is as much true of the whole room as it is of the person inside. One can see this point by extending the thought experiment. Imagine that I memorize the contents of the baskets and the rule book, and I do all the calculations in my head. You can even imag-

ine that I work out in the open. There is nothing in the ''system'' that is not in me, and since I don't understand Chinese, neither does the system.

The Churchlands in their companion piece produce a variant of the systems reply by imagining an amusing analogy. Suppose that someone said that light could not be electromagnetic because if you shake a bar magnet in a dark room, the system still will not give off visible light. Now, the Churchlands ask, is not the Chinese room argument just like that? Does it not merely say that if you shake Chinese symbols in a semantically dark room, they will not give off the light of Chinese understanding? But just as later investigation showed that light was entirely constituted by electromagnetic radiation, could not later investigation also show that semantics are entirely constituted of syntax? Is this not a question for further scientific investigation?

Arguments from analogy are notoriously weak, because before one can make the argument work, one has to establish that the two cases are truly analogous. And here I think they are not. The account of light in terms of electromagnetic radiation is a causal story right down to the ground. It is a causal account of the physics of electromagnetic radiation. But the analogy with formal symbols fails because formal symbols have no physical, causal powers. The only power that symbols have, qua symbols, is the power to cause the next step in the program when the machine is running. And there is no question of waiting on further research to reveal the physical, causal properties of 0's and 1's. The only relevant properties of 0's and 1's are abstract computational properties, and they are already well known.

The Churchlands complain that I am "begging the question" when I say that uninterpreted formal symbols are not identical to mental contents. Well, I certainly did not spend much time arguing for it, because I take it as a logical truth. As with any logical truth, one can quickly see that it is true, because one gets inconsistencies if one tries to imagine the converse. So let us try it. Suppose that in the Chinese room some undetectable Chinese thinking really is going on. What exactly is supposed to make the manipulation of the syntactic elements into specifically Chinese thought contents? Well, after all, I am assuming that the programmers were Chinese speakers, programming the system to process Chinese information.

Fine. But now imagine that as I am sitting in the Chinese room shuffling the Chinese symbols, I get bored with just shuffling the—to me—meaningless symbols. So, suppose that I decide to interpret the symbols as standing for moves in a chess game. Which semantics is the system giving off now? Is it giving off a Chinese semantics or a chess semantics, or both simultaneously? Suppose there is a third person looking in through the window, and she decides that the symbol manipulations can all be interpreted as stock-market predictions. And so on. There is no limit to the

number of semantic interpretations that can be assigned to the symbols because, to repeat, the symbols are purely formal. They have no intrinsic semantics.

Is there any way to rescue the Churchlands' analogy from incoherence? I said above that formal symbols do not have causal properties. But of course the program will always be implemented in some hardware or another, and the hardware will have specific physical, causal powers. And any real computer will give off various phenomena. My computers, for example, give off heat, and they make a humming noise and sometimes crunching sounds. So is there some logically compelling reason why they could not also give off consciousness? No. Scientifically, the idea is out of the question, but it is not something the Chinese room argument is supposed to refute, and it is not something that an adherent of strong AI would wish to defend, because any such giving off would have to derive from the physical features of the implementing medium. But the basic premise of strong AI is that the physical features of the implementing medium are totally irrelevant. What matters are programs, and programs are purely formal.

The Churchlands' analogy between syntax and electromagnetism, then, is confronted with a dilemma; either the syntax is construed purely formally in terms of its abstract mathematical properties, or it is not. If it is, then the analogy breaks down, because syntax so construed has no physical powers and hence no physical, causal powers. If, on the other hand, one is supposed to think in terms of the physics of the implementing medium, then there is indeed an analogy, but it is not one that is relevant to strong AI.

Because the points I have been making are rather obvious—syntax is not the same as semantics, brain processes cause mental phenomena—the question arises, How did we get into this mess? How could anyone have supposed that a computer simulation of a mental process must be the real thing? After all, the whole point of models is that they contain only certain features of the modeled domain and leave out the rest. No one expects to get wet in a pool filled with Ping-Pong-ball models of water molecules. So why would anyone think a computer model of thought processes would actually think?

Part of the answer is that people have inherited a residue of behaviorist psychological theories of the past generation. The Turing test enshrines the temptation to think that if something behaves as if it had certain mental processes, then it must actually have those mental processes. And this is part of the behaviorists' mistaken assumption that in order to be scientific, psychology must confine its study to externally observable behavior. Paradoxically, this residual behaviorism is tied to a residual dualism. Nobody thinks that a computer simulation of digestion would actually digest anything, but where cognition is concerned, people are willing to believe in such a miracle because they fail to recognize that the mind is just as much a biological phenomenon as digestion. The mind, they suppose, is something formal and abstract, not a part of the wet and slimy stuff in our heads. The polemical literature in AI usually contains attacks on something the authors call dualism, but what they fail to see is that they themselves display dualism in a strong form, for unless one accepts the idea that the mind is completely independent of the brain or of any other physically specific system, one could not possibly hope to create minds just by designing programs.

Historically, scientific developments in the West that have treated humans as just a part of the ordinary physical, biological order have often been opposed by various rearguard actions. Copernicus and Galileo were opposed because they denied that the earth was the center of the universe; Darwin was opposed because he claimed that humans had descended from the lower animals. It is

best to see strong AI as one of the last gasps of this antiscientific tradition, for it denies that there is anything essentially physical and biological about the human mind. The mind according to strong AI is independent of the brain. It is a computer program and as such has no essential connection to any specific hardware.

Many people who have doubts about the psychological significance of AI think that computers might be able to understand Chinese and think about numbers but cannot do the crucially human things, namely—and then follows their favorite human specialty—falling in love, having a sense of humor, feeling the angst of postindustrial society under late capitalism, or whatever. But workers in AI complain—correctly—that this is a case of moving the goalposts. As soon as an AI simulation succeeds, it ceases to be of psychological importance. In this debate both sides fail to see the distinction between simulation and duplication. As far as simulation is concerned, there is no difficulty in programming my computer so that it prints out, "I love you, Suzy"; "Ha ha"; or "I am suffering the angst of postindustrial society under late capitalism." The important point is that simulation is not the same as duplication, and that fact holds as much import for thinking about arithmetic as it does for feeling angst. The point is not that the computer gets only to the 40-yard line and not all the way to the goal line. The computer doesn't even get started. It is not playing that game.

31. *Could a Machine Think?*

PAUL M. CHURCHLAND AND PATRICIA S. CHURCHLAND

In the previous selection, Searle claims human consciousness will not be understandable merely as a program for manipulating symbols. In this companion article, Paul and Patricia Churchland respond to Searle's argument. They focus on the question Could a machine think? They agree with Searle that serial, digital computers are unlikely to be able to be conscious in the sense of constituting semantic phenomena. They suggest, however, it is possible that new kinds of computers (with architectures using parallel processing) and discoveries about how the brain works may lead to the construction of artificial brains. In keeping with the strategy of eliminative materialism, they point out the possibility that a neurally grounded theory of meaning may call for a revision of the intuitions about meaning that support Searle's conclusion. Then, if it is possible to build a machine that thinks, this may illuminate the nature of human thinking, or "solve the problem of consciousness." Both Patricia and Paul Churchland are professors of philosophy at the University of California, San Diego.

Artificial-intelligence research is undergoing a revolution. To explain how and why, and to put John R. Searle's argument in perspective, we first need a flashback.

By the early 1950's the old, vague question, Could a machine think? had been replaced by the more approachable question, Could a machine that manipulated physical symbols according to structure-sensitive rules think? This question was an improvement because formal logic and computational theory had seen major developments in the preceding half-century. Theorists had come to appreciate the enormous power of abstract systems of symbols that undergo rule-governed transformations. If those systems could just be automated, then their abstract computational power, it seemed, would be displayed in a real physical system. This insight spawned a well-defined research program with deep theoretical underpinnings.

Could a machine think? There were many reasons for saying yes. One of the earliest and deepest reasons lay in two important results in computational theory. The first was Church's thesis, which states that every effectively computable function is recursively computable. Effectively computable means that there is a "rote" procedure for determining, in finite time, the output of the function for a given input. Recursively computable means more specifically that there is a finite set of operations that can be applied to a given input, and then applied again and again to the successive results of such applications, to yield the function's output in finite time. The notion of a rote procedure is nonformal and intuitive; thus, Church's thesis does not admit of a formal proof. But it does go to the heart of what it is to compute, and many lines of evidence converge in supporting it.

The second important result was Alan M. Turing's demonstration that any recursively computable function can be computed in finite time by a maximally simple sort of symbol-manipulating machine that has come to be called a universal Turing machine. This machine is guided by a set of recursively applicable rules that are sensitive to the identity, order and arrangement of the elementary symbols it encounters as input.

These two results entail something remarkable, namely that a standard digital computer, given only the right program, a large enough memory and sufficient time, can compute *any* rule-governed input-output function. That is, it can display any systematic pattern of responses to the environment whatsoever.

More specifically, these results imply that a suitably programmed symbol-manipulating machine (hereafter, SM machine) should be able to pass the Turing test for conscious intelligence. The Turing test is a purely behavioral test for conscious intelligence, but it is a very demanding test even so. (Whether it is a fair test will be addressed below, where we shall also encounter a second and quite different "test" for conscious intelligence.) In the original version of the Turing test, the inputs to the SM machine are conversational questions and remarks typed into a console by you or me, and the outputs are typewritten responses from the SM machine. The machine passes this test for conscious intelligence if its responses cannot be discriminated from the typewritten responses of a real, intelligent person. Of course, at present no one knows the function that would produce the output behavior of a conscious person. But the Church and Turing results assure us that, whatever that (presumably effective) function might be, a suitable SM machine could compute it.

This is a significant conclusion, especially since Turing's portrayal of a purely teletyped interaction is an unnecessary restriction. The same conclusion follows even if the SM machine interacts with the world in more complex ways: by direct vision, real speech and so forth. After all, a more complex recursive function is still Turing-computable. The only remaining problem is to identify the undoubtedly complex function that governs the human pattern of response to the environment and then write the program (the set of recursively applicable rules) by which the SM machine will compute it. These goals form the fundamental research program of classical AI.

Initial results were positive. SM machines with clever programs performed a variety of ostensibly cognitive activities. They responded to complex instructions, solved complex arithmetic, algebraic and tactical problems, played checkers and chess, proved theorems and engaged in simple dialogue. Performance continued to improve with the appearance of larger memories and faster machines and with the use of longer and more cunning programs. Classical, or "program-writing," AI was a vigorous and successful research effort from almost every perspective. The occasional denial that an SM machine might eventually think appeared uninformed and ill motivated. The case for a positive answer to our title question was overwhelming.

There were a few puzzles, of course. For one thing, SM machines were admittedly not very brainlike. Even here, however, the classical approach had a convincing answer. First, the physical material of any SM machine has nothing essential to do with what function it computes. That is fixed by its program. Second, the engineering details of any machine's functional architecture are also irrelevant, since different architectures running quite different programs can still be computing the same input-output function.

Accordingly, AI sought to find the input-output *function* characteristic of intelligence and the most efficient of the many possible programs for computing it. The idiosyncratic way in which the brain computes the function just doesn't matter, it was said. This completes the rationale for classical AI and for a positive answer to our title question.

Could a machine think? There were also some arguments for saying no. Through the 1960's interesting negative arguments were relatively rare. The objection was occasionally made that thinking was a nonphysical process in an immaterial soul. But such dualistic resistance was neither evolutionarily nor explanatorily plausible. It had a negligible impact on AI research.

A quite different line of objection was more successful in gaining the AI community's attention. In 1972 Hubert L. Dreyfus published a book that was highly critical of the parade-case simulations of cognitive activity. He argued for their inadequacy as simulations of genuine cognition, and he pointed to a pattern of failure in these attempts. What they were missing, he suggested, was the vast store of inarticulate background knowledge every person possesses and the commonsense capacity for drawing on relevant aspects of that knowledge as changing circumstance demands. Dreyfus did not deny the possibility that an artificial physical system of some kind might think, but he was highly critical of the idea that this could be achieved solely by symbol manipulation at the hands of recursively applicable rules.

Dreyfus's complaints were broadly perceived

within the AI community, and within the discipline of philosophy as well, as shortsighted and unsympathetic, as harping on the inevitable simplifications of a research effort still in its youth. These deficits might be real, but surely they were temporary. Bigger machines and better programs should repair them in due course. Time, it was felt, was on AI's side. Here again the impact on research was negligible.

Time was on Dreyfus's side as well: the rate of cognitive return on increasing speed and memory began to slacken in the late 1970's and early 1980's. The simulation of object recognition in the visual system, for example, proved computationally intensive to an unexpected degree. Realistic results required longer and longer periods of computer time, periods far in excess of what a real visual system requires. This relative slowness of the simulations was darkly curious; signal propagation in a computer is roughly a million times faster than in the brain, and the clock frequency of a computer's central processor is greater than any frequency found in the brain by a similarly dramatic margin. And yet, on realistic problems, the tortoise easily outran the hare.

Furthermore, realistic performance required that the computer program have access to an extremely large knowledge base. Constructing the relevant knowledge base was problem enough, and it was compounded by the problem of how to access just the contextually relevant parts of that knowledge base in real time. As the knowledge base got bigger and better, the access problem got worse. Exhaustive search took too much time, and heuristics for relevance did poorly. Worries of the sort Dreyfus had raised finally began to take hold here and there even among AI researchers.

At about this time (1980) John Searle authored a new and quite different criticism aimed at the most basic assumption of the classical research program: the idea that the appropriate manipulation of structured symbols by the recursive application of structure-sensitive rules could constitute conscious intelligence.

Searle's argument is based on a thought experiment that displays two crucial features. First, he describes a SM machine that realizes, we are to suppose, an input-output function adequate to sustain a successful Turing test conversation conducted entirely in Chinese. Second, the internal structure of the machine is such that, however it behaves, an observer remains certain that neither the machine nor any part of it understands Chinese. All it contains is a monolingual English speaker following a written set of instructions for manipulating the Chinese symbols that arrive and leave through a mail slot. In short, the system is supposed to pass the Turing test, while the system itself lacks any genuine understanding of Chinese or real Chinese semantic content [see (preceding article) "Is the Brain's Mind a Computer Program?" by John R. Searle].

The general lesson drawn is that any system that merely manipulates physical symbols in accordance with structure-sensitive rules will be at best a hollow mock-up of real conscious intelligence, because it is impossible to generate "real semantics" merely by cranking away on "empty syntax." Here, we should point out, Searle is imposing a nonbehavioral test for consciousness: the elements of conscious intelligence must possess real semantic content.

One is tempted to complain that Searle's thought experiment is unfair because his Rube Goldberg system will compute with absurd slowness. Searle insists, however, that speed is strictly irrelevant here. A slow thinker should still be a real thinker. Everything essential to the duplication of thought, as per classical AI, is said to be present in the Chinese room.

Searle's paper provoked a lively reaction from AI researchers, psychologists and philosophers alike. On the whole, however, he was met with an even more hostile reception than Dreyfus had experienced. In his companion piece in this volume, Searle forthrightly lists a number of these critical responses. We think many of them are reasonable, especially those that "bite the bullet" by insisting that, although it is appallingly slow, the overall system of the room-plus-contents does understand Chinese.

We think those are good responses, but not because we think that the room understands Chinese. We agree with Searle that it does not. Rather they are good responses because they reflect a refusal to accept the crucial third axiom of Searle's argument: *"Syntax by itself is neither constitutive of nor sufficient for semantics."* Perhaps this axiom is true, but Searle cannot rightly pretend to know that it is. Moreover, to assume its truth is tantamount to begging the question against the research program of classical AI, for that program is predicated on the very interesting assumption that if one can just set in motion an appropriately structured internal dance of syntactic elements, appropriately connected to inputs and outputs, it can produce the same cognitive states and achievements found in human beings.

The question-begging character of Searle's axiom 3 becomes clear when it is compared directly with his conclusion 1: "*Programs are neither constitutive of nor sufficient for minds.*" Plainly, his third axiom is already carrying 90 percent of the weight of this almost identical conclusion. That is why Searle's thought experiment is devoted to shoring up axiom 3 specifically. That is the point of the Chinese room.

Although the story of the Chinese room makes axiom 3 tempting to the unwary, we do not think it succeeds in establishing axiom 3, and we offer a parallel argument below in illustration of its failure. A single transparently fallacious instance of a disputed argument often provides far more insight than a book full of logic chopping.

Searle's style of skepticism has ample precedent in the history of science. The 18th-century Irish bishop George Berkeley found it unintelligible that compression waves in the air, by themselves, could constitute or be sufficient for objective sound. The English poet-artist William Blake and the German poet-naturalist Johann W. von Goethe found it inconceivable that small particles by themselves could constitute or be sufficient for the objective phenomenon of light. Even in this century, there have been people who found it beyond imagining that inanimate matter by itself, and however organized, could ever constitute or be sufficient for life. Plainly, what people can or cannot imagine often has nothing to do with what is or is not the case, even where the people involved are highly intelligent.

To see how this lesson applies to Searle's case, consider a deliberately manufactured parallel to his argument and its supporting thought experiment.

Axiom 1. *Electricity and magnetism are forces.*

Axiom 2. *The essential property of light is luminance.*

Axiom 3. *Forces by themselves are neither constitutive of nor sufficient for luminance.*

Conclusion 1. *Electricity and magnetism are neither constitutive of nor sufficient for light.*

Imagine this argument raised shortly after James Clerk Maxwell's 1864 suggestion that light and electromagnetic waves are identical but before the world's full appreciation of the systematic parallels between the properties of light and the properties of electromagnetic waves. This argument could have served as a compelling objection to Maxwell's imaginative hypothesis, especially if it were accompanied by the following commentary in support of axiom 3.

"Consider a dark room containing a man holding a bar magnet or charged object. If the man pumps the magnet up and down, then, according to Maxwell's theory of artificial luminance (AL), it will initiate a spreading circle of electromagnetic waves and will thus be luminous. But as all of us who have toyed with magnets or charged balls well know, their forces (or any other forces for that matter), even when set in motion, produce no luminance at all. It is inconceivable that you might constitute real luminance just by moving forces around!"

THE CHINESE ROOM

Axiom 1. Computer programs are formal (syntactic).

Axiom 2. Human minds have mental contents (semantics).

Axiom 3. Syntax by itself is neither constitutive of nor sufficient for semantics.

Conclusion 1. Programs are neither constitutive of nor sufficient for minds.

THE LUMINOUS ROOM

Axiom 1. Electricity and magnetism are forces.

Axiom 2. The essential property of light is luminance.

Axiom 3. Forces by themselves are neither constitutive of nor sufficient for luminance.

Conclusion 1. Electricity and magnetism are neither constitutive of nor sufficient for light.

Oscillating electromagnetic forces constitute light even though a magnet pumped by a person appears to produce no light whatsoever. Similarly, rule-based symbol manipulation might constitute intelligence even though the rule-based system inside John R. Searle's "Chinese room" appears to lack real understanding.

How should Maxwell respond to this challenge? He might begin by insisting that the "luminous room" experiment is a misleading display of the phenomenon of luminance because the frequency of oscillation of the magnet is absurdly low, too low by a factor of 10^{15}. This might well elicit the impatient response that frequency has nothing to do with it, that the room with the bobbing magnet already contains everything essential to light, according to Maxwell's own theory.

In response Maxwell might bite the bullet and claim, quite correctly, that the room really is bathed in luminance, albeit a grade or quality too feeble to appreciate. (Given the low frequency with which the man can oscillate the magnet, the wavelength of the electromagnetic waves produced is far too long and their intensity is much too weak for human retinas to respond to them.) But in the climate of understanding here contemplated—the 1860's—this tactic is likely to elicit laughter and hoots of derision. "Luminous room, my foot, Mr. Maxwell. It's pitch-black in there!"

Alas, poor Maxwell has no easy route out of this predicament. All he can do is insist on the following three points. First, axiom 3 of the above argument is false. Indeed, it begs the question despite its intuitive plausibility. Second, the luminous room experiment demonstrates nothing of interest one way or the other about the nature of light. And third, what is needed to settle the prob-

lem of light and the possibility of artificial luminance is an ongoing research program to determine whether under the appropriate conditions
the behavior of electromagnetic waves does indeed
mirror perfectly the behavior of light.

This is also the response that classical AI
should give to Searle's argument. Even though
Searle's Chinese room may appear to be "semantically dark," he is in no position to insist, on the
strength of this appearance, that rule-governed
symbol manipulation can never constitute semantic phenomena, especially when people have only
an uninformed commonsense understanding of
the semantic and cognitive phenomena that need
to be explained. Rather than exploit one's understanding of these things, Searle's argument freely
exploits one's ignorance of them.

With these criticisms of Searle's argument in
place, we return to the question of whether the
research program of classical AI has a realistic
chance of solving the problem of conscious intelligence and of producing a machine that thinks. We
believe that the prospects are poor, but we rest this
opinion on reasons very different from Searle's.
Our reasons derive from the specific performance
failures of the classical research program in AI and
from a variety of lessons learned from the biological brain and a new class of computational models
inspired by its structure. We have already indicated some of the failures of classical AI regarding
tasks that the brain performs swiftly and efficiently. The emerging consensus on these failures
is that the functional architecture of classical SM
machines is simply the wrong architecture for the
very demanding jobs required.

What we need to know is this: How does the
brain achieve cognition? Reverse engineering is a
common practice in industry. When a new piece of
technology comes on the market, competitors find
out how it works by taking it apart and divining its
structural rationale. In the case of the brain, this
strategy presents an unusually stiff challenge, for
the brain is the most complicated and sophisticated
thing on the planet. Even so, the neurosciences
have revealed much about the brain on a wide
variety of structural levels. Three anatomic points
will provide a basic contrast with the architecture
of conventional electronic computers.

First, nervous systems are parallel machines,
in the sense that signals are processed in millions of
different pathways simultaneously. The retina, for
example, presents its complex input to the brain
not in chunks of eight, 16 or 32 elements, as in a
desktop computer, but rather in the form of almost
a million distinct signal elements arriving simultaneously at the target of the optic nerve (the lateral
geniculate nucleus), there to be processed collectively, simultaneously and in one fell swoop.
Second, the brain's basic processing unit, the neuron, is comparatively simple. Furthermore, its response to incoming signals is analog, not digital,
inasmuch as its output spiking frequency varies
continuously with its input signals. Third, in the
brain, axons projecting from one neuronal population to another are often matched by axons returning from their target population. These descending
or recurrent projections allow the brain to modu-
late the character of its sensory processing. More
important still, their existence makes the brain a
genuine dynamical system whose continuing behavior is both highly complex and to some degree
independent of its peripheral stimuli.

Highly simplified model networks have been
useful in suggesting how real neural networks
might work and in revealing the computational
properties of parallel architectures. For example,
consider a three-layer model consisting of neuron-
like units fully connected by axonlike connections
to the units at the next layer. An input stimulus
produces some activation level in a given input
unit, which conveys a signal of proportional
strength along its "axon" to its many "synaptic"
connections to the hidden units. The global effect is
that a pattern of activations across the set of input
units produces a distinct pattern of activations
across the set of hidden units.

The same story applies to the output units. As
before, an activation pattern across the hidden
units produces a distinct activation pattern across
the output units. All told, this network is a device
for transforming any one of a great many possible
input vectors (activation patterns) into a uniquely
corresponding output vector. It is a device for computing a specific function. Exactly which function it
computes is fixed by the global configuration of its
synaptic weights.

There are various procedures for adjusting the
weights so as to yield a network that computes
almost any function—that is, any vector-to-vector
transformation—that one might desire. In fact, one
can even impose on it a function one is unable to
specify, so long as one can supply a set of examples
of the desired input-output pairs. This process,

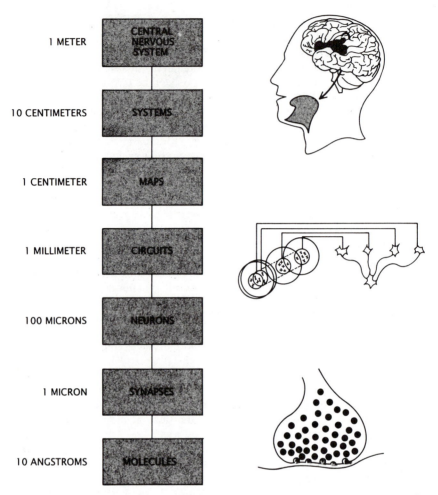

Nervous systems span many scales of organization, from neurotransmitter molecules (*bottom*) to the entire brain and spinal cord. Intermediate levels include single neurons and circuits made up of a few neurons, such as those that produce orientation selectivity to a visual stimulus (*middle*), and systems made up of circuits such as those that subserve language (*top right*). Only research can decide how closely an artificial system must mimic the biological one to be capable of intelligence.

called "training up the network," proceeds by successive adjustment of the network's weights until it performs the input-output transformations desired.

Although this model network vastly oversimplifies the structure of the brain, it does illustrate several important ideas. First, a parallel architecture provides a dramatic speed advantage over a conventional computer, for the many synapses at each level perform many small computations simultaneously instead of in laborious sequence. This advantage gets larger as the number of neurons increases at each layer. Strikingly, the speed of processing is entirely independent of both the number of units involved in each layer and the complexity of the function they are computing. Each layer could have four units or a hundred million; its configuration of synaptic weights could be computing simple one-digit sums or second-order differential equations. It would make no difference. The computation time would be exactly the same.

Second, massive parallelism means that the system is fault-tolerant and functionally persistent;

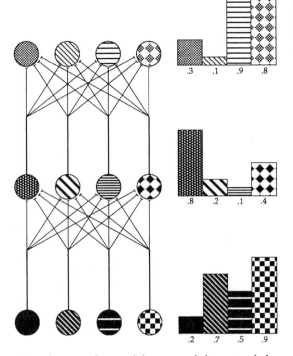

Neural networks model a central feature of the brain's microstructure. In this three-layer net, input neurons (*bottom left*) process a pattern of activations (*bottom right*) and pass it along weighted connections to a hidden layer. Elements in the hidden layer sum their many inputs to produce a new pattern of activations. This is passed to the output layer, which performs a further transformation. Overall the network transforms any input pattern into a corresponding output pattern as dictated by the arrangement and strength of the many connections between neurons.

the loss of a few connections, even quite a few, has a negligible effect on the character of the overall transformation performed by the surviving network.

Third, a parallel system stores large amounts of information in a distributed fashion, any part of which can be accessed in milliseconds. That information is stored in the specific configuration of synaptic connection strengths, as shaped by past learning. Relevant information is "released" as the input vector passes through—and is transformed by—that configuration of connections.

Parallel processing is not ideal for all types of computation. On tasks that require only a small input vector, but many millions of swiftly iterated recursive computations, the brain performs very badly, whereas classical SM machines excel. This class of computations is very large and important, so classical machines will always be useful, indeed, vital. There is, however, an equally large class of computations for which the brain's architecture is the superior technology. These are the computations that typically confront living creatures: recognizing a predator's outline in a noisy environment; recalling instantly how to avoid its gaze, flee its approach or fend off its attack; distinguishing food from nonfood and mates from nonmates; navigating through a complex and ever-changing physical/social environment; and so on.

Finally, it is important to note that the parallel system described is not manipulating symbols according to structure-sensitive rules. Rather symbol manipulation appears to be just one of many cognitive skills that a network may or may not learn to display. Rule-governed symbol manipulation is not its basic mode of operation. Searle's argument is directed against rule-governed SM machines; vector transformers of the kind we describe are therefore not threatened by his Chinese room argument even if it were sound, which we have found independent reason to doubt.

Searle is aware of parallel processors but thinks they too will be devoid of real semantic content. To illustrate their inevitable failure, he outlines a second thought experiment, the Chinese gym, which has a gymnasium full of people organized into a parallel network. From there his argument proceeds as in the Chinese room.

We find this second story far less responsive or compelling than his first. For one, it is irrelevant that no unit in his system understands Chinese, since the same is true of nervous systems: no neuron in my brain understands English, although my whole brain does. For another, Searle neglects to mention that his simulation (using one person per neuron, plus a fleet-footed child for each synaptic connection) will require at least 10^{14} people, since the human brain has 10^{11} neurons, each of which averages over 10^3 connections. His system will require the entire human populations of over 10,000 earths. One gymnasium will not begin to hold a fair simulation.

On the other hand, if such a system were to be assembled on a suitably cosmic scale, with all its pathways faithfully modeled on the human case, we might then have a large, slow, oddly made but still functional brain on our hands. In that case the default assumption is surely that, given proper inputs, it would think, not that it couldn't. There is no guarantee that its activity would constitute real thought, because the vector-processing theory sketched above may not be the correct theory of how brains work. But neither is there any a priori guarantee that it could not be thinking. Searle is once more mistaking the limits on his (or the reader's) current imagination for the limits on objective reality.

The brain is a kind of computer, although most of its properties remain to be discovered. Characterizing the brain as a kind of computer is neither trivial nor frivolous. The brain does compute functions, functions of great complexity, but not in the classical AI fashion. When brains are said to be computers, it should not be implied that they are serial, digital computers, that they are programmed, that they exhibit the distinction between hardware and software or that they must be symbol manipulators or rule followers. Brains are computers in a radically different style.

How the brain manages meaning is still unknown, but it is clear that the problem reaches beyond language use and beyond humans. A small mound of fresh dirt signifies to a person, and also to coyotes, that a gopher is around; an echo with a certain spectral character signifies to a bat the presence of a moth. To develop a theory of meaning, more must be known about how neurons code and transform sensory signals, about the neural basis of memory, learning and emotion and about the interaction of these capacities and the motor system. A neurally grounded theory of meaning may require revision of the very intuitions that now seem so secure and that are so freely exploited in Searle's arguments. Such revisions are common in the history of science.

Could science construct an artificial intelligence by exploiting what is known about the nervous system? We see no principled reason why not. Searle appears to agree, although he qualifies his claim by saying that "any other system capable of causing minds would have to have causal powers (at least) equivalent to those of brains." We close by addressing this claim. We presume that Searle is not claiming that a successful artificial mind must have *all* the causal powers of the brain, such as the power to smell bad when rotting, to

harbor slow viruses such as kuru, to stain yellow with horseradish peroxidase and so forth. Requiring perfect parity would be like requiring that an artificial flying device lay eggs.

Presumably he means only to require of an artificial mind all of the causal powers relevant, as he says, to conscious intelligence. But which exactly are they? We are back to quarreling about what is and is not relevant. This is an entirely reasonable place for a disagreement, but it is an empirical matter, to be tried and tested. Because so little is known about what goes into the process of cognition and semantics, it is premature to be very confident about what features are essential. Searle hints at various points that every level, including the biochemical, must be represented in any machine that is a candidate for artificial intelligence. This claim is almost surely too strong. An artificial brain might use something other than biochemicals to achieve the same ends.

This possibility is illustrated by Carver A. Mead's research at the California Institute of Technology. Mead and his colleagues have used analog VLSI techniques to build an artificial retina and an artificial cochlea. (In animals the retina and cochlea are not mere transducers: both systems embody a complex processing network.) These are not mere simulations in a mini-computer of the kind that Searle derides; they are real information-processing units responding in real time to real light, in the case of the artificial retina, and to real sound, in the case of the artificial cochlea. Their circuitry is based on the known anatomy and physiology of the cat retina and the barn owl cochlea, and their output is dramatically similar to the known output of the organs at issue.

These chips do not use any neurochemicals, so neurochemicals are clearly not necessary to achieve the evident results. Of course, the artificial retina cannot be said to see anything, because its output does not have an artificial thalamus or cortex to go to. Whether Mead's program could be sustained to build an entire artificial brain remains to be seen, but there is no evidence now that the absence of biochemicals renders it quixotic.

We, and Searle, reject the Turing test as a sufficient condition for conscious intelligence. At one level our reasons for doing so are similar: we agree that it is also very important how the input-output function is achieved; it is important that the right sorts of things be going on inside the artificial machine. At another level, our reasons are quite different. Searle bases his position on commonsense intuitions about the presence or absence of semantic content. We base ours on the specific behavioral failures of the classical SM machines and on the specific virtues of machines with a more brainlike architecture. These contrasts show that certain computational strategies have vast and decisive advantages over others where typical cognitive tasks are concerned, advantages that are empirically inescapable. Clearly, the brain is making systematic use of these computational advantages. But it need not be the only physical system capable of doing so. Artificial intelligence, in a nonbiological but massively parallel machine, remains a compelling and discernible prospect.

Further Reading

Addis, L. *Natural Signs: A Theory of Intentionality* (Philadelphia: Temple University Press, 1989).

Armstrong, D., and Malcolm, N. *Consciousness and Causality* (Oxford: Blackwell, 1984).

Baker, L. *Saving Belief* (Princeton, N.J.: Princeton University Press, 1987).

Block, N., ed. *Readings in Philosophy of Psychology*, Vols. I and II (Cambridge: Harvard University Press, 1980).

Borst, C., ed. *The Mind/Brain Identity Theory* (New York: St. Martin's Press, 1970).

Brentano, F. *The Psychology of Aristotle* (Berkeley: University of California Press, 1977).

Broad, C. *The Mind and Its Place in Nature* (London: Routledge & Kegan Paul, 1925).

Churchland, P. M. *Matter and Consciousness* (Cambridge: MIT Press, 1988).

Churchland, P. M. *Scientific Realism and the Plasticity of Mind* (Cambridge: MIT Press, 1979).

Churchland, P. S. *Neurophilosophy* (Cambridge: MIT Press, 1986).

Cornman, J. *Materialism and Sensations* (New Haven: Yale University Press, 1971).

Dennett, D. *Content and Consciousness* (New York: Humanities, 1969).

Dennett, D. *The Intentional Stance* (Cambridge: MIT Press, 1987).

Feigl, H. *The "Mental" and the "Physical"* (Minneapolis: University of Minnesota Press, 1967).

Flanagan, O. *The Science of Mind* (Cambridge: MIT Press, 1984).

Flew, A., ed., *Body, Mind, and Death* (New York: Macmillan, 1964).

Fodor, J. *Representations* (Cambridge: MIT Press, 1981).

Gregory, R., ed. *The Oxford Companion to the Mind* (Oxford: Oxford University Press, 1987).

Hartman, E. *Substance, Body, and Soul* (Princeton: Princeton University Press, 1977).

Haugeland, J. *Artificial Intelligence: The Very Idea* (Cambridge: MIT Press, 1985).

Haugeland, J., ed. *Mind Design* (Montgomery, Ver.: Bradford, 1981).

Hofstadter, D. *Gödel, Escher, Bach* (New York: Basic Books, 1979).

Hofstadter, D., and Dennett, D., eds. *The Mind's I* (New York: Basic Books, 1981).

Lovejoy, A. *The Revolt Against Dualism* (La Salle: Open Court, 1960).

Lycan, W. *Consciousness* (Cambridge: MIT Press, 1987).

Matson, W. *Sentience* (Berkeley: University of California Press, 1976).

McGinn, C. *The Subjective View* (Oxford: Oxford University Press, 1983).

Nagel, T. *The View from Nowhere* (Oxford: Oxford University Press, 1986).

Nelson, R. *The Logic of Mind* (Dordrecht: Reidel, 1982).

O'Connor, J., ed. *Modern Materialism: Readings on Mind-Body Identity* (New York: Harcourt, Brace & World, 1969).

Popper, K., and Eccles, J. *The Self and Its Brain* (New York: Springer, 1977).

Ryle, G. *The Concept of Mind* (New York: Barnes & Noble, 1949).

Searle, J. *Intentionality* (Cambridge: Cambridge University Press, 1983).

Smith, D., and McIntyre, R., eds. *Husserl and Intentionality* (Dordrecht: Reidel, 1982).

Strawson, P. *Individuals* (Garden City, N.Y.: Doubleday, 1963).

Woodfield, A., ed. *Thought and Object* (Oxford: Oxford University Press, 1982).

Part IV

Freedom

At this moment, you are reading this book; yet you could have been doing something else. You could have chosen to watch television, go to the movies, play tennis, or do any number of things other than read this book. Your reading this book seems to result from an act of free will, and it seems to be in your power to choose to continue or to refrain from reading it. Although these remarks seem obvious, reflection on certain other commonly accepted beliefs have led some philosophers to deny it is ever within our power to do

anything other than what we in fact do. That is, they deny the reality of freedom.

Metaphysically, the attacks on freedom have come from several directions. One argument is based on general reflections about truth and logic. According to the law of excluded middle, every proposition is either true or it is false. Thus, for example, the proposition "You will finish reading this introduction tonight" is either now true or now false. If, however, it is now true that you will finish it tonight, then the fact that you will finish it tonight must already exist. If that fact already exists, then you are powerless to not finish it. If, on the other hand, it is now false that you will finish it tonight, then the belief that you can is illusory. In either case, "nothing is or takes place fortuitously, either in the present or in the future, and there are no real alternatives; everything takes place of necessity and is fixed." Although Aristotle himself is at pains to avoid this conclusion, he sees that the argument suggests the law of excluded middle poses a serious challenge to the view that people have free will. The argument says that no person has it within his or her power to alter the course of history. This view is known as *logical fatalism*. Fatalism in this sense should be distinguished from the popular conception of fatalism according to which everything is *fated* or predetermined (by God?) regardless of human choices.

The problem of reconciling a law of logic with human freedom is closely connected with the theological problem of reconciling divine foreknowledge with human freedom. For if God knew *before* you were born that, say, you would finish reading this introduction tonight, then it must have been true before you were born that you would finish it tonight; and so you cannot bring about any alternative. This problem has been the subject of theological and philosophical reflection for centuries, and the selections by Augustine and Rowe contain discussions of the principal solutions to it.

A third attack on freedom comes, not from logic or religion, but from nature, or more specifically, from the connections most people believe exist among events in nature. Most people believe events have causes, and the causes of events "necessitate" the occurrence of those events. That is, given certain laws and initial conditions, then what happens is determined. Thus, hitting a wine glass causes it to shatter. Now, although science

has not discovered all the laws governing human actions, it would appear human behavior, like nonhuman behavior, is causally determined. The most basic laws of modern physics are not all deterministic. It is a feature of quantum mechanics that, in the microworld, some events are random (or certain initial conditions do not necessitate specific later states). But these quantum indeterminacies do not usually affect the behavior of large collections of particles like human bodies and brains. If, then, human actions are causally determined, it might seem people, contrary to common beliefs, cannot really do other than what they in fact do. Logic, religion, and science each suggest arguments that deny people are really free.

The topic of freedom is related to several of the metaphysical issues presented in Parts I, II, and III. For example, Steven Cahn argues that the metaphysical view of time defended by Bertrand Russell and D. C. Williams is "logically incompatible with man's free will. If this view of time is a truism, then so is fatalism." Consequently, he maintains that to avoid fatalism one must adopt a tensed theory of time and truth. Regarding the issue of the nature of persons, Thomas Reid and Roderick Chisholm argue that the only way to preserve belief in human freedom is to suppose the self is a substance whose actions are outside the sphere of determinism. On the other hand, if persons are deterministic physical processes, then philosophers must try to find some other analysis of freedom that does justice to the distinction between free acts and compelled acts.

Metaphysical disputes about freedom have important practical and ethical implications. People often praise or blame and reward or punish people for their actions. Philosophical theories about what makes it right to do this involve the notion of responsibility, and the idea of responsibility is usually tied to a person's being free. For example, punishment in the form of retribution is clearly wrong if one cannot do other than what one does (for example, if one is compelled or forced). Punishment whose rationale is correction or prevention of undesirable behavior, however, may be congenial even to determinism. Which social practices should be adopted may then depend upon what kind of freedom, if any, is real.

The selections in Part IV are concerned with articulating and discussing the challenging claim that freedom is not real. The first selection by Aristotle and the selection by Cahn deal with fatalism and the implications that ways of avoiding it might have for time and truth. In the selection from the *Nicomachean Ethics*, Aristotle offers an analysis of voluntary acts. For Aristotle, voluntary acts have their origins *in the agent*, and the voluntary is that which allows for the possibility of alternative action.

The readings by St. Augustine and Rowe concern the challenge to freedom represented by divine foreknowledge, whereas the selections by Aquinas, Hume, Reid, Moore, and Chisholm concern the challenge to freedom represented by causal determinism. Aquinas first raises the issue of how actions motivated by causes outside of us can be voluntary. Hume's classic discussion in "On Liberty and Necessity" together with Russell's analysis of the notions of "cause," "necessity," and "determinism" are attempts to dispel that worry. The essays by Frankfurt and Dennett are recent attempts to render the fact of causal determinism, if it is a fact, irrelevant to the topic of freedom.

32. *Fatalism, Voluntary Action, and Choice*

ARISTOTLE

In the first selection from *On Interpretation*, Aristotle raises a typical metaphysical conundrum, a paradox that results from apparently well-grounded intuitions about the world. On the one hand, people usually believe the future is open, in the sense that there are numerous *alternative* courses of actions still open for them to pursue. On the other hand, given any pair of contradictory propositions, say, *X* will occur and *X* will not occur, one is true and the other is false. But if a prediction about the future (*x will* occur) is already true, then the future seems fixed and unavoidable. Conversely, if there are genuine alternatives open in the future, then are some propositions about the future neither true nor false now? Aristotle's response to the dilemma has implications for issues concerning time and truth. (See, for example, the following article by Steven Cahn.)

In the selection from the *Nicomachean Ethics*, Aristotle analyzes the nature of voluntary actions and discusses the nature of choice and the role deliberation plays in making choices. Voluntary actions are those in which *"the moving principle is in the agent himself,"* whereas involuntary acts take place under compulsion, *"and that is compulsory of which the moving principle is outside. . . ."*

On Interpretation

In the case of that which is or which has taken place, propositions, whether positive or negative, must be true or false. Again, in the case of a pair of contradictories, either when the subject is universal and the propositions are of a universal character, or when it is individual, as has been said, one of the two must be true and the other false; whereas when the subject is universal, but the propositions are not of a universal character, there is no such necessity.

When the subject, however, is individual, and that which is predicated of it relates to the future,

Reprinted from W. D. Ross, ed., *The Oxford Translation of Aristotle.* By permission of Oxford University Press. The selections from *On Interpretation* and the *Nicomachean Ethics* originally appeared in Richard McKeon, ed., *The Basic Works of Aristotle.* (New York: Random House, 1941), pp. 45–48 and 364–69.

the case is altered. For if all propositions whether positive or negative are either true or false, then any given predicate must either belong to the subject or not, so that if one man affirms that an event of a given character will take place and another denies it, it is plain that the statement of the one will correspond with reality and that of the other will not. For the predicate cannot both belong and not belong to the subject at one and the same time with regard to the future.

Thus, if it is true to say that a thing is white, it must necessarily be white; if the reverse proposition is true, it will of necessity not be white. Again, if it is white, the proposition stating that it is white was true; if it is not white, the proposition to the opposite effect was true. And if it is not white, the man who states that it is is making a false statement; and if the man who states that it is white is making a false statement, it follows that it is not white. It may therefore be argued that it is necessary that affirmations or denials must be either true or false.

Now if this be so, nothing is or takes place fortuitously, either in the present or in the future, and there are no real alternatives; everything takes place of necessity and is fixed. For either he that affirms that it will take place or he that denies this is in correspondence with fact, whereas if things did not take place of necessity, an event might just as easily not happen as happen; for the meaning of the word 'fortuitous' with regard to present or future events is that reality is so constituted that it may issue in either of two opposite directions.

Again, if a thing is white now, it was true before to say that it would be white, so that of anything that has taken place it was always true to say 'it is' or 'it will be.' But if it was always true to say that a thing is or will be, it is not possible that it should not be or not be about to be, and when a thing cannot not come to be, it is impossible that it should not come to be, and when it is impossible that it should not come to be, it must come to be. All, then, that is about to be must of necessity take place. It results from this that nothing is uncertain or fortuitous, for if it were fortuitous it would not be necessary.

Again, to say that neither the affirmation nor the denial is true, maintaining, let us say, that an event neither will take place nor will not take place, is to take up a position impossible to defend. In the first place, though facts should prove the one proposition false, the opposite would still be untrue. Secondly, if it was true to say that a thing was both white and large, both these qualities must necessarily belong to it; and if they will belong to it the next day, they must necessarily belong to it the next day. But if an event is neither to take place nor not to take place the next day, the element of chance will be eliminated. For example, it would be necessary that a sea-fight should neither take place nor fail to take place on the next day.

These awkward results and others of the same kind follow, if it is an irrefragable law that of every pair of contradictory propositions, whether they have regard to universals and are stated as universally applicable, or whether they have regard to individuals, one must be true and the other false, and that there are no real alternatives, but that all that is or takes place is the outcome of necessity. There would be no need to deliberate or to take trouble, on the supposition that if we should adopt a certain course, a certain result would follow, while, if we did not, the result would not follow. For a man may predict an event ten thousand years beforehand, and another may predict the reverse; that which was truly predicted at the moment in the past will of necessity take place in the fullness of time.

Further, it makes no difference whether people have or have not actually made the contradictory statements. For it is manifest that the circumstances are not influenced by the fact of an affirmation or denial on the part of anyone. For events will not take place or fail to take place because it was stated that they would or would not take place, nor is this any more the case if the prediction dates back ten thousand years or any other space of time. Wherefore, if through all time the nature of things was so constituted that a prediction about an event was true, then through all time it was necessary that that prediction should find fulfilment; and with regard to all events, circumstances have always been such that their occurrence is a matter of necessity. For that of which someone has said truly that it will be, cannot fail to take place; and of that which takes place, it was always true to say that it would be.

Yet this view leads to an impossible conclusion; for we see that both deliberation and action are causative with regard to the future, and that, to speak more generally, in those things which are not continuously actual there is a potentiality in either direction. Such things may either be or not be; events also therefore may either take place or not take place. There are many obvious instances of this. It is possible that this coat may be cut in half, and yet it may not be cut in half, but wear out first. In the same way, it is possible that it should not be cut in half; unless this were so, it would not be possible that it should wear out first. So it is therefore with all other events which possess this kind of potentiality. It is therefore plain that it is not of necessity that everything is or takes place; but in some instances there are real alternatives, in which case the affirmation is no more true and no more false than the denial; while some exhibit a predisposition and general tendency in one direction or the other, and yet can issue in the opposite direction by exception.

Now that which is must needs be when it is, and that which is not must needs not be when it is not. Yet it cannot be said without qualification that all existence and non-existence is the outcome of necessity. For there is a difference between saying that that which is, when it is, must needs be, and simply saying that all that is must needs be, and similarly in the case of that which is not. In the case, also, of two contradictory propositions this holds good. Everything must either be or not be, whether in the present or in the future, but it is not always possible to distinguish and state determinately which of these alternatives must necessarily come about.

Let me illustrate. A sea-fight must either take place tomorrow or not, but it is not necessary that it should take place tomorrow, neither is it necessary that it should not take place, yet it is necessary that it either should or should not take place tomorrow. Since propositions correspond with facts, it is evident that when in future events there is a real alternative, and a potentiality in contrary directions, the corresponding affirmation and denial have the same character.

This is the case with regard to that which is not always existent or not always non-existent. One of the two propositions in such instances must be true and the other false, but we cannot say determinately that this or that is false, but must leave the alternative undecided. One may indeed be more likely to be true than the other, but it cannot be either actually true or actually false. It is therefore plain that it is not necessary that of an affirmation and a denial one should be true and the other false. For in the case of that which exists potentially, but not actually, the rule which applies to that which exists actually does not hold good. The case is rather as we have indicated.

Nicomachean Ethics, Book III

Since virtue is concerned with passions and actions, and on voluntary passions and actions praise and blame are bestowed, on those that are involuntary pardon, and sometimes also pity, to distinguish the voluntary and the involuntary is presumably necessary for those who are studying the nature of virtue, and useful also for legislators with a view to the assigning both of honours and of punishments.

Those things, then, are thought involuntary, which take place under compulsion or owing to ignorance; and that is compulsory of which the moving principle is outside, being a principle in which nothing is contributed by the person who is acting or is feeling the passion, e.g., if he were to be carried somewhere by a wind, or by men who had him in their power.

But with regard to the things that are done from fear of greater evils or for some noble object (e.g., if a tyrant were to order one to do something base, having one's parents and children in his power, and if one did the action they were to be saved, but otherwise would be put to death), it may be debated whether such actions are involuntary or voluntary. Something of the sort happens also with regard to the throwing of goods overboard in a storm; for in the abstract no one throws goods away voluntarily, but on condition of its securing the safety of himself and his crew any sensible man does so. Such actions, then, are mixed, but are more like voluntary actions; for they are worthy of choice at the time when they are done, and the end of an action is relative to the occasion. Both the terms, then, 'voluntary' and 'involuntary', must be used with reference to the moment of action. Now the man acts voluntarily; for the principle that moves the instrumental parts of the body in such actions is in him, and the things of which the moving principle is in a man himself are in his power to do or not to do. Such actions, therefore, are voluntary, but in the abstract perhaps involuntary; for no one would choose any such act in itself.

For such actions men are sometimes even praised, when they endure something base or painful in return for great and noble objects gained; in the opposite case they are blamed, since to endure the greatest indignities for no noble end or for a trifling end is the mark of an inferior person. On some actions praise indeed is not bestowed, but pardon is, when one does what he ought not under pressure which overstrains human nature and which no one could withstand. But some acts, perhaps, we cannot be forced to do, but ought rather to face death after the most fearful sufferings; for the things that 'forced' Euripides' Alcmaeon to slay his mother seem absurd. It is difficult sometimes to determine what should be chosen at what cost, and what should be endured in return for what gain, and yet more difficult to abide by our decisions; for as a rule what is expected is painful, and what we are forced to do is base, whence praise and blame are bestowed on those who have been compelled or have not.

What sort of acts, then, should be called compulsory? We answer that without qualification actions are so when the cause is in the external circumstances and the agent contributes nothing. But the things that in themselves are involuntary, but now and in return for these gains are worthy of choice, and whose moving principle is in the agent, are in themselves involuntary, but now and in return for these gains voluntary. They are more like voluntary acts; for actions are in the class of particulars, and the particular acts here are voluntary. What sort of things are to be chosen, and in return for what, it is not easy to state; for there are many differences in the particular cases.

But if some one were to say that pleasant and noble objects have a compelling power, forcing us from without, all acts would be for him compulsory; for it is for these objects that all men do everything they do. And those who act under compulsion and unwillingly act with pain, but those who do acts for their pleasantness and nobility do them with pleasure; it is absurd to make external circumstances responsible, and not oneself, as being easily caught by such attractions, and to make oneself responsible for noble acts but the pleasant objects responsible for base acts. The compulsory, then, seems to be that whose moving principle is outside, the person compelled contributing nothing.

Everything that is done by reason of ignorance is *not* voluntary; it is only what produces pain and repentance that is *in*voluntary. For the man who has done something owing to ignorance, and feels not the least vexation at his action, has not acted voluntarily, since he did not know what he was doing, nor yet involuntarily, since he is not pained. Of people, then, who act by reason of ignorance he who repents is thought an involuntary agent, and the man who does not repent may, since he is different, be called a not voluntary agent; for, since he differs from the other, it is better that he should have a name of his own.

Acting by reason of ignorance seems also to be different from acting *in* ignorance; for the man who is drunk or in a rage is thought to act as a result not of ignorance but of one of the causes mentioned, yet not knowingly but in ignorance.

Now every wicked man is ignorant of what he ought to do and what he ought to abstain from, and it is by reason of error of this kind that men become unjust and in general bad; but the term 'involuntary' tends to be used not if a man is ignorant of what is to his advantage—for it is not mistaken purpose that causes involuntary action (it leads rather to wickedness), nor ignorance of the universal (for *that* men are *blamed*), but ignorance of particulars, i.e., of the circumstances of the action and the objects with which it is concerned. For it is

on these that both pity and pardon depend, since the person who is ignorant of any of these acts involuntarily.

Perhaps it is just as well, therefore, to determine their nature and number. A man may be ignorant, then, of who he is, what he is doing, what or whom he is acting on, and sometimes also what (e.g., what instrument) he is doing it with, and to what end (e.g., he may think his act will conduce to some one's safety), and how he is doing it (e.g., whether gently or violently). Now of all of these no one could be ignorant unless he were mad, and evidently also he could not be ignorant of the agent; for how could he not know himself? But of what he is doing a man might be ignorant, as for instance people say 'it slipped out of their mouths as they were speaking,' or 'they did not know it was a secret,' as Aeschylus said of the mysteries, or a man might say he 'let it go off when he merely wanted to show its working,' as the man did with the catapult. Again, one might think one's son was an enemy, as Merope did, or that a pointed spear had a button on it, or that a stone was pumice-stone; or one might give a man a draught to save him, and really kill him; or one might want to touch a man, as people do in sparring, and really wound him. The ignorance may relate, then, to any of these things, i.e., of the circumstances of the action, and the man who was ignorant of any of these is thought to have acted involuntarily, and especially if he was ignorant on the most important points; and these are thought to be the circumstances of the action and its end. Further, the doing of an act that is called involuntary in virtue of ignorance of this sort must be painful and involve repentance.

Since that which is done under compulsion or by reason of ignorance is involuntary, the voluntary would seem to be that of which the moving principle is in the agent himself, he being aware of the particular circumstances of the action. Presumably acts done by reason of anger or appetite are not rightly called involuntary. For in the first place, on that showing none of the other animals will act voluntarily, nor will children; and secondly, is it meant that we do not do voluntarily *any* of the acts that are due to appetite or anger, or that we do the noble acts voluntarily and the base acts involuntarily? Is not this absurd, when one and the same thing is the cause? But it would surely be odd to describe as involuntary the things one ought to desire; and we ought both to be angry at certain things and to have an appetite for certain things, e.g., for health and for learning. Also what is involuntary is thought to be painful, but what is in accordance with appetite is thought to be pleasant. Again, what is the difference in respect of involuntariness between errors committed upon calculation and those committed in anger? Both are to be avoided, but the irrational passions are thought not less human than reason is, and therefore also the actions which proceed from anger or appetite are the man's actions. It would be odd, then, to treat them as involuntary.

Both the voluntary and the involuntary having been delimited, we must next discuss choice; for it is thought to be most closely bound up with virtue and to discriminate characters better than actions do.

Choice, then, seems to be voluntary, but not the same thing as the voluntary; the latter extends more widely. For both children and the lower animals share in voluntary action, but not in choice, and acts done on the spur of the moment we describe as voluntary, but not as chosen.

Those who say it is appetite or anger or wish or a kind of opinion do not seem to be right. For choice is not common to irrational creatures as well, but appetite and anger are. Again, the incontinent man acts with appetite, but not with choice; while the continent man on the contrary acts with choice, but not with appetite. Again, appetite is contrary to choice, but not appetite to appetite. Again, appetite relates to the pleasant and the painful, choice neither to the painful nor to the pleasant.

Still less is it anger; for acts due to anger are thought to be less than any others objects of choice.

But neither is it wish, though it seems near to it; for choice cannot relate to impossibles, and if any one said he chose them he would be thought silly; but there may be a wish even for impossibles, e.g., for immortality. And wish may relate to things that could in no way be brought about by one's own efforts, e.g., that a particular actor or athlete should win in a competition; but no one chooses such things, but only the things that he thinks could be brought about by his own efforts. Again, wish relates rather to the end, choice to the means; for instance, we wish to be healthy, but we choose the acts which will make us healthy, and we wish to be happy and say we do, but we cannot well say we choose to be so; for, in general, choice seems to relate to the things that are in our own power.

For this reason, too, it cannot be opinion; for opinion is thought to relate to all kinds of things, no less to eternal things and impossible things than to things in our own power; and it is distinguished by its falsity or truth, not by its badness or goodness, while choice is distinguished rather by these.

Now with opinion in general perhaps no one even says it is identical. But it is not identical even with any kind of opinion; for by choosing what is good or bad we are men of a certain character, which we are not by holding certain opinions. And we choose to get or avoid something good or bad, but we have opinions about what a thing is or whom it is good for or how it is good for him; we can hardly be said to opine to get or avoid anything. And choice is praised for being related to the right object rather than for being rightly related to it, opinion for being truly related to its object. And we choose what we best know to be good, but we opine what we do not quite know; and it is not the same people that are thought to make the best choices and to have the best opinions, but some are thought to have fairly good opinions, but by reason of vice to choose what they should not. If opinion precedes choice or accompanies it, that makes no difference; for it is not this that we are considering, but whether it is *identical* with some kind of opinion.

What, then, or what kind of thing is it, since it is none of the things we have mentioned? It seems to be voluntary, but not all that is voluntary to be an object of choice. Is it, then, what has been decided on by previous deliberation? At any rate choice involves a rational principle and thought. Even the name seems to suggest that it is what is chosen before other things.

33. *Fate, Logic, and Time*

STEVEN CAHN

In this selection, Steven Cahn, provost and vice president for academic affairs at the Graduate School and University Center of The City University of New York, explicates the metaphysical implications of Aristotle's solution to the problem of fatalism. According to Cahn, Aristotle's solution involves the (contentious) distinction between what Cahn calls the "synthetic" law of excluded middle and the "analytic" law of excluded middle. According to the synthetic law, for any proposition P, P is true, or not P is true. According to the analytic law, for any proposition P, P or not P is true. Cahn agrees with Aristotle in maintaining that the synthetic law of excluded middle does imply fatalism, but that the analytic law does not. Cahn argues that Aristotle's solution to fatalism implies propositions can change their truth value with the passage of time and, consequently, the theory of time and truth advocated by Williams (and Mellor) must be abandoned, if fatalism is to be avoided.

Fatalism, as I originally defined it, is the thesis that the laws of logic alone suffice to prove that no man has free will. . . . I have argued that, . . . if one accepts the law of excluded middle in what I have termed its "synthetic" formulation, viz., every proposition must be either true, or if not true, then false, then he is thereby logically committed to deny man's free will. . . . This law, though it has been generally accepted as a law of logic is, in fact, an empirical generalization open to serious question. It is not, as those who hold the pragmatic view of the laws of thought would have us believe, a "minimal condition for discourse." Discourse without the synthetic law of excluded middle is just as intelligible as discourse with the synthetic law of excluded middle. Furthermore, the synthetic law of excluded middle is not, as those who hold the ontological view would have us believe, an incontrovertible and indisputable fact about the world. Quite to the contrary, the synthetic law of excluded middle would be shown to be false by the occurrence of a single action which a man had within his power both to perform and not to per-

form, and whether such actions have occurred or will occur has been a source of dispute for centuries.

If one rejects the synthetic law of excluded middle as it applies to certain statements concerning future contingent events and, thereby, avoids a logical commitment to deny man's free will, is he, thereby, logically committed to deny the analytic law of excluded middle? The analytic law of excluded middle, any proposition must be either true or false, is not implied by the synthetic law of excluded middle. $LN(P \lor \sim P)$ does not imply $T(P) \lor T(\sim P)$, i.e., the logical necessity of $(P \lor \sim P)$ does not imply that P is true, or if P is not true, then $\sim P$ is true. Therefore, one can maintain the analytic law of excluded middle while rejecting the synthetic law of excluded middle.

Maintaining the analytic law of excluded middle, however, does not commit one to deny man's free will. But if one rejects the synthetic law of excluded middle, is there any reason to maintain the analytic law of excluded middle?

The analytic law of excluded middle, unlike the synthetic law of excluded middle, does appear to be an incontrovertible truth. To affirm that an event did or did not occur, that an event is or is not occurring, that an event will or will not occur, does seem to be affirming what is incontrovertibly so. It

From *Fate, Logic, and Time* by Steven M. Cahn (1967; reprinted Atascadero, Calif.: Ridgeview Publishing Company, 1982). By permission of the author.

is the analytic law of excluded middle which embodies what has been traditionally known as a "law of thought." According to the pragmatic view of the laws of thought, the analytic law of excluded middle is a necessary condition for intelligible discourse. According to the ontological view, the analytic law of excluded middle reflects an incontrovertible fact about the world. According to either of these views, however, the analytic law of excluded middle is a principle which is surely true. Consider, for instance, a man who "risks" his money by betting that a certain horse will or will not win a certain race. He is not betting that the horse will win the race. He is not betting that the horse will not win the race. What he is betting is that the horse will or will not win the race. Such a bet is surely no risk at all, for nothing could be more certain than that the horse will or will not win the race.

Thus, if one wishes to avoid fatalism and yet not violate reason itself, one must reject, as Aristotle did, the synthetic law of excluded middle and accept, as he did, the analytic law of excluded middle.[1] However, the decision to adopt Aristotle's solution to the problem of fatalism is far from the end of the matter, for this decision has many important and controversial implications.[2]

We have seen that in order to avoid fatalism, one must hold that any proposition which affirms or denies, concerning a contingent event, that it will occur is not true, though it is not false. Nevertheless, to maintain the analytic law of excluded middle, one must hold that any disjunction of such a proposition and its denial is necessarily true. For example, let P represent a proposition which affirms that a contingent event will occur. In order to avoid fatalistic implications, one must hold that (1) P is not true, (2) P is not false, (3) $\sim P$ (the contradictory of P) is not true, and (4) $\sim P$ is not false. In order to maintain the analytic law of excluded middle, one must hold that $(P \lor \sim P)$ is necessarily true, i.e., true by virtue of logic alone.

Traditional logic utilized only two truth-values. It maintained that if a proposition was not true, it must be false; and if it was not false, it must be true. The denial of the synthetic law of excluded middle with regard to certain statements concerning future contingent events would, however, seem to entail an exception to this two-valued logic, for it implies that there are certain propositions which are not true, though they also are not false. Such propositions affirm or deny, concerning a contingent event, that it will occur. Such propositions require a third truth-value.

Modern logicians have developed what is known as a three-valued logic. Such a logic provides for the case in which a proposition is not true and not false, by providing a third truth-value which such a proposition may possess. The best-known system of three-valued logic was created by the Polish logician Jan Lukasiewicz, who created his three-valued logic specifically for the purpose of providing a logical framework for Aristotle's doctrine of future contingencies.[3] This system was further developed by A. N. Prior, who also envisioned it as a logical tool for dealing with the problem of future contingencies.[4]

To see how such a three-valued logic works,[5] let us consider a proposition, represented by P, which affirms that a contingent event e will occur. According to three-valued logic, P is not true and P is not false. It is, rather, indeterminate.[6] If P is indeterminate, then $\sim P$ is also indeterminate, for if the occurrence of e is contingent, then so is the nonoccurrence of e.

It should be noted that three-valued logic does not imply an exception to the law of contradiction. That law states that if a proposition is true, then its contradictory must be false, and if a proposition is false, then its contradictory must be true. According to three-valued logic, if P is true, then $\sim P$ is false. Similarly, if $\sim P$ is true, then P is false. If P is indeterminate, then $\sim P$ is indeterminate. Thus, three-valued logic in no sense constitutes an exception to the law of contradiction.

But does three-valued logic entail an exception to the law of excluded middle? C. I. Lewis and C. H. Langford, in their discussion of Lukasiewicz' system of three-valued logic, note that such a logic "requires that the Law of Excluded Middle, 'Every proposition is either true or false,' must be repudiated as a false principle."[7]

Here again it is necessary to distinguish between the synthetic law of excluded middle and the analytic law of excluded middle. According to the synthetic law of excluded middle, every proposition must be either true, or if not true, then false, i.e., for any interpretation of P, "P" is true or "$\sim P$" is true. Three-valued logic does imply an exception to this law, for according to three-valued logic there are propositions which are *not* true and *not* false. Consider the proposition represented by P which affirms that a contingent event will occur. It is not the case that P is true, and it is not the case that *P* is false. Thus, it is not the case that *P* is either true, or if not true, then false, and the synthetic law of excluded middle is thereby repudiated.

But does a proposition which is not true and not false constitute an exception to the analytic law of excluded middle? That law states that every proposition is either true or false, i.e., for any interpretation of *P*, "*P* or ~*P*" is true. Consider again the proposition represented by *P* which affirms that a contingent event *e* will occur. *P* is *not* true. *P* is *not* false. But "*P* or ~*P*" is true, in the sense that *e* will or will not occur, though it is not true that *e* will occur and it is not true that *e* will not occur.

This does not imply, however, that either *e* will occur, or if *e* will not occur, then ~*e* (the nonoccurrence of *e*) will occur. The analytic law of excluded middle does not state either that *P* is true or that *P* is false, i.e., *e* will occur or *e* will not occur. What it does state is that *P* is either true or false, i.e., *e* will or will not occur. In other words, the analytic law of excluded middle is a limiting but not a determining principle. It limits the possibilities to the occurrence and nonoccurrence of *e*, but neither determines that *e* will occur, nor determines that *e* will not occur. The analytic law of excluded middle implies only that one of two possibilities will occur; it does not imply that one possibility will occur, nor does it imply that the other possibility will occur. To put this in terms of the symbolism, the analytic law of excluded middle, $LN(P \lor \sim P)$, implies that $T(P \lor \sim P)$, but just as $LN(P \lor \sim P)$ does not imply $LN(P) \lor LN(\sim P)$, so $T(P \lor \sim P)$ does not imply that $T(P) \lor T(\sim P)$.

It is thus possible to maintain the analytic law of excluded middle while admitting that a specific proposition is not true and not false. But if it is not true and if it is not false, it must have some other truth-value. Three-valued logic provides such a truth-value.

In order to see clearly just why the introduction of a third truth-value is necessary to avoid fatalism, consider Aristotle's example of a sea-fight tomorrow. If one affirms that a sea-fight will occur tomorrow, then he is, as we have seen, logically committed to the view that no one can prevent the occurrence of a sea-fight tomorrow; if one affirms that a sea-fight will not occur tomorrow, then he is logically committed to the view that no one can bring about the occurrence of a sea-fight tomorrow.[8] But if it is not true that a sea-fight will occur tomorrow, and if it is also not false that a sea-fight will occur tomorrow, what truth-value does the proposition "there will be a sea-fight tomorrow" have? It must have a truth-value to be meaningful, and it certainly is a meaningful proposition.[9] It implies that the present situation is compatible with someone bringing about the occurrence of a sea-fight tomorrow and the present situation is also compatible with someone preventing the occurrence of a sea-fight tomorrow, and empirical evidence is certainly relevant to verifying or disconfirming this description of the present situation. For instance, if all ships on both sides of a war have been sunk, that would constitute strong evidence against anyone's having it within his power to bring about a sea-fight tomorrow. Thus, the proposition "there will be a sea-fight tomorrow" is clearly meaningful. But if a proposition is to be meaningful, it must have a truth-value. If it is not true and it is not false, it must have a third truth-value, and it is such a truth-value which three-valued logic provides.

Aristotle's solution to the problem of fatalism thus implies a three-valued logic. But, Aristotle's solution has other consequences which are equally as important and equally as controversial, if not more controversial, than a three-valued logic. These consequences strike at the heart of certain generally accepted views of the nature of propositions as well as the nature of time.

Most modern logic utilizes only propositions which do not change their truth-value from one time to another. If a proposition is true, it has always been true and will always be true. If a proposition is false, it has always been false and will always be false. As Quine puts it:

> Logical analysis is facilitated by requiring rather that each *statement* be true once and for all or false once and for all, independently of time. This can be effected by rendering verbs tenseless and then resorting to explicit chronological descriptions when need arises for distinctions of time. The sentence, "The Nazis will annex Bohemia," uttered as true on May 9, 1936, corresponds to the statement, "The Nazis annex [tenseless] Bohemia after May 9, 1936"; and this statement is true once and for all, regardless of date of utterance.[10]

Quine is hardly alone in this opinion. His position has been supported by Bertrand Russell,[11] Ayer,[12] and J. N. Findlay, the last declaring that "if we avoided the adverbs 'here' and 'there,' if we purged our language of tenses, and talked exclusively in terms of dates and tenseless participles, we should never be involved in difficulties."[13]

However, the program advocated by Quine and those who agree with him that attempts to render all propositions tenseless without altering their meaning is doomed to failure. A proposition's tense may be shifted from the verb to an adverbial phrase, but the tense cannot be altogether eliminated without altering the meaning of the proposition. A proposition's tense is thus an integral and uneliminable part of the proposition.

This may seem to be an uninteresting logical point, but, in fact, it has serious repercussions for fatalism. Aristotle's solution to the problem of fatalism depends on a proposition's tense being an uneliminable part of the proposition, for Aristotle's solution implies that a proposition can have two different truth-values, depending on the tense of the proposition. If Quine's view were correct, a proposition's tense could have no effect on the proposition's truth-value, for the tense would be, in principle, eliminable. Therefore, Aristotle's solution to the problem of fatalism would be impossible and, as we have seen, Aristotle's solution is the only way of avoiding fatalism while still preserving logic.

In order to see just why Aristotle's solution to the problem of fatalism depends upon a proposition's changing its truth-value,[14] consider a proposition, represented by P, which affirms that a sea-fight occurs on September 7, 1948 ("occurs" to be understood tenselessly). If it was true on Sept. 6, 1948, that a sea-fight would occur on Sept. 7, 1948, then, as we have seen, it was fated on Sept. 6 that a sea-fight would occur on Sept. 7.[15] If it was true on Sept. 6 that a sea-fight would not take place on Sept. 7, then it was fated on Sept. 6 that a sea-fight would not take place on Sept. 7. But, if neither the occurrence of a sea-fight on Sept. 7 nor the nonoccurrence of a sea-fight on Sept. 7 was fated on Sept. 6, then it was not true and it was not false on Sept. 6 that a sea-fight would occur on Sept. 7. But the proposition "a sea-fight occurs on Sept. 7, 1948" must have had a truth-value on Sept. 6. This is the truth-value which I have chosen to call "indeterminate."

But, on Sept. 8, 1948, the proposition "a sea-fight occurs on Sept. 7, 1948" must be either true, or if not true, then false, for if it were indeterminate on Sept. 8 whether a sea-fight occurred on Sept. 7,

it would be within a man's power on Sept. 8 to prevent a sea-fight on Sept. 7 and it would also be within a man's power on Sept. 8 to bring about a sea-fight on Sept. 7, and this is absurd. Therefore, if it is not fated on Sept. 6 that a sea-fight will occur on Sept. 7, the proposition "a sea-fight occurs on Sept. 7, 1948" is indeterminate on Sept. 6 and either true, or if not true, then false on Sept. 8. In either case the proposition changes its truth-value from Sept. 6 to Sept. 8.

Thus, if one is to avoid fatalism and preserve logic, a proposition's truth-value must be subject to change. Indeed, this is not all a proposition must be able to change. A proposition's modality must also be subject to change. This is another idea which is unacceptable to many modern logicians. For instance, Donald Williams writes as follows:

> Even if we adopt the debatable maxim that the more absurd an idea is, the less likely it is to have been espoused by Aristotle, the idea which I impute would have to go far to vie with what Mr. Linsky imputes, viz., that the modality of a proposition, instead of depending on its logical form or other intrinsic character, depends on the *date*, so that exactly the same proposition which at 11:59 A.M. is contingent, at noon is necessary.[16]

It is important to note, however, that a proposition can have more than one kind of modality. Aristotle's solution to the problem of fatalism does *not* imply that a proposition which is logically contingent (i.e., a synthetic proposition) at one time may be logically necessary (i.e., an analytic proposition) at another time.

The term "necessary" as used in the context of the issue of fatalism has the following meaning: an event is necessary if no man has it within his power to prevent the occurrence of the event; similarly, a proposition is necessary if no man has it within his power to falsify the proposition.

The term "contingent" as used in the context of the issue of fatalism has a similar meaning: an event is contingent if it is not the case that the occurrence of the event is necessary and if it is not the case that the nonoccurrence of the event is necessary (i.e., if a man has it within his power to prevent the occurrence of the event, and if a man has it within his power to bring about the occurrence of the event); a proposition is contingent if it is not the case that the proposition is necessary and if it is not the case that the contradictory of the proposition is necessary (i.e., if a man can falsify the proposition, and if a man can falsify the contradictory of the proposition). Thus, what Aristotle's solution to the problem of fatalism does imply is that a proposition may be falsifiable at one time and not falsifiable at another time.

In order to see clearly just why Aristotle's solution does imply that a proposition's modality must be subject to change, consider again the proposition (P) "A sea-fight occurs on Sept. 7, 1948" ("occurs" to be considered tenselessly). If it was true on Sept. 6 that a sea-fight would occur on Sept. 7, then as we have seen, no man could on Sept. 6 prevent the occurrence of a sea-fight on Sept. 7, and it would not be within any man's power on Sept. 6 to falsify P. If it was true on Sept. 6 that a sea-fight would not take place on Sept. 7, then, as we have seen, no man could on Sept. 6 bring about the occurrence of a sea-fight on Sept. 7, and it would not be within anyone's power on Sept. 6 to render P true. Thus, whether P is true on Sept. 6 or whether P is false on Sept. 6, either the occurrence of a sea-fight on Sept. 7 is fated on Sept. 6 or the nonoccurrence of a sea-fight on Sept. 7 is fated on Sept. 6.

Neither one is fated on Sept. 6 *only* if on Sept. 6 P is not true and P is not false, but P is indeterminate. If it is indeterminate on Sept. 6 whether a sea-fight will occur on Sept. 7, then it is within some man's power on Sept. 6 to bring about the occurrence of a sea-fight on Sept. 7, and it is also within some man's power on Sept. 6 to prevent a sea-fight on Sept. 7. Thus, if it is indeterminate on Sept. 6 whether a sea-fight will occur on Sept. 7, P, as well as ~P, is a contingent proposition on Sept. 6, for on Sept. 6 it is within some man's power to falsify P and it is also within some man's power to render P true. Thus, if a sea-fight on Sept. 7 is not fated on Sept. 6, P is a contingent proposition on Sept. 6.

As we have seen before, however, it is not up to anyone on Sept. 8 whether or not a sea-fight occurred on Sept. 7, for if this were the case, it would be within a man's power on Sept. 8 to prevent a sea-fight on Sept. 7, and it would also be within a man's power on Sept. 8 to bring about a sea-fight on Sept. 7, and this is absurd. Therefore, on Sept. 8 either P is necessary or ~P is necessary.

So, if it is not fated on Sept. 6 that a sea-fight will occur on Sept. 7, the proposition (P) "A sea-fight occurs on Sept. 7, 1948" is contingent on Sept.

6 as is the proposition (~P) "A sea-fight does not occur on Sept. 7, 1948." But, on Sept. 8 either P is necessary or ~P is necessary.[17] In either case a proposition has changed its modality. Indeed, both P and ~P have changed their modality, for whichever proposition is necessary, the other proposition is impossible, i.e., it is not within any man's power to render the proposition true. For instance, if a sea-fight actually occurred on Sept. 7, then on Sept. 8 the proposition P is necessary and the proposition ~P is impossible, for on Sept. 8 no man can falsify P and no man can render ~P true. Thus, if one is to avoid fatalism and preserve logic, a proposition's modality must be subject to change.

These possible changes in a proposition's truth-value and modality are not merely logical peculiarities. The possibility of such changes is logically incompatible with at least two commonly held metaphysical theories of the nature of time.

The first of these theories is expressed by Bertrand Russell:

> There is some sense, easier to feel than to state, in which time is an unimportant and superficial characteristic of reality. Past and future must be acknowledged to be as real as the present, and a certain emancipation from slavery to time is essential to philosophic thought.[18]

This "emancipation from slavery to time" was so eloquently expressed by Spinoza:

> Things are conceived by us as actual in two ways—either in so far as we conceive them to exist with relation to a fixed time and place or in so far as we conceive them to be contained in God and to follow from the necessity of the divine nature. But those things which are conceived in this second way as true or real we conceive under the form of eternity, and their ideas involve the eternal and infinite essence of God.[19]

This same idea of time as a mere "superficial" aspect of reality underlies the metaphysical position defended by Donald Williams:

> I do wish to defend the view of the world, or the manner of speaking about it, which treats the totality of being, of facts, or of events, as spread out eternally in the dimension of time as well as the dimensions of space . . . there "exists" an

eternal world total in which past and future events are as determinately located, characterized, and truly describable as are southern events and western events.[20]

Williams does not specifically state that time is unimportant or "superficial," but his position obviously implies that the future is just as real as the past, and that time is of no importance in evaluating what are "facts" and what are not "facts."

A similar metaphysical thesis lies at the heart of Quine's program to require "that each statement be true once and for all or false once and for all, independently of time." Indeed, Quine utilizes the term "eternal sentence" to refer to a sentence "whose truth-value stays fixed through time and from speaker to speaker," and he argues that any sentence can be transformed without loss of meaning to an "eternal sentence."[21]

This metaphysical thesis, however, is logically incompatible with the possibility of a proposition changing its truth-value or modality depending upon the time at which it is stated, and, as we have seen, it is just such a possibility which provides the only logical escape from fatalism. If time is but a "superficial" aspect of reality, if a true proposition must be eternally true, if the "facts" are "spread out eternally," then the time at which a proposition is stated has no relevance to its truth-value or modality.

Note that I am not here referring to propositions which are incomplete due to a lack of specification of time, place, or person. "It is raining," "I am swimming," or "Jones is running" are incomplete propositions whose truth-value or modality can change without in any way casting doubt upon the metaphysical theory which declares time to be a "superficial" aspect of reality. For instance, "It is raining" may be true in New York, but false in Boston. It may be true at noon, but false at midnight. "I am swimming" may be true of one person, but false of another. "Jones is running" is necessary when Jones is running, but impossible when Jones is dead.

However, it is not such incomplete propositions to which I am referring when I argue that the possibility of a proposition's truth-value or modality being subject to change is logically incompatible with the metaphysical theory of the superficiality of time. I am referring, rather, to propositions such as "George Washington is crossing the Delaware River at 12:00 A.M. on December 25, 1776" ("is crossing" to be considered tenselessly), which are

complete as to time, place, and person. If we are to preserve logic and avoid fatalism, such a proposition's truth-value and modality must be subject to change. However, according to the view of time propounded by Russell, Williams, Quine, and others, such a change is impossible, for the "facts" are all there already, the "facts" are "eternal," and time is a "superficial" aspect of reality which does not affect these "eternal facts." Thus, this view of time, which Williams confidently refers to as a "truism,"[22] is logically incompatible with man's free will. If this view of time is a truism, then so is fatalism.

There is a second commonly held theory of time which is logically incompatible with the possibility of a proposition's truth-value or modality being subject to change. This theory does not claim that time is a superficial aspect of reality. It claims that time is no aspect of reality, for time is not real.

The view that time is unreal has a long and distinguished history in philosophic thought. One of the first philosophers to argue formally for this thesis was St. Augustine.[23] He argued that "if the present were always present and never flowed into the past, it would not be time at all, but eternity."[24] Since, according to St. Augustine, the "past" must be identified with memory and the "future" with expectation, and since memory and expectation are both present facts, all "time" is present, and thus is not time, but eternity. What are usually identified as past, present, and future should, according to St. Augustine, be properly identified as "a present of things past, a present of things present, a present of things future."[25]

A similar view of time was expressed by Immanuel Kant in his *Critique of Pure Reason*. He argued that "time [is] merely the subjective condition under which all our intuitions take place."[26] F. H. Bradley, expressing a similar view, referred to time as "illusory,"[27] and J. M. E. McTaggert likewise referred to time as a mere "appearance."[28]

This is an even more extreme metaphysical view than that supported by Russell, Williams, and Quine. Russell, though he considers time to be a "superficial" aspect of reality, does admit that "past and future must be acknowledged to be as real as the present." But though the view of time espoused by St. Augustine, Kant, Bradley, and others is contrary to that of Russell, it is, as is Russell's view, logically incompatible with Aristotle's solution to the problem of fatalism.

As we have seen, Aristotle's solution requires

that a proposition's truth-value and modality depend upon the time at which the proposition is stated. According to Aristotle's solution, a proposition may be indeterminate at one time and true, or if not true, then false at another time. Similarly, according to Aristotle's solution, a proposition may be contingent at one time and either necessary, or if not necessary, then impossible at another time. But if time is unreal, then it cannot affect a proposition's truth-value or modality, and if time cannot affect a proposition's truth-value or modality, we must either accept fatalism or reject logic.

Aristotle's solution to the problem of fatalism thus has at least three metaphysical implications concerning the nature of time. First, time is real. According to Aristotle's solution, the truth-value and modality of a proposition depend upon the time at which the proposition is stated. If time is not real, it could not affect the truth-value or modality of a proposition, and Aristotle's solution would be erroneous.

Second, time is "efficacious," i.e., time alone can affect a man's powers or abilities. According to Aristotle's solution, certain events in the future are contingent, whereas all events in the past are, by virtue of their pastness alone, necessary, i.e., it is not within any man's power to prevent their occurrence. Thus, future possibilities, which are at one time within a man's power to realize and also within his power not to realize, cease to be possibilities due to the mere lapse of time. Time alone thus can decrease a man's powers or abilities. If time were not efficacious, Aristotle's solution would be erroneous, for either all future events would be necessary, or else some past events would be contingent.

Third, time has an intrinsic sense of asymmetry. According to Aristotle's solution, the future differs from the past, and not merely in the sense that it comes later. Possibilities exist in the future in a sense in which no possibilities exist in the past. I can exert some measure of control over what will happen in the future, whereas I can exert no such control over what has happened in the past. This is commonly expressed by saying that the past is "closed," while the future is, in part, "open." If this were not the case, Aristotle's solution would be erroneous.

C. D. Broad once wrote that philosophy enables us "to replace a vague belief by a clear and analysed one, and a merely instinctive belief by one that has passed the fire of criticism."[29] Almost all men are firmly convinced that fatalism is false. However, in order to maintain this belief logically, and not merely instinctively, one must distinguish between two forms of the law of excluded middle.

What I have referred to as the synthetic law of excluded middle does logically imply that no man has free will. But to term the synthetic law of excluded middle a "law of logic" seems to me a distortion. The truth of the synthetic law of excluded middle can be decided only on empirical grounds, not on logical grounds. Fatalism, which depends for its plausibility on the fact that it utilizes premises which are indubitable and undeniable laws of logic, cannot be sustained by utilizing as a premise the synthetic law of excluded middle which is not a law of logic.

On the other hand, what I have referred to as the analytic law of excluded middle is an indubitable and undeniable law of logic. It does not, however, logically imply that no man has free will, and it does not, therefore, suffice to prove that fatalism is true.

Thus, if one wishes to preserve logic and yet avoid fatalism, one must adopt the solution presented by Aristotle more than two thousand years ago, viz., rejecting the synthetic law of excluded middle, accepting the analytic law of excluded middle, and accepting all the meta-logical and meta-temporal implications of such a position.

Endnotes

[1] Aristotle rejected the synthetic law of excluded middle both as a logical principle and as an empirical fact. However, in order to avoid fatalism one need only reject it as a logical principle. But to reject it as a logical principle one must also reject certain generally accepted views which will be discussed in the remainder of this chapter.

[2] A penetrating discussion of this aspect of the problem is to be found in Ronald J. Butler's "Aristotle's Sea Fight and Three-Valued Logic," *The Philosophical Review*, 64 (1955), 264–74.

[3] The system and its relation to Aristotle's views can be found in Jan Lukasiewicz, "Philosophische Bemerkungen zu mehrwertigen Systemen des Aussagenkalkuls," *Comptes Rendus des Séances de la Société des Sciences et des Lettres de Varsovie (Sprawozdania z pozesieden Towarzystwa Naukowego Warszawskiego)*, Classe III, Vol. XXIII (1930), Fascicule 1–3, pp. 51–77.

[4] Arthur Prior, *Formal Logic* (Oxford, 1962), pt. III, no. II.

[5] It should be noted that in order to avoid the fatalistic

conclusions of the arguments it is not necessary to adopt any one particular system of a three-valued logic. What I am proposing is the adoption of a third truth-value, and this is consistent with the adoption of any one of many three-valued logical systems. One such system is suggested in Storrs McCall's perceptive article, "Temporal Flux," *American Philosophical Quarterly*, 3 (1966), 270–81.

[6] Prior uses the term "neuter." I prefer the more descriptive term "indeterminate."

[7] Clarence Irving Lewis and Cooper Harold Langford, *Symbolic Logic* (New York, 1959), p. 222.

[8] Editors' note: Cahn's interpretation of Aristotle's argument is as follows:

Argument I:

1. Every proposition must be either true, or if not true, then false.

2. Assume that one man affirms today that an event of a given character (e.g., a sea-fight) will occur tomorrow and another denies this.

3. The statement of the one man corresponds with reality and that of the other does not.

4. But in that case it must already be true that a sea-fight will take place tomorrow, such that there is now no possibility that it might not, or else it must already be true that a sea-fight will not take place tomorrow, such that there is now no possibility that it might.

5. In either case "nothing is or takes place fortuitously, either in the present or in the future, and there are no real alternatives; everything takes place of necessity and is fixed . . . for the meaning of the world 'fortuitous' in regard to present or future events is that reality is so constituted that it may issue in either of two opposite directions" (Aristotle, *De Interpretatione*, 18^b, 5–9. All quotations are from *The Basic Works of Aristotle*, ed. Richard McKeon [New York, 1941]).

[9] It might be argued that "there will be a sea-fight tomorrow" is not a proposition at all, but rather a prediction, proposal, promise, etc. I see no reason to adopt such an approach, however, since it offers no real advantages while creating unnecessary difficulties. For example, if the sea-fight is necessary (whether or not the speaker knows it) the speaker is predicting, proposing, etc. If the sea-fight is not necessary, the speaker is uttering a proposition. This would be most peculiar, since I should think that whether a man is predicting or proposing or promising depends to a great extent on his intention and not on the contingency of a future event, a contingency of which he may be totally unaware. In addition, this approach would have the odd consequence of denying that "there will be a sea-fight tomorrow" is a proposition,

while affirming that "there was a sea-fight yesterday" *is* a proposition.

[10] W. V. O. Quine, *Elementary Logic* (New York, 1965), p. 6.

[11] Bertrand Russell, *An Inquiry into Meaning and Truth* (London, 1940), p. 113.

[12] A. J. Ayer, *Philosophical Essays* (London, 1963), p. 186.

[13] J. N. Findlay, "Time: A Treatment of Some Puzzles," in Anthony Flew, ed., *Logic and Language*, p. 58.

[14] It seems to me that regardless of my previous analysis, anyone committed to man's free will is committed to a proposition being able to change its truth-value. For example, if it is true that I will do A at t_1, then the proposition "I will do A at t_1" is true. If I can refrain from A at t_1, then I can render the proposition "I will do A at t_1" false, and thus I can change its truth-value, even if I don't exercise that option.

[15] In other words it was not within anyone's power to prevent a sea-fight on Sept. 7.

[16] Donald Williams, "Professor Linsky on Aristotle," *The Philosophical Review*, 63 (1954), 255.

[17] "Necessary," of course, in the sense that no one can prevent its occurrence.

[18] Bertrand Russell, *Our Knowledge of the External World* (London, 1929), p. 171.

[19] Benedict De Spinoza, *Ethics*, ed. James Gutmann (New York, 1957), Part Five, Proposition XXIX, Note.

[20] Williams, "The Sea Fight Tomorrow," pp. 282, 305–06.

[21] Quine, *Word and Object* (Cambridge, Mass., 1960), p. 193.

[22] Williams, p. 282.

[23] It is not my purpose here to discuss the philosophy of St. Augustine or of any other thinker whose views I quote subsequently. I am only alluding to them to show some implications of Aristotle's thesis concerning future contingencies.

[24] St. Augustine, *The Confessions of St. Augustine*, trans. F. J. Sheed (New York, 1943). Book Eleven, section XIV, p. 271.

[25] Ibid., Book Eleven, section XX, p. 276.

[26] Immanuel Kant, *Critique of Pure Reason*, trans. J. M. D. Meiklejohn (New York, 1901), p. 73.

[27] F. H. Bradley, *Appearance and Reality* (Oxford, 1959), p. 183.

[28] J. M. E. McTaggert, "The Unreality of Time," in *Philosophical Studies* (London, 1934), p. 131.

[29] C. D. Broad, *Scientific Thought* (Paterson, N.J., 1959), p. 15.

34. *Whether There Is Anything Voluntary in Human Acts?*

THOMAS AQUINAS

St. Thomas Aquinas (1225–1274) was born in the Castle of Roccasecca, near Aquino, Italy. In addition to his theological writings, of which *The Summa Theologica* is his most famous, he wrote commentaries on Boethius and almost the whole Aristotelian corpus. The brief selection included here considers three objections to Aristotle's definition of "voluntary." These objections set the stage for causal and theological problems of freedom.

We proceed thus to the First Article:

Objection 1. It would seem that there is nothing voluntary in human acts. For that is voluntary *which has its principle within itself*, as Gregory of Nyssa,[1] Damascene[2] and Aristotle[3] declare. But the principle of human acts is not in man himself, but outside him, since man's appetite is moved to act by the appetible object which is outside him, and which is as a *mover unmoved.*[4] Therefore there is nothing voluntary in human acts.

Obj. 2. Further, the Philosopher proves that in animals no new movement arises that is not preceded by another and exterior motion.[5] But all human acts are new, since none is eternal. Consequently, the principle of all human acts is from outside man, and therefore there is nothing voluntary in them.

Obj. 3. Further, he that acts voluntarily can act of himself. But this is not true of man, for it is written (*John* xv. 5): *Without Me you can do nothing.* Therefore there is nothing voluntary in human acts.

On the contrary, Damascene says that *the voluntary is an act consisting in a rational operation.*[6] Now such are human acts. Therefore there is something voluntary in human acts.

I answer that, There must needs be something voluntary in human acts. In order to make this clear, we must take note that the principle of some acts is within the agent, or in that which is moved;

whereas the principle of some movements or acts is outside. For when a stone is moved upwards, the principle of this movement is outside the stone; whereas, when it is moved downwards, the principle of this movement is in the stone. Now of those things that are moved by an intrinsic principle, some move themselves, some not. For since every agent or thing moved acts or is moved for an end, as was stated above,[7] those are perfectly moved by an intrinsic principle whose intrinsic principle is one not only of movement but of movement for an end. Now in order that a thing be done for an end, some knowledge of the end is necessary. Therefore, whatever so acts or is so moved by an intrinsic principle that it has some knowledge of the end, has within itself the principle of its act, so that it not only acts, but acts for an end. On the other hand, if a thing has no knowledge of the end, even though it have an intrinsic principle of action or movement, nevertheless, the principle of acting or being moved for an end is not in that thing, but in something else, by which the principle of its action towards an end is imprinted on it. Therefore such things are not said to move themselves, but to be moved by others. But those things which have a knowledge of the end are said to move themselves because there is in them a principle by which they not only act but also act for an end. And, consequently, since both are from an intrinsic principle, *i.e.,* that they act and that they act for an end, the movements and acts of such things are said to be voluntary; for the term *voluntary* signifies that their movements and acts are from their own inclination. Hence it is that, according to the definitions of Aristotle,[8] Gregory of Nyssa[9] and Damascene,[10] the voluntary is defined not only as having *a*

From *Introduction to St. Thomas Aquinas,* ed., with an introduction by Anton C. Pegis, Random House, Inc., 1948. Reprinted by permission of the estate of Anton C. Pegis.

principle within the agent, but also as implying *knowledge*. Therefore, since man especially knows the end of his work, and moves himself, in his acts especially is the voluntary to be found.

Reply Obj. 1. Not every principle is a first principle. Therefore, although it is of the nature of the voluntary act that its principle be within the agent, nevertheless, it is not contrary to the nature of the voluntary act that this intrinsic principle be caused or moved by an extrinsic principle; for it is not of the nature of the voluntary act that its intrinsic principle be a first principle.—Nevertheless, it must be observed that a principle of movement may happen to be first in a genus, but not first absolutely. Thus, in the genus of things subject to alteration, the first principle of alteration is the body of the heavens, which nevertheless is not the first mover absolutely, but is moved locally by a higher mover. And so the intrinsic principle of the voluntary act, *i.e.*, the cognitive and appetitive power, is the first principle in the genus of appetitive movement, although it is moved by an extrinsic principle according to other species of movement.

Reply Obj. 2. New movements in animals are indeed preceded by a motion from without; and this in two respects. First, in so far as by means of an extrinsic motion an animal's senses are confronted with something sensible, which, on being apprehended, moves the appetite. Thus a lion, on seeing the approach of the stag through its movement, begins to be moved towards the stag.— Secondly, in so far as some extrinsic motion produces a physical change in an animal's body, for example, through cold or heat; and when the body is thus affected by the motion of an exterior body, the sensitive appetite likewise, which is the power of a bodily organ, is moved accidentally. Thus, it happens that through some alteration in the body the appetite is roused to the desire of something. But this is not contrary to the nature of voluntariness, as was stated above, for such movements caused by an extrinsic principle are of another genus of movement.

Reply Obj. 3. God moves man to act, not only by proposing the appetible to the senses, or by effecting a change in his body, but also by moving the will itself; for every movement both of the will and of nature proceeds from God as the First Mover. And just as it is not incompatible with nature that the movement of nature be from God as the First Mover, inasmuch as nature is an instrument of God moving it, so it is not contrary to the character of a voluntary act that it proceed from God, inasmuch as the will is moved by God. Nevertheless, both natural and voluntary movements have this in common, that it belongs to the nature of both that they should proceed from a principle within the agent.

Endnotes

[1] Cf. Nemesius, *De Nat. Hom.*, XXXII (PG 40, 728).

[2] *De Fide Orth.*, II, 24 (PG 94, 953).

[3] *Eth.*, III, 1 (1111a 23).

[4] Aristotle, *De An.*, III, 10 (433b 11).

[5] *Phys.*, VIII, 2 (253a 11).

[6] *De Fide Orth.*, II, 24 (PG 94, 953).

[7] Q. 1, a. 2.

[8] *Eth.*, III, 1 (1111a 23).

[9] Cf. Nemesius, *De Nat. Hom.*, XXXII (PG 40, 728).

[10] *De Fide Orth.*, II, 24 (PG 94, 953).

35. *God's Foreknowledge and Human Freedom*

ST. AUGUSTINE

Augustine considers the question Does God's knowledge of what people will do make their choices illusory? Many theists want to answer no since the existence of free will is required by some religious tenets (for example, Why would God punish Adam and Eve if they were not free?). Accordingly, Augustine argues that foreknowledge and human freedom are compatible. He does so by claiming that if God knows one freely chooses to perform a certain action, then one must indeed choose freely. Thus, what one does is the basis for God's knowledge rather than the other way around.

God's Foreknowledge Does Not Exclude Man's Freedom in Sinning

AUGUSTINE:
Surely this is the question that troubles and perplexes you: how can the following two propositions, that [1] God has foreknowledge of all future events, and that [2] we do not sin by necessity but by free will, be made consistent with each other? "If God foreknows that man will sin," you say, "it is necessary that man sin." If man must sin, his sin is not a result of the will's choice, but is instead a fixed and inevitable necessity. You fear now that this reasoning results either in the blasphemous denial of God's foreknowledge or, if we deny this, the admission that we sin by necessity, not by will. Or does some other point bother you?

ERODINS:
No, nothing else right now.

A:
You think that all things of which God has foreknowledge come about by necessity, and not by will?

E:
Absolutely.

Reprinted with permission of Macmillan Publishing Company from *On Free Choice of the Will* by St. Augustine, translated by Benjamin & Hackstaff. Copyright © 1985 by Macmillan Publishing Company; © 1964.

A:
Now pay careful attention. Look at yourself a little and tell me this, if you can: how are you going to will tomorrow, to sin or to act rightly?

E:
I do not know.

A:
Do you think that God does not know either?

E:
Of course I do not.

A:
If God knows what you are going to will tomorrow and foresees how all men who exist now or will exist are going to will in the future, He foresees much more what He will do about just men and about wicked ones.

E:
Yes. If God foreknows my deeds, I would say much more confidently that He foreknows His own deeds and foresees most certainly what He will do.

A:
If everything of which God has foreknowledge happens, not by will, but by necessity, shouldn't you be careful lest you say that God does what He is going to do by necessity too, and not by will?

E:
When I said that everything that God foreknows happens by necessity, I meant only those things

which occur in His creation, not what occurs in Himself, since these latter are eternal.

A:

By this reasoning, God is not involved in His own creation.

E:

He has decided once and for all how the order of the universe He created is to be carried out, and does not arrange anything by a new act of will.

A:

Does He not make anyone happy?

E:

Yes, He does.

A:

Then He is responsible when someone becomes happy.

E:

Yes.

A:

If, then, for example, you are to be happy a year from now, He will make you happy a year from now.

E:

Yes.

A:

Therefore, God foreknows today what He will do in a year.

E:

He has always foreknown this. I also agree that He also foreknows it now if it is going to be so.

A:

Please tell me: it is not the case, is it, that you are not His creature? Won't your happiness occur in you?

E:

Of course! I am His creature and my happiness will occur in me.

A:

Therefore, your happiness will come about in you, not by will, but by the necessity of God's action.

E:

God's will is my necessity.

A:

So you will be happy against your will!

E:

Had I the power to be happy, I would surely be happy now. I wish to be happy now, and am not, because it is God, not I, who makes me happy.

A:

How clearly truth cries out from you! For you could not maintain that anything is in our power except actions that are subject to our own will. Therefore, nothing is so completely in our power as the will itself, for it is ready at hand to act immediately, as soon as we will. Thus we are right in saying that we grow old by necessity, not by will; or that we die by necessity, not by will, and so on. Who but a madman would say that we do not will with the will?

Therefore, though God foreknows what we shall will in the future, this does not prove that we do not will anything voluntarily. In regard to happiness, you said (as if I would deny it) that you do not make yourself happy. I say, however, that when you are to be happy, you shall not be happy against your will, but because you will to be happy. When, therefore, God foreknows that you will be happy, it cannot be otherwise, or else there would be no such thing as foreknowledge. Nevertheless, we are not forced to believe, as a consequence of this, that you are going to be happy when you do not want to be. This is absurd and far from the truth. Moreover, just as God's foreknowledge, which today is certain of tomorrow's happiness, does not take from you the will to be happy when you begin to be happy; in the same way, a will which deserves blame, if it is going to be blameworthy, will nonetheless remain a will, since God foreknew that it would be so.

See, please, how blindly a man says, "If God has foreknown my will, it is necessary that I will what God foreknows, since nothing can occur except as he has foreknown it. If, moreover, my act of will is subject to necessity, we must admit that I willed it not by will, but by necessity." Strange foolishness! How could it be that nothing happens otherwise than as God foreknew, if He foreknows that something is going to be willed when nothing is going to be willed? I pass over the equally astounding assertion that I just said this man makes: "It is necessary that I will in this way." By assuming necessity, he tries to exclude will. If it is necessary that he will, how can he will, if there is no will?

If he says, in another way, that since it is necessary that he will, this very will is not in his power, he is to be answered with what I just said when I asked whether you would be happy with- out wiling it. You answered that you would be happy if it were in your power to be happy, and that you wanted to, but were not yet able. Then I interposed that the truth had cried out from you because we cannot deny that we have the power, unless we cannot obtain what we will through an act of will or unless the will is absent. When we will, if the will itself is lacking in us, we surely do not will. If it cannot happen that when we will we do not will, then the will is present in the one who wills. And nothing else is in our power except what is present to us when we will. Our will, therefore, is not a will unless it is in our power. And since it is indeed in our power, it is free in us. What we do not, or cannot, have in our power is not free for us. So it follows that we do not deny that God has foreknowledge of all things to be, and yet that we will what we will. For when He has foreknowledge of our will, it is going to be the will that He has foreknown. Therefore, the will is going to be a will because God has foreknowledge of it. Nor can it be a will if it is not in our power. Therefore, God also has knowledge of our power over it. So the power is not taken from me by His foreknowledge; but because of His foreknowledge, the power to will will more certainly be present in me, since God, whose foreknowledge does not err, has foreknown that I shall have the power.

E:

I no longer deny that whatever God foreknows must come to be, and that he foreknows our sins in such a way that our will still remains free in us and lies in our power.

God's Knowledge That Man Will Sin Is Not the Cause of Sin. Hence Punishment for Sin Is Just

A:

What is it, then, that bothers you? Have you per- haps forgotten what our first argument accom- plished? Will you deny that we sin by will and not under compulsion from anyone, either higher, lower, or equal?

E:

Of course I do not dare deny any of these points. Yet I still cannot see how God's foreknowledge of our sins can be reconciled with our free choice in sinning. God must, we admit, be just and have

foreknowledge. But I would like to know by what justice God punishes sins which must be; or how it is that they do not have to be, when He foreknows that they will be; or why anything which is neces- sarily done in His creation is not to be attributed to the Creator.

A:

Why do you think that our free choice is opposed to God's foreknowledge? Is it simply because it *is* foreknowledge or, rather, because it is God's fore- knowledge?

E:

Because it is God's.

A:

If you foreknew that someone was going to sin, would it not be necessary for him to sin?

E:

Yes, he would have to sin, for my foreknowledge would not be genuine unless I foreknew what was certain.

A:

Then it is not because it is God's foreknowledge that what He foreknew had to happen, but only because it is foreknowledge. It is not fore- knowledge if it does not foreknow what is certain.

E:

I agree. But why are you making these points?

A:

Because unless I am mistaken, your foreknowledge that a man will sin does not of itself necessitate the sin. Your foreknowledge did not force him to sin even though he was, without doubt, going to sin; otherwise you would not foreknow that which was to be. Thus, these two things are not contradic- tories. As you, by your foreknowledge, know what someone else is going to do of his own will, so God forces no one to sin; yet He foreknows those who will sin by their own will.

Why cannot He justly punish what He does not force to be done, even though He foreknows it? Your recollection of events in the past does not compel them to occur. In the same way God's fore- knowledge of future events does not compel them to take place. As you remember certain things that you have done and yet have not done all the things that you remember, so God foreknows all the things of which He Himself is the Cause, and yet He is not the Cause of all that He foreknows. He is not the evil cause of these acts, though He justly avenges them. You may understand from this, therefore, how justly God punishes sins; for He does not do the things which He knows will happen. Besides, if He ought not to exact punishment from sinners because He foresees that they will sin, He ought not to reward those who act rightly, since in the same way He foresees that they will act

rightly. On the contrary, let us acknowledge both that it is proper to His foreknowledge that nothing should escape His notice and that it is proper to His justice that a sin, since it is committed voluntarily, should not go unpunished by His judgment, just as it was not forced to be committed by His foreknowledge.

---

36. *Predestination, Divine Foreknowledge, and Human Freedom*

WILLIAM L. ROWE

There are two problems William Rowe, professor of philosophy at Purdue University, addresses in his essay. The first concerns understanding how God could have *ordained* for all eternity what comes to pass, including one's choices; and, at the same time, believing choices are freely chosen. The second problem concerns the conflict between freedom and God's *knowing* from eternity what one will do. Rowe considers various classical solutions to these problems and shows how each of them hinges on definite conceptions of freedom and eternity.

Human Freedom and Divine Predestination

As a seventeen-year-old convert to a quite orthodox branch of Protestantism, the first theological problem to concern me was the question of Divine Predestination and Human Freedom. Somewhere I read the following line from the Westminster Confession: "God from all eternity did . . . freely and unchangeably ordain whatsoever comes to pass." In many ways I was attracted to this idea. It seemed to express the majesty and power of God over all that he had created. It also led me to take an optimistic view of events in my own life and the lives of others, events which struck me as bad or unfor-

tunate. For I now viewed them as planned by God before the creation of the world—thus they must serve some good purpose unknown to me. My own conversion, I reasoned, must also have been ordained to happen, just as the failure of others to be converted must have been similarly ordained. But at this point in my reflections, I hit upon a difficulty, a difficulty that made me think harder than I ever had before in my life. For I also believed that I had chosen God out of my own free will, that each of us is responsible for choosing or rejecting God's way. But how could I be responsible for a choice which, from eternity, God had ordained I would make at that particular moment in my life? How can it be that those who reject God's way do so of their own free will, if God, from eternity, destined them to reject his way? The Westminster Confession itself seemed to recognize the difficulty. For its next line read: "Yet . . . thereby is no violence offered to the will of the creatures."

For a time I accepted both Divine Predestination and human freedom and responsibility. I felt that although I could not see how both could be

From William L. Rowe, *Philosophy of Religion: An Introduction*, pp. 154–69. © 1978 by Dickenson Publishing Company, Inc. Reprinted by permission of Wadsworth, Inc.

true, they, nevertheless, might both be true, so I accepted them both on faith. But the longer I thought about it the more it seemed to me that they couldn't both be true. That is, I came to the view, rightly or wrongly, that I not only could not see how both could be true, I *could see* that they could not both be true. Slowly I abandoned the belief that before eternity God ordained whatever comes to pass. I took the view, instead, that before eternity God knew whatever comes to pass, including our free choices and acts, but that those choices and acts were not determined in advance.

What I did not know in those early years was that the topics of Predestination, Divine Foreknowledge and Human Freedom had been the focus of philosophical and theological reflection for centuries. In this chapter we shall acquaint ourselves with the various views that have emerged from those centuries of intellectual endeavor, thus enlarging our understanding of the theistic concept of God and one of the problems that has emerged in connection with it.

Freedom of Will or Choice

Perhaps it's best to begin with the idea of human freedom. For, as we shall see, there are two quite different ways in which this idea has been understood, and which way we follow makes a great deal of difference to the topic under consideration. According to the first idea, *acting freely consists in doing what you want or choose to do.* If you want to leave the room but are forcibly restrained from doing so, we certainly would agree that *staying in the room* is not something you do freely. You do not freely stay in the room because it is not what you choose or want to do, it happens against your will.

Suppose we accept this first idea of human freedom, whereby acting freely consists in doing what you want or choose to do. The problem of divine predestination and human freedom will then turn out to be not much of a problem at all. Why so? Well, to take the example of my youthful conversion, my conversion was free if it was something I wanted to do, chose to do, did not do against my will. Let's suppose, as I believe is true, that my conversion was something I chose to do, wanted to do. Is there any difficulty in believing also that before eternity God ordained that at that particular moment in my life I would be converted? It doesn't seem that there is. For God could simply

have ordained also that at that particular moment in my life I would *want* to choose Christ, to follow God's way. If so, then, on our first idea of human freedom, my act of conversion was both a free act on my part and ordained by God from eternity. On our first idea of human freedom, then, there does not seem to be any real conflict between the doctrine of divine predestination and human freedom. Is our first idea of human freedom correct? One reason for thinking that it is not was provided by the English philosopher John Locke (1632–1704). Locke asks us to suppose that a man is brought into a room while asleep. The door, which is the only way out of the room, is then securely bolted from the outside. The man does not know that the door is bolted, does not know, therefore, that he *cannot* leave the room. He awakens, finds himself in the room, looks about and notices that there are friendly people in the room with whom he would like to converse. Accordingly, he decides to stay in the room rather than leave.[1]

What are we to say of this man? Is his act *staying in the room* something he does *freely*? Well, according to our first idea of human freedom, it would seem that it is. For staying in the room is what he wants to do. He considers leaving, not knowing that he cannot leave, but rejects it because he prefers to stay in the room and engage in friendly conversation. But can we really believe that staying in the room is something he does *freely*? After all, it is the only thing that can be done. He stays in the room of *necessity*, for leaving the room is something that is not in his power to do. What is the difference between him and a second man, similarly placed, who wants to leave, but being unable to leave, also stays in the room of necessity? Is the difference that the first man does something freely, whereas, the second man does not? Or is it, rather, that the first man is just more *fortunate* than the second? Each does what he does (stay in the room) of necessity, not freely, but the first man is more fortunate in that what he *must do* turns out to be the very thing that he wants to do. Locke concludes that the first man is not more free than the second, only more fortunate. For freedom, Locke contends, consists in more than simply doing what one wants or chooses, it also must be that *it was in one's power to do otherwise.* And the reason why the first man, no less than the second, did not stay in the room freely is because it was not in his power to do otherwise, to leave the room.

The Power to Do Otherwise

The second idea of human freedom is that we do something freely only if, at the time just before we do it, it is in our power to do otherwise. And I think that on reflection we can see that the second idea is more adequate than the first. Consider, for example, growing old. This is something we do of necessity, not freely. The mere fact that someone prefers to grow old, wants to grow old, is not sufficient for it being true that he or she grows old *freely*—at best we might say that he or she grows old gracefully. Suppose, however, a process is discovered and made available whereby each of us has the power not to grow old in the sense of physical aging. Although time continues to pass, the aging process in our bodies can now be slowed enormously. Under these conditions it could be true that someone grows old freely, for one would not then grow old of necessity, it being in a person's power to do otherwise. The first idea of freedom must be abandoned in favor of the second, more adequate idea.

It is the second idea of freedom that appears to be in conflict with the idea of divine predestination. For if God has determined, from eternity, that I will be converted at a certain moment on a particular day, how can it be in my power just prior to that moment to refrain from being converted? To ascribe such a power to me is to ascribe to me the power to prevent from taking place something that God from eternity has ordained to take place. Surely if from eternity God has determined that something will happen it cannot be in some creature's power to prevent that thing from taking place. Therefore, if from eternity God did ordain whatever comes to pass then there is nothing that happens which we could have prevented from happening. So, since whatever I do has been ordained by God to take place, it is never in my power to do otherwise. And if it is never in my power to do otherwise, then nothing I do is done freely. Human freedom, it seems, is inconsistent with divine predestination.

If the above argument is correct, as I'm inclined to believe it is, the theist must either abandon the belief in human freedom or the doctrine of divine predestination. And it seems reasonable that between the two, the doctrine of divine predestination should be given its walking papers. That God has *ultimate control* over the destiny of his creation and that he *knows* in advance of its happening everything that will happen are ideas that preserve the majesty of God and provide for some degree of human optimism, without requiring that God has *decreed* to happen whatever does happen. And on the surface at least, it does not appear that the doctrine of divine foreknowledge conflicts with human freedom. So perhaps the reasonable thing to do is to reject the doctrine of divine predestination, while preserving the belief in human freedom and the doctrine of divine foreknowledge.

The Conflict Between Human Freedom and Divine Foreknowledge

But if God has not ordained from eternity everything that will happen, how is it possible for him to have known from eternity everything that happens? Doesn't the doctrine of divine foreknowledge presuppose the doctrine of divine predestination? Having decreed that something will happen at a certain time would be a way in which God could know in advance that it will happen. But it is not the only way in which God might have possessed such knowledge. We possess telescopes, for example, that enable us to know what is happening at places some distance away, because by means of the telescope we can see them happening. Imagine that God has something like a *time* telescope, a telescope that enables one to see what is happening at times some distance away. By turning the lens one focuses on a certain time, say a thousand years from now, and sees the events that are occurring at that time. With some such image as this we might account for God's foreknowledge without supposing that his knowledge is derived from his prior decree that the events in question will occur. He knows in advance the events that will take place by *foreseeing* them, not by *foreordaining* them. The doctrine of divine foreknowledge, then, does not presuppose the doctrine of divine predestination. And, as we noted earlier, there does not appear to be any conflict between divine foreknowledge and human freedom. For although God's *foreordaining* something makes that something happen, his *foreknowing* does not make it happen. Things occur not because God foreknows them; rather, he foreknows them because they occur.

Unfortunately, things are not so simple as that. There is a serious problem about divine foreknowledge and human freedom. And although we may not be able to solve this problem, it will be instructive to try to understand the problem and see what the various "solutions" are that have been advanced by important philosophers and theologians. Perhaps the best way to start is by stating the problem in the form of an argument, an argument that begins with the doctrine of divine foreknowledge and ends with the denial of human freedom. Once we understand the major premises of the argument, as well as the reasons given in support of them, we will have come to an understanding of one of the major problems theologians have wrestled with for almost two thousand years: the problem of reconciling the doctrine of divine foreknowledge with the belief in human freedom.

1. God knows before we are born everything we will do.

2. If God knows before we are born everything we will do, then it is never in our power to do otherwise.

3. If it is never in our power to do otherwise, then there is no human freedom.

Therefore,

4. There is no human freedom.

The first premise of the argument expresses an apparent implication of the doctrine of divine foreknowledge. The third premise simply states an implication of the second idea of freedom we considered earlier. According to that idea, we do something freely only if, at the time just before we do it, it is in our power to do otherwise. Thus, we concluded that the act of staying in the room was freely done only if, at the time of the decision to stay in the room, it was in the person's power to do otherwise, that is, to leave the room. Since the door was securely bolted from the outside, we concluded that he did not *freely* stay in the room. Now premise (3) merely draws the logical conclusion from this second idea of freedom: if it is *never* in our (any human being's) power to do otherwise, then there is no human freedom. Since the argument is clearly valid, the remaining question concerns premise (2): if God knows before we are born everything we will do then it is never in our power to do otherwise. Why should we accept this premise? Clearly if we replaced the word "knows" with the word "ordains" the statement would be true. But the whole point of abandoning divine predesti-

nation in favor of divine foreknowledge was that although (a) if God *ordains* before we are born everything we will do, then it is never in our power to do otherwise, seems surely true, it does not seem to be true that (b) if God *knows* before we are born everything we will do then it is never in our power to do otherwise. Since premise 2 is the same as b why should we now accept it as true? What is the reasoning by which the proponent of this argument hopes to convince us that 2 is true?

The reasoning in support of 2 is complex, so it will be best to develop it by means of an example. Let's suppose it is 2:00 p.m. on a particular Tuesday and that you have a class in philosophy of religion that meets at 2:30. Your friends ask you to go with them to an afternoon movie, but, after considering the proposal, you somehow manage to resist temptation, and elect to attend class instead. It is now 2:45 and your instructor is carrying on about foreknowledge and free will. Somewhat bored, you now wish that you had gone to the movie instead of coming to class. You realize, however, that although you now regret your decision there is nothing that you can do about it. Of course, you could get up from your seat and rush off to see what is left of the movie. But you cannot now, at 2:45, bring it about that you did not go to class at 2:30, you cannot *now* bring it about that you actually went to the movie instead. You can regret what you did, and resolve never to make that mistake again, but, like it or not, you are stuck with the fact that instead of going to the movie you went to class at 2:30. You are stuck with it because it is a *fact about the past* and you cannot *alter the past*. Our inability to alter the past is enshrined in the colloquialism, "There's no use crying over spilt milk." Within limits, however, the future seems open, pliable; we can make it to be one way or another. You believe, for example, that on Thursday, when the class meets again, it will be in your power to go to class and it will be in your power to go to a movie instead. But the past is not open, it is closed, solid like granite, and in no way within your power to alter. As Aristotle observed:

> No one deliberates about the past but only about what is future and capable of being otherwise, while what is past is not capable of not having taken place; hence Agathon is right in saying: "For this alone is lacking, even in God, to make undone things that have once been done."[2]

There are, of course, a large number of facts about the past relative to 2:45 on Tuesday. In addition to the fact that at 2:30 you came to class, there is the fact of your birth, the fact that you became a college student, the fact that Nixon resigned from the Presidency, indeed, all the facts of past history. And what you now know is that at 2:45 it is not in your power to alter *any* of them. There is nothing that is now in your power to do such that were you to do it any of these facts about the past would not have been facts about the past. Pondering your powerlessness over the past, you notice that your instructor has written on the board another fact about the past:

F. Before you were born God knew that you would come to class at 2:30 this Tuesday.

If God exists and the doctrine of divine foreknowledge is true, F is certainly a fact about the past, and it has been a fact about the past at every moment of your life. It is a fact about the past *now*—at 2:45 on Tuesday—it was a fact about the past *yesterday*, and it will be a fact about the past *tomorrow*. At this point your instructor turns and asks: "Was it in your power at 2:00 to have refrained from coming to class today?" You certainly think that it was—indeed, you now regret that you did not exercise that power—so the instructor writes on the board:

A. It was in your power at 2:00 to do something other than come to class at 2:30 this Tuesday.

But now let's think for a bit about F and A. At 2:00, F was a fact about the past. But according to A, it was in your power at 2:00 to do something (go to a movie, say) such that had you done it, what is a fact about the past (F) would not have been a fact about the past. For, clearly, if you had *exercised* your power to refrain from coming to class at 2:30 what God would have known before you were born is not what he in fact knew, that you would come to class this Tuesday, but something quite different, that you would do something else. And this in turn means that if F is a fact about the past— as it surely is if the doctrine of divine foreknowledge is true—and if A is true, then it was in your power at 2:00 this Tuesday to *alter the past*; it was in your power to do something (go to a movie) such that had you done it, what *is* a fact about the

past (F) would not have been a fact about the past. If then, *it is never in our power to alter a fact about the past*, it cannot be both that F was a fact about the past and also that it was in your power at 2:00 to refrain from coming to class at 2:30 this Tuesday.

What we have just seen is that given the doctrine of divine foreknowledge and the claim that it is in our power to have done something we did not do, it follows that it was in our power to have altered the past. For given the doctrine of divine foreknowledge it follows that *before you were born* God knew that you would come to class at 2:30 this Tuesday. And if we now claim that *at 2:00* it was in your power to have done otherwise, we imply that at 2:00 it was in your power to alter a fact about the past, the fact that before you were born God knew that you would come to class at 2:30. But we earlier concluded that we are powerless over the past, that facts about the past are not within our power to alter. If we keep to this conviction—as it seems we must—then we must conclude that if God did know before you were born that you would be in class at 2:30 (this Tuesday) then it was *not* in your power at 2:00 to do otherwise. And generalizing from this particular example, we can conclude that if it is never in our power to alter the past, then if God knows before we are born everything we will do then it is never in our power to do otherwise.

We have worked our way through the rather complex reasoning that can be used to support premise 2 of the argument designed to show a conflict between divine foreknowledge and human freedom. That premise, as you recall, says that if God knows before we are born everything we will do then it is never in our power to do otherwise. Reduced to its simplest terms, the reasoning given in support of 2 consists in arguing that if 2 is not true then it is in our power to alter the past. But it is never in our power to alter the past, so 2 must be true. From (i) God knows before we are born everything we will do, and (ii) it is sometimes in our power to do otherwise it follows, so the reasoning goes, that it is sometimes in our power to alter the past. Since it is never in our power to alter the past, premises i and ii can't both be true. Hence, if i is true then ii is false. But to say that ii is false is just to say that it is *never* in our power to do otherwise. So if i is true then it is *never* in our power to do otherwise—and this is exactly what premise 2 says.

Some Solutions to the Conflict

We've had a look at perhaps the strongest argument for the view that the doctrine of divine foreknowledge, no less than the doctrine of divine predestination, is in fundamental conflict with the belief in human freedom, an argument that has troubled philosophers and theologians for centuries. It is now time to consider the various "solutions" that have been offered and to assess their strengths and weaknesses.

The argument itself limits the number of possible solutions that can be advanced to the following four:

I. *Rejection of premise 3*: denies that we do something freely only if it is in our power to do otherwise.

II. *Rejection of premise 2*: denies that divine foreknowledge implies that it is never in our power to do otherwise.

III. *Rejection of premise 1*: denies that God has foreknowledge of future events.

IV. *Acceptance of the conclusion 4*: denies that we have human freedom.

Solutions III and IV are "radical" solutions since they amount to a denial either of the doctrine of divine foreknowledge or of human freedom. No theist seriously proposes IV, so we may safely dismiss it. III, however, as we shall see, is the solution preferred by a number of important theologians, including Boethius and Aquinas. Let's consider, then, the first three solutions to this perplexing problem.

The Definition of Freedom

The first solution rejects premise 3 of the argument, charging that 3 expresses a mistaken idea of human freedom. As we saw earlier, there are two different ideas of freedom. According to the first idea, acting freely consists in no more than doing what you want or choose to do; freedom does not require the power to do otherwise. Those who accept this idea of human freedom rightly see no conflict between it and divine foreknowledge. Indeed, as we noted earlier, there is no conflict between this idea of human freedom and the doctrine

of divine predestination. A solution along these lines was developed most fully by the American theologian, Jonathan Edwards (1703–58). The adequacy of this solution depends entirely on whether its idea of what human freedom consists in can be defended against the criticisms philosophers have advanced against it.[3] However, having rejected this idea of freedom in favor of the second idea—the idea that we do something freely only if it is in our power to do otherwise—we shall not pursue further this first solution to the problem of divine foreknowledge and human freedom. For given the second idea of human freedom, premise 3 must be accepted as true.

Power to Alter the Past

The second major solution rejects premise 2, thereby denying that divine foreknowledge implies that it is never in our power to do otherwise. Actually, what this solution shows, if successful, is not that 2 is false, but that the reasoning given in support of it is mistaken. What is that reasoning? Well, reduced to its briefest terms, the reasoning is that if 2 is not true then it is in our power to alter facts about the past—facts about what God knew before we were even born. But, so the reasoning goes, it is never in anyone's power to alter the past, therefore 2 must be true. The second solution challenges the claim that it is never in our power to alter the past, arguing that we do have the power to alter certain facts about the past, including certain facts about what God knew before we were even born. This solution was suggested by the most influential philosopher of the fourteenth century, William of Ockham (1285–1349).

The basic point on which the second solution rests involves a distinction between two types of facts about the past: facts which are *simply* about the past, and facts which are *not simply* about the past. To illustrate this distinction, let's consider two facts about the past, facts about the year 1941.

f_1: In 1941 Japan attacks Pearl Harbor.
f_2: In 1941 a war begins between Japan and the United States that lasts five years.

Relative of 1976, f_1 and f_2 are both *simply* about the past. But suppose we consider the year 1943. Relative to 1943, f_1 is a fact that is simply about the past, but f_2 is not simply about the past; f_2 is a fact about the past relative to 1943, for f_2 is, in part, a fact about 1941, and 1941 lies in 1943's past. But f_2, unlike f_1, implies a certain fact about 1944; namely.

f₃: In 1944 Japan and the United States are at war.

Since f_2 implies f_3, a fact about the future relative to 1943, we can say that relative to 1943 f_2 is a fact about the past, but not simply a fact about the past. We have then three facts, f_1, f_2, and f_3, about which we can say that relative to 1976 each is a fact simply about the past. Relative to 1943, however, only f_1 is simply about the past, we are now in a position to simply about the past, and f_3 is not about the past at all.

Having illustrated the distinction between a fact which, relative to a certain time t, is simply about the past and a fact which, relative to t, is not simply about the past, we are now in a position to appreciate its importance. Think of 1943 and the groups of persons then in power in both Japan and the United States. Neither group had it in its power to do anything about f_1. Both groups may have regretted the actions which brought it about that f_1 is a fact about the past. But it is abundantly clear that among all the things which, in 1943, it was in their power to do, none is such that had they done it, f_1 would not have been a fact about the past. It makes no sense to look back upon *1943* and say that if only one of these groups had *then* done such-and-such, f_1 would never have been a fact about the past. It makes no sense precisely because, relative to 1943, f_1 is a fact *simply* about the past. Nothing that could have been done by anyone in 1943 would have in any way altered the fact that in 1941 Japan attacked Pearl Harbor.

But what about f_2, the fact that in 1941 a war begins between Japan and the United States that lasts five years. We know that in 1943 neither group did anything that altered this fact about 1941. The question, however, is whether there were things that were not done in 1943, things which, nevertheless, were in the power of one or both of the groups to do, and which, had they been done, a certain fact about 1941, f_2, would not have been a fact at all. Perhaps there were not. Perhaps the momentum of the war was such that neither group had the power to bring it to an end in 1943. Most of us, I suppose, think otherwise. We think that there probably were certain actions that were not, but could have been, taken by one or both of

the groups in 1943, actions which had they been taken would have brought the war to an end in 1943. If what we think to be so is so, then it was in the power of one or both of the groups in 1943 to alter a fact about the past; it was in their power in 1943 to do something such that had they done it a certain fact about 1941, f_2, would not have been a fact about 1941. The basic reason why in 1943 f_2 may have been in their power to alter, whereas f_1 certainly was not, is that, unlike f_1, f_2 is not simply about the past relative to 1943, for f_2 implies a certain fact about 1944, that in 1944, Japan and the United States are at war (f_3).

What the above reasoning suggests is that our conviction that the past is beyond our power to affect is certainly true, so far as facts which are simply about the past are concerned. Facts which are about the past, but *not simply* about the past, may not, however, be beyond our power to affect. And what Ockham saw is that the facts about divine foreknowledge which are used as the basis for denying human freedom are facts about the past, but *not simply* about the past. Consider again the fact that before you were born, God knew that you would be in class at 2:30 this Tuesday. We want to believe that at 2:00 it was in your power to do otherwise, to refrain from coming to class at 2:30. To ascribe this power to you implies that it was in your power at 2:00 to alter a fact about the past, the fact that before you were born God knew that you would be in class at 2:30. This fact about the past, however, is not, relative to 2:00, a fact simply about the past. For it implies a fact about the future relative to 2:00, namely, that at 2:30 you are in class. And the solution we are exploring holds that such a fact about the past was in your power to alter if it was in your power at 2:00, as we believe it was, to have gone to a movie instead of coming to class. For it was then in your power to have done something such that had you done it what *is* a fact about a time before you were born *would not have been* a fact at all—instead it would have been a fact that before you were born God knew that you would not be in class at 2:30. Of course, there will still be many facts about God's foreknowledge that are not in your power to alter: all those facts, for example, that relative to the time you are at, are facts simply about the past. The very fact which may have been in your power to alter at 2:00—the fact that before you were born God knew you would be in class at 2:30—is, at 2:45 when you are sitting in class regretting that you did not go to a movie, a fact that cannot *then* (at 2:45) be altered, because at 2:45 it is a fact simply about the past. And there are many facts involving divine foreknowledge that are not simply about the past, which, nevertheless, are not in your power to alter, for the facts that they imply about the future do not fall within the scope of your power. For example, God knew before you were born that the sun would rise tomorrow. This fact about the past is not simply about the past because it implies a fact about tomorrow, that the sun will rise. It is nevertheless, a fact which is not in your power to alter.

We have been considering the second solution to the problem of divine foreknowledge and human freedom. As we saw, this solution consists in denying the reasoning supporting the second premise of the argument by means of which the problem was developed, the premise stating that if God knows before we are born everything we will do it is never in our power to do otherwise. According to the reasoning in support of this premise, given divine foreknowledge, it is in our power to do otherwise only if it is in our power to alter some fact about the past, a fact about what God knew before we were born. The solution we have been considering accepts this point in the reasoning given in support of premise 2, but denies the next point: that it is never in our power to alter the past. The solution argues that some facts about the past are not simply about the past, that some such facts may be within our power to alter, and that the facts about divine foreknowledge used in the reasoning for premise 2 are examples of such facts. So according to the second major solution, we have no good reasons for accepting the second premise of the argument leading from divine foreknowledge to the denial of human freedom. And without such reasons, it has yet to be shown that there is any real difficulty in holding both that God knows before we are born everything we will do and that we sometimes have the power to do otherwise.

The Denial of Foreknowledge

The third and final solution we shall consider rejects premise 1 of the argument, thereby denying that God has foreknowledge of the future events. Earlier I called this a "radical" solution since, unlike the first two solutions, instead of trying to reconcile divine foreknowledge with human freedom, it appears to deny that there is any fore-

knowledge at all. But, as we shall see, this was the solution preferred by a number of important theologians within the western religious tradition.

There are two different forms of the third solution. According to the first form, statements about certain events in the future, events which might or might not happen, are neither true nor false; they become true (false) when the events they are about actually occur (don't occur). For example, the statement, "You will attend class at a certain hour on a certain day next week" is, on the view we are considering not now true, nor is it false. When next week comes and the hour of that particular day occurs, then the statement will become true if you attend class, and false if you do not. This view concerning statements about the future, a view often ascribed to Aristotle, has the consequence that God does not *now* know whether or not you will attend class at that hour next week, that God does not have foreknowledge of such future events. For knowledge is of what is *true*, and if statements about the future are neither true nor false, they cannot then be known.

The more widely accepted form of the third solution rests upon the idea that God is "eternal" in the second of the two senses introduced in chapter one. There we noted that to be eternal in the first sense is to have infinite duration in both temporal directions. To be eternal in the second sense, however, is to exist outside of time and, therefore, independent of the fundamental law of time according to which every being in time, even an everlasting being, has its life divided into temporal parts. As Boethius wrote:

> For whatever lives in time lives in the present, proceeding from past to future, and nothing is so constituted in time that it can embrace the whole span of its life at once. It has not yet arrived at tomorrow, and it has already lost yesterday; even the life of this day is lived only in each moving, passing moment.[4]

In contrast to things in time, God is viewed as having his infinite, endless life wholly present to himself, all at once. As such, God must be outside of time altogether. For, as we've just seen, whatever is in time has its life divided into temporal parts, only one of which can be present to it at any one time.

The idea that God is eternal in the sense of being outside of time has a direct bearing on the doctrine of divine foreknowledge. For the notion of *fore*knowledge naturally suggests that a being *located* at one point in time knows something that is to take place at some later point in time. Thus we speak of God knowing *at a time before you were born* what you would do at 2:30 this Tuesday. But if God is outside of time then we cannot say that he has a *fore*knowledge of future events, if to do so implies he is located at some point in time and at that point knows what will take place at some *later* point in time. According to Boethius, Aquinas, and a number of other theologians who hold that God is eternal in the second sense, there is nothing that happens in time that is unknown to God. Every moment in time is ever *present* to God in just the way that what is happening at this particular moment within the field of our vision is present to us. God's knowledge of what to us is past and future is just like the knowledge that we may have of something that is happening in the present. Being above time, God takes in *all* time with one glance just as we who are in time may with a glance take in something that is happening in the present. Speaking of God's knowledge of what takes place in time, Boethius tells us:

> It encompasses the infinite sweep of past and future, and regards all things in its simple comprehension as if they were now taking place. Thus, if you will think about the foreknowledge by which God distinguishes all things, you will rightly consider it to be not a foreknowledge of future events, but knowledge of a never changing present. For this reason, divine foreknowledge is called providence, rather than prevision, because it resides above all inferior things and looks out on all things from their summit.[5]

According to Boethius, God does not, strictly speaking, have *fore*knowledge, for he is not in the position of knowing that something will occur *in advance* of its occurring. And yet God knows everything that has occurred, is occurring, and will occur. But he knows them in the way in which we know what occurs in the present. Perhaps we can clarify his position if we distinguish two senses of "foreknowledge," foreknowledge$_1$ and foreknowledge$_2$. A being foreknows$_1$ some event x, we shall say, provided that the being exists at a certain

time *earlier* than when x occurs and knows at that time that x will occur at some later time. This is the sort of foreknowledge which God cannot have if he is eternal in the second sense, for he will not then exist at a certain moment of time, but will be completely outside of time. A being foreknows$_2$ some event x, we shall say, provided that the occurrence of x is *present* to that being but is such that its occurrence is at a moment later than the moment at which we (who are in time) *now* exist. Given that God is eternal in the second sense he cannot have foreknowledge$_1$ of any event, but this does not preclude his having a complete foreknowledge$_2$ of all those events which, from the position of those who exist in time, are yet to come.

We can now see how Boethius and Aquinas solve the problem of divine foreknowledge and human freedom. As we saw, the problem is that to assert both implies that it is sometimes in our power to alter a fact about the past, a fact about what God knew at a time before we were born. If we hold that it is never in our power to alter any fact about the past, it seems we must deny either divine foreknowledge or human freedom. What Boethius and Aquinas point out is that this is a genuine problem only if it is foreknowledge$_1$ that is being ascribed to God. For if God has foreknowledge$_1$, there will be facts about some past time which, if we have human freedom, would have to be within our power to alter. But according to them, we cannot ascribe foreknowledge$_1$ to God, for such ascription implies that God exists in time. God has foreknowledge$_2$ of everything that is yet to come to pass. But foreknowledge$_2$ does not imply that there is some fact about some past time. For God does not exist in time at all. His foreknowledge$_2$ of some event in time is really no different from the knowledge that your instructor had at 2:30 on Tuesday when she saw you entering the classroom. No one thinks that the knowledge obtained by seeing you come into the classroom takes away the power you had earlier to have done something else. Similarly God's foreknowledge$_2$, since it looks down from above time and sees what is future *in time*, but *present* from God's vantage point, imposes no necessity on what it sees. For there is no *past fact* involving God's knowledge which you would have had to alter if you had exercised your power to do otherwise.

In this chapter we have studied one of the ageless problems for theism, the problem of divine foreknowledge and human freedom, and considered in detail the principal solutions which have emerged in the centuries of reflection on the problem. Of the three solutions we've considered only the last two are tenable if, as I've suggested, the first rests on an inadequate idea of human freedom. The last solution, based as it is on the idea that God exists outside of time, will suffer from any defects associated with that idea. Some philosophers have thought that the idea itself is incoherent, and others have argued that while the idea may be coherent, any being that is eternal in the sense of existing outside of time could never *act within time*, and, therefore, could not create a world or bring about a miracle—activities generally ascribed to the theistic God. We cannot, however, pursue these matters here.[6]

The second solution fits well with the idea that God is eternal in the first sense introduced in chapter one, eternal in the sense of being everlasting, having infinite duration in both temporal directions. On this view, foreknowledge is ascribed to God, but it is argued that insofar as we act freely we do have the power to alter some facts about the past. If both the second and third solutions are successful, then, whether God is held to be eternal in the first or second sense, the problem of divine foreknowledge and human freedom is not an insoluble problem for theism.

Endnotes

[1] John Locke, *An Essay Concerning Human Understanding*, Book II, Chapter XXI, paragraph 10, ed. Peter H. Nidditch (London: Oxford University Press, 1975), p. 238.

[2] Aristotle, *Nicomachean Ethics* VII, 2. 1139^b in *The Basic Works of Aristotle*, ed. Richard McKeon (New York: Random House, 1941).

[3] For a brilliant defense of the first idea of freedom, as well as a response to the objections raised against it, see Jonathan Edwards, *Freedom of the Will*, eds. A. S. Kaufman and W. K. Frankena (Indianapolis: The Bobbs-Merrill Co., 1969).

[4] Boethius, *The Consolation of Philosophy*, Prose VI, tr. Richard Green (New York: The Bobbs-Merrill Company, Inc., 1962).

[5] Boethius, *The Consolation of Philosophy*, Prose VI.

[6] For an excellent study of these problems see Nelson Pike, *God and Timelessness* (New York: Schocken Books Inc., 1970).

37. On Liberty and Necessity

DAVID HUME

In this classic discussion, Hume argues that the truth of causal determinism (what he calls "necessity") does not pose any threat to human freedom (what he calls "liberty"). Hume's position is called "soft determinism" or "compatibilism." According to Hume, all actions are caused, the difference between free and unfree action concerns simply whether or not one can act in accordance with one's will. In his discussion, Hume offers arguments for determinism and for the incompatibility of indeterminism and responsibility.

Part I

It might reasonably be expected, in questions which have been canvassed and disputed with great eagerness since the first origin of science and philosophy, that the meaning of all the terms, at least, should have been agreed upon among the disputants, and our inquiries, in the course of two thousand years, been able to pass from words to the true and real subject of the controversy. For how easy may it seem to give exact definitions of the terms employed in reasoning, and make these definitions, not the mere sound of words, the object of future scrutiny and examination? But if we consider the matter more narrowly, we shall be apt to draw a quite opposite conclusion. From this circumstance alone, that a controversy has been long kept on foot and remains still undecided, we may presume that there is some ambiguity in the expression, and that the disputants affix different ideas to the terms employed in the controversy. For as the faculties of the mind are supposed to be naturally alike in every individual—otherwise nothing could be more fruitless than to reason or dispute together—it were impossible, if men affix the same ideas to their terms, that they could so long form different opinions of the same subject,

especially when they communicate their views and each party turn themselves on all sides in search of arguments which may give them the victory over their antagonists. It is true, if men attempt the discussion of questions which lie entirely beyond the reach of human capacity, such as those concerning the origin of worlds or the economy of the intellectual system or region of spirits, they may long beat the air in their fruitless contests and never arrive at any determinate conclusion. But if the question regard any subject of common life and experience, nothing, one would think, could preserve the dispute so long undecided, but some ambiguous expressions which keep the antagonists still at a distance and hinder them from grappling with each other.

This has been the case in the long-disputed question concerning liberty and necessity, and to so remarkable a degree that, if I be not much mistaken, we shall find that all mankind, both learned and ignorant, have always been of the same opinion with regard to this subject, and that a few intelligible definitions would immediately have put an end to the whole controversy. I own that this dispute has been so much canvassed on all hands, and has led philosophers into such a labyrinth of obscure sophistry, that it is no wonder if a sensible reader indulge his ease so far as to turn a deaf ear to the proposal of such a question from which he can expect neither instruction nor entertainment. But the state of the argument here proposed may, perhaps, serve to renew his attention, as it has more novelty, promises at least some decision of the

From David Hume, *An Inquiry Concerning Human Understanding*, Sec. 8. First published in 1748.

controversy, and will not much disturb his ease by any intricate or obscure reasoning.

I hope, therefore, to make it appear that all men have ever agreed in the doctrine both of necessity and of liberty, according to any reasonable sense which can be put on these terms, and that the whole controversy has hitherto turned merely upon words. We shall begin with examining the doctrine of necessity.

It is universally allowed that matter, in all its operations, is actuated by a necessary force, and that every natural effect is so precisely determined by the energy of its cause that no other effect, in such particular circumstances, could possibly have resulted from it. The degree and direction of every motion is, by the laws of nature, prescribed with such exactness that a living creature may as soon arise from the shock of two bodies, as motion, in any other degree or direction than what is actually produced by it. Would we, therefore, form a just and precise idea of *necessity*, we must consider whence that idea arises when we apply it to the operation of bodies.

It seems evident that, if all the scenes of nature were continually shifted in such a manner that no two events bore any resemblance to each other, but every object was entirely new, without any similitude to whatever had been seen before, we should never, in that case, have attained the least idea of necessity or of a connection among these objects. We might say, upon such a supposition, that one object or event has followed another, not that one was produced by the other. The relation of cause and effect must be utterly unknown to mankind. Inference and reasoning concerning the operations of nature would, from that moment, be at an end; and the memory and senses remain the only canals by which the knowledge of any real existence could possibly have access to the mind. Our idea, therefore, of necessity and causation arises entirely from the uniformity observable in the operations of nature, where similar objects are constantly conjoined together, and the mind is determined by custom to infer the one from the appearance of the other. These two circumstances form the whole of that necessity which we ascribe to matter. Beyond the constant *conjunction* of similar objects and the consequent *inference* from one to the other, we have no notion of any necessity of connection.

If it appear, therefore, that all mankind have ever allowed, without any doubt or hesitation, that these two circumstances take place in the voluntary actions of men and in the operations of mind, it must follow that all mankind have ever agreed in the doctrine of necessity, and that they have hitherto disputed merely for not understanding each other.

As to the first circumstance, the constant and regular conjunction of similar events, we may possibly satisfy ourselves by the following considerations. It is universally acknowledged that there is a great uniformity among the actions of men, in all nations and ages, and that human nature remains still the same in its principles and operations. The same motives always produce the same actions; the same events follow from the same causes. Ambition, avarice, self-love, vanity, friendship, generosity, public spirit—these passions, mixed in various degrees and distributed through society, have been, from the beginning of the world, and still are, the source of all the actions and enterprises which have ever been observed among mankind. Would you know the sentiments, inclinations, and course of life of the Greeks and Romans? Study well the temper and actions of the French and English: you cannot be much mistaken in transferring to the former *most* of the observations which you have made with regard to the latter. Mankind are so much the same, in all times and places, that history informs us of nothing new or strange in this particular. Its chief use is only to discover the constant and universal principles of human nature by showing men in all varieties of circumstances and situations, and furnishing us with materials from which we may form our observations and become acquainted with the regular springs of human action and behavior. These records of wars, intrigues, factions, and revolutions are so many collections of experiments by which the politician or moral philosopher fixes the principles of his science, in the same manner as the physician or natural philosopher becomes acquainted with the nature of plants, minerals, and other external objects, by the experiments which he forms concerning them. Nor are the earth, water, and other elements examined by Aristotle and Hippocrates more like to those which at present lie under our observation than the men described by Polybius and Tacitus are to those who now govern the world.

Should a traveler, returning from a far country, bring us an account of men wholly different from any with whom we were ever acquainted, men who were entirely divested of avarice, ambition, or revenge, who knew no pleasure but friendship, generosity, and public spirit, we should immediately, from these circumstances, detect the falsehood and prove him a liar with the same certainty as if he had stuffed his narration with stories of centaurs and dragons, miracles and prodigies. And if we would explode any forgery in history, we cannot make use of a more convincing argument than to prove that the actions ascribed to any person are directly contrary to the course of nature, and that no human motives, in such circumstances, could ever induce him to such a conduct. The veracity of Quintus Curtius is as much to be suspected when he describes the supernatural courage of Alexander by which he was hurried on singly to attack multitudes, as when he describes his supernatural force and activity by which he was able to resist them. So readily and universally do we acknowledge a uniformity in human motives and actions as well as in the operations of body.

Hence, likewise, the benefit of that experience acquired by long life and a variety of business and company, in order to instruct us in the principles of human nature and regulate our future conduct as well as speculation. By means of this guide we mount up to the knowledge of men's inclinations and motives from their actions, expressions, and even gestures, and again descend to the interpretation of their actions from our knowledge of their motives and inclinations. The general observations, treasured up by a course of experience, give us the clue of human nature and teach us to unravel all its intricacies. Pretexts and appearances no longer deceive us. Public declarations pass for the specious coloring of a cause. And though virtue and honor be allowed their proper weight and authority, that perfect disinterestedness, so often pretended to, is never expected in multitudes and parties, seldom in their leaders, and scarcely even in individuals of any rank or station. But were there no uniformity in human actions, and were every experiment which we could form of this kind irregular and anomalous, it were impossible to collect any general observations concerning mankind, and no experience, however accurately digested by reflection, would ever serve to any purpose. Why is the aged husbandman more skillful in his calling than the young beginner, but because there is a certain uniformity in the operation of the sun, rain, and earth toward the production of vegetables, and experience teaches the old practitioner the rules by which this operation is governed and directed?

We must not, however, expect that this uniformity of human actions should be carried to such a length as that all men, in the same circumstances, will always act precisely in the same manner, without making any allowance for the diversity of characters, prejudices, and opinions. Such a uniformity, in every particular, is found in no part of nature. On the contrary, from observing the variety of conduct in different men we are enabled to form a greater variety of maxims which still suppose a degree of uniformity and regularity.

Are the manners of men different in different ages and countries? We learn thence the great force of custom and education, which mold the human mind from its infancy and form it into a fixed and established character. Is the behavior and conduct of the one sex very unlike that of the other? It is thence we become acquainted with the different characters which nature has impressed upon the sexes, and which she preserves with constancy and regularity. Are the actions of the same person much diversified in the different periods of his life from infancy to old age? This affords room for many general observations concerning the gradual change of our sentiments and inclinations, and the different maxims which prevail in the different ages of human creatures. Even the characters which are peculiar to each individual have a uniformity in their influence, otherwise our acquaintance with the persons, and our observations of their conduct, could never teach us their dispositions or serve to direct our behavior with regard to them.

I grant it possible to find actions which seem to have no regular connection with any known motives and are exceptions to all the measures of conduct which have ever been established for the government of men. But if we could willingly know what judgment should be formed of such irregular and extraordinary actions, we may consider the sentiments commonly entertained with regard to those irregular events which appear in the course of nature and the operations of eternal objects. All causes are not conjoined to their usual effects with like uniformity. An artificer who handles only dead matter may be disappointed of his aim, as well as the politician who directs the conduct of sensible and intelligent agents.

The vulgar, who take things according to their first appearance, attribute the uncertainty of events to such an uncertainty in the causes as makes the latter often fail of their usual influence, though they meet with no impediment in their operation. But philosophers, observing that almost in every part of nature there is contained a vast variety of springs and principles which are hid by reason of their minuteness or remoteness, find that it is at least possible the contrariety of events may not proceed from any contingency in the cause but from the secret operation of contrary causes. This possibility is converted into certainty by further observation, when they remark that, upon an exact scrutiny, a contrariety of effects always betrays a contrariety of causes and proceeds from their mutual opposition. A peasant can give no better reason for the stopping of any clock or watch than to say that it does not commonly go right. But an artist easily perceives that the same force in the spring or pendulum has always the same influence on the wheels, but fails of its usual effect perhaps by reason of a grain of dust which puts a stop to the whole movement. From the observation of several parallel instances philosophers form a maxim that the connection between all causes and effects is equally necessary, and that its seeming uncertainty in some instances proceeds from the secret opposition of contrary causes.

Thus, for instance, in the human body, when the usual symptoms of health or sickness disappoint our expectation, when medicines operate not with their wonted powers, when irregular events follow from any particular cause, the philosopher and physician are not surprised at the matter, nor are ever tempted to deny, in general, the necessity and uniformity of those principles by which the animal economy is conducted. They know that a human body is a mighty complicated machine, that many secret powers lurk in it which are altogether beyond our comprehension, that to us it must often appear very uncertain in its operations, and that, therefore, the irregular events which outwardly discover themselves can be no proof that the laws of nature are not observed with the greatest regularity in its internal operations and government.

The philosopher, if he be consistent, must apply the same reasonings to the actions and volitions of intelligent agents. The most irregular and unexpected resolutions of men may frequently be accounted for by those who know every particular circumstance of their character and situation. A person of an obliging disposition gives a peevish answer; but he has the toothache, or has not dined. A stupid fellow discovers an uncommon alacrity in his carriage; but he has met with a sudden piece of good fortune. Or even when an action, as sometimes happens, cannot be particularly accounted

for, either by the person himself or by others, we know, in general that the characters of men are to a certain degree inconstant and irregular. This is, in a manner, the constant character of human nature, though it be applicable, in a more particular manner, to some persons who have no fixed rule for their conduct, but proceed in a continual course of caprice and inconstancy. The internal principles and motives may operate in a uniform manner, notwithstanding these seeming irregularities—in the same manner as the winds, rains, clouds, and other variations of the weather are supposed to be governed by steady principles, though not easily discoverable by human sagacity and inquiry.

Thus it appears not only that the conjunction between motives and voluntary actions is as regular and uniform as that between the cause and effect in any part of nature, but also that this regular conjunction has been universally acknowledged among mankind and has never been the subject of dispute either in philosophy or common life. Now, as it is from past experience that we draw all inferences concerning the future, and as we conclude that objects will always be conjoined together which we find to have always been conjoined, it may seem superfluous to prove that this experienced uniformity in human actions is a source whence we draw *inferences* concerning them. But in order to throw the argument into a greater variety of lights, we shall also insist, though briefly, on this latter topic.

The mutual dependence of men is so great in all societies that scarce any human action is entirely complete in itself or is performed without some reference to the actions of others, which are requisite to make it answer fully the intention of the agent. The poorest artificer who labors alone expects at least the protection of the magistrate to insure him the enjoyment of the fruits of his labor. He also expects that when he carries his goods to market and offers them at a reasonable price, he shall find purchasers and shall be able, by the money he acquires, to engage others to supply him with those commodities which are requisite for his subsistence. In proportion as men extend their dealings and render their intercourse with others more complicated, they always comprehend in their schemes of life a greater variety of voluntary actions which they expect, from the proper motives, to co-operate with their own. In all these conclusions they take their measures from past experience, in the same manner as in their reasonings concerning external objects, and firmly believe that men, as well as all the elements, are to continue in their operations the same that they have ever found them. A manufacturer reckons upon the labor of his servants for the execution of any work as much as upon the tools which he employs, and would be equally surprised were his expectations disappointed. In short, this experimental inference and reasoning concerning the actions of others enters so much into human life that no man, while awake, is ever a moment without employing it. Have we not reason, therefore, to affirm that all mankind have always agreed in the doctrine of necessity, according to the foregoing definition and explication of it?

Nor have philosophers ever entertained a different opinion from the people in this particular. For, not to mention that almost every action of their life supposes that opinion, there are even few of the speculative parts of learning to which it is not essential. What would become of *history* had we not a dependence on the veracity of the historian according to the experience which we have had of mankind? How could *politics* be a science if laws and forms of government had not a uniform influence upon society? Where would be the foundation of *morals* if particular characters had no certain or determinate power to produce particular sentiments, and if these sentiments had no constant operation on actions? And with what pretense could we employ our *criticism* upon any poet or polite author if we could not pronounce the conduct and sentiments of his actors either natural or unnatural to such characters and in such circumstances? It seems almost impossible, therefore, to engage either in science or action of any kind without acknowledging the doctrine of necessity, and this *inference* from motives to voluntary action, from characters to conduct.

And, indeed, when we consider how aptly *natural* and *moral* evidence link together and form only one chain of argument, we shall make no scruple to allow that they are of the same nature and derived from the same principles. A prisoner who has neither money nor interest discovers the impossibility of his escape as well when he considers the obstinacy of the jailer as the walls and bars with which he is surrounded, and in all attempts for his freedom chooses rather to work upon the stone and iron of the one than upon the inflexible nature of the other. The same prisoner, when conducted to the scaffold, foresees his death as certainly from the constancy and fidelity of his guards as from the operation of the ax or wheel. His mind runs along a certain train of ideas: the refusal of the soldiers to consent to his escape; the action of the executioner; the separation of the head and body; bleeding, convulsive motions, and death. Here is a connected chain of natural causes and voluntary actions, but the mind feels no difference between them in passing from one link to another, nor is less certain of the future event than if it were connected with the objects present to the memory or senses by a train of causes cemented together by what we are pleased to call a "physical" necessity. The same experienced union has the same effect on the mind, whether the united objects be motives, volition, and actions, or figure and motion. We may change the names of things, but their nature and their operation on the understanding never change.

Were a man whom I know to be honest and opulent, and with whom I lived in intimate friendship, to come into my house, where I am surrounded with my servants, I rest assured that he is not to stab me before he leaves it in order to rob me of my silver standish; and I no more suspect this event than the falling of the house itself, which is new and solidly built and founded.—*But he may have been seized with a sudden and unknown frenzy.*— So may a sudden earthquake arise, and shake and tumble my house about my ears. I shall, therefore, change the suppositions. I shall say that I know with certainty that he is not to put his hand into the fire and hold it there till it be consumed. And this event I think I can foretell with the same assurance as that, if he throw himself out of the window and meet with no obstruction, he will not remain a moment suspended in the air. No suspicion of an unknown frenzy can give the least possibility to the former event which is so contrary to all the known principles of human nature. A man who at noon leaves his purse full of gold on the pavement at Charing Cross may as well expect that it will fly away like a feather as that he will find it untouched an hour after. Above one-half of human reasonings contain inferences of a similar nature, attended with more or less degrees of certainty, proportioned to our experience of the usual conduct of mankind in such particular situations.

I have frequently considered what could possibly be the reason why all mankind, though they have ever, without hesitation, acknowledged the doctrine of necessity in their whole practice and reasoning, have yet discovered such a reluctance to acknowledge it in words, and have rather shown a propensity, in all ages, to profess the contrary opinion. The matter, I think, may be accounted for after the following manner. If we examine the operations of body and the production of effects from their causes, we shall find that all our faculties can never carry us further in our knowledge of this relation than barely to observe that particular objects are *constantly conjoined* together, and that the mind is carried, by a *customary transition*, from the appearance of the one to the belief of the other. But though this conclusion concerning human ignorance be the result of the strictest scrutiny of this subject, men still entertain a strong propensity to believe that they penetrate further into the powers of nature and perceive something like a necessary connection between the cause and the effect. When, again, they turn their reflections toward the operations of their own minds and *feel* no such connection of the motive and the action, they are thence apt to suppose that there is a difference between the effects which result from material force and those which arise from thought and intelligence. But being once convinced that we know nothing further of causation of any kind than merely the *constant conjunction* of objects and the consequent *inference* of the mind from one to another, and finding that these two circumstances are universally allowed to have place in voluntary actions, we may be more easily led to own the same necessity common to all causes. And though this reasoning may contradict the systems of many philosophers in ascribing necessity to the determinations of the will, we shall find, upon reflection, that they dissent from it in words only, not in their real sentiments. Necessity, according to the sense in which it is here taken, has never yet been rejected, nor can ever, I think, be rejected by any philosopher. It may only, perhaps, be pretended that the mind can perceive in the operations of matter some further connection between the cause and effect, and a connection that has not place in the voluntary actions of intelligent beings. Now, whether it be so or not can only appear upon examination, and it is incumbent on these philosophers to make good their assertion by defining or describing that necessity and pointing it out to us in the operations of material causes.

It would seem, indeed, that men begin at the wrong end of this question concerning liberty and necessity when they enter upon it by examining the faculties of the soul, the influence of the understanding, and the operations of the will. Let them first discuss a more simple question, namely, the question of body and brute unintelligent matter, and try whether they can there form any idea of causation and necessity, except that of a constant conjunction of objects and subsequent inference of the mind from one to another. If these circumstances form, in reality, the whole of that necessity which we conceive in matter, and if these circumstances be also universally acknowledged to take place in the operations of the mind, the dispute is at an end; at least, must be owned to be thenceforth merely verbal. But as long as we will rashly suppose that we have some further idea of necessity and causation in the operations of external objects, at the same time that we can find nothing further in the voluntary actions of the mind, there is no possibility of bringing the question to any determinate issue while we proceed upon so erroneous a supposition. The only method of undeceiving us is to mount up higher, to examine the narrow extent of science when applied to material causes, and to convince ourselves that all we know of them is the constant conjunction and inference above mentioned. We may, perhaps, find that it is with difficulty we are induced to fix such narrow limits to human understanding, but we can afterwards find no difficulty when we come to apply this doctrine to the actions of the will. For as it is evident that these have a regular conjunction with motives and circumstances and character, and as we always draw inferences from one to the other, we must be obliged to acknowledge in words that necessity which we have already avowed in every deliberation of our lives and in every step of our conduct and behavior.[1]

But to proceed in this reconciling project with regard to the question of liberty and necessity—the most contentious question of metaphysics, the most contentious science—it will not require many words to prove that all mankind have ever agreed in the doctrine of liberty as well as in that of necessity, and that the whole dispute, in this respect also, has been hitherto merely verbal. For what is meant by liberty when applied to voluntary actions? We cannot surely mean that actions have so little connection with motives, inclinations, and circumstances that one does not follow with a certain degree of uniformity from the other, and that one affords no inference by which we can conclude the existence of the other. For these are plain and acknowledged matters of fact. By liberty, then, we can only mean *a power of acting or not acting according to the determinations of the will*; that is, if we choose to remain at rest, we may; if we choose to move, we also may. Now this hypothetical liberty is universally allowed to belong to everyone who is not a prisoner and in chains. Here then is no subject of dispute.

Whatever definition we may give of liberty, we should be careful to observe two requisite circumstances: *first*, that it be consistent with plain matter of fact; *secondly*, that it be consistent with itself. If we observe these circumstances and render our definition intelligible, I am persuaded that all mankind will be found of one opinion with regard to it.

It is universally allowed that nothing exists without a cause of its existence, and that chance, when strictly examined, is a mere negative word and means not any real power which has anywhere a being in nature. But it is pretended that some causes are necessary, some not necessary. Here then is the advantage of definitions. Let anyone *define* a cause without comprehending, as a part of the definition, a *necessary connection* with its effect, and let him show distinctly the origin of the idea expressed by the definition, and I shall readily give up the whole controversy. But if the foregoing explication of the matter be received, this must be absolutely impracticable. Had not objects a regular conjunction with each other, we should never have entertained any notion of cause and effect; and this regular conjunction produces that inference of the understanding which is the only connection that we can have any comprehension of. Whoever attempts a definition of cause exclusive of these circumstances will be obliged either to employ unintelligible terms or such as are synonymous to the term which he endeavors to define.[2] And if the definition above mentioned be admitted, liberty, when opposed to necessity, not to constraint, is the same thing with chance, which is universally allowed to have no existence.

Part II

There is no method of reasoning more common, and yet none more blamable, than in philosophical disputes to endeavor the refutation of any hypothesis by a pretense of its dangerous consequences to religion and morality. When any opinion leads to absurdity, it is certainly false; but it is not certain that an opinion is false because it is of dangerous consequence. Such topics, therefore, ought entirely to be forborne as serving nothing to the discovery of truth, but only to make the person of an antagonist odious. This I observe in general, without pretending to draw any advantage from it. I frankly submit to an examination of this kind, and shall venture to affirm that the doctrines both of necessity and liberty, as above explained, are not only consistent with morality, but are absolutely essential to its support.

Necessity may be defined two ways, conformably to the two definitions of *cause* of which it makes an essential part. It consists either in the constant conjunction of like objects or in the inference of the understanding from one object to another. Now necessity, in both these senses (which, indeed, are at bottom the same), has universally, though tacitly, in the schools, in the pulpit, and in common life been allowed to belong to the will of man, and no one has ever pretended to deny that we can draw inferences concerning human actions, and that those inferences are founded on the experienced union of like actions, with like motives, inclinations, and circumstances. The only particular in which anyone can differ is that either perhaps he will refuse to give the name of necessity to this property of human actions—but as long as the meaning is understood I hope the word can do no harm—or that he will maintain it possible to discover something further in the operations of matter. But this, it must be acknowledged, can be of no consequence to morality or religion, whatever it may be to natural philosophy or metaphysics. We may here be mistaken in asserting that there is no idea of any other necessity or connection in the actions of the body, but surely we ascribe nothing to the actions of the mind but what everyone does and must readily allow of. We change no circumstance in the received orthodox system with regard to the will, but only in that with regard to material objects and causes. Nothing, therefore, can be more innocent at least than this doctrine.

All laws being founded on rewards and punishments, it is supposed, as a fundamental principle, that these motives have a regular and uniform influence on the mind and both produce the good and prevent the evil actions. We may give to this influence what name we please; but as it is usually conjoined with the action, it must be esteemed a *cause* and be looked upon as an instance of that necessity which we would here establish.

The only proper object of hatred or vengeance is a person or creature endowed with thought and consciousness; and when any criminal or injurious actions excite that passion, it is only by their relation to the person, or connection with him. Actions are, by their very nature, temporary and perishing; and where they proceed not from some *cause* in the character and disposition of the person who performed them, they can neither redound to his honor if good, nor infamy if evil. The actions themselves may be blamable; they may be contrary to all the rules of morality and religion; but the person is not answerable for them and, as they proceeded from nothing in him that is durable and constant and leave nothing of that nature behind them, it is impossible he can, upon their account, become the object of punishment or vengeance. According to the principle, therefore, which denies necessity and, consequently, causes, a man is as pure and untainted, after having committed the most horrid crime, as at the first moment of his birth, nor is his character anywise concerned in his actions, since they are not derived from it; and the wickedness of the one can never be used as a proof of the depravity of the other.

Men are not blamed for such actions as they perform ignorantly and casually, whatever may be the consequences. Why? But because the principles of these actions are only momentary and terminate in them alone. Men are less blamed for such actions as they perform hastily and unpremeditately than for such as proceed from deliberation. For what reason? But because a hasty temper, though a constant cause or principle in the mind, operates only by intervals and infects not the whole character. Again, repentance wipes off every crime if attended with a reformation of life and manners. How is this to be accounted for? But by asserting that actions render a person criminal merely as they are proofs of criminal principles in the mind; and when, by an alteration of these principles, they cease to be just proofs, they likewise cease to be criminal. But, except upon the doctrine of necessity, they never were just proofs, and consequently never were criminal.

It will be equally easy to prove, and from the same arguments, that *liberty*, according to that definition above mentioned, in which all men agree, is also essential to morality, and that no human actions, where it is wanting, are susceptible of any

moral qualities or can be the objects of approbation or dislike. For as actions are objects of our moral sentiment so far only as they are indications of the internal character, passions, and affections, it is impossible that they can give rise either to praise or blame where they proceed not from these principles, but are derived altogether from external violence.

I pretend not to have obtained or removed all objections to this theory with regard to necessity and liberty. I can foresee other objections derived from topics which have not here been treated of. It may be said, for instance, that if voluntary actions be subjected to the same laws of necessity with the operations of matter, there is a continued chain of necessary causes, preordained and predetermined, reaching from the Original Cause of all to every single volition of every human creature. No contingency anywhere in the universe, no indifference, no liberty. While we act, we are at the same time acted upon. The ultimate Author of all our volitions is the Creator of the world, who first bestowed motion on this immense machine and placed all beings in that particular position whence every subsequent event, by an inevitable necessity, must result. Human actions, therefore, either can have no moral turpitude at all, as proceeding from so good a cause, or if they have any turpitude, they must involve our Creator in the same guilt, while he is acknowledged to be their ultimate cause and Author. For as a man who fired a mine is answerable for all the consequences, whether the train he employed be long or short, so, wherever a continued chain of necessary causes is fixed, that Being, either finite or infinite, who produces the first is likewise the author of all the rest and must both bear the blame and acquire the praise which belong to them. Our clear and unalterable ideas of morality establish this rule upon unquestionable reasons when we examine the consequences of any human action; and these reasons must still have greater force when applied to the volitions and intentions of a Being infinitely wise and powerful. Ignorance or impotence may be pleaded for so limited a creature as man, but those imperfections have no place in our Creator. He foresaw, he ordained, he intended all those actions of men which we so rashly pronounce criminal. And we must, therefore, conclude either that they are not criminal or that the Deity, not man, is accountable for them. But as either of these positions is absurd and impious, it follows that the doctrine from which they are deduced cannot possibly be true, as being liable to all the same objections. An absurd consequence, if necessary, proves the original doctrine to be absurd in the same manner as criminal actions render criminal the original cause if the connection between them be necessary and inevitable.

This objection consists of two parts, which we shall examine separately:

First, that if human actions can be traced up, by a necessary chain, to the Deity, they can never be criminal, on account of the infinite perfection of that Being from whom they are derived, and who can intend nothing but what is altogether good and laudable. Or, *secondly,* if they be criminal, we must retract the attribute of perfection which we ascribe to the Deity and must acknowledge him to be the ultimate author of guilt and moral turpitude in all his creatures.

The answer to the first objection seems obvious and convincing. There are many philosophers who, after an exact scrutiny of the phenomena of nature, conclude that the WHOLE, considered as one system, is, in every period of its existence, ordered with perfect benevolence; and that the utmost possible happiness will, in the end, result to all created beings without any mixture of positive or absolute ill and misery. Every physical ill, say they, makes an essential part of this benevolent system, and could not possibly be removed, by even the Deity himself, considered as a wise agent, without giving entrance to greater ill or excluding greater good which will result from it. From this theory some philosophers, and the ancient Stoics among the rest, derived topic of consolation under all afflictions, while they taught their pupils that those ills under which they labored were in reality goods to the universe, and that to an enlarged view which could comprehend the whole system of nature every event became an object of joy and exultation. But though this topic be specious and sublime, it was soon found in practice weak and ineffectual. You would surely more irritate than appease a man lying under the racking pains of the gout by preaching up to him the rectitude of those general laws which produced the malignant humors in his body and led them through the proper canals to the sinews and nerves, where they now excite such acute torments. These enlarged views may, for a moment, please the imagination of a speculative man who is placed in ease and security, but neither can they dwell with constancy on his mind, even though undisturbed by the emotions of

pain or passion, much less can they maintain their ground when attacked by such powerful antagonists. The affections take a narrower and more natural survey of their object and, by an economy more suitable to the infirmity of human minds, regard alone the beings around us, and are actuated by such events as appear good or ill to the private system.

The case is the same with *moral* as with *physical* ill. It cannot reasonably be supposed that those remote considerations which are found of so little efficacy with regard to the one will have a more powerful influence with regard to the other. The mind of man is so formed by nature that, upon the appearance of certain characters, dispositions, and actions, it immediately feels the sentiment of approbation or blame; nor are there any emotions more essential to its frame and constitution. The characters which engage our approbation are chiefly such as contribute to the peace and security of human society, as the characters which excite blame are chiefly such as tend to public detriment and disturbance; whence it may reasonably be presumed that the moral sentiments arise, either mediately or immediately, from a reflection on these opposite interests. What though philosophical meditations establish a different opinion or conjecture that everything is right with regard to the whole, and that the qualities which disturb society are, in the main, as beneficial, and are as suitable to the primary intention of nature, as those which more directly promote its happiness and welfare? Are such remote and uncertain speculations able to counterbalance the sentiments which arise from the natural and immediate view of the objects? A man who is robbed of a considerable sum, does he find his vexation for the loss anywise diminished by these sublime reflections? Why, then, should his moral resentment against the crime be supposed incompatible with them? Or why should not the acknowledgement of a real distinction between vice and virtue be reconcilable to all speculative systems of philosophy, as well as that of a real distinction between personal beauty and deformity? Both these distinctions are founded in the natural sentiments of the human mind; and these sentiments are not to be controlled or altered by any philosophical theory or speculation whatsoever.

The *second* objection admits not of so easy and satisfactory an answer, nor is it possible to explain distinctly how the Deity can be the immediate cause of all the actions of men without being the author of sin and moral turpitude. These are mysteries which mere natural and unassisted reason is very unfit to handle; and whatever system she embraces, she must find herself involved in inextricable difficulties, and even contradictions, at every step which she takes with regard to such subjects. To reconcile the indifference and contingency of human actions with prescience or to defend absolute decrees, and yet free the Deity from being the author of sin, has been found hitherto to exceed all the power of philosophy. Happy, if she be thence sensible of her temerity, when she pries into these sublime mysteries, and, leaving a scene so full of obscurities and perplexities, return with suitable modesty to her true and proper province, the examination of common life, where she will find difficulties enough to employ her inquiries without launching into so boundless an ocean of doubt, uncertainty, and contradiction.

Endnotes

[1] The prevalence of the doctrine of liberty may be accounted for from another cause, viz., a false sensation, or seeming experience, which we have, or may have, of liberty or indifference in many of our actions. The necessity of any action, whether of matter or of mind, is not, properly speaking, a quality in the agent but in any thinking or intelligent being who may consider the action; and it consists chiefly in the determination of his thoughts to infer the existence of that action from some preceding objects; as liberty, when opposed to necessity, is nothing but the want of that determination, and a certain looseness or indifference which we feel in passing, or not passing, from the idea of one object to that of any succeeding one. Now we may observe that though, in *reflecting* on human actions, we seldom feel such a looseness or indifference, but are commonly able to infer them with considerable certainty from their motives, and from the disposition of the agent; yet it frequently happens that, in *performing* the actions themselves, we are sensible of something like it; and as all resembling objects are readily taken for each other, this has been employed as a demonstrative and even intuitive proof of human liberty. We feel that our actions are subject to our will on most occasions, and imagine we feel that the will itself is subject to nothing, because, when by a denial of it we are provoked to try, we feel that it moves easily every way, and produces an image of itself (or a "velleity," as it is called in the schools), even on that side on which it did not settle. This image, or faint motion, we persuade ourselves, could at that time have been completed into the thing itself, because, should that be denied, we find upon a second trial that at present it can. We consider not that the fantastical desire of showing liberty is here the motive of our actions. And it seems certain that however we may imagine we feel a liberty within ourselves, a spectator can commonly infer our actions from our motives and character; and even where he cannot, he concludes in general that he might, were he perfectly acquainted with every circumstance of our situation and temper, and the most secret springs of our complexion and disposition. Now this is the very essence of necessity, according to the foregoing doctrine.

[2] Thus, if a cause be defined, *that which produces anything*, it is easy to observe that *producing* is synonymous to *causing*. In like manner, if a cause be defined, *that by which anything exists*, this is liable to the same objection. For what is meant by these words, "*by which*"? Had it been said that a cause is *that* after which *anything constantly exists*, we should have understood the terms. For this is, indeed, all we know of the matter. And this constancy forms the very essence of necessity, nor have we any other idea of it.

38. Of the Liberty of Moral Agents

THOMAS REID

In contrast to Hume, Reid maintains that some actions are not caused or determined by a person's character, motives, heredity, or background. Reid reasons that if an action is caused by anything other than the agent—Reid's "substantial self"—then it is not one's own will that determines choices; in such cases one's actions are not really free. In Part II, Reid argues for a substantialist conception of the self and its identity through time. Here, Reid connects that notion of the self with a denial that a free self can be caused and a rejection of Hume's views on causation. (See also the Hume selection in Part V.)

The Notions of Moral Liberty and Necessity Stated

By the *liberty* of a moral agent, I understand, a power over the determinations of his own will.

If, in any action, he had power to will what he did, or not to will it, in that action he is free. But if, in every voluntary action, the determination of his will be the necessary consequence of something involuntary in the state of his mind, or of something in his external circumstances, he is not free; he has not what I call the liberty of a moral agent, but is subject to necessity.

This liberty supposes the agent to have understanding and will; for the determinations of the will are the sole object about which this power is employed; and there can be no will, without, at least, such a degree of understanding as gives the conception of that which we will.

The liberty of a moral agent implies, not only a conception of what he wills, but some degree of practical judgment or reason.

For, if he has not the judgment to discern one determination to be preferable to another, either in itself, or for some purpose which he intends, what can be the use of a power to determine? his determinations must be made perfectly in the dark, without reason, motive, or end. They can neither be right nor wrong, wise nor foolish. Whatever the consequences may be, they cannot be imputed to the agent, who had not the capacity of foreseeing them, or of perceiving any reason for acting otherwise than he did.

We may perhaps be able to conceive a being endowed with power over the determinations of his will, without any light in his mind to direct that power to some end. But such power would be given in vain. No exercise of it could be either blamed or approved. As nature gives no power in vain, I see no ground to ascribe a power over the determinations of the will to any being who has no judgment to apply it to the direction of his conduct, no discernment of what he ought or ought not to do.

For that reason, in this Essay, I speak only of the liberty of moral agents, who are capable of acting well or ill, wisely or foolishly, and this, for distinction's sake, I shall call *moral liberty*.

What kind, or what degree of liberty belongs to brute animals, or to our own species, before any use of reason, I do not know. We acknowledge that they have not the power of self-government. Such of their actions as may be called *voluntary*, seem to be invariably determined by the passion or appetite, or affection or habit, which is strongest at the time.

This seems to be the law of their constitution, to which they yield, as the inanimate creation does, without any conception of the law, or any intention of obedience.

From Reid's *Essays on the Active Powers of the Human Mind*, Essay IV, Chapters 1 and 9. First published in 1815.

But of civil or moral government, which are addressed to the rational powers, and require a conception of the law and an intentional obedience, they are, in the judgment of all mankind, incapable. Nor do I see what end could be served by giving them a power over the determinations of their own will, unless to make them intractable by discipline, which we see they are not.

The effect of moral liberty is, that it is in the power of the agent to do well or ill. This power, like every other gift of God, may be abused. The right use of this gift of God is to do well and wisely, as far as his best judgment can direct him, and thereby merit esteem and approbation. The abuse of it is to act contrary to what he knows, or suspects to be his duty and his wisdom, and thereby justly merit disapprobation and blame.

By *necessity*, I understand the want of that moral liberty which I have above defined.

If there can be a better and a worse in actions on the system of necessity, let us suppose a man necessarily determined in all cases to will and to do what is best to be done, he would surely be innocent and inculpable. But, as far as I am able to judge, he would not be entitled to the esteem and moral approbation of those who knew and believed this necessity. What was, by an ancient author, said of Cato, might indeed be said of him. *He was good because he could not be otherwise.* But this saying, if understood literally and strictly, is not the praise of Cato, but of his constitution, which was no more the work of Cato, than his existence.

On the other hand, if a man be necessarily determined to do ill, this case seems to me to move pity, but not disapprobation. He was ill, because he could not be otherwise. Who can blame him? Necessity has no law.

If he knows that he acted under this necessity, has he not just ground to exculpate himself? The blame, if there be any, is not in him, but in his constitution. If he be charged by his Maker with doing wrong, may he not expostulate with him, and say, why hast thou made me thus? I may be sacrificed at thy pleasure, for the common good, like a man that has the plague, but not for ill desert; for thou knowest that what I am charged with is thy work, and not mine.

Such are my notions of moral liberty and necessity, and of the consequences inseparably connected with both the one and the other.

This moral liberty a man may have, though it do not extend to all his actions, or even to all his voluntary actions. He does many things by instinct, many things by the force of habit without any thought at all, and consequently without will. In the first part of life, he has not the power of self-government any more than the brutes. That power over the determinations of his own will, which belongs to him in ripe years, is limited, as all his powers are; and it is perhaps beyond the reach of his understanding to define its limits with precision. We can only say, in general, that it extends to every action for which he is accountable.

This power is given by his Maker, and at his pleasure whose gift it is, it may be enlarged or diminished, continued or withdrawn. No power in the creature can be independent of the Creator. His hook is in its nose; he can give it line as far as he sees fit, and, when he pleases, can restrain it, or turn it withersoever he will. Let this be always understood, when we ascribe liberty to man, or to any created being.

Supposing it therefore to be true, that man is a free agent, it may be true, at the same time, that his liberty may be impaired or lost, by disorder of body or mind, as in melancholy, or in madness; it may be impaired or lost by vicious habits; it may, in particular cases, be restrained by divine interposition.

We call man a free agent in the same way as we call him a reasonable agent. In many things he is not guided by reason, but by principles similar to those of the brutes. His reason is weak at best. It is liable to be impaired or lost, by his own fault, or by other means. In like manner, he may be a free agent, though his freedom of action may have many similar limitations.

The liberty I have described has been represented by some philosophers as inconceivable, and as involving an absurdity.

"Liberty," they say, "consists only in a power to act as we will; and it is impossible to conceive in any being a greater liberty than this. Hence it follows, that liberty does not extend to the determinations of the will, but only to the actions consequent to its determination, and depending upon the will. To say that we have power to will such an action, is to say, that we may will it, if we will. This supposes the will to be determined by a prior will; and, for the same reason, that will must be determined by a will prior to it, and so on in an infinite series of wills, which is absurd. To act freely, therefore, can mean nothing more than to act voluntarily; and this is all the liberty that can be conceived in man, or in any being."

This reasoning, first, I think, advanced by Hobbes, has been very generally adopted by the defenders of necessity. It is grounded upon a definition of liberty totally different from that which I have given, and therefore does not apply to moral liberty, as above defined.

But it is said that this is the only liberty that is possible, that is conceivable, that does not involve an absurdity.

It is strange indeed! if the word *liberty* has no meaning but this one. I shall mention three, all very common. The objection applies to one of them, but to neither of the other two.

Liberty is sometimes opposed to external force or confinement of the body. Sometimes it is opposed to obligation by law, or by lawful authority. Sometimes it is opposed to necessity.

First, it is opposed to confinement of the body by superior force. So we say a prisoner is set at liberty when his fetters are knocked off, and he is discharged from confinement. This is the liberty defined in the objection; and I grant that this liberty extends not to the will, neither does the confinement, because the will cannot be confined by external force.

Secondly, liberty is opposed to obligation, by law, or lawful authority. This liberty is a right to act one way or another, in things which the law has neither commanded nor forbidden; and this liberty is meant when we speak of a man's natural liberty, his civil liberty, his christian liberty. It is evident that this liberty, as well as the obligation opposed to it, extends to the will: for it is the will to obey that makes obedience; the will to transgress that makes a transgression of the law. Without will there can be neither obedience nor transgression. Law supposes a power to obey or to transgress; it does not take away this power, but proposes the motives of duty and of interest, leaving the power to yield to them, or to take the consequence of transgression.

Thirdly, liberty is opposed to necessity, and in this sense it extends to the determinations of the will only, and not to what is consequent to the will.

In every voluntary action, the determination of the will is the first part of the action, upon which alone the moral estimation of it depends. It has been made a question among philosophers, whether, in every instance, this determination be the necessary consequence of the constitution of the person, and the circumstances in which he is placed? or whether he had not power, in many cases, to determine this way or that?

This has, by some, been called the *philosophical* notion of liberty and necessity; but it is by no means peculiar to philosophers. The lowest of the vulgar have, in all ages, been prone to have recourse to this necessity, to exculpate themselves or their friends in what they do wrong, though, in the general tenor of their conduct, they act upon the contrary principle.

Whether this notion of moral liberty be conceivable or not, every man must judge for himself. To me there appears no difficulty in conceiving it. I consider the determination of the will as an effect. This effect must have a cause which had power to produce it; and the cause must be either the person himself, whose will it is, or some other being. The first is as easily conceived as the last. If the person was the cause of that determination of his own will, he was free in that action, and it is justly imputed to him, whether it be good or bad. But, if another being was the cause of this determination, either by producing it immediately, or by means and instruments under his direction, then the determination is the act and deed of that being, and is solely imputable to him.

But it is said, "That nothing is in our power but what depends upon the will, and therefore the will itself cannot be in our power."

I answer, that this is a fallacy arising from taking a common saying in a sense which it never was intended to convey, and in a sense contrary to what it necessarily implies.

In common life, when men speak of what is, or is not, in a man's power, they attend only to the external and visible effects, which only can be perceived, and which only can affect them. Of these, it is true, that nothing is in a man's power, but what depends upon his will, and this is all that is meant by this common saying.

But this is so far from excluding his will from being in his power, that it necessarily implies it. For to say that what depends upon the will is in a man's power, but the will is not in his power, is to say that the end is in his power, but the means necessary to that end are not in his power, which is a contradiction.

In many propositions which we express universally, there is an exception necessarily implied, and therefore always understood. Thus when we say that all things depend upon God, God himself is necessarily excepted. In like manner, when we say, that all that is in our power depends upon the will, the will itself is necessarily excepted; for if the will be not, nothing else can be in our power. Every effect must be in the power of its cause. The determination of the will is an effect, and therefore must be in the power of its cause, whether that cause be the agent himself, or some other being.

From what has been said in this chapter, I hope the notion of moral liberty will be distinctly understood, and that it appears that this notion is neither inconceivable, nor involves any absurdity or contradiction.

Arguments for Necessity

Another argument that has been used to prove liberty of action to be impossible is, that it implies "an effect without a cause."

To this it may be briefly answered, that a free action is an effect produced by a being who had power and will to produce it; therefore it is not an effect without a cause.

To suppose any other cause necessary to the production of an effect, than a being who had the power and the will to produce it, is a contradiction; for it is to suppose that being to have power to produce the effect, and not to have power to produce it.

But as great stress is laid upon this argument by a late zealous advocate for necessity, we shall consider the light in which he puts it.

He introduces this argument with an observation to which I entirely agree: it is, that to establish this doctrine of necessity, nothing is necessary but that, throughout all nature, the same consequences should invariably result from the same circumstances.

I know nothing more that can be desired to establish universal fatality throughout the universe. When it is proved that, through all nature, the same consequences invariably result from the same circumstances, the doctrine of liberty must be given up.

To prevent all ambiguity, I grant, that, in reasoning, the same consequences, throughout all nature, will invariably follow from the same premises: because good reasoning must be good reasoning in all times and places. But this has nothing to do with the doctrine of necessity. The thing to be proved, therefore, in order to establish that doctrine, is, that, through all nature, the same events invariably result from the same circumstances.

Of this capital point, the proof offered by that author, is that an event not preceded by any circumstances that determined it to be what it was, would be *an effect without a cause.* Why so? "For," says he, "a *cause* cannot be defined to be any thing but *such previous circumstances as are constantly followed by a certain effect*; the constancy of the result making us conclude, that there must be a *sufficient reason*, in the nature of things, why it should be produced in those circumstances."

I acknowledge that, if this be the only definition that can be given of a cause, it will follow, that an event not preceded by circumstances that determined it to be what it was, would be, not an *effect* without a cause, which is a contradiction in terms, but an *event* without a cause, which I hold to be impossible. The matter therefore is brought to this issue, whether this be the only definition that can be given of a cause?

With regard to this point, we may observe, *first*, that this definition of a cause, bating the phraseology of putting a *cause* under the category of *circumstances*, which I take to be new, is the same, in other words, with that which Mr. Hume gave, of which he ought to be acknowledged the inventor. For I know of no author before Mr. Hume, who maintained, that we have no other notion of a cause, but that it is something prior to the effect, which has been found by experience to be constantly followed by the effect. This is a main pillar of his system; and he has drawn very important consequences from this definition, which I am far from thinking this author will adopt.

Without repeating what I have before said of causes in the first of these Essays, and in the second and third chapters of this, I shall here mention some of the consequences that may be justly deduced from this definition of a cause, that we may judge of it by its fruits.

First, it follows from this definition of a cause, that night is the cause of day, and day the cause of night. For no two things have more constantly followed each other since the beginning of the world.

Secondly, it follows from this definition of a cause, that, for what we know, any thing may be the cause of any thing, since nothing is essential to a cause but its being constantly followed by the effect. If this be so, what is unintelligent may be the cause of what is intelligent; folly may be the cause of wisdom, and evil of good; all reasoning from the nature of the effect to the nature of the cause, and all reasoning from final causes, must be given up as fallacious.

Thirdly, from this definition of a cause, it follows, that we have no reason to conclude, that every event must have a cause: for innumerable events happen, when it cannot be shown that there were certain previous circumstances that have constantly been followed by such an event. And though it were certain, that every event we have had access to observe had a cause, it would not follow, that every event must have a cause: for it is contrary to the rules of logic to conclude, that, because a thing has always been, therefore it must be; to reason from what is contingent, to what is necessary.

Fourthly, from this definition of a cause, it would follow, that we have no reason to conclude that there was any cause of the creation of this world: for there were no previous circumstances that had been constantly followed by such an effect. And, for the same reason, it would follow from the definition, that whatever was singular in its nature, or the first thing of its kind, could have no cause.

Several of these consequences were fondly embraced by Mr. Hume, as necessarily following from his definition of a cause, and as favourable to his system of absolute skepticism. Those who adopt the definition of a cause, from which they follow, may choose whether they will adopt its consequences, or show that they do not follow from the definition.

A *second* observation with regard to this argument is, that a definition of a cause may be given, which is not burdened with such untoward consequences.

Why may not an efficient cause be defined to be a being that had power and will to produce the effect? The production of an effect requires active power, and active power, being a quality, must be in a being endowed with that power. Power without will produces no effect; but, where these are conjoined, the effect must be produced.

This, I think, is the proper meaning of the word *cause*, when it is used in metaphysics; and particularly when we affirm, that every thing that begins to exist must have a cause; and when, by reasoning, we prove, that there must be an eternal First Cause of all things.

Was the world produced by previous circumstances which are constantly followed by such an effect? or, was it produced by a Being that had power to produce it, and willed its production?

In natural philosophy, the word *cause* is often used in a very different sense. When an event is produced according to a known law of nature, the law of nature is called the cause of that event. But a law of nature is not the efficient cause of any event. It is only the rule, according to which the efficient cause acts. A law is a thing conceived in the mind of a rational being, not a thing that has a real existence; and, therefore, like a motive, it can neither act nor be acted upon, and consequently cannot be an efficient cause. If there be no being that acts according to the law, it produces no effect.

This author takes it for granted, that every voluntary action of man was determined to be what it was by the laws of nature, in the same sense as mechanical motions are determined by the laws of motion; and that every choice, not thus determined, "is just as impossible, as that a mechanical motion should depend upon no certain law or rule, or that any other effect should exist without a cause."

It ought here to be observed, that there are two kinds of laws, both very properly called *laws of nature*, which ought not to be confounded. There are moral laws of nature, and physical laws of nature. The first are the rules which God has prescribed to his rational creatures for their conduct. They respect voluntary and free actions only; for no other actions can be subject to moral rules. These laws of nature ought to be always obeyed, but they are often transgressed by men. There is therefore no impossibility in the violation of the moral laws of nature, nor is such a violation an effect without a cause. The transgressor is the cause, and is justly accountable for it.

The physical laws of nature are the rules according to which the Deity commonly acts in his natural government of the world; and, whatever is done according to them, is not done by man, but by God, either immediately, or by instruments under his direction. These laws of nature neither restrain the power of the Author of nature, nor bring him under any obligation to do nothing beyond their sphere. He has sometimes acted contrary to them, in the case of miracles, and, perhaps, often acts without regard to them, in the ordinary course of his providence. Neither miraculous events, which are contrary to the physical laws of nature, nor such ordinary acts of the Divine administration as are without their sphere, are impossible, nor are they *effects without a cause*. God is the cause of them, and to him only they are to be imputed.

That the moral laws of nature are often transgressed by man, is undeniable. If the physical laws of nature make his obedience to the moral laws to be impossible, then he is, in the literal sense, *born under one law, bound unto anther*, which contradicts every notion of a righteous government of the world.

But though this supposition were attended with no such shocking consequence, it is merely a supposition; and until it be proved that every choice, or voluntary action of man, is determined by the physical laws of nature, this argument for necessity is only the taking for granted the point to be proved.

Of the same kind is the argument for the impossibility of liberty, taken from a balance, which cannot move but as it is moved by the weights put into it. This argument, though urged by almost every writer in defence of necessity, is so pitiful, and has been so often answered, that it scarce deserves to be mentioned.

Every argument in a dispute, which is not grounded on principles granted by both parties, is that kind of sophism which logicians call *petitio principii*; and such, in my apprehension, are all the arguments offered to prove that liberty of action is impossible.

It may further be observed, that every argument of this class, if it were really conclusive, must extend to the Deity, as well as to all created beings; and necessary existence, which has always been considered as the prerogative of the Supreme Being, must belong equally to every creature and to every event, even the most trifling.

This I take to be the system of Spinoza, and of those among the ancients, who carried fatality to the highest pitch.

39. *On the Notion of Cause*

BERTRAND RUSSELL

Bertrand Russell (1872–1970) was a British philosopher who wrote prolifically on many aspects of philosophy and social reform. Early in his career, while teaching at Cambridge University, he did fundamental work in logic and mathematics, attempting to show that the laws of mathematics could be derived from axioms of logic. His work influenced the course of twentieth-century philosophy in many ways, *e.g.*, the development of logical positivism and the work of his student Ludwig Wittgenstein. In 1950, Russell was awarded the Nobel Prize for Literature. In this article, Russell attempts to clarify the concept of causality, which he claims is important to modern science. He feels that advanced sciences, like physics, attempt to discover laws that articulate functional relations between kinds of events. He claims that philosophical problems about determinism and freedom often stem from people attempting to think about causes according to anthropomorphic models of human volition and compulsion. Russell does not feel that scientific determinism and necessity (if any, and if properly understood) are threats to human freedom.

In the following paper I wish, first, to maintain that the word "cause" is so inextricably bound up with misleading associations as to make its complete extrusion from the philosophical vocabulary desirable; secondly, to inquire what principle, if any, is employed in science in place of the supposed "law of causality" which philosophers imagine to be employed; thirdly, to exhibit certain confusions, especially in regard to teleology and determinism, which appear to me to be connected with erroneous notions as to causality.

All philosophers, of every school, imagine that causation is one of the fundamental axioms or postulates of science, yet, oddly enough, in advanced sciences such as gravitational astronomy, the word "cause" never occurs. Dr. James Ward, in his *Naturalism and Agnosticism*, makes this a ground of complaint against physics: the business of science, he apparently thinks, should be the discovery of causes, yet physics never even seeks them. To me

it seems that philosophy ought not to assume such legislative functions, and that the reason why physics has ceased to look for causes is that, in fact, there are no such things. The law of causality, I believe, like much that passes muster among philosophers, is a relic of a bygone age, surviving, like the monarchy, only because it is erroneously supposed to do no harm.

In order to find out what philosophers commonly understand by "cause," I consulted Baldwin's *Dictionary*, and was rewarded beyond my expectations, for I found the following three mutually incompatible definitions:—

"Causality. (1) The necessary connection of events in the time-series. . . .

"Cause (notion of). Whatever may be included in the thought or perception of a process as taking place in consequence of another process. . . .

"Cause and Effect. (1) Cause and effect. . . . are correlative terms denoting any two distinguishable things, phases, or aspects of reality, which are so related to each other, that whenever the first ceases to exist, the second comes into existence immediately after, and whenever the second comes into existence, the first has ceased to exist immediately before."

From Bertrand Russell, "On the Notion of Cause," *Proceedings of the Aristotelian Society*, for 1912, pp. 1–26. © The Aristotelian Society, 1912. Reprinted by courtesy of the editor.

Let us consider these three definitions in turn. The first, obviously, is unintelligible without a definition of "necessary." Under this head, Baldwin's *Dictionary* gives the following:—

"Necessary. That is necessary which not only is true, but would be true under all circumstances. Something more than brute compulsion is, therefore, involved in the conception; there is a general law under which the thing takes place."

The notion of cause is so intimately connected with that of necessity that it will be no digression to linger over the above definition, with a view to discovering, if possible, *some* meaning of which it is capable; for, as it stands, it is very far from having any definite signification.

The first point to notice is that, if any meaning is to be given to the phrase "would be true under all circumstances," the subject of it must be a propositional function, not a proposition.[1] A proposition is simply true or false, and that ends the matter: there can be no question of "circumstances." "Charles I's head was cut off" is just as true in summer as in winter, on Sundays as on Mondays. Thus when it is worth saying that something "would be true under all circumstances," the something in question must be a propositional function, *i.e.*, an expression containing a variable, and becoming a proposition when a value is assigned to the variable; the varying "circumstances" alluded to are then the different values of which the variable is capable. Thus if "necessary" means "what is true under all circumstances," then "if x is a man, x is mortal" is necessary, because it is true for any possible value of x. Thus we should be led to the following definition:—

"Necessary is a predicate of a propositional function, meaning that it is true for all possible values of its argument or arguments."

Unfortunately, however, the definition in Baldwin's *Dictionary* says that what is necessary is not only "true under all circumstances" but is also "true." Now these two are incompatible. Only propositions can be "true," and only propositional functions can be "true under all circumstances." Hence the definition as it stands is nonsense. What is meant seems to be this: "A proposition is necessary when it is a value of a propositional function which is true under all circumstances, *i.e.*, for all values of its argument or arguments." But if we adopt this definition, the same proposition will be necessary or contingent according as we choose one or other of its terms as the argument to our propositional function. For example, "if Socrates is a man, Socrates is mortal," is necessary if Socrates is chosen as argument, but not if *man* or *mortal* is chosen. Again, "if Socrates is a man, Plato is mortal," will be necessary if either Socrates or *man* is chosen as argument, but not if Plato or *mortal* is chosen. However, this difficulty can be overcome by specifying the constituent which is to be regarded as argument, and we thus arrive at the following definition:

"A proposition is *necessary* with respect to a given constituent if it remains true when that constituent is altered in any way compatible with the proposition remaining significant."

We may now apply this definition to the definition of causality quoted above. It is obvious that the argument must be the time at which the earlier event occurs. Thus an instance of causality will be such as: "If the event e_1 occurs at the time t_1, it will be followed by the event e_2." This proposition is intended to be necessary with respect to t_1, *i.e.*, to remain true however t_1 may be varied. Causality, as a universal law, will then be the following: "Given any event e_1 there is an event e_2 such that, whenever e_1 occurs, e_2 occurs later." But before this can be considered precise, we must specify how much later e_2 is to occur. Thus the principle becomes:

"Given any event e_1, there is an event e_2 and a time-interval τ such that, whenever e_1 occurs, e_2 follows after an interval τ."

I am not concerned as yet to consider whether this law is true or false. For the present, I am merely concerned to discover what the law of causality is supposed to be. I pass, therefore, to the other definitions quoted above.

The second definition need not detain us long, for two reasons. First, because it is psychological: not the "thought or perception" of a process, but the process itself, must be what concerns us in considering causality. Secondly, because it is circular: in speaking of a process as "taking place in consequence of" another process, it introduces the very notion of cause which was to be defined.

The third definition is by far the most precise; indeed as regards clearness it leaves nothing to be desired. But a great difficulty is caused by the temporal contiguity of cause and effect which the definition asserts. No two instants are contiguous, since the time-series is compact; hence either the cause or the effect or both must, if the definition is correct, endure for a finite time; indeed, by the wording of the definition it is plain that both are assumed to endure for a finite time. But then we are faced with a dilemma: if the cause is a process involving change within itself, we shall require (if causality is universal) causal relations between its earlier and later parts; moreover, it would seem that only the later parts can be relevant to the effect, since the earlier parts are not contiguous to the effect, and therefore (by the definition) cannot influence the effect. Thus we shall be led to diminish the duration of the cause without limit, and however much we may diminish it, there will still remain an earlier part which might be altered without altering the effect, so that the true cause, as defined, will not have been reached, for it will be observed that the definition excludes plurality of causes. If, on the other hand, the cause is purely static, involving no change within itself, then, in the first place, no such cause is to be found in nature, and in the second place, it seems strange—too strange to be accepted, in spite of bare logical possibility—that the cause, after existing placidly for some time, should suddenly explode into the effect, when it might just as well have done so at any earlier time, or have gone on unchanged without producing its effect. This dilemma, therefore, is fatal to the view that cause and effect can be contiguous in time; if there are causes and effects, they must be separated by a finite time-interval τ, as was assumed in the above interpretation of the first definition.

What is essentially the same statement of the law of causality as the one elicited above from the first of Baldwin's definitions is given by other philosophers. Thus John Stuart Mill says:—

"The Law of Causation, the recognition of which is the main pillar of inductive science, is but the familiar truth, that invariability of succession is found by observation to obtain between every fact in nature and some other fact which has preceded it."[2]

And Bergson, who has rightly perceived that the law as stated by philosophers is worthless, nevertheless continues to suppose that it is used in science. Thus he says:—

"Now, it is argued, this law [the law of causality] means that every phenomenon is determined by its conditions, or, in other words, that the same causes produce the same effects."[3]

And again:—

"We perceive physical phenomena, and these phenomena obey laws. This means: (1) That phenomena a, b, c, d, previously perceived, can occur again in the same shape; (2) that a certain phenom-enon P, which appeared after the conditions a, b, c, d, and after these conditions only, will not fail to recur as soon as the same conditions are again present."[4]

A great part of Bergson's attack on science rests on the assumption that it employs this principle. In fact, it employs no such principle, but philosophers—even Bergson—are too apt to take their views on science from each other, not from science. As to what the principle is, there is a fair consensus among philosophers of different schools. There are, however, a number of difficulties which at once arise. I omit the question of plurality of causes for the present, since other graver questions have to be considered. Two of these, which are forced on our attention by the above statement of the law, are the following:

1. What is meant by an "event"?

2. How long may the time-interval be between cause and effect?

1. An "event," in the statement of the law, is obviously intended to be something that is likely to recur, since otherwise the law becomes trivial. It follows that an "event" is not a particular, but some universal of which there may be many instances. It follows also that an "event" must be something short of the whole state of the universe, since it is highly improbable that this will recur. What is meant by an "event" is something like striking a match, or dropping a penny into the slot of an automatic machine. If such an event is to recur, it must not be defined too narrowly: we must not state with what degree of force the match is to be struck, nor what is to be the temperature of the penny. For if such considerations were relevant, our "event" would occur at most once, and the law would cease to give information. An "event," then, is a universal defined sufficiently widely to admit of many particular occurrences in time being instances of it.

2. The next question concerns the time-interval. Philosophers, no doubt, think of cause and effect as contiguous in time, but this, for reasons already given, is impossible. Hence, since there are no infinitesimal time-intervals, there must be some finite lapse of time τ between cause and effect. This, however, at once raises insuperable difficulties. However short we make the interval τ, something may happen during this interval which prevents the expected result. I put my penny in the

slot, but before I can draw out my ticket there is an earthquake which upsets the machine and my calculations. In order to be sure of the expected effect, we must know that there is nothing in the environment to interfere with it. But this means that the supposed cause is not, by itself, adequate to insure the effect. And as soon as we include the environment, the probability of repetition is diminished, until at last, when the whole environment is included, the probability of repetition becomes almost *nil*.

In spite of these difficulties, it must, of course, be admitted that many fairly dependable regularities of sequence occur in daily life. It is these regularities that have suggested the supposed law of causality; where they are found to fail, it is thought that a better formulation could have been found which would have never failed. I am far from denying that there may be such sequences which in fact never do fail. It may be that there will never be an exception to the rule that when a stone of more than a certain mass, moving with more than a certain velocity, comes in contact with a pane of glass of less than a certain thickness, the glass breaks. I also do not deny that the observation of such regularities, even when they are not without exceptions, is useful in the infancy of a science: the observation that unsupported bodies in air usually fall was a stage on the way to the law of gravitation. What I deny is that science assumes the existence of invariable uniformities of sequence of this kind, or that it aims at discovering them. All such uniformities, as we saw, depend upon a certain vagueness in the definition of the "events." That bodies fall is a vague qualitative statement; science wishes to know how fast they fall. This depends upon the shape of the bodies and the density of the air. It is true that there is more nearly uniformity when they fall in a vacuum; so far as Galileo could observe, the uniformity is then complete. But later it appeared that even there the latitude made a difference, and the altitude. Theoretically, the position of the sun and moon must make a difference. In short, every advance in a science takes us farther away from the crude uniformities which are first observed, into greater differentiation of antecedent and consequent, and into a continually wider circle of antecedents recognized as relevant.

The principle "same cause, same effect," which philosophers imagine to be vital to science, is therefore utterly otiose. As soon as the antecedents have been given sufficiently fully to enable the consequent to be calculated with some exactitude, the antecedents have become so complicated that it is very unlikely they will ever recur. Hence, if this were the principle involved, science would remain utterly sterile.

The importance of these considerations lies partly in the fact that they lead to a more correct account of scientific procedure, partly in the fact that they remove the analogy with human volition which makes the conception of cause such a fruitful source of fallacies. The latter point will become clearer by the help of some illustrations. For this purpose I shall consider a few maxims which have played a great part in the history of philosophy.

1. "Cause and effect must more or less resemble each other." This principle was prominent in the philosophy of occasionalism, and is still by no means extinct. It is still often thought, for example, that mind could not have grown up in a universe which previously contained nothing mental, and one ground for this belief is that matter is too dissimilar from mind to have been able to cause it. Or, more particularly, what are termed the nobler parts of our nature are supposed to be inexplicable, unless the universe always contained something at least equally noble which could cause them. All such views seem to depend upon assuming some unduly simplified law of causality; for, in any legitimate sense of "cause" and "effect," science seems to show that they are usually very widely dissimilar, the "cause" being, in fact, two states of the whole universe, and the "effect" some particular event.

2. "Cause is analogous to volition, since there must be an intelligible *nexus* between cause and effect." This maxim is, I think, often unconsciously in the imaginations of philosophers who would reject it when explicitly stated. It is probably operative in the view we have just been considering, that mind could not have resulted from a purely material world. I do not profess to know what is meant by "intelligible"; it seems to mean "familiar to imagination." Nothing is less "intelligible," in any other sense, than the connection between an act of will and its fulfilment. But obviously the sort of nexus desired between cause and effect is such as could only hold between the "events" which the supposed law of causality contemplates; the laws which replace causality in such a science as physics leave no room for any two events between which a nexus could be sought.

3. "The cause *compels* the effect in some sense

in which the effect does not compel the cause."
This belief seems largely operative in the dislike of
determinism; but, as a matter of fact, it is connected
with our second maxim, and falls as soon as that is
abandoned. We may define "compulsion" as
follows:—"Any set of circumstances is said to compel A when A desires to do something which the
circumstances prevent, or to abstain from something which the circumstances cause." This presupposes that some meaning has been found for
the word "cause"—a point to which I shall return
later. What I want to make clear at present is that
compulsion is a very complex notion, involving
thwarted desire. So long as a person does what he
wishes to do, there is no compulsion, however
much his wishes may be calculable by the help of
earlier events. And where desire does not come in,
there can be no question of compulsion. Hence it
is, in general, misleading to regard the cause as
compelling the effect.

A vaguer form of the same maxim substitutes
the word "determine" for the word "compel": we
are told that the cause *determines* the effect in a
sense in which the effect does not *determine* the
cause. It is not quite clear what is meant by "determining"; the only precise sense, so far as I know, is
that of a function or one-many relation. If we admit
plurality of causes, but not of effects, that is, if we
suppose that, given the cause, the effect must be
such and such, but, given the effect, the cause may
have been one of many alternatives, then we may
say that the cause determines the effect, but not the
effect the cause. Plurality of causes, however, results only from conceiving the effect vaguely and
narrowly and the cause precisely and widely.
Many antecedents may "cause" a man's death,
because his death is vague and narrow. But if we
adopt the opposite course, taking as the "cause"
the drinking of a dose of arsenic, and as the "effect" the whole state of the world five minutes
later, we shall have plurality of effects instead of
plurality of causes. Thus the supposed lack of symmetry between "cause" and "effect" is illusory.

4. "A cause cannot operate when it has ceased
to exist, because what has ceased to exist is nothing." This is a common maxim, and a still more
common unexpressed prejudice. It has, I fancy, a
good deal to do with the attractiveness of Bergson's
"durée": since the past has effects now, it must still
exist in some sense. The mistake in this maxim
consists in the supposition that causes "operate" at
all. A volition "operates" when what it wills takes

place; but nothing can operate except a volition.
The belief that causes "operate" results from assimilating them, consciously or unconsciously, to
volitions. We have already seen that, if there are
causes at all, they must be separated by a finite
interval of time from their effects, and thus cause
their effects after they have ceased to exist.

It may be objected to the above definition of a
volition "operating" that it only operates when it
"causes" what it wills, not when it merely happens to be followed by what it wills. This certainly
represents the usual view of what is meant by a
volition "operating," but as it involves the very
view of causation which we are engaged in combat-
ing, it is not open to us as a definition. We may say
that a volition "operates" when there is some law
in virtue of which a similar volition in rather similar
circumstances will usually be followed by what it
wills. But this is a vague conception, and introduces ideas which we have not yet considered.
What is chiefly important to notice is that the usual
notion of "operating" is not open to us if we reject,
as I contend that we should, the usual notion of
causation.

5. "A cause cannot operate except where it is."
This maxim is very widespread; it was urged
against Newton, and has remained a source of
prejudice against "action at a distance." In philosophy it has led to a denial of transeunt action, and
thence to monism or Leibnizian monadism. Like
the analogous maxim concerning temporal contiguity, it rests upon the assumption that causes
"operate," *i.e.*, that they are in some obscure way
analogous to volitions. And, as in the case of temporal contiguity, the inferences drawn from this
maxim are wholly groundless.

I return now to the question, What law or laws
can be found to take the place of the supposed law
of causality?

First, without passing beyond such uniformities of sequence as are contemplated by the
traditional law, we may admit that, if any such
sequence has been observed in a great many cases,
and has never been found to fail, there is an inductive probability that it will be found to hold in
future cases. If stones have hitherto been found to
break windows, it is probable that they will continue to do so. This, of course, assumes the inductive principle, of which the truth may reasonably be questioned; but as this principle is not our
present concern, I shall in this discussion treat it as
indubitable. We may then say, in the case of any

such frequently-observed sequence, that the earlier event is the *cause* and the later event the *effect*.

Several considerations, however, make such special sequences very different from the traditional relation of cause and effect. In the first place, the sequence, in any hitherto unobserved instance, is no more than probable, whereas the relation of cause and effect was supposed to be necessary. I do not mean by this merely that we are not sure of having discovered a true case of cause and effect; I mean that, even when we have a case of cause and effect in our present sense, all that is meant is that, on grounds of observation, it is probable that when one occurs the other will also occur. Thus in our present sense, A may be the cause of B even if there actually are cases where B does not follow A. Striking a match will be the cause of its igniting, in spite of the fact that some matches are damp and fail to ignite.

In the second place, it will not be assumed that *every* event has some antecedent which is its cause in this sense; we shall only believe in causal sequences where we find them, without any presumption that they always are to be found.

In the third place, *any* case of sufficiently frequent sequence will be causal in our present sense; for example, we shall not refuse to say that night is the cause of day. Our repugnance to saying this arises from the ease with which we can imagine the sequence to fail, but owing to the fact that cause and effect must be separated by a finite interval of time, *any* such sequence *might* fail through the interposition of other circumstances in the interval. Mill, discussing this instance of night and day, says:—

"It is necessary to our using the word cause, that we should believe not only that the antecedent always *has* been followed by the consequent, but that as long as the present constitution of things endures, it always *will* be so."[5]

In this sense, we shall have to give up the hope of finding causal laws such as Mill contemplated; any causal sequence which we have observed may at any moment be falsified without a falsification of any laws of the kind that the more advanced sciences aim at establishing.

In the fourth place, such laws of probable sequence, though useful in daily life and in the infancy of a science, tend to be displaced by quite different laws as soon as a science is successful. The law of gravitation will illustrate what occurs in any advanced science. In the motions of mutually gravitating bodies, there is nothing that can be called a cause, and nothing that can be called an effect; there is merely a formula. Certain differential equations can be found, which hold at every instant for every particle of the system, and which, given the configuration and velocities at one instant, or the configurations at two instants, render the configuration at any other earlier or later instant theoretically calculable. That is to say, the configuration at any instant is a function of that instant and the configurations at two given instants. This statement holds throughout physics, and not only in the special case of gravitation. But there is nothing that could be properly called "cause" and nothing that could be properly called "effect" in such a system.

No doubt the reason why the old "law of causality" has so long continued to pervade the books of philosophers is simply that the idea of a function is unfamiliar to most of them, and therefore they seek an unduly simplified statement. There is no question of repetitions, of the "same" cause producing the "same" effect; it is not in any sameness of causes and effects that the constancy of scientific laws consists, but in sameness of relations. And even "sameness of relations" is too simple a phrase; "sameness of differential equations" is the only correct phrase. It is impossible to state this accurately in non-mathematical language; the nearest approach would be as follows:—"There is a constant relation between the state of the universe at any instant and the rate of change in the rate at which any part of the universe is changing at that instant, and this relation is many-one, *i.e.*, such that the rate of change in the rate of change is determinate when the state of the universe is given." If the "law of causality" is to be something actually discoverable in the practice of science, the above proposition has a better right to the name than any "law of causality" to be found in the books of philosophers.

In regard to the above principle, several observations must be made—

1. No one can pretend that the above principle is *a priori* or self-evident or a "necessity of thought." Nor is it, in any sense, a premiss of science: it is an empirical generalization from a number of laws which are themselves empirical generalizations.

2. The law makes no difference between past and future: the future "determines" the past in exactly the same sense in which the past

"determines" the future. The word "determine," here, has a purely logical significance: a certain number of variables "determine" another variable if that other variable is a function of them.

3. The law will not be empirically verifiable unless the course of events within some sufficiently small volume will be approximately the same in any two states of the universe which only differ in regard to what is at a considerable distance from the small volume in question. For example, motions of planets in the solar system must be approximately the same however the fixed stars may be distributed, provided that all the fixed stars are very much farther from the sun than the planets are. If gravitation varied directly as the distance, so that the most remote stars made the most difference to the motions of the planets, the world might be just as regular and just as much subject to mathematical laws as it is at present, but we could never discover the fact.

4. Although the old "law of causality" is not assumed by science, something which we may call the "uniformity of nature" is assumed, or rather is accepted on inductive grounds. The uniformity of nature does not assert the trivial principle "same cause, same effect," but the principle of the permanence of laws. That is to say, when a law exhibiting, *e.g.*, an acceleration as a function of the configuration has been found to hold throughout the observable past, it is expected that it will continue to hold in the future, or that, if it does not itself hold, there is some other law, agreeing with the supposed law as regards the past, which will hold for the future. The ground of this principle is simply the inductive ground that it has been found to be true in very many instances; hence the principle cannot be considered certain, but only probable to a degree which cannot be accurately estimated.

The uniformity of nature, in the above sense, although it is assumed in the practice of science, must not, in its generality, be regarded as a kind of major premiss, without which all scientific reasoning would be in error. The assumption that *all* laws of nature are permanent has, of course, less probability than the assumption that this or that particular law is permanent; and the assumption that a particular law is permanent for all time has less probability than the assumption that it will be valid up to such and such a date. Science, in any given case, will assume what the case requires, but no more. In constructing the *Nautical Almanac* for 1915

it will assume that the law of gravitation will remain true up to the end of that year; but it will make no assumption as to 1916 until it comes to the next volume of the almanac. This procedure is, of course, dictated by the fact that the uniformity of nature is not known *a priori*, but is an empirical generalization, like "all men are mortal." In all such cases, it is better to argue immediately from the given particular instances to the new instance, than to argue by way of a major premiss; the conclusion is only probable in either case, but acquires a higher probability by the former method than by the latter.

In all science we have to distinguish two sorts of laws: first, those that are empirically verifiable but probably only approximate; secondly, those that are not verifiable, but may be exact. The law of gravitation, for example, in its applications to the solar system, is only empirically verifiable when it is assumed that matter outside the solar system may be ignored for such purposes; we believe this to be only approximately true, but we cannot empirically verify the law of universal gravitation which we believe to be exact. This point is very important in connection with what we may call "relatively isolated systems." These may be defined as follows:—

A system relatively isolated during a given period is one which, within some assignable margin of error, will behave in the same way throughout that period, however the rest of the universe may be constituted.

A system may be called "practically isolated" during a given period if, although there *might* be states of the rest of the universe which would produce more than the assigned margin of error, there is reason to believe that such states do not in fact occur.

Strictly speaking, we ought to specify the respect in which the system is relatively isolated. For example, the earth is relatively isolated as regards falling bodies, but not as regards tides; it is *practically* isolated as regards economic phenomena, although, if Jevons' sun-spot theory of commercial crises had been true, it would not have been even practically isolated in this respect.

It will be observed that we cannot prove in advance that a system is isolated. This will be inferred from the observed fact that approximate uniformities can be stated for this system alone. If the complete laws for the whole universe were known, the isolation of a system could be deduced from them; assuming, for example, the law of universal gravitation, the practical isolation of the solar system in this respect can be deduced by the help of the fact that there is very little matter in its neighbourhood. But it should be observed that isolated systems are only important as providing a possibility of *discovering* scientific laws; they have no theoretical importance in the finished structure of a science.

The case where one event A is said to "cause" another event B, which philosophers take as fundamental, is really only the most simplified instance of a practically isolated system. It may happen that, as a result of general scientific laws, whenever A occurs throughout a certain period, it is followed by B; in that case, A and B form a system which is practically isolated throughout that period. It is, however, to be regarded as a piece of good fortune if this occurs; it will always be due to special circumstances, and would not have been true if the rest of the universe had been different though subject to the same laws.

The essential function which causality has been supposed to perform is the possibility of inferring the future from the past, or, more generally, events at any time from events at certain assigned times. Any system in which such inference is possible may be called a "deterministic" system. We may define a deterministic system as follows:—

A system is said to be "deterministic" when, given certain data, $e_1, e_2, \ldots, e_n$, at times $t_1, t_2, \ldots, t_n$ respectively, concerning this system, if E_t is the state of the system at any time t, there is a functional relation of the form

$$E_t = f(e_1, t_1, e_2, t_2, \ldots, e_n, t_n, t) \qquad \text{(A)}$$

The system will be "deterministic throughout a given period" if t, in the above formula, may be any time within that period, though outside that period the formula may be no longer true. If the universe, as a whole, is such a system, determinism is true of the universe; if not, not. A system which is part of a deterministic system I shall call "determined"; one which is not part of any such system I shall call "capricious."

The events $e_1, e_2, \ldots, e_n$ I shall call "determinants" of the system. It is to be observed that a system which has one set of determinants will in general have many. In the case of the motions of the planets, for example, the configurations of the

solar system at any two given times will be determinants.

We may take another illustration from the hypothesis of psycho-physical parallelism. Let us assume, for the purposes of this illustration, that to a given state of brain a given state of mind always corresponds, and *vice versa*, *i.e.*, that there is a one-one relation between them, so that each is a function of the other. We may also assume, what is practically certain, that to a given state of a certain brain a given state of the whole material universe corresponds, since it is highly improbable that a given brain is ever twice in exactly the same state. Hence there will be a one-one relation between the state of a given person's mind and the state of the whole material universe. It follows that, if n states of the material universe are determinants of the material universe, then n states of a given man's mind are determinants of the whole material and mental universe—assuming, that is to say, that psycho-physical parallelism is true.

The above illustration is important in connection with a certain confusion which seems to have beset those who have philosophized on the relation of mind and matter. It is often thought that, if the state of the mind is determinate when the state of the brain is given, and if the material world forms a deterministic system, then mind is "subject" to matter in some sense in which matter is not "subject" to mind. But if the state of the brain is also determinate when the state of the mind is given, it must be exactly as true to regard matter as subject to mind as it would be to regard mind as subject to matter. We could, theoretically, work out the history of mind without ever mentioning matter, and then, at the end, deduce that matter must meanwhile have gone through the corresponding history. It is true that if the relation of brain to mind were many-one, not one-one, there would be a one-sided dependence of mind on brain, while conversely, if the relation were one-many, as Bergson supposes, there would be a one-sided dependence of brain on mind. But the dependence involved is, in any case, only logical; it does not mean that we shall be compelled to do things we desire not to do, which is what people instinctively imagine it to mean.

As another illustration we may take the case of mechanism and teleology. A system may be defined as "mechanical" when it has a set of determinants that are purely material, such as the positions of certain pieces of matter at certain times. It is an open question whether the world of mind and matter, as we know it, is a mechanical system or not; let us suppose, for the sake of argument, that it is a mechanical system. This supposition—so I contend—throws no light whatever on the question whether the universe is or is not a "teleological" system. It is difficult to define accurately what is meant by a "teleological" system, but the argument is not much affected by the particular definition we adopt. Broadly, a teleological system is one in which purposes are realized, *i.e.*, in which certain desires—those that are deeper or nobler or more fundamental or more universal or what not—are followed by their realization. Now the fact—if it be a fact—that the universe is mechanical has no bearing whatever on the question whether it is teleological in the above sense. There might be a mechanical system in which all wishes were realized, and there might be one in which all wishes were thwarted. The question whether, or how far, our actual world is teleological, cannot, therefore, be settled by proving that it is mechanical, and the desire that it should be teleological is no ground for wishing it to be not mechanical.

There is, in all these questions, a very great difficulty in avoiding confusion between what we can infer and what is in fact determined. Let us consider, for a moment, the various senses in which the future may be "determined." There is one sense—and a very important one—in which it is determined quite independently of scientific laws, namely, the sense that it will be what it will be. We all regard the past as determined simply by the fact that it has happened; but for the accident that memory works backward and not forward, we should regard the future as equally determined by the fact that it will happen. "But," we are told, "you cannot alter the past, while you can to some extent alter the future." This view seems to me to rest upon just those errors in regard to causation which it has been my object to remove. You cannot make the past other than it was—true, but this is a mere application of the law of contradiction. If you already know what the past was, obviously it is useless to wish it different. But also you cannot make the future other than it will be; this again is an application of the law of contradiction. And if you happen to know the future—*e.g.*, in the case of a forthcoming eclipse—it is just as useless to wish it different as to wish the past different. "But," it will be rejoined, "our wishes can *cause* the future, sometimes, to be different from what it would be if

they did not exist, and they can have no such effect upon the past." This, again, is a mere tautology. An effect being *defined* as something subsequent to its cause, obviously we can have no *effect* upon the past. But that does not mean that the past would not have been different if our present wishes had been different. Obviously, our present wishes are conditioned by the past, and therefore could not have been different unless the past had been different; therefore, if our present wishes were different, the past would be different. Of course, the past cannot be different from what it was, but no more can our present wishes be different from what they are; this again is merely the law of contradiction. The facts seem to be merely (1) that wishing generally depends upon ignorance, and is therefore commoner in regard to the future than in regard to the past, (2) that where a wish concerns the future, it and its realization very often form a "practically independent system," *i.e.*, many wishes regarding the future are realized. But there seems no doubt that the main difference in our feelings arises from the fact that the past but not the future can be known by memory.

Although the sense of "determined" in which the future is determined by the mere fact that it will be what it will be is sufficient (at least so it seems to me) to refute some opponents of determinism, notably M. Bergson and the pragmatists, yet it is not what most people have in mind when they speak of the future as determined. What they have in mind is a formula by means of which the future can be exhibited, and at least theoretically calculated, as a function of the past. But at this point we meet with a great difficulty, which besets what has been said above about deterministic systems, as well as what is said by others.

If formulae of any degree of complexity, however great, are admitted, it would seem that any system, whose state at a given moment is a function of certain measurable quantities, *must* be a deterministic system. Let us consider, in illustration, a single material particle, whose co-ordinates at time t are x_t, y_t, z_t. Then, however, the particle moves, there must be, theoretically, functions f_1, f_2, f_3, such that

$$x_t = f_1(t) \qquad y_t = f_2(t) \qquad z_t = f_3(t)$$

It follows that, theoretically, the whole state of the material universe at time t must be capable of being exhibited as a function of t. Hence our universe will be deterministic in the sense defined above. But if this be true, no information is conveyed about the universe in stating that it is deterministic. It is true that the formulae involved may be of strictly infinite complexity, and therefore not practically capable of being written down or apprehended. But except from the point of view of our knowledge, this might seem to be a detail: in itself, if the above considerations are sound, the material universe *must* be deterministic, *must* be subject to laws.

This, however, is plainly not what was intended. The difference between this view and the view intended may be seen as follows. Given some formula which fits the facts hitherto—say the law of gravitation—there will be an infinite number of other formulae, not empirically distinguishable from it in the past, but diverging from it more and more in the future. Hence, even assuming that there are persistent laws, we shall have no reason for assuming that the law of the inverse square will hold in future; it may be some other hitherto indistinguishable law that will hold. We cannot say that *every* law which has held hitherto must hold in the future, because past facts which obey one law will also obey others, hitherto indistinguishable but diverging in future. Hence there must, at every moment, be laws hitherto unbroken which are now broken for the first time. What science does, in fact, is to select the *simplest* formula that will fit the facts. But this, quite obviously, is merely a methodological precept, not a law of Nature. If the simplest formula ceases, after a time, to be applicable, the simplest formula that remains applicable is selected, and science has no sense that an axiom has been falsified. We are thus left with the brute fact that, in many departments of science, quite simple laws have hitherto been found to hold. This fact cannot be regarded as having any *a priori* ground, nor can it be used to support inductively the opinion that the same laws will continue; for at every moment laws hitherto true are being falsified, though in the advanced sciences these laws are less simple than those that have remained true. Moreover it would be fallacious to argue inductively from the state of the advanced sciences to the future state of the others, for it may well be that the advanced sciences are advanced simply because, hitherto, their subject-matter has obeyed simple and easily-ascertainable laws, while the subject-matter of other sciences has not done so.

The difficulty we have been considering seems to be met partly, if not wholly, by the principle that the *time* must not enter explicitly into our formulae. All mechanical laws exhibit acceleration as a function of configuration, not of configuration and time jointly; and this principle of the irrelevance of the time may be extended to all scientific laws. In fact we might interpret the "uniformity of nature" as meaning just this, that no scientific law involves the time as an argument, unless, of course, it is given in an integrated form, in which case *lapse* of time, though not absolute time, may appear in our formulae. Whether this consideration suffices to overcome our difficulty completely, I do not know; but in any case it does much to diminish it.

It will serve to illustrate what has been said if we apply it to the question of free will.

1. Determinism in regard to the will is the doctrine that our volitions belong to some deterministic system, *i.e.*, are "determined" in the sense defined above. Whether this doctrine is true or false, is a mere question of fact; no *a priori* considerations (if our previous discussions have been correct) can exist on either side. On the one hand, there is no *a priori* category of causality, but merely certain observed uniformities. As a matter of fact, there are observed uniformities in regard to volitions; thus there is some empirical evidence that volitions are determined. But it would be very rash to maintain that the evidence is overwhelming, and it is quite possible that some volitions, as well as some other things, are not determined, except in the sense in which we found that everything must be determined.

2. But, on the other hand, the subjective sense of freedom, sometimes alleged against determinism, has no bearing on the question whatever. The view that it has a bearing rests upon the belief that causes compel their effects, or that nature enforces obedience to its laws as governments do. These are mere anthropomorphic superstitions, due to assimilation of causes with volitions and of natural laws with human edicts. We feel that our will is not compelled, but that only means that it is not other than we choose it to be. It is one of the demerits of the traditional theory of causality that it has created an artificial opposition between determinism and the freedom of which we are introspectively conscious.

3. Besides the general question whether volitions are determined, there is the further question whether they are *mechanically* determined, *i.e.*, whether they are part of what was above defined as

a mechanical system. This is the question whether they form part of a system with purely material determinants, *i.e.*, whether there are laws which, given certain material data, make all volitions functions of those data. Here again, there is empirical evidence up to a point, but it is not conclusive in regard to all volitions. It is important to observe, however, that even if volitions are part of a mechanical system, this by no means implies any supremacy of matter over mind. It may well be that the same system which is susceptible of material determinants is also susceptible of mental determinants; thus a mechanical system may be determined by sets of volitions, as well as by sets of material facts. It would seem, therefore, that the reasons which make people dislike the view that volitions are mechanically determined are fallacious.

4. The notion of *necessity*, which is often associated with determinism, is a confused notion not legitimately deducible from determinism. Three meanings are commonly confounded when necessity is spoken of:—

(α) An *action* is necessary when it will be performed however much the agent may wish to do otherwise. Determinism does not imply that actions are necessary in this sense.

(β) A *propositional function* is necessary when all its values are true. This sense is not relevant to our present discussion.

(γ) A *proposition* is necessary with respect to a given constituent when it is the value, with that constituent as argument, of a necessary propositional function, in other words, when it remains true however that constituent may be varied. In this sense, in a deterministic system, the connection of a volition with its determinants is necessary, if the time at which the determinants occur be taken as the constituent to be varied, the time-interval between the determinants and the volition being kept constant. But this sense of necessity is purely logical, and has no emotional importance.

We may now sum up our discussion of causality. We found first that the law of causality, as usually stated by philosophers, is false, and is not employed in science. We then considered the nature of scientific laws, and found that, instead of stating that one event A is always followed by another event B, they stated functional relations between certain events at certain times, which we called determinants, and other events at earlier or later times or at the same time. We were unable to find any *a priori* category involved: the existence of scientific laws appeared as a purely empirical fact, not necessarily universal, except in a trivial and scientifically useless form. We found that a system with one set of determinants may very likely have other sets of a quite different kind, that, for example, a mechanically determined system may also be teleologically or volitionally determined. Finally we considered the problem of free will: here we found that the reasons for supposing volitions to be determined are strong but not conclusive, and we decided that even if volitions are mechanically determined, that is no reason for denying freedom in the sense revealed by introspection, or for supposing that mechanical events are not determined by volitions. The problem of free will *versus* determinism is therefore, if we were right, mainly illusory, but in part not yet capable of being decisively solved.

Endnotes

[1] A propositional function is an expression containing a variable, or undetermined constituent, and becoming a proposition as soon as a definite value is assigned to the variable. Examples are: "A is A," "*x* is a number." The variable is called the *argument* of the function.

[2] *Logic*, Bk. III, Chap. V, § 2.

[3] *Time and Free Will*, p. 199.

[4] *Ibid.*, p. 202.

[5] *Loc. cit.*, § 6.

40. Free Will

GEORGE E. MOORE

George Edward Moore (1873–1958) taught philosophy at Cambridge University. Early in his career, he and Bertrand Russell led an attack on the metaphysical idealism of Bradley and McTaggart. Moore went on to develop a style of analytical philosophy that gives prominence to commonsense beliefs. In this selection, Moore presents such an analysis of "could have done otherwise." Freedom and responsibility seem to require that it be true that one could, in some sense, do otherwise than what one does. Is determinism compatible with this ability? Moore claims that the important sense of "could have done otherwise" is simply that "one *would* have done otherwise if one had chosen to do otherwise." Moore argues that people have this ability and that it is compatible with determinism.

Let us begin with the question: Is it ever true that a man *could* have done anything else, except what he actually did do? And, first of all, I think I had better explain exactly how this question seems to me to be related to the question of Free Will. For it is a fact that, in many discussions about Free Will, this precise question is never mentioned at all; so that it might be thought that the two have really nothing whatever to do with one another. And indeed some philosophers do, I think, definitely imply that they *have* nothing to do with one another: they seem to hold that our wills can properly be said to be free even if we *never* can, in any sense at all, do anything else except what, in the end, we actually do do. But this view, if it is held, seems to me to be plainly a mere abuse of language. The statement that we have Free Will is certainly ordinarily understood to imply that we really sometimes have the power of acting differently from the way in which we actually do act; and hence, if anybody tells us that we have Free Will, while at the same time he means to deny that we ever have such a power, he is simply misleading us. We certainly have *not* got Free Will, in the ordinary sense of the word, if we never really *could*, in any sense at all, have done anything else than what we did do; so that, in this respect, the two questions certainly are connected. But, on the other hand, the mere fact (if it is a fact)

that we sometimes *can*, in *some* sense, do what we don't do, does not necessarily entitle us to say that we *have* Free Will. We certainly *haven't* got it, *unless* we can; but it doesn't follow that we *have* got it, even if we *can*. Whether we have or not will depend upon the precise sense in which it is true that we can. So that even if we do decide that we really *can* often, in *some* sense, do what we don't do, this decision by itself does not entitle us to say that we have Free Will.

And the first point about which we can and should be quite clear is, I think, this: namely, that we certainly often *can*, in *some* sense, do what we don't do. It is, I think, quite clear that this is so; and also very important that we should realize that it is so. For many people are inclined to assert, quite without qualification: No man ever *could*, on any occasion, have done anything else than what he actually did do on that occasion. By asserting this quite simply, without qualification, they imply, of course (even if they do not mean to imply), that there is *no* proper sense of the word 'could', in which it is true that a man *could* have acted differently. And it is this implication which is, I think, quite certainly absolutely false. For this reason, anybody who asserts, without qualification, 'Nothing ever *could* have happened, except what actually did happen', is making an assertion which is quite unjustifiable, and which he himself cannot help constantly contradicting. And it is important to insist on this, because many people do make this unqualified assertion, without seeing how

Reprinted from *Ethics*, 1965, by G. E. Moore by permission of Oxford University Press.

violently it contradicts what they themselves, and all of us, believe, and rightly believe, at other times. If, indeed, they insert a qualification—if they merely say 'In *one* sense of the word *"could"* nothing ever *could* have happened, except what did happen', then, they may perhaps be perfectly right: we are not disputing that they may. All that we are maintaining is that, in *one* perfectly proper and legitimate sense of the word 'could', and that one of the very commonest senses in which it is used, it is quite certain that some things which didn't happen *could* have happened. And the proof that this is so, is simply as follows.

It is impossible to exaggerate the frequency of the occasions on which we *all* of us make a distinction between two things, neither of which *did* happen—a distinction which we express by saying, that whereas the one *could* have happened, and other could *not.* No distinction is commoner than this. And no one, I think, who fairly examines the instances in which we make it, can doubt about three things: namely (1) that very often there really is *some* distinction between the two things, corresponding to the language which we use; (2) that this distinction, which really *does* subsist between the things, is *the* one which we mean to express by saying that the one was possible and the other impossible; and (3) that this way of expressing it is a perfectly proper and legitimate way. But if so, it absolutely follows that one of the commonest and most legitimate usages of the phrases 'could' and 'could not' is to express a difference, which often really does hold between two things *neither* of which did actually happen. Only a few instances need be given. I *could* have walked a mile in 20 minutes this morning, but I certainly could *not* have run two miles in five minutes. I did not, *in fact*, do either of these two things; but it is pure nonsense to say that the mere fact that I *did* not, does away with the distinction between them, which I express by saying that the one was within my powers, whereas the other was *not. Although* I did neither, yet the one was certainly *possible* to me in a sense in which the other was totally *im*possible. Or, to take another instance: It is true, as a rule, that cats *can* climb trees, whereas dogs *can't.* Suppose that on a particular afternoon neither A's cat nor B's dog *do* climb a tree. It is quite absurd to say that this mere fact proves that we must be wrong if we say (as we certainly often should say) that the cat *could* have climbed a tree, though she didn't, whereas the dog *couldn't.* Or, to take an instance

which concerns an inanimate object. Some ships *can* steam 20 knots, whereas others *can't* steam more than 15. And the mere fact that, on a particular occasion, a 20-knot steamer *did* not *actually* run at this speed certainly does not entitle us to say that she *could* not have done so, in the sense in which a 15-knot one *could* not. On the contrary, we all can and should distinguish between cases in which (as, for instance, owing to an accident to her propeller) she did not, *because* she could not, and cases in which she did not, *although* she *could.* Instances of this sort might be multiplied quite indefinitely; and it is surely quite plain that we all of us do *continually* use such language: we continually, when considering two events, neither of which *did* happen, distinguish between them by saying that whereas the one *was* possible, though it didn't happen, the other was *im*possible. And it is surely quite plain that what we mean by this (whatever it may be) is something which is often perfectly true. But, if so, then anybody who asserts, without qualification, 'Nothing ever *could* have happened, except what did happen', is simply asserting what is false.

It is, therefore, quite certain that we often *could* (in *some* sense) have done what we did not do. And now let us see how this fact is related to the argument by which people try to persuade us that it is *not* a fact.

The argument is well known: it is simply this. It is assumed (for reasons which I need not discuss) that absolutely everything that happens has a *cause* in what precedes it. But to say this is to say that it follows *necessarily* from something that preceded it; or, in other words, that, once the preceding events which are its cause had happened, it was absolutely *bound* to happen. But to say that it was *bound* to happen, is to say that nothing else *could* have happened instead; so that, if *everything* has a cause, *nothing* ever could have happened except what did happen.

And now let us assume that the premise of this argument is correct: that everything really *has* a cause. What really follows from it? Obviously all that follows is that, in *one* sense of the word 'could', nothing ever *could* have happened, except what did happen. This really *does* follow. But, *if* the word 'could' is ambiguous—if, that is to say, it is used in different senses on different occasions—it is obviously quite possible that though, in *one* sense, nothing ever could have happened except what did happen, yet in *another* sense, it may at the same time be perfectly true that some things which did not happen *could* have happened. And can anybody undertake to assert with certainty that the word 'could' is *not* ambiguous? that it may not have more than one legitimate sense? *Possibly* it is not ambiguous; and, *if* it is not, then the fact that some things, which did not happen, *could* have happened, really would contradict the principle that everything has a cause; and, in that case, we should, I think, have to give up this principle, because the fact that we often *could* have done what we did not do, is so certain. But the assumption that the word 'could' is *not* ambiguous is an assumption which certainly should not be made without the clearest proof. And yet I think it often is made, without any proof at all; simply because it does not occur to people that words often are ambiguous. It is, for instance, often assumed, in the Free Will controversy, that the question at issue is solely as to whether everything is caused, or whether acts of will are sometimes uncaused. Those who hold that we *have* Free Will, think themselves bound to maintain that acts of will sometimes have *no* cause; and those who hold that everything is caused think that this proves completely that we have not Free Will. But, in fact, it is extremely doubtful whether Free Will is at all inconsistent with the principle that everything is caused. Whether it is or not, all depends on a very difficult question as to the meaning of the word 'could'. All that is certain about the matter is (1) that, if we have Free Will, it must be true, in *some* sense, that we sometimes *could* have done, what we did not do; and (2) that, if everything is caused, it must be true, in *some* sense, that we *never could* have done, what we did not do. What is very uncertain, and what certainly needs to be investigated, is whether these two meanings of the word 'could' are the same.

Let us begin by asking: What is the sense of the word 'could', in which it is so certain that we often *could* have done, what we did not do? What, for instance, is the sense in which I *could* have walked a mile in 20 minutes this morning, though I did not? There is one suggestion, which is very obvious: namely, that what I mean is simply after all that I could, *if* I had chosen; or (to avoid a possible complication) perhaps we had better say 'that I *should*, if I had chosen'. In other words, the suggestion is that we often use the phrase '*I could*' simply and solely as a short way of saying 'I *should*, if I had chosen.' And in all cases, where it is certainly true that we *could* have done, what we did

not do, it is, I think, very difficult to be quite sure that this (or something similar) is *not* what we mean by the word 'could'. The case of the ship may seem to be an exception, because it is certainly not true that she would have steamed 20 knots if *she* had chosen; but even here it seems possible that what we mean is simply that she *would, if the men on board of her* had chosen. There are certainly good reasons for thinking that we *very often* mean by 'could' merely 'would, if so and so had chosen.' And if so, then we have a sense of the word 'could' in which the fact that we often *could* have done what we did not do, is perfectly compatible with the principle that everything has a cause: for to say that, *if* I had performed a certain act of will, I should have done something which I did not do, in no way contradicts this principle.

And an additional reason for supposing that this *is* what we often mean by 'could', and one which is also a reason why it is important to insist on the obvious fact that we very often really *should* have acted differently, *if* we had willed differently, is that those who deny that we ever *could* have done anything, which we did not do, often speak and think as if this really did involve the conclusion that we never should have acted differently, even *if* we had willed differently. This occurs, I think, in two chief instances—one in reference to the future, the other in reference to the past. The first occurs when, because they hold that nothing *can* happen, except what *will* happen, people are led to adopt the view called Fatalism—the view that *whatever we will*, the result will always be the same; that it is, therefore, *never* any use to make one choice rather than another. And this conclusion will really follow if by 'can' we mean '*would* happen, even *if* we were to will it'. But it is certainly untrue, and it certainly does not follow from the principle of causality. On the contrary, reasons of exactly the same sort and exactly as strong as those which lead us to suppose that everything has a cause, lead to the conclusion that if we choose one course, the result will *always* be different in *some* respect from what it would have been, if we had chosen another; and we know also that the difference would *sometimes* consist in the fact that *what* we chose would come to pass. It is certainly often true of the future, therefore, that whichever of two actions we *were* to choose, *would* actually be done, although it is quite certain that only one of the two *will* be done.

And the second instance, in which people are

apt to speak and think, as if, *because* no man ever *could* have done anything but what he did do, it follows that he would not, even *if* he had chosen, is as follows. Many people seem, in fact, to conclude directly from the first of these two propositions, that we can never be justified in praising or blaming a man for anything that he does, or indeed for making any distinction between what is right or wrong, on the one hand, and what is lucky or unfortunate on the other. They conclude, for instance, that there is never any reason to treat or to regard the voluntary commission of a crime in any different way from that in which we treat or regard the involuntary catching of a disease. The man who committed the crime *could* not, they say, have helped committing it any more than the other man could have helped catching the disease; both events were equally inevitable; and though both may of course be great *misfortunes*, though both may have very bad consequences and equally bad ones—there is no justification whatever, they say, for the distinction we make between them when we say that the commission of the crime was *wrong*, or that the man was morally to blame for it, whereas the catching of the disease was *not* wrong and the man was not to blame for it. And this conclusion, again, will really follow if by 'could not' we mean 'would not, even if he had willed to avoid it.' But the point I want to make is, that it follows *only* if we make this assumption. That is to say, the mere fact that the man *would* have succeeded in avoiding the crime, *if* he had chosen (which is certainly often true), whereas the other man would *not* have succeeded in avoiding the disease, *even if* he had chosen (which is certainly also often true) gives an ample justification for regarding and treating the two cases differently. It gives such a justification, because, where the occurrence of an event *did* depend upon the will, there, by acting on the will (as we may do by blame or punishment) we have often a reasonable chance of preventing similar events from recurring in the future; whereas, where it did *not* depend upon the will, we have no such chance. We may, therefore, fairly say that those who speak and think, as if a man who brings about a misfortune *voluntarily* ought to be treated and regarded in exactly the same way as one who brings about an equally great misfortune *involuntarily*, are speaking and thinking *as if* it were not true that we ever should have acted differently, even *if* we had willed to do so. And that is why it is extremely important to insist on the absolute cer-

tainty of the fact that we often really *should* have acted differently, *if* we had willed differently.

There is, therefore, much reason to think that when we say that we *could* have done a thing which we did not do, we *often* mean merely that we *should* have done it, *if* we had chosen. And if so, then it is quite certain that, in *this* sense, we often really *could* have done what we did not do, and that this fact is in no way inconsistent with the principle that everything has a cause. And for my part I must confess that I cannot feel certain that this may not be *all* that we usually mean and understand by the assertion that we have Free Will; so that those who deny that we have it are really denying (though, no doubt, often unconsciously) that we ever *should* have acted differently, even if we had willed differently. It has been sometimes held that this *is* what we mean; and I cannot find any conclusive argument to the contrary. And if it is *what* we mean, then it absolutely follows that we really *have* Free Will, and also that this fact is quite consistent with the principle that everything has a cause; and it follows also that our theory will be perfectly right, when it makes right and wrong depend on what we *could* have done, *if* we had chosen.

But, no doubt, there are many people who will say that this is *not* sufficient to entitle us to say that we have Free Will; and they will say this for a reason, which certainly has some plausibility, though I cannot satisfy myself that it is conclusive. They will say, namely: Granted that we often *should* have acted differently, *if* we had chosen differently, yet it is not true that we have Free Will, unless it is *also* often true in such cases that we *could* have *chosen* differently. The question of Free Will has been thus represented as being merely the question whether we ever *could* have chosen, what we did not choose, or ever *can* choose, what, in fact, we shall not choose. And since there is some plausibility in this contention, it is, I think, worth while to point out that here again it is absolutely certain that, in two different senses, at least, we often *could* have chosen, what, in fact, we did not choose; and that in neither sense does this fact contradict the principle of causality.

The first is simply the old sense over again. If by saying that we *could* have done, what we did not do, we often mean merely that we *should* have done it, *if* we had chosen to do it, then obviously, by saying that we *could* have *chosen* to do it, we may mean merely that we *should* have so chosen, *if* we had chosen *to make the choice*. And I think there is no doubt it is often true that we should have chosen to do particular thing *if* we had chosen to make the choice; and that this is a very important sense in which it is often in our power to make a choice. There certainly is such a thing as making an effort to induce ourselves to *choose* a particular course; and I think there is no doubt that often if we *had* made such an effort, we *should* have made a choice, which we did not in fact make.

And besides this, there is another sense in which, whenever we have several different courses of action in view, it is *possible* for us to choose any one of them; and a sense which is certainly of some practical importance, even if it goes no way to justify us in saying that we have Free Will. This sense arises from the fact that in such cases we can hardly ever *know for certain* beforehand, *which* choice we actually *shall* make; and one of the commonest senses of the word 'possible' is that in which we call an event 'possible' when no man can *know for certain* that it will *not* happen. It follows that almost, if not quite always, when we make a choice, after considering alternatives, it *was* possible that we should have chosen one of these alternatives, which we did not actually choose; and often, of course, it was not only possible, but highly probable, that we should have done so. And this fact is certainly of practical importance, because many people are apt much too easily to assume that it is quite certain that they *will not* make a given choice, which they know they ought to make, if it were possible; and their belief that they *will* not make it tends, of course, to prevent them from mak-

ing it. For this reason it is important to insist that they can hardly ever know for certain with regard to any given choice that they will *not* make it.

It is, therefore, quite certain (1) that we often *should* have *acted* differently, if we had chosen to; (2) that similarly we often should have *chosen* differently, *if* we had chosen so to choose; and (3) that it was almost always *possible* that we should have chosen differently, in the sense that no man could know for certain that we should *not* so choose. All these three things are facts, and all of them are quite consistent with the principle of causality. Can anybody undertake to say for certain that none of these three facts and *no* combination of them will justify us in saying that we have Free Will? Or, suppose it granted that we have not Free Will, unless it is often true that we *could* have chosen, what we did not choose:—Can any defender of Free Will, or any opponent of it, show conclusively that what he means by 'could have chosen' in this proposition, is anything different from the two certain facts, which I have numbered (2) and (3), or some combination of the two? Many people, no doubt, will still insist that these two facts alone are by no means sufficient to entitle us to say that we have Free Will: that it must be true that we were *able* to choose, in some quite other sense. But nobody, so far as I know, has ever been able to tell us exactly what that sense is. For my part, I can find no conclusive argument to show either that some such other sense of 'can' is necessary, or that it is not.

41. *Human Freedom and the Self*

RODERICK M. CHISHOLM

Chisholm argues that to be justified in holding persons responsible for their acts, it must be true that the self is an agent that is not always caused to act by prior events (or by prior desires or motives). He reasons that, if human actions are caused by something prior, then no one could do other than what he or she does. On the other hand, if some actions are uncaused, they are capricious. In either case, it seems wrong to hold people responsible for what they do. Chisholm introduces a special causality—agent (or "immanent") causality—and a special entity—the substantial self—to explain human freedom. In his discussion, Chisholm offers a critique of Moore's compatibilist analysis of "could have done otherwise."

A staff moves a stone, and is moved by a hand, which is moved by a man (Aristotle, *Physics*, 256a).

The metaphysical problem of human freedom might be summarized in the following way: Human beings are responsible agents; but this fact appears to conflict with a deterministic view of human action (the view that every event that is involved in an act is caused by some other event); and it *also* appears to conflict with an indeterministic view of human action (the view that the act, or some event that is essential to the act, is not caused at all.) To solve the problem, I believe, we must make somewhat far-reaching assumptions about the self or the agent—about the man who performs the act.

Perhaps it is needless to remark that, in all likelihood, it is impossible to say anything significant about this ancient problem that has not been said before.[1]

Let us consider some deed, or misdeed, that may be attributed to a responsible agent: one man, say, shot another. If the man *was* responsible for what he did, then, I would urge, what was to happen at the time of the shooting was something

that was entirely up to the man himself. There was a moment at which it was true, both that he could have fired the shot and also that he could have refrained from firing it. And if this is so, then, even though he did fire it, he could have done something else instead. (He didn't find himself firing the shot 'against his will', as we say.) I think we can say, more generally, then, that if a man is responsible for a certain event or a certain state of affairs (in our example, the shooting of another man), then that event or state of affairs was brought about by some act of his, and the act was something that was in his power either to perform or not to perform.

But now if the act which he *did* perform was an act that was also in his power *not* to perform, then it could not have been caused or determined by any event that was not itself within his power either to bring about or not to bring about. For example, if what we say he did was really something that was brought about by a second man, one who forced his hand upon the trigger, say, or who, by means of hypnosis, compelled him to perform the act, then since the act was caused by the *second* man it was nothing that was within the power of the *first* man to prevent. And precisely the same thing is true, I think, if instead of referring to a second man who compelled the first one, we speak instead of the *desires* and *beliefs* which the first man happens to have had. For if what we say he did was really something that was brought about by his own beliefs and desires, if these beliefs and desires in the particular situation in which he happened to have

From the Lindley Lecture, 1964, pp. 3–15. Copyright © 1964 by the Department of Philosophy, University of Kansas. Reprinted by permission of the author and the Department of Philosophy, University of Kansas, Lawrence, Kansas.

found himself caused him to do just what it was that we say he did do, then, since *they* caused it, *he* was unable to do anything other than just what it was that he did do. It makes no difference whether the cause of the deed was internal or external; if the cause was some state or event for which the man himself was not responsible, then he was not responsible for what we have been mistakenly calling his act. If a flood caused the poorly constructed dam to break, then, given the flood and the constitution of the dam, the break, we may say, *had to* occur and nothing could have happened in its place. And if the flood of desire caused the weakwilled man to give in, then he, too, had to do just what it was that he did do and he was no more responsible than was the dam for the results that followed. (It is true, of course, that if the man is responsible for the beliefs and desires that he happens to have, then he may also be responsible for the things they lead him to do. But the question now becomes: *is* he responsible for the beliefs and desires he happens to have? If he is, then there was a time when they were within his power either to acquire or not to acquire, and we are left, therefore, with our general point.)

One may object: But surely if there were such a thing as a man who is really *good*, then he would be responsible for things that he would do; yet, he would be unable to do anything other than just what it is that he does do, since, being good, he will always choose to do what is best. The answer, I think, is suggested by a comment that Thomas Reid makes upon an ancient author. The author had said of Cato, 'He was good because he could not be otherwise', and Reid observes: 'This saying, if understood literally and strictly, is not the praise of Cato, but of his constitution, which was no more the work of Cato than his existence'.[2] If Cato was himself responsible for the good things that he did, then Cato, as Reid suggests, was such that, although he had the power to do what was not good, he exercised his power only for that which was good.

All of this, if it is true, may give a certain amount of comfort to those who are tenderminded. But we should remind them that it also conflicts with a familiar view about the nature of God—with the view that St. Thomas Aquinas expresses by saying that 'every movement both of the will and of nature proceeds from God as the Prime Mover'.[3] If the act of the sinner *did* proceed from God as the Prime Mover, then God was in the position of the second agent we just discussed—the man who forced the trigger finger, or the hypnotist—and the sinner, so-called, was *not* responsible for what he did. (This may be a bold assertion, in view of the history of western theology, but I must say that I have never encountered a single good reason for denying it.)

There is one standard objection to all of this and we should consider it briefly.

The objection takes the form of a stratagem—one designed to show that determinism (and divine providence) is consistent with human responsibility. The stratagem is one that was used by Jonathan Edwards and by many philosophers in the present century, most notably, G. E. Moore.[4]

One proceeds as follows: The expression

1. He could have done otherwise,

it is argued, means no more nor less than

2. If he had chosen to do otherwise, then he would have done otherwise.

(In place of 'chosen,' one might say 'tried', 'set out', 'decided', 'undertaken', or 'willed'.) The truth of statement (2), it is then pointed out, is consistent with determinism (and with divine providence); for even if all of the man's actions were causally determined, the man could still be such that, *if* he had chosen otherwise, then he would have done otherwise. What the murderers saw, let us suppose, along with his beliefs and desires, *caused* him to fire the shot; yet he was such that if, just then, he had chosen or decided *not* to fire the shot, then he would not have fired it. All of this is certainly possible. Similarly, we could say, of the dam, that the flood caused it to break and also that the dam was such that, *if* there had been no flood or any similar pressure, then the dam would have remained intact. And therefore, the argument proceeds, if (2) is consistent with determinism, and if (1) and (2) say the same thing, then (1) is also consistent with determinism; hence we can say that the agent *could* have done otherwise even though he was caused to do what he did do; and therefore determinism and moral responsibility are compatible.

Is the argument sound? The conclusion follows from the premises, but the catch, I think, lies in the first premise—the one saying that statement (1) tells us no more nor less than what statement (2) tells us. For (2), it would seem, could be true while (1) is false. That is to say, our man might be such that, if he had chosen to do otherwise, then he would have done otherwise, and yet *also* such that he could not have done otherwise. Suppose, after all, that our murderer could not have *chosen*, or could not have *decided*, to do otherwise. Then the fact that he happens also to be a man such that, if he had chosen not to shoot he would not have shot, would make no difference. For if he could *not* have chosen *not* to shoot, then he could not have done anything other than just what it was that he did do. In a word: from our statement (2) above ('If he had chosen to do otherwise, then he would have done otherwise'), we cannot make an inference to (1) above ('He could have done otherwise') unless we can *also* assert:

3. He could have chosen to do otherwise.

And therefore, if we must reject this third statement (3), then, even though we may be justified in asserting (2), we are not justified in asserting (1). If the man could not have chosen to do otherwise, then he would not have done otherwise—*even if* he was such that, if he *had* chosen to do otherwise, then he would have done otherwise.

The stratagem in question, then, seems to me not to work, and I would say, therefore, that the ascription of responsibility conflicts with a deterministic view of action.

Perhaps there is less need to argue that the ascription of responsibility also conflicts with an indeterministic view of action—with the view that the act, or some event that is essential to the act, is not caused at all. If the act—the firing of the shot—was not caused at all, if it was fortuitous or capricious, happening so to speak out of the blue, then, presumably, no one—and nothing—was responsible for the act. Our conception of action, therefore, should be neither deterministic nor indeterministic. Is there any other possibility?

We must not say that every event involved in the act is caused by some other event; and we must not say that the act is something that is not caused at all. The possibility that remains, therefore, is this: We should say that at least one of the events that are involved in the act is caused, not by any other events, but by something else instead. And this something else can only be the agent—the man. If there is an event that is caused, not by other events, but by the man, then there are some events involved in the act that are not caused by other events. But if the event in question is caused by the man then it *is* caused and we are not committed to

saying that there is something involved in the act that is not caused at all.

But this, of course, is a large consequence, implying something of considerable importance about the nature of the agent or the man.

If we consider only inanimate natural objects, we may say that causation, if it occurs, is a relation between *events* or *states of affairs*. The dam's breaking was an event that was caused by a set of other events—the dam being weak, the flood being strong, and so on. But if a man is responsible for a particular deed, then, if what I have said is true, there is some event, or set of events, that is caused, *not* by other events or states of affairs, but by the agent, whatever he may be.

I shall borrow a pair of medieval terms, using them, perhaps, in a way that is slightly different from that for which they were originally intended. I shall say that when one event or state of affairs (or set of events or states of affairs) causes some other event or state of affairs, then we have an instance of *transeunt* causation. And I shall say that when an *agent*, as distinguished from an event, causes an event or state of affairs, then we have an instance of *immanent* causation.

The nature of what is intended by the expression 'immanent causation' may be illustrated by this sentence from Aristotle's *Physics*: 'Thus, a staff moves a stone, and is moved by a hand, which is moved by a man' (VII, 5, 256a, 6–8). If the man was responsible, then we have in this illustration a number of instances of causation—most of them transeunt but at least one of them immanent. What the staff did to the stone was an instance of transeunt causation, and thus we may describe it as a relation between events: 'The motion of the staff caused the motion of the stone.' And similarly for what the hand did to the staff: 'The motion of the hand caused the motion of the staff'. And, as we know from physiology, there are still other events which caused the motion of the hand. Hence we need not introduce the agent at this particular point, as Aristotle does—we *need* not, though we *may*. We *may* say that the hand was moved by the man, but we may *also* say that the motion of the hand was caused by the motion of certain muscles; and we may say that the motion of the muscles was caused by certain events that took place within the brain. But some event, and presumably one of those that took place within the brain, was caused by the agent and not by any other events.

There are, of course, objections to this way of

putting the matter; I shall consider the two that seem to me to be most important.

One may object, firstly: 'If the *man* does anything, then, as Aristotle's remark suggests, what he does is to move the *hand*. But he certainly does not *do* anything to his brain—he may not even know that he *has* a brain. And if he doesn't do anything to the brain, and if the motion of the hand was caused by something that happened within the brain, then there is no point in appealing to "immanent causation" as being something incompatible with "transeunt causation"—for the whole thing, after all, is a matter of causal relations among events or states of affairs.'

The answer to this objection, I think, is this: It is true that the agent does not *do* anything with his brain, or to his brain, in the sense in which he *does* something with his hand and does something to the staff. But from this it does not follow that the agent was not the immanent cause of something that happened within his brain.

We should note a useful distinction that has been proposed by Professor A. I. Melden—namely, the distinction between 'making something A happen' and 'doing A'.[5] If I reach for the staff and pick it up, then one of the things that I *do* is just that—reach for the staff and pick it up. And if it is something that I do, then there is a very clear sense in which it may be said to be something that I know that I do. If you ask me, 'Are you doing something, or trying to do something, with the staff?' I will have no difficulty in finding an answer. But in doing something with the staff, I also make various things happen which are not in this same sense things that I do: I will make various air-particles move; I will free a number of blades of grass from the pressure that had been upon them; and I may cause a shadow to move from one place to another. If these are merely things that I make happen, as distinguished from things that I do, then I may know nothing whatever about them; I may not have the slightest idea that, in moving the staff, I am bringing about any such thing as the motion of air-particles, shadows, and blades of grass.

We may say, in answer to the first objection, therefore, that it is true that our agent does nothing to his brain or with his brain; but from this it does not follow that the agent is not the immanent cause of some event within his brain; for the brain event may be something which, like the motion of the air-particles, he made happen in picking up the

staff. The only difference between the two cases is this: in each case, he made something happen when he picked up the staff; but in the one case—the motion of the air-particles or of the shadows—it was the motion of the staff that caused the event to happen; and in the other case—the event that took place in the brain—it was this event that caused the motion of the staff.

The point is, in a word, that whenever a man does something A, then (by 'immanent causation') he makes a certain cerebral event happen, and this cerebral event (by 'transeunt causation') makes A happen.

The second objection is more difficult and concerns the very concept of 'immanent causation', or causation by an agent, as this concept is to be interpreted here. The concept is subject to a difficulty which has long been associated with that of the prime mover unmoved. We have said that there must be some event A, presumably some cerebral event, which is caused not by any other event, but by the agent. Since A was not caused by any other event, then the agent himself cannot be said to have undergone any change or produced any other event (such as 'an act of will' or the like) which brought A about. But if, when the agent made A happen, there was no event involved other than A itself, no event which could be described as *making* A happen, what did the agent's causation consist of? What, for example, is the difference between A's just happening, and the agent's *causing* A to happen? We cannot attribute the difference to any event that took place within the agent. And so far as the event A itself is concerned, there would seem to be no discernible difference. Thus Aristotle said that the activity of the prime mover is nothing in addition to the motion that it produces, and Suarez said that 'the action is in reality nothing but the effect as it flows from the agent'.[6] Must we conclude, then, that there is no more to the man's action in causing event A than there is to the event A's happening by itself? Here we would seem to have a distinction without a difference—in which case we have failed to find a *via media* between a deterministic and an indeterministic view of action.

The only answer, I think, can be this: That the difference between the man's causing A, on the one hand, and the event A just happening, on the other, lies in the fact that, in the first case but not the second, the event A *was* caused and was caused by the man. There was a brain event A; the agent did, in fact, cause the brain event; but there was nothing that he did to cause it.

This answer may not entirely satisfy and it will be likely to provoke the following question: 'But what are you really *adding* to the assertion that A happened when you utter the words "the agent *caused* A to happen"?' As soon as we have put the question this way, we see, I think, that whatever difficulty we may have encountered is one that may be traced to the concept of causation generally—whether 'immanent' or 'transeunt'. The problem, in other words, is not a problem that is peculiar to our conception of human action. It is a problem that must be faced by anyone who makes use of the concept of causation at all; and therefore, I would say, it is a problem for everyone but the complete indeterminist.

For the problem, as we put it, referring just to 'immanent causation,' or causation by an agent, was this: 'What is the difference between saying, of an event A, that A just happened and saying that someone caused A to happen?' The analogous problem, which holds for 'transeunt causation,' or causation by an event, is this: 'What is the difference between saying, of two events A and B, that B happened and then A happened, and saying that B's happening was the *cause* of A's happening?' And the only answer that one can give is this—that in the one case the agent was the cause of A's happening and in the other case event B was the cause of A's happening. The nature of transeunt causation is no more clear than is that of immanent causation.

But we may plausibly say—and there is a respectable philosophical tradition to which we may appeal—that the notion of immanent causation, or causation by an agent, is in fact more clear than that of transeunt causation, or causation by an event, and that it is only by understanding our own causal efficacy, as agents, that we can grasp the concept of *cause* at all. Hume may be said to have shown that we do not derive the concept of *cause* from what we perceive of external things. How, then, do we derive it? The most plausible suggestion, it seems to me, is that of Reid, once again: namely that 'the conception of an efficient cause may very probably be derived from the experience we have had . . . of our own power to produce certain effects.'[7] If we did not understand the concept of immanent causation, we would not understand that of transeunt causation.

It may have been noted that I have avoided the term 'free will' in all of this. For even if there is such a faculty as 'the will', which somehow sets our acts agoing, the question of freedom, as John Locke said, is not the question *'whether the will be free'*; it is the question *'whether a man be free'*.[8] For if there is a 'will', as a moving faculty, the question is whether the man is free to will to do these things that he does will to do—and also whether he is free *not* to will any of those things that he does will to do, and, again, whether he is free to will any of those things that he does not will to do. Jonathan Edwards tried to restrict himself to the question—'Is the man free to do what it is that he wills?'—but the answer to this question will not tell us whether the man is responsible for what it is that he *does* will to do. Using still another pair of medieval terms, we may say that the metaphysical problem of freedom does not concern the *actus imperatus*; it does not concern the question whether we are free to accomplish whatever it is that we will or set out to do; it concerns the *actus elicitus*, the question whether we are free to will or to set out to do those things that we do will or set out to do.

If we are responsible, and if what I have been trying to say is true, then we have a prerogative which some would attribute only to God: each of us, when we act, is a prime mover unmoved. In doing what we do, we cause certain events to happen, and nothing—or no one—causes us to cause those events to happen.

If we are thus prime movers unmoved and if our actions, or those for which we are responsible, are not causally determined, then they are not causally determined by our *desires*. And this means that the relation between what we want or what we desire, on the one hand, and what it is that we do, on the other, is not as simple as most philosophers would have it.

We may distinguish between what we might call the 'Hobbist approach' and what we might call the 'Kantian approach' to this question. The Hobbist approach is the one that is generally accepted at the present time, but the Kantian approach, I believe, is the one that is true. According to Hobbism, if we *know*, of some man, what his beliefs and desires happen to be and how strong they are, if we know what he feels certain of, what he desires more than anything else, and if we know the state of his body and what stimuli he is being subjected to, then we may *deduce*, logically, just what it is that he will do—or, more accurately, just what it is that he will try, set out, or undertake to do. Thus Professor Melden has said that 'the connection between wanting and doing is logical'.[9] But according to the Kantian approach to our problem, and this is the one that I would take, there is no such logical connection between wanting and doing, nor need there even be a causal connection. No set of statements about a man's desires, beliefs, and stimulus situation at any time implies any statement telling us what the man will try, set out, or undertake to do at that time. As Reid put it, though we may 'reason from men's motives to their actions and, in many cases, with great probability', we can never do so 'with absolute certainty'.[10]

This means that, in one very strict sense of the terms, there can be no science of man. If we think of science as a matter of finding out what laws happen to hold, and if the statement of a law tells us what kinds of events are caused by what other kinds of events, then there will be human actions which we cannot explain by subsuming them under any laws. We cannot say, 'It is causally necessary that, given such and such desires and beliefs, and being subject to such and such stimuli, the agent will do so and so'. For at times the agent, if he chooses, may rise above his desires and do something else instead.

But all of this is consistent with saying that, perhaps more often than not, our desires do exist under conditions such that those conditions necessitate us to act. And we may also say, with Leibniz, that at other times our desires may 'incline without necessitating'.

Leibniz's phrase presents us with our final philosophical problem. What does it mean to say that a desire, or a motive, might 'incline without necessitating'? There is a temptation, certainly, to say that 'to incline' means to cause and that 'not to necessitate' means not to cause, but obviously we cannot have it both ways.

Nor will Leibniz's own solution do. In his letter to Coste, he puts the problem as follows: 'When a choice is proposed, for example to go out or not to go out, it is a question whether, with all the circumstances, internal and external, motives, perceptions, dispositions, impressions, passions, inclinations taken together, I am still in a contingent state, or whether I am necessitated to make the choice, for example, to go out; that is to say, whether this proposition true and determined in fact, *In all these circumstances taken together I shall choose to go out*, is contingent or necessary'.[11] Leibniz's answer might

be put as follows: In one sense of the terms 'necessary' and 'contingent', the proposition 'In all these circumstances taken together I shall choose to go out', may be said to be contingent and not necessary, and in another sense of these terms, it may be said to be necessary and not contingent. But the sense in which the proposition may be said to be contingent, according to Leibniz, is only this: There is no logical contradiction involved in denying the proposition. And the sense in which it may be said to be necessary is this: Since 'nothing ever occurs without cause or determining reason', the proposition is causally necessary. 'Whenever all the circumstances taken together are such that the balance of deliberation is heavier on one side than on the other, it is certain and infallible that that is the side that is going to win out'. But if what we have been saying is true, the proposition 'In all these circumstances taken together I shall choose to go out', may be causally as well as logically contingent. Hence we must find another interpretation for Leibniz's statement that our motives and desires may incline us, or influence us, to choose without thereby necessitating us to choose.

Let us consider a public official who has some moral scruples but who also, as one says, could be had. Because of the scruples that he does have, he would never take any positive steps to receive a bribe—he would not actively solicit one. But his morality has its limits and he is also such that, if we were to confront him with a *fait accompli* or to let him see what is about to happen ($10,000 in cash is being deposited behind the garage), then he would succumb and be unable to resist. The general situation is a familiar one and this is one reason that people pray to be delivered from temptation. (It also justifies Kant's remark: 'And how many there are who may have led a long blameless life, who are only *fortunate* in having escaped so many temptations'.)[12] Our relation to the misdeed that we contemplate may not be a matter simply of being able to bring it about or not to bring it about. As St. Anselm noted, there are at least four possibilities. We may illustrate them by reference to our public official and the event which is his receiving the bribe, in the following way: (i) he may be able to bring the event about himself (*facere esse*), in which case he would actively cause himself to receive the bribe; (ii) he may be able to refrain from bringing it about himself (*non facere esse*), in which case he would not himself do anything to insure that he receive the bribe; (iii) he may be able to do something to prevent the event from occurring (*facere non esse*), in which case he would make sure that the $10,000 was *not* left behind the garage; or (iv) he may be unable to do anything to prevent the event from occurring (*non facere non esse*), in which case, though he may not solicit the bribe, he would allow himself to keep it.[13] We have envisaged our official as a man who can resist the temptation to (i) but cannot resist the temptation to (iv): he can refrain from bringing the event about himself, but he cannot bring himself to do anything to prevent it.

Let us think of 'inclination without necessitation', then, in such terms as these. First we may contrast the two propositions:

1. He can resist the temptation to do something in order to make A happen;

2. He can resist the temptation to allow A to happen (i.e., to do nothing to prevent A from happening).

We may suppose that the man has some desire to have A happen and thus has a motive for making A happen. His motive for making A happen, I suggest, is one that *necessitates* provided that, because of the motive, (1) is false; he cannot resist the temptation to do something in order to make A happen. His motive for making A happen is one that *inclines* provided that, because of the motive, (2) is false; like our public official, he cannot bring himself to do anything to prevent A from happening. And therefore we can say that this motive for making A happen is one that *inclines but does not necessitate* provided that, because of the motive, (1) is true and (2) is false; he can resist the temptation to make it happen but he cannot resist the temptation to allow it to happen.

Endnotes

[1] The general position to be presented here is suggested in the following writings, among others: Aristotle, *Eudemian Ethics*, bk. ii ch. 6; *Nicomachean Ethics*, bk iii, ch. 1–5; Thomas Reid, *Essays on the Active Powers of Man*; C. A. Campbell, "Is 'Free Will' a Pseudo-Problem?" *Mind*, 1951, 441–65; Roderick M. Chisholm, "Responsibility and Avoidability," and Richard Taylor, "Determination and the Theory of Agency," in *Determinism and Freedom in the Age of Modern Science*, ed. Sidney Hook (New York, 1958).

[2] Thomas Reid, *Essays on the Active Powers of Man*, essay iv, ch. 4 (*Works*, 600).

[3] *Summa Theologica*, First Part of the Second Part, qu. vi ('On the Voluntary and Involuntary').

[4] Jonathan Edwards, *Freedom of the Will* (New Haven, 1957); G. E. Moore, *Ethics* (Home University Library, 1912), ch. 6.

[5] A. I. Melden, *Free Action* (London, 1961), especially ch. 3. Mr. Melden's own views, however, are quite the contrary of those that are proposed here.

[6] Aristotle, *Physics*, bk. iii, ch. 3; Suarez, *Disputations Metaphysicae*, Disputation 18, s. 10.

[7] Reid, *Works*, 524.

[8] *Essay Concerning Human Understanding*, bk. ii, ch. 21.

[9] Melden, 166.

[10] Reid, *Works*, 608, 612.

[11] 'Lettre à Mr. Coste de la Nécessité et de la Contingence' (1707) in *Opera Philosophica*, ed. Erdmann, 447–9.

[12] In the Preface to the *Metaphysical Elements of Ethics*, in *Kant's Critique of Practical Reason and Other Works on the Theory of Ethics*, ed. T. K. Abbott (London, 1959), 303.

[13] Cf. D. P. Henry, 'Saint Anselm's *De "Grammatico,"' Philosophical Quarterly*, x (1960), 115–26. St. Anselm noted that (i) and (iii), respectively, may be thought of as forming the upper left and the upper right corners of a square of opposition, and (ii) and (iv) the lower left and the lower right.

42. *Freedom of the Will and the Concept of a Person*

HARRY FRANKFURT

Harry Frankfurt, professor of philosophy at Princeton University, responds to an objection to the compatibilist analysis of freedom. It has been argued that freedom cannot consist merely in being able to do what one wants or desires because desires may themselves be controlled by internal forces. For example, drug addicts may want to take drugs, may desire drugs, and may be unimpeded in their pursuit of drugs, but one might very well be reluctant to say that their choice to take drugs is always a *free* choice. The choice, at an advanced stage of addiction, is no longer within their control and does not seem to be free. Frankfurt attempts to deal with this difficulty by defining a free action as one in which what one does results from a second-order want that one or another first-order want be acted upon.

What philosophers have lately come to accept as analysis of the concept of a person is not actually analysis of *that* concept at all. Strawson, whose usage represents the current standard, identifies the concept of a person as 'the concept of a type of entity such that *both* predicates ascribing states of consciousness *and* predicates ascribing corporeal characteristics . . . are equally applicable to a single individual of that single type'.[1] But there are many entities besides persons that have both mental and physical properties. As it happens—though it seems extraordinary that this should be so—there is no common English word for the type of entity Strawson has in mind, a type that includes not only human beings but animals of various lesser species as well. Still, this hardly justifies the misappropriation of a valuable philosophical term.

Whether the members of some animal species are persons is surely not to be settled merely by determining whether it is correct to apply to them, in addition to predicates ascribing corporeal characteristics, predicates that ascribe states of consciousness. It does violence to our language to endorse the application of the term 'person' to those numerous creatures which do have both psychological and material properties but which are mani-

From *Journal of Philosophy* 68, no. 1 (January 1971): 5–20. Reprinted by permission of the author and the *Journal of Philosophy*.

festly not persons in any normal sense of the word. This misuse of language is doubtless innocent of any theoretical error. But although the offence is 'merely verbal', it does significant harm. For it gratuitously diminishes our philosophical vocabulary, and it increases the likelihood that we will overlook the important area of inquiry with which the term 'person' is most naturally associated. It might have been expected that no problem would be of more central and persistent concern to philosophers than that of understanding what we ourselves essentially are. Yet this problem is so generally neglected that it has been possible to make off with its very name almost without being noticed and, evidently, without evoking any widespread feeling of loss.

There is a sense in which the word 'person' is merely the singular form of 'people' and in which both terms connote no more than membership in a certain biological species. In those senses of the word which are of greater philosophical interest, however, the criteria for being a person do not serve primarily to distinguish the members of our own species from the members of other species. Rather, they are designed to capture those attributes which are the subject of our most humane concern with ourselves and the source of what we regard as most important and most problematical in our lives. Now these attributes would be of equal significance to us even if they were not in fact peculiar and common to the members of our own species. What interests us most in the human condition would not interest us less if it were also a feature of the condition of other creatures as well.

Our concept of ourselves as persons is not to be understood, therefore, as a concept of attributes that are necessarily species-specific. It is conceptually possible that members of novel or even of familiar non-human species should be persons; and it is also conceptually possible that some members of the human species are not persons. We do in fact assume, on the other hand, that no member of another species is a person. Accordingly, there is a presumption that what is essential to persons is a set of characteristics that we generally suppose— whether rightly or wrongly—to be uniquely human.

It is my view that one essential difference between persons and other creatures is to be found in the structure of a person's will. Human beings are not alone in having desires and motives, or in making choices. They share these things with the members of certain other species, some of whom even appear to engage in deliberation and to make decisions based upon prior thought. It seems to be peculiarly characteristic of humans, however, that they are able to form what I shall call 'second-order desires' or 'desires of the second order'.

Besides wanting and choosing and being moved *to do* this or that, men may also want to have (or not to have) certain desires and motives. They are capable of wanting to be different, in their preferences and purposes, from what they are. Many animals appear to have the capacity for what I shall call 'first-order desires' or 'desires of the first order', which are simply desires to do or not to do one thing or another. No animal other than man, however, appears to have the capacity for reflective self-evaluation that is manifested in the formation of second-order desires.[2]

———

I

The concept designated by the verb 'to want' is extraordinarily elusive. A statement of the form 'A wants to X'—taken by itself, apart from a context that serves to amplify or to specify its meaning— conveys remarkably little information. Such a statement may be consistent, for example, with each of the following statements: (a) the prospect of doing X elicits no sensation or introspectible emotional response in A; (b) A is unaware that he wants to X; (c) A believes that he does not want to X; (d) A wants to refrain from X-ing; (e) A wants to Y and believes that it is impossible for him both to Y and to X; (f) A does not 'really' want to X; (g) A *would rather die than X*; and so on. It is therefore hardly sufficient to formulate the distinction between first-order and second-order desires, as I have done, by suggesting merely that someone has a first-order desire when he wants to do or not to do such-and-such, and that he has a second-order desire when he wants to have or not to have a certain desire of the first order.

As I shall understand them, statements of the form 'A wants to X' cover a rather broad range of possibilities.[3] They may be true even when statements like (a) through (g) are true: when A is unaware of any feelings concerning X-ing, when he is unaware that he wants to X, when he deceives himself about what he wants and believes falsely that he does not want to X, when he also has other desires that conflict with his desire to X, or when he is ambivalent. The desires in question may be conscious or unconscious, they need not be univocal, and A may be mistaken about them. There is a further source of uncertainty with regard to statements that identify someone's desires, however, and here it is important for my purposes to be less permissive.

Consider first those statements of the form 'A wants to X' which identify first-order desires—that is, statements in which the term 'to X' refers to an action. A statement of this kind does not, by itself, indicate the relative strength of A's desire to X. It does not make it clear whether this desire is at all likely to play a decisive role in what A actually does or tries to do. For it may correctly be said that A wants to X even when his desire to X is only one among his desires and when it is far from being paramount among them. Thus, it may be true that A wants to X when he strongly prefers to do something else instead; and it may be true that he wants to X despite the fact that, when he acts, it is not the desire to X that motivates him to do what he does. On the other hand, someone who states that A wants to X may mean to convey that it is this desire that is motivating or moving A to do what he is actually doing or that A will in fact be moved by this desire (unless he changes his mind) when he acts.

It is only when it is used in the second of these

ways that, given the special usage of 'will' that I propose to adopt, the statement identifies A's will. To identify an agent's will is either to identify the desire (or desires) by which he is motivated in some action he performs or to identify the desire (or desires) by which he will or would be motivated when or if he acts. An agent's will, then, is identical with one or more of his first-order desires. But the notion of the will, as I am employing it, is not coextensive with the notion of first-order desires. It is not the notion of something that merely inclines an agent in some degree to act in a certain way. Rather, it is the notion of an *effective* desire—one that moves (or will or would move) a person all the way to action. Thus the notion of the will is not coextensive with the notion of what an agent intends to do. For even though someone may have a settled intention to do X, he may none the less do something else instead of doing X because, despite his intention, his desire to do X proves to be weaker or less effective than some conflicting desire.

Now consider those statements of the form 'A wants to x' which identify second-order desires—that is, statements in which the term 'to X' refers to a desire of the first order. There are also two kinds of situation in which it may be true that A wants to want to X. In the first place, it might be true of A that he wants to have a desire to X despite the fact that he has a univocal desire, altogether free of conflict and ambivalence, to refrain from x-ing. Someone might want to have a certain desire, in other words, but univocally want that desire to be unsatisfied.

Suppose that a physician engaged in psychotherapy with narcotics addicts believes that his ability to help his patients would be enhanced if he understood better what it is like for them to desire the drug to which they are addicted. Suppose that he is led in this way to want to have a desire for the drug. If it is a genuine desire that he wants, then what he wants is not merely to feel the sensations that addicts characteristically feel when they are gripped by their desires for the drug. What the physician wants, in so far as he wants to have a desire, is to be inclined or moved to some extent to take the drug.

It is entirely possible, however, that, although he wants to be moved by a desire to take the drug, he does not want this desire to be effective. He may not want it to move him all the way to action. He need not be interested in finding out what it is like

to take the drug. And in so far as he now wants only to *want* to take it, and not to *take* it, there is nothing in what he now wants that would be satisfied by the drug itself. He may now have, in fact, an altogether univocal desire *not* to take the drug; and he may prudently arrange to make it impossible for him to satisfy the desire he would have if his desire to want the drug should in time be satisfied.

It would thus be incorrect to infer, from the fact that the physician now wants to desire to take the drug, that he already does desire to take it. His second-order desire to be moved to take the drug does not entail that he has a first-order desire to take it. If the drug were now to be administered to him, this might satisfy no desire that is implicit in his desire to want to take it. While he wants to want to take the drug, he may have *no* desire to take it; it may be that *all* he wants is to taste the desire for it. That is, his desire to have a certain desire that he does not have may not be a desire that his will should be at all different than it is.

Someone who wants only in this truncated way to want to X stands at the margin of preciosity, and the fact that he wants to want to X is not pertinent to the identification of his will. There is, however, a second kind of situation that may be described by 'A wants to X'; and when the statement is used to describe a situation of this second kind, then it does pertain to what A wants his will to be. In such cases the statement means that A wants the desire to X to be the desire that moves him effectively to act. It is not merely that he wants the desire to X to be among the desires by which, to one degree or another, he is moved or inclined to act. He wants this desire to be effective—that is, to provide the motive in what he actually does. Now when the statement that A wants to want to X is used in this way, it does entail that A already has a desire to X. It could not be true both that A wants the desire to X to move him into action and that he does not want to X. It is only if he does want to X that he can coherently want the desire to X not merely to be one of his desires but, more decisively, to be his will.[4]

Suppose a man wants to be motivated in what he does by the desire to concentrate on his work. It is necessarily true, if this supposition is correct, that he already wants to concentrate on his work. This desire is now among his desires. But the question of whether or not his second-order desire is fulfilled does not turn merely on whether the desire he wants is one of his desires. It turns on whether this desire is, as he wants it to be, his effective desire or will. If, when the chips are down, it is his desire to concentrate on his work that moves him to do what he does, then what he wants at that time is indeed (in the relevant sense) what he wants to want. If it is some other desire that actually moves him when he acts, on the other hand, then what he wants at that time is not (in the relevant sense) what he wants to want. This will be so despite the fact that the desire to concentrate on his work continues to be among his desires.

II

Someone has a desire of the second order either when he wants simply to have a certain desire or when he wants a certain desire to be his will. In situations of the latter kind, I shall call his second-order desires 'second-order volitions' or 'volitions of the second order'. Now it is having second-order volitions, and not having second-order desires generally, that I regard as essential to being a person. It is logically possible, however unlikely, that there should be an agent with second-order desires but with no volitions of the second order. Such a creature, in my view, would not be a person. I shall use the term 'wanton' to refer to agents who have first-order desires but who are not persons because, whether or not they have desires of the second order, they have no second-order volitions.[5]

The essential characteristic of a wanton is that he does not care about his will. His desires move him to do certain things, without its being true of him either that he wants to be moved by those desires or that he prefers to be moved by other desires. The class of wantons includes all non-human animals that have desires and all very young children. Perhaps it also includes some adult human beings as well. In any case, adult humans may be more or less wanton; they may act wantonly, in response to first-order desires concerning which they have no volitions of the second order, more or less frequently.

The fact that a wanton has no second-order volitions does not mean that each of his first-order desires is translated heedlessly and at once into action. He may have no opportunity to act in accor-

dance with some of his desires. Moreover, the translation of his desires into action may be delayed or precluded either by conflicting desires of the first order or by the intervention of deliberation. For a wanton may possess and employ rational faculties of a high order. Nothing in the concept of a wanton implies that he cannot reason or that he cannot deliberate concerning how to do what he wants to do. What distinguishes the rational wanton from other rational agents is that he is not concerned with the desirability of his desires themselves. He ignores the question of what his will is to be. Not only does he pursue whatever course of action he is most strongly inclined to pursue, but he does not care which of his inclinations is the strongest.

Thus a rational creature, who reflects upon the suitability to his desires of one course of action or another, may none the less be a wanton. In maintaining that the essence of being a person lies not in reason but in will, I am far from suggesting that a creature without reason may be a person. For it is only in virtue of his rational capacities that a person is capable of becoming critically aware of his own will and of forming volitions of the second order. The structure of a person's will presupposes, accordingly, that he is a rational being.

The distinction between a person and a wanton may be illustrated by the difference between two narcotics addicts. Let us suppose that the physiological condition accounting for the addiction is the same in both men, and that both succumb inevitably to their periodic desires for the drug to which they are addicted. One of the addicts hates his addiction and always struggles desperately, although to no avail, against its thrust. He tries everything that he thinks might enable him to overcome his desires for the drug. But these desires are too powerful for him to withstand, and invariably, in the end, they conquer him. He is an unwilling addict, helplessly violated by his own desires.

The unwilling addict has conflicting first-order desires: he wants to take the drug, and he also wants to refrain from taking it. In addition to these first-order desires, however, he has a volition of the second order. He is not a neutral with regard to the conflict between his desire to take the drug and his desire to refrain from taking it. It is the latter desire, and not the former, that he wants to constitute his will; it is the latter desire, rather than the former, that he wants to be effective and to provide the purpose that he will seek to realize in what he actually does.

The other addict is a wanton. His actions reflect the economy of his first-order desires, without his being concerned whether the desires that move him to act are desires by which he wants to be moved to act. If he encounters problems in obtaining the drug or in administering it to himself, his reponses to his urges to take it may involve deliberation. But it never occurs to him to consider whether he wants the relation among his desires to result in his having the will he has. The wanton addict may be an animal, and thus incapable of being concerned about his will. In any event he is, in respect of his wanton lack of concern, no different from an animal.

The second of these addicts may suffer a first-order conflict similar to the first-order conflict suffered by the first. Whether he is human or not, the wanton may (perhaps due to conditioning) both want to take the drug and want to refrain from taking it. Unlike the unwilling addict, however, he does not prefer that one of his conflicting desires should be paramount over the other; he does not prefer that one first-order desire rather than the other should constitute his will. It would be misleading to say that he is neutral as to the conflict between his desires, since this would suggest that he regards them as equally acceptable. Since he has no identity apart from his first-order desires, it is true neither that he prefers one to the other nor that he prefers not to take sides.

It makes a difference to the unwilling addict, who is a person, which of his conflicting first-order desires wins out. Both desires are his, to be sure; and whether he finally takes the drug or finally succeeds in refraining from taking it, he acts to satisfy what is in a literal sense his own desire. In either case he does something he himself wants to do, and he does it not because of some external influence whose aim happens to coincide with his own but because of his desire to do it. The unwilling addict identifies himself, however, through the formation of a second-order volition, with one rather than with the other of his conflicting first-order desires. He makes one of them more truly his own and, in so doing, he withdraws himself from the other. It is in virtue of this identification and withdrawal, accomplished through the formation of a second-order volition, that the unwilling ad-

dict may meaningfully make the analytically puzzling statements that the force moving him to take the drug is a force other than his own, and that it is not of his own free will but rather against his will that this force moves him to take it.

The wanton addict cannot or does not care which of his conflicting first-order desires wins out. His lack of concern is not due to his inability to find a convincing basis for preference. It is due either to his lack of the capacity for reflection or to his mindless indifference to the enterprise of evaluating his own desires and motives.[6] There is only one issue in the struggle to which his first-order conflict may lead: whether the one or the other of his conflicting desires is the stronger. Since he is moved by both desires, he will not be altogether satisfied by what he does no matter which of them is effective. But it makes no difference to *him* whether his craving or his aversion gets the upper hand. He has no stake in the conflict between them and so, unlike the unwilling addict, he can neither win nor lose the struggle in which he is engaged. When a *person* acts, the desire by which he is moved is either the will he wants or a will he wants to be without. When a *wanton* acts, it is neither.

III

There is a very close relationship between the capacity for forming second-order volitions and another capacity that is essential to persons—one that has often been considered a distinguishing mark of the human condition. It is only because a person has volitions of the second order that he is capable both of enjoying and of lacking freedom of the will. The concept of a person is not only, then, the concept of a type of entity that has both first-order desires and volitions of the second order. It can also be construed as the concept of a type of entity for whom the freedom of its will may be a problem. This concept excludes all wantons, both infrahuman and human, since they fail to satisfy an essential condition for the enjoyment of freedom of the will. And it excludes those suprahuman beings, if any, whose wills are necessarily free.

Just what kind of freedom is the freedom of the will? This question calls for an identification of the special area of human experience to which the concept of freedom of the will, as distinct from the concepts of other sorts of freedom, is particularly germane. In dealing with it, my aim will be primarily to locate the problem with which a person is most immediately concerned when he is concerned with the freedom of his will.

According to one familiar philosophical tradition, being free is fundamentally a matter of doing what one wants to do. Now the notion of an agent who does what he wants to do is by no means an altogether clear one: both the doing and the wanting, and the appropriate relation between them as well, require elucidation. But although its focus needs to be sharpened and its formulation refined, I believe that this notion does capture at least part of what is implicit in the idea of an agent who *acts* freely. It misses entirely, however, the peculiar content of the quite different idea of an agent whose *will* is free.

We do not suppose that animals enjoy freedom of the will, although we recognize that an animal may be free to run in whatever direction it wants. Thus, having the freedom to do what one wants to do is not a sufficient condition of having a free will. It is not a necessary condition either. For to deprive someone of his freedom of action is not necessarily to undermine the freedom of his will. When an agent is aware that there are certain things he is not free to do, this doubtless affects his desires and limits the range of choices he can make. But suppose that someone, without being aware of it, has in fact lost or been deprived of his freedom of action. Even though he is no longer free to do what he wants to do, his will may remain as free as it was before. Despite the fact that he is not free to translate his desires into actions or to act according to the determinations of his will, he may still form those desires and make those determinations as freely as if his freedom of action had not been impaired.

When we ask whether a person's will is free we are not asking whether he is in a position to translate his first-order desires into actions. That is the question of whether he is free to do as he pleases. The question of the freedom of his will does not concern the relation between what he does and what he wants to do. Rather, it concerns his desires themselves. But what question about them is it?

It seems to me both natural and useful to construe the question of whether a person's will is free in close analogy to the question of whether an

agent enjoys freedom of action. Now freedom of action is (roughly, at least) the freedom to do what one wants to do. Analogously, then, the statement that a person enjoys freedom of the will means (also roughly) that he is free to want what he wants to want. More precisely, it means that he is free to will what he wants to will, or to have the will he wants. Just as the question about the freedom of an agent's action has to do with whether it is the action he wants to perform, so the question about the freedom of his will has to do with whether it is the will he wants to have.

It is in securing the conformity of his will to his second-order volitions, then, that a person exercises freedom of the will. And it is in the discrepancy between his will and his second-order volitions, or in his awareness that their coincidence is not his own doing but only a happy chance, that a person who does not have this freedom feels its lack. The unwilling addict's will is not free. This is shown by the fact that it is not the will he wants. It is also true, though in a different way, that the will of the wanton addict is not free. The wanton addict neither has the will he wants nor has a will that differs from the will he wants. Since he has no volitions of the second order, the freedom of his will cannot be a problem for him. He lacks it, so to speak, by default.

People are generally far more complicated than my sketchy account of the structure of a person's will may suggest. There is as much opportunity for ambivalence, conflict, and self-deception with regard to desires of the second order, for example, as there is with regard to first-order desires. If there is an unresolved conflict among someone's second-order desires, then he is in danger of having no second-order volition; for unless this conflict is resolved, he has no preference concerning which of his first-order desires is to be his will. This condition, if it is so severe that it prevents him from identifying himself in a sufficiently decisive way with *any* of his conflicting first-order desires, destroys him as a person. For it either tends to paralyse his will and to keep him from acting at all, or it tends to remove him from his will so that his will operates without his participation. In both cases he becomes, like the unwilling addict though in a different way, a helpless bystander to the forces that move him.

Another complexity is that a person may have, especially if his second-order desires are in conflict, desires and volitions of a higher order than the second. There is no theoretical limit to the length of the series of desires of higher and higher orders; nothing except common sense and, perhaps, a saving fatigue prevents an individual from obsessively refusing to identify himself with any of his desires until he forms a desire of the next higher order. The tendency to generate such a series of acts of forming desires, which would be a case of humanization run wild, also leads toward the destruction of a person.

It is possible, however, to terminate such a series of acts without cutting it off arbitrarily. When a person identifies himself *decisively* with one of his first-order desires, this commitment 'resounds' throughout the potentially endless array of higher orders. Consider a person who, without reservation or conflict, wants to be motivated by the desire to concentrate on his work. The fact that his second-order volition to be moved by this desire is a decisive one means that there is no room for questions concerning the pertinence of desires or volitions of higher orders. Suppose the person is asked whether he wants to want to concentrate on his work. He can properly insist that this question concerning a third-order desire does not arise. It would be a mistake to claim that, because he has not considered whether he wants the second-order volition he has formed, he is indifferent to the question of whether it is with this volition or with some other that he wants his will to accord. The decisiveness of the commitment he has made means that he has decided that no further question about his second-order volition, at any higher order, remains to be asked. It is relatively unimportant whether we explain this by saying that this commitment implicitly generates an endless series of confirming desires of higher orders, or by saying that the commitment is tantamount to a dissolution of the pointedness of all questions concerning higher orders of desire.

Examples such as the one concerning the unwilling addict may suggest that volitions of the second order, or of higher orders, must be formed deliberately and that a person characteristically struggles to ensure that they are satisfied. But the conformity of a person's will to his higher-order volitions may be far more thoughtless and spontaneous than this. Some people are naturally moved by kindness when they want to be kind, and by nastiness when they want to be nasty, without any explicit forethought and without any need for energetic self-control. Others are moved by nastiness when they want to be kind and by kindness when they intend to be nasty, equally without forethought and without active resistance to these violations of their higher-order desires. The enjoyment of freedom comes easily to some. Others must struggle to achieve it.

IV

My theory concerning the freedom of the will accounts easily for our disinclination to allow that this freedom is enjoyed by the members of any species inferior to our own. It also satisfies another condition that must be met by any such theory, by making it apparent why the freedom of the will should be regarded as desirable. The enjoyment of a free will means the satisfaction of certain desires—desires of the second or of higher orders—whereas its absence means their frustration. The satisfactions at stake are those which accrue to a person of whom it may be said that his will is his own. The corresponding frustrations are those suffered by a person of whom it may be said that he is estranged from himself, or that he finds himself a helpless or a passive bystander to the forces that move him.

A person who is free to do what he wants to do may yet not be in a position to have the will he wants. Suppose, however, that he enjoys both freedom of action and freedom of the will. Then he is not only free to do what he wants to do; he is also free to want what he wants to want. It seems to me that he has, in that case, all the freedom it is possible to desire or to conceive. There are other good things in life, and he may not possess some of them. But there is nothing in the way of freedom that he lacks.

It is far from clear that certain other theories of the freedom of the will meet these elementary but essential conditions: that it be understandable why we desire this freedom and why we refuse to ascribe it to animals. Consider, for example, Roderick Chisholm's quaint version of the doctrine that human freedom entails an absence of causal determination.[7] Whenever a person performs a free action, according to Chisholm, it's a miracle. The motion of a person's hand, when the person moves it, is the outcome of a series of physical causes; but some event in this series, 'and presumably one of those that took place within the brain, was caused by the agent and not by any other events'. A free agent has, therefore, 'a prerogative which some would attribute only to God: each of us, when we act, is a prime mover unmoved'.

This account fails to provide any basis for doubting that animals of subhuman species enjoy the freedom it defines. Chisholm says nothing that makes it seem less likely that a rabbit performs a miracle when it moves its leg than that a man does so when he moves his hand. But why, in any case, should anyone *care* whether he can interrupt the natural order of causes in the way Chisholm describes? Chisholm offers no reason for believing that there is a discernible difference between the experience of a man who miraculously initiates a series of causes when he moves his hand and a man who moves his hand without any such breach of the normal causal sequence. There appears to be no concrete basis for preferring to be involved in the one state of affairs rather than in the other.[8]

It is generally supposed that, in addition to satisfying the two conditions I have mentioned, a satisfactory theory of the freedom of the will necessarily provides an analysis of one of the conditions of moral responsibility. The most common recent approach to the problem of understanding the freedom of the will has been, indeed, to inquire what is entailed by the assumption that someone is morally responsible for what he has done. In my view, however, the relation between moral responsibility and the freedom of the will has been very widely misunderstood. It is not true that a person is morally responsible for what he has done only if his will was free when he did it. He may be morally responsible for having done it even though his will was not free at all.

A person's will is free only if he is free to have the will he wants. This means that, with regard to any of his first-order desires, he is free either to make that desire his will or to make some other first-order desire his will instead. Whatever his will, then, the will of the person whose will is free could have been otherwise; he could have done otherwise than to constitute his will as he did. It is a vexed question just how 'he could have done otherwise' is to be understood in contexts such as this one. But although this question is important to the theory of freedom, it has no bearing on the theory of moral responsibility. For the assumption that a person is morally responsible for what he has done does not entail that the person was in a position to have whatever will he wanted.

This assumption *does* entail that the person did what he did freely, or that he did it of his own free will. It is a mistake, however, to believe that someone acts freely only when he is free to do whatever he wants or that he acts of his own free will only if his will is free. Suppose that a person has done what he wanted to do, that he did it because he wanted to do it, and that the will by which he was moved when he did it was his will because it was the will he wanted. Then he did it freely and of his own free will. Even supposing that he could have done otherwise, he would not have done otherwise; and even supposing that he could have had a different will, he would not have wanted his will to differ from what it was. Moreover, since the will that moved him when he acted was his will because he wanted it to be, he cannot claim that his will was forced upon him or that he was a passive bystander to its constitution. Under these conditions, it is quite irrelevant to the evaluation of his moral responsibility to inquire whether the alternatives that he opted against were actually available to him.[9]

In illustration, consider a third kind of addict. Suppose that his addiction has the same physiological basis and the same irresistible thrust as the addictions of the unwilling and wanton addicts, but that he is altogether delighted with his condition. He is a willing addict, who would not have things any other way. If the grip of his addiction should somehow weaken, he would do whatever he could to reinstate it; if his desire for the drug should begin to fade, he would take steps to renew its intensity.

The willing addict's will is not free, for his desire to take the drug will be effective regardless of whether or not he wants this desire to constitute his will. But when he takes the drug, he takes it freely and of his own free will. I am inclined to understand his situation as involving the overdetermination of his first-order desire to take the drug. This desire is his effective desire because he is physiologically addicted. But it is his effective desire also because he wants it to be. His will is outside his control, but, by his second-order desire that his desire for the drug should be effective, he has made this will his own. Given that it is therefore not only because of his addiction that his desire for the drug is effective, he may be morally responsible for taking the drug.

My conception of the freedom of the will appears to be neutral with regard to the problem of determinism. It seems conceivable that it should be causally determined that a person is free to want what he wants to want. If this is conceivable, then it might be causally determined that a person enjoys a free will. There is no more than an innocuous appearance of paradox in the proposition that it is determined, ineluctably and by forces beyond their control, that certain people have free wills and that others do not. There is no incoherence in the proposition that some agency other than a person's own is responsible (even *morally* responsible) for the fact that he enjoys or fails to enjoy freedom of the will. It is possible that a person should be morally responsible for what he does of his own free will and that some other person should also be morally responsible for his having done it.[10]

On the other hand, it seems conceivable that it should come about by chance that a person is free to have the will he wants. If this is conceivable, then it might be a matter of chance that certain people enjoy freedom of the will and that certain others do not. Perhaps it is also conceivable, as a number of philosophers believe, for states of affairs to come about in a way other than by chance or as the outcome of a sequence of natural causes. If it is indeed conceivable for the relevant states of affairs to come about in some third way, then it is also possible that a person should in that third way come to enjoy the freedom of the will.

Endnotes

[1] P. F. Strawson, *Individuals* (London: Methuen, 1959), 101–2. Ayer's usage of 'person' is similar: 'it is characteristic of persons in this sense that besides having various physical properties . . . they are also credited with various forms of consciousness' [A. J. Ayer, *The Concept of a Person* (New York: St. Martin's, 1963), 82]. What concerns Strawson and Ayer is the problem of understanding the relation between mind and body, rather than the quite different problem of understanding what it is to be a creature that not only has a mind and a body but is also a person.

[2] For the sake of simplicity, I shall deal only with what someone wants or desires, neglecting related phenomena such as choices and decisions. I propose to use the verbs 'to want' and 'to desire' interchangeably, although they are by no means perfect synonyms. My motive in forsaking the established nuances of these words arises from the fact that the verb 'to want,' which suits my purposes better so far as its meaning is concerned, does not lend itself so readily to the formation of nouns as does the verb 'to desire.' It is perhaps acceptable, albeit graceless, to speak in the plural of someone's 'wants.' But to speak in the singular of someone's 'want' would be an abomination.

[3] What I say in this paragraph applies not only to cases in which 'to X' refers to a possible action or inaction. It also applies to cases in which 'to X' refers to a first-order desire and in which the statement that '*A* wants to X' is therefore a shortened version of a statement—'*A* wants to want X'—that identifies a desire of the second order.

[4] It is not so clear that the entailment relation described here holds in certain kinds of cases, which I think may fairly be regarded as non-standard, where the essential difference between the standard and the non-standard cases lies in the kind of description by which the first-order desire in question is identified. Thus, suppose that *A* admires *B* so fulsomely that, even though he does not know what *B* wants to do, he wants to be effectively moved by whatever desire effectively moves *B*; without knowing what *B*'s will is, in other words, *A* wants his own will to be the same. It certainly does not follow that *A* already has, among his desires, a desire like the one that constitutes *B*'s will. I shall not pursue here the questions of whether there are genuine counterexamples to the claim made in the text or of how, if there are, that claim should be altered.

[5] Creatures with second-order desires but no second-order volitions differ significantly from brute animals, and, for some purposes, it would be desirable to regard them as persons. My usage, which withholds the designation 'person' from them, is thus somewhat arbitrary. I adopt it largely because it facilitates the formulation of some of the points I wish to make. Hereafter, whenever I consider statements of the form '*A* wants to want to X', I shall have in mind statements identifying second-order volitions and not statements identifying second-order desires that are not second-order volitions.

[6] In speaking of the evaluation of his own desires and motives as being characteristic of a person, I do not mean to suggest that a person's second-order volitions necessarily manifest a *moral* stance on his part toward his first-order desires. It may not be from the point of view of morality that the person evaluates his first-order desires. Moreover, a person may be capricious and irresponsible in forming his second-order volitions and give no serious consideration to what is at stake. Second-order volitions express evaluations only in the sense that they are preferences. There is no essential restrictions on the kind of basis, if any, upon which they are formed.

[7] Freedom and Action,' in *Freedom and Determinism*, ed. Keith Lehrer, (New York: Random House, 1966), 11–44. Essay II.

[8] I am not suggesting that the alleged difference between these two states of affairs is unverifiable. On the contrary, physiologists might well be able to show that Chisholm's conditions for a free action are not

satisfied, by establishing that there is no relevant brain event for which a sufficient physical cause cannot be found.

[9] For another discussion of the considerations that cast doubt on the principle that a person is morally responsible for what he has done only if he could have done otherwise, see my 'Alternate Possibilities and Moral Responsibility', *Journal of Philosophy*, 1969, 829–39.

[10] There is a difference between being *fully* responsible and being *solely* responsible. Suppose that the willing addict has been made an addict by the deliberate and calculated work of another. Then it may be that both the addict and this other person are fully responsible for the addict's taking the drug, while neither of them is solely responsible for it. That there is a distinction between full moral responsibility and sole moral responsibility is apparent in the following example. A certain light can be turned on or off by flicking either of two switches, and each of these switches is simultaneously flicked to the 'on' position by a different person, neither of whom is aware of the other. Neither person is solely responsible for the light's going on, nor do they share the responsibility in the sense that each is partially responsible; rather, each of them is fully responsible.

43. *Understanding Free Will*

MICHAEL SLOTE

In this selection, Michael Slote, who teaches philosophy at the University of Maryland at College Park, explains how the analysis of free will offered by Frankfurt can be developed to avoid the problems raised by coercion (for example, a case in which a bank clerk is held up at gunpoint and reluctantly hands over the money to the robber). He also argues that such a view implies that free will is not necessary for moral responsibility. Slote concludes, though, by criticizing Frankfurt in much the same way Reid criticized Hume: relevant to free will is the question of how the second-order desire that a first-order desire be acted on has occurred. Since one may be manipulated into wanting one's own desires, the conformity of second-order volitions with first-order desires may not be sufficient for free will.

In recent years, Harry Frankfurt, Wright Neely, and Gary Watson have offered accounts of free will and free agency that play down the challenge of determinism and equate freedom with a kind of rationality in action.[1]

I believe that the approach taken by Frankfurt, Neely, and Watson (FNW, for short) represents, in

From *Journal of Philosophy* 77, no. 3 (March 1980): 136– 51. Copyright © 1980 by the *Journal of Philosophy*. Reprinted by permission of the author and publisher.

its conceptual sophistication and explanatory power, a genuine advance over previous rationality theories of freedom like that of Spinoza. But I also believe that FNW have themselves misunderstood, or failed to see clearly, the nature and implications of their own theories, and that the theories they present must borrow ideas from Spinoza in order to escape implausibility and attain their fullest development. In the end, however, I shall argue that no available rationality conception fully captures our intuitions about what it is to act of one's own free will.

I

Let me first give a rough sketch of some of the important features of FNW's approach, for the most part concentrating on Frankfurt's theory, which has been the most elaborately and systematically developed, but indicating differences among the theories when it seems important to do so.

All three philosophers focus upon cases of irrational addiction as paradigms of unfreedom.[2] Frankfurt and Neely both characterize the typical unwilling addict as someone who (e.g.) has a second-order desire not to *desire* some drug and a second-order desire (or volition) not to *give in* to his (or her) first-order desire for the drug, but who (irrationally) gives in to his first-order desire for the drug, nonetheless.[3] In a slightly different vein, Watson characterizes the unwilling addict as someone who (e.g.) puts no (positive) value upon (getting) a certain drug, but who (irrationally) acts upon his strong desire for the drug, nonetheless. In the light of such examples, they then claim, roughly, that a person acts freely when and only when his actions flow from his higher-, or highest-, order desires/volitions, rather than opposing them; alternatively, in Watson's conception, a person acts freely when and only when his actions express his values and not just his (strongest) desires or wants. At this point, I think at least some of the connection between FNW's theories and Spinoza's rationality conception of freedom should be apparent: the addictive people that the former treat as unfree are clearly also cases of Spinozan "human bondage."

Frankfurt makes the further claim that a bank clerk who reluctantly hands over money to a holdup man who threatens him with a gun will typically count, on the account he has offered, as having acted freely.[4] Such a man, he says, would prefer not to have to make the choice that faces him; but, faced with that choice, he is satisfied to be moved by his desire to hand over the money and acts in accordance with a second-order volition. And although Frankfurt also holds that the clerk will resent the intruder and be actively discontented, presumably because he feels loyalty to the bank or to its clients, he seems to feel that such descriptions do not conflict with his characterization of the act as free by the lights of his own theory. To say that such a bank clerk acts freely

has, Frankfurt admits, a jarring sound; and he thinks it a prima facie condition on the adequacy of a theory of free action that someone acting under duress in the manner of his bank clerk be judged not to have acted freely (or, presumably, of his own free will). But he attempts to mitigate the presumed implausibility of his theory not by modifying the theory, but by positing a second sense of 'free action' in which the bank clerk does *not* act freely. Neely makes the very same response to cases of duress: he does not see how his own theory can handle them and claims that there is another sense of 'free' that can.[5]

But it seems both ad hoc and self-indulgent to respond to the inability of an analysis to account for certain cases not by reformulating the analysis, but by holding on to it and claiming that the problem cases only demonstrate that there are two senses of the term or expression one is trying to define. Moreover, there is also good reason to believe that the difficulties Frankfurt and Neely think cases of duress present to their theories are themselves more imagined than real. I think it can be shown that Frankfurt and Neely's own theories, suitably supplemented, can actually *explain* why the everyday cases of duress they have in mind are not cases in which (it is natural to say that) a person acts of his own free will.

As Frankfurt and Neely describe the relevant cases of coercion, the person who reluctantly complies with a threat is reasonable to do so. So, given the emphasis their theories place on certain elements of rationality in the concept of free action, it might easily seem that they would be committed to saying that Frankfurt's bank clerk hands over the money of his own free will. But although it may be reasonable, or rational, for the clerk *to* comply with the robber's threat, he may not act rationally *in* complying with it. He may, for example, be overly frightened, or panicked; and he almost certainly will resent the intruder, if, as Frankfurt seems to assume, he has any loyalty either to the bank or to the people it serves. But does this resentment not signify a desire (or wish) for retaliation or defiance: that is, not merely a desire that the would-be robber should somehow be punished, but a desire to do something oneself to punish him or, at least, to show him what one thinks of him? Even if heroism is not widely treated as a moral obligation, most of us have a deep tendency to treat it as an ideal to be emulated. And so I think that if the clerk resents the robber, he will have various momentary/

fragmentary fantasies of heroic defiance, or foiling, or retaliation, with appropriate accompanying thoughts.

But then someone who fulfills Frankfurt's description of the bank clerk and about whom the above things are also true will qualify as *ambivalent*, if he ends up complying with the intruder's threat: ambivalent, in particular, about his own compliance. On the one hand, to the very extent that the aforementioned resentment, wishes, and fantasies exist, he will tend, both before and after the fact, to reproach himself for saving his own skin.[6] When he complies with the robber's threat, such a person acts from a desire by which he wishes not to be moved to act, even *given* the alternatives he confronts. There is in him a conflict between a first-order desire to comply (and play it safe) and an ultimately frustrated second-order volition that that desire not be effective and that, in particular, he should overcome that safe-playing desire through appropriate heroics or defiance. And so he will count at not having acted freely, on Frankfurt's own theory.[7] But, on the other hand, the bank clerk will also, presumably, have an opposing second-order volition that his desire to play it safe should be effective and his tendencies toward defiance and heroics restrained, based on the value he places on his own self-presevation. And it is just this conflict of second-order volitions that qualifies the clerk's attitude toward his compliance as ambivalence. Frankfurt ignores the possibility that his bank clerk might have to be ambivalent, given the descriptions he furnishes and normal human background assumptions. But once we recognize the ambivalence of the typical bank clerk in the situation imagined, we can see that there is no need to reformulate Frankfurt and Neely's theories or postulate a second meaning of 'freedom' in order to explain our reluctance to characterize most people who act under duress as acting freely.[8]

In saying that someone who is ambivalent about his own actions in the way described above does not act freely—either on FNW's theories or in actual fact—I do not, however, mean to suggest that *whenever* we choose among desires that cannot, in certain circumstances, be jointly realized, we do not act of our own free will. The choice of one out of an incompatible set of alternatives need not involve one in ambivalence about one's choice. If, for example, I have a hankering for Italian food and a stronger hankering for Chinese food that eventually "wins out," I may not in any way wish

that my desire for Chinese food had not been effective, even though my hankering for Italian food has not been satisfied or entirely disappeared. For simply to have a desire for something is not, automatically, to want (wish) that other, incompatible desires not exist or be fulfilled. In ambivalence, then, we have conflicting second-order desires/volitions about a first-level desire or want: wanting the first-level desire to exist or issue in action and, at the same time, wanting this not to be so. And there seems to be no reason to suppose that this phenomenon must be present when we (simply) choose between jointly unrealizable desires on the basis, say, of the greater strength of one of those desires.

Certain kinds of ambivalence, then, disqualify one from acting of one's own free will. But that is not to say that all cases of irrational, unfree action involve ambivalence. The heroin addict may not have conflicting second-order volitions in the manner of the bank clerk; he may desire heroin, wish that desire were not effective, and in no way want the desire to be effective or even to exist. To put the matter in Watson's terminology, he may place no value on realizing his desire for heroin, whereas the ambivalent bank clerk seems to place a value both on fulfilling his desire to take no chances and on overcoming that desire in heroism. However, the bank clerk and the addict do fail to act from one of their highest-order desires. And it is this common failure that makes them seem to fall short of rationality-in-action in a way that someone who merely acts from the strongest of his jointly unrealizable desires does not.[9]

II

I have so far touched upon only one central case of acting under threat or duress. For ideological or personal reasons, however, some bank clerk might be quite *willing* to hand over money to an armed robber. But then he would be unlikely to be ambivalent about handing over the money, and there would be little reason to deny that he did so of his own free will.

It also seems to be possible for someone to comply with an initially unwelcome threat without being ambivalent, and this fact must be accounted for and brought to bear on the theories of free agency we have been discussing. Consider a man told by a king whom he dislikes that if he does not visit him at the palace in a month's time, he will be sent to prison. Is it not possible that the man should reasonably decide that compliance was the sensible course of action under the circumstances and should reconcile himself to the visit—so that when the time came for him to go to the palace, he neither resented the king for forcing such a choice upon him nor wished, at some level, that he could somehow defy or disobey him? Such a person responds to the king's threat, calmly and unambivalently, as if it were some sort of *physical* obstacle, and that may give us reason to say that when he finally does visit the palace, he does so of his own free will.[10] For someone who (e.g.) comes to a large lake while on a long journey may well be faced with a choice—between detouring around the lake and turning back—that he would have preferred not to have to make. But typically, when faced with such a physical obstacle, a traveler will ungrumblingly and automatically adjust his plans; and we would normally think of such a traveler as going around the lake of his own free will, even though the location of the lake clearly does make his options worse than he might have expected. And if the man whom the king threatens has an "objective" and ungrumbling attitude toward the consequent deterioration of his options—I assume that he would generally prefer not to visit such a king, even if he knows he is in no danger in doing so—then I believe he too counts as acting of his own free will if and when he finally visits the palace on the appointed day. Certainly, there is a long tradition, exemplified by Spinoza, in which the ability to reconcile oneself to the inevitable without bitterness, or personalizing, or self-recrimination, is taken as a major aspect of what is involved in being a free person. Indeed, the ability to have such an attitude to the necessities of choice, event, and circumstance that the world imposes is quite commonly considered to mark one as being "philosophical" in that widespread use of the term that everyone but philosophers seems to use.

Now although FNW pay no particular attention to cases of acting "philosophically," on their theories the man we have just described clearly counts as acting freely. But despite Frankfurt and Neely's mistaken opinion to the contrary, those theories allow for the possibility of free rational compliance with an (initially) unwelcome threat *only in certain cases*, the very cases about which

Spinoza and, I think, we ourselves would be most inclined to say that freedom was exemplified. I would not, however, want to minimize the doubts that can arise about whether freedom really does exist in cases where someone has a "philosophical" attitude in complying with a threat. One might well feel that the king in our earlier example has so effectively intervened in the life of his "philosophical" subject, that the latter's act of visiting the palace is to a significant extent attributable to the king who has changed his options and thus not really, or fully, his own. One may feel, in other words, that however philosophical someone may be, he does not act of his own free will if the acts of another person play such an important role in determining his behavior. (One will presumably still maintain that the "intervention" of natural obstacles does not deprive people of free agency in this way, since, to ordinary ways of thinking, a person may in the course of a journey go around a lake of his own free will, even if the lake has worsened his options and led him to act as he does.)

I can see some force in these claims, but I also think that if one accepts them, one raises problems for oneself that the claims themselves are powerless to deal with (even if one grants the causal distinction between human and nonhuman "interventions" on which they are based). In particular, if we say that a threatener takes away the agency of someone who complies with his threat and that the threatened individual—whatever his inner attitude—does not, in complying, act of his own free will, we will have a problem understanding why highly attractive offers are not usually thought of as depriving us of freedom. For an attractive offer changes our options dramatically, and it seems as reasonable to attribute "ultimate agency" to someone who makes an effective offer as to someone who makes an effective threat. So I think we should be suspicious of the view that effective threats automatically deprive one of free will. What is needed, instead, is a theory of acting freely that can explain why our earlier bank clerk does not hand over the money of his own free will, but also allow for effective offers that do not deprive one of freedom. And what is also needed is a theory of free agency that can accommodate our feeling that some offers are so "coercive" and humiliating that if we do take advantage of them, we act no more freely than the bank clerk—a theory, that is, that can explain why some effective offers render us less free as agents than certain others.

I believe that FNW's conception(s) of freedom can achieve these results, once we take into account the sorts of psychological phenomena mentioned earlier and ignored, for the most part, by FNW. Their theory can explain the unfreedom of the original bank clerk in terms of his ambivalence and, ultimately, of the conflict between his effective first-order desire and one of his second-order volitions. And the difference between offers that deprive of free agency and offers that do not can, I believe, be explained in similar terms. If someone offers us an opportunity that offends none of our deeply felt values and that we feel worthy of, then if we take advantage of the opportunity, we presumably do so without ambivalence and (barring other factors that might prejudice the issue) of our own free will. But consider someone who is offered a million dollars if he will lick the offerer's boots. Almost any person who took advantage of such an offer would resent the person who had made such a "coercive" offer and be somewhat ambivalent about taking advantage of it. Most of us have some ideal notion of ourselves as not being the kind of person who can be made to lower and humiliate himself for a price. So even someone who feels that it is rational and worth while for him to lick the boots will also think less of himself for being willing to be rational in this way and wish that he were somehow above this sort of thing; and it is this state of ambivalent conflict that accounts for our intuitive judgment that such a person does not lick the boots of his own free will.

The theories of FNW thus enable us to explain important intuitive distinctions concerning the freedom or lack of freedom involved in typical responses to various sorts of offers and threats. The assumption that an effective threat always deprives of freedom, on the other hand, seems, if anything, to make such distinctions impossible of explanation. Since, moreover, the FNW theories entail that certain people who are philosophical about the threats they comply with act of their own free will, the explanatory and distinction-making power of those theories give us reasons of simplicity and system to deny that effective threats always deprive of free agency. We are, instead, given reason to accept the Spinozistic view that one is free to the extent that one responds calmly and unresentfully to the necessities the world imposes and rationally, without self-recrimination, chooses the good in the light of such necessities.[11]

Of course, there are other reasons already alluded to for thinking that someone who has a philosophical attitude in complying with a threat acts freely. Such a person does, after all, depersonalize things and treat the threat he confronts in the way that most people treat ordinary physical obstacles. Since accommodation to a physical obstacle seems in no way, intuitively, to deprive an agent of his freedom, we have some reason to say the same thing about someone who complies philosophically with a threat. It is important in this connection, however, to avoid overly strong claims about the human capacity for being philosophical, and acting freely, while complying with a threat. Even someone with a capacity for philosophical calm and acceptance may not have the time to cultivate such an attitude if—like our earlier bank clerk or any robbery victim who is told "your money or your life"—he is faced with a threat that requires immediate compliance. The Stoics (and perhaps even Spinoza) seem to have thought both that it was possible to be philosophical and free even in response to such abrupt and immediate threats and that one should cultivate the capacity for such response.[12] But it is at just this point that I find myself in deepest disagreement with the Stoics—and with Spinoza, to the extent that he agrees with them.

Consider the loyal bank clerk of our earlier example. It is a contradiction in terms to suppose that he can have an emotional attitude like loyalty and yet also be able to pick and choose among his emotional *reactions* in such a way as to (decide to) be calm and unresentful at the prospect of handing over the bank's money to an armed intruder. If someone whom we knew to have this sort of loyalty told us that he felt completely detached and emotionless in handing over money to a holdup man, we would very likely conclude that for some reason he was refusing to face his deepest feelings. And all this would also hold, a fortiori, of someone who had to give his own patiently accumulated savings to a holdup man. Faced with threats that require immediate action and that lower our expectations significantly, we cannot be completely philosophical and are incapable of free compliance. It takes time to work through resentment and reluctance, and only if a threat requires action in the relatively distant future will one's capacity for being philosophical have time to take hold. Only with such a temporal breathing space can one work through the inevitable initial reactions and come to accept the necessity of the adverse choice with which one is presented in such a way that, in complying with the threat, one acts of one's own free will.

The Stoic (or Spinoza) will claim that these considerations only show how emotionally attached to worldly things we actually are. If only we cultivated our capacity for emotional detachment, we could learn to respond to immediate threats without ambivalence or emotion and thus to act freely whether we complied with them or not. But I think that what the Stoic says is possible is not really possible, for us. Another, higher sort of being that never went through the dependency of prolonged childhood might never need or want love. But we are not beings of that sort: we seek love from the start and never really outgrow that quest or its urgency. Thus the Stoic or Spinozan ideal of emotional detachment is an illusion for us, an ideal perhaps, but one that we are simply not capable of. And if we make this assumption, then the injunction to cultivate detachment to the greatest extent possible will seem highly problematic, and the Stoic or Spinozan who claims to have achieved emotional detachment will be thought to be papering over his or her own deep (possibly thwarted) yearnings for love.

To the extent, moreover, that we love particular things or persons, we must be capable of resentment, sorrow, and anger. If threats against a loved one really leave one calm and philosophical from the start, the claim actually to love that person may be irretrievably undermined. In the abstract, the capacity to respond to threats philosophically may well be an ideal thing, a perfection. And since love for individuals by its very nature undercuts this capacity, love, as well as the need or desire for love, may constitute human weaknesses. But if these things are weaknesses, they are *basic* human weaknesses. By that I mean that they are weaknesses so endemic to our nature that if one seeks, like the Stoic, to avoid being subject to them, one is likely to get oneself into a worse position than one would have been in if one had simply accepted the weakness in oneself.[13] Love and our tendency to feel sorrow and resentment may be basic human weaknesses in this sense, because if one attempts not to love anyone and not to resent or be sad at anything, no matter how badly one is treated, one may cover up these sorts of feelings, but will also, in doing so, give them all sorts of free rein for subterranean mischief and eventual destructive effect within one's life.

Of course, some of these considerations might incline one to go to the opposite extreme from the Stoics and claim that resentment at the loss of things one loves or values may sink into the depths of our minds, but never completely dissolves. I do not see why we should believe this to be true, but, even if it is, there is no need to modify the conception of free action offered by FNW. It will simply turn out that all cases of complying with an unwelcome threat will qualify as unfree on their own theories, and we will be spared the burden of having to argue for the freedom of those who have a philosophical attitude in complying with threats. On the other hand, if the Stoics are right, and someone really could accommodate himself to all threats immediately and without emotion, there will still be no need to modify the theories of FNW.[14]

III

I would like now to show that the theories of FNW, properly understood and supported, have the important consequence that acting of one's own free will—what we shall for brevity sometimes call "free will"—is not necessary to moral responsibility, blameworthiness, and the like. In our earlier example of the reluctant bank clerk, the clerk does not hand over the money of his own free will because he acts from a desire he wishes he could rise above. But nothing in our description precludes that he acts thoughtlessly, forgetting that there is an alarm button nearby that he can push to foil the robber. And if that is his situation, then we will feel that he shouldn't hand over the money and is not only morally responsible but blameworthy for doing so.[15]

Frankfurt too believes that his bank clerk can be morally responsible and blameworthy for the way he acts under duress.[16] He also holds that it is one requisite of a good account of free action that moral responsibility should come out entailing freedom, and says that his own theory has that consequence. But it does not have that consequence, if, as we have argued, Frankfurt is mistaken in thinking that his theory commits him to calling his bank clerk a free agent. Even prescinding from Frankfurt's interpretation of his theory for cases of duress, it is not clear that Frankfurt can easily maintain that acting freely is necessary to moral responsibility. For on his account, someone struggling against a strong desire (e.g., an incipient addiction) who in the end gives in to that desire fails to act of his own free will. But nothing in this description forces us to say that the person who succumbs to his desire had to behave as he did, was compulsive rather than morally weak or, more generally, weak-willed. So, once again, Frankfurt will have to allow for cases where his definition of free will is not met but an agent is nonetheless morally responsible and even blameworthy for what he does, unless he takes the risky step of altogether denying the possibility of (blameworthy) moral weakness.

Note further that it sounds jarring and unnatural to say the (reluctant) clerk hands over the money of his own free will quite independently of any assumptions we make about whether he *had* to hand the money over or was *compelled* to do so. But this tends to show how important it is to bring in something like FNW's theories to explain our intuitive judgments about the clerk. For those theories explain why, even if he could have done otherwise, the bank clerk is judged not to act of his own free will. Of course, if the clerk for some reason really cannot do otherwise, then we may say he is not morally responsible for his actions. But as we have just seen, the judgment that someone can do otherwise does not entail the judgment that he acts of his own free will. So even if being able to do otherwise is necessary to moral responsibility, that has no tendency to show that we must act of our own free will in order to be responsible for our actions.

Despite what we have said, it might nonetheless be objected at this point that moral responsibility requires freedom in *some* customary (philosophical) sense, even if it does not entail that one act *of one's own free will*. But even if such a sense of 'freedom' exists, why should it be considered immediately relevant to *freedom of will*? Perhaps the free-will problem is simply different from the problem of the conditions of moral responsibility and the contrary opinion only arises from the misconception that the importance of free will depends on its being necessary to moral responsibility.[17] More important still, if such a (further) sense of 'freedom' really were immediately at issue in the free-will question, it would follow that any proof that we sometimes (never) do things of our own free will would by itself be insufficient to show that

we had (lacked) free will. And this consequence will surely seem counterintuitive to philosophers in the English-speaking tradition. After all, Paradigm Case "solutions" to the free-will problem are considered objectionable because they are based on the Paradigm Case Argument, not because they assume the special relevance of the notion of acting of one's own free will to the traditional problem of free will. So it cannot perhaps be an objection to the approach of the present paper that it rests on a similar assumption.

IV

Although I have all along been defending rationality theories, I do not, in the end, think that any of them offers a totally adequate conception of freedom of will. I think they offer us necessary, but not sufficient, conditions of freedom and that the conditions they omit are among the most important for understanding why free will has been such a perennial problem for philosophers.

In "Freedom of the Will and the Concept of a Person," Frankfurt makes clear his commitment to the sufficiency of his conditions for acting freely and claims, in particular, that the existence of free will or agency does not depend on how such freedom comes about. It is precisely here that I (and others) disagree with Frankfurt: certain ways of coming to fulfill Frankfurt's conditions of freedom seem, intuitively, to *deprive* one of free agency. Consider the following example. Robert, who is genuinely undecided between two conflicting first-order desires X and Y, is visited by a hypnotist who decides to "solve" his problem by putting him in a trance and inducing in him a second-order volition in favor of X; as a result of having this second-order volition, Robert then acts to satisfy X, never suspecting that his decisiveness has been induced by the hypnotist. The example may bear the marks of science fiction, but it seems adequate, nonetheless, to point up the conceptual insufficiency of "rationality" conditions of free action. For we would all surely deny that Robert acts of his own free will, when he acts from the second-order volition induced by the hypnotist.

But it is important to consider why we want to say this. We would, after all, describe Robert as having *willingly* satisfied desire X; so in denying that he acts *of his own free will*, we must be implicitly assuming that so acting involves something more than willingness taken together with our previous rationality conditions. And I believe that this further condition, in simplest terms, comes down to the requirement that our actions be fully *our own*. The feeling that Robert does not, in satisfying X, act of his own free will reflects, I think, our belief that because of the particular way the hypnotist has intervened in his life, his act is not fully his own.[18] And the assumption that acting of one's own free will requires that one's actions be fully one's own also helps us to explain what the words 'one's own' are doing in the phrase 'of one's own free will'[19] and to understand the force of our intuitive distinction, in the above example, between freedom of will and mere willingness.

In order to act of one's *own* free will, then, one's actions must be fully one's own; one must in some sense act autonomously. But these locutions, however intuitive, are extremely vague, and, at this point, there are several problems that must be faced if we are to advance our understanding of free will. We will, to begin with, want to know whether anything more definite can be said about this autonomy that seems necessary to free will but not to be implied by anything in rationality theories. But we must also ask whether such a spelling out of the notion of autonomy can help us to understand the relevance of determinism to freedom of will. FNW's theories make it difficult to see how anyone could think that determinism ever presented a challenge to free will. And it is surely some sort of problem for those theories that they seem to offer no way to make sense of the age-old belief in such a challenge. (After all, for many of us "the problem of free will" is just an ellipsis for "the problem of free will and determinism.") If, however, some sort of autonomy is, as we have claimed, necessary to freedom of will, further specification of that notion may help to explain why determinism makes free will problematic by making it clear why determinism represents a challenge to autonomy thus specified.

Of course, it might turn out that the theories of FNW, even supplemented by an appropriately elaborate conception of autonomy, did not offer sufficient conditions for freedom of will, and that some further condition, e.g., being able to do otherwise, was necessary to freedom and was the aspect of free will on which the relevance of determinism depended.[20] But this suggestion must be treated with caution, since there have long been and even now continue to be important challenges to the notion that the ability to do otherwise is necessary to acting freely. Thus if what I have just been saying is correct, a good part of the free-will problem remains up in the air. The theories of FNW offer significant necessary conditions of free will, and they have an explanatory power (and important implications) that even their proponents fail to recognize. But they leave other problems untouched; and I only hope that what we have said here may give some indication of the directions we must take in order to make further progress in understanding free will.

Endnotes

[1] See Neely, "Freedom and Desire," *Philosophical Review*, LXXXIII, 1 (January 1974): 32–54; Watson, "Free Agency," *Journal of Philosophy*, LXXII, 8 (April 1975): 205–220; Frankfurt, "Freedom of the Will and the Concept of a Person," Chapter 42 above, and "Coercion and Moral Responsibility," in T. Honderich, ed., *Essays in Freedom of Action* (London: Routledge & Kegan Paul, 1973), pp. 65–86; and "Three Concepts of Free Action: II," *Proceedings of the Aristotelian Society*, suppl. vol. XLIX (1975): 113–125. Also cf. Gerald Dworkin, "Acting Freely," *Noûs*, IV, 4 (November 1970): 367–383, for a similar approach to freedom which I shall not specifically discuss.

[2] The expressions 'freedom', 'free agency', '(acting) freely', and '(acting) of one's own free will' all occur in the papers of FNW. But among such expressions, the phrase 'of one's (his) own free will' has, for English-speaking philosophers, the distinct advantage of indicating that what one is saying is relevant to the traditional problem of free will. This particular phrase, then, will be canonical for the present essay, and any other expressions I use *in propria persona* will be merely stylistic variants. Although I shall often make use of FNW's particular terminologies in reporting their views, I believe that our own canonical phraseology can be used to report those views without undue distortion. After all, they too want their ideas to be relevant to the traditional problem of free will.

[3] For Frankfurt, second-order volitions are a particular kind of second-order desire: desires that one or another first-order desire be (or not be) acted upon, i.e., effective in action. Chapter 42 above and "Three Concepts of Free Action: II," p. 114.

[4] "Three Concepts of Free Action: II," pp 113–117 and 122–124.

[5] "Freedom and Desire," pp. 35, 50.

[6] It is a psychological commonplace that anger or resentment against a given person tends to displace itself onto other (inappropriate) targets when it cannot be directed against its original object. So perhaps we can draw a more direct connection between the clerk's resentment of the intruder and his later self-reproach, by arguing that if he does hand over the money and has any compunction about blaming innocent associates, his unsatisfied anger at the intruder is apt to turn inward (*sub specie* his ideas of heroism). For more on how resentment against others may be turned against the self, compare Nietzsche's fascinating speculations in *The Genealogy of Morals*.

[7] "Three Concepts of Free Action: II," pp. 114, 117.

[8] If we assume that no *given* act can really express an ambivalent person's values, then Watson too can account for the lack of free agency in typical cases of duress.

[9] Neely (*op. cit.*, p. 48f.) says that anyone with conflicting desires is to that extent less free; but this very statement gives us reason to suspect that he is characterizing not our ordinary concept of acting of one's own free will, but some other, related notion, or ideal, of freedom. I shall ignore this divergence in what follows.

[10] It is less natural to say that he complies with the king's threat of his own free will than that he goes to the palace of his own free will. "Of his own free will" entails "knowingly" and "intentionally" and possesses the intensionality of these latter concepts; so although one may in doing X also be doing Y, it can still be the case that one is doing X of one's own free will but not doing Y of one's own free will. It sounds somewhat odd to say that someone complies with a threat of his own free will, because it suggests that the person involved is consciously aware that he is acting as he does because of a threat; for this, in turn, suggests rather too much dwelling on the particular source of his action to make it plausible to think that he really is reconciled and "objective" about his situation or thus acting freely. It stands in favor of our account, of course, that it can explain our tendency to make these fine distinctions. But, for ease of exposition, I shall sometimes use phrases that suggest that 'of his own free will' is not intensional.

[11] I here follow Spinoza in assuming that there are some occasions when a rational and self-respecting individual will comply with a threat, rather than defy it, without reproaching himself for doing so. (See the *Ethics*, Book 4, props. XX, LXV, and LXIX, proof, corollary, and note.) Frankfurt's clerk may reproach himself for not acting heroically only because he is *not* calm, unangry, and "philosophical" about his situation. Cf. footnote 6, above; and remember, too, that most of us conceive heroism as an ideal to emulate, rather than as a moral obligation.

[12] In what follows, I shall play down certain differences between Spinoza and the Stoics, but on the whole the Stoics seem much more committed than Spinoza to the idea that reason can control emotion. In fact, Spinoza explicitly asserts a difference of this kind between his own view and that of the Stoics. (In the *Ethics*, Book 5, preface; but also see Book 5, Proposition X, proof and note; Book 5, Proposition VI; Book 4, Proposition LXXIII.) On the other hand, there are major differences among the Stoics themselves about the extent to which reason can control passion and emotion. The doctrine of total control was advocated by Chrysippus, but Posidonius seems to have held that emotions and passions were in some measure autonomous and not under the direct, immediate control of reason. [On this see F. H. Sandbach, *The Stoics* (London: Chatto & Windus, 1975), pp. 59–67, esp. p. 65.]

[13] Cf. Pascal's aphorism: "Men are so necessarily mad, that not to be mad would amount to another form of madness," in the *Pensées*, ed. T. S. Eliot (New York: Dutton, 1958), sec. 414, p. 110.

[14] I shall not consider whether someone who is philosophical in complying with an effective threat must be thought to act under duress or to have been coerced into doing what he does.

[15] We may be tempted to say that he is (fully) responsible or blameworthy not for handing over the money, but only for not pushing the alarm button. However, since we would not naturally say that the clerk omits the button pushing of his own free will (cf. footnote 8, above), we are still left with a case of moral responsibility and culpability for a non-free act (omission). (I am indebted here to Bernard Berofsky.) For a different attempt to argue for the possibility of being morally responsible for negligence or thoughtlessness in a situation where one does not act freely, see Don Locke, "Three Concepts of Free Action: I," *Proceedings of the Aristotelian Society*, suppl. vol. IL (1975): 95–112, p. 109.

[16] "Three Concepts of Free Action: II," pp. 115, 123.

[17] In the title essay of *In Defence of Free Will* (London: Allen & Unwin, 1967, p. 36), C. A. Campbell claims that free will is important only if it is necessary to moral responsibility. But the theories of FNW militate against Campbell's conclusion by pointing up how intrinsically undesirable certain sorts of unfreedom can be. If we accept their conception of freedom, then the cases of unwilling addiction and of "philosophical" calm-in-action both illustrate the importance free will has independently of its connection with moral action and moral responsibility.

I am not, however, proposing a complete dissociation of free will and moral responsibility. In the next section, we shall discuss a condition of autonomy in action which is necessary to free will and which seems necessary to moral responsibility as well. This common necessary condition can easily seem incompatible with determinism, and so it is also no part of my intention to deny that determinism poses a threat both to free will and to moral responsibility.

[18] Some kinds of intervention do *not* seem to deprive an agent of his freedom. If, instead of inducing a second-order volition in a given person, someone softens the force of one of his addictions—through a surgical intervention he is unaware of—so that he later finds it easier to resist the addiction, we might not want to deny that the person involved acted of his own free will in successfully resisting the addiction. Note too that the inducing of second-order volitions provides a much better example of an intervention that deprives an agent of freedom by rendering his actions

not fully his own, than do the effective threats (or offers) we discussed earlier. I think this has something to do with the fact that someone who complies with a threat (or offer) *knows about the intervention of another person in the situation* and *himself makes a decision to do what that person wants*; neither of these things seems to be true of the person whose second-order volition is induced in the manner of our example.

[19] Cf. W. F. R. Hardie, "My Own Free Will," *Philosophy*, XXXII, 120 (January 1957): 21–23.

[20] It also might turn out that they did offer sufficient conditions for freedom of will, that those conditions were also sufficient for being able to do otherwise and that the relevance of determinism depended on this latter fact.

---

44. I *Could Not Have Done Otherwise*: So What?

DANIEL C. DENNETT

Many philosophers believe that a necessary condition of a free action is that it be within one's power, in some sense, to do otherwise than what one does. In this provocative article, Dennett argues that this commonly accepted principle does not deserve our allegiance. His thesis, if true, would tend to undercut much of the worry about determinism and criticism of compatibilism.

Wherever progress is stalled on a philosophical problem, a tactic worth trying is to find some shared (and hence largely unexamined) assumption and deny it. The problem of free will is such a problem, and, as Peter van Inwagen notes:

> . . . almost all philosophers agree that a necessary condition for holding an agent responsible for an act is believing that the agent *could have* refrained from performing that act.[1]

Perhaps van Inwagen is right; perhaps most philosophers agree on this. If so, this shared assump-

From *Journal of Philosophy* 81, no. 10 (October 1984): 553–65. Reprinted by permission of the author and the *Journal of Philosophy*.

tion, which I will call CDO (for "could have done otherwise"), is a good candidate for denial, especially since there turns out to be so little to be said in support of it, once it is called in question. I will argue that, just like those people who are famous only for being famous, this assumption owes its traditional high regard to nothing more than its traditional high regard. It is almost never questioned. And the tradition itself, I will claim, is initially motivated by little more than inattentive extrapolation from familiar cases.

To engage the issue, I assert that it simply does not matter at all to moral responsibility whether the agent in question could have done otherwise in the circumstances. Now how does a friend of CDO set about showing that I am obviously wrong? Not by reminding me, unnecessarily, of the broad consensus in philosophy in support of the CDO principle, or by repeating it, firmly and knowingly. The inertia of a tradition is by itself scant recommendation, and if it is claimed that the assumption is not questioned because it is obvious or self-evident, I can at least ask for some supporting illustration of the self-evidence of the assumption in application to familiar cases. Can anyone give me an example of someone withholding a judgment of responsibility until he has determined (to his own satisfaction) whether the agent could have done otherwise?

It will perhaps appear that I must be extraordinarily inattentive to the topics of daily conversation if I can ask that question with a straight face. A prominent feature of many actual inquiries into the responsibility of particular agents is the asking of the question "Could he have done otherwise?" The question is raised in trials, both civil and criminal, and much more frequently in the retrospective discussions between individuals concerning blame or excuse for particular regretted acts of omission or commission.

Before turning to a closer examination of those cases, it is worth noting that the question plays almost no role in discussions of praise or reward for felicitous, unregretted acts—except in the formulaic gracious demurrer of the one singled out for gratitude or praise: "What else could I do?" ("Anyone else would have done the same." "Shucks; 'twarn't nothin'.") And in these instances we do not take the agent to be disavowing responsibility at all, but just declaring that being responsible under those conditions was not difficult.

Perhaps one reason we do not ask "Could he have done otherwise?" when trying to assess responsibility for good deeds and triumphs is that (thanks to our generosity of spirit) we give agents the benefit of the doubt when they have done well by us, rather than delving too scrupulously into facts of ultimate authorship. Such a charitable impulse may play a role, but there are better reasons, as we shall see. And we certainly do ask the question when an act is up for censure. But when we do, we never use the familiar question to inaugurate the sort of investigation that would actually shed light on the traditional philosophical issue the question has been presumed to raise. Instead we proceed to look around for evidence of what I call a pocket of *local fatalism*: a particular circumstance in the relevant portion of the past which ensured that the agent would not have done otherwise (during the stretch of local fatalism) *no matter what he had*

tried, or wanted, to do. A standard example of local fatalism is being locked in a room.[2]

If the agent was locked in a room (or in some other way had his will rendered impotent), then independently of the truth or falsity of determinism and no matter what sort of causation reigns within the agent's brain (or Cartesian soul, for that matter), we agree that "he could not have done otherwise." The readily determinable empirical fact that an agent was a victim of local fatalism terminates the inquiry into causation. (It does not always settle the issue of responsibility, however, as Harry Frankfurt shows[3]; under special circumstances an agent may still be held responsible.) And if our investigation fails to uncover any evidence of such local fatalism, this also terminates the inquiry. We consider the matter settled: the agent was responsible after all; "he could have done otherwise." Proving a negative existential is not generally regarded as a problem here. We can typically count on the agent himself to draw our attention to any evidence of local fatalism he is aware of (for if he can show that "his hands were tied" this will tend to exculpate him), so his failures to come forward with any such evidence is taken to be a reliable (but not foolproof) sign that the case is closed.

The first point I wish to make is that if the friends of CDO look to everyday practice for evidence for the contention that *ordinary people* "agree that a necessary condition for holding an agent responsible for an act is believing that the agent *could have* refrained from performing that act," they in fact will find no such support. When the act in question is up for praise, people manifestly ignore the question and would seem bizarre if they didn't. And when assessing an act for blame, although people do indeed ask "Could he have done otherwise?", they show no interest in pursuing that question beyond the point where they have satisfied their curiosity about the existence or absence of local fatalism—a phenomenon that is entirely neutral between determinism or indeterminism. For instance, people never withhold judgment about responsibility until after they have consulted physicists (or metaphysicians or neuroscientists) for their opinions about the ultimate status—deterministic or indeterministic—of the neural or mental events that governed the agent's behavior. And so far as I know, no defense attorney has ever gone into court to mount a defense based on an effort to establish, by expert testimony, that the accused was determined to make the decision that led to the dreadful act, and hence could not have done otherwise, and hence ("obviously") is not to be held responsible for it.

So the CDO principle is not something "everybody knows" even if most philosophers agree on it. The principle requires supporting argument. My second point is that any such supporting argument must challenge an abundance of utterly familiar evidence suggesting that often, when we seem to be interested in the question of whether the agent could have done otherwise, it is because we wish to draw the opposite conclusion about responsibility from that which the philosophical tradition endorses.

"Here I stand," Luther said. "I can do no other." Luther claimed that he could do no other, that his conscience made it *impossible* for him to recant. He might, of course, have been wrong, or have been deliberately overstating the truth, but even if he was—perhaps especially if he was—his declaration is testimony to the fact that we simply do not exempt someone from blame or praise for an act because we think he could do no other. Whatever Luther was doing, he was not trying to duck responsibility.

There are cases where the claim "I can do no other" is an avowal of frailty: suppose what I ought to do is get on the plane and fly to safety, but I stand rooted on the ground and confess I can do no other—because of my irrational and debilitating fear of flying. In such a case I can do no other, I claim, because my rational control faculty is impaired. This is indeed an excusing condition. But in other cases, like Luther's, when I say I cannot do otherwise I mean that I cannot because I see so clearly what the situation is and because my rational control faculty is *not* impaired. It is too obvious what to do; reason dictates it; I would have to be mad to do otherwise, and, since I happen not to be mad, I cannot do otherwise.

I hope it is true—and think it very likely is true—that it would be impossible to induce me to torture an innocent person by offering me a thousand dollars. "Ah"—comes the objection—"but what if some evil space pirates were holding the whole world ransom, and promised not to destroy the world if only you would torture an innocent person? Would that be something you would find impossible to do?" Probably not, but so what? That is a vastly different case. If what one is interested in is whether *under the specified circumstances* I could

have done otherwise, then the other case mentioned is utterly irrelevant. I claimed it would not be possible to induce me to torture someone *for a thousand dollars*. Those who hold the CDO principle dear are always insisting that we should look at whether one could have done otherwise in *exactly* the same circumstances. I claim something stronger; I claim that I could not do otherwise even in any roughly similar case. I would *never* agree to torture an innocent person for a thousand dollars. It would make no difference, I claim, what tone of voice the briber used, or whether I was tired and hungry, or whether the proposed victim was well illuminated or partially concealed in shadow. I am, I hope, immune to all such offers.

Now why would anyone's intuitions suggest that, if I am right, then if and when I ever have occasion to refuse such an offer, my refusal would not count as a responsible act? Perhaps this is what some people think: they think that if I were right when I claimed I could not do otherwise in such cases, I would be some sort of zombie, "programmed" always to refuse thousand-dollar bribes. A genuinely free agent, they think, must be more volatile somehow. If I am to be able to listen to reason, if I am to be flexible in the right way, they think, I mustn't be too dogmatic. Even in the most preposterous cases, then, I must be able to see that "there are two sides to every question." I must be able to pause, and weigh up the pros and cons of this suggested bit of lucrative torture. But the only way I could be constituted so that I can always "see both sides"—no matter how preposterous one side is—is by being constituted so that *in any particular case* "I could have done otherwise."

That would be fallacious reasoning. Seeing both sides of the question does not require that one not be overwhelmingly persuaded, in the end, by one side. The flexibility we want a responsible agent to have is the flexibility to recognize the one-in-a-zillion case in which, thanks to that thousand dollars, not otherwise obtainable, the world can be saved (or whatever). But the general capacity to respond flexibly in such cases does not at all require that one could have done otherwise in the particular case, or in any particular case, but only that under some variations in the circumstances— the variations that matter—one would do otherwise. Philosophers have often noted, uneasily, that the difficult moral problem cases, the decisions that "might go either way", are not the only, or even the most frequent, sorts of decisions for which we hold people responsible. They have seldom taken the hint to heart, however, and asked whether the CDO principle was simply wrong.

If our responsibility really did hinge, as this major philosophical tradition insists, on the question of whether we ever could do otherwise than we in fact do *in exactly those circumstances*, we would be faced with a most peculiar problem of ignorance: it would be unlikely in the extreme, given what now seems to be the case in physics, that anyone would ever know whether anyone has ever been responsible. For today's orthodoxy is that indeterminism reigns at the subatomic level of quantum mechanics; so, in the absence of any general and accepted argument for universal determinism, it is possible for all we know that our decisions and actions truly are the magnified, macroscopic effects of quantum-level indeterminacies occurring in our brains. But it is also possible for all we know that, even though indeterminism reigns in our brains at the subatomic quantum-mechanical level, our macroscopic decisions and acts are all themselves determined; the quantum effects could just as well be self-canceling, not amplified (as if by organic Geiger counters in the neurons). And it is extremely unlikely, given the complexity of the brain at even the molecular level (a complexity for which the word 'astronomical' is a vast understatement), that we could ever develop good evidence that any particular act was such a large-scale effect of a critical subatomic indeterminacy. So if someone's responsibility for an act did hinge on whether, at the moment of decision, that decision was (already) determined by a prior state of the world, then barring a triumphant return of universal determinism in microphysics (which would rule out all responsibility on this view), the odds are very heavy that we will never have *any* reason to believe of any particular act that it was or was not responsible. The critical difference would be utterly inscrutable from every macroscopic vantage point and practically inscrutable from the most sophisticated microphysical vantage point imaginable.

We have already seen that ordinary people, when interested in assigning responsibility, do not in fact pursue inquiries into whether their fellows could have done otherwise. Now we see a reason why they would be unwise to try: the sheer impossibility of conducting any meaningful investigation into the question—except in cases where macroscopic local fatalism is discovered. What then can people think they are doing when they ask the

CDO question in particular cases? Are they really asking the philosophers' metaphysical question about whether the agent was determined to do what he did, but just giving up as soon as the investigation gets difficult and the prospects get dim of striking a lucky negative answer (with the discovery of some local fatalism)? No, for there is a better question they can have been asking all along, a question that stops *for principled reasons* with the conclusion that local fatalism is ruled out (or in). It is better for two reasons: it is usually empirically answerable, and its answer matters. For not only is the traditional metaphysical question unanswerable; its answer, even if you knew it, would be useless.

What good would it do to know, about a particular agent, that on some occasion (or on every occasion) he could have done otherwise than he did? Or that he could not have done otherwise than he did? Let us take the latter case first. Suppose you knew (because God told you, presumably) that when Jones pulled the trigger and murdered his wife at time *t*, he could *not* have done otherwise. That is, given Jones's microstate at *t* and the complete microstate of Jones's environment (including the gravitational effects of distant stars, etc.) at *t*, no other Jones-trajectory was possible than the trajectory he took. If Jones were ever put back into exactly that state again, in exactly that circumstance, he would pull the trigger again—and if he were put in that state a million times, he would pull the trigger a million times.

Now if you learned this, would you have learned anything important about Jones? Would you have learned anything about his character, for instance, or his likely behavior on merely similar occasions? No. Although people are physical objects which, like atoms or ball bearings or bridges, obey the laws of physics, they are not only more complicated than anything else we know in the universe; they are also designed to be so sensitive to the passing show that they never can be in the same microstate twice. One doesn't even have to descend to the atomic level to establish this. People learn, and remember, and get bored, and shift their attention, and change their interests so incessantly, that it is as good as infinitely unlikely that any person is ever in the same (gross) *psychological* or *cognitive* state on two occasions. And this would be true even if we engineered the surrounding environment to be "utterly the same" on different occasions—if only because the second time around the agent would no doubt think something that went unthought the first time, like "Oh my, this all seems so utterly familiar; now what did I do last time?"

Learning (from God, again) that a particular agent was *not* thus determined to act would be learning something equally idle, from the point of view of character assessment or planning for the future. A genuinely undetermined agent is no more flexible, versatile, sensitive to nuances, or reformable than a deterministic near-duplicate would be.[4]

So if anyone at all is interested in the question of whether one could have done otherwise in *exactly* the same circumstances (and internal state) this will have to be a particularly pure metaphysical curiosity—that is to say, a curiosity so pure as to be utterly lacking in any ulterior motive, since the answer could not conceivably make any noticeable difference to the way the world went.

If it is unlikely that it matters whether a person could have done otherwise—when we look microscopically closely at the causation involved—what is the other question that we are (and should be) interested in when we ask "But could he have done otherwise"? Consider a similar question that might arise about a robot, destined (by hypothesis) to live its entire life as a deterministic machine on a deterministic planet. Even though this robot is, by hypothesis, completely deterministic, it can be controlled by "heuristic" programs that invoke "random" selection—of strategies, policies, weights, or whatever—at various points. All it needs is a pseudo-random number generator, either a preselected list or table of pseudo-random numbers to consult deterministically when the occasion demands or an algorithm that generates a pseudo-random sequence of digits. Either way it can have a sort of bingo-parlor machine for providing it with a patternless and arbitrary series of digits on which to pivot some of its activities.

Whatever this robot does, it could not have done otherwise, if we mean that in the strict and metaphysical sense of those words that philosophers have concentrated on. Suppose then that one fine Martian day it makes a regrettable mistake: it concocts and executes some scheme that destroys something valuable—another robot, perhaps. I am not supposing, for the moment, that *it* can regret anything, but just that its designers, back on Earth, regret what it has done and find themselves wondering a wonder that might natu-

rally be expressed: *Could it have done otherwise?* Let us suppose that they first satisfy themselves that no obvious local fatalism (locked room, dead battery) has afflicted their robot. But still they press their question: Could it have done otherwise? They know it is a deterministic system, of course; so they know better than to ask the metaphysical question. Their question concerns the design of the robot; for in the wake of this regrettable event they may wish to redesign it slightly, to make this *sort* of event less likely in the future.[5] What they want to know, of course, is what information the robot was relying on, what reasoning or planning it did, and whether it did "enough" of the right sort of reasoning or planning.

Of course in one sense of 'enough' they know the robot did not do enough of the right sort of reasoning; if it had, it would have done the right thing. But it may be that the robot's design in this case could not really be improved. For it may be that it was making optimal use of optimally designed heuristic procedures—but this time, unluckily, the heuristic chances it took didn't pay off. Put the robot in a *similar* situation in the future, and, thanks to no more than the fact that its pseudo-random number generator is in a different state, it will do something different; in fact it will usually do the right thing. It is tempting to add: it *could* have done the right thing on this occasion— meaning by this that it was well enough designed, at the time, to have done the right thing (its "character" is not impugned): its failure depended on nothing but the fact that something *undesigned* (and unanticipatable) happened to intervene in the process in a way that made an unfortunate difference.

A heuristic program is not guaranteed to yield the "right" or sought-after result. Some heuristic programs are better than others; when one fails, it may be possible to diagnose the failure as assignable to some characteristic weakness in its design, but even the best are not foolproof, and when they fail, as they sometimes must, there may be no *reason* at all for the failure; as Cole Porter would say, it was just one of those things.

Such failures are not the only cases of failures that will "count" for the designers as cases where the system "could have done otherwise." If they discover that the robot's failure, on this occasion, was due to a "freak" bit of dust that somehow drifted into a place where it could disrupt the system, they may decide that this was such an unlikely event that there is no call to redesign the system to guard against its recurrence.[6] They will note that, in the microparticular case (as always) their robot could not have done otherwise; moreover, if (by remotest possibility) it ever found itself in exactly the same circumstances again, it would fail again. But the designers will realize that they have no rational interest in doing anything to improve the design of the robot. It failed on the occasion, but its design is nevertheless above reproach. There is a difference between being optimally designed and being infallible.

Consider yet another sort of case. The robot has a ray gun that it fires with 99.9% accuracy. That is to say, sometimes, over long distances, it fails to hit the target it was aiming at. Whenever it misses, the engineers want to know something about the miss: was it due to some *systematic* error in the controls, some foible or flaw that will keep coming up, or was it just one of those things—one of those "acts of God" in which, in spite of an irreproachable execution of an optimally designed aiming routine, the thing just narrowly missed? There will always be such cases; the goal is to keep them to a minimum—consistent with cost-effectiveness, of course. Beyond a certain point it isn't worth caring about errors. W. V. Quine notes that engineers have a concept of more than passing philosophical interest: the concept of "don't-cares"—the cases one is rational to ignore.[7] When they are satisfied that a particular miss was a don't-care, they may shrug and say: "Well, it could have been a hit."

What concerns the engineers when they encounter misperformance in their robot is whether the misperformance is a telling one: Does it reveal something about a pattern of systematic weakness, likely to recur, or an inappropriate and inauspicious linking between sorts of circumstances and sorts of reactions? Is this *sort* of thing apt to happen again, or was it due to the coincidental convergence of fundamentally independent factors, highly unlikely to recur? So long as their robot is *not* misperforming but rather making the "right" decisions, the point in asking whether it could have done otherwise is to satisfy themselves that the felicitous behavior was not a fluke or mere coincidence but rather the outcome of good design. They hope that their robot, like Luther, will be imperturbable in its mission.

To get evidence about this they ignore the micro-details, which will never be the same again in any case, and just average over them, analyzing the robot into a finite array of *macro*scopically defined states, organized in such a way that there are links between the various degrees of freedom of the system. The question they can then ask is this: Are the links the right links for the task?

This rationale for ignoring micro-determinism (wherever it may "in principle" exist) and squinting just enough to blur such fine distinctions into probabilistically related states and regions that can be *treated as* homogeneous is clear, secure, and unproblematic in science, particularly in engineering and biology. That does not mean, of course, that this is also just the right way to think of people, when we are wondering whether they have acted responsibly. But there is a lot to be said for it.

Why do we ask "Could he have done otherwise"? We ask it because something has happened that we wish to interpret. An act has been performed, and we wish to understand how the act came about, why it came about, and what meaning we should attach to it. That is, we want to know what conclusions to draw from it about the future. Does it tell us anything about the agent's character, for instance? Does it suggest a criticism of the agent that might, if presented properly, lead the agent to improve his ways in some regard? Can we learn from this incident that this is or is not an agent who can be trusted to behave *similarly* on *similar* occasions in the future? If one held his character constant, but changed the circumstances in minor—even major—ways, would he almost always do the same lamentable sort of thing? Was what we observed a fluke, or was it a manifestation of a robust trend—a trend that persists, or is constant, over an interestingly wide variety of conditions?[8]

When the agent in question is oneself, this rationale is even more plainly visible. Suppose I find I have done something dreadful. *Who cares* whether, in exactly the circumstances and state of mind I found myself, I could have done something else? I didn't do something else, and it's too late to undo what I did. But when I go to interpret what I did, what do I learn about myself? Ought I to practice the sort of maneuver I botched, in hopes of making it more reliable, less vulnerable to perturbation, or would that be wasted effort? Would it be a good thing, so far as I can tell, for me to try to adjust my habits of thought in such sorts of cases in the future? Knowing that I will always be somewhat at the mercy of the considerations that merely happen to occur to me as time rushes on, knowing that I cannot entirely control this process of deliberation, I may take steps to bias the likelihood of certain sorts of considerations routinely "coming to mind" in certain critical situations. For instance, I might try to cultivate the habit of counting to ten in my mind before saying anything at all about Ronald Reagan, having learned that the deliberation time thus gained pays off handsomely in cutting down regrettable outbursts of intemperate commentary. Or I might decide that, no matter how engrossed in conversation I am, I must learn to ask myself how many glasses of wine I have had every time I see someone hovering hospitably near my glass with a bottle. This time I made a fool of myself; if the situation had been quite different, I certainly would have done otherwise; if the situation had been virtually the same, I might have done otherwise and I might not. The main thing is to see to it that I will jolly well do otherwise in (merely) similar situations in the future.

That, certainly, is the healthy attitude to take toward the regrettable parts of one's recent past. It is the self-applied version of the engineers' attitude toward the persisting weaknesses in the design of the robot. Of course, if I would rather find excuses than improve myself, I may dwell on the fact that I don't *have* to "take" responsibility for my action, since I can always imagine a more fine-grained standpoint from which my predicament looms larger than I do. (If you make yourself really small, you can externalize virtually everything.) But we wisely discourage this refuge in finer-grained visions of our embedding in the world, for much the same reason it is shunned by the engineers: what we might learn from such an investigation is never of any consequence. It simply does not matter whether one could have done otherwise.

It does not matter for the robot, someone may retort, because a robot could not *deserve* punishment or blame for its moments of malfeasance. For us it matters because we are candidates for blame and punishment, not mere redesign. You can't *blame* someone for something he did, if he could not have done otherwise. This, however, is just a reassertion of the CDO principle, not a new consideration, and I am denying that principle from the outset. Why indeed shouldn't you blame someone for doing something he could not have refrained from doing? After all, if he did it, what difference does it make that he was determined to do it?

"The difference is that if he was determined to do it, then he *had no chance not to do it*." But this is

simply a *non sequitur*, unless one espouses an extremely superstitious view of what a chance is. Compare the following two lotteries for fairness. In Lottery A, after all the tickets are sold, their stubs are placed in a suitable mixer, and, after suitable mixing (involving some genuinely—quantum-mechanically—random mixing if you like), the winning ticket is blindly drawn. In Lottery B, this mixing and drawing takes place *before* the tickets are sold, but otherwise the lotteries are conducted the same. Many people think the second lottery is unfair. It is unfair, they think, because the winning ticket is determined before people even buy their tickets; one of those tickets is *already* the winner; the other tickets are so much worthless paper, and selling them to unsuspecting people is a sort of fraud. But in fact, of course, the two lotteries are equally fair: *everyone has a chance of winning.* The timing of the selection of the winner is an utterly inessential feature. The reason the drawing in a lottery is typically postponed until after the sale of the tickets is to provide the public with first-hand eyewitness evidence that there have been no shenanigans. No sneaky agent with inside knowledge has manipulated the distribution of the tickets, because the knowledge of the winning ticket did not (and could not) exist in any agent until after the tickets were sold.

It is interesting that not all lotteries follow this practice. Publishers' Clearinghouse and Reader's Digest mail out millions of envelopes each year that say in bold letters on them "YOU MAY ALREADY HAVE WON"—a million dollars or some other prize. Surely these expensive campaigns are based on market research that shows that in general people do think lotteries with pre-selected winners are fair so long as they are honestly conducted. But perhaps people go along with these lotteries uncomplainingly because they get their tickets for free. Would many people *buy* a ticket in a lottery in which the winning stub, sealed in a special envelope, was known to be deposited in a bank vault from the outset? I suspect that most ordinary people would be untroubled by such an arrangement, and would consider themselves to have a real opportunity to win. I suspect, that is, that most ordinary people are less superstitious than those philosophers (going back to Democritus and Lucretius) who have convinced themselves that, without a continual supply of genuinely random *cruces* to break up the fabric of causation, there cannot be any real opportunities or chances.

If our world is determined, then we have pseudo-random number generators in us, not Geiger counter randomizers. That is to say, if our world is determined, all our lottery tickets were drawn at once, eons ago, put in an envelope for us, and doled out as we needed them through life. "But that isn't fair!" some say, "for some people will have been dealt more winners than others." Indeed, on any particular deal, some people have more high cards than others, but one should remember that the luck averages out. "But if all the drawings take place before we are born, some people are *destined* to get more luck than others!" But that will be true even if the drawings are held not before we are born, but periodically, on demand, throughout our lives.

Once again, it makes no difference—this time to fairness and, hence, to the question of desert—whether an agent's decision has been determined for eons (via a fateful lottery ticket lodged in his brain's decision-box, waiting to be used), or was indeterministically fixed by something like a quantum effect at, or just before, the moment of ultimate decision.

It is open to friends of the CDO principle to attempt to provide other grounds for allegiance to the principle, but since at this time I see nothing supporting that allegiance but the habit of allegiance itself, I am constrained to conclude that the principle should be dismissed as nothing better than a long-lived philosophical illusion. I may be wrong to conclude this, of course, but under the circumstances I cannot do otherwise.

Endnotes

[1] "The Incompatibility of Free Will and Determinism," *Philosophical Studies*, XXVII, 3 (March 1975): 185–99, p. 188; reprinted in Gary Watson, ed., *Free Will* (New York: Oxford, 1982): 46–58, p. 50.

[2] The misuse of this standard example—e.g., in the extrapolation to the theme that, if determinism is true, the whole world's a prison—is described in my *Elbow Room: The Varieties of Free Will Worth Wanting* (Cambridge, Mass.: Bradford/MIT Press, 1984), from which portions of the present argument are drawn.

[3] "Alternate Possibilities and Moral Responsibility," *Journal of Philosophy*, LXV, 23 (Dec. 4, 1969): 829–833.

[4] This is shown in "Designing the Perfect Deliberator," in *Elbow Room*, op. cit.

[5] "We are scarcely ever interested in the performance of a communication-engineering machine for a single input. To function adequately it must give a satisfactory performance for a whole class of inputs, and this means a statistically satisfactory performance for the class of inputs which it is statistically expected to receive." Norbert Wiener, *Cybernetics* (Cambridge, Mass.: Technology Press; New York: Wiley, 1948), p. 55.

[6] Strictly speaking, the recurrence of an event *of this general type*; there is no need to guard against the recurrence of the particular event (that is, logically impossible) or against the recurrence of an event of *exactly* the same type (that is, nomologically impossible).

[7] *Word and Object* (Cambridge, Mass.: MIT Press, 1960), pp. 182, 259.

[8] We are interested in trends and flukes in both directions (praiseworthy and regretted); if we had evidence that Luther was just kidding himself, that his apparently staunch stand was a sort of comic-opera coincidence, our sense of his moral strength would be severely diminished. "He's not so stalwart," we might say. "He could well have done otherwise."

Further Reading

Ayer, A. J. *Philosophical Essays*. London: Macmillan, 1954, Chapter 12.

Ayers, M. R. *The Refutation of Determinism*. London: Methuen, 1968.

Berofsky, B. *Freedom from Necessity: The Metaphysical Basis of Responsibility*. Boston: Routledge & Kegan Paul, 1989.

Berofsky, B., ed. *Free Will and Determinism*. Princeton, N.J.: Princeton University Press, 1972.

Craig, W. L. *The Only Wise God: The Compatibility of Divine Foreknowledge and Human Freedom*. Grand Rapids, Mich.: Baker Book House, 1987.

Dennett, D. *Elbow Room*. Cambridge, Mass.: MIT Press, 1984.

Dworkin, G., ed. *Determinism, Free Will, and Moral Responsibility*. Englewood Cliffs, N.J.: Prentice-Hall, 1970.

Fischer, J. M., ed. *Moral Responsibility*. Ithaca, N.Y.: Cornell University Press, 1986.

Forman, F. *The Metaphysics of Liberty*. Dordrecht: Klewer Academic Publishers, 1989.

Frankfurt, H. G. *The Importance of What We Care About: Philosophical Essays*. New York: Cambridge University Press, 1988.

Hampshire, S. *Freedom of the Individual*. New York: Harper & Row, 1965.

Honderich, T. *A Theory of Determinism*. Oxford: Clarendon Press, 1988.

Honderich, T., ed. *Essay on Freedom of Action*. London: Routledge & Kegan Paul, 1973.

Kane, R. *Free Will and Values*. New York: State University of New York Press, 1985.

Kenny, A. *Free Will and Responsibility*. Boston: Routledge & Kegan Paul, 1988.

Lehrer, K., ed. *Freedom and Determinism*. New York: Random House, 1966.

Morgenbesser, S., and Walsh, J. J., eds. *Free Will*. Englewood Cliffs, N.J.: Prentice-Hall, 1962.

Pike, N. *God and Timelessness*. New York: Schocken Books, 1970.

Salmon, W. *Scientific Explanation and the Causal Structure of the World*. Princeton, N.J.: Princeton University Press, 1984.

Taylor, R. *Action and Purpose*. Englewood Cliffs, N.J.: Prentice-Hall, 1960.

Thorton, M. *Do We Have Free Will?* New York: St. Martin's Press, 1989.

van Inwagen, P. *An Essay on Free Will*. Oxford: Oxford University Press, 1983.

Watson, G., ed. *Free Will*. Oxford: Oxford University Press, 1982.

Williams, B. *How Free Does the Will Need to Be?* Lawrence: University of Kansas Philosophy Department, 1986.

Williams, C. *Free Will and Determinism: A Dialogue*. Indianapolis: Hackett, 1980.

Zimmerman, M. *An Essay on Human Action*. New York: Peter Lang Publishing, 1984.

Part V

Knowing Reality

In the preceding chapters, philosophers have debated the nature or reality of: time, identity, mind, and freedom. Along the way, several other topics surfaced, for example, Platonic Forms (or universals), God, and causality. Metaphysics has such an ambitious scope—to provide general understanding of reality—that philosophers are bound to reflect on the enterprise itself. Is metaphysics possible? How should one try to achieve a general account of reality? When philosophers ask these questions, controversies pertaining to the nature of knowledge are bound to arise. In history, one can find many patterns of interaction among theories of knowledge and metaphysics: a philosopher, enthusiastic about some way of knowing, claims his or her method leads to a radically new view of reality; another is skeptical about this view, and that skepticism may undermine not only the radical view but also people's ordinary picture of reality; a third philosopher argues against skepticism and restores some legitimacy for at least an ordinary view of reality.

Though such patterns are oversimplifica-
tions, the writings in Part V consist of works
that reflect some such process at work.

Gottfried Leibniz is an example of an enthusiastic seventeenth-century rationalist
who proposed that reality is radically different from how it appears. He thought he could
prove, using just logic and a few self-evident
principles, that reality consists of an infinity
of indivisible souls arranged by God to constitute the best of all possible worlds. David
Hume raised skeptical doubts about rationalist metaphysics, doubts that were based on
his insistence that ideas should be analyzed
and justified in terms of sensory experience.
But Hume's skepticism not only deflated rationalistic metaphysics, it also suggested
that ordinary beliefs about enduring material
objects and persons were little more than unavoidable habits. Immanuel Kant then responded to Hume's challenge by arguing that
metaphysics might discover important necessary truths if it investigated the conditions
(the prerequisites) of experience. Kant conducted such a study and claimed to prove we
must perceive and think about reality in the
ways we ordinarily do. Though Kant denied
that people can have "transcendent" knowledge of "things-in-themselves," he thought
he had restored a priori confidence in the empirical reality of the ordinary world.

Early in the twentieth century, metaphysics underwent several crises. Some nineteenth-century philosophers attempted to
circumvent Kant's restriction of knowledge to
empirical reality by advocating a variety of
idealism; they saw reality as an aspect or
product of the mind. The selection by Hegel,
Chapter 48, reflects this tendency. Empirically minded philosophers viewed these systems with suspicion, but advances in science
itself generated more trouble for metaphysics.
The discovery that non-Euclidean geometries
are as consistent as Euclidean geometry, the

success of Einstein's theory of relativity, and
the counterintuitive claims of quantum mechanics all indicated Kant was wrong when
he claimed he had proven we must think
about reality in accordance with the a priori
propositions he had defended. Many philosophers adopted a stern form of empiricism,
called logical positivism, both to distance
themselves from nineteenth-century idealism
and to try to make sense out of the new scientific ideas. Central to their approach was the
use of the methods of symbolic logic to attempt to reduce controversial metaphysical
claims to propositions about language and
about what could be observed directly. The
selection by Rudolf Carnap is a strong
statement of this position. Other philosophers, though not accepting all the tenets of
logical positivism, came to agree that the
clarification of meaning and language was
very important. For some, metaphysics became the philosophy of language; for others,
the philosophy of language became the way
to try to dissolve metaphysical problems. Still
others, however, remained true to the spirit
of Hegel (see the Heidegger selection, Chapter 50).

By the 1960s, it was becoming clear that
the philosophy of language was no panacea.
Old metaphysical problems, assumptions,
and positions reappeared in philosophical
arguments about meaning and language.
And traditional metaphysical questions did
not go away—questions like How can the
solid brown table one sees really be a cloud of
invisible particles? The contemporary selections in Part V, all published after 1960, represent some recent *general* approaches to
metaphysics.

Wilfrid Sellars takes seriously the claim
that evolving science produces increasingly
better pictures of reality. So, ultimately, it is
science that decides what is real. Sellars believes the concepts one uses, including those

that interpret perceptual experience, are a product of the theories and languages one learns. Sellars does not believe there is any epistemological obstacle to accepting theoretical scientific entities as real, and he attempts to anticipate how beliefs about persons will be transformed in what he calls the scientific image of reality.

Sellars's metaphysics qualifies as optimistic in the sense that he sees science as converging to some definite picture of reality. It also qualifies as revisionary because he claims reality is quite different from how people ordinarily conceive it. By comparison, the selection by Willard Quine might seem skeptical. Though Quine is an advocate for science and approaches meaning from the perspective of a behaviorist, he maintains what one means— what one is talking or theorizing about—is, in an important way, indeterminate. Not only is meaning dependent on the language (or the-

ory) one is using, but it is always vulnerable to reinterpretation in some other language (or theory). Such "ontological relativity" suggests one should not attach too much metaphysical significance to any particular interpretation of one's language or theories.

Some readers may find Sellars's realism too stark, and some may find Quine's skepticism about meaning too opaque. Such readers will find comfort in the selection by Richard Rorty. Rorty is a pragmatist who believes most of our beliefs must be true and no language can be so different that one could not translate it into one's own. Though the title of his article is "The World Well Lost," the world Rorty is willing to lose is the remote world of the metaphysician—the one that may or may not correspond to alternative languages or conceptual schemes. Rorty is willing to lose that world so he can hold onto the ordinary world in which most of our beliefs are true.

45. *Monadology*

GOTTFRIED LEIBNIZ

Gottfried Leibniz (1646–1716) was a German philosopher who also had a distinguished career as a scientist, mathematician, and diplomat. He was an enthusiastic proponent of the view that reason can discover the nature of reality. He articulated a number of basic logical and metaphysical principles and used them to construct a comprehensive metaphysical system. The "Monadology" is a brief presentation of this system. In this work, he relies on such principles as composite substances consist of simple (noncomposite) substances and every fact must have a reason why it is so (the principle of "sufficient reason") to argue that reality consists of a multitude of more or less perceptive atoms (monads) that, though they do not interact, nevertheless are so created by God that they reflect the rest of the universe. The reader should be aware that Leibniz expounded his views in more detail in his other works and that he made lasting contributions to metaphysical topics not treated in the "Monadology." For example, he argued against the Newtonian view that space and time are absolute. The "Monadology" is an example of the rationalistic metaphysics that was criticized by Hume and Kant.

1. The *monad* of which we shall here speak is merely a simple substance, which enters into composites; *simple*, that is to say, without parts.

2. And there must be simple substances, since there are composites; for the composite is only a collection or *aggregatum* of simple substances.

3. Now where there are no parts, neither extension, nor figure, nor divisibility is possible. And these monads are the true atoms of nature, and, in a word, the elements of all things.

4. Their dissolution also is not at all to be feared, and there is no conceivable way in which a simple substance can perish naturally.

5. For the same reason there is no conceivable way in which a simple substance can begin naturally, since it cannot be formed by composition.

6. Thus it may be said that the monads can only begin or end all at once, that is to say, they can only begin by creation and end by annihilation; whereas that which is composite begins or ends by parts.

7. There is also no way of explaining how a monad can be altered or changed in its inner being by any other creature, for nothing can be transposed within it, nor can there be conceived in it any internal movement which can be excited, directed, augmented or diminished within it, as can be done in composites, where there is change among the parts. The monads have no windows through which anything can enter or depart. The accidents cannot detach themselves nor go about outside of substances, as did formerly the sensible species of the Schoolmen. Thus neither substance nor accident can enter a monad from outside.

8. Nevertheless, the monads must have some qualities, otherwise they would not even be entities. And if simple substances did not differ at all in their qualities there would be no way of perceiving any change in things, since what is in the compound can only come from the simple ingredients, and the monads, if they had no qualities, would be indistinguishable from one another, seeing also they do not differ in quantity. Consequently, a plenum being supposed, each place would always receive, in any motion, only the equivalent of what it had had before, and one state of things would be indistinguishable from another.

9. It is necessary, indeed, that each monad be different from every other. For there are never in nature two beings which are exactly alike and in which it is not possible to find an internal difference, or one founded upon an intrinsic quality.

10. I take it also for granted that every created being, and consequently the created monad also, is subject to change, and even that this change is continuous in each.

11. It follows from what has just been said, that the natural changes of the monads proceed from an *internal principle*, since an external cause could not influence their inner being.

12. But, besides the principle of change, there must be an individuating *detail of changes*, which forms, so to speak, the specification and variety of the simple substances.

13. This detail must involve a multitude in the unity or in that which is simple. For since every natural change takes place by degrees, something changes and something remains; and consequently, there must be in the simple substance a plurality of affections and of relations, although it has no parts.

14. The passing state, which involves and represents a multitude in unity or in the simple substance, is nothing else than what is called *perception*, which must be distinguished from apperception or consciousness, as will appear in what follows. Here it is that the Cartesians especially failed, having taken no account of the perceptions of which we are not conscious. It is this also which made them believe that spirits only are monads and that there are no souls of brutes or of other entelechies. They, with most people, have failed to distinguish between a prolonged state of unconsciousness and death strictly speaking, and have therefore agreed with the old scholastic prejudice of entirely separate souls, and have even confirmed ill-balanced minds in the belief in the mortality of the soul.

15. The action of the internal principle which causes the change or the passage from one perception to another, may be called *appetition*; it is true

that desire cannot always completely attain to the whole perception to which it tends, but it always attains something of it and reaches new perceptions.

16. We experience in ourselves a multiplicity in a simple substance, when we find that the most trifling thought of which we are conscious involves a variety in the object. Thus all those who admit that the soul is a simple substance ought to admit this multiplicity in the monad, and M. Bayle ought not to have found any difficulty in it, as he has done in his Dictionary, article *Rorarius*.

17. It must be confessed, moreover, that *perception* and that which depends on it *are inexplicable by mechanical causes*, that is, by figures and motions. And, supposing that there were a machine so constructed as to think, feel and have perception, we could conceive of it as enlarged and yet preserving the same proportions, so that we might enter it as into a mill. And this granted, we should only find on visiting it, pieces which push one against another, but never anything by which to explain a perception. This must be sought for, therefore, in the simple substance and not in the composite or in the machine. Furthermore, nothing but this (namely, perceptions and their changes) can be found in the simple substance. It is also in this alone that all the *internal activities* of simple substances can consist.

18. The name of *entelechies* might be given to all simple substances or created monads, for they have within themselves a certain perfection; there is a certain sufficiency which makes them the sources of their internal activities, and so to speak, incorporeal automata.

19. If we choose to give the name *soul* to everything that has *perceptions* and *desires* in the general sense which I have just explained, all simple substances or created monads may be called souls, but as feeling is something more than a simple perception, I am willing that the general name of monads or entelechies shall suffice for those simple substances which have only perception, and that those substances only shall be called *souls* whose perception is more distinct and is accompanied by memory.

20. For we experience in ourselves a state in which we remember nothing and have no distinguishable perception, as when we fall into a swoon

or when we are overpowered by a profound and dreamless sleep. In this state the soul does not differ sensibly from a simple monad; but as this state is not continuous and as the soul comes out of it, the soul is something more than a mere monad.

21. And it does not at all follow that in such a state the simple substance is without any perception. This is indeed impossible, for the reasons mentioned above; for it cannot perish, nor can it subsist without some affection, which is nothing else than its perception; but when there is a great number of minute perceptions, in which nothing is distinct, we are stunned; as when we turn continually in the same direction many times in succession, whence arises a dizziness which may make us swoon, and which does not let us distinguish anything. And death may produce for a time this condition in animals.

22. And as every present state of a simple substance is naturally the consequence of its preceding state, so its present is big with its future.

23. Therefore, since on being awakened from a stupor, we are *aware* of our perceptions, we must have had them immediately before, although we were not unconscious of them; for one perception can come in a natural way only from another perception, as a motion can come in a natural way only from a motion.

24. From this we see that if there were nothing distinct, nothing, so to speak, in relief and of a higher flavor in our perceptions, we should always be in a dazed state. This is the condition of simply bare monads.

25. We also see that nature has given to animals heightened perceptions, by the pains she has taken to furnish them with organs which collect many rays of light or many undulations of air, in order to render these more efficacious by uniting them. There is something of the same kind in odor, in taste, in touch and perhaps in a multitude of other senses which are unknown to us. And I shall presently explain how that which takes place in the soul represents that which occurs in the organs.

26. Memory furnishes souls with a sort of *consecutiveness* which imitates reason, but which ought to be distinguished from it. We observe that animals, having the perception of something which strikes them and of which they have had a similar perception before, expect, through the rep-

resentation in their memory, that which was associated with it in the preceeding perception, and experience feelings similar to those which they had had at that time. For instance, if we show dogs a stick, they remember the pain it has caused them and whine and run.

27. And the strong imagination which impresses and moves them, arises either from the magnitude or the multitude of preceding perceptions. For often a strong impression produces all at once the effect of a long-continued *habit*, or of many oft-repeated moderate perceptions.

28. Men act like the brutes, in so far as the association of their perceptions results from the principle of memory alone, resembling the empirical physicians who practice without theory; and we are simple empirics in three-fourths of our actions. For example, when we expect that there will be daylight to-morrow, we are acting as empirics, because that has up to this time always taken place. It is only the astronomer who judges of this by reason.

29. But the knowledge of necessary and eternal truths is what distinguishes us from mere animals and furnishes us with *reason* and the sciences, raising us to a knowledge of ourselves and of God. This is what we call the rational soul or *spirit* in us.

30. It is also by the knowledge of necessary truths, and by their abstractions, that we rise to *acts of reflection*, which make us think of that which calls itself "I", and to observe that this or that is within *us*; and it is thus that, in thinking of ourselves, we think of being, of substance, simple or composite, of the immaterial and of God himself, conceiving that what is limited in us is in him without limits. And these reflective acts furnish the principal objects of our reasonings.

31. Our reasonings are founded on *two great principles, that of contradiction,* in virtue of which we judge that to be *false* which involves contradiction, and that *true,* which is opposed or contradictory to the false.

32. And *that of sufficient reason,* in virtue of which we hold that no fact can be real or existent, no statement true, unless there be a sufficient reason why it is so and not otherwise, although most often these reasons cannot be known to us.

33. There are also two kinds of *truths*, those of *reasoning* and those of *fact*. Truths of reasoning are necessary and their opposite is impossible, and those of *fact* are contingent and their opposite is possible. When a truth is necessary its reason can be found by analysis, resolving it into more simple ideas and truths until we reach those which are primitive.

34. It is thus that mathematicians by analysis reduce speculative *theorems* and practical *canons* to *definitions*, *axioms* and *postulates*.

35. And there are finally simple ideas, definitions of which cannot be given; there are also axioms and postulates, in a word, *primary principles*, which cannot be proved, and indeed need no proof; and these are *identical propositions*, whose opposite involves an express contradiction.

36. But there must also be a *sufficient reason* for *contingent truths*, or those *of fact*—that is, for the sequence of things diffused through the universe of created objects—where the resolution into particular reasons might run into a detail without limits, on account of the immense variety of the things in nature and the division of bodies *ad infinitum*. There is an infinity of figures and of movements, present and past, which enter into the efficient cause of my present writing, and there is an infinity of slight inclinations and dispositions, past and present, of my soul, which enter into the final cause.

37. And as all this *detail* only involves other contingents, anterior or more detailed, each one of which needs a like analysis for its explanation, we make no advance: and the sufficient or final reason must be outside of the sequence or *series* of this detail of contingencies, however infinite it may be.

38. And thus it is that the final reason of things must be found in a necessary substance, in which the detail of changes exists only eminently, as in their source; and this is what we call God.

39. Now this substance, being a sufficient reason of all this detail, which also is linked together throughout, *there is but one God, and this God is sufficient*.

40. We may also conclude that his supreme substance, which is unique, universal and necessary, having nothing outside of itself which is independent of it, and being a pure consequence of possible being, must be incapable of limitations and must contain as much of reality as is possible.

41. Whence it follows that God is absolutely perfect, *perfection* being only the magnitude of positive reality taken in its strictest meaning, setting aside the limits or bounds in things which have them. And where there are no limits, that is, in God, perfection is absolutely infinite.

42. It follows also that the creatures have their perfections from the influence of God, but that their imperfections arise from their own nature, incapable of existing without limits. For it is by this that they are distinguished from God.

43. It is also true that in God is the source not only of existences but also of essences, so far as they are real, or of that which is real in the possible. This is because the understanding of God is the region of eternal truths, or of the ideas on which they depend, and because, without him, there would be nothing real in the possibilities, and not only nothing existing but also nothing possible.

44. For, if there is a reality in essences or possibilities or indeed in the eternal truths, this reality must be founded in something existing and actual, and consequently in the existence of the necessary being, in whom essence involves existence, or with whom it is sufficient to be possible in order to be actual.

45. Hence God alone (or the necessary being) has this prerogative, that he must exist if he is possible. And since nothing can hinder the possibility of that which possesses no limitations, no negation, and consequently, no contradiction, this alone is sufficient to establish the existence of God *a priori*. We have also proved it by the reality of the eternal truths. But we have a little while ago proved it also *a posteriori*, since contingent beings exist, which can only have their final or sufficient reason in a necessary being who has the reason of his existence in himself.

46. Yet we must not imagine, as some do, that the eternal truths, being dependent upon God, are arbitrary and depend upon his will, as Descartes seems to have held, and afterwards M. Poiret. This is true only of contingent truths, the principle of which is *fitness* or the choice of the *best*, whereas necessary truths depend solely on his understanding and are its internal object.

47. Thus God alone is the primitive unity or the original simple substance; of which all created or derived monads are the products, and are generated, so to speak, by continual fulgurations of the Divinity, from moment to moment, limited by the receptivity of the creature, to whom limitation is essential.

48. In God is *Power*, which is the source of all; then *Knowledge*, which contains the detail of ideas; and finally *Will*, which effects changes or products according to the principle of the best. These correspond to what in created monads form the subject or basis, the perceptive faculty, and the appetitive faculty. But in God these attributes are absolutely infinite or perfect; and in the created monads or in the *entelechies*, they are only imitations proportioned to the perfection of the monads.

49. The creature is said to *act* externally in so far as it has perfection, and to be *acted on* by another in so far as it is imperfect. Thus *action* is attributed to the monad in so far as it has distinct perceptions, and *passivity* in so far as it has confused perceptions.

50. And one creature is more perfect than another, in this that there is found in it that which serves to account *a priori* for what takes place in the other, and it is in this way that it is said to act upon the other.

51. But in simple substances the influence of one monad upon another is purely *ideal* and can have its effect only through the intervention of God, inasmuch as in the ideas of God a monad may demand with reason that God in regulating the others from the commencement of things, have regard to it. For since a created monad can have no physical influence upon the inner being of another, it is only in this way that one can be dependent upon another.

52. And hence it is that the actions and passive reactions of creatures are mutual. For God, in comparing two simple substances, finds in each one reasons which compel him to adjust the other to it, and consequently that which in certain respects is active, is according to another point of view, passive; *active* in so far as that what is known distinctly in it, serves to account for that which takes place in another; and *passive* in so far as the reason for what takes place in it, is found in that which is distinctly known in another.

53. Now, as there is an infinity of possible universes in the ideas of God, and as only one of them can exist, there must be a sufficient reason for the choice of God, which determines him to select one rather than another.

54. And this reason can only be found in the *fitness*, or in the degrees of perfection, which these worlds contain, each possible world having a right to claim existence according to the measure of perfection which it possesses.

55. And this is the cause of the existence of the Best; namely, that his wisdom makes it known to God, his goodness makes him choose it, and his power makes him produce it.

56. Now this *connection*, or this adaptation, of all created things to each and of each to all, brings it about that each simple substance has relations which express all the others, and that, consequently, it is a perpetual living mirror of the universe.

57. And as the same city looked at from different sides appears entirely different, and is as if multiplied *perspectively*; so also it happens that, as a result of the infinite multitude of simple substances, there are as it were so many different universes, which are nevertheless only the perspectives of a single one, according to the different *points of view* of each monad.

58. And this is the way to obtain as great a variety as possible, but with the greatest possible order; that is, it is the way to obtain as much perfection as possible.

59. Moreover, this hypothesis (which I dare to call demonstrated) is the only one which brings into relief the grandeur of God. M. Bayle recognized this, when in his Dictionary (article *Rorarius*) he raised objections to it; in which indeed he was disposed to think that I attributed too much to God and more than is possible. But he can state no reason why this universal harmony, which brings it about that each substance expresses exactly all the others, through the relations which it has to them, is impossible.

60. Besides, we can see, in what I have just said, the *a priori* reasons why things could not be otherwise than they are. Because God, in regulating all, has had regard to each part, and particularly to each monad, whose nature being representative, nothing can limit it to representing only a part of things; although it may be true that this representation is but confused as regards the detail of the whole universe, and can be distinct only in the case of a small part of things, that is to say, in the case of those which are nearest or greatest in relation to each of the monads; otherwise each monad would be a divinity. It is not as regards the object but only as regards the modification of the knowledge of the object, that monads are limited. They all tend confusedly toward the infinite, toward the whole; but they are limited and differentiated by the degrees of their distinct perceptions.

61. And composite substances are analogous in this respect with simple substances. For since the world is a *plenum*, rendering all matter connected, and since in a plenum every motion has some effect on distant bodies in proportion to their distance, so that each body is affected not only by those in contact with it, and feels in some way all that happens to them, but also by their means is affected by those which are in contact with the former, with which it itself is in immediate contact, it follows that this intercommunication extends to any distance whatever. And consequently, each body feels all that happens in the universe, so that he who sees all, might read in each that which happens everywhere, and even that which has been or shall be, discovering in the present that which is removed in time as well as in space; . . . . But a soul can read in itself only that which is distinctly represented in it. It cannot develop its laws all at once, for they reach into the infinite.

62. Thus, although each created monad represents the entire universe, it represents more distinctly the body which is particularly attached to it, and of which it forms the entelechy; and as this body expresses the whole universe through the connection of all matter in a plenum, the soul also represents the whole universe in representing this body, which belongs to it in a particular way.

63. The body belonging to a monad, which is its entelechy or soul, constitutes together with the entelechy what may be called a *living being*, and together with the soul what may be called an *animal*. Now this body of a living being or of an animal is always organic, for since every monad is in its way a mirror of the universe, and since the universe is regulated in a perfect order, there must also be an order in the representative, that is, in the

perceptions of the soul, and hence in the body, through which the universe is represented in the soul.

64. Thus each organic body of a living being is a kind of divine machine or natural automaton, which infinitely surpasses all artificial automata. Because a machine which is made by man's art is not a machine in each one of its parts; for example, the teeth of a brass wheel have parts or fragments which to us are no longer artificial and have nothing in themselves to show the special use to which the wheel was intended in the machine. But nature's machines, that is, living bodies, are machines even in their smallest parts *ad infinitum*. Herein lies the difference between nature and art, that is, between the divine art and ours.

65. And the author of nature has been able to employ this divine and infinitely marvellous artifice, because each portion of matter is not only divisible *ad infinitum*, as the ancients recognized, but also each part is actually endlessly subdivided into parts, of which each has some motion of its own: otherwise it would be impossible for each portion of matter to express the whole universe.

66. Whence we see that there is a world of creatures, of living beings, of animals, of entelechies, of souls, in the smallest particle of matter.

67. Each portion of matter may be conceived of as a garden full of plants, and as a pond full of fishes. But each branch of the plant, each member of the animal, each drop of its humors is also such a garden or such a pond.

68. And although the earth and air which lies between the plants of the garden, or the water between the fish of the pond, is neither plant nor fish, they yet contain more of them, but for the most part so tiny as to be imperceptible to us.

69. Therefore there is nothing fallow, nothing sterile, nothing dead in the universe, no chaos, no confusion except in appearance; somewhat as a pond would appear from a distance, in which we might see the confused movement and swarming, so to speak, of the fishes in the pond, without discerning the fish themselves.

70. We see thus that each living body has a ruling entelechy, which in the animal is the soul; but the members of this living body are full of other living beings, plants, animals, each of which has also its entelechy or governing soul.

71. But it must not be imagined, as has been done by some people who have misunderstood my thought, that each soul has a mass or portion of matter belonging to it or attached to it forever, and that consequently it possesses other inferior living beings, destined to its service forever. For all bodies are, like rivers, in a perpetual flux, and parts are entering into them and departing from them continually.

72. Thus the soul changes its body only gradually and by degrees, so that it is never deprived of all its organs at once. There is often a metamorphosis in animals, but never metempsychosis nor transmigration of souls. There are also no entirely *separate* souls, nor *genii* without bodies. God alone is wholly without body.

73. For which reason also, it happens that there is, strictly speaking, neither absolute birth nor complete death, consisting in the separation of the soul from the body. What we call *birth* is envelopment and diminution.

74. Philosophers have been greatly puzzled over the origin of forms, entelechies, or souls; but to-day, when we know by exact investigations upon plants, insects and animals, that the organic bodies of nature are never products of chaos or putrefaction, but always come from seeds, in which there was undoubtedly some *pre-formation*, it has been thought that not only the organic body was already there before conception, but also a soul in this body, and, in a word, the animal itself; and that by means of conception this animal has merely been prepared for a great transformation, in order to become an animal of another kind. Something similar is seen outside of birth, as when worms become flies, and caterpillars become butterflies.

75. The *animals*, some of which are raised by conception to the grade of larger animals, may be called *spermatic*; but those among them, which remain in their class, that is, the most part, are born, multiply, and are destroyed like the large animals, and it is only a small number of chosen ones which pass to a larger theatre.

76. But this is only half the truth. I have, therefore, held that if the animal never commences by natural means, neither does it end by natural means; and that not only will there be no birth, but also no utter destruction or death, strictly speaking. And these reasonings, made *a posteriori* and drawn from experience, harmonize perfectly with my principles deduced *a priori*, as above.

77. Thus it may be said that not only the soul (mirror of an indestructible universe) is indestructible, but also the animal itself, although its mechanism often perishes in part and takes on or puts off organic coatings.

78. These principles have given me the means of explaining naturally the union or rather the conformity of the soul and the organic body. The soul follows its own peculiar laws and the body also follows its own laws, and they agree in virtue of the *pre-established harmony* between all substances, since they are all representations of one and the same universe.

79. Souls act according to the laws of final causes, by appetitions, ends and means. Bodies act in accordance with the laws of efficient causes or of motion. And the two realms, that of efficient causes and that of final causes, are in harmony with each other.

80. Descartes recognized that souls cannot impart any force to bodies, because there is always the same quantity of force in matter. Nevertheless he believed that the soul could change the direction of bodies. But this was because, in his day, the law of nature which affirms also the conservation of the same total direction in matter, was not known. If he had known this, he would have lighted upon my system of pre-established harmony.

81. According to this system, bodies act as if (what is impossible) there were no souls, and that souls act as if there were no bodies, and that both act as if each influenced the other.

82. As to *spirits* or rational souls, although I find that the same thing which I have stated (namely, that animals and souls begin only with the world and end only with the world) holds good at bottom with regard to all living beings and animals, yet there is this peculiarity in rational animals, that their spermatic animalcules, as long as they remain such, have only ordinary or sensitive souls; but as soon as those which are, so to speak, elected, attain by actual conception to human nature, their sensitive souls are elevated to the rank of reason and to the prerogative of spirits.

83. Among other differences which exist between ordinary souls and minds, some of which I have already mentioned, there is also, this, that souls in general are the living mirrors or images of the universe of creatures, but minds or spirits are in addition images of the Divinity itself, or of the author of nature, able to know the system of the universe and to imitate something of it by architectonic samples, each mind being like a little divinity in its own department.

84. Hence it is that spirits are capable of entering into a sort of society with God, and that he is, in relation to them, not only what an inventor is to his machine (as God is in relation to other creatures), but also what a prince is to his subjects, and even a father to his children.

85. Whence it is easy to conclude that the assembly of all spirits must compose the City of God, that is, the most perfect state which is possible, under the most perfect of monarchs.

86. This City of God, this truly universal monarchy, is a moral world within the natural world, and the highest and most divine of the works of God; it is in this that the glory of God truly consists, for he would have none if his greatness and goodness were not known and admired by spirits. It is, too, in relation to this divine city that he properly has goodness; whereas his wisdom and his power are everywhere manifest.

87. As we have above established a perfect harmony between two natural kingdoms, the one of efficient, the other of final causes, we should also notice here another harmony between the physical kingdom of nature and the moral kingdom of grace; that is, between God considered as the architect of the mechanism of the universe and God considered as monarch of the divine city of spirits.

88. This harmony makes things progress toward grace by natural means. This globe, for example, must be destroyed and repaired by natural means, at such times as the government of spirits may demand it, for the punishment of some and the reward of others.

89. It may be said, farther, that God as architect satisfies in every respect God as legislator, and that therefore sins, by the order of nature and perforce even of the mechanical structure of things, must carry their punishment with them; and that in the same way, good actions will obtain their rewards by mechanical ways through their relations to bodies, although this cannot and ought not always happen immediately.

90. Finally, under this perfect government, there will be no good action unrewarded, no bad action unpunished; and everything must result in the well-being of the good, that is, of those who are not disaffected in this great State, who, after having done their duty, trust in providence, and who love and imitate, as is meet, the author of all good, finding pleasure in the contemplation of his perfections, according to the nature of truly *pure love*, which takes pleasure in the happiness of the beloved. This is what causes wise and virtuous persons to work for all which seems in harmony with the divine will, presumptive or antecedent, and nevertheless to content themselves with that which God in reality brings to pass by his secret, consequent and decisive will, recognizing that if we could sufficiently understand the order of the universe, we should find that it surpasses all the wishes of the wisest, and that it is impossible to render it better than it is, not only for all in general, but also for ourselves in particular, if we are attached, as we should be, to the author of all, not only as to the architect and efficient cause of our being, but also as to our master and final cause, who ought to be the whole aim of our will, and who, alone, can make our happiness.

46. *An Enquiry Concerning Human Understanding*

DAVID HUME

David Hume (1711–1776) was a Scottish philosopher who was impressed by the success of Newtonian science and who wanted to apply its methods to the study of psychology and the "moral" sciences. As Newton presented his experimental method, he claimed to be against postulating unobservable causes of phenomena; for example, he claimed to discover only the equation for gravity, not its cause. Hume believed all ideas consist of copies of sense impressions, so he analyzed metaphysical ideas (like causality, substance, and God) in terms of sensory experience. Hume also believed the only way to know truths that are not just definitions or truths of logic is by means of perceptual experience. He claimed the analysis of metaphysical ideas and the examination of the adequacy of perceptual support for metaphysical beliefs would lead to skepticism about metaphysics.

. . . [O]bscurity in the profound and abstract philosophy, is objected to, not only as painful and fatiguing, but as the inevitable source of uncertainty and error. Here indeed lies the justest and most plausible objection against a considerable part of metaphysics, that they are not properly a science; but arise either from the fruitless efforts of human vanity, which would penetrate into subjects utterly inaccessible to the understanding, or from the craft of popular superstitions, which, being unable to defend themselves on fair ground, raise these entangling brambles to cover and protect their weakness. Chased from the open country, these robbers fly into the forest, and lie in wait to break in upon every unguarded avenue of the mind, and overwhelm it with religious fears and prejudices. The stoutest antagonist, if he remit his watch a moment, is oppressed. And many, through cowardice and folly, open the gates to the enemies, and willingly receive them with reverence and submission, as their legal sovereigns.

But is this a sufficient reason, why philosophers should desist from such researches, and leave superstition still in possession of her retreat?

Is it not proper to draw an opposite conclusion, and perceive the necessity of carrying the war into the most secret recesses of the enemy? In vain do we hope, that men, from frequent disappointment, will at last abandon such airy sciences, and discover the proper province of human reason. For, besides, that many persons find too sensible an interest in perpetually recalling such topics; besides this, I say, the motive of blind despair can never reasonably have place in the sciences; since, however unsuccessful former attempts may have proved, there is still room to hope, that the industry, good fortune, or improved sagacity of succeeding generations may reach discoveries unknown to former ages. Each adventurous genius will still leap at the arduous prize, and find himself stimulated, rather than discouraged, by the failures of his predecessors; while he hopes that the glory of achieving so hard an adventure is reserved for him alone. The only method of freeing learning, at once, from these abstruse questions, is to enquire seriously into the nature of human understanding, and show, from an exact analysis of its powers and capacity, that it is by no means fitted for such remote and abstruse subjects. We must submit to this fatigue, in order to live at ease ever after: And must cultivate true metaphysics with some care, in order to destroy the false and adulterate. . . .

From Hume's *Enquiry Concerning Human Understanding*, first published in 1748.

Of the Origin of Ideas

Everyone will readily allow that there is a considerable difference between the perceptions of the mind when a man feels the pain of excessive heat or the pleasure of moderate warmth, and when he afterwards recalls to his memory this sensation or anticipates it by his imagination. These faculties may mimic or copy the perceptions of the senses, but they never can entirely reach the force and vivacity of the original sentiment. The utmost we say of them, even when they operate with greatest vigor, is that they represent their object in so lively a manner that we could *almost* say we feel or see it. . . .

Here, therefore, we may divide all the perceptions of the mind into two classes or species, which are distinguished by their different degrees of force and vivacity. The less forcible and lively are commonly denominated "thoughts" or "ideas." The other species want a name in our language, and in most others; I suppose, because it was not requisite for any but philosophical purposes to rank them under a general term or appellation. Let us, therefore, use a little freedom and call them "impressions," employing that word in a sense somewhat different from the usual. By the term "impression," then, I mean all our more lively perceptions, when we hear, or see, or feel, or love, or hate, or desire, or will. And impressions are distinguished from ideas, which are the less lively perceptions of which we are conscious when we reflect on any of those sensations or movements above mentioned.

Nothing, at first view, may seem more unbounded than the thought of man, which not only escapes all human power and authority, but is not even restrained within the limits of nature and reality. To form monsters and join incongruous shapes and appearances costs the imagination no more trouble than to conceive the most natural and familiar objects. And while the body is confined to one planet, along which it creeps with pain and difficulty, the thought can in an instant transport us into the most distant regions of the universe, or even beyond the universe into the unbounded chaos where nature is supposed to lie in total confusion. What never was seen or heard of, may yet be conceived, nor is anything beyond the power of thought except what implies an absolute contradiction.

But though our thought seems to possess this unbounded liberty, we shall find upon a nearer examination that it is really confined within very narrow limits, and that all this creative power of the mind amounts to no more than the faculty of compounding, transposing, augmenting, or diminishing the materials afforded us by the senses and experience. When we think of a golden mountain, we only join two consistent ideas, "gold" and "mountain," with which we were formerly acquainted. A virtuous horse we can conceive, because, from our own feeling, we can conceive virtue; and this we may unite to the figure and shape of a horse, which is an animal familiar to us. In short, all the materials of thinking are derived either from our outward or inward sentiment; the mixture and composition of these belongs alone to the mind and will, or, to express myself in philosophical language, all our ideas or more feeble perceptions are copies of our impressions or more lively ones.

To prove this, the two following arguments will, I hope, be sufficient. *First*, when we analyze our thoughts or ideas, however compounded or sublime, we always find that they resolve themselves into such simple ideas as were copied from a precedent feeling or sentiment. Even those ideas which at first view seem the most wide of this origin are found, upon a nearer scrutiny, to be derived from it. The idea of God, as meaning an infinitely intelligent, wise, and good Being, arises from reflecting on the operations of our own mind and augmenting, without limit, those qualities of goodness and wisdom. We may prosecute this inquiry to what length we please; where we shall always find that every idea which we examine is copied from a similar impression. Those who would assert that this position is not universally true, nor without exception, have only one, and that an easy, method of refuting it by producing that idea which, in their opinion, is not derived from this source. It will then be incumbent on us, if we would maintain our doctrine, to produce the impression or lively perception which corresponds to it.

Secondly, if it happen, from a defect of the organ, that a man is not susceptible of any species of sensation, we always find that he is as little susceptible of the correspondent idea. A blind man can form no notion of colors, a deaf man of sounds. Restore either of them that sense in which he is deficient by opening this new inlet for his sensations, you also open an inlet for the ideas, and he finds no difficulty in conceiving these objects. The case is the same if the object proper for exciting any sensation has never been applied to the organ. A Laplander . . . has no notion of the relish of wine. And though there are few or no instances of a like deficiency in the mind where a person has never felt or is wholly incapable of a sentiment or passion that belongs to his species, yet we find the same observation to take place in a less degree. A man of mild manners can form no idea of inveterate revenge or cruelty, nor can a selfish heart easily conceive the heights of friendship and generosity. It is readily allowed that other beings may possess many senses of which we can have no conception, because the ideas of them have never been introduced to us in the only manner by which an idea can have access to the mind, to wit, by the actual feeling and sensation. . . .

Here, therefore, is a proposition which not only seems in itself simple and intelligible, but, if a proper use were made of it, might render every dispute equally intelligible, and banish all that jargon which has so long taken possession of metaphysical reasonings and drawn disgrace upon them. All ideas, especially abstract ones, are naturally faint and obscure. The mind has but a slender hold of them. They are apt to be confounded with other resembling ideas; and when we have often employed any term, though without a distinct meaning, we are apt to imagine it has a determinate idea annexed to it. On the contrary, all impressions, that is, all sensations either outward or inward, are strong and vivid. The limits between them are more exactly determined, nor is it easy to fall into any error or mistake with regard to them. When we entertain, therefore, any suspicion that a philosophical term is employed without any meaning or idea (as is but too frequent), we need but inquire, *from what impression is that supposed idea derived?* And if it be impossible to assign any, this will serve to confirm our suspicion. By bringing ideas in so clear a light, we may reasonably hope to remove all dispute which may arise concerning their nature and reality.[1]

Skeptical Doubts Concerning the Operations of the Understanding

Part I

All the objects of human reason or inquiry may naturally be divided into two kinds, to wit, "Rela-

tions of Ideas," and "Matters of Fact." Of the first kind are the sciences of Geometry, Algebra, and Arithmetic, and, in short, every affirmation which is either intuitively or demonstratively certain. *That the square of the hypotenuse is equal to the square of the two sides* is a proposition which expresses a relation between these figures. *That three times five is equal to the half of thirty* expresses a relation between these numbers. Propositions of this kind are discoverable by the mere operation of thought, without dependence on what is anywhere existent in the universe. Though there never were a circle or triangle in nature, the truths demonstrated by Euclid would forever retain their certainty and evidence.

Matters of fact, which are the second objects of human reason, are not ascertained in the same manner, nor is our evidence of their truth, however great, of a like nature with the foregoing. The contrary of every matter of fact is still possible, because it can never imply a contradiction and is conceived by the mind with the same facility and distinctness as if ever so conformable to reality. *That the sun will not rise tomorrow* is no less intelligible a proposition and implies no more contradiction than the affirmation *that it will rise.* We should in vain, therefore, attempt to demonstrate its falsehood. Were it demonstratively false, it would imply a contradiction and could never be distinctly conceived by the mind.

It may, therefore, be a subject worthy of curiosity to inquire what is the nature of that evidence which assures us of any real existence and matter of fact beyond the present testimony of our senses or the records of our memory. This part of philosophy, it is observable, had been little cultivated either by the ancients or moderns; and, therefore, our doubts and errors in the prosecution of so important an inquiry may be the more excusable while we march through such difficult paths without any guide or direction. They may even prove useful by exciting curiosity and destroying that implicit faith and security which is the bane of all reasoning and free inquiry. The discovery of defects in the common philosophy, if any such there be, will not, I presume, be a discouragement, but rather an incitement, as is usual, to attempt something more full and satisfactory than has yet been proposed to the public.

All reasonings concerning matter of fact seem to be founded on the relation of *cause* and *effect*. By means of that relation alone we can go beyond the evidence of our memory and senses. If you were to ask a man why he believes any matter of fact which is absent, for instance, that his friend is in the country or in France, he would give you a reason, and this reason would be some other fact: as a letter received from him or the knowledge of his former resolutions and promises. A man finding a watch or any other machine in a desert island would conclude that there had once been men in that island. All our reasonings concerning fact are of the same nature. And here it is constantly supposed that there is a connection between the present fact and that which is inferred from it. Were there nothing to bind them together, the inference would be entirely precarious. The hearing of an articulate voice and rational discourse in the dark assures us of the presence of some person. Why? Because these are the effects of the human make and fabric, and closely connected with it. If we anatomize all the other reasonings of this nature, we shall find that they are founded on the relation of cause and effect, and that this relation is either near or remote, direct or collateral. Heat and light are collateral effects of fire, and the one effect may justly be inferred from the other.

If we would satisfy ourselves, therefore, concerning the nature of that evidence which assures us of matters of fact, we must inquire how we arrive at the knowledge of cause and effect.

I shall venture to affirm, as a general proposition which admits of no exception, that the knowledge of this relation is not, in any instance, attained by reasonings *a priori*, but arises entirely from experience, when we find that any particular objects are constantly conjoined with each other. Let an object be presented to a man of ever so strong natural reason and abilities—if that object be entirely new to him, he will not be able, by the most accurate examination of its sensible qualities, to discover any of its causes or effects. Adam, though his rational faculties be supposed, at the very first, entirely perfect, could not have inferred from the fluidity and transparency of water that it would suffocate him, or from the light and warmth of fire that it would consume him. No object ever discovers, by the qualities which appear to the senses, either the causes which produced it or the effects which will arise from it; nor can our reason, unassisted by experience, ever draw any inference concerning real existence and matter of fact.

This proposition, *that causes and effects are discoverable, not by reason, but by experience*, will readily be admitted with regard to such objects as we remember to have once been altogether unknown to us, since we must be conscious of the utter inability

which we then lay under of foretelling what would arise from them. Present two smooth pieces of marble to a man who has no tincture of natural philosophy; he will never discover that they will adhere together in such a manner as to require great force to separate them in a direct line, while they make so small a resistance to a lateral pressure. Such events as bear little analogy to the common course of nature are also readily confessed to be known only by experience, nor does any man imagine that the explosion of gunpowder or the attraction of a loadstone could ever be discovered by arguments *a priori*. In like manner, when an effect is supposed to depend upon an intricate machinery or secret structure of parts, we make no difficulty in attributing all our knowledge of it to experience. Who will assert that he can give the ultimate reason why milk or bread is proper nourishment for a man, not for a lion or tiger?

But the same truth may not appear at first sight to have the same evidence with regard to events which have become familiar to us from our first appearance in the world, which bear a close analogy to the whole course of nature, and which are supposed to depend on the simple qualities of objects without any secret structure of parts. We are apt to imagine that we could discover these effects by the mere operation of our reason without experience. We fancy that, were we brought on a sudden into this world, we could at first have inferred that one billiard ball would communicate motion to another upon impulse, and that we needed not to have waited for the event in order to pronounce with certainty concerning it. Such is the influence of custom that where it is strongest it not only covers our natural ignorance but even conceals itself, and seems not to take place, merely because it is found in the highest degree.

But to convince us that all the laws of nature and all the operations of bodies without exception are known only by experience, the following reflections may perhaps suffice. Were any object presented to us, and were we required to pronounce concerning the effect which will result from it without consulting past observation, after what manner, I beseech you, must the mind proceed in this operation? It must invent or imagine some event which it ascribes to the object as its effect; and it is plain that this invention must be entirely arbitrary. The mind can never possibly find the effect in the supposed cause by the most accurate scrutiny and examination. For the effect is totally different from the cause, and consequently can never be discovered in it. Motion in the second billiard ball is a distinct event from motion in the first, nor is there anything in the one to suggest the smallest hint of the other. A stone or piece of metal raised into the air and left without any support immediately falls. But to consider the matter *a priori*, is there anything we discover in this situation which can beget the idea of a downward rather than an upward or any other motion in the stone or metal?

And as the first imagination or invention of a particular effect in all natural operations is arbitrary where we consult not experience, so must we also esteem the supposed tie or connection between the cause and effect which binds them together and renders it impossible that any other effect could result from the operation of that cause. When I see, for instance, a billiard ball moving in a straight line toward another, even suppose motion in the second ball should by accident be suggested to me as the result of their contact or impulse, may I not conceive that a hundred different events might as well follow from that cause? May not both these balls remain at absolute rest? May not the first ball return in a straight line or leap off the second in any line or direction? All these suppositions are consistent and conceivable. Why, then, should we give the preference to one which is no more consistent or conceivable than the rest? All our reasonings *a priori* will never be able to show us any foundation for this preference.

In a word, then, every effect is a distinct event from its cause. It could not, therefore, be discovered in the cause, and the first invention or conception of it *a priori*, must be entirely arbitrary. And even after it is suggested, the conjunction of it with the cause must appear equally arbitrary, since there are always many other effects which, to reason, must seem fully as consistent and natural. In vain, therefore, should we pretend to determine any single event or infer any cause or effect without the assistance of observation and experience.

Hence we may discover the reason why no philosopher who is rational and modest has ever pretended to assign the ultimate cause of any natural operation, or to show distinctly the action of that power which produces any single effect in the universe. It is confessed that the utmost effort of human reason is to reduce the principles productive of natural phenomena to a greater simplicity, and to resolve the many particular effects into a few general causes, by means of reasonings from analogy, experience, and observation. But as to the causes of these general causes, we should in vain attempt their discovery, nor shall we ever be able to satisfy ourselves by any particular explication of them. These ultimate springs and principles are totally shut up from human curiosity and inquiry. Elasticity, gravity, cohesion of parts, communication of motion by impulse—these are probably the ultimate causes and principles which we shall ever discover in nature; and we may esteem ourselves sufficiently happy if, by accurate inquiry and reasoning, we can trace up the particular phenomena to, or near to, these general principles. The most perfect philosophy of the natural kind only staves off our ignorance a little longer, as perhaps the most perfect philosophy of the moral or metaphysical kind serves only to discover larger portions of it. Thus the observation of human blindness and weakness is the result of all philosophy, and meets us, at every turn, in spite of our endeavors to elude or avoid it.

Nor is geometry, when taken into the assistance of natural philosophy, ever able to remedy this defect or lead us into the knowledge of ultimate causes by all that accuracy of reasoning for which it is so justly celebrated. Every part of mixed mathematics proceeds upon the supposition that certain laws are established by nature in her operations, and abstract reasonings are employed either to assist experience in the discovery of these laws or to determine their influence in particular instances where it depends upon any precise degree of distance and quantity. Thus it is a law of motion, discovered by experience, that the moment or force of any body in motion is in the compound ratio or proportion of its solid contents and its velocity, and, consequently, that a small force may remove the greatest obstacle or raise the greatest weight if by any contrivance or machinery we can increase the velocity of that force so as to make it an overmatch for its antagonist. Geometry assists us in the application of this law by giving us the just dimensions of all the parts and figures which can enter into any species of machine, but still the discovery of the law itself is owing merely to experience; and all the abstract reasonings in the world could never lead us one step toward the knowledge of it. When we reason *a priori* and consider merely any object or cause as it appears to the mind, independent of all observation, it never could suggest to us the notion of any distinct object, such as its effect, much less show us the inseparable and inviolable connection between them. A man must be very sagacious who could discover by reasoning that crystal is the effect of heat, and ice of cold, without being previously acquainted with the operation of these qualities.

Part II

But we have not yet attained any tolerable satisfaction with regard to the question first proposed. Each solution still gives rise to a new question as difficult as the foregoing and leads us on to further inquiries. When it is asked, *What is the nature of all our reasonings concerning matter of fact?* the proper answer seems to be, That they are founded on the relation of cause and effect. When again it is asked, *What is the foundation of all our reasonings and conclusions concerning that relation?* it may be replied in one word, *experience*. But if we still carry on our sifting humor and ask, *What is the foundation of all conclusions from experience?* this implies a new question which may be of more difficult solution and explication. Philosophers that give themselves airs of superior wisdom and sufficiency have a hard task when they encounter persons of inquisitive dispositions, who push them from every corner to which they retreat, and who are sure at last to bring them to some dangerous dilemma. The best expedient to prevent this confusion is to be modest in our pretensions and even to discover the difficulty ourselves before it is objected to us. By this means we may make a kind of merit of our very ignorance.

I shall content myself in this section with an easy task and shall pretend only to give a negative answer to the question here proposed. I say, then, that even after we have experience of the operations of cause and effect, our conclusions from that experience are *not* founded on reasoning or any process of understanding. This answer we must endeavor both to explain and to defend.

It must certainly be allowed that nature has kept us at a great distance from all her secrets and has afforded us only the knowledge of a few superficial qualities of objects, while she conceals from us those powers and principles on which the influence of these objects entirely depends. Our senses inform us of the color, weight, and consistency of bread, but neither sense nor reason can ever inform us of those qualities which fit it for the nourishment and support of the human body. Sight or feeling conveys an idea of the actual motion of bodies, but as to what wonderful force or power which would carry on a moving body forever in a continued change of place, and which bodies never

lose but by communicating it to others, of this we cannot form the most distant conception. But notwithstanding this ignorance of natural powers[2] and principles, we always presume when we see like sensible qualities that they have like secret powers, and expect that effects similar to those which we have experienced will follow from them. If a body of like color and consistency with that bread which we have formerly eaten be presented to us, we make no scruple of repeating the experiment and foresee with certainty like nourishment and support. Now this is a process of the mind or thought of which I would willingly know the foundation. It is allowed on hands that there is no known connection between the sensible qualities and the secret powers, and, consequently, that the mind is not led to form such a conclusion concerning their constant and regular conjunction by anything which it knows of their nature. As to past *experience*, it can be allowed to give *direct* and *certain* information of those precise objects only, and that precise period of time which fell under its cognizance: But why this experience should be extended to future times and to other objects which, for aught we know, may be only in appearance similar, this is the main question on which I would insist. The bread which I formerly ate nourished me; that is, a body of such sensible qualities was, at that time, endued with such secret powers. But does it follow that other bread must also nourish me at another time, and that like sensible qualities must always be attended with like secret powers? the consequence seems nowise necessary. At least, it must be acknowledged that there is here a consequence drawn by the mind, a certain step taken, a process of thought, and an inference which wants to be explained. These two propositions are far from being the same: *I have found that such an object has always been attended with such an effect*, and *I foresee that other objects which are in appearance similar will be attended with similar effects*. I shall allow, if you please, that the one proposition may justly be inferred from the other: I know, in fact, that it always is inferred. But if you insist that the inference is made by a chain of reasoning, I desire you to produce that reasoning. The connection between these propositions is not intuitive. There is required a medium which may enable the mind to draw such an inference, if indeed it be drawn by reasoning and argument. What that medium is I must confess passes my comprehension; and it is incumbent on those to produce it who assert that it really exists and is the original of all our conclusions concerning matter of fact.

This negative argument must certainly, in process of time, become altogether convincing if many penetrating and able philosophers shall turn their inquiries this way, and no one be ever able to discover any connecting proposition or intermediate step which supports the understanding in this conclusion. But as the question is yet new, every reader may not trust so far to his own penetration as to conclude, because an argument escapes his inquiry, that therefore it does not really exist. For this reason it may be requisite to venture upon a more difficult task, and, enumerating all the branches of human knowledge, endeavor to show that none of them can afford such an argument.

All reasonings may be divided into two kinds, namely, demonstrative reasoning, or that concerning relations of ideas, and moral reasoning, or that concerning matter of fact and existence. That there are no demonstrative arguments in the case seems evident, since it implies no contradiction that the course of nature may change and that an object, seemingly like those which we have experienced, may be attended with different or contrary effects. May I not clearly and distinctly conceive that a body, falling from the clouds and which in all other respects resembles snow, has yet the taste of salt or feeling of fire? Is there any more intelligible proposition than to affirm that all the trees will flourish in December and January, and will decay in May and June? Now, whatever is intelligible and can be distinctly conceived implies no contradiction and can never be proved false by any demonstrative argument or abstract reasoning *a priori*.

If we be, therefore, engaged by arguments to put trust in past experience and make it the standard of our future judgment, these arguments must be probable only, or such as regard matter of fact and real existence, according to the division above mentioned. But that there is no argument of this kind must appear if our explication of that species of reasoning be admitted as solid and satisfactory. We have said that all arguments concerning existence are founded on the relation of cause and effect, that our knowledge of that relation is derived entirely from experience, and that all our experimental conclusions proceed upon the supposition that the future will be conformable to the past. To endeavor, therefore, the proof of this last supposition by probable arguments, or arguments

regarding existence, must be evidently going in a circle and taking that for granted which is the very point in question.

In reality, all arguments from experience are founded on the similarity which we discover among natural objects, and by which we are induced to expect effects similar to those which we have found to follow from such objects. And though none but a fool or madman will ever pretend to dispute the authority of experience or to reject that great guide of human life, it may surely be allowed a philosopher to have so much curiosity at least as to examine the principle of human nature which gives this mighty authority to experience and makes us draw advantage from that similarity which nature has placed among different objects. From causes which appear similar, we expect similar effects. This is the sum of our experimental conclusions. Now it seems evident that, if this conclusion were formed by reason, it would be as perfect at first, and upon one instance, as after ever so long a course of experience; but the case is far otherwise. Nothing so like as eggs, yet no one, on account of this appearing similarity, expects the same taste and relish in all of them. It is only after a long course of uniform experiments in any kind that we attain a firm reliance and security with regard to a particular event. Now, where is that process of reasoning which, from one instance, draws a conclusion so different from that which it infers from a hundred instances that are nowise different from that single one? This question I propose as much for the sake of information as with an intention of raising difficulties. I cannot find, I cannot imagine any such reasoning. But I keep my mind still open to instruction if anyone will vouchsafe to bestow it on me.

Should it be said that, from a number of uniform experiments, we *infer* a connection between the sensible qualities and the secret powers, this, I must confess, seems the same difficulty, couched in different terms. The question still occurs, On what process of argument is this *inference* founded? Where is the medium, the interposing ideas which join propositions so very wide of each other? It is confessed that the color, consistency, and other sensible qualities of bread appear not of themselves to have any connection with the secret powers of nourishment and support; for otherwise we could infer these secret powers from the first appearance of these sensible qualities without the aid of experience, contrary to the sentiment of all philosophers, and contrary to plain matter of fact. Here, then, is our natural state of ignorance with regard to the powers and influence of all objects. How is this remedied by experience? It only shows us a number of uniform effects resulting from certain objects, and teaches us that those particular objects, at that particular time, were endowed with such powers and forces. When a new object endowed with similar sensible qualities is produced, we expect similar powers and forces, and look for a like effect. From a body of like color and consistency with bread, we expect like nourishment and support. But this surely is a step or progress of the mind which wants to be explained. When a man says, *I have found, in all past instances, such sensible qualities, conjoined with such secret powers*, and when he says, *similar sensible qualities will always be conjoined with similar secret powers*, he is not guilty of a tautology, nor are these propositions in any respect the same. You say that the one proposition is an inference from the other; but you must confess that the inference is not intuitive, neither is it demonstrative. Of what nature is it then? To say it is experimental is begging the question. For all inferences from experience suppose, as their foundation, that the future will resemble the past and that similar powers will be conjoined with similar sensible qualities. If there be any suspicion that the course of nature may change, and that the past may be no rule for the future, all experience becomes useless and can give rise to no inference or conclusion. It is impossible, therefore, that any arguments are founded on the supposition of that resemblance. Let the course of things be allowed hitherto ever so regular, that alone, without some new argument or inference, proves not that for the future it will continue so. In vain do you pretend to have learned the nature of bodies from your past experience. Their secret nature, and consequently all their efforts and influence, may change without any change in their sensible qualities. This happens sometimes, and with regard to some objects. Why may it not happen always, and with regard to all objects? What logic, what process of argument secures you against this supposition? My practice, you say, refutes my doubts. But you mistake the purport of my question. As an agent, I am quite satisfied in the point; but as a philosopher who has some share of curiosity, I will not say skepticism, I want to learn the foundation of this inference. No reading, no inquiry has yet been able to remove my difficulty or give me satisfaction in a matter of such

importance. Can I do better than propose the difficulty to the public, even though, perhaps, I have small hopes of obtaining a solution? We shall at least, by this means, be sensible of our ignorance, if we do not augment our knowledge. . . .

Skeptical Solution of These Doubts

The passion for philosophy, like that for religion, seems liable to this inconvenience, that though it aims at the correction of our manners and extirpation of our vices, it may only serve, by imprudent management, to foster a predominant inclination and push the mind with more determined resolution toward that side which already *draws* too much by the bias and propensity of the natural temper. It is certain that, while we aspire to the magnanimous firmness of the philosophic sage and endeavor to confine our pleasures altogether within our own minds, we may, at last, render our philosophy, like that of Epictetus and other Stoics, only a more refined system of selfishness, and reason ourselves out of all virtue as well as social enjoyment. While we study with attention the vanity of human life and turn all our thoughts toward the empty and transitory nature of riches and honors, we are, perhaps, all the while flattering our natural indolence which, hating the bustle of the world and drudgery of business, seeks a pretense of reason to give itself a full and uncontrolled indulgence. There is, however, one species of philosophy which seems little liable to this inconvenience, and that because it strikes in with no disorderly passion of the human mind, nor can mingle itself with any natural affection or propensity; and that is the Academic or Skeptical philosophy. The Academics always talk of doubt and suspense of judgment, of danger in hasty determinations, of confining to very narrow bounds the inquiries of the understanding, and of renouncing all speculations which lie not within the limits of common life and practice. Nothing, therefore, can be more contrary than such a philosophy to the supine indolence of the mind, its rash arrogance, its lofty pretensions, and its superstitious credulity. Every passion is mortified by it, except the love of truth; and that passion never is nor can be carried to too high a degree. It is surprising, therefore, that this philosophy, which in almost every instance must be harmless and innocent, should be the subject of so much groundless reproach and obloquy. But, perhaps, the very circumstance which renders it so innocent is what chiefly exposes it to the public hatred and resentment. By flattering no irregular passion, it gains few partisans. By opposing so many vices and follies, it raises to itself abundance of enemies who stigmatize it as libertine, profane, and irreligious.

Nor need we fear that this philosophy, while it endeavors to limit our inquiries to common life, should ever undermine the reasonings of common life and carry its doubts so far as to destroy all action as well as speculation. Nature will always maintain her rights and prevail in the end over any abstract reasoning whatsoever. Though we should conclude, for instance, as in the foregoing section, that in all reasonings from experience there is a step taken by the mind which is not supported by any argument or process of the understanding, there is no danger that these reasonings, on which almost all knowledge depends, will ever be affected by such a discovery. If the mind be not engaged by argument to make this step, it must be induced by some other principle of equal weight and authority; and that principle will preserve its influence as long as human nature remains the same. What that principle is may well be worth the pains of inquiry.

Suppose a person, though endowed with the strongest faculties of reason and reflection, to be brought on a sudden into this world; he would, indeed, immediately observe a continual succession of objects and one event following another, but he would not be able to discover anything further. He would not at first, by any reasoning, be able to reach the idea of cause and effect, since the particular powers by which all natural operations are performed never appear to the senses; nor is it reasonable to conclude, merely because one event in one instance precedes another, that therefore the one is the cause, the other the effect. The conjunction may be arbitrary and casual. There may be no reason to infer the existence of one from the appearance of the other: and, in a word, such a person without more experience could never employ his conjecture or reasoning concerning any matter of fact or be assured of anything beyond what was immediately present to his memory or senses.

Suppose again that he has acquired more experience and has lived so long in the world as to have observed similar objects or events to be constantly conjoined together—what is the consequence of this experience? He immediately infers the existence of one object from the appearance of the other, yet he has not, by all his experience, acquired any idea or knowledge of the secret power by which the one object produces the other, nor is it by any process of reasoning he is engaged to draw this inference; but still he finds himself determined to draw it, and though he should be convinced that his understanding has no part in the operation, he would nevertheless continue in the same course of thinking. There is some other principle which determines him to form such a conclusion.

This principle is *custom* or *habit*. For whatever the repetition of any particular act or operation produces a propensity to renew the same act or operation without being impelled by any reasoning or process of the understanding, we always say that this propensity is the effect of *custom*. By employing that word we pretend not to have given the ultimate reason of such a propensity. We only point out a principle of human nature which is universally acknowledged, and which is well known by its effects. Perhaps we can push our inquiries no further or pretend to give the cause of this cause, but must rest contented with it as the ultimate principle which we can assign of all our conclusions from experience. It is sufficient satisfaction that we can go so far without repining at the narrowness of our faculties, because they will carry us no further. And it is certain we here advance a very intelligible proposition at least, if not a true one, when we assert that after the constant conjunction of two objects, heat and flame, for instance, weight and solidity, we are determined by custom alone to expect the one from the appearance of the other. This hypothesis seems even the only one which explains the difficulty why we draw from a thousand instances an inference which we are not able to draw from one instance that is in no respect different from them. Reason is incapable of any such variation. The conclusions which it draws from considering one circle are the same which it would form upon surveying all the circles in the universe. But no man, having seen only one body move after being impelled by another, could infer that every other body will move after a like impulse. All inferences from experience, therefore, are effects of custom, not of reasoning.[3]

Custom, then, is the great guide of human life. It is that principle alone which renders our experience useful to us and makes us expect, for the future, a similar train of events with those which have appeared in the past. Without the influence of custom we should be entirely ignorant of every matter of fact beyond what is immediately present to the memory and senses. We should never know how to adjust means to ends or to employ our natural powers in the production of any effect. There would be an end at once of all action as well as of the chief part of speculation. . . .

Of the Idea of Necessary Connection

The great advantage of the mathematical sciences above the moral consists in this, that the ideas of the former, being sensible, are always clear and determinate, the smallest distinction between them is immediately perceptible, and the same terms are still expressive of the same ideas without ambiguity or variation. An oval is never mistaken for a circle, nor a hyperbola for an ellipsis. The isosceles and scalenum are distinguished by boundaries more exact than vice and virtue, right and wrong. If any term be defined in geometry, the mind readily, of itself substitutes on all occasions the definition for the term defined, or, even when no definition is employed, the object itself may be presented to the senses and by that means be steadily and clearly apprehended. But the finer sentiments of the mind, the operations of the understanding, the various agitations of the passions, though really in themselves distinct, easily escape us when surveyed by reflection, nor is it in our power to recall the original object as often as we have occasion to contemplate it. Ambiguity, by this means, is gradually introduced into our reasonings: similar objects are readily taken to be the same, and the conclusion becomes at last very wide of the premises.

One may safely, however, affirm that if we consider these sciences in a proper light, their advantages and disadvantages nearly compensate each other and reduce both of them to a state of equality. If the mind, with greater facility, retains the ideas of geometry clear and determinate, it must carry on a much longer and more intricate chain of reasoning and compare ideas much wider of each other in order to reach the abstruser truths of that science. And if moral ideas are apt, without extreme care, to fall into obscurity and confusion, the inferences are always much shorter in these disquisitions, and the intermediate steps which led to the conclusion much fewer than in the sciences which treat of quantity and number. In reality, there is scarcely a proposition in Euclid so simple as not to consist of more parts than are to be found in any moral reasoning which runs not into chimera and conceit. Where we trace the principles of the human mind through a few steps, we may be very well satisfied with our progress, considering how soon nature throws a bar to all our inquiries concerning causes and reduces us to an acknowledgment of our ignorance. The chief obstacle, therefore, to our improvements in the moral or metaphysical sciences is the obscurity of the ideas and ambiguity of the terms. The principal difficulty in the mathematics is the length of inferences and compass of thought requisite to the forming of any conclusion. And, perhaps, our progress in natural philosophy is chiefly retarded by the want of proper experiments and phenomena, which are often discovered by chance and cannot always be found when requisite, even by the most diligent and prudent inquiry. As moral philosophy seems hitherto to have received less improvement than either geometry or physics, we may conclude that if there be any difference in this respect among these sciences, the difficulties which obstruct the progress of the former require superior care and capacity to be surmounted.

There are no ideas which occur in metaphysics more obscure and uncertain than those of "power," "force," "energy," or "necessary connection," of which it is every moment necessary for us to treat in all our disquisitions. We shall, therefore, endeavor in this Section to fix, if possible, the precise meaning of these terms and thereby remove some part of that obscurity which is so much complained of in this species of philosophy.

It seems a proposition which will not admit of much dispute that all our ideas are nothing but copies of our impressions, or, in other words, that it is impossible for us to *think* of anything which we have not antecedently *felt*, either by our external or internal senses. I have endeavored to explain and prove this proposition, and have expressed my hopes that by a proper application of it men may reach a greater clearness and precision in philosophical reasonings than what they have hitherto been able to attain. Complex ideas may, perhaps, be well known by definition, which is nothing but an enumeration of those parts or simple ideas that compose them. But when we have pushed up definitions to the most simple ideas and find still some ambiguity and obscurity, what resources are we then possessed of? By what invention can we throw light upon these ideas and render them altogether precise and determinate to our intellectual view? Produce the impressions or original sentiments from which the ideas are copied. These impressions are all strong and sensible. They admit not of ambiguity. They are not only placed in a full light themselves, but may throw light on their correspondent ideas, which lie in obscurity. And by this means we may perhaps obtain a new microscope or species of optics by which, in the moral sciences, the most minute and most simple ideas may be so enlarged as to fall readily under our apprehension and be equally known with the grossest and most sensible ideas that can be the object of our inquiry.

To be fully acquainted, therefore, with the idea of power or necessary connection, let us examine its impression and, in order to find the impression with greater certainty, let us search for it in all the sources from which it may possibly be derived.

When we look about us toward external objects and consider the operation of causes, we are never able, in a single instance, to discover any power or necessary connection, any quality which binds the effect to the cause and renders the one an infallible consequence of the other. We only find that the one does actually in fact follow the other. The impulse of one billiard ball is attended with motion in the second. This is the whole that appears to the *outward* senses. The mind feels no sentiment or *inward* impression from this succession of objects; consequently, there is not, in any single particular instance of cause and effect, anything which can suggest the idea of power or necessary connection.

From the first appearance of an object we never can conjecture what effect will result from it. But were the power or energy of any cause discoverable by the mind, we could foresee the effect, even without experience, and might, at first, pronounce with certainty concerning it by the mere dint of thought and reasoning.

In reality, there is no part of matter that does ever, by its sensible qualities, discover any power or energy, or give us ground to imagine that it could produce anything, or be followed by any other object, which we could denominate its effect. Solidity, extension, motion—these qualities are all complete in themselves and never point out any other event which may result from them. The scenes of the universe are continually shifting, and one object follows another in an uninterrupted succession; the power or force which actuates the whole machine is entirely concealed from us and never discovers itself in any of the sensible qualities of body. We know that, in fact, heat is a constant attendant of flame; but what is the connection between them we have no room so much as to conjecture or imagine. It is impossible, therefore, that the idea of power can be derived from the contemplation of bodies in single instances of their operation, because no bodies ever discover any power which can be the original of this idea.[4]

Since, therefore, external objects as they appear to the senses give us no idea of power or necessary connection by their operation in particular instances, let us see whether this idea be derived from reflection on the operations of our own minds and be copies from any internal impression. It may be said that we are every moment conscious of internal power while we feel that, by the simple command of our will, we can move the organs of our body or direct the faculties of our mind. An act of volition produces motion in our limbs or raises a new idea in our imagination. This influence of the will we know by consciousness. Hence we acquire the idea of power or energy, and are certain that we ourselves and all other intelligent beings are possessed of power. This idea, then, is an idea of reflection since it arises from reflecting on the operations of our own mind and on the command which is exercised by will both over the organs of the body and faculties of the soul.

We shall proceed to examine this pretension and, first, with regard to the influence of volition over the organs of the body. This influence, we may observe, is a fact which, like all other natural events, can be known only by experience, and can never be foreseen from any apparent energy or power in the cause which connects it with the effect and renders the one an infallible consequence of the other. The motion of our body follows upon the command of our will. Of this we are every moment conscious. But the means by which this is effected, the energy by which the will performs so extraordinary an operation—of this we are so far from being immediately conscious that it must forever escape our most diligent inquiry.

For, *first*, is there any principle in all nature more mysterious than the union of soul with body, by which a supposed spiritual substance acquires such an influence over a material one that the most refined thought is able to actuate the grossest matter? Were we empowered by a secret wish to remove mountains or control the planets in their orbit, this extensive authority would not be more extraordinary, nor more beyond our comprehension. But if, by consciousness, we perceived any power or energy in the will, we must know this power; we must know its connection with the effect; we must know the secret union of soul and body, and the nature of both these substances by which the one is able to operate in so many instances upon the other.

Secondly, we are not able to move all the organs of the body with a like authority, though we cannot assign any reason, besides experience, for so remarkable a difference between one and the other. Why has the will an influence over the tongue and fingers, not over the heart or liver? This question would never embarrass us were we conscious of a power in the former case, not in the latter. We should then perceive, independent of experience, why the authority of the will over the organs of the body is circumscribed within such particular limits. Being in that case fully acquainted with the power or force by which it operates, we should also know why its influence reaches precisely to such boundaries, and no further.

A man suddenly struck with a palsy in the leg or arm, or who had newly lost those members, frequently endeavors, at first, to move them and employ them in their usual offices. Here he is as much conscious of power to command such limbs as a man in perfect health is conscious of power to actuate any member which remains in its natural state and condition. But consciousness never deceives. Consequently, neither in the one case nor in the other are we ever conscious of any power. We learn the influence of our will from experience alone. And experience only teaches us how one event constantly follows another, without instructing us in the secret connection which binds them together and renders them inseparable.

Thirdly, we learn from anatomy that the immediate object of power in voluntary motion is not the member itself which is moved, but certain muscles and nerves and animal spirits, and, perhaps,

something still more minute and more unknown, through which the motion is successively propagated ere it reach the member itself whose motion is the immediate object of volition. Can there be a more certain proof that the power by which this whole operation is performed, so far from being directly and fully known by an inward sentiment or consciousness, is to the last degree mysterious and unintelligible? Here the mind wills a certain event; immediately another event, unknown to ourselves and totally different from the one intended, is produced. This event produces another, equally unknown, till, at last, through a long succession the desired event is produced. But if the original power were felt, it must be known; were it known, its effect must also be known, since all power is relative to its effect. And, *vice versa*, if the effect be not known, the power cannot be known nor felt. How indeed can we be conscious of a power to move our limbs when we have no such power, but only that to move certain animal spirits which, though they produce at last the motion of our limbs, yet operate in such a manner as is wholly beyond our comprehension?

We may therefore conclude from the whole, I hope, without any temerity, though with assurance, that our idea of power is not copied from any sentiment or consciousness of power within ourselves when we give rise to animal motion or apply our limbs to their proper use and office. . . .

But to hasten to a conclusion of this argument, which is already drawn out to too great a length: We have sought in vain for an idea of power or necessary connection in all the sources from which we would suppose it to be derived. It appears that in single instances of the operation of bodies we never can, by our utmost scrutiny, discover anything but one event following another, without being able to comprehend any force or power by which the cause operates or any connection between it and its supposed effect. The same difficulty occurs in contemplating the operations of mind on body, where we observe the motion of the latter to follow upon the volition of the former, but are not able to observe or conceive the tie which binds together the motion and volition, or the energy, by which the mind produces this effect. The authority of the will over its own faculties and ideas is not a whit more comprehensible, so that, upon the whole, there appears not, throughout all nature, any one instance of connection which is conceivable by us. All events seem entirely loose and separate. One event follows another, but we never can observe any tie between them. They seem *conjoined*, but never *connected*. But as we can have no idea of anything which never appeared to our outward sense or inward sentiment, the necessary conclusion *seems* to be that we have no idea of connection or power at all, and that these words are absolutely without any meaning when employed either in philosophical reasonings or common life.

But there still remains one method of avoiding this conclusion, and one source which we have not yet examined. When any natural object or event is presented, it is impossible for us, by any sagacity or penetration, to discover, or even conjecture, without experience, what event will result from it, or to carry our foresight beyond that object which is immediately present to the memory and senses. Even after one instance or experiment where we have observed a particular event to follow upon another, we are not entitled to form a general rule or foretell what will happen in like cases, it being justly esteemed an unpardonable temerity to judge the whole course of nature from one single experiment, however accurate or certain. But when one particular species of events has always, in all instances, been conjoined with another, we make no longer any scruple of foretelling one upon the appearance of the other, and of employing that reasoning which can alone assure us of any matter of fact or existence. We then call the one object "cause," the other "effect." We suppose that there is some connection between them, some power in the one by which it infallibly produces the other and operates with the greatest certainty and strongest necessity.

It appears, then, that this idea of a necessary connection among events arises from a number of similar instances which occur, of the constant conjunction of these events; nor can that idea ever be suggested by any one of these instances surveyed in all possible lights and positions. But there is nothing in a number of instances, different from every single instance, which is supposed to be exactly similar, except only that after a repetition of similar instances the mind is carried by habit, upon the appearance of one event, to expect its usual attendant and to believe that it will exist. This connection, therefore, which we *feel* in the mind, this customary transition of the imagination from one object to its usual attendant, is the sentiment or impression from which we form the idea of power

or necessary connection. Nothing further is the case. Contemplate the subject on all sides, you will never find any other origin of that idea. This is the sole difference between one instance, from which we can never receive the idea of connection, and a number of similar instances by which it is suggested. The first time a man saw the communication of motion by impulse, as by the shock of two billiard balls, he could not pronounce that the one event was *connected*, but only that it was *conjoined* with the other. After he has observed several instances of this nature, he then pronounces them to be *connected*. What alteration has happened to give rise to this new idea of *connection*? Nothing but that he now *feels* these events to be *connected* in his imagination, and can readily foretell the existence of one from the appearance of the other. When we say, therefore, that one object is connected with another, we mean only that they have acquired a connection in our thought and gave rise to this inference by which they become proofs of each other's existence—a conclusion which is somewhat extraordinary, but which seems founded on sufficient evidence. Nor will its evidence be weakened by any general diffidence of the understanding or skeptical suspicion concerning every conclusion which is new and extraordinary. No conclusions can be more agreeable to skepticism than such as make discoveries concerning the weakness and narrow limits of human reason and capacity.

And what stronger instance can be produced of the surprising ignorance and weakness of the understanding than the present? For surely, if there be any relation among objects which it imports us to know perfectly, it is that of cause and effect. On this are founded all our reasonings concerning matter of fact or existence. By means of it alone we attain any assurance concerning objects which are removed from the present testimony of our memory and senses. The only immediate utility of all sciences is to teach us how to control and regulate future events by their causes. Our thoughts and inquiries are, therefore, every moment employed about this relation; yet so imperfect are the ideas which we form concerning it that it is impossible to give any just definition of cause, except what is drawn from something extraneous and foreign to it. Similar objects are always conjoined with similar. Of this we have experience. Suitably to this experience, therefore, we may define a cause to be *an object followed by another, and where all the objects, similar to the first, are followed by objects similar to the second.* Or, in other words, *where, if the first object had not been, the second never had existed.* The appearance of a cause always conveys the mind, by a customary transition, to the idea of the effect. Of this also we have experience. We may, therefore, suitably to this experience, form another definition of cause and call it *an object followed by another, and whose appearance always conveys the thought to that other.* But though both these definitions be drawn from circumstances foreign to the cause, we cannot remedy this inconvenience or attain any more perfect definition which may point out that circumstance in the cause which gives it a connection with its effect. We have no idea of this connection, nor even any distinct notion what it is we desire to know when we endeavor at a conception of it. We say, for instance, that the vibration of this string is the cause of this particular sound. But what do we mean by that affirmation? We either mean *that this vibration is followed by this sound, and that all similar vibrations have been followed by similar sounds; or, that this vibration is followed by this sound, and that, upon the appearance of one, the mind anticipates the senses and forms immediately an idea of the other.* We may consider the relation of cause and effect in either of these two lights; but beyond these we have no idea of it.[5]

To recapitulate, therefore, the reasonings of this Section: Every idea is copied from some preceding impression or sentiment; and where we cannot find any impression, we may be certain that there is no idea. In all single instances of the operation of bodies or minds there is nothing that produces any impression, nor consequently can suggest any idea, of power or necessary connection. But when many uniform instances appear, and the same object is always followed by the same event, we then begin to entertain the notion of cause and connection. We then *feel* a new sentiment or impression, to wit, a customary connection in the thought or imagination between one object and its usual attendant; and this sentiment is the original of that idea which we seek for. For as this idea arises from a number of similar instances, and not from any single instance, it must arise from that circumstance in which the number of instances differ from every individual instance. But this customary connection or transition of the imagination is the only circumstance in which they differ. In every other particular they are alike. The first instance which we saw of motion, communicated by the shock of two billiard balls (to return to this obvious illustration), is exactly similar to any instance that may at present occur to us, except only that we could not at first *infer* one event from the other, which we are enabled to do at present, after so long a course of uniform experience. I know not whether the reader will readily apprehend this reasoning. I am afraid that, should I multiply words about it or throw it into a greater variety of lights, it would only become more obscure and intricate. In all abstract reasonings there is one point of view which, if we can happily hit, we shall go further toward illustrating the subject than by all the eloquence and copious expression in the world. This point of view we should endeavor to reach, and reserve the flowers of rhetoric for subjects which are more adapted to them. . . .

The chief objection against all *abstract* reasonings is derived from the ideas of space and time; ideas, which, in common life and to a careless view, are very clear and intelligible, but when they pass through the scrutiny of the profound sciences (and they are the chief object of these sciences) afford principles, which seem full of absurdity and contradiction. No priestly *dogmas,* invented on purpose to tame and subdue the rebellious reason of mankind, ever shocked common sense more than the doctrine of the infinite divisibility of extension, with its consequences; as they are pompously displayed by all geometricians and metaphysicians, with a kind of triumph and exultation. A real quantity, infinitely less than any finite quantity, containing quantities infinitely less than itself, and so on *in infinitum*; this is an edifice so bold and prodigious, that it is too weighty for any pretended demonstration to support, because it shocks the clearest and most natural principles of human reason.[6] But what renders the matter more extraordinary, is, that these seemingly absurd opinions are supported by a chain of reasoning, the clearest and most natural; nor is it possible for us to allow the premises without admitting the consequences. . . .

The absurdity of these bold determinations of the abstract sciences seems to become, if possible, still more palpable with regard to time than extension. An infinite number of real parts of time, passing in succession, and exhausted one after another, appears so evident a contradiction, that no man, one should think, whose judgment is not corrupted, instead of being improved, by the sciences, would ever be able to admit of it.

Yet still reason must remain restless, and unquiet, even with regard to that scepticism, to which she is driven by these seeming absurdities and contradictions. How any clear, distinct idea can contain circumstances, contradictory to itself, or to any other clear, distinct idea, is absolutely incomprehensible; and is, perhaps, as absurd as any proposition, which can be formed.

. . . [H]ere is the chief and most confounding objection to *excessive* scepticism, that no durable good can ever result from it; while it remains in its full force and vigour. We need only ask such a sceptic, *What his meaning is? And what he proposes by all these curious researches?* He is immediately at a loss, and knows not what to answer. A Copernican or Ptolemaic, who supports each his different system of astronomy, may hope to produce a conviction, which will remain constant and durable, with his audience. A Stoic or Epicurean displays principles, which may not only be durable, but which have an effect on conduct and behaviour. But a Pyrrhonian cannot expect, that his philosophy will have any constant influence on the mind: Or if it had, that its influence would be beneficial to society. On the contrary, he must acknowledge, if he will acknowledge any thing, that all human life must perish, were his principles universally and steadily to prevail. All discourse, all action would immediately cease; and men remain in a total lethargy, till the necessities of nature, unsatisfied, put an end to their miserable existence. It is true; so fatal an event is very little to be dreaded. Nature is always too strong for principle. And though a Pyrrhonian may throw himself or others into a momentary amazement and confusion by his profound reasonings; the first and most trivial event in life will put to flight all his doubts and scruples, and leave him the same, in every point of action and speculation, with the philosophers of every other sect, or with those who never concerned themselves in any philosophical researches. When he awakes from his dream, he will be the first to join in the laugh against himself, and to confess, that all his objections are mere amusement, and can have no other tendency than to show the whimsical condition of mankind, who must act and reason and believe; though they are not able, by their most diligent enquiry, to satisfy themselves concerning the foundation of these operations, or to remove the objections, which may be raised against them.

There is, indeed, a more *mitigated* scepticism or *academical* philosophy, which may be both durable and useful, and which may, in part, be the result of this Pyrrhonism, or *excessive* scepticism, when its undistinguished doubts are, in some measure, corrected by common sense and reflection. The greater part of mankind are naturally apt to be affirmative and dogmatical in their opinions; and while they see objects only on one side, and have no idea of any counterpoising argument, they throw themselves precipitately into the principles, to which they are inclined; nor have they any indulgence for those who entertain opposite sentiments. To hesitate or balance perplexes their understanding, checks their passion, and suspends their action. They are, therefore, impatient till they escape from a state, which to them is so uneasy; and they think, that they can never remove themselves far enough from it, by the violence of their affirmations and obstinacy of their belief. But could such dogmatical reasoners become sensible of the strange infirmities of human understanding, even in its most perfect state, and when most accurate and cautious in its determinations; such a reflection would naturally inspire them with more modesty and reserve, and diminish their fond opinion of themselves, and their prejudice against antagonists. The illiterate may reflect on the disposition of the learned, who, amidst all the advantages of study and reflection, are commonly still diffident in their determinations: And if any of the learned be inclined, from their natural temper, to haughtiness and obstinacy, a small tincture of Pyrrhonism might abate their pride, by showing them, that the few advantages, which they may have attained over their fellows, are but inconsiderable, if compared with the universal perplexity and confusion, which is inherent in human nature. In general, there is a degree of doubt, and caution, and modesty, which, in all kinds of scrutiny and decision, ought for ever to accompany a just reasoner.

Another species of *mitigated* scepticism, which may be of advantage to mankind, and which may be the natural result of the Pyrrhonian doubts and scruples, is the limitation of our enquiries to such subjects as are best adapted to the narrow capacity of human understanding. The *imagination* of man is naturally sublime, delighted with whatever is remote and extraordinary, and running, without control, into the most distant parts of space and time in order to avoid the objects, which custom has rendered too familiar to it. A correct *Judgment* observes a contrary method, and avoiding all distant and high enquiries, confines itself to common life, and to such subjects as fall under daily practice and experience; leaving the more sublime topics to the embellishment of poets and orators, or to the arts of priests and politicians. To bring us to so salutary a determination, nothing can be more serviceable, than to be once thoroughly convinced of the force of the Pyrrhonian doubt, and of the impossibility, that any thing, but the strong power of natural instinct, could free us from it. Those who have a propensity of philosophy, will still continue their researches; because they reflect, that, besides the immediate pleasure, attending such an occupation, philosophical decisions are nothing but the reflections of common life, methodized and corrected. But they will never be tempted to go beyond common life, so long as they consider the imperfection of those faculties which they employ, their narrow reach, and their inaccurate operations. While we cannot give a satisfactory reason, why we believe, after a thousand experiments, that a stone will fall, or fire burn; can we ever satisfy ourselves concerning any determination, which we may form, with regard to the origin of worlds, and the situation of nature, from, and to eternity?

This narrow limitation, indeed, of our enquiries, is, in every respect, so reasonable, that it suffices to make the slightest examination into the natural powers of the human mind, and to compare them with their objects, in order to recommend it to us. We shall then find what are the proper subjects of science and enquiry.

It seems to me, that the only objects of the abstract sciences or of demonstration are quantity and number, and that all attempts to extend this more perfect species of knowledge beyond these bounds are mere sophistry and illusion. As the component parts of quantity and number are entirely similar, their relations become intricate and involved; and nothing can be more curious, as well as useful, than to trace, by a variety of mediums, their equality or inequality, through their different appearances. But as all other ideas are clearly distinct and different from each other, we can never advance farther, by our utmost scrutiny, than to observe this diversity, and, by an obvious reflection, pronounce one thing not to be another. Or if there be any difficulty in these decisions, it proceeds entirely from the undeterminate meaning of words, which is corrected by juster definitions. That *the square of the hypothenuse is equal to the squares of the other two sides*, cannot be known, let the terms be ever so exactly defined, without a train of reasoning and enquiry. But to convince us of this proposition, *that where there is no property, there can be no injustice*, it is only necessary to define the terms, and explain injustice to be a violation of property. This proposition is, indeed, nothing but a more imperfect definition. It is the same case with all those pretended syllogistical reasonings, which may be found in every other branch of learning, except the sciences of quantity and number; and these may safely, I think, be pronounced the only proper objects of knowledge and demonstration.

All other enquiries of men regard only matter of fact and existence; and these are evidently incapable of demonstration. Whatever *is* may *not be*. No negation of a fact can involve a contradiction. The non-existence of any being, without exception, is as clear and distinct an idea as its existence. The proposition, which affirms it not to be, however false, is no less conceivable and intelligible, than that which affirms it to be. The case is different with the sciences, properly so called. Every proposition, which is not true, is there confused and unintelligible. That the cube root of 64 is equal to the half of 10, is a false proposition, and can never be distinctly conceived. But that Caesar, or the angel Gabriel, or any being never existed, may be a false proposition, but still is perfectly conceivable, and implies no contradiction.

The existence, therefore, of any being can only be proved by arguments from its cause or its effect; and these arguments are founded entirely on experience. If we reason *a priori*, any thing may appear able to produce any thing. The falling of a pebble may, for aught we know, extinguish the sun; or the wish of a man control the planets in their orbits. It is only experience, which teaches us the nature and bounds of cause and effect, and enables us to infer the existence of one object from that of another.[7] Such is the foundation of moral reasoning, which forms the greater part of human knowledge, and is the source of all human action and behaviour.

Moral reasonings are either concerning particular or general facts. All deliberations in life regard the former; as also all disquisitions in history, chronology, geography, and astronomy.

The sciences, which treat of general facts, are politics, natural philosophy, physics, chemistry, etc., where the qualities, causes and effects of a whole species of objects are enquired into.

Divinity or Theology, as it proves the existence of a Deity, and the immortality of souls, is composed partly of reasonings concerning particular, partly concerning general facts. It has a foundation in *reason*, so far as it is supported by experience. But its best and most solid foundation is *faith* and divine revelation.

Morals and criticism are not so properly objects of the understanding as of taste and sentiment. Beauty, whether moral or natural, is felt, more properly than perceived. Or if we reason concerning it, and endeavour to fix its standard, we regard a new fact, to wit, the general taste of mankind, or some such fact, which may be the object of reasoning and enquiry.

When we run over libraries, persuaded of these principles, what havoc must we make? If we take in our hand any volume; of divinity or school metaphysics, for instance; let us ask, *Does it contain any abstract reasoning concerning quantity or number?* No. *Does it contain any experimental reasoning concerning matter of fact and existence?* No. Commit it then to the flames: For it can contain nothing but sophistry and illusion.

Endnotes

[1] It is probable that no more was meant by those who denied innate ideas than that all ideas were copies of our impressions, though it must be confessed that the terms which they employed were not chosen with such caution, nor so exactly defined, as to prevent all mistakes about their doctrine. For what is meant by "innate"? If "innate" be equivalent to "natural," then all the perceptions and ideas of the mind must be allowed to be innate or natural, in whatever sense we take the latter word, whether in opposition to what is uncommon, artificial, or miraculous. If by innate he meant contemporary to our birth, the dispute seems to be frivolous, nor is it worth while to inquire at what time thinking begins, whether before, at, or after our birth. Again, the word "idea" seems to be commonly taken in a very loose sense by Locke and others, as standing for any of our perceptions, our sensations and passions, as well as thoughts. Now, in this sense, I should desire to know what can be meant by asserting that self-love, or resentment of injuries, or the passion between the sexes is not innate?

But admitting these terms "impressions" and "ideas" in the sense above explained, and understanding by "innate" what is original or copied from no precedent perception, then may we assert that all our impressions are innate, and our ideas not innate.

To be ingenuous, I must own it to be my opinion that Locke was betrayed into this question by the schoolmen, who, making use of undefined terms, draw out their disputes to a tedious length without ever touching the point in question. A like ambiguity and circumlocution seem to run through that philosopher's reasonings, on this as well as most other subjects.

[2] The word "power" is here used in a loose and popular sense. The more accurate explication of it would give additional evidence to this argument.

[3] Nothing is more usual than for writers, even on *moral, political,* or *physical* subjects, to distinguish between *reason* and *experience,* and to suppose that these species of argumentation are entirely different from each other. The former are taken for the mere result of our intellectual faculties, which, by considering a priori the nature of things, and examining the effects that must follow from their operation, establish particular principles of science and philosophy. The latter are supposed to be derived entirely from sense and observation, by which we learn what has actually resulted from the operation of particular objects, and are thence able to infer what will for the future result from them. Thus, for instance, the limitations and restraints of civil government and a legal constitution may be defended, either from *reason,* which, reflecting on the great frailty and corruption of human nature, teaches that no man can safely be trusted with unlimited authority; or from *experience* and history, which inform us of the enormous abuses that ambition in every age and country has been found to make of so imprudent a confidence.

The same distinction between reason and experience is maintained in all our deliberations concerning the conduct of life, while the experienced statesman, general physician, or merchant, is trusted and followed, and the unpracticed novice, with whatever natural talents endowed, neglected and despised. Though it be allowed that reason may form very plausible conjectures with regard to the consequences of such a particular conduct in such particular circumstances, it is still supposed imperfect without the assistance of experience, which is alone able to give stability and certainty to the maxim derived from study and reflection.

But notwithstanding that this distinction be thus universally received, both in the active and speculative scenes of life, I shall not scruple to pronounce that it is, at bottom, erroneous, or at least superficial.

If we examine those arguments which, in any of the sciences above mentioned, are supposed to be the mere effects of reasoning and reflection, they will be found to terminate at last in some general principle or conclusion for which we can assign no reason but observation and experience. The only difference between them and those maxims which are vulgarly esteemed the result of pure experience is that the former cannot be established without some process of thought, and some reflection on what we have observed, in order to distinguish its circumstances and trace its consequences—whereas, in the latter, the experienced event is exactly and fully similar to that which we infer as the result of any particular situation. The history of a Tiberius or a Nero makes us dread a like tyranny, were our monarchs freed from the restraints of laws and senates: but the observation of any fraud or cruelty in private life is sufficient, with the aid of a little thought, to give us the same apprehension, while it serves as an instance of the general corruption of human nature, and shows us the danger which we must incur by reposing an entire confidence in mankind. In both cases, it is experience which is ultimately the foundation of our inference and conclusion.

There is no man so young and inexperienced as not to have formed from observation many general and just maxims concerning human affairs and the conduct of life; but it must be confessed that when a man comes to put these in practice he will be extremely liable to error, till time and further experience both enlarge these maxims, and teach him their proper use and application. In every situation or incident there are many particular and seemingly minute circumstances which the man of greatest talents is at first apt to overlook, though on them the justness of his conclusions, and consequently the prudence of his conduct, entirely depend. Not to mention that, to a young beginner, the general observations and maxims occur not always on the proper occasions, nor can be immediately applied with due calmness and distinction. The truth is, an inexperienced reasoner could be no reasoner at all were he absolutely inexperienced; and when we assign that character to anyone, we mean it only in a comparative sense, and suppose him possessed of experience in a smaller and more imperfect degree.

4 Mr. Locke says that, finding from experience that there are several new productions in matter, and concluding that there must somewhere be a power capable of producing them, we arrive at last by this reasoning at the idea of power. But no reasoning can ever give us a new, original simple idea, as this philosopher himself confesses. This, therefore, can never be the origin of that idea.

5 According to these explications and definitions, the idea of *power* is relative as much as that of *cause*; and both have a reference to an effect, or some other event constantly conjoined with the former. When we consider the *unknown* circumstance of an object by which the degree or quantity of its effect is fixed and determined, we call that its power. And accordingly, it is allowed by all philosophers that the effect is the

measure of the power. But if they had any idea of power as it is in itself, why could they not measure it in itself? The dispute, whether the force of a body in motion be as its velocity, or the square of its velocity; this dispute, I say, needed not be decided by comparing its effects in equal or unequal times, but by direct mensuration and comparison.

As to the frequent use of the words "force," "power," "energy," etc., which everywhere occur in common conversation as well as in philosophy, that is no proof that we are acquainted, in any instance, with the connecting principle between cause and effect, or can account ultimately for the production of one thing by another. These words, as commonly used, have very loose meanings annexed to them, and their ideas are very uncertain and confused. No animal can put external bodies in motion without the sentiment of a *nisus* or endeavor; and every animal has a sentiment or feeling from the stroke or blow of an external object that is in motion. These sensations, which are merely animal, and from which we can *a priori* draw no inference, we are apt to transfer to inanimate objects, and to suppose that they have some such feelings whenever they transfer or receive motion. With regard to energies, which are exerted without our annexing to them any idea of communicated motion, we consider only the constant experienced conjunction of the events; and as we *feel* a customary connection between the ideas, we transfer that feeling to the objects, as nothing is more usual than to apply to external bodies every internal sensation which they occasion.

6 Whatever disputes there may be about mathematical points, we must allow that there are physical points; that is, parts of extension, which cannot be divided or lessened, either by the eye or imagination. These images, then, which are present to the fancy or senses, are absolutely indivisible, and consequently must be allowed by mathematicians to be infinitely less than any real part of extension; and yet nothing appears more certain to reason, than that an infinite number of them composes an infinite extension. How much more an infinite number of those infinitely small parts of extension, which are still supposed infinitely divisible?

7 That impious maxim of the ancient philosophy, *Ex nihilo, nihil fit* [From nothing, nothing comes], by which the creation of matter was excluded, ceases to be a maxim, according to this philosophy. Not only the will of the supreme Being may create matter; but, for aught we know *a priori*, the will of any other being might create it, or any other cause, that the most whimsical imagination can assign.

47. *Prolegomena to Any Future Metaphysics*

IMMANUEL KANT

Immanuel Kant (1724–1804) was a German philosopher who attempted to rescue philosophy from Hume's skepticism. Whereas rationalists viewed general ideas (innate or God-given) as the key to knowledge and empiricists emphasized sensory experience as the basis of beliefs about reality, Kant claimed to have found a new approach. He believed all experience is a synthesis of concepts and sensory material; and he asked the "transcendental question": What are the necessary (or "transcendental") conditions for experience? By investigating the structure of experience, Kant attempted to elucidate and ground general beliefs about many traditional metaphysical topics, such as space, time, substance, and causality. Though he hoped to rescue knowledge of these things from skepticism, Kant himself was skeptical of any transcendent metaphysics that attempts to describe things-in-themselves apart from experience; and he denied that concepts applied to "noumenal" reality (things-in-themselves).

Although criticized, Kant's work has been very influential. Some nineteenth-century philosophers hoped to go beyond Kant and to find a way to know things-in-themselves, and many twentieth-century philosophers have seen revolutionary developments in science as evidence that one does not have to conceptualize reality in the ways Kant thought were necessary.

Preface

My object is to persuade all those who think metaphysics worth studying that it is absolutely necessary to pause a moment and, disregarding all that has been done, to propose first the preliminary question, "Whether such a thing as metaphysics be at all possible?"

If it is a science, how does it happen that it cannot, like other sciences, obtain universal and permanent recognition? If not, how can it maintain its pretensions and keep the human understanding in suspense with hopes never ceasing, yet never fulfilled? Whether then we demonstrate our knowledge or our ignorance in this field, we must come once for all to a definite conclusion respecting the nature of this so-called science, which cannot possibly remain on its present footing. It seems almost ridiculous, while every other science is continually advancing, that in this, which pretends to be wisdom incarnate, for whose oracle every one inquires, we should constantly move round the same spot, without gaining a single step. And so its supporters having melted away, we do not find that men who are confident of their ability to shine in other sciences venture their reputation here, where everybody, however ignorant in other matters, presumes to deliver a final verdict, inasmuch as in this domain there is as yet no standard weight and measure to distinguish soundness from shallow talk.

After all, it is nothing extraordinary in the elaboration of a science, when men begin to wonder how far it has advanced, that the question should at last occur as to whether and how in

Reprinted by permission of Hackett Publishing Company from the Paul Carus translation of Kant's *Prolegomena to Any Future Metaphysics*, revised by James W. Ellington. Copyright © 1977 by Hackett Publishing Company, Inc., Indianapolis, IN.

general such a science is possible? Human reason so delights in constructions that it has several times built up a tower and then razed it to examine the nature of the foundation. It is never too late to become reasonable and wise; but if the insight comes late, there is always more difficulty in starting the change. . . .

Since the *Essays* of Locke and Leibnitz, or rather since the origin of metaphysics so far as we know its history, nothing has ever happened which could have been more decisive to its fate than the attack made upon it by David Hume. He threw no light on this kind of knowledge; but he certainly struck a spark from which light might have been obtained, had it caught some inflammable substance and had its smouldering fire been carefully nursed and developed.

Hume started mainly from a single but important concept in metaphysics, namely, that of the connection of cause and effect (including its derivative concepts of force and action, etc.). He challenged reason, which pretends to have given birth to this concept of herself, to answer him by what right she thinks anything could be so constituted that if that thing be posited, something else also must necessarily be posited; for this is the meaning of the concept of cause. He demonstrated irrefutably that it was entirely impossible for reason to think *a priori* and by means of concepts such a combination as involves necessity. We cannot at all see why, in consequence of the existence of one thing, another must necessarily exist, or how the concept of such a combination can arise *a priori.* Hence he inferred that reason was altogether deluded with reference to this concept, which she erroneously considered as one of her children, whereas in reality it was nothing but a bastard of imagination, impregnated by experience, which subsumed certain representations under the law of association, and mistook a subjective necessity (custom) for an objective necessity arising from insight. Hence he inferred that reason had no power to think such connections, even in general, because her concepts would then be purely fictitious and all her pretended *a priori* cognitions nothing but common experiences marked with a false stamp. This is as much as to say that there is not, and cannot be, any such thing as metaphysics at all.[1] . . .

I openly confess that my remembering David Hume was the very thing which many years ago first interrupted my dogmatic slumber and gave

my investigations in the field of speculative philosophy a quite new direction. I was far from following him in the conclusions to which he arrived by considering, not the whole of his problem, but a part, which by itself can give us no information. If we start from a well-founded, but undeveloped, thought which another has bequeathed to us, we may well hope by continued reflection to advance further than the acute man to whom we owe the first spark of light.

So I tried first whether Hume's objection could not be put into a general form, and soon found that the concept of the connection of cause and effect was by no means the only concept by which the understanding thinks the connection of things *a priori*, but rather that metaphysics consists altogether of such concepts. I sought to ascertain their number; and when I had satisfactorily succeeded in this by starting from a single principle, I proceeded to the deduction of these concepts, which I was now certain were not derived from experience, as Hume had tried, but sprang from the pure understanding. This deduction (which seemed impossible to my acute predecessor and had never even occurred to any one else, though no one had hesitated to use the concepts without investigating the basis of their objective validity) was the most difficult task ever undertaken in the service of metaphysics; and the worst was that metaphysics, such as it then existed, could not assist me in the least because this deduction alone can render metaphysics possible. But as soon as I had succeeded in solving Hume's problem, not merely in a particular case, but with respect to the whole faculty of pure reason, I could proceed safely, though slowly, to determine the whole sphere of pure reason completely and from universal principles, in its boundaries as well as in its contents. This was required for metaphysics in order to construct its system according to a sure plan. . . .

Preamble on the Peculiarities of All Metaphysical Cognition

Of the Sources of Metaphysics

If it becomes desirable to present any cognition as science, it will be necessary first to determine exactly its differentia, which no other science has in common with it and which constitutes its peculiarity; otherwise the boundaries of all sciences become confused, and none of them can be treated thoroughly according to its nature.

The peculiar features of a science may consist of a simple difference of object, or of the sources of cognition, or of the kind of cognition, or perhaps of all three conjointly. On these features, therefore, depends the idea of a possible science and its territory.

First, as concerns the sources of metaphysical cognition, its very concept implies that they cannot be empirical. Its principles (including not only its basic propositions but also its basic concepts) must never be derived from experience. It must not be physical but metaphysical knowledge, i.e., knowledge lying beyond experience. It can therefore have for its basis neither external experience, which is the source of physics proper, nor internal, which is the basis of empirical psychology. It is therefore *a priori* cognition, coming from pure understanding and pure reason.

But so far metaphysics would not be distinguishable from pure mathematics; it must therefore be called pure philosophical cognition; and for the meaning of this term I refer to the *Critique of Pure Reason* ("Methodology", Chap. 1, Sec. 1), where the distinction between these two employments of reason is sufficiently explained. So much for the sources of metaphysical cognition.

Concerning the Kind of Cognition Which Can Alone Be Called Metaphysical

Of the Distinction between Analytic and Synthetic Judgments in General. The peculiarity of its sources demands that metaphysical cognition must consist of nothing but *a priori* judgments. But whatever be their origin or their logical form, there is a distinction in judgments, as to their content, according to which they are either merely *explicative*, adding nothing to the content of the cognition, or *ampliative*, increasing the given cognition: the former may be called *analytic*, the latter *synthetic*, judgments.

Analytic judgments express nothing in the predicate but what has been already actually thought in the concept of the subject, though not so clearly and with the same consciousness. If I say: "All bodies are extended," I have not amplified in the least my concept of body, but have only analysed it, as extension was really thought to belong to that concept before the judgment was made,

though it was not expressed; this judgment is therefore analytic. On the other hand, this judgment, "All bodies have weight," contains in its predicate something not actually thought in the universal concept of body; it amplifies my knowledge by adding something to my concept, and must therefore be called synthetic.

The Common Principle of All Analytic Judgments Is That of Contradiction. All analytic judgments depend wholly on the principle of contradiction, and are in their nature *a priori* cognitions, whether the concepts that supply them with matter be empirical or not. For the predicate of an affirmative analytic judgment is already thought in the concept of the subject, of which it cannot be denied without contradiction. In the same way its opposite is necessarily denied of the subject in an analytic, but negative, judgment, by the same principle of contradiction. Such is the case of the judgments: "All bodies are extended," and "No bodies are unextended (i.e., simple)."

For this very reason all analytic judgments are *a priori* even when the concepts are empirical, as, for example, "Gold is a yellow metal"; for to know this I require no experience beyond my concept of gold, which contained the thought that this body is yellow and metal. It is, in fact, this thought that constituted my concept; and I need only analyze it, without looking beyond it elsewhere.

Synthetic Judgments Require a Different Principle from That of Contradiction. There are synthetic *a posteriori* judgments of empirical origin; but there are also others which are certain *a priori*, and which spring from pure understanding and reason. Yet they both agree in this, that they cannot possibly spring from the principle of analysis, namely, the principle of contradiction, alone, but require another quite different principle. But whatever principle they may be deduced from, they must be subject to the principle of contradiction, which must never be violated, even though everything cannot be deduced from it. I shall first classify synthetic judgments.

1. *Judgments of Experience* are always synthetic. For it would be absurd to base an analytic judgment on experience, as our concept suffices for the purpose without requiring any testimony from experience. That a body is extended is a judgment which holds *a priori*, and is not a judgment of experience. For before appealing to experience, we al-

ready have all the conditions for the judgment in the concept, from which we have then but to elicit the predicate according to the principle of contradiction, and thereby to become conscious of the necessity of the judgment, which experience could not at all teach us.

2. *Mathematical Judgments* are all synthetic. This fact seems hitherto to have altogether escaped the observation of those who have analysed human reason; it even seems directly opposed to all their conjectures, though it is incontestably certain and most important in its consequences. For as it was found that the conclusions of mathematicians all proceed according to the principle of contradiction (as is demanded by all apodeictic certainty), men persuaded themselves that the fundamental propositions were known from the principle of contradiction. This was a great mistake, for a synthetic proposition can indeed be comprehended according to the principle of contradiction, but only by presupposing another synthetic proposition from which it follows, but never in and by itself.

First of all, we must observe that properly mathematical propositions are always judgments *a priori*, and not empirical, because they carry with them necessity, which cannot be obtained from experience. But if this be not conceded to me, very well; I shall confine my assertion to *pure mathematics*, the very concept of which implies that it contains pure *a priori* and not empirical cognition.

It might at first be thought that the proposition $7 + 5 = 12$ is a mere analytic judgment, following from the concept of the sum of seven and five, according to the principle of contradiction. But on closer examination it appears that the concept of the sum of $7 + 5$ contains merely their union in a single number, without its being at all thought what the particular number is that unites them. The concept of twelve is by no means thought by merely thinking of the combination of seven and five; and, analyze this possible sum as we may, we shall not discover twelve in the concept. We must go beyond these concepts by calling to our aid some intuition corresponding to one of them, i.e., either our five fingers or five points (as Segner[2] has it in his *Arithmetic*); and we must add successively the units of the five given in the intuition to the concept of seven. Hence our concept is really amplified by the proposition $7 + 5 = 12$, and we add to the first concept a second one not thought in it. Arithmetical judgments are therefore synthetic, and the more plainly according as we take larger

numbers; for in such cases it is clear that, however closely we analyze our concepts without calling intuition to our aid, we can never find the sum by such mere analysis.

All principles of geometry are no less analytic. That a straight line is the shortest path between two points is a synthetic proposition. For my concept of straight contains nothing of quantity, but only a quality. The concept of the shortest is therefore altogether additional and cannot be obtained by any analysis of the concept of the straight line. Here, too, intuition must come to aid us. It alone makes the synthesis possible.

(Some other principles, assumed by geometers, are indeed actually analytic and depend on the principle of contradiction; but they only serve, as identical propositions, as a method of concatenation, and not as principles, e.g., $a = a$, the whole is equal to itself, or $a + b > a$, the whole is greater than its part. And yet even these, though they are recognised as valid from mere concepts, are only admitted in mathematics because they can be presented in some intuition.)

What actually makes us believe that the predicate of such apodeictic judgments is already contained in our concept, and that the judgment is therefore analytic, is the duplicity of the expression. We must think a certain predicate as joined to a given concept, and this necessity inheres in the concepts themselves. But the question is not what we must join in thought *to* the given concept, but what we actually think together with and in it, though obscurely; and so it is manifest that the predicate belongs to this concept necessarily indeed, yet not directly but indirectly by means of a necessarily present intuition.[3]

The essential and distinguishing feature of pure mathematical cognition among all other *a priori* cognitions is that it cannot at all proceed from concepts, but only by means of the construction of concepts (see *Critique of Pure Reason*, "Methodology", Chap. I, Sect. 1). As therefore in its judgments it must proceed beyond the concept to that which its corresponding intuition contains, these judgments neither can, nor ought to arise analytically, by dissecting the concept, but are all synthetic.

I cannot refrain from pointing out the disadvantage resulting to philosophy from the neglect of this easy and apparently insignificant observation. Hume, feeling the call (which is worthy of a philosopher) to cast his eye over the whole field of *a priori* cognitions in which human understanding claims such mighty possessions, heedlessly severed from it a whole, and indeed its most valuable, province, viz., pure mathematics. For he imagined that its nature, or, so to speak, the constitution of this province, depended on totally different principles, namely, on the principle of contradiction alone, and although he did not divide judgments in this manner formally and universally and did not use the same terminology as I have done here, what he said was equivalent to this: that pure mathematics contains only analytic, but metaphysics synthetic, *a priori* judgments. In this, however, he was greatly mistaken, and the mistake had a decidedly injurious effect upon his whole conception. But for this, he would have extended his question concerning the origin of our synthetic judgments far beyond the metaphysical concept of causality and included in it the possibility of mathematics *a priori* also; for this latter he must have assumed to be equally synthetic. And then he could not have based his metaphysical judgments on mere experience without subjecting the axioms of mathematics equally to experience, a thing which he was far too acute to do. The good company into which metaphysics would thus have been brought would have saved it from the danger of a contemptuous ill-treatment; for the thrust intended for it must have reached mathematics, which was not and could not have been Hume's intention. Thus that acute man would have been led into considerations which must needs be similar to those that now occupy us, but which would have gained inestimably from his inimitably elegant style.

Metaphysical Judgments, properly so-called, are all synthetic. We must distinguish judgments belonging to metaphysics from metaphysical judgments properly so-called. Many of the former are analytic, but they only afford the means to metaphysical judgments, which are the whole aim of the science and which are always synthetic. For if there be concepts belonging to metaphysics (as, for example, that of substance), the judgments springing from simple analysis of them also belong to metaphysics, as, for example, substance is that which only exists as subject, etc. By means of several such analytic judgments we seek to arrive at the definition of a concept. But as the analysis of a pure concept of the understanding (such as metaphysics contains) does not proceed in any different manner from the dissection of any other, even empirical, concepts, not belonging to metaphysics

(such as, air is an elastic fluid, the elasticity of which is not destroyed by any known degree of cold), it follows that the concept indeed, but not the analytic judgment, is properly metaphysical. This science has something special and peculiar to itself in the production of its *a priori* cognitions, which must therefore be distinguished from the features it has in common with other rational knowledge. Thus the judgments that all the substance in things is permanent is a synthetic and properly metaphysical judgment.

If the *a priori* concepts which constitute the materials and building blocks of metaphysics have first been collected according to fixed principles, then their analysis will be of great value. It might be taught as a particular part (as a *philosophia definitiva*), containing nothing but analytic judgments pertaining to metaphysics, and could be treated separately from the synthetic which constitute metaphysics proper. For indeed these analyses are not elsewhere of much value except in metaphysics, i.e., as regards the synthetic judgments which are to be generated out of these previously analyzed concepts.

The conclusion drawn in this section then is that metaphysics is properly concerned with synthetic propositions *a priori*, and these alone constitute its end, for which it indeed requires various dissections of its concepts, viz., analytic judgments, but wherein the procedure is not different from that in every other kind of cognition, in which we merely seek to render our concepts distinct by analysis. But the generation of *a priori* cognition by intuition as well as by concepts, in fine, of synthetic propositions *a priori* in philosophical cognition, constitutes the essential content of metaphysics. . . .

The General Question of the Prolegomena: Is Metaphysics at All Possible?

Were a metaphysics, which could maintain its place as a science, really in existence, could we say: here is metaphysics, learn it, and it will convince you irresistibly and irrevocably of its truth? This question would be useless, and there would only remain that other question (which would rather be a test of our acuteness than a proof of the existence of the thing itself): how is the science possible, and how does reason come to attain it? But human reason has not been so fortunate in this case. There is no single book to which you can point, as you do to Euclid, and say: this is metaphysics; here you may find the noblest aim of this science, namely, the knowledge of a highest being, and of a future existence, proved from principles of pure reason. We can be shown indeed many judgments, apodeictically certain, and never questioned; but these are all analytic, and rather concern the materials and the scaffolding for metaphysics than the extension of knowledge, which is our proper object in studying it. Even supposing you point to synthetic judgments (such as the principles of sufficient reason, which you have never proved, as you ought to, from pure reason *a priori*, though we gladly concede its truth), you lapse, when you try to use them for your principal purpose, into such inadmissible and uncertain assertions that in all ages one metaphysics has contradicted another, either in its assertions or their proofs, and thus has itself destroyed its own claim to lasting assent. Nay, the very attempts to set up such a science are the main cause of the early appearance of scepticism, a way of thinking in which reason treats itself with such violence that it could never have arisen save from complete despair of ever satisfying our most important aspirations. For long before men began to inquire into nature methodically, they consulted abstract reason, which had to some extent been exercised by means of ordinary experience; for reason is ever present, while laws of nature must usually be discovered with labor. So metaphysics floated to the surface, like foam, which dissolved the moment it was scooped off. But immediately there appeared a new supply on the surface, to be ever eagerly gathered up by some; while others, instead of seeking in the depths the cause of the phenomenon, thought they showed their wisdom by ridiculing the idle labor of their neighbors.

Weary therefore of dogmatism, which teaches us nothing, and of scepticism, which does not even promise us anything, not even to rest in permitted ignorance; disquieted by the importance of knowledge so much needed; and, lastly, rendered suspicious by long experience of all knowledge which we believe we possess or which offers itself under the title of pure reason—we have left but one critical question upon whose answer depends our future conduct, viz., *is metaphysics at all possible?* But this question must be answered not by sceptical objections to the asseverations of some actual system of metaphysics (for we do not as yet admit such a thing to exist), but from the conceptions, as yet only problematic, of a science of this sort. . . .

But it happens, fortunately, that though we cannot assume metaphysics to be an actual science, we can say with confidence that certain pure *a priori* synthetic cognitions are actual and given, namely, pure mathematics and pure physics; for both contain propositions which are everywhere recognized as apodeictically certain, partly by mere reason, partly by universal agreement from experience, and yet as independent of experience. We have therefore some, at least uncontested, synthetic knowledge *a priori*, and need not ask *whether* it be possible (for it is actual) but *how* it is possible, in order that we may deduce from the principle which makes the given knowledge possible the possibility of all the rest. . . .

Remarks

Whatever is given us as object must be given us in intuition. All our intuition, however, takes place only by means of the senses; the understanding intuits nothing but only reflects. And as we have just shown that the senses never and in no manner enable us to know things in themselves, but only their appearances, which are mere representations of the sensibility, we conclude that "all bodies, together with the space in which they are, must be considered nothing but mere representations in us, and exist nowhere but in our thoughts." Now is not this manifest idealism?

Idealism consists in the assertion that there are none but thinking beings; all other things which we believe are perceived in intuition are nothing but representations in the thinking beings, to which no object external to them in fact corresponds. On the contrary, I say that things as objects of our senses existing outside us are given, but we know nothing of what they may be in themselves, knowing only their appearances, i.e., the representations which they cause in us by affecting our senses. Consequently, I grant by all means that there are bodies without us, that is, things which, though quite unknown to us as to what they are in themselves, we yet know by the representations which their influence on our sensibility procures us, and which we call bodies. This word merely means the appearance of the thing, which is unknown to us but is not therefore less real. Can this be termed idealism? It is the very contrary.

Long before Locke's time, but assuredly since him, it has been generally assumed and granted without detriment to the actual existence of external things that many of their predicates may be said to belong, not to the things in themselves, but to their appearances, and to have no proper existence outside our representation. Heat, color, and taste, for instance, are of this kind. Now, if I go further and, for weighty reasons, rank as mere appearances also the remaining qualities of bodies, which are called primary—such as extension, place, and, in general, space, with all that which belongs to it (impenetrability or materiality, shape, etc.)—no one in the least can adduce the reason of its being inadmissible. As little as the man who admits colors not to be properties of the object in itself but only to be modifications of the sense of sight should on that account be called an idealist, so little can my doctrine be named idealistic merely because I find that more, nay, *all the properties which constitute the intuition of a body belong merely to its appearance*. The existence of the thing that appears is thereby not destroyed, as in genuine idealism, but it is only shown that we cannot possibly know it by the senses as it is in itself.

I should be glad to know what my assertions must be in order to avoid all idealism. Undoubtedly, I should say that the representation of space is not only perfectly conformable to the relation which our sensibility has to objects—that I have said—but that it is completely like the object—an assertion in which I can find as little meaning as if I said that the sensation of red has a similarity to the property of cinnabar which excites this sensation in me.

Hence we may at once dismiss an easily foreseen but futile objection, "that by our admitting the ideality of space and of time the whole sensible world would be turned into mere illusion." After all philosophical insight into the nature of sensuous cognition was spoiled by making the sensibility merely a confused mode of representation, according to which we still know things as they are, but without being able to reduce everything in this our representation to a clear consciousness; whereas on the contrary proof is offered by us that sensibility consists, not in this logical distinction of clearness and obscurity, but in the genetic one of the origin of cognition itself. For sensuous perception represents things not at all as they are, but only the mode in which they affect our senses; and consequently by sensuous perception appearances only, and not things themselves, are given to the understanding for reflection. After this necessary correction, an objection rises from an unpardonable and almost intentional misconception, as if my doctrine turned all the things of the world of sense into mere illusion.

When an appearance is given us, we are still quite free as to how we should judge the matter. The appearance depends upon the senses, but the judgment upon the understanding; and the only question is whether in the determination of the object there is truth or not. But the difference between truth and dreaming is not ascertained by the nature of the representations which are referred to objects (for they are the same in both cases), but by their connection according to those rules which determine the coherence of the representations in the concept of an object, and by ascertaining whether they can subsist together in experience or not. And it is not the fault of the appearances if our cognition takes illusion for truth, i.e., if the intuition, by which an object is given us, is taken for the concept of the thing or even of its existence, which the understanding only can think. The senses represent to us the paths of the planets as now progressive, now retrogressive; and herein is neither falsehood nor truth, because as long as we hold this to be nothing but appearance we do not judge of the objective nature of their motion. But as a false judgment may easily arise when the understanding is not on its guard against this subjective mode of representation being considered objective, we say they appear to move backward; it is not the senses however which must be charged with the illusion, but the understanding, whose province alone it is to make an objective judgment on appearances.

Thus, even if we did not at all reflect on the origin of our representations, whenever we connect our intuitions of sense (whatever they may contain) in space and in time, according to the rules of the coherence of all cognition in experience, illusion or truth will arise according as we are negligent or careful. It is merely a question of the use of sensuous representations in the understanding, and not of their origin. In the same way, if I consider all the representations of the senses, together with their form, space and time, to be nothing but appearances, and space and time to be a mere form of the sensibility, which is not to be met with in objects out of it, and if I make use of these representations in reference to possible experience only, there is nothing in my regarding them as appearances that can lead astray or cause illusion. For all that, they can correctly cohere according to rules of truth in experience. Thus all the propositions of geometry hold good of space as well as of all the objects of the senses, consequently, of all possible experience, whether I consider space as a mere form of the sensibility or as something adhering to the things themselves. In the former case, however, I comprehend how I can know *a priori* these propositions concerning all the objects of external intuition. Otherwise, everything else as regards all possible experience remains just as if I had not departed from the ordinary view.

But if I venture to go beyond all possible experience with my concepts of space and time, which I cannot refrain from doing if I proclaim them qualities inherent in things in themselves (for what should prevent me from letting them hold good of the same things, even though my senses might be different, and unsuited to them?), then a grave error may arise due to illusion, in which I proclaim to be universally valid what is merely a subjective condition of the intuition of things and certain only for all objects of sense, viz., for all possible experience; I would refer this condition to things in themselves, and not limit it to the conditions of experience.

My doctrine of the ideality of space and of time, therefore, far from reducing the whole sensible world to mere illusion, is the only means of securing the application of one of the most important cognitions (that which mathematics propounds *a priori*) to actual objects and of preventing its being regarded as mere illusion. For without this observation it would be quite impossible to make out whether the intuitions of space and time, which we borrow from no experience and which yet lie in our representation *a priori*, are not mere phantasms of our brain to which no objects correspond, at least not adequately; and, consequently, whether we have been able to show geometry's unquestionable validity with regard to all the objects of the sensible world just because they are mere appearances.

Secondly, though these many principles make appearances of the representations of the senses, they are so far from turning the truth of experience into mere illusion that they are rather the only means of preventing the transcendental illusion, by which metaphysics has been deceived hitherto and misled into childish efforts of catching at bubbles, because appearances, which are mere representations, were taken for things in themselves. Here originated the remarkable event of the antinomy of reason, which I shall mention later on and which is cancelled by the single observation that appearance, as long as it is employed in experience, produces truth, but the moment it transgresses the bounds of experience, and consequently becomes transcendent, produces nothing but illusion.

Inasmuch, therefore, as I leave to things as we obtain them by the senses their actuality and only limit our sensuous intuition of these things to this—that it represents in no respect, not even in the pure intuitions of space and of time, anything more than mere appearance of those things, but never their constitution in themselves—so is this position of mine not a sweeping illusion invented by me for nature. My protestation, too, against all charges of idealism is so valid and clear as even to seem superfluous, were there not incompetent judges who, while they would have an old name for every deviation from their perverse though common opinion and never judge of the spirit of philosophic nomenclature, but cling to the letter only, are ready to put their own conceits in the place of well-defined concepts, and thereby deform and distort them. I have myself given this my theory the name of transcendental idealism, but that cannot authorise anyone to confound it either with the empirical idealism of Descartes (indeed, his was only an insoluble problem, owing to which he thought every one at liberty to deny the existence of the corporeal world because it could never be proved satisfactorily), or with the mystical and visionary idealism of Berkeley (against which and other similar phantasms, our *Critique* contains the proper antidote). My idealism concerns not the existence of things (the doubting of which, however, constitutes idealism in the ordinary sense), since it never came into my head to doubt it; but it concerns the sensuous representation of things, to which space and time especially belong. Regarding space and time and, consequently, regarding all appearances in general, I have only shown that they are neither things (but are mere modes of representation) nor are they determinations belonging to things in themselves. But the word "transcendental," which for me never means a reference of our cognition to things, but only to our faculty of cognition, was meant to obviate this misconception. Yet rather than give further occasion to it by this word, I now retract it and desire this idealism of mine to be called "critical." But if it be really an objectionable idealism to convert actual things (not appearances) into mere representations, by what name shall we call that which, conversely, changes mere representations into things? It may, I think, be called *dreaming* idealism, in contradistinction to the former, which may be called *visionary* idealism, both of which are to be refuted by my transcendental, or better, *critical* idealism.

How Is Pure Natural Science Possible?

Nature is the *existence* of things, so far as it is determined according to universal laws. Should nature signify the existence of things in themselves, we could never cognise it either *a priori* or *a posteriori*. Not *a priori*, for how can we know what belongs to things in themselves, since this never can be done by the dissection of our concepts (in analytic judgments)? For I do not want to know what is contained in my concept of a thing (for that belongs to its logical being), but what in the actuality of the thing is superadded to my concept and by what the thing itself is determined in its existence outside the concept. My understanding and the conditions on which alone it can connect the determinations of things in their existence do not prescribe any rule to things in themselves; these do not conform to my understanding, but it would have to conform to them; they would therefore have to be first given to me in order to gather these determinations from them, wherefore they would not be cognised *a priori*.

A cognition of the nature of things in themselves *a posteriori* would be equally impossible. For if experience is to teach us laws to which the existence of things is subject, these laws, if they refer to things in themselves, would have to refer to them of necessity even outside our experience. But experience teaches us what exists and how it exists, but never that it must necessarily exist so and not otherwise. Experience therefore can never teach us the nature of things in themselves.

We nevertheless actually possess a pure natural science in which are propounded, *a priori* and with all the necessity requisite to apodeictic propositions, laws to which nature is subject. I need only call to witness that propaedeutic to natural knowledge which, under the title of universal natural science, precedes all physics (which is founded upon empirical principles). In it we have mathematics applied to appearances, and also merely discursive principles (from concepts), which constitute the philosophical part of the pure cognition of nature. But there is much in it which is not quite pure and independent of empirical sources, such as the concept of *motion*, that of *impenetrability* (upon which the empirical concept of matter rests), that of *inertia*, and many others, which prevent its being called a quite pure [transcendental] natural science. Besides, it only refers to objects of the external senses, and therefore does not give an example of a universal natural science in the strict sense; for such a science must bring nature in general, whether it regards the object of the external senses or that of the internal sense (the object of physics as well as psychology), under universal laws. But among the principles of this universal physics there are a few which actually have the required universality; for instance, the propositions that "substance is permanent," and that "every event is determined by a cause according to constant laws," etc. These are actually universal laws of nature, which subsist completely *a priori*. There is then in fact a pure [transcendental] natural science, and the question arises: how is it possible?

The word *nature* assumes yet another meaning, which determines the object, whereas in the former sense it only denotes the conformity to law of the determinations of the existence of things generally. Nature considered *materialiter* is the *totality of all objects of experience*. And with this only are we now concerned; for, besides, things which can never be objects of experience, if they were to be cognised as to their nature, would oblige us to have recourse to concepts whose meaning could never be given *in concreto* (by any example of possible experience). Consequently, we would have to form for ourselves a list of concepts of their nature, the reality whereof (i.e., whether they actually referred to objects or were mere creations of thought) could never be determined. The cognition of what cannot be an object of experience would be hyperphysical, and with things hyperphysical we are here not concerned, but only with the cognition of nature, the actuality of which can be confirmed by experience, though this cognition is possible *a priori* and precedes all experience.

The formal aspect of nature in this narrower

sense is therefore the conformity to law of all the objects of experience and, so far as it is cognised *a priori*, their necessary conformity. But it has just been shown that the laws of nature can never be cognised *a priori* in objects so far as they are considered, not in reference to possible experience, but as things in themselves. And our inquiry here extends, not to things in themselves (the properties of which we pass by), but to things as objects of possible experience, and the totality of these is properly what we here call nature. And now I ask, when the possibility of cognition of nature *a priori* is in question, whether it is better to arrange the problem thus: how can we cognise *a priori* that things as objects of experience necessarily conform to law? or thus: how is it possible to cognise *a priori* the necessary conformity to law of experience itself as regards all its objects generally?

Closely considered, the solution of the question represented in either way amounts, with regard to the pure cognition of nature (which is the point of the question at issue), entirely to the same thing. For the subjective laws, under which alone an empirical cognition of things is possible, hold good of these things as objects of possible experience (not as things in themselves, which are not considered here). Either of the following statements means quite the same: a judgment of perception can never rank as experience without the law that, whenever an event is observed, it is always referred to some antecedent, which it follows according to a universal rule; or else, everything of which experience teaches that it happens must have a cause.

It is, however, more convenient to choose the first formula. For we can *a priori* and before all given objects have a cognition of those conditions on which alone experience of them is possible, but never of the laws to which things may in themselves be subject, without reference to possible experience. We cannot, therefore, study the nature of things *a priori* otherwise than by investigating the conditions and the universal (though subjective) laws, under which alone such a cognition as experience (as to mere form) is possible, and we determine accordingly the possibility of things as objects of experience. For if I should choose the second formula and seek the *a priori* conditions under which nature as an object of experience is possible, I might easily fall into error and fancy that I was speaking of nature as a thing in itself, and then move round in endless circles, in a vain search

for laws concerning things of which nothing is given me.

Accordingly, we shall here be concerned merely with experience and the universal conditions of its possibility, which are given *a priori*. Thence we shall determine nature as the whole objects of all possible experience. I think it will be understood that I here do not mean the rules of the observation of a nature that is already given, for these already presuppose experience. I do not mean how (through experience) we can study the laws of nature; for these would not then be laws *a priori* and would yield us no pure natural science; but [I mean to ask] how the conditions *a priori* of the possibility of experience are at the same time the sources from which all the universal laws of nature must be derived.

In the first place we must state that while all judgments of experience are empirical (i.e., have their ground in immediate sense-perception), yet conversely, all empirical judgments are not therefore judgments of experience; but, besides the empirical, and in general besides what is given to sensuous intuition, special concepts must yet be superadded—concepts which have their origin quite *a priori* in the pure understanding, and under which every perception must be first of all subsumed and then by their means changed into experience.

Empirical judgments, so far as they have objective validity, are *judgments of experience*; but those which are only subjectively valid I name mere *judgments of perception*. The latter require no pure concept of the understanding, but only the logical connection of perception in a thinking subject. But the former always require, besides the representation of the sensuous intuition, special *concepts originally generated in the understanding*, which make the judgment of experience objectively valid.

All our judgments are at first merely judgments of perception; they hold good only for us (i.e., for our subject), and we do not till afterwards give them a new reference (to an object) and want that they shall always hold good for us and in the same way for everybody else; for if a judgment agrees with an object, all judgments concerning the same object must likewise agree with one another, and thus the objective validity of the judgment of experience signifies nothing else than its necessary universal validity. And, conversely, if we have reason to hold a judgment to be necessarily universally valid (which never rests on perception, but on the pure concept of the understanding under which the perception is subsumed), we must consider it to be objective also, that is, that it expresses not merely a reference of our perception to a subject, but a quality of the object. For there would be no reason for the judgments of other men necessarily to agree with mine, if it were not the unity of the object to which they all refer and with which they accord; hence they must all agree with one another.

Therefore objective validity and necessary universal validity (for everybody) are equivalent concepts, and though we do not know the object in itself, yet when we consider a judgment as universally valid, and hence necessary, we understand it thereby to have objective validity. By this judgment we cognise the object (though it remains unknown as it is in itself) by the universally valid and necessary connection of the given perceptions. As this is the case with all objects of sense, judgments of experience take their objective validity, not from the immediate cognition of the object (which is impossible), but merely from the condition of the universal validity of empirical judgments, which, as already said, never rests upon empirical or, in short, sensuous conditions, but upon a pure concept of the understanding. The object in itself always remains unknown; but when by the concept of the understanding the connection of the representations of the object, which are given by the object to our sensibility, is determined as universally valid, the object is determined by this relation, and the judgment is objective.

To illustrate the matter: when we say, "The room is warm, sugar sweet, and wormwood nasty,"[4] we have only subjectively valid judgments. I do not at all expect that I or any other person shall always find it as I now do; each of these sentences only expresses a reference of two sensations to the same subject, i.e., myself, and that only in my present state of perception; consequently, they are not intended to be valid of the object. Such are judgments of perception. Judgments of experience are of quite a different nature. What experience teaches me under certain circumstances, it must always teach me and everybody; and its validity is not limited to the subject nor to its state at a particular time. Hence I pronounce all such judgments as being objectively valid. For instance, when I say the air is elastic, this judgment is as yet a judgment of perception only—I do nothing but refer two sensations in my senses to one an-

other. But if I would have it called a judgment of experience, I require this connection to stand under a condition which makes it universally valid. I desire therefore that I and everybody else should always necessarily connect the same perceptions under the same circumstances.

We must therefore analyze experience in general in order to see what is contained in this product of the senses and of the understanding, and how the judgment of experience itself is possible. The foundation is the intuition of which I become conscious, i.e., perception (*perceptio*), which pertains merely to the senses. But in the next place, there is judging (which belongs only to the understanding). But this judging may be twofold: first, I may merely compare perceptions and connect them in a consciousness of my state; or, secondly, I may connect them in consciousness in general. The former judgment is merely a judgment of perception and is of subjective validity only; it is merely a connection of perceptions in my mental state, without reference to the object. Hence it is not, as is commonly imagined, enough for experience to compare perceptions and connect them in consciousness through judgment; there arises no universal validity and necessity, by virtue of which alone consciousness can become objectively valid and be called experience.

Quite another judgment therefore is required before perception can become experience. The given intuition must be subsumed under a concept which determines the form of judging in general with regard to the intuition, connects the empirical consciousness of the intuition in consciousness in general, and thereby procures universal validity for empirical judgments. A concept of this nature is *a pure a priori* concept of the understanding, which does nothing but determine for an intuition the general way in which it can be used for judging. Let the concept be that of cause; then it determines the intuition which is subsumed under it, e.g., that of air, with regard to judging in general, viz., the concept of air as regards its expansion serves in the relation of antecedent to consequent in a hypothetical judgment. The concept of cause accordingly is a pure concept of the understanding, which is totally disparate from all possible perception and only serves to determine the representation contained under it with regard to judging in general, and so to make a universally valid judgment possible.

Before, therefore, a judgment of perception

can become a judgment of experience, it is requisite that the perception should be subsumed under some such concept of the understanding; for instance, air belongs under the concept of cause, which determines our judgment about it with regard to its expansion as hypothetical.[5] Thereby the expansion of the air is represented, not as merely belonging to the perception of the air in my present state or in several states of mine, or in the state of perception of others, but as belonging to it necessarily. The judgment that air is elastic becomes universally valid and a judgment of experience only because certain judgments precede it which subsume the intuition of air under the concepts of cause and effect; and they thereby determine the perceptions, not merely as regards one another in me, but as regards the form of judging in general (which is here hypothetical), and in this way they render the empirical judgment universally valid.

If all our synthetic judgments are analyzed so far as they are objectively valid, it will be found that they never consist of mere intuitions connected only (as is commonly supposed) by comparison into a judgment; but that they would be impossible were not a pure concept of the understanding superadded to the concepts abstracted from intuition, under which pure concept these latter concepts are subsumed and in this manner only combined into an objectively valid judgment. Even the judgments of pure mathematics in their simplest axioms are not exempt from this condition. The principle that a straight line is the shortest distance between two points presupposes that the line is subsumed under the concept of quantity, which certainly is no mere intuition but has its seat in the understanding alone and serves to determine the intuition (of the line) with regard to the judgments which may be made about it in respect to the quantity, that is, to plurality (as *judica plurativa*).[6] For under them it is understood that in a given intuition there is contained a plurality of homogeneous parts.

To prove, then, the possibility of experience so far as it rests upon pure *a priori* concepts of the understanding, we must first represent what belongs to judgments in general and the various moments (functions) of the understanding in them, in a complete table. For the pure concepts of the understanding must run parallel to these moments, inasmuch as such concepts are nothing more than concepts of intuitions in general, so far as these are determined by one or other of these moments of

judging, in themselves, i.e., necessarily and universally. Hereby also the *a priori* principles of the possibility of all experience, as objectively valid empirical cognition, will be precisely determined. For they are nothing but propositions which subsume all perception (conformably to certain universal conditions of intuition) under those pure concepts of the understanding.

Logical Table of Judgments

1 *As to quantity*	2 *As to quality*
Universal	Affirmative
Particular	Negative
Singular	Infinite

3 *As to relation*	4 *As to modality*
Categorical	Problematic
Hypothetical	Assertoric
Disjunctive	Apodeictic

Transcendental Table of the Concepts of the Understanding

1 *As to quantity*	2 *As to quality*
Unity (Measure)	Reality
Plurality (Quantity)	Negation
Totality (Whole)	Limitation

3 *As to relation*	4 *As to modality*
Substance	Possibility
Cause	Existence
Community	Necessity

Pure Physiological Table of the Universal Principles of Natural Science

1	2
Axioms of intuition	Anticipations of perception

3	4
Analogies of experience	Postulates of empirical thought in general

In order to comprise the whole matter in one idea, it is first necessary to remind the reader that we are discussing, not the origin of experience, but what lies in experience. The former pertains to empirical psychology and would even then never be adequately developed without the latter, which belongs to the critique of cognition, and particularly of the understanding.

Experience consists of intuitions, which belong to the sensibility, and of judgments, which are entirely a work of the understanding. But the judgments which the understanding makes entirely out of sensuous intuitions are far from being judgments of experience. For in the one case the judgment connects only the perceptions as they are given in sensuous intuition, while in the other the judgments must express what experience in general and not what the mere perception (which possesses only subjective validity) contains. The judgment of experience must therefore add to the sensuous intuition and its logical connection in a judgment (after it has been rendered universal by comparison) something that determines the synthetic judgment as necessary and therefore as universally valid. This can be nothing but that concept which represents the intuition as determined in itself with regard to one form of judgment rather than another, viz., a concept of that synthetic unity of intuitions which can only be represented by a given logical function of judgments.

The sum of the matter is this: the business of the senses is to intuit, that of the understanding is to think. But thinking is uniting representations in a consciousness. This unification originates either merely relative to the subject and is contingent and subjective, or it happens absolutely and is necessary or objective. The uniting of representations in a consciousness is judgment. Thinking therefore is the same as judging, or referring representations to judgments in general. Hence judgments are either merely subjective when representations are referred to a consciousness in one subject only and are united in it, or they are objective when they are united in a consciousness in general, that is, necessarily. The logical moments of all judgments are so many possible ways of uniting representations in consciousness. But if they serve as concepts, they are concepts of the necessary unification of representations in a consciousness and so are principles of objectively valid judgments. This uniting in a consciousness is either analytic by identity, or synthetic by the combination and addition of various representations one to another. Experience consists in the synthetic connection of appearances (perceptions) in consciousness, so far as this con-

nection is necessary. Hence the pure concepts of the understanding are those under which all perceptions must first be subsumed before they can serve for judgments of experience, in which the synthetic unity of the perceptions is represented as necessary and universally valid.[7]

Judgments, when considered merely as the condition of the unification of given representations in a consciousness, are rules. These rules, so far as they represent the unification as necessary, are rules *a priori*, and so far as they cannot be deduced from higher rules, are principles. But in regard to the possibility of all experience, merely in relation to the form of thinking in it, no conditions of judgments of experience are higher than those which bring the phenomena, according to the different form of their intuition, under pure concepts of the understanding, and render the empirical judgments objectively valid. These are therefore the *a priori* principles of possible experience.

The principles of possible experience are then at the same time universal laws of nature, which can be cognised *a priori*. And thus the problem in our question: How is pure natural science possible? is solved. For the systematization which is required for the form of a science is to be met with in perfection here, because, beyond the above-mentioned formal conditions of all judgments in general and of all rules in general, that are offered in logic, no others are possible, and these constitute a logical system. The concepts grounded thereupon, which contain the *a priori* conditions of all synthetic and necessary judgments, accordingly constitute a transcendental system. Finally, the principles by means of which all appearances are subsumed under these concepts constitute a physiological system, that is, a system of nature, which precedes all empirical cognition of nature, first makes it possible, and hence may in strictness be called the universal and pure natural science.

The first[8] of the physiological principles[9] subsumes all appearances, as intuitions in space and time, under the concept of *quantity*, and is so far a principle of the application of mathematics to experience. The second[10] subsumes the strictly empirical element, viz., sensation, which denotes the real in intuitions, not indeed directly under the concept of *quantity*, because sensation is not an intuition that *contains* either space or time, though it puts the object corresponding to sensation in both space and time. But still there is between reality (sense-representation) and zero, or total lack of intuition in time, a difference which has a quantity. For between any given degree of light and darkness, between any degree of heat and complete cold, between any degree of weight and absolute lightness, between any degree of occupied space and of totally empty space, ever smaller degrees can be thought, just as even between consciousness and total unconsciousness (psychological darkness) ever smaller degrees obtain. Hence there is no perception that can show an absolute absence; for instance, no psychological darkness that cannot be regarded as a consciousness only surpassed by a stronger consciousness. This occurs in all cases of sensation; and so the understanding can anticipate sensations, which constitute the peculiar quality of empirical representations (appearances), by means of the principle that they all have a degree, consequently, that what is real in all appearance has a degree. Here is the second application of mathematics (*mathesis intensorum*) to natural science.

As regards the relation of appearances merely with a view to their existence, the determination is not mathematical but dynamical, and can never be objectively valid and fit for experience, if it does not come under *a priori* principles[11] by which the cognition of experience relative to appearances first becomes possible. Hence appearances must be subsumed under the concept of substance, which as a concept of the thing itself is the foundation of all determination of existence; or, secondly—so far as a succession is found among appearances, that is, an event—under the concept of an effect with reference to cause; or, lastly—so far as coexistence is to be known objectively, that is, by a judgment of experience—under the concept of community (action and reaction). Thus *a priori* principles form the basis of objectively valid, though empirical, judgments—that is, of the possibility of experience so far as it must connect objects as existing in nature. These principles are properly the laws of nature, which may be called dynamical.

Finally[12] the cognition of the agreement and connection, not only of appearances among themselves in experience, but of their relation to experience in general, belongs to judgments of experience. This relation contains either their agreement with the formal conditions which the understanding cognises, or their coherence with the material of the senses and of perception, or combines both into one concept and consequently contains possibility, actuality, and necessity according to universal laws of nature. This would constitute the physi-

ological doctrine of method (distinction between truth and hypotheses, and the bounds of the reliability of the latter).

The third table of principles drawn from the nature of the understanding itself according to the critical method shows an inherent perfection, which raises it far above every other table which has hitherto, though in vain, been tried or may yet be tried by analyzing the objects themselves dogmatically. It exhibits all synthetic *a priori* principles completely and according to one principle, viz., the faculty of judging in general, which constitutes the essence of experience as regards the understanding, so that we can be certain that there are no more such principles. This affords a satisfaction such as can never be attained by the dogmatic method. Yet this is not all; there is a still greater merit in it.

We must carefully bear in mind the ground of proof which shows the possibility of this cognition *a priori* and, at the same time, limits all such principles to a condition which must never be lost sight of, if they are not to be misunderstood and extended in use beyond what is allowed by the original sense which the understanding places in them. This limit is that they contain nothing but the conditions of possible experience in general so far as it is subjected to laws *a priori*. Consequently, I do not say that things *in themselves* possess a quantity, that their reality possesses a degree, their existence a connection of accidents in a substance, etc. This nobody can prove, because such a synthetic connection from mere concepts, without any reference to sensuous intuition on the one side or connection of such intuition in a possible experience on the other, is absolutely impossible. The essential limitation of the concepts in these principles, then, is that all things stand necessarily *a priori* under the aforementioned conditions only *as objects of experience*.

Hence there follows, secondly, a specifically peculiar mode of proof of these principles; they are not directly referred to appearances and to their relation, but to the possibility of experience, of which appearances constitute the matter only, not the form. Thus they are referred to objectively and universally valid synthetic propositions, in which we distinguish judgments of experience from those of perception. This takes place because appearances, as mere intuitions *occupying a part of space and time*, come under the concept of quantity, which synthetically unites their multiplicity *a priori* according to rules. Again, insofar as the perception contains, besides intuition, sensation, and between the latter and nothing (i.e., the total disappearance of sensation), there is an ever-decreasing transition, it is apparent that the real in appearances must have a degree, so far as it (viz., the sensation) *does not itself occupy any part of space or of time*.[13] Still the transition to sensation from empty time or empty space is only possible in time. Consequently, although sensation, as the quality of empirical intuition in respect of its specific difference from other sensations, can never be cognised *a priori*, yet it can, in a possible experience in general, as a quantity of perception be intensively distinguished from every other similar perception. Hence the application of mathematics to nature, as regards the sensuous intuition by which nature is given to us, is first made possible and determined.

Above all, the reader must pay attention to the mode of proof of the principles which occur under the title of Analogies of Experience. For these do not refer to the generation of intuitions, as do the principles of applying mathematics to natural science in general, but to the connection of their existence in experience; and this can be nothing but the determination of their existence in time according to necessary laws, under which alone the connection is objectively valid and thus becomes experience. The proof, therefore, does not turn on the synthetic unity in the connection of things in themselves, but merely of perceptions, and of these, not in regard to their content, but to the determination of time and of the relation of their existence in it according to universal laws. If the empirical determination in relative time is indeed to be objectively valid (i.e., experience), these universal laws thus contain the necessity of the determination of existence in time generally (viz., according to a rule of the understanding *a priori*). Since these are prolegomena I cannot further descant on the subject, but my reader (who has probably long been accustomed to consider experience as a mere empirical synthesis of perceptions, and hence has not considered that it goes much beyond them since it imparts to empirical judgments universal validity, and for that purpose requires a pure and *a priori* unity of the understanding) is recommended to pay special attention to this distinction of experience from a mere aggregate of perceptions and to judge the mode of proof from this point of view.

Now we are prepared to remove Hume's doubt. He justly maintains that we cannot comprehend by reason the possibility of causality, that is, of the reference of the existence of one thing to the existence of another which is necessitated by the former. I add that we comprehend just as little the concept of subsistence, that is, the necessity that at the foundation of the existence of things there lies a subject which cannot itself be a predicate of any other thing; nay, we cannot even form a concept of the possibility of such a thing (though we can point out examples of its use in experience). The very same incomprehensibility affects the community of things, as we cannot comprehend how from the state of one thing an inference to the state of quite another thing beyond it, and *vice versa*, can be drawn, and how substances which have each their own separate existence should depend upon one another necessarily. But I am very far from holding these concepts to be derived merely from experience, and the necessity represented in them to be fictitious and a mere illusion produced in us by long habit. On the contrary, I have amply shown that they and the principles derived from them are firmly established *a priori* before all experience and have their undoubted objective rightness, though only with regard to experience.

Though I have no conception of such a connection of things in themselves, how they can either exist as substances, or act as causes, or stand in community with others (as parts of a real whole) and I can just as little think such properties in appearances as such (because those concepts contain nothing that lies in the appearances, but only what the understanding alone must think), we have yet a concept of such a connection of representations in our understanding and in judgments generally. This is the concept that representations belong in one sort of judgments as subject in relation to predicates; in another as ground in relation to consequent; and, in a third, as parts which constitute together a total possible cognition. Further we know *a priori* that without considering the representation of an object as determined with regard to one or the other of these moments, we can have no valid cognition of the object; and, if we should occupy ourselves with the object in itself, there is not a single possible attribute by which I could know that it is determined with regard to one or the other of these moments, that is, belonged under the concept of substance, or of cause, or (in relation to other substances) of community, for I have no conception of the possibility of such a connection of existence. But the question is not how things in themselves but how the empirical cognition of things is determined, as regards the above moments of judgments in general, that is, how things, as objects of experience, can and must be subsumed under these concepts of the understanding. And then it is clear that I completely comprehend, not only the possibility, but also the necessity, of subsuming all appearances under these concepts, that is, of using them as principles of the possibility of experience.

In order to put to a test Hume's problematic concept (his *crux metaphysicorum*), the concept of cause, we have, in the first place, given *a priori* by means of logic the form of a conditional judgment in general, i.e., we have one given cognition as antecedent and another as consequent. But it is possible that in perception we may meet with a rule of relation which runs thus: that a certain appearance is constantly followed by another (though not conversely); and this is a case for me to use the hypothetical judgment and, for instance, to say that if the sun shines long enough upon a body it grows warm. Here there is indeed as yet no necessity of connection, or concept of cause. But I proceed and say that if this proposition, which is merely a subjective connection of perceptions, is to be a judgment of experience, it must be regarded as necessary and universally valid. Such a proposition would be that the sun is by its light the cause of heat. The empirical rule is now considered as a law, and as valid not merely of appearances but valid of them for the purposes of a possible experience which requires universal and therefore necessarily valid rules. I therefore easily comprehend the concept of cause as a concept necessarily belonging to the mere form of experience, and its possibility as a synthetic unification of perceptions in a consciousness in general; but I do not at all comprehend the possibility of a thing in general as a cause, inasmuch as the concept of cause denotes a condition not at all belonging to things, but to experience. For experience can only be an objectively valid cognition of appearances and of their succession, only so far as the antecedent appearances can be conjoined with the consequent ones according to the rule of hypothetical judgments.

Hence if the pure concepts of the understanding try to go beyond objects of experience and be referred to things in themselves (*noumena*), they have no meaning whatever. They serve, as it were, only to spell out appearances, so that we may be able to read them as experience. The principles which arise from their reference to the sensible world only serve our understanding for use in experience. Beyond this they are arbitrary combinations without objective reality; and we can neither cognise their possibility *a priori*, nor verify their reference to objects, let alone make such reference understandable, by any example, because examples can only be borrowed from some possible experience, and consequently the objects of these concepts can be found nowhere but in a possible experience.

This complete (though to its originator unexpected) solution of Hume's problem rescues for the pure concepts of the understanding their *a priori* origin and for the universal laws of nature their validity as laws of the understanding, yet in such a way as to limit their use to experience, because their possibility depends solely on the reference of the understanding to experience, but with a completely reversed mode of connection which never occurred to Hume: they are not derived from experience, but experience is derived from them.

This is, therefore, the result of all our foregoing inquiries: "All synthetic principles *a priori* are nothing more than principles of possible experience" and can never be referred to things in themselves, but only to appearances as objects of experience. And hence pure mathematics as well as pure natural science can never be referred to anything more than mere appearances, and can only represent either that which makes experience in general possible, or else that which, as it is derived from these principles, must always be capable of being represented in some possible experience.

And thus we have at last something determinate upon which to depend in all metaphysical enterprises, which have hitherto, boldly enough but always at random, attempted everything without discrimination. That the goal of their exertions should be set up so close struck neither the dogmatic thinkers nor those who, confident in their supposed sound common sense, started with concepts and principles of pure reason (which were legitimate and natural, but destined for mere empirical use) in search of insights for which they neither knew nor could know any determinate bounds, because they had never reflected nor were able to reflect on the nature or even on the possibility of such a pure understanding.

Many a naturalist of pure reason (by which I mean the man who believes he can decide in matters of metaphysics without any science) may pretend that he, long ago, by the prophetic spirit of his sound sense, not only suspected but knew and comprehended what is here propounded with so much ado, or, if he likes, with prolix and pedantic pomp: "that with all our reason we can never reach beyond the field of experience." But when he is questioned about his rational principles individually, he must grant that there are many of them which he has not taken from experience and which are therefore independent of it and valid *a priori*. How then and on what grounds will he restrain both himself and the dogmatist, who makes use of these concepts and principles beyond all possible experience because they are recognised to be independent of it? And even he, this adept in sound sense, in spite of all his assumed and cheaply acquired wisdom, is not exempt from wandering inadvertently beyond objects of experience into the field of chimeras. He is often deeply enough involved in them, though in announcing everything as mere probability, rational conjecture, or analogy, he gives by his popular language a color to his groundless pretensions.

Since the oldest days of philosophy, inquirers into pure reason have thought that, besides the things of sense, or appearances (*phenomena*), which make up the sensible world, there were certain beings of the understanding (*noumena*), which should constitute an intelligible world. And as appearance and illusion were by those men identified (a thing which we may well excuse in an undeveloped epoch), actuality was only conceded to the beings of the understanding.

And we indeed, rightly considering objects of sense as mere appearances, confess thereby that they are based upon a thing in itself, though we know not this thing as it is in itself but only know its appearances, viz., the way in which our senses are affected by this unknown something. The understanding therefore, by assuming appearances, grants also the existence of things in themselves, and thus far we may say that the representation of such things as are the basis of appearances, consequently of mere beings of the understanding, is not only admissible but unavoidable.

Our critical deduction by no means excludes things of that sort (*noumena*), but rather limits the principles of the Aesthetic[14] in such a way that they shall not extend to all things (as everything would then be turned into mere appearance) but that they shall hold good only of objects of possible experi-

ence. Hereby, then, beings of the understanding are admitted, but with the inculcation of this rule which admits of no exception: that we neither know nor can know anything determinate whatever about these pure beings of the understanding, because our pure concepts of the understanding as well as our pure intuitions extend to nothing but objects of possible experience, consequently to mere things of sense; and as soon as we leave this sphere, these concepts retain no meaning whatever.

There is indeed something seductive in our pure concepts of the understanding which tempts us to a transcendent use—a use which transcends all possible experience. Not only are our concepts of substance, of power, of action, of reality, and others, quite independent of experience, containing nothing of sense appearance, and so apparently applicable to things in themselves (*noumena*), but, what strengthens this conjecture, they contain a necessity of determination in themselves, which experience never attains. The concept of cause contains a rule according to which one state follows another necessarily; but experience can only show us that one state of things often or, at most, commonly follows another, and therefore affords neither strict universality nor necessity.

Hence concepts of the understanding seem to have a deeper meaning and content than can be exhausted by their merely empirical use, and so the understanding inadvertently adds for itself to the house of experience a much more extensive wing which it fills with nothing but beings of thought, without ever observing that it has transgressed with its otherwise legitimate concepts the bounds of their use. . . . .

How Is Metaphysics in General Possible?

Pure mathematics and pure natural science had no need for such a deduction (as has been made for both) for the sake of their own safety and certainty. For the former rests upon its own evidence, and the latter (though sprung from pure sources of the understanding) upon experience and its thorough confirmation. Pure natural science cannot altogether refuse and dispense with the testimony of experience; hence with all its certainty it can never, as philosophy, rival mathematics. Both sciences therefore stood in need of this inquiry, not for themselves, but for the sake of another science, namely, metaphysics.

Metaphysics has to do not only with concepts of nature, which always find their application in experience, but also with pure rational concepts, which never can be given in any possible experience whatsoever. Consequently, the objective reality of these concepts (viz., that they are not mere chimeras) and also the truth or falsity of metaphysical assertions cannot be discovered or confirmed by any experience. This part of metaphysics, however, is precisely what constitutes its essential end, to which the rest is only a means, and thus this science is in need of such a deduction for its own sake. The third question now proposed relates therefore, as it were, to the root and peculiarity of metaphysics, i.e., the occupation of reason merely with itself and the supposed knowledge of objects arising immediately from this brooding over its own concepts, without requiring experience or indeed being able to reach that knowledge through experience.[15]

Without solving this question, reason will never be satisfied. The empirical use to which reason limits the pure understanding does not fully satisfy reason's own proper destination. Every single experience is only a part of the whole sphere of its domain, but the absolute totality of all possible experience is itself not experience. Yet it is a necessary problem for reason, the mere representation of which requires concepts quite different from the pure concepts of the understanding, whose use is only immanent, i.e., refers to experience so far as it can be given. Whereas the concepts of reason aim at the completeness, i.e., the collective unity of all possible experience, and thereby go beyond every given experience. Thus they become *transcendent*.

As the understanding stands in need of categories for experience, reason contains in itself the ground of ideas, by which I mean necessary concepts whose object *cannot* be given in any experience. The latter are inherent in the nature of reason, as the former are in that of the understanding. While the ideas carry with them an illusion likely to mislead, this illusion is unavoidable though it certainly can be kept from misleading us.

Since all illusion consists in holding the subjective ground of our judgments to be objective, a self-knowledge of pure reason in its transcendent (hyperbolical) use is the only safeguard against the aberrations into which reason falls when it mistakes its destination, and transcendently refers to the object in itself that which only concerns reason's own subject and its guidance in all immanent use.

The distinction of *ideas*, i.e., of pure concepts of reason, from the categories, or pure concepts of the understanding, as cognitions of a quite different species, origin, and use is so important a point in founding a science which is to contain the system of all these *a priori* cognitions that, without this distinction, metaphysics is absolutely impossible or is at best a random, bungling attempt to build a castle in the air without a knowledge of the materials or of their fitness for one purpose or another. Had the *Critique of Pure Reason* done nothing but first point out this distinction, it would thereby have contributed more to clear up our conception of, and to guide our inquiry in, the field of metaphysics than all the vain efforts which have hitherto been made to satisfy the transcendent problems of pure reason; for one never even suspected that he was in quite another field from that of the understanding, and hence that he was classing concepts of the understanding and those of reason together, as if they were of the same kind.

All pure cognitions of the understanding have the feature that the concepts can be given in experience, and the principles can be confirmed by it; whereas the transcendent cognitions of reason cannot either, as ideas, be given in experience or, as propositions, ever be confirmed or refuted by it. Hence whatever errors may slip in unawares can only be discovered by pure reason itself—a discovery of much difficulty, because this very reason naturally becomes dialectical by means of its ideas; and this unavoidable illusion cannot be limited by any objective and dogmatic inquiries into things, but only by a subjective investigation of reason itself as a source of ideas.

In the *Critique of Pure Reason* it was always my greatest care to endeavor, not only carefully to distinguish the several kinds of cognition, but to derive concepts belonging to each one of them from their common source. I did this in order that by knowing whence they originated, I might determine their use with safety and also have the invaluable, but never previously anticipated, advantage of knowing the completeness of my enumeration, classification, and specification of concepts *a priori*, and of knowing it according to principles. Without this, metaphysics is mere rhapsody, in which no one knows whether he has enough or whether and where something is still wanting. We can indeed have this advantage only in pure philosophy, but of this philosophy it constitutes the very essence.

As I had found the origin of the categories in the four logical functions of all judgments of the understanding, it was quite natural to seek the origin of the ideas in the three functions of syllogisms. For as soon as these pure concepts of reason (the transcendental ideas) are given, they could hardly, except they be held innate, be found anywhere else than in the same activity of reason, which, so far as it regards mere form, constitutes the logical element of syllogisms; but, so far as it represents judgments of the understanding as determined with respect to one or another form *a priori*, constitutes transcendental concepts of pure reason.

The formal difference of syllogisms makes their division into categorical, hypothetical, and disjunctive necessary. The concepts of reason founded on them contain therefore, first, the idea of the complete subject (the substantial); secondly, the idea of the complete series of conditions; thirdly, the determination of all concepts in the idea of a complete complex of that which is possible.[16] The first idea is psychological, the second cosmological, the third theological; and, as all three give occasion to dialectic, yet each in its own way, the division of the whole dialectic of pure reason into its paralogism, its antinomy, and its ideal was arranged accordingly. Through this derivation we may feel assured that all the claims of pure reason are completely represented and that none can be wanting, because the faculty of reason itself, whence they all take their origin, is thereby completely surveyed.

In these general considerations it is also remarkable that the ideas of reason, unlike the categories, are of no service to the use of our understanding in experience, but quite dispensable, and become even an impediment to the maxims of a rational cognition of nature. Yet in another aspect still to be determined they are necessary. Whether the soul is or is not a simple substance is of no consequence to us in the explanation of its phenomena. For we cannot render the concept of a simple being understandable sensuously and concretely by any possible experience. The concept is therefore quite void as regards all hoped-for insight into the cause of appearances and cannot at all serve as a principle of the explanation of that

which internal or external experience supplies. Likewise the cosmological ideas of the beginning of the world or of its eternity (*a parte ante*) cannot be of any service to us for the explanation of any event in the world itself. And finally we must, according to a right maxim of the philosophy of nature, refrain from all explanation of the design of nature as being drawn from the will of a Supreme Being, because this would not be natural philosophy but an admission that we have come to the end of it. The use of these ideas, therefore, is quite different from that of those categories by which (and by the principles built upon which) experience itself first becomes possible. But our laborious analytic of the understanding would be superfluous if we had nothing else in view than the mere cognition of nature as it can be given in experience; for reason does its work, both in mathematics and in natural science, quite safely and well without any of this subtle deduction. Therefore our critique of the understanding combines with the ideas of pure reason for a purpose which lies beyond the empirical use of the understanding; but we have above declared the use of the understanding in this respect to be totally inadmissible and without any object or meaning. Yet there must be a harmony between the nature of reason and that of the understanding, and the former must contribute to the perfection of the latter and cannot possibly upset it.

The solution of this question is as follows. Pure reason does not in its ideas point to particular objects which lie beyond the field of experience, but only requires completeness of the use of the understanding in the complex of experience. But this completeness can be a completeness of principles only, not of intuitions and of objects. In order, however, to represent the ideas definitely, reason conceives them after the fashion of the cognition of an object. This cognition is, as far as these rules are concerned, completely determined; but the object is only an idea invented for the purpose of bringing the cognition of the understanding as near as possible to the completeness indicated by that idea.

Prefatory Remark to the Dialectic of Pure Reason

We have above shown that the purity of the categories from all admixture of sensuous determinations may mislead reason into extending their use be yond all experience to things in themselves; for though these categories themselves find no intuition which can give them meaning or sense *in concreto*, they, as mere logical functions, can represent a thing in general, but not give by themselves alone a determinate concept of anything. Such hyperbolical objects are distinguished by the appellation of *noumena*, or pure beings of the understanding (or better, beings of thought)—such as, for example, "substance," but conceived without permanence in time; or "cause," but not acting in time, etc. Here predicates that only serve to make the conformity-to-law of experience possible are applied to these concepts, and yet they are deprived of all the conditions of intuition on which alone experience is possible, and so these concepts lose all significance.

There is no danger, however, of the understanding spontaneously making an excursion so very wantonly beyond its own bounds into the field of the mere beings of thought, unless being impelled by alien laws. But when reason, which cannot be fully satisfied with any empirical use of the rules of the understanding, as being always conditioned, requires a completion of this chain of conditions, then the understanding is forced out of its sphere. And then reason partly represents objects of experience in a series so extended that no experience can grasp it, partly even (with a view to complete the series) it seeks entirely beyond experience *noumena*, to which it can attach that chain; and so, having at last escaped from the conditions of experience, reason makes its hold complete. These are then the transcendental ideas, which, (though in accord with the true but hidden ends of the natural determination of our reason) may aim, not at extravagant concepts, but at an unbounded extension of their empirical use, yet seduce the understanding by an unavoidable illusion to a transcendent use, which, though deceitful, cannot be restrained within the bounds of experience by any resolution, but only by scientific instruction and with much difficulty.

The Psychological Ideas[17]

People have long since observed that in all substances the subject proper, that which remains after all the accidents (as predicates) are abstracted, hence the substantial itself, remains unknown, and various complaints have been made concerning

these limits to our insight. But it will be well to consider that the human understanding is not to be blamed for its inability to know the substance of things, i.e., to determine it by itself, but rather for demanding to cognise it determinately as though it were a given object, it being a mere idea. Pure reason requires us to seek for every predicate of a thing its own subject, and for this subject, which is itself necessarily nothing but a predicate, its subject, and so on indefinitely (or as far as we can reach). But hence it follows that we must not hold anything at which we can arrive to be an ultimate subject, and that substance itself never can be thought by our understanding, however deep we may penetrate, even if all nature were unveiled to us. For the specific nature of our understanding consists in thinking everything discursively, i.e., by concepts, and so by mere predicates, to which, therefore, the absolute subject must always be wanting. Hence all the real properties by which we cognise bodies are mere accidents, not even excepting impenetrability, which we can only represent to ourselves as the effect of a force for which the subject is unknown to us.

Now we appear to have this substance in the consciousness of ourselves (in the thinking subject), and indeed in an immediate intuition; for all the predicates of an internal sense refer to the *ego*, as a subject, and I cannot conceive myself as the predicate of any other subject. Hence completeness in the reference of the given concepts as predicates to a subject—not merely an idea, but an object—that is, the *absolute subject* itself, seems to be given in experience. But this expectation is disappointed. For the ego is not a concept,[18] but only the indication of the object of the internal sense, so far as we cognise it by no further predicate. Consequently, it cannot be itself a predicate of any other thing; but just as little can it be a determinate concept of an absolute subject, but is, as in all other cases, only the reference of the internal phenomena to their unknown subject. Yet this idea (which serves very well as a regulative principle totally to destroy all materialistic explanations of the internal phenomena of the soul) occasions by a very natural misunderstanding a very specious argument, which infers the nature of the soul from this supposed cognition of the substance of our thinking being. This argument is specious insofar as the knowledge of this substance falls quite without the complex of experience.

But though we may call this thinking self (the soul) substance, as being the ultimate subject of thinking which cannot be further represented as the predicate of another thing, it remains quite empty and inconsequential if permanence—the quality which renders the concept of substances in experience fruitful—cannot be proved of it.

But permanence can never be proved of the concept of a substance as a thing in itself, but only for the purposes of experience. This is sufficiently shown by the first Analogy of Experience,[19] and whoever will not yield to this proof may try for himself whether he can succeed in proving, from the concept of a subject which does not exist itself as the predicate of another thing, that its existence is thoroughly permanent and that it cannot either in itself or by any natural cause come into being or pass out of it. These synthetic *a priori* propositions can never be proved in themselves, but only in reference to things as objects of possible experience.

If, therefore, from the concept of the soul as a substance we would infer its permanence, this can hold good as regards possible experience only, not of the soul as a thing in itself and beyond all possible experience. Now life is the subjective condition of all our possible experience; consequently we can only infer the permanence of the soul in life, for the death of man is the end of all the experience that concerns the soul as an object of experience, except the contrary be proved—which is the very question in hand. The permanence of the soul can therefore only be proved (and no one cares for that) during the life of man, but not, as we desire to do, after death. This is so because the concept of substance, insofar as it is to be considered as necessarily combined with the concept of permanence, can be so combined only according to the principles of possible experience, and therefore for the purposes of experience only.[20]

That there is something real outside us which not only corresponds but must correspond to our external perceptions can likewise be proved to be, not a connection of things in themselves, but for the sake of experience. This means that there is something empirical, i.e., some appearance in space outside us, that admits of a satisfactory proof; for we have nothing to do with other objects than those which belong to possible experience, because objects which cannot be given us in any experience are nothing for us. Empirically outside me is that which is intuited in space; and space, together with all the appearances which it contains, belongs to the representations whose con-

nection, according to laws of experience, proves their objective truth, just as the connection of the appearances of the internal sense proves the actuality of my soul (as an object of the internal sense). By means of external experience I am conscious of the actuality of bodies as external appearances in space, in the same manner as by means of internal experience I am conscious of the existence of my soul in time; but this soul is cognised only as an object of the internal sense by appearances that constitute an internal state and of which the being in itself, which forms the basis of these appearances, is unknown. Cartesian idealism therefore does nothing but distinguish external experience from dreaming and the conformity to law (as a criterion of its truth) of the former from the irregularity and the false illusion of the latter. In both it presupposes space and time as conditions of the existence of objects, and it only inquires whether the objects of the external senses which we, when awake, put in space are as actually to be found in it as the object of the internal sense, the soul, is in time; that is, whether experience carries with it sure criteria to distinguish it from imagination. This doubt, however, may easily be disposed of, and we always do so in common life by investigating the connection of appearances in both space and time according to universal laws of experience; and we cannot doubt, when the representation of external things throughout agrees therewith, that they constitute truthful experience. Material idealism, in which appearances are considered as such only according to their connection in experience may accordingly be very easily refuted; and it is just as sure an experience that bodies exist outside us (in space) as that I myself exist according to the representation of the internal sense (in time), for the concept "outside us" only signifies existence in space. However, as the ego in the proposition "I am" means not only the object of internal intuition (in time) but the subject of consciousness, just as body means not only external intuition (in space) but the thing in itself which is the basis of this appearance, then the question whether bodies (as appearances of the external sense) exist as bodies in nature apart from my thoughts may without any hesitation be denied. But the question whether I myself as an appearance of the internal sense (the soul according to empirical psychology) exist apart from my faculty of representation in time is an exactly similar question and must likewise be answered in the negative. And in this manner everything, when it is reduced to its true meaning, is decided and certain. The formal (which I have also called transcendental) actually abolishes the material, or Cartesian, idealism. For if space be nothing but a form of my sensibility, it is as a representation in me just as actual as I myself am, and nothing but the empirical truth of the appearances in it remains for consideration. But if this is not the case, if space and the appearances in it are something existing outside us, then all the criteria of experience outside our perception can never prove the actuality of these objects outside us. . . .

Solution of the General Question of the Prolegomena: How Is Metaphysics Possible as Science?

Metaphysics, as a natural disposition of reason, is actual; but if considered by itself alone (as the analytical solution of the third principal question showed), it is dialectical and illusory. If we think of taking principles from it, and in using them follow the natural, but on that account not less false, illusion, we can never produce science, but only a vain dialectical art, in which one school may outdo another but none can ever acquire a just and lasting approbation.

In order that as a science metaphysics may be entitled to claim, not mere fallacious plausibility, but insight and conviction, a critique of reason must itself exhibit the whole stock of *a priori* concepts, their division according to their various sources (sensibility, understanding, and reason), together with a complete table of them, the analysis of all these concepts, with all their consequences and especially the possibility of synthetic cognition *a priori* by means of the deduction of these concepts, the principles and bounds of their use, all in a complete system. Critique, therefore, and critique alone contains in itself the whole well-proved and well-tested plan, and even all the means required to establish metaphysics as a science; by other ways and means it is impossible. The question here, therefore, is not so much how this performance is possible as how to set it going and induce men of clear heads to quit their hitherto perverted and fruitless cultivation for one that will not deceive, and how such a union for the common end may best be directed.

This much is certain: whoever has once tasted critique will be ever after disgusted with all dogmatical twaddle which he formerly put up with because his reason had to have something and could find nothing better for its support. Critique stands in the same relation to the common metaphysics of the schools as chemistry does to alchemy, or as astronomy to the astrology of the fortune teller. I pledge myself that nobody who has thought through and grasped the principles of critique, even only in these *Prolegomena*, will ever return to that old and sophistical pseudoscience; but he will, rather, with a certain delight look forward to a metaphysics which is now indeed in his power, requiring no more preparatory discoveries, and now at last affording permanent satisfaction to reason. For here is an advantage upon which, of all possible sciences, metaphysics alone can with certainty reckon: that it can be brought to such completion and fixity as to require no further change or be capable of any augmentation by new discoveries, because here reason has the sources of its knowledge in itself, not in objects and their observation, by which its stock of knowledge could be further increased. When, therefore, it has exhibited the fundamental laws of its faculty completely and so determinately as to avoid all misunderstanding, there remains nothing more for pure reason to cognise *a priori*; nay, there is even no ground to raise further questions. The sure prospect of knowledge so determinate and so compact has a peculiar charm, even though we should set aside all its advantages, of which I shall hereafter speak.

All false art, all vain wisdom, lasts its time but finally destroys itself, and its highest culture is also the epoch of its decay. That this time is come for metaphysics appears from the state into which it has fallen among all learned nations, despite all the zeal with which other sciences of every kind are prosecuted. The old arrangement of our university studies still preserves its shadow; now and then an academy of science tempts men by offering prizes to write essays on it, but it is no longer numbered among sound sciences; and let anyone judge for himself how a sophisticated man, if he were called a great metaphysician, would receive the compliment, which may be well meant but is scarcely envied by anybody.

Yet, though the period of the downfall of all dogmatic metaphysics has undoubtedly arrived, we are yet far from being able to say that the period of its regeneration is come by means of a thorough and complete critique of reason. All transitions from an inclination to its contrary pass through the stage of indifference, and this moment is the most dangerous for an author but, in my opinion, the most favorable for the science. For when party spirit has died out by a total dissolution of former connections, minds are in the best state to listen to several proposals for an organisation according to a new plan.

When I say that I hope these *Prolegomena* will excite investigation in the field of critique and afford a new and promising object to sustain the general spirit of philosophy, which seems on its speculative side to want sustenance, I can imagine beforehand that everyone whom the thorny paths of my *Critique* have tired and put out of humor will ask me upon what I found this hope. My answer is: upon the irresistible law of necessity.

That the human spirit will ever give up metaphysical researches is as little to be expected as that we should prefer to give up breathing altogether, in order to avoid inhaling impure air. There will, therefore, always be metaphysics in the world; nay, everyone, especially every reflective man, will have it and, for want of a recognised standard, will shape it for himself after his own pattern. What has hitherto been called metaphysics cannot satisfy any critical mind, but to forego it entirely is impossible; therefore a critique of pure reason itself must now be attempted or, if one exists, investigated and brought to the full test, because there is no other means of supplying this pressing want which is something more than mere thirst for knowledge.

Ever since I have come to know critique, whenever I finish reading a book of metaphysical contents which, by the determination of its concepts, by variety, order, and an easy style, was not only entertaining but also helpful, I cannot help asking, "Has this author indeed advanced metaphysics a single step?" The learned men whose works have been useful to me in other respects and always contributed to the culture of my mental powers will, I hope, forgive me for saying that I have never been able to find either their essays or my own less important ones (though self-love may recommend them to me) to have advanced the science of metaphysics in the least, and why? Here is the very obvious reason: metaphysics did not then exist as a science, nor can it be gathered piecemeal; but its germ must be fully preformed in critique. But in order to prevent all misconception, we must remember what has already been said—that

by the analytic treatment of our concepts the understanding gains indeed a great deal, but the science (of metaphysics) is thereby not in the least advanced because these analyses of concepts are nothing but the materials from which the intention is to carpenter our science. Let the concepts of substance and of accident be ever so well analyzed and determined; all this is very well as a preparation for some future use. But if we cannot prove that in all which exists the substance endures and only the accidents vary, our science is not the least advanced by all our analyses. Metaphysics has hitherto never been able to prove *a priori* either this proposition or that of sufficient reason, still less any more complex theorem such as belongs to psychology or cosmology, or indeed any synthetic proposition. By all its analyzing, therefore, nothing is affected, nothing obtained or forwarded; and the science, after all this bustle and noise, still remains as it was in the days of Aristotle, though far better preparations were made for it than of old if only the clue to synthetic cognitions had been discovered.

If anyone thinks himself offended, he is at liberty to refute my charge by producing a single synthetic proposition belonging to metaphysics which he would prove dogmatically *a priori*; for until he has actually performed this feat, I shall not grant that he has truly advanced the science, even though this proposition should be sufficiently confirmed by common experience. No demand can be more moderate or more equitable and, in the (inevitably certain) event of its nonperformance, no assertion more just than that hitherto metaphysics has never existed as a science.

But there are two things which, in case the challenge be accepted, I must deprecate: first, trifling about probability and conjecture, which are suited as little to metaphysics as to geometry; and secondly, a decision by means of the magic wand of so-called sound common sense, which does not convince everyone but accommodates itself to personal peculiarities.

For as to the former, nothing can be more absurd than in metaphysics, a philosophy from pure reason, to try to ground our judgments upon probability and conjecture. Everything that is to be cognised *a priori* is thereby announced as apodeictically certain, and must therefore be proved in this way. We might as well try to ground geometry or arithmetic upon conjectures. As to the calculus of probabilities in the latter, it does not contain probable but perfectly certain judgments concerning the degree of the possibility of certain cases under given uniform conditions, which, in the sum of all possible cases, must infallibly happen according to the rule, though it is not sufficiently determined as regards every single instance. Conjectures (by means of induction and analogy) can be suffered in an empirical natural science only, yet even there at least the possibility of what we assume must be quite certain.

The appeal to common sense is even more absurd, when concepts and principles are said to be valid, not insofar as they hold with regard to experience, but outside the conditions of experience. For what is common sense? It is normal good sense, so far as it judges right? What is normal good sense? It is the faculty of the knowledge and use of rules *in concreto*, as distinguished from the speculative understanding, which is a faculty of knowing rules *in abstracto*. Common sense can hardly understand the rule that every event is determined by means of its cause and can never comprehend it thus generally. It therefore demands an example from experience; and when it hears that this rule means nothing but what is always thought when a pane was broken or a kitchen-utensil missing, it then understands the principle and grants it. Common sense, therefore, is only of use so far as it can see its rules (though they actually are *a priori*) confirmed by experience; consequently, to comprehend them *a priori*, or independently of experience, belongs to the speculative understanding and lies quite beyond the horizon of common sense. But the province of metaphysics is entirely confined to the latter kind of knowledge, and it is certainly a bad sign of common sense to appeal to it as a witness, for it cannot here form any opinion whatever, and men look down upon it with contempt until they are in trouble and can find in their speculation neither advice nor help.

It is a common subterfuge of those false friends of common sense (who occasionally prize it highly, but usually despise it) to say that there must surely be at all events some propositions which are immediately certain and of which there is no occasion to give any proof, or even any account at all, because we otherwise could never stop inquiring into the grounds of our judgments. But if we except the principle of contradiction, which is not sufficient to show the truth of synthetic judgments, they can never adduce, in proof of this privilege, anything else indubitable which they can immediately ascribe to common sense, except

mathematical propositions, such as twice two make four, between two points there is but one straight line, etc. But these judgments are radically different from those of metaphysics. For in mathematics I can by thinking construct whatever I represent to myself as possible by a concept: I add to the first two the other two, one by one, and myself make the number four, or I draw in thought from one point to another all manner of lines, equal as well as unequal; yet I can draw one only which is like itself in all its parts. But I cannot, by all my power of thinking, extract from the concept of a thing the concept of something else whose existence is necessarily connected with the former, but I must call upon experience. And though my understanding furnishes me *a priori* (yet only in reference to possible experience) with the concept of such a connection (i.e., causation), I cannot exhibit it *a priori* in intuition, like the concepts of mathematics, and to show its possibility *a priori*. This concept, together with the principles of its application, always requires, if it is to hold *a priori*—as is requisite in metaphysics—a justification and deduction of its possibility, because we cannot otherwise know how far it holds good and whether it can be used in experience only or beyond it also. Therefore in metaphysics, as a speculative science of pure reason, we can never appeal to common sense, but may do so only when (in certain matters) we are forced to surrender it and renounce all pure speculative cognition, which must always be theoretic knowledge, and therefore are forced to forego metaphysics itself and its instruction for the sake of adopting a rational faith which alone may be possible for us, sufficient to our wants, and perhaps even more salutary than knowledge itself. For then the shape of the thing is quite altered. Metaphysics must be science, not only as a whole but in all its parts; otherwise it is nothing at all, because as speculation of pure reason it finds a hold only on universal insights. Beyond its field, however, probability and common sense may be used advantageously and justly, but on quite special principles, the importance of which always depends on their reference to the practical.

This is what I hold myself justified in requiring for the possibility of metaphysics as a science.

Endnotes

[1] Nevertheless Hume called such destructive philosophy metaphysics and attached to it great value. "Metaphysics and morals," he says, "are the most important branches of science; mathematics and natural philosophy are not half so important" [*Essays Morals, Political, and Literary* (edited by Green and Grose) vol. I, p. 187. Essay XIV: Of the Rise and Progress of the Arts and Sciences]. But the acute man merely regarded the negative use arising from the moderation of extravagant claims of speculative reason, and the complete settlement of the many endless and troublesome controversies that mislead mankind. He overlooked the positive injury which results if reason be deprived of its most important prospects, which can alone supply to the will the highest aim for all its endeavors.

[2] J. A. Segner, *Elementa Arithmeticae et Geometriae, Göttingen*, 1739.

[3] In the next several pages the order of the German text as it appears in the *Philosophische Bibliothek* Edition of Kant's *Works* is followed rather than the *Akademie* Edition.

[4] I freely grant that these examples do not represent such judgments of perception as ever could become judgments of experience, even though a concept of the understanding were superadded, because they refer merely to feeling, which everybody knows to be merely subjective and which, of course, can never be attributed to the object and, consequently, never can become objective. I only wished to give here an example of a judgment that is merely subjectively valid, containing no ground for necessary universal validity and thereby for a relation to the object. An example of the judgments of perception which become judgments of experience by superadded concepts of the understanding will be given in the next note.

[5] As an easier example, we may take the following: when the sun shines on the stone, it grows warm. This judgment, however often I and others may have perceived it, is a mere judgment of perception and contains no necessity; perceptions are only usually conjoined in this manner. But if I say: the sun warms the stone, I add to the perception a concept of the understanding, viz., that of cause, which necessarily connects with the concept of sunshine that of heat, and the synthetic judgment becomes of necessity universally valid, viz., objective, and is converted from a perception into experience.

[6] This name seems preferable to the term *particularia*, which is used for these judgments in logic. For the latter already contains the thought that they are not universal. But when I start from unity (in singular judgments) and proceed to totality, I must not (even indirectly and negatively) include any reference to totality. I think plurality merely without totality, and not the exclusion of totality. This is necessary, if the logical moments are to underlie the pure concepts of the understanding. In logical usage one may leave things as they were.

[7] But how does the proposition that judgments of experience contain necessity in the synthesis of perceptions agree with my statement so often before inculcated that experience, as cognition *a posteriori*, can afford contingent judgments only? When I say that experience teaches me something, I mean only the perception that lies in experience—for example, that heat always follows the shining of the sun on a stone; consequently, the proposition of experience is always so far contingent. That this heat necessarily follows the shining of the sun is contained indeed in the judgment of experience (by means of the concept of cause), yet is a fact not learned by experience; for, conversely, experience is first of all generated by this addition of the concept of the understanding (of cause) to perception. How perception attains this addition may be seen by referring in the *Critique* itself to the section on the transcendental faculty of judgment, B 176 *et seq.*

[8] The three following paragraphs will hardly be understood unless reference be made to what the *Critique* itself says on the subject of the principles; they will, however, be of service in giving a general view of the principles, and in fixing the attention on the main moments. [See *Critique*, B 187–294.]

[9] The Axioms of Intuition. See *Critique*, B 202–207.

[10] The Anticipations of Perception. See *ibid.*, B 207–218.

[11] The Analogies of Experience. See *ibid.*, B 218–265.

[12] The Postulates of Empirical Thought. See *ibid.*, B 265–294.

[13] Heat and light are in a small space just as large, as to degree, as in a large one; in like manner the internal representations, pain, consciousness in general, whether they last a short or a long time, need not vary as to the degree. Hence the quantity is here in a point and in a moment just as great as in any space or time, however great. Degrees are thus quantities not in intuition but in mere sensation (or the quantity of the content of an intuition). Hence they can only be estimated quantitatively by the relation of 1 to 0, viz., by their capability of decreasing by infinite intermediate degrees to disappearance, or of increasing from naught through infinite gradations to a determinate sensation in a certain time.

[14] The principles of sensibility (space and time). See *Critique* of *Pure Reason*, B 33–B 73.

[15] If we can say that a science is actual, at least in the idea of all men, as soon as it appears that the problems which lead to it are proposed to everybody by the nature of human reason, and hence that at all times many (though faulty) endeavors are unavoidably made in its

behalf; then we are bound to say that metaphysics is subjectively (and indeed necessarily) actual, and then we justly ask how is it (objectively) possible.

[16] In disjunctive judgments we consider all possibility as divided in respect to a particular concept. By the ontological principle of the thoroughgoing determination of a thing in general, I understand the principle that either the one or the other of all possible contradictory predicates must be assigned to any object. This is at the same time the principle of all disjunctive judgments, constituting the foundation of the totality of all possibility, and in it the possibility of every object in general is considered as determined. This may serve as a brief explanation of the above proposition: that the activity of reason in disjunctive syllogisms is formally the same as that by which it fashions the idea of a totality of all reality, containing in itself the positive member of all contradictory predicates.

[17] See *Critique of Pure Reason*, "The Paralogisms of Pure Reason," A 341/B 399–A 405/B 432.

[18] Were the representation of the apperception (the ego) a concept by which anything could be thought, it could be used as a predicate of other things or contain predicates in itself. But it is nothing more than the feeling of an existence without the slightest concept and is only the representation of that to which all thinking stands in relation (*relatione accidentis*).

[19] Cf. *Critique*, B. 224–232.

[20] It is indeed very remarkable how carelessly metaphysicians have always passed over the principle of the permanence of substances without ever attempting a proof of it; doubtless because they found themselves abandoned by all proofs as soon as they began to deal with the concept of substance. Common sense, which felt distinctly that without this presupposition no union of perceptions in experience is possible, supplied the want by a postulate. From experience itself it never could derive such a principle, partly because material objects (substances) cannot be so traced in all their alterations and dissolutions that the matter can always be found undiminished, partly because the principle contains *necessity*, which is always the sign of an *a priori* principle. People then boldly applied this postulate to the concept of soul as a *substance*, and concluded a necessary continuance of the soul after the death of man (especially as the simplicity of this substance, which is inferred from the indivisibility of consciousness, secured it from destruction by dissolution). Had they found the genuine source of this principle—a discovery which requires deeper researches than they were ever inclined to make—they would have seen that the law of the permanence of substances finds a place for the purposes of experience only, and hence can hold good of things so far as they are to be cognised and conjoined with others in experience, but never independently of all possible experience, and consequently cannot hold good of the soul after death.

48. Excerpts from the Introduction and Logic Section of Encyclopedia of the Philosophical Sciences in Outline

G. W. F. HEGEL

After Kant, some philosophers were not satisfied with the restriction of metaphysics to the exploration of the necessary form of human experience. Some thought that there might be intuitive ways to know the "in-itself," or that consciousness might be "absolute." Hegel (1770–1831) produced a systematic, all-encompassing idealism that made a virtue of the historical contradictions in philosophy. Whereas Kant had taken such dialectical antinomies as a sign that human reason cannot fathom the "in-itself," Hegel attempted to incorporate them into a vision of Geist (mind or spirit) becoming more comprehensive and self-knowing: philosophies are cultural products that evolve by means of negating and subsuming their rivals. Hegel thought he saw such dialectical relations everywhere: in history and society, in philosophy, in science, and in logic. Though Hegel was an unabashed idealist, seemingly caught up in the metaphor of a universal life force manifesting itself in all things (the poet, Hölderlin, was his college roommate), it should be noted that he criticized other post-Kantian idealists for being merely intuitive or emotional. Hegel wanted philosophical understanding to be scientific. The selection reprinted here shows Hegel's view that metaphysics is a kind of logic.

1. Philosophy lacks an advantage enjoyed by the other sciences. It cannot like them presuppose its objects on the immediate admissions of conception, nor can it assume that its method of cognition, either for beginning or continuing, is already accepted. The objects of philosophy, it is true, are to begin with the same as those of religion. In both the object is truth, in that supreme sense in which God and God alone is truth. Both then go on to consider the finite realm of nature and the human mind, with their relation to each other and to their truth in God. Thus philosophy may—indeed must—presume some acquaintance with its objects, and an interest in them besides, if only for the reason that in point of time consciousness forms *conceptions* of objects before it forms *concepts* of them, and that it is only through conception, and

by recourse to it, that the thinking mind rises to know and comprehend *thinkingly.*

But in the thinking study of things, it soon becomes clear that it involves the requirement of showing the *necessity* of its content, of demonstrating the being of its objects, as well as their determinations. Our original acquaintance with them thus appears inadequate. We can assume nothing, and assert nothing dogmatically; nor can we accept the assertions and assumptions of others. Yet we must make a beginning; and a beginning, as immediate, involves, or rather is, an assumption. Thus it is difficult to *begin* at all.

2. This *thinking study of objects* may serve in general as a definition of philosophy. But the definition is too wide. If it is correct to say that thought makes the difference between man and animals, then everything human is human for the sole and simple reason that it is due to the operation of thought. Philosophy, on the other hand, is a peculiar mode of thinking, a mode in which thinking becomes knowledge, and conceptual knowledge. Thus however great the identity and essential unity of the two modes of thought, the philosophical mode will be *different* from the thinking that is active in all that is human and gives humanity its distinctive character. This difference relates to the fact that the strictly human and thought-induced contents of consciousness do not originally appear in the form of a thought, but as feeling, intuition, conception—all of which forms must be distinguished from the form of thought proper.

According to an old prejudice, which has become a commonplace, it is thought that marks man off from animals. Yet trivial as this old belief may seem, it must, strangely enough, be recalled to mind in view of a prejudice of the present day. This prejudice sets feeling and thought so far apart as to make them opposites, and supposes them to be so antagonistic that feeling, particularly religious feeling, is contaminated, perverted and even annihilated by thought, and religion and religiosity do not essentially grow out of and rest on thinking. But those who make this separation forget that only man has the capacity for religion, and animals no more have religion than law and morality.

Those who insist on this separation of religion from thinking usually have in mind the sort of thinking that may be called "meta-thinking," reflective thinking that considers thoughts as thoughts and brings them into consciousness. Failure to see and observe this definite distinction that philosophy draws in respect of thinking is the source of the crudest ideas and reproaches against philosophy. Man, just because it is his essence to think, is the only being that possesses law, religion, and ethics. In these spheres, therefore, thinking, in the guise of feeling, faith, or conception, has not been inactive; its activity and productions are present and contained in them. But it is one thing to have such feelings and conceptions determined and permeated by thought, and another to have thoughts about them. The thoughts to which meta-thinking on those modes of consciousness gives rise are what comprise reflection, argumentation, and the like, as well as philosophy itself.

Neglect of this distinction has led to another frequent misunderstanding. Such meta-thinking has often been held to be the condition, or even the only way, of attaining a conception and certainty of the eternal and true. The (now somewhat antiquated) metaphysical proofs of God's existence, for example, have been treated as if knowledge of them and a conviction of their validity were the sole and essential means of producing a belief and conviction that there is a God. This claim would find its parallel, if we said that eating was impossible before we had acquired a knowledge of the chemical, botanical, and zoological characters of our food; and that we must delay digestion until we have completed the study of anatomy and physiology. Were it so, these sciences in their field, like philosophy in its, would gain greatly in utility; in fact, their utility would rise to absolute and universal indispensableness. Or rather, instead of being indispensable, they would not exist at all.

3. The *content*, of whatever kind, that fills our consciousness, constitutes the *determinacy* of our feelings, intuitions, images, and ideas; of our aims and duties; and of our thoughts and concepts. Thus feeling, intuition, image, etc. are the *forms* assumed by these contents. The contents remain the same whether they are felt, intuited, represented or willed, and whether they are merely felt, or felt with an admixture of thoughts, or merely and simply thought. In any one of these forms, or in the mixture of several, the content is consciousness' *object*. But when they are thus objects of consciousness, the *determinacies of these forms* ally themselves with the content, so that each form seems to give rise to a particular object. Thus, what is at bottom the same may look like a different content.

The determinacies of feeling, intuition, desire, and will, so far as we are *aware* of them, are in general called "ideas" or "conceptions"; and, roughly speaking, philosophy puts thoughts, categories, or, more precisely, concepts, in the place of ideas. Ideas in general may be regarded as metaphors of thoughts and concepts. But to have these ideas does not imply that we appreciate their meaning for thinking, i.e., their thoughts and concepts. Conversely, it is one thing to have thoughts and concepts, and another to know what ideas, intuitions, and feelings correspond to them.

This explains in part what people call the "unintelligibility" of philosophy. The difficulty lies partly in an incapacity—which in itself is just want of habit—for abstract thinking, an inability to grasp pure thoughts and move about in them. In our ordinary consciousness the thoughts are clothed in and combined with familiar sensuous and spiritual material; and in meta-thinking, reflection, and argumentation we introduce a blend of thoughts into feelings, ideas, and intuitions. (Thus in propositions where the content is wholly sensuous—e.g., "This leaf is green"—such categories as being and individuality are introduced.) But to make thoughts pure and simple our object is a different matter.

But there is also another reason for the complaint that philosophy is unintelligible: an impatience to have before one as an idea that which is in consciousness as a thought or concept. When people are asked to apprehend some concept, they often complain that they do not know what they are supposed to *think*. In a concept there is nothing more to be thought than the concept itself. What the phrase reveals is a hankering after an idea with which we are already familiar. Consciousness, denied its familiar ideas, feels the ground where it once stood firm and at home taken from it, and, when transported into the pure region of concepts, cannot tell where in the world it is. Thus authors, preachers, and orators are found most intelligible when they speak of things that their readers or hearers already know by rote, which are familiar to them and are understood as a matter of course.

4. In connection with our ordinary consciousness, philosophy will first have to prove and even to awaken the need for its peculiar mode of knowledge. But in connection with the objects of religion, with truth in general, it will have to show that it is capable of knowing them from its own resources; and if a difference from religious conceptions comes to light, it will have to *justify* the points in which it diverges.

5. To give a preliminary explanation of this distinction and of the connected insight that the real content of our consciousness is retained, and even put in its proper light for the first time, when translated into the form of the thought and the concept, it may be well to recall another old prejudice: that to learn the truth of any object or event, even of feelings, intuitions, opinions, and ideas, we must first think it over. Now in any case to think things over is at least to transform feelings, ideas, etc., into thoughts.

Nature has given everyone an ability to think. But thought is all that philosophy claims as the form proper to her business: and thus neglect of the distinction stated in §3 leads to a new delusion, the reverse of the complaint about the unintelligibility of philosophy. This science must often submit to the slight of hearing even people who have never taken any trouble with it talk as if they thoroughly understood all about it. With no preparation beyond an ordinary education they do not hesitate, especially under the influence of religious

feelings, to philosophize and to criticize philosophy. Everybody allows that to know any other science you must have first studied it, and that you can express a judgement on it only in virtue of such knowledge. Everybody allows that to make a shoe you must have learned and practised the craft of the shoemaker, though every man has a model in his own foot, and possesses in his hands the natural endowments for the operations required. For philosophy alone, it is supposed, such study, care, and application are not requisite. This comfortable view has recently received corroboration through the theory of immediate or intuitive knowledge.

6. So much for the form of philosophical knowledge. It is no less desirable, on the other hand, that philosophy should understand that its content is no other than *actuality*, that content which, originally produced and producing itself within the precincts of the living mind, has become the *world*, the inward and outward world, of consciousness. At first we become aware of these contents in what we call experience. Even a judicious consideration of the world, of the wide range of inward and outward existence, enables us to distinguish mere appearance, transient and meaningless, from what in itself really deserves the name of actuality. As it is only in form that philosophy is distinguished from other modes of attaining an awareness of this same content, it must necessarily be in harmony with actuality and experience. In fact, this harmony may be viewed as at least an extrinsic test of the truth of a philosophy. Similarly it may be held the highest and final aim of philosophic science to bring about, by knowledge of this harmony, a reconciliation of the self-conscious reason with the reason that is in the world, with actuality.

In the preface to my *Philosophy of Right*, are found the propositions:

> What is rational is actual;
>   and,
> What is actual is rational.

These simple statements have given rise to expressions of surprise and hostility, even in quarters where it would be reckoned an insult to presume absence of philosophy, and still more of religion. Religion at least need not be brought in evidence; its doctrines of the divine government of the world affirm these propositions too decidedly. For their philosophic sense, we must presuppose cultivation enough to know, not only that God is actual, that He is the supreme actuality, that He alone is truly actual; but also, as regards the formal side, that existence is in part appearance, and only in part actuality. In common life, any brain wave, error, evil, and everything of the nature of evil, as well as every degenerate and transitory existence whatever, gets indiscriminately called an actuality. But even our ordinary feelings forbid a contingent existence getting the emphatic name of an actual; for the contingent is an existence that has no greater value than that of something possible, which may as well not be as be. As for the term 'actuality,' these critics would have done well to consider the sense in which I employ it. In a detailed Logic I have treated among other things of actuality, and accurately distinguished it not only from the contingent, which, after all, has existence, but more precisely from determinate being, existence, and other determinations.

The actuality of the rational is opposed by the notion that Ideas and ideals are nothing but chimeras, and philosophy a mere system of such figments. It is also opposed by the contrary notion that Ideas and ideals are too excellent to have actuality, too impotent to procure it for themselves. This divorce between idea and reality is especially dear to the understanding that regards its dream-like abstractions as something true and real, and prides itself on the 'ought,' which it takes especial pleasure in prescribing even in the field of politics. As if the world had waited on it to learn how it ought to be, and was not! For, if it were as it ought to be, what would come of the precocious wisdom of that 'ought'? When understanding turns this 'ought' against trivial external and transitory objects, against social regulations or conditions, which very likely possess a great relative importance for a certain time and special circles, it may often be right, and in such a case may find much that fails to satisfy general requirements: for who is not acute enough to see a great deal in his own surroundings which is really far from being as it ought to be? But such acuteness is mistaken to imagine that, in these objects and their 'ought,' it is dealing with questions of philosophical interest. The sole concern of philosophy is the Idea: and the Idea is not so impotent that it merely ought to be without actually being. The object of philosophy is an actuality of which those objects, social regulations, and conditions, are only the superficial surface.

7. Thus meta-thinking in general contains

the principle (which also means the beginning) of philosophy, and when it arose again in its independence in modern times, after the epoch of the Lutheran Reformation, it did not, as in the philosophical beginnings among the Greeks, stand merely aloof and abstract, but at once turned its energies also on the apparently illimitable material of the phenomenal world. In this way the name 'philosophy' came to be applied to all those branches of knowledge that are engaged in ascertaining the fixed measure and universal in the ocean of empirical individualities, as well as the necessity, the laws, in the apparent disorder of the endless masses of the contingent; and which thus derive their content from their own intuition and perception of the external and internal world, from the very presence of nature and of the mind and heart of man.

The principle of experience involves the infinitely important condition that, to accept and believe any fact the person must be present; or, more exactly, that he must find the fact unified and combined with the certainty of his own self. He must himself be present, whether only with his external senses, or else with his profounder mind, his essential self-consiousness. This principle is the same as that which has in the present day been termed faith, immediate knowledge, the revelation in the outward world, and, above all, in our own heart. Those sciences, which thus got the name of philosophy, we call *empirical* sciences, since they take their departure from experience. Still the essential results that they aim at and provide, are laws, general propositions, a theory—the thoughts of what is found existing. Thus Newtonian physics was called Natural Philosophy. Hugo Grotius, again, by putting together and comparing the behavior of nations toward each other in history, set up, with the help of the ordinary general reasoning, general principles, a theory that may be termed the Philosophy of International Law. In England this is still the usual signification of the term philosophy. Newton continues to be celebrated as the greatest of philosophers: and the name goes down as far as the price-lists of instrument makers. All instruments, such as the thermometer and barometer, that do not come under the special head of magnetic or electric apparatus are styled philosophical instruments. Surely thought, and not a mere combination of wood, iron, etc. ought to be called the instrument of philosophy! The recent science of Political Economy in particular is also called philosophy—what we are wont to call 'rational' political economy, or, perhaps, the political economy of *intelligence*.

8. In its own field this knowledge may at first give satisfaction; but in two ways it falls short. In the first place there is another realm of objects that it does not embrace—freedom, spirit, and God. They are excluded, not because it can be said that they have nothing to do with experience; for though they are certainly not experiences of the senses, it is quite a tautological proposition to say that whatever is in consciousness is experienced. The reason for their exclusion is that in their *content* these objects evidently show themselves as infinite.

There is an old dictum often wrongly attributed to Aristotle, and supposed to express the general tenor of his philosophy, '*Nihil est in intellectu quod non fuerit in sensu*': there is nothing in thought that has not been in sense, in experience. If speculative philosophy refused to admit this maxim, it can have done so only by a misunderstanding. It will, however, conversely, also assert: '*Nihil est in sensu quod non fuerit in intellectu.*' And this in two senses: in the general sense that *nous* or spirit (the more profound counterpart of *nous*) is the cause of the world; and in the specific sense (§2) that the feeling of right, ethics and religion is a feeling (and thus an experience) of such content as can only spring from and rest on thought.

9. In the second place in point of *form* the subjective reason requires further satisfaction; this form is, in general, necessity (§1). The method of empirical science exhibits two defects. The first is that the universal contained in it—the genus, etc.—is, on its own account, indeterminate, and therefore not on its own account connected with the particular. Each is external and accidental to the other; and it is the same with the particulars that are brought into union: each is external and accidental to the others. The second defect is that the beginnings are in every case data and postulates, neither accounted for nor deduced. In both these points the form of necessity fails to get its due. Hence meta-thinking, whenever it sets itself to remedy these defects, becomes speculative thinking, strictly philosophical thinking. As a species of meta-thinking, therefore, that, though it has much in common with the first variety, is nevertheless different from it, it thus possesses, in addition to the common forms, some forms of its own, of which the concept is the universal one.

The relation of speculative science to the other sciences is just this. It does not neglect the empirical content of the sciences, but recognizes and adopts it; it recognizes and applies to its own content the universal of these sciences, their laws and classifications: but besides all this, into the categories of science it introduces and applies other categories. The difference thus relates only to this change of categories. Speculative logic contains all previous logic and metaphysics: it preserves the same forms of thought, laws, and objects—while at the same time remodeling and expanding them with further categories.

From concept in the speculative sense we should distinguish what is ordinarily called a concept. The claim that no concept can comprehend the infinite, a claim that has been repeated over and over again till it has grown axiomatic, is based on this ordinary, one-sided sense of 'concept.'

10. The thinking involved in philosophical knowledge itself calls for explanation. We must understand in what way it possesses necessity, and its claim to be able to apprehend absolute objects (God, spirit, freedom) must be substantiated. Such an insight, however, is itself a philosophical cognition and thus falls within philosophy itself. A preliminary attempt to make matters plain would only be unphilosophical, and consist of a tissue of assumptions, assertions, and inferential pros and cons, of dogmatism without cogency, against which there would be an equal right of counter-dogmatism.

A main line of argument in the Critical Philosophy bids us pause before proceeding to inquire into God or the essence of things, and first of all examine the faculty of cognition and see whether it is equal to the task. We ought, says Kant, to become acquainted with the instrument, before we undertake the work for which it is to be employed; for if the instrument be insufficient, all our trouble will be in vain. The plausibility of this thought has won general assent and admiration; the result of which has been to withdraw cognition from an interest in its objects and absorption in them, and to direct it back to itself, to the question of form. Unless we wish to be deceived by words, it is easy to see through this. In the case of other instruments, we can examine and assess them in other ways than by setting about the special work for which they are destined. But the examination of knowledge can only be carried out by *knowing*. To examine this so-called instrument is the same thing as to know it. But to seek to know before we know is as absurd as the wise resolution of the scholastic, not to venture into the water until he had learned to swim. . . .

11. The need for philosophy may be specified thus. The mind, when it feels or intuits, finds its object in something sensuous; when it imagines, in an image; when it wills, in an aim. But in contrast to, or it may be only in distinction from, these forms of its existence and of its objects, the mind has also to gratify its highest and most inward life, *thought*. Thus the mind renders thought its object. In the deepest meaning of the phrase, it comes *to itself*; for thought is its principle, its unadulterated self. But while thus occupied, thought entangles itself in contradictions, loses itself in the hard-and-fast nonidentity of thoughts, and so, instead of reaching itself, is caught in its opposite. This result of the thinking of the mere understanding is resisted by the higher need, which is grounded in the perseverance of thought, which continues true to itself, even in this conscious loss of its consonance with itself, 'that it may overcome' and work out in thinking itself the solution of its own contradictions.

To see that thought in its very nature is dialectical, and that, as understanding, it must fall into contradictions, the negative of itself, forms one of the main lessons of logic. When thought despairs of achieving, by its own means, the solution of the contradiction that it has brought upon itself, it turns back to those solutions with which the mind has learned to console itself in some of its other modes and forms. Unfortunately, however, the retreat of thought has led it, as Plato noticed even in his time, to an unnecessary 'misology'; and it then takes up against itself that hostile attitude of which an example is seen in the doctrine that immediate knowledge, as it is called, is the exclusive form in which we are conscious of the truth.

12. The rise of philosophy is due to this need. Its point of departure is experience; our immediate and our inferential consciousness. Awakened by this stimulus, thought's essential procedure is to raise itself above natural consciousness, above the senses and inferences, into its own unadulterated element, and to assume, accordingly, at first a stand-aloof, negative attitude toward that beginning. Its first satisfaction it finds in itself, in the Idea of the universal essence of these phenomena: this Idea (the absolute, God) may be more or less abstract. Conversely, the experiential sciences con-

tain a stimulus to overcome the form in which their varied contents are presented, and to elevate these contents to necessity. For these contents have the form of a vast conglomerate, one thing side by side with another, as if they were merely given and immediate—as in general contingent. This stimulus drags thought out of that universality and its merely *implicit* guarantee of satisfaction, and impels it on to a development out of itself. This development involves, on the one hand, merely receiving the content and the determinations that it presents; but, on the other, it also gives the content a new form: it lets it emerge freely, in the sense of original thinking and in accordance only with the necessity of the subject-matter itself.

On the relation between 'immediacy' and 'mediation' in consciousness we shall speak later, expressly and with more detail. Here it may suffice that, though the two moments present themselves as distinct, still neither of them can be absent, nor can one exist apart from the other. Thus the knowledge of God, as of every supersensible reality, is essentially an elevation above sensations or intuitions: it consequently involves a negative attitude to the initial data, and to that extent mediation. For to mediate is to begin and to go on to a second thing; so that the existence of this second thing depends on our having reached it from something other than it. In spite of this, the knowledge of God is no less independent of the empirical phase: in fact, its independence is essentially secured through this negation and elevation. If we attach an unfair prominence to mediation, and represent it as conditionedness, it may be said—not that it would amount to much—that philosophy is the child of experience, of the *a posteriori*. (In fact, thinking is the negation of what we have immediately before us.) With as much truth, however, we may be said to owe eating to the means of nourishment, for we cannot eat without them. If we take this view, eating is certainly represented as ungrateful: it devours that to which it owes itself. Thinking, in this sense, is equally ungrateful.

But there is also an *a priori* aspect of thought, where by a mediation, not made by anything external but by a reflection into self, we have that immediacy that is universality, the self-containment of thought that is so much at home with itself that it feels an innate indifference to particularization, and thus to development of itself. It is thus also with religion, which, whether it be rude or elaborate, whether it be developed to scientific consciousness or confined to the simple faith of the heart, possesses the same intensive nature of contentment and felicity. But if thought gets no further than the universality of Ideas, as was perforce the case in the first philosophies (e.g., Eleatic being, or Heraclitus' becoming), it is open to the charge of formalism. Even in a developed philosophy, we may find a mastery merely of abstract propositions or determinations such as, 'In the absolute all is one,' and 'Subject and object are identical,' which are only repeated when it comes to particulars. In respect of this first period of thought, the period of mere generality, we may safely say that experience is the real author of *growth* and *advance* in philosophy. For, first, the empirical sciences do not stop short at the mere perception of the individual features of a phenomenon. By the aid of thought, they have met philosophy with materials prepared for it, in the form of general uniformities, laws, and classifications of phenomena. Thus the content of the particular is made ready to be received into philosophy. This, second, implies a compulsion on thought itself to proceed to these concrete determinations. The reception of these contents, now that thought has removed their immediacy and made them cease to be mere data, forms at the same time a development of thought out of itself. Philosophy, then, owes its development to the empirical sciences. In return it gives their contents the most essential form: the *freedom* (the *a priori*) of thinking. The contents are now warranted necessary, and no longer depend on the evidence of facts merely, that they were so found and so experienced. The fact as experienced thus becomes an illustration and a copy of the original and completely self-supporting activity of thought.

13. In the peculiar form of external history the origin and development of philosophy is presented as the history of the science. The stages in the evolution of the Idea there seem to follow each other by accident, and to present merely a number of different and unconnected principles, which the several philosophies develop. But for thousands of years the same architect has directed the work: the one living mind whose nature is to think, to bring to consciousness what it is, and, with this thus set as object before it, to be at the same time raised above it, and so to reach a higher stage of its own being. The different systems that the history of philosophy presents are, first, only one philosophy at different degrees of maturity; second, the particular principle, which is the groundwork of each system, is but a branch of one and the same whole. The last philosophy in time is the result of all the systems that preceded it, and must include their principles; and so, if indeed it is philosophy, will be the fullest, most comprehensive, and most adequate philosophy.

The spectacle of so many and so various philosophies suggests the necessity of defining strictly the universal and the particular. When the universal is taken formally and *coordinated* with the particular, it sinks into a particular itself. Even common sense in everyday matters is above the absurdity of setting a universal *beside* the particulars. Would anyone who wished for fruit reject cherries, pears, and grapes, on the ground that they were cherries, pears, or grapes, and not fruit? But when philosophy is in question, the excuse of many is that philosophies are so different, and none of them is *the* philosophy, each is only *a* philosophy. Such a plea is assumed to justify contempt for philosophy. And yet cherries too are fruit. Often, too, a system, of which the principle is the universal, is put on a level with another of which the principle is a particular, and with theories that deny the existence of philosophy altogether. Such systems are said to be only different views of philosophy. With equal justice, light and darkness might be styled different kinds of light.

14. The same development of thought that is exhibited in the history of philosophy is presented in philosophy itself, only *purely in the element of thinking* and freed of that historical externality. The free and genuine thought is internally concrete, and is thus an Idea; and in its whole universality, it is *the* Idea or *the absolute*. The science of it is essentially a *system*. For the truth is concrete; it unfolds within itself, and gathers and holds itself together in unity; that is, it is a totality; and the freedom of the whole, as well as the necessity of its distinct moments, are possible only when these are discriminated and defined.

Unless it is a system, philosophy is not in the least scientific. Unsystematic philosophising can only express personal pecularities of mind, and is contingent in its contents. Apart from the whole of which it is a moment, a content lacks justification, and is a baseless assumption, or personal conviction. Yet many philosophical treatises confine themselves to such an exposition of opinions and sentiments.

The term '*system*' is often misunderstood. It does not denote a philosophy, the principle of which is narrow and distinguished from others. On the contrary, a genuine philosophy makes it a principle to include every particular principle. . . .

18. As only the whole of science can exhibit the Idea, it is impossible to give a preliminary general conception of a philosophy. Nor can the division of philosophy be intelligible, except in connection with the Idea. A preliminary division, like the conception from which it comes, can only be an anticipation. But the Idea turns out to be the thinking that is completely identical with itself and this also in its activity of setting itself over against itself, so as to be for itself, and of being in full possession of itself in this other. Thus philosophy falls into three parts:

I. Logic, the science of the Idea in and for itself

II. The Philosophy of Nature: the science of the Idea in its otherness

III. The Philosophy of Mind, of the Idea come back to itself out of that otherness

First Part: *Science of Logic* *Preliminary Concept*

19. Logic is the science of the pure Idea, that is, the Idea in the abstract medium of thought.

This definition, and the others that occur in this introductory concept, derive from and are subsequent to a survey of the whole. This applies to all prefatory concepts whatever about philosophy.

Logic might be defined as the science of thought, and of its laws and determinations. But thought, as thought, constitutes only the medium, or universal determinacy, that renders the Idea logical. If the Idea is thought, thought must not be taken as formal, but as the self-developing totality of its laws and peculiar determinations. These laws are given by thought to itself, and not something it finds in itself and already has.

From different points of view, logic is both the hardest and the easiest science. Logic is hard, because it deals not with intuitions, nor, like geometry, with representations of the senses, but with pure abstractions; and it demands a force and facil-

ity of withdrawing into pure thought, of keeping hold of it, and of moving in such an element. Logic is easy, because its content is nothing but our own thought and its familiar determinations; and these are the acme of simplicity, the a b c of everything else. They are also what we are best acquainted with: being and nothing; quality and magnitude: being-for-self and being-in-itself; one, many, and so on. But such an acquaintance only adds to the difficulties of the study; for while, on the one hand, we readily think it not worth bothering any longer with things so familiar, on the other hand, the problem is to become acquainted with them in a new way, quite opposite to that in which we are already.

The utility of logic concerns its bearings on the student, and the training it gives for other purposes. This logical training consists in exercise in thinking (for this science is the thinking of thinking); and storing his head with thoughts. But the logical, being the absolute form of truth, and, even more, the pure truth itself, is far more than merely useful. Yet if what is noblest, most free, and independent is also most useful, logic can be so conceived. Its utility must then be estimated otherwise than as merely formal exercise in thinking.

20. If we take our *prima facie* idea of thought, we find first (a) that, in its usual subjective meaning, thought is one out of many activities or faculties of the mind, coordinate with such others as sensation, intuition, imagination, desire, volition. The product of this activity, the form or determinacy of the thought, is the *universal*, or, in general, the abstract. Thought, as an *activity*, is thus the *active* universal, and, since the deed, its product, is just the universal, it is the *self*-actuating universal. Thought conceived as a *subject* is a thinker, and the subject existing as a thinker is simply expressed as 'I.' . . .

The difference between conception and thought is of special importance, because philosophy can be said to do nothing but transform conceptions into thoughts—though it goes on to transform the mere thought into the concept.

The sensuous has been characterized by determinations of individuality and mutual externality. We can add that these determinations are themselves thoughts and universals. It will be shown in the Logic that thought and the universal is just this: it lets nothing escape it, but outflanking its other, is that other and itself. Language is the work of thought; hence all that is said in language must be universal. What I only *mean* is *mine*: it belongs to me—this particular individual. But language expresses nothing but universality; and so I cannot say what I merely *mean*. And the unutterable—feeling, sensation—far from being the highest truth, is the most unimportant and untrue. If I say 'The individual,' 'This individual,' 'here,' 'now,' all these are universal terms. Everything and anything is an individual, a 'this,' and, if it be sensible, here and now. Similarly when I say, 'I,' I *mean* myself to the exclusion of all others: but what I *say*, 'I,' is just everyone: I, which excludes all others from itself. In an awkward expression Kant said that I *accompany* all my conceptions—sensations, too, desires, actions, etc. I is in essence and act the universal, and community is also a form, though an external form, of universality. All other men have it in common with me to be I; just as it is common to all my sensations and conceptions to be mine. But I, in the abstract, as such, is pure self-relation, in which we abstract from conception and feeling, from every state and every peculiarity of nature, talent, and experience. To this extent, I is the existence of wholly *abstract* universality, of the abstractly free. Hence the I is thought as a subject, and since I am at the same time in all my sensations, conceptions, and states, the thought is everywhere present, and is a category that runs through all these determinations.

21. (b) If thinking is taken as active in relation to objects, as meta-thinking about something, then the universal or product of its activity contains the value of the thing, the essential, inward, and true core of it.

In §5 the old belief was quoted that the reality in object, circumstance, or event, the intrinsic worth or essence, the thing on which everything depends, is not an immediate datum of consciousness, or coincident with the first appearance and impression of the object; that, on the contrary, meta-thinking is required to discover the real constitution of the object, and that by meta-thinking it will be ascertained.

22. (c) By meta-thinking something is altered in the way in which the content first occurs in sensation, intuition, or conception. Thus an alteration must be interposed before the true nature of the object can come to consciousness.

23. (d) The real nature of the object comes to light in meta-thinking; but this thinking is my activity. Thus the real nature is a *product of my* mind, in its character of thinking subject, of me in my

simple universality, as the simply self-collected I, or of my freedom.

'Think for yourself' is a phrase often used as if it had some significance. In fact no one can think for another, any more than he can eat or drink for him; the expression is a pleonasm. To think is *ipso facto* to be free, for thought as the activity of the universal is an abstract relating of self to self, which, being self-contained and, as regards subjectivity, utterly featureless, finds it content only in the subject-matter and its determinations. If therefore humility or modesty consists in ascribing to subjectivity no particularity of act or quality, it is easy to solve the question concerning the humility or pride of philosophy. For in content thought is only true insofar as it sinks itself in the subject-matter, and in form is no particular state or act of the subject, but rather that attitude of consciousness where the abstract I, freed from all the particularity of its ordinary states or qualities, restricts itself to the universal in which it is identical with all individuals. Thus philosophy may be acquitted of pride. When Aristotle urges us to be worthy of that attitude, consciousness becomes worthy by letting go all particular opinions and prejudices, and submitting to the subject-matter.

24. These determinations entitle us to call thoughts 'objective thoughts,' which also include the forms primarily discussed in the common logic, which are usually treated as forms of *conscious* thought only. *Logic therefore coincides with metaphysics, the science of things grasped in thoughts*—thoughts accredited able to express the essentialities of things.

The relation of such forms as concept, judgment, and syllogism to others, such as causality, is a matter for the science itself. But this much is evident beforehand. If thought tries to form a concept of things, this concept (and thus its most immediate forms, the judgment and syllogism) cannot consist of determinations and relations that are alien and irrelevant to the things. Meta-thinking, we said, leads to the universal of things: which universal is itself one of the conceptual moments. To say that reason, understanding is in the world, is equivalent to the phrase 'objective thought.' The phrase however has the inconvenience that 'thought' is too often confined to the mind or consciousness, while 'objective' is applied primarily only to the nonmental.

25. The term 'objective thoughts' indicates the *truth*—the truth that is to be the absolute *object* of philosophy, and not merely its goal. But the expression reveals an opposition, to characterize and evaluate which is the main interest of contemporary philosophy and which forms the nub of the question of truth and of our knowledge of it. If the thought-forms are burdened with a fixed antithesis, *i.e.*, if they are only of a finite character, they are unsuitable for the truth that is absolutely in and for itself, and truth can find no place in thought. Thought that produces only finite categories and proceeds by their means, is, in the strict sense, understanding. The finitude of these categories lies in two points. First, they are only subjective, and have a permanent antithesis in the objective. Second, they are of restricted content, and so persist in antithesis to one another and still more to the absolute. To explain the position and import here attributed to logic, the attitudes in which thought is supposed to stand to objectivity will next be examined by way of further introduction. . . .

26. The first attitude is the naive procedure that has no awareness of the opposition of thinking in and against itself. It involves the *belief* that the truth is *known* by meta-thinking, and objects brought before consciousness as they really are. In this belief, thinking heads straight for objects, transforms the content of sensations and intuitions into a content of thought, and is satisfied with this as the truth. All philosophy in its beginnings, all sciences, and even the daily activities of consciousness, live in this belief.

27. This thinking is not aware of its antithesis; thus there is nothing to prevent it from possessing a genuinely philosophical and speculative content, though it is just as possible that it may never get beyond finite categories, or the still unresolved opposition. In this introduction the main question is to observe this attitude of thought in its extreme form, and thus first to examine its second form. The clearest instance of it, and one lying nearest to ourselves, is the old, pre-Kantian metaphysics. It is, however, only for the history of philosophy that this metaphysic belongs to the past: the thing is always to be found, as the view that the mere understanding takes of the objects of reason. It is here that the real and immediate good lies of a closer examination of its main content and its *modus operandi*.

28. This science took the determinations of thought to be the fundamental determinations of things. It assumed that to think what is, is to know in itself; to that extent it occupied higher ground

than the critical philosophy that succeeded it. But (1) *these determinations were cut off from their connection*; each was believed valid by itself and a possible predicate of the truth. It was a general assumption of this metaphysic that a knowledge of the absolute was gained by assigning predicates to it. It investigated neither the peculiar content and value of the determinations of the understanding, nor even this way of determining the absolute by assigning predicates to it.

Examples of such predicates are: 'existence,' in the proposition, 'God has existence'; 'finitude' or 'infinity,' as in the question, 'Is the world finite or infinite?'; 'simple' and 'complex,' in the proposition. 'The soul is simple' or again, 'The thing is a unity, a whole,' etc. Nobody asked whether such predicates had any intrinsic and independent truth, or if the judgmental form could be a form of truth.

29. Predicates of this kind, taken individually, have a restricted content, and evidently fall short of the fullness of conception (of God, nature, spirit, etc.), which they in no way exhaust. Besides, though their being predicates of one subject supplies them with connection, their contents keep them apart: and so each is brought in from outside in relation to the others.

The first of these defects the Orientals sought to remedy, when, for example, they defined God by attributing to Him many names; but still the number of names was supposed to be infinite.

30. (2) Their objects were no doubt totalities that intrinsically belong to reason, to the thinking of the internally concrete universal. But these totalities—God, the soul, the world—were taken by the metaphysician as subjects made and ready, to form the basis for an application of the categories of the understanding. They were adopted from conception. Accordingly, conception was the only criterion for whether or not the predicates were suitable and sufficient.

31. The conceptions of God, the soul, the world, may be supposed to afford thought a firm footing. But besides having a particular, subjective character clinging to them, and thus leaving room for great variety of interpretation, they themselves first require a firm definition by thought. This may be seen in any proposition where the predicate, or in philosophy the category, needs to indicate *what* the subject, or the conception we start with, is.

In such a sentence as 'God is eternal,' we begin with the conception of God, not knowing as yet what he is; to tell us that is the business of the predicate. In logic, accordingly, where the content is determined in the form of thought only, it is not merely superfluous to make these categories predicates of propositions in which God, or, still vaguer, the absolute, is the subject, but it would also have the disadvantage of suggesting another criterion than the nature of thought. Besides, the form of the proposition, or, more precisely, judgment, is not suited to express the concrete—and the true is concrete—or the speculative. The judgment is by its form one-sided and, to that extent, false.

32. (3) *This metaphysics turned into dogmatism.* By the nature of finite determinations, it had to assume that of two opposite assertions, such as the above propositions, one must be true and the other false.

33. The *first* part of this metaphysic in its systematic form is ontology, the doctrine of the abstract determinations of the essence. The multitude of these determinations and their finite validity lack a principle. They have in consequence to be enumerated empirically and contingently, and their detailed content can be founded only on conceptions, on assertions that words are used in a particular sense, and even perhaps on etymology. If experience pronounces the list to be complete, and if linguistic usage, by its agreement, shows the analysis to be correct, the metaphysician is satisfied; and the truth and necessity of such determinations is never investigated in its own right.

To ask if being, existence, finitude, simplicity, complexity, etc. are intrinsically and independently true concepts must surprise those who believe that questions of truth concern only propositions (whether a concept is or is not with truth to be attributed, as the phrase is, to a subject), and that untruth lies in the contradiction between the subject of the idea, and the concept to be predicated of it. Now as the concept is concrete, it and every determinacy in general is essentially a self-contained unity of distinct determinations. If truth, then, were nothing more than absence of contradiction, it would be first necessary in the case of every concept to examine whether it, taken individually, contains such an intrinsic contradiction.

34. The *second* branch was rational psychology or pneumatology. It dealt with the metaphysical nature of the soul—that is, of the mind regarded as a thing. It expected to find immortality in a sphere dominated by composition, time, qualitative change, and quantitative increase or decrease.

35. The *third* branch, cosmology, considered the world, its contingency, necessity, eternity, limitation in time and space; the formal laws of its changes; the freedom of man and the origin of evil.

Here it applied supposedly absolute contrasts: contingency and necessity; external and internal necessity; efficient and final cause, or causality in general and design; essence or substance and appearance; form and matter; freedom and necessity; happiness and pain; good and evil.

36. The *fourth* branch, natural or rational theology, considered the concept of God, or God as a possibility, the proofs of his existence, and his properties.

(a) When understanding thus considers God, its main purpose is to find what predicates correspond or do not to our *conception* of God. In so doing it assumes the contrast between reality and negation as absolute; hence, in the end, nothing is left for the concept as understanding takes it, but the empty abstraction of indeterminate essence, of pure reality or positivity, the lifeless product of modern enlightenment.

(b) The *demonstration* employed in finite cognition in general leads to an inversion of the true order. For it requires the statement of some objective ground for God's being, which thus presents itself as *mediated* by something else. This mode of proof, guided as it is by the understanding's notion of identity, is embarrassed by the difficulty of passing from the finite to the infinite. Either the finitude of the existing world, which remains positive, clings to God, and God has to be defined as the immediate substance of that world (pantheism); or He remains an object set over against the subject, and in this way, finite (dualism).

(c) The attributes of God, which ought to be various and determinate, actually disappeared in the abstract concept of pure reality, of indeterminate essence. Yet in our conception the finite world continues still to be a true being, with God as its antithesis; and thus arises the further conception of different relations of God to the world. These, formulated as properties, must, on the one hand, as relations to finite states, themselves be finite (e.g., just, gracious, mighty, wise, etc.); on the other hand they should be infinite. On this level of thought the contradiction admits of only the nebulous solution of quantitative exaltation of the properties, forcing them into indeterminateness, into the *sensus eminentior*. But this expedient really destroyed the property and left a mere name. . . .

79. In form the logical has three aspects: (α) the abstract or that of understanding; (β) the dialectical, or that of negative reason; (γ) the speculative, or that of positive reason.

These three aspects do not make three *parts* of logic, but are moments in every logical entity, that is, of every concept and truth whatever. They may all be put under the first stage, that of understanding, and so kept isolated from each other; but this would not give their truth. The statement of the division and determinations of logic is here only historical and anticipatory.

80. (α) Thought, as *understanding*, sticks to the fixed determinacy and its distinctiveness from others; every such limited abstract it treats as having a substance and being of its own.

81. (β) In the dialectical moment these finite determinations supersede *themselves*, and pass into their opposites.

(1) When the dialectical is taken by the understanding separately and independently, especially as shown in scientific concepts, it constitutes skepticism; this contains mere negation as the result of the dialectical.

(2) It is customary to view dialectic as an external art, which willfully introduces confusion and a mere semblance of contradictions into determinate concepts, so that the semblance is a nullity, while the true reality is the determinations of understanding. Often, indeed, dialectic is nothing more than a subjective seesaw of arguments *pro* and *con*, where the absence of substance is disguised by the subtlety that produces the arguments. But in its proper character, dialectic is the very nature and essence of the determinations of understanding, of things and of the finite as a whole. In the first instance, reflection is that movement beyond the isolated determinacy that connects it, and brings it into relation, while in other respects leaving it its isolated validity. But dialectic is the immanent movement beyond, in which the one-sidedness and limitation of the determinations of understanding is seen in its true light, as their negation. To be finite is just to sublimate itself. Thus the dialectical constitutes the life and soul of scientific progress, the principle that alone gives immanent connection and necessity to the content of science; and in it lies the true, as opposed to the external, elevation above the finite.

82. (γ) The speculative or positively rational apprehends the unity of determinations in their opposition, the affirmative that is involved in their disintegration and in their transition.

(1) The result of dialectic is positive, because it has a definite content, or because its result is not empty, abstract nothing, but the negation of certain determinations that are contained in the result, for the very reason that it is a result and not an immediate nothing. (2) Thus this rational, though it be a thought and abstract, is still a concrete, being not a plain formal unity, but a unity of distinct determinations. Bare abstractions or formal thoughts are therefore no business of philosophy, only concrete thoughts. (3) The logic of mere understanding is involved in speculative logic, and can at will be elicited from it, by simply omitting the dialectical and rational. Then it becomes what the common logic is, a descriptive collection of sundry thought-determinations, which, finite though they are, are taken to be something infinite.

83. Logic is subdivided into three parts:

I. The Doctrine of Being

II. The Doctrine of Essence

III. The Doctrine of the Concept and Idea

That is, into the doctrine of the thought:

I. In its immediacy: the concept in itself

II. In its reflection and mediation: being-for-self and show of the concept

III. In its return into itself, and its developed abiding by itself: the concept in and for itself

---

First Subdivision of Logic: The Doctrine of Being

84. Being is the concept implicit only: its determinations are beings: when they are distinguished they are each of them an other; and the form of the dialectical, *i.e.*, their further determination, is a passing over into another. This further determination is at once a forth-putting, and in that way an unfolding, of the implicit concept; and at the same time the withdrawing of being inwards, its sinking deeper into itself. The explication of the concept in the sphere of being does two things: it brings out the totality of being, and it abolishes the immediacy of being, or the form of being as such.

85. Being itself and the determinations of it that follow, as well as those of logic in general, may be viewed as definitions of the absolute, as metaphysical definitions of God; but strictly only the first and third in every sphere—the first, simple determination, and the third, the return from differentiation to simple self-relation. For a metaphysical definition of God is the expression of His nature in thoughts as such: and logic embraces all thoughts so long as they continue in the form of thought. The second determination, where the sphere is in its differentiation, is, on the other hand, a definition of the finite. The objection to the form of definition is that it implies in the mind's eye a substrate of conception. Thus even the absolute (though it purports to express God in the sense and form of thought) in relation to its predicate (the real and determinate expression in thought) is as yet only a putative thought, an indeterminate substrate. The thought, which is here the only matter of importance, is contained only in the predicate: hence the propositional form, like the said subject, is a mere superfluity (cf. §31, and below, on the judgment).

Being

86. Pure being makes the beginning: because it is both a pure thought, and immediacy, simple and indeterminate; and the first beginning cannot be anything mediated or futher determined.

All doubts about, and admonitions against, beginning science with abstract empty being, disappear, if we only perceive what a beginning naturally implies. It is possible to define being as 'I = I,' as absolute indifference or identity, and so on. Where we need to begin either with what is absolutely certain, *i.e.*, the certainty of oneself, or with a definition or intuition of the absolute truth, these and other forms of the kind may be viewed as if they must be the first. But each of these forms contains mediation, and hence cannot be the real first; mediation is an advance from a first on to a second, and an emergence from distinct items. If I = I, or even intellectual intuition, is really taken only as the first, they are in this pure immediacy just being; conversely, pure being, if abstract no longer, but involving mediation, is pure thinking or intuition.

If we enunciate being as a predicate of the absolute, we get the first definition of it: 'the absolute is being.' This is (in the thought) the absolutely initial, definition, the most abstract and poor. It is the definition of the Eleatics, but at the same time is also the familiar definition of God as the sum of all realities. We are to set aside that limitation that is in every reality, so that God shall be only the real in all reality, the superlatively real. Since reality implies a reflection, we get a more immediate statement of this when Jacobi says that the God of Spinoza is the *principium* of being in all existence.

87. But this pure being, as it is pure abstraction, is therefore the absolutely negative: which taken similarly immediately, is nothing.

(1) From this follows the second definition of the absolute: The absolute is nothing. In fact this definition is implied in saying that the thing-in-itself is the indeterminate, utterly without form and so without content, or that God *is* only the supreme essence and nothing more; for this is declaring Him to be the same negativity. The nothing that Buddhists make the principle as well as the final aim and goal, of everything, is the same abstraction.

(2) If the opposition is stated in this immediacy as being and nothing, the shock of its nullity is too great not to stimulate the attempt to fix being and secure it against transition. In this regard, meta-thinking inevitably hits on the plan of finding a fixed determination for being, to distinguish it from nothing. Thus being is taken as what persists in all change, as infinitely determinable matter, or even, unreflectingly, as some individual existence, any chance sensuous or mental entity. But all such further and more concrete determinations make being more than the pure being which it is here immediately in the beginning. Only in and because of this indeterminacy is it nothing—something inexpressible; its distinction from nothing is a mere *meaning*.

All that is wanted is to realize that these beginnings are nothing but these empty abstractions, one as empty as the other. The urge to find a fixed meaning in being or in both is the very necessity that leads to the onward movement of being and nothing, and gives them a true or concrete meaning. This advance is the logical exposition and the movement exhibited later. The meta-thinking that finds profounder determinations for them is the logical thinking through which such determinations emerge, not, however, in a contingent, but a necessary way. Every meaning, therefore, which they afterwards acquire, is only a more precise determination and truer definition of the absolute. Here emptily abstract being and nothing are replaced by a concrete in which both are elements. The supreme form of nothing in itself would be freedom: but freedom is negativity when it sinks self-absorbed to supreme intensity, and is itself an affirmation, an *absolute* affirmation.

88. Nothing as thus immediate and equal to itself, is also conversely the same as being is. The truth of being and of nothing is accordingly the unity of the two: this unity is becoming.

(1) The proposition 'Being and nothing are the same' seems so paradoxical to conception or understanding that it is perhaps taken for a joke. And indeed it is one of the hardest things thought expects of itself; for being and nothing are the antithesis in all its immediacy, that is, without the one being invested with a determination that would involve its connection with the other. They involve, however, as this paragraph points out, this determination—the determination that is just the same in both. So far the deduction of their unity is completely analytical: Indeed the whole progress of philosophizing in general, if it be methodical—that is, necessary—merely renders explicit what is implicit in a concept. It is as correct, however, to say that being and nothing are altogether different, as to assert their unity. The one is *not* what the other is. But since the distinction has not yet become determinate (being and nothing are still the immediate), it is, in the way that they have it, something unutterable, which we merely mean.

(2) No great expenditure of wit is needed to make fun of the proposition that being and nothing are the same, or rather to adduce absurdities that, it is falsely asserted, are consequences and applications of that proposition: e.g., that it makes no difference whether my home, my property, the air I breathe, this city, the sun, law, mind, God, are or not. In some of these cases, they introduce private aims, the utility a thing has for me, and ask, whether it be the same to me if the thing is or is not. In fact the teaching of philosophy is precisely to free man from the endless crowd of finite aims and intentions, by making him so indifferent to them that their being or non-being is all the same to him. But in general, reference to a content at once establishes a connection with other existences and other purposes that are assumed valid: It is now made to depend on such assumptions whether the being or not-being of a determinate content is all the same

or not. A substantial distinction is in these cases substituted for the empty distinction of being and nothing. In other cases, it is implicitly essential purposes, absolute existences, and Ideas that are placed in the mere category of being or not-being. But there is more to be said of these concrete objects than that they merely are or are not. Barren abstractions, like being and nothing—the initial categories that, for that reason, are the scantiest to be found—are utterly inadequate to the nature of these objects. Genuine content is far above these abstractions and their opposition. In general when a concrete is substituted for being and not-being, thoughtlessness makes its usual mistake of speaking about, and having in conception, something other than what is in question: and here the question is abstract being and nothing.

(3) It may be said that nobody can comprehend the unity of being and nothing. But the concept of it is stated in the sections preceding, and that is all there is to it. What they really mean by 'comprehension' is more than the strict concept: They want a richer and more complex consciousness, a conception that presents the concept as a concrete case, more familiar to the ordinary operations of thought. Insofar as incomprehensibility means only want of habituation in holding onto abstract thoughts, free from all sensuous admixture, and grasping speculative propositions, the reply is just that philosophical knowledge certainly differs in kind from the knowledge usual in common life, as well as from that dominant in the other sciences. But if non-comprehension merely means that we cannot form a conception of the unity of being and nothing, this is far from true; everyone has countless conceptions of this unity. To say that we have no such conception can only mean that in none of these conceptions do we recognize the concept in question, and we are not aware that they exemplify it. The readiest example is becoming. Everyone has a conception of becoming, and will even allow that it is *one* idea; he will further allow that, when analyzed, it involves the determination of being, and also the very other of being, nothing; and that these two determinations lie undivided in the one idea: so that becoming is the unity of being and nothing. Another obvious example is a beginning. In its beginning, the thing is not yet, but it is more than merely nothing, for its being is already in the beginning. Beginning is itself a case of becoming; only it involves a reference to the further advance. If we were to adapt logic to the more usual method

of the sciences, we might start with the representation of a beginning as abstractly thought, or with beginning as such, and analyze this representation; and perhaps people would more readily admit, as a result of this analysis, that being and nothing present themselves as undivided in unity.

(4) It remains to note that such phrases as 'Being and nothing are the same,' or 'The unity of being and nothing'—like all other such unities, that of subject and object, and others—give rise to reasonable objection. They misrepresent the case, by giving an exclusive prominence to the unity, and leaving the difference that undoubtedly lies in it (because it is being and nothing, for example, the unity of which is posited) with no express mention or notice. It accordingly seems as if the diversity is unduly abstracted from and neglected. In fact no speculative determination can be correctly expressed by any such propositional form, for the unity has to be conceived *in* the diversity, which is all the while present and explicit. Becoming is the true expression for the result of being and nothing; it is the unity of the two; but not only is it the unity, it is also inherent unrest—the unity that is no mere connection-with-self and therefore motionless, but, through the diversity of being and nothing that is in it, at war with itself. Determinate being, on the other hand, is this unity, or becoming in this form of unity: hence determinate being is one-sided and finite. The opposition seems to have vanished; it is only implied in the unity, it is not explicitly put in it.

(5) The proposition of becoming, that being is the passage into nothing, and nothing the passage into being, is countered by the proposition of pantheism, of the eternity of matter: 'From nothing comes nothing,' and 'Something only comes out of something.' The ancients made the simple reflection that the proposition 'From nothing comes nothing, from something something,' really abolishes becoming: for what it comes from and what it becomes are one and the same: it is just the proposition of the abstract identity of the understanding. It cannot but seem strange, therefore, to hear the propositions 'Out of nothing comes nothing: Out of something only comes something,' calmly taught in these days, with no awareness that they are the basis of pantheism, or that the ancients have exhausted all that is to be said about them.

Determinate Being

89. In becoming, the being that is one with nothing, and the nothing that is one with being are only vanishing factors; by its inherent contradiction becoming collapses into itself, into the unity in which the two are absorbed. Its result is accordingly determinate being.

In this first example we must call to mind, once for all, what was stated [earlier]: the only way to secure development and advance in knowledge is to hold results fast in their truth. In anything whatever we can and must point to contradiction or opposite determinations; the abstraction made by understanding is a forcible insistence on one determinacy, and an effort to obscure and remove all consciousness of the other determinacy involved. Whenever such contradiction, then, is discovered in any object or notion, the usual inference is, *Hence* this object is *nothing*. Thus Zeno, who first showed the contradiction in motion, concluded that there is no motion: and the ancients, who recognized origin and decease, the two species of becoming, as untrue categories, made use of the expression that the one or absolute neither arises nor perishes. Such dialectic looks only at the negative aspect of its result, and fails to notice, what is at the same time really present, the determinate result, here a pure nothing, but a nothing that includes being, and, in like manner, a being that includes nothing. Hence being determinate is (1) the unity of being and nothing, in which the immediacy of these determinations, and their contradiction vanishes in their connection, a unity in which they are now only moments. (2) Since the result is the sublimated contradiction, it is in the form of simple unity with itself; it also is being, but being with negation or determinateness; it is becoming expressly put in the form of one of its elements, being.

90. (α) Determinate being is being with a determinacy—which simply *is*; this immediate determinacy is quality. As reflected into itself in this its determinacy, determinate being is something, a determinate entity. The categories that develop in determinate being need be mentioned only briefly.

91. Quality, as determinateness that *is*, as contrasted with the negation involved in it but distinguished from it, is reality. Negation is no longer abstract nothing, but, as determinate being and something, is only a form in it—it is as otherness. Since this otherness, though a determination of quality itself, is in the first instance distinct from it, quality is being-for-another—an expanse of determinate being, of something. The being as such of quality, contrasted with this connection with an other, is being-in-self.

92. (β) Being, if kept distinct from determinateness, being-in-itself, would be only the empty abstraction of being. In determinate being, the determinateness is one with being; yet at the same time, when explicitly made a negation, it is a limit, a barrier. Hence otherness is not something indifferent outside it, but a moment proper to it. Something is by its quality, first finite, second, alterable; so that finitude and variability pertain to its being.

93. Something becomes an other; this other is itself a something, so it likewise becomes an other, and so *ad infinitum*.

94. This infinity is bad or negative infinity: it is only negation of the finite; but the finite rises again the same as ever, and is never sublimated. Or this infinity only expresses the *'ought'* of the sublimation of finitude. The progression to infinity never gets further than a statement of the contradiction involved in the finite, that it is something as well as its other. It sets up with endless iteration the alternation between these determinations, each of which calls up the other.

95. (γ) What we now in fact have is that something comes to be an other, and the other in general comes to be an other. In relation to another, something is itself already an other against it; since what is passed into is quite the same as what passes over (both have one and the same determination, to be an other), so something in its passage into other only joins with itself. To be thus self-related in the passage, and in the other, is genuine infinity. Or, seen negatively: what is altered is the other, it becomes the other of the other. Thus being, but as negation of the negation, is restored again: it is now being-for-self.

Dualism, in putting an insuperable opposition between finite and infinite, fails to make the simple observation that the infinite is thereby only one of two, and is reduced to a particular, to which the finite is the other particular. Such an infinite, which is only a particular, is alongside the finite, in which it thus has its limit, barrier: it is not what it ought to be, not the infinite, but is only finite. In such a relation, where the finite is on this side and the infinite on that, the one here and the other there, an equal dignity of permanence and independence is ascribed to finite and to infinite. The being of the finite is made an absolute being, and in this dualism it stands firm on its own. Touched, so to speak, by the infinite, it would be annihilated. But it is supposed not to be able to be touched by the infinite. There must be an abyss, an impassable gulf between the two, with the infinite abiding on that side and the finite on this. Those who assert that the finite firmly persists over against the infinite are not, as they imagine, far above metaphysic: they are still on the level of the most ordinary metaphysic of understanding. For the same thing occurs here as the infinite progression expresses. At one time it is admitted that the finite has no independent actuality, no absolute being, is not in and for itself, but is only a transient. But the very next moment this is forgotten; the finite, merely over against the infinite, wholly separated from it, and rescued from annihilation, is conceived as persistent in its independence. While thought thus imagines itself elevated to the infinite, it meets with the opposite: it comes to an infinite that is only a finite, and the finite, which it had left behind, is still retained and made an absolute.

After this examination (with which we could usefully compare Plato's *Philebus*) of the nullity of the distinction made by understanding between the finite and the infinite, we are again liable to hit on the expression that the infinite and the finite are therefore one, and that genuine infinity, the truth, must be defined and expressed as unity of the finite and infinite. This is to some extent correct; but is just as perverse and false as the unity of being and nothing already noticed. Besides it may fairly be charged with reducing the infinite to finitude, with a *finite* infinite. For in the expression the finite seems left in place, it is not expressly expressed as sublimated. Or, if we reflect that the finite, when united with the infinite, certainly cannot remain what it was out of such unity, and will at least suffer some change in its determination (as an alkali combined with an acid loses some of its properties), the same will happen to the infinite, which, as the negative, will on its part also get blunted on the other. This in fact happens to the abstract, one-sided infinite of understanding. The genuine infinite, however, does not merely behave like the one-sided acid; it preserves itself. The negation of negation is not a neutralization: The infinite is the affirmative, and only the finite is sublimated.

In being-for-self enters the category of ideality. Determinate being, in the first instance apprehended only in its being or affirmation, has reality; thus even finitude in the first instance is in the determination of reality. But the truth of the finite is rather its ideality. Similarly, the infinite of understanding, which is coordinated with the finite, itself only one of two finites, is untrue, ideal. This ideality of the finite is the chief maxim of philosophy; and for that reason every genuine philosophy is idealism. But everything depends on not taking for the infinite what, in its very determination, is at once made a particular and finite. For this reason we have paid more attention to this distinction. The fundamental concept of philosophy, the genuine infinite, depends on it. The distinction is cleared up by these simple, and for that reason seemingly insignificant, but incontrovertible reflections.

Being-for-self

96. (α) Being-for-self, as connection with itself, is immediacy, and as connection of the negative with itself, is *a* being-for-self, the one, which, being without distinction in itself, thus excludes the other from itself.

97. (β) The connection of the negative with itself is a negative connection, and so a distinguishing of the one from itself, the repulsion of the one; that is, a positing of many ones. The being-for-self is also immediate, and hence these many are *beings;* and the repulsion of the ones that *are* becomes to that extent their repulsion against each other as entities at hand or reciprocal exclusion.

98. (γ) But each one of the many is what the other is: each is one, or even one of the many; they are consequently one and the same. Or, considered in itself, repulsion, as negative behavior of many ones to one another, is just as essentially their connection with each other; and as what the one connects with in its repelling are ones, in them it connects itself with itself. The repulsion therefore is just as essentially attraction; and the exclusive one, or being-for-self, sublimates itself. The qualitative determinacy that in the one has attained to its determinedness in and for itself, has thus passed into the determinacy as sublimated, into being as quantity.

The philosophy of atomism is this standpoint where the absolute is as being-for-self, as one, and many ones. And the repulsion that appears in the concept of the one is taken as their fundamental force. But instead of attraction, it is chance—that is, mere absence of thought—that is supposed to bring them together. Since the one is fixed as one, it is certainly impossible to regard its congression with others as anything but external. The void, which is assumed as the complementary principle to the atoms, is repulsion itself, represented as the nothing that *is*, between the atoms. Modern atomism—and physics still retains this principle— has given up the atoms insofar as it keeps to molecules or small particles. Thus it has come closer to sensuous conception, but has abandoned the determination of thought. Besides, when an attractive is placed by the side of a repulsive force, the opposition is certainly made complete; and much stress has been laid on the discovery of this natural force, as it is called. But the connection between the two, which constitutes what is true and concrete in them, would have to be rescued from the obscurity and confusion in which they were left even in Kant's *Metaphysical Principles of Natural Science*. In modern times the atomic theory is even more important in politics than in physics. According to it, the will of individuals as such is the principle of the state: The attracting force consists of the particularity of needs and inclinations; and the universal, the state itself, is the external relation of a compact. . . .

49. *The Elimination of Metaphysics Through Logical Analysis of Language*

RUDOLF CARNAP

Rudolf Carnap (1891–1970) was a leading figure in the logical empiricist (or logical positivist) movement that flourished in Vienna in the 1920s and 1930s. He came to America in 1935 and taught at the University of Chicago until 1952 and at the University of California at Los Angeles until 1961. Carnap was skeptical about post-Kantian metaphysics, especially the variety represented by Hegel and Heidegger (see Chapter 50). With other logical empiricists, Carnap diagnosed metaphysical problems as stemming from a misuse of language. He believed philosophers have often been misled by apparent logical or semantic form, so they do not realize their problems are really "pseudoproblems" and their profound-sounding theses mere "pseudostatements." Carnap devoted much of his career to the logical analysis of science. He thought this analysis could be performed either in the vocabulary of sensation terms or in the vocabulary of external-object terms, so he was neutral about such metaphysical debates as idealism versus realism. He believed one's ontology depends on the language one chooses to analyze science.

1. *Introduction*

There have been many *opponents of metaphysics* from the Greek skeptics to the empiricists of the 19th century. Criticisms of very diverse kinds have been set forth. Many have declared that the doctrine of metaphysics is *false*, since it contradicts our empirical knowledge. Others have believed it to be *uncertain*, on the ground that its problems transcend the limits of human knowledge. Many anti-metaphysicians have declared that occupation with metaphysical questions is *sterile*. Whether or not these questions can be answered, it is at any rate unnecessary to worry about them; let us devote ourselves entirely to the practical tasks which confront active men every day of their lives!

The development of *modern logic* has made it possible to give a new and sharper answer to the question of the validity and justification of metaphysics. The researches of applied logic or the theory of knowledge, which aim at clarifying the cognitive content of scientific statements and thereby the meanings of the terms that occur in the statements, by means of logical analysis, lead to a positive and to a negative result. The positive result is worked out in the domain of empirical science; the various concepts of the various branches of science are clarified; their formal-logical and epistemological connections are made explicit. In the domain of *metaphysics*, including all philosophy of value and normative theory, logical analysis yields the negative result *that the alleged statements in this domain are entirely meaningless.* Therewith a radical elimination of metaphysics is attained, which was not yet possible from the earlier anti-metaphysical standpoints. It is true that related ideas may be found already in several earlier trains of thought, e.g., those of a nominalistic kind; but it is only now when the development of logic during recent decades provides us with a sufficiently sharp tool that the decisive step can be taken.

In saying that the so-called statements of

Reprinted with permission of The Free Press, a Division of Macmillan, Inc., from *Logical Positivism*, A. J. Ayer, editor. Copyright © 1959 by The Free Press; copyright renewed 1987. Originally published in *Erkenntnis* (1932); translated by Arthur Pap.

metaphysics are *meaningless*, we intend this word in its strictest sense. In a loose sense of the word a statement or a question is at times called meaningless if it is entirely sterile to assert or ask it. We might say this for instance about the question "what is the average weight of those inhabitants of Vienna whose telephone number ends with '3'?" or about a statement which is quite obviously false like "in 1910 Vienna had 6 inhabitants" or about a statement which is not just empirically, but logically false, a contradictory statement such as "persons A and B are each a year older than the other." Such sentences are really meaningful, though they are pointless or false; for it is only meaningful sentences that are even divisible into (theoretically) fruitful and sterile, true and false. In the strict sense, however, a sequence of words is *meaningless* if it does not, within a specified language, constitute a statement. It may happen that such a sequence of words looks like a statement at first glance; in that case we call it a *pseudo-statement*. Our thesis, now, is that logical analysis reveals the alleged statements of metaphysics to be pseudo-statements.

A language consists of a vocabulary and a syntax, i.e., a set of words which have meanings and rules of sentence formation. These rules indicate how sentences may be formed out of the various sorts of words. Accordingly, there are two kinds of pseudo-statements: either they contain a word which is erroneously believed to have meaning, or the constituent words are meaningful, yet are put together in a counter-syntactical way, so that they do not yield a meaningful statement. We shall show in terms of examples that pseudo-statements of both kinds occur in metaphysics. Later we shall have to inquire into the reasons that support our contention that metaphysics in its entirety consists of such pseudo-statements.

---

2. The Significance of a Word

A word which (within a definite language) has a meaning, is usually also said to designate a concept; if it only seems to have a meaning while it really does not, we speak of a "pseudo-concept." How is the origin of a pseudo-concept to be explained? Has not every word been introduced into the language for no other purpose than to express something or other, so that it had a definite mean-

ing from the very beginning of its use? How, then, can a traditional language contain meaningless words? To be sure, originally every word (excepting rare cases which we shall illustrate later) had a meaning. In the course of historical development a word frequently changes its meaning. And it also happens at times that a word loses its old sense without acquiring a new one. It is thus that a pseudo-concept arises.

What, now, is *the meaning of a word*? What stipulations concerning a word must be made in order for it to be significant? (It does not matter for our investigation whether these stipulations are explicitly laid down, as in the case of some words and symbols of modern science, or whether they have been tacitly agreed upon, as is the case for most words of traditional language.) First, the *syntax* of the word must be fixed, i.e., the mode of its occurrence in the simplest sentence form in which it is capable of occurring; we call this sentence form its *elementary sentence*. The elementary sentence form for the word "stone" e.g., is "x is a stone"; in sentences of this form some designation from the category of things occupies the place of "x," e.g., "this diamond," "this apple." Secondly, for an elementary sentence S containing the word an answer must be given to the following question, which can be formulated in various ways:

(1) What sentences is S *deducible* from, and what sentences are deducible from S?

(2) Under what conditions is S supposed to be true, and under what conditions false?

(3) How is S to be *verified*?

(4) What is the *meaning* of S?

(1) is the correct formulation; formulation (2) accords with the phraseology of logic, (3) with the phraseology of the theory of knowledge, (4) with that of philosophy (phenomenology). Wittgenstein has asserted that (2) expresses what philosophers mean by (4): the meaning of a sentence consists in its truth-condition. ((1) is the "metalogical" formulation; it is planned to give elsewhere a detailed exposition of metalogic as the theory of syntax and meaning, i.e., relations of deducibility.)

In the case of many words, specifically in the case of the overwhelming majority of scientific words, it is possible to specify their meaning by reduction to other words ("constitution," definition). E.g., " 'arthropodes' are animals with segmented bodies and jointed legs." Thereby the above-mentioned question for the elementary sentence form of the word "arthropode," that is for the sentence form "the thing x is an arthropode," is answered: it has been stipulated that a sentence of this form is deducible from premises of the form "x is an animal," "x has a segmented body," "x has jointed legs," and that conversely each of these sentences is deducible from the former sentence. By means of these stipulations about deducibility (in other words: about the truth-condition, about the method of verification, about the meaning) of the elementary sentence about "arthropode" the meaning of the word "arthropode" is fixed. In this way every word of the language is reduced to other words and finally to the words which occur in the so-called "observation sentences" or "protocol sentences." It is through this reduction that the word acquires its meaning.

For our purposes we may ignore entirely the question concerning the content and form of the primary sentences (protocol sentences) which has not yet been definitely settled. In the theory of knowledge it is customary to say that the primary sentences refer to "the given"; but there is no unanimity on the question what it is that is given. At times the position is taken that sentences about the given speak of the simplest qualities of sense and feeling (e.g., "warm," "blue," "joy" and so forth); others incline to the view that basic sentences refer to total experiences and similarities between them; a still different view has it that even the basic sentences speak of things. Regardless of this diversity of opinion it is certain that a sequence of words has a meaning only if its relations of deducibility to the protocol sentences are fixed, whatever the characteristics of the protocol sentences may be; and similarly, that a word is significant only if the sentences in which it may occur are reducible to protocol sentences.

Since the meaning of a word is determined by its criterion of application (in other words: by the relations of deducibility entered into by its elementary sentence-form, by its truth-conditions, by the method of its verification), the stipulation of the criterion takes away one's freedom to decide what one wishes to "mean" by the word. If the word is to receive an exact meaning, nothing less than the criterion of application must be given; but one cannot, on the other hand, give more than the criterion of application, for the latter is a sufficient determi-

nation of meaning. The meaning is implicitly contained in the criterion; all that remains to be done is to make the meaning explicit.

Let us suppose, by way of illustration, that someone invented the new word "teavy" and maintained that there are things which are teavy and things which are not teavy. In order to learn the meaning of this word, we ask him about its criterion of application: how is one to ascertain in a concrete case whether a given thing is teavy or not? Let us suppose to begin with that we get no answer from him: there are no empirical signs of teavyness, he says. In that case we would deny the legitimacy of using this word. If the person who uses the word says that all the same there are things which are teavy and there are things which are not teavy, only it remains for the weak, finite intellect of man an eternal secret which things are teavy and which are not, we shall regard this as empty verbiage. But perhaps he will assure us that he means, after all, something by the word "teavy." But from this we only learn the psychological fact that he associates some kind of images and feelings with the word. The word does not acquire a meaning through such associations. If no criterion of application for the word is stipulated, then nothing is asserted by the sentences in which it occurs, they are but pseudo-statements.

Secondly, take the case when we are given a criterion of application for a new word, say "toovy"; in particular, let the sentence "this thing is toovy" be true if and only if the thing is quadrangular. (It is irrelevant in this context whether the criterion is explicitly stated or whether we derive it by observing the affirmative and the negative uses of the word). Then we will say: the word "toovy" is synonymous with the word "quadrangular." And we will not allow its users to tell us that nevertheless they "intended" something else by it than "quadrangular"; that though every quadrangular thing is also toovy and conversely, this is only because quadrangularity is the visible manifestation of toovyness, but that the latter itself is a hidden, not itself observable property. We would reply that after the criterion of application has been fixed, the synonymy of "toovy" and "quadrangular" is likewise fixed, and that we are no further at liberty to "intend" this or that by the word.

Let us briefly summarize the result of our analysis. Let "a" be any word and "S(a)" the elementary sentence in which it occurs. Then the sufficient and necessary condition for "a" being meaningful may be given by each of the following formulations, which ultimately say the same thing:

1. The *empirical criteria* for a are known.

2. It has been stipulated from what protocol sentences "S(a)" is *deducible*.

3. The *truth-conditions* for "S(a)" are fixed.

4. The method of *verification* of "S(a)" is known.[1]

3. Metaphysical Words Without Meaning

Many words of metaphysics, now, can be shown not to fulfill the above requirement, and therefore to be devoid of meaning.

Let us take as an example the metaphysical term "principle" (in the sense of principle of being, not principle of knowledge or axiom). Various metaphysicians offer an answer to the question which is the (highest) "principle of the world" (or of "things," of "existence," of "being"), e.g., water, number, form, motion, life, the spirit, the idea, the unconscious, activity, the good, and so forth. In order to discover the meaning of the word "principle" in this metaphysical question we must ask the metaphysician under what conditions a statement of the form "x is the principle of y" would be true and under what conditions it would be false. In other words: we ask for the criteria of application or for the definition of the word "principle." The metaphysician replies approximately as follows: "x is the principle of y" is to mean "y arises out of x," "the being of y rests on the being of x," "y exists by virtue of x" and so forth. But these words are ambiguous and vague. Frequently they have a clear meaning; e.g., we say of a thing or process y that it "arises out of" x when we observe that things or processes of kind x are frequently or invariably followed by things or processes of kind y (causal connection in the sense of a lawful succession). But the metaphysician tells us that he does not mean this empirically observable relationship. For in that case his metaphysical theses would be merely empirical propositions of the same kind as those of physics. The expression "arising from" is not to mean here a relation of temporal and causal sequence, which is what the

word ordinarily means. Yet, no criterion is specified for any other meaning. Consequently, the alleged "metaphysical" meaning, which the word is supposed to have here in contrast to the mentioned empirical meaning, does not exist. If we reflect on the original meaning of the word "principium" (and of the corresponding Greek word ἀρχή), we notice the same development. The word is explicitly deprived of its original meaning "beginning"; it is not supposed to mean the temporally prior any more, but the prior in some other, specifically metaphysical, respect. The criteria for this "metaphysical respect," however, are lacking. In both cases, then, the word has been deprived of its earlier meaning without being given a new meaning; there remains the word as an empty shell. From an earlier period of significant use, it is still associatively connected with various mental images; these in turn get associated with new mental images and feelings in the new context of usage. But the word does not thereby become meaningful; and it remains meaningless as long as no method of verification can be described.

Another example is the word "God." Here we must, apart from the variations of its usage within each domain, distinguish the linguistic usage in three different contexts or historical epochs, which however overlap temporally. In its *mythological* use the word has a clear meaning. It, or parallel words in other languages, is sometimes used to denote physical beings which are enthroned on Mount Olympus, in Heaven or in Hades, and which are endowed with power, wisdom, goodness and happiness to a greater or lesser extent. Sometimes the word also refers to spiritual beings which, indeed, do not have manlike bodies, yet manifest themselves nevertheless somehow in the things or processes of the visible world and are therefore empirically verifiable. In its *metaphysical* use, on the other hand, the word "God" refers to something beyond experience. The word is deliberately divested of its reference to a physical being or to a spiritual being that is immanent in the physical. And as it is not given a new meaning, it becomes meaningless. To be sure, it often looks as though the word "God" had a meaning even in metaphysics. But the definitions which are set up prove on closer inspection to be pseudo-definitions. They lead either to logically illegitimate combinations of words (of which we shall treat later) or to other metaphysical words (e.g., "primordial basis," "the absolute," "the unconditioned," "the autonomous," "the self-dependent" and so forth), but in no case to the truth-conditions of its elementary sentences. In the case of this word not even the first requirement of logic is met, that is the requirement to specify its syntax, i.e., the form of its occurrence in elementary sentences. An elementary sentence would here have to be of the form "x is a God"; yet, the metaphysician either rejects this form entirely without substituting another, or if he accepts it he neglects to indicate the syntactical category of the variable x. (Categories are, for example, material things, properties of things, relations between things, numbers etc.)

The *theological* usage of the word "God" falls between its mythological and its metaphysical usage. There is no distinctive meaning here, but an oscillation from one of the mentioned two uses to the other. Several theologians have a clearly empirical (in our terminology, "mythological") concept of God. In this case there are no pseudo-statements; but the disadvantage for the theologian lies in the circumstance that according to this interpretation the statements of theology are empirical and hence are subject to the judgment of empirical science. The linguistic usage of other theologians is clearly metaphysical. Others again do not speak in any definite way, whether this is because they follow now this, now that linguistic usage, or because they express themselves in terms whose usage is not clearly classifiable since it tends towards both sides.

Just like the examined examples "principle" and "God," most of the other *specifically metaphysical terms are devoid of meaning*, e.g., "the Idea," "the Absolute," "the Unconditioned," "the Infinite," "the being of being," "non-being," "thing in itself," "absolute spirit," "objective spirit," "essence," "being-in-itself," "being-in-and-for-itself," "emanation," "manifestation," "articulation," "the Ego," "the non-Ego," etc. These expressions are in the same boat with "teavy," our previously fabricated example. The metaphysician tells us that empirical truth-conditions cannot be specified; if he adds that nevertheless he "means" something, we know that this is merely an allusion to associated images and feelings which, however, do not bestow a meaning on the word. The alleged statements of metaphysics which contain such words have no sense, assert nothing, are mere pseudo-statements. Into the explanation of their historical origin we shall inquire later.

4. *The Significance of a Sentence*

So far we have considered only those pseudo-statements which contain a meaningless word. But there is a second kind of pseudo-statement. They consist of meaningful words, but the words are put together in such a way that nevertheless no meaning results. The syntax of a language specifies which combinations of words are admissible and which inadmissible. The grammatical syntax of natural languages, however, does not fulfill the task of elimination of senseless combinations of words in all cases. Let us take as examples the following sequences of words:

1. "Caesar is and"

2. "Caesar is a prime number"

The word sequence (1) is formed countersyntactically; the rules of syntax require that the third position be occupied, not by a conjunction, but by a predicate, hence by a noun (with article) or by an adjective. The word sequence "Caesar is a general," e.g., is formed in accordance with the rules of syntax. It is a meaningful word sequence, a genuine sentence. But, now, word sequence (2) is likewise syntactically correct, for it has the same grammatical form as the sentence just mentioned. Nevertheless (2) is meaningless. "Prime number" is a predicate of numbers; it can be neither affirmed nor denied of a person. Since (2) looks like a statement yet is not a statement, does not assert anything, expresses neither a true nor a false proposition, we call this word sequence a "pseudo-statement." The fact that the rules of grammatical syntax are not violated easily seduces one at first glance into the erroneous opinion that one still has to do with a statement, albeit a false one. But "a is a prime number" is false if and only if a is divisible by a natural number different from a and from 1; evidently it is illicit to put here "Caesar" for "a." This example has been so chosen that the nonsense is easily detectable. Many so-called statements of metaphysics are not so easily recognized to be pseudo-statements. The fact that natural languages allow the formation of meaningless sequences of words without violating the rules of grammar, indicates that grammatical syntax is, from a logical point of view, inadequate. If grammatical syntax corresponded exactly to logical syntax, pseudo-statements could not arise. If grammatical syntax differentiated not only the word-categories of nouns, adjectives, verbs, conjunctions etc., but within each of these categories made the further distinctions that are logically indispensable, then no pseudo-statements could be formed. If, e.g., nouns were grammatically subdivided into several kinds of words, according as they designated properties of physical objects, of numbers etc., then the words "general" and "prime number" would belong to grammatically different word-categories, and (2) would be just as linguistically incorrect as (1). In a correctly constructed language, therefore, all nonsensical sequences of words would be of the kind of example (1). Considerations of grammar would already eliminate them as it were automatically; i.e., in order to avoid nonsense, it would be unnecessary to pay attention to the meanings of the individual words over and above their syntactical type (their "syntactical category," e.g., thing, property of things, relation between things, number, property of numbers, relation between numbers, and so forth). It follows that if our thesis that the statements of metaphysics are pseudo-statements is justifiable, then metaphysics could not even be expressed in a logically constructed language. This is the great philosophical importance of the task, which at present occupies the logicians, of building a logical syntax.

5. *Metaphysical Pseudo-statements*

Let us now take a look at some examples of metaphysical pseudo-statements of a kind where the violation of logical syntax is especially obvious, though they accord with historical-grammatical syntax. We select a few sentences from that metaphysical school which at present exerts the strongest influence in Germany.[2]

"What is to be investigated is being only and—*nothing* else; being alone and further—*nothing*; solely being, and beyond being—*nothing*. *What about this Nothing?* . . . *Does the Nothing exist only because the Not, i.e. the Negation, exists? Or is it the other way around? Does Negation and the Not exist only because the Nothing exists?* . . . We assert: *the Nothing is prior to the Not and the Negation.* . . . Where do we seek the Nothing? How do we find the Nothing. . . . We know the Nothing. . . .

Anxiety reveals the Nothing. . . . That for which and because of which we were anxious, was 'really'—nothing. Indeed: the Nothing itself—as such—was present. . . . *What about this Nothing?—The Nothing itself nothings.*"

In order to show that the possibility of forming pseudo-statements is based on a logical defect of language, we set up the schema below. The sentences under I are grammatically as well as logically impeccable, hence meaningful. The sentences under II (excepting B3) are in grammatical respects perfectly analogous to those under I. Sentence form IIA (as question and answer) does not, indeed, satisfy the requirements to be imposed on a logically correct language. But it is nevertheless meaningful, because it is translatable into correct language. This is shown by sentence IIIA, which has the same meaning as IIA. Sentence form IIA then proves to be undesirable because we can be led from it, by means of grammatically faultless operations, to the meaningless sentence forms IIB, which are taken from the above quotation. These forms cannot even be constructed in the correct language of Column III. Nonetheless, their nonsensicality is not obvious at first glance, because one is easily deceived by the analogy with the meaningful sentences IB. The fault of our language identified here lies, therefore, in the circumstance that, in contrast to a logically correct language, it admits of the same grammatical form for meaningful and meaningless word sequences. To each sentence in words we have added a corresponding formula in the notation of symbolic logic; these formulae facilitate recognition of the undesirable analogy between IA and IIA and therewith of the origin of the meaningless constructions IIB.

I.	II. Transition from Sense to Nonsense in Ordinary Language	III.
Meaningful Sentences of Ordinary Language	*Sense to Nonsense in Ordinary Language*	*Logically Correct Language*
A. What is outside? $Ou(?)$ Rain is outside $Ou(r)$	A. What is outside? $Ou(?)$ Nothing is outside $Ou(no)$	A. There is nothing (does not exist anything) which is outside. $\sim(\exists x).\ Ou(x)$

B. What about this rain? (i.e., what does the rain do? or: what else can be said about this rain? ?(r)	B. "What about this Nothing?" ?(no)	B. None of these forms can even be constructed.
1. We know the rain K(r)	1. "We seek the Nothing" "We find the Nothing" "We know the Nothing" K(no)	
2. The rain rains R(r)	2. "The Nothing nothings" No(no)	
	3. "The Nothing exists only because . . ." $\exists x(no)$	

On closer inspection of the pseudo-statements under IIB, we also find some differences. The construction of sentence (1) is simply based on the mistake of employing the word "nothing" as a noun, because it is customary in ordinary language to use it in this form in order to construct a negative existential statement (see IIA). In a correct language, on the other hand, it is not a particular *name*, but a certain *logical form* of the sentence that serves this purpose (see IIIA). Sentence IIB2 adds something new, viz., the fabrication of the meaningless word "to nothing." This sentence, therefore, is senseless for a twofold reason. We pointed out before that the meaningless words of metaphysics usually owe their origin to the fact that a meaningful word is deprived of its meaning through its metaphorical use in metaphysics. But here we confront one of those rare cases where a new word is introduced which never had a meaning to begin with. Likewise sentence IIB3 must be rejected for two reasons. In respect of the error of

using the word "nothing" as a noun, it is like the previous sentences. But in addition it involves a contradiction. For even if it were admissible to introduce "nothing" as a name or description of an entity, still the existence of this entity would be denied in its very definition, whereas sentence (3) goes on to affirm its existence. This sentence, therefore, would be contradictory, hence absurd, even if it were not already meaningless.

In view of the gross logical errors which we find in sentences IIB, we might be led to conjecture that perhaps the word "nothing" has in Heidegger's treatise a meaning entirely different from the customary one. And this presumption is further strengthened as we go on to read there that anxiety reveals the Nothing, that the Nothing itself is present as such in anxiety. For here the word "nothing" seems to refer to a certain emotional constitution, possibly of a religious sort, or something or other that underlies such emotions. If such were the case, then the mentioned logical errors in sentences IIB would not be committed. But the first sentence of the quotation at the beginning of this section proves that this interpretation is not possible. The combination of "only" and "nothing else" shows unmistakably that the word "nothing" here has the usual meaning of a logical particle that serves for the formulation of a negative existential statement. This introduction of the word "nothing" is then immediately followed by the leading question of the treatise: "What about this Nothing?"

But our doubts as to a possible misinterpretation get completely dissolved as we note that the author of the treatise is clearly aware of the conflict between his questions and statements, and logic. "*Question and answer* in regard to the Nothing are equally *absurd* in themselves. . . . The fundamental rule of thinking commonly appealed to, the law of prohibited contradiction, general 'logic,' destroys this question." All the worse for logic! We must abolish its sovereignty: "If thus the power of the *understanding* in the field of questions concerning Nothing and Being is broken, then the fate of the sovereignty of 'logic' within philosophy is thereby decided as well. The very idea of 'logic' dissolves in the whirl of a more basic questioning." But will sober science condone the whirl of counter-logical questioning? To this question too there is a ready answer: "The alleged sobriety and superiority of science becomes ridiculous if it does not take the Nothing seriously." Thus we find here a good confirmation of our thesis; a metaphysician himself here states that his questions and answers are irreconcilable with logic and the scientific way of thinking.

The difference between our thesis and that of the *earlier antimetaphysicians* should now be clear. We do not regard metaphysics as "mere speculation" or "fairy tales." The statements of a fairy tale do not conflict with logic, but only with experience; they are perfectly meaningful, although false. Metaphysics is not *"superstition"*; it is possible to believe true and false propositions, but not to believe meaningless sequences of words. Metaphysical statements are not even acceptable as *"working hypotheses"*; for an hypothesis must be capable of entering into relations of deducibility with (true or false) empirical statements, which is just what pseudo-statements cannot do.

With reference to the so-called *limitation of human knowledge* an attempt is sometimes made to save metaphysics by raising the following objection: metaphysical statements are not, indeed, verifiable by man nor by any other finite being; nevertheless they might be construed as conjectures about the answers which a being with higher or even perfect powers of knowledge would make to our questions, and as such conjectures they would, after all, be meaningful. To counter this objection, let us consider the following. If the meaning of a word cannot be specified, or if the sequence of words does not accord with the rules of syntax, then one has not even asked a question. (Just think of the pesudo-questions: "Is this table teavy?", "is the number 7 holy?", "which numbers are darker, the even or the odd ones?".) Where there is no question, not even an omniscient being can give an answer. Now the objector may say: just as one who can see may communicate new knowledge to the blind, so a higher being might perhaps communicate to us metaphysical knowledge, e.g., whether the visible world is the manifestation of a spirit. Here we must reflect on the meaning of "new knowledge." It is, indeed, conceivable that we might encounter animals who tell us about a new sense. If these beings were to prove to us Fermat's theorem or were to invent a new physical instrument or were to establish a hitherto unknown law of nature, then our knowledge would be increased with their help. For this sort of thing we can test, just the way even a blind man can understand and test the whole of physics (and therewith any statement made by those who can

see). But if those hypothetical beings tell us something which we cannot verify, then we cannot understand it either; in that case no information has been communicated to us, but mere verbal sounds devoid of meaning though possibly associated with images. It follows that our knowledge can only be quantitatively enlarged by other beings, no matter whether they know more or less or everything, but no knowledge of an essentially different kind can be added. What we do not know for certain, we may come to know with greater certainty through the assistance of other beings; but what is unintelligible, meaningless for us, cannot become meaningful through someone else's assistance, however vast his knowledge might be. Therefore no god and no devil can give us metaphysical knowledge.

6. *Meaninglessness of All Metaphysics*

The examples of metaphysical statements which we have analyzed were all taken from just one treatise. But our results apply with equal validity, in part even in verbally identical ways, to other metaphysical systems. That treatise is completely in the right in citing approvingly a statement by Hegel ("pure Being and pure Nothing, therefore, are one and the same"). The metaphysics of Hegel has exactly the same logical character as this modern system of metaphysics. And the same holds for the rest of the metaphysical systems, though the kind of phraseology and therewith the kind of logical errors that occur in them deviate more or less from the kind that occurs in the examples we discussed.

It should not be necessary here to adduce further examples of specific metaphysical sentences in diverse systems and submit them to analysis. We confine ourselves to an indication of the most frequent kinds of errors.

Perhaps the majority of the logical mistakes that are committed when pseudo-statements are made, are based on the logical faults infecting the use of the words "to be" in our language (and of the corresponding words in other languages, at least in most European languages). The first fault is the ambiguity of the words "to be." It is sometimes used as copula prefixed to a predicate ("I am hungry"), sometimes to designate existence ("I am"). This mistake is aggravated by the fact that metaphysicians often are not clear about this ambiguity. The second fault lies in the form of the verb in its second meaning, the meaning of *existence*. The verbal form feigns a predicate where there is none. To be sure, it has been known for a long time that existence is not a property (cf. Kant's refutation of the ontological proof of the existence of God). But it was not until the advent of modern logic that full consistency on this point was reached: the syntactical form in which modern logic introduces the sign for existence is such that it cannot, like a predicate, be applied to signs for objects, but only to predicates (cf., e.g., sentence IIIA in the above table). Most metaphysicians since antiquity have allowed themselves to be seduced into pseudo-statements by the verbal, and therewith the predicative form of the word "to be," e.g., "I am," "God is."

We meet an illustration of this error in Descartes' "cogito, ergo sum." Let us disregard here the material objections that have been raised against the premise—viz., whether the sentence "I think" adequately expresses the intended state of affairs or contains perhaps an hypostasis—and consider the two sentences only from the formal-logical point of view. We notice at once two essential logical mistakes. The first lies in the conclusion "I am." The verb "to be" is undoubtedly meant in the sense of existence here; for a copula cannot be used without predicate; indeed, Descartes' "I am" has always been interpreted in this sense. But in that case this sentence violates the above-mentioned logical rule that existence can be predicated only in conjunction with a predicate, not in conjunction with a name (subject, proper name). An existential statement does not have the form "*a* exists" (as in "I am," i.e., "I exist"), but "there exists something of such and such a kind." The second error lies in the transition from "I think" to "I exist." If from the statement "P(a)" ("a has the property P") an existential statement is to be deduced, then the latter can assert existence only with respect to the predicate P, not with respect to the subject *a* of the premise. What follows from "I am a European" is not "I exist," but "a European exists." What follows from "I think" is not "I am" but "there exists something that thinks."

The circumstance that our languages express existence by a verb ("to be" or "to exist") is not in itself a logical fault; it is only inappropriate, dangerous. The verbal form easily misleads us into the misconception that existence is a predicate. One then arrives at such logically incorrect and hence senseless modes of expression as were just examined. Likewise such forms as "Being" or "Not-Being," which from time immemorial have played a great role in metaphysics, have the same origin. In a logically correct language such forms cannot even be constructed. It appears that in the Latin and the German languages the forms "ens" or "das Seiende" were, perhaps under the seductive influence of the Greek example, introduced specifically for use by metaphysicians; in this way the language deteriorated logically whereas the addition was believed to represent an improvement.

Another very frequent violation of logical syntax is the so-called "*type confusion*" of concepts. While the previously mentioned mistake consists in the predicative use of a symbol with non-predicative meaning, in this case a predicate is, indeed, used as predicate yet as predicate of a different type. We have here a violation of the rules of the so-called theory of types. An artificial example is the sentence we discussed earlier: "Caesar is a prime number." Names of persons and names of numbers belong to different logical types, and so do accordingly predicates of persons (e.g., "general") and predicates of numbers ("prime number"). The error of type confusion is, unlike the previously discussed usage of the verb "to be," not the prerogative of metaphysics but already occurs very often in conversational language also. But here it rarely leads to nonsense. The typical ambiguity of words is here of such a kind that it can be easily removed.

> *Example:* 1. "This table is larger than that."
> 2. "The height of this table is larger than the height of that table." Here the word "larger" is used in (1) for a relation between objects, in (2) for a relation between numbers, hence for two distinct syntactical categories. The mistake is here unimportant; it could, e.g., be eliminated by writing "larger1" and "larger2"; "larger1" is then defined in terms of "larger2" by declaring statement form (1) to be synonymous with (2) (and others of a similar kind).

Since the confusion of types causes no harm in conversational language, it is usually ignored entirely. This is, indeed, expedient for the ordinary use of language, but has had unfortunate consequences in metaphysics. Here the conditioning by everyday language has led to confusions of types which, unlike those in everyday language, are no longer translatable into logically correct form. Pseudo-statements of this kind are encountered in especially large quantity, e.g., in the writings of Hegel and Heidegger. The latter has adopted many peculiarities of the Hegelian idiom along with their logical faults (e.g., predicates which should be applied to objects of a certain sort are instead applied to predicates of these objects or to "being" or to "existence" or to a relation between these objects).

Having found that many metaphysical statements are meaningless, we confront the question whether there is not perhaps a core of meaningful statements in metaphysics which would remain after elimination of all the meaningless ones.

Indeed, the results we have obtained so far might give rise to the view that there are many dangers of falling into nonsense in metaphysics, and that one must accordingly endeavor to avoid these traps with great care if one wants to do metaphysics. But actually the situation is that meaningful metaphysical statements are impossible. This follows from the task which metaphysics sets itself: to discover and formulate a kind of knowledge which is not accessible to empirical science.

We have seen earlier that the meaning of a statement lies in the method of its verification. A statement asserts only so much as is verifiable with respect to it. Therefore a sentence can be used only to assert an empirical proposition, if indeed it is used to assert anything at all. If something were to lie, in principle, beyond possible experience, it could be neither said nor thought nor asked.

Meaningful statements are divided into the following kinds. First there are statements which are true solely by virtue of their form ("tautologies" according to Wittgenstein; they correspond approximately to Kant's "analytic judgments"). They say nothing about reality. The formulae of logic and mathematics are of this kind. They are not themselves factual statements, but serve for the transformation of such statements. Secondly there are the negations of such statements ("contradictions"). They are self-contradictory, hence false by virtue of their form. With respect to all other statements the decision about truth or falsehood lies in the protocol sentences. They are therefore (true or false) *empirical statements* and belong to the domain of empirical science. Any statement one desires to construct which does not fall within

these categories becomes automatically meaningless. Since metaphysics does not want to assert analytic propositions, nor to fall within the domain of empirical science, it is compelled to employ words for which no criteria of application are specified and which are therefore devoid of sense, or else to combine meaningful words in such a way that neither an analytic (or contradictory) statement nor an empirical statement is produced. In either case pseudo-statements are the inevitable product.

Logical analysis, then, pronounces the verdict of meaninglessness on any alleged knowledge that pretends to reach above or behind experience. This verdict hits, in the first place, any speculative metaphysics, any alleged knowledge by *pure thinking* or by *pure intuition* that pretends to be able to do without experience. But the verdict equally applies to the kind of metaphysics which, starting from experience, wants to acquire knowledge about that which *transcends experience* by means of special *inferences* (e.g., the neo-vitalist thesis of the directive presence of an "entelechy" in organic processes, which supposedly cannot be understood in terms of physics; the question concerning the "essence of causality," transcending the ascertainment of certain regularities of succession; the talk about the "thing in itself"). Further, the same judgment must be passed on all *philosophy of norms*, or *philosophy of value*, on any ethics or esthetics as a normative discipline. For the objective validity of a value or norm is (even on the view of the philosophers of value) not empirically verifiable nor deducible from empirical statements; hence it cannot be asserted (in a meaningful statement) at all. In other words: Either empirical criteria are indicated for the use of "good" and "beautiful" and the rest of the predicates that are employed in the normative sciences, or they are not. In the first case, a statement containing such a predicate turns into a factual judgment, but not a value judgment; in the second case, it becomes a pseudo-statement. It is altogether impossible to make a statement that expresses a value judgment.

Finally, the verdict of meaninglessness also hits those metaphysical movements which are usually called, improperly, epistemological movements, that is *realism* (insofar as it claims to say more than the empirical fact that the sequence of events exhibits a certain regularity, which makes the application of the inductive method possible) and its opponents: subjective *idealism*, solipsism, phenomenalism, and *positivism* (in the earlier sense).

But what, then, is left over for *philosophy*, if all statements whatever that assert something are of an empirical nature and belong to factual science? What remains is not statements, nor a theory, nor a system, but only a *method*: the method of logical analysis. The foregoing discussion has illustrated the negative application of this method: in that context it serves to eliminate meaningless words, meaningless pseudo-statements. In its positive use it serves to clarify meaningful concepts and propositions, to lay logical foundations for factual science and for mathematics. The negative application of the method is necessary and important in the present historical situation. But even in its present practice, the positive application is more fertile. We cannot here discuss it in greater detail. It is the indicated task of logical analysis, inquiry into logical foundations, that is meant by "*scientific philosophy*" in contrast to metaphysics.

The question regarding the logical character of the statements which we obtain as the result of a logical analysis, e.g., the statements occurring in this and other logical papers, can here be answered only tentatively: such statements are partly analytic, partly empirical. For these statements about statements and parts of statements belong in part to pure *metalogic* (e.g., "a sequence consisting of the existence-symbol and a noun, is not a sentence"), in part to descriptive metalogic (e.g., "the word sequence at such and such a place in such and such a book is meaningless"). Metalogic will be discussed elsewhere. It will also be shown there that the metalogic which speaks about the sentences of a given language can be formulated in that very language itself.

7. Metaphysics as Expression of an Attitude toward Life

Our claim that the statements of metaphysics are entirely meaningless, that they do not assert anything, will leave even those who agree intellectually with our results with a painful feeling of strangeness: how could it be explained that so many men in all ages and nations, among them eminent minds, spent so much energy, nay veritable fervor, on metaphysics if the latter consisted of nothing but mere words, nonsensically juxtaposed? And how could one account for the fact that metaphysical books have exerted such a strong influence on readers up to the present day, if they contained not even errors, but nothing at all? These doubts are justified since metaphysics does indeed have a content; only it is not theoretical content. The (pseudo)statements of metaphysics do not serve for the *description of states of affairs*, neither existing ones (in that case they would be true statements) nor non-existing ones (in that case they would be at least false statements). They serve for the *expression of the general attitude of a person towards life* ("Lebenseinstellung, Lebensgefühl").

Perhaps we may assume that metaphysics originated from *mythology*. The child is angry at the "wicked table" which hurt him. Primitive man endeavors to conciliate the threatening demon of earthquakes, or he worships the deity of the fertile rains in gratitude. Here we confront personifications of natural phenomena, which are the quasi-poetic expression of man's emotional relationship to his environment. The heritage of mythology is bequeathed on the one hand to poetry, which produces and intensifies the effects of mythology on life in a deliberate way; on the other hand, it is handed down to theology, which develops mythology into a system. Which, now, is the historical role of metaphysics? Perhaps we may regard it as a substitute for theology on the level of systematic, conceptual thinking. The (supposedly) transcendent sources of knowledge of theology are here replaced by natural, yet supposedly transempirical sources of knowledge. On closer inspection the same content as that of mythology is here still recognizable behind the repeatedly varied dressing: we find that metaphysics also arises from the need to give expression to a man's attitude in life, his emotional and volitional reaction to the environment, to society, to the tasks to which he devotes himself, to the misfortunes that befall him. This attitude manifests itself, unconsciously as a rule, in everything a man does or says. It also impresses itself on his facial features, perhaps even on the character of his gait. Many people, now, feel a desire to create over and above these manifestations a special expression of their attitude, through which it might become visible in a more succinct and penetrating way. If they have artistic talent they are able to express themselves by producing a work of art. Many writers have already clarified the way in which the basic attitude is manifested through the style and manner of a work of art (e.g., Dilthey and his students). [In this connection the term "world view" ("Weltanschauung") is often used; we prefer to avoid it because of its ambiguity, which blurs the difference between attitude and theory, a difference which is of decisive importance for our analysis.] What is here essential for our considerations is only the fact that art is an adequate, metaphysics an inadequate means for the expression of the basic attitude. Of course, there need be no intrinsic objection to one's using any means of expression one likes. But in the case of metaphysics we find this situation: through the form of its works it pretends to be something that it is not. The form in question is that of a system of statements which are apparently related as premises and conclusions, that is, the form of a theory. In this way the fiction of theoretical content is generated, whereas, as we have seen, there is no such content. It is not only the reader, but the metaphysician himself who suffers from the illusion that the metaphysical statements say something, describe states of affairs. The metaphysician believes that he travels in territory in which truth and falsehood are at stake. In reality, however, he has not asserted anything, but only expressed something, like an artist. That the metaphysician is thus deluding himself cannot be inferred from the fact that he selects language as the medium of expression and declarative sentences as the form of expression; for lyrical poets do the same without succumbing to self-delusion. But the metaphysician supports his statements by arguments, he claims assent to their content, he polemicizes against metaphysicians of divergent persuasion by attempting to refute their assertions in his treatise. Lyrical poets, on the other hand, do not try to refute in their poem the statements in a poem by some other lyrical poet; for they know they are in the domain of art and not in the domain of theory.

Perhaps music is the purest means of expression of the basic attitude because it is entirely free from any reference to objects. The harmonious feeling or attitude, which the metaphysician tries to express in a monistic system, is more clearly expressed in the music of Mozart. And when a metaphysician gives verbal expression to his dualistic-heroic attitude towards life in a dualistic system, is it not perhaps because he lacks the ability of a Beethoven to express this attitude in an adequate medium? Metaphysicians are musicians without musical ability. Instead they have a strong

inclination to work within the medium of the theoretical, to connect concepts and thoughts. Now, instead of activating, on the one hand, this inclination in the domain of science, and satisfying, on the other hand, the need for expression in art, the metaphysician confuses the two and produces a structure which achieves nothing for knowledge and something inadequate for the expression of attitude.

Our conjecture that metaphysics is a substitute, albeit an inadequate one, for art, seems to be further confirmed by the fact that the metaphysician who perhaps had artistic talent to the highest degree, viz., Nietzsche, almost entirely avoided the error of that confusion. A large part of his work has predominantly empirical content. We find there, for instance, historical analyses of specific artistic phenomena, or an historical-psychological analysis of morals. In the work, however, in which he expresses most strongly that which others express through metaphysics or ethics, in *Thus Spake Zarathustra*, he does not choose the misleading theoretical form, but openly the form of art, of poetry.

Remarks by the Author (1957)

To section 1, "metaphysics." This term is used in this paper, as usually in Europe, for the field of alleged knowledge of the essence of things which transcends the realm of empirically founded, inductive science. Metaphysics in this sense includes systems like those of Fichte, Schelling, Hegel, Bergson, Heidegger. But it does not include endeavors towards a synthesis and generalization of the results of the various sciences.

To section 1, "meaning." Today we distinguish various kinds of meaning, in particular cognitive (designative, referential) meaning on the one hand, and noncognitive (expressive) meaning components, e.g., emotive and motivative, on the other. In the present paper, the word "meaning" is always understood in the sense of "cognitive meaning." The thesis that the sentences of metaphysics are meaningless, is thus to be understood in the sense that they have no cognitive meaning, no assertive content. The obvious psychological fact that they have expressive meaning is thereby not denied; this is explicitly stated in Section 7.

To section 6, "metalogic." This term refers to the theory of expressions of a language and, in particular, of their logical relations. Today we would distinguish between logical syntax as the theory of purely formal relations and semantics as the theory of meaning and truth-conditions.

   To section 6, realism and idealism. That both the affirmative and the negative theses concerning the reality of the external world are pseudo-statements, I have tried to show in the monograph *Scheinprobleme in der Philosophie: Das Fremdpsychische und der Realismusstreit*, Berlin, 1928. The similar nature of the ontological theses about the reality or unreality of abstract entities, e.g., properties, relations, propositions, is discussed in "Empiricism, Semantics, and Ontology," *Revue Intern. de Philos.* 4, 1950, 20–40, reprinted in: *Meaning and Necessity*, second edition, Chicago, 1956.

Endnotes

[1] For the logical and epistemological conception which underlies our exposition, but can only briefly be intimated here, cf. Wittgenstein, *Tractatus Logico-Philosophicus*, 1922, and Carnap, *Der logische Aufbau der Welt*, 1928.

[2] The following quotations (original italics) are taken from M. Heidegger, *Was Ist Metaphysik?* 1929. We could just as well have selected passages from any other of the numerous metaphysicians of the present or of the past; yet the selected passages seem to us to illustrate our thesis especially well.

50. *Letter on Humanism*

MARTIN HEIDEGGER

Martin Heidegger (1889–1976) was first a student, then successor, of the phenomenologist Edmund Husserl at the University of Freiburg. He became famous as one of the founders of twentieth-century existentialism, which has as one of its central tenets the thesis that people can be self-creating beings. According to the slogan "Existence precedes essence," people have no fixed essence, but can make their own through their choices and actions. Though Heidegger rejected the existentialist label, much of his work analyzes a broad range of human concerns, for example, temporality, death, technology, and authentic living. Heidegger's writing is notoriously difficult; it is not merely Hegelian in spirit, but it also uses many controversial German and Greek neologisms.

The preceding selection by Rudolf Carnap contains a criticism, from an empiricist perspective, of one of his early writings. Heidegger, however, shares the logical empiricist view that something is wrong with traditional metaphysics and that, somehow, language is to blame. But whereas the logical empiricists want to clarify philosophical language on the model of logic and science, Heidegger is interested in the "liberation of language from grammar." Akin to a mystical prophet, Heidegger shows his faith, in this selection, that people have some extrascientific way of coming to terms with reality: "If man is to find his way once again into the nearness of Being he must first learn to exist in the nameless."

We are still far from pondering the essence of action decisively enough. We view action only as causing an effect. The actuality of the effect is valued according to its utility. But the essence of action is accomplishment. To accomplish means to unfold something into the fullness of its essence, to lead it forth into this fullness—*producere*. Therefore only what already is can really be accomplished. But what "is" above all is Being. Thinking accomplishes the relation of Being to the essence of man. It does not make or cause the relation. Thinking brings this relation to Being solely as something handed over to it from Being. Such offering consists in the fact that in thinking Being comes to language. Language is the house of Being. In its home man dwells. Those who think and those who create with words are the guardians of this home. Their guardianship accomplishes the manifestation of Being insofar as they bring the manifestation to language and maintain it in language through their speech. Thinking does not become action only because some effect issues from it or because it is applied. Thinking acts insofar as it thinks. Such action is presumably the simplest and at the same time the highest, because it concerns the relation of Being to man. But all working or effecting lies in Being and is directed toward beings. Thinking, in contrast, lets itself be claimed by Being so that it can say the truth of Being. Thinking accomplishes this letting. Thinking is *l'engagement par l'Être pour l'Être* [engagement by Being for Being]. I do not know whether it is linguistically possible to say both of these ("*par*" and "*pour*") at once, in this way: *penser, c'est l'engagement de l'Être* [thinking is the engagement of Being]. Here the possessive form "*de l'* . . ." is supposed to express both subjective and objective genitive. In this regard "subject" and "object" are inappropriate terms of metaphysics, which very early on in the form of Occidental "logic" and "grammar" seized control of the interpretation of language. We today can only begin to descry what is concealed in that occurrence. The liberation of language from grammar into a more original essential framework is reserved for thought and poetic creation. Thinking is not merely *l'engagement dans l'action* for and by beings, in the sense of the actuality of the present situation. Thinking is *l'engagement* by and for the truth of Being. The history of Being is never past but stands ever before; it sustains and defines every *condition et situation humaine*. In order to learn how to experience the aforementioned essence of thinking purely, and that means at the same time to carry it through, we must free ourselves from the technical interpretation of thinking. The beginnings of that interpretation reach back to Plato and Aristotle. They take thinking itself to be a *technē*, a process of reflection in service to doing and making. But here reflection is already seen from the perspective of *praxis* and *poiēsis*. For this reason thinking, when taken for itself, is not "practical." The characterization of thinking as *theōria* and the determination of knowing as "theoretical" behavior occur already within the "technical" interpretation of thinking. Such characterization is a reactive attempt to rescue thinking and preserve its autonomy over against acting and doing. Since then "philosophy" has been in the constant predicament of having to justify its existence before the "sciences." It believes it can do that most effectively by elevating itself to the rank of a science. But such an effort is the abandonment of the essence of thinking. Philosophy is hounded by the fear that it loses prestige and validity if it is not a science. Not to be a science is taken as a failing which is equivalent to being unscientific. Being, as the element of thinking, is abandoned by the technical interpretation of thinking. "Logic," beginning with the Sophists and Plato, sanctions this explanation. Thinking is judged by a standard that does not measure up to it. Such judgment may be compared to the procedure of trying to evaluate the nature and powers of a fish by seeing how long it can live on dry land. For a long time now, all too long, thinking has been stranded on dry land. Can then the effort to return thinking to its element be called "irrationalism"?

You ask: *Comment redonner un sens au mot 'Humanisme'*? [How can we restore meaning to the word "humanism"?] This question proceeds from your intention to retain the word "humanism." I wonder whether that is necessary. Or is the damage caused by all such terms still not sufficiently obvious? True, "-isms" have for a long time now been suspect. But the market of public opinion continually demands new ones. We are always prepared to supply the demand. Even such names as "logic," "ethics," and "physics" begin to flourish only when original thinking comes to an end. During the time of their greatness the Greeks thought without such headings. They did not even call thinking "philosophy." Thinking comes to an end when it slips out of its element. The element is what enables thinking to be a thinking. The element is what properly enables: the enabling [*das Vermögen*]. It embraces thinking and so brings it into its essence. Said plainly, thinking is the thinking of Being. The genitive says something twofold. Thinking is of Being inasmuch as thinking, coming to pass from Being, belongs to Being. At the same time thinking is of Being insofar as thinking, belonging to Being, listens to Being. As the belonging to Being that listens, thinking is what it is according to its essential origin. Thinking *is*—this says: Being has fatefully embraced its essence. To embrace a "thing" or a "person" in its essence means to love it, to favor it. Thought in a more original way such favoring [*Mögen*] means to bestow essence as a gift. Such favoring is the proper essence of enabling, which not only can achieve this or that but also can let something essentially unfold in its provenance, that is, let it be. It is on the "strength" of such enabling by favoring that something is properly able to be. This enabling is what is properly "possible" [*das "Mögliche"*], that whose essence resides in favoring. From this favoring Being enables thinking. The former makes the latter possible. Being is the enabling-favoring, the "may be" [*das "Mög-liche"*]. As the element, Being is the "quiet power" of the favoring-enabling, that is, of the possible. Of course, our words *möglich* [possible] and *Möglichkeit* [possibility], under the dominance of "logic" and "metaphysics," are thought solely in contrast to "actuality"; that is, they are thought on the basis of a definite—the metaphysical—interpretation of Being as *actus* and *potentia*, a distinction identified with the one between *existentia* and *essentia*. When I speak of the "quiet power of the possible" I do not mean the *possibile* of a merely represented *possibilitas*, nor *potentia* as the *essentia* of an *actus* of *existentia*; rather, I mean Being itself, which in its favoring presides over thinking and hence over the essence of humanity, and that means over its relation to Being. To enable something here means to preserve it in its essence, to maintain it in its element.

When thinking comes to an end by slipping out of its element it replaces this loss by procuring a validity for itself as *technē*, as an instrument of education and therefore as a classroom matter and later a cultural concern. By and by philosophy becomes a technique for explaining from highest causes. One no longer thinks; one occupies himself with "philosophy." In competition with one another, such occupations publicly offer themselves as "-isms" and try to offer more than the others. The dominance of such terms is not accidental. It rests above all in the modern age upon the peculiar dictatorship of the public realm. However, so-called "private existence" is not really essential, that is to say free, human being. It simply insists on negating the public realm. It remains an offshoot that depends upon the public and nourishes itself by a mere withdrawal from it. Hence it testifies, against its own will, to its subservience to the public realm. But because it stems from the dominance of subjectivity the public realm itself is the metaphysically conditioned establishment and authorization of the openness of individual beings in their unconditional objectification. Language thereby falls into the service of expediting communication along routes where objectification— the uniform accessibility of everything to everyone—branches out and disregards all limits. In this way language comes under the dictatorship of the public realm which decides in advance what is intelligible and what must be rejected as unintelligible. . . . The widely and rapidly spreading devastation of language not only undermines aesthetic and moral responsibility in every use of language; it arises from a threat to the essence of humanity. A merely cultivated use of language is still no proof that we have as yet escaped the danger to our essence. These days, in fact, such usage might sooner testify that we have not yet seen and cannot see the danger because we have never yet placed ourselves in view of it. Much bemoaned of late, and much too lately, the downfall of language is, however, not the grounds for, but already a consequence of, the state of affairs in which language

under the dominance of the modern metaphysics of subjectivity almost irremediably falls out of its element. Language still denies us its essence: that it is the house of the truth of Being. Instead, language surrenders itself to our mere willing and trafficking as an instrument of domination over beings. Beings themselves appear as actualities in the interaction of cause and effect. We encounter beings as actualities in a calculative business-like way, but also scientifically and by way of philosophy, with explanations and proofs. Even the assurance that something is inexplicable belongs to these explanations and proofs. With such statements we believe that we confront the mystery. As if it were already decided that the truth of Being lets itself at all be established in causes and explanatory grounds or, what comes to the same, in their incomprehensibility.

But if man is to find his way once again into the nearness of Being he must first learn to exist in the nameless. In the same way he must recognize the seductions of the public realm as well as the impotence of the private. Before he speaks man must first let himself be claimed again by Being, taking the risk that under this claim he will seldom have much to say. Only thus will the preciousness of its essence be once more bestowed upon the word, and upon man a home for dwelling in the truth of Being.

But in the claim upon man, in the attempt to make man ready for this claim, is there not implied a concern about man? Where else does "care" tend but in the direction of bringing man back to his essence? What else does that in turn betoken but that man (*homo*) become human (*humanus*)? Thus *humanitas* really does remain the concern of such thinking. For this is humanism: meditating and caring, that man be human and not inhumane, "in-human," that is, outside his essence. But in what does the humanity of man consist? It lies in his essence.

But whence and how is the essence of man determined? Marx demands that "man's humanity" be recognized and acknowledged. He finds it in "society." "Social" man is for him "natural" man. In "society" the "nature" of man, that is, the totality of "natural needs" (food, clothing, reproduction, economic sufficiency) is equably secured. The Christian sees the humanity of man, the *humanitas* of *homo*, in contradistinction to *Deitas*. He is the man of the history of redemption who as a "child of God" hears and accepts the call of the

Father in Christ. Man is not of this world, since the "world," thought in terms of Platonic theory, is only a temporary passage to the beyond.

Humanitas, explicitly so called, was first considered and striven for in the age of the Roman Republic. *Homo humanus* was opposed to *homo barbarus*. *Homo humanus* here means the Romans, who exalted and honored Roman *virtus* through the "embodiment" of the *paideia* [education] taken over from the Greeks. These were the Greeks of the Hellenistic age, whose culture was acquired in the schools of philosophy. It was concerned with *eruditio et institutio in bonas artes* [scholarship and training in good conduct]. *Paideia* thus understood was translated as *humanitas*. The genuine *romanitas* of *homo romanus* consisted in such *humanitas*. We encounter the first humanism in Rome: it therefore remains in essence a specifically Roman phenomenon which emerges from the encounter of Roman civilization with the culture of late Greek civilization. The so-called Renaissance of the fourteenth and fifteenth centuries in Italy is a *renascentia romanitatis*. Because *romanitas* is what matters, it is concerned with *humanitas* and therefore with Greek *paideia*. But Greek civilization is always seen in its later form and this itself is seen from a Roman point of view. The *homo romanus* of the Renaissance also stands in opposition to *homo barbarus*. But now the in-humane is the supposed barbarism of gothic Scholasticism in the Middle Ages. Therefore a *studium humanitatis*, which in a certain way reaches back to the ancients and thus also becomes a revival of Greek civilization, always adheres to historically understood humanism. For Germans this is apparent in the humanism of the eighteenth century supported by Winckelmann, Goethe, and Schiller. On the other hand, Hölderlin does not belong to "humanism" precisely because he thought the destiny of man's essence in a more original way than "humanism" could.

But if one understands humanism in general as a concern that man become free for his humanity and find his worth in it, then humanism differs according to one's conception of the "freedom" and "nature" of man. So too are there various paths toward the realization of such conceptions. The humanism of Marx does not need to return to antiquity any more than the humanism which Sartre conceives existentialism to be. In this broad sense Christianity too is a humanism, in that according to its teaching everything depends on man's salvation (*salus aeterna*); the history of man

appears in the context of the history of redemption. However different these forms of humanism may be in purpose and in principle, in the mode and means of their respective realizations, and in the form of their teaching, they nonetheless all agree in this, that the *humanitas* of *homo humanus* is determined with regard to an already established interpretation of nature, history, world, and the ground of the world, that is, of beings as a whole. Every humanism is either grounded in a metaphysics or is itself made to be the ground of one. Every determination of the essence of man that already presupposes an interpretation of being without asking about the truth of Being, whether knowingly or not, is metaphysical. The result is that what is peculiar to all metaphysics, specifically with respect to the way the essence of man is determined, is that it is "humanistic." Accordingly, every humanism remains metaphysical. In defining the humanity of man humanism not only does not ask about the relation of Being to the essence of man; because of its metaphysical origin humanism even impedes the question by neither recognizing nor understanding it. On the contrary, the necessity and proper form of the question concerning the truth of Being, forgotten in and through metaphysics, can come to light only if the question "What is metaphysics?" is posed in the midst of metaphysics' domination. Indeed every inquiry into Being, even the one into the truth of Being, must at first introduce its inquiry as a "metaphysical" one.

The first humanism, Roman humanism, and every kind that has emerged from that time to the present, has presupposed the most universal "essence" of man to be obvious. Man is considered to be an *animal rationale*. This definition is not simply the Latin translation of the Greek *zōon logon echon* but rather a metaphysical interpretation of it. This essential definition of man is not false. But it is conditioned by metaphysics. The essential provenance of metaphysics, and not just its limits, became questionable in *Being and Time*. What is questionable is above all commended to thinking as what is to be thought, but not at all left to the gnawing doubts of an empty skepticism.

Metaphysics does indeed represent beings in their Being, and so it thinks the Being of beings. But it does not think the difference of both.[1] Metaphysics does not ask about the truth of Being itself. Nor does it therefore ask in what way the essence of man belongs to the truth of Being. Metaphysics has not only failed up to now to ask this question, the question is inaccessible to metaphysics as such. Being is still waiting for the time when it will become thought-provoking to man. With regard to the definition of man's essence, however one may determine the *ratio* of the *animal* and the reason of the living being, whether as a "faculty of principles," or a "faculty of categories," or in some other way, the essence of reason is always and in each case grounded in this: for every apprehending of beings in their Being, Being itself is already illumined and comes to pass in its truth. So too with *animal, zōon,* an interpretation of "life" is already posited which necessarily lies in an interpretation of beings as *zōē* and *physis,* within which what is living appears. Above and beyond everything else, however, it finally remains to ask whether the essence of man primordially and most decisively lies in the dimension of *animalitas* at all. Are we really on the right track toward the essence of man as long as we set him off as one living creature among others in contrast to plants, beasts, and God? We can proceed in that way; we can in such fashion locate man within being as one being among others. We will thereby always be able to state something correct about man. But we must be clear on this point, that when we do this we abandon man to the essential realm of *animalitas* even if we do not equate him with beasts but attribute a specific difference to him. In principle we are still thinking of *homo animalis*—even when *anima* [soul] is posited as *animus sive mens* [spirit or mind], and this in turn is later posited as subject, person, or spirit [*Geist*]. Such positing is the manner of metaphysics. But then the essence of man is too little heeded and not thought in its origin, the essential provenance that is always the essential future for historical mankind. Metaphysics thinks of man on the basis of *animalitas* and does not think in the direction of his *humanitas.*

Metaphysics closes itself to the simple essential fact that man essentially occurs only in his essence, where he is claimed by Being. Only from that claim "has" he found that wherein his essence dwells. Only from this dwelling "has" he "language"as the home that preserves the ecstatic for his essence.[2] Such standing in the lighting of Being I call the ek-sistence of man. This way of Being is proper only to man. Ek-sistence so understood is not only the ground of the possibility of reason, *ratio,* but is also that in which the essence of man preserves the source that determines him.

Ek-sistence can be said only of the essence of man, that is, only of the human way "to be." For as far as our experience shows, only man is admitted to the destiny of ek-sistence. Therefore ek-sistence can also never be thought of as a specific kind of living creature among others—granted that man is destined to think the essence of his Being and not merely to give accounts of the nature and history of his constitution and activities. Thus even what we attribute to man as *animalitas* on the basis of comparison with "beast" is itself grounded in the essence of ek-sistence. The human body is something essentially other than an animal organism. Nor is the error of biologism overcome by adjoining a soul to the human body, a mind to the soul, and the *existentiell* to the mind, and then louder than before singing the praises of the mind—only to let everything relapse into "life-experience," with a warning that thinking by its inflexible concepts disrupts the flow of life and that thought of Being distorts existence. The fact that physiology and physiological chemistry can scientifically investigate man as an organism is no proof that in this "organic" thing, that is, in the body scientifically explained, the essence of man consists. That has as little validity as the notion that the essence of nature has been discovered in atomic energy. It could even be that nature, in the face she turns toward man's technical mastery, is simply concealing her essence. Just as little as the essence of man consists in being an animal organism can this insufficient definition of man's essence be overcome or offset by outfitting man with an immortal soul, the power of reason, or the character of a person. In each instance essence is passed over, and passed over on the basis of the same metaphysical projection.

What man is—or, as it is called in the traditional language of metaphysics, the "essence" of man—lies in his ek-sistence. But ek-sistence thought in this way is not identical with the traditional concept of *existentia,* which means actuality in contrast to the meaning of *essentia* as possibility. In *Being and Time* (p. 42) this sentence is italicized: "The 'essence' of Dasein lies in its existence." However, here the opposition between *existentia* and *essentia* is not under consideration, because neither of these metaphysical determinations of Being, let alone their relationship, is yet in question. Still less does the sentence contain a universal statement about *Dasein,* since the word came into fashion in the eighteenth century as a name for "object," intending to express the metaphysical concept of the actuality of the actual. On the contrary, the sentence says: man occurs essentially in such a way that he is the "there" [*das "Da"*], that is, the lighting of Being. The "Being" of the *Da*, and only it, has the fundamental character of ek-sistence, that is, of an ecstatic inherence in the truth of Being. The ecstatic essence of man consists in ek-sistence, which is different from the metaphysically conceived *existentia*. Medieval philosophy conceives the latter as *actualitas*. Kant represents *existentia* as actuality in the sense of the objectivity of experience. Hegel defines *existentia* as the self-knowing Idea of absolute subjectivity. Nietzsche grasps *existentia* as the eternal recurrence of the same. Here it remains an open question whether through *existentia*—in these explanations of it as actuality, which at first seem quite different—the Being of a stone or even life as the Being of plants and animals is adequately thought. In any case living creatures are as they are without standing outside their Being as such and within the truth of Being, preserving in such standing the essential nature of their Being. Of all the beings that are, presumably the most difficult to think about are living creatures, because on the one hand they are in a certain way most closely related to us, and on the other are at the same time separated from our ek-sistent essence by an abyss. However, it might also seem as though the essence of divinity is closer to us than what is foreign in other living creatures, closer, namely, in an essential distance which however distant is nonetheless more familiar to our ek-sistent essence than is our appalling and scarcely conceivable bodily kinship with the beast. Such reflections cast a strange light upon the current and therefore always still premature designation of man as *animal rationale*. Because plants and animals are lodged in their respective environments but are never placed freely in the lighting of Being which alone is "world," they lack language. But in being denied language they are not thereby suspended worldlessly in their environment. Still, in this word "environment" converges all that is puzzling about living creatures. In its essence language is not the utterance of an organism; nor is it the expression of a living thing. Nor can it ever be thought in an essentially correct way in terms of its symbolic character, perhaps not even in terms of the character of signification. Language is the lighting-concealing advent of Being itself.

Ek-sistence, thought in terms of *ecstasis*, does not coincide with *existentia* in either form or content. In terms of content ek-sistence means standing out into the truth of Being. *Existentia (existence)* means in contrast *actualitas*, actuality as opposed to mere possibility as Idea. Ek-sistence identifies the determination of what man is in the destiny of truth. *Existentia* is the name for the realization of something that is as it appears in its Idea. The sentence "Man ek-sists" is not an answer to the question of whether man actually is or not; rather, it responds to the question concerning man's "essence." We are accustomed to posing this question with equal impropriety whether we ask what man is or who he is. For in the *Who?* or the *What?* we are already on the lookout for something like a person or an object. But the personal no less than the objective misses and misconstrues the essential unfolding of ek-sistence in the history of Being. That is why the sentence cited from *Being and Time* (p. 42) is careful to enclose the word "essence" in quotation marks. This indicates that "essence" is now being defined from neither *esse essentiae* nor *esse existentiae* but rather from the ek-static character of Dasein. As ek-sisting, man sustains Da-sein in that he takes the *Da*, the lighting of Being, into "care." But Da-sein itself occurs essentially as "thrown." It unfolds essentially in the throw of Being as the fateful sending.

But it would be the ultimate error if one wished to explain the sentence about man's ek-sistent essence as if it were the secularized transference to human beings of a thought that Christian theology expresses about God (*Deus est suum esse* [God is His Being]); for ek-sistence is not the realization of an essence, nor does ek-sistence itself even effect and posit what is essential. If we understand what *Being and Time* calls "projection" as a representational positing, we take it to be an achievement of subjectivity and do not think it in the only way the "understanding of Being" in the context of the "existential analysis" of "being-in-the-world" can be thought—namely as the ecstatic relation to the lighting of Being. . . .

By way of contrast, Sartre expresses the basic tenet of existentialism in this way: Existence precedes essence. In this statement he is taking *existentia* and *essentia* according to their metaphysical meaning, which from Plato's time on has said that *essentia* precedes *existentia*. Sartre reverses this statement. But the reversal of a metaphysical statement remains a metaphysical statement. With it he stays with metaphysics in oblivion of the truth of Being. For even if philosophy wishes to determine the relation of *essentia* and *existentia* in the sense it had in medieval controversies, in Leibniz's sense, or in some other way, it still remains to ask first of all from what destiny of Being this differentiation in Being as *esse essentiae* and *esse existentiae* comes to appear to thinking. We have yet to consider why the question about the destiny of Being was never asked and why it could never be thought. Or is the fact that this is how it is with the differentiation of *essentia* and *existentia* not at all a sign of forgetfulness of Being? We must presume that this destiny does not rest upon a mere failure of human thinking, let alone upon a lesser capacity of early Western thinking. Concealed in its essential provenance, the differentiation of *essentia* (essentiality) and *existentia* (actuality) completely dominates the destiny of Western history and of all history determined by Europe.

Sartre's key proposition about the priority of *existentia* over *essentia* does, however, justify using the name "existentialism" as an appropriate title for a philosophy of this sort. But the basic tenet of "existentialism" has nothing at all in common with the statement from *Being and Time*—apart from the fact that in *Being and Time* no statement about the relation of *essentia* and *existentia* can yet be expressed since there it is still a question of preparing something precursory. As is obvious from what we have just said, that happens clumsily enough. What still today remains to be said could perhaps become an impetus for guiding the essence of man to the point where it thoughtfully attends to that dimension of the truth of Being which thoroughly governs it. But even this could take place only to the honor of Being and for the benefit of Dasein which man eksistingly sustains; not, however, for the sake of man so that civilization and culture through man's doings might be vindicated. . . .

Man is rather "thrown" from Being itself into the truth of Being, so that ek-sisting in this fashion he might guard the truth of Being, in order that beings might appear in the light of Being as the beings they are. Man does not decide whether and how beings appear, whether and how God and the gods or history and nature come forward into the lighting of Being, come to presence and depart. The advent of beings lies in the destiny of Being. But for man it is ever a question of finding what is fitting in his essence which corresponds to such destiny; for in accord with this destiny man as ek-sisting has to guard the truth of Being. Man is

the shepherd of Being. It is in this direction alone that *Being and Time* is thinking when ecstatic existence is experienced as "care" (cf. section 44 C, pp. 226 ff.).

Yet Being—what is Being? It is It itself. The thinking that is to come must learn to experience that and to say it. "Being"—that is not God and not a cosmic ground. Being is farther than all beings and is yet nearer to man than every being, be it a rock, a beast, a work of art, a machine, be it an angel or God. Being is the nearest. Yet the near remains farthest from man. Man at first clings always and only to beings. But when thinking represents beings as beings it no doubt relates itself to Being. In truth, however, it always thinks only of beings as such; precisely not, and never, Being as such. The "question of Being" always remains a question about beings. It is still not at all what its elusive name indicates: the question in the direction of Being. Philosophy, even when it becomes "critical" through Descartes and Kant, always follows the course of metaphysical representation. It thinks from beings back to beings with a glance in passing toward Being. For every departure from beings and every return to them stands already in the light of Being.

But metaphysics recognizes the lighting of Being either solely as the view of what is present in "outward appearance" (*idea*) or critically as what is seen as a result of categorial representation on the part of subjectivity. This means that the truth of Being as the lighting itself remains concealed for metaphysics. However, this concealment is not a defect of metaphysics but a treasure withheld from it yet held before it, the treasure of its own proper wealth. But the lighting itself is Being. Within the destiny of Being in metaphysics the lighting first affords a view by which what is present comes into touch with man, who is present to it, so that man himself can in apprehending (*noein*) first touch upon Being (*thigein*, Aristotle, *Met.* IX, 10). This view first gathers the aspect to itself. It yields to such aspects when apprehending has become a setting-forth-before-itself in the *perceptio* of the *res cogitans* taken as the *subiectum* of *certitudo*.

But how—provided we really ought to ask such a question at all—how does Being relate to ek-sistence? Being itself is the relation to the extent that It, as the location of the truth of Being amid beings, gathers to itself and embraces ek-sistence in its existential, that is, ecstatic, essence. Because man as the one who ek-sists comes to stand in this relation that Being destines for itself, in that he ecstatically sustains it, that is, in care takes it upon himself, he at first fails to recognize the nearest and attaches himself to the next nearest. He even thinks that this is the nearest. But nearer than the nearest and at the same time for ordinary thinking farther than the farthest is nearness itself: the truth of Being. . . .

The *esti gar einai* ["for there is Being"] of Parmenides is still unthought today. That allows us to gauge how things stand with the progress of philosophy. When philosophy attends to its essence it does not make forward strides at all. It remains where it is in order constantly to think the Same. Progression, that is, progression forward from this place, is a mistake that follows thinking as the shadow which thinking itself casts. Because Being is still unthought, *Being and Time* too says of it, "there is/it gives." Yet one cannot speculate about this *il y a* precipitously and without a foothold. This "there is/it gives" rules as the destiny of Being. Its history comes to language in the words of essential thinkers. Therefore the thinking that thinks into the truth of Being is, as thinking, historical. There is not a "systematic" thinking and next to it an illustrative history of past opinions. Nor is there, as Hegel thought, only a systematics which can fashion the law of its thinking into the law of history and simultaneously subsume history into the system. Thought in a more primordial way, there is the history of Being to which thinking belongs as recollection of this history that unfolds of itself. Such recollective thought differs essentially from the subsequent presentation of history in the sense of an evanescent past. History does not take place primarily as a happening. And its happening is not evanescence. The happening of history occurs essentially as the destiny of the truth of Being and from it.[3] Being comes to destiny in that It, Being, gives itself. But thought in terms of such destiny this says: it gives itself and refuses itself simultaneously. Nonetheless, Hegel's definition of history as the development of "Spirit" is not untrue. Neither is it partly correct and partly false. It is as true as metaphysics, which through Hegel first brings to language its essence—thought in terms of the absolute—in the system. Absolute metaphysics, with its Marxian and Nietzschean inversions, belongs to the history of the truth of Being. Whatever stems from it cannot be countered or even cast aside by refutations. It can only be taken up in such a way that its truth is more primordially

sheltered in Being itself and removed from the domain of mere human opinion. All refutation in the field of essential thinking is foolish. Strife among thinkers is the "lovers' quarrel" concerning the matter itself. It assists them mutually toward a simple belonging to the Same, from which they find what is fitting for them in the destiny of Being. . . .

Homelessness ["the abandonment of Being by beings"] is coming to be the destiny of the world. Hence it is necessary to think that destiny in terms of the history of Being. What Marx recognized in an essential and significant sense, though derived from Hegel, as the estrangement of man has its roots in the homelessness of modern man. This homelessness is specifically evoked from the destiny of Being in the form of metaphysics and through metaphysics is simultaneously entrenched and covered up as such. Because Marx by experiencing estrangement attains an essential dimension of history, the Marxist view of history is superior to that of other historical accounts. But since neither Husserl nor—so far as I have seen till now—Sartre recognizes the essential importance of the historical in Being, neither phenomenology nor existentialism enters that dimension within which a productive dialogue with Marxism first becomes possible.

For such dialogue it is certainly also necessary to free oneself from naïve notions about materialism, as well as from the cheap refutations that are supposed to counter it. The essence of materialism does not consist in the assertion that everything is simply matter but rather in a metaphysical determination according to which every being appears as the material of labor. The modern metaphysical essence of labor is anticipated in Hegel's *Phenomenology of Spirit* as the self-establishing process of unconditioned production, which is the objectification of the actual through man experienced as subjectivity. The essence of materialism is concealed in the essence of technology, about which much has been written but little has been thought. Technology is in its essence a destiny within the history of Being and of the truth of Being, a truth that lies in oblivion. For technology does not go back to the *technē* of the Greeks in name only but derives historically and essentially from *technē* as a mode of *alētheuein*, a mode, that is, of rendering beings manifest [*Offenbarmachen*]. As a form of truth technology is grounded in the history of metaphysics, which is itself a distinctive and up to now the only perceptible phase of the history of Being. No matter which of the various positions one chooses to adopt toward the doctrines of communism and to their foundation, from the point of view of the history of Being it is certain that an elemental experience of what is world-historical speaks out in it. Whoever takes "communism" only as a "party" or a "Weltanschauung" is thinking too shallowly, just as those who by the term "Americanism" mean, and mean derogatorily, nothing more than a particular lifestyle. The danger into which Europe as it has hitherto existed is ever more clearly forced consists presumably in the fact above all that its thinking—once its glory—is falling behind in the essential course of a dawning world destiny which nevertheless in the basic traits of its essential provenance remains European by definition. No metaphysics, whether idealistic, materialistic, or Christian, can in accord with its essence, and surely not in its own attempts to explicate itself, "get a hold on" this destiny yet, and that means thoughtfully to reach and gather together what in the fullest sense of Being now is.

In the face of the essential homelessness of man, man's approaching destiny reveals itself to thought on the history of Being in this, that man find his way into the truth of Being and set out on this find. Every nationalism is metaphysically an anthropologism, and as such subjectivism. Nationalism is not overcome through mere internationalism; it is rather expanded and elevated thereby into a system. Nationalism is as little brought and raised to *humanitas* by internationalism as individualism is by an ahistorical collectivism. The latter is the subjectivity of man in totality. It completes subjectivity's unconditioned self-assertion, which refuses to yield. Nor can it be even adequately experienced by a thinking that mediates in a one-sided fashion. Expelled from the truth of Being, man everywhere circles round himself as the *animal rationale*.

But the essence of man consists in his being more than merely human, if this is represented as "being a rational creature." "More" must not be understood here additively as if the traditional definition of man were indeed to remain basic, only elaborated by means of an existentiell postscript. The "more" means: more originally and therefore more essentially in terms of his essence. But here something enigmatic manifests itself: man is in thrownness. This means that man, as the eksisting counter-throw [*Gegenwurf*] of Being, is more than *animal rationale* precisely to the extent

that he is less bound up with man conceived from subjectivity. Man is not the lord of beings. Man is the shepherd of Being. Man loses nothing in this "less'''; rather, he gains in that he attains the truth of Being. He gains the essential poverty of the shepherd, whose dignity consists in being called by Being itself into the preservation of Being's truth. The call comes as the throw from which the thrownness of Da-sein derives. In his essential unfolding within the history of Being, man is the being whose Being as ek-sistence consists in his dwelling in the nearness of Being. Man is the neighbor of Being. . . .

"Logic" understands thinking to be the representation of beings in their Being, which representation proposes to itself in the generality of the concept. But how is it with meditation on Being itself, that is, with the thinking that thinks the truth of Being? This thinking alone reaches the primordial essence of *logos* which was already obfuscated and lost in Plato and in Aristotle, the founder of "logic." To think against "logic" does not mean to break a lance for the illogical but simply to trace in thought the *logos* and its essence which appeared in the dawn of thinking, that is, to exert ourselves for the first time in preparing for such reflection. Of what value are even far-reaching systems of logic to us if, without really knowing what they are doing, they recoil before the task of simply inquiring into the essence of *logos*? If we wished to bandy about objections, which is of course fruitless, we could say with more right: irrationalism, as a denial of *ratio*, rules unnoticed and uncontested in the defense of "logic," which believes it can eschew meditation on *logos* and on the essence of *ratio* which has its ground in *logos*. . . .

But now in what relation does the thinking of Being stand to theoretical and practical behavior? It exceeds all contemplation because it cares for the light in which a seeing, as *theoria*, can first live and move. Thinking attends to the lighting of Being in that it puts its saying of Being into language as the home of eksistence. Thus thinking is a deed. But a deed that also surpasses all *praxis*. Thinking towers above action and production, not through the grandeur of its achievement and not as a consequence of its effect, but through the humbleness of its inconsequential accomplishment.

For thinking in its saying merely brings the unspoken word of Being to language.

The usage "bring to language" employed here is now to be taken quite literally. Being comes, lighting itself, to language. It is perpetually under way to language. Such arriving in its turn brings ek-sisting thought to language in a saying. Thus language itself is raised into the lighting of Being. Language *is* only in this mysterious and yet for us always pervasive way. To the extent that language which has thus been brought fully into its essence is historical, Being is entrusted to recollection. Ek-sistence thoughtfully dwells in the house of Being. In all this it is as if nothing at all happens through thoughtful saying.

But just now an example of the inconspicuous deed of thinking manifested itself. For to the extent that we expressly think the usage "bring to language," which was granted to language, think only that and nothing further, to the extent that we retain this thought in the heedfulness of saying as what in the future continually has to be thought, we have brought something of the essential unfolding of Being itself to language.

What is strange in the thinking of Being is its simplicity. Precisely this keeps us from it. For we look for thinking—which has its world-historical prestige under the name "philosophy"—in the form of the unusual, which is accessible only to initiates. At the same time we conceive of thinking on the model of scientific knowledge and its research projects. We measure deeds by the impressive and successful achievements of *praxis*. But the deed of thinking is neither theoretical nor practical, nor is it the conjunction of these two forms of behavior.

Through its simple essence the thinking of Being makes itself unrecognizable to us. But if we become acquainted with the unusual character of the simple, then another plight immediately befalls us. The suspicion arises that such thinking of Being falls prey to arbitrariness; for it cannot cling to beings. Whence does thinking take its measure? What law governs its deed?

Here the third question of your letter must be entertained: *Comment sauver l'élément d'aventure que comporte toute recherche sans faire de la philosophie une simple aventuriére?* [How can we preserve the element of adventure that all research contains without simply turning philosophy into an adventuress?] I shall mention poetry now only in passing. It is confronted by the same question, and in the same manner, as thinking. But Aristotle's words in the *Poetics*, although they have scarcely been pondered, are still valid—that poetic composition is truer than exploration of beings.

But thinking is an *aventure* not only as a search and an inquiry into the unthought. Thinking, in its essence as thinking of Being, is claimed by Being. Thinking is related to Being as what arrives (*l'avenant*[4]). Thinking as such is bound to the advent of Being, to Being as advent. Being has already been dispatched to thinking. Being *is* as the destiny of thinking. But destiny is in itself historical. Its history has already come to language in the saying of thinkers.

To bring to language ever and again this advent of Being which remains, and in its remaining waits for man, is the sole matter of thinking. For this reason essential thinkers always say the Same. But that does not mean the identical. Of course they say it only to him who undertakes to think back on them. Whenever thinking, in historical recollection, attends to the destiny of Being, it has already bound itself to what is fitting for it, in accord with its destiny. To flee into the identical is not dangerous. To risk discord in order to say the Same is the danger. Ambiguity threatens, and mere quarreling.

The fittingness of the saying of Being, as of the destiny of truth, is the first law of thinking—not the rules of logic which can become rules only on the basis of the law of Being. To attend to the fittingness of thoughtful saying does not only imply, however, that we contemplate at every turn *what* is to be said of Being and *how* it is to be said. It is equally essential to ponder *whether* what is to be thought is to be said—to what extent, at what moment of the history of Being, in what sort of dialogue with this history, and on the basis of what claim, it ought to be said. The threefold thing mentioned in an earlier letter is determined in its cohesion by the law of the fittingness of thought on the history of Being: rigor of meditation, carefulness in saying, frugality with words.

It is time to break the habit of overestimating philosophy and of thereby asking too much of it. What is needed in the present world crisis is less philosophy, but more attentiveness in thinking; less literature, but more cultivation of the letter.

The thinking that is to come is no longer philosophy, because it thinks more originally than metaphysics—a name identical to philosophy. However, the thinking that is to come can no longer, as Hegel demanded, set aside the name "love of wisdom" and become wisdom itself in the form of absolute knowledge. Thinking is on the descent to the poverty of its provisional essence. Thinking gathers language into simple saying. In this way language is the language of Being, as clouds are the clouds of the sky. With its saying, thinking lays inconspicuous furrows in language. They are still more inconspicuous than the furrows that the farmer, slow of step, draws through the field.

Endnotes

[1] Cf. Martin Heidegger, *Vom Wesen des Grundes* (1929), p. 8; *Kant and the Problem of Metaphysics*, trans. J. Churchill (Bloomington, Ind.: Indiana University Press, 1962), p. 243; and *Being and Time*, section 44, p. 230.

[2] In *Being and Time* "ecstatic" (from the Greek *ekstasis*) means the way Dasein "stands out" in the various moments of the temporality of care, being "thrown" out of a past and "projecting" itself toward a future by way of the present. The word is closely related to another Heidegger introduces now to capture the unique sense of man's Being—*ek-sistence*. This too means the way man "stands out" into the truth of Being and so is exceptional among beings that are on hand only as things of nature or human production. Cf. Heidegger's definition of "existence" in *Being and Time*, p. 54, above. [D. F. Krell's note.]

[3] See the lecture on Hölderlin's hymn, "Wie wenn am Feiertage. . ." in Martin Heidegger, *Erläuterungen zu Hölderlins Dichtung*, fourth, expanded ed. (Frankfurt am Main: V. Klostermann, 1971), p. 76.

[4] *L'avenant* (cf. the English *advenient*) is most often used as an adverbial phrase, *à l'avenant*, to be in accord, conformity, or relation to something. It is related to *l'aventure*, the arrival of some unforeseen challenge, and *l'avenir*, the future, literally, what is to come. Thinking is in relation to Being insofar as Being advenes or arrives. Being as arrival or presence is the "adventure" toward which Heidegger's thought is on the way. [Krell's note.]

51. *Philosophy and the Scientific Image of Man*

WILFRID SELLARS

Modern science has stimulated contemporary philosophy in many ways. Are scientific theories successful because they truly describe reality (scientific realism) or are they just useful tools for predicting observable phenomena (instrumentalism)? If scientific theories purport to describe reality, then what should one conclude when they seem to conflict with traditional beliefs that have become deeply embedded in our ordinary view of reality? This problem has been a recurrent theme in Parts I–IV. In "Philosophy and the Scientific Image of Man," Wilfrid Sellars diagnoses the general problem. He claims ordinary views of reality have their roots in what he calls the "manifest image"—a network of beliefs that originally centered on the concept of a person. The "scientific image," in contrast, consists of a description of reality "derived from the fruits of postulational theory construction." Sellars interprets a variety of historically important philosophical positions in terms of different ways the scientific image might be thought to be related to the manifest image.

Providing an account of persons becomes the chief obstacle to the completeness and superiority of the scientific image. Regarding persons, Sellars offers a functionalist account of thinking, and he suggests that science will evolve to accommodate sensory qualities. He denies that normative descriptions of persons can be reduced to scientific descriptions, but claims it will be possible to enrich the scientific image with normative language without jeopardizing the scientific image's claim to be a complete description of reality. Sellars (1912–1989) taught philosophy at the University of Pittsburgh.

The Philosophical Quest

The aim of philosophy, abstractly formulated, is to understand how things in the broadest possible sense of the term hang together in the broadest possible sense of the term. Under 'things in the broadest possible sense' I include such radically different items as not only 'cabbages and kings', but numbers and duties, possibilities and finger

This work originally appeared as "Philosophy and the Scientific Image of Man" by Wilfrid Sellars, in *Frontiers of Science and Philosophy*, Robert G. Colodny, editor. Published in 1962 by the University of Pittsburgh Press. Used by permission of the publisher.

snaps, aesthetic experience and death. To achieve success in philosophy would be, to use a contemporary turn of phrase, to 'know one's way around' with respect to all these things, not in that unreflective way in which the centipede of the story knew its way around before it faced the question, 'how do I walk?' but in that reflective way which means that no intellectual holds are barred.

Knowing one's way around is, to use a current distinction, a form of 'knowing *how*' as contrasted with 'knowing *that*'. There is all the difference in the world between knowing *how* to ride a bicycle and knowing *that* a steady pressure by the legs of a balanced person on the pedals would result in forward motion. Again, to use an example somewhat closer to our subject, there is all the difference in the world between knowing *that* each step of a given proof in mathematics follows from the preceding steps, and knowing *how* to find a proof. Sometimes being able to find a proof is a matter of being able to follow a set procedure; more often it is not. It can be argued that anything which can be properly called 'knowing how to do something' presupposes a body of knowledge *that*; or, to put it differently, knowledge of truth or facts. If this were so, then the statement that 'ducks know *how* to swim' would be as metaphorical as the statement that they know *that* water supports them. However this may be, knowing how to do something at the level of characteristically human activity presupposes a great deal of knowledge *that*, and it is obvious that the reflective knowing one's way around in the scheme of things, which is the aim of philosophy, presupposes a great deal of reflective knowledge of truths.

Now the subject-matter of this knowledge of truths which is presupposed by philosophical 'know-how', falls, in a sense, completely within the scope of the special disciplines. Philosophy in an important sense has no special subject-matter which stands to it as other subject-matters stand to other special disciplines. If philosophers did have such a special subject-matter, they could turn it over to a new group of specialists as they have turned other special subject-matters to nonphilosophers over the past 2500 years, first with mathematics, more recently psychology and sociology, and, currently, certain aspects of theoretical linguistics. What is characteristic of philosophy is not a special subject-matter, but the aim of knowing one's way around with respect to the subject-matters of all the special disciplines.

Now the special disciplines know their way around in their subject-matters, and each learns to do so in the process of discovering truths about its own subject-matter. But each special discipline must also have a sense of how its bailiwick fits into the countryside as a whole. This sense in many cases amounts to a little more than the unreflective 'knowing one's way around' which is a common possession of us all. Again, the specialist must have a sense of how not only his subject-matter, but also the methods and principles of his thinking about it fit into the intellectual landscape. Thus, the historian reflects not only on historical events themselves, but on what it is to think historically. It is part of his business to reflect on his own thinking—its aim, its criteria, its pitfalls. In dealing with historical questions, he must face and answer questions which are not, themselves, in a primary

sense historical questions. But he deals with these questions as they arise in the attempt to answer specifically historical questions.

Reflection on any special discipline can soon lead one to the conclusion that the *ideal* practitioner of that discipline would see his special subject-matter and his thinking about it in the light of a reflective insight into the intellectual landscape as a whole. There is much truth in the Platonic conception that the special disciplines are perfected by philosophy, but the companion conception that the philosopher must know his way around in each discipline as does the specialist, has been an ever more elusive ideal since the scientific revolution began. Yet if the philosopher cannot hope to know his way around in each discipline as does the specialist, there is a sense in which he can know his way around with respect to the subject-matter of that discipline, and must do so if he is to approximate to the philosophic aim.

The multiplication of sciences and disciplines is a familiar feature of the intellectual scene. Scarcely less familiar is the unification of this manifold which is taking place by the building of scientific bridges between them. I shall have something to say about this unification later in this chapter. What is not so obvious to the layman is that the task of 'seeing all things together' has itself been (paradoxically) broken down into specialities. And there *is* a place for specialization in philosophy. For just as one cannot come to know one's way around in the highway system as a whole without knowing one's way around in the parts, so one can't hope to know one's way around in 'things in general,' without knowing one's way around in the major groupings of things.

It is therefore, the 'eye on the whole' which distinguishes the philosophical enterprise. Otherwise, there is little to distinguish the philosopher from the persistently reflective specialist; the philosopher of history from the persistently reflective historian. To the extent that a specialist is more concerned to reflect on how his work as a specialist joins up with other intellectual pursuits, than in asking and answering questions within his speciality, he is said, properly, to be philosophically minded. And, indeed, one can 'have one's eye on the whole' without staring at it all the time. The latter would be a fruitless enterprise. Furthermore, like other specialists, the philosopher who specializes may derive much of his sense of the whole from the pre-reflective orientation which is our common heritage. On the other hand, a philosopher could scarcely be said to have his eye on the whole in the relevant sense, unless he has reflected on the nature of philosophical thinking. It is this reflection on the place of philosophy itself, in the scheme of things which is the distinctive trait of the philosopher as contrasted with the reflective specialist; and in the absence of this critical reflection on the philosophical enterprise, one is at best but a potential philosopher.

It has often been said in recent years that the aim of the philosopher is not to discover new truths, but to 'analyse' what we already know. But while the term 'analysis' was helpful in its implication that philosophy as such makes no *substantive* contribution to what we know, and is concerned in some way to improve the *manner* in which we know it, it is most misleading by its contrast to 'synthesis'. For by virtue of this contrast these statements suggest that philosophy is ever more myopic, tracing parts within parts, losing each in turn from sight as new parts come into view. One is tempted, therefore, to contrast the analytic conception of philosophy as myopia with the synoptic vision of true philosophy. And it must be admitted that if the contrast between 'analysis' and 'synthesis' were the operative connotation in the metaphor, then a purely analytic philosophy would be a contradiction in terms. Even if we construe 'analysis' on the analogy of making ever smaller scale maps of the same overall terrain, which does more justice to the synoptic element, the analogy disturbs because we would have to compare philosophy to the making of small-scale maps from an original large-scale map; and a smaller scale map in this sense is a triviality.

Even if the analogy is changed to that of bringing a picture into focus, which preserves the synoptic element and the theme of working within the framework of what is already known while adding a dimension of gain, the analogy is disturbing in two respects. (*a*) It suggests that the special disciplines are confused; as though the scientist had to wait for the philosopher to clarify his subject-matter, bring it into focus. To account for the creative role of philosophy, it is not necessary to say that the scientist doesn't know his way around in his own area. What we must rather say is that the specialist knows his way around in his own neighbourhood, as his neighbourhood, but doesn't know his way around in it in the same way *as a part of the landscape as a whole.*

(*b*) It implies that the essential change brought about by philosophy is the standing out of detail within a picture which is grasped as a whole from the start. But, of course, to the extent that there is *one* picture to be grasped reflectively as a whole, the unity of the reflective vision is a task rather than an initial datum. The search for this unity at the reflective level is therefore more appropriately compared to the contemplation of a large and complex painting which is not seen as a unity without a prior exploration of its parts. The analogy, however, is not complete until we take into account a *second* way in which unity is lacking in the original datum of the contemporary philosopher. For he is confronted not by one picture, but, *in principle*, by *two* and, in fact, by *many*. The plurality I have in mind is not that which concerns the distinction between the fact finding, the ethical, the aesthetic, the logical, the religious, and other aspects of experience, for these are but aspects of one complex picture which is to be grasped reflectively as a whole. As such, it constitutes one term of a crucial duality which confronts the contemporary philosopher at the very beginning of his enterprise. Here the most appropriate analogy is stereoscopic vision, where two differing perspectives on a landscape are fused into one coherent experience.

For the philosopher is confronted not by one complex many-dimensional picture, the unity of which, such as it is, he must come to appreciate; but by *two* pictures of essentially the same order of complexity, each of which purports to be a complete picture of man-in-the-world, and which, after separate scrutiny, he must fuse into one vision. Let me refer to these two perspectives, respectively, as the *manifest* and the *scientific* images of man-in-the-world. And let me explain my terms. First, by calling them images I do not mean to deny to either or both of them the status of 'reality.' I am, to use Husserl's term, 'bracketing' them, transforming them from ways of experiencing the world into objects of philosophical reflection and evaluation. The term 'image' is usefully ambiguous. On the one hand it suggests the contrast between an object, e.g., a tree, and a projection of the object on a plane, or its shadow on a wall. In this sense, an image is as much an existent as the object imaged, though, of course, it has a dependent status.

In the other sense, an 'image' is something imagined, and that which is imagined may well not exist, although the imagining of it does—in which case we can speak of the image as *merely* imaginary or unreal. But the imagined *can* exist; as when one imagines that someone is dancing in the next room, and someone is. This ambiguity enables me to imply that the philosopher is confronted by two projections of man-in-the-world on the human understanding. One of these projections I will call the manifest image, the other the scientific image. These images exist and are as much a part and parcel of the world as this platform or the Constitution of the United States. But in addition to being confronted by these images as existents, he is confronted by them as images in the sense of 'things imagined'—or, as I had better say at once, *conceived*; for I am using 'image' in this sense as a metaphor for conception, and it is a familiar fact that not everything that can be conceived can, in the ordinary sense, be imagined. The philosopher, then, is confronted by two conceptions, equally public, equally non-arbitrary, of man-in-the-world and he cannot shirk the attempt to see how they fall together in one stereoscopic view.

Before I begin to explain the contrast between 'manifest' and 'scientific' as I shall use these terms, let me make it clear that they are both 'idealizations' in something like the sense in which a frictionless body or an ideal gas is an idealization. They are designed to illuminate the inner dynamics of the development of philosophical ideas, as scientific idealizations illuminate the development of physical systems. From a somewhat different point of view they can be compared to the 'ideal types' of Max Weber's sociology. The story is complicated by the fact that each image has a history, and while the main outlines of what I shall call the manifest image took shape in the mists of prehistory, the scientific image, promissory notes apart, has taken shape before our very eyes.

The Manifest Image

The 'manifest' image of man-in-the-world can be characterized in two ways, which are supplementary rather than alternative. It is, first, the framework in terms of which man came to be aware of himself as man-in-the-world. It is the framework in terms of which, to use an existentialist turn of phrase, man first encountered himself—which is, of course, when he came to be man. For it is no merely incidental feature of man that he has a conception of himself as man-in-the-world, just as it is obvious, on reflection, that 'if man had a radically different conception of himself he would be a radically different kind of man'.

I have given this quasi-historical dimension of our construct pride of place, because I want to highlight from the very beginning what might be called the paradox of man's encounter with himself, the paradox consisting of the fact that man couldn't be man until he encountered himself. It is this paradox which supports the last stand of Special Creation. Its central theme is the idea that anything which can properly be called conceptual thinking can occur only within a framework of conceptual thinking in terms of which it can be criticized, supported, refuted, in short, evaluated. To be able to think is to be able to measure one's thoughts by standards of correctness, of relevance, of evidence. In this sense a diversified conceptual framework is a whole which, however sketchy, is prior to its parts, and cannot be construed as a coming together of parts which are already conceptual in character. The conclusion is difficult to avoid that the transition from pre-conceptual patterns of behaviour to conceptual thinking was a holistic one, a jump to a level of awareness which is irreducibly new, a jump which was the coming into being of man.

There is a profound truth in this conception of a radical difference in level between man and his precursors. The attempt to understand this difference turns out to be part and parcel of the attempt to encompass in one view the two images of man-in-the-world which I have set out to describe. For, as we shall see, this difference in level appears as an irreducible discontinuity in the *manifest* image, but as, in a sense requiring careful analysis, a reducible difference in the *scientific* image.

I have characterized the manifest image of man-in-the-world as the framework in terms of which man encountered himself. And this, I believe, is a useful way of characterizing it. But it is also misleading, for it suggests that the contrast I am drawing between the manifest and the scientific images, is that between a pre-scientific, uncritical, naïve conception of man-in-the-world, and a reflected, disciplined, critical—in short a scientific—conception. This is not at all what I have in mind. For what I mean by the manifest image is a refinement or sophistication of what might be called the 'original' image; a refinement to a degree which makes it relevant to the contemporary intellectual scene. This refinement or sophistication can be construed under two headings; (*a*) empirical; (*b*) categorial.

By empirical refinement, I mean the sort of refinement which operates within the broad framework of the image and which, by approaching the world in terms of something like the canons of inductive inference defined by John Stuart Mill, supplemented by canons of statistical inference, adds to and subtracts from the contents of the world as experienced in terms of this framework and from the correlations which are believed to obtain between them. Thus, the conceptual framework which I am calling the manifest image is, in an appropriate sense, itself a scientific image. It is not only disciplined and critical; it also makes use of those aspects of scientific method which might be lumped together under the heading 'correlational induction'. There is, however, one type of scientific reasoning which it, by stipulation, does *not* include, namely that which involves the postulation of imperceptible entities, and principles pertaining to them, to explain the behaviour of perceptible things.

This makes it clear that the concept of the manifest image of man-in-the-world is not that of an historical and bygone stage in the development of man's conception of the world and his place in it. For it is a familiar fact that correlational and postulational methods have gone hand in hand in the evolution of science, and, indeed, have been dialectically related; postulational hypotheses presupposing correlations to be explained, and suggesting possible correlations to be investigated. The notion of a purely correlational scientific view of things is both an historical and a methodological fiction. It involves abstracting correlational fruits from the conditions of their discovery, and the theories in terms of which they are explained. Yet it is a useful fiction (and hence no *mere* fiction), for it will enable us to define a way of looking at the world which, though disciplined and, in a limited sense, scientific, contrasts sharply with an image of man-in-the-world which is implicit in and can be constructed from the postulational aspects of contemporary scientific theory. And, indeed, what I have referred to as the 'scientific' image of man-in-the-world and contrasted with the 'manifest' image, might better be called the 'postulational' or 'theoretical' image. But, I believe, it will not be too misleading if I continue, for the most part, to use the former term.

Now the manifest image is important for our purpose, because it defines one of the poles to which philosophical reflection has been drawn. It is not only the great speculative systems of ancient and medieval philosophy which are built around the manifest image, but also many systems and quasi-systems in recent and contemporary thought, some of which seem at first sight to have little if anything in common with the great classical systems. That I include the major schools of contemporary Continental thought might be expected. That I lump in with these the trends of contemporary British and American philosophy which emphasize the analysis of 'common sense' and 'ordinary usage', may be somewhat more surprising. Yet this kinship is becoming increasingly apparent in recent years and I believe that the distinctions that I am drawing in this chapter will make possible an understanding and interpretation of this kinship. For all these philosophies can, I believe, be fruitfully construed as more or less adequate accounts of the manifest image of man-in-the-world, which accounts are then taken to be an adequate and full description in general terms of what man and the world really are.

Let me elaborate on this theme by introducing another construct which I shall call—borrowing a term with a not unrelated meaning—the perennial philosophy of man-in-the-world. This construct, which is the 'ideal type' around which philosophies in what might be called, in a suitably broad sense, the Platonic tradition cluster, is simply the manifest image endorsed as real, and its outline taken to be the large-scale map of reality to which science brings a needle-point of detail and an elaborate technique of map-reading.

It will probably have occurred to you by now that there are negative over-tones to both constructs: the 'manifest image' and the 'perennial philosophy'. And, in a certain sense, this is indeed the case. I *am* implying that the perennial philosophy is analogous to what one gets when one looks through a stereoscope with one eye dominating. The manifest image dominates and mislocates the scientific image. But if the perennial philosophy of man-in-the-world is in this sense distorted, an important consequence lurks in the offing. For I have also implied that man is *essentially* that being which conceives of itself *in terms of the image which the perennial philosophy refines and endorses*. I seem, therefore, to be saying that man's conception of himself in the world does not easily accommodate the scientific image; that there is a genuine tension between them; that man is not the sort of thing he conceives himself to be; that his existence is in some measure built around error. If this were what I wished to say, I would be in distinguished company. One thinks, for example, of Spinoza, who contrasted man as he falsely conceives himself to be with man as he discovers himself to be in the scientific enterprise. It might well be said that Spinoza drew a distinction between a 'manifest' and a 'scientific' image of man, rejecting the former as false and accepting the latter as true.

But if in Spinoza's account, the scientific image, as he interprets it, dominates the stereoscopic view (the manifest image appearing as a tracery of explainable error), the very fact that I use the analogy of stereoscopic vision implies that as I see it the manifest image is not overwhelmed in the synthesis.

But before there can be any point to these comparisons, I must characterize these images in more detail, adding flesh and blood to the bare bones I have laid before you. I shall devote the remainder of this section and the following section to developing the manifest image. In the concluding sections I shall characterize the scientific image, and attempt to describe certain key features of how the two images blend together in a true stereoscopic view.

I distinguished above between two dimensions of the refinement which turned the 'original' image into the 'manifest' image: the empirical and the categorial. Nothing has been said so far about the latter. Yet it is here that the most important things are to be said. It is in this connection that I will be able to describe the general structure of the manifest image.

A fundamental question with respect to any conceptual framework is 'of what sort are the basic objects of the framework?' This question involves, on the one hand, the contrast between an object and what can be true of it in the way of properties, relations, and activities; and, on the other, a contrast between the basic objects of the framework and the various kinds of groups they can compose. The basic objects of a framework need not be things in the restricted sense of perceptible physical objects. Thus, the basic objects of current theoretical physics are notoriously imperceptible and unimaginable. Their basic-ness consists in the fact that they are not properties or groupings of anything more basic (at least until further notice). The

questions, 'are the basic objects of the framework of physical theory *thing-like*? and if so, to what extent?' are meaningful ones.

Now to ask, 'what are the basic objects of a (given) framework?' is to ask not for a *list*, but a *classification*. And the classification will be more or less 'abstract' depending on what the purpose of the inquiry is. The philosopher is interested in a classification which is abstract enough to provide a synoptic view of the contents of the framework but which falls short of simply referring to them as objects or entities. Thus we are approaching an answer to the question, 'what are the basic objects of the manifest image?' when we say that it includes persons, animals, lower forms of life and 'merely material' things, like rivers and stones. The list is not intended to be complete, although it is intended to echo the lower stages of the 'great chain of being' of the Platonic tradition.

The first point I wish to make is that there is an important sense in which the primary objects of the manifest image are *persons*. And to understand how this is so, is to understand central and, indeed, crucial themes in the history of philosophy. Perhaps the best way to make the point is to refer back to the construct which we called the 'original' image of man-in-the-world, and characterize it as a framework in which *all* the 'objects' are persons. From this point of view, the refinement of the 'original' image into the manifest image, is the gradual 'de-personalization' of objects other than persons. That something like this has occurred with the advance of civilization is a familiar fact. Even persons, it is said (mistakenly, I believe), are being 'depersonalized' by the advance of the scientific point of view.

The point I now wish to make is that although this gradual depersonalization of the original image is a familiar idea, it is radically misunderstood, if it is assimilated to the gradual abandonment of a superstitious belief. A primitive man did not *believe* that the tree in front of him was a person, in the sense that he thought of it both as a tree *and* as a person, as I might think that this brick in front of me is a doorstop. If this were so, then when he abandoned the idea that trees were persons, his concept of a tree could remain unchanged, although his beliefs about trees would be changed. The truth is, rather, that *originally* to be a tree was *a way of being a person*, as, to use a close analogy, to be a woman is a way of being a person, or to be a triangle is a way of being a plane figure. That a woman is a person is not something that one can be said to *believe*; though there's enough historical bounce to this example to make it worth-while to use the different example that one cannot be said to believe that a triangle is a plane figure. When primitive man ceased to think of what we called trees as persons, the change was more radical than a change in belief; it was a change in category.

Now, the human mind is not limited in its categories to what it has been able to refine out of the world view of primitive man, any more than the limits of what we can conceive are set by what we can imagine. The categories of theoretical physics are not essences distilled from the framework of perceptual experience, yet, if the human mind can conceive of *new* categories, it can also refine the old; and it is just as important not to over-estimate the role of creativity in the development of the framework in terms of which you and I experience the world, as it is not to under-estimate its role in the scientific enterprise.

I indicated above that in the construct which I have called the 'original' image of man-in-the-world, all 'objects' are persons, and all kinds of objects ways of being persons. This means that the sort of things that are said of objects in this framework are the sort of things that are said of persons. And let me make it clear that by 'persons', I do not mean 'spirit' or 'mind'. The idea that a man is a team of two things, a mind *and* a body, is one for which many reasons of different kinds and weights have been given in the course of human intellectual development. But it is obvious, on reflection, that whatever philosophers have made of the idea of a *mind*, the pre-philosophical conception of a 'spirit', where it is found, is that of a ghostly *person*, something analogous to flesh and blood persons which 'inhabits' them, or is otherwise intimately connected with them. It is, therefore, a development *within the framework of persons*, and it would be incorrect to construe the manifest image in such a way that persons are composite objects. On the other hand, if it is to do its work, the manifest framework must be such as to make meaningful the assertion that what we ordinarily call persons are composites of a person proper and a body—and, by doing so, make meaningful the contrary view that although men have many different types of ability, ranging from those he has in common with the lowest of things, to his ability to engage in scientific and philosophical reflection, he nevertheless is one object and not a team. For we shall see

that the essential dualism in the manifest image is not that between mind and body as substances, but between two radically different ways in which the human individual is related to the world. Yet it must be admitted that most of the philosophical theories which are dominated by the manifest image are dualist in the substantive sense. There are many factors which account for this, most of which fall outside the scope of this essay. Of the factors which concern us, one is a matter of the influence of the developing scientific image of man, and will be discussed in the following section. The other arises in the attempt to make sense of the manifest image in its own terms.

Now to understand the manifest image as a refinement or depersonalization of the 'original' image, we must remind ourselves of the range of activities which are characteristic of persons. For when I say that the objects of the manifest image are primarily persons, I am implying that what the objects of this framework primarily *are* and *do*, is what persons are and do. Thus persons are 'impetuous' or 'set in their ways'. They apply old policies or adopt new ones. They do things from habit or ponder alternatives. They are immature or have an established character. For my present purposes, the most important contrasts are those between actions which are expressions of character and actions which are *not* expressions of character, on the one hand, and between habitual actions and deliberate actions, on the other. The first point that I want to make is that only a being capable of deliberation can properly be said to act, either impulsively or from habit. For in the full and non-metaphorical sense an action is the sort of thing that can be done deliberately. We speak of actions as *becoming* habitual, and this is no accident. It is important to realize that the use of the term 'habit' in speaking of an earthworm as acquiring the habit of turning to the right in a T-maze, is a metaphorical extension of the term. There is nothing dangerous in the metaphor until the mistake is made of assuming that the habits of persons are the same sort of thing as the (metaphorical) 'habits' of earthworms and white rats.

Again, when we say that something a person did was an expression of his character, we mean that it is 'in character'—that it was to be expected. We do not mean that it was a matter of *habit*. To be *habitual* is to be 'in character', but the converse is not true. To say of an action that it is 'in character', that it was to be expected, is to say that it was predictable—*not*, however, predictable 'no holds barred,' but predictable with respect to evidence pertaining to what the person in question has done in the past, and the circumstances as he saw them in which he did it. Thus, a person cannot, *logically* cannot, *begin* by acting 'in character', any more than he can *begin* by acting from habit.

It is particularly important to see that while to be 'in character' is to be predictable, the converse is not true. It does not follow from the fact that a piece of human behaviour is predictable, that it is an expression of character. Thus the behaviour of a burnt child with respect to the fire is predictable, but not an expression of character. If we use the phrase, 'the nature of a person', to sum up the predictabilities *no holds barred* pertaining to that person, then we must be careful not to equate the *nature* of a person with his *character*, although his character will be a 'part' of his nature in the broad sense. Thus, if everything a person did were predictable (in principle), given sufficient knowledge about the person and the circumstances in which he was placed, and was, therefore, an 'expression of his nature,' it would not follow that everything the person did was an expression of his *character*. Obviously, to say of a person that everything that he does is an expression of his character is to say that his life is simply a carrying out of formed habits and policies. Such a person is a type only approximated to in real life. Not even a mature person always acts in character. And as we have seen, it cannot possibly be true that he has always acted in character. Yet, if determinism is true, everything he has done has been an expression of his 'nature'.

I am now in a position to explain what I mean when I say that the primary objects of the manifest image are persons. I mean that it is the modification of an image in which *all* the objects are capable of *the full range* of personal activity, the modification consisting of a gradual pruning of the implications of saying with respect to what *we* would call an inanimate object, that it *did* something. Thus, in the original image to say of the wind that it blew down one's house would imply that the wind *either* decided to do so with an end in view, and might, perhaps, have been persuaded not to do it, *or* that it acted thoughtlessly (either from habit or impulse), or, perhaps, inadvertently, in which case other appropriate action on one's part might have awakened it to the enormity of what it was about to do.

In the early stages of the development of the manifest image, the wind was no longer conceived as acting deliberately, with an end in view; but rather from habit or impulse. Nature became the locus of 'truncated persons'; that which things could be expected to do, its habits; that which exhibits no order, its impulses. Inanimate things no longer 'did' things in the sense in which persons do them—not, however, because a *new* category of impersonal things and impersonal processes has been achieved, but because the category of *person* is now applied to these things in a pruned or truncated form. It is a striking exaggeration to say of a person, that he is a 'mere creature of habit and impulse', but in the early stages of the development of manifest image, the world includes truncated persons which *are* mere creatures of habit, acting out routines, broken by impulses, in a life which never rises above what ours is like in our most unreflective moments. Finally, the sense in which the wind 'did' things was pruned, save for poetic and expressive purposes—and, one is tempted to add, for philosophical purposes—of implications pertaining to 'knowing what one is doing' and 'knowing what the circumstances are'.

Just as it is important not to confuse between the 'character' and the 'nature' of a person, that is to say, between an action's being predictable with respect to evidence pertaining to prior action, and its being predictable no holds barred, so it is important not to confuse between an action's being *predictable* and its being *caused*. These terms are often treated as synonyms, but only confusion can arise from doing so. Thus, in the 'original' image, one person causes another person to do something he otherwise would not have done. But most of the things people do are not things they are *caused* to do, even if what they do is highly predictable. For example: when a person has well-established habits, what he does in certain circumstances is highly predictable, but it is not for that reason *caused*. Thus the category of causation (as contrasted with the more inclusive category of predictability) betrays its origin in the 'original' image. When all things were persons it was certainly not a framework conception that everything a person did was caused; nor, of course, was it a framework principle that everything a person did was predictable. To the extent that relationships between the truncated 'persons' of the manifest framework were analogous to the causal relationships between persons, the category itself continued to be used, although pruned of its implications with respect to plans, purposes, and policies. The most obvious analogue at the inanimate level of causation in the original sense is one billiard ball causing another to change its course, but it is important to note that no one who distinguishes between causation and predictability would ask, 'what *caused* the billiard ball on a smooth table to continue in a straight line?' The distinctive trait of the scientific revolution was the conviction that all events are predictable from relevant information about the context in which they occur, not that they are all, in any ordinary sense, caused.

Classical Philosophy and the Manifest Image

I have characterized the concept of the manifest image as one of the poles towards which philosophical thinking is drawn. This commits me, of course, to the idea that the manifest image is not a mere external standard, by relation to which one interested in the development of philosophy classifies philosophical positions, but has in its own way an objective existence in philosophical thinking itself, and, indeed, in human thought generally. And it can influence philosophical thinking only by having an existence which transcends in some way the individual thought of individual thinkers. I shall be picking up this theme shortly, and shall ask how an image of the world, which, after all, is a way of thinking, *can* transcend the individual thinker which it influences. (The general lines of the answer must be obvious, but it has implications which have not always been drawn.) The point I wish to make now is that since this image has a being which transcends the individual thinker, *there is truth and error with respect to it, even though the image itself might have to be rejected, in the last analysis, as false.*

Thus, whether or not the world as we encounter it in perception and self-awareness is ultimately real, it is surely incorrect, for example, to say as some philosophers have said that the physical objects of the encountered world are 'complexes of sensations' or, equally, to say that apples are not *really* coloured, or that mental states are 'behavioural dispositions', or that one cannot intend to do something without knowing that one intends to do

it, or that to say that something is good is to say that one likes it, etc. For there is a correct and an incorrect way to describe this objective image which we have of the world in which we live, and it is possible to evaluate the correctness or incorrectness of such a description. I have already claimed that much of academic philosophy can be interpreted as an attempt by individual thinkers to delineate the manifest image (not recognized, needless to say, as such) an image which is both immanent in and transcendent of their thinking. In this respect, a philosophy can be evaluated as perceptive or imperceptive, mistaken or correct, even though one is prepared to say that the image they delineate is but one way in which reality appears to the human mind. And it is, indeed, a task of the first importance to delineate this image, particularly in so far as it concerns man himself, for, as was pointed out before, man is what he is because he thinks of himself in terms of this image, and the latter must be understood before it is proper to ask, 'to what extent does manifest man survive in the synoptic view which does equal justice to the scientific image which now confronts us?'

I think it correct to say that the so-called 'analytic' tradition in recent British and American philosophy, particularly under the influence of the later Wittgenstein, has done increasing justice to the manifest image, and has increasingly succeeded in isolating it in something like its pure form, and has made clear the folly of attempting to replace it *piecemeal* by fragments of the scientific image. By doing so, it is made apparent, and has come to realize, its continuity with the perennial tradition.

Now one of the most interesting features of the perennial philosophy is its attempt to understand the status in the individual thinker of the framework of ideas in terms of which he grasps himself as a person in the world. How do individuals come to be able to think in terms of this complex conceptual framework? How do they come to have this image? Two things are to be noticed here: (1) The manifest image does not present conceptual thinking as a complex of items which, considered in themselves and apart from these relations, are not conceptual in character. (The most plausible candidates are images, but all attempts to construe thoughts as complex patterns of images have failed, and, as we know, were bound to fail.) (2) Whatever the ultimate constituents of conceptual thinking, the process itself as it occurs in the individual mind must echo, more or less adequately, the intelligible structure of the world.

There was, of course, a strong temptation not only to think of the constituents of thinking as qualitatively similar to the constituents of the world, but also to think of the world as causing constituents to occur in patterns which echo the patterns of events. The attempt, by precursors of scientific psychology, to understand the genesis of conceptual thinking in the individual in terms of an 'association' of elemental processes which were not themselves conceptual, by a direct action of the physical environment on the individual—the paradigm case being the burnt child fearing the fire— was a premature attempt to construct a scientific image of man.

The perennial tradition had no sympathy with such attempts. It recognized (*a*) that association of *thoughts* is not association of images, and, as presupposing a framework of conceptual thinking, cannot account for it; (*b*) that the direct action of perceptible nature, *as perceptible*, on the *individual* can account for associative connection, *but not the rational connections of conceptual thinking*.

Yet somehow the world *is* the cause of the individual's image of the world, and, as is well-known, for centuries the dominant conception of the perennial tradition was that of a direct causal influence of the world as intelligible on the individual mind. This theme, initiated by Plato, can be traced through Western thought to the present day. In the Platonic tradition this mode of causation is attributed to a being which is analogous, to a greater or lesser degree, to a person. Even the Aristotelian distinguishes between the way in which sensations make available the intelligible structure of things to man, and the way in which contingencies of perceptual experience establish expectations and permit a non-rational accommodation of animals to their environment. And there is, as we know today, a sound core to the idea that while reality is the 'cause' of the human conceptual thinking which represents it, this causal role cannot be equated with a conditioning of the individual by his environment in a way which could in principle occur without the mediation of the family and the community. The Robinson Crusoe conception of the world as generating conceptual thinking directly in the individual is too simple a model. The perennial tradition long limited itself to accounting for the presence in the individual of the framework of conceptual thinking in terms of a unique kind of

action of reality as intelligible on the individual mind. The accounts differed in interesting respects, but the main burden remained the same. It was not until the time of Hegel that the essential role of the group as a mediating factor in this causation was recognized, and while it is easy for us to see that the immanence and transcendence of conceptual frameworks with respect to the individual thinker is a social phenomenon, and to find a recognition of this fact implicit in the very form of our image of man in the world, it was not until the nineteenth century that this feature of the manifest image was, however inadequately, taken into account.

The Platonic theory of conceptual abilities as the result of the 'illumination' of the mind by intelligible essences limited the role of the group and, in particular, the family to that of calling these abilities into play—a role which could, in principle, be performed by perceptual experience—and to that of teaching the means of giving verbal expression to these abilities. Yet the essentially social character of conceptual thinking comes clearly to mind when we recognize that there is no thinking apart from common standards of correctness and relevance, which relate what *I do* think to what *anyone ought to* think. The contrast between '*I*' and 'anyone' is essential to rational thought.

It is current practice to compare the inter-subjective standards without which there would be no thinking, to the inter-subjective standards without which there would be no such a thing as a game; and the acquisition of a conceptual framework to learning to play a game. It is worth noting, however, that conceptual thinking is a unique game in two respects: (*a*) one cannot learn to play it by being told the rules; (*b*) whatever else conceptual thinking makes possible—and without it there is nothing characteristically human—it does so by virtue of containing a way of representing the world.

When I said that the individual as a conceptual thinker is essentially a member of a group, this does not mean of course, that the individual cannot exist apart from the group, for example as sole survivor of an atomic catastrophe, any more than the fact that chess is a game played by two people means that one can't play chess with oneself. A group isn't a group in the relevant sense unless it consists of a number of individuals each of which thinks of himself as '*I*' in contrast to 'others'. Thus a group exists in the way in which members of the group represent themselves. Conceptual thinking is not by accident that which is *communicated* to others, any more than the decision to move a chess piece is by accident that which finds an expression in a move on a board between two people.

The manifest image must, therefore, be construed as containing a conception of itself as a group phenomenon, the group mediating between the individual and the intelligible order. But any attempt to *explain* this mediation within the framework of the manifest image was bound to fail, for the manifest image contains the resources for such an attempt only in the sense that it provides the foundation on which scientific theory can build an explanatory framework; and while conceptual structures of this framework are *built on* the manifest image, they are not definable within it. Thus, the Hegelian, like the Platonist of whom he is the heir, was limited to the attempt to understand the relation between intelligible order and individual minds in analogical terms.

It is in the *scientific* image of man in the world that we begin to see the main outlines of the way in which man came to have an image of himself-in-the-world. For we begin to see this as a matter of evolutionary development, as a group phenomenon, a process which is illustrated at a simpler level by the evolutionary development which explains the correspondence between the dancing of a worker bee and the location, relative to the sun, of the flower from which he comes. This correspondence, like the relation between man's 'original' image and the world, is incapable of explanation in terms of a direct conditioning impact of the environment on the individual as such.

I have called attention to the fact that the manifest image involves two types of causal impact of the world on the individual. It is, I have pointed out, this duality of causation and the related irreducibility, within the manifest image of conceptual thinking in all its forms to more elementary processes, which is the primary and essential dualism of the perennial philosophy. The dualistic conception of mind and body characteristic of, but by no means an invariable feature of, *philosophia perennis*, is in part an inference from this dualism of causation and of process. In part, however, as we shall see, it is a result of the impact of certain themes present in even the smallest stages of the developing scientific image.

My primary concern in this essay is with the question, 'in what sense, and to what extent, does the manifest image of man-in-the-world survive the attempt to unite this image in one field of intellectual vision with man as conceived in terms of the postulated objects of scientific theory? The bite to this question lies, we have seen, in the fact that man is that being which conceives of itself in terms of the manifest image. To the extent that the manifest does not survive in the synoptic view, to that extent man himself would not survive. Whether the adoption of the synoptic view would transform man in bondage into man free, as Spinoza believed, or man free into man in bondage, as many fear, is a question that does not properly arise until the claims of the scientific image have been examined.

The Scientific Image

I devoted my attention in the previous sections to defining what I called the 'manifest' image of man-in-the-world. I argued that this image is to be construed as a sophistication and refinement of the image in terms of which man first came to be aware of himself as man-in-the-world; in short, came to be man. I pointed out that in any sense in which this image, in so far as it pertains to man, is a 'false' image, this falsity threatens man himself, inasmuch as he is, in an important sense, the being which has this image of himself. I argued that what has been called the perennial tradition in philosophy—*philosophia perennis*—can be construed as the attempt to understand the structure of this image, to know one's way around in it reflectively with no intellectual holds barred. I analysed some of the main features of the image and showed how the categories in terms of which it approaches the world can be construed as progressive prunings of categories pertaining to the person and his relation to other persons and the group. I argued that the perennial tradition must be construed to include not only the Platonic tradition in its broadest sense, but philosophies of 'common sense' and 'ordinary usage'. I argued what is common to all these philosophies is an acceptance of the manifest image as the *real*. They attempt to understand the achievements of theoretical science in terms of this framework, subordinating the categories of theoretical science to its categories. I suggested that the most fruitful way of approaching the problem of integrating theoretical science with the framework of sophisticated common sense into one comprehensive synoptic vision is to view it not as a piecemeal task—e.g., first a fitting together of the common sense conception of physical objects with that of theoretical physics, and then, as a separate venture, a fitting together of the common sense conception of man with that of theoretical psychology—but rather as a matter of articulating two whole ways of seeing the sum of things, two images of man-in-the-world and attempting to bring them together in a 'stereoscopic' view.

My present purpose is to add to the account I have given of the manifest image, a comparable sketch of what I have called the scientific image, and to conclude this essay with some comments on the respective contributions of these two to the unified vision of man-in-the-world which is the aim of philosophy.

The scientific image of man-in-the-world is, of course, as much an idealization as the manifest image—even more so, as it is still in the process of coming to be. It will be remembered that the contrast I have in mind is not that between an *unscientific* conception of man-in-the-world and a *scientific* one, but between that conception which limits itself to what correlational techniques can tell us about perceptible and introspectible events and that which postulates imperceptible objects and events for the purpose of explaining correlations among perceptibles. It was granted, of course, that in point of historical fact many of the latter correlations were suggested by theories introduced to explain previously established correlations, so that there has been a dialectical interplay between correlational and postulational procedures. (Thus we might not have noticed that litmus paper turns red in acid, until this hypothesis had been suggested by a complex theory relating the absorption and emission of electromagnetic radiation by objects to their chemical composition; yet in principle this familiar correlation could have been, and, indeed, was, discovered before any such theory was developed.) Our contrast then, is between two ideal constructs: (*a*) the correlational and categorial refinement of the 'original image', which refinement I am calling the manifest image; (*b*) the image derived from the fruits of postulational theory construction which I am calling the scientific image.

It may be objected at this point that there is no such thing as *the* image of man built from postulated entities and processes, but rather as many images as there are sciences which touch on aspects of human behaviour. And, of course, in a sense this is true. There *are* as many scientific images of man as there are sciences which have something to say about man. Thus, there is man as he appears to the theoretical physicist—a swirl of physical particles, forces, and fields. There is man as he appears to the biochemist, to the physiologist, to the behaviourist, to the social scientist; and all of these images are to be contrasted with man as he appears to himself in sophisticated common sense, the manifest image which even today contains most of what he knows about himself at the properly human level. Thus the conception of *the* scientific or postulational image is an idealization in the sense that it is a conception of an integration of a manifold of images, each of which is the application to man of a framework of concepts which have a certain autonomy. For each scientific theory is, from the standpoint of methodology, a structure which is built at a different 'place' and by different procedures within the intersubjectively accessible world of perceptible things. Thus 'the' scientific image is a construct from a number of images, each of which is *supported by* the manifest world.

The fact that each theoretical image is a construction on a foundation provided by the manifest image, and *in this methodological sense* presupposes the manifest image, makes it tempting to suppose that the manifest image is prior in a *substantive* sense; that the categories of a theoretical science are logically dependent on categories pertaining to its methodological foundation in the manifest world of sophisticated common sense in such a way that there would be an absurdity in the notion of a world which illustrated its theoretical principles *without also illustrating the categories and principles of the manifest world*. Yet, when we turn our attention to 'the' scientific image which emerges from the several images proper to the several sciences, we note that although the image is *methodologically* dependent on the world of sophisticated common sense, and in this sense does not stand on its own feet, yet it purports to be a *complete* image, i.e., to define a framework which could be the *whole truth* about that which belongs to the image. Thus although methodologically a development *within* the manifest image, the scientific image presents itself as a *rival* image. From its point of view the manifest image on which it rests is an 'inadequate' but pragmatically useful likeness of a reality which at first finds its adequate (in principle) likeness in the scientific image. I say, 'in principle', because the scientific image is still in the process of coming into being—a point to which I shall return at the conclusion of this chapter.

To all of which, of course, the manifest image or, more accurately, the perennial philosophy which endorses its claims, replies that the scientific image cannot replace the manifest without rejecting its own foundation.

But before attempting to throw some light on the conflicting claims of these two world perspectives, more must be said about the constitution of *the* scientific image from the several scientific images of which it is the supposed integration. There is relatively little difficulty about telescoping *some* of the 'partial' images into one image. Thus, with due precaution, we can unify the biochemical and the physical images; for to do this requires only an appreciation of the sense in which the objects of biochemical discourse can be equated with complex patterns of the objects of theoretical physics. To make this equation, of course, is not to equate the sciences, for as sciences they have different procedures and connect their theoretical entities via different instruments to intersubjectively accessible features of the manifest world. But diversity of this kind is compatible with intrinsic 'identity' of the theoretical entities themselves, that is, with saying that biochemical compounds are 'identical' with patterns of sub-atomic particles. For to make this 'identification' is simply to say that the *two* theoretical structures, each with its own connection to the perceptible world, could be replaced by *one* theoretical framework connected *at two levels of complexity* via different instruments and procedures to the world as perceived.

I distinguished above between the unification of the postulated *entities* of two sciences and the unification of the *sciences*. It is also necessary to distinguish between the unification of the theoretical *entities* of two sciences and the unification of the theoretical *principles* of the two sciences. For while to say that biochemical substances are complexes of physical particles is in an important sense to imply that the laws obeyed by biochemical substances are 'special cases' of the laws obeyed by physical particles, there is a real danger that the sense in which this is so may be misunderstood. Obviously a specific pattern of physical particles cannot obey different laws in biochemistry than it does in physics. It may, however, be the case that the behaviour of very complex patterns of physical particles is related in no simple way to the behaviour of less complex patterns. Thus it may well be the case that the only way in which the laws pertaining to those complex systems of particles which are biochemical compounds could be *discovered* might be through the techniques and procedures of biochemistry, i.e., techniques and procedures appropriate to dealing with biochemical substances.

There is, consequently, an ambiguity in the statement: The laws of biochemistry are 'special cases' of the laws of physics. It may mean: (*a*) biochemistry needs no variables which cannot be defined in terms of the variables of atomic physics; (*b*) the laws relating to certain complex patterns of sub-atomic particles, the counterparts of biochemical compounds, are related in a simple way to laws pertaining to less complex patterns. The former, of course, is the only proposition to which one is committed by the identification of the theoretical objects of the two sciences in the sense described above.

Similar considerations apply, *mutatis mutandis*, to the physiological and biochemical images of man. To weld them into one image would be to show that physiological (particularly neurophysiological) entities can be equated with complex biochemical systems, and, therefore, that in the weaker sense, at least, the theoretical principles which pertain to the former can be interpreted as 'special cases' of principles pertaining to the latter.

More interesting problems arise when we consider the putative place of man as conceived in behaviouristics in 'the' scientific image. In the first place, the term 'behaviouristic psychology' has more than one meaning, and it is important for our purpose to see that in at least one sense of the term, its place is not in the scientific image (in the sense in which I am using the term) but rather in the continuing correlational sophistication of the manifest image. A psychology is behaviouristic in the broad sense, if, although it permits itself the use of the full range of psychological concepts belonging to the manifest framework, it always confirms hypotheses about psychological events in terms of behavioural criteria. It has no anxieties about the concepts of sensation, image, feeling, conscious or unconscious thought, all of which belong to the manifest framework; but requires that the occurrence of a feeling of pain, for example, be asserted only on behavioural grounds. Behaviourism, thus construed, is simply good sense. It is not necessary to redefine the language of mental events in terms of behavioural criteria in order for it to be true that observable behaviour provides evidence for mental events. And, of course, even in the common sense world, even in the manifest image, perceptible behaviour is the only *intersubjective* evidence for mental events.

Clearly 'behaviourism' in this sense does not preclude us from paying attention to what people say about themselves. For *using autobiographical statements as evidence for* what a person is thinking and feeling is different from simply *agreeing with* these statements. It is part of the force of autobiographical statements in ordinary discourse—not unrelated to the way in which children learn to make them—that, other things being equal, if a person says, 'I am in state ψ', it is reasonable to believe that he is in state ψ; the probability ranging from almost certainty in the case of, 'I have a toothache', to considerably less than certainty in the case of, 'I don't hate my brother'. The discounting of verbal and non-verbal behaviour as evidence is not limited to professional psychologists.

Thus, behaviourism in the first sense is simply a sophistication within the manifest framework which relies on pre-existent evidential connections between publicly observable verbal and non-verbal behaviour on the one hand and mental states and processes on the other, and should, therefore, be considered as belonging to the manifest rather than the scientific image as I have defined in these terms. Behaviourism in a second sense not only restricts its evidential base to publicly observable behaviour, but conceives of its task as that of finding correlations between constructs which it introduces and defines in terms of publicly accessible features of the organism and its environment. The interesting question in this connection is: 'Is there reason to think that a framework of correlation between constructs of this type could constitute a scientific understanding of human behaviour?' The answer to this question depends in part on how it is interpreted, and it is important to see why this is so.

Consider first the case of animal behaviour. Obviously, we know that animals are complex physiological systems and, from the standpoint of a finer-grained approach, biochemical systems. Does this mean that a science of animal behaviour has to be formulated in neurophysiological or biochemical terms? In one sense the answer is 'ob-

viously not'. We bring to our study of animal behaviour a background knowledge of some of the relevant large-scale variables for describing and predicting the behaviour of animals in relation to their environments. The fact that these large-scale variables (the sort of thing that are grouped under such headings as 'stimulus', 'response', 'goal behaviour', 'deprivation', etc.) are such that we can understand the behaviour of the animal in terms of them is something which is not only suggested by our background knowledge, but is, indeed, *explained* by evolutionary theory. But the correlations themselves can be discovered by statistical procedures; and, of course, it is important to establish these correlations. Their discovery and confirmation by the procedures of behaviouristics must, of course, be distinguished from their *explanation* in terms of the postulated entities and processes of neurophysiology. And, indeed, while physiological considerations may *suggest* correlations be tested, the correlations themselves must be establishable independently of physiological consideration, if, and this is a 'definitional' point, they are to belong to a distinguishable science of behaviour.

Thus if we mean by 'earthworm behaviouristics' the establishing of correlations in large-scale terms pertaining to the earthworm and its environment, there may not be much to it, for a correlation does not belong to 'earthworm behaviouristics' unless it is a correlation in these large-scale terms. On the other hand, it is obvious that not every scientific truth about earthworms is a part of earthworm behaviouristics, unless the latter term is so stretched as to be deprived of its distinctive sense. It follows that one cannot explain everything an earthworm does in terms of earthworm behaviouristics *thus defined*. Earthworm behaviouristics works within a background knowledge of 'standard conditions'—conditions in which correlations in terms of earthworm behaviour categories *are* sufficient to explain and predict what earthworms do in so far as it can be described in these categories. This background knowledge is obviously an essential part of the scientific understanding of what earthworms do, though not a part of earthworm behaviouristics, for it is simply the application to earthworms of physics, chemistry, parasitology, medicine, and neurophysiology.

We must also take into consideration the fact that most of the interesting constructs of correlational behaviouristics will be 'iffy' properties of organisms, properties to the effect that *if* at that time a certain stimulus *were* to occur, a certain response *would be* made. Thus, to use an example from another field, we are able to correlate the fact that a current has been run through a helix in which a piece of iron has been placed, with the 'iffy' property of being such that if an iron filing *were* placed near it, the latter *would be* attracted.

Now it may or may not be helpful at a given stage of scientific development, to suppose that 'iffy' properties of organisms are connected with states of a postulated system of entities operating according to certain postulated principles. It is helpful, if the postulated entities are sufficiently specific and can be connected to a sufficient diversity of large-scale behavioural variables to enable the prediction of new correlations. The methodological utility of postulational procedures for the behaviouristics of lower organisms has, perhaps, been exaggerated, primarily because until recently little was known in neurophysiology which was suited to throw much light on correlations at the large-scale level of behaviouristics. In human behaviouristics, however, the situation has been somewhat different from the start, for an important feature of characteristically human behaviour is that any two successive pieces of observable behaviour *essentially* involve complex, very complex, 'iffy' facts about what the person *would have said or done* at each intervening moment *if he had been asked certain questions*; and it happens that our background knowledge makes reasonable the supposition that these 'iffy' facts obtain *because an inner process is going on which is, in important respects, analogous to overt verbal behaviour, and each stage of which would find a natural expression in overt speech.*

Thus it *does* prove helpful in human behaviouristics to postulate an inner sequence of events in order to interpret what could *in principle* be austerely formulated as correlations between behavioural states and properties, including the *very* important and, indeed, *essential* 'iffy' ones. But, and this is an important point, the postulated episodes are not postulated on neurophysiological grounds—at least this was not true until very recently, but because of our background knowledge that something analogous to speech goes on while people are sitting 'like bumps on a log'.

For our present purposes it does not make too much difference whether we say that human behaviouristics *as such* postulates inner speechlike processes, or that whatever their contribution to

explanation or discovery, these processes fall by definition outside behaviouristics proper. Whether or not human behaviouristics, as a distinctive science, includes any statements about postulated entities, the correlations it establishes must find their counterparts in the postulational image, as was seen to be true in the case of the correlations established by earthworm behaviouristics. Thus, the scientific explanation of human behaviour must take account of those cases where the correlations characteristic of the organism in 'normal' circumstances break down. And, indeed, no behaviourist would deny that the correlations he seeks and establishes are in some sense the counterparts of neurophysiological and, consequently, biochemical connections, nor that the latter are special cases within a spectrum of *biochemical* connections (pertaining to human organisms), many of which are reflected in observable phenomenon which, *from the standpoint of behaviouristics*, represent breakdowns in explanation. I shall, therefore, provisionally assume that although behaviouristics and neurophysiology remain distinctive sciences, the correlational content of behaviouristics points to a structure of postulated processes and principles which telescope together with those of neurophysiological theory, with all the consequences which this entails. On this assumption, if we trace out these consequences, the scientific image of man turns out to be that of a complex physical system.

The Clash of the Images

How, then, are we to evaluate the conflicting claims of the manifest image and the scientific image thus provisionally interpreted to constitute *the* true and, in principle, *complete* account of man-in-the-world?

What are the alternatives? It will be helpful to examine the impact of the earlier stages of postulational science on philosophy. Some reflections on the Cartesian attempt at a synthesis are in order, for they bring out the major stresses and strains involved in any attempt at a synoptic view. Obviously, at the time of Descartes theoretical science had not yet reached the neurophysiological level, save in the fashion of a clumsy promissory note. The initial challenge of the scientific image was directed at the manifest image of inanimate nature. It proposed to construe physical things, in a manner already adumbrated by Greek atomism, as systems of imperceptible particles, lacking the perceptible qualities of manifest nature. Three lines of thought seemed to be open: (1) Manifest objects are identical with systems of imperceptible particles in that simple sense in which a forest is identical with a number of trees. (2) Manifest objects are what really exist; systems of imperceptible particles being 'abstract' or 'symbolic' ways of representing them. (3) Manifest objects are 'appearances' to human minds of a reality which is constituted by systems of imperceptible particles. Although (2) merits serious consideration, and has been defended by able philosophers, it is (1) and (3), particularly the latter, which I shall be primarily concerned to explore.

First, some brief remarks about (1). There is nothing immediately paradoxical about the view that an object can be both a perceptible object with perceptible qualities *and* a system of imperceptible objects, none of which has perceptible qualities. Cannot systems have properties which their parts do not have? Now the answer to this question is 'yes', if it is taken in a sense of which a paradigm example would be the fact that a system of pieces of wood can be a ladder, although none of its parts is a ladder. Here one might say that for the system as a whole to be a ladder is for its parts to be of such and such shapes and sizes and to be related to one another in certain ways. Thus there is no trouble about systems having properties which its parts do not have *if these properties are a matter of the parts having such and such qualities and being related in such and such ways.* But the case of a pink ice cube, it would seem clear, cannot be treated in this way. It does not seem plausible to say that for a system of particles to be a pink ice cube is for them to have such and such imperceptible qualities, and to be so related to one another as to make up an approximate cube. *Pink* does not seem to be made up of imperceptible qualities in the way in which being a ladder is made up of being cylindrical (the rungs), rectangular (the frame), wooden, etc. The manifest ice cube presents itself to us as something which is pink through and through, as a pink continuum, all the regions of which, however small, are pink. It presents itself to us as *ultimately homogeneous;* and an ice cube variegated in colour is, though not homogeneous in its specific colour, 'ultimately homogeneous', in the sense to which I am calling attention, with respect to the generic trait of being coloured.

Now reflection on this example suggests a principle which can be formulated approximately as follows:

> If an object is *in a strict sense* a system of objects, then every property of the object must consist in the fact that its constituents have such and such qualities and stand in such and such relations or, roughly, every property of a system of objects consists of properties of, and relations between, its constituents.

With something like this principle in mind, it was argued that if a physical object is *in a strict sense* a system of imperceptible particles, then it cannot as a whole have the perceptible qualities characteristic of physical objects in the manifest image. It was concluded that manifest physical objects are 'appearances' *to human perceivers* of systems of imperceptible particles which is alternative (3) above.

This alternative, (3), however, is open to an objection which is ordinarily directed not against the alternative itself, but against an imperceptive formulation of it as the thesis that the perceptible things around us 'really have no colour'. Against *this* formulation the objection has the merit of calling attention to the fact that in the manifest framework it is as absurd to say that a visible object has no colour, as it is to say of a triangle that it has no shape. However, against the above formulation of alternative (3), namely, that *the very objects themselves* are appearances to perceivers of systems of imperceptible particles, the objection turns out on examination to have no weight. The objection for which the British 'common sense' philosopher G. E. Moore is directly or indirectly responsible, runs:

> Chairs, tables, etc., as we ordinarily think them to be, can't be 'appearances' of systems of particles lacking perceptible qualities, because we *know* that there are chairs, tables, etc., and it is a framework feature of chairs, tables, etc., that they have perceptible qualities.

It simply *disappears* once it is recognized that, properly understood, the claim that physical objects do not really have perceptible qualities is not analogous to the claim that something generally believed to be true about a certain kind of thing is actually false. It is not the denial of a belief *within a framework,* but a challenge to the framework. It is the claim that although the framework of perceptible objects, the manifest framework of everyday life, is adequate for the everyday purposes of life, it is ultimately inadequate and should not be accepted as an account of what there is *all things considered*. Once we see this, we see that the argument from 'knowledge' cuts no ice, for the reasoning:

> We know that there are chairs, pink ice cubes, etc. (physical objects). Chairs, pink ice cubes are coloured, are perceptible objects with perceptible qualities.
> Therefore, perceptible physical objects with perceptible qualities exist

operates *within* the framework of the manifest image and cannot *support* it. It fails to provide a point of view outside the manifest image from which the latter can be evaluated.

A more sophisticated argument would be to the effect that we successfully find our way around in life by using the conceptual framework of coloured physical objects in space and time, therefore, this framework represents things as they really are. This argument has force, but is vulnerable to the reply that the success of living, thinking, and acting in terms of the manifest framework can be accounted for by the framework which proposes to replace it, by showing that there are sufficient structural similarities between manifest objects and their scientific counterparts to account for this success.[1]

One is reminded of a standard move designed to defend the reality of the manifest image against *logically* rather than *scientifically* motivated considerations. Thus it has been objected that the framework of physical objects in space and time is incoherent, involving antinomies or contradictions, and that therefore this framework is unreal. The counter to this objection has often been, not a painstaking refutation of the arguments claiming to show that the framework is incoherent, but rather something along the following lines:

> *We know* that this collision occurred at a different place and time than that collision.
>
> Therefore, the statement that the first collision occurred at a different place and time from the other collision *is true*.
>
> Therefore, the statement that the two collisions occurred at different times and places *is consistent*.

> Therefore, statements about events happening at various times and places are, as such, consistent.

This argument, like the one we have already considered, does not prove what it sets out to prove, because it operates within the framework to be evaluated, and does not provide an external point of view from which to defend it. It makes the tacit assumption that if a framework is inconsistent, its incoherence must be such as to lead to retail and immediate inconsistencies, as though it would force people using it to contradict themselves on every occasion. This is surely false. The framework of space and time could be internally inconsistent, and yet be a successful conceptual tool at the retail level. We have examples of this in mathematical theory, where inconsistencies can be present which do not reveal themselves in routine usage.

I am not, however, concerned to argue that the manifest image is unreal because ultimately incoherent in a narrowly conceived logical sense. Philosophers who have taken this line have either (a) left it at that (Hume; scepticism), or (b) attempted to locate the source of the inconsistency in features of the framework, and interpreted reality as an inadequately known structure *analogous* to the manifest image, but lacking just those features which are responsible for the inconsistency. In contrast to this, the critique of the manifest image in which we are engaged is based on logical considerations in a broader and more constructive sense, one which compares this image unfavourably with a *more* intelligible account of what there is.

It is familiar fact that those features of the manifest world which play no role in mechanical explanation were relegated by Descartes and other interpreters of the new physics to the minds of the perceiver. Colour, for example, was said to exist only in sensation; its *esse* to be *percipi*. It was argued, in effect, that what scientifically motivated reflection recognizes to be states of the perceiver are conceptualized in ordinary experience as traits of independent physical things, indeed that these supposed independent coloured things are actually conceptual constructions which ape the mechanical systems of the real world.

The same considerations which led philosophers to deny the reality of perceptible things led them to a dualistic theory of man. For if the human body is a system of particles, the body cannot be the subject of thinking and feeling, *unless thinking and feeling are capable of interpretation as complex interactions of physical particles*; unless, that is to say, the manifest framework of man as *one* being, a *person* capable of doing radically different kinds of things can be replaced without loss of descriptive and explanatory power by a postulational image in which he is a complex of physical particles, and all his activities a matter of the particles changing in state and relationship.

Dualism, of course, denied that either sensation or feeling or conceptual thinking could in this sense be construed as complex interactions of physical particles, or man as a complex physical system. They were prepared to say that a *chair* is really a system of imperceptible particles which 'appears' in the manifest framework as a 'coloured solid' (cf., our example of the ice cube), but they were not prepared to say that man himself was a complex physical system which 'appears' to itself to be the sort of thing man is in the manifest image.

Let us consider in more detail the Cartesian attempt to integrate the manifest and the scientific images. Here the interesting thing to note is that Descartes took for granted (in a promissory-note-ish kind of way) that the scientific image would include items which would be the counterparts of the sensations, images, and feelings of the manifest framework. These counterparts would be complex states of the brain which, obeying purely physical laws, would resemble and differ from one another in a way which corresponded to the resemblances and differences between the conscious states with which they were correlated. Yet, as is well-known, he denied that there were brain states which were, in the same sense, the cerebral counterparts of conceptual thinking.

Now, if we were to ask Descartes, 'Why can't we say that sensations "really are" complex cerebral processes as, according to you, we *can* say that physical objects "really are" complex systems of imperceptible particles?' he would have a number of things to reply, some of which were a consequence of his conviction that sensation, images, and feelings belong to the same family as believing, choosing, wondering, in short are low-grade examples of conceptual thinking and share its supposed irreducibility to cerebral states. But when the chips are down there would remain the following argument:

We have pulled perceptible qualities out of the physical environment and put them into sensations. If we now say that all there really is to sensation is a complex interaction of cerebral particles, then we have taken them out of our world picture altogether. We will have made it unintelligible how things could even *appear* to be coloured.

As for conceptual thinking, Descartes not only refused to identify it with neurophysiological process, he did not see this as a live option, because it seemed obvious to him that no complex neurophysiological process could be sufficiently analogous to conceptual thinking to be a serious candidate for being what conceptual thinking 'really is'. It is not as though Descartes granted that there might well be neurophysiological processes which are strikingly analogous to conceptual thinking, but which it would be philosophically incorrect to *identify* with conceptual thinking (as he had identified physical objects of the manifest world with systems of imperceptible particles). He did not take seriously the idea that there *are* such neurophysiological processes.

Even if he had, however, it is clear that he would have rejected this identification on the ground that we had a 'clear and distinct', well-defined idea of what conceptual thinking is before we even suspected that the brain had anything to do with thinking. Roughly: we know what thinking is without conceiving of it as a complex neurophysiological process, therefore, it cannot *be* a complex physiological process.

Now, of course, the same is true of physical objects. We knew what a physical object was long before we knew that there were imperceptible physical particles. By parity of reasoning we should conclude that a physical object cannot *be* a complex of imperceptible particles. Thus, if Descartes had had reason to think that neurophysiological processes strikingly analogous to conceptual thinking exist, it would seem that he should *either* have changed his tune with respect to physical objects *or* said that conceptual thinking *really is* a neurophysiological process.

Now in the light of recent developments in neurophysiology, philosophers have come to see that there is no reason to suppose there can't be neurophysiological processes which stand to conceptual thinking as sensory states of the brain stand to conscious sensations. And, indeed, there have not been wanting philosophers (of whom Hobbes was, perhaps, the first) who have argued that the analogy should be viewed philosophically as an *identity*, i.e., that a world picture which includes *both* thoughts *and* the neurophysiological counterparts of thoughts would contain a redundancy; just as a world picture which included *both* the physical objects of the manifest image *and* complex patterns of physical particles would contain a redundancy. But to this proposal the obvious objection occurs, that just as the claim that 'physical objects are complexes of imperceptible particles' left us with the problem of accounting for the status of the perceptible qualities of manifest objects, so the claim that 'thoughts, etc., are complex neurophysiological processes' leaves us with the problems of accounting for the status of the *introspectable qualities* of thoughts. And it would seem obvious that there is a vicious regress in the claim that these qualities exist in introspective awareness of the thoughts which seem to have them, but not in the thoughts themselves. For, the argument would run, surely introspection is itself a form of thinking. Thus one thought (Peter) would be robbed of its quality only to pay it to another (Paul).

We can, therefore, understand the temptation to say that even if there are cerebral processes which are strikingly analogous to conceptual thinking, they are processes which *run parallel* to conceptual thinking (and cannot be identified with it) as the sensory states of the brain *run parallel* to conscious sensation. And we can, therefore, understand the temptation to say that all these puzzles arise from taking seriously the claim of *any* part of the scientific image to be *what really is*, and to retreat into the position that reality is the world of the manifest image, and that all the postulated entities of the scientific image are 'symbolic tools' which function (something like the distance-measuring devices which are rolled around on maps) to help us find our way around in the world, but do not themselves describe actual objects and processes. On this view, the theoretical counterparts of *all* features of the manifest image would be *equally* unreal, and that philosophical conception of man-of-the-world would be correct which endorsed the manifest image and located the scientific image within it as a conceptual tool used by manifest man in his capacity as scientist.

The Primacy of the Scientific Image: A Prolegomenon

Is this the truth of the matter? Is the manifest image, subject, of course, to continual empirical and categorial refinements, the measure of what there really is? I do not think so. I have already indicated that of the three alternatives we are considering with respect to the comparative claims of the manifest and scientific images, the first, which, like a child, says 'both', is ruled out by a principle which I am not defending in this chapter, although it does stand in need of defence. The second alternative is the one I have just reformulated and rejected. I propose, therefore, to re-examine the case against the third alternative, the primacy of the scientific image. My strategy will be to argue that the difficulty, raised above, which seems to stand in the way of the identification of thought with cerebral processes, arises from the mistake of supposing that in self-awareness conceptual thinking presents itself to us in a qualitative guise. Sensations and images *do*, we shall see, present themselves to us in a qualitative character, a fact which accounts for the fact that they are stumbling blocks in the attempt to accept the scientific image as real. *But* one scarcely needs to point out these days that however intimately conceptual thinking is related to sensations and images, it cannot be equated with them, nor with complexes consisting of them.

It is no accident that when a novelist wishes to represent what is going on in the mind of a person, he does so by 'quoting' the person's thoughts as he might quote what a person says. For thoughts not only are the sort of things that find overt expression in language, we conceive of them as analogous to overt discourse. Thus, *thoughts* in the manifest image are conceived not in terms of their 'quality', but rather as inner 'goings-on' which are analogous to speech, and find their overt expression in speech—though they can go on, of course, in the absence of this overt expression. It is no accident that one learns to think in the very process of learning to speak.

From this point of view one can appreciate the danger of misunderstanding which is contained in the term 'introspection'. For while there is, indeed, an analogy between the direct knowledge we have of our own thoughts and the perceptual knowledge we have of what is going on in the world around us, the analogy holds only in as much as both self-awareness and perceptual observation are basic forms of non-inferential knowledge. They differ, however, in that whereas in perceptual observation we know objects as being of a certain quality, in the direct knowledge we have of what we are thinking (e.g., I am thinking that it is cold outside) what we know non-inferentially is that *something analogous to and properly expressed by the sentence, 'It is cold outside', is going on in me.*

The point is an important one, for if the concept of a thought is the concept of an inner state analogous to speech, this leaves open the possibility that the inner state conceived in terms of this analogy is *in its qualitative character* a neurophysiological process. To draw a parallel: if I begin by thinking of the cause of a disease as a substance (to be called 'germs') which is analogous to a colony of rabbits, in that it is able to reproduce itself in geometrical proportion, but, unlike rabbits, imperceptible and, when present in sufficient number in the human body, able to cause the symptoms of disease, and to cause epidemics by spreading from person to person, there is no logical barrier to a subsequent identification of 'germs' thus conceived with the *bacilli* which microscopic investigation subsequently discovers.

But to point to the analogy between conceptual thinking and overt speech is only part of the story, for of equally decisive importance is the analogy between speech and what sophisticated computers can do, and finally, between computer circuits and conceivable patterns of neurophysiological organization. All of this is more or less speculative, less so now than even a few years ago. What interests the philosopher is the matter of principle; and here the first stage is decisive—the recognition that the concept of a thought is a concept by analogy. Over and above this all we need is to recognize the force of Spinoza's statement: 'No one has thus far determined what the body can do nor no one has yet been taught by experience what the body can do merely by the laws of nature insofar as nature is considered merely as corporeal and extended' (*Ethics*, Part Three, Prop. II [note]).

Another analogy which may be even more helpful is the following: suppose we are watching the telegraphic report of a chess game in a foreign country.

White	Black
P—K3	P—QB3

And suppose that we are sophisticated enough to know that chess pieces can be made of all shapes and sizes, that chess boards can be horizontal or vertical, indeed, distorted in all kinds of ways provided that they preserve certain topological features of the familiar board. Then it is clear that while we will think of the players in the foreign country as moving kings, pawns, etc., castling and check-mating, our concepts of the pieces they are moving and the moving of them will be simply the concept of items and changes which play a role analogous to the pieces and moves which take place when *we* play chess. We know that the items must have some intrinsic quality (shape, size, etc.), but we think of these qualities as 'those which make possible a sequence of changes which are structurally similar to the changes which take place on our own chess boards'.

Thus our concept of 'what thoughts are' might, like our concept of what a castling is in chess, be abstract in the sense that it does not concern itself with the *intrinsic* character of thoughts, *save as items which can occur in patterns of relationships which are analogous to the way in which sentences are related to one another and to the contexts in which they are used.*

Now if thoughts are items which are conceived in terms of the roles they play, then there is no barrier *in principle* to the identification of conceptual thinking with neurophysiological process. There would be no 'qualitative' remainder to be accounted for. The identification, curiously enough, would be even more straightforward than the identification of the physical things in the manifest image with complex systems of physical particles. And in this key, if not decisive, respect, the respect in which both images are concerned with conceptual thinking (which is the distinctive trait of man), *the manifest and scientific images could merge without clash in the synoptic view.*

How does the situation stand in respect to sensation and feeling? Any attempt at identification of these items with neurophysiological process runs into a difficulty to which reference has already been made, and which we are now in a position to make more precise. This difficulty accounts for the fact that, with few exceptions, philosophers who have been prepared to identify conceptual thinking with neurophysiological process have *not* been prepared to make a similar identification in the case of sensation.

Before restating the problem let us note that curiously enough, there is more similarity between the two cases than is commonly recognized. For it turns out on reflection that just as conceptual thinking is construed in the manifest image by analogy with overt speech, so sensation is construed by analogy with its external cause, sensations being the states of persons which correspond, in their similarities and differences to the similarities and differences of the objects which, in standard conditions, bring them about. Let us assume that this is so. But if it is so, why not suppose that the inner-states which *as sensations* are conceived by analogy with their standard causes, are *in propria persona* complex neurophysiological episodes in the cerebral cortex? To do so would parallel the conclusion we were prepared to draw in the case of conceptual thinking.

Why do we feel that there would be something extremely odd, even absurd, about such a supposition? The key to the answer lies in noticing an important difference between identifying thoughts with neurophysiological states and identifying sensations with neurophysiological states. Whereas both thoughts and sensations are conceived by analogy with publicly observable items, in the former case the analogy concerns the *role* and hence leaves open the possibility that thoughts are radically different *in their intrinsic character* from the verbal behaviour by analogy with which they are conceived. But in the case of sensations, the analogy concerns the quality itself. Thus a 'blue and triangular sensation' is conceived by analogy with the blue and triangular (facing) surface of a physical object which, when looked at in daylight, is its cause. The crucial issue then is this: can we define, in the framework of neurophysiology, states which are sufficiently analogous in their *intrinsic* character to sensations to make identification plausible?

The answer seems clearly to be 'no'. This is not to say that neurophysiological states cannot be defined (in principle) which have a high degree of analogy to the sensations of the manifest image. That this can be done is an elementary fact in psycho-physics. The trouble is, rather, that the feature which we referred to as 'ultimate homogeneity', and which characterizes the perceptible qualities of things, e.g., their colour, seems to be essentially lacking in the domain of the definable states of nerves and their interactions. Putting it crudely, colour expanses in the manifest world consist of regions which are themselves colour expanses, and these consist in their turn of regions which are colour expanses, and so on; whereas the state of a group of neurons, though it has regions which are also states of groups of neurons, has ultimate regions which are *not* states of groups of neurons but rather states of single neurons. And the same is true if we move to the finer grained level of biochemical process.

Nor do we wish to say that the ultimate homogeneity of the sensation of a red rectangle is a matter of each physical particle in the appropriate region of the cortex *having* a colour; for whatever other difficulties such a view would involve, it doesn't make sense to say of the particles of physical theory that they are coloured. And the principle of reducibility, which we have accepted without argument, makes impossible the view that groups of particles can have properties which are not 'reducible to' the properties and relations of the members of the group.

It is worth noting that we have here a recurrence of the essential features of Eddington's 'two tables' problem—the two tables being, in our terminology, the table of the manifest image and the table of the scientific image. There the problem was to 'fit together' the manifest table with the scientific table. Here the problem is to fit together the manifest sensation with its neurophysiological counterpart. And, interestingly enough, the problem in both cases is essentially the same: *how to reconcile the ultimate homogeneity of the manifest image with the ultimate non-homogeneity of the system of scientific objects.*

Now we are rejecting the view that the scientific image is a mere 'symbolic tool' for finding our way around in the manifest image; and we are accepting the view that the scientific account of the world is (in principle) the adequate image. Having, therefore, given the perceptible qualities of manifest objects their real locus in sensation, we were confronted with the problem of choosing between dualism or identity with respect to the relation of conscious sensations to their analogues in the visual cortex, and the above argument seems to point clearly in the dualistic direction. The 'ultimate homogeneity' of perceptible qualities, which, among other things, prevented *identifying* the perceptible

qualities of physical objects with complex properties of systems of physical particles, stands equally
in the way of *identifying*, rather than *correlating*,
conscious sensations with the complex neural
processes with which they are obviously connected.

But such dualism is an unsatisfactory solution,
because *ex hypothesi* sensations are essential to the
explanation of how we come to construct the 'appearance' which is the manifest world. They are
essential to the explanation of how there even *seem*
to be coloured objects. But the scientific image
presents itself as a closed system of explanation,
and *if the scientific image is interpreted as we have
interpreted it up to this point* the explanation will be
in terms of the constructs of neurophysiology,
which, according to the argument, *do not involve the
ultimate homogeneity, the appearance of which in the
manifest image is to be explained*.

We are confronted, therefore, by an antinomy,
either, (a) the neurophysiological image is *incomplete*, and must be supplemented by new objects ('sense fields') which do have ultimate homogeneity, and which somehow make their presence
felt in the activity of the visual cortex as a system of
physical particles; or, (b) the neurophysiological
image is complete and the ultimate homogeneity of
the sense qualities (and, hence, the sense qualities,
themselves) is *mere appearance* in the very radical
sense of not existing in the spatiotemporal world
at all.

Is the situation irremediable? Does the assumption of the reality of the scientific image lead
us to a dualism of particles and sense fields? of
matter and 'consciousness'? If so, then, in view of
the obviously intimate relation between sensation
and conceptual thinking (for example, in perception), we must surely regress and take back the
identification or conceptual thinking with neurophysiological process which seemed so plausible a
moment ago. We could then argue that although in
the absence of other considerations it would be
plausible to equate conceptual thinking with neurophysiological process, when the chips are *all*
down, we must rather say that although conceptual thinking and neurophysiological process are
each analogous to verbal behaviour as a public social phenomenon (the one by virtue of the very way
in which the very notion of 'thinking' is formed;
the other as a scientifically ascertained matter of
fact), they are also *merely* analogous to one another
and cannot be identified. If so, the manifest and the
scientific conception of *both* sensations *and* concep-

tual thinking would fit into the synoptic view as
parallel processes, a dualism which could only be
avoided by interpreting the scientific image *as a
whole* as a 'symbolic device' for coping with the
world as it presents itself to us in the manifest
image.

Is there any alternative? As long as the ultimate constituents of the scientific image are particles forming ever more complex systems of particles, we are inevitably confronted by the above
choice. But the scientific image is not yet complete;
we have not yet penetrated all the secrets of nature.
And if it should turn out that particles instead of
being the primitive entities of the scientific image
could be treated as singularities in a space-time
continuum which could be conceptually 'cut up'
without significant loss—*in inorganic contexts, at
least*—into interacting particles, then we would not
be confronted at the level of neurophysiology with
the problem of understanding the relation of *sensory consciousness* (with its ultimate homogeneity)
to *systems of particles*. Rather, we would have the
alternative of saying that although for many purposes the central nervous system can be construed
without loss as a complex system of physical particles, *when it comes to an adequate understanding of the
relation of sensory consciousness to* neurophysiological process, we must penetrate to the non-
particulate foundation of the particulate image,
and recognize that in this non-particulate image
the qualities of sense are a dimension of natural
process which occurs only in connection with
those complex physical processes which, when
'cut up' into particles in terms of those features
which are the least common denominators of physical process—present in inorganic as well as organic processes alike—become the complex system of particles which, in the current scientific
image, *is* the central nervous system.

Putting Man into the Scientific Image

Even if the constructive suggestion of the
preceding section were capable of being elaborated
into an adequate account of the way in which the
scientific image could recreate in its own terms the
sensations, images, and feelings of the manifest
image, the thesis of the primacy of the scientific
image would scarcely be off the ground. There
would remain the task of showing that categories

pertaining to man as a *person* who finds himself confronted by standards (ethical, logical, etc.) which often conflict with his desires and impulses, and to which he may or may not conform, can be reconciled with the idea that man is what science says he is.

At first sight there would seem to be only one way of recapturing the specifically human within the framework of the scientific image. The categories of the person might be reconstructed without loss in terms of the fundamental concepts of the scientific image in a way analogous to that in which the concepts of biochemistry are (in principle) reconstructed in terms of sub-atomic physics. To this suggestion there is, in the first place, the familiar objection that persons as responsible agents who make genuine choices between genuine alternatives, and who could on many occasions have done what in point of fact they did not do, simply *can't* be construed as physical systems (even broadly interpreted to include sensations and feelings) which evolve in accordance with laws of nature (statistical or non-statistical). Those who make the above move can be expected to reply (drawing on distinctions developed in the first section) that the concepts in terms of which we think of a person's 'character', or the fact that 'he could have done otherwise,' or that 'his actions are predictable' would appear in the reconstruction as extraordinarily complex defined concepts not to be confused with the concepts in terms of which we think of the 'nature' of NaCl, or the fact that 'system X would have failed to be in state S given the same initial conditions' or that 'it is predictable that system X will assume state S given these initial conditions.' And I think that a reply along these lines could be elaborated which would answer *this* objection to the proposed reconstruction of categories pertaining to persons.

But even if the proposed reconstruction could meet what might be called the 'free will' objection, it fails decisively on another count. For it can, I believe, be conclusively shown that such a reconstruction is *in principle* impossible, the impossibility in question being a strictly logical one. (I shall not argue the point explicitly, but the following remarks contain the essential clues.) If so, that would seem to be the end of the matter. Must we not return to a choice between (*a*) a dualism in which men as scientific objects are constrasted with the 'minds' which are the source and principle of their existence as persons; (*b*) abandoning the reality of persons as well as manifest physical ob-

jects in favour of the exclusive reality of scientific objects; (*c*) returning once and for all to the thesis of the merely 'calculational' or 'auxiliary' status of theoretical frameworks and to the affirmation of the primacy of the manifest image?

Assuming, in accordance with the drift of the argument of this chapter, that none of these alternatives is satisfactory, is there a way out? I believe there is, and that while a proper exposition and defence would require at least the space of this whole volume, the gist can be stated in short compass. To say that a certain person desired to do A, thought it his duty to do B but was forced to do C, is not to *describe* him as one might describe a scientific specimen. One does, indeed, describe him, but one does something more. And it is this something more which is the irreducible core of the framework of persons.

In what does this something more consist? First, a relatively superficial point which will guide the way. To think of a featherless biped as a person is to think of it as a being with which one is bound up in a network of rights and duties. From this point of view, the irreducibility of the personal is the irreducibility of the 'ought' to the 'is.' But even more basic than this (though ultimately, as we shall see, the two points coincide), is the fact that to think of a featherless biped as a person is to construe its behaviour in terms of actual or potential membership in an embracing group each member of which thinks of itself as a member of the group. Let us call such a group a 'community'. Once the primitive tribe, it is currently (almost) the 'brotherhood' of man, and is potentially the 'republic' of rational beings (cf., Kant's 'Kingdom of Ends'). An individual may belong to many communities, some of which overlap, some of which are arranged like Chinese boxes. The most embracing community to which he belongs consists of those with whom he can enter into meaningful discourse. The scope of the embracing community is the scope of 'we' in its most embracing non-metaphorical use. 'We', in this fundamental sense (in which it is equivalent to the French '*on*' or English '*one*'), is no less basic than the other 'persons' in which verbs are conjugated. Thus, to recognize a featherless biped or dolphin or Martian as a person is to think of oneself and it as belonging to a community.

Now, the fundamental principles of a community, which define what is 'correct' or 'incorrect', 'right' or 'wrong', 'done' or 'not done', are the most general common *intentions* of that community with respect to the behaviour of members of the group. It follows that to recognize a featherless biped or dolphin or Martian as a person requires that one think thoughts of the form, 'We (one) shall do (or abstain from doing) actions of kind A in circumstances of kind C.' To think thoughts of this kind is not to *classify* or *explain*, but to *rehearse an intention*.[2]

Thus the conceptual framework of persons is the framework in which we think of one another as sharing the community intentions which provide the ambience of principles and standards (above all, those which make meaningful discourse and rationality itself possible) within which we live our own individual lives. A person can almost be defined as a being that has intentions. Thus the conceptual framework of persons is not something that needs to be *reconciled with* the scientific image, but rather something to be *joined* to it. Thus, to complete the scientific image we need to enrich it *not* with more ways of saying what is the case, but with the language of community and individual intentions, so that by construing the actions we intend to do and the circumstances in which we intend to do them in scientific terms, we *directly* relate the world as conceived by scientific theory to

our purposes, and make it *our* world and no longer an alien appendage to the world in which we do our living. We can, of course, as matters now stand, realize this direct incorporation of the scientific image into our way of life only in imagination. But to do so is, if only in imagination, to transcend the dualism of the manifest and scientific images of man-in-the-world.

Endnotes

[1] It might seem that the manifest framework accounts for the success of the scientific framework, so that the situation is symmetrical. But I believe that a more penetrating account of theoretical explanation than I have been able to sketch in this chapter would show that this claim is illusory.

[2] Community intentions ('One shall . . .') are not just private intentions (I shall . . .') which everybody has. (This is another way of putting the above mentioned irreducibility of 'we.') There is, however, a logical connection between community and private intentions. For one does not really share a community intention unless, however often one may rehearse it, it is reflected, where relevant, in the corresponding private intention.

---

52. *Ontological Relativity*

WILLARD V. O. QUINE

Rationalists were confident reason could grasp the meaning of ideas and show that some beliefs correspond to reality. Empiricists like Hume doubted one could know anything about the causes of ideas beyond their relations to other components of experience, like sensations; but they too were confident that an analysis of ideas would result in definite knowledge of their meaning of ideas and that some knowledge of the relations among them could be a priori. Much twentieth-century philosophy shared this optimism about meaning, though the focus shifted from meaning as a psychological phenomenon to meaning as it is expressed in languages. Philosophers hoped the analysis of language (whether "ordinary language," scientific languages, or ideal languages constructed with the aid of formal logic) would help settle metaphysical disputes. Frequently, however, these analyses embodied controversial metaphysical assumptions, as has been made clear by the work of Willard Van Orman Quine, an emeritus professor of philosophy at Harvard University.

Quine is a logician who approached language from a naturalistic point of view—skeptical about both abstract Platonic entities and private mental entities. In 1951, he published "Two Dogmas of Empiricism," an influential paper that denied there are any analytic truths (beliefs that might be known a priori to be true just by virtue of meaning); and he has continued to argue that there is no a priori knowledge of meaning that solves metaphysical problems. Quine insists theories of meaning should be based on data consisting of overt behavior, but then theories of meaning encounter many of the philosophical problems that other scientific theories face—for example, theories are "underdetermined by data" in the sense that several different theories could be compatible with (or explain) the data. In "Ontological Relativity," Quine shows how his important theses about meaning (indeterminancy of translation and inscrutibility of reference) lead to the conclusion that there is no absolute way to say what a language (or a scientific or formal theory) is about. Thus, ontological claims are always *relative*: "It makes no sense to say what the objects of a theory are, beyond saying how to interpret or reinterpret the theory in another." And there are numerous alternative theories, which, Quine hopes, evolve in accordance with scientific principles.

I

I listened to Dewey on Art as Experience when I was a graduate student in the spring of 1931. Dewey was then at Harvard as the first William James Lecturer. I am proud now to be at Columbia as the first John Dewey Lecturer.

Philosophically I am bound to Dewey by the naturalism that dominated his last three decades. With Dewey I hold that knowledge, mind, and meaning are part of the same world that they have to do with, and that they are to be studied in the same empirical spirit that animates natural science. There is no place for a prior philosophy.

When a naturalistic philosopher addresses himself to the philosophy of mind, he is apt to talk of language. Meanings are, first and foremost, meanings of language. Language is a social art which we all acquire on the evidence solely of other people's overt behavior under publicly recognizable circumstances. Meanings, therefore, those very models of mental entities, end up as grist for the behaviorist's mill. Dewey was explicit on the

point: "Meaning . . . is not a psychic existence; it is primarily a property of behavior."[1]

Once we appreciate the institution of language in these terms, we see that there cannot be, in any useful sense, a private language. This point was stressed by Dewey in the twenties. "Soliloquy," he wrote, "is the product and reflex of converse with others." Further along he expanded the point thus: "Language is specifically a mode of interaction of at least two beings, a speaker and a hearer; it presupposes an organized group to which these creatures belong, and from whom they have acquired their habits of speech. It is therefore a relationship." Years later, Wittgenstein likewise rejected private language. When Dewey was writing in this naturalistic vein, Wittgenstein still held his copy theory of language.

The copy theory in its various forms stands closer to the main philosophical tradition, and to the attitude of common sense today. Uncritical semantics is the myth of a museum in which the exhibits are meanings and the words are labels. To switch languages is to change the labels. Now the naturalist's primary objection to this view is not an objection to meanings on account of their being mental entities, though that could be objection enough. The primary objection persists even if we take the labeled exhibits not as mental ideas but as Platonic ideas or even as the denoted concrete objects. Semantics is vitiated by a pernicious mentalism as long as we regard a man's semantics as somehow determinate in his mind beyond what might be implicit in his dispositions to overt behavior. It is the very facts about meaning, not the entities meant, that must be construed in terms of behavior.

There are two parts to knowing a word. One part is being familiar with the sound of it and being able to reproduce it. This part, the phonetic part, is achieved by observing and imitating other people's behavior, and there are no important illusions about the process. The other part, the semantic part, is knowing how to use the word. This part, even in the paradigm case, is more complex than the phonetic part. The word refers, in the paradigm case, to some visible object. The learner has now not only to learn the word phonetically, by hearing it from another speaker; he also has to see the object; and in addition to this, in order to capture the relevance of the object to the word, he has to see that the speaker also sees the object. Dewey summed up the point thus: "The characteristic theory about *B*'s understanding of *A*'s sounds is that he responds to the thing from the standpoint of *A*." Each of us, as he learns his language, is a student of his neighbor's behavior; and conversely, insofar as his tries are approved or corrected, he is a subject of his neighbor's behavioral study.

The semantic part of learning a word is more complex than the phonetic part, therefore, even in simple cases: we have to see what is stimulating the other speaker. In the case of words not directly ascribing observable traits to things, the learning process is increasingly complex and obscure; and obscurity is the breeding place of mentalistic semantics. What the naturalist insists on is that, even in the complex and obscure parts of language learning, the learner has no data to work with but the overt behavior of other speakers.

When with Dewey we turn thus toward a naturalistic view of language and a behavioral view of meaning, what we give up is not just the museum figure of speech. We give up an assurance of determinacy. Seen according to the museum myth, the words and sentences of a language have their determinate meanings. To discover the meanings of the native's words we may have to observe his behavior, but still the meanings of the words are supposed to be determinate in the native's *mind*, his mental museum, even in cases where behav-

ioral criteria are powerless to discover them for us. When on the other hand we recognize with Dewey that "meaning . . . is primarily a property of behavior," we recognize that there are no meanings, nor likenesses nor distinctions of meaning, beyond what are implicit in people's dispositions to overt behavior. For naturalism the question whether two expressions are alike or unlike in meaning has no determinate answer, known or unknown, except insofar as the answer is settled in principle by people's speech dispositions, known or unknown. If by these standards there are indeterminate cases, so much the worse for the terminology of meaning and likeness of meaning.

To see what such indeterminacy would be like, suppose there were an expression in a remote language that could be translated into English equally defensibly in either of two ways, unlike in meaning in English. I am not speaking of ambiguity within the native language. I am supposing that one and the same native use of the expression can be given either of the English translations, each being accommodated by compensating adjustments in the translation of other words. Suppose both translations, along with these accommodations in each case, accord equally well with all observable behavior on the part of speakers of the remote language and speakers of English. Suppose they accord perfectly not only with behavior actually observed, but with all dispositions to behavior on the part of all the speakers concerned. On these assumptions it would be forever impossible to know of one of these translations that it was the right one, and the other wrong. Still, if the museum myth were true, there would be a right and wrong of the matter; it is just that we would never know, not having access to the museum. See language naturalistically, on the other hand, and you have to see the notion of likeness of meaning in such a case simply as nonsense.

I have been keeping to the hypothetical. Turning now to examples, let me begin with a disappointing one and work up. In the French construction "ne . . . rien" you can translate "rien" into English as "anything" or as "nothing" at will, and then accommodate your choice by translating "ne" as "not" or by construing it as pleonastic. This example is disappointing because you can object that I have merely cut the French units too small. You can believe the mentalistic myth of the meaning museum and still grant that "rien" of itself has no meaning, being no whole label; it is part of "ne . . . rien," which has its meaning as a whole.

I began with this disappointing example because I think its conspicuous trait—its dependence on cutting language into segments too short to carry meanings—is the secret of the more serious cases as well. What makes other cases more serious is that the segments they involve are seriously long: long enough to be predicates and to be true of things and hence, you would think, to carry meanings.

An artificial example which I have used elsewhere[2] depends on the fact that a whole rabbit is present when and only when an undetached part of a rabbit is present; also when and only when a temporal stage of a rabbit is present. If we are wondering whether to translate a native expression "gavagai" as "rabbit" or as "undetached rabbit part" or as "rabbit stage," we can never settle the matter simply by ostension—that is, simply by repeatedly querying the expression "gavagai" for the native's assent or dissent in the presence of assorted stimulations.

Before going on to urge that we cannot settle the matter by non-ostensive means either, let me belabor this ostensive predicament a bit. I am not worrying, as Wittgenstein did, about simple cases of ostension. The color word "sepia," to take one of his examples,[3] can certainly be learned by an ordinary process of conditioning, or induction. One need not even be told that sepia is a color and not a shape or a material or an article. True, barring such hints, many lessons may be needed, so as to eliminate wrong generalizations based on shape, material, etc., rather than color, and so as to eliminate wrong notions as to the intended boundary of an indicated example, and so as to delimit the admissible variations of color itself. Like all conditioning, or induction, the process will depend ultimately also on one's own inborn propensity to find one stimulation qualitatively more akin to a second stimulation than to a third; otherwise there can never be any selective reinforcement and extinction of responses.[4] Still, in principle nothing more is needed in learning "sepia" than in any conditioning or induction.

But the big difference between "rabbit" and "sepia" is that whereas "sepia" is a mass term like "water," "rabbit" is a term of divided reference. As such it cannot be mastered without mastering its

principle of individuation: where one rabbit leaves off and another begins. And this cannot be mastered by pure ostension, however persistent.

Such is the quandary over "gavagai": where one gavagai leaves off and another begins. The only difference between rabbits, undetached rabbit parts, and rabbit stages is in their individuation. If you take the total scattered portion of the spatiotemporal world that is made up of rabbits, and that which is made up of undetached rabbit parts, and that which is made up of rabbit stages, you come out with the same scattered portion of the world each of the three times. The only difference is in how you slice it. And how to slice it is what ostension or simple conditioning, however persistently repeated, cannot teach.

Thus consider specifically the problem of deciding between "rabbit" and "undetached rabbit part" as translation of "gavagai." No word of the native language is known, except that we have settled on some working hypothesis as to what native words or gestures to construe as assent and dissent in response to our pointings and queryings. Now the trouble is that whenever we point to different parts of the rabbit, even sometimes screening the rest of the rabbit, we are pointing also each time to the rabbit. When, conversely, we indicate the whole rabbit with a sweeping gesture, we are still pointing to a multitude of rabbit parts. And note that we do not have even a native analogue of our plural ending to exploit, in asking "gavagai?" It seems clear that no even tentative decision between "rabbit" and "undetached rabbit part" is to be sought at this level.

How would we finally decide? My passing mention of plural endings is part of the answer. Our individuating of terms of divided reference, in English, is bound up with a cluster of interrelated grammatical particles and constructions: plural endings, pronouns, numerals, the "is" of identity, and its adaptations "same" and "other." It is the cluster of interrelated devices in which quantification becomes central when the regimentation of symbolic logic is imposed. If in his language we could ask the native, "Is this *gavagai* the same as that one?" while making appropriate multiple ostensions, then indeed we would be well on our way to deciding between "rabbit," "undetached rabbit part," and "rabbit stage." And of course the linguist does at length reach the point where he can ask what purports to be that question. He develops a system for translating our pluralizations, pronouns, numerals, identity, and related devices contextually into the native idiom. He develops such a system by abstraction and hypothesis. He abstracts native particles and constructions from observed native sentences and tries associating these variously with English particles and constructions. Insofar as the native sentences and the thus associated English ones seem to match up in respect of appropriate occasions of use, the linguist feels confirmed in these hypotheses of translation —what I call *analytical hypotheses*.[5]

But it seems that this method, though laudable in practice and the best we can hope for, does not in principle settle the indeterminacy between "rabbit," "undetached rabbit part," and "rabbit stage." For if one workable overall system of analytical hypotheses provides for translating a given native expression into "is the same as," perhaps another equally workable but systematically different system would translate that native expression rather into something like "belongs with." Then when in the native language we try to ask "Is this *gavagai* the same as that?" we could as well be asking "Does this *gavagai* belong with that?" Insofar, the native's assent is no objective evidence for translating "gavagai" as "rabbit" rather than "undetached rabbit part" or "rabbit stage."

This artificial example shares the structure of the trivial earlier example "ne . . . rien." We were able to translate "rien" as "anything" or as "nothing," thanks to a compensatory adjustment in the handling of "ne." And I suggest that we can translate "gavagai" as "rabbit" or "undetached rabbit part" or "rabbit stage," thanks to compensatory adjustments in the translation of accompanying native locutions. Other adjustments still might accommodate translation of "gavagai" as "rabbit-hood," or in further ways. I find this plausible because of the broadly structural and contextual character of any considerations that could guide us to native translations of the English cluster of interrelated devices of individuation. There seem bound to be systematically very different choices, all of which do justice to all dispositions to verbal behavior on the part of all concerned.

An actual field linguist would of course be sensible enough to equate "gavagai" with "rabbit," dismissing such perverse alternatives as "undetached rabbit part" and "rabbit stage" out of hand. This sensible choice and others like it would help in turn to determine his subsequent hypotheses as to what native locutions should answer to the English apparatus of individuation, and thus everything would come out all right. The implicit maxim guiding his choice of "rabbit," and similar choices for other native words, is that an enduring and relatively homogeneous object, moving as a whole against a contrasting background, is a likely reference for a short expression. If he were to become conscious of this maxim, he might celebrate it as one of the linguistic universals, or traits of all languages, and he would have no trouble pointing out its psychological plausibility. But he would be wrong; the maxim is his own imposition, toward settling what is objectively indeterminate. It is a very sensible imposition, and I would recommend no other. But I am making a philosophical point.

It is philosophically interesting, moreover, that what is indeterminate in this artificial example is not just meaning, but extension; reference. My remarks on indeterminacy began as a challenge to likeness of meaning. I had us imagining "an expression that could be translated into English equally defensibly in either of two ways, unlike in meaning in English." Certainly likeness of meaning is a dim notion, repeatedly challenged. Of two predicates which are alike in extension, it has never been clear when to say that they are alike in meaning and when not; it is the old matter of featherless bipeds and rational animals, or of equiangular and equilateral triangles. Reference, extension, has been the firm thing; meaning, intension, the infirm. The indeterminacy of translation now confronting us, however, cuts across extension and intension alike. The terms "rabbit," "undetached rabbit part," and "rabbit stage" differ not only in meaning; they are true of different things. Reference itself proves behaviorally inscrutable.

Within the parochial limits of our own language, we can continue as always to find extensional talk clearer than intensional. For the indeterminacy between "rabbit," "rabbit stage," and the rest depended only on a correlative indeterminacy of translation of the English apparatus of individuation—the apparatus of pronouns, pluralization, identity, numerals, and so on. No such indeterminacy obtrudes so long as we think of this apparatus as given and fixed. Given this apparatus, there is no mystery about extension; terms have the same extension when true of the same things. At the level of radical translation, on the other hand, extension itself goes inscrutable.

My example of rabbits and their parts and stages is a contrived example and a perverse one, with which, as I said, the practicing linguist would have no patience. But there are also cases, less bizarre ones, that obtrude in practice. In Japanese there are certain particles, called "classifiers," which may be explained in either of two ways. Commonly they are explained as attaching to numerals, to form compound numerals of distinctive styles. Thus take the numeral for 5. If you attach one classifier to it you get a style of "5" suitable for counting animals; if you attach a different classifier, you get a style of "5" suitable for counting slim things like pencils and chopsticks; and so on. But another way of viewing classifiers is to view them not as constituting part of the numeral, but as constituting part of the term—the term for "chopsticks" or "oxen" or whatever. On this view the classifier does the individuative job that is done in English by "sticks of" as applied to the mass term "wood," or "head of" as applied to the mass term "cattle."

What we have on either view is a Japanese phrase tantamount say to "five oxen," but consisting of three words;[6] the first is in effect the neutral numeral "5," the second is a classifier of the animal kind, and the last corresponds in some fashion to "ox." On one view the neutral numeral and the classifier go together to constitute a declined numeral in the "animal gender," which then modifies "ox" to give, in effect, "five oxen." On the other view the third Japanese word answers not to the individuative term "ox" but to the mass term "cattle"; the classifier applies to this mass term to produce a composite individuative term, in effect "head of cattle"; and the neutral numeral applies directly to all this without benefit of gender, giving "five head of cattle," hence again in effect "five oxen."

If so simple an example is to serve its expository purpose, it needs your connivance. You have to understand "cattle" as a mass term covering only bovines, and "ox" as applying to all bovines. That these usages are not the invariable usages is beside the point. The point is that the Japanese phrase comes out as "five bovines," as desired, when parsed in either of two ways. The one way treats the third Japanese word as an individuative term true of each bovine, and the other way treats that word rather as a mass term covering the unindividuated totality of beef on the hoof. These are two very different ways of treating the third Japanese word; and the three-word phrase as a whole turns out all right in both cases only because of compensatory differences in our account of the second word, the classifier.

This example is reminiscent in a way of our trivial initial example, "ne . . . rien." We were able to represent "rien" as "anything" or as "nothing," by compensatorily taking "ne" as negative or as vacuous. We are able now to represent a Japanese word either as an individuative term for bovines or as a mass term for live beef, by compensatorily taking the classifier as declining the numeral or as individuating the mass term. However, the triviality of the one example does not quite carry over to the other. The early example was dismissed on the ground that we had cut too small; "rien" was too short for significant translation on its own, and "ne . . . rien" was the significant unit. But you cannot dismiss the Japanese example by saying that the third word was too short for significant translation on its own and that only the whole three-word phrase, tantamount to "five oxen," was the significant unit. You cannot take this line unless you are prepared to call a word too short for significant translation even when it is long enough to be a term and carry denotation. For the third Japanese word is, on either approach, a term: on one approach a term of divided reference, and on the other a mass term. If you are indeed prepared thus to call a word too short for significant translation even when it is a denoting term, then in a back-handed way you are granting what I wanted to prove: the inscrutability of reference.

Between the two accounts of Japanese classifiers there is no question of right and wrong. The one account makes for more efficient translation into idiomatic English; the other makes for more of a feeling for the Japanese idiom. Both fit all verbal behavior equally well. All whole sentences, and even component phrases like "five oxen," admit of the same net overall English translations on either account. This much is invariant. But what is philosophically interesting is that the reference or extension of shorter terms can fail to be invariant. Whether that third Japanese word is itself true of each ox, or whether on the other hand it is a mass term which needs to be adjoined to the classifier to make a term which is true of each ox—here is a question that remains undecided by the totality of human dispositions to verbal behavior. It is indeterminate in principle; there is no fact of the matter. Either answer can be accommodated by an account of the classifier. Here again, then, is the inscrutability of reference—illustrated this time by a humdrum point of practical translation.

The inscrutability of reference can be brought closer to home by considering the word "alpha," or again the word "green." In our use of these words and others like them there is a systematic ambiguity. Sometimes we use such words as concrete general terms, as when we say the grass is green, or that some inscription begins with an alpha. Sometimes on the other hand we use them as abstract singular terms, as when we say that green is a color and alpha is a letter. Such ambiguity is encouraged by the fact that there is nothing in ostension to distinguish the two uses. The pointing that would be done in teaching the concrete general term "green," or "alpha," differs none from the pointing that would be done in teaching the abstract singular term "green" or "alpha." Yet the objects referred to by the word are very different under the two uses; under the one use the word is true of many concrete objects, and under the other use it names a single abstract object.

We can of course tell the two uses apart by seeing how the word turns up in sentences: whether it takes an indefinite article, whether it takes a plural ending, whether it stands as singular subject, whether it stands as modifier, as predicate complement, and so on. But these criteria appeal to our special English grammatical constructions and particles, our special English apparatus of individuation, which, I already urged, is itself subject to indeterminacy of translation. So, from the point of view of translation into a remote language, the distinction between a concrete general and an abstract singular term is in the same predicament as the distinction between "rabbit," "rabbit part," and "rabbit stage." Here then is another example of the inscrutability of reference, since the difference between the concrete general and the abstract singular is a difference in the objects referred to.

Incidentally we can concede this much indeterminacy also to the "sepia" example, after all. But this move is not evidently what was worrying Wittgenstein.

The ostensive indistinguishability of the abstract singular from the concrete general turns upon what may be called "deferred ostension," as opposed to direct ostension. First let me define direct ostension. The *ostended point*, as I shall call it, is the point where the line of the pointing finger first meets an opaque surface. What characterizes *direct ostension*, then, is that the term which is being ostensively explained is true of something that contains the ostended point. Even such direct ostension has its uncertainties, of course, and these are familiar. There is the question how wide an

environment of the ostended point is meant to be covered by the term that is being ostensively explained. There is the question how considerably an absent thing or substance might be allowed to differ from what is now ostended, and still be covered by the term that is now being ostensively explained. Both of these questions can in principle be settled as well as need be by induction from multiple ostensions. Also, if the term is a term of divided reference like "apple," there is the question of individuation: the question where one of its objects leaves off and another begins. This can be settled by induction from multiple ostensions of a more elaborate kind, accompanied by expressions like "same apple" and "another," if an equivalent of this English apparatus of individuation has been settled on; otherwise the indeterminacy persists that was illustrated by "rabbit," "undetached rabbit part," and "rabbit stage."

Such, then, is the way of direct ostension. Other ostension I call *deferred*. It occurs when we point at the gauge, and not the gasoline, to show that there is gasoline. Also it occurs when we explain the abstract singular term "green" or "alpha" by pointing at grass or a Greek inscription. Such pointing is direct ostension when used to explain the concrete general term "green" or "alpha," but it is deferred ostension when used to explain the abstract singular terms; for the abstract object which is the color green or the letter alpha does not contain the ostended point, nor any point.

Deferred ostension occurs very naturally when, as in the case of the gasoline gauge, we have a correspondence in mind. Another such example is afforded by the Gödel numbering of expressions.[7] Thus if 7 has been assigned as Gödel number of the letter alpha, a man conscious of the Gödel numbering would not hesitate to say "Seven" on pointing to an inscription of the Greek letter in question. This is, on the face of it, a doubly deferred ostension: one step of deferment carries us from the inscription to the letter as abstract object, and a second step carries us thence to the number.

By appeal to our apparatus of individuation, if it is available, we can distinguish between the concrete general and the abstract singular use of the word "alpha"; this we saw. By appeal again to that apparatus, and in particular to identity, we can evidently settle also whether the word "alpha" in its abstract singular use is being used really to name the letter or whether, perversely, it is being used to name the Gödel number of the letter. At any rate we can distinguish these alternatives if also we have located the speaker's equivalent of the numeral "7" to our satisfaction; for we can ask him whether alpha *is* 7.

These considerations suggest that deferred ostension adds no essential problem to those presented by direct ostension. Once we have settled upon analytical hypotheses of translation covering identity and the other English particles relating to individuation, we can resolve not only the indecision between "rabbit" and "rabbit stage" and the rest, which came of direct ostension, but also any indecision between concrete general and abstract singular, and any indecision between expression and Gödel number, which come of deferred ostension. However, this conclusion is too sanguine. The inscrutability of reference runs deep, and it persists in a subtle form even if we accept identity and the rest of the apparatus of individuation as fixed and settled; even, indeed, if we forsake radical translation and think only of English.

Consider the case of a thoughtful protosyntactician. He has a formalized system of first-order proof theory, or protosyntax, whose universe comprises just expressions, that is, strings of signs of a specified alphabet. Now just what sorts of things, more specifically, are these expressions? They are types, not tokens. So, one might suppose, each of them is the set of all its tokens. That is, each expression is a set of inscriptions which are variously situated in space-time but are classed together by virtue of a certain similarity in shape. The concatenate $x \frown y$ of two expressions x and y, in a given order, will be the set of all inscriptions each of which has two parts which are tokens respectively of x and y and follow one upon the other in that order. But $x \frown y$ may then be the null set, though x and y are not null; for it may be that inscriptions belonging to x and y happen to turn up head to tail nowhere, in the past, present, or future. This danger increases with the lengths of x and y. But it is easily seen to violate a law of protosyntax which says that $x = z$ whenever $x \frown y = z \frown y$.

Thus it is that our thoughtful protosyntactician will not construe the things in his universe as sets of inscriptions. He can still take his atoms, the single signs, as sets of inscriptions, for there is no risk of nullity in these cases. And then, instead of taking his strings of signs as sets of inscriptions, he can invoke the mathematical notion of sequence and take them as sequences of signs. A familiar way of taking sequences, in turn, is as a mapping of things on numbers. On this approach an expression or string of signs becomes a finite set of pairs each of which is the pair of a sign and a number.

This account of expressions is more artificial and more complex than one is apt to expect who simply says he is letting his variables range over the strings of such and such signs. Moreover, it is not the inevitable choice; the considerations that motivated it can be met also by alternative constructions. One of these constructions is Gödel numbering itself, and it is temptingly simple. It uses just natural numbers, whereas the foregoing construction used sets of one-letter inscriptions and also natural numbers and sets of pairs of these. How clear is it that at just *this* point we have dropped expressions in favor of numbers? What is clearer is merely that in both constructions we were artificially devising models to satisfy laws that expressions in an unexplicated sense had been meant to satisfy.

So much for expressions. Consider now the arithmetician himself, with his elementary number theory. His universe comprises the natural numbers outright. Is it clearer than the protosyntactician's? What, after all, is a natural number? There are Frege's version, Zermelo's, and von Neumann's, and countless further alternatives, all mutually incompatible and equally correct. What we are doing in any one of these explications of natural number is to devise set-theoretic models to satisfy laws which the natural numbers in an unexplicated sense had been meant to satisfy. The case is quite like that of protosyntax.

It will perhaps be felt that any set-theoretic explication of natural number is at best a case of *obscurum per obscurius*; that all explications must assume something, and the natural numbers themselves are an admirable assumption to start with. I must agree that a construction of sets and set theory from natural numbers and arithmetic would be far more desirable than the familiar opposite. On the other hand our impression of the clarity even of the notion of natural number itself has suffered somewhat from Gödel's proof of the impossibility of a complete proof procedure for elementary number theory, or, for that matter, from Skolem's and Henkin's observations that all laws of natural numbers admit nonstandard models.[8]

We are finding no clear difference between *specifying* a universe of discourse—the range of the variables of quantification—and *reducing* that universe to some other. We saw no significant difference between clarifying the notion of expression and supplanting it by that of number. And now to say more particularly what numbers themselves are is in no evident way different from just dropping numbers and assigning to arithmetic one or another new model, say in set theory.

Expressions are known only by their laws, the laws of concatenation theory, so that any constructs obeying those laws—Gödel numbers, for instance—are *ipso facto* eligible as explications of expression. Numbers in turn are known only by their laws, the laws of arithmetic, so that any constructs obeying those laws—certain sets, for instance—are eligible in turn as explications of number. Sets in turn are known only by their laws, the laws of set theory.

[Bertrand] Russell pressed a contrary thesis, long ago. Writing of numbers, he argued that for an understanding of number the laws of arithmetic are not enough; we must know the applications, we must understand numerical discourse embedded in discourse of other matters. In applying number, the key notion, he urged, is *Anzahl*: there are *n* so-and-sos. However, Russell can be answered. First take, specifically, *Anzahl*. We can define "there are *n* so-and-sos" without ever deciding what numbers are, apart from their fulfillment of arithmetic. That there are *n* so-and-sos can be explained simply as meaning that the so-and-sos are in one-to-one correspondence with the numbers up to *n*.[9]

Russell's more general point about application can be answered too. Always, if the structure is there, the applications will fall into place. As paradigm it is perhaps sufficient to recall again this reflection on expressions and Gödel numbers: that even the pointing out of an inscription is no final evidence that our talk is of expressions and not of Gödel numbers. We can always plead deferred ostension.

It is in this sense true to say, as mathematicians often do, that arithmetic is all there is to number. But it would be a confusion to express this point by saying, as is sometimes said, that numbers are any things fulfilling arithmetic. This formulation is wrong because distinct domains of objects yield distinct models of arithmetic. Any progression can be made to serve; and to identify all progressions with one another, e.g., to identify the progression of odd numbers with the progression of evens, would contradict arithmetic after all.

So, though Russell was wrong in suggesting that numbers need more than their arithmetical

properties, he was right in objecting to the definition of numbers as any things fulfilling arithmetic. The subtle point is that any progression will serve as a version of number so long and only so long as we stick to one and the same progression. Arithmetic is, in this sense, all there is to number: there is no saying absolutely what the numbers are; there is only arithmetic.[10]

II

I first urged the inscrutability of reference with the help of examples like the one about rabbits and rabbit parts. These used direct ostension, and the inscrutability of reference hinged on the indeterminacy of translation of identity and other individuative apparatus. The setting of these examples, accordingly, was radical translation: translation from a remote language on behavioral evidence, unaided by prior dictionaries. Moving then to deferred ostension and abstract objects, we found a certain dimness of reference pervading the home language itself.

Now it should be noted that even for the earlier examples the resort to a remote language was not really essential. On deeper reflection, radical translation begins at home. Must we equate our neighbor's English words with the same strings of phonemes in our own mouths? Certainly not; for sometimes we do not thus equate them. Sometimes we find it to be in the interests of communication to recognize that our neighbor's use of some word, such as "cool" or "square" or "hopefully," differs from ours, and so we translate that word of his into a different string of phonemes in our idiolect. Our usual domestic rule of translation is indeed the homophonic one, which simply carries each string of phonemes into itself; but still we are always prepared to temper homophony with what Neil Wilson has called the "principle of charity." We will construe a neighbor's word heterophonically now and again if thereby we see our way to making his message less absurd.

The homophonic rule is a handy one on the whole. That it works so well is no accident, since imitation and feedback are what propagate a language. We acquired a great fund of basic words and phrases in this way, imitating our elders and encouraged by our elders amid external circumstances to which the phrases suitably apply. Homophonic translation is implicit in this social method of learning. Departure from homophonic translation in this quarter would only hinder communication. Then there are the relatively rare instances of opposite kind, due to divergence in dialect or confusion in an individual, where homophonic translation incurs negative feedback. But what tends to escape notice is that there is also a vast mid-region where the homophonic method is indifferent. Here, gratuitously, we can systematically reconstrue our neighbor's apparent references to rabbits as really references to rabbit stages, and his apparent references to formulas as really references to Gödel numbers and vice versa. We can reconcile all this with our neighbor's verbal behavior, by cunningly readjusting our translations of his various connecting predicates so as to compensate for the switch of ontology. In short, we can reproduce the inscrutability of reference at home. It is of no avail to check on this fanciful version of our neighbor's meanings by asking him, say, whether he really means at a certain point to refer to formulas or to their Gödel numbers; for our question and his answer—"By all means, the numbers"—have lost their title to homophonic translation. The problem at home differs none from radical translation ordinarily so called except in the willfulness of this suspension of homophonic translation.

I have urged in defense of the behavioral philosophy of language, Dewey's, that the inscrutability of reference is not the inscrutability of a fact; there is no fact of the matter. But if there is really no fact of the matter, then the inscrutability of reference can be brought even closer to home than the neighbor's case; we can apply it to ourselves. If it is to make sense to say even of oneself that one is referring to rabbits and formulas and not to rabbit stages and Gödel numbers, then it should make sense equally to say it of someone else. After all, as Dewey stressed, there is no private language.

We seem to be maneuvering ourselves into the absurd position that there is no difference on any terms, interlinguistic or intralinguistic, objective or subjective, between referring to rabbits and referring to rabbit parts or stages; or between referring to formulas and referring to their Gödel numbers. Surely this is absurd, for it would imply that there is no difference between the rabbit and each of its parts or stages, and no difference between a formula and its Gödel number. Reference would seem now to become nonsense not just in radical translation but at home.

Toward resolving this quandary, begin by picturing us at home in our language, with all its predicates and auxiliary devices. This vocabulary includes "rabbit," "rabbit part," "rabbit stage," "formula," "number," "ox," "cattle"; also the two-place predicates of identity and difference, and other logical particles. In these terms we can say in so many words that this is a formula and that a number, this a rabbit and that a rabbit part, this and that the same rabbit, and this and that different parts, *in just those words*. This network of terms and predicates and auxiliary devices is, in relativity jargon, our frame of reference, or coordinate system. Relative to *it* we can and do talk meaningfully and distinctively of rabbits and parts, numbers and formulas. Next, as in recent paragraphs, we contemplate alternative denotations for our familiar terms. We begin to appreciate that a grand and ingenious permutation of these denotations, along with compensatory adjustments in the interpretations of the auxiliary particles, might still accommodate all existing speech dispositions. This was the inscrutability of reference, applied to ourselves; and it made nonsense of reference. Fair enough; reference *is* nonsense except relative to a coordinate system. In this principle of relativity lies the resolution of our quandary.

It is meaningless to ask whether, in general, our terms "rabbit," "rabbit part," "number," etc., really refer respectively to rabbits, rabbit parts, numbers, etc., rather than to some ingeniously permuted denotations. It is meaningless to ask this absolutely; we can meaningfully ask it only relative to some background language. When we ask, "Does 'rabbit' really refer to rabbits?" someone can counter with the question: "Refer to rabbits in what sense of 'rabbits'?" thus launching a regress; and we need the background language to regress into. The background language gives the query sense, if only relative sense; sense relative in turn to it, this background language. Querying reference in any more absolute way would be like asking for absolute position, or absolute velocity, rather than position or velocity relative to a given frame of reference. Also it is very much like asking whether our neighbor may not systematically see everything upside down, or in complementary color, forever undetectably.

We need a background language, I said, to regress into. Are we involved now in an infinite regress? If questions of reference of the sort we are considering make sense only relative to a background language, then evidently questions of reference for the background language make sense in turn only relative to a further background language. In these terms the situation sounds desperate, but in fact it is little different from questions of position and velocity. When we are given position and velocity relative to a given coordinate system, we can always ask in turn about the placing of origin and orientation of axes of that system of coordinates; and there is no end to the succession of further coordinate systems that could be adduced in answering the successive questions thus generated.

In practice of course we end the regress of coordinate systems by something like pointing. And in practice we end the regress of background languages, in discussions of reference, by acquiescing in our mother tongue and taking its words at face value.

Very well; in the case of position and velocity, in practice, pointing breaks the regress. But what of position and velocity apart from practice? what of the regress then? The answer, of course, is the relational doctrine of space; there is no absolute position or velocity; there are just the relations of coordinate systems to one another, and ultimately of things to one another. And I think that the parallel question regarding denotation calls for a parallel answer, a relational theory of what the objects of theories are. What makes sense is to say not what the objects of a theory are, absolutely speaking, but how one theory of objects is interpretable or reinterpretable in another.

The point is not that bare matter is inscrutable: that things are indistinguishable except by their properties. That point does not need making. The present point is reflected better in the riddle about seeing things upside down, or in complementary colors; for it is that things can be inscrutably switched even while carrying their properties with them. Rabbits differ from rabbit parts and rabbit stages not just as bare matter, after all, but in respect of properties; and formulas differ from numbers in respect of properties. What our present reflections are leading us to appreciate is that the riddle about seeing things upside down, or in complementary colors, should be taken seriously and its moral applied widely. The relativistic thesis to which we have come is this, to repeat: it makes no sense to say what the objects of a theory are, beyond saying how to interpret or reinterpret that theory in another. Suppose we are working within a theory and thus treating of its objects. We do so

by using the variables of the theory, whose values those objects are, though there be no ultimate sense in which that universe can have been specified. In the language of the theory there are predicates by which to distinguish portions of this universe from other portions, and these predicates differ from one another purely in the roles they play in the laws of the theory. Within this background theory we can show how some subordinate theory, whose universe is some portion of the background universe, can by a reinterpretation be reduced to another subordinate theory whose universe is some lesser portion. Such talk of subordinate theories and their ontologies *is* meaningful, but only relative to the background theory with its own primitively adopted and ultimately inscrutable ontology.

To talk thus of theories raises a problem of formulation. A theory, it will be said, is a set of fully interpreted sentences. (More particularly, it is a deductively closed set: it includes all its own logical consequences, insofar as they are couched in the same notation.) But if the sentences of a theory are fully interpreted, then in particular the range of values of their variables is settled. How then can there be no sense in saying what the objects of a theory are?

My answer is simply that we cannot require theories to be fully interpreted, except in a relative sense, if anything is to count as a theory. In specifying a theory we must indeed fully specify, in our own words, what sentences are to comprise the theory, and what things are to be taken as values of the variables, and what things are to be taken as satisfying the predicate letters; insofar we do fully interpret the theory, *relative* to our own words and relative to our overall home theory which lies behind them. But this fixes the objects of the described theory only relative to those of the home theory; and these can, at will, be questioned in turn.

One is tempted to conclude simply that meaninglessness sets in when we try to pronounce on everything in our universe; that universal predication takes on sense only when furnished with the background of a wider universe, where the predication is no longer universal. And this is even a familiar doctrine, the doctrine that no proper predicate is true of everything. We have all heard it claimed that a predicate is meaningful only by contrast with what it excludes, and hence that being true of everything would make a predicate meaningless. But surely this doctrine is wrong. Surely self-identity, for instance, is not to be rejected as meaningless. For that matter, any statement of fact at all, however brutally meaningful, can be put artificially into a form in which it pronounces on everything. To say merely of Jones that he sings, for instance, is to say of everything that it is other than Jones or sings. We had better beware of repudiating universal predication, lest we be tricked into repudiating everything there is to say.

Carnap took an intermediate line in his doctrine of universal words, or *Allwörter*, in *The Logical Syntax of Language*. He did treat the predicating of universal words as "quasi-syntactical"—as a predication only by courtesy, and without empirical content. But universal words were for him not just any universally true predicates, like "is other than Jones or sings." They were a special breed of universally true predicates, ones that are universally true by the sheer meanings of their words and no thanks to nature. In his later writing this doctrine of universal words takes the form of a distinction between "internal" questions, in which a theory comes to grips with facts about the world, and "external" questions, in which people come to grips with the relative merits of theories.

Should we look to these distinctions of Carnap's for light on ontological relativity? When we found there was no absolute sense in saying what a theory is about, were we sensing the infactuality of what Carnap calls "external questions"? When we found that saying what a theory is about did make sense against a background theory, were we sensing the factuality of internal questions of the background theory? I see no hope of illumination in this quarter. Carnap's universal words were not just any universally true predicates, but, as I said, a special breed; and what distinguishes this breed is not clear. What I said distinguished them was that they were universally true by sheer meanings and not by nature; but this is a very questionable distinction. Talking of "internal" and "external" is no better.

Ontological relativity is not to be clarified by any distinction between kinds of universal predication—unfactual and factual, external and internal. It is not a question of universal predication. When questions regarding the ontology of a theory are meaningless absolutely, and become meaningful relative to a background theory, this is not in general because the background theory has a wider universe. One is tempted, as I said a little while back, to suppose that it is; but one is then wrong.

What makes ontological questions meaningless when taken absolutely is not universality but circularity. A question of the form "What is an F?" can be answered only by recourse to a further term: "An F is a G." The answer makes only relative sense: sense relative to the uncritical acceptance of "G."

We may picture the vocabulary of a theory as comprising logical signs such as quantifiers and the signs for the truth functions and identity, and in addition descriptive or nonlogical signs, which, typically, are singular terms, or names, and general terms, or predicates. Suppose next that in the statements which comprise the theory, that is, are true according to the theory, we abstract from the meanings of the nonlogical vocabulary and from the range of the variables. We are left with the logical form of the theory, or, as I shall say, the *theory form*. Now we may interpret this theory form anew by picking a new universe for its variables of quantification to range over, and assigning objects from this universe to the names, and choosing subsets of this universe as extensions of the one-place predicates, and so on. Each such interpretation of the theory form is called a model of it, if it makes it come out true. Which of these models is meant in a given actual theory cannot, of course, be guessed from the theory form. The intended references of the names and predicates have to be learned rather by ostension, or else by paraphrase in some antecedently familiar vocabulary. But the first of these two ways has proved inconclusive, since, even apart from indeterminacies of translation affecting identity and other logical vocabulary, there is the problem of deferred ostension. Paraphrase in some antecedently familiar vocabulary, then, is our only recourse; and such is ontological relativity. To question the reference of all the terms of our all-inclusive theory becomes meaningless, simply for want of further terms relative to which to ask or answer the question.

It is thus meaningless within the theory to say which of the various possible models of our theory form is our real or intended model. Yet even here we can make sense still of there being many models. For we might be able to show that for each of the models, however unspecifiable, there is bound to be another which is a permutation or perhaps a diminution of the first.

Suppose for example that our theory is purely numerical. Its objects are just the natural numbers. There is no sense in saying, from within that theory, just which of the various models of number theory is in force. But we can observe even from within the theory that, whatever 0, 1, 2, 3, etc. may be, the theory would still hold true if the 17 of this series were moved into the role of 0, and the 18 moved into the role of 1, and so on.

Ontology is indeed doubly relative. Specifying the universe of a theory makes sense only relative to some background theory, and only relative to some choice of a manual of translation of the one theory into the other. Commonly of course the background theory will simply be a containing theory, and in this case no question of a manual of translation arises. But this is after all just a degenerate case of translation still—the case where the rule of translation is the homophonic one.

We cannot know what something is without knowing how it is marked off from other things. Identity is thus of a piece with ontology. Accordingly it is involved in the same relativity, as may be readily illustrated. Imagine a fragment of economic theory. Suppose its universe comprises persons, but its predicates are incapable of distinguishing between persons whose incomes are equal. The interpersonal relation of equality of income enjoys, within the theory, the substitutivity property of the identity relation itself; the two relations are indistinguishable. It is only relative to a background theory, in which more can be said of personal identity than equality of income, that we are able even to appreciate the above account of the fragment of economic theory, hinging as the account does on a contrast between persons and incomes.

A usual occasion for ontological talk is reduction, where it is shown how the universe of some theory can by a reinterpretation be dispensed with in favor of some other universe, perhaps a proper part of the first. I have treated elsewhere[12] of the reduction of one ontology to another with help of a *proxy function*: a function mapping the one universe into part or all of the other. For instance, the function "Gödel number of" is a proxy function. The universe of elementary proof theory or protosyntax, which consists of expressions or strings of signs, is mapped by this function into the universe of elementary number theory, which consists of numbers.

The proxy function used in reducing one ontology to another need not, like Gödel numbering, be one-to-one. We might, for instance, be confronted with a theory treating of both expressions and ratios. We would cheerfully reduce all this to the universe of natural numbers, by invoking a proxy function which enumerates the expressions in the Gödel way, and enumerates the ratios by the classical method of short diagonals. This proxy function is not one-to-one, since it assigns the same natural number both to an expression and to a ratio. We would tolerate the resulting artificial convergence between expressions and ratios, simply because the original theory made no capital of the distinction between them; they were so invariably and extravagantly unlike that the identity question did not arise. Formally speaking, the original theory used a two-sorted logic.

For another kind of case where we would not require the proxy function to be one-to-one, consider again the fragment of economic theory lately noted. We would happily reduce its ontology of persons to a less numerous one of incomes. The proxy function would assign to each person his income. It is not one-to-one; distinct persons give way to identical incomes. The reason such a reduction is acceptable is that it merges the images of only such individuals as never had been distinguishable by the predicates of the original theory. Nothing in the old theory is contravened by the new identities.

If on the other hand the theory that we are concerned to reduce or reinterpret is straight protosyntax, or a straight arithmetic of ratios or of real numbers, then a one-to-one proxy function is mandatory. This is because any two elements of such a theory are distinguishable in terms of the theory. This is true even for the real numbers, even though not every real number is uniquely specifiable; any two real numbers x and y are still distinguishable, in that $x < y$ or $y < x$ and never $x < x$. A proxy function that did not preserve the distinctness of the elements of such a theory would fail of its purpose of reinterpretation.

One ontology is *always* reducible to another when we are given a proxy function f that is one-to-one. The essential reasoning is as follows. Where P is any predicate of the old system, its work can be done in the new system by a new predicate which we interpret as true of just the correlates fx of the old objects x that P was true of. Thus suppose we take fx as the Gödel number of x, and as our old system we take a syntactical system in which one of the predicates is "is a segment of." The corresponding predicate of the new or numerical system, then, would be one which amounts, so far as its extension is concerned, to the words "is the Gödel number of a segment of that whose Gödel number is." The numerical predicate would not be given this devious form, of course, but would be rendered as an appropriate purely arithmetical condition.

Our dependence upon a background theory becomes especially evident when we reduce our universe U to another V by appeal to a proxy function. For it is only in a theory with an inclusive universe, embracing U and V, that we can make sense of the proxy function. The function maps U into V and hence needs all the old objects of U as well as their new proxies in V.

The proxy function need not exist as an object in the universe even of the background theory. It may do its work merely as what I have called a "virtual class,"[13] and Gödel has called a "notion."[14] That is to say, all that is required toward a function is an open sentence with two free variables, provided that it is fulfilled by exactly one value of the first variable for each object of the old universe as value of the second variable. But the point is that it is only in the background theory, with its inclusive universe, that we can hope to write such a sentence and have the right values at our disposal for its variables.

If the new objects happen to be among the old, so that V is a subclass of U, then the old theory with universe U can itself sometimes qualify as the background theory in which to describe its own ontological reduction. But we cannot do better than that; we cannot declare our new ontological economies without having recourse to the uneconomical old ontology.

This sounds, perhaps, like a predicament: as if no ontological economy is justifiable unless it is a false economy and the repudiated objects really exist after all. But actually this is wrong; there is no more cause for worry here than there is in *reductio ad absurdum*, where we assume a falsehood that we are out to disprove. If what we want to show is that the universe U is excessive and that only a part exists, or need exist, then we are quite within our rights to assume all of U for the space of the argument. We show thereby that if all of U were needed then not all of U would be needed; and so our ontological reduction is sealed by *reductio ad absurdum*.

Toward further appreciating the bearing of ontological relativity on programs of ontological reduction, it is worth while to reexamine the philosophical bearing of the Löwenheim-Skolem theorem. I shall use the strong early form of the theorem,[15] which depends on the axiom of choice. It says that if a theory is true and has an indenumerable universe, then all but a denumerable part of that universe is dead wood, in the sense that it can be dropped from the range of the variables without falsifying any sentences.

On the face of it, this theorem declares a reduction of all acceptable theories to denumerable ontologies. Moreover, a denumerable ontology is reducible in turn to an ontology specifically of natural numbers, simply by taking the enumeration as the proxy function, if the enumeration is explicitly at hand. And even if it is not at hand, it exists; thus we can still think of all our objects as natural numbers, and merely reconcile ourselves to not always knowing, numerically, which number an otherwise given object is. May we not thus settle for an all-purpose Pythagorean ontology outright?

Suppose, afterward, someone were to offer us what would formerly have qualified as an ontological reduction—a way of dispensing in future theory with all things of a certain sort S, but still leaving an infinite universe. Now in the new Pythagorean setting his discovery would still retain its essential content, though relinquishing the form of an ontological reduction; it would take the form merely of a move whereby some numerically unspecified numbers were divested of some property of numbers that corresponded to S.

Blanket Pythagoreanism on these terms is unattractive, for it merely offers new and obscurer accounts of old moves and old problems. On this score again, then, the relativistic proposition seems reasonable: that there is no absolute sense in speaking of the ontology of a theory. It very creditably brands this Pythagoreanism itself as meaningless. For there is no absolute sense in saying that all the objects of a theory are numbers, or that they are sets, or bodies, or something else; this makes no sense unless relative to some background theory. The relevant predicates—"number," "set," "body," or whatever—would be distinguished from *one another* in the background theory by the roles they play in the laws of that theory.

Elsewhere [*The Way of Paradox*] I urged in answer to such Pythagoreanism that we have no ontological reduction in an interesting sense unless we can specify a proxy function. Now where does the strong Löwenheim-Skolem theorem leave us in this regard? If the background theory assumes the axiom of choice and even provides a notation for a general selector operator, can we in these terms perhaps specify an actual proxy function embodying the Löwenheim-Skolem argument?

The theorem is that all but a denumerable part of an ontology can be dropped and not be missed. One could imagine that the proof proceeds by partitioning the universe into denumerably many equivalence classes of indiscriminable objects, such that all but one member of each equivalence class can be dropped as superfluous; and one would then guess that where the axiom of choice enters the proof is in picking a survivor from each equivalence class. If this were so, then with help of Hilbert's selector notation we could indeed express a proxy function. But in fact the Löwenheim-Skolem proof has another structure. I see in the proof even of the strong Löwenheim-Skolem theorem no reason to suppose that a proxy function can be formulated anywhere that will map an indenumerable ontology, say the real numbers, into a denumerable one.

On the face of it, of course, such a proxy function is out of the question. It would have to be one-to-one, as we saw, to provide distinct images of distinct real numbers; and a one-to-one mapping of an indenumerable domain into a denumerable one is a contradiction. In particular it is easy to show in the Zermelo-Fraenkel system of set theory that such a function would neither exist nor admit even of formulation as a virtual class in the notation of the system.

The discussion of the ontology of a theory can make variously stringent demands upon the background theory in which the discussion is couched. The stringency of these demands varies with what is being said about the ontology of the object theory. We are now in a position to distinguish three such grades of stringency.

The least stringent demand is made when, with no view to reduction, we merely explain what things a theory is about, or what things its terms denote. This amounts to showing how to translate part or all of the object theory into the background theory. It is a matter really of showing how we *propose*, with some arbitrariness, to relate terms of the object theory to terms of the background theory; for we have the inscrutability of reference to allow for. But there is here no requirement that the background theory have a wider universe or a stronger vocabulary than the object theory. The theories could even be identical; this is the case when some terms are clarified by definition on the basis of other terms of the same language.

A more stringent demand was observed in the case where a proxy function is used to reduce an ontology. In this case the background theory needed the unreduced universe. But we saw, by considerations akin to *reductio ad absurdum*, that there was little here to regret.

The third grade of stringency has emerged now in the kind of ontological reduction hinted at by the Löwenheim-Skolem theorem. If a theory has by its own account an indenumerable universe, then even by taking that whole unreduced theory as background theory we cannot hope to produce a proxy function that would be adequate to reducing the ontology to a denumerable one. To find such a proxy function, even just a virtual one, we would need a background theory essentially stronger than the theory we were trying to reduce. This demand cannot, like the second grade of stringency above, be accepted in the spirit of *reductio ad absurdum*. It is a demand that simply discourages any general argument for Pythagoreanism from the Löwenheim-Skolem theorem.

A place where we see a more trivial side of ontological relativity is in the case of a finite universe of named objects. Here there is no occasion for quantification, except as an inessential abbreviation; for we can expand quantifications into finite conjunctions and alternations. Variables thus disappear, and with them the question of a universe of values of variables. And the very distinction between names and other signs lapses in turn, since the mark of a name is its admissibility in positions of variables. Ontology thus is emphatically meaningless for a finite theory of named objects, considered in and of itself. Yet we are now talking meaningfully of such finite ontologies. We are able to do so precisely because we are talking, however vaguely and implicitly, within a broader containing theory. What the objects of the finite theory are, makes sense only as a statement of the background theory in its own referential idiom. The answer to the question depends on the background theory, the finite foreground theory, and, of course, the particular manner in which we choose to translate or embed the one in the other.

Ontology is internally indifferent also, I think, to any theory that is complete and decidable.

Where we can always settle truth values mechanically, there is no evident internal reason for interest in the theory of quantifiers nor, therefore, in values of variables. These matters take on significance only as we think of the decidable theory as embedded in a richer background theory in which the variables and their values are serious business.

Ontology may also be said to be internally indifferent even to a theory that is not decidable and does not have a finite universe, if it happens still that each of the infinitely numerous objects of the theory has a name. We can no longer expand quantifications into conjunctions and alternations, barring infinitely long expressions. We can, however, revise our semantical account of the truth conditions of quantification, in such a way as to turn our backs on questions of reference. We can explain universal quantifications as true when true under all substitutions; and correspondingly for existential. Such is the course that has been favored by Leśniewski and by Ruth Marcus.[16] Its nonreferential orientation is seen in the fact that it makes no essential use of namehood. That is, additional quantifications could be explained whose variables are placeholders for words of any syntactical category. *Substitutional* quantification, as I call it, thus brings no way of distinguishing names from other vocabulary, nor any way of distinguishing between genuinely referential or value-taking variables and other place-holders. Ontology is thus meaningless for a theory whose only quantification is substitutionally construed; meaningless, that is, insofar as the theory is considered in and of itself. The question of its ontology makes sense only relative to some translation of the theory into a background theory in which we use referential quantification. The answer depends on both theories and, again, on the chosen way of translating the one into the other.

A final touch of relativity can in some cases cap this, when we try to distinguish between substitutional and referential quantification. Suppose again a theory with an infinite lot of names, and suppose that, by Gödel numbering or otherwise, we are treating of the theory's notations and proofs within the terms of the theory. If we succeed in showing that every result of substituting a name for the variable in a certain open sentence is true in the theory, but at the same time we disprove the universal quantification of the sentence,[17] then certainly we have shown that the universe of the the-

ory contained some nameless objects. This is a case where an absolute decision can be reached in favor of referential quantification and against substitutional quantification, without ever retreating to a background theory.

But consider now the opposite situation, where there is no such open sentence. Imagine on the contrary that, whenever an open sentence is such that each result of substituting a name in it can be proved, its universal quantification can be proved in the theory too. Under these circumstances we can construe the universe as devoid of nameless objects and hence reconstrue the quantifications as substitutional, but we need not. We could still construe the universe as containing nameless objects. It could just happen that the nameless ones are *inseparable* from the named ones, in this sense: it could happen that all properties of nameless objects that we can express in the notation of the theory are shared by named objects.

We could construe the universe of the theory as containing, e.g., all real numbers. Some of them are nameless, since the real numbers are indenumerable while the names are denumerable. But it could still happen that the nameless reals are inseparable from the named reals. This would leave us unable within the theory to prove a distinction between referential and substitutional quantification.[18] Every expressible quantification that is true when referentially construed remains true when substitutionally construed, and vice versa.

We might still make the distinction from the vantage point of a background theory. In it we might specify some real number that was nameless in the object theory; for there are always ways of strengthening a theory so as to name more real numbers, though never all. Further, in the background theory, we might construe the universe of the object theory as exhausting the real numbers. In the background theory we could, in this way, clinch the quantifications in the object theory as referential. But this clinching is doubly relative: it is relative to the background theory and to the interpretation or translation imposed on the object theory from within the background theory.

One might hope that this recourse to a background theory could often be avoided, even when the nameless reals are inseparable from the named reals in the object theory. One might hope by indirect means to show within the object theory that there are nameless reals. For we might prove within the object theory that the reals are indenumerable and that the names are denumerable and hence that there is no function whose arguments are names and whose values exhaust the real numbers. Since the relation of real numbers to their names would be such a function if each real number had a name, we would seem to have proved within the object theory itself that there are nameless reals and hence that quantification must be taken referentially.

However, this is wrong; there is a loophole. This reasoning would prove only that a relation of all real numbers to their names cannot exist as an entity in the universe of the theory. This reasoning denies no number a name in the notation of the theory, as long as the name relation does not belong to the universe of the theory. And anyway we should know better than to expect such a relation, for it is what causes Berry's and Richard's and related paradoxes.

Some theories can attest to their own nameless objects and so claim referential quantification on their own; other theories have to look to background theories for this service. We saw how a theory might attest to its own nameless objects, namely, by showing that some open sentence became true under all constant substitutions but false under universal quantification. Perhaps this is the only way a theory can claim referential import for its own quantifications. Perhaps, when the nameless objects happen to be inseparable from the named, the quantification used in a theory cannot meaningfully be declared referential except through the medium of a background theory. Yet referential quantification is the key idiom of ontology. Thus ontology can be multiply relative, multiply meaningless apart from a background theory. Besides being unable to say in absolute terms just what the objects are, we are sometimes unable even to distinguish objectively between referential quantification and a substitutional counterfeit. When we do relativize these matters to a background theory, moreover, the relativization itself has two components: relativity to the choice of background theory and relativity to the choice of how to translate the object theory into the background theory. As for the ontology in turn of the background theory, and even the referentiality of its quantification—these matters can call for a background theory in turn.

There is not always a genuine regress. We saw

that, if we are merely clarifying the range of the variables of a theory or the denotations of its terms, and are taking the referentiality of quantification itself for granted, we can commonly use the object theory itself as background theory. We found that when we undertake an ontological reduction, we must accept at least the unreduced theory in order to cite the proxy function; but this we were able cheerfully to accept in the spirit of *reductio ad absurdum* arguments. And now in the end we have found further that if we care to question quantification itself, and settle whether it imports a universe of discourse or turns merely on substitution at the linguistic level, we in some cases have genuinely to regress to a background language endowed with additional resources. We seem to have to do this unless the nameless objects are separable from the named in the object theory.

Regress in ontology is reminiscent of the now familiar regress in the semantics of truth and kindred notions—satisfaction, naming. We know from Tarski's work how the semantics, in this sense, of a theory regularly demands an in some way more inclusive theory. This similarity should perhaps not surprise us, since both ontology and satisfaction are matters of reference. In their elusiveness, at any rate—in their emptiness now and again except relative to a broader background—both truth and ontology may in a suddenly rather clear and even tolerant sense be said to belong to transcendental metaphysics.[19,20]

Endnotes

[1] J. Dewey, *Experience and Nature* (La Salle, Ill.: Open Court, 1925, 1958), pp. 170–185.

[2] Quine, *Word and Object* (Cambridge, Mass.: MIT Press, 1960), §12.

[3] L. Wittgenstein, *Philosophical Investigations* (New York: Macmillan, 1953), p. 14.

[4] Cf. *Word and Object*, §17.

[5] *Word and Object*, §15.

[6] To keep my account graphic I am counting a certain postpositive particle as a suffix rather than a word.

[7] [Gödel numbering is a way of using numbers as a code for symbols.—Ed.]

[8] See Leon Henkin, ''Completeness in the theory of types,'' *Journal of Symbolic Logic* 15 (1950), 81–91, and references therein.

[9] For more on this theme see my *Set Theory and Its Logic* (Cambridge, Mass.: Harvard, 1963, 1969), §11.

[10] Paul Benacerraf, "What numbers cannot be," *Philosophical Review* 74 (1965), 47–73, develops this point. His conclusions differ in some ways from those I shall come to.

[11] N. L. Wilson, "Substances without substrata," *Review of Metaphysics* 12 (1959), 521–539, p. 532.

[12] Quine, *The Ways of Paradox* (New York: Random House, 1966), pp. 204 ff.; or see *Journal of Philosophy*, 1964, pp. 214 ff.

[13] Quine, *Set Theory and Its Logic*, §2 ff.

[14] Kurt Gödel, *The Consistency of the Continuum Hypothesis* (Princeton, N.J.: The University Press, 1940), p. 11.

[15] Thoralf Skolem, "Logisch-kombinatorische Untersuchungen über die Erfüllbarkeit oder Beweisbarkeit mathematischer Sätze nebst einem Theorem über dichte Mengen," *Skrifter utgit av Videnskapsselskapet i Kristiania*, 1919, 37 pp. Translation in Jean van Heijenoort, ed., *From Frege to Gödel: Source Book in the History of Mathematical Logic* (Cambridge, Mass.: Harvard, 1967), pp. 252–263.

[16] Ruth B.Marcus, "Modalities and intensional languages," *Syntheses* 13 (1961), 303–322. I cannot locate an adequate statement of Stanislaw Leśniewski's philosophy of quantification in his writings; I have it from his conversations. E. C. Luschei, in *The Logical Systems of Leśniewski* (Amsterdam: North-Holland, 1962), pp. 108 ff. confirms my attribution but still cites no passage.

[17] Such is the typical way of a numerically insegregative system, misleadingly called "ω-inconsistent." See my *Selected Logic Papers* (New York: Random House, 1966), pp. 118 ff., or *Journal of Symbolic Logic*, 1953, pp. 122 ff.

[18] This possibility was suggested by Saul Kripke.

[19] In developing these thoughts I have been helped by discussions with Saul Kripke, Thomas Nagel, and especially Burton Dreben.

[20] [Note added later.] Besides such ontological reduction as is provided by proxy functions (cf. pp. 526–528), there is that which consists simply in dropping objects whose absence will not falsify any truths expressible in the notation. Commonly this sort of deflation can be managed by proxy functions, but R. E. Grandy has shown me that sometimes it cannot. Let us by all means recognize it then as a further kind of reduction. In the background language we must, of course, be able to say what class of objects is dropped, just as in other cases we had to be able to specify the proxy function. This requirement seems sufficient still to stem any resurgence of Pythagoreanism on the strength of the Löwenheim-Skolem theorem.

53. *The World Well Lost*

RICHARD RORTY

Scientific realists like Sellars suggest reality may be quite different from how we ordinarily perceive and think it to be. But "ontological relativists" like Quine point out that there may be deep reasons why any theory or language can be reinterpreted in terms of other theories or languages, and this may give the impression that any claim to say what is real is just one of many equally cogent rival interpretations. Should one, then, be skeptical of claims about what the world really is? How should one choose which interpretation or which theory to believe among all the rivals that are equally compatible with the data?

In "The World Well Lost," Richard Rorty, professor of philosophy at the University of Virginia, argues that the skepticism generated by the idea of radically different conceptual frameworks (or languages) is mistaken. Rorty thinks most beliefs must be true and will survive conceptual change. If so, the challenge of radically different conceptual frameworks is overrated. He diagnoses the skeptical threat as stemming, in part, from the idea of the world as a remote Kantian thing-in-itself, which makes different frameworks true or false, and recommends abandoning this notion of the world. As a pragmatist, he is content to continue working with the world as conceived in the bulk of our beliefs.

The notion of alternative conceptual frameworks has been a commonplace of our culture since Hegel. Hegel's historicism gave us a sense of how there might be genuine novelty in the development of thought and of society. Such a historicist conception of thought and morals was, we may see by hindsight, rendered possible by Kant, himself the least historicist of philosophers. For Kant perfected and codified the two distinctions that are necessary to develop the notion of an "alternative conceptual framework"—the distinction between spontaneity and receptivity and the distinction between necessary and contingent truth. Since Kant, we find it almost impossible not to think of the mind as divided into active and passive faculties, the former using concepts to "interpret" what "the world" imposes on the latter. We also find it difficult not to distinguish between those concepts which the mind could hardly get along without and those which it can take or leave alone—and we think of truths about the former concepts as "necessary" in the most proper and paradigmatic sense of the term. But as soon as we have this picture of the mind in focus, it occurs to us, as it did to Hegel, that those all-important a priori concepts, those which determine what our experience or our morals will be, might have been different. We cannot, of course, imagine what an experience or a practice *that* different would be like, but we can abstractly suggest that the men of the Golden Age, or the inhabitants of the Fortunate Isles, or the mad, might shape the intuitions that are our common property in different molds, and might thus be conscious of a different "world."

Various attacks on the contrast between the observed and the theoretical (in, e.g., Kuhn, Feyerabend, and Sellars) have led recently to a new appreciation of Kant's point that to change one's concepts would be to change what one experi-

From Richard Rorty, *Consequences of Pragmatism*. Originally published in the *Journal of Philosophy*, vol. lxix (1972), pp. 649–665. Copyright © 1982 by the University of Minnesota Press. Reprinted by permission of the University of Minnesota.

ences, to change one's "phenomenal world." But this appreciation leads us to question the familiar distinction between spontaneity and receptivity. The possibility of different conceptual schemes highlights the fact that a Kantian unsynthesized intuition can exert no influence on how it is to be synthesized—or, at best, can exert only an influence we shall have to describe in a way as relative to a chosen conceptual scheme as our description of everything else. Insofar as a Kantian intuition is effable, it is just a perceptual judgment, and thus not *merely* "intuitive." Insofar as it is ineffable, it is incapable of having an explanatory function. This dilemma—a parallel to that which Hegelians raised concerning the thing-in-itself—casts doubt on the notion of a faculty of "receptivity." There seems no need to postulate an intermediary between the physical thrust of the stimulus upon the organ and the full-fledged conscious judgment that the properly programmed organism forms in consequence. Thus there is no need to split the organism up into a receptive wax tablet on the one hand and an "active" interpreter of what nature has there imprinted on the other. So the Kantian point that different a priori concepts would, if there could be such things, give a different phenomenal world gives place either to the straightforward but paradoxical claim that different concepts give us different worlds, or to dropping the notion of "conceptual framework" altogether. 'Phenomenal' can no longer be given a sense, once Kantian "intuitions" drop out. For the suggestion that our concepts shape neutral material no longer makes sense once there is nothing to serve as this material. The physical stimuli themselves are not a useful substitute, for the contrast between the "posits" which the inventive mind constructs to predict and control stimuli, and the stimuli themselves, can be no more than a contrast between the effable world and its ineffable cause.[1]

The notion of *alternative* conceptual frameworks thus contains the seeds of doubt about the root notion of "conceptual framework," and so of its own destruction. For once the faculty of receptivity and, more generally, the notion of neutral material becomes dubious, doubt spreads easily to the notion of conceptual thought as "shaping" and thus to the notion of the World-Spirit moving from one set of a priori concepts to the next.

But the doubts about the Hegelian picture produced by an attack on the given/interpretation distinction are vague and diffuse by comparison with those which result from attacking the necessary/contingent distinction. Quine's suggestion that the difference between a priori and empirical truth is merely that between the relatively difficult to give up and the relatively easy brings in its train the notion that there is no clear distinction to be drawn between questions of meaning and questions of fact. This, in turn, leaves us (as Quine has pointed out in criticizing Carnap) with no distinction between questions about alternative "theories" and questions about alternative "frameworks."[2] The philosophical notion of "meaning," against which Quine is protesting is, as he says, the latest version of the "idea idea"—a philosophical tradition one of whose incarnations was the Kantian notion of "concept." The notion of a choice among "meaning postulates" is the latest version of the notion of a choice among alternative conceptual schemes. Once the necessary is identified with the analytic and the analytic is explicated in terms of meaning, an attack on the notion of what Harman has called the "philosophical" sense of 'meaning' becomes an attack on the notion of "conceptual framework" in any sense that assumes a distinction of kind between this notion and that of "empirical theory."[3]

So far we have seen how criticisms of givenness and of analyticity both serve to dismantle the Kantian notion of "conceptual framework"—the notion of "concepts necessary for the constitution of experience, as opposed to concepts whose application is necessary to control or predict experience." I have been arguing that without the notions of "the given" and of "the a priori" there can be no notion of "the constitution of experience." Thus there can be no notion of alternative experiences, or alternative worlds, to be constituted by the adoption of new a priori concepts. But there is a simpler and more direct objection to the notion of "alternative conceptual framework," to which I now wish to turn. This objection has recently been put forward, in connection with Quine's thesis of indeterminacy, by Davidson and Stroud.[4] The argument is verificationist, and turns on the unrecognizability of persons using a conceptual framework different from our own (or, to put it another way, the unrecognizability as a *language* of anything that is not translatable into English). The connection between Quine's attack on "conventionalist" notions of meaning and this verificationist argument is supposed to be as follows: if one thinks of "meaning" in terms of the discovery of the speech dispositions of foreigners rather than in terms of mental essences (ideas, concepts, chunks of the crystalline structure of thought), then one will not be able to draw a clear distinction between the foreigner's using words different in meaning from any words in our language and the foreigner's having many false beliefs. We can and must play off awkward translations against ascriptions of quaint beliefs, and vice versa, but we will never reach the limiting case of a foreigner all or most of whose beliefs must be viewed as false according to a translating scheme that pairs off all or most of his terms as identical in meaning with some terms of English. We will not reach this case (so the Davidsonian argument goes) because any such translation scheme would merely show that we had not succeeded in finding a translation at all.

But (to extend Davidson's argument a bit) if we can never find a translation, why should we think that we are faced with language users at all? It is, of course, possible to imagine humanoid organisms making sounds of great variety at one another in very various circumstances with what appear to be various effects upon the interlocutors' behavior. But suppose that repeated attempts systematically to correlate these sounds with the organisms' environment and behavior fail. What should we say? One suggestion might be that the analytic hypotheses we are using in our tentative translation schemes use concepts that we do not share with the natives—because the natives "carve up the world" differently, or have different "quality spaces" or something of the sort. But could there be a way of deciding between this suggestion and the possibility that the organisms' sounds are *just* sounds? Once we imagine different ways of carving up the world, nothing could stop us from attributing "untranslatable languages" to *anything* that emits a variety of signals. But, so this verificationist argument concludes, this degree of openendedness shows us that the purported notion of an untranslatable language is as fanciful as that of an invisible color.

It is important to note that Quinean arguments against analyticity and for the indeterminacy of translation are not necessary for this argument. The argument stands on its own feet—Quine's only contribution to it being to disparage the possibility that 'meaning' can mean something more than what is contextually defined in the process of predicting the foreigner's behavior. To adopt this view of meaning is all that is required to suggest that the notion of "people who speak our language but believe nothing that we believe" is incoherent.[5] To *show* that it is incoherent, however—to complete the argument—one would have to show in detail that no amount of nonlinguistic behavior by the foreigner could be sufficient to underwrite a translation that made all or most of his beliefs false.[6] For it might be the case, for example, that the way in which the foreigner dealt with trees while making certain sounds made it clear that we had to translate some of his utterances as "These are not trees," and so on for everything else with which he had dealings. Some of his utterances might be translated as: "I am not a person," "These are not words," "One should never use *modus ponens* if one wishes valid arguments," "Even if I were thinking, which I am not, that would not show that I exist." We might ratify these translations by showing that his nonlinguistic ways of handling himself and others showed that he actually did hold such paradoxical beliefs. The only way to show that this suggestion cannot work, would be actually to tell the whole story about this hypothetical foreigner. It might be that a story could be told to show the coherence of these false beliefs with each other and with his actions, or it might not. To show that Davidson and Stroud were right would be to show that, indeed, no such story was tellable.

There is, I think, no briefer way to decide on the soundness of this a priori argument against the possibility of alternative conceptual frameworks than to run over such possible stories. But this inconclusiveness is a feature this argument has in common with all interesting verificationist antiskeptical arguments. It conforms to the following pattern: (1) the skeptic suggests that our own beliefs (about, e.g., other minds, tables and chairs, or how to translate French) have viable alternatives which unfortunately can never be known to hold but which justify the suspension of judgment; (2) the anti-skeptic replies that the very meaning of the terms used shows that the alternatives suggested are not merely dubious but in principle unverifiable, and thus not reasonable alternatives at all; (3) the skeptic rejoins that verificationism confuses the *ordo essendi* with the *ordo cognoscendi* and that it may well be that some alternative is true even though we shall never know that it is; (4) the anti-skeptic replies that the matter is not worth debating until the skeptic spells out the suggested alternative in full detail, and insinuates that this cannot be done; (5) the controversy degenerates into a dispute about assuming the burden of proof, with the skeptic claiming that it is not up to him to build up a coherent story around his suggested alternative but rather up to the anti-skeptic to show a priori that this cannot be done.

In the case at hand, the skeptic is the fan of "alternative conceptual frameworks," practicing his skepticism on a global scale by insinuating that our entire belief structure might dissolve, leaving not a wrack behind, to be replaced by a complete but utterly dissimilar alternative. The Davidsonian anti-skeptic is in the position of asking how one could come to call any pattern of behavior evidence for such an alternative. The skeptic replies that perhaps we could *never* come to do so, but this merely shows how complete our egocentric predicament is. And so it goes.[7]

In this case, however (unlike the case of limited skepticism about whether, e.g., 'pain' or 'red' means to me what it does to you) the skeptic's global approach gives him a significant dialectical advantage. For he can here sketch what might bring about the actualization of his suggested alternative without being caught up in disagreement about how to interpret concrete experimental results. He can simply refer us to ordinary scientific and cultural progress extrapolated just beyond the range of science fiction. Consider, he will say, the following view of man's history and prospects. Our views about matter and motion, the good life for man, and much else have changed in subtle and complicated ways since the days of the Greeks. Many of the planks in Neurath's boat have been torn up and relaid differently. But since (1) we can describe why it was "rational" for each such change to have occurred, and (2) *many* more of our beliefs are the same as Greek beliefs than are different (e.g., our belief that barley is better than nettles and freedom than slavery, that red is a color, and that lightning often precedes thunder), we should not yet wish to talk about "an alternative conceptual framework." And yet we must admit that even the relatively slight refurbishings of the boat which have occupied the past two thousand years are enough to give us considerable difficulty in knowing just *how* to translate some Greek sentences, and just *how* to explain the "rationality" of the changes that have intervened. Again, the various shifts that have taken place in our understanding of the subject matter of the beliefs we purportedly "share" with the Greeks (resulting from, e.g., the development of new strains of nettles, new forms of slav-

ery, new ways of producing color perceptions, and new explanations of the sound of the thunder and the look of the lightning) make us a little dubious about the claim to shared belief. They create the feeling that here too we may be imposing on history rather than describing it. Let us now extrapolate from ourselves to the Galactic civilization of the future, which we may assume to have moved and reshaped 10^{50} planks in the boat we are in, whereas since Aristotle we have managed to shift only about 10^{20}. Here the suggestion that we interpret these changes as a sequence of rational changes in views about a common matter seems a bit forced, and the fear that even the most empathic Galactic historians of science "won't really understand us properly" quite appropriate. So, our skeptic concludes, the Davidson-Stroud point that to describe in detail the Galactic civilization's beliefs is automatically to make them merely alternative theories within a common framework is not enough. Granting this point, we can still see that it is rational to expect that the incommunicably and unintelligibly novel will occur, even though, *ex hypothesi*, we can neither write nor read a science-fiction story that describes Galactic civilization. Here, then, we have a case in which there really is a difference between the *ordo cognoscendi* and the *ordo essendi*, and no verificationist argument can apply.

To intensify the antinomy we confront here, let us agree for the sake of argument that it is a necessary condition for an entity to be a person that it have or once have had the potentiality for articulating beliefs and desires comparable in quantity and complexity to our own. The qualifications are required if we are to include infants and the insane while excluding dogs and the simpler sort of robots. But the same qualifications will, of course, give trouble when we come to cases where it is not clear whether we are educating a person by developing his latent potentialities (as by teaching a child a language) or transforming a thing into a person (as by clamping some additional memory units onto the robot). Bating this difficulty for the moment, however, let us simply note that this formulation has the consequence that ascribing personhood, ascribing a language, and ascribing beliefs and desires go hand in hand. So, if Davidson is right, ascribing personhood and ascribing mostly the *right* beliefs and mostly the *appropriate* desires go hand in hand. This means that we shall never be able to have evidence that there exist persons who speak languages in principle untranslatable into

English or hold beliefs all or most of which are incompatible with our own.

Despite this, however, we can extrapolate to a story about how just such persons might come into existence. So it seems that the world may come to be full of persons whom we could never conceivably recognize as such. A Galactic time-traveler come among us, we now realize, would eventually be forced to abandon his original presumption that we were persons when he failed to correlate our utterances with our environment in any way that enabled him to construct an English-Galactic lexicon. Our initial assumption that the Galactic emissary was a person would be frustrated by the same sort of discovery. How sad that two cultures who have so much to offer each other should fail to recognize each other's existence! What pathos in the thought that we, time-traveling among our Neanderthal ancestors, might stand to them as the Galactic stands to us! But the situation is even worse than that, for reasons I hinted at earlier. We can now see that, for all we know, our *contemporary* world is filled with unrecognizable persons. Why should we ignore the possibility that the trees and the bats and the butterflies and the stars all have their various untranslatable languages in which they are busily expressing their beliefs and desires to one another? Since their organs suit them to receive such different stimuli and to respond in such different ways, it is hardly surprising that the syntax and the primitive predicates of their languages bear no relation to our own.

The inclusion of this last possibility may suggest that something has gone wrong. Perhaps we should not have been so ready to admit the possibility of extrapolation. Perhaps we were too hasty in thinking that attributions of personhood and of articulate belief went hand in hand—for surely we know in advance that butterflies are not persons and therefore know in advance that they will have no beliefs to express. For myself, however, I see nothing wrong with the proposed extrapolation, and I do not see what 'known in advance not to be a person' could mean when applied to the butterfly save that the butterfly doesn't seem human. But there is no particular reason to think that our remote ancestors or descendants would seem human right off the bat either. Let the notion of a person be as complex and multiply criterioned as you please, still I do not think that it will come unstuck from that of a complex interlocked set of beliefs and desires, nor that the latter notion can be separated

from that of the potentiality for translatable speech. So I think that to rule the butterflies out is to rule out the Galactics and the Neanderthals, and that to allow extrapolation to the latter is to allow for the possibility that the very same beliefs and desires which our Galactic descendants will hold are being held even now by the butterflies. We can dig in our heels and say that terms like 'person', 'belief', 'desire', and 'language' are ultimately as token-reflexive as 'here' and 'now' or 'morally right', so that in each case essential reference is made to where *we* are. But that will be the *only* way of ruling out the Galactic, and thus the *only* way of ruling out the butterfly.

If this seems puzzling, I think it will seem less so if we consider some parallels. Suppose we say that there is no poetry among the Patagonians, no astronomy among the aborigines, and no morality among the inhabitants of the planet Mongo. And suppose a native of each locale, protesting against our parochial view, explains that what they have is a *different* sort of poetry, astronomy, or morals, as the case may be. For the Patagonian, neither Homer nor Shelley nor Mallarmé nor Dryden look in the least like poets. He admits, however, that Milton and Swinburne are both faintly reminiscent, in the same only vaguely describable respect, of the paradigms of Patagonian poesy. Those paradigms strike him as clearly fulfilling some of the roles in his culture which our poets fulfill in ours, though not all. The aborigine knows nothing of the equinoxes and the solstices, but he does distinguish planets from stars. However, he uses the same term to refer to planets, meteors, comets, and the sun. The stories he tells about the movements of these latter bodies are bound up with a complicated set of stories about divine providence and cure of diseases, whereas the stories told about the stars have to do exclusively with sex. The inhabitants of the planet Mongo appear shocked when people tell the truth to social equals, and surprised and amused when people refrain from torturing helpless wanderers. They seem to have no taboos at all about sex, but a great many about food. Their social organizations seem held together half by a sort of lottery, and half by brute force. The inhabitants of Mongo, however, profess to be revolted by the Earthlings' failure to grasp the moral point of view, and by our apparent confusion of morality with etiquette and with expedients for ensuring social order.

In the three cases just cited the question, Is it a

different *sort* of poetry (or astronomy, or morality), or do they simply have *none*? is obviously not the sort of question it is very important to answer. I suggest that the question, Are the Galactics, or the butterflies, different sorts of persons than ourselves or not persons at all? is also not very important. In the three cases mentioned, one can extend the argument indefinitely by pressing for further details. In the global case, where *ex hypothesi* no translation scheme will work, we cannot. But in the global case (having beliefs *tout court*), as in the particular cases of having beliefs about astronomy or about right and wrong, what is in question is just the best way of predicting, controlling, and generally coping with the entities in question. In the course of figuring this out, we encounter some of the same hard questions I referred to above—the questions that arise when coping with such border-line cases as fetuses, prelinguistic infants, computers, and the insane—Do they have civil rights? Must we try to justify ourselves to them? Are they thinking or acting on instinct? Are they holding beliefs or merely responding to stimuli? Is that a word to which they assign a sense, or are they just sounding off on cue? I doubt that many philosophers believe any longer than procedures for answering such questions are built into "our language" waiting to be discovered by "conceptual analysis." But if we do not believe this, perhaps we can be content to say, in the global case, that the question, Might there be alternative conceptual frameworks to our own, held by persons whom we could never recognize as persons? is the same case. I doubt that we can ever adumbrate general ways of answering questions like, Is it a conceptual framework very different from our own, or is it a mistake to think of it as a language at all? Is it a person with utterly different organs, responses, and beliefs, with whom communication is thus forever impossible, or rather just a complexly behaving thing?

This "don't-care" conclusion is all I have to offer concerning the antinomy created by the Davidson-Stroud argument on the one hand and the skeptic's extrapolation on the other. But this should not be thought of as denigrating the importance of what Davidson and Stroud are saying. On the contrary, I think that, having seen through this antinomy and having noticed the relevance of the original argument to our application of the notion of "person," we are now in a better position to see the importance that it has. This importance can be

brought out by (a) looking at the standard objection to the coherence theory of truth ("it cuts truth off from the world") and (b) recurring to our previous discussion of the Kantian roots of the notion of "conceptual framework."

Consider first the traditional objection to coherence theories of truth which says that, although our only *test* of truth must be the coherence of our beliefs with one another, still the *nature* of truth must be "correspondence to reality." It is thought a sufficient argument for this view that Truth is One, whereas alternative equally coherent sets of beliefs are Many.[8] In reply to this argument, defenders of coherence and pragmatic theories of truth have argued that our so-called "intuition" that Truth is One is simply the expectation that, if all perceptual reports were in, there would be one optimal way of selecting among them and all other possible statements so as to have one ideally proportioned system of true beliefs. To this reply, the standard rebuttal is that there would clearly be many such possible systems, among which we could choose only on aesthetic grounds. A further, and more deeply felt, rebuttal is that it is the *world* that determines the truth. The accident of which glimpses of the world our sense organs have vouchsafed us, and the further accidents of the predicates we have entrenched or the theories whose proportions please us, may determine what we have a right to believe. But how could they determine the *truth*?[9]

Now the Davidson-Stroud argument supplies a simple, if temporizing, answer to this standard objection to the coherence theory. Since most of our beliefs (though not any particular one) simply *must* be true—for what could count as evidence that the vast majority of them were not?—the specter of alternative conceptual frameworks shrinks to the possibility that there might be a number of equally good ways to modify slightly our present set of beliefs in the interest of greater predictive power, charm, or what have you. The Davidson-Stroud point makes us remember, among other things, what a very small proportion of our beliefs are changed when our paradigms of physics, or poetry, or morals, change—and makes us realize how few of them *could* change. It makes us realize that the number of beliefs that changed among the educated classes of Europe between the thirteenth and the nineteenth centuries is ridiculously small compared to the number that survived intact. So this argument permits us to say: it is just not the case that there are "alternative" coherent global sets of beliefs. It is perfectly true that there will always be areas of inquiry in which alternative incompatible sets of beliefs are "tied." But the fact that we shall *always* be holding mostly true beliefs and, thus, presumably be "in touch with the world" the vast majority of the time makes this point seem philosophically innocuous. In particular, the claim that, since Truth is One and, therefore, is "correspondence," we must resurrect a foundationalist epistemology to explain "how knowledge is possible" becomes otiose.[10] We shall automatically be "in touch with the world" (most of the time) whether or not we have any incorrigible, or basic, or otherwise privileged or foundational statements to make.

But this way of dealing with the claim that "it is the *world* that determines what is true" may easily seem a fraud. For, as I have been using it, the Davidson-Stroud view seems to perform the conjuring trick of substituting the notion of "the unquestioned vast majority of our beliefs" for the notion of "the world." It reminds us of such coherence theorists as Royce, who claim that our notion of "the world" is just the notion of the ideally coherent contents of an ideally large mind, or of the pragmatists' notion of "funded experience"—those beliefs which are not at the moment being challenged, because they present no problems and no one has bothered to think of alternatives to them. In all these cases—Davidson and Stroud, Royce, Dewey—it may well seem that the issue about truth is just being ducked. For our notion of the world—it will be said—is not a notion of unquestioned beliefs, or unquestionable beliefs, or ideally coherent beliefs, but rather of a hard, unyielding, rigid *être-en-soi* which stands aloof, sublimely indifferent to the attentions we lavish upon it. The true realistic believer will view idealisms and pragmatisms with the same suspicion with which the true believer in the God of our Fathers will view, for example, Tillich's talk of an "object of ultimate concern."[11]

Now, to put my cards on the table, I think that the realistic true believer's notion of the world is an obsession rather than an intuition. I also think that Dewey was right in thinking that the only intuition we have of the world as determining truth is just the intuition that we must make our new beliefs conform to a vast body of platitudes, unquestioned perceptual reports, and the like. So I am happy to interpret the upshot of the Davidson-Stroud argument in a Deweyan way.

But I have no arguments against the true believer's description of our so-called "intuitions." All that can be done with the claim that "only the *world* determines truth" is to point out the equivocation in the realists' own use of 'world'. In the sense in which "the world" is just whatever that vast majority of our beliefs not currently in question are currently thought to be about, there is of course no argument.[12] If one accepts the Davidson-Stroud position, then "the world" will just be the stars, the people, the tables, and the grass—all those things which nobody except the occasional "scientific realist" philosopher thinks might not exist. The fact that the vast majority of our beliefs must be true will, on this view, guarantee the existence of the vast majority of the things we now think we are talking about. So in one sense of 'world'—the sense in which (except for a few fringe cases like gods, neutrinos, and natural rights) we now know perfectly well what the world is like and could not possibly be wrong about it—there is no argument about the point that it is the world that determines truth. All that "determination" comes to is that our belief that snow is white is true because snow is white, that our beliefs about the stars are true because of the way the stars are laid out, and so on.

But this trivial sense in which "truth" is "correspondence to reality" and "depends upon a reality independent of our knowledge" is, of course, not enough for the realist.[13] What he wants is precisely what the Davidson-Stroud argument prevents him from having—the notion of a world *so* "independent of our knowledge" that it might, for all we know, prove to contain none of the things we have always thought we were talking about. He wants to go from, say, "we might be wrong about what the stars are" to "none of the things we talk about might be anything like what we think they are." Given this projection from, as Kant would say, the "conditioned" to the "unconditioned," it is no wonder that antinomies are easily generated.

The notion of "the world" as used in a phrase like 'different conceptual schemes carve up the world differently' must be the notion of something *completely* unspecified and unspecifiable—the thing-in-itself, in fact. As soon as we start thinking of "the world" as atoms and the void, or sense data and awareness of them, or "stimuli" of a certain sort brought to bear upon organs of a certain sort, we have changed the name of the game. For we are now well within some particular theory about how the world is. But for purposes of developing a controversial and nontrivial doctrine of truth as correspondence, only an utterly vague characterization in some such terms as 'cause of the impacts upon our receptivity and goal of our faculty of spontaneity' will do. "Truth" in the sense of "truth taken apart from any theory" and "world" taken as "what determines such truth" are notions that were (like the terms 'subject' and 'object', 'given' and 'consciousness') made for each other. Neither can survive apart from the other.

To sum up this point, I want to claim that "the world" is either the purely vacuous notion of the ineffable cause of sense and goal of intellect, or else a name for the objects that inquiry at the moment is leaving alone: those planks in the boat which are at the moment not being moved about. It seems to me that epistemology since Kant has shuttled back and forth between these two meanings of the term 'world', just as moral philosophy since Plato has shuttled back and forth between 'the Good" as a name for an ineffable touchstone of inquiry which might lead to the rejection of *all* our present moral views, and as a name for the ideally coherent synthesis of as many of those views as possible. This equivocation seems to me essential to the position of those philosophers who see "realism" or "the correspondence theory of truth" as controversial or exciting theses.

To remove altogether the "realistic" temptation to use the word 'world' in the former vacuous sense, we should need to eschew once and for all a whole galaxy of philosophical notions that have encouraged this use—in particular, the Kantian distinctions I discussed at the outset. For suppose we have a simple theory of the eye of the mind either getting, or failing to get, a clear view of the natures of kinds of things—the sort of theory we get, say, in parts of Aristotle's *Posterior Analytics*. Then the notion of alternative sets of concepts will make no clear sense. *Noûs* cannot err. It is only when we have some form of the notion that the mind is split between "simple ideas" or "passively received intuitions" on the one hand and a range of complex ideas (some signifying real, and some only nominal, essences) on the other, that *either* the coherence theory of truth *or* the standard objections to it can begin to look plausible. Only then is the notion plausible that inquiry consists in getting our "representations" into shape, rather than simply describing the world. If we no longer have a

view about knowledge as the result of manipulating *Vorstellungen*, then I think we can return to the simple Aristotelian notion of truth as correspondence with reality with a clear conscience—for it will now appear as the uncontroversial triviality that it is.

To develop this claim about the way in which Kantian epistemology is linked with the notion of a nontrivial correspondence theory of truth and thus with the "realist's" notion of "the world" would require another paper, and I shall not try to press it further. Instead I should like to conclude by recalling some of the historical allusions I have made along the way, in order (as Sellars says) to place my conclusions in philosophical space. I said at the outset that the notion of "conceptual framework" and, thus, that of "alternative conceptual framework" depend upon presupposing some standard Kantian distinctions. These distinctions have been the common target of Wittgenstein, Quine, Dewey, and Sellars. I can now express the same point by saying that the notion of "the world" that is correlative with the notion of "conceptual framework" is simply the Kantian notion of a thing-in-itself, and that Dewey's dissolution of the Kantian distinctions between receptivity and spontaneity and between necessity and contingency thus leads naturally to the dissolution of the true realistic believer's notion of "the world." If you start out with Kant's epistemology, in short, you will wind up with Kant's transcendental metaphysics. Hegel, as I suggested earlier, kept the epistemology, but tried to drop the thing-in-itself, thus making himself, and idealism generally, a patsy for realistic reaction. But Hegel's historical sense—the sense that nothing, including an a priori concept, is immune from cultural development—provided the key to Dewey's attack on the epistemology that Hegel shared with Kant. This attack was blunted by Dewey's use of the term 'experience' as an incantatory device for blurring every possible distinction, and so it was not until more sharply focused criticisms were formulated by Wittgenstein, Quine, and Sellars that the force of Dewey's point about "funded experience" as the "cash-value" of the notion of "the world" could be seen. But now that these criticisms have taken hold, the time may have come to try to recapture Dewey's "naturalized" version of Hegelian historicism. In this historicist vision, the arts, the sciences, the sense of right and wrong, and the institutions of society are not attempts to embody or formulate truth or goodness or beauty. They are attempts to solve problems—to modify our beliefs and desires and activities in ways that will bring us greater happiness than we have now. I want to suggest that this shift in perspective is the natural consequence of dropping the receptivity/spontaneity and intuition/concept distinctions, and more generally of dropping the notion of "representation" and the view of man that Dewey has called "the spectator theory" and Heidegger, the "identification of *physis* and *idea*." Because the idealists kept this general picture and occupied themselves with redefining the "object of knowledge," they gave idealism and the "coherence theory" a bad name—and realism and the "correspondence theory" a good one. But if we can come to see both the coherence and correspondence theories as noncompeting trivialities, then we may finally move beyond realism and idealism. We may reach a point at which, in Wittgenstein's words, we are capable of stopping doing philosophy when we want to.

Endnotes

[1] T. S. Kuhn, "Reflections on My Critics," in I. Lakatos and A. Musgrave, eds., *Criticism and the Growth of Knowledge* (New York: Cambridge, 1970), p. 276, says that "the stimuli to which the participants in a communication breakdown respond are, under pain of solipsism, the same" and then continues by saying that their "programming" must be so also, since men "share a history . . . a language, an everyday world, and most of a scientific one." On the view I should like to support, the *whole* anti-solipsist burden is borne by the "programming," and the "stimuli" (like the noumenal unsynthesized intuitions) drop out. If a stimulus is thought of as somehow "neutral" in respect to different conceptual schemes, it can be so only, I would argue, by becoming "a wheel that can be turned though nothing else moves with it." (Cf. Ludwig Wittgenstein, *Philosophical Investigations* [New York: Macmillan, 1958], I, 271.)

[2] See W. V. Quine, "On Carnap's View on Ontology," in *The Ways of Paradox* (New York: Random House, 1966), pp. 126–134.

[3] See Gilbert Harman, "Quine on Meaning and Existence, I," *Review of Metaphysics*, XXI, 1 (September 1967): 124–151, p. 142.

[4] I first became aware of this argument, and of the importance of the issues I am here discussing, on reading the sixth of the Locke Lectures which Davidson gave at Oxford in 1970. These lectures are at present still unpublished, and I am most grateful to Davidson for permission to see the manuscript, and also the manuscript of his 1971 University of London Lectures on "Conceptual Relativism"—the more especially as I want to turn Davidson's argument to purposes for which he would have slim sympathy. After reading Davidson's unpublished material, I read Barry Stroud's presentation of a partially similar argument in "Conventionalism and the Indeterminacy of Translation," in *Words and Objections: Essays on the Work of W. V. Quine*, ed. Davidson and J. Hintikka (Doredrecht: Reidel, 1969), esp. pp. 89–96. Stroud and Davidson concur in rejecting the notion of "alternative conceptual frameworks," but Davidson goes on to draw explicitly the radical conclusion that "most of our beliefs must be true." It is this latter conclusion on which I shall be focusing in this paper. (Addendum, 1981: Although Davidson has not yet published his Locke Lectures in full, the material most relevant to this paper has appeared in his "On the Very Idea of a Conceptual Scheme," *Proceedings of the American Philocophical Association*, 17 (1973–74), pp. 5–20.)

[5] I have argued elsewhere ("Indeterminancy of Translation and of Truth," *Synthese*, 23 [1972]: 443–462) that Quine's doctrine that there is no "matter of fact" for translations to be right or wrong about, is philosophical overkill, and that the "idea idea" is adequately discredited by attacks on the Kantian distinctions discussed above.

[6] The importance of this point was shown me by Michael Friedman. I am grateful also to Michael Williams for ctiricisms of my general line of argument.

[7] I have tried to develop this view of the course of the argument between verificationists and skeptics in "Verificationism and Transcendental Argument, *Noûs*, V, 1 (February 1971); 3–14; and in "Criteria and Necessity," *Noûs*, VIII, 4 (November 1973): 313–329.

[8] For a formulation of this objection, see John L. Pollock, "Perceptual Knowledge," *Philosophical Review*, LXXX, 3 (July 1971): 290–292.

[9] This sort of question is at the root of the attempt to distinguish between a "theory of truth" and a "theory of evidence" in reply to such truth-as-assertibility theorists as Sellars—see Harman's criticism of Sellars on this point in "Sellars' Semantics," *Philosophical Review*, LXXIX, 3 (July 1970): 404–419, pp. 409ff., 417ff.

[10] See Pollock, op. cit., for a defense of the claim that, once we reject a coherence theory of justification, such an explanation in foundationalist terms becomes necessary.

[11] For examples of the programmatic passion that realism can inspire, see the "Platform of the Association for Realistic Philosophy" in *The Return to Reason*, ed.

John Wild (Chicago: Henry Regnery, 1953); and the "Program and First Platform of Six Realists," in Edwin B. Holt et al., *The New Realism* (New York: Macmillan, 1912), pp. 471ff.

[12] I say "are currently thought to be about" rather than "are about" in order to skirt an issue that might be raised by proponents of a "causal theory of reference." Such a theory might suggest that we are in fact now talking about (referring to) what the Galactics will be referring to, but that the Galactics might know what this was and we might not. (The relevance of such theories of reference was pointed out to me by Michael Friedman and by Fred Dretske.) My own view, which I cannot develop here, is that an attempt to clarify epistemological questions by reference to "reference" will always be explaining the obscure by the more obscure—explicating notions ("knowledge," "truth") which have some basis in common speech in terms of a contrived and perpetually controversial philosophical notion.

[13] I do not wish to be taken as suggesting the triviality of Tarski's semantic theory, which seems to me not a theory relevant to epistemology (except perhaps, as Davidson has suggested, to the epistemology of language learning). I should regard Tarski as founding a new subject, not as solving an old problem. I think that Davidson is right in saying that, in the sense in which Tarski's theory is a correspondence theory, "it may be the case that no battle is won, or even joined between correspondence theories and others" ("True to the Facts," *Journal of Philosophy*, LXVI, 21 [Nov. 6, 1969]: 748–764, p. 761). The philosophically controversial "correspondence theory of truth" to which coherence and pragmatic theories were supposed alternatives is not the theory Strawson (quoted by Davidson, op. cit., p. 763) identifies as "to say that a statement is true is to say that a certain speech-episode is related in a certain conventional way to something in the world exclusive of itself." For this latter view would, as far as it goes, be perfectly acceptable to, e.g., Blanshard or Dewey.

Further Reading

Aune, B., *Metaphysics: The Elements* (Minneapolis: University of Minnesota Press, 1985).

Ayer, A. J., *Philosophy in the Twentieth Century* (New York: Vintage, 1984).

Benardete, José, *Metaphysics: The Logical Approach* (New York: Oxford University Press, 1989).

Bergmann, G., *Logic and Reality* (Madison: University of Wisconsin Press, 1964).

Campbell, K., *Metaphysics: An Introduction* (Belmont, Calif.: Dickenson, 1976).

Carr, B., *Metaphysics: An Introduction* (Atlantic Highlands, N.J.: Humanities Press, 1988).

Churchland, P., and Hooker, C., eds., *Images of Science* (Chicago: University of Chicago Press, 1985).

Coburn, R., *The Strangeness of the Ordinary: Problems and Issues in Contemporary Metaphysics* (Savage, Maryland: Barnes and Noble Imports, 1990).

Cornman, J., *Metaphysics, Reference, and Language* (New Haven, Conn.: Yale University Press, 1966).

Davidson, D., and Hintikka, J., eds., *Words and Objections: Essays on the Work of W. V. Quine* (Dordrecht: Reidel, 1969).

Delaney, C., Loux, M., Gutting, G., and Solomon, W., *The Synoptic Vision: Essays in the Philosophy of Wilfrid Sellars* (Notre Dame, Ind.: University of Notre Dame Press, 1977).

Evans, G., and McDowell, J., eds., *Truth and Meaning: Essays in Semantics* (Oxford: Oxford University Press, 1976).

Feigl, H., Sellars, W., and Lehrer, K., eds., *New Readings in Philosophical Analysis* (New York: Appleton-Century-Crofts, 1972).

Goodman, N., *Languages of Art* (New York: Bobbs-Merrill, 1968).

Goodman, N., *Ways of Wordmaking* (Indianapolis: Hackett, 1978).

Hacking, I., *Why Does Language Matter to Philosophy?* (Cambridge: Cambridge University Press, 1975).

Hahn, L., and Schilpp, P., eds., *The Philosophy of W. V. Quine*, Vol. XVIII, The Library of Living Philosophers (La Salle, Ill.: Open Court, 1986).

Hamlyn, D., *Metaphysics* (Cambridge: Cambridge University Press, 1984).

Heidegger, M., *Introduction to Metaphysics* (Garden City, N.Y.: Doubleday & Co., 1961).

Heidegger, M., *Being and Time*. (J. Macquarrie and E. Robinson, trans.) (New York: Harper and Row, 1962).

Korner, S., *Metaphysics: Its Structure and Function* (New York: Cambridge University Press, 1984).

Lewis, D., *Philosophical Papers*, Vol. I & II (New York: Oxford University Press, 1983).

Passmore, J., *A Hundred Years of Philosophy* (New York: Basic Books, 1966).

Passmore, J., *Recent Philosophers* (La Salle, Ill.: Open Court, 1985).

Putnam, H., *The Many Faces of Realism* (La Salle, Ill.: Open Court, 1987).

Putnam, H., *Realism and Reason, Philosophical Papers*, Vol. 3 (New York: Cambridge University Press, 1983).

Quine, W., *From a Logical Point of View* (Cambridge, Mass.: Harvard University Press, 1953).

Quine, W., *Ontological Relativity and Other Essays* (New York: Columbia University Press, 1969).

Quine, W., *Roots of Reference* (La Salle, Ill.: Open Court, 1973).

Quine, W., *Word and Object* (Cambridge: Massachusetts Institute of Technology Press, 1960).

Romanos, G., *Quine and Analytic Philosophy* (Cambridge: Massachusetts Institute of Technology Press, 1983).

Rorty, R., *Consequences of Pragmatism* (Minneapolis: University of Minnesota Press, 1982).

Rorty, R., *Contingency, Irony, and Solidarity* (New York: Cambridge University Press, 1989).

Rorty, R., ed., *The Linguistic Turn* (Chicago: University of Chicago Press, 1967).

Rorty, R., *Philosophy and the Mirror of Nature* (Princeton: Princeton University Press, 1979).

Rosenberg, J., *Linguistic Representation* (Dordrecht: Reidel, 1974).

Russell, B., *Problems of Philosophy* (New York: Oxford University Press, 1959).

Schilpp, P. A., ed., *The Philosophy of Rudolf Carnap*, Vol. XI, The Library of Living Philosophers, (La Salle, Ill.: Open Court, 1963).

Sellars, W., *Science, Perception, and Reality* (New York: Routledge & Kegan Paul, 1963).

Sellars, W., *Science and Metaphysics* (London: Routledge & Kegan Paul, 1968).

Solomon, R. C., *From Rationalism to Existentialism* (New York: Harper & Row, 1972).

Solomon, R. C., *Continental Philosophy Since 1750* (Oxford: Oxford University Press, 1988).

van Fraassen, B., *The Scientific Image* (New York: Oxford University Press, 1980).